Facilitating Freedom of Religion or Belief: A Deskbook

Published by the Oslo Coalition on Freedom of Religion or Belief in celebration of the 20th anniversary of the Declaration on the Elimination of All Forms of Intolerance and of Discrimination Based on Religion or Belief

Editors: Tore Lindholm
W. Cole Durham, Jr.
Bahia G. Tahzib-Lie

Associate Editors: Elizabeth A. Sewell
Lena Larsen

BYU International Center for Law and Religion Studies
Provo, Utah, USA

The Norwegian Centre for Human Rights
University of Oslo
Norway

The Royal Norwegian Ministry of Foreign Affairs

Springer-Science+Business Media, B.V.

A C.I.P. Catalogue record for this book is available from the Library of Congress.

Printed on acid-free paper.

ISBN 978-90-04-13783-7 ISBN 978-94-017-5616-7 (eBook)
DOI 10.1007/978-94-017-5616-7

Originally published by Martinus Nijhoff Publishers in 2004
Softcover reprint of the hardcover 1st edition 2004

Koninklijke Brill NV incorporates the imprint Martinus Nijhoff Publishers.
http://www.brill.nl

Cover illustration: Pablo Picasso, "Dance of Youth"

To Defenders of Freedom of Religion or Belief
and
To Victims of Intolerance

"Is it not true, my friend, that the river has very many voices? Has it not the voice of a king, of a warrior, of a bull, of a nightbird, of a pregnant woman and a sighing man, and a thousand other voices?" "It is so," nodded Vasudeva, "the voices of all living creatures are in its voice."

–Hermann Hesse, *Siddhartha*

Any royalties of this book will be used to support the efforts of the Oslo Coalition on Freedom of Religion or Belief.

Contents

Part III: Freedom of Religion or Belief and the State

Part IV: Women, Parents, and Children

Part V: Changing Beliefs and the Tensions of Tolerance

Part VI: Contexts for Facilitating Freedom of Religion or Belief

APPENDICES

Foreword

By the Norwegian Minister of Foreign Affairs
March 2000–October 2001

Thorbjørn Jagland

Human rights know no borders. More than fifty years after the adoption of the Universal Declaration of Human Rights, we have only just begun to understand the true impact of recognizing the universality of human rights—"human rights for all." This means that the struggle for freedom of religion or belief for every individual is every government's struggle and every government's responsibility.

Religion is a powerful force. Freedom of religion or belief includes the freedom, either alone or in community with others, in public or in private, to practice one's religion or belief, whether through worship, observance of religious customs or teaching. Freedom of religion or belief also includes the right not to have a religion or belief, and to change one's religion.

Every society benefits from the full and unhindered practice of religion or belief. Full respect for this basic human right can be a powerful force for preventing, quelling and ending conflicts. Experience has shown that peaceful coexistence across religious, ethnic or national borders is only possible if the freedom to have different religious views is ensured, both formally and in practice.

This requires direct involvement on the part of religious leaders and communities, and also governments. Thus, dialogue between leaders and other trusted members of religious communities, NGOs, scholars and representatives of governments should be encouraged.

In order to be successful, such dialogues must be open and frank and they must address real issues. Exchanges like this help communities to see themselves through the eyes of others and to gain new insight into other religions or beliefs as well as their own. Discussing common concerns, listening to others and exchanging ideas promote tolerance and freedom of religion or belief. Such dialogues also give us an opportunity to analyze the obstacles to the unhindered practice of religion or belief. Since progress in the field of human rights is measured in terms of implementation, the objective of dialogue and discussion must be the fulfillment, safeguarding and defense of freedom of religion or belief.

Tore Lindholm, W. Cole Durham, Jr., Bahia G. Tahzib-Lie (eds.), Facilitating Freedom of Religion or Belief: A Deskbook, *xiii–xiv.*

I congratulate the Oslo Coalition on Freedom of Religion or Belief on producing this book, which will be a valuable tool for anyone desiring to understand and contribute to the promotion of such freedom. The book is a fruit of the Oslo Conference on Freedom of Religion and Belief, which was held in August 1998 and co-sponsored by the Norwegian Government. I hope the reader will find this collection of articles stimulating and challenging and that it will serve the cause of freedom of religion or belief everywhere.

Foreword

By the United Nations Special Rapporteur on Freedom of Religion or Belief

Abdelfattah Amor

The United Nations Commission on Human Rights continues to be alarmed that serious instances of intolerance and discrimination on the grounds of religion or belief, including acts of violence, intimidation and coercion motivated by religious intolerance, occur in many parts of the world and threaten the enjoyment of human rights and fundamental freedoms. For years the Commission has been reiterating its concern in its annual resolutions on the elimination of all forms of religious intolerance, most recently Resolution 2001/42.

The international community must, therefore, react by fighting against such acts and especially by preventing them. This book, published by the Oslo Coalition on Freedom of Religion or Belief on the occasion of the twentieth anniversary of the 1981 United Nations Declaration on the Elimination of All Forms of Intolerance and of Discrimination Based on Religion or Belief, is integral to this reaction. The great variety and the quality of contributions assembled here witness the necessity of greater recognition of violations of freedom of religion or belief and the importance and urgency that exist to combat every manifestation of intolerance and discrimination, and especially to prevent them. This publication contributes significantly to the reinforcement and the development of the right to freedom of religion or belief, a right underlying the establishment of the mandate on freedom of religion or belief, formerly referred to as the mandate on religious intolerance, and the evolution of action associated with it.

◆ ◆ ◆

By Resolution 1986/20 of 10 March 1986 the Commission on Human Rights decided to appoint a special rapporteur charged with examining incidents and governmental actions in all parts of the world which are inconsistent with the provisions of the 1981 Declaration on the Elimination of All Forms of Intolerance and of Discrimination Based on Religion or Belief, and recommending measures to remedy such situations. Fourteen years later, by Resolution 2000/33, the Commission on

Tore Lindholm, W. Cole Durham, Jr., Bahia G. Tahzib-Lie (eds.), Facilitating Freedom of Religion or Belief: A Deskbook, *xv–xviii.*

Human Rights decided to change the title of the mandate of the Special Rapporteur on Religious Intolerance at the next extension of the Special Rapporteur's mandate, in 2001.

The new title of Special Rapporteur on Freedom of Religion and Belief came into effect at the 57th session of the Commission in March–April 2001.

The 1981 Declaration guarantees freedom of religion and belief, and elaborates the relevant norms enshrined in other international human rights instruments. These instruments include the International Covenant on Civil and Political Rights, in particular article 18, and the International Covenant on Economic, Social, and Cultural Rights, in particular article 13. From these instruments it can be inferred that the right to have, adopt or change freedom of religion or belief is absolute. It is also clear that manifestations of religion or belief may only be subject to certain specific limitations. The United Nations Committee on Human Rights has detailed in General Comment No. 22 of 20 July 1993 that restrictions on the freedom to manifest religion or belief are only permitted if limitations are prescribed by law and necessary to protect public safety, order, health or morals, or the fundamental rights and freedoms of others. The Committee has also pointed out that limitations imposed must not be applied in a manner that would vitiate the right to freedom of thought, conscience, and religion. The Committee has maintained that limitations may be applied only for those purposes for which they were prescribed and must be directly related and proportionate to the specific need on which they are predicated. Restrictions may not be imposed for discriminatory purposes or applied in a discriminatory manner.

• • •

Within the scope of the mandate on freedom of religion or belief, it has been noted for several years that manifestations of intolerance and discrimination based on religion or belief persist in countries that are in various stages of development and that have various political, social, and cultural systems—despite the multitude of established norms and the diversity of mechanisms in place to counteract them.

The identified infractions are diverse and concern violations of nondiscrimination and tolerance of religion and belief in the following areas: freedom of thought and conscience; freedom to practice one's religion or belief; freedom regarding the disposition of religious property; and, more generally, a person's right to life, bodily integrity, and health. Women, in the eyes of religion, or of considerations imputed to religion, continue to bear the brunt of violations.

The victims of such intolerance and discrimination are also diverse. Whether it involves believers or nonbelievers, religious communities, or society in general, those who are most affected are vulnerable groups. This implicates women on the one hand and minorities on the other. Minorities in this sense include new religious movements, for which freedom of religion or belief must be guaranteed. At the same time, it is necessary to guard against invoking the cloak of religious freedom as an alibi for purposes contrary to human rights.

Major challenges are emerging in the face of increasing manifestations of hatred, intolerance, and violence based upon extremism. Religious extremism may, in some cases, lead to situations that are difficult to control, even compromising the right to peace. Afghanistan was until recently the site of one of the most intolerable examples of extremism, but the challenge of religious extremism belongs to no particular society, state, or religion.

◆ ◆ ◆

In order to counter an alarming assessment regarding tolerance and nondiscrimination based on religion or belief, I suggest going beyond everyday management of these phenomena. Prevention by means of open communication, urgent calls for action addressed to states, and on-site visits are of vital importance to break the vicious circle of violations of freedom of religion or belief. This prevention depends primarily upon education and inter-religious dialogue. As the Preamble of UNESCO's Constitution states, "since wars begin in the minds of men, it is in the minds of men that the defenses of peace must be constructed."

◆ ◆ ◆

The teaching of tolerance and nondiscrimination must be oriented along various lines; including the family, society, religious communities, political parties, and the media. I have also been inclined to believe that training in school is especially suited to ensure that values supporting human rights are internalized and to foster a culture of tolerance and human rights.

This proposed education explains the initiative, taken within the framework of the mandate, to organize together with the Spanish Government an international consultative conference on school education in relation to freedom of religion or belief. This conference took place in Madrid in November 2001 to celebrate the twentieth anniversary of the adoption of the 1981 Declaration.

The conference developed an international, school-based strategy for students at elementary and secondary education levels. Additionally, the conference considered a set of recommendations to shed light on the establishment of programs and scholarly manuals, regarding education on tolerance and nondiscrimination in the areas of religion and belief.

◆ ◆ ◆

Inter-religious dialogue is essential for the prevention of misunderstandings, conflicts, and violations of freedom of religion or belief. As the United Nations High Commissioner for Human Rights so rightly pointed out in her 21 September 1999 address, marking the 950th anniversary of the City of Nuremberg and its conference on peace and human rights, "The full title of the conference, namely, 'Human Rights: Favored by Religions, Threatened by Religions,' illustrates the fact that religion's message of peace and love can be distorted to become an instrument of hatred and conflict. Religion can and should play an important role in conflict prevention and post-conflict reconciliation." At stake in the promotion and protection of freedom of religion or belief is not so much the search for one unique and exclusive truth, but rather a search to promote greater respect for the rights of individuals, groups, and communities. To this end, measures applied at national and international levels should overlap at the point of constructive dialogue among members of religious communities, and between different religious communities and public powers in a spirit of tolerance and respect.

There is good reason to celebrate initiatives that promote this dialogue, such as the Geneva Spiritual Appeal, which was delivered and signed by representatives of various religions and by the International Committee of the Red Cross (ICRC), the Office of the United Nations High Commissioner for Human Rights (OHCHR), the United Nations High Commissioner for Refugees (UNHCR), and the World Health Organization (WHO) during an interconfessional service held in Geneva on 24 October 1999 as part of United Nations Day. Furthermore, UNESCO has established the World Council on Inter-Religious Dialogue. Finally, hope is generated by the efforts of the United Nations Year of Dialogue between Civilizations, 2001.

In sum, education and inter-religious dialogue constitute two essential axes destined to prevent violations throughout the world. It must be remembered that the representation of one's own image hinges on the respect one bears toward the self-image of others. "The encounter with alterity is the encounter with ourselves," writes Federico Mayor, who adds, "the path that leads to the realization that 'others, they are us' is strewn with pitfalls."

Foreword

By the United Nations High Commissioner for Human Rights

September 1997–September 2002

Mary Robinson

The sense of shared purpose and commitment I witnessed at the Oslo Conference on Freedom of Religion or Belief, held 12–15 August 1998, was impressive. I welcome the initiative arising from the Oslo Conference to publish this book, *Facilitating Freedom of Religion or Belief*, growing out of papers submitted at the conference and based on the work of experts in the field.

The 1981 United Nations Declaration on the Elimination of All Forms of Intolerance and Discrimination Based on Religion or Belief elaborated on the basic rights and freedoms set out in article 18 of the Universal Declaration of Human Rights and other relevant provisions, and called on states to take all effective measures necessary to prevent and eliminate discrimination and appropriate measures to combat intolerance on the grounds of religion or other beliefs. The Declaration further expressed the conviction of the international community that freedom of religion or belief can contribute to the attainment of world peace, social justice and friendship among people.

The recent Millennium Peace Summit of Religions and Spiritual Leaders, which opened at the United Nations on 28 August 2000, affirmed the importance of dialogue and discussion between the world's religions in the pursuit of the fundamental purposes of the United Nations Charter.

It is evident that tolerance and respect for other religions and beliefs will make the world a more peaceful place. The opposite is also clear: that bigotry, prejudice and discrimination are a sure recipe for conflict and even war. There is an onus on all of us to defend the rights of all persons to follow their own religion or belief without hindrance. Religions themselves have responsibilities too. As I said at Oslo:

> The major religions, while concerned with ultimate questions, frequently present themselves as protectors and promoters of human dignity. They see themselves in particular as defenders of the deprived, the poor, the discriminated against. So their religious freedom is a freedom in society not merely to believe and to worship but also to uphold the cause of the deprived. In these circumstances they must ensure that their own internal practices are not discriminatory on grounds of gender or race or class. They have to learn from the good practice of wider society as well as teach it.

Tore Lindholm, W. Cole Durham, Jr., Bahia G. Tahzib-Lie (eds.), Facilitating Freedom of Religion or Belief: A Deskbook, *xix–xx.*

The Oslo Conference was noteworthy, not only because it brought together such a distinguished group of experts from academia, governments, international organizations, and NGOs, but because it forged an enduring coalition of interested parties to carry on the work of defending freedom of religion or belief. The launch of this book makes a significant contribution to that ongoing work by providing all of the actors involved with a valuable tool to help better understand the root causes of intolerance and discrimination and to learn more about how to combat these ills.

ACKNOWLEDGEMENTS

This volume would not have been possible without the dedicated efforts and assistance of many. The Royal Norwegian Ministry of Foreign Affairs has provided steadfast encouragement and generous financial support, making possible the wide distribution of the book to students, NGOs, and activists in developing countries. We are also indebted to the Norwegian Centre for Human Rights, the Oslo Coalition on Freedom of Religion or Belief, and the International Center for Law and Religion Studies at Brigham Young University for providing generous financial backing in the editorial process and for freeing up the time of Tore Lindholm, Cole Durham, and Elizabeth Sewell for their part of the work on the book. Many thanks are also in order to the Bahá'í community of the Netherlands for their hospitality during meetings held in The Hague.

The editors also gratefully acknowledge the research and editorial contributions of many talented students in both Oslo and Provo. Thanks to Christian Moe, Turid Smith Polfus, Lincoln T. Peterson, Patrick J. Thurston, Ann Elizabeth Gedicks, Hannah Clayson Smith, James and Jaimee Macanas Neel, Howard Baik, Gabe S. Clark, Claire Foley, Sarah and Carter Chow, Joshua D. Jewkes, Rana Lehr Lehnardt, Christopher R. Preston, Lance S. Lehnhof, Michael Monson, John Valentine, Natalie Peterson, Jonathon Tichy, Matthew Jarman, Jed K. Burton, Cory Talbot, David Garner, Eric Hunter, Erika Rowberry, Marc Porter, Michael Lopez, Nathan Jensen, Robert Roe, Tessa Santiago, Rod Andreason, Michele I. Cheney, Devaughn Fraser, and Richard Hawkins for their excellent assistance. We also are grateful to Professor Daryl Lee for his able English translations of the foreword by Special Rapporteur Abdelfattah Amor and the chapter by Doudou Diene. Most of all, we are thankful for the contributions of the various authors and for their patience through the editorial process.

The preproduction editing and formatting process would not have come together without the dedication, attention to detail, and hours of intensive labor of Kristen M. Bahlmann, Robert P. Schwartz, Rebecca S. Kellogg, Barbara Fuller, Peter Jasinki, and Christine Brown. Many thanks are also in order to the support and administrative team in Provo that helped push the book through to completion: Deborah Wright, Christine Scott, Kimberly Mantz, Marné Pieper, and Anthony Haws. We also appreciate

Tore Lindholm, W. Cole Durham, Jr., Bahia G. Tahzib-Lie (eds.), Facilitating Freedom of Religion or Belief: A Deskbook, *xxi–xxii.*

the support of Lindy Melman and Peter Buschman at Martinus Nijhoff/Brill. Finally, but certainly not least, we express appreciation for the great support, encouragement, and patience of our spouses and family members during the editorial and writing process.

We also would like to acknowledge the Artists Rights Society of New York, which granted us permission to use a copy of Picasso's *Dance of Youth* (© 2001 Estate of Pablo Picasso/Artists Rights Society [ARS], New York) on the cover of this book.

–The Editors

List of Abbreviations

1965 Convention	The United Nations Convention on the Elimination of All Forms of Racial Discrimination (1965)
1981 Declaration	Declaration on the Elimination of All Forms of Intolerance and of Discrimination Based on Religion or Belief (1981)
1990 Charter of Paris	Charter of Paris for a New Europe (1990)
ACHR	American Convention on Human Rights (1969)
African Charter	The African Charter on Human and Peoples' Rights (1981)
American Convention	American Convention on Human Rights (1969)
BCLR	Butterworths Constitutional Law Reports
BDPA	Beijing Declaration and Platform for Action of the Fourth World Conference on Women
Beijing +5 document	Report of the Ad Hoc Committee of the Whole of the 23rd special session of the UN General Assembly entitled Women 2000: Gender Equality, Development and Peace for the Twenty-First Century (2000)
BJP	Bharatiya Janata Party
BPA	Beijing Platform for Action of the Fourth World Conference on Women
CEC	Conference of European Churches
CEDAW	Convention on the Elimination of All Forms of Discrimination Against Women (1979)
CERD	Committee on the Elimination of Racial Discrimination
CESNUR	Centro Studi sulle Nuove Religioni (Center for Studies on New Religions)
CIS	Commonwealth of Independent States
COE	Council of Europe
Concluding Document of the Vienna Meeting	Concluding Document of the Vienna Meeting of Representatives of the Participating States of the Conference on Security and Co-operation in Europe (1986)

Convention of Belém do Pará Inter	American Convention on the Prevention, Punishment and Eradication of Violence against Women (1994)
Copenhagen Document	Document of the Copenhagen Meeting of Representatives of the Participating States of the Conference on the Human Dimension of the Conference on Security and Co-operation in Europe (1990)
CPCs	Countries of particular concern
CRC	Convention on the Rights of the Child
CSBMs	Confidence and Security Building Measures
CSCE	Conference for Security and Co-operation in Europe (now OSCE)
CTS	Consolidated Treaty Series
DEVAW	Declaration on the Elimination of Violence against Women (1993)
DRL	Bureau of Democracy, Human Rights and Labor in the US State Department
EC	European Communities
ECHR	European Convention on Human Rights (1950)
ECJ	European Court of Justice
EComHR	European Commission of Human Rights
ECOSOC	Economic and Social Council of the United Nations
ECR	European Court Reports
ECtHR	European Court of Human Rights
ETS	European Treaty Series
EU	European Union
European Convention	European Convention for the Protection of Human Rights and Fundamental Freedoms (1950)
FCRA	Foreign Contributions Regulation Act (1976)
FGM	female genital mutilation
FORB	freedom of religion or belief
Fourth Geneva Convention	Geneva Convention Relative to the Protection of Civilian Persons in Time of War (1949)
Framework Convention	Framework Convention for the Protection of National Minorities (1995)
FRY	Federal Republic of Yugoslavia
FSC	Forum for Security Co-operation
FYR Macedonia	Former Yugoslav Republic of Macedonia
GDR	German Democratic Republic
Geneva Convention I	Geneva Convention for the Amelioration of the Condition of the Wounded and Sick in Armed Forces in the Field (1949)
Geneva Convention II	Geneva Convention for the Amelioration of the Condition of Wounded, Sick and Shipwrecked Members of Armed Forces at Sea (1949)
Geneva Convention III	Geneva Convention Relative to the Treatment of Prisoners of War (1949)
Geneva Convention IV	Geneva Convention Relative to the Protection of Civilian Persons in Time of War (1949)

Genocide Convention	International Convention on the Prevention and Punishment of the Crime of Genocide (1948)
GONGO	governmental NGO
HCNM	High Commissioner on National Minorities
ICCPR	International Covenant on Civil and Political Rights (1966)
ICESCR	International Covenant on Economic, Social and Cultural Rights (1966)
ICJ	International Court of Justice
ICTR Statute	Statute of the International Criminal Tribunal for the Prosecution of Persons Responsible for Genocide and Other Serious Violations of International Humanitarian Law Committed in the Territory of Rwanda and Rwandan Citizens Responsible for Genocide and Other Such Violations Committed in the Territory of Neighboring States between 1 January 1994 and 31 December 1994 (1994)
ILC	International Law Commission of the United Nations
ILO	International Labor Organization
Implementation Report of the Secretary General	UN Secretary General, Implementation of the Declaration of on the Elimination of All Forms of Religious Intolerance and of Discrimination Based on Religion or Belief (1996)
INFORM	Information Network Focus on Religious Movements
Inter-American Commission	Inter-American Commission on Human Rights
Inter-Am Com HR	Inter-American Commission on Human Rights
IRF	Office of International Religious Freedom in the US State Department
IRFA	International Religious Freedom Act of 1998
ISKCON	International Society for Krishna Consciousness
LNTS	League of Nations Treaty Series
MILS	Mission interministérielle de lutte contre les sectes (French Interministerial Mission to Combat Sects)
Minorities Declaration	Declaration on the Rights of Persons Belonging to National or Ethnic, Religious, and Linguistic Minorities
NAACP	National Association for the Advancement of Colored People
NATO	North Atlantic Treaty Organization
NGO	Non-governmental organization
NIS	newly Independent States
NRM	new religious movement
OAS	Organization of American States
OAU	Organization of African Unity
ODIHR	Office for Democratic Institutions and Human Rights of the OSCE
OHR	Office of the High Representative of the International Community (in Bosnia)
OSCE	Organization for Security and Cooperation in Europe
QUANGO	quasi-NGO
RE	religious education

Rome Statute	Rome Statute of the International Criminal Court UN Doc. (2002)
SA	South Africa
SALR	South African Law Reports
SARA	State Administration of Religious Affairs
SFOR	Stabilisation Force in Bosnia and Herzegovina
Siracusa Principles	Siracusa Principles on the Limitation and Derogation Provisions in the International Covenant on Civil and Political Rights (1984)
The Hague Convention IV	The Hague Convention Respecting the Laws and Customs of War on Law (1907)
UDHR	Universal Declaration of Human Rights (1948)
UN Charter	United Nations Charter (1976)
UNDP	United Nations Development Programme
UNESCO	United Nations Educational, Scientific and Cultural Organization
UNFPA	United Nations Population Fund
UNHCHR	United Nations High Commissioner for Human Rights
UNHCR	United Nations High Commissioner for Refugees
UN HR Com	United Nations Human Rights Commission
UNICEF	United Nations International Children's Emergency Fund
UNIMIK	United Nations Interim Mission in Kosovo
Universal Declaration	Universal Declaration of Human Rights (1948)
USIP	United States Institute of Peace
WCC	World Council of Churches
WCRP	World Conference on Religion and Peace
WHO	World Health Organisation

Introduction

The Editors, with Nazila Ghanea

The Renewed Salience of Religion and Freedom of Religion or Belief

The challenge of freedom of religion or belief is as old as history, yet as current as today's headlines. It occupies some of humankind's most ancient narratives: Cain slew Abel following a dispute about the proper form of sacrifice;[1] Antigone buried Polyneices in a classic encounter of conscience with state power;[2] Prince Siddhartha Gautama had to turn from the allures of his father's court to follow the path of asceticism and ultimately enlightenment;[3] early in Islamic history exiled Muslims fleeing from persecution by the Quraysh tribe were given freedom to practice their religion under the protection of the Christian Emperor of Abyssinia.[4] But the challenge is more general. It arises wherever differences of fundamental beliefs create tensions in families or in communities, which seems to be virtually inescapable.

The underlying problems can take mild or acute forms, but they pervade human life, and the challenge has not receded with time. Contemporary struggles replicate ancient tragedies, too often on a far more massive scale. Witness the events of September 11, 2001 in the United States, March 11, 2004 in Spain, the litany of interreligious warfare in all too many countries, or recurrences of genocide that mock the post-holocaust motto, "never again." Other conflicts may be less life threatening, but if left to simmer too long, or under too much pressure, they also can explode.

As this volume was going to press, there were major public debates in several Western European countries about the acceptability of Muslim women (and girls) wearing the *hijab*, or Islamic head scarf. In France major legislation prohibiting the wearing of *hijab*, or comparable religious symbols, in public settings is in process. Taking just this one example, who can see all the ramifications of tensions and state

---

[1] Genesis 4:3–8.

[2] Sophocles, *Antigone*.

[3] E. H. Johnstone, *The Buddhacarita or Acts of the Buddha* (Calcutta, 1939).

[4] Muhammad Ibn Ishaq, *The Life of Muhammad*, trans. A. Guillaume (Islamabad: Oxford University Press, 1967).

Tore Lindholm, W. Cole Durham, Jr., Bahia G. Tahzib-Lie (eds.), Facilitating Freedom of Religion or Belief: A Deskbook, *xxvii–lxxiv.*

action regarding the wearing of Muslim scarves that are currently arising in families, schools, employment, and countless other settings, in private and public, both in Europe and (by way of reaction and reverberation) throughout the Muslim world?

In the new millennium, the challenge seems at once greater and more urgent than ever before. It pervades the crucial sectors of modern life—from culture and civil society, to politics and identity, to security and conflict. Contrary to the prognostications of secularization theory, religion is not withering away. Rather, it is making a pronounced comeback in many parts of the world. But it is returning in many forms, and yielding a highly plural brew, particularly when viewed from a global perspective. Whatever one thinks of Huntington's "clash of civilizations" thesis, and the inevitability of conflict along religiously-based, civilizational lines,[5] the renewed prominence of religion has catapulted issues of freedom of religion or belief to center stage. From previously having been largely a specialist issue of interest to relatively few at the international level, its import can now scarcely be overestimated.

In the cultural sphere, the importance of this issue is evident in the tension between particularist claims and the view that human rights are genuinely universal. Some of the most contested problems in this context arise precisely in the field of freedom of religion or belief. These include issues of proselytism, the right to change one's religion, and the role of women as affected by religion. Impasse on these cultural issues helps to explain why the 1981 UN Declaration on the Elimination of All Forms of Intolerance and of Discrimination Based on Religion or Belief has been stalemated as a declaration and has not evolved into a legally binding covenant. Similarly, the 1993 Vienna World Conference on Human Rights did not succeed in crafting a new understanding on the universality or particularity of human rights. It merely acknowledged disagreement through its compromise language, giving continued recognition to the universality of human rights while accepting cultural and religious particularities as well.[6]

The significance of religion and belief and the freedom that protects them is also evident at the level of civil society. The associational rights that protect civil society organizations overlap with and reinforce the rights and freedoms that protect belief communities. The latter play a critical role in motivating, organizing, staffing, supporting, and partnering with civil society organizations to carry out countless projects that benefit society. Belief communities are a major repository of altruism and moral commitment. Civil society organizations, of course, reflect the full range of plurality of the societies in which they are found, and their interests may coincide with or diverge from those of religious organizations or the state. Sometimes this may lead to cooperation between public, religious, and governmental sectors. This is often the case in Europe and more recently has been evidenced in the United States by faith-based initiatives encouraged by United States President

---

[5] Samuel P. Huntington, *The Clash of Civilizations and the Remaking of World Order* (New York: Simon and Schuster, 1996).

[6] The Vienna Declaration and Programme of Action states in operative paragraph 5, "All human rights are universal, indivisible and interdependent and interrelated.... While the significance of national and regional particularities and various historical, cultural and religious backgrounds must be borne in mind, it is the duty of States, regardless of their political, economic and cultural systems, to promote and protect all human rights and fundamental freedoms."

George W. Bush.[7] Sometimes, however, alignments with religious communities can be divisive and can entrench conflicting cleavages. A potential remedy in this area is to encourage joint action that brings the efforts of different communities to bear on shared concerns. For example, the 2001 Cantle report on "Community Cohesion," commissioned by the Home Office in the United Kingdom, recommended that funds be allocated in such a way as to maximize contact, awareness, and activities *between* communities.[8]

The resurgence of religion is perhaps even more evident in politics. In this regard one thinks of the rise of the religious right and the significance of abortion politics in the United States, the rise of political Islam in many countries around the world, the significance of religion to the political movements that brought down communism in country after country in Eastern Europe, and so forth. In addition to these macro-political events, there is the constant flow of religion-related events that attract political interest and concern: the clergy sex abuse scandals in the United States are just one particularly sordid example.

Identity politics is yet another area implicating religion in major ways. Ethnicity and religion are often closely linked and have a long history of spawning conflict: Serb and Croat in Yugoslavia, Sunni and Shia in Iraq, Christian and Muslim in Indonesia. Identity politics is also in the emerging politics of sexual orientation. Issues of same-sex marriage have emerged as a major issue in United States presidential politics. Liberalization in this area is an emerging pattern in many parts of Europe. Sexual orientation has also become a significant issue in internal church politics in many denominations. To give only one example, the consecration of an openly active homosexual, Bishop Gene Robinson in New Hampshire, may yet split the worldwide Anglican Church.

Conflict and security have emerged as particularly urgent arenas in which religion has long been recognized as an important factor. Whether conflict is ***motivated*** by religion or ***aggravated*** by politicians who exploit religious identities is an ongoing discussion. However, the link itself is undeniable, and is illustrated by all too many recent episodes. Intercommunal violence led to the killing of twenty-one Copts in al-Kosheh in Upper Egypt in January 2000. Horrific bloodshed resulted from the violence between religious groups in Gujarat, India in spring 2002. In autumn 2002 sectarian violence left hundreds dead when violence was unleashed in Nigeria during the attempted hosting of the Miss World beauty contest. The decade of the 1990s witnessed interreligious conflicts in the former Yugoslavia, intercommunal killings in Northern Ireland, and slaughters in Algeria and the Sudan. The potential link between religion and

[7] January 2001 saw President George Bush expand government funding to faith-based organizations. He also set up a new White House Office of Faith-Based and Community Initiatives to give such organizations greater access to federal funds.

[8] The Home Office commissioned the Cantle report of December 2001 in response to the summer 2001 riots in the northern English towns that left hundreds injured and community relations in tatters. Cantle found that the towns where the riots occurred had been deeply polarized with segregated ethnic communities living "a series of parallel lives." It criticized the funding of separate and distinct community interests, as this tended to reinforce cultural differences. The report instead recommended that a government funding regime be set up to create an ethos "which constantly promotes joint work and collaboration" across communities. It recommended that funding bodies should require collaborative working and generally be provided both on a thematic basis and based on needs across communities.

violence has been evidenced in another way by suicides and attacks that have arisen from time to time in connection with unusual new religious movements in the United States, Japan, Switzerland, France, and Belgium.

While the dark side of religion and violence cannot be ignored, it is vital to remember that belief communities also play a potent role in conflict prevention, conflict resolution, post-conflict reconciliation, and general social stabilization. Religions have been guilty of contributing to tensions leading to war, but their fundamental message is peace. As Rüdiger Noll's chapter in this volume notes, religious leaders have often played particularly courageous roles in helping to find ways to resolve conflicts. They are often vital to achieving spiritual reconciliation, which is a necessary precondition to other more tangible forms of rebuilding after conflict. More generally, religion plays critical roles in inculcating habits of honesty, industry, loyalty, and numerous other traits without which societies would have difficulty functioning. The resurgence of religion around the world reflects most fundamentally the attractions of these positive sides of religion.

The tragic events of September 11, 2001 have prompted a tectonic shift in thinking about the relationship of religion, freedom, and security. These events provided a powerful reminder of the vulnerability of civilization—vulnerability that has been hammered home by bomb blasts in many other parts of the world, emphasizing that no homeland is secure. But in too many cases, this shared international experience has prompted overreaction. Human rights have been sacrificed to the supposed necessities of security. History's lesson, echoed in the key United Nations declaration on point, is too often forgotten: "the disregard and infringement of human rights and fundamental freedoms, in particular of the right to freedom of thought, conscience, religion or whatever belief, have brought, directly or indirectly, wars and great suffering to mankind. . . ."[9] What the rush to protect security forgets is that security purchased with the suppression of rights is only a stopgap. Temporary expedients may be necessary, but a solution that fails to protect rights is at best an illusion, and an illusion without a future. Injustice lacks long-term stability.

Far from withering away, then, religion has assumed new salience. But this has stirred new anxieties. The "ambivalence of the sacred"[10]—the fact that religion spawns both good and evil—has led on the one hand to a global resurgence of religion and on the other to global pressures to mitigate religious hazards. This in turn has given new urgency to questions of how to structure the freedom of religion or belief. In our pluralistic world, the alternatives are stark. Either we must find ways for groups with differing beliefs to live together (which appears to be possible only by respecting freedom of religion or belief, whether through state-enforced protections or through internalizing norms of respect for the dignity and religious choices of others), or we must face constant friction, all too frequent warfare, and the ultimate risk of nuclear Armageddon.

---

[9] Preamble, United Nations Declaration on the Elimination of All Forms of Intolerance and of Discrimination Based on Religion or Belief (hereinafter "1981 Declaration").

[10] See R. Scott Appleby, *The Ambivalence of the Sacred: Religion, Violence, and Reconciliation* (Oxford: Rowman & Littlefield Publishers, 2000).

Faced with these ineluctable alternatives, the right to freedom of religion or belief has the complex task of protecting religion and its potential for good while permitting certain limitations designed to filter out religion's negative hazards. In this sense, the right to freedom of religion or belief addresses both poles of the ambivalence of the sacred. It also bridges both universal and particular: it constitutes a ***universal*** call to respect ***particular*** world views and requires ***particular*** faiths to endorse ***universal*** religious freedom. But recognition that the right to freedom of religion or belief is designed to address these polarities—the ambivalence of the sacred and the tension of universal and particular—does not mean that translating it into practice is easy or automatic. Rather, it calls for continual striving to find sensitive ways to facilitate accommodation of religious and cultural differences within a broad framework of interpersonal and intercultural respect.

Facilitating Freedom of Religion or Belief

The present volume is the outgrowth of efforts to foster just such "continual striving" to facilitate freedom of religion or belief. The original impetus for the book came from the 1998 Oslo Conference on Freedom of Religion or Belief, a remarkable conference that was originally organized as part of efforts to celebrate the fiftieth anniversary of the Universal Declaration of Human Rights. This book is just one of many contributions that continue to flow from that seminal conference, and, indeed, the length of its gestation is attributable in no small part to the fact that its editors and authors have been at the forefront of a wide range of initiatives that exemplify the kind of "continual striving" that is needed. Some of these initiatives have followed as a direct result of the Oslo Conference; others have been part of broader efforts at the national and international level that the Oslo Conference hoped to support. Direct involvement of our authors in the unfolding course of events as noted in the following paragraphs has enriched the sense of engagement throughout the volume, sharpening awareness both of the issues that need to be addressed and of the measures that make a difference.

Funded by the Norwegian government and organized in association with the Council for Religious and Life Stance Communities in Norway, the Oslo Conference was a unique gathering of government officials, experts, intergovernmental actors, and representatives of various NGOs. The aim of the conference was to re-energize efforts aimed at effective enforcement of article 18 of the Universal Declaration of Human Rights. The conference used a networking methodology, reflected in the many differing voices and organizations it brought together, to focus on both the substance of the right and the modalities of its implementation.

The unique blend of deep understanding of the issues combined with commitment to finding practical ways forward among conference participants is reflected in the concluding document of the conference, the Oslo Declaration on Freedom of Religion or Belief (included as Appendix F to this volume). Framed by participants at the conference, the Oslo Declaration was also subsequently signed by representatives of twenty-five religious and life-stance communities in Norway on November 8, 2001. Even now, rereading this Declaration recalls the energy and commitment of the Oslo Conference. Beyond reassertion of the core values codified in international norms on freedom of religion or belief, the Oslo Declaration exudes commitment to make a difference. It identifies the key international norms as "a universal standard around which we wish to *rally*." It recognizes practical needs for additional financial and personnel support for those in international institutions tasked with working on tolerance and freedom of religion or belief. At the same time, it calls for greater efficiency in use of resources that are available. It inventories the range of bodies that can make a difference, and challenges them to create educational and other programs that can contribute in practical ways to building a culture of tolerance. And so forth.

One of the most significant results of the Conference was that the participants, in the second recital of the Oslo Declaration, "accepted the challenge to build an international coalition and to develop a strategic plan of action to achieve substantial progress in and give practical support to the implementation of Article 18 . . . ." Responding to this challenge and the final paragraph of the Declaration, the organizers and sponsors of the Oslo Conference created the Oslo Coalition on Freedom of Religion or Belief. While based in Norway, the Coalition has maintained a broad outlook and international connections from the beginning. Among other things, it has a distinguished International Advisory Council; some of its members have authored chapters for this volume or have participated in other Oslo Coalition projects.

From the beginning, the Oslo Coalition has been committed to action, and in particular to practical action likely to have broad impact supportive of other international initiatives. It has aimed to facilitate freedom of religion or belief within a genuinely international framework—the level at which its activities are concentrated. The Oslo Coalition generally does not focus on the interests of particular individuals or religious groups, nor is it engaged in carrying out monitoring activities. While such activities are clearly vital, the Oslo Coalition has sought to avoid duplicating the work of other international organizations and NGOs that already carry out these tasks.

Rather, the Coalition has undertaken a number of projects with far broader impact. For example, the Coalition has played a significant role in supporting the UN's International Consultative Conference on School Education in Relation with Freedom of Religion and Belief, Tolerance and Non-discrimination held in Madrid from November 21–23, 2001. Prior to the conference, the Coalition took an active role in reviewing and commenting on documents. Also, in April 2001 it organized a side meeting in Geneva at the time of the UN Commission on Human Rights annual session entitled "Religious Education in Pluralistic Societies: Aims and Challenges." The objective was to help prepare and deepen thinking in advance of the November Conference. The Coalition has organized follow-up efforts aimed at acting on recommendations from the conference. Jolanta Ambrosewicz-Jacobs describes the recommendations of the conference in chapter 37, and Ingvill Plesner uses data from the conference as part of the basis for her analysis in chapter 36 of ways that tolerance can be promoted in the context of education. Coalition work in this area has now grown into an impressive ongoing program, including a major conference in September of 2004 and global networking efforts to identify appropriate models and best practices for teaching tolerance.[11]

---

[11] See the website of the Oslo Coalition, <http://www.oslocoalition.org/html/project_school_education/index.html> (last visited March 20, 2004), for an overview on current programs.

The Oslo Coalition has also been actively involved in conferences promoting improved implementation of freedom of religion or belief among religious leaders and government officials charged with making and administering public policy in Central Asia and the Caucasus. This initiative started with co-sponsorship of conferences with the Russian Academy of State Service in Moscow in 2000 and 2001. The Coalition's involvement made it possible to bring officials to Moscow from some of the outlying areas. Connections from these early conferences rapidly became the basis for projects in Azerbaijan (2000, 2002, 2003), the northern Caucasus (2002), and Central Asia (2003).

In addition to taking advantage of opportunities to work directly with key government officials and religious leaders in these projects, the Coalition has played a distinctive role by sharing the Norwegian experience with interfaith dialogue. This experience is described in considerable detail by Inge Eidsvåg, Tore Lindholm, and Barbro Sveen in chapter 35. In particular, in the various regional conferences, Coalition representatives laid recurrent emphasis on the fact that finding common projects that different religious groups can work on jointly is often much more effective in building trust and understanding than formal dialogues on theological themes. Significantly, that experience was being applied in practice in various settings in the former Soviet Union at the same time the chapter describing the Norwegian experience was being written, resulting in valuable synergies. In retrospect, the Oslo Conference itself can be seen as an application of this methodology—bringing numerous groups together to work on the common project of promoting freedom of religion or belief for all—and the initial methodological insight is having a significant impact in other areas.

The Coalition has also undertaken major projects in China and Indonesia, which have added both geographic and substantive scope to its efforts. The China initiative has involved a series of exchanges with Chinese experts aimed at promoting dialogue on freedom of religion and belief issues. The Coalition is acutely aware of some of the areas and religions of China that have suffered most from violations of freedom of religion or belief. The Coalition's work in China has demonstrated its ability to build constructive channels for sensitive dialogue on human rights performance. In Indonesia, against the background of tragic violence associated with interreligious tensions, similar exchanges have focused on establishing relationships between faith groups and academics with the aim of adding conflict resolution efforts to the Coalition's repertoire of promoting interfaith dialogue and human rights compliance. These efforts have sought to apply in practice many of the ideas highlighted by Rüdiger Noll in chapter 33, on "The Role of Religion and Religious Freedom in Contemporary Conflict Situations."

In 2002 the Coalition added another major initiative of tremendous potential significance: the Project on New Directions in Islamic Thought and Practice. Here efforts are aimed at "creating a forum where Muslim reform thinkers may present and discuss ideas and develop strategies for further action."[12] As in so many other areas, this initiative couples academic expertise, networking, and a strong interest in allowing groups to

---

[12] Oslo Coalition website, <http://www.oslocoalition.org/html/project_new_horizons/index.html> (last visited March 20, 2004).

think through their own issues in dialogue within a religious tradition and across traditional divides. One important sub-theme for this project is Islam, Women, and Religious Freedom. Islam is sometimes used as an argument for practices that flout standards of human rights. Conflicts and tensions with respect to CEDAW provisions are well known. Not so widely known is the fact that Muslim women's issues raise questions of freedom of religion or belief. Several major challenges regarding Muslim women hinge on contestable interpretations of Islam. Solutions may be sought by way of new readings and interpretation, as proposed by Shirin Ebadi, Nobel Peace Prize Laureate for 2003.

In 2004 the Coalition initiated a project on Proselytism and Human Rights. This has become an urgent religious freedom topic, in a time of post-colonialism, post-communism, and religious resurgence. The project addresses questions about human rights as well as broader concerns about appropriate behavior and ethical standards for the conduct of missionary activity.

Of course, it is not only the activities of the Oslo Coalition itself that have absorbed the energies of our authors. The years since the Oslo Conference have witnessed a number of significant developments affecting freedom of religion or belief, and these have engaged our authors in countless ways. Many have vast experience in United Nations settings. Professor Theo van Boven, author of chapter 7 on the UN Commission on Human Rights, for example, has vast experience, having served for many years on various United Nations human rights bodies, including his current appointment for the Commission as Special Rapporteur on the question of torture and other cruel, inhuman or degrading treatment or punishment. Martin Scheinin, author of chapter 8 on the UN Human Rights Committee, currently serves as a member of that Committee. Manfred Nowak, co-author of chapter 6 on limitations clauses, has also served in many positions dealing with human rights in the UN system. Doudou Diene, author of chapter 9 on "UNESCO's Facilitation of Freedom of Religion or Belief," has worked in various capacities at UNESCO ever since his days as Senegal's representative to UNESCO in the 1970s. In particular, he has had many high-level assignments involving him in UNESCO dialogue projects. Many of the other authors, such as Natan Lerner and Johan van der Vyver, are well-known experts on human rights norms, both in the United Nations and other settings.

Other authors have had significant experience in other emerging institutional settings. For example, the Organization for Security and Cooperation in Europe (OSCE) has been an important energy center for freedom of religion or belief over the past five years. Norway assumed the Chairmanship of the OSCE in 1999, shortly after the Oslo Conference, allowing many of the ideas from the conference to have direct influence. Janne Haaland Matlary was State Secretary for Foreign Affairs of Norway during this period and was thus in a particularly good position to write chapter 12, in which she gives an account of how implementation of religious freedom norms could best be advanced from within the Chairmanship. Bahia Tahzib-Lie also had an insider's perspective while working at the Human Rights Division of the Human Rights and Peacebuilding Department of the Dutch Ministry of Foreign Affairs. She played a major role in organizing a seminar on "Freedom of Religion or Belief in the OSCE Region: Challenges to Law and Practice" that was sponsored by the Foreign Ministry of the Netherlands in The Hague in June 2001 in cooperation with the Romanian Chair-in-Office of the OSCE.

Another significant development over the last five years has been the work of the Advisory Panel on Freedom of Religion or Belief, created under the auspices of the OSCE's Office of Democratic Institutions and Human Rights. The Advisory Panel has emerged as a significant resource for strengthening religious freedom commitments in OSCE participating states. Several of our authors have played significant roles in this regard. Rüdiger Noll has served as overall chair for the Panel and has co-chaired the working group on conflict resolution with Bahia Tahzib-Lie. Cole Durham has served as a co-chair on legislative matters, with Karen Lord, Jeremy Gunn, and Roman Podoprigora serving with his working group. Jolanta Ambrosewicz-Jacobs has been a co-chair regarding educational issues, with Urban Gibson serving as one of the members of the working group on education.

Still another significant institutional development over the past five years was the passage of the International Religious Freedom Act in the United States. Passed just a few weeks after the Oslo Conference in 1998, this led to the creation of an office in the US State Department headed by an Ambassador-at-Large charged with responsibility for religious freedom matters, establishment of the United States Commission on International Religious Freedom, and new requirements for annual reports by the US State Department on the compliance of nations around the world with international standards governing freedom of religion or belief. This development has been controversial both within the United States and abroad, but at a minimum it has helped focus attention on religious freedom issues and, since US embassies around the world are charged with collecting information for these reports, has provided an impetus for dialogue on current issues in every country. Jeremy Gunn, who served as a principal adviser to the first Ambassador-at-Large and also as the first director of research for the Commission on International Religious Freedom, was uniquely placed to write chapter 32, which gives a more detailed picture of how the new United States institutions emerged and what they were designed to do. Tad Stahnke, author of chapter 27 on "The Right to Engage in Religious Persuasion," also has significant background with the Commission, serving as Deputy Director for Policy for the Commission as this volume goes to press.

Of course, it is not only institutions but also particular issues that have attracted the engagement of our authors. This will be described in due course. The point is that the book has benefited immeasurably from the immersion of its authors in the practical realities of building more effective mechanisms for implementing this fundamental freedom. Moreover, in large part because of direct engagement with developments in the field, the book has evolved in significant ways since it was first envisioned.

The original intention had been just to publish a selection of the conference papers presented in 1998. However, as the project developed the editors realized the need for a work with more comprehensive coverage that could serve as a consolidated reference to all aspects of freedom of religion or belief. About a year after the original conference, the idea of publishing a "deskbook" emerged. This entailed totally revamping the organization of the volume to be published and recruiting busy scholars already immersed in activities such as those described above. Active engagement continued to suggest new topics that led to expanding the scope of the volume. One of the inevitable results has been that different chapters have been completed at very different times. Between the crush of pressures on the editors and the complexity of managing a volume with so many authors from so many countries, it has simply not been possible to assure that every article could take into account all events up to a uniform cutoff date. Our sense, however, is that this is not a critical problem. Our aim has not been to provide an up-to-the-minute report on developments, but rather to provide a comprehensive picture of the full complex of ideas, applicable norms, institutional leverage points, key emerging issues, and contexts relevant to facilitating freedom of religion or belief. This the various chapters amply provide. If the lives of those working on the book had been less busy and less intensively engaged in furthering the aims of the book in practical settings, the book would no doubt have appeared earlier. We hope there will be understanding for the trade-offs we have been forced to make.

It goes without saying that the authors in this volume each have their own views, and disagree with each other on many points. In this sense, the deskbook itself has been an example of the kind of dialogue that the Oslo Coalition fosters. It is important to emphasis that the views of each of the authors are theirs alone and do not necessarily represent the views of the Oslo Coalition, the editors, or other authors. The deskbook is a collaborative project aimed at identifying core notions of freedom of religion or belief and ideas for better implementing its ideals. The deskbook responds itself to this ideal recognizing the importance of respecting the range of views held by the different authors in the volume, coming as they do from many different countries and belief traditions.

One shortcoming of the volume of which we are acutely conscious is that despite strenuous efforts, the overwhelming majority of the chapters are written by experts from the West. No one working on the project had any doubt that understanding of the issues would be deepened by interaction with experts from other parts of the world. While it has not been possible to satisfactorily address this concern within the actual pages of the book, it is anticipated that the Oslo Coalition, working with partners from other regions, will sponsor conferences and other activities designed to stimulate the kind of trans-cultural dialogue on freedom of religion or belief that has not been adequately captured in the book. Our hope, then, is that the book will be viewed as a starting point for deepened dialogue on the relevant issues, and not as an incomplete endpoint of discussion.

The Normative Core of Freedom of Religion or Belief

Before turning to a more detailed overview of the contents of this volume, it seems appropriate to identify briefly what we have come to regard as the normative core of the right to freedom of religion or belief. As we have worked with the range of issues covered by this volume, we have come to a fuller understanding of the complexity of the values involved. We understand that the issues involved arise in a host of different historical and cultural contexts, and that the institutional arrangements in any particular society will inevitably vary in many ways. But there are certain core values that will be protected and features that a regime will exhibit if freedom of religion or belief is respected. These constitute a set of minimum standards; obviously, many systems go much further in building genuine cultures of tolerance and mutual respect.

Freedom of religion or belief, in its current historical form,[13] is a universally applicable *human right* codified in international human rights instruments. At the normative level, it has been clear from the beginning of the modern human rights era that freedom of religion or belief is a *fundamental* right,[14] and indeed one of the preeminent fundamental rights. Emerging from the ashes of the Second World War, the right has been articulated most authoritatively in article 18 of both the Universal Declaration of Human Rights and the International Covenant on Civil and Political Rights. Individuals—all human beings everywhere in the world—are the primary holders and beneficiaries of this freedom; states—ideally under continual critical scrutiny by informed citizens—are the primary addressees and thus the primary holders of the correlative obligations. Beyond the religious freedom provisions of the Universal Declaration and the ICCPR, key elaborations and specifications of the human right to freedom of religion or belief are provided by, inter alia, the 1981 Declaration, the European Convention for the Protection of Human Rights and Fundamental Freedoms, the American Convention on Human Rights, the Concluding Document of the Vienna Meeting of Representatives of the Participating States of the CSCE (particularly its principles 16 and 17). The United Nations Human Rights Committee General Comment No. 22 (48) provides normative substance to article 18 of the ICCPR.

The normative core of the human right to freedom of religion or belief may be condensed to eight components:[15]

1. *Internal freedom:* Everyone has the right to freedom of thought, conscience and religion; this right includes freedom for all to have, adopt, maintain or change[16] religion or belief.[17]

---

[13] See Evans, chapter 1 of this volume.

[14] One clear sign of this is the fact that religious freedom protections are nonderogable.

[15] The key provisions drawn on are article 18 of the Universal Declaration; article 18.1 to 18.4, article 2.2 and article 4.2 of the ICCPR and article 14 of the CRC. See also the 1981 Declaration; article 9 of the ECHR; article 12 of the ACHR; article 8 of the ACHPR; and Principles 16 and 17 of the Concluding Document of the Vienna Meeting of Representatives of the Participating States of the CSCE. Component 6 differs from the other eight, in that it is implied from rather than directly stated in the express language of the relevant treaties. See note 21 below.

[16] While the notion that freedom of religion or belief includes the right to "have or adopt" a religion is undisputed, there has been considerable controversy about whether it includes the right to "change." The Universal Declaration (article 18) and major regional treaties (ECHR, art. 9[1]; ACHR, art 12[1]), as well as leading commentaries recognize that this is an integral part of freedom of religion or belief. See, e.g., John P. Humphrey, "Political and Related Rights," in ***Human Rights in International Law: Legal and Policy Issues***, ed. Theodor Meron (Oxford: Clarendon Press, 1984), 171, 179; Richard B. Lillich, "Civil Rights," in ***Human Rights in International Law: Legal and Policy Issues***, ed. Theodor Meron (Oxford: Clarendon Press, 1984), 115, 159; Manfred Nowak, ***U.N. Covenant on Civil and Political Rights, CCPR Commentary*** (Kehl/Strasbourg/Arlington: N.P. Engel, 1993), 316; Karl Josef Partsch, "Freedom of Conscience and Expression, and Political Freedoms," ***The International Bill of Rights: The Covenant on Civil and Political Rights***, ed. Louis Henkin (New York: Columbia University Press, 1981), 209, 211. Commenting on the "have or adopt" locution that was settled upon in the ICCPR in an effort to avoid controversy with Muslim countries over the word "change." The UN Human Rights Committee has observed that "the freedom to "have or to adopt" a religion or belief necessarily entails the freedom to choose a religion or belief, including, inter alia, the right to replace one's current religion or belief with another or to adopt atheistic views, as well as the right to retain one's religion or belief." General Comment 22 (48), para. 5; see also Ghanea, chapter 29, 670–75. In our view, this is tantamount to saying that freedom of religion implicitly includes the

2. *External freedom:* Everyone has the freedom, either alone or in community with others, in public or private, to manifest his or her religion or belief in teaching, practice, worship and observance.[18]
3. *Noncoercion:* No one shall be subject to coercion that would impair his or her freedom to have or to adopt a religion or belief of his or her choice.[19]
4. *Nondiscrimination:* States are obliged to respect and to ensure to all individuals within their territory and subject to their jurisdiction the right to freedom of religion or belief without distinction of any kind, such as race, color, sex, language, religion or belief, political or other opinion, national or other origin, property, birth or other status.[20]
5. *Rights of parents and guardians:* States are obliged to respect the liberty of parents, and, when applicable, legal guardians to ensure the religious and moral education of their children in conformity with their own convictions, subject to providing protection for the rights of each child to freedom of religion or belief consistent with the evolving capacities of the child.[21]
6. *Corporate freedom and legal status:* A vital aspect of freedom of religion or belief, particularly in contemporary settings, is for religious communities to have standing and institutional rights to represent their rights and interests as communities. That is, religious communities themselves have freedom of religion or belief, including a right to autonomy in their own affairs. While religious communities may not wish to avail themselves of formal legal entity status, it is now widely recognized that they have a right

---

freedom to change without using the word. Thus, while we understand that there may be disagreement, we believe that freedom of religion or belief in the present-day world necessarily includes the right to change religion or life stance. At the same time, we note that a particular religion or religious community is free to take the position that a person who has changed religion and departed from the faith may be excluded from the religious community and be the subject of religious discipline, but the individual's civil and political rights should not be reduced as a result.

[17] The HRC General Comment to article 18 of the ICCPR clarifies that, "Article 18 protects theistic, non-theistic and atheistic beliefs, as well as the right not to profess any religion or belief." The human right to freedom of religion or belief is therefore intended to equally protect believers and nonbelievers, religions and beliefs.

[18] ICCPR, art. 18(1); ECHR, art. 9(1).

[19] ICCPR, art. 18(2).

[20] Antidiscrimination norms, and in particular, norms that bar discrimination on the basis of freedom of religion or belief, pervade the key international instruments. See, e.g., UDHR, art. 2; ICCPR, art. 2(1); ECHR, art. 14 ("the rights and freedoms set forth in this Convention shall be secured without discrimination on any ground such as . . . religion"); ACHR, art. 1(1)(States Parties undertake to ensure "free and full exercise of those rights and freedoms, without any discrimination for reasons of . . . religion"). Moreover, as the UN Human Rights Committee has noted, restrictions on religious freedom "may not be imposed for discriminatory purposes or applied in a discriminatory manner." UN Human Rights Committee, General Comment No. 22(48), para. 8. Thus, the nondiscrimination norm is built into the requirement that limitations on religious freedom be "necessary" in order to be permissible under article 18 of the ICCPR. Similarly, articles 2 and 3 of the 1981 Declaration make it clear that discrimination is inconsistent with freedom of religion or belief. In general, the emphasis on nondiscrimination is so pervasive that one might almost conclude not only that non-discrimination is central to the normative core of freedom of religion or belief, but that the norm in question is *only* an equality norm. In our view, however, as emphasized by listing nondiscrimination along with the other elements of the normative core, it is vital not to forget the *freedom* dimension of the right, acknowledging of course that this is a freedom all are equally entitled to claim.

[21] ICCPR, art. 18(4); CRC, art. 14. See also chapter 24 in this volume.

to acquire legal entity status as part of their right to freedom of religion or belief and in particular as an aspect of the freedom to manifest religious beliefs not only individually, but in community with others.[22]

7. *Limits of permissible restrictions on external freedom:* Freedom to manifest one's religion or belief may be subject only to such limitations as are prescribed by law and are necessary to protect public safety, order, health, or morals or the fundamental rights of others.[23]
8. *Nonderogability:* States may make no derogation from the right to freedom of religion or belief, not even in times of public emergency.[24]

These eight components of the human right to freedom of religion or belief can be identified from amongst the complex body of mutually supporting, internationally codified, human rights norms. When applied to particular contexts and for practical

---

[22] The corporate dimension of freedom of religion or belief is analyzed in much greater depth in chapters 14 (Roland Minnerath's treatment of religious autonomy) and 15 (Cole Durham's analysis of religious association laws). See, especially, Minnerath, chapter 14, 291–93; Durham, chapter 15, 321–25, 356–57, 365–66, 370–77. The key treaty language from the ICCPR states that the right to "freedom of thought conscience and religion . . . shall include . . . freedom, either individually *or in community with others* and in public or private, to manifest his religion . . . ." ICCPR, art. 18 (emphasis added). We believe that the binding status of the corporate freedom component of the normative core is implicitly recognized in article 18, and can be deduced from existing standards, the factual necessities of protecting individual rights, and the jurisprudence that has emerged. See, e.g., Metropolitan Church of Bessarabia v. Moldova, ECtHR, App. No. 45701/99, 13 December 2001. There has been disagreement over the years as to whether freedom of religion or belief has the corporate, "group rights" dimension identified in this sixth component of the normative core. The alternative was to hold that the international instruments created only individual rights, and that to the extent religious groups were granted standing to represent rights of religious communities, they were doing so only in a derivative capacity. In many respects, this is merely a metaphysical dispute, because as a functional matter, the rights of religious communities have been consistently recognized and protected. In fact, freedom of religion or belief has collective dimensions that cannot be fully protected without an institutional rights bearer (typically with some type of corporate form or legal entity status) that can stand for and express the rights of the community. See generally chapters 16 and 17. Accordingly, we have concluded that there is a corporate dimension that belongs to the normative core of freedom of religion or belief. Even if there is a disagreement on the point whether collectivities can themselves be right bearers, there can be no doubt that there is a collective dimension to the religious freedom rights held in common by the many members of religious communities.

[23] ICCPR, art. 18(3); ECHR, art. 9(2); UN Human Rights Committee, General Comment No. 22 (48), adopted by the UN Human Rights Committee on July 20, 1993, UN Doc. CCPR/C/21/Rev.1/Add.4 (1993), reprinted in UN Doc. HRI/GEN/1/Rev.1 at 35 (1994). It is important to emphasize that while some limitations on the scope of freedom of religion or belief are necessary, they are to be construed very narrowly in order to maximize the scope of the freedom. The strictness of the constraints on limitations is analyzed in depth by Manfred Nowak and Tanja Vospernik in chapter 6 of this volume. Failure to understand the strictly limited nature of the limitations can itself pose a hazard to the freedom.

[24] ICCPR, art. 4(2). The right to freedom of religion or belief was not listed among the nonderogable rights under the ECHR, but all parties to the ECHR have subsequently ratified the ICCPR, and are thereby obligated to recognize the nonderogable character of the right to freedom of religion or belief. ECHR, art. 15(1) provides that derogations are permissible "under this Convention [only] to the extent strictly required by the exigencies of the situation, provided that such measures are not inconsistent with its other obligations under international law." Thus, freedom of religion or belief would now appear, at least indirectly, to be a nonderogable right under the ECHR. Of course, the fact that the right to freedom of religion or belief is nonderogable does not mean that limitations may not be imposed on manifestations in that limited range of circumstances where the limitations clauses of international instruments permit.

purposes, these norms may need further interpretation and elaboration. For example, early doubts about whether freedom of religion or belief necessarily implied that religious communities could be rights bearers and that these rights could have a corporate dimension have now been largely resolved in favor of the existence of such institutional rights. Within the Council of Europe and the OSCE, for example, it is now recognized with particular clarity that the right to freedom of religion and the right to freedom of association entail the right of religious communities to acquire legal entity status in order to carry out their affairs.[25] Similarly, it is clear that religious communities are to enjoy broad autonomy.[26] In addition to receiving additional elaboration, the elements of the normative core receive independent reinforcement from other human rights norms that often have vital significance for the exercise and enjoyment of religious freedom,[27] notably freedom of expression, freedom of assembly, freedom of association, and freedom of movement.[28]

While freedom of religion or belief applies to ***individual human beings,*** it also includes protection of ***community activities*** (component 2 above) and ***intergenerational relations*** (component 5 above). Religion or belief ***communities*** benefit from the protection granted community activities. States are burdened with the correlative obligation to safeguard collective as well as institutional religious group rights.[29]

As the enumeration of the core elements of freedom of religion or belief makes clear, this is a complex right, containing sub-elements that overlap with a variety of values protected by other human rights. This has led to tendencies to interpret freedom of religion or belief through the conceptual filter of other norms to which the various sub-elements of religious freedom are linked, such as equality or freedom of expression or the rule of law. Some have gone even further, recommending that freedom of religion be reduced to or supplanted by one of these other norms. These tendencies impoverish our understanding of freedom of religion or belief and fail to understand the extent to which the differing values constitute a seamless web crucial as a whole to protecting the fragile yet vital interactions of belief, action, and community that constitute belief systems.

Clearly facilitating the human right to freedom of religion or belief is not limited exclusively to providing legal protection for the eight core components identified above. Furthermore, there is more to freedom of religion or belief than human rights protection. Many countries provide additional, more concrete protections in

---

[25] See Sidiropoulos v. Greece, ECtHR, App. No. 26695/95, 10 July 1998; Hasan and Chaush v. Bulgaria, ECtHR, Application No. 30985/96, 26 October 2000; Canea Catholic Church v. Greece, ECtHR, App. No. 25528/94, 16 December 1997; Freedom and Democracy Party v. Turkey, ECtHR, App. No. 23885/94, 8 December 1999.

[26] See principle 16, Vienna Concluding Document; Hasan and Chaush v. Bulgaria, ECtHR, Application No. 30985/96, 26 October 2000; Serif v. Greece, ECtHR, App. No. 38178/97, 14 December 1999; Bessarabian Metropolitan Church v. Moldova, ECtHR, App. No. 45701/99, 13 December 2001.

[27] Most chapters in the present volume are devoted to the study of specific aspects of freedom of religion or belief, examining issues of international law, domestic legislation, administrative structures and functions, as well as particular historical, social, and cultural contexts.

[28] ICCPR articles 19, 21, 22, and 12 respectively.

[29] For the distinction between individual, collective, and institutional group rights, see chapter 4 of this volume. The rights of religious groups are spelled out in article 6 of the 1981 Declaration and in articles 16 and 17 of the Vienna Concluding Document.

their constitutional or legal orders. Such national elaborations are largely shaped by the religion-state structure, which stretches from various forms of "separation" through to establishment of religion and identification of the state with a particular religion. Countries that provide for "separation" of religion and state do so in different formats and to different effects. This can range from the benign neutrality in the United States, through various types of *laïcité* or secularism, to the harsh separation that existed in former socialist bloc regimes. Countries that allow for various degrees of "establishment" of religion may make legal provision for significant cooperation with, and financial support of, religious institutions.

The institutional configuration of religion-state relations reflects diverse histories, cultures, and political compromises. The core values protected under the auspices of freedom of religion or belief allow for a broad range of options in the ways that different states structure the relationship with religion, belief communities, and individual believers.[30] However, there is a core set of values, including at least the eight identified above, that constitute the ***minimum*** requirements for a just society and for protection of the universal right to freedom of religion or belief.

The large majority of the world's nations, including those containing the overwhelming majority of the world's population, have ratified the key international instruments affirming this right. Even if this were not the case, however, the right to freedom of religion or belief is so fundamental and so widely accepted that it is generally held to be protected as part of customary international law.[31]

---

[30] See UN Human Rights Committee, General Comment 22 (48), para. 9.

[31] See, e.g., Philip Alston, "The Universal Declaration at 35: Western and Passé or Alive and Universal," *The Review of the International Commission of Jurists* 31 (1983): 60, 69 (arguing that the Universal Declaration is customary law); Richard Bilder, "The Status of International Human Rights Law: An Overview," in *International Human Rights Law and Practice,* ed. James Tuttle (Chicago: American Bar Association, 1978), 1, 8 (arguing that the Universal Declaration is customary law); Derek Davis, "The Evolution of Religious Freedom as a Universal Human Right: Examining the Role of the 1981 United Nations Declaration on the Elimination of all Forms of Intolerance and of Discrimination Based on Religion or Belief," *BYU Law Review* (2002): 217, 230 (arguing that the 1981 Declaration is customary law); Louis Henkin, *The Age of Rights* (New York: Columbia University Press, 1990), 19 (arguing that the Universal Declaration is customary law); John Humphrey, *No Distant Millennium: The International Law of Human Rights* (Paris: UNESCO, 1989), 155 (arguing that the Universal Declaration is customary law); John Humphrey, "The International Bill of Rights: Scope and Implementation," *William and Mary Law Review* 17 (1976): 527, 529 (arguing that the Universal Declaration is customary law); Richard B. Lillich, "Civil Rights," in *Human Rights in International Law: Legal and Policy Issues,* ed. Theodor Meron (Oxford: Clarendon Press, 1984), 115, 116 (arguing that the Universal Declaration is customary law); A. H. Robertson and J. G. Merrills, *Human Rights in the World,* 3d ed. (Manchester: Manchester University Press, 1989), 96 (arguing that the Universal Declaration is customary law); Louis B. Sohn, "The Human Rights Law of the Charter," *Texas International Law Journal* 12 (1977): 129, 133 (arguing that the Universal Declaration is customary law); Bahiyyih G. Tahzib, *Freedom of Religion or Belief: Ensuring Effective International Legal Protection* (Boston: Martinus Nijhoff, 1996), 184–85 (arguing that the 1981 Declaration is customary law); Patrick Thornberry, *International Law and the Rights of Minorities* (Oxford: Clarendon Press, 1991), 237–38 (arguing that the Universal Declaration is customary law); Humphrey Waldock, "Human Rights in Contemporary International Law and the Significance of the European Convention," *The European Convention of Human Rights* (Brit. Inst. Int'l & Comp. L.) (Ser. No. 5, 1965): 1, 15 (arguing that the Universal Declaration is customary law). See also Hurst Hannum, "The Status of the Universal Declaration of Human Rights in National and International Law," *Georgia Journal of International and Comparative Law* 25 (1995/1996): 287, 317–52 (summarizing statements of constituents of several states and international bodies as well as influential authors holding that the Universal Declaration of Human Rights is customary law).

Despite broad acceptance of international norms affirming freedom of religion or belief, experience at the level of implementation has born sad testament to the challenges of effectively protecting this right. Egregious violations remain all too common:

- the genocide of religious groups
- the incarceration and punishment of individuals primarily for reasons of religion and conscience
- the abuse of antiterrorism and national security laws to suppress religious minorities across the continents
- discrimination and attacks on new religious movements
- the incitement of hatred along religious lines—particularly Islamophobia and anti-Semitism

Of course, not all recurrent denials of this freedom are of the order of those endangering life or other extreme violations. The spectrum of discrimination and intolerance in the field of religion or belief is vast. Stringent registration laws, for example, can severely restrict the activities of groups, as can unwarranted interference in the internal organization of communities by government officials. Barriers to the religious education of children hinder the conveyance of the belief to the next generation and may continue the wider public's ignorance about the particular group involved. Discrimination can severely impact all areas of life for individual believers as well as the group as a whole, and may reveal itself in a variety of avenues such as political life, employment, and legal access. Whereas such denials may not seem to "qualify" as being particularly severe human rights violations, as compared with torture, disappearances, and the like, they can lead to longstanding grievances, simmering under the surface, and possibly later erupt into violence. It is of critical importance that such issues are dealt with effectively and early by governments acting in good faith towards their human rights obligations. Of course, different levels of violation deserve different levels of response. Dealing with other rights violations can sometimes take higher priority. But care must be taken to assure that in prioritizing other urgent matters, religious freedom issues are not allowed to slip off the list altogether. While protection of religious rights sometimes appears to be a back-burner item, it is one that we neglect at our peril, because of the high risk that simmering tensions today may boil over tomorrow.

Overview of the Book

We turn now to the task of providing an introduction to the structure and contents of the book. As noted above, this volume was reconceived early in its history as a "deskbook." That is, the aim was to produce a work that could serve as a comprehensive resource for anyone seriously engaged in the task of facilitating freedom of religion or belief. With this in mind, our objective here is to provide a guide to the contents of the book, and to suggest some of the ways it might most effectively be used.

Before proceeding to a chapter-by-chapter analysis, a few words on the broad structure of the volume may be helpful. The book brings together many voices, coming from different religious, national, and cultural backgrounds, each speaking for themselves and often disagreeing with others in the book. It goes without saying that each author is responsible solely for his or her own contribution.

The "deskbook" vision has shaped the book in several ways that are reflected in the broad divisions of the book. In the first place, it meant that we wanted the book to be useful as a practical matter for human rights workers. That meant that our aim was not so much to unravel new theoretical reflections on this subject as to provide a sound understanding of the ideas, institutions, and issues that shape the field. At the same time, this objective required some introduction to the historical and philosophical issues involved. Our solution was to call on two individuals with strong activist credentials—Malcolm Evans and Tore Lindholm—who could describe the "Origins and Grounds of Freedom of Religion or Belief" in part I of the book in a way that connects directly with practical issues.

The second key element of the deskbook is a thorough exposition of the relevant "International Norms and Institutions." The idea behind this part of the book was that serious human rights workers need access to high-level commentaries on the array of relevant norms and on the international institutions charged with implementing these norms. Thus, part II aspires to guide the reader through the complex web of norms, institutions, and procedures set up to protect freedom of religion or belief. The volume of relevant international legal materials is expanding to the point of being unmanageable. From this perspective, Natan Lerner's chapter provides an immensely useful overview of the entire body of relevant norms. This is supplemented by Johan van der Vyver's analysis of the relationship of religious freedom norms to other human rights and by Llewellyn and Condé's chapter addressing the often-overlooked implications of religious freedom rights for international humanitarian law and the emerging field of international criminal law. These contributions are then rounded out by the chapter by Nowak and Vospernik on permissible limitations. In many ways this is one of the most crucial chapters in the volume, because for the most part, encroachments on religious freedom occur not because government officials question the existence of the right to freedom of religion or belief, but because they (erroneously) believe that the particular limitation they impose is justified.

Discussion of the substantive norms is then augmented by a series of chapters describing the array of institutions charged with implementing freedom of religion or belief. Accordingly, there are chapters written by leading experts on the United Nations Commission on Human Rights (van Boven), the UN Human Rights Committee (Scheinin), UNESCO (Diene), the Council of Europe, including the European Court of Human Rights, (Martínez-Torron and Navarro-Valls), and the Organization for Security and Cooperation in Europe (Gibson, Lord, and Matlary). A major objective in this part is to provide background on the institutional and procedural levers available at the international level to help facilitate better protection of freedom of religion or belief.

Part III of the book turns to a series of key issues concerning the relationship of religion and the state. This section opens with José de Sousa e Brito's analysis of the importance of protecting conscientious objection not only in military, but also in a variety of other contexts in which conscience confronts the state. This is followed by a general essay on the importance of religious autonomy by Archbishop Roland Minnerath, and a more detailed chapter by Cole Durham analyzing the implications of religious freedom norms for religious association laws. These two chapters are particularly significant for the legal issues faced by religious institutions in their interactions with the state. Lee Boothby then addresses the unique issues that arise in state-controlled environments such as prisons, hospitals, and the military. This is followed by Roman Podoprigora's analysis of the constraints religious freedom norms impose on exercise of official discretion in granting or denying approvals for various types of religious activity. Finally, Jean Baubérot describes one of the major models of the place of religion in public life: the French laicist approach. Each of these chapters explores crucial dimensions of the interface between religion and the state. Each national order invariably has its own institutional arrangements; the deskbook is designed to illuminate the key problem areas, noting where international human rights norms leave flexibility and drawing attention to areas where they set minimum standards.

Part IV recognizes that changing attitudes toward gender, family, and children are raising a host of new issues for freedom of religion and belief. While our treatment of these questions cannot hope to be exhaustive, the authors of chapters 19–24 provide an impressive opening to dialogue in this area. Bahia Tahzib-Lie sketches the range of issues that "dissenting women" face. Özlem Denli's essay on the Islamic scarf controversy, while focused on Turkey, raises broader issues relevant to similar controversies in other parts of the world. Juliet Sheen, who helped identify a range of women's issues in her work as co-editor with Kevin Boyle of the world report on freedom of religion or belief,[32] analyzes burdens that women face in asserting their rights to freedom of religion or belief. Ursula King brings years of academic experience to her study of "Hinduism and Women." Similarly, Kari Elisabeth Børresen brings distinguished academic credentials to her critique of the normative status of women within her own (Roman Catholic) tradition. Finally, Geraldine van Bueren, writing as both an academic and as an active participant in the framing of children's rights instruments, provides a particularly helpful view of the belief rights of children.

No set of chapters can be fully representative of the range of issues percolating in this area. Our hope was that we could raise some of the salient issues, remembering that while women and children have sometimes suffered most at the hands of religion, in many settings they are also its largest class of devotees, its greatest beneficiaries, and in the case of women, its most ardent defenders. Here, perhaps more than in any other area, there is an urgent need for religious freedom to succeed in its above-noted task of protecting religion and its potential for good while filtering out religion's negative hazards and finding sensitive ways to facilitate accommodation of religious and cultural differences within a broad framework of interpersonal and intercultural respect.

Part V deals with two major areas of particular sensitivity for freedom of religion or belief: issues concerning religious "sects" or "cults," and issues regarding religious persuasion. Each of the chapters in this part of the book is connected more or less directly to questions concerning the right to "have or adopt" or to "change" religion. The chapters on "sects" and "cults" are ultimately about the protections that accrue to those who "have or adopt" a religion that may appear unfamiliar or strange. In recent years, there has been a substantial volume of legislation prompted by fears based on stereotypical images of new religious movements. This trend has been paralleled in many ways by legislation prompted by fears of "religious extremists" from

---

[32] Kevin Boyle and Juliet Sheen, eds., *Freedom of Religion or Belief: A World Report* (London: Routledge, 1997).

various traditions. While events of recent years leave no doubt that genuine problems exist, legal reactions are often overbroad, imposing constraints on legitimate groups that are inconsistent with religious freedom norms. Eileen Barker, an internationally acclaimed sociologist and one of the world's leading experts on these phenomena, helps to dispel some of the myths and stereotypes. For their part, Fautré, Garay, and Nidegger provide a case study in the French-speaking countries of Europe. These chapters are vital because the real test of religious freedom always comes down to how the unfamiliar and unpopular groups are treated. Tolerance for the popular is no challenge.

The remaining chapters in part V focus on long-running debates on the right to engage in religious persuasion on the one hand and issues of protecting religious and cultural identity on the other. Tad Stahnke's chapter provides a helpful analytic framework for sorting out the differences between protected witnessing of one's faith and "improper proselytism," arguing in the end for broad protections for religious persuasion. Makau Mutua, on the other hand, is sharply critical of most traditional missionary efforts, viewing them as inappropriate assertions of cultural power that undermine traditional cultural identities. Nazila Ghanea focuses on the Muslim doctrine proscribing apostasy from Islam. These issues are vital to an understanding of current international religious freedom norms, because they constitute one of the critical areas of disagreement concerning the scope of religious freedom norms: whether religious freedom includes the right to "change [one's] religion or belief," as many in the Christian world believe and as stated in the Universal Declaration of Human Rights and the European and American Conventions, or whether it would constitute impermissible apostasy (at least in the case of conversion from Islam). It may be possible to reach greater consensus on this point once political loyalty and religious affiliation are clearly differentiated, since within contemporary Muslim discourse, new approaches to religious freedom are being discussed that recognize that apostasy is primarily a religious issue that triggers religious but not necessarily civil and political sanctions. Such approaches leave choice of religion to the individual where change of religion is not taken as entailing disloyalty to the state.

Part VI focuses on a variety of "Contexts for Facilitating Freedom of Religion or Belief." What ties the chapters in this section together is that each addresses practical settings and practical methodologies that are important for ameliorating implementation of religious freedom norms. Several of the chapters focus on bridge building and dialogue between religious communities (i.e., those of Archbishop Anastasios, Leonard Swidler, and the Norwegian coauthors Inge Eidsvåg, Tore Lindholm, and Barbro Sveen). Rüdiger Noll addresses the increasingly significant positive role that religion can play in conflict situations. Babu Gogineni and Lars Gule, as leaders of humanist organizations, draw attention to the "or belief" half of "freedom of religion or belief," emphasizing the rights of nonreligious belief and life-stance groups. Chapters discussed earlier dealing with education (by Jolanta Ambrosewicz-Jacobs and Ingvill Plesner) and the mechanisms associated with the United States International Religious Freedom Act (by Jeremy Gunn) also belong to this "Contexts" section. Finally, Elizabeth Sewell's chapter provides useful insights into ways that NGOs can facilitate freedom of religion or belief.

The conclusion and the appendices constitute an important final element of the "deskbook" plan. The conclusion draws together many of the practical recommendations made throughout the volume. We hope it will stand as an open-ended agenda for continued action. Key documents and provisions are provided in Appendices A and B, along with a list of relevant treaties in Appendix C. The book would be impossibly long if the full texts of all relevant documents were included, but sufficient information is provided to make it easy to access relevant texts online at websites such as www.religlaw.org. Relevant General Comments of the UN Human Rights Committee are included in Appendices D and E, followed by the text of the Oslo Declaration on Freedom of Religion or Belief in Appendix F. Finally, we hope that the list of NGOs working in the field provided by Appendix G (including contact information) will make a contribution to networking among those working to facilitate freedom of religion or belief.

In what follows a more detailed guide to the contents of the various chapters is provided. This follows the structure of the book's table of contents. We highlight contents of the various chapters not so much to summarize them as to suggest reasons why someone working in the field might find each chapter helpful.

Part I: Origins and Grounds of Freedom of Religion or Belief

The historical overview provided in the opening chapter by *Malcolm Evans* helps to place all the other chapters in the book in historical perspective. The timescale considered in his chapter stretches from the Roman Empire to the present. But the real focus is on identifying different major phases in the international law of freedom of religion or belief. Evans shows that concern by political authorities for religious freedom is much older than the modern state system. For the most part, religious freedom has not been promoted as an end in itself, but as a technique for preserving stability, limiting conflict, or as a pretext for intervention. Through much of history, granting religious freedom has been used as means of avoiding conflict, whereas limiting its enjoyment has been a source of conflict. In general, there has been a shift away from the practice of attempting to ensure civil harmony by keeping people of different religions apart towards providing a common institutional framework for facilitating peaceful coexistence. This is most evident in the modern regime of internationally codified universal human rights.

After tracing some of the failures of premodern experience, such as the role reversal that transformed Christianity from a victim of persecution into a source of state intolerance, Evans identifies three major configurations in the modern evolution of freedom of religion: (1) the "*cuius regio, eius religio*" model, in which the prince determined the religion of his people; (2) the minority protection model, in which international treaties provided protection for religious minorities; and (3) the contemporary human rights model. Each of these fundamental approaches to religious freedom is portrayed in significant detail.

Somewhat surprisingly, in light of the fact that the historical progression associated with the historical succession of the three approaches is toward strengthening of individual religious freedom protections, Evans argues that the past fifty years have witnessed a diminution of the political importance attached to achieving freedom of religion or belief. His point is that in contrast to the early days during and immediately after World War II, when the foundational role of religious freedom was clearly recognized, freedom of religion or belief tends now to be seen simply as one of many protections tucked away in the panoply of human rights. Moreover, its strength is further weakened by the fact that its protections are balanced against a welter of other social values. The claim that religious freedom values are eroding is surely a controversial point, and no doubt intended as such, but it is the kind of question that historical perspective entitles an author to ask. Has the right to freedom of religion or belief been subject to steady attrition, or to overshadowing as other rights have been built up? Has there been a "relativizing" political approach to religion? Are these trends a reflection of secularization and of shifting perceptions of the role of religion in society that could be reversed as religion becomes more salient? What do the long-term trends mean for the ability of freedom of religion or belief to meet the challenges of an increasingly pluralized world?

Tore Lindholm's chapter on *Philosophical and Religious Justifications of Freedom of Religion or Belief* attempts to answer at least one of the questions left by Evans' historical chapter: is religious freedom relegated to playing an essentially passive role in acknowledging and perhaps sanctifying the relativizing of values that pervades our age? Or can it provide social structures within which deeply divided worldviews can live together? In order for the latter option to be a possibility, it is vital to be able to elucidate public justification(s) of the universally applicable human right to freedom of religion or belief in a religiously, philosophically, and culturally division-prone world. A solution to this problem needs to go beyond being intellectually well-grounded and socially stable. It must facilitate *both* mutual respect and solidarity across religious and life-stance divides *and* the unflinching integrity of each normative tradition. For Lindholm, the task of philosophy in approaching this challenge is "meta-facilitation" of freedom of religion carried out by assuming the role of a Lockean "under-labourer" tasked with clearing conceptual ground rather than that of the Platonic "philosopher-king." In Lindholm's view, the major contemporary approaches to the dilemmas of religious plurality, difference, and conflict—traditional half-hearted toleration, religious relativism or skepticism, salvific pluralism, privatization or marginalization of religious commitment, and exclusion of religion from the public square (whether by strident laicist politics or by a hegemonic secularist culture)—are all found wanting. Lindholm's alternative is to draw on the emerging worldwide public commitment to human dignity as a shared focus for overlapping justification of freedom of religion or belief. Arguing the case for an expressly pluralist approach, he contends that the challenge is for every life stance (whether religious or secular) to generate and publicize espousals of the human right to freedom of religion or belief by embracing the doctrine of inherent dignity while remaining well-grounded in the heartland of their particular normative traditions. Once our differing, perhaps even incompatible, *justificatory platforms* are publicly recognized to converge in stable and internally legitimate support of this *justificandum*, prudentially based toleration will no longer be seen to suffice, and the inadequate halfway houses posed by relativism, skepticism, salvific pluralism, privatization, or exclusivist secularism will no longer be compelling ways out of the dilemmas of religious and life-stance difference. The dynamics of *overlapping justification* (as opposed to mere overlapping consensus) make it possible for one group to come to understand and trust another group's commitment to freedom of religion or belief and mutual respect, even if the premises of the justification are not totally shared. This in turn makes it possible to achieve "mutual respect with uncompromised integrity."

Lindholm's argument in this short form sounds abstract, but in fact it is enlivened with historical, sociological, and theological considerations, drawing on many of the great pioneers in articulating particular religious groundings for the universal value of religious freedom, from Emperor Ashoka to Pope John XXIII. In the spirit of contributing to the practical aims of the deskbook, the chapter concludes with a section advocating the priority of cooperation across religious divides as a means for the realization of a common commitment to—and enjoyment of—the human right to freedom of religion or belief.

Part II: Freedom of Religion or Belief: International Norms and Institutions

Natan Lerner's chapter offers a comprehensive overview of *The Nature and Minimum Standards of Freedom of Religion or Belief* in international law. He traces the evolution of this freedom in the array of international instruments that have been adopted, from the Universal Declaration in 1948 to the end of the twentieth century. Of the three aspects of freedom of religion or belief encapsulated in article 18 of the Universal Declaration ([i] the *forum internum*, [ii] conversion and proselytizing and [iii] the *forum externum*), Lerner focuses most of his attention on the latter, for the obvious reason that manifestations of religion are most likely to face limitations in practice. The ICCPR is highlighted as the only binding treaty applicable worldwide that specifically and coherently protects religious rights. For this reason, Lerner devotes particular attention to article 18 and emphasizes the need to pay close attention to the UN Human Rights Committee's General Comment 22, which interprets this key provision on freedom of religion or belief. He also provides a valuable analysis of the 1981 Declaration, which he describes as being ambitious in its achievement, imprecise in a number of respects, but "reasonably good" in its text, and amounting to "a very positive step" overall. The balance of the chapter surveys regional and other international documents bearing on freedom of religion or belief. As a practical matter, Lerner's chapter is particularly useful in providing an overview of the proliferating set of documents that codify international religious freedom norms. Despite the seeming abundance of international instruments, Lerner contends that there is still a strong need to *better* protect religious groups from discrimination, persecution, and other violations of freedom of religion or belief.

Johan van der Vyver's chapter undertakes the complex task of analyzing *The Relationship of Freedom of Religion or Belief Norms to Other Human Rights.* This includes examining both areas where religious freedom and other human rights are mutually supportive and overlap, and areas where they can come into conflict. The overlaps pose few problems: freedom of expression and association, for example, provide "double protection" in areas such as religious persuasion and the right to acquire legal entity status. The areas of conflict are more controversial. Van der Vyver explores a rich range of examples from around the world illustrating the different types of conflicts with other rights. The chapter repays reading simply for the plenitude of situations it addresses. But the chapter goes further in putting forward a number of principles that are pertinent to the resolution of such conflicts.

At the outset van der Vyver addresses the potential conflicts that arise from internal disputes within a religious community. Among other things, he notes the significance of institutional group rights to freedom of religion vesting in religious institutions themselves, as opposed to collective group rights, which vest in the individual members of a group.[33] This has significant implications for the rights of religious institutions to religious autonomy and to legal entity status, as described in more detail in chapters 14 and 15 (by Minnerath and Durham, respectively). In this domain, he invokes principles drawn from the general analytic structure of "sphere sovereignty," which recognizes the exclusive competence of religious institutions to determine their own organization structure, dogma, procedures, activities, and internal disciplinary measures. To this he adds the state responsibility to respect the self-determination of religious communities. Whereas the principle of sphere sovereignty is described as an "institutional group right," which vests in a social institution, the right to self-determination is described as a "collective group right," which is afforded to individual persons belonging to that category and can be exercised separately and jointly with others of that group.

The distinction between collective and institutional rights is important and enlightening. However, couching that discussion in terms highly reminiscent of the right of peoples to self-determination might cause misunderstanding. The right of peoples to self-determination, addressed in the parallel articles 1 of the ICCPR and the ICESCR, addresses rather different matters: its *holders* are peoples and the *goods* protected by the peoples' rights to self-determination are external independence and internal democratic self-rule. Of course, van der Vyver does not intend to elevate religious communities to political peoples, nor to accord them the right to political independence (i.e., secession), nor to impose internal democratic self-rule on religious organizations that have other modes of internal ordering. The basic principle is surely sound; it may be helpful to use the language of religious autonomy to avoid confusion, but van der Vyver may believe this sounds too much like an institutional right, when it is the partially overlapping collective dimension of an associational right that he wants to bring out.

Another area van der Vyver focuses on is the interaction of equality norms with religious freedom. Often, of course, equality norms reinforce religious freedom protections. Indeed, as noted above, nondiscrimination norms are part of the normative core of freedom of religion or belief. Van der Vyver takes a strong position in this regard against privileged relationships of particular religious communities with the state, contending that such privileging discriminates against the religions and beliefs that are thereby disadvantaged, condescends towards those it "tolerates," and interferes in the internal affairs of the supposedly privileged religion.[34] This position will clearly be controversial in the many countries that continue to have official state churches or other strong forms of cooperation with particular religious denominations. Benefited groups are likely to be critical of the position; smaller and less popular groups are likely to concur. The significant point is that the strength of the equality norm in contemporary society imposes a burden of justification where privileging occurs.

[33] Van der Vyver, chapter 4, 91.
[34] Ibid., 106–07

Yet there are other situations in which religious freedom protections may collide with equality norms. Examples cited by van der Vyver include discrimination by some religions against women and against gays and lesbians.[35] Van der Vyver appears to assume that sphere sovereignty will protect doctrinally based internal practices,[36] but absent that, he appears to endorse placing equality ahead of liberty: "countries founded on libertarian principles which permit freedom of religion or belief to trump individual rights founded on human dignity and equality are at odds with the international standards of human rights protection."[37] The tension between liberty and equality is well known, and can have particularly significant ramifications for freedom of religion. Not everyone will accept van der Vyver's position on these issues, but his chapter is a significant starting point for discussion.

A final section of van der Vyver's chapter deals with permissible limitations on freedom of religion or belief. Here his analysis is conceptual, focusing on (1) "inherent limitations," (2) limitations determined by the rights and freedoms of others, and (3) limitations "in the general interest." What van der Vyver provides in this section is analysis of the type that is more typical at the level of the constitutional law of a state, in contrast to Nowak and Vospernik's discussion in chapter 6 of limitation clause issues at the level of international norms.

The next chapter, by *David Llewellyn* and *Victor Condé* considers an area which has received little scholarly attention thus far—that of *Freedom of Religion or Belief under International Humanitarian Law and International Criminal Law*. The authors argue for the fundamental importance of this matter, because not only does religious need and interest escalate during times of war or armed conflict, but religion may be deeply implicated in the violence, and solutions may be impossible without respecting religious rights. To make their point, the authors compare human rights norms regarding freedom of religion or belief with corresponding norms under international humanitarian and international criminal law. Despite the very different origins and purposes of these three areas of international law, the relevant norms reveal a close degree of correlation and resemblance. As a practical matter, the chapter underscores an idea that is often expressed, but that seldom finds more compelling vindication: freedom of religion or belief is nonderogable under all circumstances, from peace time to war to armed conflicts to post-war situations.

It is through the interplay of the principle of freedom of religion or belief and its restrictions that the *actual* scope of freedom of religion or belief is determined. Thus, the chapter on *Permissible Restrictions on Freedom of Religion or Belief* by *Manfred Nowak* and *Tanja Vospernik* is particularly critical for the volume. The authors undertake a rigorous analysis of the typical limitation clauses found in international instruments. Focusing on issues of "brainwashing" and religious persuasion, they raise questions about the borders of the *forum internum*, which is supposed to be totally exempt from limitations. They then work through the various legitimating grounds for imposing constraints on manifestations of religion listed in article 18 of the ICCPR: protection of "public safety, order, health, or morals or the fundamental rights and freedoms of others."

---

[35] Ibid., 114.
[36] Ibid., 115.
[37] Ibid., 120.

Particularly noteworthy is the treatment of "public order." This is often taken to be the most expansive justification for imposing limitations on freedom of religion, since many assume that what is intended is the broad notion of "*ordre public*" in French law used to describe a generalized sense of prevailing public policies. The authors point out that both the English and French versions of the ICCPR make it clear that in context, the phrase "public order" is intended to justify incursions on religious freedom only in the narrow sense of preventing public disturbances.[38] "Morals" as a ground of limitation is considered to be the least clear and most controversial of the grounds, because of the risk that one religion-based moral principle may be invoked to override another religious belief.

Moving beyond the formal legitimating factors, Nowak and Vospernik focus attention on nondiscrimination as an additional factor that is vital if a limitation is to be justified. As noted by the UN Human Rights Committee, discriminatory treatment invalidates a finding that a particular limitation is necessary, even if it falls within an otherwise legitimate category. Unfortunately, genuine neutrality is all too rare a commodity and the "differential" treatment meted out often amounts to outright discrimination.

A final practical critique of the handling of limitations clauses is that international and regional human rights bodies are often too deferential in assessing state limitations. The European Court, for example, has sometimes afforded governments an unnecessarily broad margin of appreciation. More could no doubt have been said about the fact that even if one of the permissible grounds for legislation is present, it is still necessary to demonstrate that the limitation in question is strictly necessary and proportionate. But in general the authors do an excellent job of stressing the narrowness of the grounds for permissible limitations, thereby facilitating protection of a broader sphere of freedom of religion or belief.

The next chapter, *Theo van Boven's* essay on *The United Nations Commission on Human Rights and Freedom of Religion or Belief*, launches the set of six chapters in the deskbook addressing the institutional mechanisms available to foster protection of the right. The author identifies three phases in the work of the Commission with respect to freedom of religion or belief: (i) standard setting from 1946–55, (ii) the (painstaking) elaboration of these standards from 1960–81, and (iii) the implementation phase from 1986 to the present. Van Boven describes in detail the evolving and growing role of the Commission's Special Rapporteur on Religious Intolerance, since 2001 referred to as the Special Rapporteur on Freedom of Religion or Belief. In van Boven's view, the Special Rapporteur has been "the main actor" in the recent contribution of the Commission to this field. The means at the Rapporteur's disposal have included the preparation of annual and interim reports to the UN regarding the state of freedom of religion or belief, the setting up of an urgent appeals procedure to respond to more serious violations, the carrying out of *in-situ* visits to observe the phenomenon of intolerance more closely and to pursue dialogue with relevant parties, and a visit follow-up procedure to pursue the matters arising from the *in-situ* visits. In the attempt to contribute to the elimination of intolerance in this field, the Rapporteur has identified particular priority issues (most notably, education for tolerance), identified categories of violations, and also undertaken the initiative of visiting major religious communities and institutions.

---

[38] Nowak and Vospernik, chapter 6, 152.

While van Boven is positive about the efficacy of the activities of the Special Rapporteur, he is critical of the Commission as a whole. Despite being "the central human rights policy organ of the United Nations," the Commission fails to deliberate constructively on freedom of religion or belief. Its annual resolution on religious intolerance tends to be repetitive. Insufficient time is given to the presentation of the Special Rapporteur's report and scant attention is paid to it in subsequent discussion under the relevant religious intolerance item on the Commission's agenda. To van Boven it is clear that the Special Rapporteur makes a more "substantial and coherent contribution to the cause of freedom of religion" than the Commission itself. The Special Rapporteur is therefore described as being "the investigative, intellectual, and operational arm of the Commission." Van Boven urges the Commission to make a more substantial and coherent contribution to the area of freedom of religion or belief, to more seriously consider the reports of the Special Rapporteur, and to further strengthen his mandate. Despite limitations on the Special Rapporteur's resources, his position remains one of the most significant channels as a practical matter to bring religious freedom problems to the attention of the United Nations.

In the next chapter, *The Human Rights Committee and Freedom of Religion or Belief, Martin Scheinin* tackles the second key international human rights body in the United Nations system. Scheinin reminds us that article 18 is not the only relevant provision of the ICCPR regarding freedom of religion or belief. Articles 2(1), 4(2), 24(1), 26, and 27 are also relevant in offering further protection and clarifying nonderogation and nondiscrimination. Scheinin looks at the three primary functions of the Human Rights Committee in turn, describing how each of these has been used to advance freedom of religion or belief. First, he analyzes the impact of the Committee in considering periodic state reports. Second, he notes that the Committee has had significant influence through its General Comments. The most significant of these in the field of freedom of religion or belief has unquestionably been its General Comment 22, providing what amounts to an official interpretation and elaboration of the meaning of article 18 of the ICCPR. Thirdly and finally, he assesses the case law emerging from individual complaints alleging violation of freedom or religion or belief. Although this case law remains sparse and underdeveloped in Scheinin's view, the resources in this area may be richer than appears at first blush, since related issues have been explored in connection with other provisions of the ICCPR. Overall, the Committee has special significance in relation to freedom of religion or belief because its jurisdiction is universal and its procedures are sufficiently flexible for it to be able to deal with the entire range of religious freedom issues.

Doudou Diene's chapter, *UNESCO's Facilitation of Freedom of Religion or Belief,* considers an institution that contributes in significant ways to real-world cultivation of tolerance, but is sometimes overlooked because its role is less legalistic and less focused on the vindication of rights. UNESCO's emphasis has been on intercultural dialogue and, more particularly, on interreligious dialogue. This is a reflection of the renewed recognition of the importance that religions and spiritual traditions have in addressing the essential questions of our time. The recent reemphasis of such matters signals a return to the most fundamental impetus behind the founding of UNESCO—that it is "in the minds of men that the defenses of peace must be constructed." Against this background, Diene outlines the relevant UNESCO declarations, activities, and projects that help foster effective implementation of the ideals of religious freedom. Through these initiatives, UNESCO has tried to reinforce the value of interaction, the experience of cultural and spiritual proximity, and the acknowledgement of pluralism, each of which contribute to the overall facilitation of freedom of religion or belief.

Turning from the United Nations to the most effective of the regional human rights systems, we have the chapter of *Javier Martínez-Torrón* and *Rafael Navarro-Valls* on *The Protection of Religious Freedom in the System of the Council of Europe.* The central focus is on the European Convention for the Protection of Human Rights and Fundamental Freedoms, and the associated European Court of Human Rights, located in Strasbourg. The Court, which now has jurisdiction over roughly 800,000,000 people, has become the premier human rights tribunal in the world. In contrast with so many other human rights institutions, which are essentially "soft law" institutions, the Court is in the relatively unique position among international bodies of being able to issue binding and enforceable decisions. With this in mind, it is surprising and perhaps a little disappointing that no cases were decided by the Court squarely under the religion provision of the European Convention (article 9) until 1993. A number of cases were decided by the European Commission of Human Rights, pursuant to the older procedure whereby the Commission filtered cases going to the Court, but none were decided by the Court itself. Particularly since 1998, however, when the new court structure and procedures went into effect,[39] the volume of case law on religion issues has been steadily increasing. This is important not only for those within the jurisdiction of the Court, but for the world at large, because the provision the Court is interpreting (article 9 of the ECHR) is almost exactly parallel to the key provisions of article 18 of the ICCPR, and the Court's decisions are an extremely credible source of persuasive authority on human rights issues.

The chapter on the Council of Europe is thus extremely important because of the overview it provides of the Court's burgeoning article 9 jurisprudence. While the primary focus of the chapter is on this case law, the authors do include a section on initiatives of the Council of Europe's Parliamentary Assembly and Committee of Ministers,[40] the most interesting of which relate to new religious movements. The ultimate outcome of these deliberations was a recommendation that called for the establishment of "information centers on 'groups of a religious, esoteric or spiritual nature,'" but at the same time urged governments "to use the normal procedures of criminal and civil law against illegal practices carried out in the name" of such groups.[41]

After a brief description of the structure and procedure of the Court, the authors turn to an exposition of its case law (as well as that of earlier Commission decisions). This goes into much greater depth and detail than can be repeated here, but a few of the particularly vital issues and potential problems the authors identify deserve mention.

A first major feature of the Court's jurisprudence is its implicit recognition that there is a "margin of appreciation" that defers to historically established structures of the relationship between religion and the state.[42] This is a practical recognition of the

[39] Martínez-Torrón and Navarro-Valls, chapter 10, 214.
[40] Ibid., 211–14.
[41] Ibid., 213–14.
[42] Ibid., 215.

diverse structures—ranging from states with established churches, to states with strong cooperationist regimes, to those with a strong laicist separation of church and state. As the authors state the apparent principle:

> Equality (article 14 of the European Convention) must be applied rigorously in many contexts to preserve religious freedom, but some flexibility is permissible in structuring cooperation with religious communities, particularly where failure to do so would disrupt long-established patterns and expectations. . . . In other words, article 9 of the European Convention is aimed at providing an adequate guarantee of the right to freedom of religion and belief. Its purpose, however, is not to establish certain uniform criteria for church-state relations in the Council of Europe members states nor—even less—to impose a compulsory secularism (*laïcité*).[43]

Established churches are permissible so long as membership in the official church is not mandatory. The Court has also made it clear that the sensitivities of dominant religious communities deserve respect.[44]

Turning from treatment of dominant to minority religious groups, the authors address cases interpreting the equality principle, worship, proselytism, and internal autonomy. They note a certain irony in the fact that while the wording of the European Convention tends to focus primarily on the rights of individuals, the European system has disregarded the individual dimension of freedom of religion or belief more often than its corporate dimension.[45] In part, this is the result of a much narrower interpretation of the notion of protected religious "practice" under the Convention, derived from earlier Commission decisions, than the interpretation that the UN Human Rights Committee has recommended with respect to the parallel language of the ICCPR.[46] Specifically, the Commission construed the notion of practice narrowly so that it covered only actions *manifesting* religion in the strict sense, as opposed to conduct *motivated* by religion.[47]

A second major concern with European Court case law has to do with ostensibly neutral laws that impose indirect restrictions on religious freedom.[48] The tendency to assume that neutral laws necessarily override conscience was more pronounced in the decisions of the Commission, but is a discernible trend (if not a confirmed position) in some of the decisions of the Court. In the view of the authors, the better position is that "freedom to practice one's religion or belief must be understood as protecting, in principle, every act of the individual when he obeys the dictates of his own conscience"[49]—thus offering the maximum presumptive protection under article 9(1). To the extent that limitations of this right are necessary, they must be justified under article 9(2), with the state having the burden of proof regarding the legitimacy and the necessity of any limitations. The authors find that the restrictions permitted to

[43] Ibid., 216.
[44] Ibid., 217.
[45] Ibid., 228.
[46] Ibid.
[47] Ibid., 229–30.
[48] The issue here is parallel to that raised by the much-criticized decision of the United States Supreme Court in Employment Division v. Smith, 494 US 872 (1990), which held that any neutral and general law that does not directly target a particular religious group (or groups) can override religious freedom claims.
[49] Martínez-Torrón and Navarro-Valls, chapter 10, 233.

date are much more skewed toward state initiatives, and that this has the effect of restricting manifestation of religion or belief and freedom of conscience. In their view, this may lead to a kind of secular fundamentalism or indoctrination, which can be as dangerous to pluralism and to minorities in particular as more blatant forms of religious fundamentalism.[50] They conclude that in the effort to eliminate intolerance, it is as important to avoid the dangers of "secularism-oriented intolerance" as it is to prevent "religion-oriented intolerance."[51]

The next two chapters consider the work of the Organization for Security and Cooperation in Europe ("OSCE"). Originally known as the Conference for Security and Cooperation, or the "Helsinki Process" because of its establishment pursuant to the 1975 Helsinki Final Act, the OSCE is currently the largest regional security and human rights organization in the world, with fifty-five member states in North America, Europe, and Central Asia. With respect to the OSCE, *Urban Gibson* and *Karen Lord* look at *Advancements in Standard Setting: Religious Liberty and OSCE Commitments. Janne Haaland Matlary* focuses more specifically on *Implementing Freedom of Religion in the OSCE: Experiences from the Norwegian Chairmanship.* Both chapters discuss the history, emergence, institutional structure, norms, and influence of the OSCE. OSCE standards in the field of freedom of religion or belief are particularly advanced, detailed, instructive, and precise. Gibson and Lord describe these commitments to be "by far the clearest delineation of religious liberty commitments in the international arena"[52] and argue that they serve as a universal example as they "represent the aspirations of millions who seek to worship and live freely as their conscience dictates."[53] They pay particular attention to the 1989 Vienna Concluding Document[54] and note a series of OSCE seminars and the creation of the Advisory Panel on Freedom of Religion or Belief, on which both authors have served.[55]

Acknowledging that OSCE commitments are "politically" rather than "legally binding," Matlary's chapter provides both practical insight into the internal workings of OSCE institutions and theoretical insight into the significance of the "soft power" instruments utilized in the OSCE. Her chapter is an important reminder to those working in the field of religious human rights that instruments of "soft power" can often be as effective and sometimes even more so than "hard law."[56] These instruments include persuasion, legal and political aid, as well as both open and discreet criticism. Among other things, precisely because they are not legally binding, OSCE commitments can be considerably more detailed and comprehensive than legally binding commitments, and this has substantially augmented their force. They link human rights more clearly to democracy and the rule of law and provide policy prescriptions that can help guide practical realization of religious freedom ideals.

Matlary also discusses how OSCE missions and various monitoring mechanisms come together to ensure the implementation of commitments. During the Norwegian Chairmanship of the organization in 1999, the goals of mainstreaming consideration of

---

50 Ibid., 235–36.
51 Ibid., 236
52 Gibson and Lord, chapter 11, 254.
53 Ibid.
54 Ibid., 248–51.
55 Ibid., 252–54.
56 Matlary, chapter 12, 259–61.

religious freedom into OSCE missions and highlighting the importance of freedom of religion in conflict resolution were uppermost. Matlary reports setbacks and some persistent failures in the field of religious freedom. Even so, the experience from the Norwegian Chairmanship of the OSCE bears out the case for political promotion of religious freedom through work with an array of soft power mechanisms and initiatives, and in close cooperation with religious communities, with NGOs, and with academia. In this respect, Matlary's chapter complements in interesting ways that of Elizabeth Sewell (chapter 38) on facilitating freedom of religion or belief through NGOs. The examples of how religious dialogue was used as a strategy in conflict prevention or resolution should also be of particular interest.

Part III: Freedom of Religion or Belief and the State

The next part of the deskbook addresses various key aspects of the interface between religion and the state. *Conscientious Objection*, the topic of the chapter by *José de Sousa e Brito*, has always been one of the most dramatic and crucial of these interaction points. Too often the subject of conscientious objection has been assumed to arise only in the context of objection to military service, but it can also include objection to performing abortions,[57] participating in flag ceremonies,[58] or taking oaths in the name of God.[59] Conscientious objection refers to the refusal to obey a legal duty in the name of individual conscience. Its acceptance, therefore, requires upholding the inviolability of conscience over the application of the law, thereby, in Sousa e Brito's words, transforming "the principle of tolerance, which is prior to and a social precondition of the constitutional state, into a human right."[60] While freedom of conscience is intimately related to freedom of religion or belief, the two freedoms differ according to Sousa e Brito in that only individuals can claim conscientious objection. Conscientious objection to military service is recognized as a constitutional right in some countries, whereas in others it is covered only at the statutory level, as a part of laws stipulating conditions upon which exemption from military service will be granted. Even where recognized in principle, its extension to conscientious objection based on secular ethical convictions or to selective opposition to particular wars or weaponry remains controversial. In general, a balance obviously needs to be struck between the claims of conscience and the interests of the state. But Sousa e Brito is critical of what he refers to as an "unfortunate American retrogression" that has reverted to nineteenth-century precedent and rejected intervening developments which had insisted that ordinary laws could override religious freedom only where there was a compelling state interest that could not be advanced in some less burdensome way.[61]

Archbishop *Roland Minnerath*'s chapter on *The Right to Autonomy in Religious Affairs* addresses the general right of religious communities and institutions to autonomy in structuring their own affairs. It thus elaborates one of the ideas belonging

[57] Sousa e Brito, chapter 13, 284.
[58] Ibid, 285–86.
[59] Ibid., 286. The general point that conscientious objection extends beyond military contexts is also addressed by Martínez-Torrón and Navarro-Valls, chapter 10, 232 & n. 83.
[60] Sousa e Brito, chapter 13, 274.
[61] See ibid., 289.

to the normative core of freedom of religion or belief as described earlier in this introduction. It also correlates in significant ways with the idea of sphere sovereignty elaborated in the chapter by van der Vyver.[62] Not surprisingly, then, Minnerath finds the autonomy of religious or belief communities to structure their own affairs to be "one of the crucial features of any system of freedom of religion or belief."[63] This is because the ecclesiastical or social structures of such communities are often "themselves the focus of deeply held beliefs."[64] Without this right, therefore, religious authenticity would be compromised and communal autonomy impaired. Because the religious life of individuals is generally interwoven with the broader life of a religious community, breaches of religious autonomy will violate not only collective and institutional rights, but individual rights as well.

Minnerath maintains that the boundary of religious autonomy goes "beyond matters that are strictly internal to the life of a religious community"[65] to include a broader range of the community's "own affairs"—i.e., the realm over which the state has no competence. Minnerath traces the grounds for the right to religious autonomy in the classic human rights instruments, and shows how these guarantee the corporate right of religious organizations to exist and to be protected in their internal autonomy. Through a detailed historical analysis of various models of autonomy, including a careful analysis of developments in the United States,[66] Europe,[67] and the European Court of Human Rights[68] dealing with disputes within religious communities, the author shows how autonomy has emerged as a right in both constitutional and international law. Minnerath then demonstrates how the right to autonomy applies with respect to matters of doctrine and teaching; faith and order; freedom in appointing, disciplining, and dismissing religious personnel; and the operation of charitable and educational organizations.

Cole Durham's chapter on *Facilitating Freedom of Religion or Belief through Religious Association Laws* contains an extensive analysis of the bearing of human rights norms on laws that govern the process of acquiring legal entity status. Because these laws are such a routine feature of the legal landscape of most countries, their significance from a human rights standpoint is often overlooked. But in fact, this turns out to be one of the most significant areas for facilitating freedom of religion or belief, both because difficulties at the stage of acquiring entity status through incorporation or registration can have such profound impact on the ability to exercise religious beliefs, and because this is an area in which reform is relatively easy.

One of the difficulties in this area is that while virtually all states have laws governing acquisition of legal entity status, these laws can be applied in very different ways. Countries with strong human rights records characteristically view such laws primarily as vehicles for facilitating religious freedom. The laws provide readily accessible legal forms that religious communities can use to structure their own affairs. In other countries,

[62] Van der Vyver, chapter 4, 94–99.
[63] Minnerath, chapter 14, 291.
[64] Ibid.
[65] Ibid., 292.
[66] Ibid., 296–300.
[67] Ibid., 305–09.
[68] Ibid., 309–14.

however, a "control" mentality continues to lead to restrictive applications of religious association laws. The contrast of "facilitation" and "control" orientations is a thread running through the entire chapter.

The chapter provides a comparative overview of the types of legal entities available within and across legal systems.[69] It then turns to an analysis of the implications of key international human rights norms for various features of religious association laws.[70] In effect, the chapter shows how analysis from many of the other chapters in the book is relevant to recurrent problems that emerge in the formulation and application of the basic laws governing the creation of legal entities for religious communities. The main focus in this area is on the requirements of substantive religious freedom norms.[71] However, particularly in light of the emerging recognition that freedom of association entails a right to acquire legal entity status, attention is paid to the implications of freedom of association for religious association law.[72] The relevance of several other human rights norms, including nondiscrimination, freedom from arbitrary decision making, and the right to effective remedies, is also noted.[73] The chapter then identifies a number of recurrent practical problems that arise in connection with religious association laws and need to be avoided.[74] In the overall design of the deskbook, this chapter is intended to provide a comprehensive guide to analyzing the practical problems that arise when religious association laws are being adopted or revised.

Lee Boothby looks at *Protecting Freedom of Religion or Belief in Restricted or Institutional Settings*—such as prisons, the military, and state-operated medical facilities. The focus is on the US experience of the past forty years, but the discussion is clearly of wider interest. The rights that may be compromised are most often those of manifestation of religion or belief through dress, headgear, diet, compulsion to work on holy days, or being denied the facilities for prayer or other religious practices. Boothby highlights the importance of upholding this freedom in institutional settings, as the persons concerned have a particularly acute need for the support of their beliefs, and such protection can help reinforce the objectives these various institutions strive to attain. The tensions in US case law relating to the extent to which individual beliefs should be accommodated in prison settings have largely been clarified with recent legislation. The Bureau of Prisons insists on the religious neutrality of the Bureau itself and on providing inmates of all faiths with opportunities to participate in their religious beliefs and practices (within the budgetary and security constraints of the prison system). The Congressional Religious Land Use and Institutionalized Persons Act of 2000 goes further and insists that no substantial burden be placed on religious exercise even if the burden results from a general rule, unless the government demonstrates a compelling interest and it is the least restrictive means of furthering that compelling governmental interest. To Boothby this demonstrates that toleration of religious diversity and neutrality is possible in such settings, even in a separationist system such as that of the United States.

---

[69] Durham, chapter 15, 337–47.
[70] Ibid., 347–84.
[71] Ibid., 350–66.
[72] Ibid., 366–77.
[73] Ibid., 378–84.
[74] Ibid., 384–400.

Roman Podoprigora focuses on a key interaction between religion and the state that is characteristic of (but not limited to) administrative law: *Freedom of Religion and Belief and Discretionary State Approval of Religious Activity.* Discretionary approvals can result in restrictions on registration, juristic personality, worship facilities, tax status, visas, or approval to run schools—to name just a few possibilities. Whereas these approvals may come from different bodies, often at relatively low levels, and may reflect the burdens of overworked bureaucracies rather than intentional discrimination, abuse of discretion in these areas can seriously curtail religious freedom. This is particularly true with respect to the activities of smaller and less popular communities. The author addresses a range of different types of problems: unreasonable delay, denial by inaction, and outright refusals stemming from either express or more frequently undisclosed bias. When such abuse of discretion occurs, it violates not only freedom of religion and belief, but fundamental rule of law values as well. Podoprigora argues it is essential that the discretionary authority of governments that can impede religious activities be wielded on a well-defined and principled basis. This is the only way that freedom of religion and belief can be fully assured.

In *The Place of Religion in Public Life: The Lay Approach, Jean Baubérot* explores one of the major models of the appropriate nature of the relationship between religion and the state. He explains in detail the French lay approach to the place of religion in public life. Drawing on a historical account of *laïcité* (French-style separation of church and state) over the two centuries since the French Revolution, Baubérot's chapter illustrates how deeply this historical background has molded the current place religion holds in the public sphere within France. In contrast to the United States and northern Europe, where "religion has been integral to the emergence of modernity," in France "modernity erected itself against religion."[75] The historical conflict over religion's place in French society has produced an acute sensitivity verging on allergic reaction to any reference to religion in the public sphere. Though some manifestations of traditional religion manage to avoid this reaction, the general picture in France is one in which society remains leery of religion in public space. In effect, the nineteenth-century restructuring of public institutions outside the control of religion produced a new "secular clergy" of professionals in fields such as education and medicine. While Baubérot's chapter was completed before the latest round of public debate on the Islamic scarf in France, his chapter helps contextualize French disquiet over "the veil affair." It also helps to explain attitudes toward Jehovah's Witnesses and other smaller groups. Without condoning some of the more prejudiced reactions, Baubérot indicates that these can be understood at least in part by the loss of prestige within the ranks of the "secular clergy" in areas such as education and medicine. Other aspects of the French reaction, including the rise of government subsidized anti-sect associations and the concomitant stigmatization of numerous smaller groups, no doubt stem from fear of the unknown—from "a sense of helplessness in the face of so many new sectarian movements that we do not yet understand."[76] In the end, these issues are taking on new forms as a result of new social pressures coming from increased pluralization and the heightened role of the media. These are obviously forces that are exerting a transformative influence on relations of religion, state, and society not only in France, but around the globe.

---

[75] Baubérot, chapter 18, 441.
[76] Ibid., 452.

Part IV: Women, Parents, and Children

The fourth part of the deskbook deals with a range of issues of extraordinary importance and profound controversy: the encounter of religious rights and religious vision (including all-too-human failures of vision) with the rights of women and children and the politics of gender. Some feminists, such as Juliet Sheen, believe that "[r]eligion is so heavily masculinized that the tenets and extensions of religious belief are sometimes, in and of themselves, violations of women's human rights."[77] In her view, "[a]rguments of religious liberty cannot legitimately be used to trump women's rights."[78] Others are less inclined to assume that women's rights automatically override religious freedom claims. Thus, though Kari Børresen is deeply critical of her own (Catholic) tradition on an array of sensitive issues, including ordination of women, she acknowledges that "it is certainly not a human right to be ordained a priest or a bishop. . . ."[79] This appears to imply that though the doctrinal foundation for the religious position is "perfectly unconvincing,"[80] and though she would work intensely to bring about change within her tradition, it does not automatically follow that international or national norms should be allowed to coerce change. On the other hand, there are positions such as that of Özlem Denli, who is troubled by a secularist state that disallows the wearing of religious symbols.[81] Still others are troubled by the fact that (typically secularist) concerns about religion-sourced discrimination seem so much more prevalent than (religiously based) concerns for incursions on women's right to freedom of religion or belief. Bahia Tahzib-Lie illustrates the multiple contexts in which women may respond to the call of conscience and examines which violations are specifically directed against women and which women are particularly vulnerable.[82] Because of the range of views in this area and the intensity with which such views are held, it is inevitable that various positions taken by our authors will attract sharp and differing disagreements from people holding a wide range of views. But we are convinced that the chapters in this part contribute more light than heat.

Three of the chapters look at the conflict between religion, religious rights, and women's rights in the context of major world religions: Hinduism (Ursula King), Catholicism (Kari Elisabeth Børresen), and Islam (Özlem Denli). Nazila Ghanea's chapter on apostasy belongs substantively to part V with its focus on changing beliefs, but sociologically it has much to say about problems that Muslim women in particular face in changing religion. The other chapters take a more general human rights approach: Bahia Tahzib-Lie focuses on the extent to which and circumstances under which questions of gender are directly or indirectly relevant to the area of freedom of religion or belief; Juliet Sheen talks about conflicts of women's and religious rights; and Geraldine Van Bueren discusses children's rights.

By focusing on the connecting thread of dissent, *Bahia Tahzib-Lie* is able to distill out many of the distinctive types of violations of freedom of religion or belief that women suffer, whether as dissenters within dominant religious traditions, dissenters

---

[77] Sheen, chapter 21, 513.
[78] Ibid., 521.
[79] Børresen, chapter 23, 555.
[80] Ibid.
[81] Denli, 510.
[82] Tahzib-Lie, chapter 19, 493.

from majority traditions who are affiliated with smaller religious communities, dissenters within or against minority traditions, believers in any tradition who dissent from the secularity of the state, dissenters from belief in general (i.e., nonbelievers), or female dissenters from male beliefs in the family context. Tahzib-Lie's chapter stands at the beginning of this part of the book, because in many ways it is the most general of the chapters dealing with women's issues, but the focus on the many settings of dissent helps contextualize all that follows. Among other things, this approach helps to bring out that international attention to women and religion thus far has been concerned almost exclusively with the protection of women against ***discriminatory*** religious norms and practices to the detriment of protecting their ***freedom.***

The author analyzes a variety of violations of freedom of religion or belief, drawn from both the "internal" and the "external" forum, and shows in case after case how a dissenting woman's right to freedom of religion or belief is violated through coercion and violence in both types of settings. One of the somewhat unexpected results is that "there may be a wider discrepancy between the protections afforded men and women with respect to their internal freedom than with respect to their external freedom."[83] Another important contribution is the chapter's recognition that the emerging international obligation to exert due diligence to protect individuals from violations of their human rights may have significant applications in the context of preventing coercion and violence against the religious freedom rights of dissenting women.[84] The due diligence principle is especially important in this context, because it affirms that certain governmental obligations may apply even when violations are perpetrated by non-state actors. In the "external forum" setting, the author provides detailed analysis of three very sensitive current issues in which state actions are directed specifically against women: female genital mutilation,[85] wearing religious garb in the workplace,[86] and the freedom not to wear religious clothing.[87] In addition, while the principle focus of the chapter is on religious freedom concerns, the author looks with some care at a number of situations in which gender-discriminatory religious norms and practices violate the human rights of women. While acknowledging the seriousness of such problems, however, she draws attention to the fact that, "in the area of women and religion or belief, there is an incongruity between the international community's intense concern for a wide set of other human rights involving women and the lesser degree of concern manifested with respect to violations of women's right to freedom of religion or belief."[88] Not content to identify a number of sensitive issues, Tahzib-Lie concludes with concrete proposals for further action by a variety of actors in the promotion of the freedom of religion or belief of "dissenting women."[89]

Özlem Denli provides an overview of the head-cover controversy in contemporary Turkey, a secular country with a Muslim majority. The state-imposed head-cover ban has far-reaching consequences for women who consider veiling in public life to be a religious obligation. Such women are excluded from the entire public sector, which

83 Ibid., 492.
84 Ibid., 460–61.
85 Ibid., 466–73.
86 Ibid., 473–83.
87 Ibid., 483–87.
88 Ibid., 488.
89 Ibid., 492–95.

is rather sizeable in Turkey. Among other things, they are deprived of the opportunity of a university education. This in turn blocks access to employment and other forms of engagement in public life. For the last two decades, this controversy has set the tone for public debate on freedom of religion or belief. More than just giving an account of the problem, however, Denli uses the concrete religious headdress issue in Turkey to provide an insightful sociological account of the tensions between laicist ideology and the resurgence of public religion in Turkey. She demonstrates how the head-cover issue has become a "nonnegotiable boundary between laicism and Islamism," and concludes that the "laicist policies of the Turkish Republic are expressions of a comprehensive doctrine that is systematically biased and exclusionist in its very makeup."[90]

Juliet Sheen is particularly dubious about claims that religious freedom can override women's rights. In her view, male dominance in the religious sphere has led to such pervasive systemic and structural inequalities that the only effect of allowing religious freedom claims to prevail over women's rights is to reinforce discrimination. Particularly suspect in her view are situations where freedom of religion is played by states and religious institutions as a trump card to justify the subordination and exclusion of women. Whereas the link between the causes of the inequalities and discrimination against women and religion may be indirect and dispersed, the results are felt in many contexts: family or personal status laws; modesty norms; expectations of obedience to husband; and so forth. These religious causes of discrimination against women are further reinforced by cultural practices that "may also be associated with religion without being sanctioned by religious law."[91] The author appeals to multifaceted strategies to reverse the denial of women's human rights due to fundamentalist demands, from education and dialogue, to sanctions and coercion against offending states.[92]

From Sheen's general critique of religious pressures to violate women's rights, we move to a highly particularized case study of India in *Ursula King's* chapter on *Hinduism and Women: Uses and Abuses of Religious Freedom.* King focuses on areas where freedom of religion or belief is in tension, or even clashes, with the human rights of Indian women. Modern interpreters use the rich but profoundly ambivalent Hindu traditions and images about the role of women to promote, as well as to obstruct, women's equal rights and status in contemporary Indian society. Whereas there have been long-standing attempts to abolish social practices such as sati, child marriage, polygamy, and the prohibition of widow remarriage, the repression of women continues. All too often, systematic and severe violations of women's rights are perpetrated in the name of religion and its free exercise, and then amplified by caste. These patterns were not helped by the colonialist's codification of Hindu law in the nineteenth century, which stripped it of ambiguities running in favor of women, translated it into the male-dominated idiom of Victorian English, and effectively locked it into a rigid anti-woman form. Nor were they assisted by the development of personal laws within which gender discrimination was prevalent. Despite these problems, King remains

[90] Denli, chapter 20, 510.
[91] Sheen, chapter 21, 519.
[92] Ibid., 520.

optimistic about the proliferation of autonomous women's groups in India since the 1970s that have helped to cultivate "genuinely Indian roots" for women's rights. However, the challenge remains enormous. Especially in light of the politicization of Hinduism in recent years, King remains deeply uncertain "whether Hinduism will allow for constructive reinterpretations within a secular framework, thereby facilitating the development of a truly universalist, inclusive spirituality that alone can affirm and empower women in a true sense." [93]

In chapter 23, *Kari Elisabeth Børresen* tackles the theme of conflicts between women's rights and normative religion in the Roman Catholic tradition. Her acerbic approach will no doubt be controversial in Catholic circles. She submits that the present-day Vatican, acting in alliance with many Muslim states and supported by vociferous fundamentalist Protestants, has launched a major campaign opposing women's human rights to control their own fertility. To explain this "retrograde alliance," she turns to an analysis of traditional Christian doctrines about the gender of the Godhead, the ensuing androcentric interpretation of preferred status for men, the denial of women's sociocultural equivalence with men, the instrumental understanding of sex as geared solely to the purpose of reproduction, and the denial of eligibility for the priesthood to women. In sum, she traces the exclusion of women from partaking in "Christ's redemptive divinisation of humanity" on equal footing with men to what she views as discredited theology. She lambasts what she calls "the current doctrinal incoherence between outdated premises and preserved conclusions."[94] Børresen finds it paradoxical that Christian feminism has first been accepted in a Protestantism that sees God's instrument of revelation primarily in the literal Bible. To the contrary, she argues, the indispensable instruments for a feminist Reformation of Christianity are still to be found in the Catholic and Orthodox traditions, when divested of androcentric distortions.

Most fascinating in Børresen's condensed and well-documented contribution is her analysis of the abiding impact of historical theological doctrines on contemporary human rights issues. This entails the need to exercise our religious freedom to probe such doctrines critically. Børresen does not call on the authority of human rights to buttress her theological agenda. As already noted, she recognizes that "it is certainly not a human right to be ordained a priest or a bishop in the Catholic Church."[95] She marshals theological and historical arguments in support of the position that all human beings are entitled to be attributed a fully Godlike humanity—and hence not be denied equal dignity, neither before God nor before humans. On her analysis, present-day Vatican doctrines simultaneously embrace freedom of religion of belief and exploit this human right to uphold anthropological and sexological tenets detrimental to women. She argues that this denial has burdened underdeveloped countries most heavily, as Catholics in most "socially advanced societies no longer respect Vatican sexology."[96]

The final chapter in this section is *Geraldine Van Bueren's The Right to be the Same, The Right to be Different: Children and Religion*. Recognizing the potential for conflict in the triangle of children's rights, parental rights and duties, and the interests

[93] King, chapter 22, 541.
[94] Børresen, chapter 23, 558.
[95] Ibid., 555.
[96] Ibid., 552.

of the state, Van Bueren contends that we need to get beyond asking what trumps what. We need to "sit down and discuss what religion can learn from human rights and how human rights can in turn be enriched by religion in ways which will better protect the rights of children."[97] Her essay is an eloquent appeal for balance: balance in understanding the best interests of the child, balance in assessing whether children have the right to be different from dominant views in their states or even in their families, balance in weighing the importance of parental authority against the autonomy of the child, balance in resolving how a child should be raised when its parents disagree on religion, balance in determining when children should be seen "as symbolizing continuity, affirmation, and the future"[98] and when the focus should be on their present.

In addressing the scope of a child's right to freedom of religion or belief, Van Bueren discloses some of the ways in which vague general norms paper over deep cultural divides. Thus, she notes that "the CRC, in contrast to the ICCPR, omits any express reference to having or adopting a religion or belief of the child's choice. . . . In addition, unlike the ICCPR, the CRC does not expressly include the freedom of a child to manifest a religion or belief in worship, observance, practice, and teaching."[99] For those who assume that the CRC simply builds on the ICCPR, the assumption is that the CRC implicitly incorporates the omitted ICCPR notions and that both children and adults have the right to "have or adopt a religion." But a number of Islamic and Catholic states "were not able to accept any provision granting children the freedom to choose and change their religion or belief."[100] Similarly, the CRC waffles to some extent on the strength of parental authority. In these areas Van Bueren believes better balancing is needed.

The chapter addresses a number of the sensitive issues concerning religion and education—religious instruction, controversial secular instruction (e.g., "factual sex education")—and how the sometimes conflicting interest of the state in educating its future citizenry is to be weighed against parental authority to control what instruction is received. Again there is a call for balance, a plea that education be "child-centered" and the implicit suggestion that it not be disrupted by religious tug-of-wars between parents (and sets of parents). Recent case law concerning corporal punishment of children is also addressed.[101]

Ultimately, Van Bueren concludes, "it is a question of balance, and the contribution of the CRC is that it has shifted the weight away from child sacrifice toward child autonomy."[102] Unstated, perhaps, is one last recognition: that the balance is shifted *toward* child autonomy, but not all the way. Children are not adults; they have "evolving capacities."[103] There are still profound reasons why adults need to judge just how much autonomy children can be given, and why (most) parents are better judges of their children's capacities and best interests than the state. Children

[97] Van Bueren, chapter 24, 561.
[98] Ibid.
[99] Ibid., 564.
[100] Ibid,, 564–65.
[101] Ibid., 568–69.
[102] Ibid., 569.
[103] CRC, art. 14.

mature; parents err and disagree. The state is left with the delicate task of balancing all these balances, and of doing so without undue interference in the lives children and their families.

Part V: Changing beliefs and the Tensions of Tolerance

Part V addresses the notion of changing beliefs in two senses: the change registered by the emergence of new religious movements and the inner individual change marked by conversion. Both lie within or near the boundary of the absolutely unregulable domain of inner belief. Yet both for a variety of reasons continue to stir controversy. This reflects the inner residuum of intolerance and the tensions it creates, even in the central stronghold of freedom of religion or belief.

Chapters 25 and 26 focus on freedom of religion or belief as relating to "New Religious Movements," or "NRMs"—a preferred way to refer to smaller religious groups without engaging in the discrimination of disparagement by referring to them as "sects" or "cults." The first chapter is a general introduction to new religious movements by *Eileen Barker,* one of the premier sociological experts in the world on these groups. The second, by *Willy Fautré, Alain Garay,* and *Yves Nidegger,* is a case study of the problematic treatment of new religious movements that has been occurring in Francophone Europe over the past several years.

Barker explores what it is about NRMs that attracts discrimination, persecution, and in general, violation of freedom of religion or belief. While noting the extraordinary diversity of NRMs, Barker outlines certain recurring characteristics of NRMs: the preponderance of first-generation members, often composed of an atypical segment of the population (young, middle class, good education); clear-cut beliefs; charismatic authority; and a tendency to create sharp social boundaries around a group, often resulting in a group's cutting itself off from the rest of society. In addition, NRMs change and evolve over time. Perhaps, Barker suggests, it is the "enthusiastic commitment, inexperience, unpredictability, and novelty"[104] that appears to pose a threat to society and lead to NRMs being treated with such suspicion and fear.

Instead of engaging in the complex process of coming to a scientifically responsible understanding of NRMs, governmental organizations and anticult groups tend to construct their perception of the reality of NRMs by relying on stereotypical images drawn from the media and other sources that often (not always) exaggerate the danger of NRMs. The images thus constructed, the reports, lists, and laws that are predicated on such stereotypes often lack credible basis in reality, and have led to extensive discrimination, and sometimes even to attacks, against the concerned groups. One of the most tenacious stereotypes is that NRMs brainwash their converts. There is now extensive research on this issue, and what it shows is that the typical groups do not use techniques that have the irresistible and irreversible impact that the idea of brainwashing conjures up.[105] Barker acknowledges that such groups often do exert pressure and sometimes impose constraints on their members, but the levels of pressure would be difficult to distinguish from legitimate groups.[106]

---

[104] Barker, chapter 25, 578.
[105] Ibid., 583–84.
[106] Ibid., 584.

In line with recurrent recommendations from the Council of Europe,[107] the authors of both chapters believe that it is counter-productive and inappropriate to adopt specialized laws that target NRMs and punish entire groups on the basis of preconceived notions about cults or on the basis of wrongful conduct perpetrated by particular members. Instead, they argue, normal criminal and civil laws equally applicable to all should be used to take effective action against *any* individuals convicted of illegal activities.

The study of Francophone Europe stresses the importance of this proposal as a counter to recent anticult initiatives in recent years in France, Belgium and Switzerland. These activities have "triggered an unprecedented wave of discrimination and intolerance" against such groups and violated international standards in the field of freedom of religion or belief. The authors are critical of the confrontational mentality used in these "Crusades" against "foreign sects," and particularly concerned about the "sect observatories" set up to study this phenomenon. Such observatories need to exert great care both to utilize scholarly methods for their activities and to avoid actions that will themselves violate international norms on freedom of religion or belief.

The next three chapters explore various dimensions of one of the more sensitive areas in the field of freedom of religion or belief—that of the right to have, adopt, or change one's religion, and the related rights to engage in persuasion, missionary work, and proselytism. *Tad Stahnke* provides a thorough and balanced overview of the scope and limits of religious persuasion. He defines proselytism as "expressive conduct undertaken with the purpose of trying to change the religious beliefs, affiliation, or identity of another."[108] It is therefore intimately linked with change in religion or belief, which is explored by *Nazila Ghanea* in her chapter on *Apostasy and Freedom to Change Religion or Belief.* The attempt to persuade covered by Stahnke's definition, if successful, results in a change of belief, and if this is a change from another belief, it will appear as apostasy to those who continue to hold the convert's original belief.

Stahnke reminds us that convictions about obligations to engage in religious persuasion and missionary work are themselves religious in nature, deserving religious freedom protection as surely as other doctrines that a missionary might teach. Stahnke also reminds us of something that, surprisingly, is often overlooked: namely, that efforts to engage in religious persuasion are covered both by freedom of religion and by freedom of expression.[109] It thus has "double" human rights protection. States restrict proselytism both directly and indirectly, intentionally and unintentionally, through their various regulations on registration and manifestation of expression and of religion or belief. Though such restrictions may be neutral in construction, they often lead to impermissible discrimination and may violate religious freedom norms in other ways.

Possible criteria for "improper proselytism" are explored by Stahnke; the touchstone he identifies in this area is the notion of coercion. This is where the emphases of Stahnke and *Makau Mutua* diverge. The former believes that the "preservation of a particular religious tradition, the official ideology of a state, or the religious character of a state's institutions—divorced from any of the other limitations expressly provided

---

[107] See discussion of this issue in Martínez-Torrón and Navarro-Valls, chapter 10, 211–14.
[108] Stahnke, chapter 27, 620.
[109] Ibid., 627.

for in international instruments—cannot support limitations on the freedom to manifest religion or belief."[110] Such one-sided protectionisms and penalties, Stahnke argues, are biased and can lead to the abuse of minorities.

Mutua's perspective on the situation is quite different. He views proselytism as a form of cultural imperialism whereby (typically) foreign missionaries demonize and deliberately destroy an indigenous belief system. This, Mutua believes, can compromise other rights and result in cultural warfare and even cultural genocide. Is there a right to be left alone, and allow the continuation of diversity of cultures? Is there a right to cultural self-preservation? If freedom of religion or belief should be protected, doesn't that mean that the religion of the "target" group should be protected as well? The example Mutua focuses on is the historical one of the spread of Islam and Christianity in Africa and the decimation of indigenous African religion where proselytizing was coupled with force and power, and therefore illegitimate. In a sense, both Stahnke and Mutua agree: proselytism that involves inappropriate levels of coercion is impermissible. The difficulty is how to define what is inappropriate. Disagreements will no doubt continue in this area, and indeed, the Oslo Coalition has undertaken a project to pursue further dialogue on this particular issue.

Whereas coercion can be coupled with proselytism, it can also be coupled with the threat against change of religion or belief. Ghanea examines international and regional standards, and finds that only the Universal Declaration, the ECHR, the American Convention on Human Rights, and various OSCE Documents explicitly protect freedom to change religion or belief. Primarily because of Muslim sensitivities, the term "change" was dropped in the ICCPR and the 1981 Declaration. Nevertheless, numerous experts, the Special Rapporteur on Freedom of Religion or Belief, and the Human Rights Committee have all found freedom to change religion or belief to constitute a legally essential component of freedom of religion or belief. Unfortunately, violence, coercion, and even death can still result from change of religion or belief. Numerous Islamic countries, for example, legally uphold penalties for apostasy. The author contends that such penalties for apostasy are not sanctioned in the Qur'an, and that the main barrier to allowing for change of religion or belief in such societies is in fact political rather than religious.

All three of the "change of religion" chapters highlight an area where delicate balancing may be required between the converter, converted, proselytizer, seeker, and those not seeking. As Ghanea argues, a more cosmopolitan and tolerant attitude needs to be nurtured, but one that is also cognizant of both the power relationships between the actors and any coercion that may be implicated.

Part VI: Contexts for Facilitating Freedom of Religion or Belief

The final section of the deskbook examines a series of contexts that are particularly important for freedom of religion or belief. It opens on the hopeful note suggested by the essay of ***Archbishop Anastasios*** of Tirana and all Albania on ***Developing Shared Values and Common Citizenship in a Secular and Pluralist Society: How Religious Communities Can Contribute***. The focus is on Christians and Muslims in a modern Europe. One of

[110] Ibid., 637.

the first duties facing Europe's Christians and Muslims is to emphasize to secular society, through their actions, that religion has a vital place in human life. This, to Archbishop Anastasios, requires them to be self-critical, admit past mistakes, reject any violence in the name of religion, and then to articulate common values and spiritual norms. The values and norms promoted by religion are eternal. It is for this reason that religious leaders should not allow religion to be politicized and manipulated for egotistical short-term motives at the expense of others. Respect for human rights, especially for freedom of conscience, can serve as the foundation for such harmonious coexistence between religious groups. However, human rights should not just be a rallying call for aggrieved minorities, quickly forgotten when majority status is achieved. In order for Europe's Christians and Muslims to progress toward serving as models of peaceful coexistence, Archbishop Anastasios promotes the need for "a dialogue of life": a dialogue focused on the most practical issues for creative interreligious understanding, such as ecology, globalization, poverty, and ethnic reconciliation. Dialogue is obviously a particularly significant context for facilitating freedom of religion or belief, as attested in several other chapters—especially 9, 33, 34, and 35.

The next chapter is an important reminder that religion is not the only context that needs to be considered: the "belief" half of "religion or belief" needs to be remembered. That is an important element in the essay on ***Humanism and Freedom from Religion*** by ***Rajaji Ramanadha Babu Gogineni*** and ***Lars Gule***. There are many world views that are not necessarily religious and yet come within the ambit of the right to "thought, conscience, and religion." The authors describe one such outlook, Humanism, as a "modern life stance rooted in rational thinking, providing a way of understanding our universe and our place in it in naturalistic terms"[111] and upholding "an open-ended and continuous interrogation about our life and the universe."[112] For Humanists, therefore, the highest priority should be given to the realization of tolerant environments conducive to free enquiry. Such environments would allow all life stances to flourish in "peaceful competition" and this, to the Humanists, crucially requires freedom *from* state-supported religion in the public sphere. Despite international standards on freedom of religion simultaneously protecting beliefs, many legal systems have not translated this into an equal protection of life stances such as Humanism. Humanists particularly face barriers in terms of their interest in the public school system, lack of media attention, and lack of toleration from the general public. Genuine state neutrality towards all religion and belief communities would mean, for example, the state not imputing religious meaning to public holidays, not making reference to religion or belief in public documents such as constitutions, not imposing religious education on children in schools, and eliminating blasphemy laws. Overall, the authors call for a strict separation of law and religion, church and state, private religion and public politics. At one point the authors state,

> It might seem like a contradiction that Humanists demand, on the one hand, recognition and even financial support from the authorities, and, on the other, freedom from religion in the public domain. However, the contradiction is only apparent, and the demands are coherent.[113]

[111] Gogineni and Gule, chapter 31, 699.
[112] Ibid.
[113] Ibid., 705.

The resolution of the contradiction comes in recognizing that Humanists and other nonbelievers should be treated equally. One can easily understand why unbelievers should not suffer discrimination due to their life stance, but it is not clear why the "realization of tolerant environments . . . crucially requires freedom *from* religion," if that means total exclusion of religion from the public square. To some, that would appear to be more like remaking public space in the humanist image along the lines of what Tore Lindholm calls "strident laicism," and contrasts with what he views as the preferred position of "universal (or nonexclusive) religious freedom."[114] In fact, however, Gogineni and Gule's approach can be given a much less strident reading. They do indeed call for "recognition and even financial support," but only to the extent this grants nonbelievers equal treatment. Ultimately, they conclude that it is "impossible to demand freedom from religion in the public space. Freedom of organization and expression as well as the freedom of religion or belief make people's right to present their religious views publicly a self-evident matter."[115] What they object to at core is state-backed support of a particular religion. They do not insist on a "strident laicist" approach calling literally for total freedom from religion. The tension between "strident laicism" and "universal (nonexclusive) religious freedom is representative of larger societal debates which are unlikely to be resolved any time soon.

The next chapter, *Jeremy Gunn's* treatment of *The United States and the Promotion of Freedom of Religion and Belief*, focuses on a rather different "context" for facilitating freedom of religion or belief: that opened up by the passage of the International Religious Freedom Act (IRFA) in the United States in October 1998. In many ways this chapter has an emphasis that parallels earlier chapters (7–12) dealing with institutions responsible for facilitating freedom of religion or belief. We have concluded that it should be treated separately, however, because it represents the initiative of one particular country (albeit an influential one) to support international religious freedom standards. In this respect the chapter is significant not only for the information it provides on the important new initiatives of the United States, but also as a reminder of the increasing importance of national initiatives in promoting freedom of religion or belief in the contemporary international human rights system. Foreign ministries around the world are constantly called upon to address religious freedom concerns, both as they deal with countries where violations occur and as they respond to concerns about their own country's practices (no one is perfect). Both Norway and the Netherlands have been particularly active in this regard. As a practical matter, those striving to improve implementation of religious freedom norms at the international level should not overlook the influence foreign ministries can have.

Having recognized that the case of the United States is just one example of the more general importance of foreign policy establishments to international religious freedom, it remains the case that the recent initiatives of the United States have been particularly significant. The passage of IRFA has made the United States "the state that most visibly promotes the rhetoric of freedom of religion in the international arena,"[116] and immediate and positive benefits from this can already be noted.

---

[114] Lindholm, chapter 2, 43–46.
[115] Gogineni and Gule, chapter 31, 718.
[116] Gunn, chapter 32, 722.

Whereas the US has a long history of contributing to the development of international norms in the field of freedom of religion or belief and of cognizance of this freedom in its foreign policy, that position has now been strengthened. The Act has required the US State Department to promote international religious freedom as part of its foreign policy, issue annual reports on the status of religious freedom in all other countries, establish an office in the State Department to oversee implementation of the law, and take actions in response to each country that violates international standards of religious freedom. Moreover, IRFA established an independent body, the US Commission on International Religious Freedom, which is charged with monitoring State Department activity in this area and making recommendations both to the president and the State Department regarding ways that US foreign policy can more effectively foster support for international religious freedom standards. All this means that religious freedom is not allowed to slip out of sight behind other priorities on human rights agendas, and as a result, the US regularly raises issues related to religious freedom in both bilateral and multilateral fora. Victims and human rights workers worldwide may do well to note that since 1998 US Embassies abroad have been instructed to pay added attention to issues of religious freedom, and are required to file an annual report on these issues. As a practical matter, one of the most significant impacts of IRFA has been that the reporting process itself opens high-profile channels in which violations of religious freedom rights can be heard and brought to the attention of domestic government leaders. This often results in quiet, back-channel diplomacy that resolves a significant volume of problems. Gunn's chapter is significant not only in describing how the various aspects of the new IRFA mechanisms work, but also in defusing misunderstandings about the motivations behind passage of IRFA. Most fundamentally, the Act is not about imposing an American agenda, but about making certain that US foreign policy is responsive to the goal of supporting *international* standards of freedom of religion or belief.

Rüdiger Noll addresses another vital context in his chapter on *The Role of Religion and Religious Freedom in Contemporary Conflict Situations.* The hope that religious leaders and communities can contribute to conflict avoidance and resolution runs through several chapters in the book, including chapter 12 on the Norwegian experience in the OSCE and chapter 38 dealing with NGOs. Rüdiger Noll brings extensive practical experience to his treatment of this theme. Anyone working with religious groups at peacemaking activities can benefit from his insights. Acknowledging that religion has too often played a negative role in violent conflict situations, Noll nonetheless challenges the view that the best means forward is to eliminate religion from politics and public life. Rather, he advances a number of reasons for thinking that religions and religious leaders can play a more positive role in preventing and resolving conflict and contributing to peace and reconciliation: their commitment to values, their competence as mediators, their structures at the local and national levels, and their long-standing presence in the field. However, in order to be able to play such a role, religions themselves need to be allowed sufficient space by states. Ensuring full implementation of freedom of religion or belief is vital to this objective. Without it there can be a dangerous escalation from discrimination to other tensions, and this can induce the negative cycle of violence rather than opening the positive potential of peacemaking.

Closely linked to the context of conflict avoidance is the theme of dialogue. This too is an idea that has emerged in several chapters in the volume (2, 9, and 30, to name just a few), but this methodology receives more specialized treatment in Leonard Swidler's chapter on *Freedom of Religion and Dialogue* and in the case study of *The Emergence of Interfaith Dialogue in Norway* submitted by *Inge Eidsvåg*, *Tore Lindholm* and *Barbro Sveen*. Swidler refers to religious freedom and dialogue as constituting "two of the most powerful transformative concepts in the history of humanity."[117] He particularly welcomes the historical emergence of neutral states committed to recognition of freedom of religion or belief. He believes that this development has been central to the "awesome, unparalleled achievements" of western civilization and its globalization.[118] In his view, uncoupling religion from the power of the state has been essential to unleashing the creative capabilities of both religion and the state. Similarly, the transformative power of dialogue constitutes a further condition for the flourishing of humanity—especially where there is "deep dialogue" where one individual or group seeks to learn from another. For effective dialogue Swidler has identified ten ground rules (the "Dialogue Decalogue"), which are detailed in his chapter.[119] He also identifies three levels at which interreligious or interideological dialogue operate: the practical, the spiritual, and the cognitive. There are, of course, voices in other parts of the world that would be more critical of Swidler's account of western civilization and globalization and the way that religious freedom has figured the rise of the West. Makau Mutua's chapter (28) with its critique of western proselytism comes to mind in this regard. But Swidler would have a ready answer on this point: more, better, and deeper dialogue.

It is at Swidler's practical level that the interreligious dialogue in Norway has concentrated its efforts, as described in the Norwegian case study. The authors of this chapter provide a detailed account of the experience of interfaith dialogue and cooperation over the past twenty years in Norway—a country where dialogue has been complicated by the fact that there is a state church that retains a number of privileges. The focus has been first on elaborating a communal ethic shared by nine Norwegian religions and life-stance communities and then on identifying foreseeable conflicts and finding constructive ways to handle them. This has involved the Norwegian Council for Religious and Life Stance Communities in dialogue and action on moral, educational, legislative, social and interethnic issues. One secret to the success of this council may have been their reliance on consensus decision making in all matters—a measure that has been key to sustaining trust and upholding a sense of equality among participating groups. This experience provides a positive example of the possibility of realizing the vision elaborated in chapters 30 and 33, that religion and belief can indeed "serve as a basis for eliminating animosities and strengthening understanding and cooperation across ethnic, ideological, and religious divides."[120]

Education is another key context for freedom of religion or belief. It is both an area where some of the major recurrent issues arise, and also a context of extraordinary importance for cultivating tolerance and mutual respect. The next two chapters

---

[117] Swidler, chapter 34, 761–62.
[118] Ibid., 765.
[119] Ibid., 772–75.
[120] Eidsvåg, Lindholm, and Sveen, chapter 35, 789.

turn to this area of endeavor. Both chapters ground their analysis in the educational initiatives of the UN Special Rapporteur on Freedom of Religion or Belief, whose activities also received attention in chapter 7. *Ingvill Thorson Plesner* considers *Promoting Tolerance through Religious Education* in general, and *Jolanta Ambrosewicz-Jacobs* concentrates on *Religious Tolerance, Freedom of Religion or Belief, and Education: Results of the 2001 UN Conference.* The question both chapters address is how religious education can be successfully delivered in our pluralistic times in ways that foster tolerance and mutual respect, without limiting the freedom of religion or belief of others. While Plesner focuses on the experience of various European countries, Ambrosewicz-Jacobs examines the findings of the 2001 UN International Consultative Conference.

Like Van Bueren's chapter (24) dealing with religion and the rights of the child, these chapters recognize the various tensions that may arise between the three-way considerations of the duty of the state to promote tolerance, the best interests of the child, and respect for the rights of parents or guardians to bring up their children in line with their religious and moral convictions. For example, the Special Rapporteur has criticized the "separation" or "ghetto" approach to religious education, which separates pupils in accordance with religious affiliation in the religious education provided by public schools. Instead he supports the "integration" approach. However, the preference of some parents is precisely to have separate denominationally-aligned religious instruction for their children. Furthermore, as Plesner suggests, the child's self-conception may also be changed by the encounter with the other, leading to further challenges by some parents or guardians. A broad dialogue about the content of religious education across religions and beliefs may be an important prerequisite to gaining support within society that can reduce opposition to the integration approach.

Both authors concur with the Special Rapporteur that schools are one of the most important arenas for fostering tolerance and laying the long-term societal foundation for freedom of religion or belief. The International Consultative Conference on School Education in Relation with Freedom of Religion and Belief, Tolerance and Non-discrimination held in Madrid in 2001, the results of which are described in the chapter by Ambrosewicz-Jacobs, focused on developing strategies towards this end. The Final Document of the conference reiterated the importance of education as a means to ensure respect for religion and belief, nondiscrimination, and tolerance. The effective implementation of its findings not only requires the cooperation of various actors such as states, NGOs, parents, and religious or belief communities, but also a range of further follow-up activities and studies. As noted earlier, the Oslo Coalition is actively engaged in implementing a number of the recommendations emerging from the Madrid conference.

The final chapter by *Elizabeth Sewell* looks at *Facilitating Freedom of Religion or Belief through NGOs.* The chapter, taken together with the list of NGOs compiled in Appendix G, is designed to extend effective NGO work on freedom of religion or belief in three ways. First, it draws on theoretical work on the role of international human rights NGOs to develop models of NGO influence. In particular, it provides an analysis of the processes whereby NGOs develop and become more (or less) effective in shaping social reality.[121] Second, it aims at highlighting the vast potential that

[121] Sewell, chapter 38, 820–26.

NGOs have to promote and further establish the right to freedom of religion or belief and the diverse array of NGOs that are contributing to this undertaking in many different ways. The NGOs may be domestic, regional, or international in scope; they may promote this freedom exclusively or as part of its larger defense of human rights in general; they may be religious organizations themselves, or academic institutions; and they could be consortia bringing together a variety of actors. Their methods vary widely, and may be colored by the above characteristics. Their key roles include "standard setting, violation reporting, providing technical advice, and lobbying and agenda setting."[122] Sewell examines each of these roles in detail, bringing examples from a variety of actors to bear on this study. Third, by sharing knowledge about what various NGOs are doing, the chapter aims to encourage cooperation and to avoid duplicative efforts. Sewell's analysis of the important roles of NGOs in facilitating freedom of religion or belief underscores the power of networking, reasonable argument, and mutually respectful dialogue in the advancement of religious liberty.

The Path Forward

Unfortunately, the need for continued facilitation of freedom of religion is not likely to diminish any time soon. Intolerance, discrimination, and persecution continue—reduced by the impact of religious freedom norms, but not abated. Most states strive to implement international standards of freedom of religion or belief, but many continue to fall short, and none are perfect. Government officials rotate in office; most are constantly learning and relearning the lessons of how to be more sensitive in respecting differing beliefs. But some are not interested in learning, and,unfortunately, some have contrary agendas. Against this often discouraging backdrop, the concluding comment about Professor Sewell's chapter deserves reiteration with respect to the contents of the deskbook and more generally with respect to its objective of facilitating freedom of religion or belief: there is great power in networking, reasonable argument, and mutually respectful dialogue.

The deskbook itself is a venture in all three. As noted earlier, its authors were brought together initially by networking through the 1998 Oslo Conference, and subsequently through additional networking as the project evolved in response to argument and dialogue. It is important to stress again that this process took time, with different chapters being finished at very different times. The result is that many of the chapters have not been able to include every late-breaking event of relevance. But the fundamental issues are amply covered. It is also important to reiterate once again that different authors come from very different backgrounds and take very different positions for which they alone are responsible. This is part of the reasonable argument and mutually respectful dialogue that is so much needed. There is much to disagree about, and yet at the same time, much to learn. Good friends disagree, and yet join again and again together to move forward.

There is much left to be done. This is not the place to go into detailed recommendations. These can be found in many of the chapters, and in addition, we have tried to collect suggestions and ideas for future effort in what we call not a conclusion,

---

[122] Ibid, 828.

but more appropriately, a "Conclusion and Agenda for the Future." There we identify additional types of support that are needed at the level of international institutions, issues that need to be addressed, monitoring that needs to be done, minimum standards that need better and more concrete formulations, websites that need to be built, literature that needs to be written, and beyond everything else, an extensive research agenda that can enable further progress. Despite the size of this volume, it provides at best a basic tool. We hope, however, that it will be a useful resource, and that it will serve as a launching pad for additional dialogue, expanded networks, and high-level reasoning that will in turn provide a powerful impetus to facilitating freedom of religion or belief.

Beyond all the tasks that demand action, there is a need for each generation to rekindle the fundamental vision of freedom of religion or belief. Sometimes the spark comes in reaction to oppression; sometimes in gratitude for the experience of freedom and respect; sometimes in the process of defending rights that are imperiled. Whatever the source of the spark, the resulting flame needs to be sustained and facilitated in the countless ways suggested in this volume. If we succeed in nurturing this flame, even in imperfect measure, we contribute to what the American founder, James Madison, once called "the lustre of our country."[123] He was writing at a time when the idea of religious freedom was young, fragile, and very much at risk, not only in his own country, but everywhere. The world has come far in the intervening centuries, though not far enough. Today the challenge is to work for this luster in all our countries, and thereby to enhance the luster of our world.

[123] James Madison, "A Memorial and Remonstrance," (1785) in *The Papers of James Madison*, ed. Robert A. Rutland et al., vol. 8 (Chicago: University of Chicago Press, 1973), 299, para. 9. This phrase has been brought to our attention by John T. Noonan's wonderful book, *The Lustre of Our Country: The American Experience of Religious Freedom* (Berkeley: University of California Press, 1998).

Part I

Origins and Grounds of Freedom of Religion or Belief

Chapter 1

Historical Analysis of Freedom of Religion or Belief as a Technique for Resolving Religious Conflict

Malcolm D. Evans

This chapter seeks to provide a brief account of the principal steps through which freedom of religion or belief has emerged in its current form. It will be shown that extending freedom of religion or belief has long been seen as a way of avoiding conflict, whilst placing limitations upon its enjoyment has led to conflict. It will also be seen that approaches taken have varied over time and that there has been, in general terms, a shift away from the practice of attempting to ensure civil harmony by keeping those of different religious persuasions apart, and towards providing tools for facilitating their peaceful coexistence within a common framework. Since the latter stages of this story are both more familiar and covered in greater detail by other contributors to this volume, they will be only lightly sketched here. The final section of this chapter will offer some reflections on current practice in the light of the material presented.

I. First Thoughts

Freedom of religion is one of the oldest and most controversial of all human rights and has been the object of international concern from the very beginnings of the modern international state system.[1] Commenting on the approach of the Romans, the historian Edward Gibbon cynically observed that:

> The policy of the emperors and the senate, as far as it concerned religion, was happily seconded by the reflections of the enlightened, and by the habits of the superstitious, part of their subjects. The various modes of worship which prevailed in the Roman world were all considered by the people as equally true; by the philosophers as equally false; and by the magistrate as equally useful. And thus toleration produced not only mutual indulgence, but even religious concord.[2]

---

[1] See Arthur Nussbaum, *A Concise History of the Law of Nations,* rev. ed. (New York: Macmillan, 1954); Malcolm D. Evans, *Religious Liberty and International Law in Europe* (Cambridge: Cambridge University Press, 1997), chap. 2.

[2] Edward Gibbon, *The Decline and Fall of the Roman Empire,* ed. David Womersley (London: Allen Lane, 1994), chap. 2; first published in 1776.

Tore Lindholm, W. Cole Durham, Jr., Bahia G. Tahzib-Lie (eds.), Facilitating Freedom of Religion or Belief: A Deskbook, *1–17.*

Christianity, however, posed a difficult problem. Like Judaism, it was monotheistic and claimed universal validity, and was hence intolerant of other religious practices. Unlike Judaism, however, it was not exclusive and became a proselytizing religion that challenged the religious pluralistic *status quo*. It was this, rather than the substance of Christian belief *per se*, that best explains the official Roman policy that veered between toleration and persecution. The crucial turning point came with the Edict of Toleration issued by Galerius on his deathbed in 311, which granted Christians the indulgence of "the rights to exist again and to set up their places of worship; provided always that they do not offend against public order."[3] This was followed by the accession of Constantine to the throne of the Western Empire. In 313, Constantine promulgated the Edict of Milan, which provided that:

> All who choose [the Christian] religion are to be allowed to continue therein, without let or hindrance and are not in any way to be molested. . . . At the same time all others are to be accorded the free and unrestricted practices of their religions; for it accords with the good order of the realm and the peacefulness of our times that each should have the freedom to worship God after his own choice; and we do not intend to detract from the honour due to any religion or its followers.[4]

Once Christianity was established as the official religion of the Roman Empire,[5] it became necessary to forge an understanding between the dictates of faith and imperial imperatives. It is rather disquieting to note that, having struggled to establish freedom for their beliefs, the interest of many theologians then shifted to the question of how the resources of the Empire could be used to deny others that same freedom.

Central to the *modus vivendi* that was forged between the Christian church and state was the Roman-law notion of the "just war." Cicero, for example, had considered that "no war is just unless it is waged after a formal demand for restoration, or unless it has been formally announced and declared beforehand."[6] The essence of the doctrine was the commission of a wrong, which, if not put to rights, would justify the use of force as the legally appropriate sanction. It came to be understood, however, that such formalities could only apply between peoples organized into civilized societies.[7] As far as Roman law was concerned, however, the worship of other gods was not a wrong and could therefore neither provide a cause of war nor justify the removal of the worshippers from the class of civilized societies. Augustine, whose writing developed the idea that the state could act as the guardian of the moral order—the Christian moral order—drew on this tradition.[8] Aquinas reworked this in the thirteenth century, concluding that a just war required "right authority," a "just cause," and a "right intent."[9]

---

[3] See Henry Bettenson and Chris Maunder, eds., *Documents of the Christian Church,* 3d ed. (Oxford: Oxford University Press, 1999), 16. The Edict also put Christians under a duty to pray for the Emperor and Empire.

[4] Ibid., 17.

[5] As a result of the *Edict of Thessalonica* (380). Bettenson and Maunder, *Documents of the Christian Church,* 24.

[6] Cicero, *De Officiis,* bk. 1, sec. 36.

[7] Cicero, *De Respublica,* bk. 1, sec. 25; Coleman Phillipson, *The International Law and Custom of Ancient Greece and Rome* (London: Macmillan, 1911), 2:195.

[8] Deane concludes that Augustine came to the position that "the church had a duty as well as a right to ask the State to punish heretics and schismatics *per se,* while Christian Kings had an obligation to use their power to protect and support the Church against heresy and schism as well as against paganism" (Herbert A.

This provided the framework for subsequent consideration of the question whether differences of religion were in themselves a just cause of war, which became a matter of particular interest in the wake of the Spanish conquest of the New World, the legality of which was examined by the Spanish writer Francisco de Vitoria (1492–1546) in *De Indis.* Rejecting the claim that the emperor or the pope enjoyed a preexisting jurisdiction, temporal or spiritual, over the New World, Vitoria considered a number of other arguments, including whether the conquest was justified on the grounds that the Indians had refused to accept the Christian faith when it had been preached to them. He accepted that the Indians were bound to listen to the preaching of the faith, and that they would commit a mortal sin if they refused to accept it, if it were presented "not once only and perfunctorily, but diligently and zealously"; but he did not believe that such a refusal justified making war.[10] Moreover, he asserted that "Christian Princes cannot, even by the authorization of the Pope, restrain the Indians from sins against the law of nature or punish them because of their sins" for "it would be a strange thing that the Pope, who cannot make law for unbelievers, can yet sit in judgment and visit punishment upon them."[11] Thus when, in *De Iure Belli*, Vitoria considered the causes of a just war, his first proposition was "Difference of Religion is not a cause of just war."[12]

This position rapidly became the orthodoxy. Alberico Gentili (1552–1608), an Italian Protestant who had fled Italy to escape the inquisition,[13] was equally clear that wars waged with religion as their sole motive were unjust. This was because a just war could only be waged as a response to a wrong, and "since the laws of religion do not properly exist between man and man, therefore no man's rights are violated by a difference in religion, nor is it lawful to make war because of religion. . . . Therefore a man cannot complain of being wronged because others differ from him in religion."[14] He took the enlightened view that:

> Religion is a matter of the mind and of the will, which is always accompanied by freedom. . . . Our minds and whatever belongs to our mind are not affected by any external power or potentate, and the soul has no master save God only, who alone can destroy the soul. Do you understand? Yet hear still one more thing. Religion ought to be free.[15]

Deane, ***The Political and Social Ideas of St Augustine*** [New York: Columbia University Press, 1963], 214–15). This, however, did not extend to forcible conversion.

[9] Aquinas, ***Summa Theologica,*** pt. 2–3, q. 40.

[10] Vitoria, *De Indis,* sec. 1, ss. 7–15.

[11] Ibid., s. 15.

[12] Vitoria, *De Iure Belli,* s. 10. Nevertheless, Vitoria made it clear that he endorsed the view that Christians had a right to preach the gospel to unbelievers and should they be resisted, "the Spaniard . . . may preach it despite their unwillingness and devote themselves to the conversion of the people in question, and if need be they may then accept or even make war, until they succeed in obtaining facilities and safety for preaching the gospel." Converts could be protected, by means of war if necessary, from attempts to reconvert them to their previous religion and, should a large number become converted, then the Pope might place a Christian ruler over them (*De Indis,* sec. 3, ss. 9–14). As Ortega puts it, "Vitoria rejected the notion of a just religious war. . . . However, in his absolute belief in the religious and cultural supremacy of Christianity, Vitoria left the Indians little scope to exercise this freedom of choice" (Martin C. Ortega, "Vitoria and the Universalist Conception of International Relations," in ***Classical Theories of International Relations,*** ed. Ian Clark and Iver B. Neumann [Basingstoke: Macmillan, 1996], 109–10).

[13] See Gesina H. J. Van der Molen, ***Alberico Gentili and the Development of International Law,*** 2d ed. (Leyden: A. W. Sijthoff, 1968), 245–56.

[14] Gentili, *De Iure Belli,* bk. 1, chap. 9.

Thus he argued that a conqueror ought not to impose his religion on a defeated people in preference to their own.[16] However, he also rejected the use of force to maintain the practice of religion within a state, arguing that "if truly the profession of a different form of religious belief by their subjects does not harm princes, we are . . . unjust . . . if we persecute those who profess another religion than our own"[17] and that "violence should not be employed against subjects who have embraced another religion than that of their ruler"[18] though subject to the qualification "unless the state suffer some harm in consequence."[19] In short, Gentili not only rejected the claim that differences of religion could justify wars between states, he also called for the toleration of religious differences within states. In the turbulent world of the late Reformation and the wars of religion that it spawned, this was more of a plea than an observation, but in making it, Gentili prefigured the emergence of the secularized society of nations which is usually associated with the Peace of Westphalia[20] that ended the Thirty Years War in 1648.

II. Religion and the European Public Order

Although the Treaties of Westphalia are usually taken to mark the commencement of the modern era, the Religious Peace of Augsburg (1555) was, perhaps, an equally important point[21] in the evolution of religious liberty within Europe. The Protestant Reformation had taken hold in many of the German territories which comprised the Holy Roman Empire, and the Peace of Augsburg recognized that Lutheran rulers should have equal status with Catholic rulers within the Empire, whilst permitting the lay (but not ecclesiastical[22]) rulers of the Empire to determine which of these two religions was to be adopted within their territories; the principle *cuius regio, eius religio.*[23] This was a significant step towards the abandonment of the theory of Empire based upon a common religion,[24] although it fell far short of a general acceptance of freedom of religion. Although Catholic or Lutheran subjects were given the right to move to a territory where the religion of the prince was more congenial,[25] this package did nothing for the position

---

[15] Ibid.

[16] Ibid., bk. 3, chap. 11, ss. 558–60. Should the defeated peoples have no religion, however, the matter would be different and "the victor . . . may most justly compel to change conduct which is contrary to nature."

[17] Ibid., bk. 1, chap. 10, s. 69.

[18] Ibid., s. 72.

[19] Ibid., chap. 11, s. 78.

[20] Comprising the *Treaty of Münster* (France and the Empire), 1 CTS 271, and the *Treaty of Osnabrück* (Sweden and the Empire), 1 CTS 119.

[21] The way had, however, already been paved by the *Peace of Nürnberg* (1532) and the *Treaty of Passau* (1552).

[22] Ecclesiastical territories that had adopted Lutheranism were required to revert to Catholicism, although the *Declaratio Ferdinandea* permitted practicing Lutherans in these territories to continue in their faith.

[23] See art. 25 and art. 16. This was further buttressed by the obligation that "no Estate shall try to persuade the subjects of other Estates to abandon their religion nor protect them against their own magistrates" (art. 23), an early example of the principle of nonintervention in the internal affairs of others (text in Gerhard Benecke, *Germany in the Thirty Years War* [London: Edwin Arnold, 1978], 8).

[24] Although this is clear now, the Peace itself was couched in terms of an interim arrangement, to take effect until some "ultimate transaction of religion" took place. Thus it was premised upon the assumptions of universality that it in fact undermined. See Geoffrey R. Elton, ed., *New Cambridge Modern History*, 2nd ed. (Cambridge: Cambridge University Press, 1990), 2:195.

of those adhering to other forms of Christian belief, and the Calvinists in particular.[26] The struggle between Catholic and Protestant, Lutheran and Calvinist was played out within Central and Northern Europe. In 1648, the enfeebled Imperial forces finally came to terms with their opponents in the Westphalia treaties concluded at Münster[27] and Osnabrück,[28] finally laying to rest the pretence of an Empire held together by, and reflective of, the universal Catholic faith.[29]

The Peace of Westphalia, then, represents a key turning point in the struggle for freedom of religion or belief within the Empire.[30] But the focus was still on the religious freedom of the state rather than that of the individual. The Treaty of Münster, concluded between the emperor and Catholic France, said little concerning religious issues, since theirs was not a religious conflict as such.[31] It did, however, affirm the religious settlement provided for in the Treaty of Osnabrück,[32] at which Lutheran Sweden took precedence.

The Treaty of Osnabrück confirmed the basic framework for religious governance set out in the Peace of Augsburg but expanded and refined it in several important respects. First, the Reformed (Calvinist) Church was now accepted as a permitted confession alongside the Lutheran and Catholic faiths.[33] Although this hardly qualifies as a recognition of freedom of religion *per se*, it was a significant advance. The application of the *cuius regio, eius religio* principle was also confirmed, although since the Treaty was, in effect, attempting to restore the religious *status quo ante* as of 1624, it is rather unclear whether the ruler was entitled to impose a faith different from that applicable at the critical date. Individuals were, however, given a five-year grace period during which both public and private worship of a different persuasion to that of the ruler was to be "patiently suffered and tolerated, without any hindrance or impediment," after which subjects of a different faith could be required to move elsewhere.[34]

Although the dominance of the state in religious governance appears to be confirmed, there are the beginnings of a shift away from restrictions upon freedom of belief and its private practice in much of the finer detail of the Treaty of Osnabrück.

---

[25] Art. 24. See Benecke, *Germany in the Thirty Years War*, 9; and Richard B. Wernham, ed., *New Cambridge Modern History* (Cambridge: Cambridge University Press, 1968), 3:491.

[26] By the 1560s Calvinism had spread from its home in Geneva and was taking hold in the Northern Provinces of the Low Countries. In the *Treaty of Union* of 1579, article 13, the seven provinces recognized that "each individual enjoys freedom of religion and no one is persecuted or questioned about his religion."

[27] *Treaty of Peace between France and the Empire,* signed 14(24) October 1648 at Münster, 1 CTS 271.

[28] *Treaty of Peace between Sweden and the Empire,* signed 14(24) October 1648 at Osnabrück, 1 CTS 119.

[29] The Papacy was not represented at the conferences, and in the bull *Zelo Domus Dei,* Pope Innocent X denounced the religious aspects of the treaties as "null, void, invalid, inequitable, unjust, condemned, reprobated, frivolous, of no force or effect." Nevertheless, the treaties were honored by the parties (Nussbaum, *A Concise History of the Law of Nations,* 116).

[30] The resolution of the conflict between the Netherlands and Spain, also concluded at Münster, did not extend religious liberties to the Catholics of those parts of Flanders, Brabant, and Limburg that passed to the Netherlands, despite the attempts of Spain. See *New Cambridge Modern History,* 4:381–82.

[31] Indeed, article 77 of the *Treaty of Münster* obliged the French king to preserve Catholicism "and abolish all innovations crept in during the war" in the territories ceded to France. Article 28, however, ensured freedom of worship for Lutherans in areas of the Palatine remaining under the control of Catholic barons.

[32] *Treaty of Münster,* art. 49.

[33] *Treaty of Osnabrück,* art. 7, secs. 1–2.

[34] Ibid., art. 5, sec. 30. Those who changed their religion subsequent to the Treaty could be required to leave after a period of three years.

This is, perhaps, best confirmed by the absence of grandiose interstate settlements of religious differences in subsequent European treaty practice. Nevertheless, there continued to be a general expectation that when territory was ceded by one sovereign to another, subjects would be allowed to continue in the private exercise of their religious beliefs or be permitted to move elsewhere.[35] This appears to represent the core minimum requirement of freedom of religion or belief necessary to preserve international peace and security at this time. In some cases, the preservation of the *status quo*, whether it be Catholic or Protestant, was required.[36] In all this, the principal motivation was the elimination of possible causes of conflict. There is no sustainable evidence of international practice motivated by the desire to promote religious liberty or tolerance as an end in itself.[37]

III. The European Powers and the Ottoman Empire

On those rare occasions when the European powers ceded territory to the Ottomans in the seventeenth and eighteenth centuries, they sought to include similar guarantees for the Christian populations.[38] In general, however, the treaty practice with the Ottomans proceeded along very different lines. Like Christianity, Islam was an aggressively universalist religion, but the system of governance within the Ottoman lands permitted a considerable degree of religious tolerance.[39] The Muslim rulers[40] also issued unilateral

---

[35] For example, by virtue of the *Treaties of Peace* concluded in 1713 at Utrecht (which brought to an end the wars of the Spanish Succession), Great Britain undertook to allow Catholics the free exercise of their religion (as far as the laws of Great Britain permitted) in those areas of Newfoundland ceded to it by France (27 CTS 475) and in Gibraltar, ceded to Great Britain by Spain (27 CTS 295). Great Britain undertook similar obligations when acquiring Canada from France and Florida from Spain under the 1763 *Peace of Paris* (42 CTS 279).

[36] See, for example, article 10 of the *Treaty of Nystadt* (1721) concerning the free exercise of the Protestant religion and the maintenance of Protestant schools in areas ceded to Russia by Sweden (31 CTS 339); article 14 of the *Treaty of Hubertusburg* (1763) in which Prussia undertook to maintain Catholicism in Silesia (ceded by Austria), whilst not "detracting from the complete freedom of conscience of the Protestant religion" (42 CTS 347); article 8 of the *Treaty of Warsaw* (1773) securing to the Catholic populations of Pomerania and other areas of Greater Poland ceded by Poland to Prussia the exercise of their religion as at September 1772 (45 CTS 253); article 8 of the *Treaty of Grodno* (1793) which secured to both the Latin and Uniate Catholic population of Lithuania (ceded by Poland to Russia) full enjoyment of their possessions and rights within the ceded territories and, in addition, the freedom of worship throughout the entire Russian Empire (52 CTS 83).

[37] That is not to say that there were no moves towards religious tolerance. On the contrary, the spirit of the Enlightenment engendered a liberalization of internal regulation of religious affairs throughout Europe. The Napoleonic reordering of the western German states further eroded the doctrinal rigidity of many of the client states. See James J. Sheehan, *Oxford History of Modern Europe: German History, 1770–1866* (Oxford: Clarendon, 1989), 268–69.

[38] When Russia returned Bessarabia, Wallachia, and Moldavia to the Ottomans, the Sublime Porte undertook "to obstruct in no manner whatsoever the free exercise of the Christian religion" in those territories (*Treaty of Kutschuk-Kainardji,* 1774, art. 16[2]). When the 1856 *Treaty of Paris* (114 CTS 409), by which the Crimea war was terminated, confirmed Ottoman suzerainty over Wallachia, Moldavia (art. 22), and Serbia (art. 28), it did so subject to a specific undertaking to preserve, *inter alia,* "full liberty of worship."

[39] The legal system of the Empire was based on Muslim religious law, which was considered not to apply to disputes between non-Muslims. This affected the entire social structure of the Empire, which was based around the various *millets,* national groups, to which all subjects belonged. Therefore, status and legal capacity in the Empire was conditioned by religious adherence. See Stanford J. Shaw, *History of the Ottoman Empire and Modern Turkey* (Cambridge: Cambridge University Press, 1976), 1:151–53.

capitulations (grants), which permitted the Christians to establish communities with considerable autonomy, including the right of free and public worship,[41] over which the foreign powers concerned exercised extensive jurisdiction. This legitimized the intrusion of European states into the Ottoman world, and as the balance of power shifted, an increasing number of European states extracted the right to act as protectors of the religious freedom of their subjects, which easily elided into a claim that they were entitled to champion the liberties, religious and otherwise, of Christians in the Empire.[42] This ultimately became a pretext for intervention on their behalf.[43]

The new states, which were created by the intervention of the major European powers, were required to guarantee the freedom of worship and toleration in the private sphere, whilst at the same time preserving any preexisting rights of particular faiths or creeds. Otherwise, general principles of nondiscrimination were to apply in the public sphere.[44] Similar principles were applied when further territories were added to these states, whether from further inroads into Ottoman possessions or when areas were later redistributed between them. Stipulations in treaties of cession, however, related only to the areas to be transferred.[45]

Subsequent uprisings against Ottoman rule or overlordship sparked a further series of conflicts and interventions, which ultimately culminated in the 1878 Treaty of Berlin[46] which laid the foundations for much of the contemporary structure of the Balkans and Eastern Europe.

The Treaty of Berlin addressed religious questions in a common formulation that provided:

---

[40] See Nussbaum, *A Concise History of the Law of Nations,* 54–58. It should not be thought that "Capitulations" were only granted by the Muslim powers in that region. Christian communities in the East (such as the Kingdom of Jerusalem and Christian Armenia) granted similar rights to Western traders. To an extent, therefore, they represented a form of local custom concerning the reception of foreign interests into the community, which transcends the purely religious (Islamic) dimension.

[41] For example, in 1535 the *First Franco–Turkish Capitulation* provided that merchants, their agents, and servants "shall have the right to practice their own religion."

[42] Thus the *Treaty of Carlowitz* and the *Treaty of Passerowitz* extended to the Austrian Emperor the right, previously enjoyed solely by the French, to intercede on behalf of all Roman Catholics, and the *Treaty of Kutschuk–Kainardji* was understood by the Russians to grant them the right to intercede on behalf of all Orthodox believers. The right of "intercession" was interpreted as placing believers—Catholic and Orthodox—under the "protection" of the relevant power. See Nussbaum, *A Concise History of the Law of Nations,* 122.

[43] See Shaw, *History of the Ottoman Empire,* 189, 250.

[44] Thus in article 1 of the *Protocol of St. Petersburg* (76 CTS 175) (1826), Russia and Great Britain agreed that Greece should become a tribute-paying dependency of the Ottomans, within which there would be "a complete liberty of Conscience." However, in 1830 the Conference of London established an independent Kingdom in which all subjects, of whatever religion, were to be eligible for all forms of public office and employment "on the footing of perfect equality, without regard to difference of creed, in all their relations, religious, civil or political" (*Third Protocol of 1930 of the Conference Relative to the Independence of Greece between France, Great Britain and Russia,* 80 CTS 327).

[45] However, the *Isahat Fermani* of 1856 promised throughout the Empire "energetic measures to ensure to each sect, whatever the numbers of its adherents, entire freedom in the exercise of religion" and outlawed discrimination on religious grounds. The free profession of any religion was to be assured and "no one shall be forced to change his religion" See Stanford J. Shaw and Ezel K. Shaw, *History of the Ottoman Empire and Modern Turkey* (Cambridge: Cambridge University Press, 1977), 2: 124–28.

[46] *Treaty between Austria-Hungary, France, Germany, Great Britain, Italy, Russia, and Turkey for the Settlement of Affairs in the East,* signed 13 July 1878 at Berlin, 153 CTS 171.

> [T]he difference of religious creeds and confessions shall not be alleged against any person as a ground for exclusion or incapacity in matters relating to the enjoyment of civil and political rights, admission to public employment, functions, and honours, or the exercise of the various professions and industries in any locality whatsoever.
>
> The freedom and outward exercise of all forms of worship shall be assured to all persons belonging to [the territorial unit concerned], as well as to foreigners, and no hindrance shall be offered either to the hierarchical organisation of the different communions, or to their relations with their spiritual chiefs.[47]

This was inserted in the sections of the Treaty which constituted Bulgaria as an autonomous principality under Ottoman suzerainty[48] and which recognized Montenegrin independence.[49] The Treaty also recognized the independence of Serbia[50] and of Romania,[51] but in both of these cases recognition was made conditional upon the stipulations concerning religion.[52] The Porte also undertook a range of obligations in respect of its remaining territories similar to those required of the newly recognized states.[53] Austria-Hungary remained in occupation of Bosnia-Herzgovina and undertook its administration.[54] In 1879, the Porte agreed that this should continue, with the proviso that the Muslim population be permitted the free practice of their faith.[55]

As the dismemberment of the Ottoman Empire unfolded, the focus of attention moved away from the rights of the Powers to represent the interests of the non-Muslim subjects of the Empire, and towards the newly established states, over which they sought influence. Religious factors played a significant role, with Russia continuing to assert itself as the champion of the Orthodox cause (Greece being manifestly unable to exert the same degree of political influence) whilst Austria-Hungary supported the Catholic interest in the west of the Balkans. The most important aspect of the Treaty of Berlin was, however, the precedent provided by making the recognition of Romania[56] and Serbia conditional upon their according religious equality and freedom of

---

[47] Ibid., art. 5.

[48] Ibid.

[49] Ibid., art. 26. All contracting states with the exception of the Porte and England had already recognized Montenegro.

[50] Ibid., art. 35.

[51] Ibid., art. 44.

[52] Ibid., art. 34 and art. 43, respectively. In the case of Romania an additional stipulation was that "the subjects and citizens of all the Powers, traders or otherwise, shall be treated in Romania, without distinction of creed, on a footing of perfect equality."

[53] Ibid., art. 62.

[54] Ibid., art. 25.

[55] *Convention between Austria-Hungary and Turkey, Relative to the Occupation of Bosnia-Herzegovina*, 1879 (155 CTS 59), art. 2: "The freedom and outward exercise of all existing religions shall be assured to persons residing or sojourning in Bosnia and the Herzegovina." This was reaffirmed following the Austro-Hungarian annexation of the territory in 1908 (*Protocol between Austria-Hungary and Turkey Relating to Bosnia-Herzegovina and the Sandjak of Novi Pazar*, 1910, art. 4, 208 CTS 355).

[56] The situation in Romania was particularly volatile since the Romanian Organic law of 1866 discriminated against non-Christians by rendering them ineligible for citizenship, and Romania possessed a large Jewish population, which was rapidly expanding due to emigration by Jews seeking to escape from Russian anti-Semitism. Making recognition conditional upon the implementation of these guarantees was intended to ensure that religious tensions would not precipitate further interventions. In fact, they very nearly precipitated the very eventuality they were designed to forestall, and the threat of intervention by Britain and

worship to all "belonging to" the territory. This added a new element to the *corpus iuris publici orientalis*, the hallmark of which was the guaranteeing of existing rights and freedoms and of ensuring that minority religious communities were not subjected to discrimination in secular matters. In addition, the obligations undertaken were to be tailored to fit the needs of the particular communities concerned where this was thought necessary. The involvement of the European Powers in the Balkans continued in a similar footing right up to the outbreak of World War I.[57] This then provided precedents that were adopted at the last of the great Conferences providing for the settlement of European territorial questions, at Paris in 1919.

IV. Developments after World War I

The fate of Jewish communities in newly recognized states forms a thread which directly connects the Treaty of Berlin with the reordering of Europe undertaken at the Paris Peace Conference of 1919. The general provisions on religious freedom in the Treaty of Berlin had proved ineffectual in Romania[58] and Jewish lobbyists were anxious to ensure that more effective mechanisms were in place to protect Jewish communities in the new Polish state.[59] The resulting Polish Minorities Treaty became a model for a series of Minorities Treaties which, in the model of the Treaty of Berlin, were imposed upon the newly created states of Poland, Yugoslavia, and Czechoslovakia at the time of their recognition, and upon Romania and Greece when they received territorial gains from the peace treaties.[60] Article 2 of the Polish (and other) Minorities Treaties and similar instruments provided:

> Poland undertakes to assure full and complete protection of life and liberty to all inhabitants of Poland without distinction of birth, nationality, language, race or religion. All inhabitants of Poland shall be entitled to the free exercise, whether public or private, of any creed, religion or belief, whose practices are not inconsistent with public order or public morals.

This obligation is couched in general terms and applied to all inhabitants. Whilst it did not offer an unfettered right to the free exercise of religion it was a significant development. However, the very fact of its being associated with a minorities treaty served to

---

France was needed to induce Romania to repeal the discriminatory provisions, following which recognition was granted by all the Contracting states. See Georges Castellan, *History of the Balkans from Mohammed the Conqueror to Stalin* (New York: Columbia University Press, 1992), 340–41.

[57] Although the treaties that terminated the Balkan Wars of 1912–13 did not contain any provision regarding the free practice of religion, the Balkan states subsequently concluded a series of bilateral treaties with Turkey, each of which included elaborate provisions dealing with the rights of the Muslim population to the free practice of their religion, the maintenance of religious foundations, and the jurisdiction of Muslim religious courts. Indeed, the Treaty that was concluded with Bulgaria even exempted the Muslim population from any obligation to pay military taxes and to undertake military service.

[58] See Jacques Fouques-Duparc, *La Protection des Minorités de Race, de Langue et de Religion* (Paris: Libraire Dalloz, 1922), 99–113.

[59] For a detailed study see Nathan Feinburg, *La Question des Minorités à la Conference de la Paix de 1919–1920 et l'action Juive en faveur de la Protection International des Minorités* (Paris: Rousseau et Cie, 1929).

[60] It also provided a model for clauses inserted into the peace treaties concluded with Germany, Austria, Hungary, and Bulgaria and for a series of declarations that were made upon their joining the League of Nations by Albania, Lithuania, Estonia, Latvia, and Iraq. See Evans, *Religious Liberty and International Law in Europe*, 135–42.

undermine its broader impact, coupled with which there were doubts as to whether it was subject to the guarantee of the League of Nations provided for in article 12 of the treaty.[61] Moreover, the primary purpose of the Polish Treaty was to offer protection to the Jewish minority in Poland. This is made clear by the special "Jewish clauses" which concerned Sabbath worship and provisions concerning educational facilities (articles 9 and 10). The other minorities treaties, too, were adapted to reflect the needs of the relevant religious communities concerned.[62]

It seems clear that the post–WW I settlement continued the tradition of being primarily concerned with securing the religious freedoms of members of a number of identified religious communities which were considered to be in a vulnerable position as a result of the territorial changes which were occurring. Once the methodology was established, it was applied with a certain degree of consistency to other states in not dissimilar positions even if the need was not as acute. The means adopted combined a number of techniques. First, there were general prohibitions of discrimination on the grounds of religion in a limited number of fields (life and liberty) combined with a general guarantee of the free exercise of religion, subject to certain restrictions. These are the same techniques which are now found in the principal human rights instruments—what has been characterized as the "right of free exercise" and the "right to nondiscrimination." They were, however, supplemented by case-specific additions and it is evident that it was the "special cases" rather than the general provisions, which were the principal focus of attention. This feature of past practice has not been carried over into the post–WW II international legal order.

It was correctly perceived that the interwar system was designed to protect either the religious rights of minorities or the rights of religious minorities, and it was as a minorities system that it was judged. Indeed, the entire period from the Peace of Westphalia to the post–WW I peace settlement can be seen—if only in retrospect—as a period in which the protection of freedom of religion or belief at the international level was founded on what would now be termed a "minorities' rights" approach. However, the seeds of an entirely different approach to the international protection of religious liberty emerged during the drafting of the Covenant of the League of Nations at the Paris Peace Conference in 1919.[63] Woodrow Wilson, President of the USA, championed the inclusion of an article in the Covenant of the League of Nations to the effect that:

---

[61] See *Acquisition of Polish Nationality*, Advisory Opinion, PCIJ Series B, No. 7:17 (1923) and *Treatment of Polish Nations and Other Persons of Polish Origins or Speech in the Danzig Territory*, Advisory Opinion, PCIJ, Series A/B, No. 44, 39 (1932), which suggest that the League's guarantee of minority rights under article 12 extended to the free exercise of religion under article 2, but not to the same rights of non-minority groups.

[62] The *Greek Minorities Treaty*, LNTS 711 (1920) contained a modified version of the "Jewish clauses" as article 10 and new articles concerning Muslim communities (art. 14), the Monks of Mount Athos (art. 13), and religious autonomy of the Vlachs of Pindus (art. 12). A separate provision relating to the Jews of Salonika was mooted, but not pressed. The *Yugoslav Minorities Treaty*, LNTS 39 (1919), contained special measures for Muslims (art. 10). The Romanians pressed hard and successfully to ensure the deletion of the Jewish clauses from the *Romanian Minorities Treaty*, LNTS 140 (1919), but it did include special measures for the Saxons and Szeklers (art. 11).

[63] See generally David H. Miller, *The Drafting of the Covenant*, 2 vols. (New York: Putnam's Sons, 1928).

> The High Contracting Parties agree that they will make no law prohibiting or interfering with the free exercise of religion, and that they will in no way discriminate, either in law or in fact, against those who practise any particular creed, religion, or belief whose practices are not inconsistent with public order or public needs.[64]

This represented a radical departure from previous practice in that it would have placed an obligation upon all members of the League of Nations, rather than on a selected range of newly created, enlarged, or defeated states. There was little enthusiasm for this article, although few seemed willing to oppose it directly. However, when the Japanese delegation proposed that the Covenant should also include an article concerning racial equality, as it seemed to them that "matters of religion and race could go well together,"[65] it was decided to drop both.[66] Nevertheless, this contributed to the pool of experience, was reflected in article 2 of the Polish, and other, Minorities Treaties, and prefigured article 18 of the Universal Declaration on Human Rights (UDHR) and subsequent international human rights instruments.

V. The Post–World War II Period

As is well known, the Second World War ushered in a period in which minorities' protection was shunned in favor of the recognition of universal and individual human rights. The right to the free exercise of religion was one of the very first to be articulated, being one of the four basic freedoms outlined by President Roosevelt and emphasized in the 1942 Declaration by the United Nations. Its inclusion in the Universal Declaration on Human Rights was never a matter of doubt. It seems, however, as if the task of defining freedom of religion or belief in an abstract fashion, and as a norm of general application, shorn from any particular context, proved more difficult than had been imagined.[67] The content of the right became a matter of some controversy, the principal points at issue being: the protection of nonreligious patterns of thought and belief, including atheism; the point at which restrictions on the exercise of freedom of religion became permissible; and the grounds upon which such interference could be justified. The issue of proselytism was an underlying concern, and a further crucial issue raised by a number of Islamic states was the question of whether freedom of religion included freedom to change one's religion. Some of these difficulties were addressed. By including "thought and conscience" alongside religion, nontheistic patterns of thought and belief are included, and the Declaration explicitly endorses freedom to change one's religion. However, on the more subtle points of interpretation it seems that although there was widespread agreement concerning the merits of

---

[64] Supplementary Agreement 7, as subsequently modified. See Miller, *The Drafting of the Covenant,* 1:53, 2:67. This, of course, owes a debt to the First Amendment to the US Constitution of 1791.

[65] Miller, ibid., 1:323–24.

[66] See Francis P. Walters, *A History of the League of Nations,* 2 vols. (London: Oxford University Press, 1952), 1:64, who observed that "the Japanese argument combined disconcertingly, from the British and American point of view, the qualities of being unanswerable and unacceptable. The only course, therefore, was to abandon both."

[67] On the drafting of article 18 of the UDHR, see Martin Scheinin, "Article 18," in *The Universal Declaration of Human Rights: A Common Standard of Achievement,* ed. Asbjørn Eide and Gudmundur Alfredsson (Boston: Martinus Nijhoff, 1999), 379–82; Evans, *Religious Liberty and International Law in Europe,* 183–93.

the text ultimately adopted, there was no real consensus concerning its meaning.[68] It is salutary to note that several of the later chapters of this book are devoted to exploring a number of unresolved difficulties.

It was always intended that the UDHR would be followed up by a legally binding Convention, and it was hoped that these problems would be addressed in that process. Unfortunately, not only was this not the case, but the corresponding article of the ICCPR—also article 18—cast some doubt on one aspect of the UDHR by replacing the explicit endorsement of freedom to change one's religion with the altogether more opaque language of freedom to "have or to adopt" a religion of one's choice.[69] Be that as it may, the twin articles 18 stand together as an attempt by the international community to forge an understanding of the content of freedom of religion or belief, an attempt which has since been taken further by the interpretive work of the Human Rights Committee with relation to the ICCPR and in particular its General Comment No. 22(48) adopted in 1993.[70]

In the early developmental work the second element of the protective scheme, the right of nondiscrimination on grounds of religion, received comparatively little attention. In the early 1960s, however, developments took place within the UN sphere which have had the effect of shifting the emphasis away from examining freedom of religion or belief and towards a consideration of discrimination on the grounds of religion or belief. The origins of this lie in the Krishnaswami Report, which was commissioned by the UN Sub-Commission on Prevention of Discrimination and Protection of Minorities and submitted to the Commission on Human Rights in 1960.[71] Although entitled "Study of Discrimination in the Matter of Religious Rights and Practices," this report ranged beyond discrimination and probed questions relating to freedom of religion or belief. It concluded with a series of "basic rules" which elaborated the meaning of article 18 of the UDHR and formed the basis of the Sub-Commission's own "Draft Principles on Freedom and Non-Discrimination in the matter of religious Rights and Freedoms." The Krishnaswami Report is itself testimony to the difficulty of examining discrimination without having a firmer grasp of what is meant by freedom of religion or belief, and in 1962 the UN Commission on Human Rights began a consideration of the Draft Principles which would have considered these in tandem

[68] For instance, the Danish member of the UNGA 3rd Committee abstained in the vote adopting the text of the article because "it could be seen that the various delegations would interpret the provisions of the declaration in different ways" (GAOR, 3rd Sess., pt. 1, 407 [1949]).

[69] On the drafting of article 18 of the ICCPR, see Marc J. Bossuyt, *Guide to the Travaux Préparatoires of the International Covenant on Civil and Political Rights* (Boston: Martinus Nijhoff, 1987), 351–71.

[70] CCPR/C/21/Rev.1/Add.4, adopted on 20 July 1993. An analysis of the work of the Human Rights Committee is beyond the scope of this paper. For detailed examinations, see Bahiyyih G. Tahzib, *Freedom of Religion or Belief: Ensuring Effective International Legal Protection* (Boston: Martinus Nijhoff, 1996), 249–375; for a more concise overview, Natan Lerner, "Religious Human Rights under the United Nations," in *Religious Human Rights in Global Perspective: Legal Perspectives,* ed. Johan D. van der Vyver and John Witte, Jr. (Boston: Martinus Nijhoff, 1996), 94–100; Evans, *Religious Liberty and International Law in Europe,* 207–26; and Malcolm D. Evans, "The United Nations and the Freedom of Religion: The Work of the Human Rights Committee," in *Law and Religion,* ed. Rex Adhar (Aldershot: Ashgate, 2000).

[71] UN Doc. E/CN.4/Sub.2/200/Rev.1. As with the *Minorities Treaties,* the origins of this report lay in pressure from Jewish lobby groups. See Natan Lerner, "Towards a Draft Declaration against Religious Intolerance and Discrimination," *Israel Yearbook of Human Rights* 11 (1981): 83.

once again. However, this was overtaken by events: Mounting Third World pressure resulted in the General Assembly requesting the Commission to prepare a Declaration and Convention on the Elimination of All Forms of Racial Discrimination.[72] As something of a *quid pro quo*, it also requested that a Declaration and Convention on the Elimination of Religious Intolerance be commenced.[73]

Although work on the Declaration and Convention on Racial Discrimination proceeded rapidly, it was not until 1981 that the Declaration on the Elimination of All Forms of Intolerance and Discrimination based on Religion or Belief was adopted.[74] Work on the Convention, originally given priority over the Declaration, has come to a standstill, with the majority of commentators believing that although such an instrument is, in principle, desirable, it is premature to proceed. As has already been mentioned, the Declaration follows the well-established pattern of combining the expression of freedom of religion or belief (article 1) with the norm of nondiscrimination (article 2). It also goes beyond previous instruments by including in article 6 a catalogue of specific forms that the freedom set out in article 1 might take. The task of securing the implementation of the Declaration falls to the UN Special Rapporteur, whose mandate was established in 1986, and his work provides the most authoritative interpretation of the Declaration.[75]

In all of this, however, there has been a dramatic shift in focus that needs to be emphasized. In his now famous 1941 Annual Address to Congress, US President Roosevelt included "freedom of worship" in his list of four "basic" freedoms and when this was omitted (along with the freedom of expression) from the "Atlantic Charter," he was prompted to observe that:

> It is unnecessary for me to point out that the declaration of principles includes of necessity the world need for freedom of religion and freedom of information. No society of the world organized under the announced principles [freedom from want and freedom from fear] could survive without these freedoms, which are a part of the whole freedom for which we strive.[76]

---

[72] UNGA Res. 1780 (17), 7 December 1962.

[73] UNGA Res. 1781 (17), 7 December 1962.

[74] The background to the 1981 Declaration and its subsequent interpretation are considered by Tahzib, *Freedom of Religion or Belief*, 122–212; Evans, *Religious Liberty and International Law in Europe*, 227–61; Lerner, "Religious Human Rights under the United Nations," 114–23; Donna Sullivan, "Advancing the Freedom of Religion or Belief through the UN Declaration on the Elimination of Religious Intolerance and Discrimination," *American Journal of International Law* 82 (1988): 487–520; Brice Dickson, "The UN and Freedom of Religion," *International and Comparative Law Quarterly* 44 (1995), 344–52.

[75] The mandate of the Special Rapporteur was established in Commision on Human Rights Resolution 1986/20 (1986). For the background, see David Weissbrodt, "The Three 'Theme' Special Rapporteurs of the UN Commission on Human Rights," *American Journal of International Law* 80 (1986): 697. It was most recently renewed for a three-year period in 2001 (see Commision on Human Rights Resolution 2001/42, [E/CN.4/RES/2001/42, adopted 23 April 2001]) and the title of the mandate changed from "Special Rapporteur on Religious Intolerance" (as it had become customary to refer to it) to "Special Rapporteur on Freedom of Religion or Belief." This is a more neutral title and the Special Rapporteur himself had requested the change some years earlier (see his *Report to the 54th Session of the Commission on Human Rights*, E/CN.4/1998/6, paras. 104–5).

[76] See Ruth B. Russell, *A History of the United Nations Charter: The Role of the United States 1940–1945*, (Washington, DC: The Brookings Institute, 1958), 41–42.

Such an approach sees the freedom of religion and belief as foundational. The entire construct of society is conditional upon its realization: it is a basic presupposition. This was then reflected in the 1942 Declaration by the United Nations, the Preamble to which provided that "complete victory over their enemies is essential to defend life, liberty, independence and religious freedom, and to preserve human rights and justice."[77] Once again, this places the protection of religious freedom on par with the preservation of human rights and justice. All these basic goods—life, liberty, independence and religious freedom, and the preservation of human rights and justice—are sought. This differs from the now familiar human rights approach which sees the freedom of religion (along with life, liberty, and independence) as an element within the overall scheme of human rights protection.[78] The last fifty years of the twentieth century have seen a diminution in the importance attached to the achievement of freedom of religion or belief, both by its incorporation *into* the human rights canon and by the manner in which it has fared *as* a human right.

VI. Concluding Thoughts

This chapter is written at the time of transition from the second to the third Christian millennium. It might be sheer coincidence, but at this time the principal national newspapers in the United Kingdom seemed to be carrying an unusually large number of items of news and comment on matters pertaining to religious belief. Much of this was concerned, not with reflections upon the content of religious belief, but rather with the consequences of religious belief for world peace and stability. This reflected the trite observation that whilst the great world religions urge their adherents to follow paths of peace, religious differences have proved a fertile ground for conflict in the past and will continue to pose a significant threat to peace in the years that lie ahead.

An exception to this was the report of a speech by the Bishop of London in which he challenged the "widely held view that religion is the most significant cause of war in human history," dubbing it "the orthodoxy of public house lounge bars."[79] However, it appears that his criticism was based on the extent to which conflict in the twentieth century was attributable to "secular messianic states, such as those under communist or fascist regimes"[80] rather than challenging the notion that religion has, historically, been a significant source of conflict.[81] Moreover, even if the Bishop's analysis is correct as regards the twentieth century, it does not automatically follow that this pattern will

---

[77] Ibid., 977.

[78] For example, the European Court of Human Rights now endorses the general proposition that "as enshrined in Article 9, freedom of thought, conscience and religion is one of the foundations of a 'democratic society' within the meaning of the Convention [ECHR]. It is, in its religious dimension, one of the most vital elements that go to make up the identity of believers and their conception of life, but it is also a precious asset for atheists, agnostics, sceptics and the unconcerned. The pluralism indissociable from a democratic society, which has been dearly won over the centuries, depends on it" (Kokkinakis v. Greece, 17 EHRR 397 [1994] [ECtHR 260-A, 25 May 1993], para. 53).

[79] *The Times,* 1 December 1999.

[80] Ibid.

[81] For a different perspective, see David Martin, *Does Christianity Cause War?* (Oxford: Clarendon, 1997), who argues that it is not so much religion but the degree of identification between the state and organized religion that conditions the extent to which religion either has, or is perceived as having, the propensity to

continue into the next. Indeed, the real question that needs to be addressed concerns the nature of the dominant forces within the international community in the years that lie ahead. Huntington has forcefully argued the thesis that the next major phase in international relations will reflect the interactions, not of nation states or of ideologies, but of civilizations.[82] Moreover, Huntington argues that of all the elements which unite to form a civilization, "the most important usually is religion."[83]

Many in the western world see this as little more than anachronistic scare-mongering, denying that religion today has that capacity to move them to violence that it apparently had in the past. Western secular modernists (and some religious apologists) will accept that there are plenty of examples of conflicts which are expressed in terms of religious difference, but they may either deny that the underlying cause of such conflict is truly religious in nature, or will draw on that as a justification for the rejection of religious values (or such versions of them). Religious beliefs which give rise to conflict or which resort to violence are considered dangerous, deviant or both. To put it starkly, many take the view that we have outgrown religiously motivated conflict, and that if others have not yet done so, they should. Private religious belief is one thing, intercommunal discord is quite another.

But what of the churches themselves? In October 1517, Martin Luther launched the Protestant reformation by posting his ninety-five theses on the Castle Church door in Wittenberg. On 31 October 1999, representatives of the Lutheran World Federation and the Catholic Church met at Augsburg to sign an Official Common Statement, endorsing a Joint Declaration on the Doctrine of Justification. Since, as the Joint Declaration notes, "[t]he doctrine of justification was of central importance for the Lutheran Reformation"[84] it is, perhaps, not entirely hyperbolic for *The Times* newspaper, in a report headed, "Catholics reconciled with Lutherans" to claim that in signing this Declaration the churches were "ending the five-century-old dispute that launched the Protestant Reformation and led to the Thirty Years War."[85]

Without attempting to explore the theological significance of the Joint Declaration, the general message that it conveys is rather surprising. At first sight, the central point appears to be that the remaining points of disagreement concerning the doctrine of justification can now be subsumed within the general agreement that now

---

"cause" war. Noting the historical drift towards greater differentiation between the state and religion, Martin takes the view that "the historical period when religion might plausibly be indicted as *itself* an issue about which men or monarchs might go to war is long past. Since the seventeenth century the involvement of religion in wars has been largely as one marker of national identity, though a major one" (104, emphasis in original).

[82] Samuel P. Huntington, *The Clash of Civilizations and the Remaking of World Order* (New York: Simon and Schuster, 1996). Subsequent page references are to the 1998 edition published in the UK by Touchstone Books.

[83] Ibid., 42. Huntington goes back to Herodotus in his support of this proposition. If some within the western world find this difficult to accept, it might be because, as Huntington notes, modern western civilization is unique among (his) civilizations in not having given birth to one of the current major world religions (54).

[84] *Joint Declaration*, Preamble, para. 1. The Joint Declaration, Official Common Statement, and other pertinent documents are available online at <http://www.lutheranworld.org/SpecialEvents/Justification/OfficialDocuments.EN.html>.

[85] *The Times*, 1 November 1999.

attaches to the reformulation that is offered.[86] However, the "disputes" are not "solved"; rather, they are now viewed in a different context, a context in which what unites is seen to be stronger than what divides. Quite how and why this shift in perspective has come about is an interesting question which cannot be pursued here. The crucial point is that the Churches are careful not to jettison the historical controversies and reject them all as ill-founded. On the contrary, the Joint Declaration stresses that "Nothing . . . is taken away from the seriousness of the condemnations related to the doctrine of justification. Some were not simply pointless."[87] It emphasizes that both churches consider that those Condemnations which they made of the others' positions during the Reformation remain as valid today as they were then, and only lose their validity when read against the newly adopted common understanding.[88] Moreover, and vitally, the Joint Declaration is "shaped by the conviction that in their respective histories [the] churches have come to new insights."[89] In other words, there is no suggestion that the entire controversy had been a ghastly mistake that could have been avoided if only the theologians had tried as hard then as they have now.[90] They might have "moved on"[91] from their past as the prevailing circumstances have changed around them, but they have not moved away from it.

Many other examples of this line of thinking could have been given, but it is particularly apposite as a conclusion to an overview of how freedom of religion or belief has evolved over time, since it takes us back to the dawning of the contemporary system born out the Peace of Westphalia. It also takes us back to the origins of our current understandings of the place of freedom of religion or belief within the international community. The purpose of this chapter was to review that story and note the options that it presents us with. It was premised upon the conviction that religion and belief are important to individuals, to nations, and to civilizations and must be approached on that basis. The Joint Declaration says that "Developments have taken place which not only make possible, but also require the churches to examine the divisive questions and condemnations and see them in a new light."[92] The gloss that must be added to the Joint Declaration is, however, that it is not just the churches which need to take stock of their position in the light of new developments.

The idea that freedom of religion or belief should be seen as a technique for avoiding religious conflict may seem paradoxical since it often seems as if differences of religion generate more conflict than they solve: Freedom of religion can be seen as

---

[86] The essence of this is set out in the *Joint Declaration*, para. 15, which reads: "Together we confess: By Grace alone, in faith in Christ's saving work and not because of any merit on our part, we are accepted by God and receive the Holy Spirit, who renews our hearts while equipping and calling us to good works."

[87] *Joint Declaration*, para. 42. At the same time, this suggests that a number of them were pointless.

[88] Ibid., para. 41. This was clearly a matter of some controversy, and the Official Common Statement, para. 2, clarified the matter by asserting that "the earlier mutual condemnations do not apply to the teaching of the dialogue partners *as presented in the Joint Declaration*" (emphasis added). See also the Annex to the Official Common Statement, para. 1.

[89] Ibid., para. 7.

[90] There is currently something of a trend for church leaders to offer apologies and seek repentance for the historic wrongs of their churches, but it seems as if the Reformation and the resistance to it is not (yet?) seen as something to be sorry for, even if the wars and devastation which followed in its wake are doubtless considered to be a matter for sorrow and regret.

[91] *Joint Declaration*, para. 7.

[92] Ibid.

part of the problem and not a part of the solution. There is, in fact, a degree of truth in this observation, since the exercise of freedom of religion or belief can indeed generate conflict with those who do not share a common belief.[93] It is therefore not surprising that one of the most common approaches to avoiding religious conflict today is to seek to balance the exercise of religion and belief against other competing values, religious or otherwise, in the belief that this will help achieve an accommodation of interests acceptable to all parties. This is certainly the current position taken within the body of international human rights law, which sees freedom of religion or belief as only one of a number of rights the enjoyment of which is to be guaranteed to individuals, a theme which is explored in a number of subsequent chapters.

Whatever the merits of this particular approach within the human rights context, it must be recognized that religious conflict also takes place at other levels, for example, when states themselves come into conflict over matters of religion and belief. In such a context the "relativising" approach of the human rights instruments has little role to play. In other words, important as this approach is, it is not the only way in which the international community has faced up to the problems posed by religious dissent and diversity. Indeed, as the earlier sections of this chapter have shown, the very structure of the contemporary international community of sovereign states is the legacy of previous attempts to "solve" these problems, but on a wholly different basis—by recognizing that facilitating the exercise of freedom of religion or belief where it is not enjoyed is indeed a way of addressing religious conflict.

Just as the manner in which the international community has addressed these issues has changed over time, so has the manner in which it perceives religious belief. As has been seen, in the middle centuries of the last millennium, religion was a dominant force in European political life. In the nineteenth century, concern for the fate of religious minorities provided the justification for foreign interventions[94] and influenced the practice of recognition of states,[95] whilst in the interwar years of the twentieth century, the Minorities Treaties system originated in the desire to protect vulnerable religious groups.[96] This chapter shows that the international interest in securing freedom of religion or belief is indeed older, and runs deeper, than the framework of human rights thinking, which simply provides the most recent vehicle through which the international community is evidencing its concern for freedom of religion or belief.

[93] Thus Martin concludes: "The great world religions together with the two or three secular universalisms (themselves metamorphoses of religious logic), are all mutually irreconcilable. To that extent the aspiration to peace is itself a source of conflict . . . we are all of us trapped in the paradox of 'wars to end wars.' It is our human condition." Martin, *Does Christianity Cause War?* 160.

[94] For example, the "French Intervention" on behalf of Maronite Christians in what is today Lebanon. See Ian Brownlie, *International Law and the Use of Force By States* (Oxford: Clarendon, 1963), 339–40.

[95] See, for example, the 1878 *Treaty of Berlin,* art. 34 and art. 43.

[96] See Evans, *Religious Liberty and International Law in Europe,* chap. 4.

Chapter 2

Philosophical and Religious Justifications of Freedom of Religion or Belief

Tore Lindholm

I. Introduction

This chapter deals with the problem of public justification of the human right to freedom of religion or belief[1] in a religiously, philosophically, and culturally division-prone world.

Validating human rights across philosophical divides may, even to a knowledgeable expert, appear an intractable task:

> The UN conception of human rights, as expressed in the Universal Declaration, gives rise to a dilemma. If this conception of human rights has a philosophical justification, this will almost certainly be controversial, since all philosophical theories of rights are controversial. However, if the concept of human rights has no philosophical justification, then its claim to have moral force is unfounded.[2]

The moral force behind the idea of modern human rights in some form is no longer a highly contested public issue. But the "why" of their moral force remains troublesome in several respects. In the first place, the range of human rights in general, as well as the content, scope, and limits of particular rights, remains highly contested. The nature of justifications may turn critically on precisely what is to be justified. Different justifications may warrant different rights and rights with different coverage and applications. Second, differing justifications may suggest different rankings and weightings of rights when competing rights come into conflict. And third, there are questions about how competing justifications are to coexist in a common social space. Such issues are particularly problematic in the domain of freedom of religion or belief. Although the existence of the right is widely recognized in the abstract, its concrete implications are

[1] The core elements of the modern, internationally recognized human right to freedom of religion or belief are outlined in the Introduction to the present volume.

[2] Michael Freeman, *Human Rights: An interdisciplinary approach* (Cambridge: Polity, 2002), 41–42. Displaying the grounds of moral validity for the particular human right to freedom of religion or belief is, I suggest below, fraught with dilemmas as recalcitrant as is justification of human rights in general.

Tore Lindholm, W. Cole Durham, Jr., Bahia G. Tahzib-Lie (eds.), Facilitating Freedom of Religion or Belief: A Deskbook, *19–61.*

often hotly contested. This is true in part because of the incredible diversity of religious phenomena, and in part because of the at times tragic conflicts that may arise between religious freedom claims and other human rights, in particular women's rights.[3] The "ambivalence of the sacred"[4] calls on the one hand for the highest order human rights protections and at the same time for some of the highest order protections against abuse.

This chapter, however, does not address specific controversies over the content, scope, limits, or relative weight of the human right to freedom of religion or belief.[5] It deals, rather, with the more basic task of spelling out the proper grounds of public legitimacy for this human right, bridging as it were recognized and abiding religious and philosophical divides. I shall argue that such public validation, in a social world that has become secular and pluralist,[6] must take the shape of overlapping justification[7] of the human right to freedom of religion or belief.

Contestable norms tend to be deemed worthy of public trust, and their political and legal implementation becomes increasingly stable, to the extent they are generally understood or perceived to enjoy well-founded, noncoerced, and widely acceptable normative legitimacy. This chapter should help clear the ground for reasonable and

---

[3] See chapters 19 through 23 of the present volume. For an insightful discussion of collisions and tensions at the intersection of religious freedom rights and women's rights see Martha Nussbaum, "The Role of Religion," chap. 3 in *Women and Human Development* (Cambridge: Cambridge University Press, 2000), 167–240. Nussbaum's analysis proceeds not in terms of human rights; rather she advocates what amounts to a human rights "proxy": a duty on all governments to recognize and implement constitutional principles safeguarding specific human capabilities "as a bare minimum of what respect for human dignity requires" (5).

[4] R. Scott Appleby, *The Ambivalence of the Sacred: Religion, Violence, and Reconciliation* (Lanham: Rowman & Littlefield Publishers, Inc., 2000).

[5] Most chapters in the present volume deal with complex and often contentious matters relating to the proper demarcation of the human right to freedom of religion or belief.

[6] I explain the conception of a secular society in subsection III.E below. Here I just note that its structure bars societal hegemony of any particular religion, ideology, or Weltanschauung. I use the terms "plural" and "plurality" to indicate the "co-presence of many," in this context the co-presence of people adhering to many diverging communities and traditions of religion and life stance; the terms "pluralist" and "pluralism" are used to indicate a cognitive or evaluative "stance to plurality." The plurality/pluralism distinction may sound strange to American ears. The distinction is used by Ian S. Markham, *Plurality and Christian Ethics*, rev. ed. (New York: Seven Ridges Press, 1999); see the review of Markham by R. J. Neuhaus in *First Things* 46 (October 1994): 74–88.

[7] The term "overlapping justification" alludes to John Rawls' doctrine of an "overlapping consensus" about the principles of social justice; see his *Political Liberalism* (New York: Columbia University Press, 1993), 131–72. Alerted by David Little ("Rethinking Human Rights: Religion, Relativism, and Other Matters," *Journal of Religious Ethics* 27 [1999]: 151–57) I prefer the term "overlapping justification" to make clear that what is at stake is justification, not just agreement (a stance shared, I believe, by Rawls most of the time in his theory of social justice). Applying Rawlsian ideas to the challenge of cross-cultural legitimation of universal human rights was proposed at the October 1989 Saskatoon Conference on Human Rights in Cross-Cultural Perspectives; see Abdullahi Ahmed An-Na'im, ed. *Human Rights in Cross-Cultural Perspectives. A Quest for Consensus* (Philadelphia: University of Pennsylvania Press, 1992), 387–435, at 400. Instead of "overlapping justification" we may, alternatively, speak about "ecumenical justification" or "plural justification." The term "ecumenical justification" is introduced, with special reference to human rights, by Joseph Chan, "A Confucian Perspective on Human Rights for Contemporary China," in *The East Asian Challenge for Human Rights*, ed. Joanne R. Bauer and Daniel A. Bell (Cambridge: Cambridge University Press, 1999), 212–37, at 212. Says Chan, "ecumenical justification . . . encourages different cultures to justify human rights in their own terms and perspectives . . ." I have argued the case for "plural justification"

stable support of freedom of religion or belief, anchored in different and competing normative commitments in the present-day world, by demonstrating how an overlapping justification may constitute a basis for mutual solidarity across the divides of diverging normative traditions.

The philosophical task I am taking up, then, might be regarded as a kind of "meta-facilitation" of freedom of religion or belief. My aim is to contribute to the overall purpose of this volume not by providing a univocal philosophical justification of the internationally recognized norms encapsulated in freedom of religion or belief, but rather by arguing the case for thinking that stability at the level of social life is not jeopardized by but *requires* plurality at the foundations of the right to freedom of religion or belief.

Thus the argument of this chapter is to encourage public espousals of differing yet overlapping justifications of the right—justifications that are well grounded in the doctrinal heartlands of contemporary religions and life stances[8]—and to show how these committed modes of discourse can provide stable footing for a universally applicable freedom of religion or belief norm. This approach is resolutely pluralist, in that it contends that the plurality of beliefs that is protected by freedom of religion or belief at the level of individual and collective life does not need to be compromised at the level of justifying the right. In this endeavor, the proper role of philosophy in my view is that of the Lockean "under-labourer" and not that of the Platonic "philosopher-king."[9]

Section II presents two dilemmas that arise once we seek to base public justification of universal norms of freedom of religion or belief on the doctrinal commitments of differing, and more or less rivaling, religions and life stances. Left unresolved both dilemmas may trigger threats to civil peace and social stability.

Section III considers historical shifts in the social forms, political contexts, and normative rationales of religious freedom. It delineates the problem-situation for principled public support of the human right to freedom of religion or belief in a world that may have become irreversibly secular and pluralist and is nevertheless experiencing hefty religious resurgence.

---

of universal human rights in Tore Lindholm, "Ethical Justification of Universal Rights across Normative Divides," in *Universal Ethics. Perspectives and Proposals from Scandinavian Scholars*, ed. G. Bexell and D. E. Andersson (The Hague: Kluwer Law International: 2002), 63–83.

8 The term "life stance" is chosen to capture nonreligious positions referred to by the term "belief" in the human rights-locution "freedom of religion or belief," e.g. in UDHR art. 18. Humanism, as presented in the chapter by Gogineni and Gule in this volume, exemplifies a nonreligious life stance: Humanists are organized at national and international levels, offer to members ceremonies of name-giving, civic confirmations, weddings, and funerals, profess a secularist creed and code of conduct, and provide members with a sense of community, in a fashion somewhat similar to that of many religious communities. Of course all human beings, including people not belonging to any religious or life-stance community and people indifferent to matters of religion or life stance, are fully entitled to, and may conceivably need, protection of their human right to freedom of religion or belief.

9 A philosopher's role in the quest for knowledge, Locke argues, may properly be that of a facilitator, in his words, "'tis ambition enough to be employed as an under-labourer in clearing ground a little, and removing some of the rubbish that lies in the way to knowledge;" (John Locke, *An Essay Concerning Human Understanding*, ed. Roger Woolhouse (London: Penguin Books, 1997 [1689]), 11. Plato, of course, leaves little doubt about his answer to the question posed in the *Republic*: "Inasmuch as philosophers only are able to grasp the eternal and unchangeable, and those who wander in the region of the many and variable are not philosophers, I must ask you which of the two classes should be the rulers of our State?" (*Republic* 484b).

Section IV addresses contemporary approaches to the dilemmas of religious freedom and religious conflict and proposes an answer to the overriding concern of the chapter. Taking for granted that human beings now and for the foreseeable future do disagree in matters of religion or life stance, my overriding concern is to grasp how we may, in the religiously discordant social world that is ours, reasonably secure both ***principled solidarity based on mutual respect across religious and life-stance divides*** and ***unflinching doctrinal integrity of, and commitment to, our differing normative traditions.*** Reasoning in a virtuous circle, my answer draws on the modern tradition of internationally recognized human rights. This tradition is, I submit, rooted in an emerging worldwide public commitment to heed as inviolable the inherent dignity of every human being.[10] Dignity is a value that may resonate within and across difference.

Section V, finally, acknowledges that generating well-grounded religious and life-stance backing of religious freedom is not in general an accomplished fact, even when such freedom is ***publicly recognized*** as an integral part of morally binding, universally applicable human rights. Well-grounded support by religious and life-stance communities of the universally applicable human right to freedom of religion or belief is still, to some extent, a *verité a faire*, "a truth to be done." Further advances in this direction may require intrareligious debate, thorny reinterpretation of doctrines, reform of traditional patterns of thought and practice, and morally dedicated cooperation, collaboration, and dialogue, not excluding respectful but candid intellectual argument across existing divides of religion and life stance. Also vital is the development of legal techniques that can forestall the recurring temptation for political actors to exploit religious identification in the pursuit of power.

II. Justifying Freedom of Religion or Belief across Normative Divides: Two Dilemmas

For the foreseeable future we may take for granted that our societies are ***plural societies***, that is to say, societies distinguished by the co-presence of several differing, and in some respects incompatible, religions and life stances ("life stances" being the secularist or nonreligious counterparts of religions[11]). Part of our problem is assessing the extent to which, and the ways in which, adherents of differing normative traditions embrace incompatible doctrines and engage in competitive communal practices.

In the context of a religiously discordant social world, two basic dilemmas arise once we try to spell out what it takes to establish generally acceptable justifications of universally applicable safeguards of freedom of religion or belief. These dilemmas are presented below and exemplify core conceptual quandaries in building social unity and stability across abiding religious and life-stance divides. In presenting the first of the dilemmas, I rely on my own Evangelical-Lutheran normative tradition, confident that my points are nevertheless amenable to critical assessment by people of diverse backgrounds.[12]

---

[10] See Lindholm, "Ethical Justification," 65–68 for a discussion of the pertinent deliberations of the founding mothers and fathers of universal human rights 1947–1948.

[11] See note 8 above.

[12] The second dilemma presented in section II is related to but not identical with the dilemma of human rights justification described by Freeman, ***Human Rights,*** and quoted in the Introduction to this chapter.

(1) ***Well-grounded mutual respect across fundamental divides.*** The first dilemma I want to draw attention to proceeds from the assumption that serious adherents of most religious or life-stance traditions hold their particular doctrine to be the Truth and their peculiar faith and/or practice to be the Path to salvation, or to paradise, or to extinction of suffering, or to an autonomous and illusion-free human life. On this assumption, if I endorse a universal moral entitlement to freedom of religion or belief, then I have to respect doctrines that claim to capture the Truth—though, as far as I can understand, they do not; and I have to respect faiths and/or practices that claim to lead to salvation/non-suffering/autonomy—though, as far as I can understand, they do not. How can I be respectful of religious or life-stance doctrines and practices that are incompatible with the Truth as understood by myself? How can I without self-betrayal and loss of integrity be bonded in mutual solidarity to people who are, for all that I know, committed to false doctrines and paths to perdition? This question is not about endorsing religious pluralism based on prudential ***modus vivendi.*** Nor is it about mutual toleration between adherents of rival doctrines and practices. The question is about the formation of authentic espousals grounded in particular religious and life-stance doctrines, of a moral entitlement of all human beings to freedom of religion or belief, regardless of their religion or life stance.[13]

The dilemma may be put as follows: How can I reasonably respect proponents of doctrines and practices that contradict my own serious commitments without, somehow, renouncing those commitments?

Many readers will balk at what they may perceive to be only an alleged (and "outdated") dilemma. Their position in this regard would be sound if the challenge of accommodating mutual respect across fundamental normative divides were already widely understood to be properly resolved. However, it is not. Surely, in many contemporary societies the problem of mutual respect across normative divides is no longer held to be a major issue. But in many contexts this remains a live issue that needs to be candidly addressed. Accordingly, we have reason not to repress or paper over the troublesome foundational question lurking beneath the pluralist surface of modern public life.

(2) ***Reasonable justification based on a plurality of incompatible grounds.***[14] Even supposing the first dilemma to be suitably settled, however, another dilemma arises: Once a comprehensive set of internally well-grounded but particular validations of freedom of religion or belief as a universal entitlement is in place, each validation will be grounded in a religious or life-stance doctrine which is incompatible or at least more or less at odds with other justificatory platforms. How can the entire set of rival justificatory platforms constitute a reasonable grounding of the right to freedom of religion or belief and, hence, a trustworthy and stable basis for its general observance?[15] The dilemma is this: A plurality of sets of incompatible premises, each of which may constitute internally well-grounded support for freedom of religion or belief, appears as a whole to be incoherent and hence not a reasonable public grounding.

The two dilemmas of justifying freedom of religion or belief across normative divides may in given circumstances trigger threats to social peace and stability. For example, the first dilemma can lead to conflict between rival "fundamentalist" communities

---

[13] See An-Na'im, ed., ***Human Rights in Cross-Cultural Perspectives***, 22–29 and passim.

[14] See Lindholm, "Ethical Justification."

[15] See David Little, "Rethinking Human Rights," 151–77.

within a larger political order. And, of course, it is not merely fundamentalist groups that may be guilty of engendering such controversies. Deeply held religious views on civil rights issues, for example, have led to substantial if healthy social conflict. The second dilemma calls attention to stability hazards of plural societies that have failed to spell out and entrench a shared public understanding of the basis for moral solidarity across religious and life-stance divides.

In the last analysis, my contention is that we are dealing here with dilemmas that are not irresolvable. Yet they need to be taken seriously, because during much of human history, they have been presumed to be valid dilemmas, and as a result, they have stood either as explicit premises or as unstated assumptions behind much of human discourse concerning freedom of religion or belief. In fact, my statement of the two dilemmas does not capture all the important assumptions about the ways that rival committed modes of discourse have been thought to jeopardize stability in a plural social world. However, in what follows we need to pay attention to the aspects highlighted by the two dilemmas, because they help identify hurdles that must be overcome, and a direction in which we need to move, to accommodate recalcitrant challenges to plural public justifications and to attain stable backing for religious and life-stance pluralism.

III. Religious Freedom: Shifting Social Forms, Contexts, and Rationales

A main goal of this section is to elucidate why religious freedom, in the present-day world, takes the form of a universally applicable human right to freedom of religion or belief. To this end the section charts some of the social and cultural background for public justification of the human right to freedom of religion or belief today, focusing on key developments leading up to the emergence in the West of a *secular social order*. Though initially a European and western social transformation, the basic structures of a secular society have made inroads into social life in almost all corners of the world through colonialism, imperialism, and globalization, as well as through the sheer and noncoercive persuasiveness of democratic human rights ideals.

Being concerned with public validation of religious liberty we may learn from the past. We also need to be aware of the peculiar problem-situations that constitute the historical context for reasoned embrace of religious freedom today. Therefore, this section first sketches the rise and historical transformations of religious freedom as it has been institutionalized historically in specific political orders. It then describes three successive phases in the evolution of religious freedom protection, thereby proposing a reading of shifting constellations of political power, religious authority, and public reason that have shaped this fundamental freedom. It next remembers some of the pioneers of principled religious support of religious freedom for all, thereby giving some sense for both the content and the existential realities of arguing for genuine respect for religious freedom for others. Finally, we go on to consider the complexities of the secular setting itself, considering first the onset of secularized international society, then the emergence of secular societies at the level of nation-states, and finally, the somewhat surprising current trend toward desecularization of domestic and transnational public discourse on politics.

A. Absence, Presence, and Transformations of Politically Instituted Religious Freedom

During the known history of organized human society, freedom of religion or belief has been the exception, not the rule. The main premodern source of political legitimacy was no doubt a given hegemonic religion. The very idea that political rulers ought to tolerate deities and religious practices of other polities would have appeared irrational in most ancient civilizations.[16] As a rule people's adherence to the given hegemonic religion could hardly be told apart from their political loyalty.

In antiquity religious toleration was nevertheless embarked upon by rulers in exceptional cases, mainly on prudential political grounds.[17] Toleration arose as a political expedient in the wake of major imperial conquests, pioneered perhaps by the Persian king Cyrus the Great in the sixth and applied by the Macedonian Alexander the Great in the fourth centuries BCE. On similar political grounds, toleration was practiced by the Roman Empire in many contexts for several centuries.

But religious toleration (or indifference) in the Roman Empire was undermined by the advent and subsequent rise of Christianity to the status of official imperial religion. During the medieval period the Roman Catholic Church, with prestigious theological arguments[18] and papal authority, called for violent crusades against infidels[19] and for persecution of heretics.[20] After the Reformation mainstream Protestants

---

[16] Malcolm Evans, *Religious Liberty and International Law in Europe* (Cambridge: Cambridge University Press, 1997), 6. See also the chapter by Evans in this volume for important materials drawn upon in the present section. For a classical statement, see Jean Jacques Rousseau's essay on civil religion in *The Social Contract*, trans. G. D. H. Cole (New York: E. P. Dutton & Co., Inc., 1950), 129–33.

[17] An exception among these exceptions was the Indian emperor Ashoka (reign appr. 265 to 238 BCE) who was unique by instituting in his vast multireligious empire religious freedom *as a matter of principle*—based, tacitly, on Buddhist doctrine; see below, subsection III.D.

[18] St. Augustine's dismal interpretation of the Gospel According to Luke 14:23, (". . . and compel them to come in, that my house may be filled") was exploited by mainstream Christian churches for fourteen centuries to justify the use of political power against heretics and infidels. See St. Augustine, *Treatise Concerning the Correction of the Donatists,* chap. 6, sec. 24. Significant portions of this text are available at the following site: <http://www.ccel.org/fathers/NPNF104/augustine/bk_correction/correction.html> (visited 23.11.02). For St. Augustine and the Donatists, see Brian Tierney, "Religious Rights: A Historical Perspective," in *Religious Liberty in Western Thought*, ed. N. B. Reynolds and W. C. Durham, Jr. (Atlanta: Scholar Press for Emory University, 1996), 33.

[19] Against infidels: "On November 25, 1095, at the Council of Clermont, Pope Urban II summoned the First Crusade. . . . The Pope urged the knights of Europe to stop fighting each other and to make common cause against the enemies of God. The Turks, he cried, are 'an accursed race, a race utterly alienated from God, a generation, forsooth, which has neither directed its heart not entrusted its spirit to God.' Killing these godless monsters was an holy act: it was a Christian duty to 'exterminate this vile race from our lands'" (Karen Armstrong, *Holy War. The Crusades and their Impact on Today's World* [New York: Doubleday/Anchor Books, 1992], 3). Armstrong quotes texts written shortly after the "success" of the First Crusade.

[20] Against heretics: "We excommunicate and anathematize every heresy that raises against the holy, orthodox and Catholic faith which we have above explained; condemning all heretics under whatever names they may be known, for while they have different faces they are nevertheless bound to each other by their tails, since in all of them vanity is a common element. Those condemned, being handed over to the secular rulers of their bailiffs, let them be abandoned, to be punished with due justice, clerics being first degraded from their orders. As to the property of the condemned, if they are laymen, let it be confiscated; if clerics, let it be applied to the churches from which they received revenues. . . . Secular authorities, whatever office they may

did no better, for a long time. Political protection of religious freedom reappeared only by fits and starts in early western modernity. From the beginning, it was based not on religious principle but on the exhaustion of combatants absorbed in seemingly interminable religious warfare between Catholic and Protestant rulers, during the sixteenth and early seventeenth centuries. Once the ferocious post-Reformation wars of religion ended in 1648, with the Peace of Westphalia, a new international order was established on notably *secular* political grounds, designed to secure peace between state parties that remained *denominational* polities—initially either Roman Catholic, or Lutheran, or Reformed.[21] At the domestic level religious toleration, not to mention religious freedom, was often extremely restricted[22] and rarely stable, as witnessed by the ominous revocation by the Roman Catholic French king in 1685 of the 1598 royal Edict of Nantes, which had granted toleration to Huguenots (French Protestants).[23] This revocation reopened the painful memory of unspeakable horrors of religious civil war in France (1560–1598).

The early Protestant pioneers of principled Christian support for religious freedom, the Anabaptists, and some other deviants from the Protestant mainstream, were literally decimated in most of post-Reformation Europe, with the Netherlands, Poland, and Russia as partial exceptions. Only in some North American colonies did principled Christian support of religious freedom gain footing, and eventually flourish, to become embodied in the path-breaking Constitution of the United States of America.[24]

For people of religious conviction it is, perhaps, small consolation that antireligious rationalist persecution of "religious superstition" in late eighteenth-century France under the banner of *Enlightenment*, and "scientific-socialist" efforts to liquidate "religious ideology" in twentieth-century Russia under the banner of *Emancipation*, attest to the fact that it is not only religious collective zealousness (or "fundamentalism") but also rationalist, laicist, and atheist ideologies that have caused severe violations of the freedom of religion or belief of those who dare to differ.

To sum up: Beginning with the 1648 Westphalian constitution of modern international society, very different political responses to religiously motivated conflict developed throughout the modern era. These responses were prompted by pressing historical

---

hold, shall be admonished and induced and if necessary compelled by ecclesiastical censure, that as they wish to be esteemed and numbered among the faithful, so for the defense of the faith they ought publicly to take an oath that they will strive in good faith and to the best of their ability to exterminate in the territories subject to their jurisdiction all heretics pointed out by the Church; so that whenever anyone shall have assumed authority, whether spiritual or temporal, let him be bound to confirm this decree by oath." From Canon 3 of *Decree of the Fourth Lateran Council* of the Roman Catholic Church, 1215. Text at <http://www.fordham.edu/halsall/basis/lateran4.html> (visited 23.11.02).

21 The secularized character of post-Westphalian international society is spelled out in subsection III.C below.

22 See subsection III.B below.

23 On the political significance of the revocation of the Edict of Nantes see Martin Kriele, *Einführung in die Staatslehre. Die geschichtlichen Legitimationsgrundlagen des demokratischen Verfassungstaates,* 5th ed. (Opladen: Westdeutscher Verlag, 1994), 48–55.

24 A good survey and general assessment of intellectual traditions leading up to the non-establishment clause in the First Amendment to the US Constitution is Noah Feldman, "The Intellectual Origins of the Establishment Clause," *N.Y.U. Law Rev.* 77 (2002): 346–428. Abiding dilemmas of an American "republic under God," bound both to non-establishment of religion and its free exercise, are instructively analyzed by Ronald F. Thiemann, *Religion in Public Life: A Dilemma for Democracy* (Washington D.C.: Georgetown University Press, 1996).

circumstances, including war and conquest, persecution and genocide, rebellion and civil war. International arrangements for protection of religious freedom were negotiated on secular terms between state parties in order to bring an end to, or in order to prevent threats of, violent conflict and were designed to reinforce international and intra-national peace, alas with uneven success.

B. The Evolution of International Protection of Religious Freedom: Three Models

International protection of religious freedom has undergone profound historical transformation over the past five centuries, exhibiting in the process significant range of variation in its social forms, substantive scope, reach of applicability, mode of implementation, and institutional stability. This obviously complicates the task of justification, since the task of moral justification clearly varies, depending on how this *justificandum* is specified.

As Malcolm Evans has demonstrated in elegant detail, international protection of religious freedom has passed through three main stages.[25] These constitute three remarkably different, successively realized, but partially overlapping models of political protection of religious liberty:

(i) The *cuius regio, eius religio*[26] model: International peace treaties providing for territorial separation of people of different religious persuasions, keeping, e.g., Catholics, Lutherans, and Reformed apart in different countries and providing for modicums of toleration of circumscribed dissidents and their right to orderly emigration should a new confession be imposed in the realm; second:

(ii) The *minority protection* model: International (bilateral or multilateral) treaties providing for protection of religious minorities within the state territory of a hegemonic ethnic or religious majority; and finally:

(iii) The *human rights* model: International (global or regional) treaties that codify international standards and provide for international monitoring of universal human rights of individual human beings and of religious or life-stance communities to freedom of religion or belief.

---

[25] See the chapter by Evans in this volume. For an extended treatment, see Malcolm Evans, *Religious Liberty and International Law in Europe* (Cambridge: Cambridge University Press, 1997), chapters 2 through 9.

[26] Literally: "whose the region (or realm), his the religion." This oft-quoted formula applied to early modern political rulers ("princes") seems to originate with Joseph Stephani, a Lutheran ecclesiastic jurist writing in the 1590s. The political model goes back to the 1555 Peace of Augsburg and is older than the famous formula. See Joseph Leclerc, "Die Religionsfreiheit im Lauf der Geschichte" [Freedom of Religion in the Course of History], *Concilium* 2 (1966): 572. This German language issue of *Concilium* has several key articles about the positions of different religions on religious freedom. The journal is also published in English; the corresponding issue in English is *Concilium* 18 (1966). It seems appropriate that a Lutheran is the source of the religio-political adage *cuius regio, eius religio*, since Lutherans in the 1530s were overwhelmed by political and military circumstances to stomach the inception of what turned out to be almost five hundred years of Lutheran "landesherrliche Kirchenregiment" ("church rule by the lord of the land"). Claiming the *cuius regio, eius religio* model to be a form of religious freedom may well be contested. It remained, well into the twentieth century, in some cases a model of religious intolerance in the land of the "Landesherr." Lutheranism is still the established state religion in Denmark and in Norway. See the chapters by Minnerath, and by Eidsvåg, Lindholm, and Sveen in this volume.

As already noted, the stability, the scope, and the reach of international and national religious freedom arrangements have been radically transformed throughout modern history. At one end of the spectrum we find revocable, ultimately self-destructive royal edicts providing, during a period of time left to royal discretion, toleration of private devotions for certain categories of heretics or dissidents in the realm. At the other end we find the regime of human rights protection "everywhere in the world" designed to protect individual as well as communal exercise, manifestation, and transgenerational reproduction of differing religious and life-stance traditions, on an equal footing for all.

As John Witte has noted, several authorities argue that religious rights were among the first to be recognized, whereas others—perhaps a minority among experts—argue that religious rights were historically among the last to be widely accepted at law.[27] Given Evans' account of the three stages through which freedom of religion or belief has emerged in its current form, both views make sense.[28] I find the minority perspective to be more perspicuous. For one thing, international recognition of a universally applicable human right to freedom of religion or belief is a very recent achievement. Only from the middle of the twentieth century onwards has a human right to freedom of religion or belief become part of international law, imposing on states a legal and political obligation for evenhanded protection for all people within their jurisdictions. As is the case with other basic human rights, the right to freedom of religion or belief is often violated, yet at the same time, violations are now increasingly recognized as just that: breaches of what present-day states and other coercive institutions owe by law and by right to every human being subject to them.

In my view, only the third model of internationally established protection of religious freedom is satisfactory in the present-day world of religious and life-stance plurality. That is to say, only a universally applicable human right to freedom of religion or belief remains adequate to the task of safeguarding liberty of faith and conviction, thereby serving peace among religions, ethnic groups, and nations, and more fundamentally: thereby protecting what respect for human dignity requires. Holding the internationally codified human right to freedom of religion or belief to be our apposite public *justificandum*, I therefore cannot fully concur with Evans' appraisal: "The last fifty years of the twentieth century has seen a diminution in the importance attached to the achievement of freedom of religion or belief, both [1] by its incorporation *into* the human rights canon and [2] by the manner in which it has fared *as* a human right."[29] I can subscribe to Evans' second point: The human right to freedom of religion or belief may still be somewhat of a stepchild of the human rights movement, having yet to be fleshed out in a special international treaty. But, incorporating protection of freedom of religion or belief as a non-derogable part of the modern human rights canon is no diminution. On the contrary, in my view this constitutes an elevation of internationally binding protection of freedom of religion or belief so as to properly fit the structural constraints and cultural dynamics of modern secular societies.

---

[27] John Witte, Jr., "Introduction," in *Religious Human Rights in Global Perspective: Religious Perspectives*, ed. John Witte, Jr. and Johan D. van der Vyver (The Hague: Martinus Nijhoff, 1996), xxxiii.

[28] See, again, the chapter by Evans in this volume.

[29] The chapter by Evans in this volume, text after footnote 78. Numbers in brackets are added.

C. The Secular Political Rationales for International Protection of Religious Liberty

What were the operative political rationales for the introduction, maintenance, and modifications of international protection of religious freedom? Against the backdrop of the three models described above, we may now review the awkward and often embarrassingly backhanded role of religion (mainly Christianity) in the development of modern safeguards of religious freedom.

It would no doubt be agreeable to the self-image of contemporary Christians to be able to claim that Christian churches prompted the modern evolution of political protection of religious toleration and, eventually, of freedom of religion or belief. However, as already noted, the 1648 peace agreement of Westphalia was struck between state parties acting on emphatically nonreligious grounds. State parties were hard-pressed to bring to an end the seemingly interminable, incredibly cruel European wars of religion that had been waged for more than a century between passionately Catholic and Protestant combatants.[30] Chiefly in this perversely indirect and ironic way did mainstream Christian churches in the West trigger the launching of the western tradition of freedom of religion. The political goal of securing peace between differing religious groups had of course been widely subscribed to, also by those Christian churches that in the circumstances of intra-Christian fragmentation were utterly unable to envisage *how*. The new-founded international society of sovereign territorial states adopted the goal of interreligious peace and toleration to the extent it was conducive to its overriding political goal of establishing peace between states parties, curbing inter-state aggression, intervention, and intra-state violence. This is the *secular political rationale* of the "cuius regio, eius religio" model and, later, of the minority protection model as well. International society was, and still is, a *secularized social order* in the specific sense that it has discarded the unitary religious legitimacy of the pre-Reformation epoch. Instead, modern sovereign states are interacting and contracting "rationally," moved by calculated "reasons of state" and no longer depending on church or other religious or life-stance approval. The growing irrelevance of religious legitimation of the emerging European Public Order is vividly exemplified by a papal statement referring to the Peace of Westphalia: "The Papacy was not represented at

[30] Writing from a different perspective, Brad S. Gregory notes: "It would be an exaggeration to say that unresolved religious disagreement caused the Enlightenment, the rise of modern science and philosophy, the early modern renaissance of skepticism, and the birth of modern relativism. Yet its important influence on all these major trajectories in modern thought is clear. Moreover, the clash of religious absolutisms in early modern Christianity was fertile soil for the growth of secular political thought and secular political institutions. Such was the logical extension of the *politique* views articulated in the sixteenth century, as for example during the French Wars of Religion. Because the prospects for peaceful coexistence among Christians were tenuous at best, and none of the parties would capitulate to the others, *only nonreligious values could serve as the basis of stable social and political life*" (*Salvation at Stake. Christian Martyrdom in Early Modern Europe* [Cambridge. Mass.: Harvard University Press, 1999], 348–49 [emphasis added]). The present chapter argues that political secularization was pioneered, as it were, by early modern international relations and was subsequently adopted domestically in the political life of a growing number of countries as a part of their in-depth structural transformations into modern secular societies. See subsection III.E below, also for a discussion of Wolfhart Pannenberg's indictment of modern secularist public culture. Pannenberg's position is close to the view Gregory labels "an exaggeration."

the [1648 Osnabrück and Münster] conferences and, in the bull *Zelo Domus Dei*, Pope Innocent X denounced the religious aspects of the treaties as 'null, void, invalid, inequitable, unjust, condemned, reprobated, frivolous, of no force or effect.' Nevertheless, the treaties were honored by the parties."[31]

It is not possible in the limited space of this chapter to describe in any detail the countless contributions of particular religious individuals,[32] or of religious communities, or of religion at large, on the subsequent evolution of international protection of religious freedom and of the ways particular minority religious communities were involved in lobbying for international minority protection treaties. The last of these was the elaborate but in the end failed system of Minority Treaties established after WWI under the auspices of the League of Nations.[33] Due to the international hegemony of Christendom in the era under discussion this subsection has dealt exclusively with the roles of Christian churches. Muslim and Jewish voices have no doubt been significant, for example in negotiations about various minority protection arrangements.

We may conclude that the launching of modern international protection of religious freedom had to proceed without the benefit of Roman Catholic or mainstream Protestant backing. By Christian default, as it were, international protection of religious liberty became a pioneering achievement of secular international "Realpolitik." Moreover, international protection of religious freedom has remained an expressly secular business conducted by state parties *etsi deus non daretur*—as if God did not exist (Grotius). The concerns of religion(s), to become effective, have had to be voiced in secular legal, political, and diplomatic space. Disqualified by their performance in the European wars of religion, mainstream Christian churches had wasted their claim to a principal public role in the shaping of modern protection of religious freedom. This damage to their political legitimacy has not begun to mend until recently.

D. Principled Religious Espousal of Freedom of Religion or Belief: Some Early Pioneers

Unwavering support of inclusive freedom of religion or belief by the authentic voices of religions is, until recently, rare. Of course, if we were examining the historical record of religious advocacy of a universal human right to freedom of religion or belief, this would be a trivial observation, since universally applicable human rights is a historically recent phenomenon. What it is stunning, however, is how exceptional, until the dawn of modern human rights in the middle of the twentieth century, is well-grounded and clearly worked out religious support of an inclusive entitlement to a freedom that transcends the divides of rival religious beliefs and secularist convictions.

It is all the more instructive, then, to call into memory pioneers of principled religious endorsement of the entitlement of *all* human beings to freedom of religion or belief. As indicated above, it is not possible to be in any sense comprehensive. Instead, in this section I shall note only a few prominent early pioneers of principled religious

[31] I have borrowed this quote from Evans; see note 28 in the chapter by Evans in this volume.

[32] We may assume that major proponents of secularized international politics, from Alberico Gentili and Hugo Grotius and onwards for a long time, were religious people. What matters here is the secular and nonreligious character of their political arguments.

[33] See sections II to IV of the chapter by Evans in this volume.

support of liberty of belief for all. The point of this exercise is partly to balance, as truth permits, the dismal picture drawn in preceding sections of religious backing of religious freedom, and partly to better understand the peculiar circumstances that have called for a religious commitment to a freedom of faith that transcends sectarian boundaries.

Ashoka: The first name to recall is that of Ashoka, the last major emperor in the Mauryan dynasty of India (reigned ca. 265 to 238 BCE). According to his own account, Ashoka conquered the country of Kalinga (today approximately Orissa State) in the eighth year of his reign. The immense sufferings this conquest inflicted on the defeated people moved Ashoka to such remorse that he henceforth renounced armed conquests. At this time he became acquainted with and adopted Buddhism. Under the influence of Buddhism he resolved to live according to and preach the dharma and to serve his subjects and all humanity adopting the policy he called "conquest by dharma." A core Buddhist concept "dharma" may be translated "principles of right life" or, using Ashoka's own words, ". . . little evil, much good, kindness, generosity, truthfulness, and purity." A devout and learned Buddhist, Ashoka did not preach nor require specifically Buddhist belief or practice from his subjects. His famous Rock Edicts (they may still be studied in several places in India, Pakistan, and Afghanistan) declare that "all religious communities shall be able to reside everywhere. For all of them desire for control of senses and purity of heart. . . ." (from Edict VII). His foremost desire for his subjects, above honors and gifts, is "that there be growth in the essentials of all religions" (from Edict XII). Ashoka makes abundantly clear to his subjects how interreligious strife is destructive of religious flourishing:

> Growth in essentials can develop in diverse ways, but at its root lies restraint in speech, so as not to praise one's own religion and denigrate the religions of others without good cause. And if there be cause for criticism, it should be done with mildness. But it is better to honor other religions on every occasion. Doing so one's own religion is served, and so is that of the other. Doing otherwise one harms one's own religion and that of others at the same time. Whoever praises his own religion, due to excessive attachment, and denigrates that of others with the thought "Let me glorify my own religion," in reality inflicts the severest injury on his own religion. Contact therefore between religions is good: One should listen to and respect the doctrines professed by others and apply what one has learned (from Edict XII).[34]

A crucial point to note about Ashoka is that his uncompromising policy of protecting religious liberty for all is tacitly based on Buddhist principles, as understood by him, and that he nevertheless did not accord political privileged status for Buddhism in his multireligious empire but urged and facilitated the flourishing of all religious communities.

---

[34] Ashoka's Edicts are quoted mainly after the following sources: *Les Inscriptions d'Asoka, traduites et commentées par Jules Bloch* (Professeur au Collège de France) (Paris: Société d'Edition "Les Belles Lettres," Collection Emile Senart, 1950); *The Edicts of King Ashoka; An English rendering by Ven S. Dhammika* (Kandy [Sri Lanka]: The Wheel Publication No. 386/387, 1993). The latter is among the translations easily found on the internet. Translations are in part somewhat uncertain, and I have taken the liberty of combining different translations. I should add here that research on Ashoka is very much in process and that interpretations of his politics on religion diverge.

Among several Muslim rulers famed for astute practice of interreligious toleration and respect, two outstanding figures are *Saladin* (of Kurd descent, born in Tikrit 1138, died 1193), the first Ayyubid sultan and famous both for having recaptured Jerusalem from the Crusaders and for his moral superiority over his Christian adversaries, and *Akbar* (born in Sind 1542, died 1605), greatest of the Mogul emperors who extended Mogul power over most of the Indian subcontinent. Unfortunately, they did not leave documents explaining or evidencing how they would have grounded their policies of interreligious freedom or toleration in Islamic doctrine.

My next case of a pioneer of principled religious support of religious liberty is a Christian clergyman and martyr for the cause of comprehensive religious freedom. *Balthasar Hubmaier* (born 1485 near Augsburg, died March 10, 1528 in Vienna) was named doctor of theology after studies at the German universities in Freiburg and Ingolstadt. He was appointed cathedral preacher at Regensburg in 1516, and he arrived in 1521 in Switzerland, where he soon became a leader of the fledgling Anabaptists. The latter are generally viewed as the most prominent movement of the radical Protestant Reformation. Persecuted even by the liberal Zwinglians for his beliefs, he was arrested in 1525 at Zürich. Released, he resumed his Anabaptist proselytizing, first in Augsburg and later in Nikolsburg, Moravia. He was especially influential through his writings and represented the more moderate strain of the movement. Prodded by the Roman Catholic Church, the agents of the emperor were constantly chasing him. Hubmaier was ultimately captured and burned at the stake as a heretic. Hubmaier's brief theological work of 1524 in defense of religious freedom, and his critique of the use of coercion against heretics or nonbelievers, bears the title *Uon ketzern vnd iren verbrennern* [On Heretics and Those Who Burn Them], subtitled *Die warhait ist vntödtlich* [Truth Is Unkillable]. I shall reproduce translations of four of its 36 articles:

> (3) Those who are . . . [heretics] should be overcome with holy instruction, not contentiously but gently, even though the Holy Scripture also includes wrath.
>
> (4) But the wrath of Scripture is truly a spiritual flame and a loving zeal, which burns only with the Word of God. . . .
>
> (22) It is fitting that secular authority puts to death the wicked (Rom. 13:14) who cause bodily harm to the defenseless. But the unbeliever should be harmed by no one should he not be willing to change and should he forsake the gospel. . . .
>
> (36) Now it appears to anyone, even a blind person, that the law [which provides] for the burning of heretics is an invention of the devil. Truth Is Unkillable.[35]

Hubmaier's Catholic and mainstream Protestant adversaries did not succeed in killing his Christian doctrine of freedom of religion or belief, though they obviously tried.[36] In essence, their successors have belatedly adopted it.

---

[35] Balthasar Hubmaier, *Schriften* (Hrsg. Gunnar Westin u. Torsten Bergsten) (Gütersloher Verlagshaus Gerd Mohn, 1962), 59–66; translation: H. Wayne Pipkin and John H. Yoder, eds., *Balthasar Hubmaier, Theologian of Anabaptism* (Scottdale, Pa.: Herald Press, 1989), 58–66.

[36] Experts are divided on whether Hubmaier in fact advocated principled universal religious freedom on Biblical grounds, which is the position attributed to him in the text.

The next figure is an American immigrant. *Roger Williams* (born ca. 1603 in London, died 1683 in Providence, Rhode Island) became a towering pioneer of universal religious liberty, in doctrine as well as in deed. The son of a shopkeeper, he was educated at Cambridge and in 1630 left England to pursue his by then completely nonconformist religious ideals in New England. Arriving in Boston in 1631, Williams refused a call to become minister of the Congregational Church because of its Anglican affiliation, and in the following year moved to the separatist Plymouth Colony. In 1633 he was back in Salem after a disagreement with Plymouth in which he insisted that the king's patent was invalid and that only direct purchase from the Indians gave a just title to the land. Invited by the church at Salem to become pastor in 1634, Williams was subsequently banished from Massachusetts Bay by the civil authorities for his dangerous views. Besides those on land rights, he held that magistrates had no right to interfere in matters of religion. Consequently, in January 1636 he set out for Narragansett Bay, and in the spring, on land purchased from the Narragansett Indians, he founded the town of Providence and the colony of Rhode Island "as an early and remarkable experiment in religious freedom."[37] Providence became a haven for Anabaptists, Quakers, and others whose beliefs were denied public expression. Williams was briefly an Anabaptist but in 1639 declared himself a Seeker. He went to England in 1643 to obtain a charter for Rhode Island and again in 1651–1654 to have it confirmed. During that visit he became a friend of the poet John Milton. He was the first president of Rhode Island under its charter and until his death always held some public office. He was of constant service to Rhode Island and neighboring colonies as a peacemaker with the Narragansett Indians, whose language he knew and whose trust he had earned. From 1636 until his death he supported himself by farming and trading.

Williams wrote comprehensive treatises arguing for universal religious freedom and insisting on the necessity of institutional separation between church and civil and political authorities. Says David Little: "Williams had his own decided theological convictions, which were strongly, if sometimes deviantly, Calvinist. He did not agree with the religious views of the American Indians or 'pagans,' as he called them, nor with the 'Mohammedans,' nor 'Papist,' nor many other Protestants, such as the Quakers. He frequently and in detail made known his objections to some of these groups; he regarded many of them as seriously in error." Boldly drawing the logical but groundbreaking practical conclusion from the traditional notion of inculpably erroneous conscience, Williams held "*they had the right to their error.*"[38] His most famous work is *The Bloudy Tenent of Persecution*, published in 1644. It opens with a list of theses, some of which I reproduce here:

> First, that the blood of so many hundred thousand souls of Protestants and Papists, spilt in wars of present and former ages, for their respective consciences, is not required nor accepted by Jesus Christ the Prince of Peace.
>
> Secondly, pregnant scriptures and arguments are throughout the work proposed against the doctrine of persecution for cause of conscience. . . .

---

[37] David Little in David Little, John Kelsay, and Abdulaziz A. Sachedina, *Human Rights and Conflict of Cultures: Western and Islamic Perspectives on Religious Liberty* (Columbia, S.C.: University of South Carolina Press, 1988), 21.

[38] Little, Kelsay, and Sachedina, *Human Rights and Conflict of Cultures,* 23.

> Fourthly, the doctrine of persecution for cause of conscience is proved guilty of all the blood of the souls crying for vengeance under the altar.
>
> Fifthly, all civil states with their officers of justice in their respective constitutions and administrations are proved essentially civil, and therefore not judges, governors, or defenders of the spiritual or Christian state and worship.
>
> Sixthly, it is the will and command of God that (since the coming of his Son the Lord Jesus) a permission of the most paganish, Jewish, Turkish, or antichristian consciences and worships, be granted to all men in all nations and countries; and they are only to be fought against with that sword which is only (in soul matters) able to conquer, to wit, the sword of God's Spirit, the Word of God.[39]

The work of Williams contributed significantly to preparing the ground for the celebrated 1791 First Amendment to the Constitution of the United States; his influence is still not sufficiently studied.[40]

The American prophet *Joseph Smith* (born Dec. 23, 1805, Sharon, Vt., killed by a mob when in jail June 27, 1844, Carthage, Ill.) became the founder of a new religious tradition. His writings, along with the Bible, provide the doctrinal foundation of the Church of Jesus Christ of Latter-day Saints (LDS Church) and other Mormon denominations.[41] Joseph Smith grew up in western New York at a time of intense religious revivalism. One day in the woods, at the age of fourteen, Joseph experienced what he conceived to be an intense spiritual revelation of God and Jesus Christ. He claimed that in 1827 an angel directed him to buried golden plates whose engraved surfaces contained a history of the earlier inhabitants of the American Continent. These were described as descendants of Hebrews who centuries earlier had sailed to North America. This *Book of Mormon* he translated from "reformed Egyptian."

Smith claimed that the LDS Church, which he organized on April 6, 1830, at Fayette, N.Y., restored the ancient, primitive Christian religion. Converts whom it attracted during the next decade followed him from New York to Ohio, then to Missouri, and finally to Illinois, where he organized the Mormon city-state of Nauvoo (1839–1846), whose population when it peaked was greater than that of Chicago at the time. The great majority of Nauvoo's inhabitants were members of the LDS Church. Before settling in Nauvoo they had been forced to press continually westward in search of economic opportunity and to escape from harsh persecution by successive neighbors, who time after time grew suspicious of the Mormons' unorthodox cooperative society, their antislavery orientation, their rule by an ecclesiastical oligarchy and their belief in access to direct revelation.

---

[39] Roger Williams, *The Bloudy Tenent of Persecution* . . . (Providence, R.I.: Publications of the Narragansett Club, 1867), 3:3–4.

[40] Feldman, eager to demonstrate the centrality of the Lockean liberty of conscience doctrine for the non-establishment clause in the US Constitution, tartly dismisses Roger Williams' role: "Roger Williams' views were not invoked at the Framing" ("The Intellectual Origins of the Establishment Clause," 427). Feldman does not address Williams' possible influence on the (much more restrictive) religious freedom doctrine of Locke. I briefly discuss Locke's doctrine in section IV.

[41] On Joseph Smith and the Mormon tradition, see Jan Shipps, *Mormonism: The Story of a New Religious Tradition* (Champaign-Urbana, Ill.: University of Illinois Press, 1987).

What was Joseph Smith's position on religious freedom? He was no doubt a strident, self-confident, and to his many vocal critics and detractors a dangerously powerful, compelling, and seductive religious and civic leader. All the more interesting, then, is his doctrine of universal religious freedom, developed and implemented during his stay in Nauvoo. I quote the Ordinance in Relation to Religious Societies in the Nauvoo Charter, drafted by Smith and enacted by the Illinois legislature:

> Be it ordained by the City Council of the City of Nauvoo, that the Catholics, Presbyterians, Methodists, Baptists, Latter-day Saints, Quakers, Episcopals, Universalists, Unitarians, Mohammedans, and all other religious sects and denominations whatever, shall have free toleration and equal privileges in this city; and should any person be guilty of ridiculing, and abusing or otherwise depreciating another in consequence of his religion . . . he shall . . . be considered a disturber of the public peace, and fined in any sum not exceeding five hundred dollars, or imprisoned not exceeding six months, or both.[42]

The religious doctrine behind this City of Nauvoo Ordinance is crucial. In a letter to John Wentworth, a friendly politician and newspaper owner in Chicago, Smith had penned a statement of Mormon doctrine that was later elevated to the status of Articles of Faith of the LDS Church. Each of the 13 Articles of Faith, except Article 11, begins "We believe . . ." Interestingly, however, Article 11 begins differently, with a claim to a right:

> We *claim the privilege* of worshiping Almighty God according to the dictates of our own conscience, *and allow all men the same privilege*, let them worship how, where, or what they may.[43]

Joseph Smith's principle of universal religious freedom, held by the LDS Church to be revealed doctrine, is articulated not as a belief but as a *right* and, applying the Golden Rule of reciprocity, this right is directly linked to principled *solidarity* with people of differing religious persuasions.

Mormons, when in majority positions, have sometimes been accused of not practicing the high standards they preach. However that may be, their revealed doctrine of inclusive or universal religious freedom, penned by their prophet Joseph Smith, appears to break new ground exemplifying an appropriate self-understanding for an emerging and proselytizing minority religious community immersed in a modern plural society.

Summing up: This subsection has called into memory a few of the pioneers of religion-based justification of the entitlement of all humans whatever their religious or life-stance affiliation to enjoy freedom of religion or belief. A striking feature of the life situations of these pioneers is that they faced critical moral and existential challenges: Large-scale violence, persecution and martyrdom, and forced emigration were among the circumstances that triggered the pioneers of religious commitment to a freedom of faith that radically transcends sectarian boundaries.

---

[42] Quoted from W. Cole Durham, Jr., *The Doctrine of Religious Freedom* (Provo, Utah: J. Reuben Clark Law School, Clark Memorandum, 2001), 12; this fine small study has interesting materials and gives further references about the LDS doctrine on religious and life-stance freedom.

[43] Durham, *The Doctrine of Religious Freedom,* 4; emphasis added.

E. The Emergence and Significance of Modern Secular Societies

Validation of the human right to freedom of religion or belief in the present-day world must take into account the perplexing relations between religion and the diverging ramifications of the "secular." This subsection addresses the notions of "secularization," "secularism," and "secular society," provisionally sorting out their benign from their malign aspects as seen from the vantage point of religions or life stances at peace with modern pluralist society. The main goal is to explicate a clear-cut conception of a *secular society*. We shall need this conception of a secular society in order to assess processes of political "desecularization" currently taking place worldwide[44] (addressed in subsection III.F below) and in order, finally, to address the overlapping and pluralist justification of modern religious liberty (section IV below).

Secularization is, generally speaking, a negation (a rupture, a weakening, or a transformation) relative to an existing form of religion or religious control or religious presence. What is crucial is the *form* of religion, control, or presence being negated, and the *way* the secularizing rupture, or weakening, or transformation takes place. This said, I note that the term "secularization" may be used to refer to very diverse, even contradictory processes: political expropriation or usurpation of religious property, political liberation from coercive religious control, decrease in popular religious adherence and practice, loss of formal or informal political power by religious leaders, alienation of public culture from (a particular) religion, transformation of religious doctrine diluting it or deepening it, establishment of autonomous areas of social life beyond the control of religious authority, and departure of believers from protected religious reservations to a life in the world ("sæculum")—to mention only some of its meanings. Unless pertinent qualifications are made, a general acceptance or a general rejection of *secularization* is likely to be ill-considered. The same goes for *secularism*, whether it is taken to mean a cognitive belief in secularization or an evaluative stance toward secularization (however qualified).[45]

Subsection III.C accounted for the secularization of *international society* after 1648 with special reference to the failure of early modern mainstream churches to support a European Public Order that was designed to protect a modicum of religious freedom across denominational divides. On this account the international society of states became and to this day remains a secular politico-legal arrangement: secular in the sense that it has discarded dependence on pre-Reformation Roman Catholic hegemony and has to this day not adopted subservience to some other religious or life-stance hegemonic authority in arranging its affairs.

With the foregoing perspectives in mind, a *secular society* is a radically new type of society that arose first in early modern western European countries and in what became the United States of America. A secular society is the outcome of secularization of

[44] See Peter L. Berger, ed, *The Desecularization of the World. Resurgent Religion and World Politics* (Washington D.C.: Ethics and Public Policy Center, 1999).

[45] The usage of the terms by religious or life-stance communities may depart from the range of meanings intimated in the text. E.g., in Roman Catholic usage "secularization" refers to church-authorized permissions given to "religious" (members of religious orders) to live outside the cloister and their order (hence, in the "sæculum"), and "secularism" refers to the modernist doctrine that man should be guided solely by considerations derived from the present life—a doctrine held to be fundamentally erroneous by the Church

premodern social order, but one that runs much deeper than the mere politico-legal secularization of international relations after 1648. This more radical secularizing transformation takes place at the level of ***particular national societies***, and what becomes secularized is hegemonic religion, the very centerpiece of premodern society, which in the process loses its hegemonic societal status and functions. Though initially a European and western revolution, the basic structures of a secular society have, with colonialism, imperialism, and globalization, by now made inroads in social existence almost everywhere on this planet.

The brief presentation below of the conception of a secular society closely follows Helge Høibraaten's two-part exposition in the essay "Secular Society: An Attempt at Initiation."[46]

In the *first part* Høibraaten describes the early modern emergence of a number of ***autonomously functioning areas of society***, that is, each operating independently of religious authority and control. Sociologically, this process may be described as a gradual functional differentiation and emancipation of various *secular spheres* from the control of religion. A first step, in the emergence of modern secular spheres, is the rise of autonomous natural science and independent scholarship in the humanities and social sciences. A second is the "rise of an economy in which religious arguments against taking interest and against social advancement through money-making lost their force . . . A third is the development of a secular state . . . which combines the monopolization of the means for the legitimate use of physical force with a neutral stance towards churches or creeds . . ."[47] A fourth and related step is the emancipation of positive law; a fifth rupture with religious hegemony comes with the rise of autonomous art; and a sixth is the development of public mandatory schools that sooner or later approximate neutrality in matters of religion. Other social areas (or "social subsystems") gaining autonomy from hegemonic religion are: medicine; the modern family; and the media.[48]

The *second part* of Høibraaten's exposition opens by stating, "a secular society is a society where options of religious disbelief and doubt are freely available, along with options of belief."[49] In other words, a secular society harbors not just the functional differentiation and emancipation of the nonreligious spheres: "Science and scholarship, the economy, the state and politics, the school system, art, the family, law . . ."[50] Secular society gives rise, also, to the ***modern religious realm***, being "the concomitant ***differentiation and specialization of religion*** within its own newly found religious sphere."[51]

---

and embraced by the nonreligious (e.g., by Humanists, see the chapter by Gogineni and Gule in this volume). Also compare the presentation of Wolfhart Pannenberg's understanding of "secularism," below.

[46] Helge Høibraaten, "Secular Society: An Attempt at Initiation," in *Islamic Law Reform and Human Rights*, ed. Tore Lindholm and Kari Vogt (Oslo: Nordic Human Rights Publications, 1993), 231–57. Høibraaten's essay is replete with references to pertinent scholarly contributions.

[47] Høibraaten, "Secular Society," 232.

[48] The structural features of secular society mentioned in the text so far are referred to in sociological terms by saying that modern society is functionally differentiated into autonomous "primary subsystems": See Niklas Luhmann, *The Differentiation of Society,* trans. Stephen Holmes and Charles Larmore (New York: Columbia University Press, 1982), 229–54 and passim.

[49] Høibraaten, "Secular Society," 239.

[50] Høibraaten, "Secular Society," 234.

[51] José Casanova, *Public Religion in the Modern World* (Chicago: The University of Chicago Press, 1994), 19 (emphasis added). Casanova's book provides an excellent but critical outline of the sociological theory of secularization (17–39 and passim).

The establishment of a free religious sphere as an integral part of secular society is epochal. Secular society now facilitates and safeguards the free exercise, reproduction, and transformation of religion or belief, in a pluralist and radically inclusive sense. In a secular society the subject matter of religion or belief has become universalized to include the conviction of "all sorts of theists, such as Christians, Jews and Muslims; atheists and anti-theists who think human autonomy and the existence of an omnipotent God irreconcilable; scientistic believers in the moral importance of a natural science world perspective where God is superfluous; . . . [and] agnostics."[52]

This modern differentiation and specialization of religion as a newly established religious sphere—the realm of religious and life-stance communities, of interreligious cooperation, communication, and even mutually respectful nonviolent polemics—also brings, it may reasonably be claimed, a societal emancipation of religion itself. In a mature secular society no particular religion, life stance, or ideology is encumbered with the status, roles, and liabilities of premodern hegemonic and more or less coercively implemented religion.[53]

Secular society's inclusive domain of religion and life stance is, of course, dependent on its being buttressed and serviced by other differentiated autonomous institutions of a modern secular society, in particular the legal system (positivized law) and the political system (democratic governance).[54] By way of constitution, legislation, policies, and administrative programs a modern secular polity repudiates religious or life-stance monopoly and privilege. More specifically, it prohibits and counteracts discrimination, coercion, or persecution on grounds of religion or belief—policies that have been pursued by regimes prodded not only by premodern religion in the past (say, Catholic clergy prodding "Louis, by the grace of God king of France and Navarre" to revoke the Edict of Nantes in 1685), but also by modern antireligious ideology (say, "scientific" socialism) and by "postmodern" religious fundamentalism (say, some versions of the ideology of an "Islamic" state[55]).

Adherents of most religions and life stances living in the present-day world have perhaps largely become secularized in this benign sense of a secular, functionally differentiated modern society. They have adapted to the modern religious sphere and

---

[52] Høibraaten, "Secular Society," 244–45. Høibraaten's inventory is even more extensive but the gist should be clear enough.

[53] There is no denying the normative implications of the conception of a secular society set forth in this section. Nour Kirabaev, at the time head of the Department of Philosophy at the Russian People's Friendship University in Moscow, in 1992 assessed the political system of the Soviet Union saying, "A socialist state is not a secular state in the same way as a democratic state. It is a sacred state. It cannot be tolerant and cannot recognize real religious freedom. It is very similar to an authoritarian theocratic state" (Lindholm and Vogt, eds., *Islamic Law Reform*, 220). Of course, antireligious state ideologies are not immune against fundamentalist excesses, be they rationalist, laicist, "scientific," or fascist.

[54] Several chapters of the present volume demonstrate this dependence to boot.

[55] Of course, a modern state may protect religious liberty and be authentically Islamic in the sense that its political legitimacy is widely accepted on Islamic grounds by Muslims. The ideology of "Islamic" state censured in the text advocates religious discrimination by the state drawing legitimacy from a particular, coercively imposed version of Islamic doctrine. An early Islamic rejection of the ideology of an "Islamic" state is Abdelwahab El-Affendi, *Who Needs an Islamic State?* (London: Grey Seal Books, 1991). The author concludes, "If the foregoing discussion has any validity, then one has to infer that the concept of an Islamic State must be completely abandoned if sanity is to return to Muslim political discourse. One should rather speak about a state for the Muslims, an Islamic political community" (93).

adopted as morally mandatory a stance of "no coercion in religion."[56] This secularization of religion, acquiescing as it were to the structural constraints of a secular society, is hardly detrimental to authentic religious flourishing.[57]

In sum, religion in a secular society has, firstly, become a *functionally specialized social sphere* harboring many differing and to some extent competing religious and life-stance convictions and communities. And secondly, accountable actors in the sphere of religion and life stance are, as a matter of course, expected to heed *interreligious pluralism*. That is to say, recognizing the fact as well as the legitimacy of the plurality of coexisting religions and life stances in the religious sphere has become mandatory for a member in good standing of secular society. Secularization understood on the paradigm of a *secular society* is, when specified with respect to its basic principles and institutions, inseparably linked to the emergence of modern, universally applicable human rights to freedom of religion or belief. Or so I want to argue by spelling out, in section IV below, the how and the why of interreligious mutual respect through human rights.

Admittedly, the presentation so far of the emergence and ramifications of the "secular" has been one-sided by focusing only on those aspects that are benign for the exercise and flourishing of freedom of religion or belief. I shall now deal with the darker side of the coin, by addressing first some ambiguities of sociological *secularization theory* and second, a somber but perceptive theological diagnosis of secularist public culture stressing its *alienation from religion*.

Secularization theory as advanced by prominent sociologists of religion in the 1950s and 1960s made three main sets of claims:[58] (1) *The twin claims of the differentiation thesis* were that societal secularization is (1a) a process of functional differentiation and emancipation of the modern secular spheres from the religious realm of hegemonic religion and (1b) the concomitant differentiation and specialization of the newly found pluralist sphere of religions and life stances;[59] (2) *The decline-of-religion thesis* postulates that the process of secularization brings in its wake the progressive shrinkage and decline of religion until (the extreme version) it eventually "withers away" or disappears; and (3) *The privatization and marginalization theses* (they are not the same but can be lumped together for our purposes) claim that the process of secularization brings about the privatization and marginalization of religion in the modern world.

Once subscribed to by most authorities in the sociology of religion, the secularization theory is now widely held to be defunct. Peter Berger claims that the key idea of secularization theory was simply mistaken: "Modernization necessarily leads to a decline of religion, both in society and in the minds of individuals. And it is precisely this key idea that has turned out to be wrong."[60] But, on José Casanova's account of

---

[56] This norm is of course enunciated in *The Holy Koran*, sura 2, aya 256.

[57] Abdullahi An-Na'im, "Synergy and Interdependence of Religion, Human Rights and Secularism," *Polylog: Forum for Intercultural Philosophizing* (2001), visited at <http://wwwpolylog.org/tehyem/2/fes7-en.htm>; Tore Lindholm, "Menneskerettigheter og religioner: konflikt eller gjensidig støtte?" [Human rights and religions: Conflict or mutual reinforcement?] *Amnesty Nytt* (Oslo: Amnesty International Norway, Sept. 1998)

[58] My summary account borrows heavily from Casanova, *Public Religion,* 11–66, concentrated at 17–20.

[59] This is, of course, the analysis presented earlier on in this section, referring to Luhmann, *The Differentiation of Society,* Høibraaten, "Secular Society," and Casanova, *Public Religion.*

[60] Peter L. Berger, ed., *The Desecularization of the World. Resurgent Religion and World Politics* (Washington D.C.: Ethics and Public Policy Center, 1999), 2–3

sociological secularization theory, only the twin structural differentiation claims (1a) and (1b) should be considered "secularization theory proper." In other words: Structural secularization of premodern social order amounts to (1a) the differentiation of autonomous social spheres *from* hegemonic religion and (1b) the concomitant differentiation *of* the modern religious sphere of differing religions and life stances. The reason for distinguishing structural secularization (the theory of differentiation and specialization of social spheres) from cultural secularization (the theory of decline, privatization, and marginalization of religion) is, of course, that the structural differentiation claims may be true and the cultural secularization claims false. And this is exactly Casanova's point: he argues that the differentiation thesis largely stands vindicated by facts as well as by recent developments.[61] But both the decline-of-religion thesis (2) and the privatization and marginalization theses (3) have turned out to be widely off the mark, being thoroughly refuted by the fact of religious resurgence worldwide.[62] Casanova makes a strong case for "secularization theory proper" (the sociological differentiation claims) in his analysis of public religion in the modern world. At the same time, Casanova explains why the decline/privatization/marginalization corollaries do not follow from modern emergence of a specialized, autonomous, and pluralist religious sphere.[63]

Secularism as alienation of public culture from religion. The distinguished German protestant theologian Wolfhart Pannenberg has recently argued a rather gloomy take on "How to Think About Secularism."[64] Pannenberg presents a normative mirror image, as it were, of the sociological decline-of-religion, marginalization, and privatization theses. Pannenberg sees cultural secularization, the roots of which he thinks were "planted in the seventeenth century," as resulting in "the present alienation of public culture from religion . . . [which in turn] is exacerbated by the cultural relativizing of the very idea of truth . . . [an idea that] is absolutely vital for the Christian faith. The destruction of that idea is key to legitimating a *secularist culture*, since the idea of truth touches on secularism's greatest vulnerability."[65] Pannenberg darkly adds that secularism has "sometimes been depicted as the consequence of apostasy from the Christian faith" and "[t]here is much to be said for that interpretation . . ."[66] Pannenberg's theological critique deals with cultural alienation from religion as a disaster befalling Christianity.

Pannenberg's diagnosis of secularism's origin does not stop with the antichurch Enlightenment philosophers who planted the roots of secularist culture in the seventeenth century. He draws our attention to the societal soil in which Enlightenment

---

[61] The general sociological argument is corroborated by Casanovas' case studies of religious structural transformation in the second half of the twentieth century in Spain, Poland, Brazil, and the United States, focusing on Catholicism in all four countries and including also Evangelical Protestantism in the US. See Casanova, *Public Religion*.

[62] Worldwide but not everywhere: some significant exceptions include the academic faculty of social science and humanities departments at elite universities in the US and the populations of European countries endowed with tenacious state church arrangements. See Berger, ed, *The Desecularization of the World*, 9–10.

[63] Casanova, *Public Religion*. Obviously, "secularization theory proper" implies the emergence of secular society as defined in this subsection but not the rise of various forms of cultural secularism.

[64] Wolfhart Pannenberg, "How to Think About Secularism," *First Things* 64 (1996): 27–32.

[65] Pannenberg, "How to Think About Secularism," 27

[66] Pannenberg, "How to Think About Secularism," 28

doctrines propounding the self-sufficient autonomy of man were planted. That European soil was made barren for religion, Pannenberg argues, by the shared memory "among thoughtful people" of unspeakable atrocities and horrors perpetrated during centuries of religious war between and within European states. Here is Pannenberg's explanation:

> When in a number of countries no religious party could successfully impose its faith upon the entire society, the *unity of the social order* had to be based on a foundation other than religion. Moreover, religious conflict had proved to be destructive of social order. In the second half of the seventeenth century, therefore, thoughtful people decided that, *if social peace was to be restored, religion and the controversies associated with religion would have to be bracketed. In that decision was the birth of modern secular culture.* It would in time lead to secular*ism* and a culture that is properly described as secularist.[67]

Pannenberg goes on to propose a cure against the calamity of secularism in terms of an intra-Christian restoration of social unity and civility:

> What Christians should learn from this is the urgency of overcoming their inherited controversies and of restoring some form of unity among themselves. In addition, the idea and practice of tolerance must be incorporated into the Christian understanding not only of freedom but of truth itself. Without these changes—changes that only Christians can bring about—it is quite unreasonable to expect modern culture to reconsider the exclusion of religion from the public square. *The memory of the role of religion in the origins of modernity powerfully reinforces the contemporary prejudice that religion in the public square is divisive, intolerant, and destructive of civil society.*[68]

Pannenberg's description of the phenomena of secularization and secularism is broadly in line with much earlier Roman Catholic censure of these modern western developments. Moreover, his general diagnosis might, if due allowance were made for his particular Christian perspective, be embraced also by many discerning non-Christians who are, likewise, deeply concerned with the menace of western secularism and modernity.

There is, I submit, significant truth in Pannenberg's and similar views of secularist culture, its causes, and its shortcomings. For instance, we may sympathize with Pannenberg when he lambasts creeping relativism about religious and metaphysical truth. And of course we may identify with his disapproval of the prejudice that privatization and marginalization of religion is still necessary to maintain civil peace and shield the public realm from religion and controversies associated with religion. Pannenberg is importantly right, too, in emphasizing that the unity of a society's order must be based on a shared and stable normative foundation, and if such a foundation cannot be provided by a particular religion it needs to be replaced. This is a crucial point to which I shall return when explaining the idea of *inherent dignity* (section IV below). And Pannenberg may be right, I believe, in his indictment of "careful trimming" of the claims and ways of religion in order not to offend people's "secular sensibilities." (But, transformation of the doctrines and practices of established religion may, of course, be authoritatively grounded in the heartland of a religious tradition.) Finally,

---

[67] Pannenberg, "How to Think About Secularism," 28, emphasis added, except for "secular*ism*."
[68] Pannenberg, "How to Think About Secularism," 30, emphasis added.

Pannenberg is crucially right when he points out the chief historical cause of the emergence of antireligious, rationalist Enlightenment philosophy and, in its wake, the antireligious biases he ascribes to contemporary secularist culture:

> The reality, I am arguing, is that the transition in question was not, or at least not chiefly, ideologically driven. *It was religious war and the destruction of social peace that made it necessary to abandon the old idea that public culture must be based on religious unity.*[69]

I have presented Pannenberg's critique of secularism understood as cultural alienation from religion both for its many insights and for the way they are linked to instructive flaws.

My first objection is that though he may be right in attributing secularism (circumscribed as public alienation from religion) to significant segments of modern western culture, Pannenberg seriously exaggerates its extent.[70] My second objection addresses Pannenberg's proposed antidote: having stated, rightly I believe, that religious wars and the destruction of social peace prompted the historical processes of secularization, Pannenberg urges that Christians overcome "their inherited controversies" and incorporate "the idea and practice of tolerance" into their "understanding not only of freedom but of truth itself." I shall now argue that this recipe is neither necessary nor sufficient for social unity and civil peace nor to earn reentry of religion to the modern secular public square.

Not necessary: Inherited intra-Christian differences and divides have arguably come to stay and Christians had better accommodate to this fact and accept its legitimacy from the vantage point of their own religious doctrines.

Not sufficient: The Lockean remedy of toleration—always a half-hearted policy—is not, or at any rate no longer, what is called for; toleration may even be held to be as much a part of the problem as it is a solution to the challenge of intrareligious and interreligious difference. The problem is that toleration does not go beyond political prudence and provide grounds for principled mutual respect across religious and life-stance divides. Hence skepticism, relativism, and liberal gag rules against public religious discourse thrive all too well under the auspices of toleration (section IV).

Finally, I object to Pannenberg's apparent oversight of the entrenched fact of religious and life-stance plurality and of the moral irreversibility of pluralism in any contemporary society (including traditionally Christian societies and certainly in Germany). Pannenberg does not take into account the religious, moral, and political upshot of the fact that contemporary interreligious and intrareligious differences cannot be eliminated peacefully, noncoercively, and without affront to human dignity and freedom. Pointedly: Social unity and civil peace today have to be expressly pluralist and publicly grounded on principles that encompass doctrinally more or less incompatible and institutionally more or less competing religions, denominations, and life stances.

The option that remains, barring a return to politically hegemonic religion or life stance, is founding social unity and civil peace on mutual solidarity and respect between many (preferably all) religions, life stances, and denominations, each party adapting to the fact of divisiveness by way of internally well-grounded espousals of the legitimacy

---

[69] Pannenberg, "How to Think About Secularism," 29, emphasis added.

[70] See note 60 above and subsection III.F below.

of a secular and pluralist order. Below I shall argue the case for such espousals through overlapping justification of universally applicable human rights to freedom of religion or belief (section IV).

F. The Return of Religion to Politics: A Legitimate Reversal of Secularization?

The causal links between religion and politics, at levels of empires, nations, political parties, ethnic minorities, social control, or social protest are complex, often substantial, and rarely absent.[71] But processes of modernization and secularization, themselves perhaps triggered and sustained by religious forces, did turn politics and religion into separate, functionally differentiated arenas of modern society and accompanied this institutional separation with a settled public conviction that politics and religion ought to be kept apart in order to safeguard civil peace, keep interreligious violence at bay, or perhaps just steer clear of futile public argument.

José Casanova's case studies of flourishing "public religion" in Europe, Latin-America, and the US, as well as numerous other studies of the recent reentry of religious voices into the public square, raise obvious questions about the factual and normative soundness of secularization doctrines.[72] Religious studies departments now teach that major parts of secularization theory fly in the face of facts. They report vigorous religious resurgence worldwide during the latter decades of the last century, most prominently within Islam and Evangelical Protestantism, but also in most other major religious communities. Moreover, they note that this trend redounds largely to the benefit of conservative religion.

On this background the quality of religion's return to the public square becomes crucial. The only issue to be dealt with in this subsection is whether, and in what manner, vigorously voiced public religious arguments, preferences, and programs, resulting in religious influence on matters political, amount to a reversal of secularization and, in particular, is a challenge to a secular society. Our answer specifies how we draw the line of demarcation between legitimate and illegitimate "reentry" of religion into modern politics. The ongoing "desecularization" of domestic and transnational public discourse about matters of public politics is, I submit, to be welcomed from the vantage point of a secular and pluralist society, to the extent the public voices of religions and life stances observe certain normative constraints. That is, it is vital that such voices do not in effect undermine the human right to freedom of religion or belief, are loyal to the principles of human rights generally, and abide by the basic standards of

[71] Steve Bruce, *Politics and Religion* (Cambridge: Polity, 2003) brings a wealth of well-documented and often fascinating facts under each of these headings. He concludes his book with a chapter on "Explanations," which are not all borne out by facts, such as, "[religions] cannot treat all people as equal irrespective of their religion" (245) or, "almost every state in which Muslims are in a large majority is theocratic" (241). How about Muslims in Indonesia? Or in Turkey? For the case of Indonesia, see Robert W. Hefner, *Civil Islam* (Princeton: Princeton University Press, 2000); for Turkey see Binnaz Toprak, "Islam and the Secular State in Turkey," in *Turkey: Political, Social and Economic Challenges in the 1990s,* ed. C. Balim et al. (London: E. J. Brill, 1995)

[72] Casanova, *Public Religion,* Berger, ed., *The Desecularization of the World,* and Torkel Brekke, *Gud i norsk politikk. Religion og politisk makt* [God in Norwegian politics. Religion and political power] (Oslo: Pax Forlag, 2002).

representative democracy, constitutionalism, the rule of law, and the separation and mutual checks of public powers. These constraints are all rooted in the emergent, globally recognized public doctrine of the inherent dignity of every human being.

Resistance to religious voice, argument, preference, and influence in political matters may, however, be justified on democratic and human rights grounds when religious or life-stance controversies threaten civil peace and undermine social solidarity across religious and life-stance divides in a secular society. And it is far from clear that the politics of all movements of religious resurgence, among Buddhists, Christians, Hindus, Jews, Muslims, and Sikhs, subscribe to and do not in effect undermine the human right to freedom of religion or belief and other principles of human rights and democracy. But what is at stake is *not* the religious or life-stance character, or language, or motives of political demands. The critical point about religious and life-stance public entries into the political realm of a secular and pluralist society is their democratic and human rights credentials, and in particular their principled espousal of the universally applicable human right to freedom of religion or belief.

We shall see that this point does not require anyone to bow passively to an established and unalterable regime. A political and legal regime has public legitimacy only if it can be reasonably endorsed by all who are party to it: hence the quest for overlapping justification of freedom of religion or belief across religious and life-stance divides.

IV. Overlapping Justification: Mutual Respect with Uncompromised Integrity

This section first lines up some familiar approaches to the challenges of religious plurality and divergence and indicates their shortcomings, in light of what has become feasible in the present-day pluralist world: namely, overlapping justification across normative divides of the human right to freedom of religion or belief. Next, the section spells out the structure and normative core of overlapping justification, starting from the justificatory argument provided by the founding mothers and fathers of universally applicable human rights. Third, it displays why overlapping justification may resolve the two dilemmas identified above[73] that arise from pluralist consent to inclusive religious freedom. And finally, it presents the paradigmatic turn of the Roman Catholic Church from principled rejection to a well-grounded doctrinal espousal of the human right to freedom of religion or belief.

Toleration is, of course, the classical and still prevailing liberal approach to the challenges to stability, civil peace, and social unity that are posed for society by religious and life-stance difference and strife. The Lockean "Revolution in Religious Liberty . . . constituted a kind of Copernican Revolution in political theory"[74] by effectively doing away with the assumptions that religious truth required state implementation of religious beliefs and that political stability presupposed religious and cultural homogeneity. Locke's celebrated arguments in *A Letter Concerning Toleration* (written in 1685, the

[73] See section II, above.

[74] W. Cole Durham, Jr., "Perspectives on Religious Liberty: A Comparative Framework," in *Religious Human Rights in Perspective. Legal Perspectives,* ed. Johan van der Vyver and John Witte, Jr. (The Hague: Martinus Nijhoff, 1996), 1–44, at 7–8

year Louis XIV had revoked the Edict of Nantes, and the Huguenots were being persecuted and forced to emigrate *en masse*) show that the machinery of political coercion cannot force a person to salvation. Locke's defense of the policy of toleration is powerful and his achievement not to be belittled. Moreover, he no doubt held toleration to accord with his Christian religion: "The toleration of those that differ from others in matters of religion, is so agreeable to the Gospel of Jesus Christ, and to the genuine reason of mankind, that it seems monstrous for men to be so blind, as not to perceive the necessity and advantage of it, in so clear a light."[75]

Yet the policy of toleration has significant shortcomings. At its core toleration constitutes a merely prudential determination to put up with other beliefs. But this prudential attitude, while extremely valuable in ruling out persecution and intervention in the religious life of others, at the same time subtly emasculates the sympathetic instinct to engage, understand, and ultimately respect others. Briefly: toleration tends to enervate serious and focused attention to genuine differences of belief by permitting apathy about others and by filtering authentic religious voice out of the public square. In preceding sections we have noted complaints about religion that have emerged with the coming of modernity. Memories of interreligious violence, war, and persecution have fed modern skepticism and relativism about serious truth claims in religious matters. The darker sides of religious discord have elicited a public culture of disbelief and generated liberal gag rules[76] against religious discourse in the public square. Each of these factors has led to religious commitment being privatized and marginalized. It is plausible to think that these modern developments have thrived all too well under the auspices of public toleration.[77] In essence a half-hearted expedient, Lockean political toleration does not envision, much less require, that parties differing in religious doctrine and ideological commitment foster and sustain internally well-grounded mutual respect, trust, and constructive cooperation among themselves. Politically sustained toleration may then have become an ambiguous survival kit for modern religion, keeping the real thing at bay, atrophied because shielded by the filter of toleration from serious public assertion and serious public criticism.

A second modern counter policy directed against troublesome religion, in particular against hegemonic religion cohabiting with established privilege, exploitation, and hypocrisy, is what might be termed ***strident laicism***, as exemplified by modern France and Turkey. While the policy of laicism protests its tolerance and neutrality, laicist politics in these countries tend to be intolerant against public manifestations of religion both traditional and new, acting as if illiberal policing of religion were mandatory for a religiously neutral state. The modern tradition of state laicism is not even consistently

[75] John Locke, *A Letter Concerning Toleration*, edited by John Horton and Susan Mendus (London and New York: Routledge, 1991), 16–17. The statement is interesting among other reasons because Locke as a matter of course introduces *two* moral tribunals for assessing toleration: both the revealed Gospel of Jesus Christ and the genuine reason of mankind, the latter implying a capacity for moral reason shared by all men.
[76] See Stephen Holmes, *Passions and Constraint. On the Theory of Liberal Democracy* (Chicago: The University of Chicago Press, 1995), 202–35.
[77] Of course, societal privatization and marginalization of religion, as well as epistemic skepticism and relativism about religious truth claims, have been endorsed as antidotes in their own right against malicious religious strife.

tolerant, hovering between religious neutrality and the substitution of antireligious "rationalism" for hegemonic religion, replacing one hegemony with another[78] rather than achieving genuine neutrality.

A third important approach has developed within religious traditions as they have addressed the challenges of religious plurality, divergence, and conflict, namely intra- and interreligious discourse about ***salvific exclusivism, salvific inclusivism,*** and ***salvific pluralism.*** Put briefly, thoughtful members of religious communities have attempted to soften "hard-line" doctrines so as to teach that salvation (or emancipation; or end to the cycle of suffering, etc.) can be reached by following differing religious paths, either equally through all approaches (salvific pluralism) or in gradations with one's own religion at the center (salvific inclusivism). Admittedly, if salvific pluralism ("all religions are equally salvific") were to become authoritatively integrated in all religious belief systems, important dimensions of interreligious strife would vanish.[79] However, conflicts within and between religions about these questions are profound and as unsettled as are other serious debates within and between religious traditions. My own view of the matter is that controversies about these questions will not end soon. In particular I want to add that religious adherents of salvific exclusivism (in line with bishop Cyprian's formula from the third century, "outside the church there is no salvation") should ***not*** be barred from the pluralist religious arena of a secular society.

What counts, I submit, is not whether religious people appreciate other beliefs and practices or whether they admit of alternative paths to salvation. What really matters is whether each, on sound internal grounds, supports the public doctrine of the equal inherent dignity and inalienable freedom of all human beings, irrespective of their religion, life stance, or any other differences, and that each reasonably understand or else trust that other similarly support general freedom of religion or belief.

The feasibility of authentic, internally well-grounded religious espousals of universal (or nonexclusive) religious freedom cannot be seriously questioned: Ashoka, Balthasar Hubmaier, Roger Williams, and Joseph Smith, despite deep and perhaps even exclusivist commitment to their own religious views, were each clearly committed to a nonexclusive notion of universal religious freedom. Today major religious communities are adhering to the examples set by these and other pioneers, and I shall present one impressive contemporary case below. But it seems that not even the pioneers of religious validations of religious liberty have developed expressly pluralist justificatory models by way of engaging in public overlapping justifications of the universally applicable human right to freedom of religion or belief.

I now turn to the task of explaining overlapping justification. The human right to freedom of religion or belief is an integrated and central part of the modern system of human rights protection, and its public validation is inseparable from the question of reasonable public endorsement of the modern human rights project as a whole. I

---

[78] Questions about a laicist (in contrast to a secular) state are addressed in chapters 18, 20, and 26 of this volume.

[79] The chapter by Leonard Swidler in this volume touches on these matters. An insightful overview of contemporary intra- and interreligious discourse about salvific exclusivism/inclusivism/pluralism, from the point of view of a Christian, is Kate McCarthy, "Reckoning with Religious Difference: Models of Interreligious Moral Dialogue," in ***Explorations in Global Ethics. Comparative Religious Ethics and Interreligious Dialogue,*** ed. Sumner B. Twiss and Bruce Grelle (Boulder: Westview Press, 1998), 73–117.

therefore start by presenting publicly recognized and entrenched values and modes of justificatory reasoning pertaining to the moral validity of modern human rights in general. Hence, I now turn to the remarkably thoughtful justification put forward by the founding mothers and fathers of modern human rights: the drafters of the Universal Declaration of Human Rights 1947–1948.[80] Their moral argument was designed to undergird and give substance to the political resolve of peoples, organized as state parties under the Charter of the United Nations, to establish a worldwide regime for the protection of human rights. The argument proceeds from two main premises. The first is an anthropological *value premise* P1 enunciating a shared commitment to heed the inherent dignity and inviolable freedom of every human being. The second is a sociological *factual premise* P2 formed as a conditional statement connecting the value premise P1 with an agreed-upon interpretation of the global circumstances—both perils and prospects—for leading human lives that are at least minimally appropriate in light of the dignity and freedom of human beings:[81]

> P1: Every human being is born free and equal in dignity (P1a); human beings are, furthermore, presumed to be sufficiently reasonable and conscientious to observe a decent public order defined in terms of human rights (P1b).
>
> P2: If peoples organized as sovereign states, under such global circumstances for human freedom and dignity as prevail in the world now and in the foreseeable future, are not to disregard their moral commitment proclaimed in P1, they are obliged to seek to agree on and establish an international regime for the domestic protection of people's dignity and freedom, by means of legally and politically codified rights, to be called "human rights."

The normative foundation of the entire edifice of modern human rights is the public doctrine of *inherent dignity* (P1a), supplemented by the public presumption of a general moral capacity to observe a decent public order (P1b).[82] Overlapping justification

---

[80] This paragraph is a severely shortened version of Lindholm, "Ethical Justification," 65–68. The public moral grounds of universally binding rights, elaborated in 1947–1948 by UN Human Rights bodies, I have earlier referred to as "a justificatory prototheory of human rights" (An-Na'im, ed., *Human Rights in Cross-Cultural Perspectives*, 395–97). Incidentally, knowledge of the Universal Declaration of Human Rights its content, intellectual background, and political context is often surprisingly shallow. A careful study of the text in its context of origin is recommended. Guidance may be found in Johannes Morsink, *The Universal Declaration of Human Rights. Origins, Drafting, and Intent* (Philadelphia: University of Pennsylvania Press, 1999); Gudmundur Alfredsson and Asbjørn Eide, eds., *The Universal Declaration of Human Rights: A Common Standard of Achievement* (The Hague: Martin Nijhoff, 1999); Mary Ann Glendon, *A World Made New: Eleanor Roosevelt and the Universal Declaration of Human Rights* (New York: Random House, 2001).

[81] The content of the two main premises is drawn from the UDHR. Premise P1 is derived from Article 1 and Article 29, and premise P2 comes from the Preamble of the UDHR and from preparatory deliberations in various UN organs at the time the UDHR was being drafted. The argument of the founders is a straightforward practical syllogism. To make the structure of the argument explicit the two premises and the conclusion would have to be put in the first person plural, giving voice to the reasoning of governments as representatives of their peoples, as in the Charter of the United Nations: "We the Peoples of the United Nations hold P1 and P2 and we therefore agree on and resolve to establish . . ." Of course, the argument is still elliptical, or incomplete; in particular, the globally prevailing social circumstances of human rights are not spelled out.

[82] International humans rights instruments use the words "freedom" and "dignity" in various configurations, always with normative intent, as the source from which human rights derive. In what follows I shall not address how the notions of dignity and freedom are conceptually linked. I shall stick to the term "inherent

across normative divides of the human right to freedom of religion or belief may, presumably, proceed from the starting point of justification for human rights in general. At the doorstep of justification any would-be party to overlapping justification is presumed to engage with the doctrine of inherent dignity.

All major international human rights instruments affirm that human rights derive from the inherent dignity of human beings, only using slight variations of language.[83] Hence, differing but overlapping justifications should be presumed to converge in providing internally well-grounded support for the notion of human dignity.

Beyond sharing in validating a doctrine of inherent human dignity on internally legitimate grounds, parties to overlapping justification have to come clear about *the link* between human dignity and human rights. Hence we must ask, how are human rights "derived" from human dignity?

Before I return to justification of religious freedom in particular I shall therefore outline major steps in a derivation, or justification, of human rights as a whole starting from the doctrine of inherent human dignity.

A good beginning to an answer is then to make the notion of inherent human dignity operational for human rights as it were, by saying that if all humans have inherent dignity, then *there is something about each and every human being* such that certain things ought not to be done to her and certain other things ought to be done for her.[84]

But, having spelled out the profoundly interrelational and practical implication that spring from embracing inherent human dignity, we are still several steps away from justifying *human rights*, that is justifying universally applicable entitlements that trump other political and moral interests.

The first step is to be clear about "the circumstances of rights." It is not a self-evident universal truth that people have rights in virtue of their inherent dignity. In a flourishing closed, small, prosperous, and morally harmonious society where people are oblivious of rights and lead fulfilling lives without rights the very introduction of rights could bring moral decline, perhaps by aggravating interpersonal conflicts. The costs of rights are not just financial, but possibly moral. Nozick's proposition, "Individuals have rights and there are things no person or group may do to them (without violating their rights)"[85] is an important truth in any modern, complex,

---

dignity." Elucidating the provenience and providing in-depth interpretation of the public doctrine of inherent human dignity is a task well beyond the present chapter. For a succinct and competent overview of the historical trajectory of the doctrine see Hubert Cancik, "'Dignity of Man' and 'Persona' in Stoic Anthropology: Some Remarks on Cicero, *De officis* I 105-107," in *The Concept of Human Dignity in Human Rights Discourse,* ed. David Kretzmer and Eckart Klein (The Hague: Kluwer Law International, 2002), 19–39. Suffice it to say here that attempts at doctrinal monopolization or "possessive embrace" of the doctrine of inherent dignity, in the name of one's own religion or life stance, should be turned down politely and firmly, in the spirit of Ashoka's dictum, "Whoever praises his own religion, due to excessive attachment, and denigrates that of others with the thought 'Let me glorify my own religion,' in reality inflicts the severest injury on his own religion."

[83] The International Covenant on Civil and Political Rights in its second preambular article reads, "*Recognizing* that these rights derive from the inherent dignity of the human person, . . ." Similar "justifcatory" language recurs throughout international human rights documents.

[84] In this and the next four paragraphs I paraphrase freely from Michael J. Perry, *The Idea of Human Rights. Four Inquiries* (Oxford: Oxford University Press, 1998), supplemented by ideas borrowed from Robert Nozick, Maurice Cranston, and James Nickel.

and plural society. It is not a *universal* moral truth, not true in all social worlds. A social world in which Nozick's proposition is true is one in which the *circumstances of rights* obtain.

A next step is to elucidate *what goods and benefits* people shall have secure access to by means of rights. The interest or values to be protected by a right must, for *a morally justified human right* to exist, be of great importance to people either generally or in significant cases and be significantly linked with people's chance to lead lives answering to human dignity. Moreover, a good or benefit, even if deemed very important for a dignified human life, should not by right be protected as a human right unless general and minimally effective and even-handed protection is, or can be made, socially feasible. Hence, to be dearly loved; to avoid early sudden death or severe conflicts; or to have a happy family life are some very cherished goods that are unsuitable for protection by rights. Jefferson in the *Declaration of Independence*, when enumerating the most important goods to be protected by natural rights, included "life, liberty and the *pursuit* of happiness." It would have been improper to proclaim a natural right to *happiness* since happiness whether as a full-fledged morally successful life or as a felicitous feel cannot properly be safeguarded by means of rights.

A reasonable counterargument to a proposal for something to be human rights-protected good would be to show that there are alternative ways of protecting the good in question that are more suitable for the purpose, or less costly, or more efficient, than rights.

Finally, in this rudimentary checklist of considerations pertaining to "the derivation of human rights from human dignity," I mention that the addressees of modern human rights, saddled by internationally binding law with the burden of implementing human rights protection for all human beings everywhere in the world, had to be modern territorial states, each state catering to people under their respective jurisdictions. In our world only states could have the requisite legitimacy, power, coercive apparatus, and other resources it takes. But for that reason, only norms and mechanisms that can attract reasonably broad international support can attain human rights status.

I submit that each of the above factors enter in the construction of legally and politically binding human rights obligations on states, and perhaps on other coercive institutions and, moreover, that this somewhat chilling realism is part and parcel of what moral, real-world respect for the inherent dignity of every human being requires.

Human rights derive, then, from the public global commitment to heed the inherent dignity of every human being but only by way of complex processes of deliberation and negotiation with moral, religious, cultural, political, economic, diplomatic, and other inputs. Human rights are not deduced by philosophy professors and theological doctors. They are generated in complex international and transnational processes of argument, bargaining, and compromise—processes to which philosophers and clerics have made significant but not always decisive contributions.[86]

---

[85] Robert Nozick, *Anarchy, State, and Utopia* (New York: Basic Books, 1974), ix.

[86] In a secular society, concern with human rights is not exclusively a political or juridical affair, but a matter potentially engaged in by all in the public square where moral, cultural, and religious, professional and lay inputs are crucial for overall legitimacy of outcomes.

The public moral legitimacy of modern human rights may be expressed by saying they have survived and are reasonably expected to survive unobstructed and informed public discussion. Though much disputed and criticized, the framework of modern human rights has so far proven its mettle under open public scrutiny. The legitimacy of international human rights norms draws also on the moral presumption for obeying the law, and more abstractly, on procedural legitimation. Hence the burden of proof is on the shoulders of their detractors. Critics of the project of universally applicable human rights can easily point to weaknesses, shortcomings, inconsistencies, and gaping double standards of implementation. But the challenge to critics and detractors is to come up with feasible alternative political, legal, and institutional measures that are arguably superior to what we already have as a globally entrenched regime: universally applicable human rights protection (though often inefficient and non-evenhanded) against pressing threats and impending perils to human freedom and dignity in the present-day world.

At this point I may usefully indicate how I conceive of justification. Justification of a problematic moral norm, at the level of the individual, does not require that the norm be deduced from unproblematic (or "certain" or "self-evident") higher principles. This ideal of justification is beautifully neat, but hardly ever reasonably practicable. We surely have moral principles that we are not willing to compromise, but their ***reasoned acceptance*** is often dependent on the wealth of moral implication we draw from them in the light of the totality of other values and beliefs we hold to, and they are often entrenched in the moral or religious traditions to which we belong. Reasonable justification has to be holistic and fallibilist: we have good reason to accept only what "best" fits into the totality of our knowledge, values, commitments, and beliefs (remembering that among our cherished commitments we may include open-mindedness, taking arguments seriously, and respect for fellow human beings and their plights). Certain beliefs and values are very strongly held, sometimes for very good reasons, and one such value commitment that is publicly articulated, defended, and shared is the doctrine of inherent human dignity. Individual convictions are often shared in the form of an entrenched living tradition. The reasonability of publicly shared traditions—of our cognitive and moral and religious culture—depends in large measure on our continual involvement in open-minded probing and questioning. But serious questioning is part and parcel of public scrutiny, discussion, argument.

So, I have no qualms speaking of deriving human rights from human dignity. But the moral and intellectual reality behind such talk is that people committed for good reasons to mutual respect and solidarity among all human beings, through informed, open-minded, and pluralist discussion and critical study, find that support and advocacy of the modern human rights project is morally compelling.

I can now return to overlapping justification across religious and life-stance divides of the human right to freedom of religion or belief. Overlapping justification, obviously, requires religious or life-stance communities, via their adherents, to engage with the doctrine of the inherent dignity of every human being and with the issues and questions that have to be addressed in deriving, and perhaps shaping, revising, and pruning, of the public conception of universally applicable human rights in the circumstances of the world in which we live. In so doing, people of faith and conviction are filling out that part of the justificatory argument that wisely was left open by the founding mothers and fathers of modern human rights exercising proper justificatory restraint.

They decided, after protracted deliberations, judiciously to leave God, Reason, Nature and Human Nature out of the foundational sources spelled out in Article 1 of the Universal Declaration of Human Rights. The completion of the universally acceptable and binding argument they did provide requires, I submit, the supplement of expressly pluralist, overlapping justification, or overlapping justifications.[87] I can now explain the idea of overlapping justification of the human right to freedom of religion or belief in two steps.

First the definition of a fully realized overlapping justification:

> *Overlapping justification of the human right to freedom of religion or belief is fully realized to the extent competent and serious adherents of each of the set of rival religious or life-stance traditions reasonably hold this universally applicable human right to be well-supported by each of the separate normative traditions in the set; in other words they reasonably hold the right to be arguably well-grounded in each particular belief- system including their own.*

Obviously, overlapping justification fully realized may demand more than what is feasible. But for our purposes we can do with much less, still requiring that each party has knowledge and understanding of the internal grounding of his or her own belief system but only requiring that he or she have reasonable trust in the cogency of the other party's espousal of the right. Hence:

> *Overlapping justification of the human right to freedom of religion or belief is not realized even at a minimum threshold level unless representative adherents of each of the set of rival religious or life-stance traditions reasonably hold this universally applicable human right to be well grounded in their own doctrine and have reasonable trust that the other normative traditions in the set hold groundings that bind their respective adherents similarly.*

Note that overlapping *justification* goes beyond mere overlapping *consensus* by requiring each party not only to adhere to but also to be knowledgeable about the grounding of the right in his or her own normative tradition.[88]

Taking for granted that human beings now and for the foreseeable future do disagree in matters of religion or life stance, my overriding concern in this chapter is, I repeat, to grasp how we may, in the religiously discordant social world that is ours, reasonably secure both *principled solidarity based on mutual respect across religious and life-stance divides* and *unflinching doctrinal integrity of, and commitment to, our differing normative traditions.* Reasoning in a virtuous circle my answer draws on the established modern tradition of internationally recognized human rights, rooted in an emerging worldwide public commitment to heed as inviolable the inherent dignity of every human being.

The public presumption or prejudice in favor of human dignity may surely resonate within and across difference. But it is now incumbent on me to spell out how overlapping justification of the human right to freedom of religion or belief among rival parties may join *principled inclusive solidarity and mutual respect* with *unflinching doctrinal integrity.*

---

[87] For the structure and principled incompleteness of the public argument for human rights supplied by the founders, see footnote 81 above.

[88] See note 7 above.

The case of freedom of religion or belief is eminently suitable to display universal solidarity of mutual recognition and respect among people adhering to doctrines that as wholes differ and are mutually incompatible. For the sake of clarity and ease of understanding I shall now present and make use of a model of a closed pluralist society with its entire population neatly and stably distributed among five rival religious or life-stance communities. I make no claim that this model is "realistic"; we are dealing with a starkly simplified model of social order that admits of a step-by-step withdrawal of simplifying assumptions, in order to study at what stage various points that can be made relative to the model collapse.

Let us call our model social order UP (say, for "United Pluralists"). Each religious community in UP is committed to a unique set of religious or life-stance doctrines, at least some of which are incompatible with beliefs held by each of the other belief communities. Members of each community tend to take their own doctrine, and the way of life associated with it, very seriously. There are no people in UP that are not adherents to one of the five belief systems along with the practices associated with these. For the purpose of the model we make no assumptions about how UP's population is carved up in belief majority or minority subpopulations. (Hence, for example, 84% of the total could belong to one belief community, but the point is that minority or majority relations are irrelevant.) For the rest, UP is assumed to be a constitutional, democratic, officially pluralist and rule-of-law regulated polity with a generally accessible and lively public sphere, befitting a secular social order as described above.[89] Now the question is: How can overlapping justification of the human right to freedom of religion or belief (defined as in the international human rights instruments dealt with in this volume) facilitate civil peace, a generally shared normative basis for UP's public institutions, and political and social stability for the citizenry of UP? The answer generally advocated in this chapter, applied to the social world of UP, is:

(a) by each religious community discovering or creating internally authoritative and well-grounded normative justifications of the universally applicable human right to freedom of religion or belief, and
(b) by each religious community making their internally grounded espousal of the human right to religious freedom public, and being ready to explain and defend their espousal of equal religious freedom for all, and
(c) by each religious community engaging in reasonable, civil, and candid public discourse with other religious communities in UP about the doctrinal cogency, trustworthiness, and doctrine/practice coherence of the way each party heeds the human right to freedom of religion or belief.

Surely, given our severely simplifying assumptions, UP would be a good *prima facie* case of stability, solidarity, and mutual respect across religious and life-stance divides *once the requirements (a) through (c) were realized.* The desiderata of social unity, civil peace, a shared commitment to heed public institutions and procedures are all in place *to the extent* religion or life-stance commitments make a difference including absolutist claims to Truth, and mutually advocacy of "extra ecclesiam non salus." But that is

---

[89] See Section III above.

just one of the points of the exercise: UPians may enjoy civil friendship across uncompromised religious divides. They have no need to tolerate one another: they respect one another in virtue of their own belief commitments, also knowing they are similarly respected by the others. And they share a mighty incentive to engage in serious, attentive, and patient public discussion about questions pertaining to religion and life stance.

From what we know about religious communities, is general realization of (a) though (c) impending? We know from experience that the discovery or construction of well-grounded and internally authoritative doctrinal foundations for embracing universal religious liberty is a reality. My own Evangelical-Lutheran community is just one case in point: Very seriously scriptural in general theological orientation, we Lutherans have discovered, but perhaps only in the latter half of the last century, that the first chapter of the first book of our Bible authoritatively grounds the doctrine of inherent human dignity and inviolable freedom. For more than four hundred years of biblical exegesis Lutherans did not hold universal human dignity, human rights, or religious freedom to derive from the book of Genesis, chapter 1, verse 27: "So God created man / in his own image, / in the image of God / he created him; / male and female / he created them." So Lutherans are far from being pioneers in the pursuit of doctrinal justification of human rights; we have rather joined the throng. And that is the more important point with respect to requirement (a): *Aggiornamento* to the circumstances, the new possibilities, and the promises of a modern, secular order is achieved or in process within many religious traditions.

Of course, I do not forget that UP is a highly simplified model of reality, and the simplifying assumptions are in part drastic. Before I address these assumptions, I shall explain why, if requirements (a) through (c) were met, the twin dilemmas of justifying freedom of religion or belief across normative divides would be resolved.

As for *well-grounded mutual respect across fundamental divides*, overlapping justification, when realized between parties adhering to rival religious doctrines, makes mutual respect and solidarity doctrinally secure. If my faith requires me to respect and stand up for your religious freedom and I know yours requires the same from you, and you and I know that we share this knowledge, then you and I stand in a relation of friendship to one another. Of course, our comprehensive religious doctrines clash, and we know this well. So UPians may, if other things do not intervene, have occasion to engage in serious interreligious argument. Good, civil and candid polemics are not off limits between people who know they are friends.

As for the dilemma of having a *reasonable justification of religious freedom based on a plurality of incompatible grounds*, I first note that in UP each party knows that all parties have reasonable and strongly held grounds for embracing the human right to freedom of religion or belief. Of course (as above) I do not hold your basic grounding to be true, but I can to my own satisfaction check its internal cogency, its trustworthiness and the doctrine/practice coherence associated with it. That is, UP citizens do share, know that they share, and (if overlapping justification is fully realized) know why and how they share a binding normative foundation for the human right to freedom of religion or belief, or alternatively (if overlapping justification is realized at the minimum level or better) have reasonable trust that they share a binding normative foundation for the human right to freedom of religion or belief. Their respective grounds for this sharing are not shared, but are publicly available for all to sort out.

What UPians do not have is a shared univocal justification of human rights generally or for the right to religious liberty (or for other principles of their political order). They do not share a justification such that the sharing runs all the way down. So be it: What the UPian normative order teaches us, I submit, is to revise any ill-founded presumptions we may have about what it takes in a religiously divided society to have a reasonably grounded and stable justification of a shared public order.

I submit, then, that the twin dilemmas that may trigger threats to civil peace and social stability are resolved by displaying how and why pluralist, reasoned support of the human right to freedom of religion or belief relieves parties from being involved in self-contradictory or doctrinally compromising positions. Of course, this conclusion depends on the simplifying assumption that only religious or life-stance commitment count, as it were. And, admittedly, citizens of UP, and people in the real world too must transform, reinterpret, or reconceptualize their religious or life-stance commitments if that is required for them to embrace the human right to freedom of religion or belief. Just that.

One way the model of UP may be useful is to ask what happens once we withdraw its simplifying assumptions and stepwise approximate our real social world, as we see it. I leave to readers (and to my own future work) the task of pinpointing assumptions that, when lifted, are liable to undermine the feasibility of social stability and solidarity based on overlapping justification of society's public normative principles, including the human right to freedom of religion or belief. The point here is to see that such overlapping justification appears to be in principle possible, and that this approach has promise of reaching a deeper level of mutual respect in a rigorously pluralistic world than can be promised by toleration, laicization, or ecumenical leveling.

I conclude this subsection with a brief presentation of the Roman Catholic Church's impressive (and wonderfully accessible!) espousal of the human right to freedom of religion or belief, based on stringent theological and natural law-grounded support of the doctrine of inherent dignity.

The case of the Catholic Church and religious freedom is a spectacular demonstration that a major and apparently conservative religious tradition can undergo profound and irreversible doctrinal transformations having very significant implications for practice.[90] For obvious reasons, the doctrinal position of the Catholic Church on human rights and freedom of religion or belief is crucial: there are one billion Catholics in the world!

The Catholic position has, over the last two centuries, shifted from outright rejection and condemnation of human rights to unqualified embrace. Pope Pius VI (Pope 1775–1799) condemned the French doctrine of human rights only two years after they had been proclaimed by the revolutionaries in 1789. He was followed by other popes who, in a number of encyclicals repeated and elaborated the rejection by the Catholic Church of rights founded on human dignity and freedom. Pope Gregory XVI (Pope 1831–1846) "denounced the concepts of freedom of conscience, freedom of the press, and separation of church and state . . ." [91] Here are some samples from

[90] The story has been told many times and I have space only for a very brief version. An excellent overview with references is Appleby, *The Ambivalence of the Sacred*, 42–48

[91] Appleby, *The Ambivalence of the Sacred*, 43

Gregory's encyclical *Mirari vos*: "This shameful font of indifferentism gives rise to that absurd and erroneous proposition which claims that liberty of conscience must be maintained for everyone." And, "Here We must include that harmful and never sufficiently denounced freedom to publish any writings whatever and disseminate them to the people, which some dare to demand and promote with so great clamor."[92] Pope Leo XIII in *Rerum novarum* 1889 made a significant move forwards by recognizing the subsidiarity-graded entitlement of wage laborers to certain economic and social benefits, but not as based on their human rights.

Only Pope John XXIII, in his encyclical *Pacem in terris*, April 1963,[93] provided theologically well-grounded support for the full range of modern human rights norms, now based squarely on the doctrine of the sacred dignity of the human person. Pope John had convoked an ecumenical council of the bishops of the Roman Catholic Church (Vatican II) and set the council's agenda of *aggiornamento* to the new political and social developments in the modern world. Pope John died soon after the council was opened, but now strong resistance to doctrinal and institutional reform gave way. Both the Vatican II declaration *Dignitatis humanae personae* (On the Right of Persons and of Communities to Social and Civil Freedom in Matters Religious) and the Vatican II pastoral constitution *Gaudium et spes* (both promulgated 7 December 1965) mark invaluable steps forward in the incorporation of human rights principles into Christian doctrine and practice. The content of the right to religious freedom defined in *Dignitatis* is reasonably consonant with the norms that were included in Article 18 of the International Covenant on Civil and Political Rights, signed March 23, 1966. As John Courtney Murray, one of the leading figures influencing the content of *Dignitatis*, has noted, its teaching on human dignity constitutes binding Catholic doctrine, whereas the arguments provided, drawn partly from human reason and partly from Christian sources, can be discussed critically and improved[94] (presumably a task primarily for Catholics). What is striking in Murray is that natural law for him is no invariant essence but "a developing tradition of ideas, commitments, and procedures that course through the social and political thoughts of a secular society that is continuously on move."[95]

---

[92] From sections14 and 15 of *Mirari vos*, Encyclical of Pope Gregory XVI, promulgated on 15 August 1832 <http://wwwewtn.com/library/encyc/g16mirar.htm> (site visited 06.11.03).

[93] Pope John XXIII, knowing he would very soon die, wrote *Pacem in terris* partly in light of the ineluctable necessity, in his view, of promoting suitable normative foundations for peaceful coexistence in the aftermath of the Cuba crisis. But in underwriting modern human rights as defined by the Universal Declaration the Holy Father could also know that "I was there": as Papal Nuncio to Paris (1943–1952) Monsignor Roncalli took part in the consultations of an advisory group to René Cassin, a prominent and influential French member of the working group of the UN Commission on Human Rights that drafted the Universal Declaration, 1946–1948.

[94] See John Courtney Murray, "Arguments for the Human Rights to Religious Freedom," chap. 4 in *Religious Liberty: Catholic Struggles with Pluralism*, by John C. Murray, edited by J. Leon Hooper, S.J. (Lousiville, Ky.: Westminster/Jon Knox Press, 1993). I highly recommend this posthumously published book to readers who want to go deeply into the impressive intellectual edifice of Catholic doctrine and argument about religious freedom and the doctrine of inherent human dignity. Murray brought to the Catholic world an innovative and penetrating understanding of the American experiment in religious freedom. A large collection of Vatican II documents with a commentary can be found in Joseph Gremillion, ed, *The Gospel of Peace and Justice. Catholic Social Teaching Since Pope John* (Maryknoll, N.Y.: Orbis Books, 1976).

[95] From Editor's introduction to Murray "Arguments for the Human Right to Religious Freedom."

One main purpose in this (all-too-short) presentation of the transformation in Catholic doctrine from outright rejection to well-grounded and authoritative doctrinal espousal of the human right to freedom of religion or belief is to demonstrate that religious traditions can change. Also significant is the fact demonstrated so well by the experience of Vatican II, that religious traditions can draw on their own resources to frame justifications for freedom of religion or belief in ways that are not only publicly accessible but even moving and persuasive across religious divides. I submit that the positive experience within the Roman Catholic Church is a possibility for religious traditions in general.

A last point is to ask: Should religious endorsements of the human right to freedom of religion or belief be required to rely upon the notion of human dignity? Perhaps not. The religious pioneers of principled religious support of religious freedom did not. In my view the doctrine of human dignity sets a presumption that may be overruled by the better arguments.

A case in point of great potential import is the project of Confucian justification of human rights argued from a reinterpretation of the foundational ethical virtue of *ren* (or *len*), the translation of which may be "two-man-mindedness" or "empathy with and concern for the other fellow." The Chinese sign for the concept is beautiful: "仁". This character represents a human being with two strokes indicating two persons, "you and I" as it were. I mention this here because the prominent Chinese member of the Commission on Human Rights, Professor P. C. Chang, proposed at a significant juncture of deliberations in 1947 that Article 1 should include *ren* among the normative grounds for the new global system of human rights. The other members, after some striving with interpretation of the Chinese term, consented and asked the Secretariat for a suitable translation. Alas, the text of draft Article 1 came back with the term "conscience" juxtaposed to "reason" in the second sentence. Professor P. C. Chang did not protest and the Chinese term in the official text of the Universal Declaration of Human Rights became not the notion of *ren* (the central virtue in classical Confucian ethics) but a modern linguistic innovation *liangxin* invented to translate the Stoic/Christian notion of "conscience." This unfortunate slip between proposal and translation may have created the mistaken impression that no authentic Chinese justification for human rights could be included in Article 1.

Today, after more than fifty years, Professor Joseph Chan of the University of Hong Kong is developing a very promising "ecumenical" justification of human rights based in the Confucian notion of *ren*[96] that may help remedy this lacuna. Here again, the rudiments of the possibilities of overlapping justification are evident.

---

96 Joseph Chan, "A Confucian Perspective on Human Rights for Contemporary China," in *The East Asian Challenge for Human Rights*, ed. Joanne R. Bauer and Daniel Bell (Cambridge: Cambridge University Press, 1999), 212–40; see also: Tommy Flakk, *Human Rights the Confucian Way. Towards International Consensus on Human Rights From Within Cultural Traditions* (Department of Political Science, University of Oslo, 2003). The story about Professor P. C. Chang, *ren*, and Article 1 of the Univeral Declaration is reported in *The Universal Declaration*, ed. Alfredsson and Eide, 43–44.

V. The Priority of Cooperation in the Pursuit of Public Justification

Thus far I have spelled out a conception of expressly pluralist support of religious freedom in terms of overlapping justification of the universally applicable human right to freedom of religion or belief; I now conclude by acknowledging that overlapping justification, full-fledged or at the minimum threshold level, or even "mere" overlapping consensus, bridging existing religious, philosophical and cultural differences, is not widely accomplished. But freedom of religion or belief, as codified in international human rights law, is almost universally accepted as legally and politically binding by states. The moral force of the idea of rights-based protection of freedom of religion or belief is no longer contestable in its general outline, and the idea enjoys widely shared public recognition as an integral part of human rights protection and observance. The publicly shared presumption as regards freedom of religion or belief is clearly in favor of safeguarding the right. But the specifics and practical import of the right are not generally appreciated. And violations, restrictions, unfounded curtailment, and neglect of the human right to freedom of religion or belief abound in the present-day world.

The appropriate demarcation of the human right to freedom of religion or belief is an exceedingly complex matter dealt with by other chapters in this volume. In this chapter my concern has been to propose, spell out, and defend a basic framework for reasonable and properly pluralist support of the universal right to religious liberty. The purpose has been to make clear why and how overlapping justification may facilitate a stable and well-grounded public regime for protection of religious freedom that is built on the reasonable endorsement by all who are or become party to it. My purpose has emphatically not been to provide a justification for the right to freedom of religion of belief that absolves adherents of any religious or life-stance community from engaging critically and constructively with the challenge of providing reasonable and internally legitimate support for the right to freedom of religion or belief.

Espousal of equal freedom and dignity is before anything else a practical—a moral and social—matter. In their ordinary social practice people tend to go by publicly entrenched values and presumptions, not all of which are benign. We may try to change public prejudices by arguments. In this chapter I have, as one example, tried to undermine the plausibility of toleration as a panacea and suitable remedy against the (presumed) threats and dangers posed by the presence of rival religious and life-stance communities in a society. My strategy has been to come up with a better conception, one that facilitates and encourages mutual respect and solidarity across normative divides based in reasonable and stable overlapping justification of the human right to freedom of religion or belief.

But as I have been arguing throughout, achieving overlapping justifications is not merely a matter of abstract theory and intellectual exchange. It depends very much on stimulating and engaging in cooperative interaction across religious and life-stance borders. We need mutual practical understanding between people with different religions and life stances. Engaging in the process of mutual understanding entails recognizing two poles of interaction:

On the one hand, SOLIDARITY:
Mutual respect, friendship, and solidarity between adherents of differing, and somehow incompatible and rivaling religious or life-stance beliefs presuppose that each person in the relationship:

- recognizes in his or her doctrine and practice the equal freedom and dignity of the other person;
- wants what is essential for the other person's enjoyment of freedom of religion or belief, knowing that the other person reciprocates;
- is willing to stand up for the other person when the other person's enjoyment of freedom of religion or belief is imperiled: practicing a standard of "all for one, one for all."

On the other hand, RIVALRY:
Our goal in reaching for interreligious understanding must include, unless we deceive ourselves, a realistic and truthful appreciation among us of our religious and life-stance differences. We must realize that metaphysical, anthropological and ethical views to which we are committed as believers are not only *not the same* but are, as far as we now know, *more or less incompatible doctrines linked with more or less rivaling practices.* In other words, religious and life-stance commitments are, for those who have them, the most important things there are and these commitments may enter into everything their possessors do. In short, despite the pull of solidarity, in virtue of our religious and life-stance commitments we are willy-nilly also at odds.

Throughout this chapter, the starting point has been that we live in irreversibly and inescapably *plural societies.* This means that the fact of plurality of religious and life-stance traditions (and sub-traditions) and communities (and subcommunities), have become essential features of our social and political orders, at local, national, and transnational levels, now and for the foreseeable future. We may, of course, hope and pray that our plural social orders will nevertheless be peaceful, non-violent, decent, and fair. But what should we as committed believers, or committed secular humanists, *do* about it?

To illustrate a prevalent attitude, let me report to you the shock, perhaps horror, voiced to me by two leading Palestinian human rights activists when I submitted to them, in 1997, that Palestinian and Israeli political leaders had consistently failed to draw on Jewish, Muslim, and Christian *religious leaders* and on people's corresponding *religious commitments* in the struggle to establish peace between Arabs and Jews.

Both Palestinian gentlemen retorted, "No way! Religion is a minefield! By all means, we must keep religion out of the picture!"

I disagreed with them then, and I disagree even more strongly today. In my view, if and to the extent religion has become a minefield for people caught up in conflict, it is a task of believers to seek to reinterpret, reform, and rebuild people's religious commitment until they are religious commitments in support of peace and understanding. Religious traditions are open to interpretation, and I now add, religious traditions have proved open, in the long run, to well-grounded and authentic reconstruction by intelligent and diligent believers.

I repeat that *genuine interreligious understanding* includes both *interreligious solidarity* and *interreligious rivalry.* And I reiterate that historical experience of talking across religious divides has often—but not always!—proved disruptive and destructive. With these points in mind I shall first present *two extremes* of talking across religious divides that both have virtues and vices, and subsequently present a *middle position* on interreligious dialogue, discussion, and cooperation. Moreover, I shall introduce what I hold to be an *optimal context* for interreligious dialogue.

First the two extremes of talking across religious divides.

I begin with what is usually called "interfaith dialogue": The exemplars of this are the achievements of the two Parliaments of the World's Religions in Chicago 1893 and again in 1993. The latter approved a "Global Ethics Declaration," drafted by Hans Küng.[97] The Global Ethics Declaration seeks to articulate a common denominator of the ethical (or metaphysical or anthropological or theological) principles of all religions.

The most serious criticism of interfaith dialogue exercises is that they succeed in reaching universal agreement at the considerable cost of being nearly void of meaningful ethical (or metaphysical or anthropological or theological) content. Another compounded objection to the "interfaith dialogue" model of talk across religious divides is that it may tend to elevate its meager lowest common denominator findings to the status of Truth.[98] This is somewhat disturbing to those who want to stick to their particular religious or life-stance convictions and commitments at least until they are convinced by better arguments that they might be wrong.

This brings me to the other extreme of talking across religious divides: "Interreligious polemics." Interreligious polemics involve adherents of differing beliefs in arguments where the parties make serious incompatible claims as to the nature of things, and what the setting for human life is, as well as serious and rivaling claims as to how human persons should respond and behave in that setting. Personally, I do sympathize with the fervent plea in favor of interreligious polemics that has been made by Paul Griffiths, an Anglican theologian and expert on Buddhist philosophy:

> polemical argument and confrontation are integral and essential to the intellectual life and . . . any attempt to remove them from that life is dangerous and in the end incoherent. . . . What goes for the intellectual life in general, and for the religious life in particular, ought to be evident also in the interactions among different religious communities, that here, too, serious and argumentative engagement ought to be part of the enterprise.[99]

Griffiths then correctly identifies one major difficulty for his plea in favor of polemics. There is a critical need for protection against threats to the physical integrity of the parties: killing, torture, "forcible conversion or whatever," directed against his interlocutor and himself. Thus, in his view, "[s]uch polemic is proper, morally speaking, *only in situations where no other threats are present.*"[100]

---

[97] Parliament of the World's Religions, *A Global Ethic: The Declaration of the Parliament of the World's Religions,* Hans Küng and Karl-Josef Kuschel, eds. (London: SCM Press, 1993), 7.

[98] For a sophisticated and well-argued case for interfaith dialogue, see the chapter by Leonard Swidler in this volume.

[99] Paul J. Griffiths, "Why We Need Religious Polemics," *First Things* 44 (June/July 1994): 31–37.

[100] Ibid. (emphasis added).

Indeed! But Griffiths does not reflect on the broader need for religious and life-stance believers—individuals as well as communities—to cater systematically and responsibly for political protection of the freedom and integrity of people engaging in serious interreligious argument.

And that brings me to what is, I submit, a morally necessary ***middle position*** on the subject of interreligious dialogue and discussion.

Between the two extremes lies an intermediate field that can be fruitfully explored. I now present a version of interreligious debate, dialogue, argument, and negotiation, which includes on the one hand catering for mutual respect, friendship and solidarity among people of rival persuasions and commitments and on the other hand the requisite element of candid appreciation of difference, incompatibility, and rivalry.

I shall propose that competent and authentic members of different religious and life-stance communities engage in extended interreligious cooperation and dialogue about a topic that brings together the two elements of solidarity and rivalry. But first I want to propose that such dialogues be conceived as part of ***a prior commitment to shared action***. Here I propose we follow a word of wisdom from the Sanskrit scriptures of the Hindu tradition:

> *Walk together*
> *Talk together*
> *All ye peoples of the world*
> *Then*
> *And only then*
> *Shall ye have peace*

In other words: I propose that we put practical ***cooperation*** between religions and life stances first, even ahead of interreligious ***dialogue***. Such cooperation may range from the lowliest level of working together in addressing pressing social problems in the local community to the level of building inclusive international coalitions between religious and life-stance communities.

In this setting, freedom of religion or belief constitutes a privileged topic of interreligious cooperation and dialogue. The internationally codified human rights norms of freedom of religion or belief, discussed at length in this volume, are perhaps not perfect. But they are, in my view, superior to anything we can hope to come up with by engineering interfaith Declarations and Deep Dialogues. Promotion of international human rights should not be left to states alone: not generally, and particularly not in the field of freedom of religion or belief. Research findings show that concerted transnational argument and advocacy for human rights do make a significant, and badly needed, difference.[101]

Experience with interreligious cooperation and dialogue from the last fifteen years in my home country, Norway, suggests it is very prudent, and perhaps even necessary to ***begin*** interreligious cooperation with the somewhat complex, simultaneously practical and doctrinal issues of freedom of religion or belief.[102]

The Norwegian experience has been that religious and life-stance minorities have very important contributions to make, partly because their freedom of religion or belief have been ignored or neglected. When minority groups understandably complain about the deficiencies in rights protection that they have suffered, inflicted as it were by the majority, then they also invite critical appraisals of the record and performance of their co-religionists in countries where they form the majority. Also, examining freedom or religion or belief norms jointly triggered critical studies of each religious tradition's historical record with respect to their toleration, respect, and solidarity with people of differing faiths. As a member of the hegemonic majority state church of Norway, I have had the privilege of witnessing the learning process in my own religious community.

This brings me to my final point: It does take an extended effort to work out, by any religious or life-stance community, properly and internally validated grounds for the principled and unwavering support of the full-fledged human right to freedom of religion or belief. But, so the argument of this chapter, it ought to be done if reversals and setbacks are to be avoided. The case of the Roman Catholic Church is extraordinary in this regard. Surely, they were latecomers to the field, but when the Roman Catholic Church finally arrived, most conspicuously and irreversibly with the work of Pope John XXIII and of Vatican II, its contribution to public justification on religious and common rationality grounds is outstanding.

Moreover, remembering past violations of the precepts of mutual respect and understanding between religions and life-stance communities, a religious community should not keep secret its internal grounding for endorsing the principles of freedom of religion or belief. It should rather invite, and probably has to expect, critical scrutiny from other religious and life-stance traditions of its internal doctrine in support of freedom of religion or belief, and of its internal interpretation of the scope, force, and limits of that right.

The case for interreligious solidarity in tandem with interreligious argument and rivalry can thus be stated simply: Once we talk serious across religious divides about the grounds of religious freedom, we cannot deny that we may disagree thoroughly, even and in particular about the foundations of our religious or life-stance commitments to protect, observe, and stand up for the religious liberty of all.

That disagreement is as it should be. Interreligious disagreement about the grounds of our commitment to freedom of religion or belief, as well as other interreligious disagreements which we may address and discuss across divides of religion and belief, is no longer a minefield, once we have all become thoroughly committed, in virtue of our rival internal grounds, to the public religious freedom principles of human rights.

---

[101] For interesting findings and arguments see Thomas Risse et al., eds., *The Power of Human Rights: International Norms and Domestic Change* (Cambridge: Cambridge Univ. Press, 1999). Also see the chapter by Elizabeth Sewell in this volume.

[102] See the chapter by Eidsvåg, Lindholm, and Sveen in this volume.

Part II

Freedom of Religion or Belief: International Norms and Institutions

Chapter 3

The Nature and Minimum Standards of Freedom of Religion or Belief

Natan Lerner

I. Introduction

This article provides an overview of the nature and scope of the minimum standards for freedom of religion or belief in the international community, as regulated by the principal international norms. Although the international community had already addressed racial discrimination, racial hatred, and other human rights issues, the United Nations did not address racial and *religious* discrimination and intolerance until the early sixties, following a series of anti-Semitic outbreaks. The United Nations separated the issues and promptly drafted a declaration and convention against racial discrimination. However, the United Nations did not draft a declaration regarding religion and belief until 1981. Moreover, it does not appear the United Nations will draft a convention regarding religion and belief any time soon, for reasons discussed hereafter.[1]

International organizations have adopted measures intended to guarantee freedom of religion or belief at the global and regional levels. These measures have also had some influence on domestic legislation. The measures address issues such as (1) the nature, scope, and other substantive aspects of freedom of religion or belief; inner- and outer-religious freedoms; the expression and manifestation of the freedom; permissible limitations and derogation of the freedom; and how the freedom clashes or interacts with other individual and collective rights, and (2) the procedural aspects available to protect individuals' fundamental rights of freedom of religion or belief,

---

[1] See part IV.C.4. Scholarly literature regarding human rights was criticized for similarly failing to sufficiently address religion, belief, and related issues. This deficiency has been remedied in recent years. Today, there are a fair number of books and articles available that address religion and beliefs and the minimum standards and norms that prevail in the area. See Malcolm D. Evans, *Religious Liberty and International Law in Europe* (Cambridge: Cambridge University Press, 1997); Natan Lerner, *Religion, Beliefs and International Human Rights* (Maryknoll, N.Y.: Orbis Books, 2000); Ted Stahnke and J. Paul Martin, eds., *Religion and Human Rights: Basic Documents* (New York: Columbia University, 1998); Johan D. van der Vyver and John Witte Jr., eds., *Religious Human Rights in Global Perspective: Legal Perspectives* (Boston: Martinus Nijhoff, 1996); Bahiyyih G. Tahzib, *Freedom of Religion or Belief: Ensuring Effective International Legal Protection* (Boston: Martinus Nijhoff, 1996).

Tore Lindholm, W. Cole Durham, Jr., Bahia G. Tahzib-Lie (eds.), Facilitating Freedom of Religion or Belief: A Deskbook, *63–83.*

including freedom *from* religion. Some countries have unilaterally addressed the second issue, while other countries have entered into special arrangements with other countries, churches, religious communities, and congregations.

This article attempts to briefly inventory these measures, which govern the sensitive issue of freedom of religion or belief. Where appropriate, this article also refers to other international instruments that indirectly impact freedom of religion or belief and to the interaction between freedom of religion or belief and other rights, including the freedoms of expression, association, and communication; gender rights; the rights of indigenous people and other special populations, such as migrant workers; educational rights; and children's rights. This article also alludes to problems concerning the relationship between the religious group and its individual members and the religious group (be it a religious congregation or community) and the state. Other articles in this volume address several of these issues in more depth.

II. The Need for the International Community to Address Freedom of Religion or Belief

With the beginning of a new millennium, the international community's continued efforts and interest in development, advancement, and technology present the ineluctable question of whether the international community is likewise ready to make additional advancements in the area of freedom of religion or belief by, perhaps, adopting a mandatory treaty based upon an existing draft or other instrument. Conversely, if the international community sees this next step as premature, undesirable, or risky, the question becomes whether it is possible to agree upon another way to place freedom of religion or belief on equal footing with other basic human rights.

None of the several suggestions and proposals to that effect adequately answer why this essential manifestation of human liberty has received less attention than other fundamental rights. Indeed, religion profoundly impacts the state of the world. Tragic events that demonstrate the powerful influence of ethnicity and religion, and in some cases require the intervention of massive international force, are but additional proof that religion plays a weighty role in xenophobia, racism, group hatred, and even territorial changes. Furthermore, religious persecution and conflicts between believers and nonbelievers; between different churches in multireligious societies; between dominating, protected, or preferred religions and religious minorities; and between newly established religions are all common phenomena. Some even argue that a shift from violence between sovereign states to conflicts between ethnic and religious groups is taking place.[2] In fact, the problem is so pervasive that the United States, the major political force in the world, considered it necessary to go through the complicated legislative process (legally and otherwise) to enact domestic legislation to protect endangered religious groups abroad.[3] These problems, and the United States' response, suggest the time is ripe for the international community to give equal attention to freedom of religion or belief.

---

[2] See Susanne Hober Rudolf and James Piscatori, eds., *Transnational Religion and Fading States* (Boulder: Westview Press, 1997), 3–4. See also Samuel Huntington, *The Clash of Civilizations and the Remaking of World Order* (New York: Simon and Schuster, 1996), which caused considerable controversy.

III. "Religion" Defined

The notion of "religion" is difficult to define in legal terms. To avoid philosophical and ideological controversy, international and human rights law have prescribed a catalog of rights and the means of protecting those rights, under the agreed heading of "freedom of thought, conscience, and religion," rather than defining the freedoms themselves. All of the basic instruments refer to these three freedoms. Moreover, most of the developed international norms protect the *manifestations* or *expressions* of the freedom of religion or belief.[4]

A major politically motivated confrontation between Western and Communist countries was avoided by inserting "belief" after "religion." The terms are intended to refer to both theistic views of the universe, as well as atheistic, agnostic, rationalistic, and other views excluding religion and religious norms.[5]

IV. The Development of Religious Rights

A. Early Protection of Religious Freedom

Historically, the protection of religious freedom preceded the protection of other rights.[6] It commenced with provisions in bilateral treaties modifying the traditional rule, *cuius regio eius religio*, a weak, limited, ad hoc system that only worked in favor of those religious minorities that a signatory state sought to protect, usually on the grounds of reciprocity.[7] Other states unilaterally extended diplomatic protection to persecuted religious minorities. Still other states adopted the principle of religious tolerance and promulgated some rules on religious freedom in their legislation.[8] The Augsburg

---

[3] See US Department of State, *Annual Report on International Religious Freedom* (1999); *International Religious Freedom Act of 1998*, Public Law No. 105–292, 112 Stat. 2787 (codified at 22 USC § 6401 [1998]).

[4] Problems exist with regard to new religious movements and sects, an issue that sparked emotional debates in many countries and led some to enact special provisions. The United Nations Rapporteur on Religious Freedom has dealt with this subject in his recent reports. See the reports submitted by Abdelfattah Amor to the Commission on Human Rights since his appointment in 1987, the last of which is, before this writing, UN Doc. E/CN.4/58 (1999). On June 22, 1999, the Council of Europe adopted the Parliamentary Assembly Recommendation 1412 (1999) on the illegal activities of sects. The Council considered it "undesirable" to enact major legislation on sects and reaffirmed its commitment to freedom of conscience and religion (ibid.).

[5] I have listed judicial attempts to define religion and references from legal dictionaries in my book, Lerner, *Religions, Beliefs and International Human Rights*, 3–4. See also Tahzib, *Freedom of Religion or Belief*, 1–3; van der Vyer and Witte, *Religious Human Rights in Global Perspective*.

[6] See John P. Humphrey, "Political and Related Rights," *Human Rights in International Law*, vol. 1, ed. Theodor Meron (Oxford: Clarendon Press, 1985), 171, 176; Karl Josef Partsch, "Freedom of Conscience and Expression, and Political Freedoms," *The International Bill of Rights*, ed. Louis Henkin (New York: Columbia University Press, 1981), 209; Paul Sieghart, *The International Law of Human Rights* (New York: Oxford University Press, 1983).

[7] At this stage (the sixteenth century) the abandonment of this traditional rule—that the sovereign's religion should be the religion of everyone under his jurisdiction—did not imply the establishment of a general freedom of religion.

[8] On these early developments, see Alessandra Luini del Russo, *International Protection of Human Rights* (Washington: Lerner Law Book Co., 1971). See also Evans, *Religious Liberty and International Law in*

(1555), Westphalia (1648), and Vienna (1815) treaties were important stages in this development, showing that the international community was relatively accepting of the principle of humanitarian intervention. Such intervention was on pragmatic grounds, however, without any philosophical or legal justification. This period culminated with the French and American Revolutions.[9]

B. Post–World War I Protection of Religious Freedom

The next relevant step toward the protection of religious freedom was the unsuccessful, but interesting, regime that developed after World War I based upon article 22 of the Covenant of the League of Nations, which guaranteed freedom of conscience and religion. Treaties' and states' unilateral statements on religious freedom sought to ensure the protection of national, ethnic, religious, cultural, and linguistic minorities.[10] This protection included individual and collective religious rights. This system failed, however, with the breakdown of the League of Nations, a consequence of the general political situation preceding World War II.

C. Post–World War II Protection of Religious Freedom

After the 1945 San Francisco Conference and the establishment of the United Nations, the international community, suspicious of the validity and genuineness of the assertion of collective and group (including religious group) rights, shifted its emphasis from protecting collective and group rights to affording protection to individual persons on the basis of individual rights and nondiscrimination. Persons whose rights were violated or jeopardized because of a group characteristic—be it race, color, religion, ethnic or national origin, culture, or language—would now be protected purely on an individual basis.[11] The issue of minority group rights, although not completely ignored, was not addressed in the early United Nations texts mainly because several member states were dealing with minority problems and the discredit of the interwar system.[12]

Europe, 42. On religious rights and minorities, see generally Lerner, "The Evolution of Minority Rights in International Law," *Peoples and Minorities in International Law,* ed. Catherine Brolmann et al. (Boston: Martinus Nijhoff, 1993), 77–101; Patrick Thornberry, *International Law and Rights of Minorities* (New York: Oxford University Press, 1991).

[9] On religious rights under national law, see Arcot Krishnaswami, *Study of Discrimination in the Matter of Religious Rights and Practices,* UN Doc. E/CN.4/Sub.2/200/rev. 1, UN Sales No. 60.XIV.2 (1960).

[10] The literature on the minority treaties is immense and cannot be listed here. Recent works include Francesco Capotorti, *Study on the Rights of Persons Belonging to Ethnic, Religious and Linguistic Minorities* (New York: United Nations, 1991), especially ch. 4; Felix Ermacora, "The Protection of Minorities Before the United Nations," in *Recueil des Cours* 182, no. 4 (1983): 247, 347; Lerner, *Group Rights and Discrimination in International Law,* 2d ed. (The Hague: Kluwer Law International, 2003); Thornberry, *International Law and Rights of Minorities*; Yoram Dinstein and Mala Tabory, eds., *The Protection of Minorities and Human Rights* (Boston: Martinus Nijhoff, 1992). On the interwar experience, see Jacob Robinson et al., *Were the Minorities Treaties a Failure?* (New York: Institute of Jewish Affairs, 1943).

[11] See Lerner, "The Evolution of Minority Rights"; Warwick McKean, *Equality and Discrimination Under International Law* (Oxford: Clarendon Press, 1983).

[12] See Lerner, "The Evolution of Minority Rights"; Thornberry, *International Law and Rights of Minorities;* Lerner, "Religious Human Rights under the United Nations," in van der Vyver and Witte, *Religious Human Rights,* 79, 85–86.

An important exception to the international community's failure to address group rights was the International Convention on the Prevention and Punishment of the Crime of Genocide ("Genocide Convention"), adopted on 9 December 1948, one day before the Universal Declaration of Human Rights.[13] Article II of the Genocide Convention specifically includes in the notion of genocide the intent to destroy, in whole or in part, a "religious group."[14] Although the victims of the crime will always be individuals, the target of the crime is the group, be it religious or otherwise. The Genocide Convention clearly addresses crimes such as those committed in the 1990s under the guise of "ethnic—meaning also religious—cleansing."[15]

1. Universal Declaration of Human Rights

Except for prohibiting the discrimination of persons on religious grounds, the United Nations Charter does not deal specifically with religious rights. The first United Nations instrument to address the subject was the 1948 Universal Declaration of Human Rights ("Universal Declaration").[16] The seminal article 18 greatly influenced the 1966 Covenant on Economic, Social, and Cultural Rights,[17] the 1966 Covenant on Civil and Political Rights,[18] the regional treaties, and the Declaration on the Elimination of All Forms of Intolerance and Discrimination Based on Religion or Belief ("1981 Declaration").[19] It reads:

> Everyone has the right to freedom of thought, conscience and religion; this right includes freedom to change his religion or belief, and freedom, either alone or in community with others and in public or private, to manifest his religion or belief in teaching, practice, worship and observance.[20]

Article 18 consists of three parts. First, it guarantees the right to freedom of thought, conscience, and religion, generally described as the *forum internum*.[21] This is a broad category, which includes the right to profess a religion or to profess none, i.e., to believe or not believe. The term "belief" twice follows the term "religion."[22] "Belief" should be interpreted strictly in connection with the word "religion." It does not refer

[13] For the text of the Genocide Convention, see Richard B. Lillich, ed., *International Human Rights Instruments,* 2d ed. (New York: W. S. Hein, 1990), 130.1. On the subject generally, see Nehemiah Robinson, *The Genocide Convention: A Commentary* (New York: Institute of Jewish Affairs, 1960).

[14] Lillich, *Human Rights Instruments,* 130.1. Article II refers to "national, ethnical, racial or religious groups, as such" (ibid.).

[15] On the international community's response to ethnic cleansing in the 1990s, see part IV.D.

[16] See Lillich, *Human Rights Instruments,* 440.1. On the Universal Declaration, see generally John P. Humphrey, "The Universal Declaration of Human Rights: Its History, Impact and Juridical Character," *Human Rights, Thirty Years After the Universal Declaration,* ed. B. G. Ramcharan (Boston: Martinus Nijhoff, 1979), 21; Nehemiah Robinson, *The Universal Declaration of Human Rights: Its Origin, Significance, Application, and Interpretation* (New York: Institute of Jewish Affairs, 1958); and Asbjørn Eide and Gudmundur Alfredsson, eds., *The Universal Declaration of Human Rights: A Commentary* (New York: Scandinavian University Press, 1992), particularly Martin Scheinin's article contained therein at 263.

[17] See Lillich, *Human Rights Instruments,* 180.1.

[18] See ibid., 170.1.

[19] See ibid., 490.1.

[20] Ibid., 490.2.

[21] See ibid., 440.4.

[22] See ibid.

to political, economic, scientific, or other beliefs. The term "belief" was incorporated into the Universal Declaration to protect the right to profess nonreligious or atheistic convictions.

It may be legitimate to consider the freedoms of conscience and religion as included in the freedom of thought. However, freedom of conscience was not universally considered a consolidated legal concept at the time of the drafting of article 18. This freedom is frequently discussed under the heading of "conscientious objection," not an exclusively religion-related issue. The reference to "freedom of conscience" was incorporated despite some opposition. The phrase refers to pacifism, obedience to superior orders, the power of the state to impose obligations in areas such as taxation, and other controversial problems regarding matters of principle for the individual.

Second, article 18 addresses conversion and religious proselyting,[23] issues that became more difficult when the 1966 Covenants and the 1981 Declaration were drafted.[24] By the time those documents were drafted, the right to teach and disseminate one's religion and to conduct proselyting activities became controversial matters. Those matters are beyond the scope of this article. They may sometimes involve a clash with rights such as privacy, interference with the integrity of some group identities—as when ethnicity and religion are closely related—and even illegal acts. Such illegal acts may include the abuse of conversion and proselyting rights, coercion of "captive audiences," and the use of improper enticements.

Third, article 18 addresses the external forum or, put another way, the manifestations of religious freedom.[25] Unlike freedom of thought and conscience, which can only be limited by complicated psychological techniques that influence the human mind, problems arise regarding manifestations of religious rights because those rights are more likely to be derogated. Given these problems, this aspect of religious freedom deserves special scrutiny.

2. The Krishnaswami Study

Arcot Krishnaswami's study,[26] submitted in 1959, was an important step in the United Nations' identification and protection of religious freedoms.[27] The study was based on information contained in eighty-two country monographs and established principles that the Sub-Commission later adopted, and which had considerable influence on future documents. The 1981 Declaration[28] and pending Draft Convention[29] incorporate many of its principles. The study did not define the term "religion" but did clarify that the term "beliefs" included attitudes concerning religion such as agnosticism, atheism, and rationalism, in addition to theistic creeds. However, these terms are not defined either.

---

[23] See ibid.

[24] For a discussion of the 1966 Covenants and the 1981 Declaration, see part IV.C.3–4.

[25] See Lillich, *Human Rights Instruments*, 440.4.

[26] Krishnaswami was appointed as Special Rapporteur by the Sub-Commission on Prevention of Discrimination and Protection of Minorities.

[27] See Krishnaswami, *Study of Discrimination in the Matter of Religious Rights and Practices.*

[28] For a discussion of the 1981 Declaration, see part IV.C.4.

[29] For a discussion of the Draft Convention, see part IV.C.4.

Krishnaswami analyzed the notions of freedom of thought, conscience, and religion as legal rights.[30] He referred to the prohibition of discrimination, dealt with the crucial issue of proselyting and conversion, and detailed the contents of the right to manifest religion, as well as permissible limitations on it.[31] He also dealt with the nature and rights of religious organizations; the relationship between those organizations and their members; and the scope of the concepts of teaching, practice, worship, and observance, embracing all possible manifestations of religion.[32] Krishnaswami stressed the collective aspects of religious rights: assembly, association, organization, and international ties and contacts.[33]

Krishnaswami's catalog of religious rights embraces worship, processions, pilgrimages, symbols, funeral practices, marriage and divorce, teaching, and appointment of personnel.[34] He also lists permissible limitations on religious rights and discusses oaths, objection to military service and other conscientious objections, compulsory medical treatment, and other particularly difficult issues.[35] Further, he discusses different approaches to the state-religion and state-religious community relationship.[36]

3. The 1966 Covenants

The United Nations took the next step in identifying and protecting religious rights when it promulgated the 1966 International Covenant on Economic, Social and Cultural Rights[37] and the 1966 International Covenant on Civil and Political Rights.[38] Eighteen years had elapsed since the adoption of the Universal Declaration. Despite the evolution of legal thought during that time, which influenced instruments such as the 1965 Convention on Racial Discrimination ("1965 Convention"),[39] the text of the 1966 Covenants reflects the Universal Declaration's general orientation and trends.[40] This can be attributed to the slow drafting process and the impact of weighty philosophical and political issues on the process, including conversion, proselyting, and the conflict between universal human rights and cultural relativism. Although several other internationally binding instruments, some of which were widely ratified, contain provisions related to religious rights,[41] the 1966 Covenant on Civil and Political Rights is

[30] See Krishnaswami, *Study of Discrimination in the Matter of Religious Rights and Practices,* 13–14.
[31] See ibid., 16–18.
[32] See ibid., 15, 18–19.
[33] See ibid., 18–19.
[34] See ibid., 26–36.
[35] See ibid., 36–39.
[36] See ibid., 39–46.
[37] See Lillich, *Human Rights Instruments,* 180.1.
[38] See ibid., 170.1. Some of the many works on the 1966 Covenants are: Philip Alston, "The Commission on Human Rights," *The United Nations and Human Rights,* ed. Philip Alston (New York: Oxford University Press, 1992), 126; Dominic McGoldrick, *The Human Rights Committee: Its Role in the Development of the International Covenant on Civil and Political Rights* (New York: Oxford University Press, 1991); Theodor Meron, ed., *Human Rights in International Law* (Oxford: Clarendon Press, 1991); and Manfred Nowak, *U.N. Covenant on Civil and Political Rights* (Arlington: N. P. Engel, 1993); Partsch, "Freedom of Conscience and Expression," 209.
[39] See Lillich, *Human Rights Instruments,* 160.1.
[40] See part IV.C.1.
[41] See Lerner, "Religious Human Rights Under the United Nations," 79.

presently the only binding treaty specifically containing a coherent articulation of such rights.[42] The Human Rights Committee, which implements the 1966 Covenant on Civil and Political Rights, also gave considerable attention to the subject, as evidenced by its issuance of a specific General Comment in 1993.[43] This comment is of great value in interpreting religious norms.

Articles 18, 19, 20, and 27 of the 1966 Covenant on Civil and Political Rights are relevant to religious rights.[44] Article 18 is seminal. The first paragraph generally tracks the language in article 18 of the Universal Declaration, with minor changes.[45] The Covenant's article 18 does not, however, explicitly refer to the right to change one's religion.[46] In an effort to compromise, it reads: "[T]he right to freedom of thought, conscience and religion [the inner forum] . . . shall include freedom to have or to adopt a religion or belief of his choice."[47] Most specialists interpret the Covenant's article 18 as fully recognizing the right to change religion, as proclaimed by the Universal Declaration.[48] But its failure to explicitly protect the right to change religion began a downward trend, which became more pronounced and very problematic during the preparation and adoption of the 1981 Declaration.

Article 18(2) prohibits "coercion" that would impair a person's freedom to have or to adopt a religion or belief.[49] The text does not define "coercion," but it should be read as meaning not only the use of force or threats but also more subtle forms of illegitimate influence, such as family considerations, public standing, and social relations. Use of such tactics is less than illegal, but so are some material enticements.

Article 18(3) deals with limitations[50] on the freedom to manifest one's religion or belief "as are prescribed by law and are necessary to protect public safety, order, health, or morals or the fundamental rights and freedoms of others."[51] Article 4 of the Covenant on Civil and Political Rights incorporates the whole of article 18 as an article that cannot be derogated even in times of public emergency.[52]

Significantly, article 18 does not mention national security as an appropriate justification for religious discrimination by a state. In a delicate area such as religious rights, limitations must be interpreted narrowly. Article 18 only permits limitations upon manifestations or the practice of religion, namely the external forum, if such limitations are prescribed by law.[53] The internal forum cannot be restricted or limited. This distinction is, of course, of the greatest importance. Judicial bodies in several countries have,

---

[42] See Lillich, *Human Rights Instruments,* 170.1.

[43] For its text, see Human Rights Committee General Comment 22 (1994), art. 18, UN Doc. HRI/GEN/1/Rev.1, 35.

[44] See Lillich, *Human Rights Instruments,* 170.7–170.8, 170.10.

[45] See ibid., 170.7.

[46] See ibid.

[47] Ibid.

[48] See Partsch, "Freedom of Conscience and Expression," 210–11; Martin Scheinin, "Article 18," in Eide and Alfredsson, *Universal Declaration of Human Rights,* 263; J. A. Walkate, "The Right of Everyone to Change His Religion or Belief," *Netherlands International Law Review* 30 (1983): 146, 153.

[49] Lillich, *Human Rights Instruments,* 170.8.

[50] On limitations in the 1966 Covenant on Civil and Political Rights, see Thomas Buergenthal, "To Respect and to Ensure: State Obligations and Permissible Derogations," in *The International Bill of Rights,* 72, 78–91, and Alexandre Charles Kiss, "Permissible Limitations on Rights," in *The International Bill of Rights,* 290, 295–310.

[51] Lillich, *Human Rights Instruments,* 170.8.

[52] See ibid., 170.2. Articles 29(2) and 29(3) of the *Universal Declaration on Human Rights* are also relevant.

[53] Lillich, *Human Rights Instruments,* 170.8.

out of necessity, intervened in religious practices such as the slaughtering of animals, the wearing of turbans, skullcaps, veils and head-coverings, the growing of beards, and work on specific days. Moreover, some religious groups' rites, customs, and rules of behavior clash with public order and morality norms of the general population in areas such as education, health, gender, and family law. This is a delicate issue, in which there may be frequent clashes between what a society may consider its minimum legal standard and minority religions' religious attitudes grounded in history and culture.[54]

The last paragraph of article 18 deals with parental rights in the field of education, a highly sensitive area.[55] The UNESCO Convention Against Discrimination in Education,[56] the 1981 Declaration,[57] the Convention on the Rights of the Child,[58] and other global and regional texts address this subject. International judicial or quasijudicial decisions on the topic have also been numerous.

Article 19 deals generally with freedom of expression.[59] Article 20(2) imposes upon states that are parties to the 1966 Covenant on Civil and Political Rights the duty to prohibit by law the advocacy of religious hatred that incites to discrimination, hostility, or violence.[60] Several states objected and entered reservations to article 20(2), seeing in it a limitation on freedom of expression.[61] Article 20(2) should be compared with article 4 of the 1965 Convention.[62] The Human Rights Committee, in its General Comment on article 20, stressed article 20(2)'s mandatory character and full compatibility with freedom of expression.[63]

Article 27 deals with minorities, including religious minorities.[64] Scholars are divided on the merits of article 27 and the scope of its protection.[65] Moreover, article 27 has, to some extent, been superseded by the 1992 United Nations Declaration on the Rights of Persons Belonging to National, Ethnic, Religious and Linguistic Minorities.[66] It can also be argued that the 1992 Declaration is a rather timid approach to the issue of minorities' rights.[67]

---

[54] For an examination of these issues, see Leon Sheleff, "Tribal Rites and Legal Rights," *Israel Yearbook on Human Rights* 18 (1988): 153; Aviam Soifer, "Freedom of Association: Indian Tribes, Workers, and Communal Ghosts," *Maryland Law Review* 48 (1989): 350; Donna J. Sullivan, "Gender Equality and Religious Freedom: Toward a Framework for Conflict Resolution," *NYU Journal of International Law and Politics* 24 (1992): 795.

[55] See Lillich, *Human Rights Instruments,* 170.8.

[56] See ibid., 330.1.

[57] See ibid., 490.1.

[58] See ibid., 423.1.

[59] See ibid., 170.8.

[60] See ibid.

[61] See Sieghart, *The International Law of Human Rights,* 450, for details of reservations and interpretations entered to article 20.

[62] See Lillich, *Human Rights Instruments,* 160.3–160.4.

[63] See Human Rights Committee General Comment 11 (1994), art. 20, UN Doc. HRI/GEN/1/Rev.1, 12.

[64] See Lillich, *Human Rights Instruments,* 170.10.

[65] The controversy primarily concerns whether article 27 protects only individuals or minority groups as well. Tomuschat takes the first view, while Ermacora, Dinstein, and Capotorti are in favor of a more group-oriented interpretation. See Lerner, *Group Rights and Discrimination in International Law,* 14, 15.

[66] See United Nations, *Human Rights: A Compilation of International Instruments,* vol. 1 (New York: United Nations Publications, 1994), 140.

[67] See Lerner, *Religion, Beliefs and International Human Rights,* 15.

The Human Rights Committee's General Comment No. 22(48) on article 18 stresses that the right to freedom of thought, conscience, and religion is "far-reaching and profound."[68] Article 18 protects theistic and atheistic beliefs, as well as the right not to profess any religion.[69] It is not limited to traditional religions.[70] It distinguishes between freedom of thought, conscience, religion, or belief—protected unconditionally—and the freedom to manifest religion or belief.[71] Paragraph 4 lists a broad range of acts encompassed in the freedom to manifest religion or belief, to be exercised individually or in community with others.[72] The freedom to "have or to adopt" a religion or belief includes the right to replace one's religion with another or to adopt atheistic views.[73] Coercion in this respect is barred.[74] Paragraph 6 regards religious education and parental rights.[75] Paragraph 7 reiterates the obligatory character of article 20 of the Covenant, which prohibits advocacy of religious hatred. Paragraph 8 permits limitations only if they are prescribed by law and are necessary to protect public safety, order, health or morals, or the fundamental rights of others.[76] Article 18(3), on limitations, should be strictly interpreted.[77] Paragraphs 9 and 10 address discrimination when there is a state religion or if a set of beliefs is treated as official ideology.[78] Conscientious objection is the subject of paragraph 11.[79]

The General Comment on article 18 should be viewed as an authoritative interpretation of the scope of article 18 by the body in charge of implementation of the Covenant on Civil and Political Rights. It is also relevant to the interpretation of the 1981 Declaration, to be discussed below.

4. The 1981 Declaration[80]

Proclaimed by the General Assembly of the United Nations on 25 November 1981, the 1981 Declaration is presently the most important global instrument regarding religious rights. Although not binding, the 1981 Declaration, like all solemn declarations of the United Nations General Assembly, implies an expectation of observance. It has its origin, together with the draft convention still pending ("Draft Convention"), in the anti-Semitic events of 1959 and 1960 ("swastika epidemics") that prompted the United Nations to start its unfinished legislative process regarding manifestations of racial and religious discrimination and intolerance.[81] The reasons for the

[68] See General Comment 22.
[69] Ibid.
[70] See ibid.
[71] See ibid.
[72] See ibid.
[73] Ibid.
[74] See ibid.
[75] See ibid.
[76] Ibid.
[77] Ibid.
[78] See ibid.
[79] See ibid.
[80] See Lillich, ***Human Rights Instruments,*** 490.1.
[81] General Assembly Resolution 1510 (XV) (1960), dated 12 December 1960. For the work of the Sub-Commission on Prevention of Discrimination and Protection of Minorities after the incidents, see UN Doc. No. E/CN.4/800, para. 163 (1960); and Resolutions 3 (XII) and 6 (XVI) on the Commission of Human

United Nations' delayed action regarding religious freedoms have been recounted repeatedly, and the reasons for the interruption of the drafting of a convention in the areas of religion or belief are well known.[82] International politics have undoubtedly played a major role. In light of this, the 1981 Declaration is clearly the United Nations' most ambitious achievement in this sphere to date, despite the fact that most of its provisions already exist in other binding instruments. The 1981 Declaration permits measures of implementation. Various Special Rapporteurs have already been appointed, and those Special Rapporteurs have produced an extremely valuable body of information. The system requires improvement, but its usefulness is obvious.

The 1981 Declaration took a clear stand with regard to the scope of the term "religion." The 1981 Declaration defines "religion" to include "beliefs," namely nontheistic convictions related to religion, such as atheism, rationalism, agnosticism, and other "beliefs," provided those convictions are related to religion.[83] Beliefs related to politics, social, or economic issues are not included. The controversy regarding issues of conversion and proselyting, present at all stages in the 1981 Declaration's preparation, threatened to prevent the General Assembly from adopting the Declaration. The controversy, however, was remedied by a compromise incorporated into article 8 of the 1981 Declaration, which preserves the applicability of the norms of the Universal Declaration and the 1966 Covenants.[84] This controversy nevertheless weakened the text of the 1981 Declaration. Two decades of protracted and difficult negotiations were required to reach a compromise. Even if one accepts the view of commentators who consider the differences in wording between the Universal Declaration and the 1981 Declaration to be insubstantial, one cannot ignore the argument that the differences may prevent the Declaration from being viewed as part of customary law applicable to some societies.

One of the deficiencies of the 1981 Declaration is the imprecise use of the terms "discrimination," clearly a legal concept, and "intolerance," a rather vague concept referring essentially to emotional, psychological, philosophical, and other attitudes likely to generate discrimination, hatred, or persecution.[85] In fact, the 1981 Declaration gives both words equivalent meaning.[86] Moreover, the 1981 Declaration, unlike the Draft Convention, does not incorporate provisions on incitement to intolerance or discrimination on religious grounds. The need and desire to compromise in drafting

---

Rights (1960). For an analysis of the 1981 Declaration, see Lerner, *Group Rights and Discrimination in International Law,* 84–108; Sullivan, "Advancing the Freedom of Religion or Belief through the UN Declaration on the Elimination of Religious Intolerance and Discrimination," *American Journal of International Law* 82 (1988): 487.

[82] See Lerner, *Group Rights and Discrimination in International Law,* 85. For the reasons why the United Nations treated religious issues differently than other human rights issues, see also Antonio Cassese, "The General Assembly: Historical Perspective 1945–1989," in *The United Nations and Human Rights,* 37.

[83] See Lerner, *Group Rights and Discrimination in International Law,* 89.

[84] See ibid.

[85] *Webster's New International Dictionary of the English Language* (1971) defines "intolerant" as "refusing to allow others the free enjoyment of their opinions or worship." Elizabeth Odio Benito in *Study of the Current Dimensions of the Problems of Intolerance and Discrimination Based on Religion or Belief,* UN Doc. E/CN.4/Sub.2/26 (1987), 3, states that manifestations of intolerance, often extending far beyond discrimination, include stirring up hatred against or even persecuting individuals or groups of a different religion or belief.

[86] See Lillich, *Human Rights Instruments,* 490.2.

the 1981 Declaration are reflected in the references to conversion, missionary activities and the right to teach and propagate a religion, and the right to leave a religion. They continue the descent already mentioned in the above discussion on the respective provisions in the 1966 Covenant on Civil and Political Rights. The prohibition of discrimination is vague and requires further elaboration. Not every preference based on religion or belief is discriminatory. For example, comparative legislation on religious rights sometimes prefers religions, treats religions differently, and draws distinctions between religions that respond to social and historic realities. In some cases, legislation may be discriminatory; in other cases, it may not. Common sense is the key, particularly since the 1981 Declaration prohibits discrimination, not only by the state, but also by institutions, groups, and persons.[87]

Despite these shortcomings, the 1981 Declaration text constitutes a far-reaching catalog of generally recognized human rights related to religion or belief. Where the 1981 Declaration is unclear, authoritative interpretations of the 1966 Covenant on Civil and Political Rights are helpful.[88] The 1981 Declaration follows the pattern of the Covenant in drawing the distinction between basic rights in the inner forum—thought, conscience, and religion—and the external manifestations of religion—worship, observance, practice, and teaching.[89] Only external manifestations, which are in some cases listed, may be limited if such limitations are prescribed by law and necessary to protect public safety, order, health or morals, or the fundamental rights of others.[90] The 1981 Declaration does not distinguish the rights of nationals and the rights of aliens.

The catalog of religious rights is listed in the comprehensive, but not exhaustive, text of article 6.[91] It includes the right to worship and assemble and to maintain places for this purpose; to establish institutions; to make, acquire, and use materials necessary to the religion; to produce relevant publications; to teach the religion in suitable places; to receive financial contributions; to train and appoint appropriate leaders; to observe days of rest and to celebrate holidays and ceremonies; and to communicate with individuals and communities on religious matters at the national and international levels.[92] Some of these same rights appear in articles 16 and 17 of the Conference on Security and Co-operation in Europe's ("CSCE") 1989 Concluding Document of the Vienna meeting.[93]

On the whole, the 1981 Declaration is a reasonably good text, which, more or less, reflects the international community's present understanding of the minimum standard for matters of religious rights. It is to be noted that the Special Rapporteurs appointed since 1986 have been performing the role usually assigned to formal mechanisms

---

[87] See ibid.

[88] See Partsch, "Freedom of Conscience and Expression"; General Comment 22.

[89] See Lillich, *Human Rights Instruments,* 490.3–490.4.

[90] See ibid., 490.2. On several occasions, the Human Rights Committee and the European Court on Human Rights dealt with the scope of permissible limitations. The European Court clarified the meaning of "morals" in Handyside v. UK, 1 EHRR 737 (ECtHR 24, 7 December 1976).

[91] See Lillich, *Human Rights Instruments,* 490.3–490.4.

[92] See ibid. However, rights considered but omitted include the rights to observe dietary practices, to make pilgrimages, and not to be coerced to take an oath of a religious nature.

[93] See Council of Europe, *Human Rights in International Law* (1995), 403 (emphasizing the rights of religious communities in Principle 16.4); see also W. Cole Durham, Jr., *Freedom of Religion or Belief: Laws*

incorporated into mandatory treaties.[94] There is certainly room for improvement, and some recommendations have been advanced to that effect. But this does not detract from the positive aspects of the document, which enlarges the scope of specific articles in the obligatory 1966 Covenants. So long as no progress is made on the Draft Convention, and there are no signs of such progress, the 1981 Declaration is a very positive step in the international effort to ensure human religious rights.

5. Other Global Provisions

International human rights should be viewed as a universal, all-embracing system of rights. The specific provisions on religion and belief must be considered in connection with other norms adopted by the international community and with regional instruments regulating religion or belief in some parts of the world. Religion is a wide-reaching spiritual, social, and political phenomenon. Many facets of life are covered by rules dealing with religion or belief.

For these reasons, after the adoption of the United Nations Charter and the early instruments directly concerned with issues involving religion or belief, such as the Genocide Convention and the Universal Declaration, many international law documents, although mainly directed toward the protection of other specific rights, also address religious rights. Among those international law documents, the following deserve mentioning:

- The Genocide Convention.[95]
- Humanitarian law, consolidated in the 1949 Geneva Conventions and 1977 Protocols.[96]
- The Declaration and Convention on the Elimination of All Forms of Racial Discrimination.[97] This is an appropriate guideline for state action in the field of religious prejudice, intolerance, and discrimination, which includes the difficult subject of prohibiting and incriminating group discrimination, incitement, and hatred in general.
- The 1979 Convention on the Elimination of All Forms of Discrimination Against Women.[98] It is impossible to ignore the clash between gender equality and religious practices difficult to eliminate from some traditions, particularly where the personal status law is part of the law of the state.[99]

Affecting the Structuring of Religious Communities (Warsaw: Organization on Security and Co-operation in Europe, 1999).

[94] Not being a treaty, the 1981 Declaration did not establish such a mechanism. The reports submitted by the Special Rapporteurs do not differ, however, from similar documents to be submitted under treaty obligations.

[95] See Lillich, *Human Rights Instruments,* 130.1. See part IV.C and part IV.E for discussions of the Genocide Convention.

[96] See Lillich, *Human Rights Instruments,* 70.1, 80.1, 90.1, 100.1, 200.1, 210.1.

[97] See ibid., 160.1.

[98] See ibid., 220.1. On the Convention generally, see Theodor Meron, *Human Rights Law-Making in the United Nations* (New York: Oxford University Press, 1986), 53.

[99] See Sullivan, "Gender Equality and Religious Freedom," 795. This article contains an extensive bibliography on women's rights. See also Kathleen E. Mahoney and Paul Mahoney, eds., *Human Rights in the Twenty-First Century* (Boston: Martinus Nijhoff, 1993), 71–117.

- The 1960 UNESCO Convention Against Discrimination in Education.[100] This contains norms on the establishment of separate educational systems for religious reasons and on parental rights.[101] These norms should be compared to those included in the Convention on the Rights of the Child[102] and have been the subject of frequent judicial or quasijudicial adjudication.[103]
- The 1958 International Labor Organization Convention (No. 111) Concerning Discrimination in Respect of Employment and Occupation.[104] The quasijudicial supervisory bodies of the International Labor Organization ("ILO") had to deal, on many occasions, with issues regarding religious rights of employees, frequently in connection with holy days and days of rest.[105] Another interesting ILO treaty in this context is the 1989 Convention (No. 169) Concerning Indigenous and Tribal Peoples in Independent Countries,[106] a partial revision of the 1957 Convention. The new instrument, strongly group-oriented, protects the identities (including religious) of indigenous populations with a view toward ensuring respect for the religious and spiritual values and practices of the interested populations as groups and as individuals.[107]
- The 1990 U.N. International Convention on the Protection of the Rights of Migrant Workers and Members of Their Families.[108] This convention contains provisions for the satisfaction of the cultural and religious needs of such migrants and contains an article inspired by article 18 of the 1966 Covenant on Civil and Political Rights.[109]
- The 1992 United Nations Declaration on the Rights of Persons Belonging to National or Ethnic, Religious and Linguistic Minorities.[110] This declaration implies some progress as compared to article 27 of the Covenant on Civil and Political Rights. Its relationship to religious rights is limited.

While many of the listed provisions are consistent with the minimum standard[111] for religious rights, contradictory rules (and in some cases even divergent principles) have developed in areas such as gender and minority rights. This, again, raises the issue of universality versus cultural relativism with respect to some major religions, new religions, and sects in particular.

---

[100] See Lillich, *Human Rights Instruments,* 330.1.
[101] See ibid., 330.2.
[102] See ibid., 423.3.
[103] See Case "Relating to Certain Aspects of the Laws on the Use of Languages in Education in Belgium" v. Belgium, App. Nos. 01474/62, 01677/62, 01691/62, 01769/63, 01994/63, 02126/64 (ECtHR 6, 23 July 1968); Kjeldsen, Busk Madsen and Pedersen v. Denmark, 1 EHRR 711 (1979–80) (ECtHR 23, 7 December 1976); Angelini v. Sweden, 10 EHRR 123 (EComHR, 1988).
[104] See Lillich, *Human Rights Instruments,* 320.1.
[105] For the work of the ILO and its struggle against discrimination, see generally N. Valticos, "The International Labor Organization," *The International Dimensions of Human Rights,* vol. 1, ed. Karel Vasak (Westport, Conn.: Greenwood Press, 1979), 363.
[106] See United Nations, *Human Rights* 1, 475. For an analysis of the 1989 Convention (No. 169) concerning Indigenous and Tribal Populations or Peoples, see Lerner, *Group Rights and Discrimination in International Law,* 111–124.
[107] See United Nations, *Human Rights,* 475.
[108] See ibid., 554.
[109] See ibid. For a critical analysis, see Ved P. Nanda, "The Protection of the Rights of Migrant Workers," *Asian and Pacific Migration Journal* 2 (1993): 161.

6. Regional Norms and Special Agreements[112]

A study of religious rights cannot ignore the following: the 1950 European Convention for the Protection of Human Rights and Fundamental Freedoms;[113] the 1969 American Convention on Human Rights;[114] the documents adopted by the Organization (formerly Conference) on Security and Co-operation in Europe;[115] and the African Charter on Human and Peoples' Rights.[116] These instruments should be compared to the global rules.

At the European level particularly, a comprehensive and important jurisprudence has developed as a consequence of the work of the European Court and former European Commission on Human Rights. These European bodies adjudicated issues such as the mandatory use of crash helmets, compulsory membership in health services, compulsory insurance, religious needs of prisoners, the status of religious congregations, the rights of the clergy, parental rights, conscientious objection, taxation, blasphemy, the status of minor and new religious groups, and the relationship between churches and their members.[117] This created an interesting body of jurisprudence and contributed to the interpretation of the basic rules concerning religious rights. The issue of new religions and sects has recently become very controversial in Europe, and a recent Council of Europe statement regarding this issue has drawn attention.[118] Principles 16 and 17 of the 1989 Concluding Document of the Vienna Meeting of the CSCE deserve special mention also because of their detailed coverage of religious rights.[119] These principles should be compared with those religious rights listed in the 1981 Declaration.

Although not precisely regional arrangements, some states have entered into bilateral agreements with churches and religious communities, providing a framework for the solution and clarification of different problems in this area. Spain, for instance,

---

[110] See United Nations, *Human Rights*, 140. For a comparison with other provisions on minorities, see Lerner, *Religion, Beliefs and International Human Rights*, 33–35; also Lerner, *Group Rights and Discrimination in International Law*, 18–25.

[111] See Abdullah Ahmed An-Naim, ed., *Human Rights in Cross-Cultural Perspectives: A Quest for Consensus* (Philadelphia: University of Philadelphia Press, 1992), 6; Fernando R. Teson, "International Human Rights and Cultural Relativism," in *Human Rights in the World Community*, 2d ed., ed. Richard Claude and Burns H. Weston (Philadelphia: University of Philadelphia Press, 1992), 42–51; Jack Donnelly, "Cultural Relativism and Universal Human Rights," *Human Rights Quarterly* 6 (1984): 400. *Human Rights Quarterly* 16, no. 2 (1994) carries several articles on the subject, see 235 in particular.

[112] An in-depth discussion of the protection of religious rights by regional instruments is beyond the scope of this article.

[113] See 213 UNTS 211 (1993). There is vast literature on the protection of human rights in Europe. For a recent comprehensive book, see Evans, *Religious Liberty and International Law in Europe*.

[114] See 9 ILM 673 (1970). On the American system generally, see Thomas Buergenthal et al., *Protecting Human Rights in the Americas* (Arlington: N. P. Engel, 1995); Scott Davidson, *The Inter-American Human Rights System* (Brookfield, Vt.: Dartmouth, 1997).

[115] For the Organization on Security and Co-operation in Europe ("OSCE") documents, see Council of Europe. For a discussion of the OSCE's work in general, see Arie Bloed, ed., *The Conference on Security and Co-operation in Europe* (Boston: Kluwer Academic, 1993). See also Durham, *Freedom of Religion or Belief*.

[116] For the African Charter on Human and Peoples' Rights, see 21 ILM 58 (1982). See also U. Oji Umozurike, *The African Charter on Human and People's Rights* (Boston: Martinus Nijhoff, 1997).

[117] See Evans, *Religious Liberty and International Law in Europe*.

[118] See "Official Press Release of the Council of Europe," *Official Gazette of the Council* (June 1999).

[119] See Council of Europe, *Human Rights in International Law*.

has entered into such agreements with different religious communities.[120] Also noteworthy is the 1993 agreement between the State of Israel and the Holy See preceding the establishment of diplomatic relations between them.[121] This agreement refers to the protection of Catholic interests in Israel and to the Catholic Church's condemnation of anti-Semitism.[122] The agreement has been described as the first agreement between the Holy See and a non-Christian state.[123]

D. Protection from Persecution

Although international law adequately addressed racial discrimination (though the issue of implementation is not always resolved satisfactorily), there remains a strongly felt need to protect religious groups from discrimination, persecution, and incitement.[124] International and domestic law must also address the defamation and libel of groups or of persons belonging to a group for their membership in the group, even though such defamation and libel are less dramatic than physical persecution.[125]

The developing trend is to make the prohibition of religious discrimination, like the prohibition of racial discrimination, a peremptory norm of international law or, in other words, *jus cogens*.[126] Hatred and intolerance, admittedly less precise terms, are mentioned in some provisions addressing incitement to hatred, intolerance, and other related evils. But it is still necessary to harmonize basic rights, such as freedom of speech or of association on the one hand, and, on the other hand, the right of collective entities and their members not to be subjected to libel, defamation, hostility, intolerance, or incitement to hatred. The highly relevant issue of whether punishment should be enhanced for crimes committed on religious or racial grounds must also be resolved.

The various instruments referenced above contain provisions to protect religious and other groups. The Genocide Convention, for example, protects religious groups' right to exist.[127] Similarly, article 19 of the 1966 Covenant on Civil and Political Rights

---

[120] See Alberto de la Hera and Rosa María Martízez de Codes, eds., *Spanish Legislation on Religious Affairs* (Madrid: Ministerio de Justicia, 1998).

[121] See "Holy See–Israel: Fundamental Agreement," 33 ILM 153 (1994).

[122] See ibid.

[123] See Silvio Ferrari, "Concordats were Born in the West," *La Porta D'Oriente* 12/13 (1998): 37–44; Lerner, "Protecting Religious Human Rights by Bilateral Arrangements," *La Porta D'Oriente* 12/13 (1998): 45–55.

[124] The controversial *International Religious Freedom Act of 1998*, Public Law No. 105–292, 112 Stat. 2787 (codified at 22 USC § 6401 [1998]), calls upon the President of the United States to take a range of diplomatic and other actions against any country that engages in or tolerates violations of religious freedom. See § 6441. See also the detailed list of violations of religious rights in many countries included in the reports of Special Rapporteur Abdelfattah Amor in note 4. See also Kevin Boyle and Juliet Sheen, eds., *Freedom of Religion and Belief: A World Report* (New York: Routledge, 1997), which covers persecution against various religious groups in different countries.

[125] On this controversial issue, see, for example, Raphael Cohen-Almagor, "Harm Principle, Offence Principle, and the Skokie Affair," *Political Studies* 41 (1993): 453; Kenneth Lasson, "Racial Defamation as Free Speech: Abusing the First Amendment," *Columbia Human Rights Law Review* 17 (1985): 11; and Natan Lerner, "Group Libel Revisited," *Israel Yearbook on Human Rights* 17 (1987): 184.

[126] See Ian Brownlie, *Principles of Public International Law*, 4th ed. (New York: Oxford University Press, 1990), 513 n. 29.

[127] See Lillich, *Human Rights Instruments*, 130.1.

authorizes limitations upon the freedom of expression to protect "the rights and reputations of others."[128] Article 20 prohibits the advocacy of national, racial, or religious hatred that constitutes incitement to discrimination, hostility, or violence.[129] The Human Rights Committee, in its General Comment on article 20, affirms that the prohibition is fully compatible with other freedoms.[130] Likewise, articles 10(2) and 11(2) of the European Convention on Human Rights restrict the freedom of expression, assembly, and association when necessary in a democratic society to "protect[] . . . the reputation . . . of others."[131] The American Convention on Human Rights refers to the right of "everyone" to have his honor and dignity respected, liability to protect the "reputations of others," and penalties for "advocat[ing] . . . national, racial, or religious hatred that constitute[s] incitement[] to lawless violence or to any other similar action against any person or group of persons on any grounds including those of race, color, religion, language, or national origin."[132] The 1981 Declaration calls upon states to take "all necessary measures . . . to . . . combat discrimination on the ground of religion or belief."[133] The 1978 UNESCO Declaration on Race and Racial Prejudice urges the mass media and all organized groups to refrain from presenting "a stereotyped, partial, unilateral or tendentious picture of individuals and of various human groups."[134] The 1990 Charter of Paris for a New Europe states the determination of its signatories "to combat all forms of racial and ethnic hatred, anti-Semitism, xenophobia, and discrimination against anyone, as well as persecution on religious and ideological grounds."[135]

The main provisions prohibiting incitement against groups, communities, and collective entities are contained in the United Nations Convention on the Elimination of All Forms of Racial Discrimination ("1965 Convention"), ratified by 158 states as of 2001.[136] Article 4 of the 1965 Convention contains provisions concerning incitement, hatred, and hostility against persons and groups.[137] It is a controversial article and was subject to criticism and formal reservations. Article 4 has, however, become an important guideline for states, and several have enacted domestic legislation in the spirit of its provisions.[138] Article 4 is undoubtedly relevant to religious rights. Its text was a compromise between, on the one hand, those who sought primarily to penalize

[128] Ibid., 170.8

[129] See ibid.

[130] Human Rights Committee General Comment 11.

[131] *European Convention for the Protection of Human Rights and Fundamental Freedom,* 3 September 1953, 213 UNTS 222, art. 10(2).

[132] *American Convention on Human Rights,* 18 July 1978, 9 ILM 673.

[133] See Lillich, *Human Rights Instruments,* 490.3.

[134] See United Nations, *Human Rights,* 132.

[135] See United Nations, *Human Rights: A Compilation of International Instruments,* vol. 2 (New York: United Nations Publications, 1994), 406.

[136] See Lillich, *Human Rights Instruments,* 160.1; see also Lerner, *The U.N. Convention on the Elimination of All Forms of Racial Discrimination* (Alphen aan den Rijn: Sijthoff & Noordhoff, 1980); G. Tenekides, "L'Action des Nationes Unies Contre la Discrimination Raciale," *Recueil des Cours III* (n.p., 1980), 269. See also the Reports of the Committee on the Elimination of Racial Discrimination ("CERD"), the most recent of which (at the time of publication of this article) is indexed as UN Doc. A/54/18 (1999).

[137] See Lillich, *Human Rights Instruments,* 160.3–160.4.

[138] See Jose D. Ingles, "Study on the Implementation of Article 4 of the Convention on the Elimination of All Forms of Racial Discrimination," UN Sales No. E.85.XIV.2 (1986).

not only "incitement to discrimination" but also the "dissemination of ideas based on racial superiority or hatred," and, on the other hand, those who considered such penalties a threat to the basic freedoms of speech and association.[139] As is frequently the case with such compromise, the text adopted is not entirely satisfactory and contains shortcomings.

Nevertheless, the obligations that article 4 imposes are considered mandatory. State parties are bound to enact implementation legislation in accordance with it, even if they allege that racial discrimination or racist organizations do not exist in their jurisdiction.[140] However, in order to avoid interpretations that states might consider incompatible with their constitutional systems, the opening paragraph of article 4 contains a sentence clarifying that measures to be adopted shall be "with due regard to the principles embodied in the Universal Declaration of Human Rights."[141] Nevertheless, where rights clash, the orientation of article 4 is that freedom of speech or association cannot be invoked to prevent a state from taking legal measures, including penal action, against violations of the 1965 Convention.

Article 4 is presently one of the most ambitious provisions in international law intended to fight not only racial discrimination but all related evils, such as racial hatred, racial propaganda, and associations with a racist purpose.[142] Even though there are few references to religion in the text of the 1965 Convention (because of the decision to separate the instruments on race from those on religion), it seems beyond any doubt that article 4 acts as a guideline to interpret the provisions of the 1981 Declaration.

E. International Criminal Law

Postwar international law had to respond to the lessons of the most costly conflict in history, in terms of human lives. Those constructing an international order to preserve peace and prevent horrendous crimes, like those committed before and during World War II, were conscious of the need to avoid the recurrence of criminal policies directed against specific groups, religious or otherwise. One of the first human rights treaties adopted by the United Nations was the Genocide Convention,[143] discussed above. The Nuremberg trials influenced the Genocide Convention. As stated by the International Court of Justice, it "was manifestly adopted for a purely humanitarian and civilizing purpose" with the intention "to condemn and punish genocide as a crime under international law involving a denial of the right of existence of entire human groups, a denial which shocks the conscience of mankind and results in great losses to humanity."[144]

Today, the prohibition of genocide is part of *jus cogens*. The Genocide Convention does not contain measures of implementation. Moreover, it has exercised little influence in preventing clear-cut genocidal situations affecting religious and other groups in various parts of the world over the past few decades. The Genocide Convention needs updating, but, on the whole, it is one of the basic instruments protecting ethnic and religious groups and addressing those groups' fundamental right to preserve their existence.

---

[139] Lerner, *Religion, Beliefs and International Human Rights*, 53.

[140] See Lillich, *Human Rights Instruments*, 160.3–160.4.

[141] Ibid.

[142] See ibid.

[143] See ibid., 130.1.

[144] "Reservations to the Convention on Genocide Case," *ICJ Reports* (1970): 23.

In the 1990s, the international community had to confront the tragic events in former Yugoslavia known as "ethnic cleansing." A large body of documents, literature, and decisions dealing with the events in this context, including those of the International Court of Justice, already exists.[145] It should be emphasized that the issue is wider than pure "ethnicity" in its strictest sense. United Nations Rapporteurs pointed out the severe damage suffered by religious and cultural monuments and sites of the different religions. "Such wanton destruction," wrote Angelo Vidal d'Almeida Ribeiro, "appears to be part of the policy of certain groups aimed at eradicating the religious and cultural base of ethnic communities living in a given area in order to encourage their departure and prevent their eventual return."[146]

As a result of these events, the Security Council established an international tribunal under Security Resolution 808 on 22 February 1993 "for the prosecution of persons responsible for serious violations of international humanitarian law committed in the territory of the former Yugoslavia since 1991."[147] The Security Council, invoking Chapter 7 of the Charter, established the international tribunal because of the threat to peace, the need for expedience, and the need to create an effective and binding obligation to take action as required.[148] The Security Council also adopted the international tribunal's statute. The Security Council followed the same procedure in establishing an international tribunal for similar crimes committed in Rwanda.[149]

Both international tribunals are *ad hoc* institutions. They are the first international courts dealing with war crimes and crimes against humanity since the Nuremberg and Tokyo trials. In 1998, an international conference convened by the United Nations in Rome decided by a large majority to create a permanent international criminal court to deal with war crimes and crimes against humanity.[150] Such crimes are frequently committed for religious or ethno-religious reasons.

V. Conclusion

This article has attempted to summarize the steps taken in international law to guarantee freedom of religion or belief. There is no generally agreed-upon definition of "religion," mainly because of the desire to avoid ideological confrontations. There is, however, agreement that in modern human rights law the word "religion," usually followed by the word "belief" refers to theistic convictions involving a transcendental

---

[145] The United Nations General Assembly and Security Council, as well as other United Nations organs and treaty bodies, adopted numerous resolutions on ethnic cleansing. See, e.g., Natan Lerner, "Ethnic Cleansing," *Israel Yearbook on Human Rights* 24 (1994): 103; Theodor Meron, "The Case for War Crimes Trials in Yugoslavia," *Foreign Affairs* 72 (1993): 122; James C. O'Brien, "The International Tribunal for Violation of International Humanitarian Law in the Former Yugoslavia," *American Journal of International Law* 87 (1993): 639.

[146] UN Doc. E/CN.4/1993/62, at 119. A spokesman for the UN High Commissioner for Refugees accused Serbians of "erasing all traces of a Muslim religious and cultural presence." Chuck Sudetic, "U.N. Says 'Ethnic Cleansing' by Serbs Intensifies," *New York Times*, 30 January 1994, A13.

[147] See 32 ILM 1159–1205 (1993), containing the Secretary General's Report and Security Council resolutions.

[148] See ibid.

[149] United Nations, *Security Council Resolution 955*, 33 ILM 1598 (1994).

[150] See UN Doc. A/CONF. 183/9 (as corrected by the *procès-verbaux* of 10 November 1998 and 12 July 1999).

view of the universe and a normative code of behavior as well as atheistic, agnostic, rationalistic, and other views in which such elements are absent. "Beliefs," in this context, always relate to religion and exclude beliefs of a different character in the political or social fields.

The international community has not adopted a specific mandatory treaty regarding religion. There is a draft that was under negotiation for several years, but it is doubtful that work on the draft will resume in the near future. The discussion about its need has been inconclusive. Different alternatives to the treaty have been submitted, anticipating that such a treaty may encounter objections from states and major religious communities. On the one hand, some fear that pushing for a convention may result in a low common denominator and a limited number of ratifications. On the other hand, some argue that there is obvious value in a treaty that goes beyond the articles on religious rights in the 1966 Covenant on Political and Civil Rights and incorporates most of the principles of the 1981 Declaration. The idea of the 1965 Convention as a model is stimulating, although the situations and factors influencing both areas are undoubtedly quite different.

Article 18 of the Universal Declaration and article 18 of the 1966 Covenant on Political and Civil Rights are the basic provisions in the global instruments addressing religious freedom. The 1981 Declaration, although not obligatory, contains widely accepted international standards. Some of those provisions are customary international law, and a few should be seen as *jus cogens*, namely a rule which cannot be altered except by the will of the international community as a whole.

There is also a monitoring system. The General Comments of the Human Rights Committee, the reports and studies submitted by U.N. Special Rapporteurs, the development of a reporting system, the judicial and quasijudicial decisions addressing some very significant issues in the area of religion, the special arrangements between some states and religious communities or religiously originated or oriented communities together provide a reasonable degree of protection and provide guarantees in the tense, delicate, and explosive area of basic religious rights.

Pending problems are numerous. They include the issue of conversion and proselyting, opting out of religious communities, conscientious objection (not necessarily a religious issue), and the clash between rights in the field of religion or belief and those in other spheres. Evidence of the tension, delicacy, and explosiveness of these issues abounds. It can be seen in the struggle of the universal acceptance and understanding of human rights and what is loosely called cultural particularism or relativism against the dangers of wars, genocide, and persecution stemming from religious sentiments or hatred, of which the horrible practices of "ethnic cleansing" have been a very recent and tragic example. Some steps in the field of international criminal law directly relate to these excesses in matters of religious rights. Indeed, the most powerful state in today's world has felt the need to enact unilateral protective measures against religious persecution abroad.

The renewed interest in the field of religious rights is a positive development that requires an adequate, practical legislative response. It presents a fascinating challenge for lawyers, political scientists, and theologians. The international community must strive to reach a consensus to incorporate rights related to religion into the widely developed system of international human rights. Such consensus was attained in other delicate areas affecting the sensibilities of large groups. The new millennium is a propitious moment to review this issue and renew work on it. No group is expected to renounce its principles and basic ideology. However, because they are so important, religion or belief deserve an intelligent, careful, and balanced accommodation in fundamental legal norms that provide a minimum standard acceptable to a large majority of mankind. The instruments discussed in this article contain many ingredients of such a standard.

Chapter 4

The Relationship of Freedom of Religion or Belief Norms to Other Human Rights

Johan D. van der Vyver

In 1996, the South African Parliament adopted legislation prohibiting corporal punishment "at a school to a learner."[1] The legislation followed an earlier decision of the Constitutional Court,[2] and the jurisprudence of several neighboring countries,[3] that flogging constitutes a cruel and inhuman punishment.

The constitutionality of the South African statute was challenged, on religious freedom grounds, by an association originally established in the United States "to promote evangelical Christian education" and which controlled 196 independent Christian schools in South Africa with an enrollment of 14,500 pupils. These schools sought to maintain an active Christian ethos, of which corporal punishment allegedly constitutes an integral part. The constitutional challenge was based on a supposition that the legislative prohibition of corporal punishment in the applicant's schools violated the individual, parental, and community rights of those associated with the applicant to freely practice their religion.

In support of that position, the applicant cited several Bible texts pertinent to the need for "corporal correction":

> Proverbs 22:6: "Train up a child in the way it should go and when he is old he will not depart from it."
>
> Proverbs 22:15: "Foolishness is bound in the heart of a child, but the rod of correction shall drive it far from him."

---

[1] *South African Schools Act,* Act 84, sec. 10 (1996).

[2] State v. Williams, 3 *South African Law Reports* (hereinafter SALR) 632 (South African Constitutional Court (hereinafter "SA Const Ct"), 1995); 7 *Butterworths Constitutional Law Reports* (hereinafter BCLR) 861 (1995).

[3] See Ex Parte Attorney-General, Namibia: In re Corporal Punishment by Organs of State, 3 SALR 76 (1991) (NmSC) in regard to Namibia; State v. F, 1 SALR 460 (1989) (Z) and State v. A Juvenile, 4 SALR 151 (1990) (ZS) in regard to Zimbabwe. Following the judgment in the latter case, the Constitution of Zimbabwe was amended to exclude the competence of a court of law to find that corporal punishment

Tore Lindholm, W. Cole Durham, Jr., Bahia G. Tahzib-Lie (eds.), Facilitating Freedom of Religion or Belief: A Deskbook, *85–123.*

> Proverbs 19:18: "Chasten thy son while there is hope and let not thy soul spare for his crying."
>
> Proverbs 23:13–14: "Do not withhold discipline from a child, if you punish with a rod he will not die. Punish him with a rod and save his soul from death."

The applicant based the divinely imposed responsibility of parents for the training and upbringing of their children on Deuteronomy 6:4–7:

> Hear, O Israel! The Lord is our God, the Lord is one!
>
> And thou shall love the Lord your God with all your heart and with all your soul and with all your might.
>
> And these words which I am commanding you today, shall be on your heart; and you shall teach them diligently to your sons and shall talk of them when you sit in your house and when you walk by the way and when you lie down and when you rise up.

The constitutionality of the contested legislation was upheld in the High Court[4] and by the Constitutional Court.[5] The Court in both instances accepted the religious sincerity of the applicant and assumed that the need for corporal correction constituted part of the religious belief it professed. However, the Biblical texts cited in support of its submissions confined the duty to chastise a child to the parents and did not provide support for the parent to delegate that responsibility to third parties, including teachers.

The significance of the judgment for purposes of the present survey is reflected in an observation of Justice Albie Sachs (in whose judgment all the other nine judges sitting in the matter concurred) noting that "a multiplicity of intersecting constitutional values and interests are involved in the present matter—some overlapping, some competing,"[6] including the right of the child to human dignity,[7] to freedom and security of the person,[8] and to be protected from maltreatment, neglect, abuse, or degradation.[9] In terms of the South African Constitution, "[a] child's best interests are of paramount importance in every matter concerning the child."[10]

In almost all situations involving freedom of religion or belief similar intersecting values and concerns will inevitably arise. The interaction between freedom of religion or belief and other basic human rights touched upon in the South African case is a recurring theme: on the one hand is the need to afford meaningful protection to freedom of religion or belief by also protecting rights and freedoms that complement the free exercise of religion or belief, and on the other is a certain tension between

---

constituted a violation of the constitutional provision prohibiting inhuman and degrading punishments. See Zimbabwe Const, Amend. 11, Act, 1990, sec. 5(3).

[4] Christian Ed. S. Afr. v. Minister of Ed., 4 SALR 1092 (SE), 9 BCLR 951 (1999).

[5] Christian Ed. S. Afr. v. Minister of Ed., 4 SALR 757 (SA Const Ct), 10 BCLR 1051 (2000).

[6] Ibid., at para. 15.

[7] Republic of South Africa Const, Act 108 of 1996, sec. 10 (hereinafter "SA Const").

[8] Ibid., sec. 12.

[9] Ibid., sec. 28(1)(d).

[10] Ibid., sec. 28(2).

basic rights and freedoms perceived by proponents of a particular religion or belief as violating the norms upon which their convictions are founded. Freedom of religion or belief cannot prosper on its own: it requires protection of collateral rights such as freedom of expression and of assembly. Many religions, conversely, as a matter of religious principle, advocate male dominance in the family and in ecclesiastical structures, or condemn homosexuality, and consequently find nondiscrimination decrees based on gender equality offensive to the tenets to which they subscribe.

This chapter will touch upon some of those overlapping and competing rights, and also seek to explore the prevailing models for reconciling or affording preference to the rights and freedoms that support or might come into conflict with freedom of religion or belief.

I. International Standard of Freedom of Religion or Belief

The standard-setting norm on freedom of religion or belief is to be found in Article 18 of the Universal Declaration of Human Rights, 1948,[11] which provides:

> Everyone has the right to freedom of thought, conscience and religion; this right includes freedom to change his religion or belief, and freedom, either alone or in community with others and in public or private, to manifest his religion or belief in teaching, practice, worship and observance.

The freedom to change one's religion or belief, combined with freedom to manifest a religion or belief in teaching and in practice, clearly sanction an entitlement to spread one's faith by persuading others, through word or deed, to subscribe to the principles of one's own belief and to associate themselves with the institutional structures of one's religion. This entitlement finds corroborative support in the right to freedom of opinion and expression, which includes "freedom to . . . seek, receive and impart information and ideas through any media and regardless of frontiers,"[12] and freedom of association, which is negatively defined in the Declaration as the right not to be compelled to belong to an association.[13]

The freedom to change one's religion or belief was transcribed in the International Covenant on Civil and Political Rights, 1966,[14] to "freedom to have or adopt a religion or belief of his own choice,"[15] and a limitations provision was added to subject (only) freedom to manifest one's religion or belief to "such limitations as are prescribed by law and are necessary to protect public safety, order, health, or morals or the fundamental rights and freedoms of others."[16] The Covenant further expressly guarantees that: "No one shall be subject to coercion which would impair his freedom to have or to adopt a religion or belief of his own choice."[17]

---

[11] UN General Assembly, *Universal Declaration of Human Rights*, UNGA Res. 217 A (III), 71, UN Doc. A/810, 3d Sess., Pt. 1 (1948) (hereinafter "UDHR").
[12] Ibid., art. 19.
[13] Ibid., art. 20(2).
[14] *1966 International Covenant on Civil and Political Rights*, 999 UNTS 171, reprinted in 6 ILM 368 (1967) (hereinafter "ICCPR").
[15] Ibid., art. 18(1).
[16] Ibid., art. 18(3).
[17] Ibid., art. 18(2).

These, then, are the international norms asserting the right of everyone to practice and to spread their religion or belief. The International Covenant on Civil and Political Rights admittedly only binds states parties to the Covenant, and it could perhaps be argued that the Universal Declaration is in itself a nonbinding instrument. However, there are compelling reasons for holding that the Universal Declaration affords substance to the concept of "human rights and fundamental freedoms" within the meaning of the Charter of the United Nations Organization;[18] and in terms of Articles 55 and 56 of the Charter, member states of the Organization have pledged themselves to take joint and separate action, in cooperation with the Organization, to promote universal respect for and observance of those rights and freedoms without distinction as to race, sex, language, or religion. The equality component of Articles 55 and 56 makes it abundantly clear that discrimination based on religion is emphatically prohibited in international law.

The Free Exercise Clause in the 1981 Declaration on the Elimination of All Forms of Intolerance and of Discrimination based on Religion or Belief,[19] mimicked the wording of the International Covenant on Civil and Political Rights—with one important exception: it omitted mention of the right to adopt a religion or belief of one's choice. This omission was insisted upon by Islamic countries, since explicit sanctioning of a "freedom . . . to adopt a religion or belief" of one's own choice was perceived to be incompatible with Muslim teaching.[20] There is, of course, much to be said for the view that provision in the 1981 Declaration for "freedom to have a religion or whatever belief of his own choice" and for "freedom . . . to manifest his religion or belief in . . . practice and teaching," combined with the proscription of "coercion which would impair his freedom to have a religion or belief of his choice," adequately endorse a right to trade in one's religion or belief for another;[21] and the Declaration in any event subordinated all of its provisions to the superior authority of the Universal Declaration of Human Rights and the International Covenants on Human Rights.[22]

In the Canadian case of *R. v. Big M. Drug Mart (Ltd.),* Dickson C.J.C. encapsulated as follows the gist of religious freedom:

> The essence of the concept of freedom of religion is the right to entertain such religious beliefs as a person chooses, the right to declare religious beliefs openly and without fear of hindrance or reprisal, and the right to manifest religious belief by worship and practice or by teaching and dissemination.[23]

---

[18] United Nations Charter, 1976 YBUN 1043; 59 Stat. 1031; UNTS 994, reprinted in 3 Bevans 1153 (hereinafter "UN Charter").

[19] UN General Assembly, *1981 Declaration on the Elimination of All Forms of Intolerance and of Discrimination Based on Religion or Belief,* UN Doc. A/36/683, UNGA 36th Sess., Supp. 51, art. 1, Res. 55 (XXXVI), 171 (1981); reprinted in 21 ILM 205 (1982) (hereinafter "1981 Declaration").

[20] Bahiyyih G. Tahzib, *Freedom of Religion or Belief: Ensuring Effective International Legal Protection* (Boston: Martinus Nijhoff, 1996), 167.

[21] E. Odio Benito, *Study of the Current Dimensions of the Problems of Intolerance and of Discrimination on Grounds of Religion or Belief,* UN Doc. E/CN.4/Sub.2/1987/26, para. 21 (1986).

[22] Article 8 of the Declaration provides: "Nothing in the present Declaration shall be construed as restricting or derogating from any rights defined in the Universal Declaration of Human Rights and the International Covenants on Human Rights."

[23] R. v. Big M. Drug Mart (Ltd.), 13 CRR 64 (1985), 95; see also State v. Lawrence; State v. Negal; State v. Solberg, 4 SALR 1176 (1997), 10 BCLR 1348 (1997) (SA Const Ct), para. 92; Christian Ed. S. Afr. v. Minister of Ed., 4 SALR 757 (SA Const Ct), 10 BCLR 1051, para. 18 (2000).

Controversies centered in particular upon the right to spread and to convert others to one's faith[24] remain a stumbling block in efforts to establish universal respect for, and adherence to, the vital components of religious freedom as contemplated by founders of the United Nations.

Within the United Nations, the struggle for supremacy of different human rights perceptions has come to be marginally addressed in the debate as to the universality of human rights. The principle proclaiming the universality of human rights is founded on the notion that all human rights apply uniformly and with equal force throughout the world. It thus opposes the doctrine of the so-called relativity of human rights, which maintains that in the application of human rights in concrete situations allowance should be made for particularities that attend cultural, ethnic, or religious varieties.[25] The principle of universality thus opposes the assumption that distinct cultural traditions or religious tenets provide justification to deny to individual members of a group certain basic human rights. It censures "adaptations" of human rights to suit nonlibertarian or nonegalitarian practices founded on customs within indigenous, ethnic, or religious communities.

Although the United Nations, in the practical application of human rights principles, is evidently sensitive to ethnic, cultural, and religious peculiarities, it does so only within the perimeters of basic human rights values. The Final Act of the United Nations World Conference on Human Rights that was held in Vienna, Austria, in June 1993 thus proclaims:

> All human rights are universal, indivisible and interdependent and interrelated. The international community must treat human rights globally in a fair and equal manner, on the same footing, and with the same emphasis. While the significance of national and regional peculiarities and various historical, cultural and religious backgrounds must be borne in mind, it is the duty of States, regardless of their political, economic and cultural systems, to promote and protect all human rights.[26]

It is important to note that international instruments for the promotion and protection of human rights only apply to states and therefore address the responsibilities of governmental institutions. Internal disputes within a religious community and intra-denominational rivalries therefore do not come within the reach of international law pre- and proscriptions pertaining to freedom of religion or belief. Within the confines of the particular generation of rights to which freedom of religion or belief belongs, the nature of internationally imposed state responsibilities is also quite restricted: the repositories of political power are in general required (negatively) ***to refrain from*** interfering in the enclave of religion or belief, ***to permit*** or ***to endure,*** and ***to afford protection*** for, the

[24] Natan Lerner identified "matters of conversion" and "opting-out from some religions or recognized religious communities" as belonging to "particularly complicated problems that continue to arouse controversy" in the context of religious freedom (Natan Lerner, "Religious Human Rights under the United Nations," *Religious Human Rights in Global Perspective: Legal Perspectives,* ed. Johan D. van der Vyver and John Witte Jr. (The Hague: Martinus Nijhoff, 1996), 133).

[25] Ann Elizabeth Mayer defined the general approach of cultural relativists as follows: "[I]n general they are inclined to condemn the notion that there are universal standards by which all cultures may be judged and to deny the legitimacy of using values taken from Western culture to judge institutions of non-Western cultures. They also tend to oppose the idea that human rights norms are universal" (Ann Elizabeth Mayer, *Islam and Human Rights* (London: Pinter Publishers, 1995), 8).

[26] *Vienna Declaration and Program of Action,* Pt. I, para. 5 at 20, A/Conf.157/24 (25 June 1993).

free exercise of religion or belief in all its manifestations. The (positive) duty of states *to provide* services, facilities or material support is as a general rule confined to the second generation of economic and social rights and solidarity rights of the third-generation kind.

The interdependent and interrelated disposition of all human rights, from the perspective of freedom of religion or belief, now calls for closer scrutiny.

II. The Right to Existence and Sovereignty of Religious Institutions

In 1925, legislation was adopted in New York for the purpose of acquiring a cathedral for the Russian Orthodox Church in North America as a place of worship "in accordance with the doctrine, discipline and worship of the Holy Apostolic Catholic Church of Eastern Confession as taught by the holy scriptures, holy tradition, seven œcumenical councils and holy fathers of the Church."[27] In consequence of strong anti-Soviet sentiments that prevailed in the United States at the time, Article 5(C) was added to the Religious Corporation Law of New York in 1945[28] (with clarifying amendments being added in 1948) with a view to transferring the control of the New York churches of the Russian Orthodox religion from the central Patriarchate in Moscow to the governing authorities of the church in America. The archbishop of New York was subsequently elected in that capacity by a Sobor of American churches to serve as head of the Metropolitan of All America and Canada. A dispute erupted as to his competence, in virtue of Article 5(C), to occupy the church property in New York. The matter was decided in favor of the Moscow Patriarchate in *Kedroff v. St. Nicholas Cathedral*, the Court holding that Article 5(C) violated the constitutional right to "the free exercise of an ecclesiastical right, the Church's choice of its hierarchy."[29] Justice Reed, speaking for the majority, referred to "a spirit of freedom for religious organizations" embracing "power to decide for themselves free from state interference, matters of church government as well as those of faith and doctrine," which freedom includes the right to select the clergy of the church.[30]

Kedroff is quite unique in American jurisprudence in that it recognized an organized religious institution, the Orthodox Church, as the repository of a constitutional right, freedom of religion. American courts had always proceeded on the assumption that the freedoms guaranteed by the Bill of Rights vest in individuals (natural persons) only. *Kedroff* deviates, or at least came close to deviating, from that assumption. *Kedroff* also calls attention to the concept of group rights. A distinction should be made in this regard between collective group rights and institutional group rights.[31]

A *collective group right* is afforded to individual persons belonging to a certain category, such as children, women, or ethnic, religious and cultural minorities.[32] The right of a religious community to peaceful assembly, freedom of association, freedom

---

[27] *New York General Code,* 1925, c. 463.

[28] New York, "'Religious Corporation' Law," 302 NY 24, 96 NE 2d 68.

[29] Kedroff v. St. Nicholas Cathedral, 344 US 94, 119 (1952).

[30] Ibid., 116.

[31] See Van der Vyver, "Constitutional Options for Post-Apartheid South Africa," *Emory Law Journal* 40 (1991): 825–28.

of expression, and freedom of thought, conscience and religion[33] thus belongs to every member of the group and can be exercised separately, or jointly with any other member(s) of the group. Collective group rights of religious communities have indeed been recognized in the United States on several occasions, for example to substantiate the payment of unemployment benefits to Sabbatarians who refused to work on their day of rest;[34] or to a Jehovah's Witness who refused to accept employment in a factory which produced parts that would be used in military armament;[35] or to exempt members of the Old Order Amish religion and of the Conservative Amish Mennonite Church from the statutory obligation to cause their children to attend formal high school education to the age of 16.[36] In international law, collective group rights find expression in the right to self-determination of peoples, which will be considered later on in this chapter.

Whereas a collective group right vests in individual members of a community of people bound together by, for example, a particular national or ethnic, linguistic, or religious allegiance, an ***institutional group right*** vests in a social institution as such and can only be exercised by that collective entity through the agency of its authorized executive organs. The special significance of *Kedroff* is the recognition by the U.S. Supreme Court in that case that the church, as a legal entity, is the bearer of the constitutional right to freedom of religion.[37]

The South African Constitution is perhaps the most advanced of all human rights instruments in affording recognition to the basic rights and freedoms of group entities such as the institutional church. Not only are juristic persons proclaimed to be duty-bound to uphold the provisions of the South African Bill of Rights "if, and to the extent that, it is applicable, taking into account the nature of the right and the nature of any duty imposed by the right,"[38] juristic persons are also "entitled to the rights in the Bill of Rights to the extent required by the nature of the rights and the nature of that juristic person."[39] Ironically, the question whether or not a religious institution as a juristic person has the right to freedom of religion, belief and opinion[40] is controversial. According to Stuart Woolman, "[c]orporations have neither conscience nor religion" within the meaning of the constitutional protection of freedom of religion,

---

[32] Yoram Dinstein defined "collective human rights" as those "afforded to human beings communally, that is to say, in conjunction with one another as a group—a people or a minority" (Yoram Dinstein, "Collective Human Rights of Peoples and Minorities," *International and Comparative Law Quarterly* 25 (1976): 102–03). See also Brian Berry, *Culture and Equality: An Egalitarian Critique of Multiculturalism* (Cambridge: Harvard University Press, 2001), 112–18.

[33] See the *European Framework Convention for the Protection of National Minorities,* art. 7, ETS 157, *reprinted in* 34 ILM 351 (1995) (hereinafter "Framework Convention").

[34] Sherbert v. Verner, 373 US 398 (1963); see also Hobbie v. Unemployment Appeals Commission of Florida, 480 US 136 (1987); Frazee v. Illinois Dept. of Employment Sec., 489 US 829 (1989).

[35] Thomas v. Review Board, Indiana Employment Sec. Div., 450 US 707 (1981).

[36] Wisconsin v. Yoder, 406 US 205 (1972).

[37] See John H. Garvey, "Churches and the Free Exercise of Religion," *Notre Dame Journal of Law, Ethics and Public Policy* 4 (1990): 578–84 (concluding with reference to *Kedroff,* at 584, that "churches as groups may also claim a right to the free exercise of religion").

[38] SA Const, sec. 8(2).

[39] Ibid., sec. 8(4).

[40] Ibid., sec. 15.

belief, and opinion.[41] Gerrit Pienaar likewise argued that faith and conscience are highly personal and cannot vest in a church.[42] E. F. J. Malherbe, on the other hand, maintains that a church institution does have a right to freedom of religion.[43] It is respectfully submitted that a doctrinal confession is an essential component of a religious community and, when under threat, can at least be vindicated by the institutional structures serving that community.

An American analyst of *Kedroff* defined the substance of the institutional group rights vesting in the Church as a matter of sphere sovereignty:

> The heart of the pluralistic thesis is the conviction that government must recognize that it is not the sole possessor of sovereignty, and that private groups within the community are entitled to lead their own free lives and exercise within the area of their competence an authority so effective as to justify labeling it a sovereign authority.[44]

The sovereignty of a structural religious institution (the church) may at different levels be implicated by state action, for example by state control through a system of registration of religious institutions, and through state interference in the internal affairs of a religious institution.

A. Registration of Religious Institutions

Perhaps the greatest assault upon the sovereignty of religious institutions derives from state-imposed regulations rendering the very existence, or at least the effective functioning, of such institutions dependent upon their registration with political authorities.[45] The mandatory registration of religious institutions is required by many states, combined in several instances with the requirement of a minimum number of adherents to the religion applying for registration.[46]

In Russia, a local religious organization may only be established by no fewer than ten citizens of the Russian Federation.[47] In Poland, the Law of 17 May 1989 on Guarantees of Freedom of Conscience and Belief[48] requires the endorsement of an application for registration as a prerequisite for "[t]he right to create churches and other religious unions"[49] by at least fifteen Polish citizens.[50] In Hungary, the registration of

---

[41] Stuart Woolman, "Application," *Constitutional Law of South Africa*, ed. Chaskalson et al (Cape Town: Juta and Co., 1999), 10.2d.

[42] Gerrit Pienaar, "Konstitutsionele Voorskrifte Rakende Regspersone," *Tydskrif vir Hedendaagse Romeins-Hollandse Reg* 60 (1997): 581; see also Gerrit Pienaar, *Legal Subjectivity and the Juristic Person* (Potchefstroom: 1999), 100 n. 2.

[43] E. F. J. Malherbe, "Die Grondwetlike Beskerming van Godsdiensvryheid," *Tydskrif vir die Suid-Afrikaanse Reg* (1998): 679.

[44] Mark DeWolfe Howe, "Foreword: Political Theory and the Nature of Liberty," *Harvard Law Review* 67 (1953): 91.

[45] In *Hasan and Chaush v. Bulgaria*, the European Court of Human Rights stopped short of deciding that formal registration of religious communities constitutes a violation of the principle of religious freedom as enunciated in the European Convention (Hasan and Chaush v. Bulgaria, App. No. 30985/96 (ECtHR, 26 October 2000), para. 77).

[46] See generally Cole Durham's chapter in this volume.

[47] Russian Federation, *Law on Freedom of Conscience and Religious Associations*, arts. 8.3, 9.1 (1997), translated by Lawrence Uzzell; reprinted in *Emory International Law Review* 12 (1998): 656–714.

[48] J.L. of 1989 No. 29, Item 155.

[49] Ibid., art. 30.

churches is conditional upon their being founded by at least 100 natural persons.[51] In Slovakia, at least 20,000 signatures must endorse the application for registration of a church.[52]

The constitutionality of the Hungarian provision requiring a minimum number of founding members of a church was contested in the Constitutional Court in 1993.[53] The application was based on Article 60(2) of the Hungarian Constitution, which guarantees the common exercise of religion, and on Article 90(3), which makes provision for the separation of church and state. The Court rejected the application because the requirement in question applied equally to all religious denominations. As far as the separation of church and state is concerned, the Court pointed out that registered churches enjoyed a greater measure of internal autonomy than other social entities in the country, and it was therefore within the (political) domain of the state to establish conditions to be satisfied by religious institutions in order to qualify for official "church" status; and churches with a smaller membership can in any event still exercise *religious* (in contradistinction to the privileged civil) functions within the body politic.

The Slovakian precondition for registration can of course be applied to stifle the activities of religious institutions with fairly substantial support in the country. In 1993, the Roman Catholic Church represented the majority religion in Slovakia with a membership of 3,187,383, followed by the Lutheran Church (Augsburg Confession) with 326,397 members, the Greek–Catholic Uniates Church with 187,733 members, the Reformed Calvinistic Church with 82,545 members, and the Orthodox Church with 37,376 members.[54] The Jehovah's Witnesses (10,501 members) and "other churches and religious institutions" (3,625 members)[55] clearly fell short of the minimum support required for their registration with the political authorities of Slovakia.

In recent times, several Eastern European countries have enacted legislation requiring re-registration of religious institutions with a view, clearly, to enforce restrictions upon those perceived to be undesirable. In Bulgaria, for example, the Persons and Family Act, which requires the registration of nonprofit associations, was amended in 1994 to mandate the re-registration of such associations and, in terms of the newly enacted Article 133a, to make consent of the Council of Ministers a prerequisite for registration. Acting pursuant to that provision, the Council of Ministers declined to approve the re-registration of, *inter alia*, the Jehovah's Witnesses.[56] In July 1997, following a decision of the Supreme Court of Bulgaria to uphold the Council's decision,[57] a complaint lodged with the European Commission of Human Rights by the Jehovah's Witnesses in this regard was held to be admissible by the Commission,[58] and subsequently a friendly settlement of the dispute was reached.

---

[50] Ibid., art. 31.

[51] Hungary, Polgári Törvénykönyv (Civil Codes), "On the Freedom of Conscience and Religion as well as the Churches," Act IV, art. 9.1.a (1990).

[52] Slovak National Council, *Collection of Laws of the Czech and Slovak Federative Republic,* Law No. 192/1992 (1992); see also Law No. 308 (1991) regulating the registration procedures.

[53] Decision No. 8, II.27 AB (1993), *Eastern European Case Reporter of Constitutional Law* 1, no. 1 (1994): 109.

[54] See *Statistical Yearbook of the Slovak Republic* (1993), 437–40.

[55] Ibid.

[56] Eastern European Council of Ministers, Decision No. 255 (28 June 1994).

[57] Case No. 733/94 (30 November 1994).

[58] See Christian Association Jehovah's Witnesses v. Bulgaria, Case No. 28626/95 (EComHR, July 3, 1997).

In terms of a statute enacted by the Austrian Parliament on 10 December 1997, a religious association, if it is to enjoy the status of a "state recognized religion," must have existed in Austria for a period of at least twenty years, including a minimum period of ten years as one that was legally recognized by the Government, and it must also have a following of not less than 16,000 adherents (0.2 percent of the population). The legislation paved the way for reducing the state-recognized religions in Austria from the previous number of twelve to no more than four. It should be noted, though, that religious associations that had been recognized prior to the entry into force of the 1997 legislation retained their recognized status even if they did not comply with the minimum membership threshold. The religions not recognized by the Government are denied certain benefits, including the right to levy taxes, to conduct religious classes in public schools, to receive state subsidies for their private schools, and to broadcast radio services. Further legislation has been enacted to regulate the granting of legal personality to such (nonrecognized) religious associations, subject to the condition that their application is supported by at least three hundred residents of Austria who are not also members of an officially recognized religious association or of another registered (nonrecognized) religious association.[59]

B. Sphere Sovereignty of Religious Institutions

In 1992, the state-appointed Directorate of Religious Denominations of Bulgaria issued a decree proclaiming that the acting Bulgarian Patriarch Maxin was not elected in accordance with the bylaws of the Bulgarian Orthodox Church, and furthermore, that the Church was not registered with the Office of Religious Affairs.[60] The Holy Synod of the Bulgarian Orthodox Church brought an action in the Supreme Court of Bulgaria to set aside, on review, an earlier judicial decision declining its protestations of the director's decree. The application was dismissed by the Supreme Court.[61] The decision was based on a legal technicality, namely that the decree of the Directorate of Religious Affairs was not an "individual administrative act" as defined in Article 2 of the Law of Administrative Procedure, and was therefore not appealable in terms of Article 37(2) of that law.

In 1992, the Directorate of Religious Denominations also declared the election in 1988 of Mr. Gendzhev as Chief Mufti of the Muslims in Bulgaria null and void and demanded his removal from office. Legal proceedings challenging this decision were unsuccessful. The National Conference of Muslims thereupon elected Mr. Fikri Sali Hasan as Chief Mufti of Bulgarian Muslims. The Directorate of Religious Denominations registered the new leadership in terms of the 1949 Religious Denominations Act, but in 1995 registered a new leadership of the Bulgarian Muslim community which included Mr. Gendzhev as president of the Supreme Holy Council. The newly registered leadership took possession of the Chief Mufti's offices in Sofia. Proceedings were eventually brought by Mr. Hasan and another before the European Court of

---

[59] "Rechtspersönlichkeit von religiösen Bekenntnissgemeinschaften," in ***Bundesgesetzblatt für die Republik Österreich*** (9 January 1998).

[60] Director of Religious Affairs to the Council of Ministers, Act No. 92/5/25/92.

[61] Decision No. 255 (Supreme Court of Bulgaria, Sofia, 5 November 1992).

Human Rights in Strasbourg to challenge state interference in the internal organization of religious communities and institutions.[62] The application was successful, the Court holding that the autonomous existence of religious communities is an indispensable component of pluralism in a democratic society and that state interference in the internal organization of the Muslim community violated the applicant's right to religious freedom.

These incidents illustrate a particular challenge that confronts religious institutions in many parts of the world: the right to function as religious institutions within the confines of the body politic, and the right to conduct their internal affairs without state interference. There are two seemingly diverse—but nevertheless closely related—forces at work in this regard. At one end of the spectrum is a question of governments doing too little to afford constitutional protection to the lifestyle and interests of religious, ethnic, or cultural minorities, thereby acting in defiance of the international-law decree proclaiming the right to self-determination of peoples. At the other end of the spectrum there is the tendency, in consequence of the absence of constitutional constraints that could place a damper on the exercise of political power, for governments to unduly regulate the internal affairs of sections of the community with distinct religious, ethnic, or cultural affiliations, thereby falling into the trap of political totalitarianism.

Totalitarianism manifests itself when the repositories of state authority take it upon themselves to unduly regulate the private lives of persons under its control, or to interfere in the internal affairs of institutions other than organs of state. In the context of the present survey, political totalitarianism signifies attempts by governmental authorities to undermine the internal sphere sovereignty of religious institutions.

The Dutch expression ***souvereiniteit in eigen sfeer*** (sovereignity in its own sphere) was first used in 1862 by a politician of the Netherlands, Guillaume Groen van Prinsterer (1801–1876), to designate the range of competencies of the church against those of the state.[63] The idea itself, however, preceded this descriptive phrase by approximately 300 years. According to Herman Dooyeweerd, "the first modern formulation of the principle of internal sphere sovereignty in the societal relationship" is to be found in a statement of the medieval Calvinistic jurist, John Althusius (1557–1638).[64] Althusius proclaimed that all distinct social entities are governed by their own laws and that those laws differ in every instance according to the typical nature of the social institution concerned.[65]

In the three hundred years that separated Althusius and Groen van Prinsterer, the concept of the internal sovereign authority of social entities surfaced from time to time, mostly in the ranks of Lutheran political scientists and by and large confined to church-state relations. Friedrich Julius Stahl (1802–1861), for example, noted that

---

[62] Hasan and Chaush v. Bulgaria, Case No. 30985/96 (ECtHR, 26 October 2000).

[63] G. Groen van Prinsterer, *Ter Nagedachtenis van Stahl* (Amsterdam, 1862), 30–31.

[64] H. Dooyeweerd, *A New Critique of Theoretical Thought,* vol. 3 (Jordan Station, Ontario: Padeia Press, 1969), 663; see also Dooyeweerd, *De Strijd om het Souvereiniteitsbegrip in de Moderne Rechtsen Staatsleer* (Amsterdam: H. J. Paris, 1950), 7–8.

[65] J. Althusius, *Politica Methodiae Digesta,* 3d ed. (Herborn: Scientia Aalen, 1614), 1.19 at 7: "Propriae leges sunt cujusque consociationis peculiares, quibus illa regitur. Atque hae in singulis speciebus consociationis iliae atque diversae sunt, prout natura cujusque postulat."

church and state occupied places of independence of one another,[66] that the church was "an institution of an altogether different kind,"[67] and that "ecclesiastical authority . . . is to be strictly distinguished from secular authority."[68]

Dutch political scientists and legal philosophers, schooled in the tradition of Calvinistic social theories, including in particular Abraham Kuyper (1837–1920), were particularly influential in extending the application of sphere sovereignty to the interrelationships of *all* (fundamentally different) structural social entities. The doctrine, as currently defined, received its final touches through the philosophy of the Cosmonomic Idea of Herman Dooyeweerd (1894–1977).[69]

The notion of sphere sovereignty finds expression in various forms in some of the constitutions of the world. Singapore confines the internal sovereignty of religious groups to managing their own religious affairs.[70] Ireland more generously proclaims the right of every religious denomination to manage its own affairs.[71] Italy affords independence and sovereignty, "each within its own ambit," to the state and the Roman Catholic Church only.[72] Romania permits the organization of religious sects "in accordance with their own statutes" but "under the conditions of the law."[73] In the Czech Republic, "[c]hurches and religious societies administer their own affairs, appoint their organs and their spiritual leaders, and establish religious orders and other church institutions, independently from organs of the state."[74] Poland defines the relationship between church and state and other religious organizations on the basis of "the principle of respect for their autonomy and the mutual independence of each in its own sphere, as well as . . . the principle of cooperation for the individual and the common good."[75]

Sensitivity in the United States to the sphere sovereignty of religious organizations is exemplified by Section 702 of the Civil Rights Act of 1964,[76] which exempts religious corporations, associations, educational institutions and societies from the

---

66 F. J. Stahl, *Der Protestantismus als politisches Prinzip* (Berlin: 2e Aufl., 1853), 16, 18.

67 Stahl, *Die Kirchenverfassung nach Lehre und Recht der Protestanten* (Erlangen: 2e Aufl., 1862), 72: "eine Institution ganz anderer Art."

68 Ibid., 13: "das Kirchenregiment . . . vom weltlichen Regiment strenge zu sondern [ist]"; see also ibid., 8, 47, 184.

69 See, in general, Dooyeweerd, *A New Critique,* 169–70; Dooyeweerd, *Het Souvereiniteitsbegrip,* 51; see also Dooyeweerd, *Verkenningen in de Wijsbegeerte, de Sociologie en de Rechtsgeschiedenis* (Amsterdam: Buijten and Schipperheijn, 1962), 80; J. Dengerink, *Critisch-Historisch Onderzoek naar de Sociologische Ontwikkeling der Beginsel der "Souvereiniteit in Eigen Kring" in de 19e en 20e Eeuw* (Kampen: J. H. Kok, 1948), 11; Gordon J. Spykman, "Sphere Sovereignty in Calvin and Calvinist Tradition" *Exploring the Tradition of John Calvin,* ed. David E. Holwerda (Grand Rapids: Baker, 1976), 163; Van der Vyver, *Die Juridiese Funksie van Staat en Kerk: 'n Kritiese Analise van die Beginsel van Soewereiniteit in Eie Kring* (Durban: Butterworths, 1972), 76–78, 91–99; Van der Vyver, "Sovereignty and Human Rights in Constitutional and International Law," *Emory International Law Review* 5 (1991): 342–55; Van der Vyver, "Legal Dimensions of Religious Human Rights: Constitutional Text," *Religious Human Rights in Global Perspective,* ix, xli–xliv.

70 Republic of Singapore Const, art. 15(3), (1963).

71 Republic of Ireland Const, art. 44(2)(5), (1937).

72 Republic of Italy Const, art. 7, (1948).

73 Romania Const, art. 29(3), (1991).

74 Czech Republic, *Fundamental Rights and Freedoms Charter,* art. 16(2), (1992).

75 Republic of Poland Const, art. 25(3), (1997).

76 United States, *Civil Rights Act,* sec. 702, 42 USC § 2000e-1(a), (1964).

Equal Employment Opportunity provisions of the Act[77] with respect to the employment of persons of a particular religion to perform work connected with the carrying on by the corporation, association, educational institution or society of its activities. The constitutionality of Section 702 was upheld in *Corporation of the Presiding Bishop of the Church of Jesus Christ of Latter-day Saints v. Amos.*[78] The Court decided that Section 702 was intended to alleviate "significant governmental interference with the ability of religious organizations to define and carry out their religious mission."[79] In that case, a building engineer working for a nonprofit gymnasium operated by religious institutions affiliated with the Church of Jesus Christ of Latter-day Saints was dismissed because he had lapsed from the church's faith. The Court upheld the legitimate competence of the church authorities to do so. In a concurring judgment, Justice Brennan endorsed the internal sovereignty of the church:

> Determining that certain activities are in furtherance of an organization's religious mission, and that only those committed to that mission should conduct them is . . . a means by which a religious community defines itself. Solicitude for a church's ability to do so reflects the idea that furtherance of the autonomy of religious organizations often furthers religious freedom as well.[80]

There is, of course, more to sphere sovereignty than just that:

- In contradistinction to the Islamic presupposition of the identity of law and religion, it proclaims church and state to be distinct social structures, each with a unique identity and the one irreducible to the other.
- As against the scholastic notion of subsidiarity, it stipulates in essence that social entities of different kinds, including church and state, do not derive their respective competencies from one another, but are in each instance endowed with an internal enclave of domestic powers that emanate from the typical structure of the social entity concerned and as conditioned by the particular function that constitutes the special destiny of that social entity.
- In opposition to the paradigm professing the separation of church and state, it recognizes the encaptic intertwinement of fundamentally different social structures,[81] and it accordingly emphasizes the mutual symbiosis of church and state as peculiarly different social structures and of law and religion as distinct modal aspects within the social environment.

It may be noted, in passing, that the notion of sphere sovereignty was not unknown in scholastic thinking. In the Papal Encyclical *Rerum Novarum* (1891), Pope Leo XIII, while defining the relationship between the state and trade unions on the basis of

---

[77] Ibid., Chapter VII, 42 USC § 2000e et seq.

[78] Corporation of the Presiding Bishop of the Church of Jesus Christ of Latter-day Saints v. Amos, 483 US 327 (1987).

[79] Ibid., 335.

[80] Ibid., 342.

[81] Dooyeweerd, *Verkenningen,* 102–03 (defining "encapsis" as "an intertwinement of intrinsically different structures").

subsidiarity—noting that private societies, including workmen's associations, "exist within the State, and are each part of the State"[82]—nevertheless afforded to Catholic trade unions greater powers of self-determination which seemingly came close to the idea of internal sphere sovereignty: referring to the analogy of ecclesiastical institutions—"[t]he administration of the State . . . have no rights over them"[83]—he said of Catholic workmen's societies:

> Let the State watch over these societies of citizens united together in the exercise of their rights; but let it not thrust itself into their peculiar concerns and their organisation; for things move and live by the soul within them, and they may be killed by the grasp of a hand from without.[84]

There is seemingly also a shift in Roman Catholic social theory toward recognizing a greater measure of sovereignty of church and state. Professor Roland Minnerath almost said it in so many words. According to him, church–state relationships ought to be based on (a) the autonomy of each of the two parties, and (b) cooperation in areas of common interest;[85] and he went on to explain:

> Recognition of the autonomy of church and state requires that each shall be sovereign and independent in its own sphere.[86]

Sphere sovereignty in church-state relations thus recognizes the exclusive competence of religious institutions to determine their own organizational structures, to define their own normative dogma, to develop their own liturgical procedures, to embark upon faith-centered activities of their own choice, to freely spread and actively seek conversions to their faith, to establish and implement their own internal disciplinary imperatives—in every instance without state prescription or interference. The entitlement of religious institutions to conduct their internal affairs without state regulation or interference is closely related to the right to privacy. In *NAACP v. Alabama ex rel. Patterson,* Justice Harlan, delivering the judgment of the Court, spoke of "[i]nviolability of privacy in group association [which] may in many circumstances be indispensable to preservation of freedom of association, particularly where a group espouses dissident beliefs."[87]

The contemporary welfare state tends, in violation of the above directive, to extend the scope of political power to regulate the private lives of individuals and the internal sphere of activities of institutions other than the state. This also applies in many countries of the world to state-imposed regulation of religion—often under pretenses of securing religious freedom.

Bulgaria may here be singled out as a country where totalitarianism in the above sense continues to prevail. Although the Constitution of Bulgaria professes to uphold the separation of religious institutions from the state,[88] it goes on to proclaim Eastern

---

[82] *Rerum Novarum,* 1891: Encyclical of Leo XIII on the Rights and Duties of Capital and Labour, para. 55, reprinted in Henry George, *The Conditions of Labour,* 163–95 (1943).
[83] Ibid., para. 57.
[84] Ibid., para. 59.
[85] Roland Minnerath, "The Doctrine of the Catholic Church," *Proceedings of the Third World Conference on Religious Liberty* (Silver Spring, Maryland: IRLA, 1989), 49, 51.
[86] Ibid. See also the chapter by Professor Minnerath in this volume.
[87] NAACP v. Alabama ex rel. Patterson, 357 US 449, 462 (1958).

Orthodox Christianity to be the "traditional religion" of the country.[89] Freedom of conscience, freedom of thought, and the right to choose a religion (or to uphold atheistic views) is guaranteed,[90] but the freedom of conscience and religion must be exercised subject to the demands, *inter alia,* of "national security [and] public order."[91] The right of churches and religious communities to freely perform their rites must be exercised "within the limits of the Constitution and the laws."[92] The Law on Religion, 1949, makes provision for the institution, as part of the state bureaucracy, of the Office of Religious Affairs, and compels church institutions to submit their appeals, circulars, and other papers or articles "of public interest" to its director, who in turn may prohibit the circulation or execution of those appeals, circulars, papers, or articles which "contradict the laws, public order or good morals."[93]

The Law on Religion, 1949, further prohibits the establishment of hospitals and charitable or other similar institutions by churches.[94] Churches require the permission of the Director of Religious Affairs to maintain contact with foreign denominations, institutions, and organizations, or with persons living or placed outside the country,[95] and also for receiving donations from abroad.[96] Proselytizing by foreign missions is absolutely forbidden.[97]

These provisions have been under review in recent years, but attempts at legal reform to secure religious freedom in the country have thus far been clouded in controversy and remain in abeyance. The laws of Bulgaria therefore continue to violate a salient norm of international law proclaiming the right to self-determination of peoples.

III. The Right to Self-Determination of Religious Communities

In the early 1970s, members of the Old Order Amish religion and a member of the Conservative Amish Mennonite Church of Green County, Wisconsin, were convicted for violating a compulsory school-attendance law which required them to send their children to a public or private school until the children reached the age of sixteen years. The defendants maintained that their children's attendance at high school, public or private, was contrary to the Amish religion and way of life. By sending the children to high school, they would therefore not only expose them to the danger of censure of the church community, but also endanger their own salvation and that of their children. The compulsory school-attendance law, according to the defendants, thus violated the free exercise of their religion. The United States Supreme Court, in *Wisconsin v. Yoder,* upheld

---

88 Republic of Bulgaria Const, art. 13(2) (1991); see also "Law on Religion," art. 3, State Gazette, No. 48 (1 March 1949).

89 Republic of Bulgaria Const, art. 13(3).

90 Ibid., art. 37(1).

91 Ibid., art. 37(2); see also "Law on Religion," art. 5 (1949). art. 4 of the "Law on Religion" further provides that "[n]o one . . . should . . . be free from executing his/her duties, imposed by the laws of the country, because he/she belongs to some church or does not belong to any."

92 "Law on Religion," art. 2.

93 Ibid., art. 15.

94 Ibid., art. 21.

95 Ibid., art. 22.

96 Ibid., art. 24.

97 Ibid., art. 23.

the latter submission, holding that the First and Fourteenth Amendments prevented the state from compelling the Amish to cause their children to attend formal high school education to the age of sixteen.[98]

The issue here is the right to self-determination of a religious community. Whereas the principle of sphere sovereignty of a social entity denotes an institutional group right, the right to self-determination of peoples is a collective group right; that is, a right belonging to individual members of a distinct community of people—here a religious community.

The right to self-determination of peoples, alongside the equality of nations, large and small, has been recognized as a basic norm of international law.[99] In terms of Article 27 of the International Covenant on Civil and Political Rights, self-determination, as currently perceived, entails the following principle:

> In those States in which ethnic, religious or linguistic minorities exist, persons belonging to such minorities shall not be denied the right, in community with the other members of their group, to enjoy their own culture, to profess and practice their own religion, or to use their own language.[100]

The right to self-determination of, among others, religious communities has been endorsed by several other international human rights instruments. The Declaration on the Rights of Persons Belonging to National or Ethnic, Religious and Linguistic Minorities[101] thus speaks of "the right [of national or ethnic, religious and linguistic minorities] to enjoy their own culture, to profess and practice their own religion, and to use their own language, in private and in public, freely and without interference or any form of discrimination." Governments, through their respective constitutional and legal systems, ought to secure the interests of distinct sections of the population that constitute minorities in the above sense. The Declaration addresses in general the duty of states in positive language where it proclaims:

> States shall take measures to create favorable conditions to enable persons belonging to minorities to express their characteristics and to develop their culture, language, religion, traditions and customs, except where specific practices are in violation of national law and contrary to international standards.[102]

The Declaration clearly spells out the obligation of states derived from this general mandate: protect, and encourage conditions for the promotion of, the concerned group identities of minorities under the jurisdiction of the duty-bound state;[103] afford to minorities the special competence to participate effectively in decisions pertinent to

---

[98] Wisconsin v. Yoder, 406 US 205 (1972).

[99] UN Charter, art. 1; see also ibid., arts. 15, 73.

[100] ICCPR, art. 27; see, in general, Felix Ermacora, "The Protection of Minorities Before the United Nations," Recueil des Cours 4 (1983): 246.

[101] *Declaration on the Rights of Persons Belonging to National or Ethnic, Religious and Linguistic Minorities,* UNGA Res. 135, 47th Sess., 2(1), 210, UN Doc. A/Res/47/135 (18 Dec. 1992); reprinted in 32 ILM 911 (1993).

[102] Ibid., art. 4(2); see also the Framework Convention, art. 5(1).

[103] *Declaration on the Rights of Persons Belonging to National or Ethnic, Religious and Linguistic Minorities,* arts. 1(1) and 4(2).

the group to which they belong;[104] do not discriminate in any way against any person on basis of his/her group identity,[105] and in fact take action to secure their equal treatment by and before the law,[106] and so on.

The Council of Europe's 1995 Framework Convention for the Protection of National Minorities encapsulated minority rights in much the same vein: it guarantees equality before the law and equal protection of the laws;[107] states parties promise to provide "the conditions necessary for persons belonging to national minorities to maintain and develop their culture, and to preserve the essential elements of their identity, namely their religion, language, traditions and cultural heritage";[108] states parties recognize the right of persons belonging to a national minority "to manifest his or her religion or belief and to establish religious institutions, organizations and associations";[109] and the Framework Convention guarantees the use of minority languages, in private and in public, orally and in writing.[110]

The South African Constitution sets a commendable example for the protection of the right to self-determination of religious communities. It provides that:

> (1) Persons belonging to a cultural, religious or linguistic community may not be denied the right, with other members of that community—
>
> (a) to enjoy their culture, practise their religion and use their language; and
>
> (b) to form, join and maintain cultural, religious and linguistic associations and other organs of civil society.
>
> (2) The rights in subsection (1) may not be exercised in a manner inconsistent with any provision of the Bill of Rights.[111]

The second clause of this provision brings to the fore the truism that the constitutional right to self-determination of religious (and the other sectional) communities is subject to limitations. However, its wording is excessively broad and could be relied upon by political authorities to restrict the right to self-determination of religious communities beyond a need dictated, as a matter of necessity, by considerations of the general interest pertinent to the protection of public safety, order, health or morals, or the fundamental rights of persons not belonging to the religious community in question.

Denial of the right to self-determination through state interference in the domestic enclave of religious communities is commonplace in many countries of the world. In Poland, for example, the Law of 17 May 1989 on Guarantees of Freedom of Conscience and Belief[112] contains a long list of competencies *afforded by the state* to citizens

---

[104] Ibid., art. 2(3).
[105] Ibid., art. 3.
[106] Ibid., art. 4(1).
[107] Framework Convention, art. 4(1).
[108] Ibid., art. 5(1).
[109] Ibid., art. 8.
[110] Ibid., art. 10(1); see also *European Charter for Regional or Minority Languages* (1992), ETS 148.
[111] SA Const, art. 31.
[112] Poland, "Law on Guarantees of Freedom of Conscience and Belief," J.L. of 1989 No. 29, Item 155 (17 May 1989).

as components of the freedom of conscience and belief:[113] the right to create churches and other religious unions and to belong or not to belong to them; to participate in religious functions and services, fulfill religious duties, and observe religious holidays; to profess their religion or convictions; to bring up their children according to their religious convictions; not to profess their religion or belief; to maintain contact with other persons of their faith and to participate in international religious organizations; to utilize information sources in matters of religion; to produce, to purchase, and to make use of objects required for religious cult purposes and religious practices; to produce, purchase and possess articles required for observing religious rites; to choose a clerical or monastic order; to establish lay organizations with a view to realizing objectives of a professed religion or conviction. Poland established, as part of the state administration, the Office for Denominational Affairs as a link, on the political front, between church and state.[114] The creation of a church or other religious union in Poland is effected through registration of the institution with the Office of Denominational Affairs,[115] supported by at least fifteen Polish citizens,[116] and including in the application all kinds of information, including details of the "basic doctrinal assumptions" of the concerned faith[117] and the applicant's statute (containing details—insisted upon by the state—of, *inter alia,* its aims and proposed activities, sources of financing and the like).[118] Church officials are required by law to notify the appropriate organ of state about the creation, change of name, seat, borders, or merger, division and annulment of a diocese or of a parish.[119] The state wants to know about the appointment or removal from office of the executive organ of a church or other religious institution.[120] The Head of the Office of Denominational Affairs may "express reservations" in regard to the appointment of a foreigner as the responsible church official entrusted with the duty of notifying the state of the above information and eventualities.[121]

In Croatia, the Law on the Legal Status of Religious Communities, 1978,[122] prescribes severe penalties for acts such as the "abuse" of religion, the religious press, religious activity, or a religious community for "political goals";[123] collecting contributions for religious purposes outside places "intended for such purposes" unless approval is obtained from the municipal authority for internal affairs;[124] organizing or engaging in social activities not directly related to the needs of the religious community for the administration of religious affairs and religious service, or for the needs of individual believers;[125] conducting religious ceremonies or administering religious affairs, without state permission, beyond the limits of areas prescribed by the law[126] for such purposes;[127] or giving religious instruction to pupils at public schools during school hours.[128]

---

[113] Ibid., art. 2.
[114] Ibid., art. 15(1).
[115] Ibid., art. 30.
[116] Ibid., art. 31.
[117] Ibid., art. 32(1)(a).
[118] Ibid., art. 32(2).
[119] Ibid., art. 14(1).
[120] Ibid., art. 14(2).
[121] Ibid., art. 14(4).
[122] Croatia, "Law on the Legal Status of Religious Communities," Official Gazette No. 14/78 (1978).
[123] Ibid., art. 23(2).
[124] Ibid., art. 24(1), read with art. 14.
[125] Ibid., art. 24 (2).

Legislation of this kind is offensive even if it happens to be permissive, because it is based on the erroneous assumption that the enjoyment of religious freedom derives from a political concession. Religious expression is not a gift of the state but vests in every individual because he or she is a human being.

IV. Religious Freedom and the Right to Equal Protection and Nondiscrimination

In September 1997, the Russian Federation enacted the Law on Freedom of Conscience and Religious Associations,[129] which mandates the re-registration of all religious institutions which have not been registered in the Russian Federation for a period of at least 15 years.[130] The infamous Article 27.3 spells out in sordid detail the restrictions imposed upon religious institutions without the fifteen-year registered tenure which fail to apply for, or to procure, re-registration:

- The members of those religious organizations entertaining conscientious objections to military service will not be allowed to do alternative service in lieu of military conscription, and their clergy will not qualify for deferment of conscription into military service and exemption from military training in peace time;[131]
- They are not entitled to create educational institutions,[132] or to teach religion to their children in municipal educational institutions;[133]
- They may not attach to themselves the representative body in Russia of a foreign religious organization;[134]
- They are not permitted to carry out religious rites in health centers and hospitals, in children's homes, in homes for the elderly and institutions for handicapped persons, or in prisons or similar institutions;[135]
- It is forbidden for them to produce, acquire, export, import and distribute religious literature, printed, audio and video material, and other articles of religious significance,[136] and they may not institute enterprises for producing liturgical literature and articles for religious services;[137]
- They are precluded from the right to create educational organizations and institutions;[138]

---

[126] Ibid., arts. 15 and 16.
[127] Ibid., art. 24(3).
[128] Ibid., art. 24(4), read with art. 17.
[129] Russian Federation, "Law on Freedom of Conscience and Religious Associations" (see note 47 in this chapter); see W. Cole Durham Jr. and Lauren B. Homer, "Russia's 1997 Law on Freedom of Conscience and Religious Associations: An Analytical Appraisal," *Emory International Law Review* 12 (1998): 101; Irana G. Basova, "Freedom Under Fire: The New Russian Religious Law," *Temple International and Comparative Law Journal* 14 (2000): 189–98.
[130] Russian Federation, "Law on Freedom of Conscience and Religious Associations," art. 27(3).
[131] Ibid., read with art. 3(4).
[132] Ibid., read with art. 5(3).
[133] Ibid., read with art. 5(4).
[134] Ibid., read with art. 13(5).
[135] Ibid., read with art. 16(3).
[136] Ibid., read with art. 17(1).
[137] Ibid., read with art. 17(2).
[138] Ibid., read with art. 18(2).

- They may not set up schools for professional religious education for the training of their clergy;[139] and
- It is forbidden for them to invite foreign citizens for professional purposes, including preaching and religious activity.[140]

To avoid these impediments, the religious institution bears the onus of producing documentary evidence of its "existence on the corresponding territory" for the critical period of fifteen years.[141] And such religious institutions must in fact re-register annually until they satisfy the fifteen years criterion. In consequence of some of the negative responses to the legislation, the fifteen year rule has been held not to apply to religious organizations that were registered at the time the 1997 legislation entered into force or to "centralized religious organizations"; that is, those that consist of no fewer than three local religious organizations of the same creed.[142] In a judgment of 23 November 1999, the Russian Constitutional Court, applying the latter directives, decided that Article 27.3, "when normatively applied," does not contravene the Constitution of the Russian Federation. The Court did find that an individual with conscientious objections against military service can invoke the constitutional provisions guaranteeing every citizen the right to nonviolent alternatives to military service. In a subsequent matter, decided on 13 April 2000, the Court again declined to declare the law unconstitutional but nevertheless ruled that the Independent Russian Region of the Society of Jesus (Jesuits) be registered as a "religious organization," even though the Jesuits did not clearly fit any of the criteria that qualified for the statutory categories for re-registration.

What is here forbidden for religious institutions without the fifteen years registered tenure in the Russian Federation (referred to in the law as "religious groups") are included in the statutory entitlements of religious institutions complying with the fifteen years requirement (referred to in the law as "religious organizations"). Distinguishing for legal purposes between these two categories of religious institutions seems arbitrary and in any event lacks a reasonable base. The differentiations founded on this classification are clearly discriminatory.

When the Russian Federation was admitted to the Council of Europe in 1998, the question as to the compatibility of its Law on Freedom of Conscience and Religious Associations became an issue. The European Convention for the Protection of Human Rights and Fundamental Freedoms guarantees to everyone "the right to freedom of thought, conscience and religion," which includes (a) the right to change one's religion or belief, and (b) the right to manifest one's religion or belief, either alone or in community with others and in private or in public, in worship, teaching, practice, and observance.[143] Freedom to manifest one's religion or belief ([b] and not [a]) can be subjected to limitations, provided the limitations are prescribed by law and are necessary in a democratic society in the interests of public safety, for the protection of public order, health or morals, or for the protection of the rights and

---

[139] Ibid., read with art. 19.

[140] Ibid., read with art. 20(2).

[141] Ibid.

[142] Ibid., art. 9(2).

[143] *European Convention on Human Rights*, 4 November 1950, art. 9(1), 213 UNTS 221, art. 9(1); ETS 5 (hereinafter "ECHR").

freedoms of others.[144] It is difficult to see how the restrictions placed upon some religions by the Russian law can be justified under the rubric of any of these contingencies. Assuming, however, that they can, the question will then arise whether the discriminatory component of the Russian law will render it censurable under the European Convention.

For purposes of the argument, nondiscrimination provisions in constitutional bills of rights and international human rights instruments can be classified into two main categories: those prohibiting discrimination *per se* based on, *inter alia*, religion; and those prohibiting discrimination in respect only of the rights and freedoms enunciated in the concerned instrument.

The nondiscrimination provisions in the International Covenant on Civil and Political Rights[145] are of the first kind, while the European Convention falls in the second category. It provides:

> The enjoyment of the rights and freedoms as set forth in this Convention shall be secured without discrimination on any grounds such as sex, race, colour, language, religion, political or other opinion, national or social origin, association with a national minority, property, birth or other status.[146]

Upon the above assumption—i.e. that the restrictions imposed by the Russian law are confined to matters of manifestation and are found to be justified under the limitations clause—there is, though unconvincingly, an argument to be made that the discrimination component of the law will not constitute a violation of the European Convention. The enjoyment of freedom of thought, conscience, and religion "as set forth in this Convention" must be understood to mean that freedom as legitimately curtailed under authority of the limitations clause; and the argument will then have it that the enjoyment of freedom of thought, conscience and religion as legitimately curtailed is granted to everyone. The alternative—and perhaps better—reasoning would be that inasmuch as limitations upon freedom of thought, conscience and religion would be justified under the criteria laid down in the European Convention, those limitations must apply equally to all religions and not only to the politically disadvantaged ones.

The European Court of Human Rights might nevertheless adopt the first-mentioned line of reasoning—if for no other reason then perhaps simply because institutionalized denominational favoritism is commonplace in Europe. The Roman Catholic Church is still an established church, or is afforded special constitutional recognition, in Liechtenstein,[147] Malta,[148] and Monaco.[149] The Evangelical Lutheran Church is an established church in Denmark,[150] Iceland,[151] and Norway.[152] The Eastern Orthodox

---

[144] Ibid., art. 9(2).
[145] ICCPR, art. 26.
[146] Ibid., art. 14 (emphasis added); see also UDHR, art. 2; 1981 Declaration, art. 2.
[147] Liechtenstein Const, art. 37 (1921).
[148] Republic of Malta Const, art. 2 (1964).
[149] Principality of Monaco Const, art. 9 (1962).
[150] Kingdom of Denmark Const, sec. 4 (1953).
[151] Iceland Const, art. 62 (1944).
[152] Kingdom of Norway Const, art. 2 (1814).

Church of Christ is singled out as "[t]he prevailing religion" in Greece,[153] and the "traditional religion" of Bulgaria.[154] The Church of England is the established church in England,[155] and the Presbyterian Church enjoys the same status in Scotland.[156]

It stands to reason that preferential treatment by the state of a particular church institution or any religion or group of religions violates the essential components of equal protection and the norm against discrimination. Nor would toleration toward church institutions and religions not singled out for preferential treatment discount these injustices. Toleration entails within itself condescending attitudes, necessitates entanglement, and obstructs sphere sovereignty.

Establishment might be seen by some as a means of protection of the state-sponsored religious institution. Sphere sovereignty condemns establishment for what it really is: state interference in the internal management of the church. Lutheran Archbishop K. G. Hamman of Uppsala, in a recent statement, therefore rightly praised the then imminent disestablishment of his church in Sweden after four hundred years of state control. Terminating appointment of church officials by political authorities was specially mentioned as a practice that is no longer acceptable in this day and age.

The current tendency in some European countries, including Austria, Belgium,[157] France,[158] and Germany, to entrust the state with the competence to identify and to outlaw so-called dangerous sects is also indicative of a denial of equal treatment and a certain degree of discrimination.[159] In 1992, the European Parliament adopted a recommendation emphasizing the undesirability, in view of the freedom of conscience and religion, of major legislation on religious cults and noting that "such legislation might well interfere with this fundamental right and harm traditional religions."[160] A subsequent *Report on Cults in the European Union,* prepared by Maria Berger of Austria, also followed a particularly cautious approach, calling on member states "to take

---

[153] Greece Const, art. 3 (1975).

[154] Republic of Bulgaria Const, art. 13(3) (1991).

[155] See Submission of the Clergy Act, 25 Hen. 8, c. 19; Act of Supremacy, 1 Eliz. 1, c. 1; see also Van der Vyver, *Die Juridiese Funksie van Staat en Kerk,* 134–40.

[156] See *Union with Scotland Act,* 5 Ann, c. 8; see also Van der Vyver, *Die Juridiese Funksie van Staat en Kerk,* 140–42.

[157] A Statute creating an Advisory and Information Center on Harmful and Dangerous Sectarian Movements was signed into law by the Belgian King on 2 June 1998. See *Belgisch Staatsblad/Moniteur Belge,* F.98-3121 (25 November 1998). Thus far, close to 200 movements have been identified as ones suspected of being harmful or dangerous cults. See Duquesne et Willems, *Documents parlementaires Chambre 1996–97,* no. 313/7 (partie I) et 313/8 (partie II).

[158] After parliamentary reports prepared in 1996 and 1999 pertaining to "dangerous cults," and following the establishment in 1998 of a governmental "Mission to Fight Against Cults," the French Senate on 16 December 1999 unanimously approved a Bill amending the French Law of 10 January 1936 and certain other laws to include religious cults or sects in the category of organizations that can be banned and dissolved by executive decree. See Sénat, Proposed Law No. 131, 14 December 1999. The banning of organizations and groups can follow upon a second conviction for a variety of offences, provided the organizations or groups are furthermore regarded as "a trouble for public order or a major danger for human personality."

[159] For further discussion of the anti-sect phenomena in the European francophone sphere, see the chapter by Fautré et al. in this volume.

[160] Parliamentary Assembly Recommendation 1178, "Sects and New Religious Movements," para. 5 (5 Feb 1992) in *Council of Europe Parliamentary Assembly, Texts Adopted by the Assembly* (1991–93). The Recommendation places emphasis on education and legislation, where this does not already exist, to afford corporate status to all sects and new religions "which have been registered."

action only on the problematic activities of cults and in connection with their specific activities if they affect people's physical and mental integrity or social and financial standing," and not to confine such action to religious organizations per se. Regrettably, this report has for all intents and purposes been shelved by the European Parliament. Recently, the European Court of Human Rights decided to give preference to an application of the Christian Federation of Jehovah's Witnesses protesting the discrimination it suffers due to its being listed in the French inventory of "dangerous sects."[161]

In the end, the Russian Law on Freedom of Conscience and Religious Associations might after all not be shielded behind the existing religious practices of a cross-section of European countries to avoid its condemnation on grounds of religious discrimination. Whereas the European countries practicing religious favoritism in general also uphold a fair degree of toleration in respect of the nonfavored religions, the impediments suffered by "religious groups" in the Russian Federation are drastic and far-reaching, and render the discriminatory component of the Law highly unreasonable.[162]

V. Freedom of Expression of Religious Communities and Institutions

In 1998, a matter came before the European Court of Human Rights, in the case of *Larissis v. Greece,* involving three officers in the Greek air force who were convicted for engaging fellow members of the air force in religious discussions, reading extracts from the Bible and encouraging the fellow members of the air force to accept the beliefs of the Pentecostal Church.[163] As members of the Pentecostal Church, the officers had a religious duty to convert others to their faith.

The Greek Constitution prohibits proselytization,[164] and the Law on Proselytism renders proselytization punishable.[165] Proselytism is defined in the Law as "any direct or indirect attempt to intrude on the religious beliefs of a person of a different religious persuasion, with the aim of undermining those beliefs, either by any kind of inducement or promise of an inducement or moral support or material assistance, or by fraudulent means or by taking advantage of the other person's inexperience, trust, need, low intellect or naivety." The question to be considered by the European Court of Human Rights was whether these provisions violated the guarantees in the European Convention to protect the freedom of thought, conscience, and religion of every person.[166]

Earlier, the European Court of Human Rights was called upon to evaluate action taken in Greece against Jehovah's Witnesses based on the above statutory proscription of proselytization. In *Kokkinakis v. Greece,*[167] the Court found that the conviction of

---

161 Christian Federation of Jehovah's Witnesses v. France, App. No. 53430/1999 (ECtHR).

162 See T. Jeremy Gunn, "Caesar's Sword: The 1997 Law of the Russian Federation on the Freedom of Conscience and Religious Associations," *Emory International Law Review* 12 (1998): 57–64.

163 Larissis and Others v. Greece, 27 EHRR 329 (1999) (ECtHR, 24 February 1998).

164 Greece Const, art. 13(2), (1975).

165 Law No. 1363/1938, as amended by Law No. 1672/1939, sec. 4.

166 ECHR, art. 9.

167 Kokkinakis v. Greece, 17 EHRR 397 (1994) (ECtHR, 25 May 1993); for a discussion of the case, see Gunn, "Adjudicating Rights of Conscience under the European Convention of Human Rights," *Religious*

the applicant and his wife for having initiated a discussion of their religion with a certain Mrs. Kyriakaki constituted a violation of their right to religious freedom as guaranteed by the European Convention. The Court was not prepared, however, to condemn the proscription of proselytization as such, holding that there might be instances of "improper proselytism" consisting of "a corruption or deformation of [true evangelism]" and which may take on the form of "activities offering material or social advantages with a view to gaining new members of a Church or exerting improper pressure on people in distress or in need." Improper proselytism, the Court went on to say, "may even entail the use of violence or brain washing" and as such it would not be compatible with "respect for the freedom of thought, conscience and religion of others."[168]

In *Larissis,* the Court upheld the conviction of the military officers for proselytization of their subordinates in the air force, but upheld their complaint under the provision of the European Convention dealing with religious freedom as far as their conviction for proselytizing civilians was concerned. Due to the hierarchical structures in the armed forces,[169] the Court held, subordinates could find it difficult to rebuff the approaches of an individual of superior rank or to withdraw from a conversation initiated by the superior officer; and this brought the missionary endeavors within the confines of "improper proselytism" under the rubric of "the offering of material or social advantage or the application of improper pressure with a view to gaining new members for a Church."[170] These considerations did not apply when a person holding military rank engaged civilians in religious talk.[171] The Court confirmed in this regard that religious freedom as such implies freedom to manifest one's religion, including the right to try to convince others of the salience of one's belief.

These decisions illustrate the complementary interaction of freedom of religion or belief with freedom of speech. In *Larissis* the Court declined to give a separate ruling on submissions of the petitioners based on freedom of speech, because "no separate issue arose" under the freedom-of-speech guarantees of the European Convention. It stands to reason that the right to spread one's religion or belief cannot be vindicated without the broadest possible free speech guarantees.

In the case of *Manoussakis and Others v. Greece,*[172] the European Court of Human Rights had occasion to censure the government of Greece for applying state-imposed legislation to sanction rigid, or indeed prohibitive, conditions to restrict the activities of faiths outside the Greek Orthodox Church. The Court noted in that case that the right to freedom of religion as guaranteed under the European Convention of Human Rights and Fundamental Freedoms excludes any discretion on the part of the state to determine whether religious beliefs or the means used to express such beliefs are legitimate. Constitutional and legislative decrees deviating from that norm is therefore, from the perspective of freedom of religion or belief, most regrettable.

Human Rights in Global Perspective, 305; Lerner, "Proselytism, Change of Religion, and International Human Rights," *Emory International Law Review* 12 (1998): 547–56; and the chapter by Stahnke in this volume.

168 Kokkinakis v. Greece, 21, para. 48.

169 Larissis v. Greece, para. 51.

170 Ibid., para. 54–55.

171 Ibid., para. 55.

172 Mannousakis and Others v. Greece, 23 EHRR 387 (1997) (ECtHR, 26 September 1996).

The Constitution of Ghana, for example, authorizes statutory limitations of "freedom of thought, conscience and belief" and the "freedom to practice any religion and to manifest such practice" for the purpose of, *inter alia,* "safeguarding the people of Ghana against teaching or propagation of a doctrine which exhibits or encourages disrespect for the nationhood of Ghana, the national symbols and emblems, or incites hatred against other members of the community"—provided the limitations are "justifiable in terms of the spirit of the Constitution."[173] Proselytization by foreign missions is absolutely forbidden in Bulgaria.[174]

It is perhaps worth noting that the Supreme Court of the Republic of Udmurt in the Russian Federation, in a decision handed down in the town of Izhevsk on 5 March 1997,[175] declared unconstitutional a law of the Udmurt Republic *On Missionary Activity on the Territory of the Udmurt Republic.*[176] The law placed severe restrictions on missionary activities and was held to violate Article 28 of the Constitution of the Russian Federation, which—as cited in the judgment—provides:

> Everyone is guaranteed freedom of conscience, freedom of confession, including the right individually and jointly with others to profess any religion or to profess none, freely to choose, to hold and to spread religious or other convictions and to act in accordance with them.

VI. Freedom of Assembly and Association of Religious Communities and Institutions

In 1990, the (political) United Communist Party (TBKP) was established in Turkey. Ten days later, the attorney general brought proceedings in the Constitutional Court for the dissolution of the TBKP on the grounds that it represented an attempt to establish the domination of one social class over the others, declared itself to be the successor to a political party that had previously been dissolved, illegally included the word "communist" in its name, and undermined the integrity of the Turkish state. On 16 July 1991, the Constitutional Court ordered the dissolution of the TBKP. An application was finally brought before the European Court of Human Rights, in the *Case of the United Communist Party of Turkey v. Turkey.*[177]

The European Convention for the Protection of Human Rights and Fundamental Freedoms contains the following guarantees pertaining to freedom of assembly and association:

> 1. Everyone has the right to freedom of peaceful assembly and to freedom of association with others, including the right to form and to join trade unions for the protection of his interests.

---

[173] Republic of Ghana Const, art. 21(4)(e) (1992).

[174] "Law on Religion," art. 23 (1949).

[175] In the case of Mashagatova Svetlana Pavlovna and Others v. Urdmurt Republic State Council (Urd. ASSR Sup. Ct.) An English translation of the judgment was reprinted in *Emory International Law Review* 12 (1998): 715–38.

[176] Russian Federation, Udmurt Republic, Law No. 221-1 (28 May 1996).

[177] United Communist Party of Turkey and Others v. Turkey (ECtHR, Jan. 30, 1998). For further discussion of this and other European Court of Human Rights cases, see the chapter in this volume by Navarro-Valls and Martínez-Torrón.

> 2. No restrictions shall be placed on the exercise of these rights other than such as are prescribed by law and are necessary in a democratic society in the interests of national security or public safety, for the prevention of disorder or crime, for the protection of health or morals or for the protection of the rights and freedoms of others. This article shall not prevent the imposition of lawful restrictions on the exercise of these rights by members of the armed forces, of the police or of the administration of the State.[178]

The European Court rejected a submission of the Turkish government that the wording of the first subsection must be taken to confine freedom of assembly and association under the Convention to trade unions and similar institutions. The right to form and join trade unions only serves as an example and reference thereto does not exclude other types of institutions such as political parties. It was further decided that the prohibition of the TBKP was not informed by any conduct on its part, since action had been taken by the authorities before the party had the chance of showing its colors. Nor could the limitations clause of the provision assist the Turkish government, particularly since multiple political parties is an essential component of democracy, and their dissolution can therefore not be said to be "necessary in a democratic society." A principal characteristic of democracy is the possibility it offers of resolving a country's problems through dialogue, without recourse to violence. Democracy, the Court proclaimed, thrives on freedom of expression. The banning of a political party was in the circumstances of the case unnecessary in a democratic society and violated the right to freedom of assembly and association of its members.

In the context of the present survey, the *Case of the United Communist Party of Turkey* is important in two respects: it illustrates that freedom of religion or belief is not confined to religious freedom; and it highlights the entanglement of freedom of religion or belief with freedom of assembly and association.[179] That entanglement is clearly implicated by that component of freedom of religion or belief comprising the "freedom, either individually or in community with others and in public or in private, to manifest his religion or belief."[180]

Freedom of assembly and of association as a precondition for the exercise of freedom of religion or belief was also in issue in *Sidiropoulos v. Greece*.[181] The case concerned refusal of the Greek authorities to register a certain nonprofit organization, called the Home of Macedonian Civilization, under Article 79 of the Greek Civil Code. The organization was founded in 1990 by a group of people of Macedonian extraction living in Florina (northern Greece) and who prided themselves on having a "Macedonian national consciousness." The Florina Court of First Instance refused the application for registration of the association on the grounds that its real aims were to promote the idea that there was a Macedonian minority in Greece, which would go against Greece's national interests and therefore be contrary to law.

The European Court of Human Rights found that refusal to register the association constituted an interference in the applicants' right to freedom of association, since it deprived the applicants of any possibility of jointly or individually pursuing the

---

[178] ECHR, art. 11.

[179] See also Freedom and Democracy Party (*ÖZDEP*) v. Turkey, App. No. 23885/94 (ECtHR, 8 December 1999).

[180] UDHR, art. 18; ICCPR, art. 18(1); 1981 Declaration, art. 1(1).

aims they sought to promote. The Greek government conceded this, but argued that it acted within the confines of the limitations provision in the European Convention that applies to freedom of assembly and association, particularly since the founders of the Home of Macedonian Civilization denied the Greek identity of Macedonia and its inhabitants and thereby undermined the territorial integrity of Greece. The European Court would have nothing of it: the right to form an association is an inherent part of the freedom of assembly and association, and the aims of the association were merely to preserve and develop the traditional folk culture of the Florina region—which in themselves are perfectly legitimate aims.[182]

VII. The Competence to Vindicate Freedom of Religion or Belief

Freedom of religion or belief would be but an empty shell if its repositories are deprived of a legal remedy to enforce that freedom. Several judgments of the European Court of Human Rights clearly make the point.

In 1987, two people living next to a cathedral in Crete of the Roman Catholic Church of the Virgin Mary demolished a wall surrounding the cathedral and made a window in their own building facing and looking into the cathedral. The Church sought a declaratory order certifying its ownership of the wall that had been demolished and an order for it to be restored to the previous situation. It turned out that the Catholic Church, which had been operating in Greece since the setting up of the Greek state in 1830, had never taken the legal steps required by law for the acquisition of legal personality. The respondents therefore argued, and the Canea Court of First Instance (sitting as an appellate division) decided, that the Church lacked *locus standi in iudicio* to bring suit in a court of law.

The European Court of Human Rights noted that the legal personality of the Greek Catholic Church and of its parish churches had never before been questioned and that the church and its parishes participated in numerous legal transactions as though they were legal subjects. All kinds of difficulties would confront the church if it should now take the legal steps required for legal subjectivity, including the implied admission that its earlier transactions were null and void for lack of legal personality of the church. By denying the church standing to protect its property, the Court not only penalized the church for failure to comply with a simple formality, it also deprived the church of a legal remedy to seek protection of its rights in a court of law.

Earlier, in *Holy Monasteries v. Greece,*[183] the European Court of Human Rights also censured a Greek law regulating matters of church property[184] for denying a church, because of its lack of legal personality, the "right to court." The issue in that case was the right of the church to manage its properties and to contest the fixing of compensation for the expropriation of church property. By preventing the monasteries from bringing before the appropriate courts any complaint they might have against the Greek state, third parties, or the Greek Church itself, or by even intervening in such

---

[181] Sidiropoulos and Others v. Greece, App. No. 26695/95 (ECtHR 1998-IV, 10 July 1998).
[182] Ibid., para. 30–47; and see also Serif v. Greece, App. No. 34369/97 (ECtHR, 14 December 1999).
[183] Holy Monasteries v. Greece, 20 EHRR 1 (1995) (ECtHR 301, 9 December 1994),
[184] Republic of Greece, Law No. 1700/1987.

proceedings, the law violated the right to a fair trial, which in terms of the European Convention includes "a fair and public hearing . . . by an independent and impartial tribunal established by law."[185]

Nonregistration of a religious institution and the consequent incapacity of the institution to own property and to exercise the entitlements of ownership was also an issue in *Institute of French Priests v. Turkey*.[186] A friendly settlement was reached in that case, the terms of which the Treasury and Directorate General Foundations afforded to the priests life tenancy, including the right to let the land (with the Treasury and Directorate General Foundations being entitled to a reasonable proportion of the rent).

Over and above the "rights to a court," the European Convention also expressly mandates the right to an effective remedy of persons whose rights and freedoms, including freedom of thought, conscience and religion, have been violated.[187] This right was an issue in two cases involving the refusal, on religious grounds, of Jehovah's Witnesses to permit their children to take part in a school parade commemorating the outbreak of the war between Greece and Italy in 1940.[188] The Court in both instances declined to find a violation of the students' freedom of religion—the obligation to take part in the school parade was not of the kind that should offend the parents' religious convictions—but decided that Article 13 of the European Convention had been violated in that the applicants had not had an effective remedy before the national authorities in order to raise the complaints which they later submitted to the European Court of Human Rights.

It stands to reason that recourse to a court of law for the vindication of one's freedom of religion or belief must be conditioned by all the due process requirements of a fair trial.

VIII. Conflicts Between Freedom of Religion or Belief and Other Human Rights

Freedom of religion or belief is intimately linked to the sphere sovereignty, as an institutional group right, of religious organizations and other institutions founded upon a common belief structure. It is also intimately linked to the right to self-determination, as a collective group right, of religious communities and other associations of people bound together by a shared conviction. Freedom of religion or belief furthermore requires the backing of the right to equal protection and nondiscrimination, freedom of expression, freedom of association, and a legal remedy for the protection of its various manifestations. However, freedom of religion or belief may in many respects also come into conflict with some of the basic and widely accepted components of the human rights paradigm.

The Islamic Republic of Iran, for example, invoked the authority of the Koran for a criminal justice system that deviates considerably from the proscription of cruel and inhuman punishments.[189] Execution by means of stoning is prescribed by the Islamic

---

[185] ECHR, art. 6(1).

[186] Institute of French Priests v. Turkey, App. No. 26308/95 (ECtHR, 14 December 2000).

[187] Ibid., art. 13.

[188] Valsamis v. Greece, 24 EHRR 294 (1997) (ECtHR, 18 December 1996); Efstratiou v. Greece, App. No. 24095/94 (ECtHR 1996-VI, 18 December 1996).

Penal Code of Iran for the crime of adultery, subject to the following decree: "In the punishment of stoning to death, the stones should not be too large so that the person dies on being hit by one or two of them; they should not be so small either that it could not be defined as stones."[190]

Punishment of a *mohareb* (enemy of Allah) occurs by way of crucifixion that could leave the convicted person on the cross for as long as three days (in the expectation that he or she would perish within that period).[191] Punishment for theft includes physical mutilation: dismemberment of four fingers of the right hand in the case of a first offender, dismemberment of the left foot of the thief in the case of a second offender, and following mandatory imprisonment of a third offender, execution of those convicted for the fourth time.[192] Flogging is prescribed for adultery,[193] taking alcohol,[194] sodomy,[195] lesbianism,[196] pimping,[197] and malicious accusation.[198] Corporal punishment, which may include eighty lashes for drinking an alcoholic beverage[199] and one hundred lashes for fornication "by a man or a woman not qualified as married,"[200] is inflicted subject to the following decree: "A man is whipped while standing and his body naked except a cover on his privy parts but a woman is whipped while sitting and her dress tied to her body."[201] Such textual fundamentalism is not confined to factions within Islam. It also filters through in the religious teachings of many Christian groups.

In South Africa, for example, the Foundation for Ethical Medicine (*Stigting vir Etiese Medisyne*) devoted a special volume of its journal to the question of capital punishment. One of the contributors presented an in-depth analysis of penal theories and Biblical texts sanctioning the death penalty to come to the following conclusion:

> The death penalty is essential, not because a vast majority (71.4%) of a democratic country such as South Africa is in favor of it, not because efforts to rehabilitate criminals have failed, not because the judge has the right to execute the revenge of society, not because the community will commit less crimes, not because it will prevent the criminal from committing further crimes. The death penalty is essential because God commanded it.
>
> The blood defileth the land [Num. 35:33] and the blood calls for retribution. God will restore His violated right, either indirectly through civil authority or directly by God Himself. God demands that the civil authority applies its criminal laws as a means of demonstrating its condemnation of crime [see Deut. 21:1–9].[202]

[189] See David Weissbrodt, Joan Fitzpatrick, and Frank Newman, *International Human Rights: Law, Policy and Process* (Cincinnati: Anderson, 2001), 168–71.
[190] Islamic Penal Code of Iran, art. 119.
[191] Ibid., art. 207.
[192] Ibid., art. 218.
[193] Ibid., arts. 100–104.
[194] Ibid., arts. 123–36.
[195] Ibid., art. 152.
[196] Ibid., arts. 159, 164.
[197] Ibid., art. 168.
[198] Ibid., arts. 176, 178, 187.
[199] Ibid., art. 131.
[200] Ibid., art. 102.
[201] Ibid., art. 132.

The Old Testament prescribes capital punishment for murder,[203] adultery and fornication,[204] bestiality,[205] homosexuality,[206] rape,[207] incest,[208] rebellious and insubordinate children and children who curse their parents,[209] defying of the Sabbath,[210] abduction and the slave trade,[211] idolatry,[212] witchcraft, false prophesy,[213] and blasphemy.[214] According to the member of the Foundation for Ethical Medicine (with reference to Matt. 5:17–19),[215] the laws of God, including the penal laws, have not been dissolved by the coming of Jesus Christ. And so much so for the proscription of cruel and inhuman punishments in human rights terms!

Certain religious groups also insist, as a matter of faith, on the transformation of the state into one, or the establishment of a political community, with a distinct denominational commitment. Many religions discriminate against women and, on scriptural grounds,[216] condemn members of the gay and lesbian community. Some members of the "Religious Right" in the United States are known to have urged the American government not to ratify the International Convention on the Rights of the Child because it allegedly undermines parental authority. Many religions of the world strongly oppose a restricted interpretation of the right to life, or an extended interpretation of sex equality, that would permit abortions on demand.

This is not the time or place to enter into a theological and/or jurisprudential discourse on any of the above religiously based submissions which gainsay the equality and nondiscrimination principles enshrined as a basic premise of the human rights ideology, or the norms seeking to promote the best interests of a child. Suffice it to say that equal treatment and nondiscrimination has been identified as a fundamental directive of the legal idea: that is, the most basic norm which ought to guide the conduct of persons in political authority and be embodied in the laws of the state. The state should, however, be cautious in imposing the directives that inform the propriety of state-imposed decrees upon the internal sphere of religious communities and nonstate institutions. The right to self-determination of religious communities and the sphere sovereignty of non-state institutions constrain the state to confine its regulation of

---

202 M. C. Durand, "Die Noodwendige Doodstraf," *Die Joernaal vir Etiese Medisyne* 1, no. 3 (2000): 13, 43 (translation from Afrikaans by the present writer).

203 Ex. 21:12; Num. 35:31.

204 Lev. 20:10; Deut. 22:21.

205 Ex. 22:19; Lev. 20:15. In Lev. 18:22, 23, banning (not death) is ordained for bestiality and sodomy.

206 Lev. 20:13.

207 Deut. 22:25.

208 Lev. 20:11, 14.

209 Ex. 21:15, 17; Deut. 31:20–23.

210 Ex. 31:14; 35:2; Num. 15:32–36.

211 Ex. 21:16; Deut. 24:7.

212 Lev. 20:2; Deut. 13:6–17.

213 Ex. 22:18; Lev. 20:27; Deut. 13:5, 18:20.

214 Lev. 24:16.

215 "Think not that I am come to destroy the law, or the prophets: I am not come to destroy, but to fulfill. For verily I say unto you, Till heaven and earth pass, one jot or one tittle shall in no wise pass from the law, till all be fulfilled. Whosoever therefore shall break one of these least commandments, and shall teach men so, he shall be called the least in the kingdom of heaven: but whosoever shall do and teach them, the same shall be called great in the kingdom of heaven" (Matt. 5:17–19).

216 See, as far as the most cited references to the Bible are concerned, Lev. 19:22 and 20:13; Rom. 1:26–27.

matters that essentially fall within the internal domain of such communities and institutions to conduct that clearly implicates public safety, order, health or morals, or the fundamental rights and freedoms of others.

Human persons find themselves in numerous structural or organized social institutions: some through voluntary accession, and others involuntarily. The state is an *institutional social entity* in the latter sense: one's submission to its authority is to a large extent not dependent on the will of its subjects. Because of that, the repository of political power ought to conduct itself, and design its laws, in a manner that would be fair to all its citizens. Any state-imposed arrangement that would prefer one religion over the other, or would discriminate against sections of its population on grounds that are beyond the control of those discriminated against, would be highly unbecoming. A single example will suffice to illustrate the point.

In a publication purporting to reflect the state of religious liberty around the world, the author expresses the view that the "radical homosexual movement" in Canada constitutes "[a]n increasing threat to religious liberty."[217] Proposed legislation that would limit "hate speech" against identifiable groups is here singled out as a manifestation of that threat.

Hate speech proscriptions would not be constitutional in countries, such as the United States, whose constitutional system is founded on libertarian principles, but in countries such as Canada, founded on the primacy of egalitarian considerations, the idea of equal protection of the laws and nondiscrimination would trump the exercise of (unbecoming) free speech. In both systems, religious institutions are permitted to discriminate in their own internal regulations and practices against gays and lesbians, or against women, since the constraints emanating from a bill of rights as a general rule do not apply to the internal household of non-state organizations.

Hate speech legislation almost invariably targets the slandering of persons for what they are, believer or advocate. The church has a special calling to speak out against sin, but sin manifests itself in conduct. Subjecting someone to ridicule or contempt merely on account of their (involuntary) gender-based orientation is as much a crime against humanity as was the condemnation of persons to an inferior status in public life because of their (involuntary) racial extraction under the apartheid system that prevailed in South Africa before 1994. If any religious institution feels constrained to discriminate against persons on the basis of gender or sexual orientation, then so be it; but for the church to demand of the state to do the same in respect to sections of its subjects would be highly inappropriate. The laws of the state ought to strive toward the principle of justice, which requires the equal protection of all by and before those laws.

IX. Restrictions on the Exercise of Freedom of Religion or Belief

The freedom to manifest religion or belief is not an absolute freedom. A distinction should be made between limitations of that freedom on the one hand, and the suspension of freedom of religion or belief on the other.

---

217 Pedro C. Moreno, ed., *Handbook on Religious Liberty Around the World* (Charlottesville: Rutherford, Institute, 1996), 311.

A. Limitations of Freedom of Religion or Belief

The limitations imposed by law on a legally protected right fall into several categories:

- Limitations inherent in the concept of the right being protected;
- Limitations determined by the rights and freedoms of others;
- Limitations in the general interest.

1. The Conceptual Confines of Freedom of Religion or Belief

Entitlements included in the freedom of religion or belief apply only to those modalities of human experience which qualify as matters of "religion" or "belief." One cannot, for example, rely on the constitutional protection of freedom of religion or belief *per se* to substantiate one's right to vote, or to fair labor practices, or for the protection of one's language and culture.

Defining religion is no easy task. The difficulties that confront courts of law when having to determine legal rights or obligations associated with "religion" may be gleaned from South African jurisprudence.

In a case dealing with the old censorship laws of the country, the Appellate Division of the Supreme Court (as it was then called) had to determine when a publication or object would be considered offensive to the religious convictions or feelings of a section of the South African population.[218] The Court decided that "religion" essentially involves the belief in, some kind of commitment to, and the serving of, a supreme being or unseen power.[219] Earlier, a governmental commission of inquiry found that the "Church of Scientology," being "a religion without God and without reverence to a higher power," cannot be regarded as a religion or a church.[220] However, in another matter involving conscientious objections to serve in the defense force, a South African court found that Theravada Buddhism, although a nontheistic religion, was nevertheless "a recognized religious denomination" within the meaning of the Defense Act.[221] More recently, the question arose whether an agnostic pupil could rely on the constitutional provision proclaiming that attendance of religious observances in a state or state-aided institution (in this instance the German School in Pretoria) is to be "free and voluntary," to contest a school rule that made attendance of religious instruction mandatory.[222] Judge Van Dijkhorst held that "religion" is not a neutral concept but denotes a "system of faith and worship [as] the human recognition of superhuman controlling power and especially of a personal God or gods entitled to obedience and worship."[223] He went on to say:

> [Religion] cannot include the concept of atheism or agnosticism which are the very antithesis of religion. The atheist and agnostic is afforded his protection under the freedom of thought, belief and opinion part of this section [on freedom of religion, belief and opinion]. There is conceptionally no room for him under the freedom of religion part. Freedom of religion does not mean freedom from religion. . . .

---

[218] *Publications Act 42,* sec. 47(2) (1974) (subsequently repealed).

[219] Publications Control Board v. Gallo (Africa) Ltd., 3 SALR 665 (S. Afr. Sup. Ct. Appel. Div), 672 (1975).

[220] *Report of the Commission of Inquiry into Scientology,* para. 13(10), R.P. 55 of 1973.

[221] Hartman v. Chairman, Board of Religious Objections, 1 SALR 922 (O)(1987).

[222] Wittmann v. Deutscher Schulverein, Pretoria, 4 SALR 423 (T)(1998).

> When therefore . . . sec. 15(2) of the Constitution permit[s] religious observances, this is a reference to the Jewish, Christian, Moslem, Buddhist and other faiths practising their religion. . . . Religious observances . . . do[] not mean a practice which neither Jew, Christian, Moslem, Buddhist, nor other faiths recognise as such; where the Supreme Being is neither the God of Israel nor the Holy Trinity nor Allah the Merciful etc but a vague nonentity.[224]

The fact that the Court included Buddhism in the list of religions while Buddhism does not believe in, worship, or recognize a "superhuman controlling power" or a "personal God or gods" must not pass unnoticed. It again illustrates the difficulty of definition. Not surprisingly, therefore, many other jurisdictions seek to avoid the dilemma of having to scrutinize the exact meaning of "religion."

In Hungary, the question of defining a religion emerged in a matter concerning the return of school buildings to churches from which those buildings had been taken during the communist regime. The Court in that case rejected an application contesting the constitutionality of restoring the property claims of the church. The argument founded on the separation of church and state[225] was rejected since the return of the buildings to the concerned church institutions did not deprive Hungarian citizens of the right to attend secular schools; a submission that the Act sanctioning the return of the school buildings[226] required adoption by a two-thirds majority, as required by Article 60(4) of the Constitution in respect of any law concerning freedom of conscience and religion, was dismissed since the Act in question did not fall within the confines of the constitutional provision; and the Court likewise rejected the applicant's contention that the law in question conflicted with the constitution and consequently amounted to a constitutional amendment. In the course of its reasoning, the Hungarian Constitutional Court stated that it was not for the state to decide which characteristics ought to be satisfied by any particular belief in order to qualify as a religion: that should be left to "self-interpretation by the churches."[227] The state "can only make appropriate general rules about religion and churches which can be used equally for all churches and religions."[228]

In a comment on Article 18 of the International Covenant on Civil and Political Rights, the Human Rights Committee preferred a wide definition of religion:

> Article 18 protects theistic, non-theistic and atheistic beliefs, as well as the right not to profess any religion or belief. . . . Article 18 is not limited in its application to traditional religions or to religions and beliefs with institutional characteristics or practices analogous to those of traditional religions.[229]

For purposes of applying the international standards of the freedom under consideration, defining "religion" may be avoided, since the same entitlements incorporated into freedom of religion also constitute the substance of freedom of belief. A belief need not be qualified by religious convictions, and the fact that it is not so qualified will not deprive it of the same protection afforded to freedom of religion.

---

[223] Ibid., at 449.

[224] Ibid.

[225] Republic of Hungary Const, Act No. XX as amended, art. 60(3), (1949).

[226] Ibid., Act No. XXXII (1991).

[227] Decision No. 4/1993(II.12) AB, *East European Case Reporter of Constitutional Law* 1, no. 1 (1994): 62.

[228] Ibid.

Whereas atheism and agnosticism will qualify as a belief, it is doubtful whether nonbelief can be said to be either a religion or a belief.

2. Limitations of Freedom of Religion or Belief by Other Rights and Freedoms

Female genital mutilation (FGM) is widely practiced in countries of central and north Africa and the Middle East. Justification for FGM is based on several grounds, including religious grounds.[230] Although the practice of FGM is mostly associated with Islamic sunna, it is also practiced by African Coptic Christians and a small group of Ethiopian Jews called Fallashas.[231] In those factions of Islam practicing FGM, the procedure is viewed as a means of protecting female modesty and chastity, and associated with the high premium placed by the Koran on virginity.[232]

FGM amounts to sexually defined physical mutilation of extreme severity and with irreversible consequences, its practice is almost exclusively inspired by male interests (prolonged sexual pleasure of the male partner), it as such constitutes sex- and gender-based discrimination of the worst kind; and since it is mostly executed while the victim is an infant, it also implicates the rights of the child. The United Nations Declaration on the Elimination of Violence Against Women (1993) mentions FGM as an instance of "violence against women."[233] This raises the question as to an appropriate criterion for balancing freedom of religion or belief with other basic human rights where that freedom comes into conflict with those other rights.

It has often been said that different human rights are equal in status, the one not being more important than any of the others.[234] In cases where the conflicting rights are of equal importance, courts should attempt to strike a fair balance between conflicting rights. The Roman-law adage *sic utere tuo ut alienum non laedas* (exercise your own rights so as not to harm other persons) is not always a useful formula for resolving conflicts of rights in the constitutional context. One could, for example, argue that the Jehovah's Witness who knocks on doors to distribute *The Watch Tower* is free to exercise her evangelical calling as long as she refrains from invading the right to privacy of other persons, or with equal force on basis of the *sic-utere-tuo* approach, that one's right to privacy reaches only as far as would not infringe upon the freedom of members of an evangelical group to spread their faith.

---

229 UN Human Rights Committee General Comment No. 22 (48), para. 2, UN Doc. CCPR/C/21/Rev.1/Add.2 (1993).

230 See Alison T. Slack, "Female Circumcision: A Critical Appraisal," *Human Rights Quarterly* 10 (1988): 446–47; Valerie Oosterveld, "Refuge Status for Female Circumcision Fugitives: Building a Canadian Precedent," *Univ Torornto Fac. of L. Rev.* 51 (1993): 282; Abbie J. Chester, "Justifying the Unjustifiable: Rite v. Wrong," *Buffalo Law Review 45* (1997): 555, 581–86; J. M. T. Labuschagne, "Circumcision and Female Genital Mutilation: A Human Rights and Antropo-Legal Evaluation," *Sou. Afr. Publ. L.* 13 (1998): 287.

231 Oosterveld, "Refuge Status for Female Circumcision Fugitives," 282.

232 Marie Bassili Assaad, "Female Circumcision in Egypt: Social Implications, Current Research, and Prospect for Change," *Studies in Family Planning* 11, no. 1 (1980): 5.

233 *Declaration on the Elimination of Violence Against Women,* 20 December 1993, UNGA Res. 48/104, 48th Sess., art. 2(a), UN Doc. A/48/49 (1994).

234 See Gardiner v. Whitaker, 2 SALR 672 (EC), 690 (1995); 5 BCLR19 (EC), 36 (1994) (Froneman, J. stating that "the Constitution creates no hierarchy of rights").

Canadian courts have attempted to resolve the problem of conflicting rights on the basis of a cost/benefit analysis: the courts assess the harm that would result from, for example, limiting freedom of speech in relation to the harm that might be caused to individuals, sections of the community, or community interests as such if freedom of speech were to be allowed to take its course to the detriment of the right to human dignity or equality.[235] Applying this approach, the Canadian Court found that a law directed against hate speech was constitutional.[236]

Many constitutional systems founded on a bill of rights proclaim the preeminence of certain constitutional rights. In probably all constitutional systems there is in fact a basic *Grundnorm*, determined by the historical circumstances and political structure of the country concerned, which permeates the entire spectrum of rights protection: in Germany, the right to human dignity;[237] in the United States, the First Amendment freedoms (freedom of speech, of the press, and of religion); in Canada, the norm of equal protection; in South Africa, human dignity, equality and freedom (in that preferential order).[238] Because the United States has a libertarian system of human rights protection, its constitutional dispensation has been described as one that sanctions "freedom from, rather than rights to. . . ."[239] Countries where freedoms reign supreme will inevitably uphold the constitutionality of hate speech and pornography, whereas those where egalitarian principles and/or human dignity constitute(s) the most basic norm will feel constrained to outlaw such unbecoming manifestations of freedom of expression. In developing countries, where the government contracted a constitutional obligation to orchestrate the reconstruction and development of society, individual rights to property and to free economic activities may have to give way to state-imposed programs *bona fide* designed and executed for the economic and social upliftment of the people.

There are clear indications in international human rights instruments that preference is to be given to egalitarian rather than libertarian principles. The Universal Declaration of Human Rights and the International Covenant on Civil and Political Rights both proclaim that "recognition of the inherent dignity and of the equal and inalienable rights of all members of the human family *is the foundation of* freedom, justice and peace in the world";[240] and the very title of the 1981 Declaration indicates that its emphasis is on "all forms of intolerance and discrimination" based on religion or belief. According to its preamble, the Declaration is founded on the basic principles of the Charter of the United Nations proclaiming "the dignity and equality inherent in all human beings."[241]

The norm to be derived from these directives is that freedom of religion may never be exercised in a manner that would violate human dignity, and that all forms of state-imposed discrimination based on religion or belief is unacceptable. Since, for example,

---

[235] See R. v. Red Hot Video Ltd., 45 Cr. Rep. (3d) 36 (BCCA) (1985).

[236] R. v. Keegstra, 3 S.Ct. 697 (1990).

[237] Germany, Grundgesetz, art. 1.

[238] SA Const, sec. 36 (defining the "new South Africa" as "an open and democratic society based on human dignity, equality and freedom"); see Van der Vyver, "Constitutional Free Speech and the Law of Defamation," *South African Law Journal* 112 (1995): 572, 593–94, 595.

[239] See S. Marks, "Emerging Human Rights: A New Generation for the 1980's," *Rutgers Law Review* 33 (1981): 438.

[240] UDHR, First Preambular Paragraph; ICCPR, First Preambular Paragraph (emphasis added).

[241] 1981 Declaration, First Preambular Paragraph.

physical mutilation implicates the dignity of the victim, and since racial segregation inevitably amounts to discrimination, the religious rationale offered by some for FGM and for apartheid cannot serve as justification for those practices.

Furthermore, countries founded on libertarian principles which permit freedom of religion or belief to trump individual rights founded on human dignity and equality are at odds with the international standards of human rights protection.

3. Limitations of Freedom of Religion or Belief in the General Interest

Sphere sovereignty of religious institutions and the right to self-determination of religious communities do not mean that such entities and communities within the body politic exist in isolation from one another or from the state structures. Religious communities, among others, may therefore fall afoul of the demands of peaceful coexistence. A critical question always surfaces when religious institutions, or their officials or members acting in the name of religion, violate the laws of the state: How ought the state to respond?

Freedom of religion or belief does not indemnify its repositories against prosecution for criminal conduct or against administrative control in (genuinely) the general interest. Fiscal fraud, extortion, and false advertising ought not to escape the power of the sword simply because such criminal conduct emanates from, or is legitimized by their perpetrators under the guise of, religion. The state must boldly accept the responsibility of regulating medical or psychological therapeutic procedures with a view to disqualifying persons not academically and professionally equipped to practice medicine or psychiatry, and should not avoid enforcing such administrative regulations where transgressions are conducted in the name of religion. Refusal of parents or guardians to submit the children in their care to medical treatment, or to afford assistance to persons in danger, calls for protective state intervention and cannot be excused simply because such omissions were prompted by religious scruples. Consumption of harmful drugs should not be tolerated by law-enforcement agencies merely because it constitutes part of a religious ritual.

The laws of most countries do criminalize unbecoming acts perpetrated under the auspices of religious claims. However, unbecoming religious practices are not always easy to identify. It is undoubtedly true that financial gain rather than spiritual concerns may inspire the missionary practices of those religious sects that promise a place in heaven to converts in exchange for their personal life savings and selfless (money-collecting) services—but who is to say? Many cults only use the guise of religion to entice a prestige- or profit-rendering following into their fold—but how can one tell? Insidious means of proselytism (creating a relationship of dependency through the deprivation of food and sleep, or down-right brainwashing) has become standard practice of several religious sects—but where exactly does one draw the line? Many self-professed "evangelists" shamelessly exploit the miseries of persons in distress, through poverty or illness, in order to secure their subservience—but what can one do?

Here, legal proscription may not be the answer, lest juridical protection were to become the tool of political repression—which simply, again, underscores the truism that the law is not always a feasible instrument for the curtailment of social evils.[242] The focus of the law in matters of religion should remain confined to acts that are clearly and widely recognized as decidedly criminal, or which in the public interest evidently require administrative regulation. Beyond those confines, the norms inherent in the right to self-determination and the principle of sphere sovereignty require that legal proscription must be avoided. There, one ought to fully apply the public's right to information and place one's trust in the powerful virtue of persuasion as a means of cultivating the kinds of conviction that will counteract religious exploitation and which at the same time can withstand moral scrutiny.

B. Suspension of Freedom of Religion or Belief

There are certain advantages attached to the merging under the same umbrella of the entitlements inherent in freedom of religion and those applying to other (nonreligious) belief structures. For one thing, the need to distinguish and to define religious belief—which seems to be quite impossible—thereby becomes almost entirely obsolete.

However, there might also be disadvantages attached to following this course. If the category becomes too expansive—the South African Constitution protects within a single rubric, freedom of conscience, religion, thought, belief, and opinion[243]—political authorities might more readily permit the suspension of the entire package of modalities compounded under a single label. While, for example, the exercise of freedom of religion might be considered a nonderogable right in times of national emergency, the manifestation of certain political beliefs might be considered undesirable if the emergency has been prompted by political insurrection.[244]

Suspension of a constitutionally protected right refers to a competence of political authorities to render those rights inoperative in times of a national emergency.

The Basic Law of Germany proclaims freedom of belief, conscience, religion, and creed to be unassailable in the sense that those freedoms may never be curtailed.[245] Limitations that could be lawfully imposed on certain other constitutional rights may in any event never derogate from the core element of the right.[246]

As internationally perceived, freedom of religion or belief includes two closely related but nevertheless clearly distinguishable entitlements: freedom to adopt a religion or belief of one's own choice; and freedom to manifest that religion or belief in worship, observance, practice, and teaching.[247] The first entitlement relates to the inner act of believing, and the latter to external acts giving expression to one's faith. The entitlement

---

[242] See Van der Vyver, "Law and Morality," *Fiat Iustitia: Essays in Memory of Oliver Deneys Shreiner*, ed. Ellison Kahn (Cape Town: Juta and Co., 1983), 350, 368–69; Van der Vyver, "The Function of Legislation as an Instrument of Social Reform," *South African Law Journal* 93 (1976): 62–67; Van der Vyver, "The State, the Individual and Society," *South African Law Journal* 94 (1977): 303–05.

[243] SA Const, sec. 15(1).

[244] In the (interim) South African Constitution of 1993, freedom of conscience, religion, thought, belief and opinion were among the non-derogable rights. SA Const, Act 200, sec. 34(5)(c) (1993). These freedoms are not listed as non-derogable rights in the (final) South African Constitution of 1996. See SA Const, sec. 37(5)(c).

[245] Germany, Grundgesetz, art. 4(1): "Die Freiheit des Glaubens, des Gewissens und die Freiheit des religiösen und weltanschaulichen Bekenntnissen sind unverletzlich."

[246] Germany, Grundgesetz, art. 19(2): "In keinem Fall darf ein Grundrecht in seinem Wesensgehalt angetasst werden."

[247] See ICCPR, art. 18(1); 1981 Declaration, art. 1(1).

to entertain the inner act of believing is absolute in nature and cannot be subjected to limitations or suspension. The external act of manifesting one's religion or belief can be subjected to limitations, provided the limitations are (1) prescribed by law, and (2) are necessary to protect public safety, order, health or morals, or the fundamental rights of others.[248] Freedom of thought, conscience and religion cannot be suspended in times of national emergency.[249] It is thus a nonderogable right.

This means, in essence, that freedom to manifest one's religion or belief can in the appropriate circumstances be curtailed where such curtailment is strictly required in the interest of public safety, order, health or morals, or the fundamental rights of others, but it can never be taken away entirely; or, to borrow a phrase from the German Basic Law, the limitations imposed upon freedom of religion or belief may never impair the core element of that freedom—not even in a state of emergency that threatens the life of a nation. The principle is stated as follows in the Universal Declaration of Human Rights: "Nothing in this Declaration may be interpreted as implying for any State, group or person any right to engage in any activity or to perform any act aimed at the destruction of any of the rights and freedoms set forth herein."[250]

This means, among other things, that the limitations imposed upon freedom of religion or belief to protect public safety, order, health or morals, or the fundamental rights of others must be proportional to the contingency that prompted the limitation. In *X & Church of Scientology v. Sweden,* the European Commission of Human Rights explained as follows the similar limitation principles that obtains under the European Convention for the Protection of Human Rights and Fundamental Freedoms (in that case in the context of freedom of expression):

> It emerges from the case law of the Convention organs that the "necessity" test cannot be applied in absolute terms, but requires the assessment of various factors. Such factors include the nature of the right involved, the degree of interference, i.e. whether it was proportionate to the legitimate aim pursued, the nature of the public interest and the degree to which it requires protection in the circumstances of the case.[251]

X. Conclusion

There are clear differences between a collection of people sharing a particular religion or belief on the one hand, and institutions created to serve that community such as a church, political party, or management committee. Freedom of religion or belief of, for example, a religious community is dependent on the right to self-determination of members of that community: the right to manifest their religion or belief, individually or in community with other members of their creed and in public or privately, in worship, observance, practice, and teaching. Organized institutions serving that community are entrusted, as against institutions of a different kind such as the state and as

[248] ICCPR, art. 18(3); 1981 Declaration, art. 1(3).

[249] ICCPR, art. 4(2); 1981 Declaration, art. 8 (subordinating the protection of freedom of religion or belief to the provisions of the ICCPR).

[250] UDHR, art. 30.

[251] X and Church of Scientology v. Sweden, App. No. 7805/77 (EComHR 511, 16 Decisions and Reports 70, 5 May 1979), para. 5.

a *sine quo non* for the meaningful exercise of freedom of religion or belief, with a sovereign range of competencies within their own respective spheres of religiously qualified or faith-based activities. Sphere sovereignty constitutes the right to privacy of religious and other faith-based institutions.

The right to self-determination of faith communities and the exercise of sphere sovereignty by the organized structures within those communities do not exist, and cannot be exercised, in isolation from a whole range of other basic human rights and fundamental freedoms, including the right to equal protection and nondiscrimination, freedom of expression, freedom of assembly and association, and an effective remedy to vindicate the freedom of religion or belief or for the protection of the integrity of members of the faith community or the property interest of its organized institutions.

Religious and other faith communities may also gainsay some of the value systems that have come to be associated with the idea of human rights protection. The scriptures of diverse religions ordained punishments which by contemporary standards are denounced as being cruel and inhuman. Proponents of a variety of religions, in defiance of the norm against totalitarianism and discrimination, insist on the establishment of political communities with a distinct commitment to their own religious persuasion. Many religions endorse gender discrimination and condemn people on basis of their sexual orientation. Pro-life protagonists mostly base their opposition to abortions on religious grounds. Child abuse occurs most commonly in fundamentalist religious households. The right to self-determination of faith communities and the sphere sovereignty of religious institutions demand that political authorities refrain from prohibiting internal religious practices merely because they do not coincide with current perceptions of human rights, but should on the other hand impose restrictions on manifestations of religion or belief, when necessary, to protect public safety, order, health or morals, or the fundamental rights of others.

The freedom to manifest one's freedom of religion or belief is thus not an absolute freedom. It is essentially limited to an enclave of entitlements determined by the conceptual meaning of "religion or belief." It must be exercised with due regard for the rights and freedoms of others and within the confines of the *general* interest. However, international law also proclaims the right to freedom of religion or belief to be a nonderogable right: it ought never to be suspended in times of national emergency. The exercise of freedom of religion or belief may thus be subjected to constraints, dictated by the demands of public safety, order, health or morals, or the fundamental rights of others. Those constraints may not impair the core element, the nucleus of meaning, of that freedom. A religion or belief per se may never be regulated, sanctioned, or proscribed by state-imposed coercive means.

CHAPTER 5

FREEDOM OF RELIGION OR BELIEF UNDER INTERNATIONAL HUMANITARIAN LAW AND INTERNATIONAL CRIMINAL LAW

David Llewellyn and H. Victor Condé

I. INTRODUCTION

Religious faith assists people to grapple with the mysteries of life and death, and life after death, to assuage the wrenching personal shocks and spiritual agonies of suffering and loss, to formalize through words and ceremonies the transitions of living friends and family to lost companions, private memories, and silent memorials. Since wars cause such suffering and loss to an exponential degree beyond normal life, religious needs and interests escalate during times of war and armed conflicts.

Or religion may be integral to the controversy and even interposed as a rationalization for violence. Whether through sincere beliefs, however misguided, or the manipulation of religious sympathies or doctrines by malicious leaders, religion often has been the definitive divisive element for disputes that degenerate into the systemic violence of rebellions, revolutions, civil wars, and both noninternational and international armed conflicts.

Heightened religious concerns during the suffering, death, and destruction of military conflicts receive recognition and protection under international humanitarian law, particularly the four Geneva Conventions of 1949 and their two additional protocols of 1977.[1]

When the frenzy of war subsides and considerations of justice resume their natural priority, some specifically antireligious acts of violence or aggression during military conflicts can be addressed through the norms and tribunals of international criminal

[1] *Geneva Convention for the Amelioration of the Condition of the Wounded and Sick in Armed Forces in the Field* (1949) (hereinafter "Geneva Convention I"); *Geneva Convention for the Amelioration of the Condition of Wounded, Sick and Shipwrecked Members of Armed Forces at Sea* (1949) (hereinafter "Geneva Convention II"); *Geneva Convention Relative to the Treatment of Prisoners of War* (1949) (hereinafter "Geneva Convention III"); *Geneva Convention Relative to the Protection of Civilian Persons in Time of War* (1949) (hereinafter "Geneva Convention IV"); *Protocol Additional to the Geneva Conventions of 12 August 1949, and Relating to the Protection of Victims of International Armed Conflicts* (1977) (hereinafter "Additional Protocol I"); *Protocol Additional to the Geneva Conventions of 12 August 1949, and Relating to the Protection of Victims of Non-International Armed Conflicts* (1977) (hereinafter "Additional Protocol II").

Tore Lindholm, W. Cole Durham, Jr., Bahia G. Tahzib-Lie (eds.), Facilitating Freedom of Religion or Belief: A Deskbook, *125–146.*

law, applying only the most salient and critical elements of humanitarian law which have become universally recognized as crimes against humanity, genocide, and those violations of the laws and customs of war identified as war crimes—as in the Rome Statute of the International Criminal Court of 1998[2] and its predecessors, the Statute of the International Criminal Tribunal for the Former Yugoslavia,[3] and the Statute of the International Criminal Tribunal for Rwanda.[4]

Religion receives varying forms of recognition and protection under international law, whether expressed in peacetime legal human rights norms, in wartime humanitarian guarantees, or in postwar criminal codes and judgments of international tribunals. These overlapping approaches have begun to yield to the inevitable centripetal pull toward convergence, presaging a time when they will be seamlessly integrated into a unified framework of uniform, natural, inalienable, and universal norms adapted to all times, circumstances, and human conditions.

Humanitarian law, arising out of its historic context and its specific purpose to promote humane treatment of people and to ameliorate their suffering during times of war, has inherent limitations to its application. The Geneva Conventions generally apply only for the duration of the armed conflict[5] and only to protected persons under the conventions, such as wounded and noncombatant members of the military, armed forces on land[6] and naval forces,[7] prisoners of war,[8] and alien civilians.[9] But the universality of the humanitarian norms underlying the laws of war is not entirely suppressed in the specifics of the Geneva Conventions. First, common article 3, identical in each

---

[2] UN Doc. A/CONF.183/9, as corrected by the procès-verbaux of 10 November 1998 and 12 July 1999. *The Rome Statute of the International Criminal Court* (hereinafter "Rome Statute") was adopted by a UN Diplomatic Conference of Plenipotentiaries on the Establishment of an International Criminal Court, Rome, 17 July 1998. The Rome Statute entered into force on July 1, 2002. Pursuant to the Final Act of the Conference, a Preparatory Commission, composed of states which have signed the treaty, is structuring the Court, drafting Rules of Procedure and Rules of Evidence, and Elements of the Crimes, and related aspects of the Court. Now that the Statute has entered into force, an Assembly of States Parties will monitor the working of the ICC. The ICC is a judicial organ independent from the United Nations but having a legal relation to the UN by express international agreement.

[3] *Statute of the International Tribunal for the Prosecution of Persons Responsible for Serious Violations of International Humanitarian Law Committed in the Territory of the Former Yugoslavia since 1991,* SC Res. 808, UN SCOR, 48th Sess., 3175th mtg., UN Doc. S/RES/808 (1993), approved by SC Res. 827, UN Doc. S/RES/827 (1993) of 25 May 1993. The International Criminal Tribunal for the Former Yugoslavia has prosecuted defendants for numerous crimes whose victims were identified in part by their religion.

[4] *Statute of the International Criminal Tribunal for the Prosecution of Persons Responsible for Genocide and Other Serious Violations of International Humanitarian Law Committed in the Territory of Rwanda and Rwandan Citizens Responsible for Genocide and Other Such Violations Committed in the Territory of Neighboring States between 1 January 1994 and 31 December 1994,* SC Res. 955, UN SCOR, 49th Sess., 3453d mtg., UN Doc. S/RES/955 (1994), adopted 8 November 1994 [hereinafter "ICTR Statute"].

[5] The conventions apply during "declared war or . . . any other armed conflict," Geneva Convention I, art. 2, and the identical language of article 2 of all four Geneva Conventions; and until "final repatriation" of protected persons, Geneva Convention I, art. 5.

[6] Geneva Convention I applies to members of the "armed forces of a Party to the conflict" (Geneva Convention I, art. 13), "who have fallen into the hands of the enemy" (Geneva Convention I, art. 5).

[7] "[T]he present Convention shall apply only to forces on board ship" (Geneva Convention II, art. 4). Forces that come ashore are subject to Geneva Convention I.

[8] Protected persons, "prisoners of war," are limited to specified people in "the power of the enemy" (Geneva Convention III, art. 4).

[9] "Persons protected" are those "in the hands of a Party to the conflict or Occupying Power of which they are not nationals" (Geneva Convention IV, art. 4).

of the four Geneva Conventions, declares three minimum standards even concerning domestic violence, during "armed conflict not of an international character," (1) requiring noncombatants to be "treated humanely, without any adverse distinction founded on race, color, religion or faith, sex, birth or wealth, or any other similar criteria"; (2) prohibiting violence, hostage taking, outrages upon personal dignity, and extrajudicial sentences and executions; and (3) requiring care for the sick and wounded. Nondiscrimination on the basis of "religion or faith" is one of the essential minimum standards of humanitarian law under all circumstances. Second, article 72 of Additional Protocol I invokes substantive human rights into the "humanitarian protection of civilians and civilian objects in the power of a Party to the conflict contained in the Fourth Convention," by incorporating "other applicable rules of international law relating to the protection of ***fundamental human rights*** during international armed conflict" (emphasis added). Third, article 75 of Additional Protocol I and article 4 of Additional Protocol II expressly protect freedom of religion or belief, not only against discrimination,[10] but also as affirmative, substantive entitlements for all noncombatants: "Each Party shall respect the person, honor, convictions and religious practices of all such persons."[11] "All persons who do not take a direct part or who have ceased to take part in hostilities . . . are entitled to respect for their person, honor and convictions and religious practices."[12]

Not only has international humanitarian law recognized and invoked human rights, but human rights instruments have crossed over into the field of humanitarian law, the theater of armed conflicts.[13] The responsibilities of all people to protect human rights and dignity, and particularly religious belief and practice, have crossed military lines already, in that human rights under the International Covenant on Civil and Political Rights (hereinafter "ICCPR") apply during times of armed conflict. This application can be seen from the unrestricted language of the descriptions of the possessors of human rights under the ICCPR, e.g., "every human being," "everyone," "all persons," and the language of the derogation clause in article 4. First, human rights can be derogated under the ICCPR only "In time of public emergency which threatens the life of the nation." [14] Human rights persist therefore even during times of armed conflict, until hostilities reach the stage of emergency that the life of the nation is jeopardized, and then human rights can be derogated only "to the extent strictly required by the exigencies of the situation" and cannot "involve discrimination solely on the ground of . . . religion."[15] Second, under the nonderogation provisions, "[n]o derogation" may be made from the right to freedom of thought, conscience, and religion protected by article 18.[16] Third, the limitations clause in the ICCPR provision regarding freedom of religion or belief[17] pointedly does not include "national security"

---

[10] "[W]ithout any adverse distinction based upon . . . religion or belief." See also Additional Protocol II, art. 2.

[11] Additional Protocol I, art. 75(1).

[12] Additional Protocol II, art. 4(1).

[13] For a survey of historical sources and trends, see H. Victor Condé, "Protection of Religious Freedoms under International Humanitarian Law and International Human Rights Law in Times of Armed Conflict," *U.C. Davis Journal of International Law and Policy* 5 (winter 1999): 95–110.

[14] ICCPR, art. 4(1).

[15] ICCPR, art. 4(2).

[16] ICCPR, art. 4(2).

[17] ICCPR, art. 18(3).

as a legitimate ground for limiting manifestation of religion or belief, although "national security" appears among the proper grounds for limitation of the rights to freedom of expression, assembly, and association.[18] Fourth, the ICCPR prohibits "[a]ny propaganda for war" and "[a]ny advocacy of national, racial or religious hatred that constitutes incitement to discrimination, hostility or violence."[19]

International humanitarian law provides the core legal basis for the international criminal tribunals and their jurisdiction. "The International Tribunal for Rwanda shall have the power to prosecute persons responsible for serious violations of international humanitarian law,"[20] "persons committing genocide,"[21] "persons responsible for the following crimes," which constitute "crimes against humanity,"[22] and "persons committing or ordering to be committed serious violations of article 3 common to the Geneva Conventions of 12 August 1949 for the Protection of War Victims, and of Additional Protocol II thereto of 8 June 1977."[23]

The worldwide reaction of abhorrence at the atrocities perpetrated against religious and other minorities during World War II provided the genesis for criminal enforcement of rights recognized under international humanitarian law. The postwar Nuremberg trials imposed criminal sanctions for war crimes based upon universally acknowledged, albeit previously only partially articulated, norms of personal responsibility which bind every human being, notwithstanding contrary domestic laws or military orders. Among the core crimes is religious persecution.[24] These supranational standards are characteristic of, and implicit in, humanitarian law, which operates despite conditions of war, martial law, and the absence of functional civil legal institutions.[25]

Genocide entered the canon of international crimes with the adoption in 1948 of the Genocide Convention, which shows the intersection of human rights, humanitarian and criminal law perspectives, declaring that "genocide is a crime under international

---

[18] ICCPR, arts. 19(3), 21, and 22(2).

[19] ICCPR, art. 20.

[20] ICTR Statute, art. 1.

[21] ICTR Statute, art. 2(1).

[22] ICTR Statute, art. 3.

[23] ICTR Statute, art. 4.

[24] The criminal norms imposed in the Nuremberg trials were declared in the "Nuremberg Charter" (also known as the "London Charter"), including "crimes against peace," "war crimes," and "crimes against humanity," defined as "murder, extermination, enslavement, deportation, and other inhumane acts committed against any civilian population, before or during war, or persecution on political, racial, or religious grounds in execution of or in connection with any crime within the jurisdiction of the tribunal, whether or not in violation of the domestic law of the country where perpetrated" (Adam Roberts and Richard Guelff, eds., *Documents on the Law of War,* 2d ed. [Oxford: Clarendon Press, 1989], 153–56).

[25] The post–World War II focus on the international protection of human rights and fundamental freedoms, which produced the Charter and organization of the United Nations (1945), the *Universal Declaration of Human Rights* (1948) (hereinafter "UDHR") and the *Convention on the Prevention and Punishment of the Crime of Genocide* (1948) (hereinafter "Genocide Convention"), provided the impetus for the restatement and expansion of international humanitarian law in the Geneva Conventions of 1949. (The UN Charter opens with the words, "We the peoples of the United Nations, determined to save succeeding generations from the scourge of war.") Humanitarian law standards at the time of the Nuremberg trials were distilled from earlier, foundational documents of humanitarian law, proceeding from such sources as the *Convention for the Amelioration of the Conditions of the Wounded Armies in the Field,* 22 August 1864, Geneva and *The Hague Convention Respecting the Laws and Customs of War on Law,* 18 October 1907 (hereinafter "The Hague Convention IV"). The Hague Convention IV, art. 18, states that "[p]risoners of war shall enjoy

law, contrary to the spirit and aims of the United Nations" and that it is punishable "whether committed in time of peace or in time of war."[26] The crime of genocide consists of acts intended to eliminate people identified with a particular "national, ethnical, racial or religious group, as such."[27]

An "international penal tribunal" for trying persons charged with genocide is postulated in the Genocide Convention, and the UN General Assembly adopting the draft convention called upon the International Law Commission "to study the desirability and possibility of establishing an international judicial organ for the trial of persons charged with genocide."[28] In 1998, this process culminated in the Rome Statute of the International Criminal Court.

The Rome Statute has as its purpose the establishment of a permanent International Criminal Court to adjudicate prosecutions of criminal violations of "the most serious crimes of concern to the international community as a whole," which are genocide, crimes against humanity, and war crimes.[29] "War crimes" means "[g]rave breaches of the Geneva Conventions of 12 August 1949" as listed in the Rome Statute "against persons or property protected under the provisions of the relevant Geneva Convention;"[30] "[o]ther serious violations of the laws and customs applicable in international armed conflict, within the established framework of international law;"[31] "[i]n the case of armed conflict not of an interational character, serious violations of article 3 common to the four Geneva Conventions;"[32] "[o]ther serious violations of the laws and customs applicable in armed conflicts not of an international character, within the established framework of international law,"[33] which may include conflicts "in the territory of a state when there is protracted armed conflict between government authorities and organized armed groups or between such groups."[34]

Religious identity and freedom are protected under each of the three categories of international crimes enforceable through the Rome Statute. First, "genocide" consists of attacks against people identified with a "national, ethnical, racial or religious group," by killing, causing serious bodily or mental harm, imposing conditions of life calculated to destroy the group physically, in whole or in part, preventing births or transferring children out of the group.[35] Second, "crimes against humanity," includes "[p]ersecution against any identifiable group or collectivity on . . . religious . . .

---

complete liberty in the exercise of their religion," and art. 46 that "religious convictions and practice must be respected."

[26] Genocide Convention, Preamble and art. I.

[27] Genocide Convention, art. II. Genocide has ripened into customary international law, a jus cogens peremptory norm binding on all nations, which no national law or international agreement can contravene and for which there is no immunity, despite official status or claims of superior orders.

[28] Genocide Convention, art. VI.

[29] Rome Statute, art. 5–8. For elements of the crimes, see the *Report of the Preparatory Commission for the International Criminal Court,* Finalized Draft Text of the Elements of Crimes, 6 July 2000, PCNICC/2000/INF/3/Add.2.

[30] Rome Statute, art. 8(2)(a).

[31] Rome Statute, art. 8(2)(b).

[32] Rome Statute, art. 8(2)(c).

[33] Rome Statute, art. 8(2)(e).

[34] Rome Statute, art. 8(2)(f).

[35] Rome Statute, art. 6. This language is taken verbatim from the Genocide Convention, art. II.

grounds."[36] International human rights law inheres in the definition of "persecution" under the Rome Statute as "the intentional and severe deprivation of fundamental rights contrary to international law by reason of the identity of the group or collectivity."[37] Religious and other persecution constitutes a "crime against humanity" under the Rome Statute "in connection with . . . any crime within the jurisdiction of the Court," without any requirement of a nexus to war or armed conflict.[38] Third, the specified "grave breaches" of the Geneva Conventions which represent "war crimes" under the Rome Statute include "[i]ntentionally directing attacks against buildings dedicated to religion,"[39] and "[i]ntentionally directing attacks against . . . personnel using the distinctive emblems of the Geneva Conventions in conformity with international law," which includes chaplains and various religious personnel and ministers of religion.[40]

Finally, international human rights law serves also as a check against any possible abuse by the International Criminal Court of its humanitarian law enforcement authority, in that the application and interpretation of the international criminal court statute "must be consistent with internationally recognized human rights" and must be applied in a nondiscriminatory manner.[41] Due process rights of criminal defendants are protected under human rights instruments and customary international human rights law, as are the rights of the accused to a fair trial without religious bias.

II. Parameters of Freedom of Religion or Belief under International Human Rights, Humanitarian, and Criminal Law

The process of the convergence of the language and implementation of rights, freedoms, human dignity, and humanitarian intervention into an integrated conceptual scheme and a functional legal whole highlights some noteworthy distinctions in approaches to matters relating to religion or belief among the various systems.[42]

---

[36] Rome Statute, art. 7(1)(h). The ICTR Statute contains an element in the definition of "crimes against humanity" which has been eliminated from the Rome Statute and which has a religious aspect. The Rome Statute, art. 7(1), states that, "For the purpose of this Statute, 'crime against humanity' means any of the following acts when committed as part of a widespread or systematic attack directed against any civilian population, with knowledge of the attack." The ICTR Statute, art. 3, omits "with knowledge of the attack" and substitutes "on national, political, ethnic, racial or religious grounds," thereby adding invidious specific intent as an element of the crime, which is omitted from the general scienter language of the Rome Statute.

[37] Rome Statute, art. 7(2)(g).

[38] Rome Statute, art. 7(1)(h).

[39] Rome Statute, arts. 8(2)(b)(ix), 8(2)(e)(iv). The protection of religious, historical, educational, cultural and similar sites reflects the provisions in the Hague Convention for the Protection of Cultural Property in the Event of Armed Conflict, art. 1(a) (1954, entry into force 1956), <http://www.unesco.org/culture/laws/hague/html_eng/fulltest.htm> (accessed 19 August 2001), which identifies "property of great importance to the cultural heritage of every people, such as monuments of architecture, art or history, whether religious or secular; archeological sites . . . works of art; manuscripts, books and other objects." See Additional Protocol I, art. 53, and Additional Protocol II, art. 16, including protection of "works of art or places of worship which constitute the cultural or spiritual heritage of peoples."

[40] Rome Statute, arts. 8(2)(b)(xxiv), 8(2)(e)(ii).

[41] Rome Statute, art. 21(3).

[42] For a historical analysis of freedom of religion or belief and the genesis of the sovereign state as the locus of legal rights, through the Protestant Reformation, see Daniel Philpott, "The Religious Roots of Modern International Relations," *World Politics* 52 (January 2000): 206–45.

A. Humanitarian Law Provides for Affirmative Intervention for People's Spiritual Welfare

Humanitarian law presumes the necessity of, and affirmatively provides for, assistance and intervention by chaplains and religious personnel for the "spiritual needs" and "spiritual welfare" of people under war conditions.[43] Religion is more than just a prohibited ground for adverse distinction or discrimination, as in the checklist of "race, color, religion or faith, sex, birth, wealth, or any other similar criteria."[44] Unlike the other categories of nondiscrimination, religion receives affirmative protection and the special assistance of religious personnel during times of armed conflict.

People need access to religious guidance during war. War brings death and intensifies questions concerning the meaning of life. Is anything in this world worth dying for? If so, why? Obviously in war the aggressor believes that something is worth killing for. Does that justify killing the aggressor and its soldiers? Or is life too sacred to participate on either side of the conflict? Do conditions of war justify actions that I would find morally repugnant, reprehensible, and inconceivable acting as a private person? Are my personal moral and religious convictions subservient to the needs and demands of the state? Am I a traitor to my country, my community, or my family if I oppose this war and refuse to serve in the military? Does God approve of this war and my participation in it? Will my actions in this conflict have eternal consequences? Everyone compelled to confront such issues by the circumstances of war surely is entitled to the assistance of religious counselors of his faith and choice to provide guidance, if desired. "Chaplains" and "religious personnel" are treated like medical personnel under humanitarian law, categories of people whose specialized expertise becomes invaluable under wartime conditions.

Protecting people against religious and other forms of discrimination and providing for freedom of religious belief and practice, to the extent possible under the constraints of a military regime, are important during war, as at all times, but it is the very nature of war that gives rise to the unique provisions under the Geneva Conventions that single out ministers, chaplains, and religious advisors for affirmative protection and assistance, unlike any provisions of human rights law.

B. Protected Religion is Intended to Serve Humanitarian Ends

Religion is not defined under international humanitarian law, criminal law, or human rights law, and it serves divergent functions in each system. The studied absence of a definition performs a useful service, but it also conceals a significant legal flaw which is manageable in current international criminal law, troublesome in human rights law, but virtually irreconcilable to humanitarian law.

The broadest range of meaning assigned to religion appears in international human rights law, where it is encompassed with the triplet phrase, "thought, conscience and religion" in article 18 of the ICCPR, which immediately adds the summary phrase "religion or belief." The breadth of these undefined terms is acknowledged and

---

[43] E.g., Geneva Convention I, art. 28. See section IV.G of the categorical analysis of the religion-related provisions of the Geneva Conventions and their Additional Protocols.

[44] Geneva Conventions, common art. 3.

emphasized in the 1981 United Nations Declaration on the Elimination of All Forms of Intolerance and of Discrimination Based on Religion or Belief (hereinafter "1981 Declaration"),[45] which states that, "Everyone shall have the right to freedom of thought, conscience and religion. This right shall include freedom to have a religion or ***whatever*** belief of his choice."[46] Clearly this indefinite terminology is intended to provide room for all belief systems religious, atheistic, secular, antireligious, and all variations thereof since all conceptions of life are deserving of protection and respect.[47] That is the theory, because to define religion inevitably means to include some conceptions and to exclude others, and who has the wisdom, authority, or arrogance to deny someone else the right to freedom of conscience and personal faith?

Nevertheless, a very real, visible, divisive, and diabolical discrepancy exists concerning the meaning of protected religion within international legal systems, particularly related to armed conflicts. What about religions that condone violence or promote war? What about religious systems that refuse to tolerate other religions and beliefs? What about religions with different conceptions of human rights, or humanitarian behavior, or criminal conduct than that espoused by international law? Alongside pronouncements extolling principles of equality and nondiscrimination before the law for freedom of thought, conscience, religion or belief in the Preamble to the 1981 Declaration appear these clashing paragraphs:

> Considering that the disregard and infringement of human rights and fundamental freedoms, in particular of the right to freedom of thought, conscience, religion or whatever belief, have brought, directly or indirectly, wars and great suffering to mankind, especially where they serve as a means of foreign interference in the internal affairs of other States and amount to kindling hatred between peoples and nations. . . .
>
> Considering that it is essential to promote understanding, tolerance and respect in matters relating to freedom of religion and belief and to ensure that the use of religion or belief for ends inconsistent with the Charter of the United Nations, other relevant instruments of the United Nations and the purposes and principles of the present Declaration is inadmissible,
>
> Convinced that freedom of religion and belief should also contribute to the attainment of the goals of world peace, social justice and friendship among peoples.

Religion is not protected simply for its own sake or for the liberty of conscience of the individual. Protected religions serve humanitarian purposes, and religions and beliefs which transgress these humanitarian ends are undeserving of protection. Such

---

[45] UN General Resolution 36/55, 36th UN GAOR Supp. (No. 51) at 171, UN Doc. A/36/684 (1981). United Nations, *Human Rights: A Compilation of International Instruments* (New York: United Nations, 1993), 122–25.

[46] 1981 Declaration, art. 1(1), emphasis added. The 1981 Declaration omits the provision in ICCPR, art. 18, of freedom to "adopt a religion or belief," and the similar provision in UDHR, art. 18, of "freedom to change his religion or belief," while it broadens the scope of "thought, conscience and religion" and "religion or belief" to embrace "whatever belief."

[47] "Considering that religion or belief, for anyone who professes either, is one of the fundamental elements in his conception of life and that freedom of religion or belief should be fully respected and guaranteed" (1981 Declaration, Preamble, para. 4).

religions are "inadmissible." Although the language of international law seems to admit all religious beliefs on terms of equality, in reality protected religion has definitive boundaries.

International criminal law can function without having to confront the unresolved dichotomy within the meaning of religion. A crime of genocide involving attacks against a religious group, by killing, causing serious bodily or mental harm, imposing conditions of life calculated to destroy the group physically, in whole or in part, preventing births or transferring children out of the group,[48] can be prosecuted even if the victimized group itself advocates religious hatred and intolerance or practices violence or even genocide. The religious status of the victim is irrelevant. Similarly, persecution against an identifiable religious group may be prosecuted as a crime against humanity,[49] even though the persecuted group itself advocates and practices persecution of others. Actual self-defense would, of course, present a different issue.

A hypothetical problem can be posed to highlight the clash of basic values and the latent controversy concerning protection of intolerant or violently aggressive religions, by considering, for example, the meaning of "[c]ausing serious . . . mental harm" or nonphysical "persecution" of members of religious groups under international criminal law.[50] Would attempts to promote a religion of tolerance to an intolerant religious minority be a potential criminal act? Or, to put it another way, might a program of human rights education which taught religious tolerance contrary to the beliefs and practices of an intolerant ethnic group be unlawful religious persecution?

International human rights law, on its face, appears to shield any system of thought or religion, "whatever belief," regardless of its teachings, yet functionally it excludes some religious beliefs and practices as "inadmissible" and unworthy of protection because of their attitudes and actions pertaining to intolerance, violence, and war. Thus human rights norms broaden the meaning of "religion" to admit conceptions of life outside belief in God, the supernatural, a moral order, doctrines, rites, or an identified community of believers, and then narrow the meaning again to affirm only belief systems that respect the peaceful, humanistic, and humanitarian ends of human rights, respect for human dignity, and the development of the human personality. In the ICCPR, freedom to manifest religion or belief may be restricted on various counts, i.e.: (1) by "such limitations as are prescribed by law and are necessary to protect public safety, order, health, or morals or the fundamental rights and freedoms of others;"[51] (2) by prohibitions against "propaganda for war" and "advocacy of national, racial or religious hatred that constitutes incitement to discrimination, hostility or violence;"[52] (3) by the rights of "ethnic, religious or linguistic minorities . . . in community with the other members of their group, to enjoy their own culture, to profess and practise their own religion, or to use their own language;"[53] and (4) by the authority of the state to restrict freedom of expression, assembly, and association "in the interests of national security."[54] What remains problematic in human rights law is

---

[48] Rome Statute, art. 6.
[49] Rome Statute, art. 7(1)(h).
[50] Rome Statute, arts. 6(b), 7(2)(g).
[51] ICCPR, art. 18(3).
[52] ICCPR, art. 20.
[53] ICCPR, art. 27.
[54] ICCPR, arts. 19, 21–22.

whether offensive belief systems and religions, which refuse to denounce war, violence, and intolerance should receive equal protection under other human rights norms, particularly (1) religious nondiscrimination and equality before the law,[55] (2) equal rights to participate in public affairs and public service without religious distinctions,[56] and (3) parental rights to direct "the religious and moral education of their children in conformity with their own convictions."[57] Religious (and religion-like) attitudes toward war and armed conflict, it thus appears, may exert an influence upon the construction and implementation of human rights norms regarding freedom of religion or belief.

In humanitarian law, undefined and unrestricted references to religion or belief, which do not distinguish intolerant and violently aggressive religious beliefs and systems, present apparently irreconcilable conflicts with aspects of the norms of the Geneva Conventions. The purpose of humanitarian conventions is to provide healing, comfort, protection, and a temporary legal order for persons under war conditions, until restoration of peace and the rule of law. The roles of chaplains, ministers, religious personnel, and their equivalents are specially protected because they contribute to the healing and comfort of the suffering. Humanitarian law does not contemplate providing special protection, facilities, and access to civilians, prisoners of war, and out-of-combat military personnel for religious counselors whose message and mission is to teach intolerance, division, and disrespect for the lives and dignity of all human beings. Like the medical attendants whose rights of safe passage and protection they share, religious workers serve only one purpose, to heal. Doctors who worsen their patients' conditions with defective medical care surely must forfeit their special status, and so must religious agents who promote hatred and animosity rather than solace and good will. Despite the commitment to equal protection "without adverse distinction founded on . . . religion,"[58] humanitarian law implicitly rejects forms of "religion or faith" which espouse inhumane attitudes and treatment of other people rather than tolerance.

III. Comparative Protections of Freedom of Religion or Belief under Humanitarian, Criminal, and Human Rights Law

A. Freedom of Thought, Conscience, and Religion

A variety of international human rights instruments, in particular the 1981 Declaration, provide a comprehensive human rights framework for observing and analyzing, by comparison, religious and belief rights and freedoms under humanitarian law, particularly the Geneva Conventions and their Protocols, and international criminal law under the Rome Statute. This section compares human rights norms regarding freedom of religion or belief with the corresponding provisions of international criminal law and international humanitarian law.

---

[55] ICCPR, art. 26.
[56] ICCPR, art. 25.
[57] ICCPR, art. 18(4).
[58] Geneva Convention, common art. 3.

1. Freedom to Have and to Choose Religion or Belief

International human rights norms provide that "Everyone shall have the right to freedom of thought, conscience and religion. This right shall include freedom to have a religion or whatever belief of his choice." [59] This is the human rights guarantee of internal freedom of religion or belief.

International criminal law implicitly recognizes freedom of belief by its protection of members of religious belief systems from genocide, persecution, and destruction of religious property.[60]

The Geneva Conventions recognize more implicitly than explicitly internal freedom. The presence of significant religious commitments and practices among military personnel, prisoners of war, and civilians is an unstated premise underlying numerous provisions in the conventions. The conventions presume the prior existence of a duty on the part of the parties to the conflict to recognize the "spiritual needs,"[61] and "spiritual . . . well being,"[62] of the people affected by the fighting. Based on this presupposition, Geneva Convention I declares that this preexisting responsibility is not diminished by the state of war. "None of the preceding provisions shall relieve the Detaining Power of the obligations imposed upon it with regard to the . . . spiritual welfare of the prisoners of war."[63]

"Prisoners' representatives shall further the . . . spiritual . . . well-being of prisoners of war."[64] "The Internee Committees shall further the . . . spiritual . . . well-being of the internees."[65]

Freedom of religion or belief does receive express recognition for civilians under Geneva Convention IV and for all noncombatants in the two Additional Protocols. "Protected persons are entitled, in all circumstances, to respect for their persons, their honor, their family rights, their religious convictions and practices, and their manners and customs."[66] Additional Protocol I affirmatively acknowledges both freedom of religious belief and religious practice, without discrimination, as the standard of all people involved in armed conflict who are not more fully protected under other provisions of the Conventions. "[P]ersons who are in the power of a Party to the conflict and who do not benefit from more favorable treatment under the Conventions or under this Protocol shall be treated humanely in all circumstances and shall enjoy, as a minimum, the protection provided by this article without any adverse distinction based upon . . . religion or belief. . . . Each Party shall respect the person, honor, convictions and religious practices of all such persons."[67] Additional Protocol II likewise affirmatively acknowledges freedom of religious belief and practice, without discrimination. "All persons who do not take a direct part or who have ceased to take part in hostilities . . . are entitled to respect for their person, honor and convictions and religious practices. They shall in all circumstances be treated humanely, without any adverse distinction."[68]

---

[59] See, e.g., 1981 Declaration, art. 1(1).
[60] Rome Statute, arts. 6–8.
[61] Geneva Convention I, art. 28.
[62] Geneva Convention III, art. 80, and Geneva Convention IV, art. 103.
[63] Geneva Convention I, art. 28.
[64] Geneva Convention III, art. 80.
[65] Geneva Convention IV, art. 103.
[66] Geneva Convention IV, art. 27.
[67] Additional Protocol I, art. 75(1).

2. Freedom to Manifest Religion or Belief[69]

Freedom of religion or belief under human rights law includes "freedom, either individually or in community with others and in public or private, to manifest his religion or belief in worship, observance, practice and teaching."[70] This is the human rights guarantee of external freedom of religion or belief.

International criminal law recognizes freedom to manifest religion, again implicitly, by its protection of members of religious groups from genocide, persecution, and destruction of religious property.[71] But interference with the religious practices of other people is not *per se* an international crime.

Under humanitarian law, freedom to manifest religion is explicitly protected for prisoners of war and civilian internees under Geneva Conventions III and IV and, for others, under the Additional Protocols:

"Prisoners of war shall enjoy complete latitude in the exercise of their religious duties."[72] "Protected persons [civilians] are entitled, in all circumstances, to respect for . . . their religious convictions and practices, and their manners and customs."[73] For "protected persons," nonrepatriated alien civilians, "the following rights will be granted to them: . . . [t]hey shall be allowed to practice their religion and to receive spiritual assistance from ministers of their faith."[74] "Internees shall enjoy complete latitude in the exercise of their religious duties, including attendance at the services of their faith."[75]

"[P]ersons deprived of their liberty for reasons related to the armed conflict . . . shall be allowed to practise their religion."[76] "Each Party shall respect the . . . religious practices of all such persons."[77]

3. Freedom from Religious or Belief Coercion

International human rights norms state that no one shall be subject to coercion which would impair his freedom to have a religion or belief of his choice.[78]

International criminal law does not utilize the term "coercion," but coercion comprises a tacit component of the "mental harm" or "conditions of life" elements of genocide, or of religious persecution.[79]

Geneva Convention IV protects against religious coercion in terms that mirror the rights of refugees seeking asylum under other norms of international law: "In no circumstances shall a protected person be transferred to a country where he or she may have reason to fear persecution for his or her . . . religious beliefs."[80]

---

[68] Additional Protocol II, art. 4(1); see art. 2.
[69] Section V elaborates on this freedom.
[70] See, e.g., 1981 Declaration, art. 1(1).
[71] Rome Statute, arts. 6–8.
[72] Geneva Convention III, art. 34.
[73] Geneva Convention IV, art. 27.
[74] Geneva Convention IV, art. 38(3).
[75] Geneva Convention IV, art. 93.
[76] Additional Protocol II, art. 5(1)(d).
[77] Additional Protocol I, art. 75(1).
[78] See, e.g., 1981 Declaration, art. 1(2).
[79] Rome Statute, arts. 6–7.

B. Legitimate Limitations on Freedom to Manifest Religion or Belief

International human rights norms clarify that freedom to manifest a religion or belief may be subject only to such limitations as are prescribed by law and are necessary to protect public safety, order, health, morals, or the fundamental rights and freedoms of others.[81] Freedom of religion or belief is, however, not subject to derogation.[82]

The Rome Statute has no provisions for states parties to limit the meaning or enforcement of any of its criminal provisions. No reservations may be made to the statute by states parties.[83]

Under the Geneva Conventions freedom of religion or belief cannot be derogated or renounced, nor can the conventions be construed to restrict, rather than enhance, freedom of religion or belief. Logistical necessities, however, may restrict manifestation of religion or belief under some circumstances. For example, "The Detaining Power may limit the number" of religious representatives in its territory, provided that "such limitation shall not hinder the effective operation of adequate relief to all prisoners of war."[84]

Freedom of religion or belief of chaplains, prisoners of war and others cannot be derogated by special agreements outside the conventions. "No special agreement shall adversely affect the situation of the wounded and sick, of members of the medical personnel or of chaplains, as defined by the present Convention, nor restrict the rights which it confers upon them."[85] "No derogation" is permitted under circumstances of military constraint, concerning substitutionary Protecting Powers.[86]

Rights under the Geneva Conventions, including the right to freedom of religion or belief, cannot be renounced by the protected persons, not even voluntarily. In this sense, Geneva Convention rights are inalienable. "Wounded and sick, as well as members of the medical personnel and chaplains, may in no circumstances renounce in part or in entirety the rights secured to them by the present Convention."[87]

The Geneva Conventions must increase and augment humanitarian protections and cannot be used to diminish the capacities of humanitarian organizations to provide relief, including the work of chaplains. "The provisions of the present Convention constitute no obstacle to the humanitarian activities . . . for the protection of wounded and sick, medical personnel and chaplains, and for their relief."[88]

---

[80] Geneva Convention IV, art. 45.

[81] See, e.g., 1981 Declaration, art. 1(3).

[82] ICCPR, art. 4(2).

[83] Rome Statute, art. 120.

[84] Geneva Convention III, art. 125.

[85] Geneva Convention I, art. 6; so also in Geneva Convention II, art. 6 ["wounded, sick and shipwrecked persons"]. Cf. "No special agreement shall adversely affect the situation of prisoners of war, as defined by the present Convention, nor restrict the rights which it confers upon them." Geneva Convention III, art. 6.

[86] Geneva Convention I, art. 10.

[87] Geneva Convention I, art. 7; so also in Geneva Convention II, art. 7: "wounded, sick and shipwrecked persons."

[88] Geneva Convention I, art. 9; so also in Geneva Convention II, art. 9: "wounded, sick and shipwrecked persons." Cf. Geneva Convention III, art. 9.

C. Prohibition of Discrimination on the Basis of Religion or Belief

International human rights norms prohibit discrimination on the basis of religion or belief, whether by government or by private actors. The 1981 Declaration, for instance, states: "No one shall be subject to discrimination by any State, institution, group of persons, or person on the grounds of religion or other belief."[89]

By itself, discrimination is not a basis for criminal prosecution under international law, but discriminatory intent is an essential element of the definitions of the crimes of genocide and unlawful persecution. Justice also requires that international criminal law must be administered "without any adverse distinction founded on . . . religion or belief."[90]

Nondiscrimination on the basis of religion or belief is integral to the Geneva Conventions, appearing not only in common article 3,[91] but in the contexts of general protections and specific injunctions. The Geneva Conventions directly address discrimination under government auspices, principally by military forces. A duty to prevent private acts of religious prejudice may be inferred from the general principles against discrimination.

Common article 3 of the Geneva Conventions provides that "Persons taking no active part in the hostilities . . . shall . . . be treated humanely, without any adverse distinction founded on . . . religion or faith." Other relevant provisions point out that the selection of medical personnel and chaplains released by an adverse party shall be made "irrespective of any consideration of . . . religion"[92] and that "[m]embers of the armed forces and other persons . . . who are wounded or sick . . . shall be treated humanely . . . without any adverse distinction founded on . . . religion."[93]

Additional Protocol I reiterates the nondiscrimination standard for the broadest possible range of protected persons. "This Part . . . shall apply to all those affected by a situation referred to in article 1, without any adverse distinction founded on . . . religion or belief."[94] Nondiscriminatory access to items used in religious ceremonies receives specific protection. The "Occupying Power shall . . . without any adverse distinction, also ensure the provision of . . . objects necessary for religious worship."[95]

Additional Protocol II maintains the nondiscrimination standards: "This Protocol shall be applied without any adverse distinction founded on . . . religion or belief."[96]

---

[89] 1981 Declaration, art. 2(1); see also arts. 2–4.

[90] Rome Statute, art. 21(3).

[91] Geneva Conventions, common art. 3(1).

[92] Geneva Convention I, art. 31.

[93] Geneva Convention I, art. 12; see also Geneva Convention II, art. 12 (naval personnel), Geneva Convention III, art. 16 (prisoners of war), and Geneva Convention IV, arts. 13, 27 (civilians).

[94] Additional Protocol I, art. 9(1) (cf. "[N]o distinction . . . founded on any grounds other than medical ones," Additional Protocol I, art. 10[2]).

[95] Additional Protocol I, art. 69(1).

[96] Additional Protocol II, art. 2(1). This "adverse distinction" principle is incorporated into Additional Protocol II, art. 4(1) (requiring people to be "treated humanely, without any adverse distinction") and art. 18(2) (requiring humanitarian relief efforts to be conducted "without any adverse distinction").

D. Rights of Parents and Children to Religion or Belief and Religious Education

International human rights norms guarantee parents the right to educate their children according to their religion or belief and guarantee children access to education consistent with the religion or belief of their parents.[97]

The form of denial of religious education rights of parents or children would have to rise to a level of persecution on religious grounds impermissible under international law to be prosecutable as a criminal violation or involve proof of "serious . . . mental harm" or forcible transfer of children to another religious group under the principles of genocide.[98] The education rights violation would be subsumed within the greater crime.

The Geneva Conventions acknowledge religious education rights of parents and children. "The Parties to the conflict" have duties to provide for children who are "orphaned or are separated from their families," particularly concerning "the exercise of their religion and their education."[99] "[T]he Occupying Power shall make arrangements for the maintenance and education, if possible by persons of their own nationality, language and religion, of children who are orphaned or separated from their parents as a result of the war."[100]

When children must be evacuated to a foreign country, "each child's education, including his religious and moral education as his parents desire, shall be provided while he is away with the greatest possible continuity." The child's identity card should include "the child's religion, if any."[101] "Children . . . shall receive an education, including religious and moral education, in keeping with the wishes of their parents."[102]

IV. Comparison of Humanitarian and Criminal Law Protection of Manifestation of Religion or Belief with Specific Human Rights Norms

Article 6 of the 1981 Declaration lists nine specific illustrations of the human right to manifest freedom of thought, conscience, religion, or belief. This section demonstrates that these illustrations are also recognized in varying degrees in humanitarian law. Each illustration provided by the 1981 Declaration is matched below with the corresponding provisions of the Geneva Conventions. Given the very different origins and purposes of these international instruments, the close degree of correlation is remarkable. Two elements of criminal persecution under the Rome Statute which protect religious places and personnel from direct military attacks also are noted, with their parallel provisions under the Protocols Additional to the Geneva Conventions.

---

[97] 1981 Declaration, art. 5. In the Declaration, parental rights are subject to the qualification that a child should be raised "in a spirit of understanding, tolerance, friendship among peoples, peace and universal brotherhood, respect for freedom of religion or belief of others, and in full consciousness that his energy and talents should be devoted to the service of his fellow men" (1981 Declaration, art. 5[3]).

[98] Rome Statute, arts. 6, 7.

[99] Geneva Convention IV, art. 24.

[100] Geneva Convention IV, art. 50.

[101] Additional Protocol I, art. 78(2).

[102] Additional Protocol II, art. 4(3)(a).

A. Freedom to Worship or Assemble in Connection with a Religion or Belief, and to Establish and Maintain Places for These Purposes[103]

Worship and assembly in proper places and with religious leaders are protected in the Geneva Conventions. As to worship services, "[p]risoners of war shall enjoy . . . attendance at the service of their faith."[104] Furthermore, "[t]he Occupying Power shall permit ministers of religion to give spiritual assistance to the members of their religious communities."[105]

As to places of worship, facilities needed to perform religious duties must be provided for captured chaplains and religious personnel. In this vein, "chaplains while retained by the Detaining Power . . . shall . . . be granted all facilities necessary to provide for the . . . religious ministration to prisoners of war."[106] "Adequate premises shall be provided where religious services may be held."[107] "The Detaining Power shall place at the disposal of interned persons, of whatever denomination, premises suitable for the holding of their religious services."[108]

Places of worship are specially protected under humanitarian law from military use and military attack. Additional Protocol I prohibits "to commit any acts of hostility directed against . . . places of worship which constitute the cultural or spiritual heritage of peoples."[109] Religious and cultural sites are granted presumptions in favor of their protection. "In case of doubt whether an object which is normally dedicated to civilian purposes, such as a place of worship" is being used for military purposes, the presumption is that it is not being so used.[110] Additional Protocol I further declares that willful attacks on various sites, including "places of worship which constitute the cultural or spiritual heritage of peoples," which places are not being used militarily by the adverse party and are not located in the immediate proximity of military objectives, resulting in their "extensive destruction," are "grave breach[es]" of the Geneva Conventions and the Additional Protocol and shall be regarded as "war crimes."[111]

Additional Protocol II repeats the prohibition against attacking historic sites, but without the references to grave breaches and war crimes: "[I]t is prohibited to commit any acts of hostility directed against historic monuments, works of art or places of worship which constitute the cultural or spiritual heritage of peoples, and to use them in support of the military effort."[112]

Under the Rome Statute, intentional military attacks against "buildings dedicated to religion" and other culturally valuable uses, in violation of the Geneva Conventions or the laws and customs of war, are "war crimes." [113]

---

[103] 1981 Declaration, art. 6(a). See also sections IV.E and IV.G on teaching and leadership.
[104] Geneva Convention III, art. 34.
[105] Geneva Convention IV, art. 58.
[106] Geneva Convention III, art. 33.
[107] Geneva Convention III, art. 34.
[108] Geneva Convention IV, art. 86.
[109] Additional Protocol I, art. 53(a).
[110] Additional Protocol I, art. 52(3).
[111] Additional Protocol I, arts. 85(4)(d), 85(5).
[112] Additional Protocol II, art. 16.
[113] Rome Statute, arts. 8(2)(b)(ix), 8(2)(e)(iv).

B. Freedom to Establish and Maintain Appropriate Charitable or Humanitarian Institutions[114]

Charitable and humanitarian institutions are not addressed directly in the Geneva Conventions, but the humanitarian and charitable functions of existing religious institutions are recognized in the permission for religious representatives to visit and assist protected persons in occupied territories. The "representatives of religious organizations . . . shall receive . . . all facilities for visiting the protected persons, for . . . religious purposes, or for assisting them. . . . Such societies or organizations may be constituted in the territory of the Detaining Power, or in any other country, or they may have an international character. The Detaining Power may limit the number of societies and organizations whose delegates are allowed to carry out their activities in its territory and under its supervision, on condition, however, that such limitation shall not hinder the supply of effective and adequate relief to all protected persons."[115]

The appointment of "a qualified layman" to serve as a chaplain, "shall take place . . . wherever necessary, with the approval of the local religious authorities of the same faith."[116]

C. Freedom to Make, Acquire, and Use to an Adequate Extent the Necessary Articles and Materials Related to the Rites or Customs of a Religion or Belief[117]

The Geneva Conventions provide for the acquisition of religious items, particularly for ceremonial rites and customs and devotional use. "Prisoners of war shall be allowed to receive . . . articles of a religious . . . character which may meet their needs, including books, devotional articles . . . and materials."[118] "Each High Contracting Party shall allow the free passage of all . . . objects necessary for religious worship intended only for civilians of another High Contracting Party, even if the latter is its adversary."[119] These rights are reaffirmed succinctly in Additional Protocol I. The "Occupying Power shall . . . without any adverse distinction, also ensure the provision of . . . objects necessary for religious worship."[120]

D. Freedom to Write, Issue, and Disseminate Relevant Publications in the Areas of Religion or Belief[121]

The Geneva Conventions contain no provisions substantially corresponding to this publication freedom.

---

[114] 1981 Declaration, art. 6(b).

[115] Geneva Convention IV, art. 142; so also in Geneva Convention III, art. 125, for prisoners of war.

[116] Geneva Convention III, art. 37.

[117] 1981 Declaration, art. 6(c).

[118] Geneva Convention III, art. 72.

[119] Geneva Convention IV, art. 23. See also Geneva Convention IV, art. 58, authorizing "books and articles required for religious needs," and Geneva Convention IV, art. 108, "books and objects of a devotional . . . character" for internees.

[120] Additional Protocol I, art. 69(1).

[121] 1981 Declaration, art. 6(d).

E. Freedom to Teach a Religion or Belief in Places Suitable for These Purposes[122]

As already observed, suitable places for assembly and worship are provided under the Geneva Conventions. Considering that people in other, less suitable and less accessible areas also need spiritual attention, the Geneva Conventions ensure rights of safe passage for "religious personnel" to a besieged or encircled area or an area of recent combat.[123] "The Parties to the conflict shall endeavor to conclude local agreements for the removal from besieged or encircled areas of [specified persons] . . . for the passage of ministers of all religions . . . on their way to such areas."[124] Chaplains are entitled to access and transportation to people also in labor units and hospitals outside a prisoner of war camp.[125]

Even criminal defendants are entitled to religious counsel. "Protected persons accused of offenses . . . shall also have the right to receive any spiritual assistance which they may require."[126]

F. Freedom to Solicit and Receive Voluntary Financial and Other Contributions from Individuals and Institutions[127]

The Geneva Conventions contain no provisions substantially corresponding to this religious solicitation freedom.

G. Freedom to Train, Appoint, Elect, or Designate by Succession Appropriate Leaders Called for by the Requirements and Standards of any Religion or Belief[128]

The Geneva Conventions specially protect chaplains and religious personnel, generally in the same manner as medical personnel are protected.[129] Unlike human rights law, which addresses primarily the structural autonomy and integrity of religious institutions and their leadership, the protections under the Geneva Conventions relate to practical functions, such as identification, safety, respect, religious work assignments, and facilities.

The "representatives of religious organizations . . . shall receive . . . all necessary facilities for visiting the prisoners, distributing . . . material, from any source, intended for religious . . . purposes, and for assisting them."[130] People who have been separated

---

[122] 1981 Declaration, art. 6(e). See also the sections IV.A and IV.G on worship and leadership.
[123] Geneva Convention I, art. 15; Geneva Convention II, art. 18.
[124] Geneva Convention IV, art. 17.
[125] Geneva Convention I, art. 28.
[126] Geneva Convention IV, art. 76.
[127] 1981 Declaration, art. 6(f).
[128] 1981 Declaration, art. 6(g). See also sections IV.A, IV.E and IV.I on worship, teaching and religious community communications.
[129] See Geneva Convention I, arts. 4, 6–7, 9–11, 15, 24, 28, 30–31, 40, 46; Geneva Convention II, arts. 5–7, 9–11, 18, 36, 37, 42, 47; Geneva Convention III, arts. 4, 11, 16, 33–37, 125; Additional Protocol I, art. 15.
[130] Geneva Convention III, art. 125.

from their religious communities by war are entitled to available religious assistance. "[P]ersons deprived of their liberty for reasons related to the armed conflict . . . shall be allowed . . . if requested and appropriate, to receive spiritual assistance from persons, such as chaplains, performing religious functions."[131]

Chaplains and religious personnel are to be accorded respect and protection "in all circumstances."[132] "The religious . . . personnel . . . shall, if they fall into the hands of the enemy, be respected and protected."[133] Part of this special respect is that religious personnel in the naval forces "may not be captured."[134] Additional Protocol I expands this protection to religious personnel on a broader range of ships.[135] Additional Protocol II enunciates that "religious personnel shall be respected and protected and shall be granted all available help for the performance of their duties."[136]

For safety purposes, chaplains and religious personnel wear the same arm emblems and carry the same special identity cards as medical personnel.[137] "Civilian religious personnel" equally receive the identification and protection afforded medical personnel.[138]

Religious leaders continue their religious duties even after their capture. The work of chaplains is to be limited to their "religious duties."[139] Chaplains "who fall into the hands of the adverse Party, shall be retained only in so far as . . . the spiritual needs and the number of prisoners of war require. . . . [T]hey shall continue to carry out . . . their . . . spiritual duties on behalf of prisoners of war, preferably those of the armed forces to which they themselves belong."[140]

Ministers of any religion "retained" by an adverse party are to be treated and to serve as chaplains. "Prisoners of war who are ministers of religion, without having officiated as chaplains to their own forces, shall be at liberty, whatever their denomination, to minister freely to the members of their community. For this purpose, they shall receive the same treatment as the chaplains retained by the Detaining Power. They shall not be obliged to do any other work."[141]

In the absence of a chaplain or prisoner of war minister, "a qualified layman, if such a course is feasible from a confessional point of view, shall be appointed" at the request and with the agreement of the "prisoners concerned" and "wherever necessary, with the approval of the local religious authorities of the same faith."[142]

---

[131] Additional Protocol II, art. 5(1)(d).
[132] Geneva Convention I, art. 24.
[133] Geneva Convention II, art. 37.
[134] Geneva Convention II, art. 36.
[135] Additional Protocol I, art. 23(5).
[136] Additional Protocol II, art. 9.
[137] Geneva Convention I, art. 40; Geneva Convention II, art. 42; Additional Protocol I, art. 18; Additional Protocol II, art. 12.
[138] Additional Protocol I, arts. 15, 66.
[139] Geneva Convention I, art. 28.
[140] Geneva Convention I, art. 28; so also in Geneva Convention II, art. 37, and Geneva Convention III, art. 35 ("amongst prisoners of war of the same religion, in accordance with their religious conscience").
[141] Geneva Convention III, art. 36.
[142] Geneva Convention III, art. 37.

Chaplains "shall not be deemed prisoners of war."[143] As protected persons, "reprisals" against chaplains and religious personnel are prohibited.[144] The protections for chaplains under the Geneva Conventions and any supplementary agreements cannot be diminished by agreements among the High Contracting Parties,[145] nor renounced by the chaplains.[146]

Religious personnel are distributed according to military identifications, languages and religious practices. "They [chaplains] shall be allocated among the various camps and labor detachments containing prisoners of war belonging to the same forces, speaking the same language or practising the same religion."[147]

The religious designations of the recipients are the primary determinants. "[P]rotected persons," nonrepatriated alien civilians under Geneva Convention IV, "shall be allowed . . . to receive spiritual assistance from ministers of their faith."[148] "The Occupying Power shall permit ministers of religion to give spiritual assistance to the members of their religious communities."[149] "Ministers of religion who are interned shall be allowed to minister freely to the members of their community," and in order to accomplish this "the Detaining Power shall ensure their equitable allocation" according to language and religion, shall provide facilities, means of transportation and authorization to visit internees, and when necessary shall allow appointment by the "local religious authorities of the same faith" of ministers or qualified laymen.[150]

"Religious personnel," as clarified by Additional Protocol I, means "military or civilian persons, such as chaplains, who are exclusively engaged in the work of their ministry and attached to various armed forces, medical and civil defense organizations, whether permanently or temporarily."[151] "Civilian religious personnel" also are entitled to respect and protection.[152] Chaplains, as noncombatants, have no right to participate directly in hostilities.[153]

Under the Rome Statute, intentional military attacks against chaplains, religious personnel, and ministers of religion who are "using the distinctive emblems of the Geneva Conventions in conformity with international law," constitute "war crimes."[154]

H. Freedom to Observe Days of Rest and to Celebrate Holidays and Ceremonies in Accordance with the Precepts of One's Religion or Belief[155]

The Geneva Conventions do not specifically recognize days of rest and holidays, although religious worship services, as previously noted, are protected. But special and explicit provision is made in the Geneva Conventions concerning funeral rites and treatment of the remains of the dead.

[143] Geneva Convention I, art. 30; so also in Geneva Convention III, art. 33, and acknowledged in art. 4.
[144] Geneva Convention I, art. 46; Geneva Convention II, art. 47.
[145] Geneva Convention I, art. 6 and Geneva Convention II, art. 6.
[146] Geneva Convention I, art. 7, and Geneva Convention II, art. 7.
[147] Geneva Convention III, art. 35.
[148] Geneva Convention IV, art. 38(3).
[149] Geneva Convention IV, art. 58.
[150] Geneva Convention IV, art. 93.
[151] Additional Protocol I, art. 8(d); see also Additional Protocol I, arts. 62–63 (religious assistance in civil defense work).
[152] Additional Protocol I, art. 15(5).

The dead are to be treated with honor and respect for their religion. Burial or cremation ceremonies are to be "based on the religion of the deceased" and the "rites of religion" to which the dead belonged.[156] "[P]risoners of war who have died in captivity are [to be] honorably buried, if possible according to the rites of the religion to which they belonged. . . . Bodies may be cremated . . . on account of the religion of the deceased."[157]

I. Freedom to Establish and Maintain Communications with Individuals and Communities in Matters of Religion and Belief at the National and International Levels[158]

Communication for purposes of religious direction and administration of religious duties is to be effectuated under the Geneva Conventions both with local military authorities and with both local and international religious authorities and organizations. First, chaplains are entitled to direct access and facilities for communication and correspondence with the authorities of the camp in order to carry out their spiritual duties.[159] Second, chaplains "shall be free to correspond, subject to censorship, on matters concerning their religious duties with the ecclesiastical authorities in the country of detention and with international religious organizations,"[160] and similar communication rights are accorded to "ministers of religion" to correspond with local and international religious officials "of their faith."[161]

V. Moral Conscience: The Source of Religion, International Human Rights, Humanitarian, and Criminal Norms

Even a brief comparative analysis of freedom of religion or belief in international humanitarian, criminal, and human rights law must acknowledge that the relevant instruments do not reveal the origins or the extent of the rights they enunciate. International humanitarian law may have come into existence as a recognized body of legal norms in the Geneva Conventions and their predecessors, human rights may date its origin as a definitive part of the international legal system from the UDHR, international criminal law may become universally enforceable under the Rome Statute, but the moral obligation to treat other human beings humanely, which is the spirit of humanitarian law, to respect the inherent human dignity of all people, which is the heart of human rights law, and to protect peaceful people from oppression and persecution because of their birth or beliefs, which is the essence of international criminal law, preexisted these documents and their legal obligations, because their truths are

---

[153] Additional Protocol I, art. 43(2).
[154] Rome Statute, arts. 8(2)(b)(xxiv), 8(2)(e)(ii).
[155] 1981 Declaration, art. 6(h).
[156] Geneva Convention I, art. 17; also incorporated into Geneva Convention II, art. 20.
[157] Geneva Convention III, art. 120; so also in Geneva Convention IV, art. 130, concerning the deaths of civilian internees.
[158] 1981 Declaration, art. 6(i). See also section IV.G on leadership.
[159] Geneva Convention I, art. 28; Geneva Convention III, art. 33.
[160] Geneva Convention III, art. 35.
[161] Geneva Convention IV, art. 93.

rooted in the human conscience. Freedom of conscience is closely linked to freedom of religion or belief, for from human conscience originates recognition of universal spiritual realities and moral values, religious consciousness, human dignity, and humanitarian concerns for suffering and injustice visited upon any member of the human family.

All of the Geneva Conventions contain explicit recognition and reliance upon the shared moral conscience of the human family. The denunciation clause of each convention states that even if a High Contracting Party denounces and withdraws from the convention, it remains bound by other inescapable, universal moral duties. "The denunciation . . . shall in no way impair the obligations which the Parties to the conflict shall remain bound to fulfill by virtue of the principles of the law of nations, as they result from the usages established among civilized peoples, from the laws of humanity and the dictates of the public conscience."[162]

Additional Protocol I restates this fundamental proposition in the following language: "In cases not covered by this Protocol or by other international agreements, civilians and combatants remain under the protection and authority of the principles of international law derived from established custom, from the principles of humanity and from dictates of public conscience."[163] Finally, the Preamble to Additional Protocol II declares the principle of prior and superintending moral law in still clearer terms of universal applicability: "Recalling that, in cases not covered by the law in force, the human person remains under the protection of the principles of humanity and the dictates of the public conscience." [164]

It is from these common moral resources, inherent in the human conscience, that religious canons, humanitarian creeds, axioms of justice, and human rights precepts derive their high calling and their supreme authority.

---

[162] Geneva Convention I, art. 63; Geneva Convention II, art. 62; Geneva Convention III, art. 142; Geneva Convention IV, art. 158.
[163] Additional Protocol I, art. 1(2).
[164] Additional Protocol II, Preamble, para. 4.

Chapter 6

Permissible Restrictions on Freedom of Religion or Belief

Manfred Nowak and Tanja Vospernik

I. Introduction

There is no doubt that freedom of thought, conscience, religion, and belief is one of the most important human rights, enjoying as it does even the privileged status of a nonderogable right. On the other hand, freedom of religion or belief protects phenomena that can be among the most controversial and dangerous in human existence, as religions and ideological belief systems can and all too often have been misused to stir up intolerance, discrimination, prejudice, hatred, and violence. When ethnic and religious criteria coincide, as for example in the former Yugoslavia, the resulting agitation can have horrendous results, including the possibilities of war and even genocide.

Governments may be key actors in such discriminatory policies by clearly siding with one (usually the majority) religion and by assisting or exploiting this religion in its policy of restricting and discriminating against other religions, beliefs, or philosophies. Governments may, however, also try to maintain a neutral position in the conflict between different religious groups. Whatever their approach, however, there will be some cases in which they will be called upon to make use of their power under international human rights law to restrict the manifestation of religion or belief.

Governmental interference might also be necessary to resolve conflicts between members of the same religion or belief or even between parents and children who adhere to the same religion. For example, if Jehovah's Witnesses, on the basis of their religious belief, refuse a life-saving blood transfusion to their six-year-old child, does the state have a right or even a duty to restrict this manifestation of religion in order to protect the child's right to life? If hundreds of adherents to a particular religious group follow the call of their leaders to commit suicide, as has recently happened in a number of highly publicized events, is this still part of the so-called *forum internum*—the internal realm in which freedom of thought, conscience, and religion reigns absolute—or is governmental interference legitimate or even obligatory?

It is surprising that many of the burning issues regarding freedom of religion or belief including the most violent religious conflicts have not given rise to more litigation before international human rights monitoring bodies. Although only the interplay

Tore Lindholm, W. Cole Durham, Jr., Bahia G. Tahzib-Lie (eds.), Facilitating Freedom of Religion or Belief: A Deskbook, *147–172.*

between the principle of freedom of religion and its restrictions truly determines the actual scope of this important right, the exact meaning of the terms used in the respective limitation clauses has only partly been clarified by international case law.

As a practical matter, human rights recognized under international law may be restricted by governments by means of, *inter alia*, reservations, declarations of interpretation, derogation (in emergency situations), deprivation in case of abuse, or specific limitation clauses.[1] In the following, we will focus on the meaning and scope of limitation clauses by analyzing relevant case law of the European Commission and Court of Human Rights, the UN Human Rights Committee, and other international and domestic bodies.

II. Is the Private Freedom of Thought, Conscience, Religion and Belief (*Forum Internum*) an Absolute Right?

The limitation clauses in Article 18(3) of the International Covenant on Civil and Political Rights (ICCPR), Article 9(2) of the European Convention on Human Rights (ECHR) and Article 12(3) of the American Convention on Human Rights (ACHR) apply only to the freedom to *manifest* one's religion or beliefs, and do not apply to the internal dimension of thought, conscience, religion, or belief. In addition, under Articles 4(2) ICCPR and 27(2) ACHR, even in times of war or public emergency, no derogation from freedom of thought, conscience, religion or belief is permitted. Although Article 9 ECHR is not among the nonderogable rights listed in Article 15(2) ECHR, scholars express doubts as to whether any derogations from the private freedom of thought, conscience, religion, or belief could be legally justified.[2] This is not likely to make much difference in practice, since all parties to the European Convention are also parties to the subsequently ratified ICCPR, and are obligated to abide by its provisions, including its nonderogation provisions. In any event, the freedoms of the *forum internum* are, therefore, widely regarded as absolute freedoms.[3] States are under an absolute obligation to refrain from interfering with the *forum internum* by means of religious or ideological indoctrination, "brainwashing," or other forms of manipulation.[4] At the same time, they have responsibility to prevent private parties,

[1] See Manfred Nowak, "Limitations on Human Rights in a Democratic Society," *Austrian–Soviet Round-Table on the Protection of Human Rights*, ed. Franz Matscher and Wolfgang Karl (Kehl, Germany: N. P. Engel Verlag, 1992), 169.

[2] See Francis G. Jacobs and Robin C. A. White, *The European Convention on Human Rights*, 2d ed. (New York: Oxford University Press, 1996), 211; Pieter van Dijk and Fried van Hoof, *Theory and Practice of the European Convention on Human Rights*, 3d ed. (The Hague: Kluwer Law International, 1998), 557. In practice, no derogations have been made in relation to both private and public freedom of religion or belief pursuant to any of the respective human rights treaties concerned. Even reservations are highly exceptional. Only Norway in 1952 entered a reservation on ECHR, Article 9 concerning its then constitutional provision of not tolerating Jesuits. The reservation was withdrawn after a respective amendment to the Constitution of 1814. Mexico made a declaration of interpretation concerning ICCPR, Article 18 to the effect that public religious acts must be performed in places of worship and that studies carried out in establishments designed for the professional education of ministers of religion are not officially recognized. The Mexican Government regarded these restrictions to be covered by the limitation clause of ICCPR, Article 18(3).

[3] Van Dijk and van Hoof, *Theory and Practice of the European Convention*, 541; Malcolm D. Evans, *Religious Liberty and International Law in Europe* (Cambridge: Cambridge University Press, 1997), 221, 317; Karl Josef Partsch, "Freedom of Conscience and Expression, and Political Freedoms," *The International Bill of*

including religious groups, from engaging in coercive, manipulative, or fraudulent forms of indoctrination.[5] This obligation is underscored by the right of everybody in Article 18(2) ICCPR and Article 12(2) ACHR not to be subjected to coercion or restrictions which would impair the freedom to have, maintain, or change one's religion or belief.[6]

The "absolute" protection of the *forum internum* against indoctrination is, however, not as absolute as it may seem at first glance. As the European Court has observed in the Greek proselytism cases, the right to manifest one's religion through teaching includes the right to try to convince one's neighbors of the truthfulness of one's own religion or belief.[7] At the same time, Muslims challenge the view that there is a right to convert from Islam to another religion. Accordingly, it is no surprise that Muslim countries, along with others having dominant religions that tend not to be actively engaged in evangelizing, have opposed an explicit right to change one's religion and the encouragement of concomitant missionary activities. How should one balance the right to teach religious views and to convince others with the "absolute" right of others not to suffer violation of their *forum internum*? At what point does the state have a right or even a duty to intervene in order to protect freedom of thought and religion?

The separate opinions of some judges in the European Court of Human Rights in the Kokkinakis case illustrate the broad range of approaches to this human rights conflict.[8] While Judge Martens argued that "there is no justification for the State to use its power 'to protect' the proselytised," Judge Valticos strongly defended state interference for the prevention of religious indoctrination. The majority opinion adopted a middle path, which recognized the permissibility of placing restrictions on this freedom in carefully delimited domains in order to reconcile the interests of the various groups and to ensure that everyone's beliefs are respected. It drew a distinction between "bearing Christian witness" and "improper proselytism" and expressed the view that while the former was "an essential mission and a responsibility of every Christian

Rights: The Covenant on Civil and Political Rights, ed. Louis Henkin (New York: Columbia University Press, 1981), 212. See also sec. 3 of Human Rights Committee General Comment 22 (1993) adopted by the UN on 20 July 1993. On the drafting history and interpretation of this General Comment see Bahiyyih G. Tahzib, *Freedom of Religion or Belief: Ensuring Effective International Legal Protection* (Boston: Martinus Nijhoff, 1996), 307.

[4] See David J. Harris, Michael O'Boyle, and Chris Warbrick, *Law of the European Convention on Human Rights* (London: Butterworths, 1995), 360; Manfred Nowak, *U.N. Covenant on Civil and Political Rights: ICCPR Commentary* (Kehl, Germany: N. P. Engel Verlag, 1993), 314.

[5] See Kokkinakis v. Greece, 17 EHRR 397 (1994) (ECtHR 260-A, 25 May 1993). See also Jochen A. Frowein and Wolfgang Peukert, *Europäische Menschenrechtskonvention: EMRK Kommentar,* 2d ed. (Kehl, Germany: N. P. Engel Verlag, 1996), 371.

[6] On the controversial question whether freedom of religion in ICCPR, Article 18 also entails the right to change one's religion see Evans, *Religious Liberty and International Law in Europe,* 201; Nowak, *U.N. Covenant on Civil and Political Rights,* 312, 317. In General Comment 22, paragraph 5, the Human Rights Committee observed that the freedom to have or to adopt a religion or belief "necessarily entails the freedom to choose a religion or belief, including the right to replace one's current religion or belief with another or to adopt atheistic views." ECHR, Article 9(1) and ACHR, Article 12(1) explicitly recognize the freedom to change one's religion.

[7] Kokkinakis v. Greece; Larissis and Others v. Greece, 27 EHRR 329 (1999) (ECtHR 1998-I, 24 February 1998). For the facts of these cases see III.E.1 in this chapter.

[8] See Kokkinakis v. Greece and Larissis and Others v. Greece; see also Evans, *Religious Liberty and International Law in Europe,* 332.

and every Church," the latter represented "a corruption or defamation of it." The *forum internum* is, therefore, only protected in cases of improper, i.e., manipulative, fraudulent, or coercive behavior.[9]

Another restriction of the *forum internum* derives from the human rights of parents, under Articles 18(4) ICCPR, 12(4) ACHR and paragraph 2 of the first protocol to the ECHR, to ensure the religious and moral education of their children in conformity with their own convictions. This right of parents to "indoctrinate" their children by means of baptizing babies or similar practices in non-Christian religions definitely imposes a restriction on the "absolute" right of everyone, including children,[10] to adopt a religion or belief of one's own choice.

These examples were selected to show that even the internal freedom of thought, conscience, religion, or belief may in fact be subject to legitimate interference from outside and needs to be balanced against the rights of parents, religious leaders, missionaries, and private or public teachers. In the following, we will, however, focus on the restrictions which states may legitimately impose on the freedom to manifest one's religion or belief through worship, observance, practice, and teaching. A comparison with similar limitation clauses regarding other human rights shows fewer grounds for restriction which means that the protection of freedom of religion or belief appears superior to that afforded by freedom of expression, assembly and association, or the right to privacy.[11]

Under Articles 18(3) ICCPR, 9(2) ECHR, and 12(3) ACHR, limitations of the freedom to manifest one's religion or beliefs are only justified if they are prescribed by law (i.e., set down in a general, abstract parliamentary act or an equivalent unwritten norm of common law which is accessible and adequately specified so that one can foresee its application); if they serve one of the five listed purposes (public safety, order, health, morals, protection of rights and freedoms of others), and if they are necessary (in Article 9[2] ECHR necessary in a democratic society), i.e., proportional and, as the European Court holds in constant jurisprudence, responding to a "pressing social need." As a general rule, limitations shall be strictly interpreted and must, of course, not be discriminatory.[12] In the following, we will attempt to shed some light on the five limitation grounds by referring to selected case law.

III. Grounds for Legislative Limitations

A. Restrictions for the Protection of Public Safety

The main purpose of the "public safety" clause is to allow restrictions on the public manifestation of religion (a religious assembly, procession, burial ceremony, etc.) if a specific danger arises threatening the safety of persons (their life, integrity, or health)

---

[9] The suggestion of Malcolm Evans to exclude "improper proselytism" from the scope of coverage of ECHR, Article 9 would, in our opinion, constitute a wrong approach (Evans, ***Religious Liberty and International Law in Europe,*** 334). Even extreme forms of missionary activities are, of course, a manifestation of religion through teaching which enjoy the protection of freedom of religion, albeit within the limits of the respective restriction clauses.

[10] See ***Convention on the Rights of the Child,*** art. 14(1).

[11] See Harris, O'Boyle, and Warbrick, ***Law of the European Convention on Human Rights,*** 358, 363.

[12] See General Comment 22, para. 8. See section IV of this chapter.

or property.[13] This is particularly the case when hostile religious groups confront each other (as, e.g., in Northern Ireland, Bosnia and Herzegovina, India, or Nigeria) or when religious customs are used to serve political interests. Where such direct religion-related threats to the safety of persons or property exist, states are authorized to take measures that are strictly necessary and proportional to protect public safety, including the prohibition or dissolution of a religious assembly, and in extreme cases, even the prohibition of particularly dangerous religious groups (above all those inciting to religious hatred or war propaganda in contravention of Article 20 ICCPR), and criminal action against the perpetrators. In the case of *M. A. v. Italy,* the Human Rights Committee deemed a criminal conviction for attempting to reorganize the dissolved fascist party in Italy a permissible interference with freedom of belief pursuant to Article 18(3) CCPR.[14] Similarly, the European Commission of Human Rights justified the conviction of an Austrian for neo-nazi activities in relation to Article 9(2) ECHR.[15]

Most cases in which governments invoke the "*public* safety" clause relate, however, to measures taken to protect the *individual* safety of those affected. In the case of *X v. UK,* the European Commission of Human Rights considered the British law requiring all motorcyclists to wear crash helmets (and the repeated criminal convictions of the applicant) as permissible for the protection of public safety, even as applied to Sikhs and even though, by the time the decision was given, the British law provided an exception in favor of Sikhs.[16] Similarly, the Human Rights Committee held in *Singh Bhinder v. Canada* that the dismissal of the Sikh applicant from the Canadian National Railway Company because of his refusal to wear safety headgear during his work was justified for reasons of public safety.[17] Both decisions are, in our opinion, wrong. First of all, it is questionable whether the "public safety" clause is here applicable at all. Mr. Singh Bhinder correctly argued that this restriction "was not necessary to protect public safety, since any safety risk ensuing from his refusal to wear safety headgear was confined to himself."[18] One should, therefore, draw a distinction between manifestations of religion or belief which might endanger the safety of other persons (public safety) and those which concern only the safety of the person in question.[19] Secondly, even if one bases such measures on the "public safety" clause, they seem to fail to meet the proportionality test. In this connection, one needs to take into account that turban

---

[13] See Nowak, *U.N. Covenant on Civil and Political Rights,* 326.

[14] M.A. v. Italy, Comm. No. 117/1981 (UN Human Rights Committee, 10 April 1984), inadmissibility decision.

[15] X v. Austria, App. No. 1747/62 (EComHR, 13 December 1963), inadmissibility decision, Yb 6, 424, 444.

[16] X v. United Kingdom, App. No. 7992/77 (EComHR, 14 Decisions and Reports 234, 12 July 1978), inadmissibility decision. See Harris, O'Boyle, and Warbrick, *Law of the European Convention on Human Rights,* 366; James E. C. Fawcett, *The Application of the European Convention on Human Rights,* 2d ed. (New York: Oxford University Press, 1987), 248; Jochen A. Frowein, "Freedom of Religion in the Practice of the European Commission and Court of Human Rights," *Zeitschrift für ausländisches öffentliches Recht und Völkerrecht* 46 (1986): 249, 259.

[17] K. Singh Bhinder v. Canada, Comm. No. 208/1986 (UN Human Rights Committee, 9 November 1989), UN Doc. A/45/40 (Vol. II), Annex IX, SE (1990).

[18] Ibid.

[19] See the correct criticism of Tahzib, *Freedom of Religion or Belief,* 296.

and beard are important religious symbols of Sikhs since the sixteenth century, that the applicants were prepared to risk their personal safety because of their religious beliefs, and that the safety of other persons was not endangered.[20] That there is no "pressing social need" is shown, e.g., by the British amendment of 1976 to exempt Sikhs from wearing crash helmets.

B. Restrictions for the Protection of Public Order

"Public order" in the English text of Articles 18(3) CCPR, 9(2) ECHR, and 12(3) ACHR differs from comparable provisions in these treaties due to the absence of the parenthetical term "ordre public." Consequently, the freedom to manifest one's religion or belief may only be restricted on this ground to avoid disturbances to the order in the narrow sense of the word.[21] "Public order" should be narrowly construed to mean the prevention of public disorder.[22] It should not be confused with a similar sounding French legal expression used in civil and administrative law and private international law, *l'ordre public,* which relates to the fundamental public policies of a society.[23] For example, the registration regulations applicable to political demonstrations are also permissible for funeral and other religious processions in order to conduct traffic and avoid disturbances of the peace.

It follows from the above distinction that mere *ordre public* rules are not permissible if they interfere with the freedom to manifest one's religion or belief. This distinction might be illustrated by a judgment of the Austrian Constitutional Court regarding ritual animal slaughtering.[24] In the Austrian State of Vorarlberg the slaughtering of animals in a conscious state—without prior anaesthetization—is in principle prohibited. Should this not be possible, one has to make sure that the animal is not suffering unnecessary pain. The applicant was convicted and sentenced to pay a fine for his participation in the slaughtering of sheep according to Islamic customs, i.e., without prior anaesthetization. The Constitutional Court found a violation of the freedom to manifest one's religion on the ground that under the heading "public

---

[20] Ibid, 297.

[21] See Nowak, *U.N. Covenant on Civil and Political Rights,* 327. Van Dijk and van Hoof, *Theory and Practice of the European Convention,* 554, argue that "public order" in ECHR, Article 9(2) only refers to the notion of "order in places accessible to everyone."

[22] For instance, principle 22 of the Siracusa Principles incorrectly states: "The expression 'public order' (ordre public) as used in the Covenant may be defined as the sum of rules which ensure the functioning of society or the set of fundamental principles on which society is founded. Respect for human rights is part of public order (ordre public)."

[23] Unlike comparable limitation clauses in other articles of the ICCPR, ICCPR, art. 18(3), lacks the parenthetical term *ordre public.* Furthermore, the French text of this provision refers to "la protection de l'ordre." This means that the expression "public order" may therefore only be used to "avoid disturbances to the order in the narrow sense" (Nowak, *CCPR Commentary,* 327; namely, "the prevention of public disorder") (UN Doc. E/CN.4/528, 59–62 [1951]) and not "to protect *ordre public* with its general connotations of national public policy" (Karl Josef Partsch, "Freedom of Conscience and Expression, and Political Freedoms," in *The International Bill of Human Rights: The Covenant on Civil and Political Rights,* ed. Louis Henkin [New York: Columbia University Press, 1981], 212–13). It should be emphasized that "the protection of public order" in ECHR, art. 9(2), which deals with limitations on external freedom of religion or belief, should also be equated with the prevention of disorder. For an explanation, see Lockwood, *Working Paper,* 56–61. See also De Jong, *Freedom of Thought,* 696 and n.23. It has also been argued that "public

order" only those restrictions are permissible which are essential for the coexistence of human beings, such as traffic regulations or provisions for the orderly conduct of burials. Although the protection of animals constitutes an increasingly important public and moral value, it is not so essential for the maintenance of public order that it could justify the prohibition of an act called for by an old religious rite and tradition. Moreover, the ritual slaughtering of sheep is not based on an aggressive attitude towards the animal.

On the basis of these considerations, one might conclude that mere *ordre public* rules, such as dress regulations that prohibit wearing headscarves for Muslim women and girls, growing beards for Buddhists, or wearing turbans for Sikhs, etc., could not be justified on the basis of the "public order" clause.[25] Case law on this subject from the European Commission of Human Rights seems, therefore, to be far too restrictive. The Commission has, for example, even denied that dress regulations in a Turkish state university prohibiting wearing Muslim headscarves constituted an interference with the applicant's freedom of religion.[26] It also accepted the somewhat curious argument of the Austrian government that the prohibition for a Buddhist prisoner to grow a beard, as prescribed by his religion, was necessary for the protection of public order so as to be able to identify him.[27]

The case of *Coeriel and Aurik v. the Netherlands* concerns two Dutch citizens who had adopted the Hindu religion and wished to study as Hindu priests ("pandits") in India. Since it is mandatory for Hindu priests to adopt Hindu names, they requested the Dutch authorities to have their surnames changed into Hindu names. This request was refused. The European Commission of Human Rights declared the complaint under Articles 9 and 14 ECHR to be manifestly ill-founded, as the applicants had not established that their religious studies would be impeded by the refusal to modify their surnames.[28] The Human Rights Committee, on the other hand, considered the grounds advanced by the Dutch authorities in refusing change of surnames (the applicants had not shown that the changes sought were essential to pursue their studies, the names had religious connotations and were not "Dutch-sounding") not to be reasonable and found a violation of the right to privacy under Article 17 ICCPR. With respect to freedom of religion, it only stated that the regulation of surnames and the change

---

order" in this provision refers only to the notion of "order in places accessible to everyone" (P. van Dijk and G. J. H. van Hoof, *Theory and Practice of the European Convention*, 554).

24 Judgment of the Austrian Constitutional Court of 17 December 1998 (Case No. B 3028/97); reprinted in *Europäische Grundrecht Zeitung* 26 (1999): 600. On this issue, see generally Walter Kälin, *Grundrechte im Kulturkonflikt, Freiheit und Gleichheit in der Einwanderungsgesellschaft* (Zürich: NZZ Verlag, 2000), 192. On ritual slaughtering, see also the judgement of the European Court of Human Rights in The Jewish Liturgical Association Cha'are Shalom Ve Tsedek v. France, App. No. 27417/95 (ECtHR, 27 June 2000).

25 See, e.g., Gabriele Kucsko-Stadlmayer, "Die Rechtsprechung des österreichischen Verfassungsgerichtshofs auf dem Gebiet der Glaubensfreiheit," *Europäische Grundrecht Zeitung* 26 (1999): 505, 506; Walter Berka, *Die Grundrechte: Grundfreiheiten und Menschenrechte in Österreich* (Vienna: Springer Verlag, 1999), 299.

26 Karaduman v. Turkey, App. No. 16278/90 (EComHR, 74 Decisions and Reports 93, 3 May 1993), inadmissibility decision.

27 X v. Austria, App. No. 1753/63 (EComHR, 15 February 1965), inadmissibility decision, Yb 8, 174. See note 35.

28 Coeriel and Aurik v. the Netherlands, App. No. 18050/91 (EComHR, 2 July 1992), inadmissibility decision; decision published in *Human Rights Law Journal* 15 (1994): 448.

thereof was "eminently a matter of public order and restrictions were therefore permissible under paragraph 3 of Article 18."[29] In our opinion, the Committee, failed to apply the proportionality test,[30] and while it correctly stated that the refusal to change surnames in the present case was an interference with the applicants' freedom to manifest their religion, the Committee erred in concluding that this limitation might be justified on the "public order" ground, because the conduct in question fails to disrupt "public order" in the narrow sense contemplated by the Covenant.

Other permissible restrictions of the freedom to manifest one's religion in the interest of public order are the requirements for religious communities to be registered as legal entities under domestic law[31] and to comply with general laws regulating public meetings or the establishment of public places of worship. If such general regulations are, however, used in an arbitrary or discriminatory manner against certain religious groups, this would amount to a violation of freedom of religion. In the case of *Manoussakis v. Greece,* the European Court of Human Rights had to rule on the compatibility of a conviction of Jehovah's Witnesses for having set up and operated a place of worship without the authorization of the Greek Minister of Education and Religious Affairs.[32] The Court held that the legal authorization requirement was consistent with Article 9 ECHR only in so far as it was intended to allow the minister to verify whether certain formal conditions were satisfied. It observed, however, that Greece had used this requirement to impose rigid, or indeed prohibitive, conditions on practice of religious beliefs by certain non-Orthodox movements. Taking into account that the applicants in 1996 still had not received an express decision on their requests of 1983 and 1984 for permission to inaugurate their place of worship, the Court decided that the conviction of the applicants constituted an interference with their freedom to manifest their religion which was not necessary in a democratic society.

From the case of *Tsavachidis v. Greece,* which also concerned the conviction of a Jehovah's Witness for having opened a place of worship without the necessary permission from the local church authorities and the Minister of Education and Religious Affairs, it became clear that Jehovah's Witnesses who manifest their religion through public worship were subject in Greece to secret surveillance. The case has been settled by means of a friendly settlement in which the Greek government undertook to guarantee, *inter alia,* that Jehovah's Witnesses "will never be subject to such surveillance in the future."[33]

In the judgement in *Serif v. Greece,* the European Court of Human Rights found a violation of Article 9 ECHR because there was no pressing social need to restrict the manifestation of Islamic religion on "public order" grounds.[34] The facts were as follows:

---

[29] Coeriel and Aurik v. The Netherlands, Comm. No. 453/1991 (UN Human Rights Committee, 31 October 1994); final views published in *Human Rights Law Journal* 15 (1994): 423.

[30] See the criticism of Tahzib, *Freedom of Religion or Belief,* 301.

[31] See Canea Catholic Church v. Greece, 27 EHRR 329 (1999) (ECtHR 1997-VIII, 16 December 1997) (violation of ECHR, arts. 6 and 14, no examination of art. 9); App. No. 25528/94 (EComHR, 3 September 1996) (violation of ECHR, arts. 9 and 14). See also the study of the Dutch Advisory Council on International Affairs, *Registration of Communities based on Religion or Belief,* The Hague (2001).

[32] Manoussakis and Others v. Greece, 23 EHRR 387 (1997) (ECtHR 1996-IV, 26 September 1996); see van Dijk and van Hoof, *Theory and Practice of the European Convention,* 555.

[33] Tsavachidis v. Greece, App. No. 28802/95 (ECtHR, 21 January 1999), friendly settlement (decision to strike case from the list of pending cases). See also the friendly settlement in Pentidis and Others v.

After one of the two Muslim leaders of Thrace, the Mufti of Rodopi, had died in 1985, the Greek president appointed a new Mufti, while the applicant was also elected Mufti by the Muslim population. Thereafter, the applicant was convicted for having usurped the functions of a religious minister and for having publicly worn the uniform of such a minister without having the right to do so. The European Court accepted that this conviction pursued the legitimate aim of protecting public order since there were two Muftis at the same time which might create tensions among the Muslims in Rodopi. It held, however, that punishing a person for the mere fact that he acted as the religious leader of a group that willingly followed him could hardly be compatible with the demands of religious pluralism in a democratic society. Rather than removing the cause of tension by eliminating pluralism, the authorities should have ensured by positive action that the competing groups tolerate each other.

The "public order" clause has often been invoked by governments to justify far-reaching restrictions on freedom of religion of prisoners. Notwithstanding the fact that maintaining prison order makes certain restrictions on the religious freedom of prisoners necessary for the protection of public order or even public safety, one cannot avoid the impression that the European Commission of Human Rights, rather than applying the limitation clause of Article 9(2) ECHR, simply relied on the ill-conceived concept of "inherent limitations."[35] It held, e.g., that a refusal by the prison authorities to provide special food required by a religion which was not the religion usually practiced in that state[36] was as justified as the prohibition for a Buddhist prisoner to grow a beard,[37] the prohibition for a Sikh prisoner to wear special clothing,[38] etc.

Finally, many applicants try to justify their noncompliance with general legal obligations by invoking freedom of conscience, religion, or belief, governments react by either questioning whether any interference with this right has occurred or by justifying it in relation to the "public order" clause. One group of cases concerns conscientious objection to the disposition by the state of the taxes it collects, in particular in relation to military expenditures. Both the European Commission of Human Rights and the Human Rights Committee regularly rejected these cases on the ground that the general obligation to contribute through taxation to arms procurement does not constitute an interference with freedom of religion or belief.[39]

A second group of cases concern conscientious objection to military service. Originally, both the European Commission of Human Rights, by reference to Article 4(3)(b) ECHR,[40] and the Human Rights Committee, by reference to Article 8(3)(c)(ii)

Greece, App. No. 23238/94 (ECtHR 1997-III, 9 June 1997), no. 39, where the facts are similar to the Manoussakis case.

[34] Serif v. Greece, App. No. 34369/97 (ECtHR, 14 December 1999). See also Hasan and Chaush v. Bulgaria, App. No. 30985/96 (ECtHR, 26 October 2000).

[35] This case law of the Commission has been strongly criticised: see van Dijk and van Hoof, *Theory and Practice of the European Convention,* 555; Evans, *Religious Liberty and International Law in Europe,* 325; Jacobs and White, *The European Convention on Human Rights,* 215.

[36] See Council of Europe, *Case-Law Topics No. 1: "Human Rights in Prison,"* 31 (1971).

[37] X v. Austria, App. No. 1753/63 (EComHR, 15 February 1965), inadmissibility decision, Yb 8, 174.

[38] X v. United Kingdom, App. No. 8231/78 (EComHR, 28 Decisions and Reports 5, 38, 6 March 1982), inadmissibility decision.

[39] For examples of these decisions see Tahzib, *Freedom of Religion or Belief,* 287.

[40] The European Commission has consistently relied on its holding in Grandrath v. Germany, App. No. 2299/64, (EComHR, 12 December 1966), inadmissibility decision, Yb 10, 626. For a critical assessment

ICCPR,[41] held that freedom of conscience and religion did not include a right to conscientious objection. In light of more recent developments in the Council of Europe and in the United Nations recognizing a right to conscientious objection, this jurisprudence is slowly changing. In its General Comment of 22 July 1993, the Human Rights Committee expressed its belief "that such a right can be derived from Article 18, inasmuch as the obligation to use lethal force may seriously conflict with the freedom of conscience and the right to manifest one's religion or belief." [42] As soon as this right is recognized in principle, every interference needs to be justified in the light of Article 18(3) ICCPR. In the case of *Westerman v. the Netherlands* the Committee had to decide whether the imposition of criminal sanctions against the applicant, who had nonetheless not been accepted as conscientious objector and who had refused to put on a uniform, to enforce the performance of military duty violated his freedom of conscience or religion.[43] The Committee first reaffirmed its General Comment and accepted that the imposition of criminal sanctions constituted an interference with Article 18 ICCPR. Rather than applying the limitation clause in Article 18(3), the Committee suddenly changed its approach and denied a violation of freedom of religion on the ground that it could not substitute its own evaluation of this issue for that of the national authorities. Six Committee members issued dissenting opinions in which they convincingly argued that Article 18 had been violated.

Another consequence of recognizing the right to conscientious objection is the obligation not to discriminate against conscientious objectors because they have failed to perform military service.[44] Several applicants have challenged the difference in duration of military and substitute service as being discriminatory. While the European Commission of Human Rights found even the Finnish system of double duration for substitute service to be nondiscriminatory, [45] the Human Rights Committee found the same system in France to violate Articles 18 and 26 of the Covenant.[46] Other applicants challenged the differential treatment between Jehovah's Witnesses (who in a number of countries are automatically exempted from military service, sometimes even also from substitute service) and other conscientious objectors. A satisfactory ruling from Strasbourg or Geneva, however, remains outstanding.[47]

A last group of cases lying at the border between public and private ordering concerns the conflict between freedom of religion or belief on the one hand and contractual obligations on the other. Governments often try to justify the legal consequences of

---

see van Dijk and van Hoof, *Theory and Practice of the European Convention*, 544; Harris, O'Boyle, and Warbrick, *Law of the European Convention on Human Rights*, 368; Jacobs and White, *The European Convention on Human Rights*, 217.

[41] L.T.K. v. Finland, Comm. No. 185/1984 (UN Human Rights Committee, 9 July 1985), inadmissibility decision. For a critical assessment see Nowak, *U.N. Covenant on Civil and Political Rights*, 322; Evans, *Religious Liberty and International Law in Europe*, 216; Tahzib, *Freedom of Religion or Belief*, 280.

[42] General Comment 22, para. 11.

[43] Westerman v. the Netherlands, Comm. No. 682/1996 (UN Human Rights Committee, 3 November 1999).

[44] General Comment 22, para. 11. On the discrimination aspect see section IV of this chapter.

[45] Autio v. Finland, App. No. 17086/90 (EComHR, 72 Decisions and Reports 245, 6 December 1991), inadmissibility decision; see the critique of Van Dijk and van Hoof, *Theory and Practice of the European Convention*, 546.

[46] Foin v. France, Comm. No. 666/1995 (UN Human Rights Committee, 9 November 1999). See also the friendly settlement of the ECHR in Stefanov v. Bulgaria, App. No. 32438/96 (ECHR, 3 May 2001).

breaching contractual obligations on religious grounds (e.g., by dismissal) with the necessity to protect public order. The case of *Delgado Páez v. Colombia* concerns a teacher of religion and ethics who was no longer allowed to teach at a public secondary school because of his '"progressive ideas in theological and social matters." The Human Rights Committee denied a violation of his freedom to manifest his religion through teaching on the ground that Colombia had a right to allow the church authorities to decide who may teach religion and in what manner.[48] According to the European Commission of Human Rights, a Muslim schoolteacher who regularly neglects his duties in order to participate in the common prayer on Friday afternoon in the mosque near the school has to make a choice between fulfilling this religious obligation and his position as a teacher.[49] On the other hand, a Jewish teacher who could not hold examinations on Saturdays because of her religious obligations complained successfully before the European Court of Justice.[50] These few selected cases show that it is very difficult to strike a fair balance between general duties deriving from laws or contractual obligations on the one hand, and the freedom to manifest one's religion on the other. Whereas freedom of religion imposes the positive duty on governments to take different religious customs and obligations into account, one also has to accept that freedom of conscience and religion does not entail an unrestricted right always to act in accordance with the rules and dictates of one's conscience and religion.[51]

C. Restrictions for the Protection of Public Health

Limitations permitted on the ground of public health are intended primarily to allow state intervention to prevent epidemic or other diseases. When a mandatory state measure, such as a vaccination duty, is necessary in the interest of public health,—i.e., the health of others—contrary religious convictions may certainly be restricted. The European Commission of Human Rights held, e.g., in *X v. the Netherlands,* that the Dutch legal requirement for dairy farmers to become members of the health service had been enacted in order to prevent tuberculosis among cattle. This justified, on the basis of the public health ground, legal measures against a Dutch Protestant farmer who for religious reasons had refused to join this mandatory state health service for his cattle.[52] The same holds true if the manifestation of a specific religion engages in activities

---

[47] See the Solomonic non-decision of the Human Rights Committee in Brinkhof v. the Netherlands, Comm. No. 402/1990 (UN Human Rights Committee, 27 July 1993) (see section IV of this chapter); see the decisions of the European Commission of Human Rights in N. v. Sweden, App. No. 10410/83 (EComHR, 40 Decisions and Reports 203, 1985), and Raninen v. Finland, App. No. 20972/92 (EComHR, 84-A Decisions and Reports 17, 1996); see van Dijk and van Hoof, *Theory and Practice of the European Convention,* 546; Tahzib, *Freedom of Religion or Belief,* 284.

[48] Delgado Páez v. Colombia, Comm. No. 195/1985 (UN Human Rights Committee, 12 July 1990); see Tahzib, *Freedom of Religion or Belief,* 292.

[49] X v. United Kingdom, App. No. 8160/78 (EComHR, 22 Decisions and Reports 27, 12 March 1981), inadmissibility decision; see van Dijk and van Hoof, *Theory and Practice of the European Convention,* 553.

[50] Prais v. EC Council (Case 130/75), 1976 ECR 1589, 2 CMLR 708; see Harris, O'Boyle, and Warbrick, *Law of the European Convention on Human Rights,* 365.

[51] See van Dijk and van Hoof, *Theory and Practice of the European Convention,* 543.

[52] X v. the Netherlands, App. No. 1068/61 (EComHR, 14 December 1962), inadmissibility decision, Yb 5, 278.

which as such are detrimental to the health of its members and possibly others as well. One may think, for example, of the practice of female genital mutilation in certain African cultures and religions or of the relationship between certain religious sects and narcotic drugs. In the case of the *"Assembly of the Church of the Universe" v. Canada,* whose religious practices necessarily involves the care, cultivation, possession, distribution, and worship of marijuana ("God's tree of life"), the Human Rights Committee had to decide whether the criminal prosecutions of members of this sect under the Canadian Narcotic Control Act amounted to a violation of their freedom to manifest their religion. The Committee declared the communication inadmissible since "a belief consisting primarily or exclusively in the worship and distribution of a narcotic drug cannot conceivably be brought within the scope of Article 18 of the Covenant."[53] This decision was rightly criticized as not being in line with the Committee's general opinion that the terms belief and religion "are to be broadly construed."[54] In our view, it would have been more appropriate to accept the practices of the "Assembly of the Church of the Universe" as falling under the terms religion or belief, and applying the limitation clause with respect to the public health or public safety criteria.

As with the "public safety" clause, one may doubt, however, whether the state also has the right to protect an individual's health against his or her own religious convictions.[55] This may arise, for example, when Jehovah's Witnesses refuse all blood transfusions, even when this may be the last possibility for saving life,[56] or when Sikhs refuse to wear safety headgear.[57]

Finally, the decision of the European Commission of Human Rights in *X v. UK* deserves a word of criticism. The applicant, a high-class Sikh, was required by British prison officials to sweep the floor of his prison cell, which he refused. The Commission was prepared to accept that his religion might require a practice of high-class Sikhs not cleaning floors and that an interference with his rights under Article 9 ECHR might have arisen. It justified this interference, however, "as necessary in a democratic society for the protection of the applicant's and other prisoners' health."[58] Although one can certainly understand the argument that, if prisoners are required to clean their own cells, all prisoners should have to do this, but it is difficult to understand why the cleaning of prison cells is necessary for the protection of "public" health, and, if that is the case, why this goal, taking into account the principle of proportionality, has to be achieved by compelling the prisoners to act in a manner that interferes with their freedom of religion.

---

[53] MAB., W.A.T. and J.-A.Y.T. v. Canada, Comm. No. 570/1993 (UN Human Rights Committee, 8 April 1994), inadmissibility decision.

[54] General Comment 22, para. 2. For the criticism of this decision see Tahzib, *Freedom of Religion or Belief,* 278.

[55] See Nowak, *U.N. Covenant on Civil and Political Rights,* 328; Tahzib, *Freedom of Religion or Belief,* 296.

[56] On this issue see the case of Hoffmann v. Austria, 17 EHRR 293 (1994) (ECtHR 255-C, 23 June 1993); see section III.E.3.

[57] See section III.A.

[58] X v. United Kingdom, App. No. 8231/78 (EComHR, 28 Decisions and Reports 5, 38, 6 March 1982), inadmissibility decision. See the criticism of Jacobs and White, *The European Convention on Human Rights,* 217; Van Dijk and van Hoof, *Theory and Practice of the European Convention,* 556.

D. Restrictions for the Protection of Morals

"Morals" is definitely the least clear and most controversial of all the legitimating grounds for justifying restrictions on the freedom to manifest one's religion or belief. As the Human Rights Committee stressed in its General Comment, "the concept of morals derives from many social, philosophical and religious traditions; consequently, limitations on the freedom to manifest a religion or belief for the purpose of protecting morals must be based on principles not deriving exclusively from a single tradition."[59] Since religions usually claim that their respective value systems constitute the most important moral guidelines, at least for those who adhere to this particular religion or belief, it seems difficult to conceive of a kind of higher and quasi universally accepted concept of morals which states could invoke to justify restrictions of religious manifestations, though one can of course imagine areas where differing religious and secular values could converge in an "overlapping consensus."[60] Given the high value attached to freedom of religion or belief, however, it is difficult to imagine moral values of sufficient magnitude to justify imposing a limitation on that freedom that would not themselves be among the constellation of values that fall within the protection of fundamental rights and freedoms of others. Thus, as a functional matter, limitations that would appropriately be justified on the ground of morals could for the most part also be justified by reference to protecting the fundamental rights of third parties.

On the other hand, it can be argued that in the absence of a uniform universal or regional standard of morals, states enjoy a fairly generous margin of appreciation when restricting religions on moral grounds.[61] In the ritual animal slaughtering case referred to above, the government of Vorarlberg had argued that the protection of animals was a moral justification for prohibiting ritual slaughtering of sheep without prior anaesthetization. The Austrian Constitutional Court held, however, that the old Jewish and Islamic tradition of slaughtering and sacrificing sheep must enjoy in fact priority over the moral value of protecting animals against unnecessary suffering.[62] This case illustrates very well the difficulties of balancing religious values with moral values. If a religious group would, however, start again with sacrificing human beings, states would definitely have a right and an obligation to interfere for the protection of the right to life. The animal and human slaughter cases represent two poles: at one end, it seems quite clear that even fairly widely held values that lie outside the range of human rights protection are not sufficient to override religious freedom; at the other extreme, no modern system can tolerate ritual sacrifice of human beings. As social settings become increasingly pluralistic, however, it is reasonable to expect that the range of situations in which some religious practices may conflict with widely shared moral values will multiply. How, for example, will Muslim polygamy be dealt with in European countries? Such problems raise a narrow version of the broader question about when the enforcement of morals is permissible: when may the state encroach not only on general

[59] General Comment 22, para. 8.

[60] John Rawls, *Political Liberalism: The John Dewey Essays in Philosophy* (New York: Columbia University Press, 1993), section 3: "The Idea of an Overlapping Consensus."

[61] See for this argument Evans, *Religious Liberty and International Law in Europe*, 324.

[62] See note 22.

freedom,[63] but on the narrower (and more highly protected domain) of religious freedom, in the name of enforcing moral values? While challenging problems may arise in this area, however, as a practical matter there are likely to be relatively few cases where states could legitimately justify this interference on the ground of protecting morals where the justification of protecting fundamental rights of others would not also apply. Let us, therefore, proceed to this most important limitation ground.

E. Restrictions for the Protection of the (Fundamental) Rights and Freedoms of Others

1. Proselytism

Since religions have the inherent tendency of interacting with other religions, sometimes in ways that can impair the religious freedom of others, states quite often feel the need to interfere with the freedom to manifest religion in order to protect religious freedom of others. As long as governments try to be neutral, these measures usually do not pose major problems. If governments follow the system of a state church and/or clearly give priority treatment to one religious community, however, the danger of arbitrary or discriminatory treatment arises. A typical example for this tendency, as the case law of the European Court of Human Rights illustrates, is the Greek system of favoring the Orthodox Church by discriminating against other religious communities, including Muslims, Catholics, or Jehovah's Witnesses.

In Greece, proselytism is regarded as impermissible interference with other religions, and indeed constitutes a criminal offence which Greek law defines as "any direct or indirect attempt to intrude on the religious beliefs of a person of a different religious persuasion, with the aim of undermining those beliefs, either by any kind of inducement or moral support or material assistance, or by fraudulent means or by taking advantage of his experience, trust, need, low intellect or naivety." The leading case on proselytism is *Kokkinakis v. Greece*.[64] The applicants, a married couple, are Jehovah's Witnesses and were convicted of that sort of evangelical activity for which this religious group is well known, i.e., going from door to door in order to persuade others to join the religion. They were particularly persistent with the wife of a cantor in the Orthodox Church who complained to the police. The European Court of Human Rights considered the relevant criteria used by the Greek legislature in adopting its antiproselyting law acceptable in so far as they pursued a legitimate aim (the protection of rights and freedoms of others) and were designed only to punish improper proselytism. It criticized, however, the judgments of the Greek courts for having not sufficiently specified in what way the accused had attempted to convince others by improper means. Therefore, the conviction was not justified by a pressing social need and violated Article 9 ECHR.[65] In *Larissis v. Greece,* the three applicants were officers

---

[63] For an exhaustive treatment of the general question, see Joel Feinberg, *The Moral Limits of the Criminal Law,* 4 vols. (New York: Oxford University Press, 1987–1990).

[64] Kokkinakis v. Greece, 17 EHRR 397 (1994) (ECtHR 260-A, 25 May 1993); see Evans, *Religious Liberty and International Law in Europe,* 332; Jacobs and White, *The European Convention on Human Rights,* 214; Harris, O'Boyle, and Warbrick, *Law of the European Convention on Human Rights,* 366.

[65] For the reasoning of the Court and its dissenting members see also section II of this essay.

in the Greek Air Force and followers of the Pentecostal Church. They were sentenced by military courts for having attempted to convert civilians as well as Orthodox airmen subordinate to them. The European Court followed its judgment in the *Kokkinakis* case and reaffirmed that freedom to manifest one's religion includes the right to try to convince one's neighbor, not, however, "improper proselytism," such as the offering of material or social advantage or the application of improper pressure with a view to gaining new members. It found no evidence that the applicants had overstepped this limit in their attempts to convert civilians and, therefore, found a violation of Article 9 in this respect. In relation to the three airmen who had felt subject to a certain degree of pressure owing to the military hierarchical structures, the Court ruled, however, that the convictions were proportional and justified for the protection of rights and freedoms of others.[66]

2. Blasphemy

While the Greek offense of proselytism aims at protecting freedom of conscience, religion, or belief against improper missionary activities by other religious groups, the criminal offence of blasphemy is meant to protect the religious feelings of individuals from being offended by others. By punishing proselytism, the state interferes with the freedom of individuals to manifest their religion through missionary activities in order to protect the religious freedom of others not to be converted. In punishing blasphemy, the state interferes with freedom of expression in order to protect religious feelings or morals, not necessarily freedom of religion. One might, therefore, question why the issue of blasphemy is dealt with in an article on permissible restrictions on freedom of religion or belief. Since the European Court of Human Rights has, however, developed a highly controversial case law of protecting religious feelings as part of the "peaceful enjoyment" of freedom of religion in Article 9 ECHR against offensive publications, we will consider this question here.

The leading case is *Otto-Preminger-Institut v. Austria* concerning the film *Das Liebeskonzil,* which was seized and forfeited as blasphemous under Austrian law.[67] The film as advertised in the applicant's cinema depicted God as a senile man, prostrating himself to the devil, erotic tension between the devil and the Virgin Mary, and Christ as a low-grade mental defective. While the European Commission of Human Rights found the film predominately satirical and its seizure and complete prohibition disproportionate and in violation of Article 10 ECHR, the Court justified the seizure and forfeiture of the film under Article 10(2) ECHR as being necessary for the protection of the right of the Roman Catholic majority population of Tyrol to proper respect for their freedom of thought, conscience, and religion as protected by Article 9 ECHR. This approach has been vehemently criticized as mistaken.[68] First of all, it is doubtful whether the right to freedom of religion contains a right to have one's religious feelings respected by others and, therefore, to be protected by the state against private interference. Of course, if private actors prevent others by means of threats or violence

---

[66] Larissis and Others v. Greece, 27 EHRR 329 (1999) (ECtHR 1998-I, No. 65, 24 February 1998).

[67] Otto-Preminger-Institut v. Austria, 19 EHRR 34 (1995) (ECtHR 295-A 20 September 1994).

[68] Van Dijk and van Hoof, *Theory and Practice of the European Convention,* 551; Evans, *Religious Liberty and International Law in Europe,* 335.

from manifesting their religion, the state is under a positive obligation to interfere and protect. It is, however, difficult to see in which way the mere screening of this film would have limited or inhibited Roman Catholics in manifesting their religion. There is no indication in the facts that the screening of the film would have led to threats or violence against Roman Catholics. The Court, in fact, has afforded freedom of religion priority over freedom of expression[69] by introducing the concept of "peaceful enjoyment of freedom of religion" (a term taken from Article 11 ECHR) against offensive or "immoral" criticism.

It is doubtful whether the Court would apply the same standard also for the protection of the feelings of a minority religion. For example, the European Commission of Human Rights in *Choudhury v. UK*, has rejected the claim of a Muslim applicant that the refusal of the British authorities to bring criminal proceedings against Salman Rushdie and the publisher of his book *Satanic Verses* would violate his religious feelings and his right to freedom of religion.[70] One of the reasons for not prosecuting Rushdie under the British law on blasphemy is the fact that this criminal offense only protects the religious feelings of Christians. The Strasbourg organs have in fact upheld convictions for blasphemy against the Christian religion under that law.[71] In the case of *Wingrove v. UK*, the Court even stated that the "fact that the law of blasphemy does not treat all religions on equal footing did not detract from the legitimacy of the aim pursued in the present context."[72] The context was as follows: Mr. Wingrove produced an eighteen-minute video entitled "Visions of Ecstasy," which shows in an erotic manner a nun's ecstatic visions of Jesus Christ fastened to the cross. The British Board of Film Classification rejected the application for a classification certificate, which means that the video was banned from being lawfully sold, hired out, or otherwise supplied to the general public. While the European Commission of Human Rights found this interference to be disproportionate to the legitimate aim of protecting the right of Christians not to be insulted in their religious feelings, the Court also in this case found no violation. It explained this reasoning as follows: "Whereas there is little scope under Article 10(2) . . . for restrictions on the political speech or on debate of questions of public interest . . . a wider margin of appreciation is generally available to the Contracting States when regulating freedom of expression in relation to matters liable to offend intimate personal convictions within the sphere of morals or, especially, religion."[73]

The case of *Malcolm Ross v. CDN* deals with the issue of "religious offense" from a somewhat different perspective. There, the applicant had been dismissed as a teacher because of expressions against the Jewish religion, which had led to a "poisoned school environment," although the applicant had strictly separated his private expressions from school teaching.[74] Again the underlying issue is whether freedom of religion or

---

[69] In this sense Harris, O'Boyle, and Warbrick, *Law of the European Convention on Human Rights,* 358.

[70] Choudhury v. United Kingdom, App. No. 17439/90 (EComHR, 5 March 1991), inadmissibility decision; decision published in *Human Rights Law Journal* 12 (1991): 172.

[71] See, e.g., the Gay News case of X Ltd. and Y v. United Kingdom, App. No. 8710/79 (EComHR, 28 Decisions and Reports 77, 7 May 1982).

[72] Wingrove v. United Kingdom, 24 EHRR 1 (1997) (ECtHR 1996-V, 25 November 1996).

[73] Ibid, para. 58; see Evans, *Religious Liberty and International Law in Europe,* 340.

[74] Ross v. CDN, Comm. No. 736/97 (UN Human Rights Committee, 18 October 2000).

belief entails an obligation to refrain from trenching on religious sensitivities. Here the offense was to a minority religion, but one that is clearly traditional and for which adherents of other more dominant traditions have clear sympathy.

In general, the case law of the European Court seems to protect moral standards which are equated with the religious feelings of the majority in the respective countries, or the feelings of minorities for which there is strong sympathy. One may detect in this approach a discriminatory element. If the Court would apply this jurisprudence, however, equally to all religious feelings, freedom of expression in this field could be heavily jeopardized.[75]

3. Additional Rights and Freedoms of Others

There is no doubt that states may, and sometimes are even under an obligation to restrict manifestations of religion or belief which endanger the fundamental rights of others, in particular the rights to life, liberty, integrity, privacy, marriage, property, health, education, equality, the prohibition of slavery and torture as well as the rights of minorities.[76] These objectives, to some extent, overlap with the other limitation grounds mentioned above. A state measure intended to protect the rights to life, health and physical integrity against violence caused by religious groups can, of course, also be justified as protecting public safety, order and health. If such measures aim, however, only at protecting the life or health of the person or persons who manifest the religion, it cannot be justified as protecting the rights of others.

This distinction can be illustrated with the well-known example of the Jehovah's Witnesses' refusal of blood transfusions. If a doctor in a state hospital forces a blood transfusion on a Jehovah's Witness against his explicit will in order to save his life, such an interference with his freedom to manifest his religion could not be justified as necessary to protect the right to life of others. Whether it can be justified in the interest of public order, health, or morals is a disputed question. In our opinion, it would in principle be a disproportionate interference with freedom of religion.[77] It also constitutes a disproportionate interference with the right to privacy which, in principle, also protects the "right to die."[78] Such interferences against an adult who is fully conscious and unambivalent about his or her decision to prefer to die rather than to accept a blood transfusion on religious grounds can, in our opinion, also not be justified by the general obligation of states, deriving from Article 2(1) ECHR, to protect everyone's right to life. If a Jehovah's Witness would, however, refuse a life-saving blood transfusion to his

---

[75] See in this sense Harris, O'Boyle, and Warbrick, *Law of the European Convention on Human Rights,* 364: "Prioritising of belief-based ideas over secular opinion is not without substantial dangers."

[76] On the meaning of the term "fundamental rights and freedoms" in ICCPR, art. 18(3); see Nowak, *U.N. Covenant on Civil and Political Rights,* 329. For examples see also the UN study of Arcot Krishnaswami, *Study of Discrimination in the Matter of Religious Rights and Practices,* UN Doc. E/CN.4/Sub.2/200/ Rev.1, UN Sales No. 60.XIV.2 (1960), 25.

[77] See sections III.A and III.C. See also Harris, O'Boyle, and Warbrick, *Law of the European Convention on Human Rights,* 370.

[78] On the questions of the "right to die" and the waiving of the right to life see also Theodore S. Orlin, "The Right to Life, The Right to Die: The Rights, Their Interrelationship and the Jurisprudential Problems," *The Jurisprudence of Human Rights Law: A Comparative Interpretive Approach,* ed. Theodore S. Orlin, Allan Rosas, and Martin Scheinin (Åbo, Turkey: Åbo Akademi University, 2000), 73.

or her child, the state (doctor), in our opinion, does not only have the right but also the duty to interfere with this manifestation of freedom of religion and exercise of parental rights in order to protect the life of the child.

The case of *Hoffmann v. Austria* touches upon the issue of balancing a child's rights against the religious rights of a parent, although the facts are somewhat different and the case was ultimately decided on other grounds.[79] Mrs. Hoffmann, originally of Roman Catholic belief, was married to a Roman Catholic and the couple had two baptized children. Subsequently she joined the Jehovah's Witnesses, but her husband did not. Following a breakdown of the marriage, she left the matrimonial home together with the children. Both parents applied for custody of the children. While the lower courts granted custody to the mother, the Austrian Supreme Court reversed this decision with reference to the religion of the mother and her total rejection of blood transfusion not only for herself but, in the absence of a court order, for her children as well. According to the Supreme Court, the practical consequences of the mother's membership of the Jehovah's Witnesses would, therefore, not be in the best interest of the children. The European Court of Human Rights considered the aim of the Supreme Court's judgment, namely the protection of the health and rights of the children, a legitimate interference with the right of the mother to the protection of her family life. But since the Supreme Court had based its judgment essentially on a difference in religion alone, the European Court found this interference disproportionate and, consequently, as a violation of Article 8 in conjunction with Article 14 ECHR. Surprisingly, it ruled that no separate issue arose under Article 9 ECHR. The case may be a study in the Court's desire to evade the extremely difficult choices that need to be made when an individual's parental and religious rights collide with the best interests of a child. In general, however, the requirements of Article 9 would appear to call for the same relief as that afforded the Jehovah's Witness mother under Article 8.

IV. Prohibition of Discrimination and Incitement to Religious Hatred

In its General Comment on the right to freedom of thought, conscience, and religion, the Human Rights Committee has put much emphasis on equality and nondiscrimination.[80] Of particular relevance to this chapter is that limitations on the freedom to manifest one's religion or belief are only permissible if they are not discriminatory (para. 8). With this in mind, it is important to note several of the principle ways in which religious discrimination occurs. State action which might otherwise be covered by a legitimating ground for limitations is not permissible if the limitation has a discriminatory purpose or effect.

With this in mind, it is useful to review some of the major concerns about discrimination that have been enunciated in the international human rights arena. Thus, the Human Rights Committee's General Comment emphasizes that the fact that a religion is recognized as a state religion or that its followers comprise the majority of the population shall not result in any privileges for this religion or discrimination against adherents to other religions or nonbelievers (para. 9). The same holds true if a set of

[79] Hoffmann v. Austria, 17 EHRR 293 (1994) (ECtHR 255-C, 23 June 1993).

[80] General Comment 22.

beliefs is treated as official ideology in constitutions or proclamations of ruling parties (para. 10). A public education system which includes instruction in a particular religion or belief is only permissible if provision is made for nondiscriminatory exemptions or alternatives (para. 6). Finally, the Human Rights Committee recalled the obligation of governments deriving from Article 20 ICCPR to prohibit any manifestation of religion or belief which amounts to propaganda for war or advocacy of national, racial, or religious hatred that constitutes incitement to discrimination, hostility, or violence (para. 7).

A. General Patterns of Discrimination

In practice, only very few governments are genuinely neutral vis-à-vis the various religious communities active in their countries. Most governments, in some way or another, provide the state, majority, or other traditional religions with certain privileges and, thereby, put other religions or beliefs in a disadvantaged position. To some extent, these differences might be explained and justified by long-standing traditions or cultural peculiarities. Of course, history and culture do not, in the absence of more, justify discrimination. All too often, however, the differential treatment results in outright discrimination, whether intended or not. In Germany, the judgment of the Federal Constitutional Court in the "*Crucifix* case," holding that the mandatory presence of the Roman Catholic crucifix in public schools of Bavaria violated freedom of religion,[81] stirred up strong resentments among the predominantly Catholic population in Bavaria. The same practice, as well as many other traditional privileges of the Roman Catholic Church in Austria and other countries with a predominantly Catholic population, has not yet resulted in any similar ruling. But the holding of the European Court of Human Rights in *Hoffmann v. Austria*[82] is only understandable if one realizes the bias in the judgment of the Austrian Supreme Court against Jehovah's Witnesses and in favor of Roman Catholics. The same bias can be seen in blasphemy cases, such as *Otto-Preminger-Institut v. Austria*,[83] even though the European Court of Human Rights found no violation by according the government a fairly broad margin of appreciation. In the United Kingdom, the law on blasphemy openly distinguishes between Christian and non-Christian religions or beliefs, and the Strasbourg organs seem to accept this distinction.[84] Most freedom of religion cases decided so far by the European Court of Human Rights are directed against Greece, i.e., a country with a state church. A combined reading of the various judgments concerning proselytism,[85] registration of places of worship, and so forth, shows a kind of systematic pattern of discrimination against Jehovah's Witnesses, Muslims, Catholics, and other religions. Many more such serious examples of religious discrimination could be cited from

---

[81] Judgement of the first senate of 16 May 1995, BVerfGE 93, 1; *Europäische Grundrecht Zeitung* 22 (1995): 359. See Klaus Dieter Bayer, *Das Grundrecht der Religions- und Gewissensfreiheit unter besonderer Berücksichtigung des Minderheitenschutzes* (Baden: Nomos Universitätsschriften, 1997), 206. See on this issue in general Walter Kälin, *Grundrechte im Kulturkonflikt*, 147.

[82] See note 75.

[83] See note 63.

[84] See section III.E.2, in particular Wingrove v. United Kingdom, 24 EHRR 1 (1997) (ECtHR 1996-V, 25 November 1996).

[85] See III.E.1 in this chapter.

other regions in the world.[86] Each of these discrimination cases, and many of those that follow, are of course violations of freedom or religion and belief in that they impose unjustifiable limitations on the freedom of action of believers and religious communities.

B. Discrimination in Education

An area where states regularly interfere, and all too often in a discriminatory manner, is education. Already in the *Danish Sex Education* case, the European Court of Human Rights held that the parental right in Article 2 of the First Protocol to the ECHR obligates the states to respect parents' religious convictions or other beliefs "throughout the entire State education programme" and to take care that "information or knowledge included in the curriculum is conveyed in an objective, critical and pluralistic manner (and does not) pursue an aim of indoctrination."[87] The Human Rights Committee held in *Hartikainen v. Finland* that mandatory public school instruction in subjects such as the general history of religions and ethics is only compatible with Article 18(4) CCPR if it is given in a neutral and objective way and respects the conviction of parents who do not believe in any religion.[88] If public schools include instruction in a particular religion or belief, it must not be mandatory and states have an obligation to provide for nondiscriminatory exemptions or alternatives.[89] Articles 18(4) ICCPR, 12(4) ACHR, and 2 of the First Protocol to the ECHR guarantee the right to found and enroll in private schools, including religious ones, and states are under no obligation to fund these schools. Moreover, in the case of *Waldman v. Canada*, the Human Rights Committee held that "if a State party chooses to provide public funding to religious schools, it should make this funding available without discrimination."[90] The communication was submitted by a Jewish father who enrolls his children in a private Jewish day school in the Canadian province of Ontario, where Roman Catholic schools are the only nonsecular schools receiving full and direct public funding. Other religious schools must fund through private sources, including tuition fees. The Canadian government argued that this distinction is based on objective and reasonable criteria as Roman Catholic schools, on the basis of privileged treatment in the constitution, are incorporated as a distinct part of the public school system. The Committee did not buy this argument and held "that the fact that a distinction is enshrined in the Constitution does not render it reasonable and objective."[91] Consequently, it

[86] See, e.g., the annual reports of the UN Special Rapporteur on the question of religious intolerance to the UN Commission on Human Rights, most recently in UN Doc. E/CN.4/2000/65. See also the judgement of the ECHR in the interstate case of Cyprus v. Turkey, App. No. 25781/94 (ECHR, 10 May 2001), paras. 241–45, 307–11.

[87] Kjeldsen, Busk Madsen and Pedersen v. Denmark, 1 EHRR 711 (1979–80) (ECtHR 23, 7 December 1976), 19 Yb 504 (1976).

[88] Hartikainen v. Finland, Comm. No. 40/1978 (UN Human Rights Committee, 9 April 1981).

[89] General Comment 22, para. 6.

[90] Waldman v. Canada, Comm. No. 694/1996 (UN Human Rights Committee, 5 November 1999). See also the inadmissibility decision five days earlier in Tadman et al. v. Canada, Comm. No. 816/1998 (UN Human Rights Committee, 29 October 1999) (lack of standing for failure to fulfill the victim requirement; but see dissenting opinions).

[91] Waldman v. Canada, U.N. Doc. CCPR/C/67/D/694/1996, para. 10.4 (see <http://www1.umn.edu/humanrts/undocs/session67/view694.htm>).

found that the applicant was a victim of violation of the right to equal and effective protection against discrimination in Article 26 ICCPR. This decision could have far-reaching consequences for many countries of the world where the state or majority religion receives privileged treatment through, *inter alia*, public funding of its schools.

C. Religious Oaths

Another area where state religions often receive a privileged treatment which may discriminate against the adherents of other religions or beliefs is the requirement of public oath before courts or other state organs. In the case of *Buscarini v. San Marino*, the European Court of Human Rights had to decide whether the legal requirement for members of Parliament to take the oath of office with a reference to the Gospels, on pain of forfeiting their seats, was compatible with freedom of conscience and religion.[92] The government emphasized the special character of San Marino, where the history and national traditions had been linked to Christianity since the Republic had been founded by a saint. The European Court held, however, that requiring the applicants to take the oath on the Gospels had been tantamount to requiring two elected representatives of the people to swear allegiance to a particular religion, a requirement which was not compatible with Article 9 ECHR. Similar violations had already much earlier been found by the Inter-American Commission on Human Rights, e.g., in relation to Jehovah's Witnesses who were prosecuted in Argentina during the military regime in the seventies for being unwilling to swear oaths of allegiance.[93] Traditionally, states have attached great significance to oath requirements, and they could arguably be justified by reference to public safety and order, but their obvious discriminatory and exclusionary impact has long made such requirements one of the classic violations of freedom of religion or belief.[94]

D. Exemptions from Military Service

Another area where states traditionally distinguish among various religions is exemption from military service. As has been shown above, states are increasingly recognizing the right of conscientious objection to military service as deriving from freedom of conscience, religion, or belief.[95] According to the UN Human Rights Committee's General Comment, when this right is recognized by law or practice, "there shall be no differentiation among conscientious objectors on the basis of the nature of their particular beliefs."[96] Despite this clear and strict language in its General Comment on this issue, the Human Rights Committee only one week later in the case of *Brinkhof v. the*

[92] Buscarini and Others v. San Marino, App. No. 24645/94 (ECtHR, 18 February 1999).

[93] See Scott Davidson, "Civil and Political Rights Protection," *The Inter-American System of Human Rights*, ed. David Harris and Stephen Livingstone (New York: Oxford University Press, 1998), 258; Torcaso v. Watkins, 367 US 488 (1964) (US Supreme Court decision holding that federal and state authorities may not impose oath requirements). See also chapter by Sousa e Brito in this volume.

[94] The provision of the United States Constitution banning religious oath requirements was part of the original constitutional document, and antedated the religion clause of the First Amendment. See US Const, art. vi.

[95] See III.B.

[96] General Comment 22, para 11.

Netherlands decided differently.[97] The communication had been submitted by a Dutch pacifist and objector to both military and substitute service who was sentenced to twelve months imprisonment under the Netherlands Military Penal Code. He complained that he was not treated in the same way as Jehovah's Witnesses who under Dutch law are exempted from military and substitute service. The Committee, after referring to its General Comment, distinguished Mr. Brinkhof's case, since he had not shown "that his convictions as a pacifist are incompatible with the system of substitute service in the Netherlands or that the privileged treatment accorded to Jehovah's Witnesses adversely affected his rights as a conscientious objector against military service." The Committee, therefore, found that he was not discriminated against. At the same time, it recommended that the Netherlands "review its relevant regulations with a view to removing any discrimination in this respect." This decision has been the subject of considerable criticism by legal scholars.[98]

While Jehovah's Witnesses are in a privileged position in the Netherlands and a few other countries with respect to conscientious objection to military service, they have more frequently found themselves in the opposite position, as the following case shows. Under a Greek law of 1998, all ministers of a "known religion," are equally exempted from military service. Although the Supreme Administrative Court of Greece had already acknowledged in 1975 that Jehovah's Witnesses were to be considered as a "known religion," the requests for exemption by the two applicants in the case of *Tsirlis and Kouloumpas v. Greece,* who were appointed religious ministers by the Central Congregation of the Christian Jehovah's Witnesses of Greece, were rejected by the Recruitment Offices. Since they refused to comply with orders from a superior to wear a uniform, they were sentenced by a military court to four years imprisonment each. The European Court of Human Rights held that this treatment was "discriminatory when contrasted with the way in which Orthodox priests were treated" and found violations of the right to personal liberty under Article 5 ECHR.[99] Here again, limitations on freedom to manifest a religious belief (here, opposition to military service), even though these might be sustained in light of the importance of the military to public safety, could not be sustained where they were administered in a discriminatory way.

E. Other Examples of Discriminatory Treatment

In the judgment concerning the interstate case of *Cyprus v. Turkey,* the European Court condemned the discriminatory treatment of Greek Cypriots on the basis of their ethnic origin, race, and religion in the enclaved Karpos region of northern

---

[97] Brinkhof v. the Netherlands, Comm. No. 402/1990 (UN Human Rights Committee, 27 July 1993); final views published in *Human Rights Law Journal* 14 (1994): 410.

[98] See Aalt Willem Heringa, "Commentaar," *NJCM-Bulletin* 18 (1993): 1010; Tahzib, *Freedom of Religion or Belief,* 284; Nowak, "Human Rights News," *Netherlands Quarterly of Human Rights* 12 (1994): 36; Nowak, "The Activities of the UN Human Rights Committee: Developments from 1 August 1992 to 31 July 1995," *Human Rights Law Journal* 16 (1995): 377, 393. On this controversial issue see also van Dijk and van Hoof, *Theory and Practice of the European Convention,* 546.

[99] Tsirlis and Kouloumpas v. Greece, 25 EHRR 198 (1997) (ECtHR 1997-III, 17 April 1996), no. 38.

Cyprus. The violations, involving severe restrictions of freedom of movement including access to worship facilities, were held to be so severe that they even constituted degrading treatment in violation of Article 3 ECHR.[100]

Finally, we would like to cite three judgements relating to a country where religious discrimination is rampant: Bosnia and Herzegovina. It is interesting to compare which type of issues the Human Rights Chamber for Bosnia and Herzegovina, a special human rights court established by the Dayton Peace Agreement of 1995,[101] has to deal with. In the well-known case of the *Islamic Community v. Republika Srpska,* the Chamber had to decide whether the refusal of the municipal authorities of Banja Luka to permit the reconstruction of mosques, which had all been destroyed in 1993, was discriminatory and violated the freedom of the Muslim population to manifest its religion. Although the fact of the destruction of the fifteen mosques during the war is outside the competence of the Chamber *ratione temporis,* it held that the Muslim believers in Banja Luka had been discriminated against (in particular, if compared to the local Serbian Orthodox majority) by the authorities in the enjoyment of their rights to freedom of religion and property. It also found a violation of freedom of religion under Article 9 ECHR in isolation and stressed the positive obligation of the authorities to protect and secure this right against interference by private persons.[102]

When the international community, in spring 2001, succeeded in forcing the Republika Srpska authorities to permit the start of reconstructing the Ferhadija mosque, this led to violent attacks by Bosnian Serbs against Muslims and representatives of the international community.

The case of *Mahmutovic v. the Republika Srpska* reveals a similar pattern of religious discrimination against the Muslim population in the Bosnian Serb Republic.[103] In 1994 the Municipality of Prnjavor decided to put the Muslim Town Cemetery in the centre of the town (close to the Serbian Orthodox and the Roman Catholic cemeteries) out of use. Although it was provided in the same decision that the burial of deceased Muslims would be performed at the new town cemetery in the eastern part of the town, this new cemetery was never established. During the war and the first years thereafter, Muslims were too afraid to carry out burials at the old Town Cemetery but rather used village cemeteries outside Prnjavor. Only in May 1998 Mr. Mahmutovic, whose family owns a parcel at that cemetery where its members had been buried for decades, buried his deceased wife at the old Town Cemetery in accordance with Muslim religious regulations and practice. Two months later, the Prnjavor Municipality Communal Inspector ordered the applicant to conduct, at his own expense, the exhumation of his late wife from the Town Cemetery, and to move her remains within fifteen days to the (nonexistent) new cemetery. The Chamber first ordered the Republika Srpska, by means of a provisional measure, to desist from implementing this decision (which was in fact complied with) and finally found that the applicant had been discriminated

---

[100] Cyprus v. Turkey, App. No. 25781/94 (ECHR, 10 May 2001).

[101] On the jurisdiction of the Human Rights Chamber in general see Nowak, "The Human Rights Chamber for Bosnia and Herzegovina Adopts Its First Judgements," *Human Rights Law Journal* 18 (1997): 174; Peter Neussl, "Bosnia and Herzegovina still far from the rule of law / Basic facts and landmark decisions of the Human Rights Chamber," *Human Rights Law Journal* 20 (1999): 290.

[103] Mahmutovic v. Republika Srpska, Case No. CH/98/892 (Human Rights Chamber, 8 October 1999), decision on admissibility and merits; decision published in *Human Rights Law Journal* 20 (1999): 328.

against in the enjoyment of his rights to private and family life as well as freedom of religion. It ordered the Republika Srpska to refrain from any steps to remove the remains of Mrs. Mahmutovic from their present place of burial and to pay to the applicant 1,000 DM in compensation for nonpecuniary damages. Although this decision has in fact been complied with by the authorities, the old Town Cemetery has nevertheless not been reopened. In February 2000 the Chamber issued another judgement on this issue where it found that the Islamic Community in Bosnia and Herzegovina as a legal entity, by being prevented from carrying out burials in the city of Prnjavor, is a victim of discrimination in the enjoyment of its right to freedom of religion. The Chamber ordered the Republika Srpska to revoke the decision of 1994 which had put the old Muslim Town Cemetery out of use, and to desist from prohibiting burials there.[104]

V. Conclusions

On the basis of international case law relating to permissible limitations on freedom of religion or belief, we can conclude that states interfere for various purposes: for the protection of legitimate public interests (such as public safety, order, health, or morals), for the protection of religious freedom and other human rights against interference by others, as well as for less legitimate interests, including the maintenance of privileges for state and majority religions, the discrimination of religious minorities, or even incitement to religious hatred and violence, as the cases in Bosnia and Herzegovina have shown.[105]

The freedom to manifest one's religion or belief as well as the internal freedom of thought, conscience, and religion are subject to all sorts of restrictions by state actors as well as private parties. As long as governments try to mediate between private religious conflicts, their restrictions usually do not go beyond the legitimate limits of state interference, and international monitoring bodies often allow them a fairly broad margin of appreciation. If governments take sides, however, with a particular (usually the state or majority) religion, their interferences soon become discriminatory and may amount to serious and systematic human rights violations.

Interferences with freedom of thought, conscience, and religion often start right from the birth of a child. If a baby would become a member of a political party or trade union, we would consider this a fairly far-reaching interference with its privacy or freedom of association. In the case of religious organizations, such interference seems to be generally accepted. If it emanates only from the parents of the baby, it is even protected by the liberty of parents to educate their children in accordance with their own religious convictions, and governments should protect this liberty against interference by others, such as schools or religious groups. There are, however, limits to this right of parents. If Jehovah's Witnesses, e.g., prevent the life of their children being saved by means of a blood transfusion, states may or even have to intervene with the liberty of parents in order to protect the life and health of the children.[106]

---

[104] Islamic Community in Bosnia and Herzegovina v. Republika Srpska, Case No. CH/99/2177 (Human Rights Chamber, 11 February 2000), decision on admissibility and merits.

[105] See notes 102 to 104.

[106] Hoffmann v. Austria, 17 EHRR 293 (1994) (ECtHR 255-C, 23 June 1993).

If governments attempt to indoctrinate children according to a given religion or ideology, international law and jurisprudence set fairly strict limits. Mandatory religious instruction in public schools is prohibited, and "ethical education" is only permitted if taught in a neutral manner.[107] Should states provide funds to private religious schools, they have to do this on an equal basis.[108]

When children become adolescents, they gradually acquire the right of their own to choose their religion or belief, which might even include the right to change their religion against the objections of their parents. States are under an obligation to provide for respective legal procedures and, if necessary, to interfere with the parents in order to protect the children's freedom of religion or belief. At this age, young people are most vulnerable to the missionary or evangelical activities of other religious groups and sects, and in particular to attempts of teachers, superiors, and other persons on whom they depend. Again, states have an obligation to protect adolescents and other vulnerable persons against improper proselytism.[109] On the other hand, too far reaching restrictions on proselytism might violate the legitimate rights of religious groups to seek to convert others.[110]

When growing up, adolescents become eligible for compulsory military service or other duties imposed on them by states that might interfere with their religious convictions. For many years, European and UN human rights treaty bodies, with questionable arguments, maintained that compulsory military service did not interfere with freedom of religion,[111] but gradually the international community has recognized the right to conscientious objection to military service as a special human right deriving from freedom of conscience and religion.[112] If states recognize substitute service, they should not discriminate against conscientious objectors as compared to soldiers, e.g., in the length of the respective services,[113] and should treat different religions equally in respect of exempting their ministers or followers from military and/or substitute service.[114]

Conscientious objection to other legal duties, such as paying taxes for military expenditures or contractual obligations has in principle either not been recognized as a right protected by freedom of religion or belief, or respective restrictions have been justified by the explicit limitation clauses. In a number of cases we are not sure whether these restrictions were really necessary for the protection of public safety, order, health, or morals, i.e., whether the proportionality test has been applied in an appropriate manner. It is, for example, questionable whether the legal or contractual obligation of

---

[107] Danish Sex Education Case: Kjeldsen, Busk Madsen and Pedersen v. Denmark, 1 EHRR 711 (1979–80) (ECtHR 23, 7 December 1976); Hartikainen et al. v. Finland, Comm. No. 40/1978 (UN Human Rights Committee, 9 April 1981).

[108] Waldman v. Canada, Comm. No. 694/1996 (UN Human Rights Committee, 5 November 1999).

[109] Larissis and Others v. Greece, 27 EHRR 329 (1999) (ECtHR 1998-I, 24 February 1998).

[110] Kokkinakis v. Greece, 17 EHRR 397 (1994) (ECtHR 260-A, 25 May 1993).

[111] Grandrath v. Germany, App. No. 2299/64, (EComHR, 12 December 1966), inadmissibility decision.

[112] See UN Commission on Human Rights Resolutions 1998/77 (1998) and 2000/34 (2000). See also the relevant Parliamentary Assembly Resolutions 337 (1967) and 816 (1977) in van Dijk and van Hoof, *Theory and Practice of the European Convention,* 544 nn. 1406–07.

[113] Westerman v. the Netherlands, Comm. No. 682/1996 (UN Human Rights Committee, 3 November 1999); Foin v. France, Comm. No. 666/1995 (UN Human Rights Committee, 9 November 1999).

[114] Brinkhof v. the Netherlands, Comm. No. 402/1990 (UN Human Rights Committee, 27 July 1993); Tsirlis and Kouloumpas v. Greece, 25 EHRR 198 (1997) (ECtHR 1997-III, 17 April 1996), No. 38.

Sikhs to wear safety headgear (rather than a turban) when driving motorbikes or working in a railway corporation was strictly required for the protection of public safety or health.[115] The same holds true for the prohibition of Muslim women to wear a headscarf in a public university.[116] With respect to prisoners, the case law seems to be even more restrictive by accepting, at least implicitly, so-called "inherent limitations."[117]

On the other hand, the European Court has accepted fairly far-reaching restrictions on freedom of expression, including the total ban of a film or video considered to be blasphemous, on the ground that the religious feelings of the adherents to the majority religion were allegedly violated.[118] This jurisprudence has rightly been criticized as in fact inventing a right to the protection of one's religious feelings, as prioritizing freedom of religion vis-à-vis freedom of expression, and as being unproportional and discriminatory.

The case law analyzed shows the difficulties of striking a fair balance between manifestations of freedom of religion on the one hand and the protection of public interests as well as human rights of private persons on the other. Some of the difficulties arise from the fact that religious groups often misuse freedom of religion and, thereby, interfere with the rights of others. Other difficulties have to do with the fact that the societies in many states have been influenced for hundreds of years by the values of one particular religion, and that their governments see nothing wrong in maintaining certain privileges for the dominant religion or religions in their states. Often the morals or values of *ordre public* which governments seek to protect are in fact based on one particular religion. This traditional attitude becomes as less acceptable as we are moving toward truly multicultural societies.[119] Even international and regional human rights monitoring bodies are sometimes influenced by moral and religious convictions and, in the event of doubts, afford governments an unnecessarily broad margin of appreciation. At a time when state-backed religious fundamentalism is increasing rather than decreasing, it will be very difficult to implement the main principle underlying the very concept of freedom of religion or belief: that states should keep a neutral position vis-à-vis all religions and should only interfere if this is absolutely necessary for mediating between conflicting religious groups or for the protection of certain public interests and human rights of others.

[115] K. Singh Bhinder v. Canada, Comm. No. 208/1986 (UN Human Rights Committee, 9 November 1989), UN Doc. A/45/40 (Vol. II), Annex IX, SE (1990); X v. United Kingdom, App. No. 7992/77 (EComHR, 14 Decisions and Reports 234, 12 July 1978), inadmissibility decision.

[116] Karaduman v. Turkey, App. No. 16278/90 (EComHR, 74 Decisions and Reports 93, 3 May 1993), inadmissibility decision.

[117] Prisoner cases (see notes 33 to 36).

[118] Otto-Preminger-Institut v. Austria, 19 EHRR 34 (1995) (ECtHR 295-A, 20 September 1994); Wingrove v. United Kingdom, 24 EHRR 1 (1997) (ECtHR 1996-V, 25 November 1996); Gay News case of X Ltd. and Y v. United Kingdom, App. No. 8710/79 (EComHR, 28 Decisions and Reports 77, 7 May 1982).

[119] See on this issue in general Walter Kälin, *Grundrechte im Kulturkonflikt* (Zürich: NZZ Buchverlag, 2000).

Chapter 7

The United Nations Commission on Human Rights and Freedom of Religion or Belief*

Theo van Boven

I. Introduction

Since its establishment in 1946, pursuant to article 68 of the United Nations Charter, the Commission on Human Rights has been actively involved in efforts to define, promote, and protect freedom of religion or belief as one of the most basic human rights and fundamental freedoms. In terms of standard setting and implementation, three stages can be distinguished in the Commission's work.

The first stage, covering the years 1946 to 1955, was characterized by solid ground work in order to lay the basis for the International Bill of Human Rights. In those years, the Commission formulated the draft texts of what became article 18 of the Universal Declaration of Human Rights and article 18 of the International Covenant on Civil and Political Rights. The standards defined in these articles set out in scope and content the essential and nonderogable normative framework relating to freedom of religion or belief. This chapter does not analyze and describe the meaning of these articles because this has been done elsewhere with great competence.[1]

The second stage stretched over more than two decades, from 1960 to 1981, and was characterized by tedious ideological and political arm wrestling in efforts to elaborate more detailed standards for the promotion and protection of freedom of religion or belief. These efforts finally resulted in the adoption and proclamation of the Declaration on the Elimination of All Forms of Intolerance and of Discrimination Based on Religion or Belief in 1981.[2] Although international instruments like the Convention on the Rights of the Child in 1989, the International Convention on the Protection of the Rights of

* The present chapter was completed in March 2000.

[1] See Bahiyyih G. Tahzib, *Freedom of Religion or Belief, Ensuring Effective International Legal Protection* (Boston: Martinus Nijhoff, 1996).

[2] For a detailed analysis of the 1981 Declaration, see Donna J. Sullivan, "Advancing the Freedom of Religion or Belief through the UN Declaration on the Elimination of Religious Intolerance and Discrimination," *American Journal of International Law* 82 (1988): 487–520.

Tore Lindholm, W. Cole Durham, Jr., Bahia G. Tahzib-Lie (eds.), Facilitating Freedom of Religion or Belief: A Deskbook, *173–188.*

All Migrant Workers and Their Families in 1990, and the Declaration on the Rights of Persons Belonging to National or Ethnic, Religious and Linguistic Minorities in 1992 have included provisions regarding freedom of religion or belief, the stage of standard-setting essentially ended in 1981, shifting UN activities to implementation measures.

Consequently, the third stage started in 1986 with the decision of the Commission on Human Rights to appoint, in view of incidents and governmental actions inconsistent with the provisions of the 1981 Declaration, a Special Rapporteur to examine such incidents and actions and to recommend remedial measures, including the promotion of a dialogue between communities of religion or belief and their governments.[3] Since 1986, the Special Rapporteur, whose mandate has been periodically renewed, has submitted annual reports to the Commission on Human Rights. Since 1994, he has also been asked to submit interim reports to the General Assembly. The first person to serve as Special Rapporteur was Mr. Angelo Vidal d'Almeida Ribeiro, a national of Portugal. After Mr. Ribeiro resigned in 1993, Mr. Abdelfattah Amor, a national of Tunisia, succeeded him as Special Rapporteur.

This chapter will focus on the more recent activities of the Commission on Human Rights in the area of freedom of religion or belief with emphasis on the work and the role of the Commission's main actor in the field, the Special Rapporteur. In order to place the work of the Commission and its Special Rapporteur in the right perspective, it is necessary to set forth at the outset the contextual framework in which the Commission operates as well as some conceptual features of the right to freedom of religion or belief.

II. Contextual Aspects and Conceptual Notions

A. The Contextual Framework of the Commission on Human Rights

The Commission on Human Rights' increasing involvement in issues relating to human rights violations in numerous countries coupled with the political implications of such involvement has caused the interests of governments to become the prevailing factor in the orientation of the Commission's work. In addition, the fact that human rights were given a more prominent place on the international political agenda in the last two decades has had a major impact on the role, the functioning, and the nature of the Commission. As was correctly stated, "[T]he Commission is therefore a *purely political body* whose course and, above all, decisions are controlled by politicians and diplomats, and in which regional group interests and differences tend to predominate."[4]

The Commission's annual sessions cover a six-week period during which it has to deal with some twenty agenda items divided into a wide range of subitems. The issue of religious intolerance is listed under "civil and political rights" with torture and detention; disappearances and summary executions; freedom of expression; independence of the judiciary, administration of justice, impunity; states of emergency; and conscientious objection to military service.[5]

---

[3] Commission on Human Rights Resolution 1986/20 (1986).

[4] *The Functioning of the United Nations Commission on Human Rights*, Netherlands Advisory Council on International Affairs, report no. 11, The Hague, September 1999, 6; emphasis added.

[5] See Commission on Human Rights, *Provisional Agenda*, 20 March–29 April 2000, UN Doc. E/CN.4/2000/1, 56th Sess. (2000).

Statistical data pertaining to the fifty-fourth session illustrate the actual, nearly unmanageable situation in which the Commission finds itself. In the fifty-fourth session, the Commission counted fifty-three member states with 609 delegation members and eighty-eight observer states with 552 delegation members. Two hundred three non-governmental organizations with 1656 persons participated in the session. Sixty-nine dignitaries addressed the Commission. It adopted eighty-four resolutions and twelve formal decisions. Four hundred seventy-nine documents were issued for the Commission with a total of 5820 pages.[6]

Further, it should be noted that the Commission is equipped with a host of thematic-specific and country-specific mechanisms, including thirty-five Special Rapporteurs, special representatives, independent experts, and working groups.[7] These people serve in their private and expert capacities. One of them is the Special Rapporteur on Religious Intolerance. The political nature of the Commission, the preponderance and diversity of governmental and other interests, the many dozens of items and issues requiring the attention of the Commission, the competing ambitions and priorities of governmental and non-governmental actors, and the large quantities of formal and informal papers are all factors that jeopardize and complicate a rational and in-depth discussion and treatment of any subject matter by the Commission. These factors cannot be ignored when examining the current role of the Commission on Human Rights with respect to freedom of religion or belief.

B. Conceptual Notions of the Right to Freedom of Religion or Belief

Before reviewing the work of the Commission on Human Rights and its Special Rapporteur on Religious Intolerance, it will be necessary, for the sake of keeping a broader perspective in mind, to outline some conceptual notions which reflect essential features of freedom of religion or belief.[8] First, in order to appreciate the full scope and the comprehensive meaning of freedom of religion or belief, one must be mindful of the fact that freedom of religion or belief can never be separated from other human rights and fundamental freedoms. Among these other human rights and fundamental freedoms are the right to life and the right to physical, mental, and moral integrity of the human person; the right to peaceful assembly and association; the right to freedom of opinion and expression; the right not to be subject to arbitrary arrest and detention; the right to leave one's country and to return to it; the right to property; the right to education, and so on. Many aspects of freedom of religion or belief have little or no meaning if other human rights are not effectively ensured.

The second basic notion pertains to the inherent link between freedom of religion or belief and the imperative standard of nondiscrimination on the grounds of religion or belief. Freedom of religion or belief is characterized by a long history in

---

[6] These figures pertain to the 1998 session of the Commission, see UN Doc. E/CN.4/1999/109.

[7] UN Economic and Social Council, Commission on Human Rights, *Provisional Agenda,* UN Doc. E/CN.4/2000/1, 56th Sess., annex (1999).

[8] See also Theo van Boven, "Religious Freedom in International Perspective; Existing and Future Standards," *Des Menschen Recht zwischen Freiheit under Verantwortung, Festschrift für Karl Josef Partsch,* ed. Jürgen Jekewitz et al. (Berlin: Duncker and Humblot, 1989), 103–13.

national and international law and progressively embraces not only persons belonging to the traditional and major Christian and non-Christian faiths but also persons adhering to indigenous beliefs, to sectarian religions, and to nonreligious beliefs, sometimes referred to as *Weltanschauungen*. Freedom of religion or belief belongs on the one hand to the realm of the mind (*forum internum*), ensuring the spiritual integrity and conscience of the human person, but it also entails freedom to manifest religion or belief in worship, teaching, practice, and observance, as spelled out in the relevant basic international standards. In addition and most noteworthy, equal importance should be attached to the right of persons and collectivities not to be discriminated against on the grounds of professing or not professing a certain religion or adhering to a certain belief. Religious nondiscrimination implies and means that nobody should be infringed in the exercise of civil and political rights (for instance, access to public office) or in the enjoyment of economic, social, and cultural rights (for instance, access to education, housing, health care, employment, or to literary or artistic facilities) on the ground that he or she belongs or does not belong to a certain religion or belief. Millions of people are not only curtailed in the exercise of their religious rights and practices, their lives and well-being are also put in jeopardy because due to their religious faith or identity they lack the enjoyment of many other human rights. It is therefore essential that the nondiscrimination imperative receive all necessary attention and emphasis.

A third fundamental notion relates to the fact that in many situations it is not the government but religious institutions, affiliations, and movements which cause religious divisions and antagonisms and incite to acts of religious extremism and violence. Inasmuch as such situations are beyond the government's control, United Nations supervisory mechanisms, which base themselves on the accountability of governments, lack an effective focus, at least in the short-term perspective. Approaches that are broader and more comprehensive than the traditional UN method of addressing governments are needed in order to cope with problems arising out of the roles and responsibility of nonstate entities. The building of understanding, respect, and tolerance between people of different religions or beliefs—and also among people of the same religion or belief—requires strenuous and persistent joint efforts by the intergovernmental and nongovernmental community alike. In this connection, interreligious dialogue must be actively pursued as a means to foster respect, understanding, and tolerance.

The fourth essential consideration addresses the notion of tolerance and respect and flows immediately from what was stated above. Too often, religious communities and denominations argue in terms of truth and error in their encounters and disputes. While truth and error may be leading notions in religious doctrine, such notions may have grave consequences for the defense of freedom of religion or belief and the promotion of tolerance, particularly when truth and error are invoked to vindicate resorting to violence. For the sake of promoting and protecting freedom of religion or belief, the respect of rights of individual persons and collectivities must be pursued first and foremost over the search for objective truth. Consequently, emphasis must be given to the promotion of constructive dialogue between religious communities themselves and between these communities and the public authorities in a spirit of tolerance and respect. As will be noted, the Special Rapporteur on Religious Intolerance takes these conceptual notions into account as leading benchmarks in the exercise of his mandate.

III. The Evolving Mandate of the Special Rapporteur

The mandate of the Special Rapporteur on Religious Intolerance, initially created in 1986 by the Commission on Human Rights, was the fourth thematic mechanism set up by the Commission. In earlier years, the Working Group on Enforced or Involuntary Disappearances (1980), the Special Rapporteur on Extrajudicial, Summary or Arbitrary Executions (1982), and the Special Rapporteur on Torture (1985) were set up. These mechanisms were created as part of the Commission's overall mandate, formulated by the Economic and Social Council and the General Assembly, to give urgent consideration to ways of improving the capacity of the United Nations to stop violations wherever they might occur.[9] These mechanisms were intended to enable the Commission to deal more effectively with violations of human rights resulting from widespread evil practices in many parts of the world. It was against this background that the Special Rapporteur on Religious Intolerance was given a mandate to examine incidents and governmental action in all parts of the world that were inconsistent with the provisions of the 1981 Declaration on the Elimination of All Forms of Intolerance and of Discrimination Based on Religion or Belief and to recommend remedial measures for such situations. It should further be recalled that the mandate of the Special Rapporteur, with its focus on violations and on practices and policies inconsistent with the 1981 Declaration, was prompted by an initiative of the United States of America that considered, at the time, a special mechanism on freedom of religion or belief to be a suitable instrument to embarrass communist regimes in the cold war context.

From the outset, the Special Rapporteur's work mainly consisted of preparing *communications* on violations of freedom of religion or belief. These communications were duly verified as to their credibility and reliability before being sent to States for their replies. This information, communications, and any replies received, were further analyzed and classified in terms of religious groups and communities whose rights had allegedly been violated with clear mention of the countries to which the communications related. Another aspect of the analysis is the identification of major problems and trends in light of the principles, rights, and freedoms enunciated in the 1981 Declaration. This exercise enables the Special Rapporteur to distinguish various types of violations occurring in a series of countries. All this information is included in the Special Rapporteur's annual reports and constitutes a fairly comprehensive account of the state of freedom of religion or belief in the world, but the information is by no means so complete that the annual reports could be considered world reports on freedom of religion or belief. The Special Rapporteur rightly observed that more resources and another methodology would be called for in order to prepare a general report that would systematically cover all States and all religions or beliefs.[10] It should be noted that in 1994, the Special Rapporteur established, in the context of work relating to communications, an *urgent appeals procedure* so as to reply more effectively and more expeditiously to particularly serious cases or situations, such as those involving threats to the right to life and the physical integrity of the human person. The method of work based on communications will be referred to in more detail below.

---

[9] UN GA Resolution 2144 A (XXI), 26 October 1966; ECOSOC Resolution 1235 (XLII), 6 June 1967.

[10] UN Economic and Social Council, Commission on Human Rights, *Civil and Political Rights, Including Religious Intolerance*, UN Doc. E/CN.4/1999/58, 55th Sess. (1999), 119–21.

Another method of work consists of *in-situ* visits by the Special Rapporteur. Such visits can only be carried out with the consent of the states concerned. The Commission on Human Rights and the General Assembly have encouraged *in-situ* visits. Thus, the Commission has repeatedly called upon all governments to cooperate fully with the Special Rapporteur, to respond favorably to requests by him to visit their countries, and to give serious consideration to inviting the Special Rapporteur to visit so as to enable him to fulfil his mandate even more effectively.[11] The Special Rapporteur emphasized the value of the *in-situ* visits by stating, "The visits enable dialogue to be initiated or pursued in greater depth with Governments and with all the parties concerned, namely, non-governmental organizations and all individuals, including victims, with a particular interest in the mandate. They also help to enhance understanding of the complexity of situations of intolerance and discrimination based on religion or belief."[12] Again, the *in-situ* visits, including the *visit follow-up procedure* introduced by the Special Rapporteur, will be further discussed below on the basis of the most recent reports of the Special Rapporteur.

While information, identification, and analysis of issues and problems relating to freedom of religion or belief as well as dialogue with governments, religious communities, and nongovernmental organizations, and immediate concern for victims of violations are principal ingredients of the Special Rapporteur's mandate, the current office holder is also mindful that his mandate, in order to lay foundations for the future, should be proactive and include a prevention strategy. Thus, for the purpose of devising a worldwide educational strategy to combat intolerance and discrimination based on religion or belief, he recommended the organization of an international conference on education as inspired by the Oslo Coalition on Freedom of Religion or Belief.[13] In addition, the Special Rapporteur indicated a number of sensitive priority issues with clear preventive implications, which require close attention in the course of the implementation of his mandate.[14] These priorities are:

- Tackling *religious extremism,* whether or not based on genuinely religious precepts, which provokes and sustains violence and causes immense suffering. One of the means recommended by the Special Rapporteur is the definition and adoption of a "minimum set of standard rules and principles of conduct and behavior in respect of religious extremism."[15]

---

[11] UN Economic and Social Council, Commission on Human Rights, *Implementation of the Declaration on the Elimination of All Forms of Intolerance and of Discrimination Based on Religion or Belief,* UN Doc. E/CN.4/RES/1999/39 (1999), 9.

[12] UN Economic and Social Council, Commission on Human Rights, *Implementation of the Declaration on the Elimination of All Forms of Intolerance and of Discrimination Based on Religion or Belief,* E/CN.4/1998/6, 54th sess. (1998), para. 22.

[13] UN Economic and Social Council, Commission on Human Rights, *Civil and Political Rights, Including Religious Intolerance,* E/CN.4/1999/58, 55th sess. (1999), 124.

[14] UN Economic and Social Council, Commission on Human Rights, *Implementation of the Declaration on the Elimination of All Forms of Intolerance and of Discrimination Based on Religion or Belief,* UN Doc. E/CN.4/1998/6, 54th Sess. (1998), 97–120; UN Economic and Social Council, Commission on Human Rights, Civil and Political Rights, Including Religious Intolerance, UN Doc. E/CN.4/1999/58, 55th Sess. (1999), 115–27.

[15] UN Economic and Social Council, Commission on Human Rights, *Implementation of the Declaration on the Elimination of All Forms of Intolerance and of Discrimination Based on Religion or Belief,* UN Doc. E/CN.4/1998/6, 54th Sess. (1998), 114.

- Tackling ***discrimination and intolerance against women***, supposedly prescribed by religion or tradition, including practices which violate the human rights of women, in response to the call of the Commission of Human Rights and the General Assembly to apply a gender perspective and to identify gender-specific abuses. To this end, the Special Rapporteur called for the formulation of practical recommendations and a plan of action for eradicating practices that violate the human rights of women.
- Examining closely the issue of ***sects or new religious movements***, which is a pressing phenomenon and which raises the crucial borderline questions of respect for the rightful exercise of freedom of religion or belief and the abuse of this freedom for purposes which conflict with health, morals, or the fundamental rights and freedoms of persons.

1. Communications Sent and Replies Received

As noted earlier, from the onset, a substantial part of the Special Rapporteur's mandate and an important chapter of the annual reports to the Commission on Human Rights have consisted of the Special Rapporteur's communications sent and replies received. It is not possible to fully describe and analyze in this chapter the wealth of information contained in the Special Rapporteur's annual reports. For illustration purposes, only a few significant features will be singled out from the Special Rapporteur's reports to the 1998 and 1999 sessions of the Commission on Human Rights.[16] In a one-year period, the Special Rapporteur sent sixty-three communications, including four urgent appeals to Iran and the Sudan, to forty-six states; twenty-two states responded to these communications.[17] In classifying communities in a variety of countries that had allegedly been victims of violations of freedom of religion or belief, the Special Rapporteur distinguished between major religions, notably Christianity, Judaism, Islam, Buddhism, and religious groups and communities such as Ahmadis, Bahá'ís, Jehovah's Witnesses, Hare Krishna, and Scientology. In a number of countries, incidents and governmental actions affected all religions and religious groups, except the official, state, or predominant religions.[18]

In his analysis of the communications from the standpoint of the principles, rights, and freedoms enunciated in the 1981 Declaration, the Special Rapporteur listed and substantiated the following categories of violations:[19]

- violations of the principle of nondiscrimination in matters of religion or belief;
- violations of the principle of tolerance in matters of religion or belief;

---

[16] UN Economic and Social Council, Commission on Human Rights, *Implementation of the Declaration on the Elimination of All Forms of Intolerance and of Discrimination Based on Religion or Belief,* UN Doc. E/CN.4/1998/6, 54th Sess. (1998); UN Economic and Social Council, Commission on Human Rights, *Civil and Political Rights, Including Religious Intolerance,* UN Doc. E/CN.4/1999/58, 55th Sess. (1999).

[17] UN Economic and Social Council, Commission on Human Rights, *Civil and Political Rights, Including Religious Intolerance,* UN Doc. E/CN.4/1999/58, 55th Sess. (1999), 24–25.

[18] UN Economic and Social Council, Commission on Human Rights, *Implementation of the Declaration on the Elimination of All Forms of Intolerance and of Discrimination Based on Religion or Belief,* UN Doc. E/CN.4/1998/6, 54th Sess. (1998), 50.

[19] UN Economic and Social Council, Commission on Human Rights, *Civil and Political Rights, Including Religious Intolerance,* UN Doc. E/CN.4/1999/58, 55th Sess., (1999), paras. 104–11.

- violations of freedom of thought, conscience, and religion or belief, including the principle of conscientious objection and freedom to change and keep one's religion and belief;
- violations of the freedom to manifest one's religion or belief;
- violations of the freedom to dispose of religious property;
- violations of physical integrity, health, and the right to life;
- violations affecting women.

The following passage effectively illustrates the findings and the analysis of the Special Rapporteur:

> This last category [violations affecting women] embraces the previous six categories of violations. The most tragic illustration is the Taliban's anti-feminine policy in Afghanistan: it is tantamount to veritable apartheid against women, as women, and on the basis of specious interpretations of Islam. This obscurantism, the product of religious extremism combining religion and politics in the interests of power, excludes women from society and consigns them to a grey area where they enjoy neither citizenship nor rights and where their submission to the all-powerful man in the name of Allah is the order of the day.[20]

2. *In-situ* Visits and Follow-up

The Special Rapporteur started his country visits in 1994 as a method to gather first-hand information and to carry on a dialogue with public authorities, religious communities, nongovernmental organizations, and directly interested persons. As noted earlier, the Commission on Human Rights and the General Assembly have repeatedly encouraged governments to invite the Special Rapporteur to visit their countries. The Special Rapporteur makes an average of two country visits per year. In the period of 1994 to 1999, eleven visits were made to a variety of important countries where delicate and sensitive issues pertaining to freedom of religion or belief and religious nondiscrimination were raised and publicly reported in addenda to the regular reports to the Commission on Human Rights and the General Assembly. The following visits took place: China (November 1994), Pakistan (June 1995), Iran (December 1995), Greece (June 1996), Sudan (September 1996), India (December 1996), Australia (February–March 1997), Germany (September 1997), United States of America (January–February 1998), Vietnam (October 1998), and Turkey (December 1999). A visit to Bangladesh was scheduled for 2000 and replies from Argentina, Indonesia, Mauritius, Israel, the Russian Federation, and North Korea are still awaited with respect to future visits. Also, a follow-up procedure has been introduced so as to continue the dialogue with the governments concerned. For this purpose the Special Rapporteur made follow-up tables reflecting in a systematic way the recommendations he made in the mission reports with the invitation to the governments concerned to send their comments and any information on action taken or envisaged to implement the recommendations.[21] Most

---

[20] Ibid., 111.

[21] UN Doc. E/CN.4/1999/58, para. 21.

governments have replied except Iran, Germany, and Australia.[22] The follow-up tables and replies are made public in the Special Rapporteur's interim reports submitted to the General Assembly. In the light of problems encountered by the Special Rapporteur during some of the missions he carried out, he felt it necessary to recall the rules and principles implicit in the special procedures mandate for inquiring into religious intolerance, in particular the Special Rapporteur's independence, freedom of movement, freedom of assembly, freedom to meet any individual or organization he feels could clarify various issues, with no constraints or repercussions whatsoever.[23] These are essential principles and conditions for independent missions and inquiries on the spot and currently the subject of work done in the UN General Assembly concerning a possible Code of Conduct for Experts on Mission and UN Officials other than Secretariat staff.

In addition to *in-situ* visits to states, the Special Rapporteur decided, as a new approach, to visit major religious communities or institutions in order to establish with them a direct dialogue on the basis of the 1981 Declaration and to discuss possible solutions relating to problems and issues of intolerance and discrimination in the area of freedom of religion or belief. The first such visit led the Special Rapporteur to the Vatican in September 1999, which was extensively reflected in his report to the fifty-sixth session of the Commission on Human Rights.[24] The discussions with the Vatican covered many important issues, including the position of the Vatican with regard to certain states as well as various aspects of interreligious dialogue with Jews, Muslims, Buddhists, Hindus, and non-Roman-Catholic Christians. Questions relating to sects and new religious movements as well as the position of the Vatican with respect to the role of women and the family and with regard to religious education and training were also discussed. Based on his discussions, overall findings, and the insights he gained over the years, the Special Rapporteur emphasized the importance of education and interreligious dialogue as key elements in preventive strategies aimed at counteracting religious extremism and intolerance.[25]

It is not yet clear how the Special Rapporteur envisages continuing the new approach he embarked upon. While he was able to arrange a visit to a well-established and hierarchical institution as the Vatican, direct contact with other religious bodies and communities that are less organized and institutionalized may be more difficult, especially when such organizations face internal divisions stemming from discord in religious doctrine and practice and from diversity in cultural and geographical settings. There will be a need for the Special Rapporteur to find valuable interlocutors with proper understanding and authority, coming from different religious communities and geographical regions, in order to promote and engage in meaningful inter-religious dialogue leading to reciprocal commitments. It should be emphasized that in all such efforts, a gender perspective has to be applied in accordance with repeated pronouncements of the Commission on Human Rights.[26]

---

[22] UN Doc. E/CN.4/2000/65, para. 118.

[23] UN Doc. E/CN.4/1999/58, para. 18.

[24] UN Doc. E/CN.4/2000/65, paras. 120–72.

[25] Ibid., paras. 178–81.

[26] UN Economic and Social Council, ***Implementation of the Declaration on the Elimination of All Forms of Intolerance and of Discrimination Based on Religion or Belief***, UN Doc. E/CN.4/RES/1999/39 (1999), 8.

3. The Title of the Mandate

In his reports of the late nineties, the Special Rapporteur proposed that the customary title of his mandate "Special Rapporteur on Religious Intolerance" be changed into "Special Rapporteur on freedom of Religion or Belief."[27] He advanced several arguments in favor of such a change. These arguments are both of a substantive and of a practical nature. First, the customary title does not adequately reflect the notion of "belief," which also covers nonreligious beliefs in terms of *Weltanschauung* in accordance with the scope of article 18 of the Universal Declaration of Human Rights and the 1981 Declaration. Moreover, in a practical sense, the customary title appears to antagonize certain interlocutors and sometimes makes dialogue difficult. The Special Rapporteur's wish to see the title of his mandate changed to Special Rapporteur on Freedom of Religion or Belief is certainly legitimate and in line with the basic notions and standards contained in widely accepted international instruments in the field of human rights. It also corresponds to the evolution of his mandate. The Commission on Human Rights noted the request of the Special Rapporteur and decided to change the title at its fifty-sixth session in 2000 and to effectuate the change at the extension of the Special Rapporteur's mandate in 2001.[28]

IV. The Role of the Commission on Human Rights

The question of religious intolerance figures annually on the agenda of the Commission on Human Rights. The principal documentation before the Commission is the report submitted by the Special Rapporteur, together with addenda relating to his country visits. In light of the political and contextual factors which determine the Commission's proceedings and which were described above, it is no surprise that the discussions in the Commission lack focus and coherence. Usually, less than one-fifth of the membership of the Commission takes part in the discussions on the question of religious intolerance. Only a few countries, notably the United States, Ireland, and Norway, make it a habit to take the floor. Nongovernmental organizations have traditionally shown a greater interest in issues relating to freedom of religion or belief, and their interventions, usually relating to particular concerns in one or more countries, outnumber those of state representatives. It is striking that, in general, few references are made to the reports of the Special Rapporteur and that even the countries that have been visited by the Special Rapporteur do not usually comment on the reports relating to these visits. This unrewarding pattern of discussions does not only characterize the Commission's dealings with the question of freedom of religion or belief but is an across-the-board phenomenon concerning the Commission's entire agenda.[29] Most

---

27 UN Economic and Social Council, Commission on Human Rights, *Implementation of the Declaration on the Elimination of All Forms of Intolerance and of Discrimination Based on Religion or Belief,* UN Doc. E/CN.4/1998/6, 54th Sess. (1998), 104–5; UN Economic and Social Council, Commission on Human Rights, *Civil and Political Rights, Including Religious Intolerance,* UN Doc. E/CN.4/1999/58, 54th Sess. (1999), 122.

28 Commission on Human Rights Resolution 2000/33, 20 April 2000, para. 11 (2000).

29 See the very informative analytical reports of the UN Commission on Human Rights and of other UN Human Rights bodies contained in issues of *Human Rights Monitor,* published by the International Service for Human Rights, Geneva (Adrien Claude Zoller, editor-in-chief).

actors in diplomatic and political forums tend to be stronger on procedure than on substance, and the question arises whether a body like the Commission on Human Rights is at all able to discuss in-depth and in an effective manner the many sensitive issues included in the Special Rapporteur's reports. In this connection, it is noteworthy that negotiations and other steps in preparation of decision-making by the Commission follow informal and pre-established patterns, and are not reflected in the Commission's public records. The most visible "product" of the Commission is its annual resolutions. Another aspect deserving attention is the linkage drawn by the Commission between racism, xenophobia, and religious intolerance and the Commission's stand against defamation of religions. These issues will be further discussed in more detail.

A. Annual Resolutions

For many years, Ireland has been the principal sponsor of the annual resolution carrying the title "Implementation of the Declaration on the Elimination of All Forms of Intolerance and of Discrimination Based on Religion or Belief." Ireland introduces the draft resolution in the public meeting, and it is assumed that this country plays the key role in the conduct of informal talks and negotiations. It is also standard practice that the annual resolutions on this matter are adopted without a vote and that the texts are cosponsored by a large number of member states and observer states of the Commission.[30] The high number of cosponsor states stands in contrast with the small number of state representatives who actually participate in the public discussions on this issue and suggests a fair degree of ritual in dealing with the matter. This suggestion is also strengthened by the fact that the annual resolutions of the Commission on Human Rights, in this area and in others, contain standard language that remains largely unchanged year after year. Only on occasion does the language reveal interesting variation.

By way of illustration, a number of features of the annual resolution adopted by the fifty-fifth session of the Commission, Resolution 1999/39, will be highlighted. As regards the work of the Special Rapporteur, the resolution:

- welcomed his report (paragraph 1);[31]
- encouraged his continuing efforts to examine incidents and governmental actions incompatible with the Declaration and to recommend remedial measures as appropriate (paragraph 6);
- invited him to contribute effectively to the preparatory process for the World Conference against Racism to be held in 2001 (paragraph 7);
- stressed the need for him to apply a gender perspective (paragraph 8);
- called upon all governments to cooperate fully with him and to respond favorably to requests from him to visit their countries (paragraph 9);

---

[30] Resolution 1998/18, adopted in 1998, was co-sponsored by forty-six states and joined by eleven more states as co-sponsors, and Resolution 1999/39, adopted in 1999, was co-sponsored by fifty-one states and subsequently co-sponsored by ten more states.

[31] The resolution, adopted in 1998, was less complimentary and simply "took note" of the report (Resolution 1998/18, para. 1). UN Economic and Social Council, Commission on Human Rights, *Implementation of the Declaration on the Elimination of All Forms of Intolerance and of Discrimination Based on Religion or Belief,* UN Doc./CN.4/RES/1998/18 (1998), 1.

- welcomed his work and reiterated the need for him to respond effectively to credible and reliable information that comes before him and invited him to carry out his work with discretion, objectivity, and independence (paragraph 10); and
- noted his request to change his title from Special Rapporteur on Religious Intolerance to Special Rapporteur on Freedom of Religion or Belief and decided to consider changing the title at its next session (paragraph 11).

As regards substantive aspects relating to freedom of religion or belief, the resolution urged states *inter alia*:

- to ensure that their constitutional and legislative systems provide adequate and effective guarantees as well as effective remedies where the right to freedom of religion or belief, including the freedom to change one's religion, is violated (paragraph 4[a]);
- to ensure that no one is deprived of the right to life or the right to security of person because of religion or belief, or is subjected to torture or arbitrary arrest or detention on that account (paragraph 4[b]);
- to take all necessary actions to combat hatred, intolerance, and acts of violence, intimidation, and coercion motivated by intolerance based on religion or belief, with particular regard to religious minorities, and also including practices which violate the human rights of women and discriminate against women (paragraph 4[c]);
- to recognize the right of all persons to worship and assemble (paragraph 4[d]);
- to ensure that members of law enforcement bodies, civil servants, educators, and other public officials respect different religions and beliefs and do not discriminate on the grounds of religion or belief (paragraph 4[e]);
- to ensure that religious places, sites, and shrines are fully respected and protected (paragraph 4[f]); and
- to promote and encourage understanding, tolerance and respect in matters relating to freedom of religion or belief (paragraph 4[g]).

It appears from the text just outlined that the Commission on Human Rights broadly lends its authority to the Special Rapporteur to carry on his work on the basis of communications and *in-situ* visits "with discretion, objectivity and independence."[32] He is also advised to apply a gender perspective. Furthermore, the Commission is sensitive to the Special Rapporteur's wish to change the title of his mandate. On the other hand, the Commission is not clearly disposed, neither in its resolutions nor in its discussions, to refer to developments and trends or other substantive matters outlined in the Special Rapporteur's annual reports and, thus, generally avoids entering into controversies. It is true that the Commission makes pronouncements, in a rather general manner, on substantive aspects relating to freedom of religion or belief, but these pronouncements do not go beyond citing or paraphrasing existing international standards and are not a direct response to the Special Rapporteur's reports. It is, however,

---

[32] UN Economic and Social Council, Commission on Human Rights, ***Implementation of the Declaration on the Elimination of All Forms of Intolerance and of Discrimination Based on Religion or Belief***, UN Doc. E/CN.4/RES/1999/39 (1999), 10.

interesting and relevant that the Commission, like the Special Rapporteur, specifically refers to the notions of freedom to change one's religion or belief; the right to life, liberty, and security of person; and the right not to be subjected to torture, arbitrary arrest, or detention because of religion or belief. This emphasis is fully warranted and deserves to be further substantiated and elaborated.

B. Racism, Xenophobia and Religious Intolerance

It is often difficult to draw a clear line between attitudes and expressions of religious intolerance and racial prejudice and hatred. Anti-Semitism may comprise elements of racial and religious intolerance, and it appears that anti-Muslim sentiments also have racial as well as religious aspects.[33] Against this background, the Commission on Human Rights requested in Resolution 1999/78 that the High Commissioner for Human Rights invite the Special Rapporteur on Religious Intolerance to participate in the preparatory process of the World Conference against Racism, Racial Discrimination, Xenophobia and Related Intolerance by initiating studies on action to combat incitement to hatred and religious intolerance. Furthermore, a similar clause was included in paragraph 7 of Commission Resolution 1999/39 concerning the Implementation of the Declaration on the Elimination of All Forms of Intolerance and of Discrimination Based on Religion or Belief, which was discussed above. The Special Rapporteur accepted this challenge and recommended that studies be prepared on the image of religious minorities in the media and the identification and measures of intolerance against ethno-religious communities.[34] In the same vein, the Special Rapporteur on Religious Intolerance and the Special Rapporteur on Racism, Racial Discrimination and Related Intolerance were requested to take into account the provisions of Resolution 1999/82 on the issue of "Defamation of religions" adopted by the Commission on Human Rights on 30 April 1999. This resolution had its origin in an initiative of the Organization of the Islamic Conference, whose spokesman from Pakistan said:

> [I]n the past few years, there had been new manifestations of intolerance and misunderstanding, not to say hatred, of Islam and Muslims in various parts of the world. It was to be feared that those manifestations might become as widespread and endemic as anti-Semitism had been in the past. There was a tendency in some countries and in the international media to portray Islam as a religion hostile to human rights, threatening to the Western world and associated with terrorism and violence.[35]

Other countries, notably members of the European Union with Germany as spokesperson, expressed reservations since the original draft text "referred exclusively to the negative stereotyping of Islam, whereas other religions had been and continued to be

---

[33] See for instance the report of the Committee on the Elimination of Racial Discrimination to the UN General Assembly, UN Doc. A/51/18, 51st Sess., para. 230, where the Committee expressed special concern over the issue of religious discrimination in connection with anti-Muslim sentiment and stated that discrimination against Muslims may be closely related to questions of race and ethnicity.

[34] Report of the Committee on the Elimination of Racial Discrimination to the UN General Assembly, UN Doc. 1/51/18, 51st Sess., para. 3; UN Economic and Social Council, Commission on Human Rights, *Civil and Political Rights, Including Religious Intolerance,* UN Doc. E/CN.4/2000/65 (2000), 56th Sess., 108.

[35] UN Economic and Social Council, Commission on Human Rights, *Summary Record of the 61st Meeting,* UN Doc. E/CN.4/1999/SR.61, 55th Sess. (1999), 1.

subjected to various forms of discrimination, intolerance, and even persecution."[36] They proposed amendments designed to broaden the issue and to deal equally with all religions. Intense negotiations led to the adoption, without a vote, of a compromise text on defamation of religions, which expressed:

- deep concern with negative stereotyping of religions;
- deep concern that Islam is frequently and wrongly associated with human rights violations and with terrorism;
- concern with any role in which the print, audio-visual or electronic media, or any other means are used to incite acts of violence, xenophobia, or related intolerance and discrimination towards Islam and any other religion.

The adoption of this resolution by the Commission on Human Rights is noteworthy for various reasons. Its introduction, discussion, and adoption in the context of the Commission's item on racism, racial discrimination, xenophobia, and all forms of discrimination, implies and recognizes that racial discrimination, xenophobia, and religious intolerance are often interlinked and require coordinated strategies in legislation, education, and other fields to prevent and eradicate such phenomena. Further, negative stereotyping of religions is rampant in many situations and places and goes hand in hand with evil acts of violence, intimidation, and coercion, often motivated by religious extremism. Quite correctly, the Special Rapporteur on Religious Intolerance noted that these phenomena not only jeopardize relations between religious communities *inter se* but also relations within religious communities. Furthermore, he expressed concern that actions against defamation of religions may be manipulated so that they counteract human rights as may be the case in laws and their applications to suppress and punish blasphemy. In this connection, the Special Rapporteur's conclusions and recommendations in his report on his visit to Pakistan are relevant. He stated there that applying the death penalty for blasphemy appears disproportionate and unacceptable.[37]

VI. Concluding Comments

The present chapter focuses on the UN Commission on Human Rights and freedom of religion or belief. Emphasis is placed on implementation, in particular, of the role of the Commission and its Special Rapporteur on Religious Intolerance in recent years, and not on standard-setting activities that the Commission was able or unable[38] to carry out. This chapter pretends in no way to cover the issue in a complete manner. It is merely indicative and illustrative and deals more with processes than with the realities of freedom of religion or belief and of religious nondiscrimination in many parts of the world. In many situations, religious nationalism and ethnicity leading to religious extremism, violence, and violations of human rights on a massive scale outweigh and

---

[36] Ibid., 3.

[37] UN Economic and Social Council, Commission on Human Rights, *Implementation of the Declaration on the Elimination of All Forms of Intolerance and of Discrimination Based on Religion or Belief*, UN Doc. E/CN.4/1996/95/Add.1, 52nd Sess. (1996), 82.

[38] It must be reminded that the *Declaration on the Elimination of All Forms of Intolerance and of Discrimination Based on Religion or Belief* is, as yet, not followed up by a convention on the same subject, as was originally envisaged by the UN GA in Resolution 1781 (XVII).

[39] See text to note 31 above, paragraph 11 of Resolution 1999/39 of the Commission on Human Rights.

overshadow the role of religion or belief as a factor and actor for peace and human rights. Numerous conflicts in the world have religious overtones and underscore the need to effectively promote understanding, tolerance, and respect in matters relating to freedom of religion or belief, as is rightly stated in the preamble of the 1981 Declaration.

In this respect, the role of the Commission on Human Rights is important inasmuch as it embeds freedom of religion or belief in the broad spectrum of the interdependence and indivisibility of all human rights and peace. The Commission on Human Rights can be considered the central human rights policy organ of the United Nations, and it has mandated Special Rapporteurs, such as the Special Rapporteur on Religious Intolerance, to function with independence and objectivity under its authority. Perusal of the Commission's documents and records proves that the Special Rapporteur, as the investigative, intellectual, and operational arm of the Commission, makes a more substantial and coherent contribution to the cause of freedom of religion or belief than the Commission itself. The Commission, as a platform of discussion and an organ of political decision making, is most reluctant to come to grips with the agonizing realities relating to freedom of religion or belief and religious intolerance and discrimination. When the Commission recently initiated a special effort on the issue of defamation of religion and implied a link between race and religion, it was clear that political overtones prevailed.

The Special Rapporteur on Religious Intolerance, whose title, as had been requested by him,[39] has been changed to Special Rapporteur on Freedom of Religion or Belief, has been able to broaden and deepen his mandate under the authority of the Commission. His country visits and efforts to carry on dialogues with religious institutions and personalities are promising. The reports of his *in-situ* visits show objectivity and understanding and do not hide practices having adverse consequences on freedom of religion or belief. Nevertheless, the ultimate test of the effectiveness of the Special Rapporteur's mandate depends on constructive and proactive cooperation, in good faith, of secular and religious authorities. Whether such cooperation is clearly and sufficiently forthcoming is still questionable.

The Special Rapporteur's mandate and role is different from that of treaty bodies, such as the Human Rights Committee, which also deal with issues relating to freedom of religion or belief and religious nondiscrimination. In addition to the fact that the Special Rapporteur can deal with cases and situations that pertain to States that have not ratified the relevant treaties, the Special Rapporteur enjoys broader margins of operation. He can initiate visits and hold on-the-spot dialogues with official authorities, nongovernmental organizations, religious institutions, and personalities. He can also promote educational programs and mobilize advisory services and technical assistance. In the area of freedom of religion or belief, where the roles and responsibilities of nonstate entities are particularly important, the function of the Special Rapporteur, unhampered by legal constraints inherent in treaty mechanisms, is crucial and complementary.

Against this background, it is desirable that the mandate of the Special Rapporteur be further strengthened. The Special Rapporteur has made a strong plea to allocate more financial, human, and technological resources to the mandate. He has also requested that a new methodology of work be adopted, which would allow him to systematically cover all states, religions, and beliefs, and that consistency be brought between the title of the Special Rapporteur's mandate and its implementation.[40] These wishes are fully legitimate. In the meantime, the Commission has changed the title of the Special Rapporteur's mandate.

In addition, the Commission on Human Rights should more substantially consider the Special Rapporteur's reports at its sessions. If the Commission were to do this with all of its special mechanisms, it would be a much more effective forum. The results of a study conducted to enhance the effectiveness of the Commission on Human Rights mechanisms focused on the important benefits that would result from having more interactive debate on the reports of the Special Rapporteurs. More specifically, the study recommended that time be made available for such debate in the course of the Commission session, immediately following the presentation of the report by the mandate holder. It was also observed, in the same context, that a more meaningful discussion could be expected if governments that received visits from rapporteurs were encouraged to comment in detail on the reports.[41] The present chapter confirms that this recommendation is pertinent to the Special Rapporteur on Religious Intolerance. Its adoption and implementation would make the role of the Commission on Human Rights more meaningful, not only in the exercise of political and moral authority, but also in serving as a platform for more constructive deliberation and dialogue.

---

[40] UN Economic and Social Council, Commission on Human Rights, *Civil and Political Rights, Including Religious Intolerance,* UN Doc. E/CN.4/1999/58, 55th Sess. (1999), 118–22.

[41] UN Economic and Social Council, Commission on Human Rights, *Report by the Working Group on Enhancing the Effectiveness of the Mechanisms of the Commission on Human Rights,* 16 February 2000, UN Doc. E/CN.4/2000/112, 56th Sess., para. 30 (2000).

Chapter 8

The Human Rights Committee and Freedom of Religion or Belief

Martin Scheinin

I. Religion or Belief under the Covenant on Civil and Political Rights

The 1966 International Covenant on Civil and Political Rights is one of the most important universal treaties on human rights. The Covenant protects, in the form of a legally binding international treaty ratified by three quarters of all states in the world,[1] a large part of the rights enshrined in the 1948 Universal Declaration of Human Rights. Many of these rights are also protected by the International Covenant on Economic, Social and Cultural Rights, a sister covenant to the Covenant on Civil and Political Rights. In some areas, the two covenants fail to protect certain rights included in the Declaration.[2] In other respects, the two covenants represent a progressive development in the understanding of human rights, since they include rights that are not mentioned in the Universal Declaration.[3] Freedom of thought, conscience, and religion is protected by article 18 of the Covenant on Civil and Political Rights and reads as follows:

> 1. Everyone shall have the right to freedom of thought, conscience and religion. This right shall include freedom to have or to adopt a religion or belief of his choice, and freedom, either individually or in community with others and in public or private, to manifest his religion or belief in worship, observance, practice and teaching.
>
> 2. No one shall be subject to coercion which would impair his freedom to have or to adopt a religion or belief of his choice.

[1] As of 2 May 2003, 149 states had ratified the Covenant. In addition, the Covenant continues to apply in Kazakhstan, Hong Kong, and Macau due to earlier ratification by the Soviet Union, the United Kingdom, and Portugal respectively. The Human Rights Committee has consistently taken the position that once the population of a territory finds itself protected by the Covenant, state succession or other forms of transfer of sovereignty over the territory do not affect the applicability of the Covenant.

[2] See *Universal Declaration of Human Rights,* art. 17 (property), and art. 14 (asylum).

[3] See ICCPR, art. 27 (rights of members of minorities).

Tore Lindholm, W. Cole Durham, Jr., Bahia G. Tahzib-Lie (eds.), Facilitating Freedom of Religion or Belief: A Deskbook, *189–202. © 2004 Koninklijke Brill NV.*

> 3. Freedom to manifest one's religion or beliefs may be subject only to such limitations as are prescribed by law and are necessary to protect public safety, order, health, or morals or the fundamental rights and freedoms of others.
>
> 4. The States Parties to the present Covenant undertake to have respect for the liberty of parents and, when applicable, legal guardians to ensure the religious and moral education of their children in conformity with their own convictions.

Paragraphs 1 and 2 cover a wide range of the various dimensions of freedom of religion or belief. Paragraph 3 allows for and conditions possible limitations on certain but not all dimensions of the said freedom, namely those dimensions that amount to the "manifestation" of religion or belief. For instance, the "internal dimension," the individual right to have or adopt a religion or belief, is not subject to limitations. Paragraph 4 includes a special clause on religious education.[4]

Within the framework of the Covenant, article 18 is the main provision related to freedom of religion or belief. Other provisions, however, add important elements to the protection of this freedom. As article 18 is listed in article 4, paragraph 2,[5] freedom of religion is among the nonderogable rights under the Covenant. These provisions of the Covenant cannot be derogated from during a state of emergency that threatens the life of the nation. The nondiscrimination clauses in article 2, paragraph 1, and article 26 specifically mention religion as one of the prohibited grounds for discrimination. A similar reference to religion is made in the rights of the child provision in article 24, paragraph 1.[6] Further protection is afforded through the minority rights clause in article 27, under which members of ethnic, religious, or linguistic minorities shall not be denied, *inter alia*, the right to profess and practice their own religion in community with the other members of the group.[7]

II. The Main Functions of the Human Rights Committee

The Human Rights Committee is the independent expert organ assigned to monitor states' compliance with the International Covenant on Civil and Political Rights. The Committee is one of the six so-called treaty bodies operating under six major United Nations human rights treaties.[8] The Committee's eighteen members come from various

---

[4] ICCPR, art. 18(4) is similar to ICESCR, art. 13(3). This is one of the issues where there is considerable interdependence between the two 1966 Covenants.

[5] ICCPR, art. 4(1) provides for derogation from obligations under the Covenant "in time of public emergency which threatens the life of the nation and the existence of which is officially proclaimed . . . provided that such measures are not inconsistent with [States Parties'] other obligations under international law and do not involve discrimination solely on the ground of race, colour, sex, language, religion or social origin." Article 4(2) states, "No derogation from articles 6, 7, 8 (paras. 1 and 2), 11, 15, 16 and 18 may be made under this provision."

[6] "Every child shall have, without any discrimination as to race, colour, sex, language, religion, national or social origin, property, or birth, the right to such measures or protection as are required by his status as a minor, on the part of his family, society and the State" (ICCPR, art. 24[1]).

[7] "In those States in which ethnic, religious or linguistic minorities exist, persons belonging to such minorities shall not be denied the right, in community with the other members of their group, to enjoy their own culture, to profess and practice their own religion, or to use their own language" (ICCPR, art. 27).

[8] The other five treaty bodies are: the Committee Against Torture, established pursuant to article 17 of the *Convention Against Torture and Other Cruel, Inhuman or Degrading Treatment or Punishment;* the

parts of the world and are elected in their individual capacity to perform the predominantly legal (or even quasi-judicial) task of interpreting the provisions of the Covenant.[9]

The Human Rights Committee has three primary functions. *First*, under article 40 of the Covenant, each state party has an obligation to submit *periodic reports* on the implementation of the Covenant. The Committee considers these reports in open hearings through dialogue between the Committee members and a delegation sent by the state party. Since 1992, the result of this procedure is a set of *concluding observations*, which are state-specific assessments of the issues arising under the Covenant and concrete recommendations by the Committee explaining how compliance with Covenant obligations should be improved. Although the actual dialogue in the hearings is conducted between the Committee and the state party only, the reporting procedure is rather transparent and open to non-governmental organizations (NGOs) and other operators who wish to address problems related to the performance of the country in question under the Covenant. For example, the Committee welcomes so-called "shadow reports" by NGOs. Presession working groups hear NGOs in formulating the questions to be posed to the state party delegation. The Committee itself meets with NGOs in lunch-hour briefings and, finally, the actual hearings are open to the public. Hence, NGOs can exert a certain influence merely through their visible presence.

A *second* main function of the Human Rights Committee was developed as a by-product of the reporting procedure. Article 40, paragraph 4, uses the notion of *general comments* when it deals with the outcome of the reporting procedure. While the Covenant is silent on the possibility of country-specific concluding observations, it does explicitly prescribe that the Committee shall submit, after studying the reports by states, "such general comments as it may consider appropriate."[10] Until 1992, several committee members, most of whom were from Eastern Europe, took the position that the Committee is precluded from making state-specific assessments of compliance with the Covenant in the context of the reporting procedure. Instead of a set of jointly decided concluding observations, each individual member expressed his or her personal conclusions at the end of the hearings. This defect in the approach taken at that time was conducive to active work on another front, namely the elaboration of general comments. Until the year 1992, the Human Rights Committee issued 21 general comments which usually

Committee on Economic, Social and Cultural Rights, established to supervise the implementation of the *International Covenant on Economic, Social and Cultural Rights;* the Committee on Elimination of Discrimination Against Women, established pursuant to article 17 of the *Convention on Elimination of All Forms of Discrimination Against Women;* the Committee on the Elimination of Racial Discrimination, established pursuant to article 8 of the *International Convention on the Elimination of All Forms of Racial Discrimination;* and the Committee on the Rights of the Child, established pursuant to article 43 of the *Convention on the Rights of the Child.* On 1 July 2003, a seventh human rights treaty will enter into force, namely the *International Convention on the Protection of the Rights of All Migrant Workers and Members of Their Families.*

[9] ICCPR, arts. 28–34 prescribe the procedures for selection of committee members. Members are nationals of states parties to the Covenant, are qualified to serve by virtue of their "high moral character and recognized competence in the field of human rights," and "serve in their personal capacity" (art. 28). Members are elected by secret ballot (art. 29) in a meeting of states parties (art. 30). The Committee includes no more than one national of the same state (art. 31). Members are elected for terms of four years and may be re-elected (art. 32).

[10] ICCPR, art. 40(4).

pertained to one specific article of the Covenant, and which consolidated the understanding of the Committee on issues of interpretation arising under that specific treaty provision.[11] Some of the general comments, however, deal with cross-cutting themes related to procedure[12] or substance.[13] The elaboration of general comments has not been discontinued after the Committee started issuing state-specific concluding observations.[14] The institution of general comments still serves a function as a method to consolidate the Committee's understanding on issues arising under the Covenant. Perhaps the main purpose of general comments currently is to serve as substantive guidelines when states parties compile their periodic reports under article 40.

Although they originated from the reporting procedure, the general comments also draw upon a *third* main function of the Human Rights Committee, namely the procedure for *individual complaints* under the Optional Protocol to the Covenant on Civil and Political Rights.[15] This is the part of the work of the Committee that is closest to judicial decision making: in concrete cases related to an individual or group of persons, the Committee, through an adversarial procedure, decides whether the state party in question has violated the complainant's human rights. The fact that the Human Rights Committee is not a court is reflected in two characteristics of the complaint procedure: (1) the procedure is conducted through written submissions by the state and the individual, rather than through oral hearings before the Committee, and (2) neither the Covenant nor its Optional Protocol includes a provision on the binding nature of the *final views* of the Committee, which are issued as the end result of the complaint procedure. This does not mean that the findings by the Committee would amount to mere "recommendations." They are legal interpretations issued by the independent international expert body established by the Covenant for the purpose of interpreting the Covenant. If a state party wishes to replace the Committee's interpretation of a specific treaty provision with a differing opinion, it must present very compelling reasons.

The individual complaint procedure is optional in the sense that it only applies to states that have ratified both the Covenant and its Optional Protocol on the system of individual communications [16] However, since the complaint procedure is clearly quasi-judicial in nature, it is highly important in developing the interpretation and understanding of the legal obligations stemming from the Covenant. Hence, the views adopted by the Human Rights Committee through the complaints procedure are also relevant to states other than those that have themselves ratified the Optional Protocol.

The procedure for individual complaints may be summarized as follows. An individual or a group of individuals (but not a separate juridical person) who claims that his/her/their rights under the Covenant have been violated through an act or omission

---

[11] For instance, General Comment 22 (1993) deals with ICCPR, art. 18 (freedom of thought, conscience and religion).

[12] General Comment 24 (1994) deals with reservations to the Covenant.

[13] The subject matter of General Comment 15 (1986) is the rights of aliens as addressed by various substantive provisions of the ICCPR.

[14] As of May 2003, the total number of general comments issued by the Human Rights Committee is thirty, some of which, however, replace an earlier general comment.

[15] See *Optional Protocol to the International Covenant on Civil and Political Rights*, arts. 1–5 (hereafter *Optional Protocol*).

[16] As of 2 May 2003, 104 states had ratified the *Optional Protocol*, leaving forty-five states that had ratified the Covenant but not the *Optional Protocol*. See note 1.

by a state party to the Covenant, is entitled to submit a complaint, or individual communication.[17] The complainant may appoint counsel for representation. NGOs are permitted to represent victims of human rights violations but only as legal representatives of named individuals, not in the form of *actio popularis*.

There are several procedural requirements that must be fulfilled before a claim is admissible to the Committee. A complaint may only be considered by the Committee if the complainant is personally affected by the alleged violation (victim requirement), the state in question has ratified the Optional Protocol allowing for individual complaints, and the complainant has exhausted all available and effective domestic remedies.[18] The exhaustion of domestic remedies may require, for instance, that the person claim a violation of the Covenant or of similar domestic provisions in the courts of the country, and if possible, take that claim to the highest national or constitutional court. Furthermore, the same issue presented by or on behalf of the same individual cannot be pending before another international human rights body, for instance the European Court of Human Rights.[19]

When dealing with a case, the Committee can issue separate decisions as to admissibility and merits, or merge the two issues into one single decision. Currently, the latter approach is more commonly employed. In some cases the complaint is declared inadmissible without hearing the state party but otherwise all final decisions are based on submissions sought equally from the two parties of the case, the complainant and the state.[20] The complaint is form free, and there is no fee for the proceedings or the final decision. No legal aid is available unless domestic law provides for legal aid "from home" in relation to international procedures. In its final views, the Human Rights Committee expresses its position as to whether the Covenant was violated and in which respects, and as to what would constitute an effective remedy for the violation.[21]

A further function of the Human Rights Committee is mentioned in article 41 of the Covenant. This provision allows for interstate complaints between states parties to the Covenant, provided that both states in question have given a separate declaration recognizing the jurisdiction of the Human Rights Committee to deal with such complaints. As of May 2003, this procedure had never been resorted to.

III. The Committee's General Comment on Article 18

In 1993 the Human Rights Committee adopted a general comment on article 18 of the Covenant.[22] The general comment sheds additional light on many dimensions of freedom of religion or belief.[23] In the general comment, the Committee emphasizes

[17] *Optional Protocol*, art. 2.

[18] Ibid., arts. 1, 2.

[19] Ibid., art. 5.

[20] *Rules of Procedure of the Human Rights Committee*, rule 94, UN Doc. CCPR/C/3/Rev.6.

[21] The remedy might include, for instance, the release of a detained person, the commutation of a death sentence or compensation. Over the years, the Committee's statements on "effective remedy" have undergone a development towards more and more concrete pronouncements. Although the Committee still has not started to give its opinion as to the specific amount of compensation, an important step in this direction was taken in the case of Vladimir Petrovich Laptsevich v. Belarus, Comm. No. 780/1997 (UN Human Rights Committee, 13 April 2000).

[22] Human Rights Committee General Comment 22. The Human Rights Committee's general comments are reproduced in UN Doc. HRI/GEN/1/Rev.4. They can also be found on various human rights websites,

that article 18 protects "theistic, non-theistic and atheistic beliefs, as well as the right not to profess any religion or belief."[24] On the issue of "new religions," the Committee follows this broad interpretation by pointing out that article 18 is "not limited to traditional religions or religions and beliefs with institutional characteristics or practices analogous to those of traditional religions." The Committee also expresses concern in relation to any tendency to discriminate against any religion or belief as they are broadly interpreted.[25]

In its general comment, the Committee clearly accepts the position that the recognition of an official or state religion is not by itself a violation of article 18, but the comment emphasizes at the same time that such recognition "shall not result in the impairment of the enjoyment of any of the rights under the Covenant, including articles 18 and 27, nor in any discrimination against adherents to other religions or non-believers."[26]

As to the notion of "manifesting" one's religion or beliefs used in paragraphs 1 and 3 of article 18, the Committee expresses its interpretation on the multitude of different forms of manifestation:

> The freedom to manifest religion or belief in worship, observance, practice and teaching encompasses a broad range of acts. The concept of worship extends to ritual and ceremonial acts giving direct expression to belief, as well as various practices integral to such acts, including the building of places of worship, the use of ritual formulae and objects, the display of symbols, and the observance of holidays and days of rest. The observance and practice of religion or belief may include not only ceremonial acts but also such customs as the observance of dietary regulations, the wearing of distinctive clothing or headcoverings, participation in rituals associated with certain stages of life, and the use of a particular language customarily spoken by a group.[27]

In relation to the prohibition of "coercion" used in article 18, paragraph 2, the Committee takes the view that both direct (e.g., physical force or penal sanctions) and indirect forms of coercion are in violation of the Covenant: "Policies or practices having the same intention or effect, such as, for example, those restricting access to education, medical care, employment or the rights guaranteed by article 25 of the Covenant[28] and other provisions of the Covenant are similarly inconsistent with article 18.2."[29]

On the issue of lawful limitations to the freedom to manifest one's religion or belief, the Committee emphasizes that article 18, paragraph 3 "is to be strictly interpreted."[30] Restrictions are allowed only on grounds enumerated in the said paragraph,

---

including the UN High Commissioner on Human Rights <www.unhchr.ch>, the Netherlands Human Rights Institute SIM <www.law.uu.nl/english/sim>, and the University of Minnesota <http://www1.umn.edu/humanrts/gencomm/hrcomms.htm>. The same websites also include collections of concluding observations and Optional Protocol cases by the Human Rights Committee. At the time of writing this chapter (October 2000), the SIM website was the most useful website, due to its broad coverage and developed search functions.

23 For a more thorough analysis of General Comment 22, see Bahiyyih G. Tahzib, *Freedom of Religion or Belief: Ensuring Effective International Legal Protection* (Boston: Martinus Nijhoff, 1996).

24 Human Rights Committee General Comment 22, para. 2.

25 Ibid.

26 Ibid., para. 9.

27 Human Rights Committee General Comment 22, para. 4.

28 Rights of political participation.

29 Human Rights Committee General Comment 22, para. 5.

not for instance, for the protection of "national security" which is mentioned in some other limitation clauses in the Covenant[31] but not in article 18. The Committee also takes a narrow view on what is meant by "morals" as a legitimate aim for limiting the freedom to manifest religion or belief. As the concept of morals derives from many philosophical and religious traditions, any limitations that serve the purpose of protecting morals "must be based on principles not deriving exclusively from a single tradition."[32]

As to religious education within the public school system, the Committee makes clear "that article 18.4 permits public school instruction in subjects such as the general history of religions and ethics if it is given in a neutral and objective way."[33] Public education that would include instruction in a particular religion or belief "is inconsistent with article 18.4 unless provision is made for non-discriminatory exemptions or alternatives that would accommodate the wishes of parents and guardians."[34]

Finally, the General Comment adopted on article 18 includes an important example of the role of the Human Rights Committee in developing understanding of the Covenant. With reference to individuals' claims based on article 18 and growing recognition by states parties, the Committee affirmed that conscientious objection to military service does enjoy protection under article 18:

> The Covenant does not explicitly refer to a right to conscientious objection, but the Committee believes that such a right can be derived from article 18, inasmuch as the obligation to use lethal force may seriously conflict with the freedom of conscience and the right to manifest one's religion or belief.[35]

IV. Case Law on Religion or Belief under the Optional Protocol

Still today, more than twenty-five years after the Covenant entered into force, the Committee's case law under article 18 remains sparse, particularly in the core areas of freedom of religion or belief.

Although the case law under article 18 itself is rather underdeveloped in quantitative or qualitative terms, it does demonstrate that *other provisions* of the Covenant include important dimensions related to the freedom of religion and belief.

In *William Eduardo Delgado Paez v. Colombia*,[36] the issue under article 18 was whether the transfer of a teacher who advocated "liberation theology" from teaching religion to teaching other subjects constituted a violation of the teacher's rights under article 18. The Committee held that the transfer, which was initiated by the Catholic Church to which the complainant belonged, was not a violation of article 18. It

---

[30] Ibid., para. 8.
[31] See ICCPR, arts. 12, 13, 14(1), 19, 21, 22.
[32] Human Rights Committee General Comment 22, para. 8.
[33] Ibid., para. 6.
[34] Ibid.
[35] Ibid., para. 11.
[36] William Eduardo Delgado Paez v. Colombia, Comm. No. 195/1985 (UN Human Rights Committee, 12 July 1990).

explained that "Colombia may, without violating this provision of the Covenant, allow the Church authorities to decide who may teach religion and in what manner it should be taught."[37]

In the case of *M.A.B., W.A.T. and J. A.Y.T. v. Canada*,[38] the Committee dismissed a complaint brought by members of a newly established, allegedly religious, group claiming that their belief consisted primarily or exclusively of the worship and distribution of cannabis. In the Committee's view, this practice could not conceivably be brought within the scope of article 18 of the Covenant.

The case of *Coeriel et al. v. The Netherlands*[39] involved persons who had converted to Hinduism and who, in order to become Hindu priests, had sought to have their surnames changed. According to the complainants, the authorities' refusal to approve the name changes violated article 18 of the Covenant and constituted unlawful or arbitrary interference with their privacy under article 17.[40] The Human Rights Committee held that the regulation of surnames and the change thereof was eminently a matter of public order and that restrictions were therefore permissible under article 18, paragraph 3. Hence, the communication was declared inadmissible in relation to article 18.[41] However, the Committee found that a violation of article 17 had been established:

> In the present case, the authors' request for recognition of the change of their first names to Hindu names in order to pursue their religious studies had been granted in 1986. The state party based its refusal of the request also to change their surnames on the grounds that the authors had not shown that the changes sought were essential to pursue their studies, that the names had religious connotations and that they were not 'Dutch sounding'. The Committee finds the grounds for so limiting the authors' rights under article 17 not to be reasonable. In the circumstances of the instant case the refusal of the authors' request was therefore arbitrary within the meaning of article 17, paragraph 1, of the Covenant.[42]

In *K. Singh Bhinder v. Canada*,[43] the complainant had been dismissed from his post as maintenance electrician of the government owned Canadian National Railway Company. The complainant, who was a Sikh by religion, had insisted on wearing a turban instead of safety headgear while at work. This refusal led to the termination of his employment contract. The Committee found no violation of the Covenant:

> If the requirement that a hard hat be worn is regarded as raising issues under article 18, then it is a limitation that is justified by reference to the grounds laid down in article 18, paragraph 3. If the requirement that a hard hat be worn is seen as a discrimination de facto against persons of the Sikh religion under article 26,[44] then, applying criteria now well established in the jurisprudence of the Committee, the

[37] Ibid., para. 5.7.

[38] M.A.B., W.A.T. and J. A.Y.T. v. Canada, Comm. No. 570/1993 (UN Human Rights Committee, 25 April 1994).

[39] Coeriel et al. v. The Netherlands, Comm. No. 453/1991 (UN Human Rights Committee, 31 October 1994).

[40] "No one shall be subjected to arbitrary or unlawful interference with his privacy, family, home or correspondence, nor to unlawful attacks on his honour and reputation" (ICCPR, art. 17[1]).

[41] Coeriel et al. v. The Netherlands, para. 6.1.

[42] Ibid., para. 10.5.

[43] K. Singh Bhinder v. Canada, Comm. No. 208/1986 (UN Human Rights Committee, 9 November 1989).

legislation requiring that workers in federal employment be protected from injury and electric shock by the wearing of hard hats is to be regarded as reasonable and directed towards objective purposes that are compatible with the Covenant.[45]

In *Clement Boodoo v. Trinidad and Tobago*,[46] the Committee found a violation of article 18 when a prisoner had been subjected to serious restrictions on his freedom to manifest religion:

> As to the author's claim that he has been forbidden from wearing a beard and from worshipping at religious services, and that his prayer books were taken from him, the Committee reaffirms that the freedom to manifest religion or belief in worship, observance, practice and teaching encompasses a broad range of acts and that the concept of worship extends to ritual and ceremonial acts giving expression to belief, as well as various practices integral to such acts. In the absence of any explanation from the State party concerning the author's allegations in paragraphs 2.3–2.6, the Committee concludes that there has been a violation of article 18 of the Covenant.[47]

In the field of ***religious education***, the leading cases decided by the Committee are *Erkki Hartikainen et al. v. Finland*[48] and *Arieh Hollis Waldman v. Canada*.[49] The fact that only the first-mentioned case was actually decided under article 18 is indicative of the far-reaching interdependence between various provisions of the Covenant.

In *Hartikainen*, it was alleged that the then applicable Finnish School System Act of 1968 violated article 18, paragraph 4, of the Covenant. The Act stipulated obligatory attendance in Finnish schools, requiring children whose parents were atheists to attend classes on the history of religion and ethics, the curriculum of which was to a high degree religious in nature. The Committee concluded with what can be described as a ***qualified nonviolation***. Although the teaching plan of history of religion and ethics was, at least in part, religious in character, the appropriate action available under article 18 of the Covenant was being taken to resolve nonreligious parents' and schoolchildren's concerns. According to the views of the Committee, instruction in the study of the history of religion and ethics was an appropriate substitute for religious instruction to students whose parents or legal guardians objected to religious instruction under article 18, paragraph 4 if such alternative course of instruction is given in a neutral and objective way and respects the convictions of parents and guardians who do not believe in any religion.

The *Waldman* case is the prime example of the importance of the nondiscrimination clause of article 26 for freedom of religion or belief. The case was brought to the Human Rights Committee by a Jewish parent who, at considerable cost, secured the

---

[44] "All persons are equal before the law and are entitled without any discrimination to the equal protection of the law. In this respect, the law shall prohibit any discrimination and guarantee to all persons equal and effective protection against discrimination on any ground such as race, colour, sex, language, religion, political, or other opinion, national or social origin, property, birth or other status" (ICCPR, art. 26).

[45] K. Singh Bhinder v. Canada, para. 6.2.

[46] Clement Boodoo v. Trinidad and Tobago, Comm. No. 721/1996 (UN Human Rights Committee, 2 April 2002).

[47] Ibid., para. 6.6.

[48] Hartikainen et al. v. Finland, Comm. No. 40/1978 (UN Human Rights Committee, 9 April 1981).

[49] Arieh Hollis Waldman v. Canada, Comm. No. 694/1996 (UN Human Rights Committee, 3 November 1999).

education of his children in a private Jewish school in Ontario. In the same province at the same time, religious Catholic schools were funded as a part of the public school system, free of cost to the parents. The coexistence of secular schools and Catholic religious schools within the publicly funded school system was a result of a constitutional arrangement dating back to 1867 and was aimed at protecting the Roman Catholic minority in Ontario.

The Committee concluded that the differential treatment experienced by Mr. Waldman, a Jewish parent who wished to secure religious education for his children, compared to the treatment afforded to members of the Roman Catholic minority amounted to discrimination in violation of article 26. The Committee's views referred to the fact that neither the Roman Catholic community nor any identifiable subsection of that community was in a disadvantaged position compared to members of the Jewish community.[50] The Committee pointed out that the complainant did not send his children to a private religious school in order to secure private education for them, but because the publicly funded school system made no provision for his religious denomination. The Committee concluded:

> [I]f a state party chooses to provide public funding to religious schools, it should make this funding available without discrimination. This means that providing funding for the schools of one religious group and not for another must be based on reasonable and objective criteria. In the instant case, the Committee concludes that the material before it does not show that the differential treatment between the Roman Catholic faith and the author's religious denomination is based on such criteria. Consequently, there has been a violation of the author's rights under article 26 of the Covenant to equal and effective protection against discrimination.[51]

Also the case of ***Malcolm Ross v. Canada***[52] related to schools. No violation of article 18 was found in that a schoolteacher had been removed from a teaching position after a causal link had been established between the teacher's public statements concerning adherents of the Jewish faith and a "poisoned school environment." The Committee reasoned:

> As regards the author's claims under article 18, the Committee notes that the actions taken against the author through the Human Rights Board of Inquiry's Order of August 1991 were not aimed at his thoughts or beliefs as such, but rather at the manifestation of those beliefs within a particular context. The freedom to manifest religious beliefs may be subject to limitations which are prescribed by law and are necessary to protect the fundamental rights and freedoms of others.[53]

As was implied above in the context of the Committee's General Comment on article 18, ***conscientious objection to military service*** is an area where the Committee's position has clearly evolved over the years. The "old approach" was visible in ***L.T.K. v. Finland***,[54] where the Committee held:

---

[50] Ibid., para. 10.4.

[51] Ibid., para. 10.6. In a concurring individual opinion, the author of the present chapter elaborates on what kind of criteria should be applied to determine in which situations states have funding obligations in relation to religious minority education (ibid., Individual Opinion, M. Scheinin [concurring]).

[52] Malcolm Ross v. Canada, Comm. No. 736/1997 (UN Human Rights Committee, 18 October 2000).

[53] Ibid., para. 16.8.

[54] L.T.K. v. Finland, Comm. No. 185/1984 (UN Human Rights Committee, 9 July 1985).

> The Covenant does not provide for the right to conscientious objection; neither article 18 nor article 19 of the Covenant, especially taking into account paragraph 3 (c) (ii) of article 8, can be construed as implying that right. The author does not claim that there were any procedural defects in the judicial proceedings against him, which themselves could have constituted a violation of any of the provisions of the Covenant, or that he was sentenced contrary to law.[55]

A change in the Committee's position can be seen in *Godefriedus Maria Brinkhof v. The Netherlands*,[56] where the Committee referred to its own general comment recognizing the applicability of article 18 to conscientious objection. In that case, the Committee stated:

> [T]he exemption of only one group of conscientious objectors and the inapplicability of exemption for all others cannot be considered reasonable. In this context, the Committee refers to its General Comment on article 18 and emphasizes that, when a right of conscientious objection to military service is recognized by a state party, no differentiation shall be made among conscientious objectors on the basis of the nature of their particular beliefs. However, in the instant case, the Committee considers that the author has not shown that his convictions as a pacifist are incompatible with the system of substitute service in the Netherlands or that the privileged treatment accorded to Jehovah's Witnesses adversely affected his rights as a conscientious objector against military service. The Committee therefore finds that Mr. Brinkhof is not a victim of a violation of article 26 of the Covenant.[57]

Finally, in *Westerman v. The Netherlands*,[58] the Committee revisited the actual article 18 issue. The complainant had been denied recognition as a conscientious objector, since his reasons for objection did not meet the conditions set forth in domestic law.[59] Although the Committee clearly recognized that a right to conscientious objection could be derived from article 18, it found no violation of that provision in the concrete case:

---

55 Ibid., para. 5.2.

56 Godefriedus Maria Brinkhof v. The Netherlands, Comm. No. 402/1990 (UN Human Rights Committee, 30 July 1993).

57 Ibid., para. 9.3. Other cases related to alleged discrimination of conscientious objectors include Järvinen v. Finland, Comm. No. 295/1988 (UN Human Rights Committee, 25 July 1990), where a longer term for conscientious objectors compared to military service was found to rest on objective and reasonable grounds. In a series of later cases against France, however, a violation of article 26 was established. See Foin v. France, Comm. No. 666/1995 (UN Human Rights Committee, 9 November 1999). The term of alternative service was 24 months, compared to then applicable 12 months in military service. The Committee reasoned:
[T]he law and practice may establish differences between military and national alternative service and that such differences may, in a particular case, justify a longer period of service, provided that the differentiation is based on reasonable and objective criteria, such as the nature of the specific service concerned or the need for a special training in order to accomplish that service. (Foin v. France, para. 10.3)
In Foin v. France, paragraph 10.3 the state party argues "that doubling the length of service was the only way to test the sincerity of an individual's convictions" and did not, in the Committee's opinion, satisfy the requirement of reasonable and objective criteria. See also Maille v. France, Comm. No. 689/1996 (UN Human Rights Committee, 31 July 2000), and Venier and Nicolas v. France, Comm. Nos. 690 and 691/1996 (UN Human Rights Committee, 10 July 2000).

58 Westerman v. The Netherlands, Comm. No. 682/1996 (UN Human Rights Committee, 3 November 1999).

59 "[I]nsurmountable objections of conscience to performing military service in person, because of the use of violent means" (ibid., para. 6.5).

> The Committee observes that the authorities of the state party evaluated the facts and arguments advanced by the author in support of his claim for exemption as a conscientious objector in the light of its legal provisions in regard to conscientious objection and that these legal provisions are compatible with the provisions of article 18.[60]

Six members of the Committee, including the present author, dissented. They emphasized that the complainant's objection constituted a legitimate exercise of his freedom of thought, conscience, and religion, and that the state party had failed to provide justification why the denial of conscientious objector status did not amount to unacceptable differentiation among conscientious objectors on the basis of their particular beliefs.[61]

The case of *Ilmari Länsman et al. v. Finland*[62] is a typical "article 27 case" brought by members of an indigenous minority community under the notion that they have a right to enjoy their culture in relation to the protection of their traditional lands, resources, and economic forms of life.[63] No violation of article 27 was found, but the Human Rights Committee established certain important principles about how states should secure the effective participation of (indigenous) minorities and work to sustain the traditional economy. The relevant issue in the present context is passing reference to the fact that Mount Riutusvaara, the subject of stone quarrying, was a sacred site in the old Sami religion. Due to the fact that the Sami of today do not continue to exercise their traditional beliefs, the point was never developed. It is, therefore, quite natural that the Human Rights Committee did not pay particular attention to the issue. However, the case is illustrative of the fact that freedom of religion or belief may potentially be at the heart of an indigenous or minority claim. It is useful to remember that article 27 refers not only to the right of minorities to enjoy their own culture but also to their right to practice their religion. For many indigenous minorities, land or specific sites are not only important as physical space for manifesting a religion, but they have sacred significance. Giving attention to indigenous conceptions of religion or belief broadens our understanding of how wide an area is actually covered by the notion of freedom of religion or belief.

Another "article 27 case" worth mentioning here is *Francis Hopu and Tepoaitu Bessert v. France*.[64] Due to a declaration made by France upon ratification of the Covenant on Civil and Political Rights that was treated as a valid reservation by the Human Rights Committee, the case was declared inadmissible under article 27.[65] Instead, the Committee found a violation of articles 17 and 23 (privacy and family life) in that the

---

[60] Ibid., para. 9.5.

[61] Ibid., dissenting opinion of P. Bhagwati, L. Henkin, C. Medina Quiroga, F, Pocar, M. Scheinin; ibid., dissenting opinion of H. Solari Yrigoyen.

[62] Ilmari Länsman et al. v. Finland, Comm. No. 511/1992 (UN Human Rights Committee, 8 November 1994).

[63] "In those States in which ethnic, religious or linguistic minorities exist, persons belonging to such minorities shall not be denied the right, in community with the other members of their group, to enjoy their own culture, to profess and practice their own religion, or to use their own language" (ICCPR, art. 27).

[64] Francis Hopu and Tepoaitu Bessert v. France, Comm. No 549/1993 (UN Human Rights Committee, 29 July 1997).

[65] Ibid., para. 4.3.

state party had allowed the construction of a hotel on the traditional burial site of indigenous Polynesians.[66] The Committee's reasoning is based on the notions of identity, history, and culture but it is quite evident that religion or belief also had or could have played a role.[67]

V. Examples of Findings on Religion or Belief through the Reporting Procedure

Since 1992, when the Human Rights Committee started issuing its concluding observations at the end of the consideration of reports by states pursuant to article 40 of the Covenant, a considerable number of concluding observations have included issues related to freedom of religion or belief. These findings add to the understanding of the Human Rights Committee's role in the protection of various aspects of freedom of religion or belief. Some illustrative examples of the findings are presented below in the form of quotations from the concluding observations.

Senegal (1997): The Committee expresses its concern at the statement in the report that "there are no minorities in Senegal," and at the failure of the state party to provide information on the recognition and protection of religious and ethnic minorities in Senegal. In that regard:

> The Committee recommends that the state party take legal and practical steps to recognize and protect religious and ethnic minorities, with a view to ensuring the rights guaranteed under article 27 of the Covenant. The Committee further suggests that the Government of Senegal take into consideration the Committee's General Comment No. 23 on this matter.[68]

Slovakia (1997): The Committee notes that Act No. 308/1991 Coll. on freedom of religion and the status of churches and religious societies and Acts No. 83/1990 Coll., 300/1990 Coll. and 62/1993 Coll. on the association of citizens require that churches, religious societies, associations, and non-governmental organizations be registered in order to function freely and/or to receive subsidies from the State. Given that prerequisites to this registration are very restrictive, some churches and religious or other associations are excluded from being legally recognized. Therefore:

> the Committee recommends that all necessary measures be adopted in order to amend the relevant legislation so as to bring it into conformity with articles 18 and 22 of the Covenant.[69]

Sudan (1997): The Committee regrets the documented cases of official action which interferes with the rights of non-Muslim religious denominations and groups to practise their religion and to carry out peaceful educational activities. Therefore:

---

[66] Ibid., para. 10.3.

[67] "It transpires from the authors' claims that they consider the relationship to their ancestors to be an essential element of their identity and to play an important role in their family life" (ibid., para. 10.3).

[68] UN Human Rights Committee, 61st session, *Concluding Observations of the Human Rights Committee: Senegal,* UN Doc. CCPR/C/79/Add.82, views adopted on 19 November 1997, para. 17.

[69] UN Human Rights Committee, 60th session, *Concluding Observations of the Human Rights Committee: Slovakia,* UN Doc. CCPR/C/79/Add.79, views adopted on 18 August 1998, para. 21.

> A mechanism should be established to protect minority religious groups from discrimination and action seeking to impede their freedom to teach and practise their religious beliefs.[70]

Israel (1998): The Committee expresses serious concern over deeply imbedded discriminatory social attitudes, practices and laws against Arab Israelis that have resulted in a lower standard of living compared with Jewish Israelis, as is evident in their significantly lower levels of education, access to health care, access to housing, land and employment. It notes with concern that most Arab Israelis, because they do not join the army, do not enjoy the financial benefits available to Israelis who have served in the army, including scholarships and housing loans. The Committee also expresses concern that the Arabic language, though official, has not been accorded equal status in practice, and that discrimination against members of the Arab minority appears to be extensive in the private sector. In this regard, the Committee urges the state party to take steps without delay to ensure equality to Arabs and to proceed as soon as possible with the planned formulation of a draft law on discrimination in the private sector and to adopt it at an early date. . . . The Committee is concerned at the preference given to the Jewish religion in the allocation of funding for religious bodies, to the detriment of Muslims, Christians, Druze and other religious groups. The Committee recommends that regulations and criteria for funding be published and applied to all religious groups on an equal basis.[71]

Norway (1999): The Committee reiterates its concern over section 2 of the Constitution which provides that individuals professing the Evangelical-Lutheran religion are bound to bring up their children in the same faith. Its inclusion in the Constitution is incompatible with the Covenant. The Committee therefore recommends that section 2 is modified to comply with article 18 of the Covenant.[72]

VI. Conclusion

In the overall framework of protecting international freedom of religion or belief, the role of the Human Rights Committee acting under the Covenant on Civil and Political Rights is special in two respects. *First,* its jurisdiction is universal in character, applying one set of standards to a wide range of circumstances that represent the full spectre of current religions, cultures, and civilizations. It is especially important that the jurisdiction and the composition of the Committee are universal in nature. *Second,* the Human Rights Committee is special because of its ability to deal with all aspects of freedom of religion or belief. The Committee is not constrained by one type of procedure (for instance, dealing only with complaints related to individual violations of human rights) but uses different procedures and dimensions through the handling of individual complaints, periodic reports by state parties, and the issuing of general comments.

---

[70] UN Human Rights Committee, 61st session, *Concluding Observations of the Human Rights Committee: Sudan,* UN Doc. CCPR/C/79/Add.85 views adopted on 19 November 1997, para. 23.
[71] UN Human Rights Committee, 63d session, *Concluding Observations of the Human Rights Committee: Israel,* UN Doc. CCPR/C/79/Add.93, views adopted on 18 August 1998, paras. 12, 28.
[72] UN Human Rights Committee, 67th session, *Concluding Observations of the Human Rights Committee: Norway,* UN Doc. CCPR/C/79/Add.112, views adopted on 5 November 1999, para. 13.

Chapter 9

UNESCO's Facilitation of Freedom of Religion or Belief

Doudou Diene[1]

I. Introduction

The beginning of the third millennium is the scene of a return to the spiritual. This return is manifest in various developments:

- The powerful claim for the centrality of the spiritual in the fields of society, politics, culture and ethics, in societies of the South as of the North, often represents a radical form of opposition to (or even rejection of) the dominant materialist culture and its values, images, and practices. But here, as in other conflicts, the division occurs not only along lines of North and South. In the so-called developed societies of the North, Fukuyama's proclamation of the "end of history"[2] and liberalism's announcement of the "final triumph" have given rise to radical opposition that also expresses itself in spiritual and religious fields. As the "religious demand" grows, it adds an increasing degree of complexity to traditional interreligious divisions and also fosters intrareligious conflicts and controversies.
- The spiritual has also become a central referent for the personal well-being of an interior life. Focusing on the importance of the interior life often translates into a rejection of ritualized forms of religion and a search for other forms of "wisdom." In this context, humanitarian activity expresses in a non-religious way what may be considered the highest form of spirituality: the act of service. Because of the social, cultural, and spiritual questioning that it creates, globalization significantly exacerbates this debate and introduces a drama in which the actors both identify with each other and oppose each other, and in which the roles are distributed and the discourses of legitimation and exclusion are contrived.
- The controversy concerning sects—when seized upon in politics, when distorted by the media, and when excluded from academic research—muddles

---

[1] I would like to thank Ehsan Naraghi, Personal Adviser to the Director General of UNESCO, for her help in preparing this article.

[2] See Francis Fukuyama, *The End of History and the Last Man* (New York: Free Press, 1992).

Tore Lindholm, W. Cole Durham, Jr., Bahia G. Tahzib-Lie (eds.), Facilitating Freedom of Religion or Belief: A Deskbook, *203–208.*

debate and hides the urgency for open, objective, and public consideration on the place and role of the spiritual in the larger issues of the moment: peace, development, and human rights.

Each of these developments is taking place in a context of cultural homogenization, of domineering materialism, and of eroding spiritual values. This context raises several questions: what are conditions for the expression of faith, and what are conditions underlying freedom of religion? Interreligious dialogue is a response to these issues.

II. The Program for Interreligious Dialogue

UNESCO began and developed a program for interreligious dialogue because it realized the significant contribution that religions and spiritual traditions can bring to today's essential questions such as peace, globalization, development, human rights, the environment, isolationism based on ethnic or religious identity, and other such questions.

UNESCO's recent commitment to the problem of interreligious dialogue represents a return to what may constitute the most fundamental message of the organization's founding fathers. Indeed, we find this fruitful intuition in the heart of UNESCO's constitution: "[S]ince wars begin in the minds of men, it is in the minds of men that the defences of peace must be constructed."[3] In an effort to influence the "minds of men" through dialogue, UNESCO, in February 1989, organized an international symposium on the contribution of religions of the world to the implementation of human rights.[4] A few years later, the effort to promote religious dialogue continued in the 1994 Declaration of Barcelona on the role of religion in the promotion of a culture of peace. The Declaration states: "Cultures give religions their language and religions give cultures their ultimate signification."

When it comes to intellectual, ideological, and political issues, UNESCO has for a long time been a sounding board and an arena for East–West and North–South confrontations. Ideology somehow managed to hide spiritual concerns during this period of confrontation, although UNESCO has always had at the center of its activity essential issues of ethics, justice, and participation, which were another way of expressing the primacy of the human spirit. Recently, the member states of UNESCO have recognized intercultural dialogue, of which interreligious dialogue is an essential dimension, as one of the Organization's priorities.

The OSCE has primarily been able to help realize dialogue between civilizations through introduction of the foundational concept of the "culture of peace" and launching associated programs of intercultural and interreligious dialogue. The interdisciplinary project "Toward a Culture of Peace" consolidates UNESCO's various activities in order to promote adherence to the values on which the "spirit of peace" is founded: respect for human rights and democratic principles; rejection of violence and of all forms of discrimination; advancement of the principles of liberty, justice, solidarity, tolerance, and comprehension, not only among peoples but also between groups and individuals, in order to support the acquisition of knowledge, skills, and attitudes that embody these values.

---

[3] UNESCO Const, Preamble. The constitution was adopted by the London Conference in November 1945 and entered into effect on 4 November 1946 after twenty states had deposited instruments of acceptance.

[4] The tone of the 1989 symposium was set by the slogan "No peace in the world without religious peace."

The Program of a Culture of Peace contains a number of specific projects, including "Routes of Faith" and "Routes of al-Andalus," as well as the "Spiritual Convergence and Intercultural Dialogue" Program.

The notion of "Routes," around which most of these programs are organized—"The Silk Route,"[5] "Routes of Faith,"[6] "The Routes of al-Andalus,"[7] etc.—adds another dimension to the concept of cultural dialogue between civilizations. For example, "The Silk Route" program gets its name from the trading routes that have crossed the Eurasian Continent through the ages. The basic objective of UNESCO's Silk Route Project is to shed light on the fertile and complex cultural interactions between East and West via these communication highways, which have made so substantial a contribution to the forging of a rich common heritage among the people of the Eurasian continent. With a multidisciplinary approach and the organization of international scientific field trips, seminars, exhibitions, and meetings, this project has stimulated much research and international cooperation. UNESCO's fundamental aim is to create the right conditions to raise people's awareness of the necessity of restoring the cultural dialogue of the Silk Roads as a way to promote a culture of peace and tolerance. For example, the *Integral Study of the Silk Road,* started in 1988 within the framework of the World Decade for Cultural Development, made inquiries directly in the field of cultural values and organized vast intercontinental scientific expeditions and decentralized meetings. The harvest from the *Silk Road* has been enormous: publications in a number of fields, four hundred hours of filmed archives, cultural aid programs for cultural tourism, and so forth.[8]

In the framework of "Routes of Faith," special attention will be given to activities concerned with the contribution of religions and spiritual traditions towards the establishment of a culture of peace. Another significant program in this regard has been the "Spiritual Convergence and Intercultural Dialogue" Program, which links the "Routes of Faith" and "Routes of al-Andalus" and highlights the complex interactive process between Judaism, Christianity, and Islam, as well as between Europe, the Arab World, and sub-Saharan Africa in an attempt to promote interreligious dialogue in concerned countries and regions. This program, launched by UNESCO in 1995, seeks to bring together personalities from different religions, spiritual traditions, and cultures so they can acknowledge, through formal declarations, the proximity of their spiritual values as well as their commitment to interreligious dialogue.[9]

[5] See Gail Larminaux, *The Silk Roads: Roads of Dialogue* (New York: UNESCO, 1997). See especially vol. 1.

[6] *Roads of Faith: The Malta Declaration* (23 September 1997), <http://www.unesco.org/cpp/uk/declarations/malta.pdf>.

[7] *The Routes of al-Andalus: Spiritual Convergence and Intercultural Dialogue* (1997) <http://www.unesco.org/culture/al-andalus/index.shtml>. Islamic, Christian, and Jewish cultures and religions coexisted for nearly eight centuries in al-Andalus. The "Routes to al-Andalus" Project seeks to highlight the processes, mechanisms, and heritage of dialogue that gradually developed in medieval Spain and to study the consequences today of the interactions that took place in that context.

[8] UNESCO was also associated with the commemoration of the five hundredth anniversary of the *Meeting of Two Worlds (1492–1992),* through the launching on the one hand of *Amerindia '92,* as a framework for reflection and dialogue with America's native peoples, and on the other the launching of *Chain Encounters.* These activities aimed at illustrating, through the project *Afroamerica,* the universal dimension of the interactive process initiated by Christopher Columbus' expedition. They find their natural extension in two projects entitled respectively, *The Maya World* and *Baroque Spaces.* The commemoration also gave birth to projects such as *Africa* and *Between Europe and America* and *Crossed Destinies.*

The "Spiritual Convergence and Intercultural Dialogue" Program has resulted in a series of Interreligious Dialogue Meetings: in Barcelona (1994), Rabat (1995 and 1998), Malta (1997), Bishkek (1999), Tashkent (2000), and Paris (2001). In addition, UNESCO chairs of "Scripture, Spiritual Traditions and their Specific Cultures" are being created in leading academic centers.[10] These bring together teachers and researchers specialized in multidisciplinary aspects of religious studies and committed to the promotion of interreligious dialogue.

What UNESCO has added to the traditional approach to dialogue through reciprocal knowledge—which, although it is pertinent, remains reductive—is the value of interaction. Reciprocal knowledge implies the recognition of identities, whereas interaction sheds light on interproductive possibilities between civilizations, and hence on cultural and spiritual proximity and pluralism.

By shedding light on the interactions and fruitful exchanges between civilizations, cultures, and spiritual traditions, it is possible to create a solid defense against withdrawal into one's identity, against spiritual isolationism, and against the daily manifestations of intolerance in several regions of the globe. For example, in an effort to focus more directly on actual conflicts, the director–general decided in 1993 to have UNESCO propose to the General Assembly of the United Nations the declaration of the year 1995 as the "International Year of Tolerance" to coincide with the fiftieth anniversary of the creation of the United Nations. On this occasion, numerous events, meetings, and publications both around the world and throughout member states made possible the study of the spiritual and cultural values of different religions. Additionally, the director-general encouraged the General Assembly of the United Nations to proclaim the year 2000 "International Year of the Culture of Peace."

Dialogue is the best means of preventing and putting an end to conflicts. It affords, in fact, the possibility of developing a better perception of the other and of recognizing that alterity can be enriching.[11] In a context of fear and withdrawal, in

---

[9] The program not only focuses on bringing to light the interaction between spiritual traditions and their specific cultures by underlining the contributions and borrowings that have taken place between different cultures, but also seeks to promote reciprocal knowledge and the discovery of a common heritage and shared values.

[10] To date, the following chairs have been established: "Chair on Reciprocal Knowledge of Religions of the Book and Education for Peace," The European University Institute Rachi de Troyes and University of Reims Champagne-Ardennes, France; "Chair in Interfaith Studies," University of Birmingham, United Kingdom; "Chair on Cultural and Religious Itineraries," Centre d'Etudes des Religions du Livre (CERL), Research Unit of the CNRS, and Ecole Practique des Hautes Etudes, Paris, France; "Chair on Comparative Study of Religions," Faculty of Letters of la Manouba, Tunis University, Tunisia; "Chair on the Study of Cultures and Religions," The Kyrgyz-Russian Slavic University, Bishkek, Kyrgyzstan; "Chair in Interfaith Studies," The Elijah School for the Study of the Wisdom of World Religions, Jerusalem, Israel and McGill University of Montreal, Canada; "Chair in Intercultural and Inter-religious Exchange," The International Academy for the Study of Cultures and Religions at the Romanian Academy, Bucharest, Romania; and "Chair on Comparative Study of World Religions," Tashkent Islamic University, Tashkent, Uzbekistan.

[11] UNESCO gives priority to intercultural and inter-religious dialogue in education and training, with the objective to further reciprocal knowledge of shared spiritual and ethical values and to highlight interactions between religions and spiritual traditions. UNESCO has sent a questionnaire to four thousand major educational institutions worldwide, in order to identify ongoing experiences being set up in various countries and to identify current needs in terms of adequate pedagogical tools and specialized teaching. The results, drawn from the collected answers and the elaboration of future programs, will be examined in workshops on a regional level. Workshops in central Asia (Kazakhstan and Kyrgyzstan) took place in 2001.

which the enemy is a neighbor, we must come to understand that identity is texture and movement. We must shed light on the dialectic of giving and receiving, and privilege the rediscovery of proximity. In the final analysis, it is a question of promoting the dialectic of universality and diversity, and, therefore, of recognizing the relation between a plurality of identities and a common world heritage.

It is significant to note that UNESCO's Program for Interreligious Dialogue is defined in the Malta Declaration on the project for "Roads of Faith":

> This dialogue, far from ignoring the differences between our respective spiritual heritages, enables us, on the contrary, to discover those differences, to become better acquainted with one another and to enrich one another. Its effect is not to cause each individual to blend into the others, but rather to reinforce his or her convictions; it is not aimed at a merging of spiritual identities, nor at developing some form of syncretism, nor again at providing a platform for proselytism, but it stands for openness, respect, and recognition of the possibilities of living together in a pluralistic context.[12]

Consequently, interreligious dialogue presupposes that each religion and spiritual tradition must assume, express and make known its own unique character. This uniqueness must be expressed in the two fundamental dimensions of each religion and spiritual tradition: the essence and its manifestation. Interreligious dialogue presupposes, therefore, both the freedom to express these unique qualities and the existence of a legal framework that allows to each the free development of its beliefs while respecting the other.

Cultural and spiritual pluralism constitutes one of the essential values of interreligious dialogue, notably in the context of globalization. Pluralism could be defined as the recognition, promotion, and respect for diversity of cultures and religions. And this recognition, promotion, and respect together presuppose the freedom of religion and belief as an essential condition. In an effort to combat the increasingly acute difficulty of dialogue between Europe and Islam, the director-general has encouraged the creation of two projects. The first project, the *Bayt al-Hikma* project, is designed to shed new light on the contribution of the Islamic civilization to the development of the scientific, cultural, and artistic heritage of humanity.[13] The second project, *AMAR-UNESCO Standing Conference: European and Islamic Civilizations: A Permanent Forum for Dialogue,* aims at establishing a bridge for a sustained dialogue and a cultural partnership between the contemporary Islamic World and the West. [14]

---

[12] *Roads of Faith: The Malta Declaration* (23 September 1997) <http://www.unesco.org/cpp/uk/declarations/malta.pdf>.

[13] A summer course was held on the *History of Sciences in the Mediterranean Under the Fatimids*, ending with an appeal to International Organizations and NGOs to intensify cooperation in order to create a common cultural, economic, and political space between the North and South. A symposium on *Medicine, Pharmacopoeia and Hospitals* in the Islamic world took place in 1999 to study the role of Islamic civilization in the development of medical sciences. On the occasion of the celebration of the nine hundredth anniversary of Omar Khayyam, the internationally renowned poet, mathematician, astronomer, and philosopher, an international symposium on Omar Khayyam and a critical edition of his mathematical work are planned. In the framework of the celebration in Tunisia of the eight hundredth anniversary of Averroes (1126–1198), UNESCO has brought its technical and financial support to the organization of an international symposium on the famous doctor-philosopher, who acted as a bridge between Islam and the West and who introduced the philosophical thought of Aristotle and Plato into Europe.

Interreligious dialogue bears as much upon the essence of religion as upon its manifestation. But history and, to be sure, current events teach us that the recognition of universal values shared by religions and spiritual traditions has often been accompanied by misunderstanding, disagreement, and hostility when it comes to the external manifestation of religious essence. Confrontations have often had more to do with the manifestation rather than the essence of religion; rituals, liturgies, dress and dietary codes, collective ceremonies, and other external expressions of religion have often been the cause or the pretext for ostracism and conflicts with terrible consequences.

III. Conclusion

UNESCO's mandate proposes therefore a project of construction over the course of time, a long and profound labor of ethics in the world's vast fields. This project focuses essentially on the promotion of ethics in the different disciplines of the mind, the promotion of scientific progress and of knowledge and information, and the construction of a culture of peace and the development of dialogue between cultures, civilizations, and religions. In a context of democracy, liberty, and pluralism, the setting for this drama is the long memory of history; its outcome depends upon securing the values of this program within everyday life, within the city, within the neighborhood . . . within man.

---

[14] The first three conferences were attended by men and women from more than seventeen countries and from many different religions. They developed two innovative projects: the *Women's Forum Dialogue,* aimed at fostering the dialogue between Muslim and European women, and the *Intercultural Business Group,* designed at promoting new ethical standards in business cooperation between Europe and the Muslim world.

Chapter 10

The Protection of Religious Freedom in the System of the Council of Europe

Javier Martínez-Torrón and Rafael Navarro-Valls

I. Introduction

The international protection of the freedom of religion and belief advanced significantly during the second half of the twentieth century.[1] Religious liberty has traveled a long way since it was solemnly recognized by the Universal Declaration of Human Rights in 1948.[2] Together with the United Nations' initiatives[3] and impelled by the 1948 Universal Declaration, other important steps have been taken by regional international organizations.

Among these regional documents, the European Convention for the Protection of Human Rights and Fundamental Freedoms (the "Convention" or the "European Convention") is especially significant.[4] The European Convention was created by the Council

[1] A good exposition of the history of the international efforts to guarantee the protection of religious freedom can be found in Bahiyyih G. Tahzib, *Freedom of Religion or Belief: Ensuring Effective International Legal Protection* (Boston: Martinus Nijhoff, 1996), 63–247, and Malcolm D. Evans, *Religious Liberty and International Law in Europe* (Cambridge: Cambridge University Press, 1997), 6–171. For a summary description of the concept of religious freedom present in international documents, see Jean Duffar, "La liberté religieuse dans les textes internationaux," *La libertad religiosa: Memoria del IX Congreso Internacional de Derecho Canónico* (México: Universidad Nacional Autónoma de México, 1996), 471–97. See also C. Evans, *Freedom of Religion Under the European Convention on Human Rights* (Oxford: Oxford University Press, 2001); Leonard M. Hammer, *The International Human Right to Freedom of Conscience* (Burlington: Ashgate, 2001).

[2] *Universal Declaration of Human Rights*, GA Res. 217A, UN Doc. A/810 (1948).

[3] After the *Universal Declaration*, there have been two main milestones in the history of UN efforts to promote the respect of religious liberty around the world. The first is the 1966 *International Covenant on Civil and Political Rights* (opened for signature 19 December 1966), 999 UNTS 171, 6 ILM 368 (especially article 18). The second is the 1981 *Declaration on the Elimination of All Forms of Intolerance and of Discrimination Based on Religion or Belief*, GA Res. 36-55, UN GAOR, 36th Sess. Agenda Item 75, Supp. No. 51, UN Doc. A/36/55.

[4] *European Convention for the Protection of Human Rights and Fundamental Freedoms* (opened for signature 4 November 1950), 213 UNTS 221 (hereafter "European Convention"). We could also mention the following: the 1969 *American Convention on Human Rights*, 22 November 1969, 9 ILM 99 (especially article 12); the 1981 *African Charter on Human and Peoples' Rights*, 27 June 1981, 21 ILM 58 (especially article 12); and some of the documents produced by the Organization (formerly Conference)

Tore Lindholm, W. Cole Durham, Jr., Bahia G. Tahzib-Lie (eds.), Facilitating Freedom of Religion or Belief: A Deskbook, *209–238. © 2004 Koninklijke Brill NV.*

of Europe in 1950 and has often been presented as a model of effectiveness in the international protection of human rights, especially because of the judicial machinery created to enforce the rights recognized in the Convention: the European Court of Human Rights (the "European Court" or the "Court"), located in Strasbourg, France. If one compares the current systems for the international protection of human rights, the prior statement is probably accurate. The European system, however, is not perfect, at least as far as the protection of the freedom of thought, conscience, and religion is concerned.

In the following pages, we will mention some initiatives of the Council of Europe related to freedom of religion or belief. This will include explaining the basic features of the European Court's composition and procedure (Part II). Next, we will attempt to describe what are, in our opinion, the main strengths and deficiencies of the case law of the European Court with regard to the freedom of religion or belief (Parts III and IV).[5] Finally, we will conclude with some recommendations on aspects of the European Court's doctrine that should be changed if the Court wants to be considered an example that should be followed in the international community.

II. The Council of Europe and Freedom of Religion or Belief

The Council of Europe was founded in 1949, in the context of the postwar movements destined to promote European unity. Its primary aim was to unify the efforts of European democratic countries in order to reinforce respect for human rights. The number of member states of the Council of Europe, initially ten,[6] has continually increased as democracy has spread throughout Europe.[7] Acceptance as a member of the Council of Europe has become a distinctive sign of being a democratic regime.

---

for Security and Cooperation in Europe (OSCE), in particular the *Concluding Document of the Vienna Meeting: Conference on Security and Cooperation in Europe,* 28 ILM 531 (especially principles 16, 17) (1989). For a more detailed analysis of these documents, see Javier Martínez-Torrón, "La protección internacional de la libertad religiosa," *Tratado de Derecho Eclesiástico* (Pamplona: Ediciones Universidad de Navarra, 1994), 141–239, as well as the bibliography there cited. For the purposes of this essay, we have reduced the bibliographical references to a minimum. Further references can be found in the books cited in note 1.

[5] In this essay, we will use the term "religious freedom" or "freedom of religion or belief" with essentially the same meaning as "freedom of thought, conscience, and religion" (the latter is the expression utilized by the European Convention). The reason is that, in our opinion, the reference to thought, conscience, and religion does not intend to separate three different rights but merely to note diverse profiles of the same fundamental right. On the other hand, as religion seems to be—historically as well as conceptually—the center around which this right has been construed, the wording "religious freedom" may be considered sufficiently expressive. For a more extensive explanation of this idea, see Martínez-Torrón, "La protección internacional," 186–93.

[6] *The Statute of the Council of Europe* was signed in London on 5 May 1949 by the representatives of Belgium, Denmark, France, Ireland, Italy, Luxembourg, the Netherlands, Norway, the United Kingdom, and Sweden.

[7] After the massive incorporation of post-socialist countries, there are currently forty-three member states of the Council of Europe. Armenia and Azerbaijan were accepted as of 25 January 2001 and are the most recent additions. They had not ratified their membership at the time this volume went to press, but are expected to do so. In addition, there are some "observers" to the Committee of Ministers—among which is the Holy See—and to the Parliamentary Assembly. Information about the Council of Europe, its organization, activities, documentation, etc., can be obtained at <http://www.coe.int>.

The first and principal achievement of the Council of Europe—its masterpiece, as has been said—was the European Convention on Human Rights, which was signed in Rome on 4 November 1950 and entered into force on 3 September 1953. The European Convention has been successively amended by several protocols. Three provisions of the Convention deal with religion. The freedom of thought, conscience, and religion is recognized in article 9 of the Convention.[8] Article 14 enshrines the principle of equality and prohibits discrimination based on religion.[9] Article 2 of the First Protocol endorses the rights of parents to choose the religious or ideological orientation of their children's education.[10]

As we said before, the main reason for the success of the European Convention is that a specific judicial body—the European Court of Human Rights—was created to guarantee the effective protection of the rights and freedoms recognized in the document. This fact has made the European Convention a unique instrument for the advancement of human rights in the international sphere. We will later describe the structure and procedure of the European Court and analyze its case law on religious freedom. But first we will note some other initiatives adopted by the Council of Europe on the subject.

A. Initiatives of the Parliamentary Assembly and the Committee of Ministers of the Council of Europe

Since the mid-1960s, the Parliamentary Assembly of the Council of Europe has showed an increasing interest in questions related to freedom of religion or belief. Its initiatives in this field have typically consisted of "resolutions" and "recommendations" requesting the Committee of Ministers of the Council of Europe to take certain measures or inviting the governments of the member states to adopt some provisions in their respective national laws.[11] Although neither recommendations nor resolutions have binding force,[12] they do express a persuasive state of opinion. Notably, these guidelines have not infrequently been followed by governments and have sometimes promoted significant changes in national legislation.

---

[8] "1. Everyone has the right to freedom of thought, conscience and religion; this right includes freedom to change his religion or belief and freedom, either alone or in community with others and in public or private, to manifest his religion or belief, in worship, teaching, practice and observance.
"2. Freedom to manifest one's religion or beliefs shall be subject only to such limitations as are prescribed by law and are necessary in a democratic society in the interests of public safety, for the protection of public order, health or morals, or for the protection of the rights and freedoms of others" (European Convention, art. 9).

[9] "The enjoyment of the rights and freedoms set forth in this Convention shall be secured without discrimination on any ground such as sex, race, colour, language, religion, political or other opinion, national or social origin, association with a national minority, property, birth or other status" (ibid., art. 14).

[10] "No person shall be denied the right to education. In the exercise of any functions which it assumes in relation to education and to teaching, the State shall respect the right of parents to ensure such education and teaching in conformity with their own religious and philosophical convictions" (*Protocol [No. 1] to the European Convention,* 20 Mar. 1952, art. 2, 213 UNTS 262).

[11] The Parliamentary Assembly is the Council of Europe's deliberative body. It has been called "Europe's democratic conscience." It is the most widely-based European assembly. Its 602 members (301 representatives and 301 substitutes) are elected or appointed by national parliaments from among their own members. Each country has a number of representatives depending on the size of its population; all the main national political parties should be represented. Nongovernmental organizations take part in a certain number of committees as observers and provide a valuable input to important events organized by

The Council of Europe's most important actions with regard to the freedom of religion and belief have focused on three subjects. First, chronologically, is conscientious objection to military service. Since 1967, the Parliamentary Assembly as well as the Committee of Ministers have put considerable pressure on European governments, urging them to recognize the right of individuals to refuse compulsory military service on conscience grounds and to allow such individuals to perform instead alternative civic service on an equal basis.[13] These efforts—both cause and effect of an increasing pacifist mentality—have indeed influenced the evolution of many national laws in Europe. By the late 1980s, most member states had tolerant legislation on the subject. However, the enlargement of the Council of Europe through the incorporation of post-socialist European countries calls for new actions.

A second set of initiatives regard the role of religion in contemporary society. In two recommendations, one from 1993 and one from 1999,[14] the Parliamentary Assembly emphasized that cooperation between religion and democracy is not only possible but necessary. The real danger to democracy is extremism, understood as a perversion of religion. The state is obliged to actively promote tolerance, especially through educational measures (such as through courses on the comparative history of religions in schools, cooperation with religious educational institutions, etc.). And, of course, the state is also bound to guarantee the efficient protection of religious freedom in its individual as well as in its institutional profiles.

It is interesting to note that the Parliamentary Assembly included a reference to a previous recommendation, from 1988,[15] which specified the rights of churches that are implicit in religious freedom (i.e., the right to have legal recognition by the state, to own

---

the Assembly. The Parliamentary Assembly elects the Council of Europe's secretary general and the judges of the European Court of Human Rights. The texts adopted by the Assembly provide guidelines for the Committee of Ministers, national governments, parliaments, and political parties. The Assembly has also initiated many European conventions, which form the basis of a truly European system of legislation.
The Committee of Ministers is the active body of the Council of Europe. It is composed of the foreign ministers of member states, who meet at least twice a year to review political issues and matters of European cooperation and to give the necessary political impetus to the Council's activities. However, the ministers' deputies are, in practice, the governments' permanent representatives to the Council of Europe; they meet once a week and have the same decision-making powers as the ministers and supervise the Council's activities. Most decisions require a two-thirds majority of votes cast, but a simple majority is sufficient for procedural questions. The Committee of Ministers' decisions are sent to governments in the form of recommendations or are embodied in European conventions and agreements, which are legally binding on states that ratify them. The Committee also adopts declarations and resolutions on current political issues. Over 170 conventions have been drawn up. They are concerned mainly with human rights but cover other areas that affirm and strengthen the Council of Europe's democratic, social, and cultural cohesion. The Committee of Ministers also ensures that conventions and agreements between member states are implemented (for instance, the Committee supervises the execution by member states of the judgments of the European Court of Human Rights).

[12] Recommendations contain proposals addressed to the Committee of Ministers, the implementation of which is within the competence of governments. Resolutions embody decisions by the Assembly on questions that it is empowered to put into effect or expressions of view for which it alone is responsible.

[13] The most relevant documents in this regard are the Parliamentary Assembly Resolution 337 (1967), and the Committee of Ministers Recommendation R (87)8 (1987).

[14] Parliamentary Assembly Recommendation 1202 (1993) on religious tolerance in a democratic society, and Parliamentary Assembly Recommendation 1396 (1999) on religion and democracy. In a similar direction, but with a wider scope, we could also cite Committee of Ministers Recommendation R (97)21 (1997) to member states, on the media and the promotion of a culture of tolerance.

places of worship, to freely disseminate their doctrines, etc.). The 1988 recommendation set out some fundamental principles with the aim of fostering respect for religious freedom in the communist countries, taking advantage of the doors opened by ***perestroika***. Nonetheless, even today the implementation of those principles continues to be necessary, as many of the former socialist countries have legislation on religious affairs that does not correspond fully with international European standards.[16]

The third notable subject is the advancement and proliferation of new movements of religious or spiritual character, which has caused a strong polemic in many European countries in recent years. This topic was first addressed by a recommendation of the Parliamentary Assembly in 1992.[17] In its Recommendation 1178 (1992), the Parliamentary Assembly concluded that major legislation on sects was undesirable on the grounds that such legislation might well interfere with the freedom of conscience and religion guaranteed by article 9.[18] Significantly, the Parliamentary Assembly also recommended introducing legislation that would grant corporate status to new religious movements which have been registered, thereby underscoring its commitment to religious freedom for such groups. At the same time, it recommended that certain educational and legislative measures were appropriate, such as inclusion in the basic curriculum of objective factual information concerning established religions and their major variants, providing of supplementary information of a similar objective nature concerning the nature and activities of new religious movements, and strengthening various kinds of child protection and social welfare legislation.[19]

Interest in the issue was rekindled as a result of a number of highly visible incidents in the mid-1990s, including the Solar Temple suicides and the subway gassings in Japan associated with Aum Shinrikyo. Several reports have been drafted, coming from different perspectives and diverse committees of the Parliamentary Assembly. The result was the unanimous adoption of a new recommendation in 1999.[20] The Parliamentary Assembly's 1999 position on new religious movements can be summarized as follows: the problems caused by some of the new movements, often referred to insensitively and disparagingly as "sects," must be addressed through educational and cultural measures rather than merely legal actions. Specifically, the Parliamentary Assembly called for the establishment of information centers on "groups of a religious, esoteric or spiritual nature" at European and national levels. At the same time, however, the Assembly urged governments of members states "to use the normal procedures of criminal and civil law against illegal practices carried out in the name of groups of a religious, esoteric or spiritual nature."[21] The Recommendation further encouraged member states to adopt an approach

---

[15] Parliamentary Assembly Recommendation 1086 (1988) on the situation of the church and freedom of religion in Eastern Europe.

[16] See Viktor Yelensky, "The Role of Religion in Eastern Europe: From Communism to Democracy," in the official publication of the Parliamentary Assembly, ***Religion and Democracy***, doc. 8270 (1999): 39–50. Among Spanish works, see María J. Roca, "La legislación sobre libertad religiosa en el Este de Europa: Especial referencia a Ucrania," ***Anuario de Derecho Eclesiástico del Estado*** 13 (1997): 189–221.

[17] Parliamentary Assembly Recommendation 1178 (1992) on sects and new religious movements.

[18] Ibid. The Parliamentary Assembly's conclusion was based in part on recognition that normal criminal laws are sufficient to address serious problems.

[19] Ibid.

[20] Parliamentary Assembly Recommendation 1412 (1999) on "Illegal activities of sects."

[21] Ibid.

"which will bring about understanding, tolerance, dialogue and resolution of conflicts," and "to take firm steps against any action which is discriminatory or which marginalizes religious or spiritual minority groups."[22]

In short, only the normal procedures of criminal and civil law are to be used against illegal practices of some groups, but specific criminal legislation on "sects" seems undesirable, as the exercise of religious freedom might be endangered. The Assembly places particular emphasis on the protection of minors against excessive influence by spiritual or religious groups and on guaranteeing the actual freedom of followers to abandon the movement at any moment, but seeks to balance this concern with cautions to make certain that the religious freedom of such groups is accorded due respect.

B. The European Court of Human Rights

The European Court of Human Rights works as a constitutional court, interpreting the European Convention, which has become in effect the "bill of rights" of democratic Europe. The Court began its activities in January 1959, but its structure and procedure has been substantially changed by Protocol 11 to the Convention, which entered into force in November 1998.[23]

The Court currently functions on a permanent basis. It is composed of one judge from each state that has signed the European Convention and consequently accepted the jurisdiction of the Court. The judges are elected for a period of six years by the Parliamentary Assembly of the Council of Europe. The Assembly chooses a judge from each member state from a list of three candidates proposed by that state.

One of the most interesting and important modifications introduced by Protocol 11 was granting to individuals the right to direct access to the Court. Before 1998, individuals were entitled only to file an application before the European Commission of Human Rights, claiming that a member state had infringed the Convention. The Commission was not a judicial body, but acted as a filter; it decided which applications deserved an examination of the merits and transmitted them to the Court, accompanied by a report on the merits of the case. The other applications were declared inadmissible.

Protocol 11 has eliminated the Commission. Today the Court may receive applications directly from any person, nongovernmental organization, or group of individuals. Each application is first examined by a committee of three judges. A committee may, by a unanimous vote, declare an individual application inadmissible either for procedural reasons or by declaring the application "manifestly ill-founded." Otherwise, a chamber of seven judges will decide on the admissibility and merits of the case. The Court may also sit in a Grand Chamber of seventeen judges if a case raises an issue of general importance—especially when a serious question affecting the interpretation of the Convention is involved or when a decision delivered by a chamber might be inconsistent with the case law of the Court. In chambers as well as in the Grand Chamber, the judge elected from the state implicated by the application sits as an *ex officio* member.

---

[22] Ibid.

[23] *Protocol No. 11 to the European Convention,* 11 May 1994, 33 ILM 960. The full text of *Protocol No. 11,* and the rest of the basic texts of the Convention, can be obtained in the website of the European Court: <http://www.echr.coe.int>. All the decisions of the Court are now available and searchable at the same website.

The Court, following the text of the Convention, has traditionally shown a preference for a friendly settlement as the best way to put an end to an application, provided that human rights are duly respected. If this is not possible, the Court will conduct its ordinary judicial proceedings and deliver a final judgment that has binding force on the states. If the Court finds that there has been a violation of the Convention, the injured party may be afforded a just satisfaction. The Committee of Ministers will supervise the execution. The experience of more than thirty years reveals that the states have normally accepted and executed the decisions of the Court.

Until 1993, the Court did not directly address the questions raised by the right to freedom of religion or belief.[24] Applications based on article 9 of the Convention were usually declared inadmissible by the Commission as manifestly ill-founded, sometimes with decisions that were longer and deeper than one would expect from a body with no judicial power and that did not seem to harmonize with the obvious lack of justification that the Commission attributed to the application.

This situation has changed remarkably in recent years. The reasons for this change are not completely clear, but the recent expansion of the Council of Europe throughout eastern Europe may have played a significant role. For several decades, most member states had high standards of protection for freedom of religion or belief. The massive incorporation of post-communist countries into the system of the European Convention might have motivated the Court to define more carefully the content and limits of the right to freedom of thought, conscience, and religion.

In any event, the decisions of the European Court of Human Rights are the only decisions under the Council of Europe system that have binding force on member states. Therefore, it is important that we analyze here the case law of the Court with regard to both the individual and institutional aspects of religious freedom. Space constraints on this chapter determine that our study be brief. However, we will also take into account the doctrine expressed by the former European Commission of Human Rights, which became extinct in 1998. Although the European Commission did not have any formal jurisdictional power, the length and reasoning of many of its decisions and reports permit us to say that there is a sort of "case law" of the Commission that parallels that of the Court. And, generally speaking, with regard to religious freedom, there has been a line of continuity between the views of the Commission and the jurisprudence of the Court after 1993.

---

[24] Indeed, the first case decided in light of article 9 was Kokkinakis v. Greece, 17 EHRR 397 (1994) (ECtHR 260-A, 25 May 1993). Until then the Court had decided only one case in which a question of religion or conscience was involved, and the decision was dealt with under article 2 of the First Protocol. See Kjeldsen, Busk Madsen and Pedersen v. Denmark, 1 EHRR 711 (1979–80) (ECtHR 23, 7 December 1976). A succinct analysis of the case law of the European Court and Commission of Human Rights can be found in Francesco Margiotta Broglio, "Religione e Stato in alcuni sistemi constituzionali atipici: Il caso della Convenzione Europea del 1950," *La libertad religiosa y de conciencia ante la justicia constitucional: Actas del VIII Congreso Internacional de Derecho Eclesiástico del Estado,* ed. Javier Martínez-Torrón (Granada: Comares, 1998), 299–310. See also Javier Martínez-Torrón, "The European Court of Human Rights and Religion," *Law and Religion*, Current Legal Issues 2001, ed. Richard O'Dair and Andrew D. Lewis, vol. 4 (Oxford: Oxford University Press, 2001), 185–204; Nikolaus Blum, *Die Gedanken-, Gewissens- und Religionsfreiheit nach Art. 9 der Europäischen Menschenrechtskonvention* (Berlin: Duncker u. H., 1990).

III. The Case Law of the European Court Regarding the Attitude of the State and Secular Law toward Religious Communities

The freedom of thought, conscience, and religion is naturally a right that belongs primarily to individuals, but it has a very significant institutional or "collective" dimension as well. In international law, it is deeply implanted that every religious confession is entitled to religious freedom, no matter whether it is a traditional major church or a recent and atypical group.[25] All religious denominations must have the freedom to act freely in any country without being the object of unjustified restriction or persecution, even if they are minority groups and even if they defend moral values that conflict with the values widely accepted by a certain society.

The case law of the European Commission and the European Court of Human Rights has specified some legal consequences of the right to religious freedom that must be extended to religious confessions.

A. The Position of the Major Churches

One of the most important assertions of the Strasbourg jurisprudence regards the political principles that determine the relationships between state and religion.

The Court has implicitly recognized that there is a certain "margin of appreciation" with respect to the ways that states structure their relations with religious communities. In particular, various forms of cooperation between the state and the religious confessions can exist, even when the state does not cooperate in a strictly equal fashion with all religions. Equality (article 14 of the European Convention) must be applied rigorously in many contexts to preserve religious freedom, but some flexibility is permissible in structuring cooperation with religious communities, particularly where failure to do so would disrupt long-established patterns and expectations. Not even privileged collaborations between states and certain churches, in the form of a hidden confessionality of the state (as in Greece) or in the form of state churches (as in England or in some Scandinavian countries), have been considered contrary to the European Convention. The important thing—in the Court's view—is that the relationships of privileged collaboration do not produce, as a side effect, significant discriminatory impact on individuals or unjustified harm to the freedom to act that the rest of the groups and individuals must enjoy in religious and ideological matters.

In other words, article 9 of the European Convention is aimed at providing an adequate guarantee of the right to freedom of religion and belief. Its purpose, however, is not to establish certain uniform criteria for church-state relations in the Council of Europe member states nor—even less—to impose a compulsory secularism (*laïcité*).

---

[25] As far as the European Convention is concerned, the European Commission affirmed, in 1979, that it is "artificial" to differentiate between the religious freedom of a church and that of its followers. A religious confession actually acts on behalf of its members when it presents an application and is consequently fully legitimated to claim a violation of article 9. Cf. Church of Scientology and Another v. Sweden, 16 Decisions and Reports 70 (ECC 511, App. No. 7805/77, 5 May 1979) (regarding an application filed by the Church of Scientology against Sweden). The Court accepted explicitly this principle in the decisions The Jewish Liturgical Association Cha'are Shalom Ve Tsedek v. France, 27 June 2000, para. 72; and Metropolitan Church of Bessarabia v. Moldova, 13 December 2001, para. 101.

The background of this approach is the idea that the state's attitude towards religion is primarily a political issue and is the result, to a large extent, of the historical tradition and the social circumstances of each country.

Thus, in the *Kokkinakis* case, after a careful scrutiny of the legal restrictions on religious proselytism in Greece—and notwithstanding the fact that the Greek government received a condemnatory judgment—the European Court did not question that the close connection of the Greek Orthodox Church with the state was a legitimate political choice.[26]

Furthermore, the Commission has explicitly affirmed that a state church system does not itself violate article 9 of the Convention as long as membership in the official church is not mandatory.[27] The Commission has also accepted, as compatible with the European Convention, various expressions of state cooperation with religious bodies that do not correspond with the principle of equality. For instance, the Commission has acknowledged that it is appropriate for states to grant financial aid to some churches, in the form of tax exemptions[28] or in the form of assigning some of the taxes collected by the state to sustain the official church[29] or the church to which the taxpayer belongs;[30] to grant to the churches standing to sue their followers before the state courts in order to enforce the payment of religious taxes;[31] and to collaborate in the teaching of Christian doctrine in the public schools by the official church, provided that this teaching is done in an objective and pluralist manner and assuming that the collaboration of the state cannot be considered "indoctrination."[32]

The position of the traditional major churches has been so notably respected that the European Court has held that the protection of the religious feelings of their faithful must prevail over certain forms of freedom of expression by others when that expression can be qualified as blasphemy. Thus, in the cases of *Otto-Preminger-Institut* and *Wingrove*, the Court upheld the ban on the commercial distribution of some films that had been considered offensive to the feelings of Christian people by the Austrian and British authorities respectively.[33]

---

[26] Kokkinakis v. Greece, 17 EHRR 397 (1994) (ECtHR 260-A, 25 May 1993). The same conclusion can be obtained from the report of the Commission in the case of Holy Monasteries v. Greece, 20 EHRR 1 (1995) (ECtHR 301, 9 December 1994), which ended with a friendly settlement (Rep. Com. 13092/87 and 13984/88, 14 January 1993; the decision of the Court, accepting the fairness of the agreement, was delivered on 1 September 1997, Reports of Judgments and Decisions 1997-V).

[27] Darby v. Sweden, Rep. Com. 11581/85 (EComHR, 9 May 1989), para. 45. It has even been accepted that in a system with a state church like Sweden the government can dismiss a minister for intentionally neglecting the civil duties attached to his religious office (Dec. Adm. 11045/84, 42 Decisions and Reports 247).

[28] El Salvador Baptist Church v. Spain, Dec. Adm. 17522/90 (arguing that the church suffered discriminatory treatment because its places of worship were not exempted from the real property taxes in Spain, as Catholic premises were).

[29] See Darby v. Sweden (concerning the payment of local taxes aimed at financially supporting the Swedish Lutheran Church).

[30] Dec. Adm. 10616/83, 40 Decisions and Reports 284 ff. (concerning the ecclesiastical tax in a Swiss town aimed at financially supporting the churches that are legally recognized; the tax had to be paid by the people who figure as members of the respective church in the civil registry).

[31] Dec. Adm. 9781/82, 37 Decisions and Reports 42 ff. (The Catholic Church in Austria took a Catholic married couple to the civil courts to claim the payment of the ecclesiastical tax that Catholics must pay in every Austrian diocese).

[32] Dec. Adm. 4733/71, 14 Y.B. EConHR 664, 674 ff. (EComHR) and Angelini v. Sweden, Dec. Adm. 10491/83, 51 Decisions and Reports 41 ff. (concerning religious education in Swedish public schools).

Nevertheless, the *Pellegrini* case demonstrates that the Court is prepared to restrict the interpretation of some traditional legal advantages of the major churches when they are applied in a way that seems to be incompatible with the rights guaranteed by the Convention. Thus, the Court affirmed that granting civil effects to an ecclesiastical judicial decision declaring a marriage null and void under the canon law—which is a long established practice in Italian law according to the concordat between the Italian state and the Holy See—was contrary to the right to a fair trial enshrined in article 6 ECHR, because, in the particular circumstances of the case, the defendant's right to prepare her defense adequately had not been duly respected in the proceedings before the ecclesiastical courts.[34]

B. The Minority Religious Groups

In recent years, the Court has paid increasing attention to the rights of minority religious groups under article 9 of the European Convention. Its fundamental approach can be condensed into a single statement: such groups are entitled to true freedom to act and not merely to toleration. The main consequences of this general idea, according to the case law of the Court, are the following.

1. The Interpretation of the Equality Principle

Some of these consequences have a direct connection with the principle of equality enshrined in article 14 of the European Convention. Under article 14 of the Convention, discrimination is forbidden.[35] Therefore, individuals have the right not to suffer

---

[33] Otto-Preminger-Institut v. Austria, 19 EHRR 34 (1995) (ECtHR 295-A, 20 September 1994); Wingrove v. United Kingdom, 24 EHRR 1 (1997) (ECtHR 1996-V, 25 November 1996). The former related to a satiric movie entitled "Council in Heaven," in which God was presented as a senile man prostrated before the devil and Jesus Christ as a mentally retarded person; an erotic relationship between the devil and the Virgin was also insinuated. The latter referred to a video of eighteen minutes duration containing a peculiar interpretation of St. Teresa of Avila's ecstasy, in a pornographic setting with homosexual connotations.

[34] Pellegrini v. Italy, 20 July 2001. The relevant part of article 6 ECHR reads: "1. In the determination of his civil rights and obligations or of any criminal charge against him, everyone is entitled to a fair and public hearing within a reasonable time by an independent and impartial tribunal established by law." For a critical commentary of the decision, written by a judge of the Vatican State Court of Appeals, see J. Llobell, "El derecho a un proceso equitativo. Notas a propósito de una sentencia de la Corte Europea de los Derechos Humanos sobre la homologación civil de una sentencia canónica de nulidad de matrimonio dictada en el marco del proceso documental canónico," *Revista General de Derecho Canónico y Derecho Eclesiástico del Estado*, no. 1 (2003) (www.iustel.com).

[35] More precisely, what article 14 prohibits is discrimination with regard to "the rights and freedoms set forth in this Convention," but not with regard to other provisions of national laws. This latter aspect, which certainly enlarges the scope of the equality principle, is the object of *Protocol No. 12 to the European Convention*; its article 1 (*General prohibition of discrimination*) provides: "(1) The enjoyment of any right set forth by law shall be secured without discrimination on any ground such as sex, race, colour, language, religion, political or other opinion, national or social origin, association with a national minority, property, birth or other status. (2) No one shall be discriminated against by any public authority on any ground such as those mentioned in paragraph 1." *Protocol No. 12* was open for signature on 4 November 2000, but is not in force yet (ten ratifications are necessary for its entry into force; twenty-six countries have signed the new Protocol but only one—Georgia—has ratified it at the moment).

discriminatory treatment on account of their membership in a minority religion, even if their belief and behavior contrast sharply with the commonly accepted social customs. Thus, in *Hoffmann*, the European Court held that there cannot be a difference in treatment on the sole ground of religion when a national court rules on the custody of children in a case of divorce.[36] Similarly, we could add, even though the doctrine of the Court has not been conclusive on this point, that members of minority religious groups cannot be kept under surveillance in the absence of a compelling justification based on something other than their mere religious membership.[37] The same rule must be applied to the confinement of people in order to subject them to a process of "deprogramming" from their membership in a "sect"; this is something that can only be done on a voluntary basis.[38]

The prohibition of discrimination embodied in article 14 of the Convention, in principle, is applicable not only to discrimination against individuals but also to discrimination against religious groups as such. However, the European Court does not seem to have interpreted this principle always with the same criteria.

A broad interpretation of the principle of equality was adopted in the case of *Canea Catholic Church.* There the Court held that every religious denomination has the right not only to be accepted as existing *de facto* but also to be granted legal personality under conditions that are fair and similar to those applied to other denominations. National governments cannot unreasonably discriminate between religious confessions with regard to the requirements they—or their institutions—must fulfill in order to be acknowledged as legal persons in the secular sphere, especially when legal personality is indispensable for claiming their rights before the civil courts. Otherwise, in addition to the implications for

---

[36] Hoffmann v. Austria, 17 EHRR 293 (1994) (ECtHR 255-C, 23 June 1993). This case was decided under articles 14 and 8 of the Convention (right to respect for private and family life). A housewife had converted to Jehovah's Witnesses and taken the children with her when the divorce proceedings were still pending. The European Court reversed the decisions of Austrian national courts, which had granted the children's custody to the father. In our opinion, although the principles stated by the European Court are right, the decision was wrong because the wife had unilaterally broken the marital agreement, according to which children had to be educated in the common religion of spouses (they were both Roman Catholics at the time). It is very significant that the decision was adopted by five votes to four. See the dissenting opinion of Judge Mifsud Bonnici. In another case related to custody of children after their parents' divorce (Ignaccolo-Zenide v. Rumania, App. No. 31679/96 [ECtHR, 25 January 2001]), the father alleged—at a certain moment of the procedures before Rumanian courts—that the mother belonged to a sect "not recognized in Rumania" (cf. para. 45); this assertion, however, seems to have had an effect on the decisions of neither the national courts nor the European Court.

[37] Tsavachidis v. Greece, App. No. 28802/95 (ECtHR, 21 January 1999). The case related to the surveillance of Jehovah's Witnesses by the National Intelligence Service. It ended with a friendly settlement in which the Greek government agreed to pay a sum of money for the costs and submitted a formal statement declaring that "the Jehovah's Witnesses are not, and will not in the future be, subject to any surveillance on account of their religious beliefs." By then the European Commission had already elaborated its report on the merits of the case and expressed the opinion that there had been a violation of article 8 (thirteen votes to four) and that there had been no violation of article 9 (nine votes to eight).

[38] Riera Blume and Others v. Spain, App. No. 37680/97 (ECtHR, 14 October 1999). This case referred to some members of the so-called "Centro Esotérico de Investigaciones." The applicants' homes were searched following a judicial order, and the applicants were subsequently confined in a hotel against their will for "deprogramming"; the confinement did not follow any judicial order and was carried out by a private association of "anti-sects" with some participation of the Catalan police. The Court avoided pronouncing any opinion under article 9 and decided in favor of the applicants under article 5(1) (right to liberty and security).

the right of religious freedom, there would be a violation of the right to a hearing by a tribunal, which is an integral part of the right to a fair trial (article 6 of the European Convention).[39] More recently, in the decision *Metropolitan Church of Bessarabia,* the Court has reaffirmed, unanimously, that article 9 ECHR includes the right of new religious denominations to obtain legal personality in conditions equal to recognized churches, especially when the refusal to register a group causes an unjustified restriction on the exercise of religious freedom in its collective dimension (e.g., with regard to internal autonomy, religious meetings, public worship, ownership of real property, commercialization of religious objects, etc.).[40]

By contrast, a recent example of a restrictive interpretation of the equality principle is the decision *Cha'are Shalom Ve Tsedek*, a complex case regarding the ritual slaughter of animals.[41] A strongly divided court—ten votes against seven[42]—considered that national authorities enjoy a margin of appreciation and give certain legal advantages to religious denominations in the course of managing relations with religious communities, so long as it is not proved that individuals' freedom to practice their religion has been impaired.

More precisely, it was held that neither the right to religious freedom nor the equality principle had been violated by the fact that French authorities granted authorization to issue administrative permits for ritual slaughter exclusively to the Jewish Consistorial Association of Paris, while denying such authorization to a minority Jewish association of ultraorthodox orientation. The Consistorial Association is an institution representing most of the main denominations within Judaism. The applicant association, Cha'are Shalom Ve Tsedek, which is not part of the Consistory, deemed that the examination performed by the inspectors of the Consistorial Association was not meticulous enough to guarantee the religious purity of food.[43] In the Court's view, the applicant's right to religious freedom

---

[39] Canea Catholic Church v. Greece, 27 EHRR 329 (1999) (ECtHR 1997-VIII, 16 December 1997). The case related to the Roman Catholic Church of the Virgin Mary in Canea, built in the thirteenth century, which is the cathedral of the Roman Catholic diocese of Crete. Two people living next to the church had demolished one of the surrounding walls and opened a window looking onto the church in the wall of their own building. The Greek courts denied legal standing to the church, as it had not complied with the formal requirements generally stated by the civil code to acquire legal personality. This denial contradicted abundant administrative and judicial practice in Greece in relation to the Roman Catholic Church. Furthermore, it constituted discrimination in light of contrasting treatment accorded to the Greek Orthodox Church and to the Jewish communities, which were granted legal personality and standing to sue without having to follow the civil formalities common to all associations. It is worth noting that the case was decided in light of article 6 (right to a fair trial), taken alone and together with article 14; as a violation of article 6 had been found, the Court declined to decide on the alleged violation of article 9.

[40] See Metropolitan Church of Bessarabia v. Moldova, 13 December 2001, especially nn. 105, 118 and 129. The case related to the creation, in 1992, of a new autonomous local Orthodox church that claimed to be the successor, in the canonical order, of the old Metropolitan Church of Bessarabia, which existed until 1944. The new church counts approximately one million members among Moldavian people, with 160 ecclesiastics, 117 communities in Moldavian territory, and some communities in other Eastern European countries. The Moldavian government had repeatedly refused to recognize the church.

[41] The Jewish Liturgical Association Cha'are Shalom Ve Tsedek v. France, App. No. 27417/95 (ECtHR, 27 June 2000).

[42] Significantly, in this case the Court was sitting as a Grand Chamber.

[43] According to the French legislation and the European Union directives, ritual slaughter constitutes an exception to the general rules aimed at guaranteeing appropriate hygienic conditions and at avoiding unnecessary suffering to animals. This exception is granted in order to respect the ritual laws of some religions, especially Judaism and Islam. Ritual slaughter may be performed only by those persons who have been authorized by the religious bodies specifically approved by the French administration. In

had not been violated, for members of the applicant association were not prevented from obtaining meat that satisfied their religious scruples, since they could buy that sort of food in a few butcher's shops in Paris or import it from Belgium. The Court held that the principle of equality had not been infringed either. French authorities had a margin of appreciation allowing them to determine that only a single institution representing all Jewish communities would be empowered to authorize ritual slaughterers exempt from otherwise applicable laws governing slaughter of animals, based on reasons of public health (to ensure due hygienic conditions) and public order (to foster reciprocal toleration between different religious options). Indeed the decision affirmed that the applicant association had the opportunity to reach an agreement with the Consistorial Association of Paris in order to have ritual slaughter performed by its own personnel. The negotiations had failed because of some differences concerning the religious tax that should be required from buyers of the certified food and paid to the Consistorial Association.

As we said, the *Cha'are Shalom Ve Tsedek* decision was strongly contested by seven judges, who considered that the restrictive interpretation of the equality principle provided by the Court in this case was unacceptable. In their view, the Court had failed to emphasize that the state is obliged to provide an analogous legal treatment as a means to guarantee pluralism, which is an indispensable condition to the exercise of freedom. The seven judges affirmed, in a joint dissenting opinion, that the Court had omitted to analyze whether the applicant association—a minority Jewish association—was in a situation analogous to the Jewish Consistorial Association of Paris, as far as the legislation on religious bodies was concerned—i.e., whether it was a body of religious nature, and whether it pursued religious aims and utilized equivalent means. If that was the case, as it seemed to be, the right approach would have been to examine whether the French administration had an "objective and reasonable justification" to grant the requested administrative permit for ritual slaughter to one Jewish association and to deny the same permit to the other. Apparently that justification did not exist, and consequently—the dissenting opinion concluded—the association Cha'are Shalom Ve Tsedek had been a victim of discrimination.[44]

France, only the Joint Rabbinical Committee (*Commission Rabbinique Intercommunautaire*) has received the administrative approval necessary to grant permits regarding ritual slaughter according to the Torah and the Talmud. That committee is part of the Jewish Consistorial Association of Paris, an institution representing most Jewish communities in France and most of the main denominations within Judaism, with the exceptions of the liberals and the ultraorthodox. The applicant Jewish liturgical association, which is of ultraorthodox orientation, considered that the persons appointed by the Joint Rabbinical Committee were too lax in applying the ritual slaughter rules established by the Jewish law, and consequently the purity of food was not sufficiently certified. For that reason, the applicant association had asked—unsuccessfully—for a separate authorization to permit for its own slaughterers.

[44] In addition, the dissenting opinion argued that the French State could not take into account either the different number of followers, or the doctrinal discrepancies in the religious requisites of "pure" food, nor the inability of both associations to reach an agreement. On the contrary, the state was obliged to provide an analogous legal treatment as a means to guarantee pluralism, which is an indispensable condition to the exercise of freedom. Moreover, in the dissenting judges' view, the European Court did not attach enough importance to two facts: first, administrative French praxis had been very different with regard to the Muslims, with respect to whom there was a remarkable diversity of representative bodies approved by the French administration to grant permits for ritual slaughter; and second, it was inaccurate to invoke reasons of public health in this case, because the hygienic conditions required by the applicant association were stricter than the ones usually existing in the slaughterhouses of the Consistorial Association.

In another recent case, *Thlimmenos*, the European Court has added a new interesting nuance to the interpretation of the equality principle. Article 14 of the Convention is violated not only when states treat persons differently in analogous situations without providing an objective and reasonable justification. According to the Court, "[t]he right not to be discriminated against in the enjoyment of the rights guaranteed under the Convention is also violated when States without an objective and reasonable justification fail to treat differently persons whose situations are significantly different."[45] In this regard, the Court held that a behavior inspired by personal beliefs constitutes a relevant differentiating factor when determining the consequences deriving from a criminal conviction. In particular, when an individual has been convicted of a felony for refusing to perform military service on account of his religious beliefs, he can legitimately claim to be exempted from the general rule that disqualifies people convicted of felony from entering the civil service.[46]

2. Worship, Proselytism and Internal Autonomy

The European Court has recognized the right of religious groups to possess and manage their own places of worship and meeting.[47] To deny this right without sufficient justification is incompatible with the European Convention, according to the doctrine of the Court in *Manoussakis* and *Pentidis*. Both cases arose from applications submitted by Jehovah's Witnesses who claimed that the Greek law on places of worship had been applied to them in a discriminatory and hostile manner. The Greek legislation prescribes that in order to open a public place of worship, civil authorities must first grant explicit permission. The alleged aim of the legislation is to ensure that the place is not run by secret sects, that there is no danger to public order or morals, and that the place of worship will not be a cover for acts of proselytism, which is explicitly forbidden by the Greek Constitution. After analyzing the relevant legislation, the European Court concluded that it granted

---

[45] Thlimmenos v. Greece, App. No. 34369/97 (ECtHR, 6 April 2000), para. 44.

[46] The applicant in the *Thlimmenos* case was a Jehovah's Witness who had been convicted of insubordination in 1983 for refusing to perform unarmed military service, at a time of general mobilization, on account of his religious beliefs. He was sentenced to four years imprisonment, and was released on parole after two years. In 1988, he passed a public examination to become a chartered accountant, a liberal profession which, until 1993, could be exercised only by those who became members of the Greek Institute of Chartered Accountants. In spite of his successful examination—he came second among sixty candidates—the Executive Board of the Institute refused to appoint him because, according to the law, a person who did not qualify for the civil service could not be appointed a chartered accountant, and conviction of felony constituted a disqualification for the civil service. The European Court considered that the Greek State had violated article 14 of the Convention in conjunction with article 9. It was true that the authorities were bound to apply the law in force and deny the applicant's appointment, but the legislation itself had failed to make the appropriate distinctions: there existed no objective and reasonable justification for not treating the applicant differently from other persons convicted of a felony, and his exclusion from the profession of chartered accountants did not pursue a legitimate aim.

[47] Naturally, this right implies the right to freely attend religious ceremonies in those places. Unjustified restriction of free access to places of worship constitutes a violation of article 9 of the Convention, for it prevents people from manifesting their religion "either alone or in community with others." See Cyprus v. Turkey, App. No. 25781/94 (ECtHR, 10 May 2001), paras. 241–47. In this case, which has many and complex political implications, the Court found a violation of the right to religious freedom of the Greek-Cypriot community of Northern Cyprus by the Turkish government (within the context of a much more extensive violation of human rights in that part of Cyprus).

an excessive discretion to Greek authorities and that there were not sufficient guarantees to ensure an objective decision on the permit—among other reasons because representatives of the Greek Orthodox Church intervened in the decision-making process.[48]

Proselytism by religious minorities has been the focus of the European Court's attention in two other cases against Greece.

In the *Kokkinakis* case, the Court held that article 9 of the Convention includes the right of individuals and religious groups to spread their doctrines and to gain new followers through proselytism, provided that they do not use abusive, fraudulent, or violent means.[49] An elderly man, a follower of the Jehovah's Witnesses, had been arrested and subsequently sentenced by the Greek courts under the law that declares proselytism a crime. This law, enacted in 1938, followed the constitutional ban on proselytism, dating back to 1844 and retained in the 1975 Constitution. Both provisions are aimed at protecting the social status of the Greek Orthodox Church.

The Court did not declare the Greek law on proselytism incompatible with the European Convention, for it was possible to construe that law as a means to protect the rights and freedom of others. However, the Court did hold that the right of individuals and groups to disseminate their beliefs was an integral part of the right to religious freedom enshrined in article 9 of the Convention. Consequently, the prohibition of Greek law was legitimate only as applied to "improper proselytism," for instance, the proselytism that entailed the use of violence, fraud, or brainwashing. After a careful scrutiny of the facts, the Court concluded that the Greek government had not supplied enough evidence to prove that Mr. Kokkinakis, who merely engaged in door-to-door evangelism, was engaged in improper proselytism, and his conviction had therefore infringed the European Convention.

More recently, in the *Larissis* case, the Court has added new, interesting nuances on this doctrine when proselytism is carried out in certain special environments, such as the armed forces. More precisely, it was held that restrictions on proselytism are legitimate when they are applied in a superior-subordinate relationship, i.e., when a superior tries to

[48] Manoussakis v. Greece, 23 EHRR 387 (1997) (ECtHR 1996-IV, 26 September 1996); Pentidis and Others v. Greece, App. No. 23238/94 (ECtHR 1997-III, 9 June 1997). In *Manoussakis,* the applicants had asked for government permission to set up a place of worship, and they began to utilize the place, as the permit had not been granted within a period of time that they considered to be excessive. Criminal proceedings were initiated against them in the Greek courts. The European Court held that there had been a violation of article 9 after evaluating three key facts: the Greek authorities had excessive discretion to estimate the need to open a place of worship; there was not a concrete term during which to decide on the permit, allowing the proceedings to be extended indefinitely; and the Greek Orthodox Church intervened in the decision-making process. The *Pentidis* case ended with a friendly settlement; after the condemnatory judgment received in *Manoussakis,* the Greek government granted the administrative authorization required by the Jehovah's Witnesses.

[49] Kokkinakis v. Greece, 17 EHRR 397 (1994) (ECtHR 260-A, 25 May 1993). For a detailed comment on this decision, see Javier Martínez-Torrón, "Libertad de proselitismo en Europa: A propósito de una reciente sentencia del Tribunal europeo de derechos humanos," *Quaderni di diritto e politica ecclesiastica,* no. 1 (1994): 59–71; Jeremy Gunn, "Adjudicating Rights of Conscience Under the European Convention on Human Rights," *Religious Human Rights in Global Perspective,* ed. Johan D. van der Vyver and John Witte (Boston: Martinus Nijhoff, 1996), 305–30. On the problems involved in determining a concept of proselytism in international law, see Natan Lerner, "Proselytism, Change of Religion, and International Human Rights," *Emory International Law Review* 12 (1998): 477–561; Tad Stahnke, "Proselytism and the Freedom to Change Religion in International Human Rights Law," *BYU Law Review,* no. 1 (1999): 251.

convert a subordinate, even if it has been done merely through respectful conversations on religious topics. Such restrictions are justified by the need to avoid the risk that the relationship can degenerate, causing subordinates to act under improper pressure from their superiors. However, restrictions on proselytism are not justified when the same kind of religious conversation takes place between an officer and a civilian, even if the latter also belongs to the military environment, because they are not linked by any superior-subordinate relationship.[50]

Turning to the rights of religious groups, it seems natural that article 9 of the European Convention should be construed to include the rights of religious groups to be recognized and to have internal autonomy and control of their own affairs. This interpretation has been recently supported by some decisions of the Court.

In the *Serif* case, the Court held that, except when there is a "pressing social need," the state is not permitted to interfere in a purely religious question that has been decided by a religious community, even when that community has become divided by opposite views on the issue and a "social tension" might subsequently arise.[51] This is one of the unavoidable effects of pluralism, which in turn is inseparable from democracy.[52] In particular, "the Court does not consider that, in democratic societies, the State needs to take measures to ensure that religious communities remain or are brought under a unified leadership."[53] The case regarded the appointment of a Muslim religious leader (*Mufti*) in a region of Greece (Thrace) with a significant Muslim population of Turkish origin. The leader in question had been elected by the Muslim community, disregarding the intervention of the state authorities prescribed by the Greek law governing the election and appointment of Muftis.[54]

A similar doctrine has been expressed by the Court in its subsequent decision *Hasan and Chaush*.[55] The facts of the case relate to the religious disputes between two different factions of the Bulgarian Muslim community and the intervention of state authorities in the election and appointment of a Muslim religious leader, within the context of the process of democratization commenced in Bulgaria at the end of 1989. According to Bulgarian law, only the Muslim leadership registered by the Directorate of Religious Denominations enjoys the legal representation of the Islamic religious community and has the right to use its property and assets. The Bulgarian government, without providing any specific ground for its decision, decided to support one of the rival religious leaders, after these proved over time to be unable to reach an agreement. The Council of Ministers even disobeyed an order of the Bulgarian Supreme Court urging it to register Mr. Hasan—the applicant—as the Chief Mufti in Bulgaria.

---

[50] Larissis and Others v. Greece, 27 EHRR 329 (1999) (ECtHR 1998-I, 24 February 1998). *Larissis* involved three officers of the Greek Air Forces who belonged to the Pentecostal Church.

[51] Serif v. Greece, App. No. 34369/97 (ECtHR, 14 December 1999).

[52] See also, among other cases, Freedom and Democracy Party (ÖZDEP) v. Turkey, App. No. 23885/94 (ECtHR, 8 December 1999), para. 37.

[53] Serif v. Greece, para. 52.

[54] It must be noted that the law had been changed a few days before the election took place and once it had been organized. The Greek government justified the state's intervention on account of the administrative and judicial functions that Muftis exercise. The case also involved some interesting issues concerning some international treaties signed by Greece in the 1910s and 1920s, but the Court decided not to express any opinion on the subject.

[55] Hasan and Chaush v. Bulgaria, App. No. 30985/96 (ECtHR, 26 October 2000).

The European Court, following its doctrine in *Serif,* reiterated that national authorities interfere in the exercise of religious freedom when they fail to remain neutral with regard to changes in the leadership of a religious community, or when they try to force the community to come together under a single leadership against its own wishes.[56] In this case, the Court held that the government's interference with the internal organization of the Islamic community could not be considered legitimate, because national legislation gave a virtually unlimited power to public authorities to decide which religious leadership was the legitimate one and had consequently the right to be registered. More specifically, the Court's conclusion was that such interference was not "prescribed by law," as this expression had been interpreted in prior decisions; i.e., domestic law must be sufficiently precise, accessible, and foreseeable, for it must constitute a protection against arbitrary interferences by public authorities. In the present case, the relevant Bulgarian legislation did not provide for any substantive criteria for the national authorities' decision, thus granting them an unfettered power.[57]

In the case of *Church of Bessarabia,*[58] the Court reiterated the principles stated in the cases *Serif* and *Hasan and Chaush.* The Moldavian government had refused to grant legal personality to the applicant church, arguing that it was merely a schismatic group within the Metropolitan Church of Moldova, which had been legally recognized. In the government's view, the religious freedom of Orthodox citizens had not been violated, for they could practice their religion within the recognized church. The Court held that the respondent government, by supporting one of the Orthodox churches in the conflict, had failed to remain neutral with regard to a dissension of purely religious nature, thus interfering with the autonomy of churches that was guaranteed by article 9 of the European Convention.

More recently, the foregoing doctrine has been emphasized by the European Court—for the fourth time in three years—in *Agga v. Greece*, a case that offered many analogies with *Serif.*[59]

The strength of protections afforded by the abovementioned religion cases is reinforced by other European Court decisions involving freedom of expression and freedom of association, such as *United Communist Party of Turkey* and other subsequent cases concerning the dissolution of political parties for allegedly opposing the Turkish Constitution's principles.[60] In those cases, the Court declared that there is a close connection between the freedom of association (article 11) and the freedom of expression

---

[56] Ibid., para. 78.

[57] Ibid., paras. 84–88. Once the Court reached that conclusion, it deemed unnecessary to continue the three-prong test of article 9(2); i.e., to judge whether the state's interference pursued a "legitimate aim" and was "necessary in a democratic society."

[58] Metropolitan Church of Bessarabia v. Moldova, 13 December 2001. See note 40 and accompanying text.

[59] Agga v. Greece, 17 October 2002.

[60] See United Communist Party of Turkey v. Turkey, App. No. 19392/92 (ECtHR 1998-I, 30 January 1998), especially paras. 42–43; Socialist Party v. Turkey, App. No. 21237/93 (ECtHR 1998-III, 25 May 1998), para. 41; Freedom and Democracy Party (ÖZDEP) v. Turkey, para. 37. The three cases were decided in favor of the applicants under article 11 of the Convention (freedom of association). See also Sidiropoulos and Others v. Greece, App. No. 26695/95 (ECtHR 1998-IV, 10 July 1998), para. 40. *Sidiropoulos* involved the refusal to register a cultural and political association aimed at promoting Macedonian autochthonous values.

(article 10). In a democratic society, protection of the freedom to express an opinion, even when those opinions "offend, shock or disturb," is one of the objectives of the freedom of assembly and association. In such a sensitive area, restrictions on freedom of association must be "construed strictly" and can be justified only by "convincing and compelling reasons." This narrow construction of the limits to freedom of association demands that national states "have only a limited margin of appreciation" to impose such restrictions, which in turn "goes hand in hand with rigorous European supervision embracing both the law and the decisions applying it." In other words, political and cultural organizations—no matter how controversial they are—can be dissolved or denied legal status only if they constitute immediate threats to the constitutional order, i.e., if national authorities demonstrate that restriction of freedom of association is required by a "pressing social need."

Naturally, this reasoning is also applicable to the freedom of thought, conscience, and religion enshrined in article 9. It follows that, in this regard, religious freedom must be construed as broadly as the European Court has construed the freedom of association. And the same is probably true with regard to the connection between the freedom of religion and the freedom of expression, because these provisions of the European Convention are all aimed at protecting pluralism, without which—as the Court has repeatedly emphasized—democracy cannot exist. By implication, any limitations on freedom of religion must be construed at least as narrowly as constraints on the expression and association values. Indeed, in *Kokkinakis* the Court affirmed that "freedom of thought, conscience and religion is one of the foundations of a 'democratic society' within the meaning of the Convention. It is, in its religious dimension, one of the most vital elements that go to make up the identity of believers and their conception of life, but it is also a precious asset for atheists, agnostics, sceptics and the unconcerned. The pluralism indissociable from a democratic society, which has been dearly won over the centuries, depends on it."[61]

The foregoing ideas seem to keep all their strength even after the Court's controverted decision in the recent case of *Refah Partisi (The Welfare Party) v. Turkey*,[62] although the decision raises some questions concerning the future interpretation of freedom of association and freedom of religion. This was the fourth case in which the European Court had to deal with the dissolution of a political party by the Turkish Constitutional Court, but this time, contrary to what occurred in the other three cases, the Court did not find that freedom of association had been violated.[63]

The *Refah Partisi* was a political party with a specific Islamist orientation. In fact, although accepting the constitutional principle of secularism (*laïcité*), the party proposed a reinterpretation of that principle, which has been considered essential to keep a peaceful political life in Turkey since the establishment of the republic. Such reinterpretation of *laïcité* included the project to promote a "multilegal system" in the country, i.e., the notion that each group would be governed by its specific religious laws. Based on diverse declarations and activities of members of the Welfare Party, the Turkish Constitutional Court inferred that there was a hidden agenda of the party itself, which aimed at setting up a political system incompatible not only with the principle of *laïcité* but also with the very notion of democracy—namely, the establishment of a theocratic system based on

---

[61] Kokkinakis v. Greece, 17 EHRR 397 (1994) (ECtHR 260-A, 25 May 1993), para. 31. See also Serif v. Greece, App. No. 34369/97 (ECtHR, 14 December 1999), para. 49.

[62] Refah Partisi (The Welfare Party) v. Turkey, 31 July 2001.

[63] The other three are cited supra, in note 60.

the *Sharia* or Islamic law, through recourse, if necessary, to the *jihad* or holy war. The European Court substantially accepted the Turkish Court's assumption and sustained that the dissolution of the Welfare Party was justified on the basis of a "pressing social need." The ruling was therefore legitimate from the Convention's perspective.

The consequences that the *Refah Partisi* decision will produce in the case law of the European Court are still uncertain. It is true that the principles governing the interpretation of freedom of association do not seem to be very much affected. In fact, the Court's decision was adopted by a narrow margin (four votes to three); the dissenting judges wrote an extensive joint opinion, in which, significantly, they did not question the general principles inspiring the Court's reasoning but rather their application to the circumstances of the case.[64] Actually these principles were substantially the same utilized in the precedent decisions rejecting the dissolution of other political parties in Turkey.

However, some particularities of the *Welfare Party* case suggest that this decision may acquire a special relevance. On the one hand, the Welfare Party, created in 1983, was a very significant party in the political spectrum of Turkey; indeed it was part of a coalition government at the moment of its dissolution and the party's president was the prime minister of Turkey. On the other hand, some of the statements of the Court might have a deep future influence on the conception of the state's power to limit the manifestations of freedom of religion and belief, especially where the Islamic religion is concerned.[65] In particular, the European Court declared that the establishment of *Sharia* or Islamic law as a political regime is not compatible with "the fundamental principles of democracy as expressed in the Convention." And the Court added: "It is difficult to declare one's respect for democracy and human rights while at the same time supporting a regime based on sharia, which clearly diverges from Convention values, particularly with regard to its criminal law and criminal procedure, its rules on the legal status of women and the way it intervenes in all spheres of private and public life in accordance with religious precepts."[66]

The *Refah Partisi* decision was appealed before the Grand Chamber of the European Court. The new decision—delivered when this paper had already been sent to print—unanimously upheld the previous judgment and substantially accepted its reasoning.[67]

---

[64] In short, the three dissenting judges considered that the Welfare Party could not be held responsible for the activities of some of its members and that the party's dissolution was not supported by enough evidence proving the existence of a "pressing social need."

[65] In fact, some state restrictions on the use of the Islamic veil by women in public places—universities and schools—had been previously sustained as legitimate by the European Commission and the European Court. See decisions on the admissibility of Karaduman v. Turkey, App. No. 16278/90 (EComHR, 74 Decisions and Reports 93, 3 May 1993); Bulut v. Turkey, App. No. 18783/91 (EComHR, 3 May 1993); and Dahlab v. Switzerland, App. No. 42393/98 (ECtHR, 15 February 2001).

[66] Refah Partisi (The Welfare Party) v. Turkey, para. 72. The dissenting opinion to the decision does not discuss this statement of the Court. This is not the first time that the Court has alluded to the difficulties of making some parts of the Islamic religious message compatible with the Western concept of democracy. In *Dahlab,* the Court declared that to wear the Islamic veil "seems to be imposed to women by a koranic prescription which ... is difficult to reconcile with the principle of equality of sexes. To wear the Islamic veil is also difficult to reconcile with the message of tolerance, of respect for others, and above all of equality and non-discrimination that every teacher must transmit to the students in a democracy." (Authors' translation: the text of the decision is available only in French in the web pages of the Court.)

[67] Refah Partisi (The Welfare Party) v. Turkey, 13 February 2003. The first decision was adopted by one of the chambers of the Court—seven judges, while the Court sitting as a Grand Chamber is composed of seventeen judges. According to article 43(1) of the Convention, "[w]ithin a period of three months from

IV. The Case Law of the European Court and the Problem with the Protection of the Religious Liberty of Individuals and of Some Religious Minorities

The European Convention, like all international documents on human rights, considers the freedom of thought, conscience, and religion as a right that belongs primarily to individuals. On a conceptual level, the right of religious groups appears to be derivative from the individual's right. Yet ironically, the strictly individual dimension of this freedom has been disregarded more often and has arguably received less protection from the Strasbourg jurisdiction than the corporate dimension of the right.

A. The Meaning of the Term "Practice" under the European Convention

The problem of insufficient protection of individual freedom of religion or belief arises from the terminology utilized by the European Convention and most other international texts that describe the content of the freedom of religion and belief. Among the aspects of this freedom that deserve protection, article 9(1) mentions the right to manifest one's religion or belief in worship, teaching, *practice*, and observance.[68] If we direct our attention to the term practice, the most obvious interpretation seems to be that article 9 guarantees the right of individuals to behave in accordance with the prohibitions and dictates of their own consciences. This guarantee should be granted whether or not these practices are based on the tenets of an institutional religion or derive from strictly personal beliefs and whether or not the individual's conscience is grounded on religious or nonreligious beliefs.[69] Of course, this guarantee is necessarily limited (article 9[2]), as the freedom to act is never absolute.

This broad construction of the right to manifest one's belief in *practice* has been proposed by the General Comment of the Committee of Human Rights on article 18 of the 1966 UN International Covenant on Human Rights.[70] We are afraid, however, that the attitudes of the European Court and Commission have been different with regard to article 9 of the European Convention. We will try to summarize their approach to this question in the following pages.[71]

The Commission and the Court's case law has stressed the need to distinguish between the internal and external aspects of religious liberty. The former is the freedom to believe, which embraces the freedom to *choose* one's beliefs—religious or nonreligious—

the date of the judgment of the Chamber, any party to the case may, in exceptional cases, request that the case be referred to the Grand Chamber"; a panel of five judges will decide upon that request. *Refah Partisi* was, of course, one of those "exceptional cases" raising "a serious question affecting the interpretation or application of the Convention or the protocols thereto, or a serious issue of general importance" (European Convention, art. 43[2]).

[68] European Convention, art. 9(1).

[69] It does not seem accurate to interpret the term *practice* as the mere practice of rites, considering that the ritual dimension of religious freedom is alluded to in other words used in article 9, in particular the terms *worship* and *observance*.

[70] The General Comment on article 18 was adopted by the Committee on 20 July 1993. For an analysis of the text, see Tahzib, *Freedom of Religion or Belief*, 307–75.

[71] On this subject, see also M. Evans, *Religious Liberty*, 293–314.

and the freedom to *change* one's religion. The latter consists of the freedom to ***manifest*** one's religion or belief. The internal dimension of religious freedom is ***absolute*** and may not be restricted, but the freedom to manifest religious beliefs in action is by its very nature ***relative*** and may be subjected to the restrictions specified in article 9(2).[72]

All this seems indisputable. It is obvious that public authorities can neither take nor permit any direct action to impel the citizens to believe or not to believe in something. For this reason, in the *Kjeldsen* case in 1976, the Court held that the state, when organizing the educational system, is not allowed to develop any activities that amount to indoctrinating the students with a particular religious or moral view of life contrary to the convictions of their parents.[73] In a similar direction, much more recently, the Court sustained, in the *Buscarini* case, that a citizen cannot be compelled to take an oath on the Gospels as a requirement to hold a public office voluntarily assumed—this would be equivalent to forcing him to express a religious belief against his will.[74]

However, the crucial issue is understanding the relative character of the freedom of individuals to *act* or *practice* according to the dictates of their own conscience, which issue is closely connected with the problem of conflicts between law and conscience, between legal and moral duties. In our opinion, the framework proposed by the European jurisdiction is not the most desirable. The Commission's approach has consisted mainly in drawing a line of separation between the concepts of ***manifestation*** and

---

[72] C. v. United Kingdom, 37 Decisions and Reports 147 (EComHR, Dec. Adm. 10358/83), in which the Commission utilizes the expression "forum internum." The same doctrine is reiterated in Dec. Adm. 10678/83, 39 Decisions and Reports 268 and Dec. Adm. 14049/88. See also Darby v. Sweden, Rep. Com. 11581/85 (EComHR, 9 May 1989), para. 44. The Court, following the Commission's approach, has subsequently alluded to this double side of religious freedom and has emphasized that the limits stated in article 9(2) are applicable only to the freedom to ***manifest*** one's religion or belief but not to the freedom to *choose* one's religion or belief. See Kokkinakis v. Greece, paras. 31, 33.

[73] Kjeldsen, Busk Madsen and Pedersen v. Denmark, 1 EHRR 711 (1979–80) (ECtHR 23, 7 December 1976). This case related to the implementation of a new system of sex education in public schools intended to prevent undesired pregnancies among teenagers. Some parents alleged conscientious objection to this teaching, as they considered that sex education was within the exclusive domain of parents. The Danish government refused to exempt those parents' children from sex education classes. *Kjeldsen* was the first case decided by the Court in which religious beliefs were concerned and the only one until *Kokkinakis* in 1993. The decision focused on the interpretation of article 2 of the First Protocol (right to education and right of parents concerning their children's education).

[74] Buscarini and Others v. San Marino, App. No. 24645/94 (ECtHR, 18 February 1999). More specifically, the Court affirmed that it was incompatible with the European Convention to deprive two elected members of Parliament of their office if they did not take their oath on the Gospels; it would be "tantamount to requiring two elected representatives of the people to swear allegiance to a particular religion" (ibid., para. 39). The law requiring newly elected members of Parliament (General Grand Council) to swear on the Gospels was changed shortly after the facts alleged in the application took place. A statute of 1993, following the practice of many European countries, introduced a choice between the traditional oath and one in which the reference to the Gospels was replaced by the words "on my honor." It is interesting to compare the Court's decision in *Buscarini* with a former decision of the Commission (Dec. Adm. 11321/85, 6 October 1986). An elected member of a regional Parliament in Spain had refused to swear allegiance to the Constitution and had been consequently deprived of his parliamentary rights (there was no religious reference in that oath, as the Spanish law, since 1979, permits the choice between swearing on God or on one's own honor). The Commission justified the possible interference in the applicant's freedom of conscience by resorting to paragraph 2d of article 9: Spanish authorities could legitimately require an oath that was essentially a symbolic expression of respect for the constitutional order; its meaning was nothing else but to agree that any intent to modify the constitutional order should be done through lawful means.

motivation. From this perspective, the European Convention would not necessarily guarantee the right to practice any particular external behavior adapted to one's belief—in other words, the term *practice* does not include each and every act motivated or influenced by a religion or belief.[75]

B. "Neutral" Laws and Moral Obligations: The Indirect Restriction of Religious Freedom

The foregoing approach seems reasonable in abstract, for behavior *obliged* by conscience—which seems to be the behavior protected by article 9—is different from behavior simply *permitted* by conscience. Nevertheless, the truth is that the case law of the Commission reveals that it has traditionally adopted a rather restrictive attitude. Namely, it has tended to consider that the protective umbrella of article 9 does not necessarily extend to an individual's behavior imposed by his own conscience; this is especially true when an individual attempts to adapt his conduct to his moral obligations in ordinary life, but his behavior does not strictly consist in religious teaching or correspond to specific ceremonial practices.[76] Moreover, the Court has stated that certain professional situations voluntarily assumed may entail additional specific restrictions on religious freedom; this occurs particularly within "a system of military discipline that by its very nature implie[s] the possibility of placing on certain of the rights and freedoms of members of the armed forces limitations incapable of being imposed on civilians."[77]

In this regard, the European Court has often drawn implicitly a distinction between states' actions that have a direct and an indirect impact on religious freedom.

In the Court's view, the state interferes with the exercise of freedom of religion or belief when an individual's behavior is prevented or punished by a law or by other state activity *directly* aimed at restricting the manifestation, the worship, or the expansion of

---

[75] This doctrine has been repeatedly stated by the Commission and assumed by the Court. With regard to the Commission's decisions, see Arrowsmith v. United Kingdom, 19 Decisions and Reports 19–20 (EComHR, Rep. Com. 7050/75 [1981], 12 June 1979) (concerning a British pacifist sentenced to a term of imprisonment for having distributed illegal leaflets among English soldiers in Northern Ireland); C. v. United Kingdom (conscientious objection to paying taxes in the percentage of the state budget aimed at military costs); Dec. Adm. 10678/83, 39 Decisions and Reports 268 (conscientious objection to contributing to the public system of pensions); Dec. Adm. 11579/85, 48 Decisions and Reports 255 (conflict between the laws governing religious and civil marriages); Dec. Adm. 14049/88 (conscientious objection to paying taxes in the percentage of the state budget aimed at financing legal abortions in France). With regard to the Court's decisions, see Kalaç v. Turkey, 27 EHRR 552 (1999) (ECtHR 1997-IV, Report of Decisions and Judgments 1199, 1 July 1997), para. 27; Hasan and Chaush v. Bulgaria, App. No. 30985/96 (ECtHR, 26 October 2000), para. 60.

[76] For further details on this approach of the Strasbourg jurisdiction, see Javier Martínez-Torrón, "La giurisprudenza degli organi di Strasburgo sulla libertà religiosa," ***Rivista internazionale di diritti dell'uomo*** (Milano: Università Cattolica del Sacro Cuore, 1993), 335–79.

[77] Kalaç v. Turkey, para. 28. The case involved the compulsory retirement of an officer of the Turkish army, decreed by the Supreme Military Council, for his membership of an Islamic fundamentalist movement supporting ideas contrary to the constitutional principle of secularism. The European Court held that the applicant had not been punished because of his religious beliefs or practices—on the contrary, he was permitted to observe the normal religious duties of Islam—but rather because his "conduct breached military discipline and infringed the principle of secularism." Therefore, the Court concluded, "the applicant's compulsory retirement did not amount to an interference with the right guaranteed by article 9 since it was not prompted by the way the applicant manifested his religion" (ibid., paras. 30–31).

certain or of all religions. In these cases, the European Convention requires that the state justify the interference on the individual's freedom according to article 9(2), especially proving that the restrictive measures are "necessary in a democratic society."

This was indeed the approach of the Court when it decided in favor of the applicant in the *Kokkinakis* case[78] because the Greek courts, based on the laws against religious proselytism, had sentenced a Jehovah's Witness without enough evidence that he had been engaged in "improper proselytism," i.e., trying to convert people through abusive or deceitful means. To apply the law indiscriminately against proselytism was equivalent to restricting, without due justification, the freedom to manifest one's religion or beliefs in teaching. The same occurred in the *Buscarini* case,[79] where the Court held that requiring newly elected members of Parliament to swear allegiance to the Constitution on the Gospels, on pain of forfeiting their parliamentary seats, was contrary to the provisions of article 9, which "entails, *inter alia*, freedom to hold or not to hold religious beliefs and to practise or not to practise a religion." The religious oath requirement could not be considered "necessary in a democratic society," for it amounted to imposing on the applicants an obligation to declare their belief in a religion that was not their own.[80]

A similar way of reasoning was followed by the Court in the *Dahlab* case when it declared inadmissible the application of a Swiss teacher in a public primary school, converted to Islam, who, in application of a cantonal law aimed at preserving the secular character of public schools, had been prohibited from wearing the traditional prescriptive veil on her head when teaching to her students.[81] Although the Court reached here a final conclusion opposite to those in *Kokkinakis* and in *Buscarini*, its analysis also began by recognizing that imposing on teachers the prohibition of carrying "strong" religious symbols constituted an interference with the applicant's religious freedom and the state had to provide a sound justification under article 9(2) of the Convention. In this case, the European Court shared the opinion of the Swiss Federal Court on the consequences of the neutrality principle (*laïcité*); namely, that this principle entailed some restrictions on the civil servants' right to manifest their religion or belief, especially in the educational environment, where students may be more easily influenced and "religious peace" must be protected with extreme care.[82]

---

[78] See note 49 and accompanying text.

[79] See note 74 and accompanying text.

[80] Buscarini v. San Marino, paras. 34, 39.

[81] Dahlab v. Switzerland, decision on the admissibility of App. No. 42393/98 (ECtHR, 15 February 2001).

[82] In our opinion, the Court showed too much respect for the state's margin of appreciation in the *Dahlab* case. First, the "religious peace" of the school does not seem to have suffered any serious threat, for the applicant wore the Islamic *foulard* during approximately five years until she was prohibited from doing so by the (female) general director of primary schools of Geneva's canton; in all those years there appears not to have been any problem caused at the school by the applicant's veil nor a single complaint of the students or of the students' parents. Second, we do not fully understand why the principle of *laïcité* (neutrality, secularism) should require, in a country enjoying religious peace as Switzerland, that no religious personal symbols are visible in the teachers' clothes, instead of permitting that students can see in their own school an evidence of the religious pluralism existing in Swiss society. As long as teachers respect the students' belief and do not attempt to proselytize them, the evidence of religious pluralism seems to be more consistent with a neutral attitude of the state and, on the other hand, more educative for students than the fictional absence of religion on the part of school personnel.

The Commission and the Court's approach has been very different with regard to "neutral" laws, i.e., laws that pursue legitimate secular goals. When the legal duties imposed by a "neutral" law collide with the moral obligations of certain individuals, these persons see their right to practice their religion or belief as being *indirectly* and nonetheless unavoidably restricted by that law—this is the case of the different types of conscientious objection.[83] The immediate consequence is that a moral burden is placed upon the shoulders of these people, as they must choose between disobedience to the law and disobedience to their conscience—one receives a worldly punishment, the other entails a spiritual sanction. In those cases, the European jurisdiction, and especially the Commission, has apparently tended to deny that article 9 offers any protection, for it could not be affirmed that there has been a state interference with religious freedom. In short, its analysis can be summarized as follows: it is not necessary to consider whether the state can provide a legitimate justification for the legislation under attack (according to article 9[2]) because the right to freedom of thought, conscience, and religion (according to the description of its content in article 9[1]) has not actually been (directly) violated.

It would be inaccurate to affirm that there is a conclusive doctrine of the European Court on the issue of conflicts between "neutral laws" and individuals' freedom of conscience, but we could mention three cases in which it is possible to observe some traces of the foregoing mode of reasoning. Significantly, all three cases referred to problems arising within the educational environment, which might lead to consider them as right to education cases rather than freedom of religion cases.

The first of them is *Kjeldsen, Busk Madsen and Pedersen*, in 1976. It concerned the opposition of some students' parents to compulsory sex education for teenagers in the public schools of Denmark. They unsuccessfully claimed an exemption from those classes for their children.[84] The case was decided in the light of article 2 of the First Protocol,[85] and the Court proposed a very restrictive interpretation of the parents' right with regard to the religious and philosophical orientation of their children's education. In brief, the Court held that the state was free to organize the educational system, and particularly the curricula of public schools, even if the religious or philosophical convictions of parents were disregarded. The fact that some parents objected, upon grounds of conscience, to certain contents of the school curriculum did not grant them any right to require of the state a special exemption of those educative contents for their children. Consequently, the state was obliged neither to grant such exemption nor to justify its refusal. The state's power to control the educational environment, as we noted before, was only limited by the prohibition of indoctrination.

---

[83] The phenomenon of conscientious objection goes far beyond the most well-known type, i.e., conscientious objection to military service. An extensive analysis of conscientious objections in international and comparative law, with numerous bibliographical and case law references, can be found in Rafael Navarro-Valls and Martínez-Torrón, *Las objeciones de conciencia en el derecho español y comparado* (Madrid: McGraw-Hill, 1997); there is also an Italian version: *Le obiezioni di coscienza: Profili di diritto comparato* (Torino: Giappichelli, 1995). The case law of the United States is especially rich in dealing with these situations. An interesting and comprehensive study of it, elaborated by a Spanish scholar, with abundant bibliographical references, is found in Rafael Palomino, *Las objeciones de conciencia: Conflictos entre conciencia y ley en el derecho norteamericano* (Madrid: Montecorvo, 1994).

[84] See note 69 and accompanying text. For a more detailed analysis of the *Kjeldsen* decision, see Navarro-Valls and Martínez-Torrón, *Las objeciones de conciencia en el derecho español y comparado,* 199–203.

[85] See note 10.

Twenty years later, the twin decisions *Efstratiou* and *Valsamis*[86] dealt with a relatively similar problem. In those cases the Court decided on the applications of two Greek secondary school students, both followers of the Jehovah's Witnesses, who refused, for religious reasons, to participate in the school parades organized during the national festival to commemorate the outbreak of war between Greece and Fascist Italy in 1940. They argued that their conscience prohibited them from being present in a civic celebration in which a war was remembered and in which military and ecclesiastical authorities took part. The two students were denied permission to be absent from the parade, and their failure to attend was punished by one day's suspension from school. The European Court decided the case in the light both of article 9 of the Convention and of article 2 of the First Protocol (as interpreted in *Kjeldsen*). The decision sustained the Greek government's position, considering especially two facts. One was the moderate punishment imposed to the students, which could not amount to a deprivation of the right to education. The other was that the Court could "discern nothing, either in the purpose of the parade or in the arrangements for it, which could offend the applicants' pacifist convictions."[87] However, the Court noted additionally that the European Commission considered, in its report on the case, that "article 9 did not confer a right to exemption from disciplinary rules which applied generally and in a neutral manner and that in the instant case there had been no interference with the applicant's right to freedom to manifest her religion or belief."[88]

In our opinion, this interpretation of article 9 inverts the logical order of concepts in this matter. It is universally accepted that human rights must be construed broadly. In order to understand the exact meaning of the freedom to manifest one's religion or belief in "practice," it seems that we should approach the question in the following sequence: (i) freedom to practice one's religion or belief must be understood as protecting, in principle, every act of the individual when he obeys the dictates of his own conscience, but (ii) paragraph 2 of article 9—the limits on religious liberty—will be utilized, when necessary, as a corrective element for a freedom that, by its own nature, tends to be exercised in an undefined and unpredictable way.

Thus, we manage to reconcile two paramount interests that are inclined to conflict with each other: the maximum degree of initial protection of the freedom of belief and the security that the legal order demands. Furthermore, we introduce an important assumption: the state has the burden of proof with regard to the necessity of a restrictive measure; i.e., it must affirmatively prove that, in a particular case of conflict, it is necessary "in a democratic society" to restrict the exercise of religious freedom. Following this approach would obstruct the development of policies that ignore the needs of religious freedom and that are especially harmful to minority groups.

In any event, the Court neither subscribed to nor rejected explicitly the Commission's interpretation of article 9 in *Efstratiou* and *Valsamis*. The Commission's view might be expressive of a certain state of mind in the Strasbourg jurisdiction, in a line of continuity with *Kjeldsen*. However, we might well assume also that the Court is hesitating about

[86] Efstratiou v. Greece, App. No. 24095/94 (ECtHR 1996-VI, 18 December 1996); Valsamis v. Greece, 24 EHRR 294 (1997) (ECtHR 1996-VI, 18 December 1996). The texts of both decisions are almost identical, as indeed were the facts in issue.

[87] Efstratiou v. Greece, para. 32; Valsamis v. Greece, para. 31.

[88] Efstratiou v. Greece, para. 37; Valsamis v. Greece, para. 36.

which path it should follow beyond the strict borders of the educational environment. In this regard, we should note that the Commission's restrictive interpretation of freedom of conscience seems to contradict the Court's own words in the recent *Hasan* case: "but for very exceptional cases, the right to freedom of religion as guaranteed under the Convention excludes any discretion on the part of the State to determine whether religious beliefs or the means used to express such beliefs are legitimate."[89] Behavior in accordance with the dictates of one's own conscience in daily life is, in our view, an evident and most important expression of freedom of religion and belief. However, it is not clear yet whether these words of the *Hasan* decision will constitute a twist in the former doctrine of the Commission, or whether they will rather be understood as applicable only to the typical expressions of religious liberty and particularly to those directly related to the internal affairs of religious communities.

C. Substituting the Individual's Judgment of Conscience

One of the aforementioned aspects of the Court's reasoning in *Efstratiou* and *Valsamis* is particularly problematic. When the Court examined the arguments of the applicants, it declared that the parades that the Jehovah's Witnesses morally disapproved of were merely civic acts without any particular political or ideological connotation, and, consequently, they could not offend the pacifist convictions of the students.[90] Thus, the Court in effect substituted its judgment for the conscience of the persons involved, defining what was "reasonable" for them to believe with regard to their participation in a national commemorative ceremony.

In our opinion, this is a dangerous mistake. This could initiate an unacceptable itinerary leading to the Court determining which beliefs are "reasonable" and which are not. Naturally, it is necessary to verify—as far as possible—that parties are not deceitfully alleging moral convictions they do not really or sincerely hold in order to avoid fulfilling a legal duty. But this does not mean that a secular court is competent to elucidate when the beliefs of a person are sufficiently consistent from an "objective" point of view. This is a slippery slope. This conviction that public authorities, in a neutral secular society, must refrain from pronouncing on the truth or falsehood of a religious dogma or a moral belief is deeply rooted in Western legal culture.[91] Indeed, the European Court itself has affirmed that "the State's duty of neutrality and impartiality ... is incompatible with any power on the State's part to assess the legitimacy of religious beliefs."[92]

In the above-mentioned decisions, the European Court did not seem to be fully aware of the fundamental philosophy underlying the protection of religious liberty in our civilization. The reason why the freedom of each individual conscience must be respected is not that it is objectively correct—the courts would then have to judge the truth of the alleged beliefs, as a sort of new Inquisition. Rather, freedom of conscience must be respected because it is considered a fundamental area of the individual's autonomy in democratic societies, and, consequently, the legal system has determined that nobody may interfere with the individual's conscience as long as other prevailing juridical interests are

[89] Hasan and Chaush v. Bulgaria, App. No. 30985/96 (ECtHR, 26 October 2000), para. 79.
[90] See Valsamis v. Greece, paras. 31, 37; Efstratiou v. Greece, paras. 32, 38.
[91] See for example United States v. Ballard, 322 US 78 (1944).
[92] Metropolitan Church of Bessarabia v. Moldova, 13 December 2001, para. 123.

not endangered. What freedom of religion or belief protects is, namely, the right to choose the truths in which one is willing to believe. Hence, article 9(2) of the European Convention provides that the state may restrict the exercise of that freedom only when it is "necessary in a democratic society."

In other words, the government is not obliged to respect and protect religious freedom because it considers the convictions of its citizens to be correct, or even convenient. It is obliged to protect the freedom to believe and to act accordingly because this freedom constitutes an essential element of a democratic system. The protection of that freedom is a paramount *public* interest and not merely a *private* interest of individuals and groups. This is something that is easily understood with regard to other liberties—for instance, the freedom of expression or the freedom of association—but is sometimes inexplicably ignored when dealing with religious liberty.

This fact is even more shocking when we realize that the European Court itself has repeatedly emphasized that an adequate protection of these three freedoms (religion, expression, association), enshrined in articles 9–11 of the Convention, is necessary to preserve pluralism, which is in turn indispensable for democracy.[93] The prejudice about the exercise of religious freedom—when compared with other fundamental liberties—might have some relationship with an old idea of the first liberalism, spread by the French Enlightenment, which appears to emerge subconsciously and intermittently in some European conceptions of human rights. According to that position, religion was a private matter that had to be confined within the individual's conscience and removed from the most significant areas of public life. This was viewed as a condition for safeguarding religious peace in society, which was an integral part of "public order" (*ordre public*). The foregoing idea may have been justified within a historical context dominated by the need to free secular society from the burden imposed by large traditional churches, but the socio-political situation in most parts of Europe is now, fortunately, very different. To maintain, implicitly or explicitly, that position in our day may amount to "secular indoctrination," and we should bear in mind that the aim of indoctrination is one of the clear limits that the state cannot exceed according to the European Court's interpretation of freedom of religion or belief. In effect, a state's failure to facilitate actual religious pluralism in society, and the corresponding external expressions of that pluralism, would be equivalent to supporting a certain belief (secularism, i.e., no-religion) over the others (religions). This is namely what occurs when a radical interpretation of the neutrality principle is held, without proving that the consequent restrictions on external manifestations of citizens' religion or beliefs are "necessary in a democratic society" by reason of a "pressing social need."[94] In our view, a too strict conception of state neutrality could easily lead to a sort of "secular fundamentalism."

---

[93] With regard to freedom of expression and freedom of association, see United Communist Party of Turkey v. Turkey, App. No. 19392/92 (ECtHR 1998-I, 30 January 1998), paras. 42–43; Socialist Party v. Turkey, App. No. 21237/93 (ECtHR 1998-III, 25 May 1998), para. 41; and Freedom and Democracy Party (ÖZDEP) v. Turkey, App. No. 23885/94 (ECtHR, 8 December 1999), para. 37. With respect to freedom of thought, conscience, and religion see Kokkinakis v. Greece, 17 EHRR 397 (1994) (ECtHR 260-A, 25 May 1993), para. 31; and Serif v. Greece, App. No. 34369/97 (ECtHR, 14 December 1999), para. 49.

[94] This type of extreme interpretation of state neutrality seems to be present in the Court's decision in *Dahlab,* for they supported the national interpretation of neutrality without evidence that the applicant's free expression of religion could endanger religious peace or the rights or freedom of others (see notes

It is therefore important that the European Court open its mind to all the consequences inherent in a global notion of pluralism, which demands a wider protection of the individual aspects of freedom of religion and belief. The outcome of the Court's approach in this area is bound to transcend the individual sphere. We said before that the European Court had positively impelled the acknowledgment of the rights of minority groups.[95] Nonetheless, we feel obliged to add that, if the Court followed the Commission's previous restrictive doctrine on individuals' right to manifest their religion or belief in practice, it would produce negative effects for some religious minorities, particularly for those minorities that defend ideas openly contrary to the ethical choices assumed by the majority of people in a certain society.

In effect, the laws considered "neutral" usually conform—as does any law—to the ethical values that are dominant in a determined social environment at a certain moment. "Neutral" laws will rarely conflict with the morals or life practices of the major churches,[96] but they can more often cause conflicts with minority religious groups that engage in conduct that is socially atypical.[97] To hold that a "neutral" law must automatically prevail and that the state is under no obligation to justify denial of exemptions from the general application of the law as a measure "necessary in a democratic society" would constitute a significant risk for the rights of minorities.

V. Conclusion: Religious and Secular Intolerance

If we analyze the different problems that the protection of religious liberty experiences in the world, we can affirm that, from the point of view of the law of the state, the main problem is intolerance. In this regard, it is important that we distinguish between two sorts of intolerance.

One is religion-oriented intolerance, in which the legal and constitutional structure of the state is designed according to the dictates of a religion, and the other religions or beliefs are either disregarded or persecuted, depending on how hostile the government and the hierarchy of the official religion are. This is currently the case, for example, in many Islamic countries and in some countries where a strong Christian Orthodox church is established (as occurs in some parts of Eastern Europe).

The other is secularism-oriented intolerance, wherein the state decides to be positively secular or laic (according to the French meaning of *laïcité*) and draws a line of separation between state and religion. This choice is normally justified either by recourse

---

81–82 and accompanying text). The Court's approach in the *Welfare Party* case was different; in this decision, the majority of judges understood that the public behavior of some members of the Refah Partisi could lead to a serious future danger for the fundamental values of democracy in Turkey; their evaluation of the facts may not be accurate, as the dissenting judges argued, but the Court actually weighted the evidence provided by both parties of the process (see notes 62–67 and accompanying text). We should note that the value of the *Welfare Party* case as precedent is much higher than *Dahlab,* for the latter is a decision declaring the application inadmissible as "manifestly ill-founded."

[95] See Part III.B of this chapter.

[96] Naturally, there are exceptions, especially when the party or parties in power are determined to change some of the ethical patterns of society through legislation—they often succeed after a few years. The laws decriminalizing abortion in the Western world constitute a good example of this.

[97] This is the reason why Muslims and Jehovah's Witnesses, for instance, experience frequent problems in European countries.

to historical reasons (i.e., France), or by arguing that it is necessary to preserve the reciprocal autonomy of the state and the churches (i.e., the United States), or by claiming that it is indispensable to keep the state free from the religious intolerance of a significant part of the population (i.e., Turkey). In any event, experience shows that these states sometimes adopt an aggressive secularism and endeavor to remove any actual reference to religious beliefs and practice from social public life. Secularism then becomes a sort of official "religion."

Religious intolerance transforms a religious dogma into the law of the state. Secular intolerance transforms the law of the state into a religious dogma. There exists a secular fundamentalism that parallels religious fundamentalism; if the latter has been called a "perversion" of religion,[98] an analogous qualification should correspond to the former. Neither of them seems to be an adequate solution to guarantee the respect for the freedom of religion or belief.

If we examine the case law of the European Court, we can conclude that it has been willing to condemn religion-oriented intolerance, but it has failed to realize that, in the Commission's doctrine on the automatic predominance of "neutral" laws over the freedom of conscience, there may be an implied and dangerous justification of secularism-oriented intolerance.

We Europeans are usually proud of the system we have built for the protection of human rights. We tend to think that ours is not merely a good system—it is the *best* system, and it is a model that should be followed everywhere. This is probably fairly accurate if we refer to the existing supranational judicial machinery for the enforcement of the rights included in the European Convention. But our conclusion may be not entirely optimistic if we focus on the substantive meaning of some of the rights, as interpreted in the case law of the Court.

As far as religious liberty is concerned, the case law of Strasbourg certainly shows a very positive side: its emphasis on the idea that the concession of privileges to the major churches must be accompanied by an acknowledgment, and a real protection, of the rights of religious minorities.[99] State cooperation with churches can occur in different degrees, but the freedom enjoyed by religious groups—and their followers—must be understood according to strict equality. Cooperation can be different, freedom cannot. The European Court seems to be very conscious of how important it is to specify the consequences of this general principle after the enlargement of the Council of Europe with the incorporation of post-communist countries. Moreover, this is an idea that can be "exported" to other countries and to other cultures.

The negative side of the Strasbourg case law, as we have seen,[100] is the inclination towards enshrining the absolute supremacy of "neutral" laws over the rights of individual conscience. The effects of this approach are harmful, not only for individuals, but also for those minority religious groups that defend moral values that do not fully correspond to the Western heritage—i.e., the values of the Judæo-Christian tradition, amalgamated with other values typical of secularism.

---

[98] Parliamentary Assembly Recommendation 1396 (1999) on religion and democracy, para. 3. See note 14 and accompanying text.

[99] See Part III of this chapter.

[100] See Part IV.B of this chapter.

The European Court has not explicitly accepted that idea but has not rejected it either. It is, of course, an idea that is difficult to "export," and should not be exported, to other countries. It would mean that our supranational judicial system had failed to design an appropriate legal framework to make possible the integration of non-Western cultures and religions into Europe. Furthermore, it is an example of what should not be done. If the European Court affirms the unconditional supremacy of "neutral" laws over the freedom of conscience, it might not have many arguments to reply to the parallel supremacy of "religious" laws in the states of religion-oriented intolerance. After all, both are laws coming from the legislative authority of the state.

Certainly, it could be discussed whether it is possible to integrate non-Western religions and cultures into Europe without breaking the social and political framework that is characteristic of our concept of democracy. One of the main problems we have in this regard is the increase in the Islamic population of Europe caused by migration, which raises the question of the extent to which Islamic religious laws are compatible with the concepts of freedom and democracy so deeply rooted in the European political conscience.[101] There is no easy answer to that question, among other reasons because there are different conceptions of Islam and not all of them are equally flexible and willing to integrate with non-Islamic cultures.

In any event, if we Europeans really do want to be viewed by other countries as an example of respect for human rights, we must endeavor to accommodate the diverse religions and cultures relentlessly arriving at and developing in European society, which is becoming more and more multicultural. Of course this has to be done with respect for non-Western ideas, but preserving at the same time the many valuable contributions that our political evolution has made to civilization—to begin with the very notions of individual freedom and human rights, which are the fundamentals of democracy. It is not easy to reach the right balance, but we are bound to try.

---

[101] As we have seen, this was one of the central questions in the two decisions on the case of Refah Partisi (The Welfare Party) v. Turkey, 31 July 2001 and 13 February 2003. See notes 62–67 and accompanying text.

Chapter 11

Advancements in Standard Setting: Religious Liberty and OSCE Commitments

Urban Gibson and Karen S. Lord

This chapter outlines the structure of the Organization for Security and Co-operation in Europe (OSCE) and highlights the standard-setting advancement in the field of religious liberty found in the commitments undertaken by the OSCE participating States.

I. Background on the OSCE

The OSCE was created in the early 1970s as a multilateral forum for dialogue and negotiation between East and West. Known as the Conference on Security and Co-operation in Europe (CSCE) until 1995, the OSCE is engaged in standard setting in fields ranging from military security to economic and environmental cooperation, to human rights and humanitarian concerns. In addition, it engages in a variety of preventive diplomacy initiatives designed to prevent, manage, and resolve conflict within and among the participating States. The history of the OSCE is twofold. From 1974 to 1990, the CSCE (as its name implies) worked as a continuous conference. The Paris Summit Meeting in 1990 marked the beginning of institutionalization, reflecting the changes in Europe and the new challenges for the post–Cold War period. Today, the OSCE comprises fifty-five participating States[1] from the region stretching from Vancouver to Vladivostok (moving east), including the United States, Canada, and all the countries of Europe and the former Soviet Union. All participating States have equal status and are represented on the basis of common interest, common rules, and norms.

---

[1] The OSCE Participating States, according to the official French alphabetical order, are: 1. Albania, 2. Germany, 3. United States of America, 4. Andorra, 5. Armenia, 6. Austria, 7. Azerbaijan, 8. Belarus, 9. Belgium, 10. Bosnia Herzegovina, 11. Bulgaria, 12. Canada, 13. Cyprus, 14. Croatia, 15. Denmark, 16. Spain, 17. Estonia, 18. Finland, 19. France, 20. Georgia, 21. United Kingdom, 22. Greece, 23. Hungary, 24. Ireland, 25. Iceland, 26. Italy, 27. Kazakhstan, 28. Kyrgyzstan, 29. Latvia, 30. the former Yugoslav Republic of Macedonia, 31. Liechtenstein, 32. Lithuania, 33. Luxembourg, 34. Malta, 35. Moldova, 36. Monaco, 37. Norway, 38. Uzbekistan, 39. Netherlands, 40. Poland, 41. Portugal, 42. Romania, 43. Russian Federation, 44. San Marino, 45. Holy See, 46. Slovak Republic, 47. Slovenia, 48. Sweden, 49. Switzerland, 50. Tajikistan, 51. Czech Republic, 52. Turkmenistan, 53. Turkey, 54. Ukraine, 55. Yugoslavia (suspended between 1992–2000). Serbia was admitted to the OSCE on 10 November 2000.

Tore Lindholm, W. Cole Durham, Jr., Bahia G. Tahzib-Lie (eds.), Facilitating Freedom of Religion or Belief: A Deskbook, *239–254.*

The origin of the OSCE can be traced to the early 1950s, with a proposal from the Soviet Union to create an all-European security conference. Finland offered Helsinki as a venue for the conference in 1969, inviting all European countries, the United States, and Canada. In 1972, the thirty-five States agreed to enter into multilateral consultations concerned with preparations for the conference, and the stage was set for the preparatory talks in Helsinki with the original thirty-five nations. In 1973, the consultations resulted in the "Blue Book," which outlined final recommendations for the scope and rules of procedure for the Organization. On 1 August 1975 in Helsinki, heads of the thirty-five participating States signed the Helsinki Final Act of the Conference on Security and Co-operation in Europe, including "the Helsinki Decalogue," for behavior among the participating States and of governments toward their citizens.

The Helsinki Final Act laid the basis for further development of the OSCE process. The document is not a treaty, but a politically binding agreement adopted on the basis of consensus. It is divided into three main categories, or "baskets" concerning: (1) questions relating to security in Europe; (2) cooperation in the field of economics, science and technology, and the environment; and (3) cooperation in humanitarian and other fields. Furthermore, it called for regular follow up meetings to review the implementation of OSCE agreements, to set new standards and norms, to expand cooperation, and to maintain political dialogue. In the 1970s and 1980s, such meetings were held in Belgrade, Madrid, and Vienna. At these meetings, all OSCE participating States agreed upon important commitments aimed at upholding human rights, and measures to build confidence among the participants through the advance notification of military activities and the exchange of military information. In addition, a number of expert meetings were held on specific topics such as democratic institutions, human rights, human contacts, peaceful settlement of disputes, environment, media, science, culture, and economic cooperation.

The Charter of Paris of November 1990 marked the turning point in the history of the OSCE in the post–Cold War era, serving as a transition for the OSCE from its role as a forum for negotiation and dialogue to an active operational structure. At the first summit meeting since Helsinki, the Heads of State or Government adopted the "Charter of Paris for a New Europe" aimed at defining the OSCE's identity in a new international environment and taking advantage of unprecedented opportunities for cooperation. New "Guidelines for the Future" were created together with standing institutions like the Conflict Prevention Centre in Vienna, the Office for Free Elections in Warsaw, and the Secretariat in Prague. The Charter also established three main political, consultative bodies: The Council of Ministers, a Committee of Senior Officials, and regular summit meetings of Heads of State or Government. Meanwhile, newly independent states from Central and Eastern Europe and the former Soviet Union applied for membership, and the number of OSCE participating States expanded to fifty-five. During the same period, an important arms control agreement, the Treaty on Conventional Armed Forces in Europe (CFE) was negotiated in the framework of the OSCE process and signed in November 1990. The CFE limits nonnuclear ground and air forces from the Atlantic to the Ural Mountains. A follow-up agreement to CFE sets limits on personnel strength in the same region. Also in 1992, the OSCE adopted a comprehensive document on Confidence and Security Building Measures as well as a declaration on the Open Skies Treaty. In September

1992, a new body, the Forum for Security Cooperation, was formed in Vienna to negotiate and consult on concrete measures aimed at strengthening security and stability throughout Europe.

Further impetus and possibilities for concerted action in the OSCE framework were outlined in the new Helsinki Document of July 1992. It established a number of practical tools to strengthen the OSCE's contribution to the protection of human rights and manage the unprecedented change underway in Europe. In particular, it called for an ambitious role for the OSCE in early warning, conflict prevention, and crisis management. The position of High Commissioner on National Minorities was created. In December 1992, the OSCE Council established a new post of Secretary General and in 1993, a strengthened Secretariat in Vienna. In December 1993, a new body, the Permanent Committee, was established in Vienna, significantly expanding the possibilities for political consultation, dialogue, and decision making on a weekly basis. The new operational profile of the OSCE expanded with the dispatch of several conflict prevention and crisis management missions in areas of potential or actual conflict.

II. OSCE Structures and Institutions

A. Summit and Review Conferences

Summits of Heads of State or Government of OSCE participating States take place, as a rule, every two years. They set priorities and provide orientation at the highest political level. Review Conferences precede the Summits. The conference delegates are tasked to review the entire range of activities within the OSCE (including a thorough implementation debate), consider further steps to strengthen the OSCE process, and draft a decision-oriented document to be adopted at the summit.

B. Implementation Meetings on Human Dimension Issues

In Helsinki in 1992, it was decided to hold Implementation Meetings in the field of the human dimension, including free elections, freedom of the media, and the protection of persons belonging to national minorities, in every year in which there is no OSCE Summit. These meetings take place in Warsaw, and the first was held in 1993. The purpose of these meetings is to achieve further progress concerning respect for all human rights and fundamental freedoms, human contacts, and other issues of a related humanitarian character, and serve as a forum for exchange of views concerning OSCE commitments in the fields of human rights and democracy. The meetings are attended by OSCE participating States, NGOs, and relevant international organizations and institutions.

C. OSCE Ministerial Council

The Council, whose members are the Foreign Ministers of the OSCE participating States, is the central decision-making and governing body of the OSCE. It considers issues relevant to the OSCE and takes appropriate decisions. It prepares the meetings of Heads of State or Government and implements tasks defined and decisions taken by these meetings. The Council meets at least once a year.

D. Senior Council (SC)

The SC (renamed from the CSO at the time the CSCE became the OSCE) is responsible for overview, management, and coordination of OSCE activities. It lays down political guidelines and makes key decisions between the annual OSCE Council Meetings. The fifty-five participating States are represented by Senior Officials (Directors) from capitals or by Vienna-based Heads of Delegations. The SC has special competencies concerning Early Warning, Conflict Prevention and Crisis Management, and Peaceful Settlement of Disputes. The SC has met semiannually in Prague and once a year as the Economic Forum; however, since 1997, the Senior Council has only been meeting as the Economic Forum. The CSO and SC met—with some exceptions—in Prague, but no meetings of the SC have taken place since 1997, with the exception of the yearly Economic Forum, which is officially also a meeting of the SC.

E. The Permanent Council (PC)

Based in Vienna, the PC is responsible for the day-to-day operational tasks of the OSCE under a representative of the Chair in Office. Its members, the Heads of Delegations of the OSCE participating States, meet weekly at the "Hofburg" Conference Center. The PC conducts comprehensive and regular consultations and makes decisions on all issues pertinent to the OSCE. It can also be convened to deal with emergency situations.

F. The Forum for Security Cooperation (FSC)

The FSC, consisting of representatives of the delegations of the OSCE participating States, is an integral part of the OSCE. It meets weekly in the Vienna "Hofburg" and negotiates and consults on concrete measures aimed at strengthening security and stability throughout Europe. Its main objectives are: (a) negotiations on arms control, disarmament, and confidence and security building; (b) regular consultations and intensive cooperation on matters related to security; and (c) the further reduction of the risks of conflicts. It is also responsible for implementing Confidence and Security Building Measures (CSBMs), preparing seminars on military doctrine, holding annual implementation assessment meetings, and providing a forum for discussion and clarification of information exchanged under agreed CSBMs.

G. Chairman-in-Office (CIO)

The CIO, who changes every year, is responsible for the coordination of and consultation on current OSCE business on behalf of the Council and the Senior Council (SC). The CIO may be assisted by the Troika, consisting of the preceding and the succeeding Chairmen. Ad Hoc Steering Groups, which may be established on a case-by-case basis, further assist the CIO, in particular in the field of conflict prevention and crisis management. Personal Representatives, which are designated by the CIO with a clear and precise mandate, are also tasked with assisting the CIO in dealing with a crisis or a conflict.

H. The Secretary General

The Secretary General is appointed by the Ministerial Council for a period of three years. Based in Vienna, the Secretary General acts as the representative of the Chairman in Office and supports the CIO in activities aimed at fulfilling the goals of the OSCE. The Secretary General's tasks also include the management of the OSCE structures and operations. The Secretary General is the OSCE's Chief Administrative Officer who works closely with the CIO in the preparation and guidance of OSCE meetings, and ensures the implementation of its decisions.

I. High Commissioner on National Minorities (HCNM)

The OSCE created the job of HCNM to respond, at the earliest possible stage, to ethnic tensions that have the potential to develop into a conflict within the OSCE region. The role of the HCNM is to identify and promote the early resolution of ethnic tensions that might endanger peace, stability, or relations between OSCE participating States. The Office of the High Commissioner is located in The Hague.

J. OSCE Representative on Freedom of Media

The post of the Representative on Freedom of Media was called for by the 1996 Lisbon Summit and was established by the Permanent Council on 5 November 1997. The task of the Representative on Freedom of Media is to assist governments in the furthering of free, independent, and pluralistic media. The Representative reports on media development in all participating States and advocates complete compliance with relevant OSCE principles and commitments.

K. The Secretariat

The Secretariat, under the Secretary General's direction, operates mainly in Vienna and consists of four departments: (a) the Department for Chairman in Office Support, which is responsible for the preparation of meetings, contacts with international organizations, press relations, and public information; (b) the Conflict Prevention Center, which is responsible for overall support of OSCE tasks (in the fields of early warning, conflict prevention, and crisis management), operational support of OSCE missions, and running the OSCE database and communications network; (c) the Department of Conference Services, which is responsible for conference services, interpretation services, documentation, and protocol; and (d) the Department for Administration and Budget, which is responsible for administrative services, personnel policies, and financial control. The office in Prague, which belongs to the Secretariat in Vienna, services the Senior Council meetings, maintains OSCE archives, and distributes documents.

L. Office for Democratic Institutions and Human Rights (ODIHR)

The Charter of Paris for a New Europe (1990) established an Office for Free Elections in Warsaw. The 1992 Ministerial Council decided to expand the functions of this office and transformed it into the ODIHR. Based in Warsaw, the ODIHR is the OSCE institution responsible for furthering human rights, democracy, and the rule of law. It provides the forum for meetings and expert seminars to address the implementation of human dimension commitments. It serves as the institutional framework for sharing and exchanging information on the building of democratic institutions and holding elections within participating States. It coordinates the monitoring of elections and provides expertise and training on constitutional and legal matters.

M. OSCE Missions

The OSCE has had missions in Kosovo (OMIK), Armenia, Azerbaijan, Bosnia and Herzegovina, Croatia, Estonia, Georgia, Latvia, Moldova, Tajikistan, and the former Yugoslav Republic of Macedonia (OSCE spillover monitor mission to Skopje).[2] There has also been an OSCE Assistance Group to Chechnya (Russian Federation), a presence in Albania, an Advisory and Monitoring Group in Belarus, an OSCE Liaison Office in Central Asia (Tashkent, Uzbekistan), OSCE Centers in Almaty (Kazakhstan), Ashgabad (Turkmenistan) and Bishkek (Kyrgyzstan), and a high-level planning group for the OSCE Peacekeeping Force for Nagorno-Karabakh. The OSCE has also had a Personal Representative of the Chairman-in-Office on the Conflict Dealt With by the OSCE Minsk Conference based in Tblisi and assisted by field assistants who are deployed on a rotating basis in Baku, Yerevan, and Stepanakert/Khankendi.

OSCE Missions serve as instruments of conflict prevention, crisis management, and postconflict rehabilitation. Their mandate generally calls for the establishment of good contacts to local representatives and the further strengthening of initiated dialogue between the parties concerned. The Missions' main tasks are: (1) fact-finding situations representing a dispute with the potential to develop into a crisis; and (2) monitoring of elections, agreements between conflicting parties, and third-party peace-keeping activities. The mandates for the respective mission, agreed upon by the Senior Council, are adjusted to the specific situation in the region where the mission is deployed.

---

[2] Southeast Europe is the area of highest concentration for OSCE field activities. In 1992, the OSCE dispatched its first mission to Kosovo, Sandjak, Vojodina, and Skopje (FYR Macedonia). The Kosovo Verification Mission, which worked from October 1998 to March 1999, was the largest with 1,400 persons working under the UN Security Council Resolutions 1160 (1998) and 1199 (1998) to verify maintenance of the ceasefire, monitor movement of forces, provide assistance in return of refugees and displaced persons, supervise elections, and help in forming elected bodies of self-administration and police forces. The mission's goal was also to promote human rights and democracy building. The mission was withdrawn by a decision of the Chairman-in-Office when situations became life-threatening for OSCE personnel. After the ceasefire, the mission was replaced by the OSCE part of the United Nations mission UNIMIK, with a similar mandate as the verification mission. The OSCE missions to Bosnia and Herzegovina, the OSCE Mission to Croatia, the spillover monitor mission to Skopje, and the OSCE presence in Albania still continue today. As of 1 September 2001, the mission to Skopje was enlarged to fifty persons.

N. Other OSCE-Related Bodies

1. The Parliamentary Assembly (PA)

In April 1991, parliamentarians from the OSCE participating States agreed to the creation of the OSCE Parliamentary Assembly. The PA meets once a year and is supported by a Secretariat in Copenhagen. The CIO stays in regular contact with the PA and reports on the work of the OSCE. The chairman of the PA regularly reports to the OSCE Implementation Meetings, Review Conferences, Ministerial Councils, and the Permanent Council.

2. Court of Conciliation and Arbitration

The Court was established by the Convention on Conciliation and Arbitration within the OSCE in December 1992. It aims at settling disputes which are submitted to it by the OSCE States that signed the convention through means of conciliation and, when appropriate, arbitration. The Court will be based in Geneva. It will be operational after the deposit of the twelfth instrument of ratification or accession. On 23 August 1994, the tenth State deposited its ratification instrument. There has never yet been a trial before the Court of Conciliation and Arbitration, although there are some calls to strengthen the Court.

III. Religious Freedom Commitments within the OSCE

Religious liberty has been an integral part of the OSCE process. From the Helsinki Final Act to the Vienna and Copenhagen Concluding Documents, the OSCE participating States have affirmed time and time again that religious liberty is a fundamental human right. The freedom to profess and practice a religion alone or in community, the freedom to meet with and exchange information with co-religionists regardless of frontiers, the freedom to freely present to others and discuss one's religious views, and the freedom to change one's religion have all been enshrined in the OSCE documents. Participating States have also committed to eliminating and preventing discrimination based on religious grounds in all fields of civil, political, economic, social, and cultural life. Noninterference in the affairs of religious communities, such as selection of personnel, is also central to the OSCE understanding of religious liberty. Religious education in any language is protected along with the right for parents to ensure religious education of their children in line with their own convictions. Participating States have also pledged to allow the training of religious personnel in appropriate institutions. Following is a detailed analysis of OSCE commitments relating to freedom of religion or belief.

A. Cold War–Era Commitments

The earliest Helsinki Process Commitments were worked out during the height of the Cold War era. What was then the Conference on Security and Co-operation in Europe (CSCE) was just getting started and was feeling its way fairly cautiously. For the first decade of its existence, the Helsinki Process was rather minimalist in its approach, and human dimension efforts in that era were quite limited. Nevertheless, some significant foundations were laid and were very much welcomed by those who started "Helsinki groups," mostly in the Communist bloc.

The starting point was the Helsinki Final Act itself. In those days, the work of the OSCE was divided in "baskets," with human dimension and human rights issues constituting one of the baskets. The seventh principle in the Principles Section of the First Basket (or "Principle VII") of the Helsinki Final Act established the following commitment with regard to respect for human rights and fundamental freedoms, including the freedom of thought, conscience, and religion or belief:

> The participating States will respect human rights and fundamental freedoms, including the freedom of thought, conscience, religion or belief, for all without distinction as to race, sex, language or religion.
>
> Within this framework the participating States will recognize and respect the freedom of the individual to profess and practice, alone or in community with others, religion or belief acting in accordance with the dictates of his own conscience.

This commitment does little more than restate the affirmative requirements of article 18 of the International Covenant on Civil and Political Rights. It is slightly different, in that it weaves antidiscrimination norms into the basic freedom of conscience protections. Also, it does not include the carefully phrased provisions from the International Covenant that address the narrow range of circumstances under which limitations may be imposed on manifestations of religion. In substance, however, these are probably not major differences, since the international instruments clearly proscribe discrimination based on religion and international limitation provisions are likely to guide interpretation of the general Helsinki process norms.[3]

Another significant contribution dating from the Helsinki Final Act is the provision in the Third Basket, Section 1d, dealing with travel for personal or professional reasons. This provision included the following language:

> [The participating States] confirm that religious faiths, institutions and organizations, practicing within the constitutional framework of the participating States, and their representatives can, in the field of their activities, have contacts and meetings among themselves and exchange information.

This provision marked a small step toward opening up freedom of religion in areas of worship and administration. This was particularly significant as a commitment being made by socialist bloc countries. The provision goes a step beyond abstract commitments regarding freedom of religion to express a commitment to allow "contacts and meetings" among believers. This was a significant step toward creating a minimalist procedural mechanism that could actually be monitored. It constituted a small entering wedge which later opened the way for broader protection of religious freedom.

B. Madrid Concluding Document

The next noteworthy commitments were specified in the Madrid Concluding Document in 1983. The section dealing with "Questions Relating to Security in Europe—Principles" stated:

> The participating States reaffirm that they will recognize, respect and furthermore agree to take the action necessary to ensure the freedom of the individual to profess and practice, alone or in community with others, religion or belief acting in accordance with the dictates of his own conscience.
>
> In this context, they will consult, whenever necessary, the religious faiths, institutions and organizations, which act within the constitutional framework of their respective countries.
>
> They will favorably consider application by religious communities of believers practicing or prepared to practice their faith within the constitutional framework of their States, to be granted the status provided for in their respective countries for religious faiths, institutions and organizations.

These commitments further expand the commitment to take measurable procedural steps that constitute significant minimum steps for actualizing freedom of religion or belief. The participating States agree that they will "recognize, respect and . . . take the action necessary to ensure the freedom of the individual to profess and practice" freedom of religion or belief. The substantive norm is essentially that of article 18 of the International Covenant, but governments are agreeing to "take action necessary" to enforce this right. Moreover, they agree to "consult, whenever necessary . . . religious faiths, institutions and organizations." This gave religious organizations a subtle lever they could exercise when governments refused to "take action necessary": it opened a channel of communication with the State and a right to complain if State doors remained closed.

Finally, participating States committed that they "will favorably consider" applications by religious groups for legal entity status. This is described rather cumbersomely as "the status provided for in their respective countries for religious faiths, institutions and organizations." In fact, the cumbersome description seems unavoidable in light of the broad range of legal entities that are used in various OSCE countries to confer legal entity status on religious groups. The commitment made here is obviously quite weak. It is not a commitment to grant such status, merely to "favorably consider" doing so. Still, this was a step along a particular important pathway. In former socialist bloc countries in particular, constraints on acquisition of legal entity status were used as an extremely important mechanism for controlling religious groups and for disallowing—even criminalizing—nonapproved activities. Even if legal entity status had not been used to restrict religious activity, however, it is obvious that access to at least some form of legal entity status is critical in a modern world for practical actualization of religious freedom rights. It is extremely difficult to rent legal facilities, acquire property for a place of worship, hire employees, run religious educational institutions, and so forth, without a legal entity. Carrying out such activities in the name of individual members is, for most groups, too inconvenient and fraught with risks to be reasonable. The Madrid Concluding Document thus made headway toward strengthening this practical aspect of religious freedom.

---

[3] See ECHR, art. 9; ICCPR, art. 18; 1981 Declaration.

In the Human Contacts Section, the Madrid Concluding Document specified that participating States

> will further implement the relevant provisions of the Final Act, so that religious faiths, institutions, organizations, and their representatives can, in the field of their activity, develop contacts and meetings among themselves and exchange information.

This provision was essentially a follow up and recommitment to the "contacts and meetings" provision that had already been made. Such repetition plays an important role in the Helsinki Process. Where there have been shortfalls, as there no doubt had been on this front, recommitment is a not-so-subtle reminder that improved implementation is expected.

C. The Vienna Concluding Document

The Vienna Meeting, which continued over a course of three years from 1986–1989, was a major landmark in the Helsinki Process. The changing world made possible by *glasnost* and *perestroika* in the east bloc translated in the CSCE context to a willingness to accept commitments with a much higher level of specificity on a whole range of issues, including freedom of religion or belief. The key provisions are contained in principles 16 and 17. For purposes of brevity, we simply quote these provisions here in indented print, and add commentary after each provision. The complete text of the commitments is contained in the appendix. Virtually all the prior commitments are reaffirmed in the Vienna Concluding Document, but by 1989, they are taken to a higher level of concreteness, and a more generous, unstinting commitment to actualize freedom of religion or belief becomes apparent.

> (16) In order to ensure the freedom of the individual to profess and practice religion or belief, the participating State will, *inter alia*,
>
> (16.1) —take effective measures to prevent and eliminate discrimination against individuals or communities on the grounds of religion or belief in the recognition, exercise and enjoyment of human rights and fundamental freedoms in all fields of civil, political, economic, social and cultural life, and to ensure the effective equality between believers and nonbelievers;

Obviously, this is the reassertion of the antidiscrimination norm. It is broadened to include elimination of discrimination not only against individuals, but also against groups. It addresses the notion of "freedom of religion *or belief*" by being very clear that the nondiscrimination principle applies to both believers and nonbelievers.

> (16.2) —foster a climate of mutual tolerance and respect between believers of different communities as well as between believers and nonbelievers;

This commitment to "foster a climate of mutual tolerance and respect" has an admittedly mushy dimension, but it helps to describe the spirit in which all the other commitments are carried out. Moreover, it provides an important rhetorical tool in cases where States continue to act in repressive ways: they can obviously be criticized on top of everything else for not promoting the climate called for by this provision.

(16.3) —grant upon their request to communities of believers, practicing or prepared to practice their faith within the constitutional framework of their States, recognition of the status provided for them in the respective countries;

This commitment takes the Madrid Concluding Document's commitment to make legal entity status available to a higher level. The commitment is no longer merely to "favorably consider" such applications; it is an outright commitment to grant such status, provided that the religious groups in question are "prepared to practice their faith within the constitutional framework" of the State in question. This has turned out to be an extremely important provision. Over the past decade, most of the countries in the former socialist bloc (and some in the West) have either considered or adopted laws dealing with religious association. The early statutes past in the initial euphoria of the collapse of communism, were fairly open. But in the years that have followed, there has been a consistent temptation to tighten the constraints on acquiring religious entity status. It has been extremely important to be able to point to principle 16.3 in opposing overly restrictive provisions in this area.

(16.4) —respect the right of these religious communities to

—establish and maintain freely accessible places of worship or assembly,

—organize themselves according to their own hierarchical and institutional structure,

—select, appoint and replace their personnel in accordance with their respective requirements and standards as well as with any freely accepted arrangement between them and their State,

—solicit and receive voluntary financial and other contributions.

Principle 16.4 contains a set of extremely important commitments that can all be grouped under the label "autonomy in a religious organization's own affairs." This basic notion is often described as the right to autonomy in "internal affairs," but as German theory recognizes on this point, the autonomy in question may extend to a range of issues that are not strictly speaking internal. At the institutional level, religious freedom is meaningless if it does not include autonomy with respect to matters of worship and doctrine, ecclesiastical polity, selection, personnel, and finance. This provision remains somewhat vague by comparison to the range of phenomena that need to be addressed, but it is much more concrete than most religious freedom norms.

(16.5) —engage in consultation with religious faiths, institutions and organizations in order to achieve a better understanding of the requirements of religious freedom;

This commitment raises the old "meetings and contacts" commitment to a new level. The wording here suggests continuing and respectful dialogue, and an active concern on the part of the State to determine the needs of religious groups so that the State is in a better position to cooperate on such matters.

(16.6) —respect the right of everyone to give and receive religious education in the language of his choice, whether individually or in association with others;

(16.7) —in this context respect, *inter alia,* the liberty of parents to ensure the religious and moral education of their children in conformity with their own convictions;

(16.8) —allow the training of religious personnel in appropriate institutions;

In a sense, the commitments expressed in principles 16.6, 16.7, and 16.8 merely extend the "meetings and contacts" commitment into the educational sphere. Prior to *glasnost* and *perestroika,* even religious education in the home had been banned. Formal educational establishments in the form of private parochial schools had clearly not been permitted, not only in the communist States, but also in some western countries. Institutions for training clergy were also sharply restricted or nonexistent. The commitment to open up education both within the family and at the institutional levels was thus extremely significant.

(16.9) —respect the right of individual believers and communities of believers to acquire, possess, and use sacred books, religious publications in the language of their choice and other articles and materials related to the practice of religion or belief;

Principle 16.9 addresses an area that had long been a sore point: the ability to have access to sacred books, other publications, and a variety of materials needed in religious life.

(16.10) —allow religious faiths, institutions and organizations to produce, import and disseminate religious publications and materials;

Principle 16.10 goes a step further in allowing believers not only to "possess and use" religious materials themselves, but "to produce, import and disseminate" them. A limited interpretation of this provision could construe this to apply to dissemination and production or importation for use wholly within a particular denomination. But the text could also be easily read as extending this right also to the use of such materials in evangelizing.

(16.11) —favorably consider the interest of religious communities to participate in public dialogue, including through the mass media.

This provision is self-explanatory, though necessarily vague. Particularly in States where media is publicly owned, it is vital for religious groups to have access to the media. Principle 16.11 is a plea for reasonable openness in this regard.

(17) The participating States recognize that the exercise of the above mentioned rights relating to the freedom of religion or belief may be subject only to such limitations as are provided by law and consistent with their obligations under international law and with their international commitments. They will ensure in their laws and regulations and in their application the full and effective exercise of the freedom of thought, conscience, religion or belief.

Principle 17 explicitly addresses the situations under which religious freedom can be restricted. Essentially, it does this by referencing already existing international standards. One drawback to simply incorporating these limitation provisions by reference is that they are often not adequately understood when clearly spelled out in explicit language; an indirect reference adds confusion caused by the "out of sight, out of mind" syndrome. If understood with the concreteness intended, and with the sharp constraints on limitations of religious freedom that the international standards specify, this is certainly a sound provision, and it is useful to have it added in to round out and clarify the other commitments.

One final provision from the Vienna Concluding Document deserves mention. Principle 32 provides:

(32) They will allow believers, religious faiths and their representatives, in groups or on an individual basis, to establish and maintain direct personal contacts and communication with each other, in their own and other countries, ***inter alia,*** through travel, pilgrimages and participation in assemblies and other religious events. In this context and commensurate with such contacts and events, those concerned will be allowed to acquire, receive and carry with them religious publications and objects related to the practice of their religion or belief.

This commitment carries the earlier "international contacts" provisions to a new level of concreteness. This provision is a far cry from the "can have contacts" notion of earlier stages in the Helsinki process. Where initially, the effort was to translate religious freedom claims into an operational concept, in a world when even the barest meetings of believers could give rise to persecution, we now have States committing that they "***will allow***" individuals, communities and their representatives to have direct contacts, at any level—individual or group, both at home and abroad, through a series of concretely described religious practices (that are obviously not an exclusive set). These much richer contact rights are also supplemented by rights to carry (and presumably share) religious publications and "objects"—i.e., any religiously relevant items—and to use them as their beliefs deem appropriate in enriching joint religious activities.

D. Copenhagen Concluding Document

The Copenhagen Concluding Document reinforces and clarifies a number of key points from the Vienna Concluding Document. The relevant provisions are as follows:

(9.1) [The participating States reaffirm that] everyone will have the right to freedom of expression including the right to communication. This right will include freedom to hold opinions and to receive and impart information and ideas without interference by public authority and regardless of frontiers. The exercise of this right may be subject only to such restrictions as are prescribed by law and are consistent with international standards.

(9.4) [The participating States reaffirm that] everyone will have the right to freedom of thought, conscience, and religion. This right includes freedom to change one's religion or belief and freedom to manifest one's religion or belief, either alone or in community with others, in public or in private, through worship, teaching, practice and observance. The exercise of these rights may be subject only to such restrictions as are prescribed by law and are consistent with international standards.

Paragraph 9.1, while dealing more generally with freedom of expression, would appear to remove any doubt about the right of religious believers to "receive and impart" information and ideas (including their religious beliefs). Significantly, they may do so "without interference by public authority" and "regardless of frontiers." It is worth stressing here that government officials who seek to restrain religious freedom, particularly with respect to evangelization, all too often forget the overlapping and mutually reinforcing protections of freedom of religion and freedom of expression in this area. Paragraph 9.4 tracks the international norms more closely and in general reconfirms what was said in paragraph 17 in Vienna.

E. Budapest Summit Declaration (1994) and Istanbul Charter (1999)

One final OSCE commitment deserves mention here: specifically Chapter VIII. (27) from the 1994 Budapest Summit Declaration, which reads as follows:

> Chapter VIII.(27) Reaffirming their commitment to ensure freedom of conscience and religion and to foster a climate of mutual tolerance and respect between believers of different communities as well as between believers and non-believers, they expressed their concern about the exploitation of religion for aggressive nationalistic ends.

This language obviously reflects the world's experience with the tragic disintegration of Yugoslavia, the siege of Bosnia, and so forth. All too often in world history, religion is exploited or abused by political leaders to exacerbate conflicts. This is a particular risk in countries hungry to establish a national identity, where traditional religion and national identity or linked. Experience has underscored the need for consistent and ongoing efforts to cultivate an atmosphere of tolerance and to avoid exploitation of religion for "aggressive nationalist ends."

OSCE member States have reaffirmed these commitments to freedom of religion or belief, such as at the Istanbul Summit in 1999. In article 19 of the *Charter for European Security*, adopted at the Istanbul Summit, OSCE member States "reaffirm[ed] that respect for human rights and fundamental freedoms, democracy and the rule of law is at the core of the OSCE's comprehensive concept of security" and "commit[ted] [themselves] to counter such threats to security as violations of human rights and fundamental freedoms, including the freedom of thought, conscience, religion or belief."[4]

IV. Implementation of Religious Liberty Commitments in the OSCE

The first fifteen years after the signing of the Helsinki Final Act witnessed an elaboration of religious liberty commitments unparalleled in the world. The task at hand is to implement these commitments, which can only be done by the participating States themselves. The OSCE institutions can simply facilitate this process. Because the Helsinki commitments are political agreements and not treaty law, the commitments are only as good as the participating States make them in practice.[5] Most States, however, have found that significant pressure to comply also comes from the potential for negative publicity from noncompliance.

By the mid-1990s, non-governmental organizations and a few delegations began to call for a focus on religious liberty issues by the OSCE Office of Democratic Institutions and Human Rights (ODIHR).[6] At the 1995 Implementation Review Meeting,

[4] *Charter for European Security* (1999) (available online at <http://www.osce.org/docs/english/1990-1999/summits/istachart99e.htm#Anchor-TH-48123>).

[5] For a current assessment of the status of religious liberty in the OSCE region, see *Helsinki Monitor* 9, no. 3 (1999).

[6] The Conference of European Churches (CEC) and the National Councils of Churches in the USA and Canada made a suggestion to the 1994 Review Conference in Budapest that the ODIHR hold a seminar "to evaluate the implementation of the CSCE commitments regarding religious freedom in newly drafted legal texts, with particular attention to southeastern Europe."

a general agreement emerged among those delegations and non-governmental organizations that discussed religious liberty that a seminar sponsored by ODIHR would be helpful in clarifying issues and further implementation of religious liberty commitments. In April 1996, a seminar on "Constitutional, Legal and Administrative Aspects of the Freedom of Religion" was organized in Warsaw by the ODIHR. Three working groups discussed issues such as the status of believers, state-sponsored churches, dialogue between state and religious communities, equality under the law for all religious communities, freedom of education, and freedom of expression and information. The discussions covered issues such as whether state registration and recognition procedures can in fact and often are used to control and intervene into the affairs of churches and religious bodies and how tolerance and free religious expression, sometimes termed "proselytism," can be reconciled. Of course, not all religious expression is proselytism, particularly if proselytism is defined narrowly to include only coercive, manipulative, fraudulent, or other bad faith efforts to influence change of religion. Difficult issues regarding the role of the state in protecting the health and safety of its citizenry were also discussed. Out of these discussions, the ODIHR gleaned valuable information and recommendations in order to assist the participating States in implementing their agreements.

As a follow-up to the 1996 seminar, the ODIHR created an Advisory Panel of Experts on Freedom of Religion to assist the ODIHR in studying the issues discussed at the seminar and to advise the ODIHR as it assists the participating States in implementing their OSCE commitments. The Panel convened twice during the year 1997 and issued a preliminary report with working materials at the 1997 Implementation Meeting on Human Rights in Warsaw. The goal of this report was to assess the current situation and suggest measures needed to strengthen implementation of the OSCE commitments in the area of freedom of religion and belief. Recommendations include conducting a comprehensive survey of existing constitutional, legal, and administrative procedures; undertaking a comparative study of models of church, state, and societal relations; compiling and disseminating applicable texts from human rights agreements; and summarizing how the texts may be invoked.

In order to further the implementation of OSCE commitments on religious liberty, Norway, as the Chair-in-Office, called a Supplementary Meeting on Religious Liberty in March 1999—the first of its kind.[7] The one-day meeting was divided into three discussion topics: (1) religion and conflict resolution; (2) religious pluralism and tolerance; and (3) OSCE Expert Panel and recommendations for action. Each topic was introduced by one to three experts who delivered short statements to help crystallize the issues for discussion.

As a result of recommendations emerging from the 1999 Supplementary Human Dimension Meeting on Freedom of Religion or Belief and with the strong encouragement of the then Chairman-in-Office (Norway), a newly restructured Advisory Panel of Experts on Freedom of Religion or Belief was established. The Panel is divided into three thematic Working Groups: Conflict Prevention and Dialogue, Legislative Issues, and Education/Awareness for Tolerance. Each Working Group has two cochairs,

---

[7] The Norwegian Chairman-in-Office also hosted a roundtable discussion on "Religion and Conflict Prevention" in Oslo on 23 June 1999, which focused on how religion can be used to prevent or end conflicts.

who together form the Contact Group, which serves as the Panel's liaison with ODIHR. The Panel is responsible to propose projects and initiatives to ODIHR and work with ODIHR on their implementation, to keep ODIHR informed of developments and concerns in the area of freedom of religion or belief, and to be a consultative body for ODHIR for advancing freedom of religion or belief.

In the initial year after its establishment, the Panel was actively involved in numerous projects to promote freedom of religion or belief in the OSCE member States. In conjunction with the Ministry of Foreign Affairs of Armenia and the OSCE Office in Yerevan, the Panel held an expert roundtable in Armenia 24–25 May 2000 on ethnic and religious tolerance, bringing together representatives of ethnic and religious groups, NGOs, state officials, and local and international experts. As a follow-up, experts of the Panel are preparing a chapter on tolerance for a new human rights textbook for Armenian secondary schools. The Panel also, at the invitation of the Constitutional Court of Azerbaijan, cosponsored a conference on freedom of religion or belief in Baku in October 2000.

The Panel has also worked closely with a range of religious leaders in Bosnia-Herzegovina to develop a legal framework for religious associations that will protect the freedom of religion or belief of all religious groups. A draft law was prepared in connection with religious leaders and members of the Bosnian Interreligious Council, which is currently being finalized and will be submitted to the Parliament of Bosnia and Herzegovina. At the invitation of OSCE offices or member States, the Panel has also been active in providing technical drafting support for legislation in other countries, such as Albania, Kazakhstan, and the Kyrgyz Republic. Other legislative projects include development, with partnering academic institutions, of an on-line database of laws of OSCE member States that affect religious activities and organizations (www.religlaw.org).

V. Conclusion

The Helsinki commitments are by far the clearest delineation of religious liberty commitments in the international arena. The commitments forged during the Cold War era have stood the test of time and continue to serve as a beacon of hope for believers and nonbelievers around the world. Although these commitments are for a distinctive region and arose at a specific time in history, they are for all humankind and represent the aspirations of millions who seek to worship and live freely as their conscience dictates.

Chapter 12

Implementing Freedom of Religion in the OSCE: Experiences from the Norwegian Chairmanship

Janne Haaland Matlary

I. Introduction: Freedom of Religion or Belief and the Bondevik Government

Freedom of religion or belief and religious dialogue were major policy goals of Norway's 1997–2000 Bondevik government, in which I served as State Secretary of Foreign Affairs. The leading party of this coalition government, the Christian Democrats, and its Foreign Minister, Knut Vollebæk, took a major interest in promoting freedom of religion as well as in engaging religious leaders in peace and reconciliation work. Thus, it was only natural that we would seek to reinvigorate this emphasis in the work of the Organization for Security and Cooperation in Europe (OSCE). During Norway's chairmanship of this organization in 1999, we took several initiatives in this regard, seeking to implement freedom of religion as a human right as well as to increase awareness of the importance of religion both as a factor in conflicts and as a source of peaceful conflict resolution.

In this article, I will present the Norwegian chairmanship's work and experiences. First, however, it is necessary to place the OSCE and its normative basis in context, and to discuss the OSCE's impact on member states. I have no illusions as to the singular importance of our initiatives—they must be seen as small building blocks in an edifice that others have built before us. Our contribution as chairman was basically to place freedom of religion and religious dialogue in conflict resolution onto the OSCE agenda in a far more definitive way than before. At the time of writing, in the year 2000, it is too early to assess the impact of the Norwegian chair's focus on religion, but putting our work in context will allow us to at least draw some preliminary conclusions.

Political scientists have paid far too little attention to the OSCE and largely assumed that it has been a very impotent organization. This I believe to be wrong, and in need of reassessment.

First, I will describe the OSCE as an international organization and present its tools of norm implementation, democratization, and conflict resolution, which are all relevant to the implementation of religious freedom. Next, I will examine the role that freedom of

Tore Lindholm, W. Cole Durham, Jr., Bahia G. Tahzib-Lie (eds.), Facilitating Freedom of Religion or Belief: A Deskbook, *255–271.*

religion or belief has played in the OSCE's normative framework, both in its norm development as well as in terms of implementation. Finally, I will present the work the Norwegian chairmanship undertook, specifically, with regard to religious freedom and religious dialogue, and I will make a preliminary assessment of its effects.

II. The OSCE: From Process to International Organization

The OSCE was originally the Conference on Security and Co-operation in Europe (CSCE). As the name indicates, the CSCE was a process rather than an organization. At the suggestion of the then Soviet Union, the CSCE commenced in 1973 as a process of *rapprochement* between East and West.[1] It retained its ad hoc status until 1990 when it became institutionalized under the Charter of Paris for a New Europe, receiving administrative and political organs.[2] It was not until 1995 that the CSCE changed its name to the OSCE and became an official international organization.[3]

The famous Helsinki process of the 1970s was a unique meeting place between East and West during the Cold War, where human rights were discussed under the less conspicuous name of the "Third Basket,"[4] later renamed the "human dimension."[5] The discussion about human rights during the Cold War continued despite political affronts—which was a major achievement in itself. The Helsinki Final Act laid down principles about security and human rights in a path-breaking manner considering the date, 1975, when the Cold War was still a reality.[6]

The OSCE is a regional security organization that employs exclusively "soft power" tools (see below) in its military and nonmilitary tasks.[7] Its security concept is comprehensive and its tools are nonmilitary, although some of its missions are backed by military presence, such as in Bosnia and Kosovo.[8] By 2000, it had become a comprehensive security and human rights organization with a wide array of instruments at its disposal, but as of yet, little attention has been paid to the assessment of the actual impact of the OSCE on its member states. It has been widely assumed that the OSCE lacks power because of its consensual decision-making style and its lack of "hard power" tools.[9] The OSCE is an understudied organization in academic literature and has in general been

---

[1] Arie Bloed, ed., *From Helsinki to Vienna: Basic Documents of the Helsinki Process* (Boston: Martinus Nijhoff, 1990), 1; Arie Bloed, ed., *The Conference on Security and Co-operation in Europe: Analysis and Basic Documents, 1972–1993* (Boston: Kluwer Academic, 1993), 4–6; OSCE, *OSCE Handbook* (Vienna: Secretariat of the OSCE, 1999), 7.

[2] Bloed, *CSCE: Basic Documents, 1972–1993,* 12.

[3] Arie Bloed, ed., *The Conference on Security and Co-operation in Europe: Analysis and Basic Documents, 1993–1995* (Boston: Kluwer Academic, 1997), xvii, 53.

[4] John J. Maresca, *To Helsinki: The Conference on Security and Co-operation in Europe 1973–1975,* Duke Press Policy Studies (Durham: Duke University Press, 1987), 27, 34, 144–45.

[5] Bloed, *CSCE: Basic Documents, 1972–1993,* 40.

[6] Maresca, *To Helsinki,* 191–98; Bloed, *From Helsinki to Vienna,* 43, 47–48; Arie Bloed et al., eds., *Monitoring Human Rights in Europe* (Boston: Martinus Njijhoff, 1993), 45, 208; Thomas Buergenthal, "Copenhagen: A Democratic Manifesto," *World Affairs* 153, no. 1 (summer 1990): 5–7.

[7] OSCE, *OSCE Handbook,* 17, 42, 117–30.

[8] OSCE, *OSCE Handbook,* 45–54; OSCE, *Kosovo/Kosova: As Seen, As Told—An Analysis of the Human Rights Findings of the OSCE Kosovo Verification Mission, October 1998 to June 1999* (Warsaw: OSCE Office for Democratic Institutions and Human Rights), available online at <http://www.osce.org/kosovo/reports/hr/part1/index.htm>.

seen as rather insignificant. However, "the CSCE mechanisms have proven to be the real workhorses of the international community in its attempts to control sub-state conflict in post-Cold War Europe. . . . [I]n reality CSCE mechanisms have been involved in managing far more potential sub-state conflicts than either of the other [NATO and European Union] organizations."[10] As we shall see, human rights norms play an important part in conflict resolution.

The Helsinki Final Act has pioneered political agreement on human rights norms despite the Cold War. But the form of government and its ideology were not discussed; they were still an internal matter.[11] Only in 1990, after the demise of the Cold War, did it become possible to discuss the political requirements for the implementation of human rights. The 1990 Copenhagen Conference on the Human Dimension marks a watershed in the sense that one could now agree that only democracy and the rule of law could ensure the realization of human rights.[12] This marks a major change in the formation of the human rights regime in Europe: It was from then on that democracy and the rule of law emerged as intrinsic companions of human rights in an integrated whole.[13] Buergenthal calls this nothing less than a "democratic public order."[14]

The implementation of freedom of religion in participating states will naturally depend on how well the OSCE aids and monitors the implementation of human rights as a whole. The particular human right of freedom of religion has arguably not played a prominent role in the OSCE until the Norwegian chairmanship. In addition, there are problems in implementing freedom of religion in states that have been atheist for many years, such as those of the Commonwealth of Independent States[15] (CIS); and in states where nationalism and religion are mixed in an unholy alliance, such as in the Balkans. Thus, at the outset one may assume that the OSCE's record on promoting freedom of religion is not too impressive.

III. Freedom of Religion or Belief in the OSCE

The OSCE norms of human rights are well developed and comprehensive. They encompass all the internationally agreed human rights, but are distinct in their clear link between human rights and democracy and the rule of law. This link can also be found in major human rights conventions and declarations in the form of political rights to vote, freedom of assembly, right to form parties, freedom of the press, and so on. But in human rights conventions, the link between democracy and human rights is less explicit.

---

[9] However, see Thomas Buergenthal, "The CSCE Rights System," *George Washington Journal of International Law and Economics* 25, no. 2 (1991): 355, 375–81 (arguing that despite nonlegally binding status, the OSCE is necessary and powerful).

[10] Gregory Flynn and Henry Farrell, "Piecing Together the Democratic Peace: The CSCE, Norms and the 'Construction' of Security in Post-Cold War Europe," *International Organization* 53, no. 3 (summer 1999): 507.

[11] Bloed, *From Helsinki to Vienna,* 45, 47 (quoting the Helsinki Final Act, 1[a][I] and 1[a][VI]).

[12] Buergenthal, "Democratic Manifesto," 7.

[13] Janne Haaland Matlary, *Soft Power, Hard Values: Intervention for Human Rights and Democracy in Europe* (London: Palgrave, 2002).

[14] Buergenthal, "Democratic Manifesto," 7.

[15] The CIS includes all of the former republics of the USSR except the Baltic states.

In OSCE documents, there is an elaboration of the necessity of rule of law and multiparty democracy for the realization of human rights, and there are also practical policy prescriptions for how this is to be achieved.

As stated, the OSCE has embraced all fundamental freedoms and human rights as they are developed in the central human rights instruments. The Helsinki Final Act, Principle VII of the "Decalogue," declares that participating states will respect freedom of religion or belief.[16] After Helsinki, the negotiations about the "human dimension" continued in the Madrid Conference, which lasted for three years. Buergenthal described the atmosphere at the Madrid Conference as being laden with conflict and reaching a near stalemate due to an ideological contest between East and West.[17] However, the most surprising and positive result came in the field of freedom of religion or belief where this right was defined in *precise* and *practical* terms: "The most significant achievement was in the area of freedom of religion."[18] The 1983 Concluding Document of Madrid elaborates on this freedom. It affirms, *inter alia*, that member states will

> recognise, respect and furthermore agree to take the action necessary to ensure the freedom of the individual to profess and practise, alone or in community with others, religion or belief, acting in accordance with the dictates of his own conscience. . . . They will favourably consider applications by religious communities of believers practising or prepared to practise their faith within the constitutional framework of their states, to be granted the status provided for in their respective countries for religious faiths, institutions, and organizations.[19]

This document from the Madrid Conference clearly says that host states are to recognize churches and religious communities and allow public worship. This specification of what freedom of religion means in practice naturally makes it more difficult to evade the obligation of implementing this right. According to Buergenthal, this method of defining what a specific human right means in practical-political terms was pioneered at the Madrid Conference, and "it has been employed with ever greater frequency and sophistication in subsequent OSCE documents and has become the hallmark of the OSCE norms-setting practice."[20]

The right to freedom of religion or belief was further elaborated in the 1989 Concluding Document of Vienna. This document requires that states take effective measures to eliminate discrimination of individuals and communities on grounds of religion, that they ensure equality between believers and nonbelievers, that they "foster a climate of tolerance between believers of different communities as well as between believers and non-believers," and finally, that they grant religious communities legal status and facilitate their work.[21]

Summing up, we see that religious freedom in the OSCE has been well defined in an implementable way. The concrete measures to be taken by states are laid out in detail in the Vienna Concluding Document. They include the substance of the United Nations "Article 18 definition" of freedom of religion or belief,[22] and derive policy implications from it.

---

[16] Bloed, *From Helsinki to Vienna,* 47 (quoting the Helsinki Final Act).

[17] Buergenthal, "Democratic Manifesto," 5–6.

[18] Buergenthal, "The CSCE Rights System," 346.

[19] Bloed, *From Helsinki to Vienna,* 134–35 (quoting the 1983 Concluding Document of Madrid).

[20] Buergenthal, "The CSCE Rights System," 347.

[21] *CSCE Concluding Document of Vienna,* Principles 16–16.11, in Bloed, *CSCE: Basic Documents, 1972–1993,* 335–37.

IV. The Importance of Soft Power in Norm Implementation

Not until the OSCE's 1990 Charter of Paris[23] do we see an explicit linkage between democracy, rule of law and human rights. These same values are, of course, implicitly embedded in various declarations and conventions, starting with the Universal Declaration of Human Rights (1948). In the OSCE documents, however, we see an elaboration of the practical aspects of human rights implementation: What does it mean, in policy terms, to implement freedom of religion? What does it mean to implement freedom of the press?

No other human rights document is this precise in instructing law- and policy-makers what to do. As we shall see below, OSCE documents lay down specific requirements for acceptable implementation of freedom of religion. Furthermore, the linkage between human rights and democracy-*cum*-rule-of-law means that it is possible to make this kind of specification. For example, freedom of the press entails that power is dispersed and that there is a separation of powers; freedom of religion means that there is respect for the apolitical character of religious communities and space for public as well as private worship. Thus one may say that the greatness of the OSCE's approach lies in its practical nature: It specifies, in very concrete terms, that a given human right entails both taking certain measures and the actual functioning of democratic and legal institutions. It does not resort to ambiguous statements that lend themselves to various types of interpretation. The fact that the OSCE had to write texts for new and learning democracies means that these texts must be a *vade mecum* for the practitioner. The OSCE documents are thus very advanced as instructions to policy-makers, and they cannot easily be manipulated. In my view, this makes them extremely attractive.

But what about the powers of the OSCE? Can it impose its normative basis? Can it induce states to follow the latter? Or must it simply rely on the goodwill of participating states? As mentioned earlier, the OSCE relies on "soft power" tools. The concept of "soft power" is relatively new and refers to *co-optive* policy tools, as opposed to *coercive* tools.[24]

Soft power has probably always been important, but seems to enjoy a special role in international politics today.[25] There is a renewed discussion about power in the post–Cold War period. As Ingebritsen notes:

> International relations . . . have begun to focus on how states exercise influence in ways that do not conform to strictly economic or military capabilities. Instead of viewing the international system as fragmented and anarchic, a new wave of scholarship examines how states become socialized into an international community or society.[26]

---

[22] Articles 18 of both the Universal Declaration of Human Rights and the International Covenant on Civil and Political Rights deal with freedom of religion or belief.

[23] See generally Charter of Paris for a New Europe, available in Bloed, *CSCE: Basic Documents, 1972–1993,* 536–66; also available online at <http://www.osce.org/docs/english/19901999/summits/paris90e.htm>.

[24] Joseph S. Nye Jr. and William A. Owens, "American's Information Edge," *Foreign Affairs* 75, no. 2 (March/April 1996): 21 n.1.

[25] See generally Joseph S. Nye Jr., *Bound to Lead: The Changing Nature of American Power* (New York: Basic Books, 1990).

[26] Christine Ingebritsen, "Scandinavia's Influence on International Norms," *Toward a New Partnership,* ed. Christine Ingebritsen and Sabrina Ramet (forthcoming).

Nye has developed this theme, coining the term "soft power" for the power that persuades rather than coerces. He argues that the United States is the leading soft power holder, even in "hard" fields like security policy, where the future belongs to those that command "technology, education, and institutional flexibility."[27]

Nye provides a very useful continuum of types of power.[28] On the most familiar end, we find coercive power, which gives us the ability to command others to follow our will. Military power is the key power source here, but economic power counts, too. Sanctions are one example of economic power that is coercive. At the other end of the continuum, we find co-optive power. This is the power to make others agree with us and desire the same things that we desire. They may be induced to do so through light pressures, such as creating incentive structures that they follow, or through "shaming" and open criticism, or threats of such. There are many diplomatic ways of arm twisting.

As we move toward the soft side of the continuum, we find the powers of "agenda-setting" and "attraction." These power sources may be even stronger; when we define a problem and set its agenda, we then have extensive control over the decision-making process. Light coercion and pressure may still be present, though hidden as a part of a "democratic" decision-making procedure.

The greatest power, that of "persuasion," implies making others accept our problem definition and the premises for subsequent decision making. They are convinced that we are right, and internalize our views, so that they think like we do and strive for the same goals.

With coercive power, we must assume that the others will turn against us and disobey us when we no longer threaten them. With co-optive power, we obtain our goal—to make the others do as we want—without physical threats. Because the other ultimately internalizes our views, there is no threat of them turning against us or our ideology.

What is new today, says Nye, is the salience of co-optive or soft power. He argues that the United States continues to be the most powerful state because it succeeds in exercising soft power in addition to traditional hard power:

> Soft co-optive power is just as important as hard command power. If a state can make its power legitimate in the eyes of others, it will encounter less resistance to its wishes. If its culture and ideology are attractive, others will more willingly follow. . . . In short, the universalism of a country's culture and its ability to establish a set of favourable rules and institutions that govern areas of international activity are critical sources of power.[29]

Thus, soft power resources enhance the promotion of values such as human rights and democracy. In fact, soft power relies on an open society with free press and public discussion. This is because soft power is typically exercised in public, as part of public diplomacy. The actors using soft power are not only states, but also non-governmental organizations (NGOs), media, and international organizations and regimes. Here the OSCE can play a much more important role than before. It has a detailed normative framework in place, as well as a "toolbox" of typically soft power tools.

---

[27] Nye and Owens, "America's Information Edge," 20–22.

[28] Ibid., 22; Nye, *Bound to Lead,* 27–31.

[29] Nye, *Bound to Lead,* 32–33.

Soft power is becoming more prevalent in acts of *intervention*. The OSCE promotes human rights through various specific forms of intervention. Intervention here refers to active policy-making inside another country or aimed at influencing the society and government of another country. Today there is a marked trend toward such interventionism, which for the most part is positive and benign. This intervention stresses carrots instead of sticks—that is, help and assistance rather than threats and sanctions.[30] Nonetheless, we speak about transgressing traditional borders and about directly challenging the norm of sovereignty and its concomitant, nonintervention.

Further, values also seem to matter in the growing number of cases of hard power intervention since 1990. Security policy in the 1990s increasingly has to grapple with the dilemma of massive human rights abuses in internal conflicts, and the number of interventions authorized by the Security Council has increased in the present period. Although the Council cannot officially justify intervention solely because of human rights abuses, the humanitarian situation clearly matters a great deal in determining whether there is a threat to "international peace and security"—the formal basis for intervention by the Council. The old issue of humanitarian intervention has again come to the fore of international security policy.

Thus, the role of human rights, democracy, and the rule of law in foreign policy merits attention, with regard to both soft and hard power intervention. The OSCE has a large "toolbox" of soft power instruments.

V. OSCE Tools of Norm Implementation

But how has freedom of religion fared in the OSCE? What tools are there to help implement this right?

The OSCE commands several types of policy tools, some of which are traditional, diplomatic ones, whereas others are missions of short or long duration in a host country. In addition, there are tools of early warning and conflict prevention, of post-conflict management and democracy-building, as well as public "shaming" in review conferences on human rights.[31]

A. OSCE Missions

The OSCE sends missions to states with democracy and human rights problems. The first long-duration missions were deployed in 1992 to the Sandjak, Vojvodina, and Kosovo.

By the year 2000, there were fourteen missions, and these were often large. For example, about 290 people currently staff the Bosnia mission. The staff is comprised of experts in democratization and election processes, as well as experts in military affairs, such as weapons collection and demobilization. The OSCE mission in Bosnia is in charge of civil implementation of the Dayton Peace Agreement, and has conducted party registration, election monitoring, press development, and other important activities.[32] The

---

[30] Ibid., 31.

[31] See generally OSCE, *OSCE Handbook* and the OSCE web page, <http://www.osce.org>.

[32] *OSCE Mission Survey: Mission to Bosnia and Herzegovina*, 17 January 2000, <http://www.osce.org/publications/survey/survey08.htm>.

Office of the High Representative (OHR) is Bosnia's highest authority until democracy is installed, and the OSCE mission has been responsible for all aspects of democracy-building. This is highly practical work that requires expert insight into how to create a multiparty system and the rule of law, as well as insight into the practical consequences of human rights such as freedom of religion or belief, when it is being violated, and how to deal with that violation.

In Bosnia, religious freedom was a major problem since the three ethnic groups largely follow religious affiliation. One is hard pressed to find a state where the nonfulfillment of freedom of religion or belief has been more pronounced. The suggestion of rebuilding mosques and Catholic churches in Republika Srpska is still seen as a provocation, and when a Catholic outdoor mass was held in Derventa in 1998, local Serbs attacked the Croats who traveled by bus to attend the celebration. SFOR intervention by the Norwegian contingent stationed in the Nordpol brigade in nearby Modrica saved the worshippers, among whom was the cardinal of Sarajevo.

Other examples of complete religious intolerance can easily be identified in other parts of Bosnia. For example, in Mostar, which used to be a sophisticated example of religious coexistence and tolerance, there is now a "war" between Catholics and Muslims: The electric clockwork of the Catholic churches sounds at maximum volume whenever the many new mosques, financed by Middle East states, turn on their electric muezzin equally loud. The sound is blasting in the narrow valley of Mostar as the religious communities engage in a competition to silence each other. The Catholic bishop and the mufti alike refuse to cooperate with the international community and its representative. When I was in Mostar in 1999, the OSCE mission leader there, an American Catholic, was frustrated that his bishop simply refused to meet him. The Croat nationalist cause has clearly become the cause of the local Catholic Church as well.

Similar problems continue throughout the Balkans: Serbs misusing the Orthodox Church for nationalist politics, Croats misusing the Catholic Church for the same purpose, Kosovars burning Orthodox churches, and Muslim Bosnians attacking churches in "their" areas—all of this has happened, and continues to happen. The OSCE has to have an integrated approach to this kind of abuse.

In the case of the Dayton Peace Agreement, the head of the OSCE mission has real powers of sanction. The long-term leader of this mission, ambassador Robert Barry, has for many years been the most important decision maker in Bosnia, next to the OHR (the Office of the High Representative of the international community) and the commander of the SFOR forces. Dayton allows the international community to cancel elections not properly held, to remove elected politicians if they do not cooperate in democracy-building, to close presses that spread nationalist and xenophobic propaganda, and to encourage other democracy-building activities.[33] In short, the OSCE in Bosnia is part of the administration of a *de facto* international protectorate. This also applies to the governance of Kosovo.

There are other missions that have been equally large, such as the mission in Croatia, with a mandate to monitor and sanction transgressions of press freedom, abuse of presidential powers, and impartiality of judges.[34] The head of the OSCE mission can act

[33] See Bureau of Public Affairs, *Summary of the Dayton Peace Agreement,* 11 December 1995, <http://www.state.gov/www/regions/eur/bosnia/dayton.html>.

[34] *OSCE Mission Survey: Mission to Croatia,* <http://www.osce.org/publications/survey/survey09.htm>.

against transgressions of democratic government, but also has to keep up a working cooperation with the host government, because it is ultimately this government that decides whether to keep a mission by renewing its mandate.

The largest OSCE mission to date has been the Kosovo Verification Mission (KVM), with a staff of nearly 2,000. After protracted negotiations with President Milosevic, the mission commenced operation in October 1998. Many voices maintained that the KVM could do nothing further in Kosovo, because it was unarmed and was increasingly the object of attack. Due to escalating violence, the Norwegian chairmanship withdrew the mission on March 20, 1999. By this time, it had become clear that there were major troop movements from Serbia into Kosovo.[35] Shortly after the withdrawal of the mission, NATO started its attack on Kosovo and Serbia.[36]

Despite the brief duration of the mission, the KVM succeeded in documenting the escalation of human rights violations. The KVM leader, ambassador William Walker, exposed the infamous Racak massacre, where forty-nine villagers were found executed in January 1999.[37] The KVM also documented many other abuses.

An OSCE mission cannot remain in place if the host state makes the mission's work impossible and mission staff is at undue personal risk. These difficulties were also the reason for the withdrawal of the mission in Chechnya, called the Assistance and Monitoring Group (AMG), in December 1998.[38] The security situation in Chechnya had become so precarious that AMG staff could not perform their functions, but had to stay in headquarters for fear of kidnapping and ambush. The AMG has continued monitoring Chechnya from its Moscow offices with the aid of native Chechnian employees living in Chechnya.[39]

Host governments sometimes contest OSCE missions. Some governments try to restrict the mandate and to make the mission a hostage to its own political goals. This was the case with the Croat governments under Tudjman, where there were several attempts to manipulate the mission and to oust it. However, international pressure, including EU pressure, which carried the most weight with Croatia, kept the mission in place. Similar situations occurred in some of the Baltic states, where the OSCE was seen as intrusive on minority issues. The contested character of the missions is also an indicator of their importance. On the one hand, it gives international legitimacy to have an independent "eye and ear" in a state; on the other hand, it is unpleasant to have monitoring inside one's own state.

B. Specific Instruments for the Implementation of Human Rights

Human rights issues also form the core of the OSCE's comprehensive security concept—there is no stable peace without democracy, rule of law, and respect for human rights. In addition to the democratization work that is intrinsic to the mandates of

---

[35] OSCE, *Kosovo/Kosova*, available online at <http://www.osce.org/kosovo/reports/hr/part1/index.htm>.

[36] OSCE, *Annual Report 1999 on OSCE Activities*, <http://www.osce.org/docs/english/misc/anrep99e.htm#1,1,5,1>.

[37] Steven Erlanger, "Kosovo Massacre Hardens Militants and Jolts the West," *New York Times*, 25 January 1999; OSCE, *Kosovo/Kosova*, available online at <http://www.osce.org/kosovo/reports/hr/part1/index.htm>.

[38] *OSCE Mission Reports on Human Dimension Activities: OSCE Assistance Group to Chechnya*, <http://www.osce.org/odihr/docs/missions00-che.htm>.

[39] Ibid.

particular missions, there are also specific instruments for the implementation of the human rights regime. These instruments include various monitoring mechanisms, the ODIHR (Office of Democratic Institutions and Human Rights) in Warsaw, and the HCNM (High Commissioner on National Minorities) in the Hague. One particular mission, the Advisory and Monitoring Group in Belarus, has a mandate exclusively concerned with implementing the human rights regime and has been the only international presence in that state since the withdrawal of western ambassadors in 1997.[40]

1. Monitoring Mechanisms

As seen above, the Helsinki Act provisions were later developed by a follow-up meeting in Vienna from 1986 to 1989. Here, western governments proposed a *mechanism to monitor compliance* with these norms, called the "human dimension mechanism." This consisted of a Conference on the Human Dimension (CHD), which was to be held in order for the eastern states to catch up in their own democratic development. The approach was to gradually enable these states to achieve western standards. Three such conferences were held in Vienna (1989), Copenhagen (1990), and Moscow (1991), and various tools were adopted. The Vienna meeting produced a *four-stage procedure for mandatory interstate dialogue on human rights*,[41] the Copenhagen delegates adopted a document that defined human rights in more detail than the Helsinki Act, especially in the field of *minority rights*;[42] and the Moscow conference further elaborated on the Vienna mechanism by making it possible to create *independent fact-finding missions*, even without the consent on the state in question.[43] In the view of one expert, "(t)he Moscow mechanism constituted significant progress, allowing for the first time third-party supervision, fact-finding, and mediation."[44] However, these mechanisms are rarely used because the OSCE tries to encourage development instead of sanctioning countries that are striving to become democratic. The very existence of such mechanisms, however, can function as a disciplining force. The reality that a fact-finding mission may be sent to a state even without its consent means that there is an ultimate threat in store.

The Paris Summit in 1990 institutionalized additional human rights mechanisms. The Office for Free Elections (OFE) was established in Warszaw, then later renamed the Office for Democratic Institutions and Human Rights (ODIHR). There was furthermore a change in the consensus procedure for decision-making in 1992, allowing for *consensus-minus-one* in order to enable the OSCE to take measures against states in cases of "clear, gross, and uncorrected violations of OSCE commitments."[45] This procedure was used against the Federal Republic of Yugoslavia when President Slobodan Milosevic refused to permit OSCE observers to enter Kosovo and persisted in violating human rights commitments in that province. The Federal Republic of Yugoslavia was suspended from the OSCE, and the OSCE missions in Kosovo, Sandjak, and Vojvodina were forced to leave. This suspension remained in force until November 2000.

---

[40] Heinz Timmermann, "The OSCE Representation in Belarus," in *OSCE Yearbook, 1998* (Baden: Nomos Verlagsgesellschaft, 1997).

[41] Bloed, *OSCE: Basic Documents, 1972–1993,* 367–68.

[42] Ibid., 441–61.

[43] Ibid., 607–22.

[44] F. Daftary, "The Third OSCE Implementation Meeting on Human Dimension Issues in Warsaw, 1997," in *OSCE Yearbook, 1998,* 252.

2. The High Commissioner on National Minorities

The OSCE created the High Commissioner on National Minorities (HCNM) in 1992.[46] Minority issues form a very large part of the typical human rights problems in OSCE participating states. The idea that ethnic minorities have rights to language, culture, and their own religion is often highly contested. The work of High Commissioner Max van der Stoel is close to a legend in current diplomacy. The former Dutch foreign minister has traveled to many conflict areas in OSCE states where national minority rights are at stake, and has solved a number of potentially violent conflicts in a peaceful manner. Especially noteworthy is his work in the Baltic states on Russian minority rights, as well as his work in the Balkans and in East Central Europe.[47] He can travel to any OSCE country and consult with the actors he finds relevant on any potential or present conflict, and he reports to OSCE meetings and institutions. In extreme cases he can issue a "solemn warning," a tool used once in Macedonia.

His work has been, and is, very important for freedom of religion or belief; he often has the task of explaining what this right means and suggesting how to implement it. The idea of pluri-religious states is quite foreign in, e.g., Central Asia, and in the Balkans the very intermixing of politics and religion makes it very hard to rediscover what religion without instrumental interests really means. In these regions, the roving diplomacy of the High Commissioner, using only soft power tools, has been very important. However, its importance is difficult to gauge, because the conflicts that have been averted by preventive measures have not surfaced. One can at least say that the High Commissioner's work is very highly regarded in each and every OSCE state, that he has automatic access to all persons of influence, and that the fact that he reports back to the OSCE's central institutions means that all the pertinent problems in a given state will be known.

3. The Office for Democratic Institutions and Human Rights

The ODIHR's tasks are threefold: promotion of free and fair elections, democracy-building through the promotion of civil society and democratic institutions, and monitoring and implementation of human dimension commitments.[48] The most well-known of these activities is undoubtedly the election supervision and monitoring. The office is directly responsible for election processes in most of the new democracies in the OSCE. Election monitoring is also security policy because an election that is believed to have been manipulated can easily lead to armed conflict, as was the case in Albania in 1996.

Normally, however, ODIHR is involved at an earlier stage, helping governments arrange free and fair elections. It gives advice on how to make an election law and how to make a voter registry, to mention just two frequent tasks.[49] To illustrate the range of activities in this field, consider the following ODIHR projects: In 1998, ODIHR helped create a voter registry in Albania, provided advice on election systems, media regulation and voter registration in Montenegro, and helped write an election law in Armenia.[50]

---

[45] Bloed, *OSCE: Basic Documents, 1972–1993,* 832.
[46] OSCE, *OSCE Handbook,* 93.
[47] Flynn and Farrell, "Democratic Peace," 522, 527–28.
[48] OSCE, *OSCE Handbook,* 105.
[49] Ibid., 109.

A major undertaking in Central Asia was a program to train and advise election officials from all five of the republics that faced parliamentary or presidential elections between 1999–2001.[51] In a single year, 1997, the ODIHR monitored elections in Bulgaria, Albania, Bosnia and Herzegovina, Serbia, Republika Srpska, Montenegro, and twice in Croatia.[52] The election monitoring takes place with observers seconded by OSCE member states as well as by other international organizations such as the European Parliament and of the Council of Europe.[53]

In the field of democracy development, too, the ODIHR has extensive activity. In 1997, Memoranda of Understanding were signed with Central Asian republics on assistance to develop their democracies, as well as on several projects in the Caucasus. In the long term mission in Croatia and Bosnia, the democratization element is absolutely essential. In order to avoid so-called "forum shopping," joint delegations have been sent to these various areas, consisting of representatives of the EU, the CoE, and the OSCE. "A joint mission also sends the message to countries in need of assistance that the international community has mutually reinforcing standards and common goals in the fields of human rights and democratization."[54]

The ODIHR's mandate was strengthened at the Prague meeting, making it the key human rights and democracy tool of the OSCE. Each year there is a review and implementation meeting of all the OSCE participating states under the auspices of the ODIHR, lasting for two to three weeks. Here states are criticized and praised, and major discussions of implementation failure take place. It is significant that NGOs, too, are allowed full participation in these meetings. There are often very heated exchanges between certain states not used to democratic criticism, and NGOs like Human Rights Watch or the Helsinki Committee. The chairman of the only NGO from a Central Asian state which criticized its own government at the review conference in 1997 was severely beaten up outside his hotel. Suspicion centered on the secret services of the home government, although in all fairness one cannot pass judgment. This example is useful because it illustrates the novelty of western institutions to many new OSCE states: These institutions and human rights must be taught rather than imposed. After all, it took many centuries to agree on and implement the human right of freedom of religion in Europe.

VI. Implementation of Religious Freedom in the OSCE States: The ODIHR Review Conferences and Other Instruments

As previously stated, the OSCE has developed several monitoring mechanisms, such as an interstate complaint procedure called the Vienna mechanism, which may be used against a noncomplying state;[55] the Moscow mechanism, whereby the OSCE can send missions of experts and *rapporteurs* to investigate a breach of commitments, even against the will of the state in question;[56] and other monitoring mechanisms, including *ad hoc* missions and the review conferences.

---

[50] OSCE, *Office for Democratic Institutions and Human Rights* [ODIHR]*: Semi-Annual Report Autumn 1998*, <http://www.osce.org/odihr/docts/sar1298.htm>.

[51] Ibid.

[52] *OSCE Yearbook, 1998*, 492.

[53] OSCE, *ODIHR: Semi-Annual Report Autumn 1998.*

[54] *OSCE Yearbook, 1998*, 388.

[55] OSCE, *OSCE Handbook*, 87.

Each year, the OSCE states meet to review their implementation of human rights—the so-called human dimension. Both states and NGOs make plenary statements in which they launch praise and criticism, naming the states in question. These meetings are unique among international conferences in allowing the equal participation of states and NGOs. However, this is a useful manner in which to present constructive criticism, as states may be reluctant to name other states in such an endeavor.

If we look at the OSCE record from the review conferences, we find that non-implementation of freedom of religion or belief has been a persistent feature.[57] At the review conference in 1999, for instance, there was strong criticism of several western states for their strict definition of sects.[58] The United States, one of the states most concerned with religious freedom, launched heavy criticism of Belgium, France, and Austria for labeling new religious groups with the pejorative term "sects" and for establishing "anti-sect" agencies tasked with the monitoring of such new groups. In the case of France, these groups were not even allowed the right of response, but were simply defined as "sects" or "cults," according to the United States' statement. The issue of what is a sect and what is a religious or belief community is surely a contentious issue, not to be further discussed here. What is of interest in this context, however, is the fact that western states, too, criticize each other in an open and frank manner in this forum.

At this 1999 Review Conference, several delegations strongly criticized the new participating states of Central Asia, Uzbekistan, the Kyrgyz Republic, and Kazakhstan. They alleged that, in these countries, Christians are persecuted and sometimes imprisoned, missionary activity is forbidden or restricted, and new religious communities are not granted legal status. The United States and the European Union maintained that in Uzbekistan, more than two hundred people were imprisoned because of their faith, and that arrests were arbitrary and abuse pervasive. Muslims, too, are harassed and arrested in Uzbekistan. The United States and the European Union reported that the Uzbek government has used terrorism charges as pretexts for these abuses.

Further, Azerbaijan was criticized for persecuting Baptist missionaries, one of whom, a Norwegian national, was arrested and imprisoned for an extended period of time. Many of these missionaries were subsequently expelled. These actions were clearly violations of religious freedom.

Some delegates also criticized Greece and Turkey on account of ill-treatment of religious minorities. Greece was criticized for maintaining laws that are used against religious minorities, despite several rulings against this practice in the European Court of Human Rights. Turkey was criticized for forbidding the wearing of religious insignia, such as head scarves, in public places, and for the restrictions on outward manifestations of religious faith.

---

[56] Ibid.

[57] Documents of the review conferences in Budapest (1994), Lisbon-Vienna (1996), and Vienna-Istanbul (1999) are available online at <http://www.osce.org/docs/english/fupreve.htm>.

[58] 1999 OSCE Review Conference: Vienna-Istanbul, <http://www.osce.org/docs/english/1990-1999/rcs/istarev99e.htm>; European Union Statement on Freedom of Religion or Belief, <http://www.cesnur.org/testi/EU_stat.htm>; United States' Statement on Freedom of Thought, Conscience, Religion, and Belief at the 1999 OSCE Review Conference, Vienna-Istanbul, 23 September 1999, <http://www.house.gov/csce/viennaspeechesnewer.htm>.

There was also persistent criticism of Russia's 1997 religion law, which privileges the Orthodox Church by creating categories of religious communities with different levels of status. This law, vague in wording and unclear in interpretation, has led to much discrimination of non-Orthodox religious communities—such as requiring local groups that do not have centralized organizations to have a presence in Russia for fifteen years before they can obtain legal status. There has been unison western criticism of Russia in this regard.

Finally, Bulgaria, Hungary, Romania, and the Ukraine were criticized for impending legislation that would lead to discrimination, and their parliaments were urged to repeal laws not in conformity with international standards.

It is difficult to assess the impact of this type of criticism. The public "shaming" effect depends on how much press was present at a particular meeting, how the criticism of a state is reflected in its national public debate, and how much the state's reputation suffers in the international diplomatic and political community as a result. To date, OSCE meetings have had very little press attention. The lack of press interest is unfortunate because public attention is an important trigger for change. There have also been few NGOs from the new OSCE participating states in the Balkans and in the CIS. The concept of the NGO is one that needs to be developed in these states, and that takes time. In order to help this process, the OSCE has financed NGO participation from such states.

If criticism at OSCE review conferences does not yet produce the desired shaming effect, there is at least an internal OSCE effect. Individual OSCE missions note the criticism voiced in the review sessions and follow up on the human dimension issues. The various missions pursue comprehensive security policies, which include democracy and human rights issues as well as political stabilization. The actual strategies for each case naturally vary with the problems at hand.

The review conference acts as a stocktaking of all human rights problems, and its conclusions are well disseminated afterwards, both in the OSCE central secretariat as well as in the states hosting OSCE missions. Thus, the review conferences provide a "diagnostic" for the participating states. However, the follow-up in the missions could probably be better integrated.

VII. Initiatives under the Norwegian Chairmanship

During the Norwegian chairmanship, we tried to "mainstream" consideration of religious freedom into the OCSE missions, as well as requiring them to consult local religious leaders on how the latter could help in conflict resolution. We decided to highlight the importance of freedom of religion in two ways: first, as a basic human right—indeed, as one of the most important rights; and second, as a basis for conflict resolution, on the logic that instrumentalized religion often plays a major role in creating and maintaining conflicts, and that it can therefore also contribute in resolving conflicts.[59]

The Norwegian chairmanship decided to arrange two major OSCE conferences on these topics. First, we arranged a supplementary human dimensions meeting on freedom of religion and belief in Vienna in March 1999.[60] This conference united experts and

---

[59] OSCE, *Annual Report 1999 on OSCE Activities*, <http://www.osce.org/docs/english/misc/anrep99e.htm#1,1,5,1>.

representatives from almost all OSCE participating states as well as nearly seventy NGOs. As mentioned before, in many OSCE meetings NGOs have equal rights of participation with states. Second, later in the year, we arranged a high-level round-table in Oslo in which religious leaders and politicians discussed the recommendations from the Vienna conference.

In the Vienna meeting, three topics were discussed: religious dialogue and conflict prevention, religious pluralism and limitations on freedom of religion, and reports from the OSCE/ODIHR Advisory Panel of Experts on Freedom of Religion or Belief including proposals for future projects for the panel.[61] Our aim for this exercise was to arrive at concrete recommendations on how the OSCE could improve its work in these areas while simultaneously alerting participating states of the importance of the obligations they had undertaken as members of the OSCE.

The Vienna meeting resulted in several proposals: the inclusion of religious leaders in conflict resolution, and using field missions in this work; more emphasis on the need to accept, help, and tolerate missionary activity in new states, where there is no tradition in this regard; and finally, strengthening the OSCE/ODIHR Advisory Panel of Experts on Freedom of Religion or Belief. Thus, the Norwegian OSCE chairmanship put a major emphasis on strengthening the human dimension, including freedom of religion or belief.

To use religious dialogue in conflict prevention was one of the Norwegian government's main strategies in various bilateral contexts. For instance, we invited church leaders from Ethiopia and Eritrea to talks in Norway several times during the war, intending the public statement of both sides to act as an incentive for peace negotiations. In addition, the closed and direct meetings between the church leaders were conducive to mutual understanding. The Norwegian government arranged this type of meeting indirectly, with a neutral NGO, in this case the Norwegian Church Aid, as the organizer. Such arrangements allowed for distance between the foreign office and the political conflict in question, but it is also true to our conception of the proper relationship between politics and religion.

The Norwegian chairmanship believes that in order to be genuinely influential, religious leaders must be independent, not puppets of some political ploy. It is only in their capacity as true religious leaders that they can wield influence. Therefore, we want to support their way of dealing with conflict and contributing to peace ***on their own terms.***

We also used this formula in OSCE work. An important example of the Norwegian chairmanship using religious dialogue in conflict resolution was the support we gave to various initiatives in the Balkans and the Middle East. Through the Communita di Sant' Egidio, the well-known Catholic layman's organization in Rome, and the World Conference for Religion and Peace in New York, we sponsored various peace initiatives through religious dialogue and direct negotiations. Before the Kosovo war broke out, we enjoyed the success of the Communita's mons. Vicenzo Paglia, whose excellent work in Serbia and Kosovo resulted in a school and university agreement in Pristina. Due to

[60] OSCE Supplementary Meeting on Freedom of Religion and Belief, Vienna 1999, <http://www.osce.org/odihr/docs/m99-religion-report.htm>.

[61] Ibid.

Paglia's unique knowledge of both the Serb and the Kosovar side, he succeeded in negotiating an agreement whereby both ethnic groups would use the premises of the University of Pristina as well as schools in Kosovo. Unfortunately, however, the agreement was never implemented on the Serb side, and thus did not take effect. The Communita did tremendously important work in other areas as well, both in Africa and the Balkans.

Through the World Conference on Religion and Peace, an NGO affiliated with the United Nations, we supported the still ongoing work to establish dialogue in the Federal Republic of Yugoslavia after the bombing. We also financed and otherwise supported similar work in Bosnia, where the international NGO works with religious leaders to encourage them to cooperate among themselves, and then to persuade them to publicize this cooperation and thus urge ethnic groups, which follow religious lines, to cooperate. This simple model proves hard to implement in Bosnia. We worked for a long time to get religious leaders in Sarajevo to accept the concept. In the end, they were more or less able to agree on a common platform. Today, we see the gradual return of minorities, and with them, their clergy and the need to reconstruct churches and mosques. Reintegration and reconstruction have been very arduous tasks.

These examples serve to introduce the work we decided to emphasize during the Norwegian chairmanship of the OSCE. The chairman, Foreign Minister Knut Vollebæk, personally took an active interest in how one could use religious dialogue and religious leaders in the quest for peace. He undertook to make the OSCE work more actively on what freedom of religion or belief really entails, and to encourage the organization to use religious dialogue in its conflict resolution work. The OSCE had not previously resorted to religious dialogue in its reconciliation efforts. In the words of Vollebæk:

> In the work on the human dimension we have also stressed the connection between culture, religion, and conflict resolution—if religious leaders cannot agree on a peace message, what chance do peace conferences then stand? . . . Culture and religion have become the symbol of conflict in many places, but true religion and culture are, in fact, the very opposite. They are therefore both important tools in conflict resolution. As chairman we have taken several steps to increase the consciousness of this within the OSCE and in particular in the missions.[62]

What were these specific initiatives? First, the Norwegian chairmanship reactivated the OSCE/ODIHR Advisory Panel of Experts on Freedom of Religion or Belief, led by Rüdiger Noll. This panel was given funding to make a list of priorities and to initiate some projects. As mentioned above, the chairmanship further arranged a special conference on religious freedom in Vienna in March 1999. This conference brought together more than 150 experts from all OSCE participating states as well as the major NGOs in the field, and led to a set of recommendations and conclusions about further work.

Later in the year, the chairman arranged a high-level conference in Oslo on freedom of religion or belief and how to use religion in conflict resolution. Representatives of the major conflicting parties in Kosovo also attended, along with actors like the Communita di Sant' Egidio.

---

[62] Knut Vollebæk, speech given to the Oslo Military Society (Oslo, Norway, 4 October 1999).

During the Norwegian chairmanship, we also decided that all missions should, as a routine task, consult religious leaders in their host countries on how they could contribute to peace building, thus aiming at integrating the monitoring and fostering of religious freedom in the missions themselves.

VIII. Conclusion

OSCE documents define the right to freedom of religion or belief in very precise terms to guide policy makers in new democracies where this right is largely unfamiliar. The OSCE has many tools at its disposal to implement this right, employing "soft power" such as persuasion, legal and political aid, and open as well as discreet criticism. Although the meaning of "implementation" in this regard has been very clearly specified, it is hard to measure the impact of the OSCE in this regard. There are persistent problems in the OSCE area in this field, such as the law on religion in Russia, the lack of understanding in Central Asia of what this right entails, the Balkan conflicts where religion is instrumentalized, and the need to further agree on what freedom of religion means in western states.

The Norwegian chairmanship sought to highlight the importance of religion in several ways: as a source of conflict when instrumentalized, as an avenue for conflict resolution, and as the object of a primary human right which the OSCE has defined in very clear terms. During the year of the Norwegian chairmanship, we moved the issue of religion to the forefront of the OSCE agenda through expert-level and political-level conferences. We also sought to streamline the follow-up on the conclusions from these conferences into the standard operating procedures of the missions. It is too early to assess the impact of these efforts, and such an assessment should in any case be left for others to make. However, it remains clear that freedom of religion is a source of much conflict and abuse in OSCE participating states, and that the OSCE, therefore, must remain seized of the issue.

Part III

Freedom of Religion or Belief and the State

Chapter 13

Conscientious Objection

José de Sousa e Brito

I. The Right to Conscientious Objection: Boundaries

In a democracy, as a general rule, minorities should obey the law, which in principle is the will of the majority. There are two main exceptions. The first is in the case of an unjust law, because it offends human rights, which are more "fundamental" than the pretended rights created by such a law. This leads to a conflict between the principle of democratic order and the principle of the rule of law. But as these are both principles of democracy, as a system of principles, the conflict is solved by considering the law invalid or subject to judicial review, exposing it to civil disobedience or to a right of resistance, or even capable of justifying revolution. The second exception occurs when the law is a just law and an unassailable expression of the general will, in spite of which affected minorities may in good faith refuse to "surrender to the popular will,"[1] in the words of Justice Stone in a famous dissenting opinion in a Supreme Court case. This is the premise of conscientious objection. It provides the basis in a modern constitutional state for minorities to be able to assert a right to tolerance. In earlier times they had only the last recourse of political dissenters: the right to emigrate,[2] which in the case of the United States could easily be correlated with a right of free movement from state to state.

The right to conscientious objection is indeed the right to refuse a legal duty in the name of individual conscience. The conflict between law and conscience is resolved in such cases, because the principle of the inviolability of conscience prevails over the principle of generality of law. It is true that the conflict, which exists *prima facie*, is formally removed when the objection is generally recognized in the Constitution and is regulated in its exercise by subsequent general laws. But if the principle of generality of law is thus formally protected, it nevertheless remains true that the legal

[1] Minersville School District v. Gobitis, 310 US 586, 601 (1940).

[2] See Jean-Jacques Rousseau, *Du contract social,* 1.3, ch. 18 (*Oeuvres completes*, t. 3, Bibliothèque de la Pleiade, Paris: Gallimard, 1964), 436.

Tore Lindholm, W. Cole Durham, Jr., Bahia G. Tahzib-Lie (eds.), Facilitating Freedom of Religion or Belief: A Deskbook, *273–289.*

exception arises for reasons which are not included in those that were the basis of the constitutional and legal deliberations that create the legal duty. Rather, the grounds for the exception directly and entirely oppose the considerations that give rise to the legal duty from which exception is taken. In other words, it is not because the reasons for imposing a duty of military service do not apply to the conscientious objector that this duty is removed. It is because the objector is allowed to make his reasons prevail over those of the law, not because the law adopts them, though in exceptional cases, but because the law tolerates them out of respect for the freedom of conscience. Conscientious objection represents the transformation of the principle of tolerance, which is prior to and a social precondition of the constitutional state, into a human right.

The right to conscientious objection is one of the elements that constitutes the freedom of conscience. Such freedom protects conscience and its decisions not only internally against undue influence from outside—by coercion, brainwashing, drugs, etc.—but also externally as freedom to act in accordance with conscience. Finally, the freedom of conscience may conflict with a legal duty and prevail. In such cases there is a right to conscientious objection.

As with freedom of conscience and in contrast to freedom of religion, only individuals can claim conscientious objection. We do not think of conscientious objection as a right of corporations, churches, or minorities, in spite of its being sociologically a concern of minorities, mainly religious minorities.

Sometimes the law allows for voluntary exceptions to a rule, opening room for action according to conscience. For example, in Portugal, the body of the dead may be used to obtain vital organs for organ transplants unless the individual expressly declines in writing prior to death. Since the rule does not impose a duty (but instead creates a presumption of consent), these are not cases of conscientious objection.

II. Historical Development: From Liberty of Religion to Liberty of Conscience and from Liberty of Conscience to Conscientious Objection

A. Early Historical Developments

The constitutional history of the right to conscientious objection is intimately interwoven with that of liberty of conscience and its relation to religious liberty. Antecedents are to be found in an older history of ideas, highlighted for example by the apostle Paul's recognition of individual conscience as a source of the supreme law of action—the law written in the hearts and coincident with the law revealed by God for those "having not the law."[3] The invocation of conscience also appears as a principle of ecclesiastical and civil disobedience in religious matters exercised by Luther in the Diet of Worms of 1521 and by the protestant princes responding in 1529 to the Diet of Speyer.[4] Already a component of the Rhode Island Charter granted in 1663 by Charles II,

[3] Romans 2:14–15.

[4] Hajo Holborn, *A History of Modern Germany: The Reformation* (New York: A. A. Knopf, 1959).

liberty of conscience was regarded as essential to religious liberty.[5] The Constitution of Pennsylvania of 1776 makes no specific mention of religious liberty, which is understood however to be sufficiently subsumed in the notion of liberty of conscience. In addition to the right to conscientious objection to military service, it recognizes a right to conscientious objection in general: "Nor can any man who is conscientiously scrupulous of bearing arms be justly compelled thereto, if he will pay such equivalent, nor are the people bound by any laws, but such as they have in like manner assented to, for their common good."[6] Afterwards, this formulation appears in virtually identical terms in the Constitution of Vermont of 1777[7] but extends only to the aspect of military service in the constitutions of Delaware of 1776 and New Hampshire of 1784.[8]

B. The Idea of Conscience in the Constitution of the United States

Madison's original proposal for what became the religion clauses of the First Amendment of the Constitution of the United States referred to the rights of conscience: "The civil rights of none shall be abridged on account of religion belief or worship, [n]or shall any national religion be established, nor shall the full and equal rights of conscience be in any manner, nor on any pretence, infringed."[9] This clause on the rights of conscience was clearly intended to encompass the free exercise of religion. In the final version endorsed by the House of Representatives, a new clause on the free exercise of religion was introduced: "Congress shall make no law establishing religion, or to prevent the free exercise thereof or to infringe the rights of conscience."[10] The Senate narrowed the establishment clause and dropped the explicit reference to the rights of conscience clause, by adopting the following reading: "Congress shall make no law establishing articles of faith or a mode of worship, or prohibiting the free exercise of religion."[11] The deletion of the reference to "rights of conscience" may have reflected a view that the second phrase was simply redundant, but more likely it reflected the view that "free exercise of religion" was broader in its coverage than "rights of conscience," both because "free exercise" covered action as well as belief, and because free exercise protected communal religious practices as well as the individual.[12] Thus, free exercise included the rights of conscience, with the possible exception that at the time, rights of conscience may have been understood as protecting only

[5] Richard L. Perry and John C. Cooper, eds., *Sources of Our Liberties* (New York: New York University Press, 1972), 170: "[A]ll and everye person and persons may, from tyme to tyme and all tymes hereafter, freelye and fully hav and enjoye his and theyre owne judgements and consciences, in matter of religious concernements."

[6] Pensylvania Const, art. 8 (1776).

[7] Vermont Const, ch. 1, art. 9 (1777).

[8] Perry and Cooper, *Sources of our Liberties,* 330, 365, 339, 393.

[9] Proposal of James Madison, 8 June 1789, in *Annals of Congress,* ed. Joseph Gales, vol. 1 (Washington, DC: Gales and Seaton, 1834), 451.

[10] Proposal of Fisher Ames, 20 August 1789, in *Annals of Congress,* 796.

[11] *Documentary history of the First Federal Congress of the United States of America, March 4, 1789–March 3, 1791,* ed. Linda Grant De Pauw, vol. 1 (Baltimore: Johns Hopkins Universtiy Press, 1972), 166 (Senate Journal).

[12] Michael McConnell, "The Origins and Historical Understanding of Free Exercise of Religion," *Harvard Law Review* 103 (1990): 1409, 1488–1500.

religious and not secular belief systems.[13] It was in the conference committee of the two bodies, chaired by Madison, that the final text was adopted including a broader establishment clause. It should be noted that laws subsidizing religion are seen as laws "respecting the establishment of religion," even though they do not directly establish a state church; on the free exercise side, in contrast, reference to conscience was dropped, so that the final text read: "Congress shall make no law respecting an establishment of religion, or prohibiting the free exercise thereof."[14]

C. Conscience in the Constitutions of Europe

The constitutional evolution in Europe occurred in three successive steps: the first step was the separation of the liberty of conscience from religious liberty. Both are guaranteed separately in the German constitution of 1849, which was approved in Paulskirche but never entered into force (sec. 144: "Volle Glaubens- und Gewissensfreiheit" [full freedom of belief and conscience]), and in the Swiss constitution of 1874, art. 49 ("la liberté de conscience et de croyance est inviolable"). The German constitution of Weimar of 1919 (art. 35) repeats the formula outlined in Paulskirche, and, among others, the Portuguese constitution of 1911, art. 3, nr. 4, closely follows the Swiss formula.

The second step was the shift from protecting the inner freedom of conscience to include its external and even public expression. A corresponding right, restricted to the free exercise of religion and limited by "the general laws" (Weimar), or "l'ordre public et les bonnes moeurs" (Swiss), is found in the above mentioned constitutions. The important innovation of the *Grundgesetz* of the Federal Republic of Germany in 1949 is that the freedom of conscience is inviolable and not subject to any express limitation by the general laws or any other clause.

The third step was the recognition of the general freedom to act in practical life without violating conscience, which implies the right to conscientious objection whenever there is a conflicting legal duty. The *Grundgesetz* of the Federal Republic of Germany in 1949 states: "no one shall be compelled to bear arms in military service against his conscience. A federal law shall regulate the details" (art. 4[3]). The Austrian constitution follows suit (art. 9[a], sec. 3, added in 1975), as do the constitutions of Portugal of 1976 (art. 41[5]), and of Spain of 1978 (art. 30[2]). The Dutch constitution of 1983 simply states that "the law articulates the conditions upon which exemption from military service will be guaranteed to serious conscientious objection" and thus avoids creating an unambiguous constitutional right.[15] Similarly, the new Swiss Constitution of 1998 states that "the law provides for alternative civil service" without recognizing a right *per se*. In the wave of new constitutions of the former communist countries, the constitutional right to conscientious objection to military

---

[13] Ibid.

[14] US Const, amend. 1. On the history of the text, see Johnny H. Killian and Leland E. Beck, eds., *The Constitution of the United States of America: Analysis and Interpretation* (Washington, DC: Government Printing Office, 1987), 963–64.

[15] Vermeulen contends that there is no such right (Ben P. Vermeulen, "Conscientious Objection in Dutch Law," in European Consortium for Church-State Research, *Conscientious Objection in the EC Countries* [Milan: Giuffrè, 1992], 273).

service is recognized in Croatia (art. 47 of the constitution of 1991), Slovenia (art. 123 of the constitution of 1991), Estonia (art. 124 of the constitution of 1992), Slovakia (art. 25[2] of the constitution of 1992), the Czech Republic (art.15[3] of the constitution of 1992), and Russia (art. 28 of the constitution of 1993), among others.[16] The constitution of Malta of 1974 recognizes the same right if conscription is introduced (art. 36[2][c]). Outside Europe we also find the same right in the constitutions of countries such as Brazil, Uruguay, Guyana, Suriname, and Zambia.[17]

A general right to conscientious objection was recognized in the constitution of a sovereign state for the first time in the Portuguese constitution in art. 41(6), which was introduced by a constitutional amendment in 1982. It states: "The right to conscientious objection is guaranteed according to law." The constitution of the Cape Verde Islands followed (art. 48[8] has the same wording and was clearly influenced by the Portuguese model).

It must be kept in mind, however, that constitutional law is not restricted to the actual textual provisions of written constitutions. There is also constitutional custom and jurisprudence. It was namely the constitutional jurisprudence of the Supreme Court of the United States, the Federal Constitutional Court of Germany, and the Constitutional Court of Italy that developed the contours of a general right to conscientious objection before it was expressly articulated for the first time in the text of a constitutional provision (1982 in Portugal). Indeed, there are many common principles and customs in constitutional jurisprudence that transcend international borders in spite of widely divergent textual formulations.

D. Non-Constitutional Developments

At a non-constitutional level, constitutional law is often further developed by ordinary legislation. For example, the general right to conscientious objection recognized in the Portuguese constitution is now elaborated in article 12 of the Portuguese Law of Religious Freedom as follows:

> 1. Freedom of conscience includes the right to object to the compliance with laws that contradict the imperative doctrines of one's own conscience, within the limits of the rights and duties imposed by the Constitution and under the terms of the laws that may govern the exercise of conscientious objection.
> 2. The doctrines of conscience that are considered as imperative are those whose infringement involves a serious offense to one's moral integrity and, consequently make it inappropriate to require any other behaviour.
> 3. Conscientious objectors to military service, without excluding those who also invoke a conscientious objection to civil service, have the right to a civil service system, which respects the doctrine of their conscience, so long as it is compatible with the principle of equality.[18]

---

[16] A French translation of most of these constitutions is given by Michel Lusage, ed., *Constitutions d'Europe centrale, orientale et balte* (Paris: La documentation française, 1995).

[17] According to the official answers summarised in the report on conscientious objection to military service of the United Nations (New York, 1985), 23.

[18] Portuguese Law of Religious Freedom, art. 12, law no. 16/2001, 21 June 2001.

It may happen that at the level of ordinary legislation, and so in the practice of law, the right to conscientious objection is recognized to an even greater extent in countries where there is no explicit provision for it in the constitution.

In the Netherlands, for example, political objections to NATO and capitalism, selective objection to service in the Dutch armed services without rejecting one's subsequent participation in the armed violence of certain liberation movements, and even conscientious objection based on the belief that NATO is dominated by the Roman Catholic Church, are recognized.[19] Such objections would probably be accepted in Danish law as falling under the concept of "a deep-rooted ethical conviction of a political nature,"[20] but it is not likely that any of these objections would be accepted in most other countries, including Portugal, which has the broadest textual constitutional consecration of conscientious objection. We have seen however that there is no specific right to conscientious objection in the Dutch constitution, and it is doubtful if there is a constitutionally based conscientious objection right there with regard to military service.

At the statutory level, the recognition of a right of conscientious objection is at first restricted to military service and to religious objection by members of historic Christian peace churches. So while the Quakers, Mennonites and Brethren came to North America fleeing persecution in Europe, the colonial governments often exempted them from the duty of bearing arms and allowed them to perform alternative service in wartime as demonstrated by the Rhode Island statute of August 13, 1673.[21] Subsequently, conscientious objection became legally accepted in most other states of the United States and eventually by the federal government. During World War I the United States and Britain were the only major powers that allowed for conscientious objection. In the United States, section 4 of the Selective Draft Act of 18 May 1917 declared that "nothing in this Act shall be construed to require or compel any person to serve in army of the forces herein provided for who is found to be a member of any well recognized religious sect or organization at present organized and existing and whose existing creeds or principles forbid its members to participate in war in any form . . . but no person so exempted shall be exempted from service in any capacity that the President shall declare to be non-combatant." But at that time there were also new religious conscientious objectors who did not even accept alternative service, namely the Seventh-Day Adventists and the Jehovah's Witnesses. In addition there were conscientious objectors from nonpacifist mainstream churches and non-religious political objectors. The accepted definition of conscientious objection was first expanded by law to include non-religious ethical objectors in Denmark (since 1917),[22] Norway, Sweden, and the Netherlands. In these countries an objector was "only he who refused to

---

[19] Quoted by Vermeulen, 276 n.42.

[20] See Erik Siesly, "Conscientious Objection in Danish Law," in *Conscientious Objection in EC Countries,* 161.

[21] See John Whiteclay Chambers II, "Conscientious Objectors and the American State from Colonial Times to the Present," in *The New Conscientious Objection: From Sacred to Secular Resistance,* ed. Charles C. Moskos and John Whiteclay Chambers II (New York: Oxford University Press, 1993), 26. For more generally regarding what follows in the text, see "The Secularization of Conscience," in ibid., 4.

[22] Henning Sorensen, "Denmark: The Vanguard of Conscientious Objection," in Moskos and Chambers, *New Conscientious Objection,* 107.

serve because of his conviction that he may never kill a human being."[23] In Norway, the objection could be "based on serious religious conviction or on other serious grounds of conscience,"[24] but neither selective objection nor politically based objection was legally acceptable.

These countries were at the forefront of expanding conscientious objection by permitting objection to non-combatant alternative military service (and transferring to civilian alternative service) or even to civilian alternative service (and permitting to choose civil service), recognizing the "objection of nuclear pacifists" (e.g., Norway in 1990), etc. In most countries, however, the law of conscientious objection admits ethical objection only if it pertains to all kinds of war, but not merely objection to a particular war or to certain kinds of weapons.

The statutes have to conform to constitutional law, and there is a clear tendency towards a common doctrine of human rights among all constitutional and international human rights courts. The main purpose of this chapter will be to explore the major features of such a common doctrine with regard to conscientious objection and also some of the reasons supporting it in constitutional jurisprudence. A warning, however, must be made; the general approach advocated in this chapter is still far from achieving universal recognition. As the recent retrogression of the jurisprudence of the Supreme Court of the United States shows, this is an area where general agreement about what is binding law has not yet been reached; still some judges acknowledge a human right to conscientious objection in cases where other judges deny it.

III. Conscientious Objection in International Law

The Universal Declaration of Human Rights of 1948 has a far-reaching provision on freedom of thought, conscience, and religion (art. 18): "Everyone has the right to freedom of thought, conscience and religion; this right includes freedom to change his religion or belief, and freedom, either alone or in community with others and in public or private, to manifest his religion or belief in teaching, practice, worship and observance." A similar provision (with only the word order of the last phrase altered to read "worship, teaching, practice and observance") is followed in the European Convention on Human Rights of 1950 (art. 9[1]) and again in the International Covenant on Civil and Political Rights of 1966 (of which art. 18[1] is almost identical to art. 9[1] of the European Convention, except that the Covenant uses the phrase "[t]his right shall include freedom to have or to adopt a religion or belief of his choice," instead of "this right includes freedom to change his religion or belief"). Both the European Convention (art. 4[3][b]) and the Covenant (art. 8[3][c][ii] makes reference to conscientious objection in that they indicate that the term "forced or compulsory labour" shall not include "[a]ny service of a military character and, in countries where conscientious objection is recognized, any national service required by law of conscientious objectors" (in the words of the Covenant). It seems to follow that those two

[23] This was the case, for example, in a 1923 Dutch law (Vermeulen, "Conscientious Objection in Dutch Law," in *Conscientious Objection in the EC Countries,* 270).

[24] N. P. Gleditsch and N. I. Agoy, "Norway: Toward Full Freedom of Choice?" in Moskos and Chambers, *New Conscientious Objection,* 116 (citing a 1922 Norwegian law).

treaties do not hold that recognizing the right of conscientious objection to military service is mandatory. This is indeed the usual interpretation of the European Convention.[25] The same could be said of the *travaux preparatoires* of the Covenant,[26] and was also declared by the early jurisprudence of the UN Human Rights Committee.[27] But the Universal Declaration contains no such reference. The United Nations Human Rights Committee however, commenting in 1993 on art. 18 of the Covenant and cognizant of the fact that this right is not universally recognized by law or in practice, stated that "the Committee believes that such a right can be derived from art. 18, inasmuch as the obligation to use lethal force may seriously conflict with freedom of conscience and the right to manifest one's religion or belief."[28] In fact, since 1987[29] the Committee has consistently appealed for recognition of the right to conscientious objection to military service as a human right. Likewise in the Council of Europe there is a movement toward the recognition of such a right which enjoys the support of the Parliamentary Assembly[30] and the Committee of Ministers.[31]

IV. The Right to Conscientious Objection: Internal Boundaries

The right to conscientious objection necessarily conflicts with the very interests protected by the law that is objected to. Establishing its boundaries is a function of balancing the seriousness of the individual objection, measured by the burden that the law imposes on the conscience, on the one hand, against the weight of the interests that the law in question intends to protect or further on the other. Let us consider the main types of cases where such a balance has been struck in constitutional and international jurisprudence on human rights. In light of the wide array of dynamics at play here (such as strong public sentiment and conflicting legal theories), each tribunal or commission approaches the problem differently and explains or justifies its actions in accordance with the overall internal and external realities of each case. Some critical comments, however, are here in place, not only from an ethical point of view, but also

---

[25] Granbath Case (EComHR, 29 June 1967), Yb 10, 675; App. No. 5591/72 (EComHR, 43 Decision and Reports 161, 2 April 1973); App. No. 7705/76 (EComHR, 9 Decisions and Reports 196, 3 July 1977); App. No. 10410/83 (EComHR, 40 Decisions and Reports 203, 11 October 1984). See for example, Francis G. Jacobs, *The European Convention on Human Rights* (Oxford: Clarendon, 1975); G. Malinervi and J. A. Frowein in Louis-Edmond Pettiti, Emmannuel Décaux, and Pierre-Henri Imbert, *La Convention Européenne des Droits de l'Homme: Commentaire article par article* (Paris: Economica, 1986), 187, 354. For a dynamic interpretation, according to which conscientious objection is a manifestation of conviction according to art. 9(1), see R. Ergec, "Les dimensions européenes de l'objection de conscience" in *Conscientious Objection in the EC Countries,* 12.

[26] See Arcot Krishnaswami, *Study of Discrimination in the Matter of Religious Rights and Practices,* UN Doc. E/CN.4/Sub.2/200/Rev.1 (1960), ch. 3(B)(ii).

[27] L.T.K. v. Finland, UN Human Rights Committee, Comm. No. 185/1984. 40th Sess., supp. no. 540, A/40/40.

[28] Human Rights Committee General Comment 22(1993), UN Doc. CCPR/C/21/rev.1/ Add.4 (1993), reprinted in UN Doc. HRI/GEN/1/Rev.1 (1994), 35.

[29] UN Human Rights Committee, Resolution 1987/46 (1987), paras. 1–2 ; UN HR Committee, Resolution 1993/84 (1993), paras. 1 and 4; UN HR Committee, Resolution 1989/59 (1989), paras. 1–2.

[30] Recommendation 816 (1977).

[31] Recommendation R (87) 8.

from the viewpoint of public or legal reason, which takes into account the sources of law that command for each tribunal or commission the method of justifying the decision in each case.

A. Conscientious Objection to Military Service

1. Evolution of the Right to Conscientious Objection to Military Service

Clearly the central cases of conscientious objection are those of objection to military service. As the UN Committee on Human Rights said, "the obligation to use lethal force may seriously conflict with freedom of conscience and the right to manifest one's religion or belief."[32] An unconditional prohibition to killing, derived from Exodus 20:13 ("Thou shalt not kill") is usually invoked, as is Jesus's command of nonresistance (Matt. 5:39–41). Because of this, conscientious objectors were sometimes called "nonresistants" in the past.[33] There are no doubts about the centrality of the prohibition to kill in almost any code of conduct, so the test of seriousness of the burden of conscience is limited to the unconditional character of the particular prohibition and to the sincerity of adherence to the system of beliefs.

In the United States, when Congress instituted compulsory conscription in 1917, it exempted those persons who were adherents of a "well-recognized religious sect or organization . . . whose existing creed or principles [forbid] its members to participate in war in any form." [34] In 1940, Congress enlarged the exemption to include any person who "by reason of religious training and belief is conscientiously opposed to participation in war in any form."[35] In 1948, Congress defined "religious training and belief" to mean "an individual's belief in a relation to a Supreme Being involving duties superior to those arising from any human relation but [not including] essentially political, sociological, or philosophical views or a merely personal moral code."[36] In 1965, in *United States v. Seeger*, the Supreme Court said that "the test of belief 'in a relation to a Supreme Being' is whether a given belief that is sincere and meaningful occupies a place in the life of its possessor parallel to that filled by the orthodox belief in God of one who clearly qualifies for the exemption."[37] This was reaffirmed by the Court in *Welsh v. United States* in 1970, by stating that opposition to the war must "stem from the registrant's moral, ethical or religious beliefs about what is right and

---

[32] General Comment No. 22(48), para. 11.

[33] Cf. Moskos and Chambers, cit., 11.

[34] The Draft Act of 1917, 40 Stat. 76, 78.

[35] Selective Training and Service Act of 1940, Act of 16 September 1940, ch. 720, 54 Stat. 885 (1940).

[36] United States v. Seeger, 380 US 163, 165 (1965).

[37] Ibid., 165–66, 176. This was the main thrust of the *Torcaso* case, also of 1965, which was not a conscription but an oath case, where the court noted that "neither a State nor the Federal Government . . . can constitutionally pass laws or impose requirements which aid all religions as against non-believers, and neither can aid those religions based on a belief in the existence of God as against those founded on different beliefs." And a footnote explained, "Among religions in this country which do not teach what would generally be considered a belief in the existence of God are Buddhism, Taoism, Ethical Culture, Secular Humanism and others" (Torcaso v. Watkins, 367 US 488, 495 n.11 [1964]).

wrong and . . . these beliefs must be held with the strength of traditional religious convictions."[38] These definitions were given as interpretations of statutory law, but I think that they are what European constitutional jurisprudence calls "interpretation[s] in conformity with the Constitution," which is indeed a way of applying the Constitution. Such applications actually contribute to an understanding of the concept of "substantial burden": a practice that violates a belief which occupies a place in life parallel to the orthodox or traditional belief in God puts the same burden on the belief holder. In this way the Supreme Court aligned the law, invoking reasons of constitutional character (as noted in *Torcaso*), with the laws of Denmark, Norway, Sweden, and the Netherlands adopted between 1917 and 1923, but stopped short of recognizing a human right to conscientious objection to military service.

2. Alternative Service

One way of testing the seriousness of individual belief is by the willingness to perform alternative service, if the latter is not less burdensome than actual military service. For example, the German Federal Constitutional Court has ruled that it is permissible to take into consideration not only the duration of basic military service, but also periods of additional service (in particular reserve duty training).[39] Furthermore, the Court found that the actual burdens of military service, such as having to be on duty at irregular intervals or quartering in barracks, should also be taken into account. Consequently, the Court ruled that a longer duration for alternative civilian service, amounting to approximately one-third of the period of compulsive military service, is not unreasonable.

In similar a manner, the United Nations Human Rights Committee decided in *Järvinen v. Finland* [40] that the prolongation of the term for alternative service from twelve to sixteen months was based on reasonable and objective criteria, since applicants are assigned to civilian service solely on the basis of their own declarations. The new arrangements were designed to facilitate the administration of alternative service and removed from conscientious objectors the often difficult task of convincing the examination board of the sincerity of their beliefs.

In apparent contrast, the Italian Constitutional Court (decision no. 470 of 31 July 1985) declared art. 15 of the Draft Law, which established a difference in the duration of the service requirement of the objector (twenty months) versus that of the standard conscript (twelve months), to be unconstitutional, because it violated the principle of equality.

These three decisions take in account not only the right to conscientious objection, but also the principle of equality and are not necessarily contradictory. Each holding is based on a variety of factors causing burden of proof on the means of proof available.

In any case, willingness to perform alternative civilian service should not be the singular test of sincerity of belief since this would exclude absolute objectors (e.g., Jehovah's Witnesses), who likewise object to alternative service, from being considered

[38] Welsh v. United States, 398 US 333, 340 (1970).
[39] BVerfGE 69, 1 (22).
[40] UN Doc. CCPR/C/SR.1247.

objectors to military service, which they clearly are. Another serious question is that of acknowledging objection to alternative service, which may be justifiably excluded or restricted on the basis of the principle of equality. The awkward solution of this issue in the Belgian Draft Law,[41] which excludes then the very objection to military service, is unacceptable.

3. The Scope of Conscientious Objection to Military Service

How far does the right to conscientious objection to military service extend? Since it is the burden upon the conscience that is at stake, it seems that the specific content of the mandates of one's conscience should be irrelevant to the law. This question has been dealt with by the German Federal Constitutional Court in a decision that departed from the characterization of "conscientious decision" as a decision that exists only if acting against it would represent a serious burden upon one's conscience: "any serious moral decision, that is, oriented by the categories of 'good' and 'evil,' of which the individual has an internal experience as being binding and unconditionally obligatory for him in such a way that he would not be capable of acting against it without a serious violence against his conscience."[42]

The German Court concluded that the objection is acceptable if it is principled so that it covers all kinds of war, even if it is eventually conditioned in time by changes in the manner of prosecuting contemporary wars, but it is against the constitution if it is conditioned by a certain situation (*situationsbedingt*), by the participation in a specific war, in certain kinds of warfare, or under special conditions or with special weapons. This last restriction has been criticized in light of some constitutional doctrine that invokes the same definition of "conscientious decision" to derive two consequences. First, it is not the freedom of acting in accordance with conscience that is protected by the law, but immunity from being coerced into a decision which is unbearable for conscience, that is guaranteed before the law. As Böckenförde says, "in so far as it is an imperative court when it hears appeals, the conscience begins to act only when the personality as such, in its identity, is critically menaced ('I can't be one of those who does it')."[43] Second, "the question of conscience cannot be limited either by subject or by the content of conscience, or by reasons or motives";[44] "the person who has the fundamental right determines by herself—within the limits of the legal order of the constitutional State, which limit each exertion of freedom—the content, the dignity and the value of her own freedom."[45] It is true that the ultimate burden upon the conscience depends on the individual. But such a burden must necessarily

---

[41] Cf. Rik Torfs, "L'objection de conscience en Belgique," in *Conscientious Objection in EC Countries,* 219. Identical provisions of the Portuguese draft law of 1992 have now been revoked by art. 12 of the Law of Religious Liberty of 2001 (Law No. 16/2001 of 22 June 2001).

[42] BVerfGE 12, 45 (55).

[43] Böckenförde, 243; in the same line, Niklas Luhmann, "Die Gewissensfreiheit und das Gewissen" (1965), republished in *Ausdifferenzierungen des Rechts* (Frankfurt am Main: Suhrkampe, 1981), 326.

[44] Böckenförde, 242.

[45] Herbert Behtge, "Gewissensfreiheit," in *Handbuch des Staatsrechts der Bundesrepublik Deutschland,* vol. 6, ed. Josef Isensee and Paul Kirchhof (Heidelberg: C. F. Müller, 1989), sec. 137, 7.

be balanced with the compelling interest of the State in ensuring due respect for the war decision of the constitutional organs and the efficacy of the country's war effort. It is therefore reasonable to consider that the burden of acting against one's principled objection to war in general is weightier than the burden of acting against one's personal reservations about the justice of a certain war in a given situation, when balancing such burdens against the State interests that are at stake.

In *Gillette v. United States* in 1971, the Supreme Court addressed the issue of whether or not Selective Service Laws, covering only those individuals who object to all wars as a principle of conscience, presented a violation of the religion clauses of the First Amendment. The petitioner's first contention was that Congress interfered with the free exercise of religion clause by failing to relieve objectors to a particular war from the duty of military service, when the objection was religious or conscientious in nature. The Court declared that its past cases did not support the proposition that a posture of conscientious objection relieves an objector from conforming with colliding duties fixed by a democratic government. The Court found that the conscription law, as applied to an objector of a particular war, is far from unjustified. The government has a legitimate and overriding interest in procuring the manpower necessary for military purposes and maintaining an equitably administered draft service; the integrity of the Selective Service system would be threatened or compromised by the added difficulty of separating sincere conscientious objectors from fraudulent claimants.[46] The *Gillette* holding further clarified the concept of "compelling interest" as it applies to both the positions of the State and the individual. Later, in his dissenting opinion in *Smith,* Justice Blackmun contended that the State's interest must be "properly narrowed"[47] to the same plane of generality as the competing interest of the objector, i.e., to the governmental interest in refusing to make an exception for the religious practice.

B. Conscientious Objection to Abortion

The prohibition to kill is also invoked by conscientious objectors to abortion. Here, the State's interest in guaranteeing the scope of the law that confers a right to an abortion to a pregnant woman, along with other related interests, are only abridged if the abortion cannot be properly performed by competent medical personnel. Only in such cases is restriction admissible.

The Italian Constitutional Court[48] upheld the constitutionality of a legal provision that did not allow conscientious objection by the competent judge to an abortion sought by a female minor or a woman deemed mentally incompetent. An analogous decision could be expected in an action challenging a provision that does not permit hospital administrators to object to the performance of an abortion in his or her facility, since the law specifically guarantees the performance of an abortion on certain conditions.

---

[46] Gillette v. United States, 401 US 437 (1971).

[47] Employment Division, Department of Human Resources of Oregon v. Smith, 494 US 872, 910 (1990).

[48] Decision No. 196 (*Corte costituzionale,* 25 May 1987) 32, 1987, 1 (1460).

C. Expression Compelled against Conscience

The first group of conscientious objection cases in which the Supreme Court of the United States recognized the existence of a human right in this area consisted of cases of objection to express oneself against conviction. In the first case the objectors refused to salute the American flag, swear to defend the country, or to swear by or in the name of God.

Lilian and William Gobitis, aged twelve and ten, were Jehovah's Witnesses who had been taught not to worship any "graven image" (Ex. 20:5: "Thou shalt not bow down thyself to them"). They therefore refused to participate in daily flag ceremonies at their school in Pennsylvania. Participation in the flag ceremony was required as a condition for attendance in the public schools and so the Gobitis children were expelled. In *Minersville School District v. Gobitis*, the Supreme Court voted 8–1 to sustain participation in the flag ceremony as a valid requirement. Only Justice Stone dissented, claiming in a famous sentence that the majority's opinion was "no more than the surrender of the constitutional protection of the liberty of small minorities to the popular will." The guarantees of the First and Fourteenth Amendments must "be deemed to withhold from the state any authority to compel belief or the expression of it where that expression violates religious convictions."[49]

Three years later, *Gobitis* was overruled by *West Virginia State Board of Education v. Barnette*. After the *Gobitis* decision the West Virginia State Board of Education required all schools to conduct daily flag ceremonies in which all teachers and pupils were required to participate. Several Jehovah's Witnesses families sued for an injunction to stop enforcement of the policy. By a 6–3 vote the Supreme Court reversed *Gobitis*. The opinion of the Court was delivered by Justice Jackson and announced on Flag Day in 1943. He wrote:

> We can have intellectual individualism and the rich cultural diversities that we owe to exceptional minds only at the price of occasional eccentricity and abnormal attitudes. When they are so harmless to others or to the State as those we deal with here, the price is not too great. But freedom to differ is not limited to things that do not matter much. That would be a mere shadow of freedom. The test of its substance is the right to differ as to things that touch the heart of the existing order. If there is any fixed star in our constitutional constellation, it is that no official, high or petty, can prescribe what shall be orthodox in politics, nationalism, religion, or other matters of opinion or force citizens to confess by word or act their faith therein. If there are any circumstances which permit an exception, they do not now occur to us.[50]

The *Barnette* Court took a very strong position by dismissing the utilitarian argument that would restrict conscientious objection to those cases when its application is harmless to others or to the State.[51]

---

[49] Minersville School District v. Gobitis, 310 US 586, 606, 604 (1940).

[50] West Virginia State Board of Education v. Barnette, 319 US 624, 641–42 (1943).

[51] These are the cases of objections against duties created by paternalistic laws, cases of objection to duties to avoid harm to others or to the State that can be satisfied by fulfilling other duties through alternative service or by indemnity and perhaps cases of public-interest laws concerned with the provision of common goods (taxation, anti-pollution laws, etc.) where the exemption of a single individual makes no significant difference to attaining the envisaged good. These are the cases allowed for by Joseph Raz, *The Authority of Law*

Another group of cases relates to the naturalization oath. Under the oath, applicants had to swear "to support and defend the Constitution and the law of the United States of America against all enemies, foreign and domestic." The naturalization service interpreted this language to require a willingness to bear arms in defense of the country as a prerequisite of citizenship, so it denied the naturalization applications of two women pacifists and a fifty-year-old Yale Divinity School professor who said that he would fight only in wars that he believed to be morally justified. In *United States v. Schwimmer* (1929) the Court upheld the position of the naturalization service as reasonable.[52] But in 1946, in *Girouard v. United States*, the Court reversed its earlier holding and stated that the oath did not expressly require persons seeking naturalization to swear to bear arms and ruled that this interpretation should not be read into the oath. Congress could not have intended to deny citizenship in a country noted for its protection of religious beliefs to persons whose religious beliefs prevented them from bearing arms.[53]

Finally, in *Torcaso v. Walkins* (1961), the Court held that the provision of the Maryland Constitution requiring a declaration of belief in the existence of God as part of a religious test for public office was unconstitutional. The Court, besides invoking the First and Fourteenth Amendments, noted that art. 6 of the United States Constitution provides that "no religious test shall ever be required as a qualification to any Office or public Trust under the United States."

D. Objection to Acting against One's Belief

The step from objection to express oneself against one's belief, to objection to acting against one's belief was only taken by the Supreme Court of the United States in the 1960s. For this the Court had to overcome a historical distinction on the basis of which the Court had upheld federal legislation against the Mormons because of their practice of polygamy in the nineteenth century. Although laws "cannot interfere with mere religious beliefs and opinions, they may with practices" said the Court in *Reynolds v. United States* in 1879.[54] In 1961, in *Braunfeld v. Brown*, Chief Justice Warren, delivering the Court's opinion, made a general assessment of this doctrine and introduced important qualifications:

> [I]n *Reynolds v. United States*, this Court upheld the polygamy conviction of a member of the Mormon faith despite the fact that an accepted doctrine of his church then imposed upon its male members the duty to practice polygamy. And, in *Prince v. Commonwealth of Massachusetts* . . . this Court upheld a statute making it a crime for a girl under eighteen years of age to sell any newspapers, periodicals or merchandise in public places despite the fact that a child of the Jehovah's Witnesses faith believed

(Oxford: Clarendon, 1983), 283–86. Raz is not a utilitarian but he admits that "the argument outlined agrees in principle with the utilitarian approach" (ibid., 281).

52 United States v. Schwimmer, 279 US 644 (1929); United States v. Macintosh, 283 US 605 (1931); United States v. Bland, 283 US 636 (1931).

53 Girouard v. United States, 328 US 61 (1946).

54 Reynolds v. United States, 98 US 145, 166 (1879). Similarly, in Davis v. Beason, 133 US 333, 345 (1890), the Court stated: "Crime is not the less odious because sanctioned by what any particular sect may designate as religion."

> that it was her religious duty to perform this work. . . . Of course, to hold unassailable all legislation regulating conduct which imposes solely an indirect burden on the observance of religion would be a gross oversimplification. If the purpose or effect of a law is to impede the observance of one or all religions or is to discriminate invidiously between religions, that law is constitutionally invalid even though the burden may be characterised as being only indirect. But if the State regulates conduct by enacting a general law within its power, the purpose and effect of which is to advance the State's secular goals, the statute is valid despite its indirect burden on religious observance unless the State may accomplish its purpose by means which do not impose such a burden.[55]

In conclusion, the Court upheld the validity of a Pennsylvania Sunday closing law challenged by an Orthodox Jew who observed the Jewish Sabbath and closed his clothing and furniture store on Saturday. The Court found that, although the law imposed an incidental burden by making certain religious practices more expensive, it advanced the secular purpose of providing citizens with a uniform day of rest.

1. Accommodating Religious Belief in the Workplace

Two years later the Court made the decisive step from belief to practice in *Sherbert v. Verner* (1963). Adell Sherbert was fired from her job at a South Carolina textile mill because, as a Seventh-Day Adventist, she refused to work on Saturdays. On the grounds that she refused to accept available work, the State denied her unemployment compensation benefit claims. Overturning the State's ruling by a 7–2 vote, the Court, speaking through Justice Brennan explained that the State's action forced Sherbert either to abandon her religious principles in order to work, or to maintain her religious precepts and forfeit unemployment compensation benefits. "Governmental imposition of such a choice puts the same kind of burden upon the free exercise of religion as would a fine imposed against appellant for her Saturday worship,"[56] Brennan wrote. "Only the gravest abuses, endangering paramount interest, give occasion for permissible limitation,"[57] he said. Prevention of fraudulent claims was the only reason the State advanced for denying benefits to *Sherbert*, Brennan noted. To justify that denial, he wrote, the State must show that "no alternative forms of regulation [aimed at preventing such fraud] would combat such abuses without infringing first amendment rights."[58] In this way *Sherbert* introduced the "*Sherbert*" test which states that governmental actions that substantially burden a religious practice must be justified by a compelling governmental interest.

2. Conscientious Objection to School Attendance

Another important application and expansion of the *Sherbert* case was made in 1972 in *Wisconsin v. Yoder* involving conscientious objection to compulsory school attendance. Old Order Amish parents refused to send their children to school beyond the

---

[55] Braunfeld v. Brown, 366 US 599, 607 (1961).
[56] Sherbert v. Verner, 374 US 398, 404 (1963).
[57] Ibid., 406, quoting Thomas v. Collins, 323 US 516, 530 (1945).
[58] Ibid., 407.

eighth grade, because a high school education engendered values contrary to traditional Amish beliefs, which hold that salvation may be obtained only by living in religious, agrarian communities separate from the world and worldly influences. The Supreme Court said that:

> [C]ompulsory school attendance to age 16 for Amish children carries with it a very real threat of undermining the Amish community and religious practice as they exist today; they must either abandon belief and be assimilated into society at large, or be forced to migrate to some other and more tolerant region. . . .
>
> The Amish alternative to formal secondary school education has enabled them to function effectively in their day-to-day life under self-imposed limitations on relations with the world, and to survive and prosper in contemporary society as a separate, sharply identifiable and highly self-sufficient community for more than 200 years in this country. In itself this is strong evidence that they are capable of fulfilling the social and political responsibilities of citizenship without compelled attendance beyond the eighth grade at the price of jeopardizing their free exercise of religious belief. . . .
>
> [A] State's interest in universal education, however highly we rank it, is not totally free from a balancing process when it impinges on fundamental rights and interests, such as those specifically protected by the Free Exercise Clause of the First Amendment. . . .
>
> Where fundamental claims of religious freedom are at stake, . . . [the Court] cannot accept such a sweeping claim . . . [that the State's interest in compulsory education is compelling] despite its admitted validity in the generality of cases. [W]e must searchingly examine the interests that the State seeks to promote . . . and the impediment to those objectives that would flow from recognizing the claimed Amish exemption.[59]

In *Yoder*, the Amish parents likewise demonstrated the existence of a substantial or severe burden, so the Court upheld the Amish parents' conscientious objection in this case. The Court accepted the claim that the Amish lifestyle and attitudes toward education are inseparable from and an integral part of the basic tenets of their religion, indeed as much a part of their religious belief and practices as baptism, the confessional, or a Sabbath may be for others. Enforcement of the State's compulsory education law would "gravely endanger if not destroy the free exercise of respondents' religious beliefs."[60] As Justice Blackmun again rightly interprets, it is not a matter of religious doctrine, but a matter of evaluating the severity of burden, to ask if it endangers or destroys free exercise or if the exception is "vital . . . to the protection of values promoted by the right of free exercise.[61]

E. Unfortunate American Retrogression

Unhappily, the inspiring advances of *Yoder,* which could help bring the American jurisprudence in line with that of Europe, were subsequently abandoned.

---

[59] Wisconsin v. Yoder, 406 US 205, 214, 218, 221, 225 (1972).
[60] Ibid., 219.

With *Employment Division, Department of Human Resources of Oregon v. Smith* (1990),[62] the Court retrogressed to the rule of *Reynolds v. United States* (1878),[63] which bluntly held that although laws "cannot interfere with mere religious beliefs and opinions, they may with practices." The *Smith* Court upheld a state law disqualifying employees for unemployment compensation because of the sacramental use of peyote at a ceremony of their Native American Church. Justice Scalia, who delivered the opinion of the Court, did not apply the *Sherbert* test, as Justice O'Connor (who concurred in judgement) proposed, saying that Oregon has a compelling interest in prohibiting the possession of peyote by its citizens. Speaking as if *Sherbert* was already dead latter, Scalia wrote, "Even if we were inclined to breathe into *Sherbert* some life beyond the unemployment compensation field, we would not apply it to require exemptions from a generally applicable criminal law."[64]

Smith, then, is a clear retrogression. The fundamental case of conscientious objection is the objection to compulsory military service, which too is undoubtedly an exemption from a generally applicable criminal law.

---

[61] Ibid., 221.
[62] 494 US 872.
[63] 98 US 145, 166.
[64] Ibid., at 890, 903.

Chapter 14

The Right to Autonomy in Religious Affairs

Roland Minnerath

I. Introduction

The autonomy of religious or belief communities in structuring their own affairs is one of the crucial features of any meaningful system of freedom of religion or belief. The ecclesiastical and social structures of religious communities are not merely accidental features that can be refashioned by the state without altering essence. Nor are they simply convenient vehicles for expression of individual belief. Often these structures are themselves the focus of deeply held beliefs. Whether there should be a pope and bishops, what the nature of religious hierarchy (or nonhierarchy) should be, how monastic life should be structured (or whether monastic life should be fostered at all), the role of priesthood and authority—these and countless similar questions have long been highly contested matters in the religious sphere. Practical matters of day-to-day administration are also infused with religious significance: who is entitled to ordain or be ordained, who defines the mission of the organization, who is charged with leadership responsibilities for the religious community, who is assigned to work in which position—these are not merely secular decisions.

Moreover, individual freedom of conscience for most is intimately tied to a community of belief, and if that community is not free to shape itself, the conscience of its individual believers is inevitably compromised. Religious authenticity, for both the individual and the community, cannot be fully achieved if communal autonomy is impaired.

Further, at the level of relations between religious institutions and the state, religious autonomy is clearly one of the central issues. The degree of separation or cooperation between belief communities and the state is partially about assuring state neutrality so that the engine of the state cannot be utilized by some either to procure privileges for themselves or to impose their beliefs on others. But it is also fundamentally about protecting the autonomy of religious communities from state intervention and the risks of lost authenticity that result from excessive attention to state incentives (whether positive or negative). Protection of the autonomy of collective, corporate religious activity is thus vital both to individual claims of conscience and to appropriate structuring of the relationship between religion and the state.

Tore Lindholm, W. Cole Durham, Jr., Bahia G. Tahzib-Lie (eds.), Facilitating Freedom of Religion or Belief: A Deskbook, *291–319.*

The aim of this chapter is to trace the emerging consensus that the right of a religious community to autonomy in its own affairs is a crucial component of freedom of religion or belief. It suggests that a consensus has been reached as to the institutional autonomy of religious organizations in the law of nations despite great variety among differing constitutional and legal traditions on the issue. In the past, this right has often been described as a right to "autonomy in *internal* religious affairs." The better thinking in this area, however, has recognized that the autonomy in question extends beyond strictly "internal" matters to include a broader range of issues involved in carrying out a religious mission. Thus, in German thought, references to autonomy in internal affairs have been largely supplanted by references to a community's "own affairs" *(eigene Angelegenheiten)*.[1] This locution does not work quite as well in English as it does in German, but the idea is clear: religious organizations should have autonomy in a sphere appropriately defined in terms of their own affairs. The term "autonomy" suggests that there are corporate religious activities over which the state acknowledges it has no competence. While the phrase "internal religious affairs" also suggests that there are religious activities that the state lacks competence to regulate, it suggests a circle with a shorter radius, not giving sufficient scope for the full range in which autonomy is necessary and appropriate to fully protect freedom of religion. But in light of the more established pattern of speaking of "internal affairs," it will suffice in this chapter to retain the older locution, while recognizing that it is intended to cover not merely the matters that are strictly internal to the life of a religious community, but also those that are internal to what can appropriately be characterized as its "own" sphere of activity.

Internal autonomy in this broader sense has two dimensions that might in theory be either linked or dissociated: 1) autonomy of belief, and 2) institutional autonomy. Autonomy of belief covers the right of a religious organization to define, elaborate, and control its own doctrine. Institutional autonomy connotes the right of a religious organization to self-administration according to the rules and demands of the religion itself. As this chapter will demonstrate, there is not a single unitary approach among nations as to the right to autonomy in internal religious affairs. Moreover, international human rights instruments tend to focus on individual rights and thus often have not expressly addressed religious autonomy as a corporate right.[2] Yet the existence of such a right is implicit in the encompassing right to freedom of religion or belief.

The idea of religious autonomy as a corporate right, as distinguished from an individual right to freedom of religion or belief, challenges the present individualist culture of human rights and related understandings of the rule of law. Individual rights protecting freedom of conscience, religion, or belief are clearly guaranteed by international law, grounded on the dignity of the human being. Not so explicitly assured are the corporate rights of religious organizations, which are often more a matter of inference and implication. When corporate rights are mentioned in international instruments, they are typically described as though they are derivative from individual rights.[3] Religious organizations

---

[1] See, e.g., Axel Freiherr von Campenhausen, "Church Autonomy in Germany," in *Church Autonomy: A Comparative Survey,* ed. Gerhard Robbers (Frankfurt am Main: Peter Lang, 2001), 77, 78–79.

[2] Note, however, that principle 16(d) of the Vienna Concluding Document in the Helsinki Process has expressly addressed key autonomy issues. Decisions of the European Court of Human Rights have also recognized the religious autonomy dimensions of freedom of religion or belief under article 9 of the European Convention. See Section III(B) of this chapter.

themselves often neglect to assert collective autonomy claims, in part because their interests are for the most part adequately protected by individual rights, and in part because other issues often claim greater urgency. But religion implies sharing the same belief in community with others. Accordingly, individual religious freedom implicitly requires a corporate or communal dimension. Indeed, while no international instrument expressly states that religious bodies or churches have an original right to exist or to protection of their internal autonomy, it is important to remember that historically, church autonomy as a corporate right preceded individual members' rights as later proclaimed in international instruments.

A. Historical Origins of the Claim for Autonomy in Internal Affairs

It is no surprise that problems of autonomy in church-state relations have arisen principally out of the Christian tradition. The demand for autonomy tends to be less important when religion is mainly a type of social and civic ritual devoid of strong conscientious beliefs. For example, in a number of ancient civilizations, civil servants managed both religious ceremonies and other secular needs of the society. Serving as a priest was often a stepping stone in a civil official's career. A claim for religious autonomy seems pointless where a religion does not call for an organization differentiated from society itself, where there is no clergy separate from other state officers, and where there is no doctrine to keep and proclaim. In contrast, by its very nature, the Christian Church from the beginning was a community that transcended ethnic, social, and cultural boundaries.[4] Christianity cannot simply be identified with a nation and even less so with a political order, even if it often was and continues to be in the Eastern churches.

But internal autonomy has not always been pursued with the same intensity in all Christian churches. For example, the Catholic Church and the Anglo-Saxon nonconformist Protestant churches of the seventeenth century have claimed autonomy in internal religious affairs, while the Eastern Orthodox and major Protestant churches have not. As this section explains, there are three principal models of autonomy that have grown out of the Christian history of church-state relations: 1) the Catholic independent papacy model, 2) the Protestant nonconformist church model, and 3) the American separation of church and state model. This section provides a historical overview of the emergence of the right to religious autonomy, first identifying the differences between the Catholic and Orthodox approaches to claims of autonomy, then discussing the historical backdrop of the Catholic Church's struggle for autonomy, and finally outlining the major features of these three models of church-state relations.

---

[3] Thus, article 18 of the ICCPR states that the right to "freedom of thought, conscience and religion" includes "freedom, either individually or in community with others and in public or private, to manifest his religion or belief in worship, observance, practice and teaching." The collective dimension is recognized, but the focus is on the individual.

[4] Judaism, in contrast, blurs ethnic and religious belonging, though autonomy has certainly been important to Jewish communities in a variety of historical settings. In Islam, the Umma is both a civil and religious community of believers. Hinduism and Confucianism are closely related to a culture and a legal system. Buddhism transcends ethnic groups but tends to call for withdrawal from the world in ways that could benefit from autonomy but tend not to lead to assertions of autonomy rights. Given the close nexus between these other religions and the communities in which they are found, it is no wonder that the claim for institutional autonomy of religious organizations comes mainly from the Christian experience.

B. Historical Differences between the Catholic and Eastern Orthodox Churches Regarding Autonomy

A striking difference between the Catholic and Orthodox understanding of the church-state relationship is revealed in their differing approaches to church autonomy. In the Byzantine Church, which evangelized the areas of central and eastern Europe, there is a clear understanding of church subordination to the political ruler. The *basileus* (Roman emperor) and later the Russian tsar were the effective heads of their respective churches.[5] Thus, the distinction between the church as a community of believers and the church as the body politic was nearly eliminated. In contrast, in the Latin West the papacy struggled to maintain the distinction between political and ecclesiastical spheres. This was a long process, but ultimately concluded in a clear understanding that the ecclesiastical body cannot absorb or be absorbed by the political one.

In the Byzantine model the church did not always have autonomy in matters of doctrine and worship, and certainly not in matters of institutional and structural policy. In the West, the church claimed to be autonomous in both respects. In the East, canon law was an autonomous ecclesiastical legal system, but it was also part of the civil law complemented, if necessary, by the *nomocanones* (civil laws on church matters). According to the Byzantine Constitution inspired by Patriarch Photios (*Eisagogè*, around 880), the Christian empire was governed by two heads—the emperor and the patriarch—in which obviously the former had the effective institutional power. In Russia, the church was even more completely governed by the tsar, who suppressed the Patriarchate and ruled over all religious issues as if the church were just one government ministry among others. Doctrine was left to the clergy, but the whole institution of the church remained in the hands of the political ruler.

What happened with the Reformation in the West? Like the Eastern Orthodox churches, churches that separated from Rome in Lutheran and Anglican realms became official state churches. The political ruler became "Head of the Church," or *summus episcopus* (highest bishop). Church affairs were administered by secular princes and later by democratically elected parliaments. Internal autonomy of these Protestant churches was extremely limited: the king appointed clergy, prayer books were approved by Parliament, and secular law determined the extent of pastoral competence. The classical Scandinavian state churches and the Anglican Church in Great Britain are examples of this lack of doctrinal and institutional autonomy.[6]

C. Historical Development of the Catholic Church's Claim to Autonomy

Under the slogan *libertas ecclesiae* (freedom for the church), the eleventh-century popes struggled to assert their autonomy from the secular princes on the issue of church autonomy. At stake was the freedom to elect bishops and abbots according to the rules of the

---

[5] Of course there were variants on this model in the West, as in the case of Denmark-Norway from 1537–1814.

[6] Not surprisingly, autonomy considerations have proven to be a major factor in the recent disestablishment of the state church in Sweden. See E. Kenneth Stegeby, "An Analysis of the Impending Disestablishment of the Church of Sweden," *BYU L. Rev.* (1999): 703. Of course, the fact that a secular ruler also served as head of the church did not necessarily entail state insensitivity to religious concerns. Some, such as

church. The significance of the so-called "Gregorian Reform" cannot be underestimated. It signaled the will of the church in the West to claim not only doctrinal autonomy, but also institutional autonomy. Later, in the era of absolutism, the Catholic Church could not escape the general trend of the European monarchies to control the institutional life of the churches. This control was particularly strict in the Portuguese and Spanish colonies overseas. Nearly everywhere, the monarchs appointed the bishops and severely limited their communications with Rome. The difference with Anglican and Lutheran monarchies was one of principle. Catholic monarchs could never claim to be the heads of their churches. Wherever they enjoyed the capacity to appoint bishops, they admitted that this was not an innate right, but a privilege bestowed on them through a concordat. The concordats of the absolutist era at least served to maintain the principle of institutional autonomy of the church. Intrusions into internal church functions by the monarchs were considered temporary concessions by the pope. While this arrangement could be considered a fiction, the fiction kept alive the church's ideals of autonomy, in the expectation of more favorable times.

During the eighteenth century, Catholic canonists developed a new approach to the captive situation imposed on the church. Their efforts were directed against both the practice of absolutism and its justification by Protestant scholars such as Samuel Pufendorf and Justus Henning Böhmer. The latter asserted that the church is nothing more than a free association of believers organized according to the rules of the state. The Catholic canonists responded that the church is an institution that goes back to Christ, and Christ himself bestowed upon the church all the means necessary for it to carry out its mission. The church in this understanding is not a free association resulting merely from the will of its members. Moreover, the rules according to which the church is organized are not secular rules. The laws of the church are genuine and true laws, and they differ in their essence from the laws of the state that aim to provide the temporal common good of society. The church itself is an original and separate juridical order, different from that of the state. The church, according to the canonists, is a "perfect society," meaning that it has all necessary features to function just as the state does. This means the church has all the legal and institutional means it needs to perform its goals. It expects no institutional help from the state. The state in this view must recognize that the church is autonomous in its own sphere, and, conversely, the church must recognize the autonomy of the state in its own realm. This doctrine was the strongest expression to date regarding the internal autonomy of the church. In short, church and state relate to each other on the basis of legal equality.

D. Three Models of Religious Autonomy

1. The Church as an Independent Sovereign

This brings us to the first and unquestionably the strongest model of religious autonomy: that associated with the history of the Catholic Church as an independent sovereign. In this model, church and state are related on the basis of legal equality. The specific qualification of the Catholic Church, attested by history and doctrine, as a

---

Christian III, were highly devout, theologically able, and had competence in this area that could have matched that of the papacy. Thus, lack of a clear distinction between church and state did not necessarily impair religious autonomy.

sovereign subject of international law, is in line with this doctrine. The Catholic Church maintains its character as a trans-national organization with an internal legal system totally independent of secular legal rules. This independence culminates in the independence of the papacy from any secular state or jurisdiction. The purpose of the creation of the Vatican City State in 1929 was precisely to give the Holy See the visible independence corresponding to its sovereignty in ecclesiastical matters. The latter has never been put in jeopardy. It flows from the self-understanding that the Catholic Church has always developed with numerous and varied political regimes. The contribution of the Catholic Church to the notion of church autonomy has provided a significant historical pattern. It can be said that this model, particularly its notion that the church is independent of and stands on equal footing with the state, has attracted the adherence of other churches or religious organizations in their understanding of church-state relations in the present conditions of the rule of law. In this field, the Catholic model has anticipated the future.

2. The Nonconformist Church Model

The second model of church autonomy is linked to the emergence of the nonconformist churches of the seventeenth century. With the Tolerance Act of 1689, Britain acknowledged other dissident churches in addition to the established church. Among those nonconformist religious groups, the Quakers, and later the Methodists, set up church organizations free from state control, but not from all state regulation. Members of many of these nonconformist churches emigrated to America, which gave birth to a radical new experiment. The first immigrants were nonconformist groups, with no king or pope, but with the Word of God. These religious communities in New England did not want to establish a religion—they wanted the freedom to worship according to conscience.

3. The American Model: Separation of Church and State

In 1791 the First Amendment of the United States Constitution outlined the aspiration for a new relationship between church and state: "Congress shall make no law respecting an establishment of religion or prohibiting the free exercise thereof."[7] This was the fruit of the American experiment of a plurality of peoples and religions deciding to live in the same state. The state must be religiously neutral, but not hostile to religion. At the same time, as the *Declaration of Independence* of 1776 clearly shows, this state would not be antireligious. It would not be confessional, but would respect all religions. In this the American State clearly found its own way to carry out the Christian enjoinder to "Render therefore unto Caesar the things which be Caesar's, and unto God the things which be God's"[8]—namely, by drawing a distinction between the religious and political order, while at the same time acknowledging, at least in the *Declaration of Independence,* the role of God as "the Creator," the "Supreme Judge," and "Divine Providence."[9] The

---

[7] United States Constitution, amend. I.

[8] Luke 20:25.

[9] Current United States Supreme Court jurisprudence has given the Establishment Clause of the First Amendment a more secularist meaning, but originally a strong case can be made that the aim of the First Amendment was to guarantee that the federal government (through Congress) would not make any laws dealing with establishments of religion that existed in the various states. See Frederick Mark Gedicks, *The*

Jeffersonian "wall of separation" was designed not only to keep religion from dominating the state, but to assure that religious autonomy would be protected so that the "garden" of the church would not be invaded by the wilderness of the state.[10]

In many ways the American experience has provided one of the richest stores of experience in protecting religious autonomy. In part because principles of religious freedom were constitutionally entrenched there earlier than in other countries, there has been a longer period during which the full range of autonomy issues could be recognized and constitutionally anchored. Because the evolution of strong protections of religious autonomy unfolded earlier in the United States than elsewhere, it will be helpful to describe this process here before proceeding to a description of European developments.

Most analyses of the law of religious freedom in the United States focus on chains of precedent deriving either from the non-establishment clause or the free exercise clause of the First Amendment to the United States Constitution. While the right to religious autonomy is obviously protected by these two clauses, the most significant cases dealing with religious autonomy form a third and independent strand in American constitutional thought that is broadly anchored in the First Amendment, but not necessarily tied exclusively to either the non-establishment or the free exercise clause.[11] The third strand of cases grows out of situations involving controversies within religious communities that reach secular courts in the form of disputes over control of church property or ecclesiastical office. Over time, these cases have forged profound and rigorous constraints on the authority of government institutions to intrude into religious affairs. Europeans, who have typically experienced the separationist model in anticlerical versions quite hostile to religion, often assume that American separationism is infused with a similar spirit. In fact, American separationism is probably better interpreted as a model in which separation of religion and state is pursued to protect religious autonomy. This is particularly evident in the religious controversy cases.

The first major case in this chain of precedents, *Watson v. Jones*,[12] involved a post–Civil War dispute in Kentucky between factions in a church that had divided over the slavery issue. A struggle ensued over which faction should own the church building.

Rhetoric of Church and State (Durham, N.C.: Duke University Press, 1995); Steven D. Smith, *Foreordained Failure: The Quest for a Constitutional Principle of Religious Freedom* (New York: Oxford University Press, 1995).

[10] Mark DeWolfe Howe, *The Garden and the Wilderness: Religion and Government in American Constitutional History* (Chicago: University of Chicago Press, 1965).

[11] Legal scholars have advanced arguments that the autonomy cases should in fact be conceptualized as deriving from one or the other of the main branches of the First Amendment religion clause. Thus, Douglas Laycock argued in a seminal article in 1981 that the religious autonomy cases should be understood as a branch of free exercise doctrine. Douglas Laycock, "Towards a General Theory of the Religion Clauses: The Case of Church Labor Relations and the Right to Church Autonomy," *Colum. L. Rev.* 81 (1981): 1373. Carl Esbeck, in contrast, has contended that the autonomy cases should be understood as an aspect of non-establishment principles. Carl Esbeck, "The Establishment Clause as a Structural Constraint on Governmental Power," *Iowa L. Rev.* 84 (1998): 1. There are also some references in Supreme Court cases linking the autonomy cases to a particular clause. See, e.g., Serbian Eastern Orthodox Diocese v. Milivojevich, 426 US 696, 734 (Rehnquist, J., dissenting); Presbyterian Church v. Mary Elizabeth Hull Memorial Presbyterian Church, 393 US 440, 449 (1969); Kedroff v. St. Nicholas Cathedral, 344 US 94, 116, 121–22 (1952). The Court has, in general, avoided grounding the autonomy cases exclusively in either the free exercise or the non-establishment clause, referring more broadly to their grounding in the First Amendment generally.

[12] 80 US 679 (1871).

The Supreme Court analyzed the case on the basis of common law principles governing civil associations. The Court rejected English precedents, which decided such issues on the basis of a "departure from doctrine" test. That is, in the case of a controversy, a group would retain control of church property if it could show that the rival group had departed from the doctrinal position characteristic of the religious body before the dispute emerged. The thought was that the property was intended to be held for the benefit of those with the original beliefs. The Court reasoned that such a view might make sense in a country with an established church, where "the Lord Chancellor . . . [is the] representative of the Established Church, . . . and whose judicial decision may be, and not unfrequently is, invoked in cases of heresy and ecclesiastical contumacy."[13] But this approach was inappropriate in a country committed to religious freedom. In what has become one of the classic statements of the principles undergirding protection of religious autonomy, the Court stated:

> In this country the full and free right to entertain any religious belief, to practice any religious principle, and to teach any religious doctrine which does not violate the laws of morality and property, and which does not infringe personal rights, is conceded to all. The law knows no heresy, and is committed to the support of no dogma, the establishment of no sect. The right to organize voluntary religious associations to assist in the expression and dissemination of any religious doctrine, and to create tribunals for the decision of controverted questions of faith within the association, and for the ecclesiastical government of all the individual members, congregations, and officers within the general association, is unquestioned. All who unite themselves to such a body do so with an implied consent to this government, and are bound to submit to it. But it would be a vain consent and would lead to the total subversion of such religious bodies, if any one aggrieved by one of their decisions could appeal to the secular courts and have them reversed. It is of the essence of these religious unions, and of their right to establish tribunals for the decision of questions arising among themselves, that those decisions should be binding in all cases of ecclesiastical cognizance, subject only to such appeals as the organism itself provides for.[14]

The Court concluded that in assessing controversies, civil courts should defer to the conflict resolution structures that have been developed by religious communities themselves and should avoid second-guessing the decisions of such bodies, including decisions as to the appropriate scope of jurisdiction of ecclesiastical decision-making bodies. "It is easy to see," the Court remarked,

> that if the civil courts are to inquire into all these matters, the whole subject of the doctrinal theology, the usages and customs, the written laws, and fundamental organization of every religious denomination may, and must, be examined into with minuteness and care, for they would become, in almost every case, the criteria by which the validity of the ecclesiastical decree would be determined in the civil court. This principle would deprive these bodies of the right of construing their own church laws, would open the way to all the evils which we have depicted as attendant upon the [British doctrine], and would, in effect, transfer to the civil courts where property rights were concerned the decision of all ecclesiastical questions.[15]

[13] 80 US at 727–28.
[14] Ibid., at 728–29.
[15] Ibid., at 733–34.

The *Watson v. Jones* decision laid the foundation for a strong tradition of insistence that governmental institutions must refrain from intervention in matters of religious doctrine and ecclesiastical polity. In 1952, in the case of *Kedroff v. St. Nicholas Cathedral*,[16] the principles enunciated in *Watson* were recognized as having constitutional status,[17] and this tradition has been elevated and broadened over time into a constitutionally protected right to religious autonomy. The *Kedroff* case underscored the strength of the autonomy principles involved. At a time when American relations with Russia were particularly strained, the Court held that legislation that transferred control of property belonging to the Russian Orthodox Church from the Moscow Patriarchate to an American Russian Orthodox group independent of Moscow violated the First Amendment.

Subsequently, the Court has made it clear that use of the "departure from doctrine" test in resolving religious controversies is inconsistent with the First Amendment because of the inevitable state intermeddling in doctrinal matters this would entail.[18] The Court reasoned that if civil courts were allowed to resolve religious controversies, "the hazards are ever present of inhibiting the free development of religious doctrine and of implicating secular interests in matters of purely ecclesiastical concern."[19] The Court has acknowledged that there are a variety of ways that states may protect religious autonomy. They can do so by deferring to the decisions of acknowledged decision-making structures in the ecclesiastical polities of different religious communities, as in *Watson* and *Kedroff*, or they may apply "neutral principles of law"—i.e., routine principles of judicial interpretation of legal documents—where religious communities have structured their affairs with secular legal instruments that can be interpreted without getting entangled in matters of religious interpretation.[20] The fundamental point, however, is that governmental institutions must respect the autonomy of religious bodies in structuring their affairs, either by deferring to religious decision-making bodies, or by applying neutral judicial methodologies to interpretation of documents framed (autonomously) by the religious community involved.

The rigor of the Court's insistence on respect for religious autonomy emerges perhaps most clearly in *Serbian Eastern Orthodox Diocese v. Milivojevich*.[21] Earlier cases had suggested that despite the general ban on judicial intervention in religious controversies, some limited scrutiny might be permissible where a religious decision resulted from "fraud, collusion or arbitrariness."[22] In *Milivojevich*, however, the Court overturned an

---

[16] 344 US 94 (1952).

[17] At the time *Watson v. Jones* was decided, the Supreme Court had not yet clearly held that the federal religion clause was applicable to the states. It was decided on the basis of general principles of federal law that were informed by the common law tradition. In *Kedroff* the Court concluded that while the *Watson* opinion was not clearly grounded in the constitution, it "radiates . . . a spirit of freedom for religious organizations, an independence from secular control or manipulation, in short, power to decided for themselves, free from state interference, matters of church government as well as those of faith and doctrine. Freedom to select the clergy, where no improper methods of choice are proven, we think, must now be said to have federal constitutional protection as a part of the free exercise of religion against state interference" (344 US at 116).

[18] Presbyterian Church v. Mary Elizabeth Blue Hull Memorial Presbyterian Church, 393 US 440 (1969).

[19] Ibid., at 449.

[20] Jones v. Wolf, 443 US 595 (1979).

[21] 426 US 696 (1976).

[22] See, e.g., Presbyterian Church v. Mary Elizabeth Blue Hull Memorial Church, 393 US 440, 451 (1969); Gonzalez v. Roman Catholic Archbishop of Manila, 280 US 1 (1929).

Illinois State Supreme Court decision that had refused to accept the decision of a hierarchical church defrocking the American leader of the Serbian Eastern Orthodox Church because of the apparent arbitrariness of the decision. The Court concluded that

> no "arbitrariness" exception in the sense of an inquiry whether the decisions of the highest ecclesiastical tribunal of a hierarchical church complied with church laws and regulations is consistent with the constitutional mandate that civil courts are bound to accept the decisions of the highest judicatories of a religious organization of hierarchical polity on matters of discipline, faith, internal organization, or ecclesiastical rule, custom, or law. For civil courts to analyze whether the ecclesiastical actions of a church judicatory are in that sense "arbitrary" must inherently entail inquiry into the procedures that canon or ecclesiastical law supposedly requires the church judicatory to follow, or else into the substantive criteria by which they are supposedly to decide the ecclesiastical question. But this is exactly the inquiry that the First Amendment prohibits; recognition of such an exception would undermine the general rule that religious controversies are not the proper subject of civil court inquiry, and that a civil court must accept the ecclesiastical decisions of church tribunals as it finds them.[23]

Strong protection of religious autonomy has worked its way out from the fundamental cases noted above to a broad range of other situations.[24] Thus, for example, there are strong constraints on litigation between clergy and their respective faith communities.[25] Faith communities are insulated from claims under federal employment discrimination law under what is known as the ministerial exception.[26] Religious organizations have broad discretion to engage in hiring practices that allow them to favor their own members and to take considerations of religious belief into account in employment decisions.[27] Religious organizations are free to structure and administer their affairs in ways that accord with their doctrine and sense of religious mission. Significantly, a major 1990 case that narrowed the interpretation of free exercise of religion in other respects did not question and indeed cited with approval the religious autonomy cases.[28]

II. Towards Institutional Freedom of Churches

The American experiment was followed in the nineteenth century by some European nations renouncing their former practice of tightly controlling church activities. On the road towards autonomy there remained two kinds of obstacles: the system of state churches and the antireligious state control of churches. The first of these continues to exist in

[23] Ibid., at 713.

[24] For a useful collection of cases in which autonomy issues arise, see Mark E. Chopko, "Constitutional Protection for Church Autonomy: A Practitioner's View," in *Church Autonomy: A Comparative Survey,* ed. Gerhard Robbers (Frankfurt: Peter Lang, 2002). See also Robert A. Destro, "The Politics of Church Autonomy in the USA," in *Legal Position of Churches and Church Autonomy,* ed. Hildegard Warnink (Leuven: Uitgeverij Peeters, 2001), 187–219.

[25] Ibid., at 105–107.

[26] McClure v. Salvation Army, 460 F2d 553 (5th Cir.), *cert. denied*, 409 US 896 (1972).

[27] See, e.g., Corporation of the Presiding Bishop of the Church of Jesus Christ of Latter-day Saints v. Amos, 483 US 327 (1987). See generally, Douglas Laycock, "Towards a General Theory of the Religion Clauses: The Case of Church Labor Relations and the Right to Church Autonomy," *Colum. L. Rev.* 81 (1981): 1373.

[28] Employment Division v. Smith, 494 US 872, 877 (1990).

some countries, but has evolved in the direction of regimes that maintain genuine tolerance and respect for nonestablished beliefs. Alternatively, formal establishment has been left behind, but strong systems of cooperation between church and state remain.

The second or laicist approach is most obvious in France and found its most radical and oppressive expressions in the harsh persecutions of religion in communist regimes. It is remarkable that revolutionary France, while proclaiming in the 1789 Declaration of the Rights of Man and of the Citizen the freedom to have religious opinions, did not institutionally separate the state from the Catholic Church. In fact it regressed to models theretofore only practiced by Orthodox or Lutheran powers. The Catholic Church became a state church in a state that was formally not Catholic. The *Civil Constitution of the Clergy* (1791) was adopted, which reorganized the territorial setting of the church, separated it from Rome, and gave it its internal laws, all without any regard to church wishes. This applied only to the Catholic Church; other churches were free to organize themselves as they wished. But with respect to the Catholic Church, the aim was clear: the French Revolutionaries sought to reduce the influence of the Catholic Church by taking drastic measures to control the internal affairs of the church.

The Concordat between France and the Holy See signed in 1801 was completed unilaterally with the Organic Articles of 1802, in exactly the same vein as the former legislation. The Articles governed all aspects of the internal organization of the church. Without being an official religion or an established church in France, the Catholic Church was actually run according to the former royal and then revolutionary concept of control of the church. The Articles even prescribed what had to be taught in Catholic seminaries. For instance, it emphasized the teaching of the so-called "Gallican Principles."[29] Old jurisdictional measures like the *placet*[30] and the *appeal ab abusu*[31] were maintained. Thus in quite a different historical, cultural, and juridical setting, the French state continued to regulate the internal affairs of the church, just as in the times of the former monarchy. Similar legal prescriptions were adopted concerning the internal affairs of the Protestant churches (1802) and the Jewish communities (1808–1844), all being "recognized cults."[32]

When France separated church and state in 1905,[33] the motivation was ideological. The idea was to eliminate the church and Christianity from society as much as possible. The result of this hostile separation was an increased internal autonomy of the former "recognized" religions, but at the same time a denial of their internal constitution with

[29] The "Gallican Principles" were set forth in the "Declaration of the Four Articles of the French Episcopate" in 1682. Francis Messner, "The Autonomy of Religious Confessions in France," in *Legal Position of Churches and Church Autonomy,* ed. Hildegard Warnink (Leuven: Uitgeverij Peeters, 2001), 112. They stated that the pope could not act against the customs of the Church of France, and that the councils were superior to the pope.

[30] A *placet* was a decision of the sovereign that permitted a document from the Holy See to be effective in the kingdom.

[31] *Appeal ab abusu* was a procedure whereby civil courts could decide whether a church pronouncement interfered with civil legislation. It could lead to annulment of such a pronouncement. See S.B. Smith, *Elements of Ecclesiastical Law,* 9th ed., (New York: Benziger Brothers, 1887), 1:226–27.

[32] Under the regime of the Concordat (1802–1905), four religious groups were "recognized cults": Roman Catholics, Lutherans, Reformed, and Jews. The first three were regulated by the *Organic Articles* (1802); the last by laws of 1808. As a practical matter, the state controlled the appointment of community leaders and the administration of their property.

[33] Law of Separation of Church and State of December 9, 1905.

respect to civil law. They had to accept the juridical form of imposed religious associations set up by the state to control their personnel and property. Strict conditions were imposed on monastic and other religious orders, and the regular clergy were forbidden to teach in public schools.

Up to the present, Belgium, Luxembourg, and Alsace-Moselle (three French administrative districts) maintained in varying degrees some elements of the Napoleonic principles. In the Kingdom of the Netherlands' Constitution of 1815, all religions were treated equally and the state continued to finance ministers.[34] But the Napoleonic Concordat remained in force in the Belgian provinces, and the Fundamental Law did not guarantee the right of religions to freely organize themselves. The Belgian Constitution of 1831, which is still in force today, was considered a vanguard liberal Fundamental Law. In matters of religion, it abolished state control over the churches.[35] Specifically, it expressly abolished one of the most appalling marks of state control over internal church life: the appointment of bishops and other ministers (art. 16).[36] Thereafter the Catholic Church could freely communicate with Rome.

The Luxembourg Constitution of 1848 was more restrictive of religious autonomy. The Napoleonic legislation has never been formally abrogated, in the expectation of a new concordat that has never been forthcoming. In Alsace-Moselle, both the Napoleonic Concordat and the Organic Articles are still in force, but most of the 77 Articles are obsolete.

As an established church, the Church of England is run by the British Parliament as its highest legislative body. In the nineteenth century, jurisdiction over marriage and probate was taken away from the church and assumed by secular tribunals. In 1919 the Church of England Assembly Act[37] created the church's legislative body, called a Synod since 1970. The Church of England was disestablished in Ireland in 1869 and in Wales in 1920. In both areas the Anglican Church became an association under private law. In Scotland the Presbyterian Church was established in the sixteenth century, and a royal commissioner takes part in its general assembly. During the nineteenth century, religious freedom was granted to Catholics, and in 1850 the Catholic hierarchy and canon law were reintroduced. Around the end of the seventeenth century, nonconformists gradually acquired institutional freedom. Their legal status, just as that of the Catholic Church, had the form of a voluntary association. England abolished restrictions on the Jews and atheists and so introduced the principle of religious freedom as a basic principle of the common law. In that configuration the nonestablished churches enjoyed more institutional freedom than the official ones. In Ireland a court decision in 1925 classified Catholic canon law as a foreign legal system.

---

[34] Netherlands Constitution (1815), arts. 190–196. See Sophie C. van Bijsterveld, "State and Church in the Netherlands," in *State and Church in the European Union,* ed. Gerhard Robbers (Baden-Baden: Nomos Verlagsgesellschaft, 1996), 211. For an overview of church autonomy in the Netherlands, see Sophie van Bijsterveld, "Church Autonomy in the Netherlands," in *Legal Position of Churches and Church Autonomy,* ed. Hildegard Warnink (Leuven: Uitgeverij Peeters, 2001), 147–163.

[35] Rik Torfs, "State and Church in Belgium," in *State and Church in the European Union,* ed. Gerhard Robbers, (Baden-Baden: Nomos Verlagsgesellschaft, 1996), 16–17.

[36] Belgium Constitution, art. 16.

[37] The Church of England Assembly (Powers) Act of 1919. See David McClean, "State and Church in the United Kingdom," in *State and Church in the European Union,* ed. Gerhard Robbers (Baden-Baden: Nomos Verlagsgesellschaft, 1996), 314.

In the Netherlands, the Reformed Church was the "dominant church" from 1572 to 1848, notwithstanding the changing political regimes. The Religious Bodies Act of 1853 granted internal freedom to the churches and remained in force until 1988. The Constitution Revision of 1972 disengaged the state from its obligation to finance wages and pensions of the clergy, as compensation for expropriation endured during the nineteenth century. The revised Constitution of 1983, in article 6, abolishes all former restrictions on the exercise of religious freedom. No church is granted special state support, and all religious organizations enjoy internal autonomy under a private legal status. They are legally juridical persons *sui generis* according to the civil code, which does not make any prescription as to the internal structure of churches, exempting them from determinations imposed on other legal persons. In case of conflict, canon law has precedence over civil law. Moreover, the civil code does not define what a church is, but rather leaves this definition to the religious body itself. Religious organizations may choose either the legal form of common associations or foundations. The law recognizes churches as they are constituted, either as centralized entities or as local units.

The Kingdom of Greece established in its first constitution (1822–1827) the principle of "coordination" between the state and the Orthodox state religion. From 1833 onward, the system was instead a form of hegemony of the state according to law.[38] State officials governed all the administrative aspects of the church, leaving only doctrinal issues to be determined by the church itself. Even the autocephalous character of the Church of Greece with respect to the Patriarchate of Constantinople was decided by the government in 1833. This regime was reinforced by constitutions dating from 1844 to 1968. The Constitution of 1975 does not embody the regime of mere "coordination," but plainly maintains control by state law over church administration and the determination by the Parliament of sacred canons in the Greek Orthodox Church.[39]

In the sixteenth century, Denmark, Norway, and Sweden established Lutheran State Churches. All Swedish born citizens were automatically members of the state church. The latter was governed by the king and later by the Parliament. Only in 1866 was a general church assembly endowed with the competence to make recommendations upon ecclesiastical laws; clergy comprised 50 percent of the membership of this general church assembly. The 1974 Constitution guarantees religious freedom for all. A new statute in 1992 gave a democratic structure to the church with only doctrinal issues being reserved to the bishops. In what was primarily an effort to strengthen church autonomy, the Swedish Church was disestablished in 2000.[40] This reform made the Church of Sweden an autonomous legal entity, but the Parliament reaffirmed a Church Act that defines its structure and doctrinal identity as an "Evangelical-Lutheran folk church."

Finland has two official churches, corresponding to its successive Lutheran and Orthodox rulers. The Church General Assembly had more autonomy than its counterparts in Scandinavia when it was founded in 1869, but remained a mixed body of church

---

[38] See Charalambos Papastathis, "State and Church in Greece," in *State and Church in the European Union*, ed. Gerhard Robbers (Baden-Baden: Nomos Verlagsgesellschaft, 1996), 75–76.

[39] Greek Constitution, art. 72.

[40] For an overview of this process, which was set in place well in advance, see Kenneth Stegeby, "An Analysis of the Impending Disestablishment of the Church of Sweden," *BYU L. Rev.* (1999): 703.

and state officials under the revision of 1965. The assembly calls for the approval of bills on ecclesiastical matters to be voted on by the Parliament. Significant reform legislation is under consideration as this chapter goes to press.

The Danish Constitution of 1849 (paragraph 4) recognizes the "Evangelical-Lutheran Church as the Danish Folk Church" and provides for its support by the state. This constitutional reference restricts the power of the Parliament to make church legislation in conflict with the doctrinal identity of the church. But the Danish Folk Church has no national synod and the Head of State (i.e., the government) has, beside the Parliament, supreme authority in ecclesiastical matters, including appointments of bishops. Forty percent of the salary of clergy is funded by the state, with the balance of church activities being supported by church taxes levied at the municipal level.

The Norwegian Constitution of 1814 states that the "Evangelical-Lutheran religion remains the public religion of the state" (para. 2) and limits the powers of the Parliament vis-à-vis the King (i.e., government)—the Head of the Church of Norway—among other things in doctrinal questions. During the last decades of the twentieth century authority has been delegated to a National Church Synod. Since 1996 local parishes have status as independent legal entities (Church Act of 1996, art. 2), with the restriction that they must be considered parts of the Church of Norway. Separation of church and state is, at the time of writing (2003), on the agenda of both church and state. Outcome and timing of these deliberations remains uncertain.[41]

Only when a state gives up its former confessional status is it able to recognize church autonomy fully. As a normative matter, church autonomy is a corollary of the general human right to religious freedom. But as a practical matter, effective protection of this corporate right depends on the self-understanding of the state as much as it is a result of the self-understanding of the churches. While the phenomenon of states with formally established churches continues to exist, the clear historical trend is away from such establishments. As has been mentioned, Sweden disestablished in 2000. None of the states emerging from communism has chosen the confessional state form (despite the centuries-long tradition of "symphony of church and state" that had preceded communism in many of these states). Even where state churches remain, broad toleration of other religious groups has tended to reinforce awareness of the significance of religious autonomy. In the modern setting, the general trend is toward recognition by the state that it lacks competence to establish rules defining the religious beliefs of its citizens. Hence it recognizes that the legal order of the state does not intrude into all the dimensions of social life. The state, under the rule of law, willingly excludes from its competence the domain in which churches are active, namely the realm of religious faith and the institutional organization of religious communities. The state nevertheless must not declare that it is not interested in religion. It must not impose a religion, but should take into account that citizens may also be believers wishing to belong to a religious organization. So the state recognizes that other juridical orders exist that are not those of the state. All churches have their own structure, constitution, mission, proceedings, rules, and order. This order, and actions motivated by efforts to carry out the vision and demands of this normative order, constitute the sphere of autonomy recognized for religious communities.

---

[41] See chapter 35 by Eidsvåg, Lindholm, and Sveen in this volume.

III. The Emergence of Autonomy as a Right

A. Autonomy in Constitutional Law

A significant shift in states' comprehension of their specific duties towards religion can be seen in the nineteenth century Austrian Empire. The countries of the former Austro-Hungarian Empire came from a tradition of strict state-controlled churches. The March Constitution of 1849 introduced individual and corporate religious freedoms for Catholics, Reformed, Lutheran, and Orthodox.[42] This measure was confirmed by the 1867 Fundamental Law on Basic Rights of Citizens.[43] This law—more clearly than the Belgian Constitution of 1831—explicitly recognizes the internal autonomy of churches and can be considered the first law to do so. The 1867 Fundamental Law states the following: "Every Church and religious society recognized by the law has the right to communal public worship, to order and administer its internal affairs autonomously, and to retain possession and enjoyment of its institutions."[44] The recognized religions were considered public law corporations. In 1874 a law on the recognition of religions opened the possibility of other religious organizations attaining the status of a recognized religion.[45] Historically there was a sharp distinction made between recognized and nonrecognized religious organizations. For a considerable period, progress in the corporate right to autonomy did not keep pace with developments in the individual right to freedom of religion and belief.[46] Until 1998, only twelve religious bodies besides the Catholic Church were "recognized," whereas other religious groups were relegated to private association status. A new federal law concerning Legal Personality of Registered Religious Communities,[47] adopted in 1998, established an intermediate status available to many religious communities. Gradually, pressures emanating from the law of international human rights, particularly the European Convention, coupled with constitutional norms requiring equal treatment that are being protected by an increasingly activist court, are leading to a more fully integrated approach that affords broad protection of religious autonomy for a wide spectrum of religious groups. The autonomy right is generally understood to include areas such as "dogma, teaching, religious service, own legislation and jurisdiction, disciplinary measures, appointment to and dismissal from a church office, conditions which are to be complied with by employees, and administration of church property."[48] Holders of the autonomy or self-determination right include not only religious organizations

[42] Constitution of 29 March 1849, section IV, art. 5, in *Die Verfassung des Deutschen Reiches vom Jahre 1849,* ed. Ludwig Bergsträsser (Bonn: 1913), 80.

[43] RGBl. 1867/142, art. 15.

[44] RGBl. 1867/142, art. 15. Cf. I. Gampl/R. Potz/B. Schinkele,1 Österreichesches Staatskirchenrecht (Wien 1990) 30 ff.

[45] Gesetz betreffend die gesetzliche Anerkennung von Religionsgesellschaften, RGBl. 1874/68; cf. Gampl/Potz/Schinkele, supra, .145 ff.; R. Potz, "State and Church in Austria," in *State and Church in the European Union,* ed. Gerhard Robbers (Baden-Baden: Nomos Verlag, 1996), 238 f.

[46] Brigitte Schinkele, "Church Autonomy in Austria," in *Church Autonomy: A Comparative Survey,* ed. Gerhard Robbers (Frankfurt: Peter Lang, 2002), 562, 563.

[47] BGBl. I 1998/19; Appendix to H. Kalb/R. Potz/B.Schinkele, Eintragung und Anerkennung von Religionsgemeinschaften nach dem Inkraftreten des Bundesgesetzes über die Rechtspersönlichkeit von religiösen Bekenntnisgemeinschaften, Österr. Archiv für Kirchenrecht (1998), 58, 97 ff.

[48] Brigitte Schinkele, "Church Autonomy in Austria," supra, 566–67.

themselves, but also other private law entities with partially religious functions, and even religious associations that have not sought secular entity status.[49] Other protections of religious autonomy are evident. For example, recognized churches and religious societies are protected in their autonomy from certain rules having to do with the organization of industrial relations, co-determination, and other regulations in order to avoid conflicts with the autonomy of religious organizations in defining their affairs.[50] To the extent discrepancies remain in the treatment of recognized and other religious associations, equalitarian and human rights principles are likely to reduce this distance over time where objective grounds for the discrimination cannot be demonstrated.[51]

The full institutional autonomy of churches appears as a fundamental principle in the German Weimar Constitution of 1919. Article 137 is exemplary in prohibiting a state church. It further states that "every religious body regulates and administers its affairs autonomously within the limits of the law valid for all. It confers its offices without the participation of the State or the civil community."[52] The Evangelical and Catholic Churches were immediately recognized as "corporate bodies under public law." Other religious organizations can apply to enjoy the same status "where their constitution and the number of their members offers an assurance of permanency."[53] The same article extends the possibility to apply for a corporate body under public law to associations cultivating a philosophical persuasion. This legal status enables churches and similar associations to levy taxes on their members with the help of the public administration. Articles 136 through 141 of the Weimar Constitution were incorporated in the Basic Law of the Federal Republic of Germany 1949.

Thus a new model emerged. Under this approach, "no particular identification between the Church and State is meant; quite the contrary, as the State's view accepts such a description as a justification for the religious communities being part of public life."[54] Further, in contrast to other public corporations, "the religious communities with this status are not integrated into the State's structure. They retain their complete autonomy."[55] This special status has been attained by a broad range of religious communities.[56] A recent decision by the German Constitutional Court involving Jehovah's Witnesses has sharply limited the grounds under which stable religious groups willing to live within the constitutional order can be denied public corporation status.[57] Moreover, even religious communities that do not acquire public corporation status are assured

---

[49] Ibid., at 567–68.

[50] Ibid., at 570.

[51] See ibid., 570–74. See also Richard Puza, "Legal Position of Churches, Church Autonomy and Tendencies in Jurisprudence," in *Legal Position of Churches and Church Autonomy,* ed. Hildegard Warnink (Leuven: Uitgeverij Peeters, 2001), 57–81.

[52] Weimar Constitution, art. 137(3), incorporated in the current German Basic Law, art. 140.

[53] Weimar Constitution, art. 137(5), incorporated in the current German Basic Law, art. 140.

[54] Gerhard Robbers, "State and Church in Germany," in *State and Church in the European Union,* ed. Gerhard Robbers (Baden-Baden: Nomos Verlagsgesellschaft, 1996), 57, 62. For further discussion of the German model, see Gerhard Robbers, "Church Autonomy in Germany Including an Attachment on Relevant European Union Law," in *Legal Position of Churches and Church Autonomy,* ed. Hildegard Warnink (Leuven: Uitgeverij Peeters, 2001), 121–27.

[55] Ibid., at 61–62.

[56] Ibid., at 61.

[57] Bundesverfassungsgericht, Decision of 19 December 2000.

broad autonomy rights. Thus, for example, in a case involving the Bahá'í, the Constitutional Court held that legal requirements that governed acquisition of status as a civil association had to be adjusted to meet the peculiarities of a religion's organizational requirements.[58] Germany has thus found a way to maintain the principle of legal separation between church and state, while at the same time accommodating the principle of juridical cooperation between both, and the internal autonomy of the church organization. The church is separated from the state and at the same time inserted into the legal framework of society.

The principles of church autonomy appear in other constitutions of the first half of the twentieth century. Ireland, a Catholic country, never had an official church. From 1800 to 1871, the Anglican Church was the established church to which Catholics also had to pay taxes. When Ireland became independent, the principle of religious freedom was fixed in the constitution.[59] Article 44 of the revised Constitution of 1937 makes clear that the state should finance no religion, and further that "every religious denomination shall have the right to manage its own affairs."[60]

The 1948 Constitution of Italy did not call for any revision of the Lateran Treaty or the Concordat of 1929 with the Holy See. In other words, Catholicism continued to be "the only religion of the State."[61] It formulated the relationship between the Catholic Church and the state in these words: "The Church and the State, each one in its own sphere, are independent and sovereign."[62] In the revised Concordat of 1984 the reference to the state religion was eliminated.[63] But article 1 retained the formulation of "independent and sovereign" taken from the constitution.[64]

In the 1965 Vatican II Constitution *Gaudium et spes*, the relationship between church and state was defined in a similar way: "The political community and the Church in their own field are independent from one another and autonomous."[65] Therefore a "healthy cooperation" between both is wished, which may vary in its form from one context to the other.[66] The doctrinal foundation of internal autonomy of churches is the right to religious freedom itself. The 1965 Vatican II Declaration *Dignitatis humanae* stressed that religious freedom by its very nature has a social or community dimension.[67] The basic principle is that religious communities should "govern themselves according to their own norms."[68] This implies that they should have the freedom to worship in public and private, teach to their own members, develop institutions through their members, and organize their life in accordance with their faith. Religious organizations should have the freedom to organize their internal structure, train and appoint their ministers according

[58] Bundesverfassungsgericht Entscheidungen 83, 341 (1991).
[59] Irish Constitution of 1922, art. 16.
[60] Irish Constitution, art. 44.
[61] Lateran Treaty of 1929, art. 1.
[62] Italian Constitution, art. 7.
[63] "Accordo tra la Santa Sede e la Repubblica Italian ache apporta modificazioni al Concordato Lateranense," in *Raccolta di Concordati 1950–1999,* José T. Martín de Agar (2000), 559 (Protocollo Addizionale all' art.1).
[64] Ibid., at 553, art. 1.
[65] *Gaudium et spes*, 76, 3.
[66] Ibid.
[67] *Dignitatis humanae*, 4.
[68] Ibid.

to their own rules, communicate with fellow members abroad, have appropriate buildings for worship, own property, organize meetings, and develop charitable programs. On September 1, 1980, Pope John Paul II wrote letters to the Heads of the States parties to the Helsinki Act in which he included a list of community rights required by religious freedom and the principle of internal autonomy.[69]

In the Catholic area since Vatican II, there has been a widespread acceptance of the principle of church autonomy for the benefit of all confessions. It is known that the Catholic Church, with the Declaration on Religious Freedom, adopted in 1965 by the Vatican II, not only supported religious freedom as a personal natural right, but also developed the collective implications of this right.[70] The Council discarded the theory of the Catholic confessional state and endorsed the notion that the state should not impose or prohibit religious belief. Rather, it should positively support the exercise of religious freedom as a civil right. Consequently, the Catholic Church encouraged the revision of those concordats that still mentioned the confessional character of the state. Accordingly, both Spain in 1976–1979 and Italy in 1984 removed the notion of state religion from their concordats, and also abolished the ecclesiastical rights previously exercised by the state. In these countries, the Catholic Church, along with other churches and religious organizations, are now totally independent and autonomous in carrying out their respective missions. The concordat tradition has no doubt contributed to the tendency in these states to reach agreements with the other religious organizations, thereby respecting the internal autonomy of other groups as well. The post–Vatican II Catholic notion of church autonomy and its recognition by the state has extended itself in this way into the juridical self-understanding of other religious organizations.

Therefore, it is no surprise that the phrase "independent and autonomous" has received an increased acceptance in more recent concordats signed by countries with the Holy See. Concordats (also called conventions, accords, or agreements) are bilateral treaties. States having concordats with the Holy See generally have parallel agreements between the state and the other religious communities, as in Spain and Italy. The concept of autonomy has become integral to common understanding of the very nature of the corporate freedom of religious communities. In the Catholic experience of the church-state relationship, the principles recalled by Vatican II and the practice of recent concordats are in continuity with the traditional requirements expressed under the general concept of "perfect society."

The following are excerpts from recent concordats from different regions and cultural backgrounds that contain the concept of "independent and autonomous" as the formulation of church-state relations vis-à-vis internal affairs. San Marino, in the preamble to its 1992 convention with the Holy See, reproposed the formula of the above-mentioned Italian revised concordat.[71] Poland, in article 1 of the 1993 Concordat, used the words "independent and autonomous,"[72] and in its Constitution of 1997 used the concept of

---

[69] Letter of Pope John Paul II to the Heads of State who Signed the Helsinki Final Act, 1 September 1980, in *Acta Apostolicae Sedis* 72 (1980) 1256–1258.

[70] *Dignitatis humanae*, 4.

[71] See "Conventio Inter Apostolicam Sedem et Rem Publicam Sancti Marini," in *Raccolta di Concordati 1950–1999,* José T. Martín de Agar (2000), 741 (preamble).

[72] "Sollemnis conventio inter Apostolicam Sedem et Poloniae rem Publicam," in *Raccolta di Concordati 1950–1999,* José T. Martín de Agar (2000), 684 (art. 1).

"autonomy and mutual independence of [state and churches] in [their] own sphere[s]."[73] Croatia, in its convention of 1996, repeated that church and state are "independent and autonomous"[74] and that the church has exclusive competence to order its internal governance.[75] Also, Kazakhstan in 1998 sustained "the principles of respect and non-interference in internal affairs."[76] In Germany where concordats were signed with the new *Länder*, the constitutional principle of "Selbsbestimmung" (autonomy of the church) was reentrenched; this was also the case in Mecklenburg-Vorpommern (1997)[77] and Thüringen (1997).[78] Saxony stated that the church "orders and manages its own affairs in an autonomous way in the framework of the laws valid for all."[79]

Some recent constitutions mention the right to autonomy of religious organizations. Spain speaks of freedom of religion for communities as well as for individuals.[80] Portugal is much more explicit and specifies that "Churches and religious communities are separate from the state and free to organize and exercise their own ceremonies and worship."[81] The 1991 Constitution of Gabon states that "religious communities order and manage their own affairs in an independent way."[82]

B. Autonomy in International Law

International instruments protecting human rights have been primarily concerned with individual rights, but the growing consensus concerning the right to religious autonomy is evident in this area as well. In major international instruments enunciating the right of individuals to freedom of conscience and religion there is no express mention of the corporate rights of religious organizations. However, these rights are suggested indirectly, albeit often through derivation from individual rights. The International Covenant on Civil and Political Rights, for example, notes that religion is practiced not only alone but also "in community with others,"[83] and that the right to manifest one's faith or belief includes the activities of "worship, observance, practice and teaching."[84] Obviously, such activities generally have a collective aspect. It is clear then that religious freedom has

[73] Poland Constitution of 1997, art. 25.
[74] "Conventio inter Sanctam Sedem et Croatiæ Rem Publicam de Iuridicialibus quæstionibus," in *Raccolta di Concordati 1950–1999,* José T. Martín de Agar (2000), 155 (art. 1).
[75] Ibid., at 156 (art. 5).
[76] "Agreement between the Republic of Kazakhstan and the Holy See on Mutual Relations," in *Raccolta di Concordati 1950–1999,* José T. Martín de Agar (2000), 612 (preamble: "desiring to develop mutual relations between the Republic of Kazakhstan and the Holy See in accordance with the principles of respect and non-interference in internal affairs").
[77] "Conventio Inter Apostolicam Sedem et Foederatam Civitatem Megaloburgi-Pomeraniæ Anterioris," in *Raccolta di Concordati 1950–1999,* José T. Martín de Agar (2000), 471 (preamble: "im gegenseitigen Respekt vor ihrem Selbstbestimmungsrecht und in Bereitschaft zur Zusammenarbeit").
[78] "Conventio Inter Apostolicam Sedem et Liberum Statum Thuringiae," in *Raccolta di Concordati 1950–1999,* José T. Martín de Agar (2000), 440 (art. 1, sec. 2: "selbständig").
[79] "Conventio Inter apostolicam Sedem et Foederatam Civitatem Saxoniae-Anhaltini," in *Raccolta di Concordati 1950–1999,* José T. Martín de Agar (2000), 486 (art. 1, para. 2).
[80] Spanish Constitution of 1978, art. 16.
[81] Portugese Constitution, art. 41 (1976).
[82] Gabon Constitution, arts. 1, 13.
[83] ICCPR, art. 18.
[84] ICCPR, art. 18.

communal dimensions. Though the ICCPR does not expressly treat religious organizations as bearers of rights, it is clear that corresponding protections can be derived from the rights granted to individuals.

Much the same can be said with regard to the 1981 UN Declaration on the Elimination of All Forms of Intolerance and Discrimination Based on Religion or Belief.[85] It repeats the notion from the ICCPR that freedom of thought, conscience, and religion find expression "either individually or in community with others."[86] It lays particular emphasis on issues of discrimination,[87] which are often linked to group membership. Significantly, virtually all of the specific examples of freedom of religion or belief enunciated in article 6 of the 1981 Declaration presuppose religious autonomy. Thus, the right noted in article 6(a) "[t]o worship or assemble in connexion with a religion or belief, and to establish and maintain places for these purposes" is inconceivable for most religious groups without collective activity by the religious community. This activity is a primary expression of religious autonomy. Similarly, the right in article 6(b) "[t]o establish and maintain appropriate charitable or humanitarian institutions" could conceivably be exercised by an individual, but in reality, it tends to be exercised by churches and religious communities acting in a corporate or associational capacity. The right to create various subsidiary entities for carrying out a religious mission is a vital dimension of religious autonomy. Article 6(c) enunciates the right "[to] make, acquire and use to an adequate extent the necessary articles and materials related to the rites or customs of a religion or belief." Of course, individuals need to be able to use religious objects, but again, this is also a vital aspect of the autonomy of religious bodies. The same can be said with respect to the rights "[t]o write, issue and disseminate relevant publications" and "[t]o teach a religion or belief in places suitable for these purposes," noted in article 6(d) and 6(e). As a practical matter, the right in article 6(f) "[t]o solicit and receive voluntary financial and other contributions from individuals and institutions" is almost always asserted by religious communities acting as corporate or associational entities. Indeed, these days an individual attempting to solicit funds in an individual capacity would typically be suspect, and not eligible for tax exempt status or other favorable tax treatment. The importance of article 6(f) is in fact primarily to stress the significance of financial independence as a core feature of religious autonomy. Article 6(g), which speaks of the right "[t]o train, appoint, elect or designate by succession appropriate leaders called for by the requirements and standards of any religion or belief" is designed to emphasize the core aspect of religious autonomy that relates to selection, assignment, supervision, and discipline of religious personnel by a religious community. Observance of church holidays and days of rest (article 6(h)) is often as much a collective as an individual matter. Finally, the significance of protecting the right "[t]o establish and maintain communications with individuals and *communities* in matters of religion and belief at the national and international level" (article 6(i)(emphasis added)) is precisely to make certain that channels of communication necessary for instituting and exercising religious autonomy are not restricted. In short, the 1981 Declaration recognizes and calls for the protection of the autonomy of religious bodies in a variety of significant ways.

An even more explicit recognition of the right to religious autonomy is evident in the Helsinki Process. In the follow-up conference held under the auspices of the Helsinki Final Act that concluded in Vienna in 1989, the scope of religious freedom was elaborated with

---

[85] UN General Assembly Res. 36/35 (25 Nov. 1981).

[86] 1981 Declaration, art. 1(1).

some precision. Principle 16 commits the then CSCE Participating states to eliminate all forms of religious discrimination against individuals or communities and to guarantee effective equality between believers and nonbelievers.[88] Further, it encourages dialogue between believers of different communities. Participating states committed that they would grant legal entity status to all religious communities who desired it and were willing to practice their faith within the constitutional framework of their states. Moreover, they committed that they would respect the following "rights of these communities": to establish and maintain places of worship; to organize themselves according to their own hierarchical and institutional structure; to choose, appoint, and replace their personnel according to their own rules and needs; and to receive financial contributions.[89] These are, of course, key features of religious autonomy. Principle 16 also commits states to protect the right to receive and dispense religious education individually or in association with others.[90] In addition, it urges states to allow the training of religious ministers in appropriate schools and respect the right of believers and communities to possess books or objects needed for religious practice.[91] It further stresses the right of "religious faiths, institutions and organizations to produce and import and disseminate religious publications and materials."[92] This document in effect constitutes a manifesto of corporate rights of religious organizations. The general right to self-government is implied and specified in considerable detail.

The right to religious autonomy has also found strong support under the European Convention for the Protection of Human Rights and Fundamental Freedoms, as manifested by decisions of the European Court of Human Rights. This may be seen at two levels. First, the Court has recognized the importance of a crucial threshold condition for autonomy by recognizing the right of religious organizations to acquire legal entity status. In a series of decisions first under article 11 (freedom of association) and then under article 9 (freedom of religion or belief), the Court has stressed the importance of this right. In *Sidiropoulos v. Greece*,[93] the Court stated categorically that "the right to form an association is an inherent part" of the right to freedom of association. It further noted that the fact that "citizens should be able to form a legal entity in order to act collectively in a field of mutual interest is one of the most important aspects of the right to freedom of association, without which the right would be deprived of any meaning."[94] Cases decided under article 9 have made it clear that the right to legal entity status applies with equal if not greater force where it is asserted by religious groups.[95] The Court underscored this point in *Metropolitan Church of Bessarabia v. Moldova*,[96] holding that

---

87 1981 Declaration, arts. 2–4.

88 Vienna Concluding Document, principle 16(a).

89 Ibid., principle 16(d).

90 Ibid., principle 16(e).

91 Ibid., principle (16(h)–(i).

92 Ibid., principle 16(j).

93 ECtHR, App. No. 26695/95, Decision of 10 July 1998.

94 Ibid., at para. 40. Additional freedom of association cases supporting this point include Freedom and Democracy Party (OZDEP) v. Turkey (ECtHR, App. No. 23885/94, Decision of 8 December 1999); United Communist Party of Turkey v. Turkey (ECtHR, App. No. 19392/92, Decision of 30 January 1998); Sidiropoulos & Others v. Greece (ECtHR, Decision of 10 July 1998).

95 Canea Catholic Church v. Greece, 27 EHRR 521 (1999)(ECtHR, App. No. 25528/94, Dec. 16, 1997)(legal personality of Roman Catholic church protected); Hasan and Chaush v. Bulgaria (ECtHR, App. No. 30985/96, Oct. 26, 2000)(interference with internal organization of Muslim community and

> since religious communities traditionally exist in the form of organised structures, Article 9 must be interpreted in the light of Article 11 of the Convention, which safeguards associative life against unjustified State interference. Seen in that perspective, the right of believers to freedom of religion, which includes the right to manifest one's religion in community with others, encompasses the expectation that believers will be allowed to associate freely, without arbitrary State intervention. ***Indeed, the autonomous existence of religious communities is indispensable for pluralism in a democratic society and is thus an issue at the very heart of the protection which Article 9 affords.***[97]

The second and deeper level of European Court protection of religious autonomy is evident in recent cases rejecting state efforts to intervene in or otherwise take sides in religious disputes. Thus, in *Serif v. Greece*,[98] the Court held that conviction of a Moslem cleric for "usurping the functions of a known religion" violated article 9 where the facts merely showed that the individual in question had been duly selected by an group of Moslems independent of the Mufti officially appointed by the state. As the Court stated, "punishing a person for the mere fact that he acted as the religious leader of a group that willingly followed him can hardly be considered compatible with the demands of religious pluralism in a democratic society."[99] The Greek government contended that it needed to intervene "in order to avoid the creation of tension among the Moslems in Rodopi and between Moslems and the Christians of the area as well as Greece and Turkey."[100] The Court responded by noting that while tension is possible and can result in divisions, "this is one of the unavoidable consequences of pluralism. The role of the authorities in such circumstances is not to remove the cause of tension by eliminating pluralism, but to ensure that the competing groups tolerate each other."[101] In short, it is inappropriate for the government to intervene in the self-structuring or autonomy of religious groups.

Similarly, in ***Hasan and Chaush v. Bulgaria***,[102] the European Court held that state intervention in a controversy between two rival leaders of Bulgarian Muslims violated freedom of religion or belief. Among other things, the Directorate of Religions had at various times recognized one of the leaders and refused to recognize the other and to register the rival group. The Court indicated that it did "not deem it necessary to decide ***in abstracto*** whether acts of formal registration of religious communities and changes in their leadership constitute an interference with the rights protected by article 9 of the Convention."[103] Nevertheless, the Court held that "facts demonstrating a failure by the authorities to remain neutral in the exercise of their powers in this domain must lead to the conclusion that the State interfered with the believers' freedom to manifest their religion."[104] According to the Court, the European Convention

---

managing its affairs violates religious freedom, and decision on grounds of freedom of association was unnecessary because freedom of religion analysis was carried out in light of freedom of association requirements).

[96] ECtHR, App. No. 45701/99, Decision of 13 Dec. 2001.

[97] Ibid., at para. 118 (emphasis added). The issue of the right to entity status is discussed in more detail in chapter 15 by Durham in this volume.

[98] ECtHR, App. No. 38178/97, Decision of 14 Dec. 1999.

[99] Ibid., at para. 51.

[100] Ibid., at para. 53.

[101] Ibid.

[102] ECtHR, App. No. 30985/96, Decision of 26 Oct. 2000.

[103] Ibid., at para. 77.

> excludes any discretion on the part of the State to determine whether religious beliefs or the means used to express such beliefs are legitimate. State action favouring one leader of a divided religious community or undertaken with the purpose of forcing the community to come together under a single leadership against its own wishes would likewise constitute an interference with freedom of religion.[105]

The Court noted that the Bulgarian practice according to which "the legitimacy and representation powers of the leadership of a religious denomination are certified by the Directorate of Denominations" had the impermissible effect of "putting an end to the first applicant's functions as Chief Mufti, removing the hitherto recognised leadership of the religious community and disallowing its statute and by-laws."[106] The Bulgarian government's response that "nothing prevented the first applicant and those supporting him from organising meetings" was not acceptable. As the Court put it, "It cannot be seriously maintained that any State action short of restricting the freedom of assembly could not amount to an interference with the rights protected by article 9 of the Convention even though it adversely affected the internal life of the religious community."[107] In the Court's view, "[t]he acts of the authorities operated, in law and in practice, to deprive the excluded leadership of any possibility of continuing to represent at least part of the Muslim community and of managing its affairs according to the will of that part of the community,"[108] and hence there was "an interference with the internal organisation of the Muslim religious community and with the applicants' right to freedom of religion as protected by article 9 of the Convention."[109]

Significantly, in *Hasan and Chaush*, the Court went on to hold that the legal structures governing the Directorate of Denomination's activities in the case failed to rise to the level of article 9's "prescribed by law" requirement—a standard generally met in most cases—because they failed to measure up to general rule of law standards in the qualitative sense. That is, they did not shield the applicant's fundamental right to freedom of religion or belief from arbitrary interferences, and they failed to provide substantive criteria that could guide state institutions in dealing with "register[ing] religious denominations and changes of their leadership in a situation of internal divisions and of conflicting claims for legitimacy."[110] Accordingly, the Court did not even reach analysis of the additional requirements posed by article 9—i.e., whether such measures could be justified in terms of legitimate state objectives and whether the particular measures were "necessary in a democratic society."

The Court further emphasized the significance of religious autonomy in *Metropolitan Church of Bessarabia v. Moldova*.[111] In this case, government authorities refused to recognize the Metropolitan Church of Bessarabia ostensibly because they viewed it not as a new denomination but merely as a part of the already recognized Orthodox Christian Church[112] and because "the creation of the applicant church had in reality been an

---

[104] Ibid., at para. 78.
[105] Ibid.
[106] Ibid., at para. 79.
[107] Ibid., at para. 81.
[108] Ibid., at para. 82.
[109] Ibid.
[110] See ibid., at paras. 84–86
[111] ECtHR, App. No. 45701/99, Decision of 13 Dec. 2001.
[112] Ibid., at para. 98.

attempt to set up a new administrative organ within the Metropolitan Church of Moldova."[113] The government also claimed that the Bessarabian Church threatened the territorial integrity and stability of Moldova since it was aligned with interests in Moldova that favored union with Romania.[114] In effect, the state attempted to argue that it could not register a dissenting group as a separate Orthodox Church as this would interfere with the internal affairs of the mother church. The Court rightly rejected this argument, recognizing that the right to autonomy in internal affairs does not carry with it the right to compel others who do not wish to do so to remain inside the church. The Court emphasized that "[i]n exercising its regulatory power in this sphere and in its relations with the various religions, denominations and beliefs, the State has a duty to remain neutral and impartial. . . .What is at stake here is the preservation of pluralism and the proper functioning of democracy."[115] The Court further observed that "the right to freedom of religion for the purposes of the Convention excludes assessment by the State of the legitimacy of religious beliefs or the ways in which those are expressed."[116] As already noted above, the Court buttressed its position by stressing that the autonomous existence of religious communities is "indispensable for pluralism in a democratic society."[117]

In short, in an ever-lengthening line of cases, the European Court has recognized that the right to religious autonomy, which can be asserted both by individuals and on their behalf by religious communities as such,[118] lies at the core of freedom of religion or belief.

IV. Features of Religious Autonomy

Religious autonomy issues arise in a wide variety of contexts, but a number of recurrent issues giving rise to special legislation and case law deserve specific mention. These include freedom to teach the faith, matters of faith and order, free appointment of ministers, and church-run charitable institutions.

A. Freedom to Teach the Faith

The clearest and most axiomatic domain of church autonomy is certainly the question of the church's freedom to teach its faith. This is not satisfactorily respected everywhere, particularly where the creed of established churches is anchored in the constitution of the state. In England, Norway, and Denmark the basic articles of faith, or the doctrinal identity of churches, have constitutional rank. In Greece, the Orthodox Church is linked by constitution to the Church of Constantinople, and the organs of church government are confirmed by the constitution.[119] Any attempt to change or develop religious beliefs in such settings would require a revision of the fundamental law.

---

[113] Ibid.

[114] Ibid., at para. 120.

[115] Ibid., at para. 116.

[116] Ibid., at para. 117.

[117] Ibid., at para. 118 (emphasis added); see text at note 97 above.

[118] Ibid., at para. 101.

[119] Greek Constitution, art. 3.

B. Matters of Faith and Order

With the exception of Sweden, which recently disestablished its church, the Lutheran Scandinavian churches are run by Parliaments, cabinets, or ministries, though matters of faith and order are increasingly delegated to church synods and local congregations. The procedure of the election of bishops and clergy has been settled by law. Also, the Church of England needs the confirmation by Parliament for internal decisions such as the revision of the *Prayer Book* (1927, 1928) or the ordaining of women. One of the ironies of established church status is that official or established churches often enjoy less internal freedom than nonrecognized churches existing on the same soil. The decision of Sweden to put an end to the secular state church in January 2000 and to grant all registered churches equal legal recognition and autonomy of government reflects the general trend of the northern European states.

C. Free Appointment of Ministers

The free appointment of ministers is a classical test for effective church autonomy. Prior to the twentieth century, the prevailing European experience was that only nonconformist churches were free to elect their ministers. In established churches the sovereign or his government chose the bishops. With respect to countries having established churches, this basically has not changed. The Church of England presents a list of two candidates for bishop to the government, which chooses and proposes the appointment to the Monarch. In Greece, the election of the Archbishop of Athens by the Holy Synod is performed in the presence of a government representative. In Catholic countries, the privilege for heads of state to interfere in the appointment of bishops was abolished by the Second Vatican Council and the post-Vatican II concordats.[120] In post World War I concordats, the general practice was to inform governments before an appointment was published, ensuring a right to express any objections. Since Vatican II, only the official notification of the appointment is generally envisaged. Alsace-Moselle is now the only area in the world where the bishops and other ministers are formally appointed by the Head of State or the government. In southern Europe, there are no longer limitations on the free designation of church ministers.[121] The right to autonomy in the selection of ecclesiastical personnel now seems to be clearly established.[122]

D. Church-Owned Charitable and Educational Institutions

More subtle is the link between church and state when the church involves itself with public services on a large scale, like working with hospitals and schools at all levels (kindergartens through theological faculties in state universities). Churches have often

---

[120] See, e.g., "Convention with Spain" (1976), in *Raccolta di Concordati 1950–1999,* José T. Martín de Agar (2000), 786 (art 1); "Convention with Monaco" (1981), in ibid., 671 (art. 2); "Concordat with Columbia" (1973), in ibid., 132 (art. 14); "Convention with Haiti" (1984), in ibid., 514 (art. 4).

[121] Until 1972, all religious ministers were financed by the state. In 1981 the state redeemed its last obligations by creating a foundation to administer capital for the sustenance of the clergy. From then on, religious bodies were treated indifferently, as common associations of private law with no fiscal exemptions.

become partners in social activities. In Germany the two main churches are among the largest employers in the country. This raises concern over labor laws and the specific goals of church-run institutions. Church employment is specifically supported by law. Employees accept being bound by church hiring and firing criteria. But churches are so narrowly woven into the net of social services that they are *de facto* restricted in their autonomy. The balance between legal autonomy and intensive cooperation in civil society is not easy to maintain. On one hand, churches observe that social or educational services belong to their mission and to the sphere of their organizational autonomy. On the other hand, the state has to foster positive activities in these areas, and may do so in ways inconsistent with the application of the principle of religious autonomy.

In Germany, Austria, and Switzerland, having the status of a public corporation, or *Körperschaft*, has major consequences. Most notable is the authority to levy church taxes. As church taxes are compulsory for all citizens who are listed as members of the *Körperschaft*, those citizens who do not want to pay church taxes have to declare that they have left their church. This approach is substantially less sensitive to issues of church autonomy in structuring relations on financial issues than the Italian and Spanish "tax check off" models, which avoid any interference between citizenship and faith. Anyone is free to specify an amount to be contributed to his or her church (or some alternative charitable purpose) in conjunction with the filing of taxes. There are no civil or canonical consequences for either choice.

Without going into detail, it is fair to say that growing respect is being accorded to religious autonomy rights in the new regimes of eastern Europe beginning in 1990, though problems obviously remain.[123] Long-entrenched patterns of tight control over religious organizations exert residual influence, even when constitutional norms radiate a new spirit. Constitutions in this region often assert separationist principles, but tend to follow the model of legal recognition and cooperation with the state. State churches are abolished, but national churches receive special treatment. Article 14 of the Russian Constitution of 1993 states that no religion may be instituted as mandatory or state-sponsored, and that all religious associations shall be separated from the state and be equal before the law.[124] The Russian Constitution also guarantees the freedom of religion, including the freedom to disseminate religious beliefs.[125] The Russian *Law on Religious Associations* of 1997[126] seems to contradict the second paragraph of article 14 of the Russian Constitution, as it appears to proscribe the registration of religious associations

---

[122] See, e.g., Hasan and Chaush v. Bulgaria, ECtHR, App. No. 30985/96, 26 Oct. 2000; Serif v. Greece, ECtHR, App. No. 38178/97, 14 Dec. 1999; Corporation of the Presiding Bishop of the Church of Jesus Christ of Latter-day Saints v. Amos, 483 US 327 (1987); Vienna Concluding Document, principle 16(d).

[123] For an overview of developments in this region, see Silvio Ferrari, W. Cole Durham, Jr. and Elizabeth A. Sewell, eds., *Law and Religion in Post-Communist Europe* (Leuven: Peeters, 2003); W. Cole Durham, Jr. and Silvio Ferrari, eds., *Religion Laws of Post-Communist Europe* (Leuven: Peeters, 2003). Electronic versions of legislation from most of these countries is available at <www.religlaw.org>.

[124] Konst. RF, art. 14.

[125] Konst. RF, art. 28.

[126] On Freedom of Conscience and Religious Associations, Fed. Law 125–FZ (Sept. 26, 1997), Ross. Gazeta, Oct. 1, 1997, LEXIS, Int'l Law Libr., RFLAW File (GARANT 71640). For discussion of the 1997 Russian Law, see W. Cole Durham, Jr. and Lauren B. Homer, "Russia's 1997 Law On Freedom of Conscience and Religious Associations: An Analytical Appraisal," *Emory Int'l L. Rev.* 12 (1998): 101; see also T. Jeremy Gunn, "Caesar's Sword: The 1997 Law of the Russian Federation on the Freedom of Conscience and Religious Associations," *Emory Int'l L. Rev.* 12 (1998): 43.

that have been present in Russia for less than fifteen years if they are not part of larger centralized organizations. Generally speaking, Russian law and that of most other former socialist bloc countries is cognizant of the importance of avoiding intervention in internal religious affairs.

V. Legal Recognition of Autonomy

To proclaim the internal autonomy of religious organizations is one thing; to give it legal effect is another. There are diverse legal mechanisms to ensure internal autonomy. What kind of legal consistency should comprise the autonomous sphere of religious life? Some concordat states give full legal effect to the institutions of the Catholic Church. In many cases the legal personality of the church and its territorial circumscriptions—parishes or dioceses or its councils, like the Conference of Bishops, that enjoy the legal personality in canon law—are recognized as juridical persons in civil law. Traditionally, this recognition was granted by the Catholic States (compare Colombia, Concordat 1973, art. 4)[127] and reformulated in more recent concordats in countries such as Spain (1979, art. 1),[128] Italy (1984, art. 7),[129] Poland (1993, art. 4),[130] and Croatia (1996), which recognize the public legal personality of the Catholic Church ***and*** of all ecclesiastical institutions enjoying this status in canon law (art. 2).[131]

But recent examples show that this recognition may also be granted by states with no Catholic background. Indeed, this would appear to be required under the European Convention.[132] But the basic principle is emerging in other areas as well. Four years after the ***Fundamental Agreement*** (1993),[133] Israel and the Holy See signed a special ***Legal Personality Agreement*** (1997)[134] that assures "full effect in Israeli law": [135] 1) to the legal personality of the Catholic Church, 2) to the legal personality of the Eastern Catholic and Latin Patriarchates, their respective dioceses, the Assembly of the Catholic bishops of the Holy Land,[136] and 3) to the Pontifical Institutes of Consecrated Life.[137] These ecclesiastical juridical persons have been created according to the legislation of the Holy

[127] "Solemnis Convention inter sanctam Sedem et Rem Publicam Columbianam in ***Raccolta di Concordati 1950–1999,*** José T. Martín de Agar (2000), 128 (art. 4).

[128] "Conventiones Inter Apostolicam Sedem et Nationem Hispanam," in ***Raccolta di Concordati 1950–1999,*** José T. Martín de Agar (2000), 790 (art. 1, secs. 3, 4).

[129] "Accordo tra la Santa Sede e la Repubblica Italiana che apporta modificazioni al Concordato Lateranense," in ***Raccolta di Concordati 1950–1999,*** José T. Martín de Agar (2000), 554 (art. 7).

[130] "Sollemnis conventio inter Apostolicam Sedem et Poloniae Rem Publicam," in ***Raccolta di Concordati 1950–1999,*** José T. Martín de Agar (2000), 684–85 (art. 4, secs. 1, 2).

[131] "Conventio inter Sanctam Sedem et Croatiæ Rem Publicam de Iuridicialibus quæstionibus," reprinted in ***Raccolta di Concordati 1950–1999,*** José T. Martín de Agar (2000), 155 (art. 2, secs. 1, 2).

[132] See, e.g., Hasan and Chaush v. Bulgaria, ECtHR, Appl No. 30985/96, Decision of 26 Oct. 2000; Canea Catholic Church v. Greece, ECtHR, App. No. 25528/94, Decision of 16 Dec. 1997.

[133] See generally, "Fundamental Agreement Between the Holy See and the State of Israel in ***Raccolta di Concordati 1950–1999,*** José T. Martín de Agar (2000), 516–25.

[134] See generally, "Agreement Between the State of Israel and the Holy See Pursuant to Article 3(3) of the Fundamental Agreement Between the State of Israel and the Holy See," in ***Raccolta di Concordati 1950–1999,*** José T. Martín de Agar (2000), 526–32.

[135] Ibid., at 526 (art. 2).

[136] Ibid., at 527 (art. 3).

[137] Ibid., at 528 (art. 5).

See, which is a sovereign in international law.[138] The provisions of article 6 make clear that the law of Israel governs any legal act made by ecclesiastical juridical persons in Israel.[139] But the canon law governs the designation of the ecclesiastical officer able to act in behalf of the legal person.[140] Any ecclesiastical legal person is deemed to have consented to sue and be sued before a judicial or administrative forum in Israel.[141]

In Estonia where Catholics are a small minority, "the Catholic Church as also its institutions which in accordance with Canon Law, have the status of either public or private juridical persons, shall enjoy juridical personality in civil law, according to the legislation of the Republic of Estonia."[142] Such institutions have to register with the Estonian authorities.[143] Gabon also recognizes the intrinsic juridical personality of the Catholic Church and the legal personality of its institutions as granted by canonical law.[144]

As a final note, an agreement was signed on February 15, 2000 with the Palestine Liberation Organization,[145] wherein, according to article 7, "full effect will be given in Palestinian Law to the legal personality of the Catholic Church and of the canonical legal persons."[146]

VI. Conclusion

The following are the three main models of how the institutional autonomy of churches interacts with the legal order of a state:

—The German model offers to the churches a civil juridical structure, namely the *Körperschaft des öffentlichen Rechts*, which gives them a possibility to behave as public actors in society, including the right to levy taxes from their members through state organizations. This status is extended to the territorial units of churches like dioceses or *Landeskirchen*.

—The model of total separation is exemplified in countries such as the United States, France, and the Netherlands, where the state wants to ignore the internal order of churches. In these systems, religious bodies have the possibility of resorting to the common law of associations or of availing themselves of legal structures established by special laws of association designed for them. In this model the church institutions themselves do not have civil effect, though suitable legal entities are available that the religious institutions can use to carry out their affairs. But case law suggests that the state cannot simply ignore the internal functioning of churches and must take into account that they have internal structures.

---

138 Ibid., at 528 (art. 6, sec. 1).

139 Ibid. (art. 6, sec. 2(a)).

140 Ibid., at 529 (art. 6, sec. 2(b)).

141 Ibid. (art. 6, sec. 4).

142 "Conventio Inter Apostolicam Sedem et Rem Publicam Estoniae," in *Raccolta di Concordati 1950–1999,* José T. Martín de Agar (2000), 197 (art. 2).

143 Ibid., art. 2 (recognition of legal personality commences "from the date of their registration with the competent Estonian authorities").

144 "Accord-cadre entre le Saint-Siège et la Republique Gabonaise sur les Principes et sur certaines Dispositions Juridiques concernant leurs Relations et leur Collaboration," in *Raccolta di Concordati 1950–1999,* José T. Martín de Agar (2000), 222 (art. 2, secs. 1, 2).

145 "Basic Agreement between the Holy See and the Palestine Liberation Organization," in *I Concordati del 2000,* José T. Martín de Agar (2001), 53–56.

146 Ibid., at 55.

—The concordat model is one in which the church institutions at canon law receive civil effect in civil law and are able to act in the juridical order of the state. Equal recognition is obviously granted by the state to other religious organizations with which it concludes special agreements. This is probably the most advanced model representing state respect of the internal autonomy of churches. This model saves the spirit of independence of church and state and fosters their mutual cooperation.

Chapter 15

Facilitating Freedom of Religion or Belief through Religious Association Laws

W. Cole Durham, Jr.

I. Introduction

A country's law and practice regarding religious entities constitutes a crucial test of its performance in facilitating freedom of religion or belief. This may seem surprising. The intricacies of the law of religious associations are clearly not the first issues that come to mind when one thinks of freedom of religion or belief. One is more likely to think of overt religious persecution, issues of conscientious objection in the military or other fields, restrictions on worship, constraints on religious speech and persuasion, interference with prescribed religious observances such as days of work or types of clothing, issues of religion and education, discrimination in employment, and so forth.

But on closer reflection, it is obvious that the law governing the creation, recognition and registration of appropriate legal entities is vital for the life of most religious communities in a modern legal setting. While there are a small number of groups that may object to being required to obtain legal entity status,[1] most groups desire to register

[1] There are a small number of religious communities that object as a matter of conscience to the requirement of being chartered by the state. For example, the International Council of Churches of Evangelical Christians/Baptists objects to registration as a matter of principle. See Felix Corley, "Estonia: Registration Transferred from Interior Ministry to Courts," *Keston News Service,* 4 July 2002, available at <http://www.religioscope.com/articles/2002/008_estonia_reg.htm> (last visited 11 November 2003). This religious organization was formed when a group of Baptists rejected compromises that the mainstream Union of Evangelical Christians-Baptists accepted in order to be registered in the Soviet regime. In 1961 these Baptists split from the mainstream Church and formed the International Council of Churches of Evangelical Christians-Baptists. Lawrence A. Uzzell, "Russian Baptists Being Punished for Independence," *The Moscow Times,* 15 September 2003, available at <http://www.themoscowtimes.com/stories/2003/09/15/006.html> (last visited 11 November 2003).
If recognition and registration laws are mandatory rather than permissive, such groups are faced with an immediate crisis of conscience. They cannot gather to worship legally and still follow their beliefs. Similar problems arise for others who, for a variety of practical reasons, decide as a matter of convenience or priority that the burdens of registration outweigh the benefits. Smaller groups may lack the legal and technical expertise necessary to craft a charter, or they may simply wish to worship together without

Tore Lindholm, W. Cole Durham, Jr., Bahia G. Tahzib-Lie (eds.), Facilitating Freedom of Religion or Belief: A Deskbook, *321–405.*

and obtain recognition, because it is only in this way that they can gain the benefits of juristic personality. The precise set of rights that is associated with such status varies from legal system to legal system, and within each system, depending on the particular type of legal entity involved.[2] But at a minimum, in the contemporary world, it is extremely difficult without entity status for a group to engage in the most rudimentary legal acts—e.g., opening a bank account, renting or acquiring property for a place of worship or for other religious uses, entering into contracts (including the array of agreements from contracts of employment with key religious personnel, to arrangements for publication of religious material or production of items needed for religious worship or observance, to mundane contracts for acquisition of supplies, electricity, heat, and other routine items needed in connection with religious life), to sue and be sued (i.e., to defend the rights of the organization by instituting legal actions,[3] and to be subject to lawsuits),[4] and so forth. These issues multiply for larger organizations that need to build and maintain multiple edifices for worship, to develop networks of pastoral care, and to establish an array of charitable and educational services—all in accordance with and rooted in sensitive patterns of conscientious belief.

Legal entity status is vital because, as a practical matter, a religious organization of any appreciable magnitude cannot operate effectively and efficiently without such status. A contemporary religious community needs to interact with the secular legal order in countless ways in order to carry out its affairs. Arranging such matters without legal entities is hopelessly cumbersome, and exposes religious communities to liability risks and legal problems that should not be imposed on religious communities against their will.[5] For example, if the property of a religious group is owned in the name of an individual, the interests of the group as a whole are put in jeopardy because there is a risk that the individual may appropriate the property for his own use, or may incur other unexpected liabilities in contract or tort that could be satisfied from the religious property.

---

going through extensive red tape. For them, mandatory registration entails an unwanted burden on the exercise of religious freedom rights that is not justified in terms of permissible grounds for limiting religious freedom rights. They are willing to forego the benefits of legal entity status and experience the requirement to seek such status as a religious freedom violation. This is even more clearly a problem where government officials deny the group the legal status required to carry out religious activities, or where the group has grounds to believe that initial or continuing efforts to acquire such status are likely to be unavailing. Problems associated with groups who object to state chartering, however, are relatively rare.

[2] Various types of entity status are described briefly near the end of section I below, but as explained there, the primary focus of this chapter is "base-level" entities, rather than the upper-tier entities such as public corporations (*Körperschaften des öffentlichen Rechts*) in Germany or recognized churches (*anerkannte Kirchen*) in Austria and many other systems.

[3] See, e.g., Lance Lehnhof, "Freedom of Religion Association: The Right of Religious Organizations to Obtain Legal Entity Status Under the European Convention," *BYU Law Review* (2002): 561–609, 562.

[4] The right to be sued would appear at first to be the antithesis of a privilege, but unless an organization can be sued, it may be difficult to obtain financing. Well-meaning legislatures sometimes immunize religious property from foreclosure actions, but this may in fact make it difficult for a religious group to obtain financing. See, e.g., *Law on the Freedom of Conscience and Religious Associations,* No. 125-FZ (1997) (amended 2000, 2002) [Russia] (hereinafter "Russian Law"), art. 21(3). Moreover, the fact that a religious organization can be sued in its own capacity may protect individual members from becoming personally liable for activities of the religious organization.

[5] Patty Gerstenblith, "Civil Court Resolution of Property Disputes among Religious Organizations," in *Religious Organizations in the United States: A Study of Legal Identity, Religious Freedom and the Law,* ed. James A. Serritella et al. (Durham: Carolina Academic Press, forthcoming, 2004).

If the individual holding the property dies, his or her heirs might inherit the religious property, regardless of their relationship to the religion. If the property is deemed to be held by an unincorporated association rather than a particular individual, problems of liability in contract or tort to third parties and issues of inheriting shares in the unincorporated association grow even more complex. Further, if the need arises to transfer property, the task of securing the consent of the association and all its members—particularly if the association has a considerable number of members and has survived over many years—becomes almost insuperable.[6]

Moreover, in many legal systems, there are a variety of additional legal issues that have substantial impact on religious life that are linked to acquiring legal entity status (or to specific types of entity status). Just a few examples will suffice to show how vital these issues can be. In many legal systems, registration is often a necessary precondition for:

- obtaining land use or other governmental permits;[7]
- inviting foreign religious leaders, workers and volunteers into a country;[8]
- arranging visits and ministries in hospitals, prisons and the military;[9]

---

[6] See, e.g., "Developments in the Law—Nonprofit Corporations," *Harvard Law Review* 105 (1992): 1578–1699; "Judicial Control of Actions of Private Associations," *Harvard Law Review* 76 (1962–63): 1055.

[7] In many instances, entity status may not be strictly necessary for obtaining various approvals of this nature. That is, laws governing land use permits may permit an individual member of a religious group to process an application. But there are a number of possible hitches. Where a land use approval is being sought for a particular piece of property, the landowner may need to submit the application, and it is much easier for an entity to own the land, for reasons described above. Also, particular members of a congregation may move in and out. Where applications take some time, it would be inconvenient for the application to lapse or to require amendment because of shifting membership. Countless other examples could be provided that would underscore the importance of having access to entity status. Moreover, as a practical matter, government officials in one office may be more comfortable granting approvals to an entity that has been approved by other officials.

[8] See, e.g., Russian Law, art. 20(2) ("Religious organizations shall have an exclusive right to invite foreign citizens for purposes of carrying on professional, including preaching, religious activities in the given organizations according to Federal Laws."); *Law on the Freedom of Conscience and Religious Organizations* (1991) (amended 1997, 2001) [Armenia] (hereinafter "Armenian Law"), art. 7(j) ("The spiritual and religious activities of Religious Organizations shall be carried out within the following clearly prescribed rights: . . . to invite their representatives . . . the above-mentioned rights will be acquired by a Religious Organization only upon its registration in the Republic of Armenia."); *Law on the Freedom of Conscience and Religious Organizations* (1991) (amended 1992, 1993, 1995, 1996) [Ukraine] (hereinafter "Ukrainian Law"), art. 24 ("The clergy, religious preachers, preceptors, other representatives of foreign organizations, who are foreign citizens temporarily staying in Ukraine, may engage in the preaching of religious doctrines, the performance of religious rites and other canonical activities only in those religious organizations that invited them, and subject to an official approval of the government authority that registered the statute of the relevant religious organization").

[9] See, e.g., *Law on Religious Organizations* (1995) (amended 1996, 1997, 1998, 2000) [Latvia] (hereinafter "Latvian Law"), art. 14(5) ("Religious organizations may engage in religious activities in hospitals, homes for the elderly and the disabled, places of detention and in the National Armed Forces, if the persons finding themselves in these institutions wish so."); Armenian Law, art. 7(c) ("The spiritual and religious activities of Religious Organizations shall be carried out within the following clearly prescribed rights: To perform religious services, rights and ceremonies in . . . religious institutions, as well as cemeteries, houses and residences of citizens, hospitals, in homes for the mentally retarded and the handicapped, detainment centers, military camps at the request off the citizens living there who are members of a given religion.").

- eligibility to establish educational institutions (whether for educating children or for training clergy);[10]
- eligibility to establish separate religiously motivated charitable organizations;[11]
- obtaining exemption from a variety of different forms of taxation and the deductibility of contributions to religious organizations.[12]

The foregoing are merely a representative set of the host of issues that may hinge on obtaining entity status.[13]

The general point is that it is extremely difficult as a practical matter to carry out the full range of a group's legitimate religious activities without access to legal entity status that carries with it sufficient corporate powers to carry out the full range of activities of a religious organization.[14] Denial of access to such entity status thus constitutes a severe burden and limitation both on a belief community's right to freedom of religion or belief

---

[10] See, e.g., Russian Law, art. 19(1) ("Religious organizations shall, acting in accordance with their charters, have the exclusive right to set up religious educational establishments to train ministers of religious worship and religious personnel."); Latvian Law, art. 13(2) ("Only registered religious associations or dioceses shall be entitled to establish educational institutions for the ecclesiastics, monasteries, missions and diaconate institutions."); Ukrainian Law, art. 19 (religious organization status needed to establish boarding schools).

[11] See, e.g., Ukrainian Law, art. 19 ("Religious organizations shall be entitled to establish . . . charitable institutions.").

[12] It is worth noting that some religious freedom problems may stem from excessively tight linkage of legal entity status and the availability of indirect benefits such as tax-exempt status and the deductibility of contributions. States have legitimate interests in making sure that rights to tax exemption are not abused and that tax funds are used for authorized purposes. If acquisition of legal entity status automatically carries with it tax benefits, state officials will quite naturally tend to monitor the acquisition of such status more closely, and may be more inclined to deny the status altogether. The unfortunate result of this approach is that legitimate religious groups may be delayed in obtaining legal entity status, or denied it altogether, because of fears about the risks of future abuse by the group itself, or by others. This is a clear case where the regulatory means used are disproportionate to the regulatory end, resulting in the inappropriate limitation of religious activity. A much better approach from the standpoint of international human rights standards is to separate issues of acquiring legal entity status from issues of eligibility for tax or other financial benefits. Procedurally, this means granting entity status readily and without delay, and dealing with issues of tax abuse after the fact (i.e., when they have actually occurred or appear likely to occur) by terminating tax-exempt status (but not necessarily entity status) of such groups. This allows entity status to be made available rapidly, facilitating the religious freedom of groups seeking the status, while safeguarding the interests of the state in a less burdensome manner.

[13] For thorough treatments of many of the relevant structural and organizational issues that arise in the law of the United States, see James A. Serritella et al., eds., *Religious Organizations in the United States: A Study of Legal Identity, Religious Freedom and the Law* (Durham: Carolina Academic Press, forthcoming, 2004); William W. Bassett, *Religious Organizations and the Law,* 2 vols. (Eagan, Minnesota: Thomson/West, 2003). For comparable analysis of relevant German law, see Joseph Listl and Dietrich Pirson, eds., *Handbuch des Staatskirchenrechts der Bundesrepublik Deutschland*, 2d rev. ed., 2 vols. (Berlin: Duncker & Humblot, 1994–95).

[14] In general, the "full range of activities" includes all those that an individual would have the right to engage in, either alone or in community with others, under international standards. See *International Covenant on Civil and Political Rights*, adopted and opened for signature by United Nations General Assembly Resolution 2200A (XXI), art. 18 (16 December 1966) (hereinafter "ICCPR"); *United Nations Declaration on the Elimination of All Forms of Intolerance and Discrimination Based on Religion or Belief,* proclaimed by United Nations General Assembly Resolution 36/55 (25 November 1981) (hereinafter "1981 Declaration").

as a collectivity, and on the rights of its individual believers. Denial of access to entity status may impose particular burdens on leaders of a religious group, who may feel thwarted in their efforts to carry out their religious responsibilities appropriately.[15] Often, such responsibilities come in the form of a religious calling or vocation, and fulfilling these obligations is felt as a matter of conscientious obligation, akin to a religious commandment. Ordinary members will be adversely impacted because the ability for the belief community to organize and structure religious life will be impaired in countless ways. Given all the foregoing considerations, it is no surprise that the right to legal entity status is now firmly grounded in human rights law.[16]

Given all the practical ramifications of entity status, official defenses of restrictive laws to the effect that religious groups may worship and practice their religions without entity status are simply not responsive. To say that religious activity is not absolutely barred without entity status does not prove that religious freedom rights and nondiscrimination rights are being satisfactorily protected. In the contemporary world, full protection of religious freedom and equality demands granting entity status sufficient to enable religious communities to "manifest [their] religion or belief in teaching, practice, worship and observance"[17]—in short, to carry out the full range of religious and charitable activities that have been associated with religious life throughout history.

These considerations also explain why the laws governing registration and incorporation of religious associations have become an important benchmark for assessing the level of religious freedom in various countries.[18] Laws governing access to religious entity status are described differently in different systems and confer a variety of different statuses and names on religious organizations.[19] In what follows, I will use the term "religious

---

[15] For example, a leader of a group may feel particular responsibility to find a place of worship, and this may prove extremely difficult to arrange if a legal entity cannot be created. In this case both the individual religious freedom of the religious leader, who is restricted in his ability to carry out his religious obligations, and the religious freedom of the group he represents, are impaired.

[16] Freedom and Democracy Party (ÖZDEP) v. Turkey (ECtHR, App. No. 23885/94, 8 December 1999); United Communist Party of Turkey v. Turkey (ECtHR, App. No. 19392/92, 30 January 1998); Sidiropoulos & Others v. Greece (ECtHR, 10 July 1998). Canea Catholic Church v. Greece, 27 EHRR 521 (1999) (ECtHR, App. No. 25528/94, 16 December 1997) (legal personality of the Roman Catholic Church protected); Hasan and Chaush v. Bulgaria (ECtHR, App. No. 30985/96, 26 October 2000); Metropolitan Church of Bessarabia v. Moldova (ECtHR, App. No. 45701/99, 13 December 2001). Refah Partisi v. Turkey (ECtHR, App. Nos. 41340/98, 41342/98, 41343/98, 41344/98, 2001), the only recent European Court case that has not sustained a right to entity status, is clearly distinguishable in that it involved the dissolution of an entity (a political party) that, in the view of the European Court, posed a serious threat to democratic values. See Lance Lehnhof, "Freedom of Religious Association: The Right of Religious Organizations to Obtain Legal Entity Status Under the European Convention," *BYU Law Review* (2002): 561, 580–88 (demonstrating that the *Refah* decision does not undermine prior European Court holdings and that under normal circumstances articles 9 and 11 of the European Convention support a right of entity status for religious groups). For further discussion of the right to entity status, see section III below.

[17] *Universal Declaration of Human Rights*, adopted and proclaimed by United Nations General Assembly Resolution 217A (III), art. 18 (10 December 1948) (hereinafter "UDHR").

[18] The annual country reports on freedom of religion or belief prepared by the US State Department, for example, assess each country's religious association laws and the extent of barriers to entity status as an important practical indicator of the level of religious freedom in each jurisdiction. See, e.g., 2003 Report, US Department of State, available online at <http://www.state.gov/g/drl/rls/irf/> (last visited 22 January 2004).

[19] See section II below for an overview of types of legal entities available in different systems.

association law" to refer broadly to the entire range of laws governing entities that religious groups or communities can use in structuring their legal affairs.[20] There are few areas where the nature of legislation has such profound implications for the life of religious communities. Religious organizations are acutely conscious of their needs in this area, and where restrictions exist, they quite predictably press for reform.[21] Because religious entity status is vital as a legal foundation for most other activities, this becomes a forefront issue of concern and surfaces as a priority demand. For long-established religions, issues of entity status are often taken for granted and forgotten, but even they cease to be apathetic when conflicts arise. The importance of juristic personality has a way of resurfacing and reminding religious communities of its importance when disputes arise.[22] Precisely because legislation in this area can so readily facilitate or restrict religious freedom, it becomes an important barometer of the general climate of freedom of religion or belief in any country.

Another reason that registration laws tend to be a key indicator of religious freedom is that they are often the vehicle that states use to respond to perceived social problems involving religion. This can take the form either of tightening the formulation or the application of registration laws. For example, France responded to perceived problems emanating from "dangerous sects" by passing a law in 2001 that allows courts to dissolve associations when they or one of their leaders has been convicted of causing harm to individuals, the illegal practice of medicine or improper handling of pharmaceuticals, or misleading publicity or fraud.[23] Similarly, local level prosecutions seeking to dissolve the

---

[20] In some countries the applicable legislation will specifically use the term "associations." In others, religious denominations object to being described as "mere associations," because they feel they should be regarded as distinct from other civil associations, such as social or sports clubs. In still other parts of the world, grouping both religious and other civil associations together is thought to insulate the state from charges of giving unfair preference to religion. In the United States, for example, grouping religious entities with other nonprofit associations for purposes of granting tax-exempt status helps insulate such tax treatment from establishment clause challenges under the First Amendment of the federal constitution. See Walz v. Tax Comm'n, 397 US 664 (1970). I use the term "religious association law" broadly to cover not only laws specifically dealing with associations, but also corporation laws, laws dealing exclusively with religious entities, and other areas of the law (e.g., trusts in common law jurisdictions) that can be used to create legal entities for managing the legal affairs of religious groups and communities as they interact with secular legal orders. In this broad sense, religious association law can be construed to include everything from treaty provisions, such as concordats that govern religious affairs, to background rules governing informal unincorporated associations. Note that religious association laws as thus defined will cover establishment of entities for secular life-stance communities as well. Thus, in the spirit of freedom of religion *or belief*, "religious association laws" as I am using the term covers legislation dealing with both religious associations and other types of belief communities.

[21] This helps to explain why issues of religious association law often attract even greater attention than other types of religious freedom infractions. By solving the critical threshold organizational issues linked to religious association law, government officials can eliminate one of the most problematic "squeaky wheels" in the overall system of protection of freedom of religion or belief.

[22] See, e.g., Canea Catholic Church v. Greece, 27 EHRR 521 (1999) (ECtHR, App. No. 25528/94, 16 December 1997) (legal personality of the Roman Catholic Church, which became relevant in a legal dispute involving the wall of a church building that was over one hundred years old, was recognized even though formal requirements for acquiring entity status had not been followed).

[23] For the full text of the law in English, see <http://www.cesnur.org/2001/fr_law_en.htm> (last visited 6 November 2003). For a more detailed discussion of this law and its background, see the chapter by Fautré, Garay, and Nidegger in this volume. For additional background, see Hannah Smith, "Liberté, Egalité, et Fraternité at Risk for New Religious Movements in France," *BYU Law Review* (2000): 1099.

Jehovah's Witnesses and the Salvation Army have been brought in Russia.[24] New legislation targeting extremism and terrorism in the aftermath of September 11, 2001 has also tended to affect religious association laws.[25] Because religion and belief communities increasingly have a transnational character, and most groups of any size have coreligionists in other countries, cases such as these almost invariably prompt international outcry.

While certain conduct carried out under the umbrella of a religious entity can be sufficiently grave to warrant denial of legal entity status,[26] for the most part the use of control mechanisms associated with religious association law tend to be overbroad, ineffective and even counterproductive. For example, in situations where a member or a leader of a religious group has engaged in criminal or fraudulent conduct, one can certainly understand why appropriate criminal sanctions or civil liability should be imposed. But it is not at all clear why other members of the belief community and the belief community as a collective entity should be deprived of access to legal entity status because of the wrongdoing of other members of the group. This result might be appropriate if all the members of the group could be shown to be complicit in the wrongdoing under normal rules of accessorial liability. In fact, however, resorting to control mechanisms in association laws typically goes far beyond what would be allowed under the law and procedure governing accessorial liability in most legal systems.[27] In general, overbroad efforts at controlling religious groups violate the religious freedom rights of those such as the innocent group members with respect to whom there is no justification for limiting access to legal entity status and the various advantages associated therewith. Freedom of religion or belief demands a more precise tailoring of regulatory means and ends if it is to be legitimate.[28]

The use of registration laws as a control mechanism has the added drawback that it is often ineffective and can be counterproductive as well. Needless to say, genuinely dangerous groups seldom describe their unlawful objectives in documents that are submitted in the registration process. Overly stringent registration standards are most likely to have the effect of simply driving such illegitimate groups underground. This often leaves the excessive burdens of registration laws to be borne primarily by the legitimate, law-abiding groups, while the targeted groups may be unaffected. There is considerable evidence in some countries that the result of harsh treatment of legitimate groups can lead to greater destabilization than the social problems a regime is trying to control in the first place.[29]

---

[24] See US Department of State, ***International Religious Freedom Report 2002: Russia,*** available at <http://www.state.gov/g/drl/rls/irf/2002/13958.htm> (last visited 15 December 2003).

[25] See, e.g., the discussion of Russia's extremism law in Brian Gross, "A Bend in the Road to Civil Society: The Effect of Russian Anti-Extremism Legislation on Not-for-Profit Organizations," ***International Journal of Not-for-Profit Law*** 6 (September 2003): 1, available online at <http://www.icnl.org/journal/vol6iss1/rel_grossprint.htm> (last visited 14 December 2003).

[26] Cf. Refah Partisi v. Turkey (ECtHR, App. Nos. 41340/98, 41342/98, 41343/98, 41344/98, 2001) (sustaining dissolution of a political party pressing an Islamic agenda).

[27] See, e.g., Sanford H. Kadish, "Complicity, Cause and Blame: A Study in the Interpretation of Doctrine," ***Cal. Law Review*** 73 (1985): 323–89; Claus Roxin, ***Täterschaft under Tatherrschaft*** (Berlin: de Gruyter, 1975).

[28] See section III(A)(6) below.

[29] See International Crisis Group, ***Radical Islam in Central Asia: Responding to Hizb ut-Tahir*** (30 June 2003), available online at <http://www.crisisweb.org/home/index.cfm?id=1441&l=1> (last visited 6 December 2003); International Crisis Group, ***Central Asia: Islam and the State*** (10 July 2003), available online at <http://www.crisisweb.org/home/index.cfm?id=1442&l=1> (last visited 6 December 2003).

Note that the various advantages associated with entity status, and no doubt many others that could be identified, are typically available in a variety of constitutional systems—both those that insist on a strong "separation" of religion and state, and those that allow strong cooperation. It is significant to bear in mind that registration and recognition can also carry with them more extensive privileges. Some of these privileges would be unconstitutional in separationist regimes such as the United States, or laicist regimes such as France or Turkey.[30] But such privileges may be not only allowed, but even constitutionally protected in many other systems.[31] These privileges include arrangements such as imposing and collecting "church tax,"[32] eligibility for various types of tax "check off" systems that contribute to financing of religious institutions,[33] funding of clergy salaries,[34] subsidies for maintenance of religious buildings,[35] cooperation in the provision of religious education,[36] and a variety of other forms of cooperation between the state and religious organizations. Even leaving financial benefits aside, it is clear in many systems that legal entity status (possibly restricted to certain classes of legal entities) confers credibility, legitimacy, respectability and prestige, which are intrinsically valuable to and desired by religious communities.[37] Depending on the country and background historical factors, these intangible benefits may be linked to acquiring specific types of formal legal status.[38] Where constitutionally permissible, the various modes of tangible cooperation interact with patterns of social prestige and legitimacy in mutually reinforcing ways that redound to the benefit of religious groups.

[30] See "Turkey" in Kevin Boyle and Juliet Sheen, eds., *Freedom of Religion and Belief: A World Report* (London: Routledge, 1997), 386–97; Brigitte Basdevant-Gaudemet, "State and Church in France," in *State and Church in the European Union*, ed. Gerhard Robbers (Baden-Baden: Nomos, 1996).

[31] With the exception of France, most European systems allow substantial cooperation of the state with religion. The United Kingdom, Norway, Finland and Denmark have established churches. Substantial cooperation, including religious education and various kinds of public cooperation and support for church finance, are evident in the German, Italian and Spanish systems. See generally Gerhard Robbers, ed., *State and Church in the European Union* (Baden-Baden: Nomos, 1996). It is accordingly no surprise that the distinctive church-state systems of the European Union are formally recognized as an area left to the law of the various members states. Declaration 11 (Declaration on the status of churches and non-confessional organizations) to the Treaty of Amsterdam (Official Journal C 340 of 10 November 1997) ("The European Union respects and does not prejudice the status under national law of churches and religious associations or communities in the Member States. The European Union equally respects the status of philosophical and non-confessional organizations.").

[32] See Gerhard Robbers "State and Church in Germany," in *State and Church in the European Union*, ed. Gerhard Robbers (Baden-Baden: Nomos, 1996), 57–74.

[33] See Iván C. Ibán, "State and Church in Spain," in *State and Church in the European Union*, ed. Gerhard Robbers (Baden-Baden: Nomos, 1996), 93–118.

[34] See *Law on the Freedom of Religious Belief and on the Status of Churches and Religious Societies*, No. 308 (1991) [Czechoslovakia] (note that this law is no longer in effect in the Czech Republic, but it is in effect [as amended] in Slovakia).

[35] Even laicist France allows this type of cooperation. Basdevant-Gaudemet, "State and Church in France," 119–46.

[36] See Ibán, "State and Church in Spain," 93–118; German Basic Law, art. 7; chapter by Plesner in this volume.

[37] This is more typical of systems in which there is a stratified set of legal entities. The higher-level entities or levels of recognition carry higher social prestige. See Silvio Ferrari, "State and Church in Italy," in *State and Church in the European Union*, ed. Gerhard Robbers (Baden-Baden: Nomos, 1996), 169–90; Ibán, "State and Church in Spain," 93–118.

[38] An example of this would be obtaining status as a Körperschaft des öffentlichen Rechts (public corporation) in Germany. See generally Robbers, "State and Church in Germany," 57–74.

The internationally recognized right to freedom of religion or belief does not necessarily preclude cooperationist approaches to structuring the relationship of religion and the state, such as those described in the preceding paragraph. Briefly stated this is because aid to or cooperation with religion does not inevitably interfere with the freedom to worship, observe, practice, or teach religion and, indeed, may have a favorable effect. From a human rights perspective, aid or cooperation only becomes problematic when it is administered in a discriminatory manner,[39] or in a way that either directly or indirectly results in "coercion which would impair . . . freedom to have or adopt a religion of [one's] choice"[40] or some other impermissible limitation on a manifestation of religion.[41]

For a variety of historical and practical reasons, systems with strong cooperationist elements almost inevitably develop dual- or multiple-tier systems of registration and recognition that help distinguish those eligible for full state cooperation from those who receive less or no support. These systems can become quite complex as they grapple with the competing pressures inherent in trying to manage massive systems of state support with deep historical roots while respecting modern axioms of equal treatment. The "upper-tier" structures tend to be very country-specific and highly sensitive to historical factors, as are the various advantages in the form of direct and indirect financial benefits, other privileges and prestige that go with this status. For example, many countries with a Roman Catholic background have agreements with the Catholic Church and increasingly with other major denominations that govern church-state relations with these groups.[42] In Germany, a number of benefits, as well as heightened prestige, flow from achieving status as a public corporation.[43] In Austria, "recognized churches" have more privileges and greater public status than a recently created category of "publicly registered belief communities,"[44] and these have various advantages over religious groups that elect to organize simply as ordinary "registered associations."

Thus far, the differential treatment of differing religious groups that is evident in such stratified systems has not been held to violate antidiscrimination norms. In part this reflects political considerations, since there is typically insufficient will to take on entrenched relationships between the state and predominant religions that have evolved over centuries. It also reflects assumptions that "there are reasonable and objective

---

39 ICCPR, arts. 2(1), 26.

40 ICCPR, art. 18(2).

41 ICCPR, art. 18(3). See section III below and the chapter by Nowak and Vospernik in this volume.

42 See Silvio Ferrari, "The Emerging Pattern of Church and State in Western Europe: The Italian Model," *BYU Law Review* (1995): 421–37; Rosa María Martínez de Codes, "The Contemporary Form of Registering Religious Entities in Spain," *BYU Law Review* (1998): 369–84; Alberto de la Hera, "Relations with Religious Minorities: The Spanish Model," *BYU Law Review* (1998): 387–400.

43 See Ernst-Lüder Solte, "Die Organisationsstruktur der übrigen als öffentliche Körperschaften verfassten Religionsgemeinschaften und ihre Stellung im Staatskirchenrecht," in *Handbuch des Staatskirchenrechts der Bundesrepublik Deutschland*, ed. Joseph Listl and Dietrich Pirson, 2d rev. ed. (Berlin: Duncker & Humblot, 1994), § 13, 1:417–36. Many smaller groups have been granted this status. See Gottfried Held, "Die Kleinen öffentlic-rechtlichen Religionsgemeinschaften im Staatskirchenrecht der Bundesrepublik," *Jus Ecclesiasticum*, vol. 22 (Munich: 1974), 19.

44 The phrase "publicly registered belief communities" is being used to translate "Bekenntnisgemeinschaften." See Herbert Kalb et al., *Religionsgemeinschaftenrecht* (Vienna: Verlag Österreich, 1998) (containing Austrian laws and commentary); see also Christopher J. Miner, "Losing My Religion: Austria's New Religion Law in Light of International and European Standards of Religious Freedom," *BYU Law Review* (1998): 607–45.

considerations, growing out of history, tradition, accrued obligations, identity forming and government limiting roles, social peacekeeping and the practicalities of dealing with major churches that justify differential treatment."[45] Economies of scale can also play a role.[46] Countries are reluctant to adopt international obligations that would require dismantling long-established and generally satisfactory church-state structures.[47] In light of these considerations, it seems unlikely that multi-tier systems will be held in principle to violate core international religious freedom standards, at least so long as all religious organizations have reasonable access to base-level entities that have sufficient powers to carry out the full range of their legitimate religious (or life-stance) activities. Of course, if particular systems go too far in privileging particular groups, human rights violations are not foreclosed.

In what follows, the emphasis will be on access to "base level" legal entity status rather than on the "upper-tier" structures that are often developed in cooperationist or established religion systems. The reason for this emphasis is straightforward: denial of access to base-level entity status causes the most significant and prevalent infringements of freedom of religion or belief. Moreover, the greatest consensus exists on this issue, and it is in this area that the clearest international norms have crystallized. While treatment of the rich diversity of structures that have developed in connection with cooperationist regimes will not be possible, it is important to remember that basic human rights principles constrain even the most deeply rooted patterns of state cooperation with or establishment of religion when these are coercive, impose undue limitations or involve impermissible discrimination.

II. Comparative Overview of Legal Structures Available to Religious Organizations

A. Overview of the Range of Available Entities and Associated Legal Benefits

In order to better appreciate the range of human rights issues that arise in connection with laws governing religious organizations, some comparative perspective on the range of entities available will be helpful. Virtually all legal systems, whether in the civilian or common law orbit, have legal provisions specifying the legal structures available to religious communities for organizing their affairs. Typically in civilian systems there is some mechanism for registering and/or recognizing such organizations, thereby endowing them with legal personality.[48] In common law jurisdictions such as the United States, a variety of devices are available, including trusts, corporations sole, nonprofit corporations,

---

[45] Cole Durham, *Freedom of Religion or Belief: Laws Affecting the Structuring of Religious Communities* (Warsaw, Poland: OSCE/ODIHR, 1999), 44.

[46] One might argue, for example, that the German church tax system, whereby churches exercise a taxing power vested in them as public corporations and the state cooperates in helping to collect the taxes as part of its normal tax collection scheme, may not be cost-effective for smaller denominations.

[47] E.g., Declaration 11 (Declaration on the status of churches and non-confessional organizations) to the Treaty of Amsterdam (Official Journal C 340 of 10 November 1997) ("The European Union respects and does not prejudice the status under national law of churches and religious associations or communities in the Member States. The European Union equally respects the status of philosophical and non-confessional organizations.").

[48] See, e.g., W. Cole Durham, Jr. and Silvio Ferrari, eds., *Religious Registration Laws in Post-Communist Europe* (Leuven: Peeters, forthcoming, 2004).

and religious corporations.[49] In the common law world, these all tend to be "base level" legal entities. There is no sense that an organization must spend time qualifying as one type of entity before it becomes eligible to move on to a "higher" status. The differing entities are not perceived as carrying with them fundamentally distinct levels of status and privilege. Rather, they are conceived essentially as a menu of legal options that religious organizations may elect to use, depending on which structure best fits their legal needs.[50] In general, the typical statutes describing how to set up a corporation would be analogous to a representative provision in a civilian legal system dealing with religious associations.

While religious association laws vary greatly in the range of issues they address, and in the way they are linked to other aspects of the legal systems of which they are a part, they tend to address the following:

(1) the individuals who are entitled to establish the legal entity;
(2) instructions for how the founders are to identify themselves;
(3) individuals who represent the entity, and how they are identified;
(4) the procedures founders must follow for founding the entity;
(5) contents of the statute, charter, articles of incorporation or other document governing the operations of the entity;
(6) criteria for governmental registration or recognition of the entity;
(7) procedures and time periods for registering the entity;

---

[49] For an excellent overview and comparison of these devices, see Patty Gerstenblith, "Associational Structures of Religious Organizations," *BYU Law Review* (1995): 439, 444–62; Patty Gerstenblith, "Civil Court Resolution Of Property Disputes Among Religious Organizations," in *Religious Organizations in the United States: A Study of Legal Identity, Religious Freedom and the Law*, ed. James A. Serritella et al. (Durham: Carolina Academic Press, forthcoming, 2004).

[50] This sentence exaggerates the situation slightly. The various types of legal entity status mentioned here are not all created equal, and each is not available in every state. Moreover, some have more attractive features than others. As a historical matter, the religious corporation is a relative latecomer, and it has been developed at least in part with an eye to giving appropriate respect to the distinctive religious liberty concerns that differentiate religious from other public benefit corporations. Thus, in the introduction to the Model Nonprofit Corporation Act, the Reporter describes typical benefits, noting that

> for sound constitutional and policy reasons the Revised Act provides religious corporations with more flexibility in structure and operations than public benefit corporations. The constitutional limitations on state regulation of religious corporations are recognized by section 1.80. Specific sections of the Revised Act are not applicable to religious corporations. For example, the provisions relating to receiverships and custodianships and to procedures on termination of members are not applicable to religious corporations. Other sections of the Revised Act may be negated by the articles or bylaws of religious corporations. These sections include: (1) the provisions relating to the removal of directors elected by members or directors; and (2) the right of members to inspect membership lists and receive financial statements (Subcommittee on the Model Nonprofit Corporation Law of the Business Law Section of the American Bar Association, Revised Model Nonprofit Corporation Act: Official Text With Official Comments and Statutory Cross-References [Michael C. Hone, Reporter] [Clifton, New Jersey: Prentice Hall Law and Business, 1987], xxix–xxx [footnotes omitted].)

While there are notable benefits to the religious corporation, there is no sense that special status is a precondition for access to this type of legal entity; any religious group may elect to organize as this type of entity, and precisely which groups qualify as religious is left for determination on a case-by-case basis (ibid, xxix).

(8) appeal procedures if the registration is denied;
(9) limitations on the permissible activities of the entity;
(10) constraints on the distribution of revenues and assets of the entity;
(11) amendments of the entity's governing documents; and
(12) dissolution provisions.

B. Facilitation vs. Control Functions

What is striking about the laws available that govern the creation of legal entities for religious groups is that they can be used in very different ways in different legal systems. Thus, in the United States and most of western Europe, laws governing the creation of religious entities are designed and used fundamentally to facilitate the organization of religious activity. In contrast, it is very clear that such laws were used in the former Soviet Union as control mechanisms. More recent legislation in most former socialist bloc countries has moved in the direction of a more facilitative approach,[51] but there are holdovers of the more control-oriented approach. For example, a very restrictive law was passed by the Belarus Parliament in October 2002,[52] and such legislation also persists in central Asia.[53] Even where legislation has been liberalized, the control orientation of government officials often remains in evidence. A number of the laws of former socialist bloc countries are either designed with control in mind, or have features that reflect the older mind set.[54] Even in the many countries from that region that have passed new legislation, old patterns of administration tend to continue.[55] Far too often, those administering laws governing religious associations continue to use them to create obstacles for religious activities instead of trying to facilitate them.

In fact, of course, all laws in this area have both facilitative and control features. Much depends on how these laws are applied in practice. Most religious association laws, for example, have provisions addressing dissolution or liquidation, and to the extent anything beyond voluntary dissolution is allowed, the potential for state intervention obviously grants some measure of control. In legal systems that respect freedom of religion or belief, the conditions under which dissolution is allowed are strictly limited.

---

[51] See Silvio Ferrari, W. Cole Durham, Jr., and Elizabeth A. Sewell, eds., *Law and Religion in Post-Communist Europe* (Leuven: Peeters, 2003); Durham and Ferrari, *Religious Registration Laws in Post-Communist Europe.*

[52] *Law on the Freedom of Religion and Religious Organizations* (2002) [Belarus] (hereinafter "Belarusian Law"), available at <www.religlaw.org> (last visited 6 December 2003).

[53] See, e.g., *Law on the Freedom of Worship and Religious Organizations* (1998) [Uzbekistan] (hereinafter "Uzbek Law"); *Law on Freedom of Religion and Religious Associations* (1992) [Kazakhstan], both available at <www.religlaw.org> (last visited 6 December 2003).

[54] See, e.g., Belarusian Law; Armenian Law; *Law on Freedom of Religious Beliefs*, No. 281 (1992) (amended 1996, 1997, 2001) [Azerbaijan] (hereinafter "Azerbaijani Law"), available at <www.religlaw.org> (last visited 6 December 2003).

[55] See, e.g., W. Cole Durham, Jr. and Lauren B. Homer, "Russia's 1997 Law on Freedom of Conscience and Religious Associations: An Analytical Appraisal," *Emory International Law Review* 12 (1998): 101, 169; US Department of State, *International Religious Freedom Report 2002: Russia*, available at <http://www.state.gov/g/drl/rls/irf/2002/13958.htm> (last visited 15 December 2003).
The tendency to retain the control orientation is often particularly pronounced at the local level, where officials have been accustomed to adopting a restrictive rather than facilitative approach for years, and where old habits of thought and practice are hard to break.

The control function is cabined in this narrow domain. Broadening the conditions for involuntary dissolution obviously broadens the potential scope of the state's control function. Even in countries where registration serves primarily a mere notice function, informing the state that the organization is operating requires submitting documents that will give the state the contact information on persons who represent the organization and who can be contacted if there are problems. This minimalist approach gives state officials a handle that can be used to contact the organization if control issues arise. But a vastly greater control function is evident where restrictive criteria govern whether entity status will be given. Granting of entity status itself becomes a control point in many countries, and as suggested above, this can lead to violations of the right to freedom of religion or belief (and the right to freedom of association) if access to entity status is obstructed unduly.

This section identifies some of the reasons why common law jurisdictions have tilted strongly toward the "facilitative approach" and then portrays the flexibility of the array of facilitative devices that are available, starting with the broad array of types of entities available in the United States, and then noting representative institutions from several other jurisdictions. Comprehensiveness in describing the full range of entities available worldwide is not possible. For example, it has not been possible to explore in any detail the types of entity structures that have emerged where Islam is the dominant religion. Because my own work has tended to concentrate primarily on the Americas, Europe and the former socialist bloc countries, it is not surprising that systems from these parts of the world receive more detailed attention in what follows. The aim in this section is to provide a broad perspective on the range of entities available in legal systems around the world that can be used to facilitate freedom of religion or belief at the level of laws governing the legal entities that religious groups can use.

The facilitative approach emerged in common law jurisdictions as part of the general evolution of the law of trusts and religious corporations, together with the general expansion of patterns of tolerance and freedom of religion. In the United States, the latter was reinforced by the constitutional commitment to freedom of religion. The private trust is a unique institution that emerged in the common law world[56] and is essentially unknown in civilian systems, although many of its functions can be duplicated using other legal devices.[57] As noted by Hansmann and Mattei, "[t]he Anglo-American concept of the trust, together with the equity jurisprudence of which it forms a part, are the fortuitous product of the peculiar historical path followed by English law."[58] In the typical

[56] The renowned English historian F. W. Maitland said of this institution: "The idea of a trust is so familiar to us all that we never wonder at it. And yet surely we ought to wonder. If we were asked what was the greatest and most distinctive achievement performed by Englishmen in the field of jurisprudence I cannot think that we could have any better answer to give than this, namely, the development from century to century of the trust idea" (Frederic William Maitland, *Collected Papers* [Cambridge: Cambridge University Press, 1911], 3:271–72).

[57] Technically, the trust emerged in equity rather than common law. There are canon law antecedents. See R. H. Helmholz, "The Early Enforcement of Uses," *Columbia Law Review* 79 (1979): 1503. Many of the key functions played by trusts can be arranged by contract or agency law. See Henry Hansmann and Hugo Mattei, "Trust Law in the United States: A Basic Study of its Special Contribution," *American Journal of Comparative Law* 46 (Supp. 1998): 133; Hansmann and Mattei, "The Functions of Trust Law: A Comparative Legal and Economic Analysis," *New York University Law Review* 73 (1998): 434; John Langbein, "The Contractarian Basis of the Law of Trusts," *Yale Law Journal* 105 (1995): 625.

[58] Hansmann and Mattei, "Trust Law in the United States," 134.

trust, a "trustor" or "settlor" transfers property to a trustee, who has the duty to hold the property and administer it for the benefit of a beneficiary. The trustee is the "legal" owner of the property; the beneficiary is its "equitable" owner.

This simple device has myriads of uses, not the least of which is that it ultimately became a significant device for holding religious property. Initially, trusts could only be enforced in favor of identifiable beneficiaries, but with the development of the idea of the charitable trust, which allowed trusts for a particular use or group, including religious uses or groups, the trust became an important early vehicle for holding religious property.[59] The most significant thing about a trust is that it "facilitates the partitioning of assets into bundles that can conveniently be pledged separately to different classes of creditors."[60] In effect, though not technically a distinct legal person or entity,[61] a trust as a functional matter has a number of the organizational attributes of a legal entity and yet can be set up by private parties with no action of any kind by the state. An analogy would be certain South African corporations that can be set up by private parties with no state approval.[62]

In England the trust has been the primary vehicle for organizing charitable activities, including religion, from the Reformation down to the present.[63] Because the creation of charitable corporations has depended on the crown, there has been somewhat greater freedom with respect to formation of charitable trusts.[64] But the basic rules governing charitable trusts and charitable corporations have been fairly consistent with each other.[65]

In the United States the situation is somewhat more complex, because some of the states repealed the English statute on which charitable trusts were assumed to be based[66] as part of the general repeal of British legislation following the Revolutionary War.[67] The consequence was that for a considerable period, at least in some states, there were some complexities in using charitable trusts, and charitable corporations were actually an easier vehicle to use.[68] This also meant that the trust and corporate forms evolved more

[59] Paul G. Kauper and Stephen C. Ellis, "Religious Corporations and the Law," *Michigan Law Review* 71 (1973): 1499, 1502.
[60] Hansmann and Mattei, "Trust Law in the United States," 134.
[61] Harry G. Henn and Michael George Pfeiffer, "Nonprofit Groups: Factors Influencing Choice of Form," *Wake Forest Law Review* 11 (1975): 181, 197.
[62] Johan van der Vyver, "Religion," in *The Law of South Africa* (LAWSA), ed. W. A. Joubert and J. A. Faris, 23 (Durban: Butterworths), para. 248 (Joan Church rev.).
[63] James J. Fishman, "The Development of Nonprofit Corporation Law and an Agenda for Reform," *Emory Law Journal* 34 (1985): 617, 620.
[64] Ibid.
[65] Ibid.
[66] The Statute of Charitable Uses of 1601, 43 Eliz. I, ch. 4 (1601). Doubts about the continued vitality of charitable trusts were at least partially dispelled by the Supreme Court in 1844, when Justice Story determined that charitable trusts had in fact been part of the common law even before the Statute of Charitable uses was enacted. Vidal v. Girard's Ex'rs, 43 US (2 How.) 127, 196 (1844).
[67] Fishman, "The Development of Nonprofit Corporation Law," 624–28.
[68] During the nineteenth century fears of (1) excessive accumulation of property in the hands of churches, (2) encumbering property with constraints imposed by the "dead hand" of past trustors, and (3) lack of adequate enforcement to assure fulfillment of trustees' duties, led to imposition of a variety of constraints on charitable and religious trusts (ibid., 627–28). These included limits on the amount of property they could hold, accounting requirements and restrictions on transfer of property (ibid., 634). Religious corporations were easier to use and emerged earlier than business corporations.

independently than in England.[69] Charitable corporations had been recognized as a vehicle for charitable giving since colonial days.[70] Religious corporations were the most numerous type of private corporation prior to the Revolution; only later did the business corporation become much more common.[71] Over time many of the earlier constraints on charitable trusts have fallen away,[72] but use of the corporate form has remained prevalent. As the modern business corporation emerged over the course of the nineteenth and twentieth centuries and came into common use in the business world, nonprofit corporation law came to be influenced more and more by business corporation models, leading to much greater flexibility in both trust and corporate forms.[73]

Because religious corporations must comply with various legislative requirements, whereas trusts are formed by exclusively private activity, the trust form has advantages in terms of flexibility at the stage of establishing a charitable or religious organization.[74] Of course, if disagreements emerge or other problems arise in connection with a trust, parties may need to resort to courts to enforce their interests, and other state officials may get involved in remedying wrongdoing.[75] But the point remains that no formal state action is required at the stage of creating a trust.[76]

---

[69] Ibid., 640–50. Because of the separate evolution, there are some significant distinctions between the two forms (ibid., 651–53).

[70] Ibid., 630–31.

[71] Ibid., 630–37.

[72] Fishman, "The Development of Nonprofit Corporation Law," 636, 653, 659–655.

[73] As Henn and Boyd have stated the relationship: "Nonprofit organizations have been the neglected stepchildren of modern organization law. The law historically has given nonprofit organizations, like Cinderellas, the hand-me-downs of their half-siblings, the business organizations" (Harry G. Henn and Jeffery H. Boyd, "Statutory Trends in the Law of Nonprofit Organizations: California, Here We Come!" *Cornell Law Review* 66 [1981]: 1103, 1104).

[74] Fishman, "The Development of Nonprofit Corporation Law," 653. In certain other respects, e.g., standards of fiduciary responsibility and ease of resigning as trustee, the trust form has some requirements that can be more stringent (ibid., 653).

[75] For an extensive discussion of the extent to which courts and other state officials should be permitted to be involved in disputes involving religious organizations and trusts, see Dallin H. Oaks, "Trust Doctrines in Church Controversies," *BYU Law Review* (1981): 805.

[76] Where there is precedent or other reason for thinking that a particular group is unlikely to qualify as the type of group for which charitable trusts are appropriate, attempts to use the trust form will ultimately prove unavailing. But where there is a legitimate religious group, the absence of a formal state action requirement lowers the barrier that might otherwise exist to creating an entity-like legal structure. Several advantages that help facilitate religious life flow from this feature of trusts. It enables a group to commence operations and to establish a track record that may help them surmount challenges to the validity of this structure at a later time. It also helps avoid hazards of stereotypical and prejudicial assessments of the group on the part of state officials. By requiring less in the way of statutory formalities, such purely private structures allow greater flexibility for sustained operation. Onerous registration requirements are problematic, because they require a group to expend resources on organizational matters before it acquires the legal structure it needs to muster such resources. Such requirements can also give government officials inappropriate leverage to pressure groups to make concessions in exchange for favorable decisions, or to obstruct group activity on the basis of prejudice. So long as there is a substantial range of cases under a trust regime according to which there is no serious legal question about the trust's validity, and the religious group using the trust form falls within that range, it is likely that in many cases no challenge to the validity of the trust will ever be brought, thereby eliminating problems of official abuse. Indeed, even for controversial groups, scarce enforcement resources may mean that only the clearly problematic trusts will be challenged. The fact that validity of trusts is ultimately reviewed by judicial officials may also be beneficial, in the sense that the judiciary may be better insulated from political

For my purposes, it is this feature of trust law that deserves particular attention. What it has meant is that in most states, a religious congregation could avoid the countless complexities that arise in attempting to hold property in an unincorporated association by conveying property to one or more trustees, to hold property in trust for the benefit of the church or congregation. Of course, these same advantages could be attained by using the corporate form. Moreover, one of the advantages of securing the corporate form is that it is clear from the moment the corporation is created that the entity established is recognized by the state. In contrast to the situation with trusts, an organization does not run the risk that a corporation that has been created by the state will later be found not to have been validly created in the first place.[77] Since access to the corporate form is now easy, the corporate form tends to be preferred. But the relative ease of establishing charitable trusts, taken together with growing experience that genuine problems can be dealt with at a later stage in the life of an entity, has helped set a threshold expectation that state involvement in the establishment of entities by religious communities should be fairly minimal.

The early history of corporations or charters in the United States followed the English pattern according to which a corporation could only be established with the express approval of the sovereign. In the colonial period many church bodies were unable to secure the corporate privilege, because this was reserved for the established church.[78] After the Revolution, in the democratic United States, the erosion of the notion of a corporation as a grant of a special sovereign favor gradually led to the demise of this "special charter" conception of incorporation.[79] The old system of special charters and religious favoritism gave way to statutes that "granted corporate form to all bodies that could comply with certain minimal prerequisites."[80] If these requirements had been set too high, the charitable trust mechanism could have been used in their stead.[81] Two types of religious corporations emerged—the trustee corporation, which simply incorporated the trustees, and the membership corporation.[82] A third form, the corporation sole, also emerged.[83] This came to be used particularly for hierarchical organizations. For example, a corporation sole could be

---

pressures linked to the unpopularity of religious groups than state officials in other branches of government. It may be that a regime that grants ready access to both the creation of trusts and religious corporations is optimally facilitative. Organizations without the wherewithal to get advance approval can use the trust form, which, even with its associated uncertainties, is still better than proceeding without any type of entity status. Other organizations can take advantage of advance clearance procedures to dispense with the risk of unfavorable subsequent determinations. Each organization can choose whichever vehicle seems best for it. Most modern facilitative systems find a way of combining these advantages in a way that grants ready access to entity status and does not impose unnecessary restraints.

[77] Of course, subsequent misconduct can lead to dissolution, but the organizers do not find out later that their legal vehicle was void *ab initio*.

[78] Paul G. Kauper and Stephen C. Ellis, "Religious Corporations and the Law," *Michigan Law Review* 71 (1973): 1507.

[79] Ibid., 1509.

[80] Ibid., 1510.

[81] This would not work, of course, in those jurisdictions that did not recognize charitable trusts or construed them so narrowly as to make them an ineffective vehicle. Even so, general experience with trusts and the growing experience with easy access to corporate status in the business world tended to encourage a facilitative approach over time. This was particularly true for religious groups, given the general commitment to religious freedom in the United States.

[82] Kauper and Ellis, "Religious Corporations and the Law," 1511.

[83] Ibid.

used to hold the property under the control of the bishop of a Catholic diocese. The point is, the evolution moved everything in the direction of simple, nondiscriminatory access to legal personality for religious bodies. As the implications of the right to freedom of religion or belief for entity status have been more fully recognized, there has been a general evolution both in trust and corporate law to facilitate access to entity status.

C. Types of Entities Available to Religious Groups in the United States

The law governing the creation of legal entities is a matter of state law in the United States, and the laws vary to a considerable extent from state to state. About fifteen of the states—typically older jurisdictions—have specific laws dealing with the organization of specific denominations.[84] This bears some analogy to the agreement system in Italy, Spain and many other countries with strong Roman Catholic influence, except that in each case there is a "default" law for "other" religions that allows any religious group to incorporate.[85] As one would expect, these laws tend to be tailored to specific needs of the denominations involved and afford them appropriate flexibility in owning property and dealing with various other issues.

The laws of eighteen states provide for trustee corporations.[86] Historically, trusteeship corporations represented the initial stage in moving from a heavy reliance on the trust form to more general use of corporate structures. In effect, the trusteeship corporation simply incorporated the trustees. Possibly because this form sometimes sets limitations on the permissible range of actions of trustees (for example, in selling property without judicial approval), this form tends to be used sparingly.[87]

Far more common today is the membership corporation, which is available in forty-three jurisdictions.[88] In thirty-one of these jurisdictions it is the only type of ecclesiastical corporation.[89] The membership corporation is analogous in many ways to the business

---

[84] The states with such laws are Connecticut, Delaware, Illinois, Kansas, Louisiana, Maine, Maryland, Massachusetts, Michigan, Minnesota, New Hampshire, New Jersey, New York, Vermont and Wisconsin. See Kauper and Ellis, "Religious Corporations and the Law," 1534, n. 173. Nevada previously had this type of statute, but has repealed it. The number of denominations covered by specific statute differs markedly from state to state. New York provides for more than thirty-five denominations. Most states with this type of statute cover no more than seven. Illinois, Louisiana and New Hampshire have special statutes only for the Orthodox Church, and Minnesota has a special law only for the Protestant Episcopal Church (Patty Gerstenblith, "Associational Structures of Religious Organizations," *BYU Law Review* (1995): 452–54, n.44). These special statutes sometimes reflect a continuation of the special charter system and a reluctance to disrupt entities formed under older laws (ibid., 452–53). In some cases special legislation may be called for because of unique needs of particular denominations (William J. Boyer, Jr., "Property Rights of Religious Institutions in Wisconsin," *Marquette Law Review* 36 [1953]: 329 [certain religious bodies could not readily revise their structures to comply with organizational patterns set forth in statutes on religious corporations]).

[85] The "default" law could be a normal not-for-profit corporation law, or it may be a generic religious corporation law. See generally Gerstenblith, "Associational Structures of Religious Organizations," 444–49.

[86] Kauper and Ellis, "Religious Corporations and the Law," 1538. Fifteen of the eighteen jurisdictions are located east of the Mississippi River.

[87] Ibid.

[88] Ibid., 1539.

[89] Ibid.

corporation, except that usually no stock certificates are issued. In effect, the members of the corporation (typically defined in the bylaws or articles of incorporation) are incorporated, and the members control the corporation. This form of organization is more democratic than other forms of organization and tends to appeal to denominations that are organized in a congregational fashion.[90]

Twenty-six states provide for corporations sole.[91] The corporation sole is a form of entity that traces its history back to the mid–fifteenth century, when it emerged as a type of entity ecclesiastical organizations could use to hold property in perpetuity.[92] The corporation sole is in effect a one-person corporation that incorporates a particular office, such as that of a bishop, and allows the current incumbent of the office to control the property owned by the corporation.[93] In the early days the corporation sole provided a vehicle for owning church property that avoided the risks of church property descending to the heirs of an ecclesiastical leader at his death. It works well for hierarchical organizations in which identifiable office holders are responsible for holding church property. Some of the impetus for the corporation sole structure came from the Roman Catholic Church.[94] Generally, corporations sole in the United States can be used only by ecclesiastical organizations.[95] The basic procedures for incorporation, the corporate powers granted, and the methods of dissolution of a corporation sole are typically similar to those for other types of nonprofit organizations.[96] What is different is that the ecclesiastical official chosen in accordance with the canons, rites, regulations or discipline of a particular religion may be incorporated and is thereupon authorized to deal with property vested in the corporation sole in accordance with principles of church governance of the religion in question.[97] Upon the death, resignation or removal of the person who is the corporation sole, the successor is automatically vested with title to and power and authority over the property on the same terms as the predecessor.[98] This significantly simplifies problems of transition by making control of property follow the office, and not the office-holder.[99]

---

[90] Ibid., 1539–40.

[91] Gerstenblith, "Associational Structures of Religious Organizations," 454.

[92] Ibid., 455–56; Kauper and Ellis, "Religious Corporations and the Law," 1540–41.

[93] Gerstenblith, "Associational Structures of Religious Organizations," 454; Kauper and Ellis, "Religious Corporations and the Law," 1540. As classically defined by Blackstone, a corporation sole is "one person only and his successors, in some particular station, who are incorporated by law, in order to give them some legal capacities and advantages, particularly that of perpetuity, which in their natural persons they could not have had" (Sir William Blackstone, ***Blackstone's Commentaries.*** With notes of reference to the Constitution and the laws of the Federal Government of the United States, and of the Commonwealth of Virginia, by St. George Tucker, vol. 2 [South Hackensack, N.J.,:Rothman Reprints, 1969], 469). See also Frederic W. Maitland, "The Corporation Sole," ***Law Quarterly Review*** 16 (1900): 335.

[94] Gerstenblith, "Associational Structures of Religious Organizations," 456; James B. O'Hara, "The Modern Corporation Sole," ***Dickinson Law Review*** 93 (1988): 23, 31.

[95] Gerstenblith, "Associational Structures of Religious Organizations," 454. One exception is Arizona, which permits formation of a corporation sole for the purpose of acquiring, holding and disposing of the property of scientific research institutions (Ariz. Rev. Stat. Ann. § 10-421 [1993]).

[96] Gerstenblith, "Associational Structures of Religious Organizations," 459.

[97] For this reason the corporation sole is particularly good at mirroring a group's internal theological structure as that is mediated through the mind and interpretation of the authorized incumbent of the office that has been incorporated (ibid., 455).

[98] Ibid., 458–59.

[99] Some statutes extend the corporation sole effects to situations where an individual has not formally incorporated as a corporation sole but in fact holds property in trust for the use or benefit of a religious

In virtually all states[100] religious groups can incorporate as simple nonprofit organizations, although they may be required to indicate (at their option) what type of nonprofit corporation they are.[101] For example, the California Nonprofit Corporation Law distinguishes between public benefit, mutual benefit and religious corporations, with public benefit entities receiving the highest degree of regulation, and with religious corporations receiving a lower degree of regulation out of respect for the religious freedom rights of these organizations.[102]

One additional source of flexibility in the United States may flow from the nature of its federal system. Along the lines suggested by business corporation laws, many states provide for the operation of corporations from other states within their borders.[103] Generally, they allow entities from other states to perform the same acts as domestic corporations.[104] This means that if a religious group does not find a legal structure that optimally fits its needs in one state, it may organize in a state that has the preferred legal form, and then function as a nonprofit entity in the state with the less attractive laws. There appears to be virtually no case law on this subject, but it suggests that federalism may expand the general facilitative orientation of the United States system.[105]

---

group. See, e.g., Alaska Stat. § 10.40.120 (1989); Ariz. Rev. Stat. Ann. § 10-427 (1988); Colo. Rev. Stat. § 7-52-105 (1990); Utah Code Ann. § 16-7-10 (Michie 1991); Wyo. Stat. § 17-8-117 (1989).

[100] The major exceptions are Virginia and West Virginia, whose constitutions, for historical reasons, prohibit the granting of incorporation to any church or religious denomination. See Va. Const, art. IV, § 14; W.Va. Const, art. VI, § 47. This limitation is rooted in strict church-state separation theory going back to Jefferson and Madison, and possibly beyond to English mortmain statutes (Gerstenblith, "Associational Structures of Religious Organizations," 462). As a practical matter this does not constitute a major practical problem for religious groups, though it affords less flexibility than the religious corporation form available in many other states. Church property can still be held in a trust. Many religious groups have incorporated a fund that is used to hold church property. This has the functional effect of providing a corporate entity for holding church property, without incorporating the denomination itself (Gerstenblith, "Associational Structures of Religious Organizations," 464 & n. 85). Also, both Virginia and West Virginia now have not-for-profit corporation laws that allow creation of nonprofit corporations for "any lawful purpose or purposes" (Va. Code Ann. § 13.1-825 [Michie 1994]; W. Va. Code § 31-1-7 [1994]). The constitutions bar incorporating a church itself, but do not ban the creation of nonprofit entities that can hold religious property and carry out religious purposes (Gerstenblith, "Associational Structures of Religious Organizations," 463–64).

[101] Ibid., 444–49. A few states require that religious organizations incorporate under religious corporation provisions; organization as a secular nonprofit appears not to be an option (Del. Code Ann. Tit. 27, § 101 [1994]; Md. Code Ann. Corps. & Ass'ns § 5-302 [1994]; N.H. Stat. Ann § 306.4 [1984]; N.C. Gen. Stat. § 55-A-3[A][3] [1990]; Ohio Rev. Code Ann. § 1702.03 [Baldwin 1995]). However, this is probably a more beneficial category and is unlikely to be experienced as a constraint by religious groups.

[102] Calif. Corp. Code §§ 5000-10841, §§ 5110-6910 (public benefit corporations); §§ 7110-8910 (mutual benefit corporations); §§ 9110-9690 (religious corporations). The section of the California code dealing with religious corporations emerged in part in response to overzealous efforts of the state attorney general to regulate the affairs of the World Wide Church of God in the late 1970s. The religious corporation provisions were designed to protect religious groups from excessive intervention in their internal affairs. See, e.g., Stanley R. Rader, *Against the Gates of Hell: The Threat to Religious Freedom in America* (New York: Everest House, 1980).

[103] Patty Gerstenblith, "Associational Structures of Religious Organizations," *BYU Law Review* (1995): 467–68.

[104] Since there is very little case law on this point, it is difficult to tell whether this recognition of entities from other jurisdictions extends to non-US jurisdictions, or is merely a reflection of the obligation of each state in the United States to give "full faith and credit" to the laws of other states under art. IV, sec. 1 of the US Constitution.

[105] Gerstenblith, "Associational Structures of Religious Organizations," 467–68.

Generally speaking, most states afford religious groups multiple options so that they can find the form most suitable to their ecclesiastical polity. Because both the trust and simple not-for-profit organization forms are always available as fallback organizational forms, practice consistently views these and other forms as devices designed to facilitate religious activity. Regardless of the form chosen, red tape in acquiring entity status is minimal. Religious groups do not face stiffer burdens in acquiring entity status than other nonprofit organizations. Indeed, they are often spared much of the regulatory burden associated with other public benefit organizations out of deference for their right to religious freedom.[106]

In the mid-1990s the DePaul Center for Church/State Studies surveyed 261 national level religious organizations in the United States to assess what type of legal structures these churches use to carry out their affairs.[107] The survey covered most major denominations in the United States and, of course, many minor ones as well. Despite the fact that approximately two-thirds of the respondents indicated that the nature of their religious organization was religiously or scripturally based, and a variety of other considerations suggested that the groups were quite diverse, the typical pattern of organization was surprisingly consistent. Respondents were asked, "Which *one* of the following would best characterize the formal legal structure of your organization?" The survey yielded the following statistics on legal form:[108]

An Unincorporated Association	8%
A Religious Not-for-Profit Corporation. . . .	87%
A Not-for-Profit Corporation	3%
A Charitable or Religious Trust	1%
A Corporation Sole	1%
A For-Profit Corporation	1%
Some other type of legal structure	1%

There is a remarkable convergence on the "religious not-for-profit" corporation, with 87% of religious communities having elected to use that form. Typically, organization as a "religious" not-for-profit corporation gives some advantages over the regular non-profit form—essentially in alleviating various reporting and other burdens out of respect for religious freedom. This form appears to be easily accessible and sufficiently flexible to meet a wide array of organizational needs.

It should be noted that the foregoing survey addressed the issue of the types of entities denominations use to organize their affairs at the national level. The results might be quite different if one were trying to determine how property is held by entities that hold property at the local level. It would still be true that "for-profit" structures would rarely be used, because of the adverse tax implications. Similarly, the use of unincorporated associations would remain rare. Other than groups who resist accepting state charters for doctrinal reasons, most groups would find some kind of entity structure more practical. Indeed,

---

[106] See, e.g., the Model Nonprofit Corporation Act, discussed in note 50 above.

[107] John Massad and Rhys H. Williams, "Religious Diversity, Civil Law and Institutional Isomorphism," in *Religious Organizations in the United States: A Study of Legal Identity, Religious Freedom and the Law*, ed. James A. Serritella et al. (Durham: Carolina Academic Press, forthcoming, 2004).

[108] See ibid.

some groups that view themselves as an unincorporated association nationally might well elect to use some entity form to hold property at the local level. Corporations sole are often used by hierarchical groups to hold property at the local level (for example, this would be true in many states for property owned by Catholic dioceses). In general, however, religious corporation status of some type has become available in most jurisdictions, and because this form often provides added protection for religious groups against various types of governmental regulation and red tape, it is not surprising that a large percentage of groups elect to organize their affairs as some type of religious corporation.

Several things should be emphasized about the range of entity options available to religious groups in the United States. First, whatever the early history of these various entity options may have been, virtually all are now easily accessible to religious groups that desire to use them.[109] Once a religious group has selected which type of entity it wishes to organize and prepares the necessary documents, approval of the documents by state officials is generally very prompt, typically taking only a few minutes, or at most, a few days. Second, the number of founders required is small—generally less than ten, and usually less than five. Third, to the extent that document filings are analogous to the registration process in Europe, the documents serve primarily a notice or informational function. They let state officials know that the organization is functioning and provide contact information for key officers, so that the state knows who to contact in the event any problems arise. State officials who accept the relevant documents are not performing a licensing or approval function; they are in effect merely taking notice of the existence of the group. Fourth, acquisition of entity status is, if anything, less burdensome than acquisition of normal nonprofit association status, among other reasons because religious groups are free to organize using trust or religious corporation statutes. Fifth, acquisition of entity status is typically not directly connected to state financial benefits such as tax-exempt status.[110] This means that whether or not an entity is eligible for financial benefits

---

[109] Of course, the denomination specific laws are open only to the denominations in question. Similarly, in some states there may be some constraints on the availability of some specialized types of entities.

[110] That is, acquiring entity status is an independent process from gaining tax-exempt status. Even more clearly, legal entity status is not a basis for obtaining more direct types of subsidy that are often available through "cooperationist" regimes, since such direct subsidies of religious organizations are constitutionally impermissible in the United States, nor is it tied to the complex problems of property restitution that have plagued legal systems throughout the former socialist bloc.

Religious organizations are exempt from federal taxation under the Internal Revenue Code IRC § 501(c)(3) (hereinafter "IRC"). Contributions to religious organizations (technically, to a "church" or "association of churches") are deductible from taxable income (IRC § 170[b][1][A][i]). Churches have a mandatory exception from the presumption of being a "private foundation" (which is subject to various strict tax requirements) (IRC § 508[c][1][A]). They are also exempt from the requirement applicable to most nonprofit organizations of filing annual informational returns (Form 990) (IRC § 6033[a][2][A]). Religious organizations also have some exemptions from requirements of paying social security taxes under the Federal Insurance Contributions Act (FICA) (26 USC § 3121[w][3]), and under the Federal Unemployment Tax Act (IRC § 3309[b]). State tax exemption rules tend to follow federal models, though they differ in detail. It is also significant to note that even when it comes to acquiring tax-exempt status, religious groups have significant advantages over other nonprofit groups. In general, to obtain tax-exempt status an organization must file Internal Revenue Service Form 1023, which requires a group to file extensive information establishing their charitable character and justifying the granting of tax-exempt status. Significantly, religious organizations do not have to file this form to be tax-exempt, though many elect to do so to obtain official documentation of their tax-exempt status from the Internal Revenue Service. See Instructions for Form 1023, available from the Internal Revenue Service at

in its interaction with the state, it is free to carry out the full range of its religious activities. With respect to a new organization, the ability to acquire entity status and move forward with religious activities does not get delayed or obstructed because of questions about eligibility for other state benefits. Finally, it is significant to note that the various structures are not viewed as instrumentalities for controlling the religious sector. This does not mean that American society is naïve about possible problems that some religious actors can create for society. It just means that association law is not viewed as the primary control mechanism. Rather, instead of trying to address potential problems before they occur through association law, actual problems are dealt with as they arise by criminal, tax or other administrative officials. This facilitates the activities of religious groups and focuses control functions on genuine problems.

What emerges, then, is a picture in which the state attitude toward religion is profoundly facilitative. The general trend of legal development has been toward making it easy for religious communities to organize their affairs and to interact easily with the secular domains of property ownership, employment, and the countless other domains in which religious groups need to interact with the secular legal order. Multiple legal structures are made available for this purpose by the state, and each of the structures has considerable flexibility. With the exception of statutes designed to work for specific denominations, most of the legal structures are sufficiently pliable that they can work for many religious groups. In general, recognizing that religious groups are entitled to religious freedom, the statutes are crafted in ways that minimize regulatory burden and that take into account the importance of avoiding intrusion into the organizational affairs of religious communities.

D. The Global Trend toward More Facilitative Religious Association Laws

While the laws of religious associations in other countries often differ in significant ways from that in the United States, it is fair to say that the broad trend of history is in the direction of more facilitative religious association laws. To cite the most dramatic example, there has been a radical shift in the laws of former socialist bloc countries over the past fifteen years.[111] Some of the "control mentality" remains in both the structure and the implementation of religion laws in these countries, but it is clear that there has been a massive transformation in the direction of facilitating freedom of religion or belief. In general, most countries in this region have laws that reaffirm constitutional provisions dealing with freedom of religion or belief, provide more detailed provisions spelling out the meaning of these constitutional norms, and, in particular, specify the requirements and procedures for acquiring religious entity status. The collapse of communism has brought with it the emergence of more democratic regimes in many other parts of the world, and this has tended to bring with it more facilitative approaches to the law of religious associations. This section highlights general trends or notable developments in other parts of the world.

<http://www.irs.gov/pub/irs-fill/k1023.pdf>. Special audit rules to avoid excessive intervention in religious affairs have been established under the Church Audit Procedure Act (IRC § 7611). For more extensive discussion of these issues, see Edward McGlynn Gaffney, Jr., "Religious Autonomy and the Exemption of Religious Organizations from Federal Taxation in the United States," in *Church Autonomy: A Comparative Survey*, ed. Gerhard Robbers (Frankfurt am Main: Peter Lang, 2001), 179, 212–25.

[111] See Silvio Ferrari, W. Cole Durham, Jr., and Elizabeth A. Sewell, eds., *Law and Religion in Post-Communist Europe* (Leuven: Peeters, 2003).

In Europe the importance of the facilitative orientation has been underscored by the line of recent European Court cases that have affirmed that the right to association includes the right to be able to acquire entity status.[112] While some of the early cases involved political and cultural associations, it is now clear that these cases protect the rights of religious communities to acquire legal entity status as well.[113] As has been noted earlier, many European countries have multi-tiered systems. In these systems it is typically possible at the "base level" for a religious group to organize as a normal nonprofit association (e.g., a registered association). Some have base-level associations specifically designed for religious communities. In some cases a special category of religious associations constitutes an intermediate category between secular nonprofit associations and "upper-tier" status, which might typically include an established church or major denomination. Thus, in Austria, there is the category of confessional communities (***Bekenntnisgemeinschaften***) between normal registered associations and upper-tier "recognized religions."[114] It is worth noting that not only is a facilitative approach evident with respect to base-level entities, but, in addition, "promotion" to higher levels is becoming easier. Thus there is a fairly large number of religious groups that have been accorded "public corporation" status in Germany.[115] A recent Constitutional Court case there appears to protect fairly broad access to "public corporation" status.[116] In countries using the agreement or concordat system, there are some efforts to broaden the number of groups that have the benefit of agreements.

---

[112] Interpreting the language of article 11 of the European Convention for the Protection of Human Rights and Fundamental Freedoms (opened for signature by the Council of Europe on 4 November 1950, entered into force 3 September 1953) (hereinafter "ECHR") (parallel to art. 22 in the ICCPR), the European Court of Human Rights has held that the right to association includes as an integral part the right to entity status, and that this applies to religious associations as well. See Freedom and Democracy Party (ÖZDEP) v. Turkey (ECtHR, 8 December 1999); United Communist Party of Turkey v. Turkey (ECtHR, 30 January 1998); Sidiropoulos & Others v. Greece (ECtHR, 10 July 1998). This reasoning extends to religious organizations. See Canea Catholic Church v. Greece, 27 EHRR 521 (1999) (ECtHR, 16 December 1997) (legal personality of the Roman Catholic Church protected); Hasan and Chaush v. Bulgaria (ECtHR, 26 October 2000) (interference with internal organization of Muslim community and managing its affairs violated religious freedom, and decision on grounds of freedom of association was unnecessary because freedom of religion analysis was carried out in light of freedom of association requirements).

[113] See a more detailed discussion in section III, below.

[114] See Herbert Kalb et al., ***Religionsgemeinschaftenrecht*** (Vienna: Verlag Österreich, 1998) (containing Austrian laws and commentary); see also Christopher J. Miner, "Losing My Religion: Austria's New Religion Law in Light of International and European Standards of Religious Freedom," ***BYU Law Review*** (1998): 607–45.

[115] Ernst-Lüder Solte, "Die Organisationsstruktur der übrigen als öffentliche Körperschaften verfassten Religionsgemeinschaften und ihre Stellung im Staatskirchenrecht," in ***Handbuch des Staatskirchenrechts der Bundesrepublik Deutschland***, ed. Joseph Listl and Dietrich Pirson, 2d rev. ed., 2 vols. (Berlin: Duncker & Humblot, 1994–95), § 13, 1:417. For a thorough but not necessarily exhaustive listing of smaller groups with public corporation status, see Gottfried Held, "Die Kleinen öffentlic-rechtlichen Religionsgemeinschaften im Staatskirchenrecht der Bundesrepublik," ***Jus Ecclesiasticum***, vol. 22 (Munich: 1974), 19.

[116] The decision reversed a determination that Jehovah's Witnesses were not entitled to public corporation status because of lack of loyalty to the state. The case was remanded to assess certain factual issues in light of the Constitutional Court's decision, but, in general, the decision signaled a broad and liberal understanding of the criteria for acquiring public entity status (Decision of the German Federal Constitutional Court of 19 December 2000 [BVerfG, 19.12.2000, Az. 2 BvR 1500/97], available at <http://www.bverfg.de>).

The situation in Latin America varies from country to country, but the broad pattern is a shift from the historical dominance of the Roman Catholic Church to systems that provide reasonable access to entity status for all religious groups.[117] As a result of the history of the region, the Catholic Church tends to have a distinctive status everywhere. It is generally recognized as an entity of public law, which gives it special status and generally makes it unnecessary for the Catholic Church to seek entity status through other channels. Entity status is in effect a given, and the Church has had considerable autonomy to operate under its own canon law.

The Catholic Church has not had totally unfettered autonomy in Latin America. Historically the power of the Church has been limited in some countries because of the historical legacy of the Patronate—the inherited legacy of Spanish and Portuguese monarchical authority over the Church granted in exchange for the monarchies' support for missionary efforts throughout South America.[118] The nature of state authority derived from this source has been transformed over time in the post-colonial era, but has meant that even long after the end of Spanish and Portuguese rule, the state could assert considerable power over the Church. In Mexico limitations on religion emanated from the aggressive secularism of the 1917 Revolution.[119] Needless to say, the communist revolution in Cuba has also drastically limited religious freedom and the freedom of religious association.

Nonetheless, the dominant pattern has been a shift from Catholic confessional states to more democratic regimes that provide genuine religious freedom, including greater flexibility for non-Catholic religious entities. As long as the Catholic Church was the established state religion, there was little need for the development of laws providing for the creation of religious legal entities or the registration of religious groups. Since World War II, however, all countries in Latin America have adopted constitutional provisions that guarantee freedom of religion.[120] Further, the sociological setting began to change

---

[117] For a valuable collection of essays placing Latin American developments in comparative perspective, see Javier Moctezuma Barragan and Alvaro Castro Estrada, eds., *Foro Internacional Sobre Libertad Religiosa: Memoria* (2003) (containing papers presented at a conference celebrating the tenth anniversary of the adoption of the Mexican law on religious associations in 1992). See also Paul E. Sigmund, ed., *Religious Freedom and Evangelization in Latin America: The Challenge of Religious Pluralism* (Maryknoll, N.Y.: Orbis Books, 1999).

[118] Mark A. Burkholder and Lyman L. Johnson, *Colonial Latin America*, 2d ed. (New York: Oxford University Press, 1994), 84; Patrick J. Thurston, "The Development of Religious Liberty in Chile, 1973–2000," *BYU Law Review* (2000): 1185, 1190–92.

[119] See Ricardo Hernandéz-Forcada, "The Effect of International Treaties on Religious Freedom in Mexico," *BYU Law Review* (2002): 301, 305–7.

[120] See Antigua and Barbuda Const, art. 11; Argentina Const, § 14, § 20; Bahamas Const, arts. 15 cl. 2, 22; Barbados Const, art. 19; Belize Const, arts. 3 cl. 2, 11; Bolivia Const, art. 182, Brazil Const, art. 5; Canada Const, Act § 2a; Chile Const, art. 19 cl. 6; Colombia Const, arts. 18, 19; Costa Rica Const, art. 75; Cuba Const, art. 8; Dominica Const, art. 9; Dominican Republic Const, art. 8 cl. 8; Ecuador Const, art. 23 cl. 11; El Salvador Const, art. 25; Grenada Const Order, art. 9; Guatemala Const, art. 36; Guyana Const, art. 145; Haiti Const, art. 30; Honduras Const, art. 77; Jamaica Const, art. 21 cl. 1; Mexico Const, art. 25; Nicaragua Const, art. 29; Panama Const, art. 35; Paraguay Const, art. 24; Peru Const, art. 2 cl. 3; Puerto Rico Const, art. 22, § 3; St. Kitts and Nevis Const, art. 11; St. Lucia Const, art. 9; St. Vincent Const, art. 9; Suriname Const, art. 18; Trinidad and Tobago Const, § 4h; Uruguay Const, art. 5; US Const, amend. 1; Venezuela Const, art. 57. Despite constitutional protections in Cuba, religious freedom has in fact been quite limited there.

dramatically. In the latter half of the twentieth century, non-Catholic religious groups began to grow rapidly and to present the need for new legal structures for religious entities.[121] Changes in the theological climate within the Catholic Church after the Second Vatican Council have also made it easier to recognize the religious freedom claims of other groups.[122]

At this point, with the exception of Cuba, religious communities are free to assemble and worship without governmental approval throughout Latin America, but as in other parts of the world, most religious groups prefer to have access to some form of religious entity. The general pattern in Latin America is to address this need of non-Catholic groups through generic laws governing civil associations. These entities are noncommercial in nature and in effect constitute the counterpart to standard nonprofit corporations in the United States. Typical laws governing civil associations allow a group of founders to form an association under written bylaws that explain the nature, purpose and structure of their association. Such associations can be formed for a number of purposes, including charitable, social, educational, cultural and religious. Normally the legal requirements to form and maintain such civil associations are not overly restrictive. The major restriction is that the entity must operate on a nonprofit basis (i.e., no proceeds or assets of the association can be transferred or distributed to the founders). In order to form such an association, the founders prepare written bylaws that are executed, notarized and filed with some agency of the government, usually the ministry of justice. Provided these generic procedural requirements are met, the entity obtains legal personality. The formation of civil associations is not normally subject to any sort of discretionary approval by the government. Once formed, the entity normally has to meet annual filing and reporting requirements or its existence may lapse.

When a religious group organizes a civil association or similar type of legal entity under which it wishes to conduct its legal affairs,[123] the entity is in fact registered with and recognized by the government. In many countries the religious entity is subject to precisely the same minimal level of governmental review that other charitable or cultural entities experience. Thus, in those Latin American countries that do not have any special or further registration of religious entities, once the civil association is formed and the relevant documents are filed with the government, the religious association has all the legal status that it needs to operate fully. This is the situation in Brazil, Uruguay, Paraguay and Venezuela, which have no national register of religions.

---

[121] See José Casanova, *Public Religions in the Modern World* (Chicago: Univ. of Chicago Press, 1994), 113–34; David Martin, *Tongues of Fire: The Explosion of Protestantism in Latin America* (Oxford: Blackwell, 1990). "[M]ost writers place the number of Protestants in Latin America at between 12 and 15 percent of the population—a dramatic increase from an estimated 1 percent in 1930 and 4 percent in 1960. The largest percentages are in Guatemala, Brazil, Chile, El Salvador, and Nicaragua, but the expansion is continent-wide" (Paul E. Sigmund, ed., "Introduction," in *Religious Freedom and Evangelization in Latin America: The Challenge of Religious Pluralism* [Maryknoll, New York: Orbis Books, 1999], 1, 2).

[122] For a discussion of the significance of these changes, see the chapter by Lindholm in this volume.

[123] In addition to the generic civil association, foundations and nonprofit corporations are other types of legal entities sometimes used by Latin American churches. Within the last few years, several countries have begun to recognize "religious associations." Mexico, Colombia and Chile all now allow the registration of specifically religious associations, as opposed to the more generic civil associations used in other Latin American countries.

Several other Latin American countries, including Chile, Argentina, Mexico and Peru, have adopted legislation that specifically addresses issues of registering religious entities.[124] These countries do not mandate registration in the sense of imposing sanctions for failure to do so. However, a variety of benefits are typically reserved for entities that do register. These benefits include various tax exemptions, support for obtaining visas for religious workers and missionaries, protection of the name and important symbols of the religion from use by unauthorized persons or groups, civil recognition of education at church schools, guaranteed access by ministers to hospitals and the military, and other similar benefits. None of these registration laws make registration difficult or overly burdensome for the applicants. While emerging legislation can be criticized in its details, the general pattern is one in which a fundamentally open and facilitative approach is emerging.[125]

Similar patterns are evident in other parts of the world. South Africa, for example, has very enlightened laws on registration. Under South African law it is possible to incorporate a religious organization without securing any state approval.[126] This is the ultimate extension of the idea born in common law countries with the law of trusts, that legal entities can be the creation of private determinations. Canada[127] and New Zealand,[128] as one would expect, have very flexible laws. Japan[129] and several Pacific nations[130] have very flexible provisions that provide appropriate access to legal entity status for religious groups.

---

[124] Chile, Law of Worship, Law N° 19.638 (2000), summary of requirements available at <http://www.minjusticia.cl/comunes.html#>; Colombia, Law of Religious Liberty and Worship, Law 133 of 1994 (23 May 1994), available at <http://www.secretariasenado.gov.co/leyes/L0133_94.HTM>; Argentina, National Registry of Religions, Law n° 21.745 (15 February 1978), see also Decree n° 2.037/79, Resolution n° 3.509/94, Resolution n° 3.510/94, Resolution n° 167/97, summary of requirements available at <http://www.mrecic.gov.ar/ministerio/sculto/tramites2.html>; Mexico, Law of Religious Associations and Public Worship (15 July 1992), full text available at: <http://info4.juridicas.unam.mx/ijure/tcfed/23.html>; Peru, Implementation of the Registry of Non-Catholic Confessions, Ministerial Resolution No. 377-2003-JUS (13 October 2003).

[125] For the overview of the Latin American situation, I am indebted to Scott E. Isaacson. For a more detailed analysis of recent legislation in Chile and Colombia, see Scott E. Isaacson, "A Practical Comparison of the Laws of Religion of Colombia and Chile," *International Journal of Not-for-Profit Law*, vol. 6 (September 2003), <http://www.icnl.org/journal/vol6iss1/rel_isaacsonprint.htm> (visited 13 December 2003). For examples of provisions deserving criticism, note the requirements in Mexico and Peru that limit registration to religious groups that have been present in the country for ten and five years, respectively (see section IV).

[126] Johan van der Vyver, "Religion," in *The Law of South Africa* (LAWSA), ed. W. A. Joubert and J. A. Faris, 23 (Durban: Butterworths), para. 248 (Joan Church rev.).

[127] Canada Corporations Act (1970). Part II of this federal law governs the incorporation of religious organizations. Department of Justice, <http://laws.justice.gc.ca/en/C-1.8/10842.html> (visited 18 June 2001); Revenue Canada, <http://www.ccra-adrc.gc.ca> (visited 19 June 2001).

[128] Charitable Trusts Act (1908) (as amended in 1957) [New Zealand]; Incorporated Societies Act (1908) (as amended in 1957) [New Zealand].

[129] 1951 Law on Religious Corporations [Japan].

[130] Charitable Trust Act [Samoa], available online at <http://www.vanuatu.usp.ac.fj/sol_adobe_documents/World/Pacific%20legislation/Samoa/Charitable%20Trusts%20Act%201965.PDF>; Charitable Trust Act [Tonga], available online at <http://www.vanuatu.usp.ac.fj/paclawmat/Paclawmat_MAIN.html>; Charitable Trust Act [Solomon Islands], available online at <http://www.vanuatu.usp.ac.fj/paclawmat/Paclawmat_MAIN.html>.

Thus, it is fair to say that the prevailing trend, at least among democratically oriented regimes, is clearly toward religious association laws that provide easy access to legal entity status and that implement these laws in a facilitative way. As will be evident from section III, this is precisely what international human rights norms demand. Unfortunately, there are still many parts of the world where religious association laws remain quite restrictive. This is a major problem throughout much of the Muslim world. Laws in China and several Southeast Asian countries remain restrictive. Moreover, in many other parts of the world—even in countries where one would expect high levels of compliance with international norms—significant areas for improvement remain. Thus, as a practical matter, while the law of religious associations may not be the most dramatic field in the overall domain of freedom of religion or belief, it is clearly one in which some of the most meaningful practical strides can be made.

III. The Implications of Relevant International Human Rights Norms

The aim of this chapter thus far has been to demonstrate why flexible religious association laws making access to legal entity status are so vital for freedom of religion or belief (section I), and then to provide a comparative overview of the range of available legal mechanisms and approaches to facilitating freedom of religion or belief through religious association law (section II). The comparative perspective acknowledges that religious association laws that are very similar in structure can have very different effects on freedom of religion or belief, depending on whether they are interpreted and administered with an eye to facilitating freedom or with the aim of using the legal system to manage or control religious activities. Recurrent problems that arise if the control orientation goes too far are the subject of section IV.

In this section the effort is to show how strands drawn from all of the international human rights instruments, as analyzed in many of the other chapters in this volume,[131] come together to ground the right of religious groups to acquire entity status. I first examine the substantive right to religious freedom, as defined and elaborated by human rights instruments and bodies. These demonstrate that religious association laws must have sufficient scope to allow religious groups (as well as other life-stance communities)[132] to carry out the full range of activities suggested by the idea of a right to "manifest [one's] religion or belief in teaching, practice, worship and observance"[133] and "either individually or in community with others."[134] I then examine the impact of free association rights, both alone and in conjunction with freedom of religion.[135] Finally, I look at other key human rights, which protect not only (1) the right to be treated equally by

[131] See, e.g., the chapters in this volume by Lerner, van der Vyver, Nowak and Vospernik, van Boven, Scheinin, Gibson and Lord, and Martínez-Torrón and Navarro-Valls.

[132] The rights discussed in this chapter cover both religious communities and, in the spirit of freedom of religion *or belief*, also other life-stance or *Weltanschauung* communities. For purposes of brevity and to avoid cumbersome repetition, it is not always convenient to refer to both types of groups. References to religious groups in what follows should be understood inclusively, as covering both religious and other types of belief communities.

[133] UDHR, art. 18; ICCPR, art. 18(1); ECHR, art. 9(1).

[134] ICCPR, art. 18(1).

[135] Section III(B).

religious association laws,[136] but also (2) the right to be guaranteed that such laws conform to fundamental requirements of the rule of law,[137] and (3) the right to fair procedures for all groups seeking religious entity status.[138]

To the extent that religious association laws interfere with the freedom of religion or belief, freedom of association, or other human rights, they constitute limitations that are permissible only if they fall within the limitation clauses of the relevant international instruments.[139] These limitation clauses must be construed narrowly to maximize freedom of religion; this means that the range of permissible limitations on religious freedom posed by religious association laws should be kept to a minimum. Full implementation of the array of international norms that bear on religious association laws, including care to make sure that these laws do not impermissibly limit freedom of religion or belief, assures a facilitative interpretation and administration of these laws.

Increasingly, because of widespread recognition of the practical ramifications of religious association law described in section I above, the significance of access to legal entity status has emerged as a forefront practical concern. The Helsinki Process has paid special attention to this issue,[140] noting its importance as early as its Madrid Meeting in 1983. At that time the Participating States indicated that they would "favourably consider applications by religious communities of believers practicing or prepared to practice their faith within the constitutional framework of their States, to be granted the status provided for in their respective countries for religious faiths, institutions and organizations."[141] This language was strengthened in the Vienna Concluding Document in 1989, which in this area as in so many others marked a crucial turning point in attitudes of East and West toward many human rights issues. The Vienna Concluding Document provided that Participating States would not only "favourably consider applications" but that they "*will* . . . *grant* upon their request to communities of believers, practicing or prepared to practice their faith within the constitutional framework of their States, recognition of the status provided for them in their respective countries."[142] The language of this commitment sounds rather vague, but the intent was clear. As section II of this chapter has

---

[136] Section III(C)(1).

[137] Section III(C)(2).

[138] Section III(C)(3).

[139] For a more detailed analysis of the limitation clauses, see the chapter by Nowak and Vospernik in this volume. The implications of limitation clauses for religious association laws are spelled out in section III(A)(6) below.

[140] For a more detailed analysis of many of the issues addressed in this section, see the background paper I prepared at the request of the OSCE's Office of Democratic Institutions and Human Rights: Cole Durham, *Freedom of Religion or Belief: Laws Affecting the Structuring of Religious Communities* (Warsaw: OSCE/ODIHR, 1999), available at <http://www.osce.org/odihr/documents/background/religion/>, and also available in Russian at <http://www.osce.org/odihr/documents/background/religion/i4_index-rus.htm>.

[141] Paragraph 14 of the Concluding Document of the Madrid Meeting (Questions Relating to Security in Europe). Helsinki Process documents are available at the OSCE website, <www.osce.org>. See also Office of Democratic Institutions and Human Rights, *OSCE Human Dimension Commitments: A Reference Guide* (Warsaw: OSCE Office of Democratic Institutions and Human Rights, 2001), available at <http://www.osce.org/odihr/documents/oscecommitments.pdf>. A Russian version is also available at <http://www.osce.org/odihr/documents/oscecommitments_ru.pdf>.

[142] *Concluding Document of the Vienna Meeting of Representatives of the Participating States of the Conference on Security and Cooperation in Europe*, Questions Relating to Security in Europe: Principle 16.3 (emphasis added) (adopted 17 January 1989) (hereinafter "Vienna Concluding Document").

demonstrated, there are a host of differently named entities that could be described in terms of "the status provided for them in their respective countries"—trusts, nonprofit corporations, religious corporations, civil associations, religious organizations, etc. The aim of the Vienna Concluding Document was to look beyond institutional form and to commit countries to grant religious groups access to entity status in a form appropriate to facilitate a religious community's efforts to carry out the full range of its activities, within "the constitutional framework of their States." Issues concerning religious association laws remained an important OSCE concern throughout the 1990s. In June of 2002 the Dutch government, in cooperation with the Romanian Chair-in-Office of the OSCE, sponsored a seminar for the OSCE region that placed a major emphasis on these issues.[143] This helped highlight continuing OSCE concerns in this area. The OSCE has done a major service to the international community by focusing attention on the importance of religious association laws. In doing so, however, the OSCE was not adding something new; it was merely emphasizing what was already inherent in the existing international norms governing freedom of religion or belief that have been accepted by a large majority of the nations of the world.

While at first blush one might think that the pronouncements of the key international human rights instruments are too abstract to reach the concrete issues that typically arise in connection with religious association laws, in fact the implications of these instruments in demanding a facilitative approach become clear once they are carefully analyzed. This analysis quickly becomes complex, however, because of the range of relevant norms and because of the multiplicity of international instruments that address the overlapping set of norms that are relevant.

One could approach analysis of the various issues on a document-by-document basis, since each international instrument articulates the relevant norms in slightly different ways, but for current purposes it will expedite analysis to proceed on an issue-by-issue basis, summarizing what each instrument adds to the treatment of the relevant norms. Because of the underlying similarities of these norms, especially on core issues affecting religious registration laws, it makes sense to interweave references to them in this discussion, despite the fact that the various instruments have slightly different meanings and levels of authority.[144]

---

[143] The proceedings of this seminar were published: OSCE, *Seminar on Freedom of Religion or Belief in the OSCE Region: Challenges to Law and Practice* (The Hague: Ministerie van Buitenlandse Zaken, 26 June 2001).

[144] A difficulty with this approach is that different instruments obviously have different levels of binding force. As a technical matter, treaties such as the ICCPR are legally binding on the numerous countries that have ratified them. In contrast, the earlier Universal Declaration of Human Rights is formally only a "Declaration," as is the 1981 Declaration on the Elimination of All Forms of Intolerance and of Discrimination Based on Religion or Belief. But in fact for all practical purposes, the language of both of these has for the most part been reduced to treaty language in the ICCPR and other instruments. Moreover, many would argue that these declarations have become customary law in any event. See Derek Davis, "The Evolution of Religious Freedom as a Universal Human Right: Examining the Role of the 1981 United Nations Declaration on the Elimination of all Forms of Intolerance and of Discrimination Based on Religion or Belief," *BYU Law Review* (2002): 217, 230 (arguing that the 1981 Declaration is customary law); Bayiyyih G. Tahzib, *Freedom of Religion or Belief: Ensuring Effective International Legal Protection* (Boston: Martinus Nijhoff, 1996), 184–85 (arguing that the 1981 Declaration is customary law); Patrick Thornberry, *International Law And The Rights of Minorities* (Oxford: Clarendon Press, 1991), 237–38 (arguing that the Universal Declaration is customary law); Louis Henkin, *The Age of Rights*

A. The Substantive Right to Freedom of Religion or Belief

The starting point for analysis of the implications of the substantive right to freedom of religion or belief is article 18 of the UDHR, which virtually all other international instruments parallel:[145]

> *Everyone has* the right to freedom of thought, conscience and *religion*; this right includes freedom to change his religion or belief, and freedom, either alone *or in community with others* and in public or private, to *manifest* his religion or belief in *teaching*, *practice*, *worship* and *observance*.[146]

I have italicized a series of the key terms in this provision that have particular significance for the law of religious associations. In what follows I consider these italicized terms in turn, using them to help mark key features of the right to freedom of religion or belief in this area.[147]

(New York: Columbia University Press, 1990), 19 (arguing that the Universal Declaration is customary law); John Humphrey, *No Distant Millennium: The International Law Of Human Rights* (Paris: UNESCO, 1989), 155 (arguing that the Universal Declaration is customary law); A. H. Robertson and J. G. Merrills, *Human Rights In The World,* 3d ed. (Manchester: Manchester University Press, 1989), 96 (arguing that the Universal Declaration is customary law); Richard B. Lillich, "Civil Rights," in *Human Rights In International Law: Legal And Policy Issues,* ed. Theodor Meron (Oxford: Clarendon Press, 1984), 115, 116 (arguing that the Universal Declaration is customary law); Philip Alston, "The Universal Declaration at 35: Western and Passé or Alive and Universal," *The Review of the International Commission of Jurists* 31 (1983): 60, 69 (arguing that the Universal Declaration is customary law); Richard Bilder, "The Status of International Human Rights Law: An Overview," in *International Human Rights Law & Practice,* ed. James Tuttle (Chicago: American Bar Association, 1978), 1, 8 (arguing that the Universal Declaration is customary law); Louis B. Sohn, "The Human Rights Law of the Charter," *Texas International Law Journal* 12 (1977): 129, 133 (arguing that the Universal Declaration is customary law); John Humphrey, "The International Bill of Rights: Scope and Implementation," *William and Mary Law Review* 17 (1976): 527, 529 (arguing that the Universal Declaration is customary law); Humphrey Waldock, "Human Rights in Contemporary International Law and the Significance of the European Convention," in *The European Convention of Human Rights* (Brit. Inst. Int'l & Comp. L., Ser. No. 5, 1965): 1, 15 (arguing that the Universal Declaration is customary law). See also Hurst Hannum, "The Status of the Universal Declaration of Human Rights in National and International Law," *Georgia Journal of International and Comparative Law* 25 (1995/1996): 287, 317–52 (summarizing statements of constituents of several states and international bodies as well as influential authors holding that the Universal Declaration of Human Rights is customary law).

Regional instruments such as the European Convention for the Protection of Human Rights and Fundamental Freedoms, the American Convention on Human Rights, and the African Charter on Human and Peoples' Rights bind only the countries in their respective regions, but interpretations of these norms, as provided for example by the European Court of Human Rights, constitute persuasive authority concerning the meaning of parallel international treaty language. Similarly, while the "political commitments" of the Helsinki Process may not be as strong as other "legally binding" commitments, they have often proven to be more effective as a practical matter, and, in any event, they also have persuasive authority.

[145] E.g., art. 18 of the ICCPR, art. 1 of the 1981 Declaration, art. 9 of the ECHR, and art. 12 of the American Convention on Human Rights (except that "in community with others" reads "together with others"). Article 8 of the African Charter on Human and People's Rights frames the issues differently, stating that "Freedom of conscience, the profession and free practice of religion shall be guaranteed. No one may, subject to law and order, be submitted to measures restricting the exercise of these freedoms." This formulation is arguably weaker than the others, but many of the points made in interpreting the UDHR, which have obvious parallels with the other instruments, ought to apply to the African Charter version as well.

[146] UDHR, art. 18 (emphasis added).

1. The Universality of the Right

"*Everyone.*" All human beings have this right.[148] All of the major international instruments are consistent on this point.[149] Even a child has this right, which in a child's case is to be respected, taking into account "the rights and duties of the parents . . . to provide direction to the child in the exercise of his or her right in a manner consistent with the evolving capacities of the child."[150] The right is not limited in its availability to citizens, or even permanent residents. Nonresident aliens and stateless persons have the right to freedom of religion or belief.[151] So do foreign religious leaders, religious personnel and missionaries. Human beings do not lose their rights by taking on religious roles.

A recurring problem with religious association laws is that they often compromise the scope of the right by limiting it to citizens or permanent residents. States may have grounds for keeping certain classes of persons from entering their country that will satisfy the requirements necessary to limit manifestations of religion (e.g., persons who are likely to be dangerous to their citizens), but these classifications should not be structured in a way that discriminates on the basis of religion alone.[152] Significantly, whereas states have some latitude in imposing restrictions on the political activity of aliens notwithstanding the general

---

[147] This analysis can be compared with the "core" notions in the right to freedom of religion or belief identified in the introduction to this volume.

[148] This is consistent with the overall philosophy underlying human rights instruments: that all human beings have these rights and that they are not merely an aspect of citizenship. See Christian Tomuschat, "Freedom of Association," in *The European System for the Protection of Human Rights*, ed. R. St. J. Macdonald, F. Matscher, and H. Petzold (Dordrecht: Martinus Nijhoff Publishers, 1993), 493, 497.

[149] ICCPR, art. 18 ("Everyone shall have the right to freedom of thought, conscience and religion"); 1981 Declaration, art. 1 ("Everyone shall have the right . . ."); ECHR, art. 9(1) ("Everyone has the right to freedom of thought, conscience and religion"); ACHR, art. 12(1) ("Everyone has the right to freedom of conscience and of religion"); African Charter on Human and Peoples' Rights, art. 8.

[150] *Convention of the Rights of the Child*, adopted and opened for signature by United Nations General Assembly Resolution 44/25 on 20 November 1989 (entered into force 2 September 1990), art. 14(2). See the chapter by van Bueren in this volume.

[151] Note that the European Convention allows states to impose restrictions on the political activity of aliens, but not on the religious activity of such aliens. Specifically, article 16 provides: "Nothing in Articles 10 [expression], 11 [association] and 14 [equal availability of fundamental rights] shall be regarded as preventing the High Contracting Parties from imposing restrictions on the political activity of aliens." See Tomuschat, "Freedom of Association," 493, 497.

[152] According to article 2(1) of the 1981 Declaration, "No one shall be subject to discrimination by any State, institution, group of persons or person on the grounds of religion or other beliefs." Article 2(2) further specifies that "the expression 'intolerance and discrimination based on religion or belief' means any distinction, exclusion, restriction or preference based on religion or belief and having as its purpose or as its effect nullification or impairment of the recognition, enjoyment or exercise of human rights and fundamental freedoms on an equal basis." Countries have great discretion in determining who shall be allowed to enter their borders, but structuring such classifications on the basis of religious criteria alone would appear to constitute impermissible discrimination under article 2, which applies to everyone and makes no distinction between citizens and foreigners. Similarly, article 26 of the ICCPR provides that "All persons are equal before the law and are entitled without any discrimination to the equal protection of the law. In this respect, the law shall prohibit any discrimination and guarantee to all persons equal and effective protection against discrimination on any ground such as . . . religion." Again, no distinction is made between persons inside or outside of a country. States are free to draw all manner of other distinctions between insiders and outsiders—they simply cannot use religion alone as a ground for exclusion.

protections of freedom of expression, freedom of association and the right to enjoy fundamental freedoms without discrimination, the rights of noncitizens with respect to freedom of religion or belief may not be subjected to parallel constraints.[153]

2. Religious Freedom Rights Are Not Created or Conferred by the State

"*Has.*" Religious freedom is not something bestowed by the state or its statutory regimes, but is something that individuals and religious groups have simply by virtue of their human nature. Because religious association laws necessarily take the form of telling individuals and groups what they must do to form various kinds of religious entities, there is a tendency on the part of some state officials to assume that the state may legitimately decide whether or not to make such status available, how entities should be structured, what degree of autonomy entities should have, what level of control the state should exert over such entities, and so forth. In fact, the history of interactions of religious communities and state institutions is filled with instances in which states have exercised power in ways that determined as a factual matter the nature of legal entities available and the scope of the freedom they would make available. But this does not prove that such assertions of state power were legitimate or consistent with human rights. The point of identifying freedom of religion or belief as a human right is that the right does not depend for its normative legitimacy on how it is factually structured by a state. In a similar vein, the right to entity status does not depend on the contingency of whether states have in fact recognized this status as they should. In the modern world, a state may limit manifestation of religion or belief just as detrimentally by constraining religious entities as it can through criminal norms or other licensing schemes. Limitations of any sort are permissible only to the extent permitted under limitation clauses such as article 18(3) ICCPR, article 9(2) ECHR and article 12(3) ACHR.[154]

3. The Need for a Broad Definition of Religion

"*Religion.*" It is incumbent on officials administering religious association laws to take a broad approach that avoids discrimination by definitional fiat. Religion and a variety of other terms that may become relevant in applying norms governing freedom of religion or belief (e.g., conscience, belief, sect, clergy, confession and countless others) are notoriously difficult to define.[155] This is in part because what counts as religion or religious is

---

[153] See, e.g., ECHR, art. 16: "Nothing in Articles 10, 11 and 14 shall be regarded as preventing the High Contracting Parties from imposing restrictions on the political activity of aliens." The fact that "national security" is a permissible ground for limitation of freedom of association and freedom of expression, but not freedom of religion, reflects a similar sense of the high priority of protecting freedom of religion or belief for "everyone." Compare arts. 19(3)(b), 21 and 22(2) ICCPR, arts. 10(2) and 11(2) ECHR, and arts. 13(2)(B), 15 and 16(2) ACHR with arts. 18(3) ICCPR, 9(2) ECHR and 12(3) ACHR.

[154] See the chapter by Nowak and Vospernik in this volume.

[155] See W. Cole Durham, Jr. and Elizabeth A. Sewell, "Defining Religion," *Religious Organizations in the United States: A Study of Legal Identity, Religious Freedom and the Law*, ed. James A. Serritella et al. (Durham: Carolina Academic Press, forthcoming, 2004). For an excellent overview of definitional issues in the international context, see T. Jeremy Gunn, "The Complexity of Religion and the Definition of Religion in International Law," *Harvard Human Rights Journal* 16 (2003): 189–215.

inherently vague, and the variation in the range of phenomena potentially described by these terms is so vast. But it is also in part because insensitive definitions by the state may themselves be inherently discriminatory and may have the practical effect of imposing limitations on beliefs that individuals and groups sincerely believe to be religious. While these definitional problems may be ultimately insolvable at the level of theory, in the overwhelming majority of cases they are relatively easy to resolve in fact. The approach promulgated by the UN Human Rights Committee in its General Comment No. 22 in 1993 is sound and should be followed. Specifically, paragraph 2 of that document provides:

> Article 18 protects theistic, non-theistic and atheistic beliefs, as well as the right not to profess any religion or belief. The terms belief and religion are to be broadly construed. Article 18 is not limited in its application to traditional religions or to religions and beliefs with institutional characteristics or practices analogous to those of traditional religions. The Committee therefore views with concern any tendency to discriminate against any religion or belief for any reasons, including the fact that they are newly established, or represent religious minorities that may be the subject of hostility by a predominant religious community.[156]

This provision recognizes the incredible diversity of religious phenomena that must be taken into account in protecting freedom of religion or belief. Religious association laws need to be drafted with the reality of this virtually boundless pluralism in mind. Whatever else religious freedom means, it is not limited to protecting "traditional religions" with which a state is comfortable. It clearly extends to smaller groups, to newly established groups, to dissenting groups within a denomination, to schismatic groups, to extremist or fundamentalist groups—in short, to all the kinds of groups that test our ability to show genuine tolerance and respect.

Unfortunately, many countries ignore the foregoing counsel and are too specific in their legal definitions of "religion." In China definitions are so strict that even traditional religions do not fit within the set of religious organizations recognized by the state.[157] More generally, the narrowness of the established criteria for a legitimate religious organization in many countries often excludes nonconventional religious organizations, whose characteristics may differ in some ways from the legal definition. For example, in the Belarusian Law the definition mentions "religious associations, monasteries, religious brotherhoods and sisterhoods, religious missions, and spiritual educational institutions."[158] This implies a structured organization of only specific types, while there are other kinds of religious associations that are not even mentioned in the provision. Estonia provides another example: it dedicates three paragraphs in its religious law to a definition of

---

[156] Human Rights Committee General Comment 22 (1993) on ICCPR art. 18, 20 July 1993, 48th Sess., para. 2.

[157] E.g., Jehovah's Witnesses, Ba'hai, The Church of Jesus Christ of Latter-day Saints (Mormons), Russian Orthodoxy and even Judaism. This reluctance to expand the universe of recognized religions stems in part from a fear of opening up a "Pandora's box" that would make it difficult for the government to deny registration or recognition to any religious group. See Kim-Kwong Chan and Eric Carlson, *Religious Freedom in China: Policy, Administration, and Regulation* (forthcoming, 2004) (manuscript on file with author), 25.

[158] *Law on the Freedom of Religion and Religious Organizations* [Belarus], art. 9, ch. 2 (2002), available at <http://www.religlaw.org>.

religious organizations, with rigid rules that imply structured hierarchical organizations.[159] In 2000 a Hungarian draft law on religious freedom proposed narrowing down possible legitimate religions by identifying them as "a structured set of beliefs" and also went further, adding to the definition a specific requirement of "focus on reality as a whole."[160] Such a provision could prevent registration and thus legitimacy of nonstructured religious associations that focus their teachings on the afterlife or a different kind of reality. Fortunately, this restrictive draft was not adopted. In Armenia an association can only be recognized as religious if it "is based on any historically canonized Holy Scriptures," if its doctrine "forms part of the international contemporary religious-ecclesiastical communities," and if "it is free from materialism and is intended for purely spiritual goals."[161] These definitions presuppose traditional religious organizations with clearly defined scriptures and familiar organizations.

In Peru it is not so much the term "religion" itself that has caused the problem, but instead unduly narrow interpretations of the terms "convents" and "monasteries."[162] This is a useful reminder that definitional problems can extend to other types of terminology that may have a particular meaning in one religion, but rather different meanings (or counterparts) in other religions.

It should be clear that the term "religion" as used in the international instruments includes "religious sects."[163] It has become all too common in recent years to stigmatize some groups by referring to them as sects. Intentional use of such terminology with the intent to disparage is itself a violation of religious freedom norms. Any claim that "sects" are not "religions" for purposes of asserting religious freedom claims adds injury to insult.

---

[159] Relevant text from the Estonian Law is as follows: ". . . [a] church is an association of at least three voluntarily joined congregations which has an episcopal structure and is doctrinally related to three ecumenical creeds or is divided into at least three congregations and which operates on the basis of its statutes, is managed by an elected or appointed management board and is entered in the register in the cases and pursuant to the procedure prescribed by this Act." See Churches and Congregations Act (2002) [Estonia] (hereinafter "Estonian Law"), ch. 1, secs. 1–3, available at <www.religlaw.org>.

[160] "[R]eligion . . . refers to a transcendent entity, has a structured set of beliefs, its doctrines focus on reality as a whole and it encompasses the totality of the personality with its particular behavioral requirements which do not violate morals and human dignity" (Amendment to Hungarian Law, ch. 1, sec. 8, para. 3, unadopted draft from 2000, available at <www.religlaw.org>.

[161] Armenian Law, art. 5, available at <www.religlaw.org>.

[162] In Peru, "a grave interpretation problem has arisen due to the fact that the terms 'convents and monasteries,' which have been understood in a restrictive manner as manner as 'canonic,' unduly exclude the property used to house the ministers of any confession, as well as property used for administrative offices. Additionally, some municipalities in Peru demand non-Catholic confessions to follow an administrative process so that each 'temple' or 'religious site' built requires express exemption to be given. This application was not the spirit of the legislation and it is not found in the text of Legislative Decree 776. The exemption is granted for a determined time and must be renewed; however, this is illegal, since the expiration of the exemption is permanent and automatic. Recently, some municipalities have denied the exemption to some non-Catholic confessions using the illegal grounds that the confessions have not been officially recognized by the Peruvian state. These applications of the law are outrageous. Tax exemptions should be extended to all religious confessions so that these confessions need not divert their material resources to burdensome fiscal obligations. In addition, there is no reason why the follower s of any confession should not receive equal tax deductions for the contributions offered to their churches" (Guillermo Garcia Montufar and Elvira Martinez Coco, "Antecedents, Perspectives, and Projections of a Legal Project about Religious Liberty in Peru," *BYU Law Review* [1999]: 503, 520).

[163] The numerous cases protecting Jehovah's Witnesses clearly demonstrate this. See, e.g., Kokkinakis v. Greece, 260-A (1993) (ECtHR, ser. A), at 15; Manoussakis and Others v. Greece, 23 EHRR 387 (1997)

Note that inclusion of a group in the category of religion does not automatically lead to the conclusion that every religious claim it asserts will automatically be vindicated. Extreme claims that threaten others with imminent and palpable injury will clearly justify state intervention. More generally, religious claims may be subjected to limitations in the narrowly described situations articulated in the relevant limitation clauses. But what occurs in such situations is justifiable state intervention that overrides a religious freedom claim, not state regulation of nonreligious conduct.

4. The Collective Dimension of Religious Rights and the Right to Religious Autonomy.

"*In Community With Others.*" A particularly important aspect of freedom of religion or belief is that it often protects activity that has a social or communal dimension. While individual religious belief and conduct is clearly imaginable, real religious life almost invariably involves interactive conduct "in community with others." The sense and reality of community is vital to much of religious "teaching, practice, worship and observance." Unduly narrow religious association laws, or restrictive implementation of such laws, necessarily interfere with this social dimension of the freedom to manifest beliefs. This in turn necessarily results in interference with individual manifestations of religion, to the extent that individual manifestations involve interaction with others.

Stated differently, religious association laws create legal frameworks that are vital for a host of practical reasons to unimpaired practice and observance of one's religion. Whatever position one takes on whether there is a group dimension to religious rights, or whether group rights are just an elaborate metaphor for individual rights, the point is that religious association laws that are easily accessible, flexible and adaptable are vital to protecting any sense of religious life that is sufficiently rich to include a meaningful experience of "community with others." The need for authentic community life, as envisioned and actualized by a religious community that is free of state influence, helps ground the community's right to religious autonomy. It is a specialized and heightened form of the right to association.[164] Once one recognizes that the right to religious autonomy is included in the core right to freedom of religion,[165] religious association laws that restrict the exercise of that autonomy obviously infringe freedom of religion or belief.

There was some early authority under the European Convention to the effect that a church, "being a legal and not a natural person, is incapable of having or exercising the rights mentioned in Article 9."[166] Profit-making entities in particular were thought to be inappropriate subjects of article 9 rights,[167] but even nonprofit entities were held to lack

(ECtHR, 26 September 1996). For discussions of the sect issue, see Jean-Marie Woehrling, "Une définition juridique des sectes?" in *Les "sectes" et le droit en France,* ed. Francis Messner (Paris: PUF, 1999), 63–90; Francis Messner et. al., eds., *Traité de droit français des religions* (Paris: 2003), 22–39, esp. 35–39.

[164] See section III(B) below.

[165] See the introduction and the chapter by Minnerath in this volume.

[166] Church of X v. United Kingdom, 29 Decisions and Reports of the European Commission of Human Rights 70 (1968) (EComHR, Application No. 3798/68), also cited in *Yearbook of the European Convention on Human Rights* (1969),12:306, 314.

[167] Company X v. Switzerland, No. 7865/77, Decisions and Reports of the European Commission of Human Rights (1979), 16:85, 87.

the ability to exercise freedom of conscience (as opposed to freedom of religion, which legal persons can assert).[168] The notion appears to have been that "[w]hereas the freedom of thought and conscience, as well as the freedom to choose a religion or belief are strictly personal freedoms, the right to freedom of religion has not only an individual but also a collective dimension, and the very functioning of churches depends on respect for this right."[169] This view is criticized by Malcolm Evans, who notes that "a church, as an organization, is neither more nor less capable of having a religion or belief than any other legal person is of having a conscience."[170]

In any event, the early view that legal entities could not assert freedom of religion or belief has since been rejected by European institutions.[171] Already in *Church of Scientology v. Sweden*, the Commission concluded that for purposes of article 9, the distinction between a church and its members was artificial, and, accordingly, a church could assert article 9 rights in its own capacity as a representative of its members.[172] This approach has been criticized on the grounds that "it merely allowed the church to 'stand in the shoes' of its members and failed to acknowledge the right of a church to manifest its religion in its own right."[173] Subsequent decisions have made it clear that churches and other similar legal persons with religious and philosophical objects can assert article 9 rights both as representatives of their members[174] and in their own capacities.[175] Indeed, the European Court has gone so far as to recognize the standing of a church to assert religious claims even though it has not complied with legal formalities for acquiring entity status, and to hold that failure to recognize such standing constitutes a deprivation of the

---

168 Verein Kontakt Information Therapie and Hagen v. Austria, Application No.11921/86, Decisions and Reports of the European Commission of Human Rights (1988), 57:81, 88. In that case the Commission rested its decision on the notion that while freedom of religion could be exercised by a legal person, freedom of conscience could not.

169 P. van Dijk and G. J. H. van Hoof, *Theory and Practice of the European Convention on Human Rights*, 3d ed. (The Hague: Kluwer International Law, 1998), 552.

170 Malcolm D. Evans, *Religious Liberty and International Law in Europe* (Cambridge: Cambridge University Press, 1997), 288.

171 Malcolm N. Shaw, "Freedom of Thought, Conscience and Religion," in *The European System for the Protection of Human Rights*, ed. R. St. J. Macdonald, F. Matscher and H. Petzold (Dordrecht: Martinus Nijhoff Publishers, 1993), 445, 450.

172 *Decisions and Reports of the European Commission of Human Rights* (Decision of 5 May 1979), 16:68, 70, para. 5.

173 Malcolm Evans, *Religious Liberty and International Law in Europe*, 287; van Dijk and van Hoof, *Theory and Practice of the European Convention on Human Rights*, 552.

174 See, e.g., Metropolitan Church of Bessarabia v. Moldova (ECtHR, Application No. 45701/99, 13 December 2001), para. 101 ("a church or ecclesiastical body may, as such, exercise on behalf of its adherents the rights guaranteed by Article 9"); Jewish Liturgical Ass'n Cha'are Shalom ve Tsedek v. France (ECtHR, Application No. 27417/95, 27 June 2000), para. 72 (" [a] religious body may, as such, exercise on behalf of its adherents the rights guaranteed by Article 9").

175 Kontakt-Information-Therapie and Hagen v. Austria, No. 11921/86, Decisions and Reports of the European Commission of Human Rights (1988), 57:81, 88; A. R. M. Chappell v. UK, No. 12587/86, Decisions and Reports of the European Commission of Human Rights (December 1987), 53:241, 246; Iglesia Bautisti 'El Salvador' and Ortega Moratilla v. Spain, No. 17522/90, Decisions and Reports of the European Commission of Human Rights (1992), 72:256; Omkarananda and the Divine Light Zentrum v. United Kingdom, No. 8118/77, Decisions and Reports of the European Commission of Human Rights (1981), 25:105 (association with religious and philosophical objects could possess and exercise right to freedom of religion or belief).

right to a hearing by a tribunal under article 6(1) ECHR.[176] The right of religious groups and entities to assert religious freedom claims on a collective basis is widely recognized in the world's legal systems.[177] In general, recognizing that religious groups and entities are rights bearers is appropriate both because such organizations are often best positioned to seek effective protection of freedom of religion or belief, and because it is appropriate for the collectivity to be vested with the ability to protect the collective dimension of the right.

5. Limitations on Entity Rights Impermissibly Constrain Manifestation of Religion

"*Manifestation.*" Laws that make it difficult to acquire entity status impose limitations on manifestation of religion in many, many ways. Among other things, they interfere with virtually every example of manifestation of religion for which the 1981 Declaration demands protection, as the following catalogue of problems (premised on article 6 of the 1981 Declaration) demonstrates. They make it difficult to secure premises where a religious community can "worship or assemble in connexion with a religion or belief."[178] They can prevent establishment of "appropriate charitable or humanitarian institutions."[179] They make it difficult for the religious community to "make, acquire and use . . . the necessary articles and materials related to the rites or customs of a religion or belief"[180] or to "issue and disseminate relevant publications."[181] In a contemporary setting, almost all of these "manifestations" presuppose legal entities that can acquire or rent property, enter into contracts and so forth. Similarly, without appropriate legal entities, a religious community's ability to "solicit and receive voluntary financial and other contributions from individuals and institutions"[182] is severely impaired. That is, virtually all the concrete examples of protected manifestations of religion enumerated in the 1981 Declaration are virtually unthinkable as a practical matter without effective access to entity status. What is true of the 1981 Declaration's examples is true more generally: curbs on entity status represent fundamental constraints on freedom of religion or belief.

"*Teaching, Practice, Worship and Observance.*" These terms appear to describe in an expansive way general types of conduct embraced within the general category of religious activity. They should be viewed as being representative, and not necessarily

---

[176] See Canea Catholic Church v. Greece (ECtHR, Application No. 25528/94, 16 December 1997), paras. 30–31. Unlike the Commission, the European Court ultimately did not ground its decision in *Canea Catholic Church* on a violation of article 14 in connection with article 9 (discrimination in protection of article 9 rights), and instead predicated its decision on impaired access of the church's right to a tribunal under article 6(1) itself, and taken together with article 14.

[177] See, e.g., Bellotti v. Baird, 443 US 622 (1979); Serbian Eastern Orthodox Diocese for the United States of America and Canada v. Milivojevich 426 US 696 (1976); BVerfGE 83, 341 [Germany]; see generally Natan Lerner, *Group Rights and Discrimination in International Law* (Dordrecht: Martinus Nijhoff, 1991); Frederick Mark Gedicks, "Toward a Constitutional Jurisprudence of Religious Group Rights," *Wisconsin Law Review* (1989): 99.

[178] 1981 Declaration, art. 6(a); see also ibid., art. 6(e) (which assures the right to "teach a religion or belief in places suitable for these purposes").

[179] Ibid., art. 6(b).

[180] Ibid., art. 6(c).

[181] Ibid., art. 6(d).

[182] Ibid., art. 6(f). See also Vienna Concluding Document, principle 16(d).

exhaustive.[183] As noted by Professor Carolyn Evans, "The United Nations material, especially the Krishnaswami study, indicates that the words were used to try to cover a wide range of manifestations of religions and beliefs and were not intended to be read in a limited manner. . . . [I]t may be safely assumed that the intention was to embrace all possible manifestations of religion or belief with the terms 'teaching, practice, worship and observance.'"[184] The terms emphasize that freedom of religion or belief goes beyond holding an "internal" belief to engaging in "external" conduct.

With respect to each of these categories, it is possible to conceive of a small group carrying out some types of "teaching, practice, worship, and observance" without acquiring legal entity status. A small group can meet in someone's home to teach or exchange ideas. Individuals in the group can attempt to practice and observe the teachings they have absorbed. They can worship together—in the home, or in some natural setting. But once the community begins to be more than de minimis—as soon as it begins to involve more than two or three families—entity status is critical in all of these domains. The instances of manifestation addressed in the prior paragraph (drawn from the examples identified in the 1981 Declaration) are all cases in point.

6. Constraints Imposed in Connection with Religious Association Laws Are Permissible Only to the Extent That They Can Be Justified under Applicable Limitation Clauses

A key feature of the substantive norm of freedom of religion or belief is that it is not unlimited. No limitations on this freedom were articulated in the Universal Declaration of Human Rights, but as soon as efforts went forward to reduce the language of the Declaration to treaty language, the need for limiting language was evident. Thus, virtually

---

[183] As stated by the UN Human Rights Committee, the "freedom to manifest religion or belief in worship, observance, practice and teaching encompasses a broad range of acts." Among other things, the Committee continues, "the practice or teaching of religion or belief includes acts integral to the conduct by religious groups of their basic affairs." (Human Rights Committee General Comment 22 [1993] on ICCPR art. 18, 20 July 1993, 48th Sess., para. 4). Prof. Nowak suggests that the ICCPR places "particular emphasis on four forms [of manifestation]" (Manfred Nowak, *U.N. Covenant on Civil and Political Rights, CCPR Commentary* [Kehl/Strasbourg/Arlington: N. P. Engel, 1993], 320, para. 23). He views worship (the "specific manner in which the ritual [of a given religion] is structured"), observance ("processions, wearing of religious clothing or beards, circumcision, prayer and all other customs and rites of the various religions"), and teaching ("every form of imparting the substance of a religion or belief") as being fairly clear in their meaning. Practice is still broader and more difficult to specify. Nowak believes that "practice" is not so broad as "every act or omission motivated by religion or belief," but that it includes "conduct obviously related to a religious conviction" (ibid., 321, paras. 24–25). Malcolm Evans appears to be critical of a narrow approach that views the four forms of manifestation as an "exhaustive catalogue" and interprets only "acts closely and directly connected with the formal practice of religious rites and customs" as falling within "manifestation," as opposed to a more flexible view which would include "[f]orms of behaviour and activities which flow from religious convictions" (Malcolm Evans, *Religious Liberty and International Law in Europe*, 216).

[184] Carolyn Evans, *Freedom of Religion under the European Convention on Human Rights* (Oxford: Oxford University Press, 2001), 105, quoting Arcot Krishnaswami, Special Rapporteur of the Sub-Commission on Prevention of Discrimination and Protection of Minorities, *Study of Discrimination in the Matter of Religious Rights and Practices*, UN Document E/Cn.4/Sub.2/200/Rev.1 (1960), 17. Carolyn Evans is critical of precedent in the Council of Europe that construes these terms as the exclusive delimiters of the meaning of manifestation, instead of taking a more inclusive approach (ibid., 106).

all of the international instruments contain limitation clauses, and these are all quite similar. Experience at the national level, even under constitutions such as that of the United States that set no express bounds on religious liberty,[185] recognized that religious liberty was not an absolute.[186] As Professor Nowak has noted, "the interplay between the principle of freedom of religion and its restrictions is what truly determines the actual scope of the individual's right."[187] Consistent with the general recognition that only high order state interests should override a right as fundamental as freedom of religion or belief,[188] limitation clauses for freedom of religion or belief have been drafted very narrowly.[189] Indeed, in many respects, the limitations allowed in connection with freedom of religion or belief are narrower than those allowed with respect to other fundamental rights.[190]

Of course, to the extent that religious association laws facilitate religious activity, they are permissible because they do not operate as limitations on freedom of religion or belief. But to the extent that such laws are used to control religion, or to the extent that they impose unnecessary restraints by being insufficiently flexible, they operate as limitations. As such, they are only permissible to the extent that the applicable limitation clauses allow such constraints.

According to the various international instruments, limitations may be imposed only on manifestations of religion or belief, not on the rights within the *forum internum* to "have or adopt" a religion.[191] In general, religious association rules deal with manifestations of

---

185 The First Amendment of the United States Constitution provides that "Congress shall make no law respecting an establishment of religion or prohibiting the free exercise thereof." (US Const, amend. I). While there is no express limitation clause in the US Constitution, the United States Supreme Court, beginning with its earliest cases construing the free exercise clause, recognized that certain limitations were necessary. By the time the international instruments were being drafted, there was already substantial case law regarding limitations, with obvious parallels to the international instruments. First, there was an absolute right to freedom with respect to internal beliefs, and only outer actions (comparable to "manifestations" under the international instruments) could be limited by the states (Reynolds v. United States, 98 US 145, 165–67 [1878]; Cantwell v. Connecticut, 310 US 296 [1940]). State interests sufficient to override religious freedom claims included: morals (Reynolds v. United States, 98 US 145 [1878]); health (Jacobson v. Massachusetts, 197 US 11 [1905]); child health and welfare (Prince v. Massachusetts, 321 US 158 [1944]); public order (Minersville School District v. Gobitis, 310 US 586 [1940]); and rights of third parties (Prince v. Massachusetts, 321 US 158, 177 [1944] [Jackson, J., dissenting]).

186 See, e.g., Charter of Fundamental Rights and Freedoms, § 1 [Canada]; Declaration of the Rights of Man and of the Citizen, arts. 4, 10 (1789) [France];Const, art. 16(1) [Spain]. Const, art. 6 [Netherlands].

187 Nowak, *U.N. Covenant on Civil and Political Rights, CCPR Commentary,* 311.

188 See, e.g., Karl Josef Partsch, "Freedom of Conscience and Expression, and Political Freedoms," *The International Bill of Rights: The Covenant on Civil and Political Rights,* ed. Louis Henkin (New York: Columbia University Press, 1981), 209, 212–14.

189 Limitation clauses are thoroughly analyzed in the chapter by Nowak and Vospernik in this volume. Treatment of this issue here draws on their analysis and focuses on types of limitations particularly likely to arise in connection with religious association laws.

190 Thus, freedom of religion or belief is typically recognized as a non-derogable right (ICCPR, art. 4[2]), whereas neither freedom of speech nor freedom of association is accorded this treatment. Freedom of religion or belief was derogable under the ECHR, but since all members of the Council of Europe have ratified the ICCPR, ECHR signatories are obligated to respect the non-derogability of freedom of religion or belief (ECHR, arts. 15[1] and 60).

191 See, e.g., Bahiyyih G. Tahzib, *Freedom of Religion or Belief: Ensuring Effective International Legal Protection* (The Hague: Martinus Nijhoff Publishers, 1996), 87–89; Malcolm Evans, *Religious Liberty and International Law in Europe* (Cambridge: Cambridge University Press, 1997), 294–98; Martin

religion in collective religious life, so that the absolute bar against intervening in the internal forum does not apply. It is worth noting, however, that the precise outer boundaries of the non-regulable ***forum internum*** have never been precisely demarcated. Accordingly, one can at least argue that matters of doctrine, beliefs about internal ecclesiastical structure, membership and discipline, a variety of other organizational matters, and possibly even beliefs about how donations should be made and administered, are all themselves matters of religious belief linked to the internal forum. The fact that these beliefs are shared by members of a religious community does not itself transmute them into limitable "manifestations" of belief. They are internal beliefs that are held in common by the community. Arguably, shared internal beliefs become limitable manifestations when they begin to have adverse effects for other parties. The collective feature of internal beliefs may help explain why states should respect religious autonomy by remaining neutral and avoiding intervention in matters of doctrine and religious polity; any other course inevitably involves inappropriate intrusion not only into internal religious affairs, but also into shared internal religious beliefs.[192] Religious association laws that confer authority to review the substantive beliefs of religious communities, including beliefs about how the association should be structured, are problematic at least in part for this reason.

Turning to manifestations of religion, limitations can only be imposed if they meet three additional sets of requirements. First, they must be "prescribed by law" in the sense of being imposed by rules that comport with the rule of law.[193] In particular, this means that rules cannot be unduly vague or subject to undue discretion in their enforcement.[194] But significantly, mustering sufficient political support to be prescribed by law does not suffice on its own to justify overriding religious freedom claims; otherwise religious freedom rights would always be at the mercy of majoritarian rule, even where majorities are insensitive to rights of religious minorities.[195] As a practical matter, religious association laws typically pass the formal requirement of being "prescribed by law." They are, after all, religious association *laws*. But problems of inartful drafting, to say nothing of bias against smaller and less popular groups, often result in provisions that fail other rule of law standards by being impermissibly vague or by otherwise permitting arbitrary or discriminatory conduct on the part of officials implementing religious association laws.[196]

Scheinin, "Article 18," in *The Universal Declaration of Human Rights: A Common Standard of Achievement,* ed. Gudmundur Alfredsson and Asbjørn Eide (The Hague: Martinus Nijhoff Publishers, 1999), 383; Nowak, *U.N. Covenant on Civil and Political Rights, CCPR Commentary*, 314–15.

[192] On the importance of religious autonomy, see the chapter by Minnerath in this volume.

[193] See, e.g., Sunday Times v. the United Kingdom (1979) (30 ECtHR, ser. A), at 30; Kokkinakis v. Greece, 260-A (1993) (ECtHR, ser. A), at 15; Carolyn Evans, *Freedom of Religion under the European Convention on Human Rights*, 138–42; Malcolm Evans, *Religious Liberty and International Law in Europe*, 319–20.

[194] Carolyn Evans, *Freedom of Religion under the European Convention on Human Rights*, 138–42; Hasan and Chaush v. Bulgaria (ECtHR, App. No. 30985/96, 26 October 2000), paras. 84–87.

[195] This is the fundamental flaw with the decision of the United States Supreme Court in Employment Division v. Smith, 494 US 872 (1990), which held that any neutral and general law can override religious freedom claims.

[196] A recent Bulgarian case was decided by the European Court of Human Rights on the basis of failure to comply with basic rule of law standards (Hasan and Chaush v. Bulgaria [ECtHR, App. No. 30985/96, 26 October 2000]).

This leads to the second area that permissible limitations must satisfy: they must fall within one of an expressly enumerated set of legitimating grounds. Thus limitations are only permissible if they further public safety, public order, health or morals, or the rights and freedoms of others. As the UN Human Rights Committee's official commentary on article 18(3) of the ICCPR points out, the language of the limitations clause is to be strictly interpreted:

> [R]estrictions are not allowed on grounds not specified there, even if they would be allowed as restrictions to other rights protected in the Covenant, such as national security. Limitations may be applied only for those purposes for which they were prescribed.[197]

While the enumerated legitimating grounds would appear to embrace a fairly broad range of potential limitations on freedom of religion or belief, there are some limitations that are clearly ruled out. Thus, a generalized sense that certain religious organizations pose a threat to national security does not constitute a permissible ground for adopting restrictive religious association laws.[198] Similarly, as already noted,[199] the right to freedom of religion or belief is not derogable even in time of emergency. Of course, where emergency situations or threats to national security constitute concrete threats to public health, safety and order, or to the rights of third persons, the limitation clauses allow proportionate interventions by state officials, but generalized appeals to national security or other state interests outside the ambit of concrete and imminent threats to the named interests do not suffice. Note that it is hard to see how the need to deal with emergency situations would necessitate building long-term restrictions into normal religious association laws.

For the most part, religious association laws are not designed to promote public health or safety, but one might argue that they contribute to public order, at least in the sense of the totality of the general policies of the community, like the notion of *ordre public* used in French public and administrative law (and other civilian legal systems). Using this notion, the contention would be that religious association laws, even those with "control" as opposed to "facilitative" effects, could be justified on the grounds that they are simply part of (and hence in furtherance of) public order. It is important to understand, however, that the international instruments do not support this reading. Significantly, the French version of the ICCPR does not use the generalized term *ordre public,* but instead *la protection de l'ordre,* terminology suggesting concrete public disturbance and disorder.[200] Since religious association laws are not generally designed to protect public order in the sense of preventing public disturbances, the public order ground is also less of a support for religious association laws than might be thought.

---

197 Human Rights Committee General Comment 22 (1993) on ICCPR art. 18, 20 July 1993, 48th Sess., para. 8.

198 Ibid. National security is consistently excluded from the list of permissible grounds for limiting freedom of religion or belief in all the major international instruments. See ICCPR, art. 18(3); ECHR, art. 9(2); ACHR, art. 12(3). This is in obvious contrast to the limitation clauses for freedom of expression: ICCPR, art. 19(2)(b); ECHR, art. 10(2); ACHR, art. 13(2)(b), assembly, ICCPR, art. 21; ECHR, art. 11; ACHR, art. 15, and association. ICCPR, art. 22(2); ECHR, art. 11; ACHR, art. 16(2).

199 See note 191 above.

200 Carolyn Evans, *Freedom of Religion under the European Convention on Human Rights*, 150. The French Conseil d'État has itself become progressively more scrupulous in its application of the doctrine of "ordre publique" in its decisions regarding religion and has recently rejected vague assertions of the doctrine (Francis Messner et. al., eds., *Traité de droit français des religions* (Paris: 2003), 190–94.

While the legitimating grounds are thus not so broad as might at first be thought, they nonetheless have a very wide scope, so that it is generally the third feature of the religious freedom limitation clauses—the requirement that the limitation be "necessary,"[201] or "necessary in a democratic society"[202]—that turns out to be most significant. That is, even if a particular limitation on freedom of religion or belief passes the "prescribed by law" and "permissible legitimating ground" tests, it is permissible as a matter of international human rights law only if it is genuinely necessary. In the words of the UN Human Rights Committee, limitations "must be directly related and proportionate to the specific need on which they are predicated. Restrictions may not be imposed for discriminatory purposes or applied in a discriminatory manner."[203]

The necessity constraint is vital as a practical matter. Public officials defending a certain limitation can often point to legislation supporting it, so that it is "prescribed by law." Moreover, they often assume that the enumerated legitimating grounds, particularly public order, were intended to be construed more broadly than is in fact the case. As a result, they assume that the legitimating grounds of the limitation clauses are broad enough that they can be used to cover virtually any potential limitation. Popular belief tends in the same direction, since government has assumed a pervasive role within the setting of contemporary social welfare states, and older assumptions about the virtues of limited government are often forgotten. The result is that both officials and citizens tend to assume that the government is free to shape religious association laws however it chooses. In this context, insistence that limitations be genuinely and strictly necessary puts crucial brakes on state action that would otherwise impose excessive limitations on manifestations of religion.

As the European Court has framed the issue, an interference with religion is necessary only when there is a "pressing social need" that is "proportionate to the legitimate aim pursued."[204] Clearly, when analyzed in these terms, the issue of necessity must be assessed on a case-by-case basis. However, certain general conclusions have emerged. First, in assessing which limitations are "proportionate," it is vital to remember that "freedom of thought, conscience and religion is one of the foundations of a 'democratic society.'"[205] That is, freedom of religion or belief must be assigned a heavy weight in the balance.

---

[201] ICCPR, art. 18(3).

[202] ECHR, art. 9(2). It is not clear how much the reference to democratic society adds to the necessity test, because in any society only certain measures are strictly necessary for public safety, health, order and so forth. In countries that are committed to democratic values, however, the reference is an added reminder that limitations need to be construed narrowly in no small part because freedom of religion and belief is a crucial dimension of democratic order.

[203] Human Rights Committee General Comment 22 (1993) on ICCPR art. 18, 20 July 1993, 48th Sess., UN Doc. CCPR/C/21/Rev.1/Add.4 (1993), reprinted in UN Doc. HRI/GEN/1/Rev.1 at 35 (1994), para. 8.

[204] See, e.g., Kokkinakis v. Greece, 17 EHRR 397 (1994) (ECtHR, 25 May 1993), para. 49; Wingrove v. United Kingdom (1996) (23 ECtHR, ser.A, 1937), para. 53; Manoussakis and Others v. Greece, 23 EHRR 387 (1997) (ECtHR, 26 September 1996), paras. 43–53; Serif v. Greece (ECtHR, App. No. 38178/97, 14 December 1997), para. 49; Metropolitan Church of Bessarabia v. Moldova (ECtHR, App. No. 45701/99, 13 December 2001), para. 119.

[205] See Metropolitan Church of Bessarabia v. Moldova (ECtHR, App. No. 45701/99, 13 December 2001), para. 114, which provides as follows:

> freedom of thought, conscience and religion is one of the foundations of a "democratic society" within the meaning of the Convention. It is, in its religious dimension, one of the most vital elements that go to make up the identity of believers and their conception of life,

Second, limitations cannot pass the necessity test if they reflect state conduct that is not neutral and impartial. This point was emphasized in *Metropolitan Church of Bessarabia v. Moldova,*[206] where the European Court of Human Rights stressed that "in exercising its regulatory power . . . in its relations with the various religions, denominations and beliefs, the State has a duty to remain ***neutral and impartial.***" [207] The neutrality and impartiality of the state is particularly significant when it comes to organizational issues. Citing one of the key association cases, the Court underscores their significance: "[w]hat is at stake here is the preservation of pluralism and the proper functioning of democracy."[208] Against any inclination that states in general (and Moldova in particular) might have to use regulatory power to control interreligious tension, the Court repeated the reminder from earlier cases that "the role of the authorities in such circumstances is not to remove the cause of tension by eliminating pluralism, but to ensure that the competing groups tolerate each other."[209] In the context of the *Bessarabian Church* case, this meant that the state could not manipulate religious association law in a way that sided with a preferred group and denied access to entity status to a less favored group.

More generally, the requirement of state neutrality and impartiality sets extremely important constraints both on the framing and the implementation of religious association law. In particular, it "excludes assessment by the State of the legitimacy of religious beliefs or the ways in which those beliefs are expressed."[210] This has important practical implications for the process of reviewing applications for entity status. States may not engage in substantive review of the doctrines or organizational features of religious communities that are grounded in religious belief. Moreover,

> State measures favouring a particular leader or specific organs of a divided religious community or seeking to compel the community or part of it to place itself, against its will, under a single leadership, would also constitute an infringement of the freedom of religion. In democratic societies the State does not need to take measures to ensure that religious communities remain or are brought under a unified leadership. . . . Similarly, where the exercise of the right to freedom of religion or of one of its aspects is subject under domestic law to a system of prior authorisation, involvement in the procedure for granting authorisation of a recognised ecclesiastical authority cannot be reconciled with the requirements of paragraph 2 of Article 9.[211]

The neutrality and impartiality requirement thus has profound implications for nonintervention in the structuring of religious associations. Not only may government not take sides in religious disputes, but, in addition, it may not use religious association law to help "unify" religious communities that are experiencing tensions or outright divisions.

---

but it is also a precious asset for atheists, agnostics, sceptics and the unconcerned. The pluralism indissociable from a democratic society, which has been dearly won over the centuries, depends on it.

206 Ibid.

207 Ibid., para. 116 (emphasis added).

208 Ibid., citing United Communist Party of Turkey v. Turkey (ECtHR, App. No. 19392/92, 30 January 1998), para. 57.

209 Ibid., citing Serif v. Greece (ECtHR, App. No. 38178/97, 14 December 1997), para. 53.

210 Ibid., para. 117.

211 Ibid.

Moreover, it cannot permit one religious authority, through express delegation or otherwise (e.g., through behind-the-scenes influence), to have a say in whether other groups are recognized.[212]

Third, limitations cannot pass the necessity test if they impose arbitrary constraints on the right to manifest religion.[213] Neither discriminatory nor arbitrary government conduct is necessary—especially not in a democratic society. Where legitimating grounds are invoked to address unfounded stereotypical conceptions of religious groups rooted in prejudice, and limitations are being imposed "for discriminatory purposes or applied in a discriminatory manner,"[214] they are not necessary and cannot be allowed. Similarly, state regulations that impose excessive and arbitrary burdens on the right to associate and worship in community with others—such as burdensome registration requirements—are impermissible.[215]

Fourth, interference with freedom of religion or belief is not necessary where the interests the state seeks to protect are not immediately or realistically threatened. Thus, in the *Bessarabian Church* case, while the Court did recognize that risks of collaboration with Romanian separatists constituted a type of danger cognizable under the public order and public safety provisions of the limitation clause of article 9, the Court ultimately concluded that there was no genuine likelihood that the averred harms were likely to come to fruition. While recognizing that the Bessarabian Church could not be judged solely by what one could read about it in its articles of association, there was nothing to indicate that the Church was doing anything other than engaging in legitimate religious activities or to link it to activities or organizations likely to bring about the harms feared by the government. Moreover, the worry that once recognized, the Church might constitute a danger to national security and territorial integrity was merely hypothetical, and not sufficient to justify denial of recognition.[216] That is, even if one assumed that the looser

---

[212] Moldova's claim that neutrality required it to stay out of what it viewed as an internal dispute within the Orthodox Church lacked credibility, at least in part because the Metropolitan Church of Bessarabia had applied for recognition prior to the Metropolitan Church of Moldova (ibid., para. 123). If the government's concern with neutrality had been sincere, it would have registered the Bessarabian Church and then applied its reasoning to preclude registration of the Moldovan Church. Obviously the government was not neutral as to the result. More generally, the government's approach involved an impermissible assessment of the legitimacy of a particular group's religious beliefs. In effect, it was relying exclusively on the Moldovan Church's assessment of the situation, according to which the Bessarabian Church "was not a new denomination" (ibid.), and was really just an internal part of the Moldovan Church. Further, the state was making recognition of the Bessarabian Church "depend on the will of an ecclesiastical authority that had been recognised—the Metropolitan Church of Moldova" (ibid). The contours of group membership for purposes of asserting the rights to freedom of religion and of association are not defined by theological fiat, but by the actual beliefs of the individuals involved. A group cannot coerce (or invoke state power to coerce) individuals to belong to it against their will. Freedom of religion and association are voluntary and entail a right of exit. A state that seeks to enforce the boundaries of a religious group by requiring or pressuring individuals to be members of a group against their will violates its obligations of neutrality. See ibid.

[213] Ibid., para. 118; Manoussakis and Others v. Greece, 23 EHRR 387 (1997) (ECtHR, 26 September 1996), paras. 43–53.

[214] Human Rights Committee General Comment 22 (1993) on ICCPR art. 18, 20 July 1993, 48th Sess., UN Doc. CCPR/C/21/Rev.1/Add.4 (1993), reprinted in UN Doc. HRI/GEN/1/Rev.1 at 35 (1994), para. 8.

[215] Metropolitan Church of Bessarabia v. Moldova (ECtHR, App. No. 45701/99, 13 December 2001), para. 118.

limitation clause of article 11 applied and permitted "national security" to be used as a permissible ground for limitation, the evidence supporting such a threat was insufficient to justify the kind of interference with article 11 rights that denial of recognition entailed.[217] *A fortiori*, grounds justifying interference with article 9 were lacking.

Perhaps most significantly from the perspective of religious association laws, where religious groups can point to alternative ways that a particular state objective can be achieved that would be less burdensome for the religious group and would substantially accomplish the state's objective, it is difficult to claim that the more burdensome alternative is genuinely necessary. Stated differently, limitations must be narrowly tailored to accomplish the objectives they seek to bring about. Denying or sharply restricting entity status is almost always an overbroad response to particular concerns covered by the permissible legitimating grounds—"public safety, order, health, or morals or the fundamental rights and freedoms of others."[218] There is almost always a more narrowly drawn approach to addressing the particular concern than denying entity status. A state can impose narrower criminal or administrative penalties for those within the belief community who actually endanger the specific concern (e.g., health or safety), rather than depriving the entire belief community of the benefits of entity status. Thus, even where such concerns are grounded in more than stereotypes or prejudice, limitations imposed as a condition to access to entity status under religious association laws can seldom be justified.

7. Summary of the Implications of Substantive Religious Freedom Norms for the Right to Legal Entity Status

Briefly stated then, the substantive norm of freedom of religion or belief, which is affirmed in all the key international human rights instruments, provides the foundation for religious groups to acquire a type of legal entity status sufficiently robust to carry out a full range of religious activities. The international instruments recognize that everyone has the right to freedom of religion or belief and that this right is not a gift bestowed by the state, but rather a right that flows from the inherent dignity of humankind. The international instruments also recognize that there is a social dimension to freedom of "thought, conscience and religion" that includes freedom to manifest religion "individually or in community with others."[219] In a modern setting, as laid out in section I above, failure of a state to make a meaningful form of entity status available entails serious interference with religious freedom rights. Such interference is permissible only under the sharply restricted situations specified in the various limitation clauses of the various

---

[216] Ibid., para. 125.

[217] See ibid. The Court does not expressly explain why it refers to national security at this point in its opinion, despite the fact that it is clear that national security is only a legitimating ground justifying limitation of freedom of association, and not freedom of religion. Compare ECHR, art. 11(2) with ECHR, art. 9(2). This may have been a slip in application of the relevant limitation clauses. But most likely what is intended is what is suggested here—that even if the looser limitation clause were applied, the facts did not warrant the interference with religious freedom and religious association rights that nonrecognition of the Bessarabian Church entailed.

[218] ICCPR, art. 18(3).

[219] ICCPR, art. 18(1).

international instruments. As a general matter, control-oriented religious association laws cannot be justified under the limitation clauses, both because the purposes served by such laws are not covered by the legitimating grounds articulated in the limitation clauses, and because the purposes involved could generally be served by state action much narrower in its focus than restricting the entity status of religious communities.

B. The Right to Association and the Law of Religious Associations

The right to entity status is protected not only by the substantive right to freedom of religion or belief, but also by the overlapping right to freedom of association. Indeed, there is a close historical connection between freedom of religion and freedom of association.[220] In its collective dimension, freedom of religion or belief can be regarded as a special form of freedom of association. As one of the key drafters of the UDHR has stated, "whatever else they may be, churches are also associations."[221] In general, an association involves "two or more persons . . . [acting] in concert with a view to pursuing specific common objectives."[222] In this sense, persons pursuing religious objectives "in community with others" constitute an association and are entitled to protection under both freedom of religion and freedom of association norms.

1. Substantive Content of the Right to Freedom of Association

Article 20 of the UDHR articulates the basic features of the freedom of association norm, providing that "[e]veryone has the right to freedom of peaceful assembly and association,"[223] and that "[n]o one may be compelled to belong to an association."[224] Protections of the rights to assembly and association were articulated jointly in both the UDHR and the ECHR,[225] but subsequent documents have separated these rights.[226] Article 16 of the ACHR expressly lists possible purposes of association, providing that "[e]veryone has the right to associate freely for ideological, religious, political, economic, labor, social, cultural, sports, or other purposes."[227] The other major international instruments do not expressly list the possible purposes, but with them as well "the protective scope is broad."[228]

---

220 John P. Humphrey, "Political and Related Rights," in *Human Rights in International Law: Legal and Policy Issues*, ed. Theodor Meron (Oxford: Clarendon Press, 1984), 171, 188, 191. Humphrey was the Director of the Secretariat's Division on Human Rights and in this capacity played a key role in developing basic drafts of the UDHR. See Johannes Morsink, *The Universal Declaration of Human Rights: Origins, Drafting, and Intent* (Philadelphia: University of Pennsylvania Press, 1999), 5.

221 Humphrey, "Political and Related Rights," 191.

222 Christian Tomuschat, "Freedom of Association," in *The European System for the Protection of Human Rights*, ed. R. St. J. Macdonald, F. Matscher, and H. Petzold (Dordrecht: Martinus Nijhoff Publishers, 1993), 493, 493.

223 UDHR, art. 20(1).

224 UDHR, art. 20(2).

225 "Everyone has the right to freedom of peaceful assembly and to freedom of association with others, including the right to form and to join trade unions for the protection of his interests" (ECHR, art. 11[1]).

226 ICCPR, arts. 21–22; ACHR, arts. 15–16.

227 ACHR, art. 16(1).

Ability to claim the right to association does not depend on the particular legal status a group has under the domestic law of a country; rather, the notion of "association" is an autonomous concept determined by the international instruments.[229] Otherwise states could manipulate the coverage of the right by restructuring the local law of associations.

Like freedom of religion, freedom of association has both individual and collective dimensions and entails positive state obligations to make entity status available. As stated by Professor Nowak,

> Freedom of association is . . . conceived of as a *subjective right of the individual* to found an association with those like-minded or to join an existing association. But it also covers the collective right of an existing association to perform activities in pursuit of the common interests of its members. The States Parties are thus obligated not to prohibit or otherwise interfere with the founding of associations or their activities.

---

[228] Manfred Nowak, *U.N. Covenant on Civil and Political Rights, CCPR Commentary* (Kehl/Strasbourg/Arlington: N. P. Engel, 1993), 386.

In fact, an early version of the UDHR provided that "[t]here shall be freedom of peaceful assembly and of association for political, religious, cultural, scientific, professional, and other purposes compatible with this Declaration." See Morsink, *The Universal Declaration of Human Rights*, 168, citing UN Doc. E/CN.4/W.2/Rev.2. As a result of pressure from trade union interests, this was subsequently expanded to include an express reference to a right to participate in trade unions. Subsequently, Eleanor Roosevelt suggested that the list of purposes be dropped. Ultimately, a compromise was reached whereby the catalogue was dropped, but the reference to trade unions was retained (ibid, 170–71). The rationale was that while "the catalogue of political, economic, religious, social and cultural rights [was] recognized by the constitutions of almost all nations of the world" (ibid., quoting Santa Cruz of Chile, E/CN.4/SR.41/p.3.), it was important to expressly recognize trade union associations, "because they had not been part of the classical eighteenth-century lists of rights" (ibid., quoting Cassin's support for Santa Cruz, E/CN.4/SR.41/p.3). The reference to trade unions eventually dropped out of the UDHR, but language expressly referencing trade unions was ultimately adopted first in the ECHR (art. 11[1]) and subsequently in the ICCPR (art. 22[1]).

The point is that it was consistently understood that freedom of association covered religious as well as other associations. Accord Tomuschat, "Freedom of Association," 493, 496. Vacillation concerning whether to expressly mention it or not, and whether or not to include mention of trade unions, cannot be taken as any indication of an intent that religious associations are not covered by the right to association. See Lance Lehnhof, "Freedom of Religious Association: The Right of Religious Organizations to Obtain Legal Entity Status under the European Convention," *BYU Law Review* (2002): 561, 568 (noting this point with respect to the ECHR). In general, the legislative history regarding trade unions reflects special political pressures regarding the rights of trade unions during the formative days of the international instruments. The resulting "prominence given to them should not be taken to mean that trade union freedom has a higher legal value than 'ordinary' freedom of association" (Tomuschat, "Freedom of Association," 493, 494). The European Court has expressly rejected the argument that the right of association was intended largely for the purpose of protecting trade unions, and therefore excluded political parties, holding that "trade unions are but one example among others of the form in which the right to freedom of association may be exercised" (United Communist Party of Turkey v. Turkey [ECtHR, Application No. 19392/92, 30 January 1998], paras. 24–25). The Court emphasized that even more persuasive than the wording of article 11 in this regard was that "political parties are a form of association essential to the proper functioning of democracy," and that there accordingly "can be no doubt that political parties come within the scope of Article 11" (ibid., para. 25). In light of the importance that the Court has attached in other contexts to the role of religious freedom to democratic values, see, e.g., Metropolitan Church of Bessarabia v. Moldova (ECtHR, App. No. 45701/99, 13 December 2001), para. 114 (noting the Court's "settled case-law to the effect that . . . freedom of thought, conscience and religion is one of the foundations of a 'democratic society'"), a parallel argument can be made that religion cannot be excluded from the scope of article 11.

[229] Tomuschat, "Freedom of Association," 493, 494.

> Because groups of persons usually seek to pursue their longer-term interests in a legally recognized form (usually as juridical persons), States Parties are also under a *positive duty* to provide the legal framework for founding juridical persons. Since freedom of association, like other political freedoms, also has effects on the *horizontal level*, States are, furthermore, obligated to protect the formation or activities of associations against interference by private parties.[230]

In short, the right to association entails the right of human beings to join together for legitimate common purposes. To respect this right, states are obligated not only to refrain from interfering with the founding and continuance of associations, but also to provide a legal framework for the establishment of juridical persons through which associations can carry out their activities,[231] as well as a legal environment in which associations will be protected from interference by third parties. Both individuals and associations themselves are bearers of the right to association. [232] The right to freedom of association embraces the right to form associations, to join them, and the right to establish an effective organizational structure consonant with the beliefs and purposes of the organization.[233] It should also be noted that as a general matter, the right of freedom of association has a negative dimension: the right to association is voluntary, and individuals and groups have a right not to be compelled to participate in private associations.[234]

2. Religious Freedom and the Right to Association

Since a group of individuals exercising the right to freedom of religion or belief "in community with others" is an association, both the individuals and the group involved can assert the rights and are entitled to the benefits of freedom of association. Certainly, the fact that they have the special protections afforded by the right to freedom of religion or belief does not diminish their right to assert freedom of association. They have at least the same rights that other associations have, and in certain respects they are entitled to heightened protection.[235]

---

230 Nowak, *U.N. Covenant on Civil and Political Rights, CCPR Commentary*, 387 (emphasis original).

231 Tomuschat, "Freedom of Association," 506; Nowak, *U.N. Covenant on Civil and Political Rights, CCPR Commentary*, 387 (commenting on the right to entity status guaranteed by art. 22 of the ICCPR); Sidiropoulos v. Greece (1998-IV ECtHR), 1594, 1614 ("The Court points out that the right to form an association is an inherent part of the right set forth in Article 11 [freedom of association]. . . . That citizens should be able to form a legal entity in order to act collectively in a field of mutual interest is one of the most important aspects of the right to freedom of association, without which that right would be deprived of any meaning.")

232 Tomuschat, "Freedom of Association," 497–98.

233 Ibid., 498–99.

234 UDHR, art. 20(2); Sigurdur A. Sigurjonsson (ECtHR, 30 June1993) (includes extensive analysis of the protection of the negative right of association); Young, James & Webster v. United Kingdom 4 EHRR 38 (1982) (44 ECtHR, ser. A, 13 August 1981) (holding that compulsory membership in certain trade unions as required by British "closed-shop" rules violated art. 11 ECHR). Certain professional associations created not only in the interests of their members but to protect the public do not fall within the coverage of freedom of association, and may accordingly be compulsory (P. van Dijk and G. J. H. van Hoof, *Theory and Practice of the European Convention on Human Rights* [The Hague: Kluwer Law International, 1998], 592–96).

235 For additional considerations arguing in favor of heightened protection, see Lehnhof, "Freedom of Religious Association," 581–600.

This heightened protection reflects certain fundamental features of the relationship between freedom of religion or belief and freedom of association. In the first place, as has already been noted,[236] the limitation clauses associated with religious freedom allow a much narrower range of intervention than those associated with freedom of association. The flip side of narrower limitation clauses is expanded protection in the religious domain.

Second, the nature of religious activities entitles them to heightened protection vis-à-vis other activities that might be pursued by associations. As a general matter, the freedom of association guarantees the right to associate in order to carry out further activities, but the other activities themselves enjoy special human rights protection only if they are covered by other rights.[237] Thus, while the right to form corporations and trade unions is protected by freedom of association, the activities of these organizations, in the absence of some independent fundamental right covering the activity, are not entitled to any special human rights protection merely because they involve collective as opposed to individual activity. In contrast, the activities of political parties and religious communities are protected by freedom of expression and freedom of religion, so that for such expressive organizations, the collective activity has independent protection.[238]

Third, religious associations are not merely instrumental devices for pursuing individual ends. In profound ways they provide contexts within which individual self-actualization unfolds.[239] They constitute mediating institutions between the individual and the state that help buffer individual life from the state and other mega-institutions of modern life.[240] At the same time, they provide the nurturing seedbeds within which the differing values and orientations of genuine pluralism can grow and flourish. They constitute communicative social settings that provide the context for finding meaning and for accepting or choosing fundamental life orientations and values. Religious organizations are not the only associations with these features. Much the same can be said for a range of expressive or intimate associations.[241] What is significant about such organizations is that they play a unique role in fostering the unfolding of human dignity. They are vital to the

---

[236] See section III(A)(6) above.

[237] Tomuschat, "Freedom of Association," 500.

[238] Ibid., 501.

[239] For the significance of the relationship of dignity and self-definition values to the grounding of a right to legal entity status under freedom of association norms, I am indebted to an unpublished paper by Michael W. Durham, "The Right to Form a Non-Profit: The Importance of Legal Entity Status to Freedom of Association" (May 28, 2002) (unpublished manuscript in possession of the author). Durham contends that it is not the importance of social settings to self-definition and protecting the collective will of an organization alone that demand legal entity status, but the fact that without such status, "group action would be no more than the temporary coincidence of individual purposes" (ibid., 17). Legal entities create structures through which individuals can bind themselves to follow collective decision-making processes that are necessary for "undertaking and accomplishing serious projects" (ibid.), while providing the vehicle for "asset partitioning" that makes it possible for associations to function efficiently. See also Henry Hansmann and Reinier Kraakman, "The Essential Role of Organizational Law," *Yale Law Journal* 110 (2000): 387. Durham's analysis was written with general nonprofit organizations in mind, but applies with equal force to religious associations.

[240] Peter Berger and Richard J. Neuhaus, *To Empower People: The Role of Mediating Institutions in Public Policy* (Washington: American Enterprise Institute for Public Policy Research, 1977).

[241] "Expressive" and "intimate" associations constitute two major areas accorded heightened protection under United States freedom of association law. See, e.g., Boy Scouts of America v. Dale, 530 US 640 (2000) (Boy Scouts had an expressive agenda that allowed exclusion of homosexual leaders); New York State Club Ass'n v. City of New York, 487 US 1 (1988); Board of Directors of Rotary Int'l v. Rotary Club,

process by which individuals define themselves by interacting with others. The German Constitutional Court's approach to grounding freedom of association rights is grounded on precisely this insight: the concept of the human person presupposed by the German commitment to human dignity "is not that of the isolated and self-sufficient individual, but that of the person who is part of a community . . . [and] who depends for his development on multiple inter-personal relations. An essential part of these are provided through associations."[242] Precisely because the collective dimension of freedom of religion and freedom of association overlap in this context, heightened protection of religious associations (and other associations with this tight linkage to human dignity) is deserved.

3. The Right to Legal Entity Status

The bottom line for religious associations is that they can lay claim to the right to entity status that has emerged as an essential feature of the modern right to freedom of association. They have at least the same right to entity status as other associations, and to the extent that religious associations are entitled to heightened protections, their claims to entity status are correspondingly stronger.

While the right to entity status and to satisfactory legal frameworks granting such status has been recognized for some time, both at the international level[243] and in national legal systems,[244] this development is nowhere more evident than in the European Court

---

481 US 537 (1987); Roberts v. United States Jaycees, 468 US 609 (1984); Note, "State Power and Discrimination by Private Clubs: First Amendment Protection for Nonexpressive Associations," *Harvard Law Review* 104 (1991): 1835. (The name of the student author is not mentioned at the end of the note.)

[242] Entscheidungen des Bundesverfassungsgerichts, 50 BVerfGE 290, 353–54 (1979), translated in Sabine Michalowski and Lorna Woods, *German Constitutional Law: The Protection of Civil Liberties* (Aldershot, Hants, England: Dartmouth Pub. Co., 1999), 278.

[243] See, e.g., Manfred Nowak, *U.N. Covenant on Civil and Political Rights, CCPR Commentary* (Kehl/Strasbourg/Arlington: N. P. Engel, 1993), 387 (commenting on the right to entity status guaranteed by art. 22 of the ICCPR).

[244] See, e.g., Federal Republic of Germany, Basic Law, art. 9(1) ("All Germans have the right to form associations and societies"); Polish Const, art. 12 ("The Republic of Poland shall ensure freedom for the creation and functioning of trade unions, socio-occupational organizations of farmers, societies, citizens' movements, other voluntary associations, and foundations."); Albanian Const, art. 46 ("Everyone has the right to organize collectively for any lawful purpose. . . . The registration of organizations or societies in court is done according to the procedure provided by law.") One of the foundational cases giving rise to more active forms of judicial review in France was by coincidence a case protecting freedom of association and the right to entity status. See Decision of the French Constitutional Council No. 71-44 of 16 July 1971, reprinted in Vicki C. Jackson and Mark Tushnet, *Comparative Constitutional Law* (New York: Foundation Press, 1999), 558–59, translation from John Bell, *French Constitutional Law* (Oxford, England: Clarendon Press, 1992), 272–73. See also ibid., 553–58, excerpting commentary by Alec Stone, *The Birth of Judicial Politics in France* (Oxford: Oxford University Press, 1992), 64–69, 257–60. See also James E. Beardsley, "The Constitutional Council and Constitutional Liberties in France," *Am. J. Comp. L.* 20 (1972): 431. The German Constitutional Court has spelled out the right to entity status as follows:

> Freedom of association is to a more or less significant extent dependent on regulations which integrate the free associations and their life has always been linked with the necessity of a statutory implementation of this freedom, without which it could not achieve its practical effectiveness. . . . [But] from the necessity of some implementation it cannot follow that any particular existing implementation attains constitutional status. On the other hand, the leg-

of Human Rights. For that reason, the case law of the European Court needs to be addressed here in greater detail. In what follows I turn first to the initial cases that recognized the right to entity status solely on the basis of freedom of association, and then to the later cases that recognized this right in the freedom of religion context.

In *Sidiropoulos v. Greece*,[245] the Court held that denial of legal entity status to a Macedonian cultural association by a Greek court violated freedom of association rights under article 11 of the ECHR. In explaining its decision, the Court stated categorically:

> [t]hat citizens should be able to form a legal entity in order to act collectively in a field of mutual interest is ***one of the most important aspects of the right to freedom of association, without which the right would be deprived of any meaning***. The way in which national legislation enshrines this freedom and its practical application by the authorities reveal the state of democracy in the country concerned. Certainly States have a right to satisfy themselves that an association's aim and activities are in conformity with the rules laid down in legislation, ***but they must do so in a manner compatible with their obligations under the Convention and subject to review by the Convention institutions***.[246]

Where *Sidiropoulos* involved the right to form an association, *United Communist Party of Turkey v. Turkey*[247] addressed the issue of dissolution of a political party. In that case the party was dissolved almost immediately after it was formed. The Court rejected the argument that association rights did not extend beyond formation, holding that freedom of association

> would be largely theoretical and illusory if it were limited to the founding of an association, since the national authorities could immediately disband the association without having to comply with the Convention. It follows that the protection afforded by Article 11 lasts for an association's entire life and that dissolution of an association by a country's authorities must accordingly satisfy the requirements of paragraph 2 of that provision.[248]

> islator cannot choose the implementation arbitrarily. . . . The legislator therefore has to make available a sufficient variety of legal structures suitable for the different types of associations, thus assuring a reasonable choice among them (50 BVerfGE 290, 358–59 [1979], translated in Michalowski and Woods, *German Constitutional Law*, 279–80).

In determining whether the relevant legal framework unduly constricts the right to association, the Federal Constitutional Court assesses whether the relevant rules compromise (1) the ability of individuals to form, join, or withdraw from associations (ibid., 356); (2) the ability of the association to function (ibid., 357); or (3) the ability of members to "determine the will" of the association without external influences (84 BVerfGE 372, 380–81 [1991]).

245 ECtHR, App. No. 26695/95, 10 July 1998.

246 Ibid., para. 40 (emphasis added). The Court further emphasized the significance of entity status in the recent case of Gorzelik v. Poland (ECtHR, App. No. 44158/98, 12 December 2001), para. 55, noting that "[t]he most important aspect of freedom of association is that citizens should have the right to create a legal entity in order to act collectively in a field of mutual interest. Without this, that right would have no practical meaning." The Court concluded that the right to association was not violated in *Gorzelik*, because the organization in question was free to reregister if it dropped certain nonvital features that would otherwise have created problems in the overall structure of Polish election law, but it clearly emphasized the significance of the right at stake.

247 ECtHR, App. No. 19392/92, 30 January 1998.

248 Ibid., para. 33.

The Court went on to hold that there was no evidence that the party bore any responsibility for terrorist activity or that either its program or its activities threatened to destroy rights protected by the ECHR.[249] Accordingly, the Court concluded that "a measure as drastic as the immediate and permanent dissolution of [a political party] . . . is disproportionate to the aim pursued and consequently unnecessary in a democratic society." [250] Thus, no violation of article 11 occurred. The Court reached essentially the same conclusion in *Freedom and Democracy Party v. Turkey*.[251]

While the initial set of cases vindicating the right to entity status dealt with political and cultural associations, it is now clear that the same logic extends to religious associations. The interplay between article 9 and article 11 ECHR in situations involving organizational issues in a religious community was addressed in considerable detail in *Hasan and Chaush v. Bulgaria*.[252] In that case, there was a division in the Bulgarian Muslim community regarding who should be the official mufti leading the community. Bulgarian political parties aligned themselves with the rival muftis as they came to power. The government was only willing to grant official status to one mufti and one affiliated Muslim organization.[253] In their arguments before the Court, the parties disagreed as to whether article 9 or article 11 should apply. The Bulgarian government sought to persuade the Court that the organizational issues raised by the case should be treated purely as freedom of association (article 11) issues;[254] the religious applicants saw their claim very much in freedom of religion (article 9) terms.[255] The Court analyzed the issue as follows:

> The Court recalls that religious communities traditionally and universally exist in the form of organised structures. They abide by rules which are often seen by followers as being of a divine origin. Religious ceremonies have their meaning and sacred value for the believers if they have been conducted by ministers empowered for that purpose in compliance with these rules. The personality of the religious ministers is undoubtedly of importance to every member of the community. Participation in the life of the community is thus a manifestation of one's religion, protected by Article 9 of the Convention.
>
> Where the organisation of the religious community is at issue, Article 9 must be interpreted in the light of Article 11 of the Convention which safeguards associative life against unjustified State interference. Seen in this perspective, the believer's right to freedom of religion encompasses the expectation that the community will be allowed to function peacefully free from arbitrary State intervention. Indeed, the autonomous existence of religious communities is indispensable for pluralism in a democratic society and is thus an issue at the very heart of the protection which Article 9 affords. It directly concerns not only the organisation of the community as such but also the effective enjoyment of the right to freedom of religion by all its active members. Were the organisational life of the community not protected by Article 9 of the Convention, all other aspects of the individual's freedom of religion would become vulnerable.[256]

---

[249] Ibid., para. 59.
[250] Ibid., para. 61.
[251] ECtHR, App. No. 23885/94, 8 December 1999.
[252] ECtHR, Application No. 30985/96, 26 October 2000.
[253] Ibid., para. 28.
[254] Ibid., paras. 57–58.
[255] Ibid., para. 56.

The Court's reasoning handed a victory to the religious applicants, but it did so by spelling out the interaction of articles 9 and 11. The court recognized that issues of religious organization are vital religious issues in their own right. Accordingly, they remain religious freedom issues, but the relevant religious freedom norms must also take into account freedom of association principles that protect the religious community from "arbitrary state intervention." In the context of religious organizational issues, this associational freedom protection translates into a concern for religious autonomy, which is both "indispensable for pluralism in a democratic society" and "at the very heart of the protection which Article 9 affords."[257] In effect, article 11 concerns are absorbed into and recognized as part of article 9 protections, where they protect both the collective and the individual dimensions of freedom of religion or belief. If the organizational issues were left unprotected, "all other aspects of the individual's freedom of religion would become vulnerable."[258] A little further on, the Court rejects the government's claim that the case would be "better dealt with solely under Article 11," holding that "[s]uch an approach would take the applicants' complaints out of their context and disregard their substance."[259] The Court's insistence that "Article 9 must be interpreted in the light of the protection afforded by Article 11"[260] is thus an insistence that the protections that have been worked out in the article 11 context should be carried over to the article 9 context and given full effect, while maintaining sensitivity to the religious context and the substance of religious freedom rights. Thus, the right to entity status initially identified under article 11 applies *a fortiori* in the article 9 setting.

This conclusion was further solidified in *Metropolitan Church of Bessarabia v. Moldova*.[261] There the Court repeated the formula requiring that article 9 be interpreted in light of article 11, but this time did so in the context of directly addressing the right to register and acquire entity status.[262] The Metropolitan Church of Bessarabia is an Eastern Orthodox Church attached to the Patriarchate of Bucharest. It is recognized by all Orthodox patriarchates with the exception of that in Moscow. [263] The political authorities in Moldova favored the Metropolitan Church of Moldova, which is subservient to the Moscow Patriarchate, and repeatedly refused to recognize the Bessarabian Church. In Moldova this refusal of recognition not only deprived the Bessarabian Church of the usual benefits of legal entity status—recognition by a formal state decision was in fact required as a matter of law for a denomination to be active in the country.[264] The government took the position, ultimately rejected by the Court, that the Bessarabian Church was not really a separate church, but rather a schismatic part of the Moldovan Church, and that registering the former would constitute impermissible intervention in the affairs of the latter.[265] The government also expressed fears that the Bessarabian Church would

---

256 Ibid., para. 62.
257 Ibid.
258 Ibid.
259 Ibid., para. 65.
260 Ibid.
261 ECtHR, App. No. 45701/99, 13 December 2001.
262 Ibid., para. 118.
263 Ibid., para. 12.
264 Ibid., paras. 13, 110. The government claimed that it tolerated the Bessarabian Church despite its illegal status, but this was belied by the record in the case.
265 See ibid., paras. 13–30.

work "hand-in-glove with Romanian interests favourable to reunification between Bessarabia and Romania, . . . thus endangering social stability and even Moldova's territorial integrity."[266] Analyzing these issues, the Court concluded that the denial of recognition constituted an interference with religious freedom,[267] albeit one that was "prescribed by law"[268] and that "pursued a legitimate aim under Article 9 § 2, namely protection of public order and public safety."[269] However, as in so many article 9 cases, the crucial issue was whether the interference was "necessary in a democratic society," and on this front the government's case foundered.

In the course of analyzing this issue, the Court provided one of the most comprehensive expositions to date of the implications of freedom of religion and freedom of association for the organizational autonomy of religious communities. Many of the key points regarding the basic features of freedom of religion or belief have already been noted above, in the discussion of the substantive right to freedom of religion or belief.[270] With respect to the specific issue of the right to entity status, the opinion does not specify from which of the two articles this particular protection is derived, but precisely because the Court expressly emphasized in the course of this analysis that "Article 9 must be interpreted in the light of Article 11,"[271] the overall analysis provided by the Court can be taken at a minimum as a definitive pronouncement of what the two rights taken together require.[272] Further, since the *Bessarabian Church* case is decided fundamentally under article 9, the case stands for the proposition that the right to entity status initially recognized under article 11 is also an inherent aspect of the right to freedom of religion or belief.

In working its way to this conclusion, the Court first emphasizes the foundational character of the rights and the importance of state neutrality and impartiality in dealing with religious associations. Then the Court turns to the importance of the associational issues per se. Reformulating slightly language drawn from *Hasan and Chaush*, the Court stated the applicable principles in this area as follows:

> since religious communities traditionally exist in the form of organised structures, Article 9 must be interpreted in the light of Article 11 of the Convention, which safeguards associative life against unjustified State interference. Seen in that perspective, the right of believers to freedom of religion, which includes the right to manifest one's religion in community with others, encompasses the expectation that believers will be allowed to associate freely, without arbitrary State intervention. Indeed, *the autonomous existence of religious communities is indispensable for pluralism in a democratic society and is thus an issue at the very heart of the protection which Article 9 affords.*[273]

---

[266] Ibid., para. 111.
[267] Ibid., paras. 102–5.
[268] Ibid., para. 110.
[269] Ibid., para. 113.
[270] See section III(A)(6) above.
[271] Ibid., para. 118.
[272] After completing its article 9 analysis, when addressing whether there had been article 6 and article 11 claims, the Court stated, "Having taken Articles 6 and 11 into account in the context of Article 9 (see paragraphs 118 and 129 above), the Court considers that there is no cause to examine them separately." Note that this not a statement that the Court does not need to reach the articles 6 and 11 issues because the case has been disposed of on a satisfactory independent ground. Here the Court makes it clear that articles 6 and 11 are significant, but they have already been taken into account in connection with the decision under article 9, which was made "in light of" articles 6 and 11.

Turning to the legal entity issue itself, the Court continued:

> one of the means of exercising the right to manifest one's religion, especially for a religious community, in its collective dimension, is the possibility of ensuring judicial protection of the community, its members and its assets, so that Article 9 must be seen not only in the light of Article 11, but also in the light of Article 6 [access to tribunals].[274]

A basic aspect of legal entity status is the recognition of legal standing in judicial processes for the entity either to pursue its rights and interests or to defend itself against claims by others. Since it is well understood that this right to sue and be sued is a typical feature of legal entity status, this passage in effect recognizes the need both for the legal framework through which legal entity status is acquired, and a viable judicial enforcement setting. The Court expanded further on this point in the course of applying these principles to the facts of the *Bessarabian Church* case. Specifically, the Court found that

> in the absence of recognition the applicant church may neither organise itself nor operate. Lacking legal personality, it cannot bring legal proceedings to protect its assets, which are indispensable for worship, while its members cannot meet to carry on religious activities without contravening the legislation on religious denominations.[275]

To the government's claim that it "tolerated" the Bessarabian Church despite the fact that it had not been recognized, the Court responded that it could not "regard such tolerance as a substitute for recognition, since recognition alone is capable of conferring rights on those concerned."[276] In the Court's view, granting of legal entity status was important both as a matter of principle, to vindicate freedom of religion and association, and as a practical matter, because the Bessarabian Church had in fact had difficulty in defending its rights without entity status.[277]

An important outer limit on the right to entity status was identified by the European Court in the recent case of *Refah Partisi v. Turkey*.[278] There the Court sustained dissolution of what had been, until its judicial demise, the largest plurality party in the Turkish parliament.[279] The *Refah Partisi* (or in English, the "Welfare Party") case can best be

---

273 Ibid., para. 118 (emphasis added).

274 Ibid.

275 Ibid., para. 129.

276 Ibid.

277 Ibid.

278 The *Refah Partisi* (*Welfare Party*) case was initially decided by a seven-member chamber of the Court that was divided on the outcome 4-3 (Welfare Party v. Turkey [ECtHR, App. Nos. 41340/98, 41342/98, 41343/98, 41344/98, 31 July 2001] [hereinafter "Refah I"]). Judges Fuhrmann, Loucaides and Sir Nicolas Bratza filed a joint dissenting opinion. The case was subsequently referred to a 17-member Grand Chamber of the Court, which filed a unanimous opinion holding that dissolution of the Welfare Party did not constitute a violation of the ECHR (Refah Partisi [Welfare Party] v. Turkey [ECtHR, 13 February 2003] [hereinafter "Refah II"]). In the most fundamental respects, Refah II did not significantly alter the position of the majority in Refah I.

279 Before its dissolution, Refah had existed as a political party for fifteen years. At the time it was dissolved, it had 158 of 450 parliamentary seats and attracted 21.4% of the popular vote in the preceding election. Before its dissolution it had ruled for almost a year in a coalition government, with its leader as prime minister. It left office peacefully when the coalition came unglued. See Christian Moe, "Refah Revisited: Strasbourg's Construction of Islam," Paper Presented at the Conference on "The Turkish Welfare Party Case: Implications for Human Rights in Europe," Central European University, Budapest, Hungary, 12–15 June 2003 (unpublished manuscript in possession of the author).

understood as a "militant democracy" decision—i.e., a case about the point at which democratic regimes can step in to prevent a potentially antidemocratic party from taking power.[280] The Court essentially viewed the Welfare Party as an Islamicist party that might ultimately unravel Turkey's secularist tradition and replace it with "a regime based on shari'ah within the framework of a plurality of legal systems [which would subject Jews to Jewish law, Muslims to shari'ah, etc.] and that Refah did not exclude recourse to force in order to implement this policy and keep the system it envisaged in place."[281] There is significant room for doubt about the accuracy of the Court's analysis of Islam; altogether too much of its reasoning rests on stereotypical thinking about Islam and fears about the place of Islam in modern Europe.[282] These issues cannot be pursued further here.

The point for present purposes is that the risk that the Refah Party had enough strength that it might actually have succeeded in bringing about its purported objectives that explains the following apparent paradox: of the four Turkish party dissolution cases that the European Court has resolved on the merits, the only dissolution it sustained was that of the party with the highest level of democratic legitimacy, as measured by electoral support. Precisely because the Refah Party had substantial support, it posed a greater threat of bringing about its objectives, and thus a graver threat to democratic order.

But this same consideration makes it clear that *Refah*, being fundamentally a militant democracy case, is sharply distinguishable from the other cases involving right to entity status, and is likely to pose no problem for typical religious association cases. Religious groups that have problems acquiring entity status are typically small and unlikely to pose serious threats to the sustainability of a democratic political order supporting a regime of human rights. They are generally much less threatening or divisive than some of the groups whose right to entity status has thus far been sustained. It is also important to remember that *Refah* dealt with a political party whose objective, as a political party, was to gain state power. Religious entities *qua* religious entities are generally not seeking political power. While the state may arguably seek to prevent anticonstitutional forces from obtaining political and governmental power, it should not need to exercise this authority over private associations of individuals, such as religious organizations, which are not threatening political takeover. Even where divisions in larger denominations are involved, such as those that have occurred in recent years within the Orthodox communities in Bulgaria and Moldova, any threat to fundamental democratic order remains remote. Far from suggesting a reversal or rethinking of the Court's line of cases vindicating the right to legal entity status, then, the *Welfare Party* case suggests that it is only when an association poses a feasible, imminent and realistic threat to democratic institutions that its association rights may be curtailed.[283] In short, the notion that the right to

---

[280] For an analysis of the notion of militant democracy, see Andras Sajo, "Militant Democracy and Transition Towards Democracy," Presented at the Conference on Militant Democracy held at Central European University, 5–6 December 2003.

[281] Refah II, para. 132.

[282] This was the theme of many of the papers at the Conference on "The Turkish Welfare Party Case: Implications for Human Rights in Europe," Central European University, Budapest, Hungary, 12–15 June 2003. Papers are being prepared for publication. From this conference, see in particular, Christian Moe, "Refah Revisited."

entity status is an "inherent part" and one of the "most important aspects of the right to freedom of association"[284] has in no sense been weakened by the *Refah* decision, particularly as it might apply to religious groups.

4. Summary

In summary, then, the right to freedom of association reinforces the right to entity status that religious communities have as a matter of freedom of religion or belief. The right to freedom of religion is at least as robust in this respect as the freedom of association right, and, as noted earlier,[285] religious communities may be entitled to greater protection in this regard than many other types of associations. For example, limitation clauses might permit denial of entity status for nonreligious associations on national security grounds that cannot be invoked under the limitation clauses applicable to freedom of religion. Moreover, as expressive associations, religious communities are entitled to greater protection in the full range of their activities. In any event, religious groups were always understood as falling within the coverage of the freedom of association right.[286] Whatever else the association right means for religious communities, it must assure them of the right to acquire a legal entity equipped with sufficient powers to enable the community to carry out the full range of its legitimate religious activities. The jurisprudence of the European Court is now quite extensive and provides powerful authority binding within its own jurisdiction (and persuasive everywhere else) that emphasizes the following points: (1) the right to form a legal entity is one of the most important aspects of the right to freedom of association, without which the right would be deprived of any meaning;[287] (2) protection of religious associations is vital to democratic and pluralistic society;[288] (3) the state must be neutral and impartial in adopting and implementing laws governing religious associations;[289] (4) believers should be allowed to associate freely in pursuit of their religious objectives, without arbitrary state intervention;[290] (5) only where religious associations pose realistic, imminent threats to public order and safety or other enumerated grounds for limiting freedom of religion may states permissibly interfere with the acquisition of legal entity status;[291] and (6) discriminatory denial of legal entity status is impermissible.[292]

---

283 See Lance Lehnhof, "Freedom of Religious Association: The Right of Religious Organizations to Obtain Legal Entity Status Under the European Convention," *BYU Law Review* (2002): 561, 580 (reaching a parallel conclusion on the basis of his analysis of Refah I).

284 Sidiropoulos v. Greece (ECtHR, App. No. 26695/95, 10 July 1998), para. 40.

285 See section III(B)(2) above.

286 See section III(B)(1) above.

287 Sidiropoulos v. Greece (ECtHR, App. No. 26695/95, 10 July 1998), para. 40.

288 Hasan and Chaush v. Bulgaria (ECtHR, Application No. 30985/96, 26 October 2000), para. 62; Metropolitan Church of Bessarabia v. Moldova (ECtHR, App. No. 45701/99, 13 December 2001), paras. 114, 118.

289 Metropolitan Church of Bessarabia v. Moldova, para. 116; see also section III(A)(6) above.

290 Hasan and Chaush v. Bulgaria, para. 62; Metropolitan Church of Bessarabia v. Moldova, para. 118.

291 Metropolitan Church of Bessarabia v. Moldova, para. 125.

292 The Court noted in the Bessarabian case that in determining whether the Bessarabian Church should be recognized, the Moldovan authorities had not used the same criteria they had applied to other religious communities, and no satisfactory justification for the differential treatment had been provided (ibid., para. 129).

C. Other Human Rights Protections Relevant to Religious Associations

A variety of other general human rights protections are relevant to certain aspects of the law of religious associations. Because these are not so directly focused on the life of religious communities as freedom of religion and freedom of association norms, they will be treated in more summary fashion. Although treated in less depth, they can provide crucial protections for religious communities in the circumstances when they become relevant.

1. Nondiscrimination Norms

Nondiscrimination is a fundamental and pervasive feature of international human rights instruments. All of the major international human rights instruments guarantee that everyone is entitled to the rights and freedoms they protect "without distinction of any kind, such as . . . religion."[293] Some of the norms address only nondiscrimination with respect to fundamental rights covered by the instrument in which the nondiscrimination norm is found. Thus, article 14 of the ECHR specifies that "[t]he enjoyment of the rights and freedoms set forth in this Convention shall be secured without discrimination."[294] Nondiscrimination in this sense can be characterized as an "accessory prohibition" reinforcing other substantive norms.[295] Other norms constitute general equal protection provisions, proscribing state action that violates equality principles. In contrast to the ECHR, the ICCPR and other regional instruments also provide for an independent right to equality.[296] Thus, the article 26 of the ICCPR provides:

> All persons are equal before the law and are entitled without any discrimination to the equal protection of the law. In this respect, the law shall prohibit any discrimination and guarantee to all persons equal and effective protection against discrimination on any ground such as race, colour, sex, language, *religion*, political or other opinion, national or social origin, property, birth or other status.[297]

Of course, most national constitutions also provide an independent equality right.[298]

---

[293] UDHR, art. 2; ICCPR, art. 2(1); ECHR, art. 14 ("the rights and freedoms set forth in this Convention shall be secured without discrimination on any ground such as . . . religion"); ACHR, art. 1(1) (States Parties undertake to ensure "free and full exercise of those rights and freedoms, without any discrimination for reasons of . . . religion").

[294] ECHR, art. 14. For a useful analysis of the coverage of article 14, see Karl Josef Partsch, "Discrimination," in *The European System for the Protection of Human Rights*, ed. R. St. J. Macdonald, F. Matscher, and H. Petzold (Dordrecht: Martinus Nijhoff Publishers, 1993), 571–92; P. van Dijk and G. J. H. van Hoof, *Theory and Practice of the European Convention on Human Rights,* 3d ed. (The Hague: Kluwer Law International, 1998), 710–30.

[295] Manfred Nowak, *U.N. Covenant on Civil and Political Rights, CCPR Commentary* (Kehl/Strasbourg/Arlington: N. P. Engel, 1993), 465.

[296] ACHR, art. 24; African Charter on Human and Peoples' Rights (adopted by the Organization of African Unity on 17 June 1981), art. 3.

[297] ICCPR, art. 26 (emphasis added).

[298] See, e.g., Nihal Jayawickrama, *The Judicial Application of Human Rights Law: National, Regional and International Jurisprudence* (Cambridge: Cambridge University Press, 2002), 816–41; Nowak, *U.N. Covenant on Civil and Political Rights, CCPR Commentary*, 459; US Const, amend. XIV; German Basic Law, art. 3.

What is significant to bear in mind with respect to religious association laws is that whether an "independent" or an "accessory" equality right is involved, making discriminatory distinctions on the basis of religion itself is likely to constitute a violation. Because the distinctions are likely to result in discriminatory impacts in the lives of individual believers, and in many cases because the norms do not permit unequal treatment of juristic persons any more than they do of natural persons, nondiscrimination provisions may provide an important source of relief. There is some tendency to assume that the distinctions made in the course of structuring religious association laws are like those made in tax laws or other legislation regulating business enterprises, where bright lines simply have to be drawn, and broad deference to the resulting classifications is the norm. The important point to bear in mind is that precisely because the fundamental right to freedom of religion or belief is involved, more rigorous scrutiny of legal classifications is required to assure that impermissible discrimination does not occur. The UN Human Rights Committee has recognized that "not every differentiation of treatment will constitute discrimination, if the criteria for such differentiation are reasonable and objective and if the aim is to achieve a purpose which is legitimate under the Covenant."[299] But precisely because religious association laws are so vital to the practice of religion "either individually or in community with others,"[300] great care must be taken to assure that distinctions made are genuinely objective, and not merely a smoke screen covering religious discrimination.

The importance of nondiscrimination was given particular emphasis in the 1981 Declaration on the Elimination of All Forms of Intolerance and of Discrimination Based on Religion or Belief. While the 1981 Declaration is, as its name suggests, a declaration rather than a formal treaty, it reaffirms norms articulated by legally binding treaties such as the ICCPR and other widely accepted international instruments. Articles 2 and 3 reaffirm the ICCPR's antidiscrimination norms. Article 2(2) defines "intolerance and discrimination based on religion or belief" as:

> [a]ny distinction, exclusion, restriction or preference based on religion or belief and having as its purpose or its effect nullification or impairment of the recognition, enjoyment or exercise of human rights and fundamental freedoms on an equal basis.[301]

This language arguably goes beyond the language of the ICCPR in that it extends to private as well as state action, but since the focus in connection with statutory schemes dealing with the grant of entity status to religious organizations is obviously a state action, the antidiscrimination norms articulated clearly fall within binding treaty obligations.

Article 27 of the ICCPR addresses discrimination issues where "ethnic, religious or linguistic minorities exist." Article 27 provides additional protection against discrimination against religious minorities, providing that "persons belonging to such minorities shall not be denied the right, in community with the other members of their group, to

---

299 Human Rights Committee General Comment 18 (1989) on Non-Discrimination, 37th Sess., para. 13.

300 ICCPR, art. 18(1).

301 1981 Declaration, art. 2(2). Similarly, article 3 of the 1981 Declaration underscores the significance of the antidiscrimination norm established by article 2, noting that "[d]iscrimination between human beings on the grounds of religion or belief constitutes an affront to human dignity and a disavowal of the principles of the Charter of the United Nations, and shall be condemned as a violation of the human rights and fundamental freedom proclaimed in the Universal Declaration of Human Rights." (ibid., art. 3).

enjoy their own culture, to profess and practice their own religion, or to use their own language." The term "minorities" is not clearly defined in the Covenant, and this provision may ultimately be limited to groups that would constitute classical ethnic minorities. But as I have argued elsewhere, the use of the word "or" in article 27 may signal broader coverage:

> Statistically speaking, there is at most one majority religion in any given country, and all others constitute minority religions. In many countries, no single group is in a majority position. There is a tendency to think of minorities as an identifiable cultural group, tied together by common language, traditions, ethnicity and so forth. But the use of the word "or" in the Covenant suggests that there may be religious minorities that are not necessarily also part of ethnic or linguistic minorities. The UN Human Rights Committee's General Comment No. 23(50) on Article 27 indicates that "the persons designed to be protected are those who belong to a group and who share in common a culture, a religion and/or a language. Those terms also indicate that the individuals designed to be protected need not be citizens of the State party."[302]

Significantly, the nondiscrimination rights covered by article 27 are not restricted to citizens. "Just as [those protected by this provision] . . . need not be nationals or citizens, they need not be permanent residents. Thus, migrant workers or even visitors in State party constituting such minorities are entitled not to be denied the exercise of those rights" [to "enjoy their own culture, to practice their religion and speak their language" in community with members of their group].[303]

The question as to whether the "minority" protection provisions of article 27 of the ICCPR should apply to religious groups that are not culturally or ethnically different from the surrounding population remains open. On the one hand, one could argue that the historical problems and tensions associated with ethnic minorities are objectively distinguishable and pose different magnitudes of risk to states than "nonethnic" religious minorities. On the other hand, it is not clear why ethnic or cultural religious groups should have greater protection or attention than smaller and often less popular religious groups. Favoritism of the ethnic and cultural religious groups clearly constitutes differential treatment vis-à-vis the smaller groups. Typically, the problems involved with "ethnic" religious minorities involve tensions between a prevailing traditional religion and another traditional religion typically associated with a minority ethnic group. This would be the problem of a Catholic Croat living in Orthodox Serbia, or an Orthodox Serb living in Catholic Croatia. In contrast, minority religions that are not linked to ethnic or cultural groups are much more likely to be new religious movements, which often suffer much more serious religious discrimination than traditional minority groups.[304] What is the objective, nondiscriminatory basis for favoring the traditional minority over the nontraditional group? This flies in the face of the UN Human Rights Committee's concern with "any tendency to discriminate against any religion or belief for any reasons, including the fact that they are newly established, or represent religious minorities that may be the

---

302 Cole Durham, *Freedom of Religion or Belief: Laws Affecting the Structuring of Religious Communities* (Warsaw: OSCE/ODIHR, 1999), 16, citing Human Rights Committee General Comment 23 (1994) on ICCPR art. 27, 50th Sess., para. 5.1. Religious and minority rights are distinguishable from political rights, which may be made to apply only to citizens under article 25 of the ICCPR.

303 Human Rights Committee General Comment 23 (1994) on ICCPR art. 27, 50th Sess., para. 5.2.

304 See the chapters by Barker and by Fautré, Garay, and Nidegger in this volume.

subject of hostility by a predominant religious community."[305] Regardless of how this question is ultimately resolved, however, it is clear that to the extent that religious minorities are recognized as minorities, they have an added layer of protection against discrimination under article 27.

2. Norms Proscribing Arbitrary Decision Making

One of the recurrent problems experienced particularly by smaller religious groups in connection with religious association laws involves arbitrary decisions by state officials—often by lower-level bureaucrats at the local level.[306] Local administrative officials often appear to be subject to behind-the-scenes pressures, either from local politicians or influential religious leaders. Because such administrative decisions can be made by relatively obscure or even anonymous officials, they may evade scrutiny by human rights observers. Precisely because of these factors, it is important to assure that religious association laws are administered in a nonarbitrary way.

Manoussakis v. Greece,[307] perhaps the leading European Court case considering arbitrariness in the religious freedom context, is instructive. *Manoussakis* involved endless bureaucratic delays in processing a request from Jehovah's Witnesses for a house of prayer permit. While the case is not squarely about religious association laws, it is precisely relevant to the all-too-typical problem of arbitrary decisions and bureaucratic delay encountered in connection with securing registration or recognition under such laws. In subjecting the pertinent Greek legal provisions to the "strict scrutiny" called for because religious freedom issues were involved,[308] the Court noted that the provisions "allow far-reaching interference by the political, administrative and ecclesiastical authorities with the exercise of religious freedom."[309] Problems included (1) conditions "which confer a very wide discretion on the police, mayor or chairman of the district council,"[310] (2) the fact that the key provision permitted the approving authority "to defer his reply indefinitely," since it "does not lay down any time limit,"[311] and (3) the fact that either inaction or refusal of authorization could occur "without explanation or without giving a valid reason."[312] The Court also noted that there appeared to be no justification for a provision empowering the approving official to "assess whether there is a 'real need' for the religious community in question to set up a church"[313] by evaluating whether fifty families living in relatively close proximity were requesting the

---

305 Human Rights Committee General Comment 22 (1993) on ICCPR art. 18, 48th Sess., para. 2.

306 This issue is addressed in much greater detail in the chapter by Podoprigora in this volume.

307 Manoussakis and Others v. Greece, 23 EHRR 387 (1997) (ECtHR, App. No. 18748/91, 26 September 1996).

308 Ibid., para. 44.

309 Ibid., para. 45.

310 Ibid.

311 Ibid.

312 Ibid.

313 Ibid., referring to section 1(1)(a) of the royal decree of 20 May/2 June 1939, which provided that in order to get authorization for construction or operation of religious facilities, an "application shall be submitted by at least fifty families, from more or less the same neighbourhood and living in an area at a great distance from a temple of the same denomination, it being assumed that the distance makes it difficult for them to observe their religious duties" (ibid., para. 23).

facility. Arbitrariness was also evident in the fact that although case law from the Supreme Administrative Court in Greece accorded "the local ecclesiastical authority [only] a purely consultative role,"[314] and even then, only in actual construction of a religious building, in fact local officials relied expressly on the lack of authorization from the local bishop of the Orthodox Church. Finally, there was some indication that the conduct of the approving authority was unfair and was attributable "to the difficulty that the latter might have had in giving legally valid reasons for an express decision refusing the authorization or to his fear that he might provide the applicants with grounds for appeal."[315]

Taking these problematic features of the Greek situation into account, the Court emphasized that "[t]he right to freedom of religion as guaranteed under the Convention excludes any discretion on the part of the State to determine whether religious beliefs or the means used to express such beliefs are legitimate."[316] It follows that requirements such as that for the Greek house of prayer permit or for approvals under religious association laws are permissible only "to verify whether the formal conditions laid down in . . . [such] enactments are satisfied."[317] The court also criticized the tendency, documented in the case, for the state "to use the possibilities afforded by the above-mentioned provisions to impose rigid, or indeed prohibitive, conditions on practice of religious beliefs by certain non-Orthodox movements, in particular Jehovah's Witnesses."[318] The Court detected "a clear tendency on the part of the administrative and ecclesiastical authorities to use these provisions to restrict the activities of faiths outside the Orthodox Church."[319] Given the various types of arbitrary conduct involved, the Court concluded that the conviction which ensued when Jehovah's Witnesses finally used their facility without approval was not "proportionate to the legitimate aim pursued [public order], nor, accordingly, as necessary in a democratic society."[320]

Freedom from arbitrary state action is at the core of what is required by the "prescribed by law" phrase that appears in several of the international limitation clauses.[321] Indeed, it is at the heart of what is meant by the ideal of "rule of law." As the European Court has stressed, phrases such as "prescribed by law" in international human rights instruments require not only that

> the impugned measure should have some basis in domestic law, but also refer to the quality of the law in question. The law should be both *adequately accessible* and *foreseeable*, that is formulated with sufficient precision to enable the individual—if need be with appropriate advice—to regulate his conduct. . . . *For domestic law to meet these requirements it must afford a measure of legal protection against arbitrary interferences by public authorities* with the rights safeguarded by the Convention. In matters affecting fundamental rights *it would be contrary to the rule of law, one of the basic principles of a democratic society enshrined in the Convention, for a legal discretion*

---

[314] Ibid, paras. 26, 47.
[315] Ibid., para. 51.
[316] Ibid., para. 47.
[317] Ibid.
[318] Ibid., para. 48.
[319] Ibid.
[320] Ibid., para. 53.
[321] See, e.g., ICCPR, art. 18(3); ECHR, art. 9(2).

> ***granted to the executive to be expressed in terms of an unfettered power.*** Consequently, the law must indicate with sufficient clarity the scope of any such discretion conferred on the competent authorities and the manner of its exercise.[322]

Significantly, then, the constraint on arbitrariness in connection with religious association laws must also be understood to preclude not only the problematic features noted in connection with ***Manoussakis***, but, more generally: (1) laws and administrative practices that are inaccessible and lack transparency; (2) retroactive legislation; (3) legislation that is so vague as to fail to give fair notice of its implications for the conduct of citizens; and (4) legislation which, through vague provisions or otherwise, leaves excessive discretion in the hands of officials.

3. The Right to Effective Remedies

Another set of implications of general human rights norms for religious association law can be summarized under the heading of a right to effective remedies. This is also rooted in general rule of law conceptions, but has found specific embodiment in a number of international norms.

At the most general level, there are a number of provisions that obligate states to give practical effect to the array of norms spelled out in international human rights law. These are obviously relevant in the area of freedom of religion or belief, and are particularly meaningful when it comes to religious association laws, because without these so many other aspects of freedom of religion or belief suffer. Thus, article 2(2) of the ICCPR obligates State Parties "to take the necessary steps . . . to adopt such legislative or other measures as may be necessary to give effect to the rights recognized in the present Covenant."[323] This is buttressed by the provisions in subparagraph 3 of article 2, which provide that "any person whose rights or freedoms as herein recognized are violated shall have an effective remedy"[324] and that this shall include the possibility of having rights to such remedies "determined by competent judicial, administrative or legislative authorities, or by any other competent authority provided for by the legal system of the State, and to develop the possibilities of judicial remedy."[325]

The right to an effective remedy in particular has significant implications in connection with religious association laws. Under the European Convention, this right is articulated both as a general matter in article 13,[326] and also with respect to the right "to a fair and public hearing within a reasonable time by an independent and impartial tribunal established by law" as specified in article 6(1).[327] As described earlier,[328] the European Court has sustained the right of a religious community to acquire entity status on the

[322] Hasan and Chaush v. Bulgaria (ECtHR, App. No. 30985/96, 26 October. 2000), para. 84 (emphasis added).
[323] ICCPR, art. 2(2).
[324] ICCPR, art. 2(3)(a).
[325] ICCPR, art. 2(3)(b).
[326] ECHR, art. 13 provides: "Everyone whose rights and freedoms as set forth in this Convention are violated shall have an effective remedy before a national authority notwithstanding that the violation has been committed by persons acting in an official capacity."
[327] ECHR, art. 6(1).
[328] See sections III(A)(6) and III(B) above.

basis of article 9, construed "in light of" article 6.[329] In the *Canea* case, the Court in effect held that article 6 required a state to hear the claim of a religious community, even though it had not complied with the formalities necessary to acquire legal personality and the associated right to sue. Even more clearly, in the *Bessarabian Church* case, the Court recognized that without entity status, the right of a religious community to defend its rights in court were prejudiced. These provide representative instances of the way that the right to an effective remedy is vital to supplementing entity rights.

One of the most important practical needs of religious associations is the right to prompt decisions and meaningful appeals to impartial judicial bodies. All too often, religious association laws neglect this crucial issue. This causes bureaucratic delay, which itself interferes with freedom of religion or belief as in *Manoussakis*.[330] It is important that religious association laws contain provisions (or are governed by administrative appeal procedures that may be specified in an administrative code or the like) that specify a reasonably short time for approval of entity status. Ideally such time periods should not exceed thirty days—sixty at the outside. After a reasonable and specified amount of time has passed, or once an adverse decision has been made, the party seeking entity status should have recourse to a prompt appeal to an impartial tribunal. It should also be clear that the standards for review should not allow courts or other state officials to engage in nonneutral, substantive review of religious beliefs, including organizational beliefs, as described earlier.[331] The right to an effective remedy requires procedures along this line.

IV. Analysis of Representative Issues That Arise in Connection with Religious Association Laws

In this section I turn to an analysis of the major features (both substantive and procedural) of the legal structures available to religious organizations in carrying out their affairs. For the most part, analysis in this section focuses on emerging legislation in former socialist countries.[332] In part this is because I have done most of my research in this part of the world. But the focus has the added advantage of taking a realistic look at

---

329 Metropolitan Church of Bessarabia v. Moldova (ECtHR, App. No. 45701/99, 13 December 2001), para. 118; Canea Catholic Church v. Greece, 27 EHRR 521 (1999) (ECtHR, App. No. 25528/94, 16 December 1997).

330 23 EHRR 387 (1997) (ECtHR, App. No. 18748/91, 26 September 1996).

331 See discussion of neutrality and impartiality requirements above.

332 For simplicity, the laws of the various socialist bloc countries are cited in full here, and will be referred to only by the short forms indicated here in the rest of this chapter. Full texts of these laws are available at <www.religlaw.org>. Law on Non-Profit Organizations, No. 8788 (2001) [Albania] (hereinafter "Albanian Non-Profit Law"); Law on the Freedom of Conscience and Religious Organizations (1991) (amended 1997, 2001) [Armenia] (hereinafter "Armenian Law"); Law on Freedom of Religious Beliefs, No. 281 (1992) (amended 1996, 1997, 2001) [Azerbaijan] (hereinafter "Azerbaijani Law"); Law on the Freedom of Religion and Religious Organizations (2002) [Belarus] (hereinafter "Belarusian Law"); Religious Denominations Act, (2002) [Bulgaria] (hereinafter "Bulgarian Law"); Law on Legal Position of Religious Communities (2002) [Croatia] (hereinafter "Croatian Law"); Law on Churches and Religious Societies (2002) [Czech Republic] (hereinafter "Czech Law"); Law on the Freedom of Religious Belief and on the Status of Churches and Religious Societies, No. 308 (1991) (amended 2000) [Czechoslovakia] (hereinafter "Czechoslovakian Law"); Churches and Congregations Act (2002) [Estonia] (hereinafter "Estonian Law"); Law on Freedom of Conscience and Religions and the Churches, Act No. IV (1990) [Hungary] (hereinafter "Hungarian Law"); Law on Religious Organizations (1995) (amended 1996, 1997, 1998, 2000) [Latvia] (hereinafter "Latvian Law"); Law on Religious Communities and Associations,

legislation clearly in the process of shifting from a "control" to a more "facilitative" approach. Thus, the section identifies not only concrete problems, but also practical realities associated with the transition to an approach more fully consistent with modern human rights standards. The aim is not to provide detailed instructions on the mechanics of setting up religious entities, or a thorough comparative study of relevant laws governing these issues. Rather, it is to identify key religious freedom issues associated with faulty laws governing the granting of entity status to belief communities.

A. Mandatory Registration Laws

For a variety of practical reasons, most religious organizations desire to obtain legal entity status,[333] which normally comes with registration or incorporation. But it is important to remember that this is not always the case. There are some individuals and groups that object to such state chartering as a matter of conscience.[334] More frequently, the lack of formal legal structure may reflect the fact that the group of believers is simply too small for burdensome legal procedures to make sense—either to the group or to public officials. Most regimes now recognize that the right to freedom of religion or belief precludes laws that make registration or the equivalent a mandatory precondition of having, adopting or manifesting religious beliefs.[335] There is also recent history of countries rejecting proposals that would have imposed such requirements.[336]

No. 89-1985 (1995) (amended 1997, 2000) [Lithuania] (hereinafter "Lithuanian Law"); Law on Religious Communities and Religious Groups, No. 35 (1997) [Macedonia] (hereinafter "Macedonian Law"); Law on Denominations, No. 979-XII (1992) (amended 1998, 2002) [Moldova] (hereinafter "Moldovan Law"); Law Regarding the Guarantees of Freedom of Religion and Belief (1989) [Poland] (hereinafter "Polish Law"); Ordinance No. 26 on Associations and Foundations (2000) [Romania] (hereinafter "Romanian Ordinance"); Law on the Freedom of Conscience and Religious Associations, No. 125-FZ (1997) (amended 2000, 2002) [Russia] (hereinafter "Russian Law"); Law on the Registration of Churches and Religious Societies, Act No.192 (1992) [Slovakia] (hereinafter "Slovakian Law"); Law on the Freedom of Conscience and Religious Organizations (1991) (amended 1992, 1993, 1995, 1996) [Ukraine] (hereinafter "Ukrainian Law"); Law on the Freedom of Worship and Religious Organizations (1998) [Uzbekistan] (hereinafter "Uzbek Law").

333 See section I above.

334 See note 1 above.

335 To my knowledge, no North or South American country (other than Cuba) and no western European country requires that religious groups register or secure prior governmental approval in order to carry out their basic religious activities. In eastern Europe, not even the rather restrictive 1997 Russian Law makes acquiring legal entity status mandatory. Groups lacking status as a legal entity (an "organization" in the Russian Law) are still clearly free to practice their religion, although there are a variety of things the group lacks legal capacity to do (Russian Law, art. 7 [recognizing the existence of religious groups that do not have entity status]; W. Cole Durham, Jr. and Lauren B. Homer, "Russia's 1997 Law on Freedom of Conscience and Religious Associations: An Analytical Appraisal," *Emory Int'l Law Review* 12 [1998]: 169).

336 For example, the attempt to pass legislation including a mandatory registration feature was headed off in Bulgaria in 2000, after the draft in question received a negative review from the Council of Europe. See also Emil Cohen, *Bulgaria: A Meeting of Religious and Human Rights Activists Denounces the Final Version of the Draft Denominations Act*, Tolerance Foundation (8 November 2000), available at <http://www.hrwf.net/html/bulgaria2000.html#BulgarijeAmeeting> (last visited 15 December 2003). In Kazakhstan, legislation requiring registration was struck down by Kazakhstan's Constitutional Court. See US Department of State, *International Religious Freedom Report 2002: Kazakhstan*, sec. II, available at <http://www.state.gov/g/drl/rls/irf/2002/13942.htm> (last visited 4 November 2003).

Unfortunately, there continue to be countries around the world taking the opposite tack, where laws proscribe practice of religion unless registration or some other form of state approval or license is obtained. The People's Republic of China, for example, recognizes only five official religions. While there is a growing tendency in practice to allow at least some other groups to function on a limited scale, religious organizations other than the five remain technically illegal and subject to state monitoring and often repression.[337] Much the same can be said of Vietnam[338] and Laos. [339] Problems along these lines also continue in some former Soviet countries. For example, although provisions of the current Belarusian Law proclaim that everyone has the right to freedom of conscience[340] and freedom of religion,[341] in fact religious groups must be registered in order to conduct religious activities or worship legally.[342] Uzbekistan[343] and Kazakhstan[344] have provisions that appear to make registration mandatory, and Moldovan law might be

---

[337] All religious activities are funneled through eight religious organizations that represent the five official religions: Daoism, Buddhism, Protestantism, Catholicism, and Islam. See Document No. 19, "The Basic Viewpoint and Policy on the Religious Question During Our Country's Socialist Period," translated in R. Lanier Britsch, "The Current Legal Status of Christianity in China," *BYU Law Review* (1995): 347; Kim-Kwong Chan and Eric Carlson, *Religious Freedom in China: Policy, Administration, and Regulation* (forthcoming, 2004) (manuscript on file with author), 15. For examples of state monitoring and repression, see Freedom House Center for Religious Freedom, "Report Analyzing Seven Secret Chinese Government Documents," available at <http://www.freedomhouse.org/religion>, and documents published by the Committee for Investigation on Persecution of Religion in China, available at <http://www.china21.org>.

[338] See Zachary Abuza, *Renovating Politics in Contemporary Vietnam* (Boulder, Colorado: Lynne Rienner, 2001). The US State Department confirms this problem. "During the period covered by this report [2002], members of unrecognized religious groups were beaten, arrested, and detained by the authorities" (US Department of State, *International Religious Freedom Report 2002: Vietnam*, available at <http://www.state.gov/g/drl/rls/irf/2002/13916.htm> [last visited 15 December 2003]).

[339] "The LFNC [Lao Front for National Construction] recognizes two Protestant groups: the Lao Evangelical Church (LEC), which is the umbrella Protestant Church, and the Seventh-Day Adventist Church. The LFNC strongly encourages all other Protestant groups to become part of the LEC church" (US Department of State, *International Religious Freedom Report 2002: Laos*, sec. I, available at <http://www.state.gov/g/drl/rls/irf/2002/13878.htm> [last visited 15 December 2003]).

[340] Belarusian Law, ch. 1, art. 1.

[341] Ibid.

[342] "Communities carry out their activities voluntarily in compliance with their statutes and are to be registered in the order provided by this law" (ibid., art. 14). "Religious organizations are subject to mandatory state registration" (ibid., art. 16). Article 38 of the Belarusian Law lists the consequences from suspension of registration of a religious organization: "In the event of suspension of activities, a religious organization loses its right to conduct religious, entrepreneurial or other activities, to speak in the capacity of a provider of mass media and other legal entities, to transfer monetary assets from current bank accounts to other legal entities, except in cases of remittance of payments to the budget, state off-budget funds and other mandatory payments, accounts previously established by citizen and labor contracts, and remuneration of damages caused by the actions of the religious organization" (ibid., art. 38).

[343] US Department of State, *International Religious Freedom Report 2002: Uzbekistan*, sec. II, available at <http://www.state.gov/g/drl/rls/irf/2002/13990.htm> (last visited 15 December 2003). Not only is religious activity by unregistered groups subject to sanction, but in addition, "[o]fficials who allow activity of non-registered religious organizations shall bear responsibility in accordance with the law" (Uzbek Law, art. 11).

[344] The 2002 US State Department Report on International Religious Freedom noted that while the "National Religion Law . . . does not require religious organizations to register with the Government[,] . . . [a] new Administrative Code [provision], which entered into force in February 2001, allows national and local authorities to suspend the activities or fine the leaders of unregistered religious organizations"

construed to the same effect.[345] In Latvia the law does not explicitly require registration, but in practice only registered organizations can carry out a variety of key religious functions.[346] In some areas, such as Uzbekistan, religious activities by unregistered groups carry substantial civil and even criminal penalties.[347] In Nagorno-Karabakh such unauthorized practice of religion has reportedly carried prison sentences of up to fifteen years.[348]

Such mandatory registration or "preapproval" requirements cannot withstand scrutiny under international human rights standards. They violate the essential notion of universally applicable human rights—that the rights are not created or bestowed by the state, but are inherent aspects of the status and dignity of being human[349]—as well as the broad language of the Universal Declaration of Human Rights[350] and other international instruments.[351]

In addition, sanctions against individuals and groups for manifesting their religion in "teaching, practice, worship and observance" merely because of failure to obtain legal entity status from the state cannot be said to be "necessary"[352] or "necessary in a democratic society."[353] Mandatory registration requirements are not only unnecessary in general

---

(US Department of State, ***International Religious Freedom Report 2002: Kazakhstan***, sec. II, available at <http://www.state.gov/g/drl/rls/irf/2002/13942.htm> [last visited 15 December 2003]).

345 The relevant provision states, "For denominations to be organized and to function they shall submit an application for organization and functioning to the State Service on Denominational Affairs, to which there shall be attached a charter (regulations) of organization and activity that shall contain information on organizational and management systems, accompanied by the fundamental principles of belief" (Moldovan Law, art. 14, para. 1). This provision may simply articulate what is required to obtain entity status, without proscribing religious activity if such status is not obtained. However, there are parts of article 14 that appear to assume that having registered status is necessary to carry out religious activities legally. The final two paragraphs of the article provide that under certain circumstances involving encroachment upon the "indepęndence, sovereignty, integrity and security of the Republic of Moldova," an organization's application for registration may be determined to be invalid, and a religious organization whose activities are limited for these reasons can "recommence its activity only after conforming to the effective court decision" (ibid., art. 14). The most reasonable construction of this provision would hold not that religious activity without registration is per se illegal, but only activities that are extremely dangerous to the state justify termination of rights of religious activity.

346 For example, only registered religious organizations are allowed to "establish educational institutions for the ecclesiastics, monasteries, missions and deaconate institutions," "engage in religious activities" in public places after obtaining authorization, and "invite foreign clergyman or missionaries to engage in religious activities in the Republic of Latvia." (Latvian Law, arts. 13[2], 14[3], 14[4]).

347 US Department of State, ***International Religious Freedom Report 2002: Uzbekistan***, sec. II, available at <http://www.state.gov/g/drl/rls/irf/2002/13990.htm> (last visited 15 December 2003).

348 Karen Ohanj, ***Societal Responses to Religious Diversity and Pluralism in Nagorno-Karabakh***, London CESNUR Conference Paper (April 2001).

349 See discussion in section III(A)(2) above.

350 UDHR, art. 18 ("***[e]veryone*** has the right to freedom of thought, conscience and religion; this right includes . . . freedom either ***alone or in community with others*** and in public or private, to manifest his religion or belief in teaching, practice, worship and observance"); see generally the discussion in section III(A) above.

351 See section III above.

352 ICCPR, art. 18(3).

353 ECHR, art. 9(2); ICCPR, art. 18(3). On the strictness with which the limitation clauses should be construed, see the chapter by Nowak and Vospernik in this volume; UN Human Rights Committee, General Comment 22(48) (1993) on ICCPR art. 18, adopted 20 July 1993, UN Doc. CCPR/C/21/Rev.1/Add.4 (1993). See the discussion in section III(A)(6) above.

(as evidenced by the fact that relatively few states insist on them); they are unnecessary in particular in that they are disproportionate. Registration is an altogether too blunt instrument to tackle the problems that may emanate from a small number of individuals and groups in connection with these legitimate state concerns. Any legitimate concerns a state may have in registration (such as being aware of the existence of religious groups in society or of who represents religious groups in public settings) can be sufficiently met by notice requirements (as opposed to state-controlled registration requirements) that do not confer on government the right to curtail religious practice.

B. Minimum Membership Requirements

The key features of typical laws dealing with registration or incorporation set forth the formal requirements that a particular organization must satisfy in order to acquire legal entity status. Typically, one of these is the minimum number of members that the organization must have.

As of the writing of this chapter, I do not have comprehensive comparative data on minimum member requirements for all countries around the globe. However, the data on the fifty-five OSCE countries is enlightening. The overwhelming majority of the participating states in the OSCE have minimum member requirements of 10 or less. In the former socialist region, only five states have minimum member requirements above 30,[354] and the majority require less than 15.[355] Similarly, most Latin American states require only the amount of founders required by the normal laws for establishing civil associations, usually only 2 or 3 members.

A number of countries with strong present or past control approaches to regulating religious entities, however, have extremely high minimum membership requirements: Slovakia requires 20,000 members,[356] the Czech Republic requires 300 members,[357] and Armenia requires 200 members for a religious group to register.[358] If an alternative for registration as a civil nonprofit organization is available, the numerical requirements for

---

[354] Armenia, 200, Armenian Law, art. 5(e); Croatia, 500, Croatian Law, para. 1, art. 21; Czech Republic, 300, Czech Law, tit. III, sec. 10, para. 2; Hungary, 100, Hungarian Law, ch. 2, sec.9, para. 1(a); Slovak Republic, 20,000, An Amendment to the Law on the Registration of Churches and Religious Societies, Act. No. 192 (1992), para. 2, available at <http://www.religlaw.org>.

[355] The Constitutional Court of the Former Yugoslav Republic of Macedonia recently struck down as unconstitutional a legislative provision setting 50 adults as the minimum necessary for recognition of a religious association (Decision of the Macedonian Constitutional Court of 23–24 December 1998, p.3 ["the requirement of such a high limit of founders . . . represents a limitation of the freedom of the religion and the freedom of association"]). Similarly, based in part on OSCE recommendations, the Constitutional Council in Kazakhstan struck down a law including a minimum member requirement of 50 in April 2002 (US Department of State, *International Religious Freedom Report 2002: Kazakhstan*, sec. II, available at <http://www.state.gov/g/drl/rls/irf/2002/13942.htm> [last visited 4 November 2003]). However, there has been some political pressure in certain countries within the OSCE to consider increasing the minimum number of members needed to establish basic legal entities through which religious organizations carry out their religious affairs. For example, this is the case with draft legislation in Croatia.

[356] See An Amendment to the Law on the Registration of Churches and Religious Societies, Act. No. 192 (1992) [Slovak Republic], para. 2, available at <http://www.religlaw.org>.

[357] Czech Law, tit. III, sec. 10, para. 2.

[358] Armenian Law, art. 5. Post-Communist countries are not the only ones that use high membership requirements as a means to control religious groups and limit entry of newer groups. The Pacific nation

religious organizations need not prevent acquisition of legal entity status. However, in some cases certain basic benefits are limited to religious entities registered as religious entities, which raises discrimination issues.[359] In any case, it is not clear why registration as a religious group should be significantly more difficult than registration as a nonprofit or charitable association. If anything, concerns for religious freedom would suggest that registration for religious organizations should be simpler.[360]

It is also important to remember in this regard that many religious communities are organized on a congregational rather than a hierarchical basis. This is not merely a matter of convenience; it is very often a matter of deep religious belief. In such organizations the congregation is the appropriate church unit for acquiring legal recognition. Because many smaller groups have relatively few members in any particular city, it is often the case that their congregations may be quite small. They may consist of a handful of families, with the result that the total number of actively participating adults may be less than 20, or even 15.

Sometimes the pressure for increasing the minimum member requirement comes from concerns to exercise better control over smaller, unknown, and sometimes dangerous groups. This was a significant concern behind proposed legislation, including a minimum membership requirement of 50, that was struck down by the Constitutional Council of Kazakhstan in April 2002.[361] This approach, however, is counterproductive. Genuinely dangerous groups will simply go underground, and the burden of registration then falls on law abiding groups for whom a minimum number of founders as high as 50 can operate as a significant burden on religious freedom rights.[362]

Increasing the number beyond ten or fifteen results in significant violations of international human rights standards, at least with respect to smaller groups organized on a congregational basis who wish to acquire legal personality for their religious community but who lack the requisite number of members. In the absence of measures designed to prevent religious meetings in homes,[363] very small groups can function informally. Once more than three or four families are involved, however, operating a congregationally based church without entity status becomes complex. Thus, for smaller religious communities, minimum membership requirements that exceed as few as 10–15 adult members can be extremely problematic.

---

of Kiribati recently amended its registration law to require a religious group to have 2% of its adult population to register (Religious Bodies Registration, Chap. 68, Vol. IV [1978], as amended by the Religious Bodies Registration [Amendment] Act [1985] [Kirbati], available online at <http://www.vanuatu.usp.ac.fj/paclawmat/Paclawmat_MAIN.html>).

359 See section III(C)(1).

360 See section II(C) and II(D) above and section IV(D) below.

361 US Department of State, ***International Religious Freedom Report 2002: Kazakhstan***, sec. II, available at <http://www.state.gov/g/drl/rls/irf/2002/13942.htm> (last visited 4 November 2003)

362 It is of course true that lack of entity status will make organizational matters more complicated for the underground group, and to that extent will constitute an incremental factor hampering its development. But to structure the law in a way that penalizes legitimate groups for the risk that some groups may be dangerous imposes an unnecessarily harsh burden on the legitimate groups. Particularly when one takes into account that normal criminal and/or administrative sanctions are available to deter genuinely dangerous conduct, the incremental "hampering effect" of strict registration rules cannot be justified when weighed against the burden such rules impose on legitimate groups.

363 China is not the only place where "house churches" are not welcome. Land use rules can often be used to make group worship in a home setting problematic. Requirements that all surrounding homeowners consent, or that rule out religious uses in residential areas, can be problematic in this regard.

Raising minimum membership requirements for religious communities creates problems of discrimination between civil and religious organizations. The Croatian Law on Associations only requires three founders,[364] whereas the new Croatian Law on Religious Communities requires a minimum of 500 members.[365] Religious communities should be granted equivalent treatment—not heavier burdens. They have a right under the European Convention to legal entity status, and particularly where smaller religious groups cannot organize as normal associations,[366] it is vital that such status be accorded them without a large number of founders.[367]

More fundamentally, excessive minimum member requirements violate both freedom of religion and freedom of association. As chronicled above,[368] recent decisions of the European Court of Human Rights have held that religious, cultural and political associations have a right to legal entity status as an inherent aspect of their right to freedom of association and freedom of religion.[369] Religious association laws that set unduly high minimum membership requirements further invade the right of religious communities to autonomy in structuring their internal affairs.[370] Perhaps most significantly, minimum member requirements clearly impose unauthorized limitations on manifestations of freedom of religion.[371]

A handful of west European states have higher minimum member requirements. However, these are only for "upper-tier" entities, not for the basic legal entity available for religious organizations.[372] They provide no persuasive authority for approving excessive minimum member requirements for acquisition of base-level entity status.

C. Minimum Duration Requirements

Some registration schemes impose the excessively burdensome requirement that groups exist in the country for an extended period of time before they can be registered. For example, in Mexico and Peru registration is limited to religious groups that have been

---

364 Law on Associations, Official Gazette of the Republic of Croatia, No. 88 (2001) [Croatia], available at <http://www.icnl.org>.

365 Croatian Law, art 21.

366 Ibid.

367 Manoussakis and Others v. Greece, 23 EHRR 387 (1997) (ECtHR, 26 September 1996), was ultimately decided on grounds of impermissible arbitrariness that was involved in withholding approval of a house of prayer permit. Interestingly, however, the decree implementing the statute under which the impermissibly arbitrary state conduct occurred was one that set a high minimum member requirement for a house of prayer permit. Specifically, it required that the application for the permit needed to be made by "at least fifty families, from more or less the same neighborhood." (ibid., para. 23).

368 See sections III(A)(6) and III(B)(3).

369 Freedom and Democracy Party (ÖZDEP) v. Turkey (ECtHR, 8 December 1999); United Communist Party of Turkey v. Turkey (ECtHR, 30 January 1998); Sidiropoulos & Others v. Greece (ECtHR, 10 July 1998), *cf.* Canea Catholic Church v. Greece, 27 EHRR 521 (1999) (ECtHR, 16 December 1997) (legal personality of Roman Catholic Church protected); Hasan and Chaush v. Bulgaria (ECtHR, 26 October 2000) (interference with internal organization of Muslim community and managing its affairs violates religious freedom, and decision on grounds of freedom of association was unnecessary because freedom of religion analysis was carried out in light of freedom of association requirements).

370 On autonomy rights, see the chapter by Minnerath in this volume.

371 See discussion in section III(A)(6). See also the chapter by Nowak and Vospernik in this volume.

372 E.g., in Austria religious organizations must have a national membership equaling at least 2% of the Austrian population to obtain the higher-level status of a recognized religion (***anerkannte Religion***)

present in the country for ten and five years, respectively.[373] Russia's 1997 Law requires groups to either be part of a centralized religious organization or have existed for fifteen years in the country to have normal legal entity status.[374]

These requirements are rationalized on the grounds that only serious religions with some kind of staying power should be registered. If registration is the gateway to tax exemptions or other government benefits, the argument is apparently that such benefits should only be conferred on groups that prove they show some permanence. But this argument is flawed. Why would the length of time a religious entity has been present in a country have a legitimate bearing on whether it qualifies for benefits enjoyed by other religions? Surely if there is fear of non-genuine groups obtaining tax exemptions, the legislation should attempt to deal directly with that concern, and not use a rather overbroad approach of saying that all groups with less than five or ten years do not qualify, regardless of the individual facts. None of the enumerated grounds in the limitation clauses identify newness of a religion as a legitimate ground for limitation. The fact that some new groups might turn out to be dangerous is far too speculative and overbroad to justify a general requirement that all groups meet a duration requirement. While some western European governments have imposed duration requirements for religious groups to obtain higher-tier status,[375] none have done so for basic legal entity status.

In practice, these time limits impose substantial burdens on new religious groups. Just as requirements of large minimum memberships violate the right to legal entity status provided by the international instruments, so too do requirements that organizations be in the country for extended periods of time. The European Court of Human

---

(Budesgesetz über die Rechtspersönlichkeith von religiösen Bekenntnisgemeinschaften, § 11.2 [BGBl I 1998/19] [Austria], reproduced in Herbert Kalb et al., *Religionsgemeinschaftenrecht* [Vienna: Verlag Österreich, 1998], 104, 108).

373 Ministerial Resolution No. 377-2003-Jus (13 October 2003), art. 3 [Peru]; Mexico Law of Religious Associations and Public Worship, art. 7, II.

374 Russian Law, art. 27.3. Article 27 states, in part, that religious associations "which do not possess a document proving their existence [in Russia for] at least 15 years are to enjoy the rights of a legal person on the condition of re-registration every year until the expiration of the indicated 15-year period. During this period, these religious [associations] are not to enjoy rights stipulated in articles 3.4, 5.3, 5.4, 13.5, 16.3, 17.1, 17.2, 18.2 (as applicable to educational institutions and mass media), 19, and 20.2 of this federal law." The Russian Constitutional Court has limited this requirement to centralized organizations registered after 1997 (Jehovah's Witnesses and Christian Church of Praise case ruled on by the Constitutional Court on 23 November 1999, No. 16-P, Institute of Religion and Law, "Religious Associations: Freedom of Conscience and Religion; Normative Acts and Judicial Decisions," Moscow, Jurisprudence, 2001, at 238).

375 E.g., Austria passed a law in 1998 that created the new intermediate status of "confessional communities" (***Bekenntnisgemeinschaften***), which is above the level of a normal registered association, but does not have the full status of a "recognized religion" (***anerkannte Religion***) (Bundesgesetz über die Rechtspersönlichkeit von religiösen Bekenntnisgemeinschaften, § 11.2 [BGBl I 1998/19] [Austria], reproduced in Herbert Kalb et al., *Religionsgemeinschaftenrecht* [Vienna: Verlag Österreich, 1998], 104–18). Under this law religious organizations must have "confessional community" status for ten years (and some entity status for twenty years) in order to apply for the status of a recognized religion. See Christopher J. Miner, "Losing My Religion: Austria's New Religion in Light of International and European Standards of Religious Freedom," *BYU Law Review* (1998): 607. In Portugal religious associations can receive the qualification that they are "settled in the country" if they have been an "organized social presence" in Portugal for over thirty years or have been established abroad for more than sixty years (Law on Religious Freedom [Law No. 16/2001] [Portugal], art. 37).

Rights has held that religious, cultural and political associations have a right to legal entity status as an inherent aspect of their right to freedom of association and freedom of religion.[376] This should not be dependent on how long those associations have existed.

Requirements that religious groups exist a number of years before they can obtain basic- level entity status also impose limitations on manifestations of freedom of religion that are not authorized within the meaning of the standard limitation clauses.[377] The legitimating grounds (public safety, order, health, etc.) are to be narrowly construed, and requirements for age of a religious tradition in a country do not fall within any of the categories that justify limiting religious freedom and are not "necessary" or "necessary in a democratic society." The fact that most European states do not have such provisions strongly suggests, at least in the absence of compelling local circumstances to the contrary, that such requirements are not "necessary in a democratic society."[378] They are not narrowly tailored to carry out their legitimate objectives; they are not necessitated by any "pressing social need;" they do not meet proportionality requirements; and, in general, they accomplish nothing other than contributing to unlawful discrimination. Nor would this seem to be an area in which European supervision should give way to a "margin of appreciation." Thus, they fail to qualify as permissible legal limitations on freedom of religion or belief.

D. Other Excessively Burdensome Requirements for Acquiring Entity Status

Many of the most significant practical problems continue to be associated with problematic requirements, criteria, and procedures associated with registration or incorporation of religious associations. There are a variety of provisions that fall in the category of unnecessarily burdensome requirements. Examples include recurrent provisions that one must run the gauntlet of official approval processes at both the national and local levels, as in the registration requirements in legislation proposed (but not adopted) in Bulgaria in 2000. Similarly burdensome are newly emerging requirements such as that proposed by another Bulgarian draft, that religious groups provide a certificate from foreign governments verifying that the association has "not been denied registration as such in member States of the Council of Europe, as well as a written declaration that no civil or criminal suits have been started against the association."[379] Fortunately the draft containing this provision is no longer likely to be adopted. Such provisions would be extremely

---

[376] Freedom and Democracy Party (ÖZDEP) v. Turkey (ECtHR, 8 December 1999); United Communist Party of Turkey v. Turkey (ECtHR, 30 January 1998); Sidiropoulos & Others v. Greece (ECtHR, 10 July 1998), *cf.* Canea Catholic Church v. Greece, 27 EHRR 521 (1999) (ECtHR, 16 December 1997) (legal personality of Roman Catholic Church protected); Hasan and Chaush v. Bulgaria (ECtHR, 26 October 2000) (interference with internal organization of Muslim community and managing its affairs violates religious freedom, and decision on grounds of freedom of association was unnecessary because freedom of religion analysis was carried out in light of freedom of association requirements).

[377] See section III(A)(6) above.

[378] Conceivably, compelling local circumstances might make a constraint necessary in one democracy that is not in another. For example, Germans might think they need greater flexibility in dealing with neo-Nazi parties than other democracies do. Whatever the merits of that particular argument, it is difficult to imagine similarly compelling arguments for an unreasonably high minimum membership requirement.

[379] See Bulgarian draft laws online at <www.religlaw.org>.

burdensome in that they require proof of a negative—something that is always difficult to do. The burden presupposes a kind of "guilty unless proven innocent" approach that is particularly inappropriate when religious freedom is involved. In China applications for registration of venues for religious activities must include an "opinion" from the local People's Government before being sent to the national Religious Affairs Bureau for approval. No further details are included as to what this "opinion" must be or the consequences of a negative opinion.[380]

Some burdensome registration laws can discriminate against particular religious beliefs. For example, the Armenian Law requires that organizations be "based on a historically canonized scripture" and be "part of the international religious community."[381] Other laws provide that the religious organization must not constitute a health hazard to its members, which seems to be an attempt to bar religious organizations that engage in extensive fasting or faith healing from having legal entity status.[382] While governments clearly have a legitimate interest in protecting the health of their citizens, they can easily do this through general legislation, such as laws requiring children to be given medical care. Banning legal entity status of a group simply because of its religious beliefs is disproportionate and unnecessary in a democratic society.

Requirements that religious organizations submit personal information on all their founding members are excessive, particularly in countries where the minimum number of members is large or where there are histories of government repression and citizens may have legitimate concerns about governmental attempts to track their religious beliefs. The 2002 Czech Law, for example, requires the full name and identity number of 300 citizens for a religious organization to be registered.[383] The 1997 Macedonian law originally required religious organizations to submit the "name of the religious community or group, data for the founders, its headquarters, subject of its operation, designation of the rooms where religious activities and rituals are performed and data for the persons in charge for operation and representation of the religious group" in order to register.[384] However, in 1998 the Macedonian Constitutional Court declared this paragraph unconstitutional, since such data about the founders of the religious group is not required by any other association of citizens.[385] The court held that this represented an impermissible limitation on freedom of religion and freedom of association.[386]

---

380 Religious Affairs Bureau, "Registration Procedures for Venues of Religious Activity," art. 3 (1994).

381 Armenian Law, art. 5.

382 See, e.g., Czech Law, sec. 5 (barring registration of religious organizations that "restrict the personal freedom of individuals, especially through the use of psychological pressure or physical force to create dependence, leading to physical, psychological, or economic harm to persons and their family members, to the disruption of their social relationships, including impairing the psychological development of minors and restricting their right to education, 383[4] and preventing or inhibiting a minor from receiving health care appropriate to their respective health needs"); Religious Bodies (Registration) Law of 1989, PN DCL No. 221 (1989), sec. 6(2) [Ghana] (religious organizations must submit "a declaration that the places and modes of worship do not constitute a health or environmental hazard to the members of the [religious] body or to the public general"). The Ghana law was subsequently rendered unconstitutional, see E. K. Quashigah, "Legislating Religious Liberty: The Ghanaian Experience," *BYU Law Review* (1999): 589, 595.

383 Czech Law, secs. 3(c), 10.2.

384 Macedonian Law, art. 11(2).

385 Macedonian Constitutional Court (Decision no. 223/97).

386 Ibid.

Still another form of excessively burdensome requirements occurs sometimes when states proscribe religious organizations from registering as secular nonprofit organizations while simultaneously imposing constraints on access to religious entity status. This can occur either because the state in question has not (yet) enacted association laws designed specifically for religious associations, or because the applicable religious association laws are too restrictive. In both situations the right to entity status is effectively denied. Often, religious organizations would prefer to organize as religious organizations, because religious association laws typically afford greater protections and in some cases greater benefits and prestige. But where a country opens the possibility for the creation of other types of nonprofit organizations, refusal to allow a group to organize under such a law merely because it is religious would constitute discrimination on the basis of religion (unless religious entity status that is at least as beneficial is made available on some other basis).[387] Moreover, if a country imposes stricter requirements on religious associations than on secular nonprofit groups as a condition for acquiring entity status, it is difficult to understand why the requirements are genuinely "necessary" or "necessary in a democratic society," thus failing to meet a crucial test under the typical limitation clauses of applicable international instruments.[388] In general, the better practice is to allow religious and other life-stance associations the option of registering either as secular or as religious entities.[389]

E. Excessive Governmental Discretion

Another recurrent problem is that government leaders are granted excessive discretion in granting approvals that are important for carrying out religious activities. Examples include a variety of grants of discretionary authority to heads of religious affairs in Romania and Bulgaria in the registration process and otherwise. This problem is compounded when legislation creates multiple discretionary barriers, such as the situation in an unadopted Bulgarian draft that required religious groups to obtain (and maintain) the approval of both local magistrates and national authorities if they were to be able to carry out their affairs. When such discretion is abused (and there are tremendous pressures operating particularly on local authorities that virtually guarantee such abuse will occur when new religious movements are involved), it violates the European Convention as explained in the *Manoussakis* case, which involved discretionary denials of house of prayer permits in Greece.[390]

In general, there is reason to think that vesting political officials with authority to approve religious entity applications may be more problematic than leaving such decisions with the judiciary. There are two major variants of the allocation of such authority to political officials. Occasionally, authority for ultimate approval is retained by a national parliament. In that situation marginal groups have difficulty over time getting parliamentary attention, much less serious and favorable consideration. The more typical nonjudicial pattern delegates decision-making authority to a particular official within one of the political branches of government. The difficulty in this scenario is that a political official may be (1) more subject to political pressures, (2) more likely to have a substantive vision

[387] See section III(C)(1) above (addressing nondiscrimination norms).
[388] See section III(A)(6) above (addressing limitation clauses).
[389] See, e.g., sections II(C) and II(D) above.
[390] Manoussakis and Others v. Greece, 23 EHRR 387 (1997) (ECtHR 1996-IV, 26 September 1996).

of how he wishes the religious sector to develop, and (3) less concerned with achieving impartiality in the essentially judicial task of determining whether a group meets various formal requirements for entity status. This risk may be magnified where local as opposed to national level political officials are involved. Of course, the decision whether to allocate such decisions to a political or judicial branch depends on the independence and impartiality of the judiciary as compared with that of the political (or civil service) official(s) in the particular country. At a minimum, this consideration underscores the need for a right of appeal to the judiciary, and for clear standards that will make it possible for the judiciary to verify that discretion is not abused.

A common area of concern for potential abuse of discretion is the time allowed governmental bodies to make decisions on registration. While most post-Socialist countries require the government to respond within one month to the religious organization's request for registration,[391] two countries require sixty days.[392] The fact that such approval periods need not be unduly protracted is indicated by a Romanian ordinance promulgated in 2000, which requires a response within three days.[393] While allowing government officials some time for processing a registration is reasonable, laws containing time limits such as six months,[394] or not containing a statutory deadline at all, are very problematic.[395] Government officials may merely stall registration of unpopular groups rather than issue a decision that could be contested in court. Unfortunately, this approach continues in some Russian regions and other post-Socialist nations.[396] A rule that provides that applications be approved by default if they have not been approved within thirty to sixty days would solve many of these problems, at least if it did not result in last-minute perfunctory denials.

Discretion in approving applications for registration can also be easily abused, particularly in countries with traditions of virtually unlimited state control. The situation in Kazakhstan, as described by a Kazakh scholar, is indicative of the situation in several parts of the post-Socialist world:

---

[391] See Armenian Law, art. 16 (one month); Azerbaijani Law, ch. 3, art. 16 (one month); Belarus Law, art. 17 (one month; however, this time period is extended to six months if the religious community is practicing an "unknown" faith); Latvian Law, art. 8(2) (one month, however, the Board of Religious Affairs may keep first-time registrant applications longer, with notification to the interested party); Moldovan Law, art. 14 (thirty days for the registration of a denomination, fifteen days for the registration of the component of the denominations); Russian Law, art. 11(8) (one month; however, if an examination by a religious expert is required, the deadline may be extended for up to six months); and Ukrainian Law, art. 14 (one month).

[392] See Hungarian Law, sec. 12 (sixty days); Polish Law, art. 33 (2 months).

[393] Romanian Law, art. 8 (three days).

[394] Lithuanian Law, art. 11; Belarus Law, art. 17 (the one-month deadline can be extended to six months if the religious community is practicing an "unknown" faith); Latvia Law, art. 8(2) (normally one month, but the Board of Religious Affairs may keep first-time registrant applications longer, with notification to the interested party); Russian Law, art. 11(8) (normally one month; however, if an examination by a religious expert is required, the deadline may be extended for up to six months).

[395] Albanian Non-Profit Law, art. 13 (no deadline; however, it is expected that this law will provide a deadline of thirty days by analogy to the registration procedures of commercial companies contained in article 24 of the 1993 Law on the Commercial Register); See also Czech Republic Law; Estonia Law; Macedonia Law; and Slovakia Law. Sometimes when there is no approval deadline in a religious association law itself, other rules in a country's procedure codes or administrative law may define a period in which a decision must be rendered.

[396] See, e.g., US Department of State, *International Religious Freedom Report 2002: Russia*, available at <http://www.state.gov/g/drl/rls/irf/2002/13958.htm> (last visited 15 December 2003).

> state administrative officials have every right to decline the registration of any religious organization on any pretext. The registration may be declined for a variety of reasons, such as finding insignificant mistakes in the registration documents or imposing upon a registrant the officials' own ideas about religious organizational structure. Sometimes the Ministry of Justice has unofficial instructions not to register certain religious organizations. In Kazakhstan such instructions have been given regarding the registration of the Jehovah's Witnesses, Korean Protestant Churches, several Moslem organizations which do not belong to the Religious Moslem Administration of Kazakhstan, the Russian Orthodox Church Abroad, and others. When such unofficial instructions have been given, it is practically impossible to register a religious organization." [397]

Discretion in registering religions can easily be cabined. Most western European countries and states of the United States allow no discretion to registering officials to look at the substance of the charter of the group to be registered. The state is obligated to maintain a neutral posture.[398] Chile's law on religious registration similarly limits discretion by stating "The Ministry of Justice shall not deny registration."[399] The Ministry of Justice can notify the applicant if the application "fails to meet some requirement," which automatically gives the applicant a cure period.[400] Since the requirements for registration are for the most part technical, there is not much room for any discretionary denial of the application. As this example suggests, the most effective method of avoiding excessive discretion in government reviews of registration application is to have minimal requirements in the first place.

Excessive discretion is also a problem in statutes that allow for de-registration or dissolution of religious entities. In recent years many of such provisions have been connected with concerns for religious extremism, such as problems with "Islamic fundamentalism" or perceived problems with "dangerous cults."[401] In both cases legal responses tend to be overbroad and insufficiently sensitive to the rights of smaller but legitimate groups. Fear of extreme sects in France led to the establishment of the Inter-Ministerial Mission in France with the primary purpose "to fight sects."[402] The mission was to analyze the activity of sects,[403] report to the Public Prosecutor the acts to be prosecuted, train public representatives to fight against sects, and inform the public of the danger that sects present.[404] The French anti-sect law permits the state to de-register religious organizations that pursue "activities which have as their purpose or effect to create, maintain or exploit the psychological or physical subjection of persons taking part in these activities,"

---

[397] Roman Podoprigora, "Religion in Kazakhstan: A General View," *BYU Law Review* (1999): 581, 587. See also the chapter by Podoprigora in this volume.

[398] Metropolitan Church of Bessarabia v. Moldova (ECtHR , App. 45701/99, 13 December 2001), paras. 116–17.

[399] Chile, Law No. 19.638 (officially published 26 May 2000), art. 11.

[400] Ibid.

[401] See the chapters by Barker and by Fautré, Garay, and Nidegger in this volume. See also Brian Gross, "A Bend in the Road to Civil Society: The Effect of Russian Anti-Extremism Legislation on Not-for-Profit Organizations," *International Journal of Not-for-Profit Law* 6 (September 2003): 1, available online at <http://www.icnl.org/journal/vol6iss1/rel_grossprint.htm> (last visited 14 December 2003).

[402] "Establishing an Inter-Ministerial Mission to Fight against Sects," Decree No. 98.890 7 (October 1998).

[403] Ibid., sec. 1.

[404] Ibid., sec. 2.

after one or more of its actual or de facto leaders have been convicted of one of a list of felonies.[405] In addition to problems of vague terms, this law provides excessive discretion to government officials, who can use the law to dissolve unpopular groups.

F. Vagueness

Problems of excessive discretion are compounded by vague or nonexistent standards in statutory mandates that guide discretion. These problems are legion in emerging legislation. Vague definitions of the notion of "sects" as "extremist groups" in draft Kazakh legislation in 2001 would be a case in point here. Another example is the Belarusian Law that grants enforcement power to local governments without defining the enforcement itself.[406] The vagueness of the enforcement thus opens up possibilities for the authorities to discriminate against religious organizations under the pretext of carrying out the law.

Another example of a vague concept is "notario arraigo," used in the Mexican law on religions,[407] which literally means "notable or notorious roots," but can probably be best translated as "widespread roots or acceptance in the community." In Mexico, only religions that possess "notario arraigo" can register under the law. There is no definition of what kind of presence in the community constitutes "widespread roots." This kind of vague requirement could easily be exploited as a basis for problematical denials of registration.

Yet another example of vagueness is an Armenian requirement that a religious organization must be "free from materialism and [be] intended for purely spiritual goals."[408] This language is not only inherently vague, but virtually invites registration authorities to use their own religious notions to assess a group's eligibility for registration.

In the Czech Republic there is a requirement that groups not use "psychological pressure" to "creat[e] dependence, leading to the physical, psychological or economic damage to persons and their dependent family members, to the destruction of their social relationships, including impairing the psychological development of minors and restricting their right to education, and precluding their receiving health care appropriate to their respective health needs." [409] This language is all too likely to be used against unpopular groups, but not against prevailing religions. Thus, even assuming a religious association law is a sufficiently narrow means for pursuing the health objective envisioned,[410] the provision appears to be impermissibly vague.

---

[405] "A bill directed to the reinforcement of prevention and repression of cultic movements which undermine human rights and fundamental freedoms" (31 May 2001).

[406] "Control of implementation of legislation of the Republic of Belarus on freedom of conscience, religion, and religious organizations at the local level is conducted by local councils of deputies, executive, and administrative bodies," art. 36, and the Republican Body of State Governance on Religious Affairs has the power to receive from local bodies "information on observance of the law of the Republic of Belarus on Freedom of Conscience, Religion, and Religious Organizations," art. 11, Law on Freedom of Religion and Religious Organizations (2002) [Belarus], available at <http://www.religlaw.org>.

[407] Law of Religious Associations and Public Worship (15 July 1992) [Mexico], art. 7(2). The term is taken from the Religious Liberty Law (1980) [Spain], Organic Law 7/1980 (BOE of 24 July), arts. 7 and 8, but there religious groups are only required to have "notario arraigo" in order to enter into agreements with the government that define access to "upper-tier" entity status that makes a group eligible for "cooperation" benefits. See the discussion of upper-tier entities at the end of section I above.

[408] Armenian Law, art. 5(d).

[409] Czech Law, tit. I, sec. 5(c).

[410] See discussion in section III(A)(6) above.

Still another example is provided by the Constitution of the People's Republic of China, which protects "normal religious activities." However, exactly what constitutes "normal" activities is not defined in either the Constitution or other legislative or administrative materials.[411]

Each of these vague provisions, in different ways, leaves the fate of a religious association at the mercy of the bias of local authorities.[412] These provisions violate fundamental rule of law constraints, as discussed earlier.[413]

G. Intervention in Internal Religious Affairs

Another major problem, made worse by vague standards and a pre-existing "control" mentality, is that some legislative initiatives appear to authorize governmental officials to intervene in the internal autonomy of religious organizations. In Azerbaijan, for example, Islamic groups are required to have one administrative center,[414] and this is certainly not the only jurisdiction where a preference for an "official," state-approved mufti has been the pattern.[415] The 2002 Bulgarian Law was in part designed to resolve a schism in the Bulgarian Orthodox Church, and in effect made it impossible for the "schismatic" group to be registered.[416] In China several legal norms require all religious activities to be funneled through and supervised by government-sanctioned "patriotic religious associations."[417]

These laws violate the fundamental norms of religious autonomy grounded in the right to freedom to manifest religion "in community with others" and in freedom of association law. Interpreting these norms, the European Court of Human Rights has repeatedly held that government entities cannot attempt to influence internal structuring of religious organizations.[418] As mentioned earlier, the hierarchical or congregational structuring of a religious organization and the choice of its leaders may reflect key elements of its belief, and must be respected.[419] Attempts by Moldova to refuse registration to the Metropolitan Church of Bessarabia, a breakoff of the Russian Orthodox Church of the Moscow Patriarchy, were rejected by the European Court of Human Rights. The

---

411 Xianfa (Constitution of the People's Republic of China), art. 36, sec. 3 (1982). One pair of commentators opined, "In the jargon used most frequently, permitted activities are called 'normal' and those of which the Party disapproves may be called 'illegal'" (Alan Hunter and Kim-Kwong Chan, ***Protestantism in Contemporary China*** [Cambridge: Cambridge Univ. Press, 1993], 50).

412 *Cf.* "In the decision making process of registration in the Register based on the request, the ministry is authorized to seek, from requester, further documents which could establish validity of the claim" (Draft Law on Religious Groups [2000] [Croatia], art. 19, sec. 2., available at <http://www.religlaw.org>).

413 See section III above.

414 1992 Azerbaijan Law, art. 9.

415 See, e.g., Serif v. Greece (ECtHR, App. No. 38178/97, 14 December 1997); Hasan and Chaush v. Bulgaria (ECtHR, App. No. 30985/96, 2000).

416 See Bulgarian Law, art. 10.

417 See, e.g., Religious Affairs Bureau, "Rules for the Implementation of the Provisions on the Administration of Religious Activities of Aliens within the Territory of the People's Republic of China," art. 10 (2000); "Regulations on Religious Affairs of the Province of Guangdong," art. 25 (2000), included in "Five Provincial Level Official Regulations on Religious Affairs," ***Chinese Law and Government*** 36, no. 3 (May–June 2003): 60–68.

418 Serif v. Greece (ECtHR, App. No. 38178/97, 14 December, 1997); Hasan and Chaush v. Bulgaria (ECtHR, App. No. 30985/96, 2000); Case of Metropolitan Church of Bessarabia v. Moldova (ECtHR, App. 45701/99, 13 December 2001). See section III above.

419 See discussion in section III(A)(6) above.

Court explained: "[T]he right to freedom of religion within the Convention excludes the evaluation by the state as to the legitimacy of religious beliefs or the ways in which they are expressed. . . . To force a religious community, or a part of a religious community, to place itself, against its will, under a single direction, would equally constitute an infringement on freedom of religion. In a democratic society, the state does not need to take measures to guarantee that religious communities are or remain under a single direction."[420]

Registration laws can also appear to authorize intrusive review of a religious organization's beliefs and internal administrative practices. This is a constant risk, particularly where religious association laws contain vague provisions describing necessary features for acquiring entity status. But review going to the substance of religious beliefs (including beliefs about organization and ecclesiastical structure) is clearly inconsistent with requirements of state neutrality.[421]

At times governments have formally or informally refused registration or other core government services based on the objections of leaders of majority religions in the area. The permission of the majority religions is deemed necessary to protect social harmony and stability. In Kazakhstan in a trial proceeding aimed at banning Jehovah's Witnesses in the city of Taraz, a case was adjourned while an expert council of Orthodox Priests and Muslim Muftis did an expert study on the religious teachings of Jehovah's Witnesses. Needless to say, such a body is not well suited to render an impartial result. Similar problems arose in the trial that considered dissolving the Jehovah's Witness organization in Moscow. Orthodox experts were asked whether the Jehovah's Witnesses' interpretation of various biblical passages was correct. Canons of religious freedom do not countenance this type of second-guessing of doctrinal beliefs by state organs. Delegation of government approvals of one group to religious leaders of other groups, or to bodies dominated by such individuals, is particularly inappropriate. The European Court has soundly rejected the view that other religious leaders or groups should be permitted to compromise the state's duty of neutrality and impartiality in registering religious groups.[422]

H. Retroactive Provisions

One of the recurring difficulties is that when new laws dealing with religious associations are passed, insufficient attention is paid to transition issues. All too often, groups that have already been registered under the prior legal regime are expected to re-register. Such has been the case when new registration regimes have been introduced in Armenia,[423] Croatia,[424] Estonia,[425] Ghana,[426] and Russia.[427]

---

420 Ibid., para. 117.

421 See section III(A)(6) above.

422 Ibid., para. 116 (by making the Bessarabian Church's legal recognition dependent on another, separate religious organization, Moldovan officials "had failed to discharge their duty of neutrality and impartiality); see also Manoussakis and Others v. Greece, 23 EHRR 387 (1997) (ECtHR 1996-IV, 26 September 1996) (striking down Greek government action against a minority church in part because of Greek Orthodox involvement).

423 Presidential Decree, following The Republic of Armenia Law On the Freedom of Conscience and on Religious Organization (21 December 1997), para. 1, available at <http://www.religlaw.org>.

424 "Religious communities that operate as legal entities in the Republic of Croatia when this Law comes into force shall register in the Register by submitting an application for registration" (Croatian Law, art. 5[1]).

Often a transparent aim of de-registering some of the less popular groups is evident. This appeared to be the objective of a legislative proposal in Hungary in 1993 that failed, and it also constituted a very problematic feature of the 1997 Russian Law,[428] which was ultimately struck down by the Russian Constitutional Court.[429] The Russian Constitutional Court held that an existing centralized organization "has all the rights prescribed to the religious organizations by the Law" and cannot be denied these through a re-registration requirement without violating the constitutional guarantee of freedom of religious association and the legal equality principle.[430]

V. Conclusion: Toward a Facilitative Approach to Religious Association Law

This chapter has documented the importance of religious association laws to the practical implementation of freedom of religion or belief (section I), depicted the types of legal structures available to religious communities for organizing their affairs, including their interactions with secular legal systems (section II), analyzed the international human rights norms that have a bearing on religious association laws (section III), and identified recurrent issues that arrive in the formulation and implementation of such legislation (section IV). Throughout the chapter attention has been paid to the fact that religious association laws can be construed and implemented either in ways that facilitate freedom of religion or belief, or in ways that emphasize a more restrictive "control" orientation. In this concluding section, the aim is to draw the various strands of the chapter together in order to provide a picture of fundamental features of religious association law that can contribute in a positive way to the facilitation of freedom of religion or belief.[431]

In the long and continuing struggle to achieve the ideals of this fundamental freedom, there are many realities that are very difficult to change: entrenched social attitudes, sometimes embedded in centuries of tension and bitterness; painful histories of discrimination and persecution; ethnic rivalries; limitations in the ability of education systems to internalize values of toleration and respect; failures on the part of religious leaders to help translate religious ideals of respect for others into religious practice; and so forth. Within this often

---

[425] All religious organizations registered before the coming into effect of Estonia's 2002 Churches and Congregations Act have to be re-registered by July 1, 2004. Religious organizations which do not re-register themselves will be liquidated as legal persons (Estonian Law, arts. 28–29).

[426] Religious Bodies (Registration) Law of 1989, PN DCL No. 221 (1989) [Ghana]. This law was subsequently rendered unconstitutional by the 1992 Ghanaian Constitution. See E. K. Quashigah, "Legislating Religious Liberty: The Ghanaian Experience," *BYU Law Review* (1999): 595.

[427] Russian Law, art. 27.

[428] See Russian Law, art. 27.

[429] See Decision of the Constitutional Court of the Russian Federation in connection with the complaint of the Jehovah's Witnesses and Christian Church of Praise (23 November 1999), No. 16-P, Institute of Religion and Law, "Religious Associations: Freedom of Conscience and Religion; Normative Acts and Judicial Decisions," Moscow, Jurisprudence, 2001, at 238. For a discussion of this case and some of the retroactivity issues, see Lev Simkin, "Church and State in Russia," in *Law and Religion in Post-Communist Europe*, ed. Silvio Ferrari, W. Cole Durham, Jr., and Elizabeth A. Sewell (Leuven: Peeters, 2003), 261, 271–74.

[430] Ibid. at 243–44.

[431] Footnotes in this section refer back to sections of this chapter where the various features of a facilitative approach are grounded in international human rights commitments and discussed in more detail, either positively or by negative implication from the analysis of problems.

discouraging landscape, progress with respect to religious association laws, though not without its own challenges, is comparatively easy and exerts powerful leverage on the more general objective of facilitating freedom of religion or belief.[432]

Progress in this area is easier than in many others because the necessary legal devices and models are easily accessible. In fact, taking the facilitative approach they entail is called for by international human rights commitments most states have already made.[433] Moreover, both religious and life-stance communities on the one hand and states on the other have interests in developing good religious association laws: the religious communities because these laws facilitate their communal life by easing interaction with the secular legal order; the states because such laws solve so many problems and remove so many irritations at the religion-state interface that can otherwise result in difficult problems for the state. Religious association laws also have tremendous symbolic power in communicating a regime's real attitudes when it comes to freedom of religion or belief. Without facilitative association laws and practices, the most impressive formal commitments to religious freedom will be seen as mere lip-service, both at home and abroad.[434] This is a major reason why progress in this area is an important litmus test not only for effective implementation of religious freedom norms,[435] but also more generally for democratization. In short, this is an area in which regimes with restrictive legislation can make dramatic strides in improving human rights compliance.

Turning to the features that facilitative laws on religious associations should have, a number of preliminary points should be fairly clear. In the first place, religious communities should be free not to acquire legal entity status in the relatively unlikely event that they prefer this course.[436] Second, in legal systems that have separate laws for religious organizations and for secular nonprofits, religious organizations should be free to choose either option.[437] Generally, separate religious association laws will have more attractive features, since such laws should be sensitive to the unique requirements of freedom of religion or belief, but it hurts nothing to leave the option open of organizing as a normal nonprofit entity. If the requirements of the religious association law are more burdensome to a particular religious group than those that apply to secular nonprofit associations, impermissible discrimination against religious organizations is almost certainly occurring.[438] This risk is ameliorated if religious groups are free to choose which form of organization they prefer.

If there are additional upper-tier entities in the country's legal system, it is important to make certain that powers and privileges vital to carrying out normal religious life are not restricted to "upper-tier" entities. Facilitative laws help assure that a religious community can carry out the full range of its activities through a base-level religious association or through the secular nonprofit organizational form.[439] At a minimum, this must include the full range of activities identified in documents such as the UN 1981 Declaration, article

[432] See sections I and II(D) above.

[433] See section III above.

[434] See section I above.

[435] Ibid.

[436] See footnote 1 above; also see section IV(A).

[437] See section IV(D).

[438] Ibid.; also see section III(C)(1) above.

[439] See Cole Durham, *Freedom of Religion or Belief: Laws Affecting the Structuring of Religious Communities* (Warsaw, Poland: OSCE/ODIHR, 1999); section III above.

6, and the Vienna Concluding Document, principle 16, and other similar rights that are routinely expected in connection with religious documents. To the extent that certain "cooperation" benefits are linked exclusively to the "upper-tier" organizational forms, there must be objective justifications of a nondiscriminatory nature for the differentiation.[440]

The number of individuals required to found a religious organization should be small—normally ten or less.[441] The state has some legitimate interest in being able to contact leaders of a religious community, and given turnover in groups, it may be important for organizational documents to identify a few such leaders. But higher minimum member requirements are not necessary in a democratic society, and unnecessarily deprive smaller religious groups of access to religious entity status.[442] This works a prejudicial hardship, particularly on congregationally organized religious groups for which higher minimum membership requirements may pose an insurmountable obstacle to accessing religious entity rights.[443] Other restrictions on founders should also be avoided. With respect to foreign founders, it is worth remembering in this regard that international instruments contemplate that governments will be able to impose some added regulation in connection with political activity of citizens under freedom of expression, freedom of association and nondiscrimination norms, but that this is not foreseen in connection with freedom of religion or belief.[444]

Flexibility should also be granted for other religious entities to be founders of religious organizations. Hierarchical organizations may wish to create sub-entities to facilitate the organization of the affairs of the overall religious community. A religious community may want to segregate some of its charitable activities, such as health care, educational institutions, humanitarian aid, and the like, into separate legal entities. Sometimes separate religious communities may wish to join together on a common project, and a legal entity may be a significant vehicle for doing so. Also, it should be remembered that not all belief-related organizations are denominational. Some may reflect secular life stances; others may reflect transdenominational organizations. Society tends to be richly benefited by the array of activities carried out by belief communities, and religious association laws should facilitate creation of the legal structures that help this occur.[445]

Other barriers to entity status, such as lengthy duration requirements prior to access to base-level entity status, should also be avoided.[446] The burdens on religious freedom associated with lack of access to entity status are real and immediate; unreasonable delays either in the form of legislative prerequisites[447] or in administrative approval processes[448] beyond short review periods (ideally not more than thirty days) should be avoided. Prompt appeal rights should also be assured.[449]

---

[440] See sections I and III(C)(1) above.
[441] Section IV(B) above.
[442] See sections III(A)(6) and IV(B) above.
[443] See sections III(B)(3) and IV(B) above.
[444] See ECHR, art. 16; section III(A)(1) above.
[445] See section III(B)(2) above.
[446] See section IV(C) above.
[447] Ibid.
[448] Ibid.
[449] See ibid.; section III(C)(4) above.

Of course, there may be individuals who will seek to abuse the rights associated with legal entity status. The solution to this problem, however, is not to raise the access barriers for all groups, both legitimate and illegitimate. A more effective approach, which avoids unnecessary interference with religious rights, is to allow fairly easy access to basic legal entity rights while reserving the right to grant and withdraw other benefits, such as tax-exempt status or other "cooperation rights," after more careful review.[450] Typically, abuses involve claiming financial or other benefits without genuine justification. Problems of this type can be dealt with by cutting off the financial or other benefit and recouping any inappropriately claimed benefits. Abuses stemming from acquisition of legal personality alone—ability to open bank accounts, to rent or acquire property, to enter into contracts, and to sue and be sued—are unlikely to create substantial risks of abuse in and of themselves. Government authorities should have substantial authority to impose sanctions on abuses when they occur or are attempted, and should be authorized to capture ill-gotten gains resulting from abuse, following appropriate hearing procedures. In general, however, problems of wrongdoing are best dealt with through criminal, administrative or civil sanctions, rather than by policing initial access to entity status.

Religious association laws need to allow belief communities significant flexibility in the way they structure their affairs.[451] Matters of ecclesiastical polity and ecclesiastical office almost always reflect doctrinal beliefs and matters of religious practice. Often the problem here is that religious association laws are drawn up with traditional religious groups and practices in mind, without allowing sufficient flexibility for other belief groups. Assumptions about the nature of clergy and religious government that are perfectly appropriate for familiar groups may create Procrustean beds for other groups. Even within familiar groups, legislation written for a church may not apply neatly to religious orders.[452] Wooden interpretation of rules by those charged with implementing them can cause further problems.

Review of applications for entity status (registration, incorporation and the like) must be structured in ways that are scrupulous in maintaining the neutrality of the state. Those conducting the review process should be limited to reviewing formal statutory requirements (e.g., that requisite information about founders is provided, that contact information is adequate, that adequate provision is made for assets in the event of dissolution, etc.). They should have no discretion to assess matters going to the substance of beliefs or religious practices. State authorities must remain neutral in assessing the truth of religious beliefs and must treat all groups impartially.

---

[450] See section II(B) above.

[451] Cole Durham, *Freedom of Religion or Belief: Laws Affecting the Structuring of Religious Communities* (Warsaw, Poland: OSCE/ODIHR, 1999).

[452] See, e.g., 13 April 2000 decision on the complaint of the religious organization "Independent Russian Region of the Society of Jesus," on an alleged violation of constitutional rights and freedoms by articles 8.3, 8.4, 8.5, 9, 13, 27.3 and 27.4 of the Federal Law "On Freedom of Conscience and Religious Associations," No. 46-O (Russian Constitutional Court), in Institute of Religion and Law, "Religious Associations: Freedom of Conscience and Religion; Normative Acts and Judicial Decisions," Moscow, Jurisprudence, 2001, 247 (invalidating rule under 1997 Russian law that prevented recognition of Jesuit order as a centralized organization because it had only two and not the requisite three subdivisions).

In particular, state officials should not meddle with a religious organization's "own" affairs.[453] As noted in principle 16(4) of the Vienna Concluding Document, to mention only one of the relevant instruments, this includes the right of a religious group to establish places of worship; to organize according to the organization's own hierarchical (or nonhierarchical) structure; to select, appoint and replace their personnel in accordance with their requirements; and to solicit and receive funds. Territorial structure is another matter generally understood to fall within a religious community's "own" affairs. The state should not second-guess a religious community's determination of how large or small its congregations ought to be, and what their territorial reach should be. A religious community may decide to have boundaries of its subunits that do not necessarily correspond with political boundaries. States should also not limit where religious organizations assign their personnel, or how they transfer them among ecclesiastical units. Different religious groups allocate their ecclesiastical personnel in different ways, and state officials should not interfere with such processes. Provisions that give state officials a right to approve (or veto) invitations to foreign coreligionists are also problematic in this regard. Of course, if there are objective, nonreligious grounds for denying a visa, that is a different case. But blocking interactions among religious believers across national frontiers for what are in reality only religious reasons is not consistent with state neutrality and with abstaining from interference in internal religious affairs.[454]

Criteria for granting approval of entity status are likely to have a number of features with respect to which similar considerations should apply. The most significant characteristic these criteria should have is that they should be drafted with precision; vague provisions that fail to give parties clear notice of what may lead to dissolution are particularly problematic.[455] Similarly, provisions that leave officials excessive discretion to review or assess the substance of religious beliefs, including organizational beliefs, are not permissible. In many respects the grounds for approval or dissolution should not impose limitations on acquisition or retention of entity status that are more burdensome than those allowed by limitation clauses in the international human rights instruments.[456]

In general, the process for acquiring legal entity status should be designed so that it is efficient and respects the dignity of the members of belief communities filing applications and awaiting approvals. Government officials involved with administering religious association laws should see their role primarily as one that supports and facilitates religious life, rather than one that aims at policing and controlling religious groups. A shift in attitude on the part of the officials administering religious association laws is often one of the most critical transformations in "fostering a climate of mutual toleration and respect."[457] Certainly it is the aspect of the interaction of religion with the state over which governments have the most direct control.

---

453 See section IV(G) for the points raised in this paragraph.
454 See section III(A)(6) above.
455 See sections III(A)(6) and IV(F) above.
456 See section III(A)(6) above.
457 Vienna Concluding Document, principle 16b.

Adopting a facilitative approach to the framing and implementation of religious association laws lays the critical legal and social foundation needed to translate the ideals of the grand pronouncements of the international law of religious freedom into action at the level of the practical lives of belief communities. This is critical to the creation of the social space within which individuals can find and shape their worldviews, and traditions can be nourished. It is vital to the process whereby authentic respect can transmute differences among groups into social stability, to the genuine public order and security of lasting peace, and to the kind of fruitful pluralism that is vital to democratic society.

Chapter 16

Protecting Freedom of Religion or Belief in Restricted or Institutional Settings

Lee Boothby

Despite meaningful advances in the recognition and protection of fundamental religious freedoms in many parts of the world, certain segments of society usually realize the benefits of social progress only with significant delay. This chapter will consider both the historical challenges and recent advances attained in upholding the religious freedoms and accommodating the sometimes diverse religious practices of individuals in restricted or institutional settings such as prisons, the military, and state-operated medical facilities. While much of the present discussion is primarily based on the experiences of the United States during the past forty years, largely parallel progress has occurred in the democratic societies in western Europe. Clearly the United States is not the only model, and its protections of religious freedom in institutional settings have not always been ideal. Nevertheless, illuminating the US system is particularly valuable. Because it generally takes a separationist and neutral approach in church-state matters, its widespread accommodations in this arena illustrate the need for government flexibility in these circumstances as well as some ways that states can accommodate individuals' religious needs in institutional settings without discriminating against minority or less-popular religions.

The challenges faced by individuals in various state-controlled settings are as diverse as their religious beliefs and practices. Some experience difficulties securing a dietary regime that conforms to their fundamental religious beliefs; they must either go hungry or violate these beliefs. Others are subject to uniform dress and grooming policies that do not permit them to wear religious garments or headwear or that require them to cut their hair and shave their beards in violation of deeply held religious beliefs. And some are forced to work on holy days or are denied the time and privacy needed for prayers and other rituals required by their religious faiths.

Although many of these concerns can be adequately resolved by merely increasing the level of institutional tolerance or incorporating religious freedom norms already commonly observed in society at large, there is little question that these norms will, of necessity, be subject to some measure of adaptation in the context of the particular restricted or institutional setting. Attainment of the overarching institutional objectives sought is usually dependent upon maintaining a rigid internal structure and uniformity

Tore Lindholm, W. Cole Durham, Jr., Bahia G. Tahzib-Lie (eds.), Facilitating Freedom of Religion or Belief: A Deskbook, *407–423.*

not customary to civilian life. This by no means suggests, however, that the religious rights of prison inmates, soldiers, and medical patients are somehow inferior—indeed, quite the opposite may be true—but merely that the exigencies of the restricted setting to which they are subject may occasionally necessitate an abridgement of these rights in order to achieve a greater overall societal purpose.

In discussing the role and scope of religious freedoms in restricted or institutional settings, it is important to bear in mind that this issue directly and intimately affects the rights and lives of human beings who may have particularly acute needs for the support that their religious beliefs and contact with coreligionists provide. In the case of prison inmates for example, religious faith may play a significant role in the rehabilitation process. For soldiers faith can provide a spiritual balance to the immense psychological and physical rigors of military service. And for medical patients faith can have significant implications in the healing process. Indeed, the tolerance and even accommodation of fundamental religious freedoms by these state institutions can greatly contribute to ultimately achieving the very objectives pursued by these institutions.

It is well known that in the United States, because of adherence to the principle of church-state separation, the state is generally prohibited from any direct involvement in religious worship and practice. But when individuals are required to live in restricted settings such as prisons, the military, and to a lesser extent hospitals, the principle of religious liberty requires the state to actively accommodate the practice of religion. Thus, the military provides for the work of chaplains, state and federal governments construct and maintain chapels for prison inmates, and special accommodations are made available to patients in state-owned medical facilities. Nevertheless, the state is still required to avoid demonstrating a preference to any particular religion or class of religions.

Inasmuch as the most restrictive setting among those considered in this examination is the prison system, it will be given primary treatment. To the degree that religious rights would apply to incarcerated individuals, at least this same measure of rights would clearly apply to those in less-restricted, state-controlled settings.

A. Inmates of Penal Institutions

Prisoners are prime candidates for unwarranted intrusions on their religious liberty. In truth, most people probably have little concern for prisoner rights, including the freedom to observe and practice their faith. However, as already noted, religious free exercise protections may be more important for prisoners than for any other segment of society, given the positive role that faith-based activity can have in the rehabilitation process.

The likelihood of government-imposed burdens on religion occurring in the prison system is particularly great, given the almost total discretionary authority granted prison administrators. In penal institutions the state controls dress, diet, grooming, work schedules, external communications, receipt of printed material, and all other personal and social aspects of an inmate's life.

Although regulations governing the conditions of incarceration are generally applicable to all inmates and may be religiously neutral on their face, the rights of some inmates may unduly suffer from the strict application of such blanket requirements. The problem is exacerbated when the prisoner is an adherent of a minority religion that includes practices not generally observed by those of larger and better-understood faiths.

1. Legal Standards Protecting Religious Freedom of Inmates

The legal basis for addressing prisoners' religious concerns in the United States flows from several court decisions and has varied somewhat over the past forty years. A review of the evolution of current policies is instructive. Tracing the development of current standards in this difficult area shows the positive impact that courts, legislatures, and executive agencies can have in promoting freedom of religion and belief. Courts and legislatures have been sensitive to the need to avoid micromanaging institutional settings, but have, on the whole, provided important protections for inmates' freedom of religion and belief.

Modern case law in the United States concerning religious freedom in prisons starts with the general holding of the Supreme Court in 1963 in *Sherbert v. Verner.* In that case the United States Supreme Court held that when government requirements conflict with an individual's religious beliefs, the individual must be accommodated unless the government can demonstrate a compelling governmental interest and that no less restrictive alternative means are available to satisfy the state's interest.[1] This standard appeared to provide significant protection for prison inmates, who quickly sought constitutional protection based on this decision. But lack of concern for prisoners' religious rights found expression in political debates, legislative halls, and even the courts. There were ongoing arguments as to what standard should be applied to prisoners and how the conflicting interests should be balanced.

An important case in determining the application of *Sherbert* was *Barnette v. Rogers,* decided by a federal court of appeals three years after *Sherbert.*[2] The basic issue in *Rogers* was whether the District of Columbia authorities were constitutionally compelled to accommodate the Muslim prisoners' dietary requirements.

The Muslim prisoners alleged that jail authorities denied their request to "be fed at least one full-course, pork-free, diet once a day."[3] The district court dismissed the complaint, saying the inmates were fed a "well balanced and wholesome diet," and "by refraining from eating those things that they considered objectionable,"[4] the Muslim prisoners could still practice their religion. Reversing the trial court, the court of appeals employed the *Sherbert* "compelling state interest/least restrictive alternative" test.[5] The court stated:

> The record supports the District Court's findings so far as they go, but an insuperable difficulty emanates from the absence of findings bearing upon the criteria that are constitutionally critical. There is no finding as to whether any particular "considerations underlying our penal system" warrant the tax on conscience that the jail's food service policies require appellants to endure. Nor is there any finding as to whether that program should be administered in such a way as to lighten or eliminate its burden on free religious exercise . . .

---

[1] Sherbert v. Verner, 374 US 398 (1963).

[2] Barnette v. Rogers, 410 F2d 995 (DC Cir 1969).

[3] Ibid., at 997.

[4] Ibid., at 999.

[5] Ibid., at 1000.

> Appellants do not seek, either for themselves or other Muslims, a full menu tailored especially to their religious beliefs. Their request . . . is essentially a plea for a modest degree of official deference to their religious obligations. Certainly if this concession is feasible from the standpoint of prison management, it represents the bare minimum that jail authorities, without specific requests, are constitutionally required to do, not only for Muslims but indeed for any group of inmates with religious restrictions on diet.[6]

Barnette represented meaningful progress for prisoners in terms of securing basic religious rights, but the conflict within the judiciary as to whether prisoners' religious rights should be given more than token recognition resurfaced in the Supreme Court in *Cruz v. Beto*,[7] a case that also involved important issues of equality, or nondiscrimination. That case involved a Buddhist adherent incarcerated in a Texas state prison. Cruz alleged that although members of other religions were allowed to use the prison chapel, he was not. He further complained that when he shared Buddhist religious material with other inmates, prison authorities reacted by placing him in solitary confinement and feeding him a diet consisting of only bread and water. He also said that he was prohibited from corresponding with his religious advisor.

The *Cruz* complaint alleged that Texas actively encouraged inmates to participate in religious programs and provided and financed chaplains of the Catholic, Jewish, and Protestant faiths and that weekly Sunday school classes and religious services were offered as well. Cruz also claimed that Jewish and Christian literature was supplied to inmates at state expense.

The federal district court denied relief without a hearing, saying that the complaint was in an area that should be left "to the sound discretion of prison administrators."[8] It went on to say that, "valid disciplinarian security reasons not known to this court may prevent the 'equality' of exercise of religious practices in prison."[9] The court of appeals affirmed.[10] In a *per curiam* opinion, the Supreme Court vacated and remanded, stating:

> Federal courts sit not to supervise prisons but to enforce the constitutional rights of all 'persons,' including prisoners. We are not unmindful that prison officials must be accorded latitude in the administration of prison affairs, and that prisoners necessarily are subject to appropriate rules and regulations. But persons in prison, like other individuals, have the right to petition the Government for redress of grievances, which, of course, includes 'access of prisoners to the courts for the purpose of presenting their complaints.'[11]

The court concluded:

> If Cruz was a Buddhist and if he was denied a reasonable opportunity of pursuing his faith comparable to the opportunity afforded fellow prisoners who adhered to conventional religious precepts, then there was palpable discrimination by the State against

[6] Ibid., at 1001.
[7] Cruz v. Beto, 445 F2d 801(1971), vacated and remanded, 405 US 319 (1972).
[8] Ibid., at 321.
[9] Ibid.
[10] Cruz v. Beto, 405 US 319 (1972).
[11] Ibid., at 321.

> the Buddhist religion .... The First Amendment, applicable to the states by reason of the Fourteenth Amendment, ... prohibits government from making a law 'prohibiting the free exercise [of religion].' If the allegations of this complaint are assumed to be true, as they must be on the motion to dismiss, Texas has violated the First and Fourteenth Amendments.[12]

While this case demonstrates that the Supreme Court has actively ensured the protection of incarcerated persons' religious freedoms, other cases also reveal its understanding that the judiciary cannot control all the details of prison reform. For example, in *Procunier v. Martinez*,[13] the Supreme Court held that "[w]hen a prison regulation or practice offends a fundamental constitutional guarantee, federal courts will discharge their duty to protect constitutional rights."[14] However, at the same time, the Court articulated a concern that "courts are ill equipped to deal with increasingly urgent problems of prison administration and reform."[15]

Despite the protections of *Barnette* and *Cruz*, the US Federal Bureau of Prisons still did not provide a specialized diet for prisoners with religious dietary needs until the US Court of Appeals for the Second Circuit's decision in *Kahane v. Carlson* in 1975. This case involved a claim brought by a prisoner, an Orthodox Jewish rabbi, who contended his free exercise rights were infringed because the prison failed to provide him with a kosher diet.[16] In *Barnette* all that was at issue was a request for a single religious-appropriate meal per day. In *Kahane* the court took the next step and held that prison officials must provide a prisoner a diet that is consistent with his religious scruples. The Second Circuit, in an insightful opinion, stated:

> We agree with the court below that the prison authorities are proscribed by the constitutional status of religious freedom from managing the institution in a manner which unnecessarily prevents Kahane's observance of his dietary obligations. The difficulties for the prisons inherent in this rule would seem surmountable in view of the small number of practicing Orthodox Jews in federal prisons (which the evidence indicate would not exceed approximately twelve), and in view of the fact that the state and city prisons provide Kosher food, that federal institutions do so on high holy day and that medical diets are not unknown in the federal system.[17]

Almost immediately after the decision in *Kahane*, the US Federal Bureau of Prisons adopted a policy of providing kosher meals to Jewish inmates.[18] But there were other inmates, such as Muslims and Seventh-Day Adventists, who also required accommodation. The Bureau of Prisons then adopted a fixed fourteen-day rotating menu. Under this "common fare" (now called "religious diet") menu, correctional institutions were still to provide a religious diet that was kosher. However, all prison inmates requiring a religiously mandated diet could participate.[19]

---

[12] Ibid., at 322.

[13] Procunier v. Martinez, 416 US 396 (1974).

[14] Ibid., at 405.

[15] Ibid.

[16] Kahane v. Carlson, 527 F2d 492 (2d Cir 1975).

[17] Ibid., at 495–496.

[18] BOP Program Statement 4746.2.

[19] BOP Operations Memorandum 253–83 (5360).

There were some practical problems with the common fare program. First, some prisons were not careful in providing kosher food or adhering to kosher food requirements. Second, smaller portions were often provided prisoners on the common fare program than provided to prisoners on the main line. Third, a hot meal was provided only three times per week. And finally, inmates who complained about violations of the Bureau of Prisons common fare requirements were sometimes penalized for complaining. But overall, the common fare program represented progress.

In addition to accommodating dietary concerns, the Bureau of Prisons also began to facilitate other religious practices. These included the possession and wearing of certain articles of religious clothing and the liberalization of grooming standards to accommodate inmates such as Jews and Muslims.

There was at least a cursory attempt under *Sherbert* at religious accommodation in US federal prisons, but two Supreme Court decisions issued in 1987 diluted the effect of the *Sherbert* test in cases affecting prison inmates. In *Turner v. Safley*,[20] the Court stated that a prison regulation is constitutional "if it is reasonably related to legitimate penological interests," [21] thus substituting a "reasonableness test" for the *Sherbert* "compelling state interest/no less restrictive alternative" test. This was immediately followed by *O'Lone v. Estate of Shabazz*,[22] which upheld a prison regulation on the basis of the *Turner* reasonableness standard.

The Court concluded that this lower standard was necessary to ensure that "courts afford appropriate deference to prison officials"[23] and to allow the officials "to anticipate security problems and to adopt innovative solutions to problems of prison administration."[24] The *Turner* Court established four factors that must be considered in such a reasonableness test:

1. Whether there is a valid, rational connection between the regulation and the legitimate governmental interest put forward to justify it.[25]
2. Whether there are alternative means of exercising the rights that remain open to prison inmates.[26]
3. The impact accommodation of the asserted constitutional right will have on guards and other inmates and on the allocation of prison resources generally.[27]
4. The absence of ready alternatives. This serves as evidence of the reasonableness of a prison regulation. The existence of simple alternatives may be evidence that the regulation is not reasonable but is an exaggerated response to prison concerns.[28]

A further blow to free exercise guarantees occurred in 1990 in *Employment Div., Dept. of Human Resources v. Smith*.[29] In *Smith* the Supreme Court in a 5 to 4 decision concluded that there was no duty to accommodate religious beliefs when

---

20 Turner v. Safley, 482 US 78 (1987).
21 Ibid., at 89.
22 O'Lone v. Estate of Shabazz, 482 US 342 (1987).
23 Ibid., at 349.
24 Ibid.
25 Turner v. Safley, 482 US 78, 89 (1987).
26 Ibid., at 90.
27 Ibid.
28 Ibid., at 90–91.

the government requirement was neutral and of general application.[30] The US Congress disagreed with the *Smith* decision and enacted the Religious Freedom Restoration Act (RFRA), which requires the government to justify substantial burdens on the free exercise of religion by demonstrating that the restrictions further a compelling governmental interest in the least restrictive means possible.[31] Although in 1997 the US Supreme Court held RFRA unconstitutional as applied to state and local government in *City of Boerne v. Flores*,[32] RFRA was deemed to still apply to federal institutions such as the Federal Bureau of Prisons.[33]

2. Implementation of Religious Freedom Norms in Prisons

With the guidance provided by this constitutional framework established by the US Supreme Court and Congress, the Federal Bureau of Prisons moved to increased accommodation of religious concerns of prisoners. In 1997 the Bureau of Prisons issued a Program Statement,[34] revised in 2001,[35] designed to provide inmates of all faiths with opportunities to participate in their religious beliefs and practices within the budgetary and security constraints of the prison system. The program objectives include:

1. The equitable distribution of religious resources;
2. The protection of the religious rights of inmates of all faiths within the parameters of the secure and orderly running of the institutions;
3. The providing of pastoral care to inmates and staff; and
4. The providing of expertise on matters of religion in the correctional environment.[36]

These objectives were accomplished through a variety of means. For example, each institution is to designate space for religious activities that is sufficient to fairly and equitably accommodate the needs of all religious groups in the inmate population.[37] The area is to include office space for each chaplain, storage space for religious materials, and lavatory facilities for staff and volunteers. Even a sweat lodge must be maintained in a suitable, secure, and private location for the spiritual needs of American Indian

---

[29] Employment Div., Dept. of Human Resources v. Smith, 494 US 872 (1990).

[30] Note that, in spite of *Smith*, the Second Circuit in *Bass v. Coughlin* held that federal courts should still require prisons to provide a prisoner a diet consistent with his religious beliefs (Bass v. Coughlin, 976 F2d 98 [2d Cir 1992] [*per curiam*]).

[31] Religious Freedom Restoration Act of 1993, 42 USC §§ 2000bb–bb4 (1993).

[32] City of Boerne v. Flores, 521 US 506 (1997).

[33] Ibid., at 534–536. Note that, in any case, many US states have enacted state-level versions of the Religious Freedom Restoration Act.

[34] BOP Program Statement 5360.07 (Religious Beliefs and Practices) (Aug. 25, 1997). Current BOP Program Statements are available online at <www.bop.gov>.

[35] BOP Program Statement 5360.08 (Religious Beliefs and Practices) (May 25, 2001) (rescinding Program Statement 5360.07).

[36] Ibid., at ¶ 3.

[37] According to the BOP Program Statement, the following religious practices and activities are never authorized: animal sacrifice, casting of spells/curses, nudity, self-mutilation, use or display of weapons, exclusion by race, paramilitary exercises, self-defense training, sexual acts, profanity, consumption of alcohol, ingestion of illegal substances, proselytizing, and encryption (ibid., at ¶ 7). "When necessary, Wardens may identify alternative practices and implement the least restrictive alternative consistent with the security and orderly running of Bureau institutions" (ibid.).

inmates, except in institutions where building design would prohibit the construction of such a facility.[38] The Program Statement includes specific provisions for religious diets, services, ceremonies, and meetings.[39]

Institutional chaplains are to be responsible for managing the religious activities within the institutions. They are employed to provide spiritual leadership and supervision of the institution's religious activities, but are not merely to assist prisoners of their own faith. When requested by an inmate, the chaplain is to facilitate arrangements for pastoral visits by a clergy person or representative of the inmate's faith.[40] The prison also makes arrangements for clergy/inmate privacy through the use of the attorney/client area of the prison if requested by either party.[41]

Unlike some other countries, the US does not limit clergy visits or prison ministry to representatives of religious organizations that are large, well-established, or historically rooted in a particular area. Indeed, such a limitation would violate the nondiscrimination principles of the First Amendment. Federal regulations require that "[n]o one may disparage the religious beliefs of an inmate, nor coerce or harass an inmate to change religious affiliation. Attendance at all religious activities is voluntary and, unless otherwise specifically determined by the Warden, open to all."[42]

Broad personal expression of religious belief is also available, within security limits, to prisoners of any religious tradition. For example, inmates are to be ordinarily allowed to wear or use personal religious items during religious services, ceremonies, and meetings in the chapel, unless the warden determines that the wearing or use of such items would threaten institutional security, safety, or good order. Also, upon request by an inmate, the warden may allow the wearing of or use of certain religious items throughout the institution, consistent with considerations of security, safety, and good order. Such religious wearing apparel includes, but is not limited to, prayer shawls and robes, kurda or ribbon shirts, medals and pendants, beads, medicine pouches, and various types of headgear.[43] The Program Statement specifically provides that religious headgear such as kufis, yarmulkes, turbans, crowns, and headbands, as well as scarves and head wraps for Orthodox Muslim and Jewish women, are to be permitted in all areas of the institution, subject to the normal considerations of security and good order.[44]

The warden is to endeavor to facilitate the observance of important religious holy days that involve special feasts, dietary regulations, or work proscriptions. But in order to obtain this accommodation, the inmate must submit a written request to the chaplain for time off from work to observe a religious holy day. The warden may request that the chaplain consult the community representatives of the inmate's faith group and/or other appropriate sources to verify the religious significance of the requested observance. The warden is to ordinarily allow an inmate to take earned vacation days or to make up for missed work or to change work assignments in order to accommodate the observance of the religious holy day.[45]

---

[38] Ibid., at ¶ 12.
[39] Ibid., at ¶ 8.
[40] Ibid., at ¶ 18.
[41] Ibid., at ¶ 18.
[42] 28 CFR § 548.15; see also BOP Program Statement 5360.08 ¶ 14.
[43] BOP Program Statement 5360.08 ¶ 15.
[44] Ibid.
[45] Ibid., at ¶ 17.

Under this Program Statement, the Bureau of Prisons is to provide inmates requesting a religious diet an equitable opportunity to observe their dietary practice within the constraints of budget limitations and the security and orderly running of the institution and the Bureau through a standardized "religious diet" menu.[46]

The Program Statement also makes provision for religious ceremonial or commemorative meals. Also, sacramental wine may be provided, but this provision only allows such consumption where the faith group's requirements only permit the ritual to be satisfied by the use of wine.[47]

Although the Federal Bureau of Prisons is involved with the providing of chaplains and chapels for inmates to accommodate inmate religious concerns, it is crucial to understand that policy requires the Bureau of Prisons to be religiously neutral. To ensure that this is the case, the Bureau may not require an inmate to profess a religious belief, and the inmate may not suffer adverse consequences for declining to designate a religious preference.[48] At the same time, any inmate may request the inclusion of a new or unfamiliar religious component to the Religious Service Program.[49] The designated space for conducting religious activities must be sufficient to accommodate the needs of all religious groups in the inmate population fairly and equitably, and religious groups are to share available time for facilities proportionately.[50] When inmates require spiritual counselors or advisors for religious needs other than those of familiar faith traditions, the prison chaplain may contract with representatives of other faith groups in the community.[51] While the prison is required to provide facilities and chaplains, and accommodate practices and beliefs, the Bureau of Prison bars the spending of BOP funds for personal religious items.[52] The Bureau of Prisons does set aside funds for a chaplaincy budget in prisons, but these funds must be spent in a nondiscriminatory manner. For example, a variety of periodicals, magazines, and media resources are to be purchased for general inmate use, and there must be parity among religious groups in the distribution and availability of religious literature.[53]

Even with substantial advances in the protection of the rights of inmates under the Program Statement, the United States Congress took the issue one step further in an attempt to vindicate the spirit of RFRA in light of the Supreme Court's action. In December 2000 the Congress passed, and the president signed into law, the Religious Land Use and Institutionalized Persons Act of 2000.[54] The law provides in relevant part:

> No state or local government shall impose a substantial burden on the religious exercise of a person residing in or confined to an institution . . . even if the burden results from a rule of general applicability, unless the government demonstrates that imposition of the burden on that person—

[46] Ibid., at ¶ 19.
[47] Ibid., at ¶ 20.
[48] Ibid., at ¶ 14.
[49] Ibid., at ¶ 11.
[50] Ibid., at ¶ 12.
[51] Ibid., at ¶ 13.
[52] Ibid., at ¶ 15.
[53] Ibid.
[54] *Religious Land Use and Institutionalized Persons Act of 2000,* 42 USC §§ 200cc–200cc5 (2000).

(1) is in furtherance of a compelling governmental interest; and

(2) is the least restrictive means of furthering that compelling governmental interest.[55]

The law specifically provides that "the government bears the burden of persuasion on any element of the claim" once the "plaintiff produces prima facie evidence to support a claim alleging a violation of the Free Exercise Clause or a violation of section 2 [of the Act]." However, "the plaintiff shall bear the burden of persuasion on whether the law (including a regulation or government practice) that is challenged by the claim substantially burdens the plaintiff's exercise of religion."[56] The legislation specifically anticipates the need for religious accommodation: it provides that "this Act may require a government to incur expenses in its own operations to avoid imposing a substantial burden on religious exercise."[57]

The US Religious Land Use and Institutionalized Persons Act of 2000 serves as a final demonstration of the need for broad action by the legislature and courts to ensure protection of freedom of religion and belief to inmates. While the US courts and legislature do not have a perfect record, the current level of protection reflects important accomplishments in ensuring protection of religious freedom of those in the most severely restricted settings. While it is certainly not the only approach, the US experience demonstrates that toleration of religious diversity and practices and neutrality is generally possible even in highly restrictive settings such as prisons.

B. Members of the Military

Because of the premium placed on uniformity and structure, those who serve in the military may experience some of the same problems as those who are incarcerated in state and federal prisons.

1. Conscientious Objection

The United States Supreme Court first dealt with religious freedom issues in the military with the issue of conscientious objection, when the United States still had compulsory military service requirements. As the Court noted in *Seeger v. United States*,[58] there has been "governmental recognition of the moral dilemma posed for persons of religious faith by [a] call to arms" when we were still British colonies.[59] By the time of the Civil War in the United States, "there existed a ... pattern of exempting conscientious objectors on religious grounds."[60]

During World War I "[t]he Draft Act of 1917 afforded exemption to conscientious objectors who were affiliated with a 'well-recognized religious sect or organization [then] organized and existing and whose existing creed or principles [forbade] its members to participate in war in any form. . . .'" Under the 1917 law, conscientious objectors were allowed to perform alternative noncombatant service.[61]

---

[55] Ibid.

[56] Ibid.

[57] Ibid.

[58] Seeger v. United States, 380 US 163 (1965).

[59] Ibid., at 175.

The scope of the exemption was found by Congress to be too narrow, and in 1948 it amended the provision to provide an exemption based upon "an individual's belief in relation to a Supreme Being involving duties superior to those arising from any human relation, but [not including] essentially political, sociological, or philosophical views or a merely personal moral code."[62]

In *Seeger*, the Court addressed a claim to an exemption from military service under § 6(j) of the Universal Military Training and Service Act, 50 USC App. § 456(j). The Court held that where the individual seeking exemption holds a "belief that is sincere and meaningful [and] occupies a place in the life of its possessor parallel to that filled by the orthodox belief in God," he qualifies for the exemption.[63]

Subsequently in *Welsh v. United States*,[64] the Court directly held that the law's exemption provision "exempts from military service all those whose conscience, spurred by deeply held moral, ethical, or religious beliefs, would give them no rest or peace if they allowed themselves to become a part of an instrument of war."[65] Thus, the early view that only those who are members of a well-recognized religious faith opposed to war in any form has been soundly rejected. The Congress and the Court focused on the individual's personal belief, not that of a corporate religious body.

Current Department of Defense regulations provide broad protection for conscientious objectors.[66] The provisions track *Seeger* and *Welsh* in allowing exemptions to those with "[a] firm, fixed and sincere objection to participation in war in any form or the bearing of arms, by reason of religious training and belief," meaning "[b]elief in an external power or being or deeply held moral or ethical belief, to which all else is subordinate or upon which all else is ultimately dependent, and which has the power or force to affect moral well-being."[67] The US Department of Defense makes provisions for conscientious objectors who oppose to participation in war in any form and for those who oppose bearing arms but whose convictions permit military service as a noncombatant.[68] Noncombatants may serve in medical units and other unarmed units. One of those who served but refused to carry a weapon was awarded the Armed Services' highest award, the Congressional Medal of Honor, for carrying a number of his wounded comrades to safety while suffering wounds of his own.

The Department of Defense also makes provision for those currently serving in the armed forces who have subsequently become conscientious objectors, allowing them the opportunity of an administrative discharge prior to completing an obligated term of service.[69] A conscientious objector's case is evaluated for sincerity and the

---

[60] Ibid., at 176.
[61] Ibid., at 171.
[62] Ibid., at 172.
[63] Seeger at 165–66.
[64] Welsh v. United States, 398 US 333 (1970).
[65] Ibid., at 344.
[66] Department of Defense Directive 1300.6 (Conscientious Objectors) (August 20, 1971), available online at <http://www.dtic.mil/whs/directives/corres/html/13006.htm>.
[67] Ibid., ¶¶ 3.1, 3.2
[68] Ibid., ¶¶ 3.1.1, 3.1.2.
[69] Ibid., ¶¶ 4.1, 6.1. But the regulations do prevent those who requested and were denied conscientious objector status before entering military service from requesting the status again based on essentially the same grounds (ibid., ¶¶ 4.1.1., 4.1.2).

depth of conviction.[70] Evaluating officers are instructed not to require church membership or adherence to particular theological tenets,[71] and to exercise particular care "not to deny the existence of bonafide beliefs simply because those beliefs are incompatible with one's own."[72] Examining officers are also instructed that "an applicant who is otherwise eligible for conscientious objector status may not be denied that status simply because his conscientious objection influences his views concerning the nation's domestic or foreign policies."[73] Finally, the Department of Defense also issues an important caution on the difficulty of adjudicating conscientious objection cases:

> Because of the personal and subjective nature of conscientious objection, the existence, honesty, and sincerity of asserted conscientious objection beliefs cannot be routinely ascertained by applying inflexible objective standards and measurements on an "across-the-board" basis. Requests for discharge or assignment to non-combatant training or service based on conscientious objection will, therefore, be handled on an individual basis with final determination made at the Headquarters of the Military Service concerned in accordance with the facts and circumstances in the particular case and the policy and procedures set forth herein.[74]

2. Chaplaincy

Like conscientious objection, chaplaincy has a well-established historical role in the United States. Drawing on British roots, chaplains were first established in the US in the Revolutionary War and have continued to the present.[75] Chaplaincy in the military is regulated by federal legislation requiring the appointment of chaplains as commissioned officers without command.[76] Chaplains do not bear arms, but are engaged in performing worship services, pastoral care, and moral leadership training.[77] One chaplain and at least one chaplain assistant is generally assigned to a deployable unit, which can number between four hundred and one thousand troops. While chaplains are expected to minister to members of their own faith, they are also responsible to "facilitate ministries appropriate to the rights and needs of persons of other faith groups in the pluralistic military environment."[78] To assist chaplains in this role, the military has instituted training to help chaplains become more knowledgeable about other faiths.

---

[70] Ibid., ¶ 5.3.
[71] Ibid., ¶¶ 5.3.3.1, 5.3.3.2.
[72] Ibid., ¶ 5.3.3.
[73] Ibid., ¶ 5.3.3.5.
[74] Department of Defense Directive 1300.6 ¶ 4.2 (Conscientious Objectors) (August 20, 1971), available online at <http://www.dtic.mil/whs/directives/corres/html/13006.htm>.
[75] For a brief overview of the history of chaplaincy and their current role in the US, see Army Regulation FM16-1 (Religious Support), Introduction (available online at <www.adtdl.army.mil/cgi-bin/atdl.dll/fm/16-1/Intro.htm>).
[76] 10 USC §§ 3073, 3581. Chaplaincy has been upheld against legal challenges that it violates the separation of church and state. *Katcoff v. Marsh*, 755 F2d 223, 225 (2d Cir 1985).
[77] Army Regulation FM16-1, chapter 1.
[78] Department of Defense Directive 1304.19 ¶ 3 (Appointment of Chaplains for Military Service) (September 18, 1993), available online at <http://www.dtic.mil/whs/directives/corres/html/130419.htm>.

The military appoints chaplains from over two hundred faith groups, roughly allocated among confessions based on their proportion of the national population. Chaplains must be not only educationally qualified, but must also be and remain certified by their religious faith group (referred to as an "ecclesiastical endorsing organization").[79] In an attempt to rectify past discrimination against nontraditional faith groups, the Department of Defense has made it extremely simple for groups to obtain recognition as an ecclesiastical endorsing organization and thus be represented by chaplains. To become an ecclesiastical endorsing organization, a group must only: (1) "Be organized exclusively or substantially to provide religious ministries to a lay constituency"; (2) "Possess ecclesiastical authority to grant or withdraw initial and subsequent ecclesiastical certification"; and (3) "Present an applicant for appointment as a chaplain . . ."[80]

The military has made it clear that the list of ecclesiastical endorsing organizations is not a list of "approved," "sanctioned," or "accepted" religions, as this would violate US standards of freedom of religion.[81] All chaplains, "regardless of their denomination, are expected to support and facilitate the faith needs of all service members, regardless of denomination," which may include working to train and facilitate lay leaders of groups not represented by chaplains.[82] Religious accommodations of military personnel are also not limited to those belonging to groups represented by chaplains.[83]

3. Accommodations of Religious Practices

While conscientious objection and chaplaincy have long historical roots in the US, accommodations of individual religious practices of military personnel by the military and courts have been more troublesome. One case is illustrative. In *Goldman v. Weinberger*,[84] the United States Supreme Court held that S. Simcha Goldman, an Orthodox Jew and ordained rabbi who was serving in the United States Air Force, could not be exempt from an Air Force regulation that stated in pertinent part, "headgear will not be worn . . . while indoors except by armed security police in the performance of their duties."

In this case Goldman wore his yarmulke, a complaint was lodged against him, and he was ordered not to wear this religious headgear while on duty. Over a strong dissent, the majority of the Supreme Court held that "the First Amendment does not require the military to accommodate such practices in the face of its view that they

---

[79] Ibid., ¶ 5.1.

[80] Ibid., ¶ 5.2. The organization must also "[p]rovide to the [military] the name, title, mailing address, and telephone number of the designated official authorized to represent the organization to the Military Services"; "[a]gree to abide by all Department of Defense issuances and Military Department regulations and policies on the qualification and endorsement of clergy for service as military chaplains"; and "[a]gree to notify the Department of Defense and the Military Department concerned of any withdrawal of an existing ecclesiastical endorsement" (ibid., ¶¶ 5.2.1.4–5.2.1.6).

[81] See Administrative Message (Public Affairs Guidance—DOD Policies Regarding Faith Groups in the Military), available online at <134.11.73.3/reserves/policyandnewsletters/faithgroup.htm>.

[82] Ibid.

[83] Ibid.

[84] Goldman v. Weinberger, 475 US 503 (1986).

would detract from the uniformity sought by the dress regulations" of the Air Force.[85] But, this judicial view was subsequently rejected by the Department of Defense in its later regulations.

The United States Department of Defense, in DOD Directive 1300.17,[86] officially articulated its policy regarding the religious accommodation of the Armed Forces. According to section 3.1 of this regulation:

> It is DOD policy that requests for accommodation of religious practices should be approved by commanders when accommodation will not have an adverse impact on military readiness, unit cohesion, standards, or discipline.

The regulation provides that "[w]orship services, holy days, and Sabbath observance should be accommodated except when precluded by military necessity."[87] It notes that under Public Law 100-180, section 508, members of the Armed Forces may wear visible items of religious apparel which are part of the doctrinal or traditional observance of the religious faith practiced by the member except under circumstances in which an item is not neat and conservative or its wearing interferes with the performance of military duties.[88]

In determining whether a certain item interferes with military duties, consideration centers on whether it impairs the safe and effective operation of weapons, military equipment, or machinery;[89] poses a health or safety factor to the wearer or others;[90] interferes with the wearing or proper functioning of protective clothing or equipment;[91] or otherwise impairs the accomplishment of the military mission.[92]

Subject to the particular circumstances of the branch of service and its present status, specific factors that aid in determining whether to grant an accommodation request include the importance of military requirements in terms of individual and unit readiness, health, safety, discipline, morale, and cohesion;[93] the religious importance of the accommodation to the requester;[94] the cumulative impact of repeated accommodations to the requestor;[95] alternative means available to meet the requested accommodation;[96] and previous treatment of the same or similar requests, including treatment of similar requests made for other than religious reasons.[97]

Again, the military accommodates those who face practical limitations on their opportunity to worship and practice their faith because of incompatible military requirements and other circumstances. But essential to this is the requirement of state

---

[85] Ibid., at 509–10.

[86] Department of Defense Directive 1300.17 (Accommodation of Religious Practices Within the Military Services) (Feb. 3, 1988), available online at <http://www.dtic.mil/whs/directives/corres/html/130017.htm>.

[87] Ibid., at 3.2.1.

[88] Ibid., at 3.2.7.

[89] Ibid., at 3.2.7.5.1.

[90] Ibid., at 3.2.7.5.2.

[91] Ibid., at 3.2.7.5.3.

[92] Ibid., at 3.2.7.5.4.

[93] Ibid., at 4.1.1.

[94] Ibid., at 4.1.2.

[95] Ibid., at 4.1.3.

[96] Ibid., at 4.1.4.

[97] Ibid., at 4.1.5.

neutrality in providing such accommodation. No faith is given preference, nor does any religion deliver spiritual assistance or provide blessings to military units as a whole. What is provided is an accommodation for the spiritual needs of individuals, both those of traditional religious viewpoints, as well as those who may hold unusual or novel religious beliefs or no religious beliefs whatsoever.

C. Patients in State-Operated Medical Facilities

The Establishment Clause of the First Amendment to the United States Constitution requires that when the state provides services to those within its borders that it does so with no religious purpose or effect, among other restrictions. As the Supreme Court stated in the context of public education in *Abington Township School District v. Schempp:*

> The place of religion in our society is an exalted one, achieved through the long tradition of reliance on the home, the church and the inviolable citadel of the human mind. We have come to recognize through bitter experience that it is not within the power of government to invade that citadel, whether its purpose or effect be to aid or oppose, to advance or retard. In the relationship between man and religion, the State is firmly committed to a position of neutrality.[98]

As the Supreme Court noted, the United States is committed to a role of neutrality, or nondiscrimination among religions. Later, in *Larson v. Valente*,[99] the Supreme Court addressed the question of unequal treatment of religious groups. The case involved legislation detrimental to a new, nontraditional religion. The Supreme Court found the legislation unconstitutional and declared, "the clearest command of the Establishment Clause is that one religious denomination cannot be officially preferred over another."[100] The Supreme Court further noted that "the government must be neutral when it comes to competition between sects."[101]

In the realm of state medical facilities, these principles of nonendorsement and nondiscrimination mandate equal access for representatives of all religious groups. Individuals confined to state-operated medical facilities are free to seek spiritual support from their own religious communities, whether through formally appointed hospital chaplains, clergy volunteers, or members of the community. Likewise, there can be no policy that would provide preference to any religious denomination to pastoral or other spiritual care to patients at such a facility. No action could be taken by the medical facility that would disparage the religious beliefs of any patient or coerce or harass a patient regarding matters of faith, and administrators or personnel may not place or display religious symbols in those facilities.

These core principles are reflected in the broadly accepted national US healthcare standards promulgated by the Joint Commission on the Accreditation of Healthcare Organizations. Patients have "a fundamental right to considerate care that safeguards their personal dignity and respects their cultural, psychosocial, and spiritual values."[102]

---

[98] Abington Township School Dist. v. Schempp, 374 US 203, 226 (1963).

[99] Larson v. Valente, 456 US 228 (1982).

[100] Ibid., at 244.

[101] Ibid., at 246.

[102] Joint Commission on the Accreditation of Healthcare Organizations, CAMH Update (1999).

Spiritual care of patients in state hospitals is provided by the patient's friends, family, and local clergy in addition to volunteer and paid chaplains. The Joint Commission on the Accreditation of Healthcare Organizations does not require that hospitals employ chaplains, although it does mandate a social services department.[103] It is interesting to note that chaplaincy has been rated by patients as the most important of the nonmedical services provided by a healthcare facility.[104] Most nonreligiously affiliated community hospitals have approximately one paid chaplain per one hundred inpatients.[105] Approximately 28% of the departmental ministry of these hospitals is carried out by volunteer chaplains.[106]

Professional chaplains are responsible for providing spiritual care to people of all faiths or no faith, and are professionally accountable to their own religious faith group, their certifying chaplaincy organization, and their employing institution. Most hospitals require that chaplains have advanced educational degrees and certification from one of the national chaplaincy organizations.[107] Certification usually requires a graduate degree, endorsement by a faith group or demonstrated connection to a recognized faith community, clinical pastoral training, fulfillment of annual education requirements, and adherence to a code of professional ethics that requires respect for all religious traditions of patients.

Responsibilities of chaplains in health care organizations usually include counseling, performing ordinances or leading religious ceremonies for patients of their own faith, contacting clergy on behalf of patients of other faiths, and assisting patients in dealing with grief, loss, or end-of-life care choices. Chaplains also serve as members of patient care teams, serve on hospital ethics committees, and assist healthcare professionals in understanding the roles of religion and spirituality in healing and medical treatment.

Traditionally, health care facilities have allowed clergy access to directories of patients that indicate the patient's religious affiliation, if the patient designated one. Federal regulations by the US Department of Health and Human Services ensure greater privacy of directories, but still permit hospitals to reveal patient religious affiliation to clergy or their designees.[108]

D. Conclusion

Special accommodation is permitted, and indeed may be required, when individuals are subject to state-ordered confinement or enjoy limited access to spiritual assistance and facilities. United States law demonstrates that the state can provide such

[103] Ibid.

[104] Larry VandeCreek et al., "Patient and Family Perceptions of Hospital Chaplains," *Hospital and Health Services Administration,* 36:3 (fall 1991): 464.

[105] Larry VandeCreek et al., "How Many Chaplains per 100 Inpatients? Benchmarks of Health Care Chaplaincy Departments," *The Journal of Pastoral Care,* 55:3 (fall 2001): 295.

[106] Ibid., at 298.

[107] VandeCreek, "Patient and Family Perceptions of Hospital Chaplains," 465. National chaplaincy certification groups include the Association for Clinical Pastoral Education, the National Association of Catholic Chaplains, the College of Chaplains of the American Protestant Health Association, and the National Association of Jewish Chaplains.

[108] See 45 C.F.R. 146.510. The regulations were enacted under the Health Insurance Portability and Accountability Act, Pub. L. No. 104-191, 110 Stat. 1936 (1996).

an accommodation in a religiously neutral manner so that no preference is given to nor detriment experienced by any religious faith. The US model is also useful to show the extent of accommodation needed in confined settings even under a general separationist church-state scheme. The examples given also illustrate the importance and feasibility of accommodation based on an individual's personal religious conviction. As part of the individual right to freedom of religion and belief, the right to reasonable accommodation of individual beliefs in restricted settings is in no way dependent upon membership in or affiliation with any specifically-organized religious body.

Chapter 17

Freedom of Religion and Belief and Discretionary State Approval of Religious Activity

Roman Podoprigora

I. Introduction

The rise of the human rights movement has placed added significance on the rule of law.[1] At its most basic level, the idea that people should be subject to the rule of law and not to the rule of men is the insistence that human beings should not be subject to the arbitrary power or discretion of others.[2] This applies with special force in the domain of religion.

The aim in this chapter will be to focus on certain recurrent types of problems that lead to violations of freedom of religion or belief. Indeed, the most typical violations take the form not of legislation, but of administrative action that prevents people from engaging in religious activities that are properly protected under international human rights agreements and under many national constitutions as well.

In a modern administrative state, the interactions of religious and state institutions involve countless, often low-level, approvals, licenses, permits, and other governmental decisions that can severely complicate the life of religious communities. Such decisions include threshold determinations of whether a religious community will be registered or recognized and enabled to acquire juristic personality, land use permits

[1] In seven case studies of the socialization of international human rights norms into domestic practices, "[t]here is not a single case in which a sustained improvement of human rights conditions was not preceded by the country's move toward the rule of law" (Thomas Risse and Stephen C. Ropp, "International Human Rights Norms and Domestic Change: Conclusions," *The Power of Human Rights: International Norms and Domestic Change*, ed. Thomas Risse, Stephen C. Ropp, and Kathryn Sikkink [Cambridge University Press, 1999], 249). See also Manfred Nowak, *U.N. Covenant on Civil and Political Rights: CCPR Commentary* (Kehl, Germany: N. P. Engel, 1993) 236–41 (emphasizing the necessity of a "common minimum standard of the 'rule of law' in civil and criminal trials"). See generally Ian Brownlie, *The Rule of Law in International Affairs* (The Hague: Martinus Nijhoff, 1998).

[2] See Ian Shapiro, "Introduction," *The Rule of Law*, ed. Ian Shapiro (New York: New York University Press, 1994), 1. See also Jürgen Habermas, *Between Facts and Norms*, trans. William Rehg (Cambridge, Mass.: MIT Press, 1994), 188–89.

Tore Lindholm, W. Cole Durham, Jr., Bahia G. Tahzib-Lie (eds.), Facilitating Freedom of Religion or Belief: A Deskbook, *425–440.*

authorizing use of specific locations for worship facilities, tax status determinations, visa approvals for travel of religious personnel, approvals in connections with educational institutions, the issuance of licenses for priests, and the authorization of public worship. Administrative decisions can restrict the presence of believers and their associations in hospitals, prisons, and educational institutions. States may have laws that inject governmental decision making into issues involving financial support for religious associations and their projects, or into the grant of special waivers from tax obligations.

At one level, such government approvals can be routine and innocuous. But depending on the applicable legal standards that govern approvals, the attitudes of relevant governmental officials, the attitudes of the wider populace, the ability of the wider populace to exert political pressures on decision-makers, and a variety of other factors, the exercise of official discretion in these contexts can potentially have a very significant adverse impact on the freedom of religion or belief, particularly when smaller or less-popular groups are involved.

It is in this way that complicated state administrative functions give rise to the risks of abuse of discretion by state bodies and officials who deal with religious activities in many countries. Despite the existence of a developed legal system and glowing formal protections of freedom of religion or belief, such abuse of discretion can compromise religious freedom norms in extremely serious ways. Of course, not every exercise of discretionary power in a religious sphere violates citizens' rights and freedoms and the organizational autonomy of religious communities. In many cases, the state makes discretionary decisions for the protection of the rights of private citizens, organizations, and society. But the risk of abuse remains and must be guarded against. Otherwise, state action may result in unjustifiable privileging of or discrimination against religious communities, or the curtailing of activities that should be protected and free.

International and legal acts and documents do not directly mention the range of ways that government permissions may encroach on religious freedom.[3] These documents simply provide that everyone should be free to exercise his or her religion or belief in any form, individually or together with others, without any restrictions by the state.[4] Similarly, constitutions and legislation in many countries around the world contain articles guaranteeing the right to exercise religion or belief without authorization from the state.[5] But as a practical matter, bureaucrats are accustomed to exercising their powers, and they may either intentionally or unintentionally tread on religious freedom as a result. Under conditions of economic development and globalization,

---

[3] See generally *International Covenant on Civil and Political Rights,* UN Doc. A/6316 (1966); *Declaration of the Elimination of All Forms of Intolerance and of Discrimination Based on Religion and Belief,* UN Doc. A/36/684 (1981); *European Convention for the Protection of Human Rights and Fundamental Freedoms,* 213 UNTS 221 (1950); *American Convention on Human Rights,* 1144 UNTS 123 (1978); *African Charter on Human and People Rights,* 21 ILM 58 (1982).

[4] Restriction can be imposed only in case of the necessity to guarantee the security, order, health, morality, rights and freedoms of other people. See, for example, ICCPR, 999 UNTS 171 (1966).

[5] For example, article 20 of the Italian Constitution of 1948 asserts: "No special restrictions shall be imposed by law upon any society or institution by reason of its ecclesiastical nature or its religious or its religious or liturgical purpose, nor shall any special fiscal burdens be imposed in respect of its constitution, its legal capacity, or its activities in any form" (Mauro Cappelletti, John Henry Merryman, and Joseph M. Perillo, *The Italian Legal System: An Introduction* [Stanford: Stanford University Press, 1967], 285).

the tendency toward proliferation of regulation is strong, and officials accustomed to regulation in other areas are all too prone to extend into the sensitive and protected realm of contracts between church and state.

In this chapter, we will first examine the leading case from the European Court of Human Rights dealing with the ways in which administrative decision-making may interfere with the freedom of religion or belief. *Manoussakis v. Greece*[6] has profound implications for a range of recurrent types of problems, dealing as it does with a variety of potential rule of law violations. Many of the problems in *Manoussakis* reflect general problems of abuse of state power in a democratic society, but they apply with added force when the domain of religion is involved. On the basis of our analysis of *Manoussakis*, we will then provide a taxonomy of some of the types of recurrent problems associated with the exercise of official discretion.

II. *Manoussakis v. Greece*

In the *Manoussakis* case, Jehovah's Witnesses appealed their criminal convictions for using an unauthorized place of worship. In March 1983 Mr. Manoussakis rented a room in the Ghazi district of the city of Heraklion. According to the private rental agreement, he intended to use the room "for all kinds of meetings, weddings, etc. of Jehovah's Witnesses." Three months later, in June, Mr. Manoussakis and his associates applied for a permit to use the facility as a place of worship. The chairman of the Ghazi District Council refused to certify the applicants' signatures. He withdrew his refusal in October 1983 at the urging of the prefect of Heraklion, the Deputy Minister of the Interior, and the Speaker of the Greek Parliament; the application thus became eligible for consideration by the Ministry of Education and Religious Affairs in October 1983.[7]

Meanwhile, on 30 July 1983, the Ghazi Orthodox Parish Church notified the Heraklion police that Jehovah's Witnesses were meeting in Mr. Manoussakis's rented room without authorization. The church authorities wanted the police to take punitive action and to prohibit further unauthorized meetings.[8]

Between November 1983 and December 1984, the Ministry of Education sent five letters to Mr. Manoussakis and his fellow Jehovah's Witnesses saying that it could not grant a permit because it "had not received all the necessary information from the other departments concerned." The Ministry took no further action on the application for a permit.[9]

In March 1986, the Heraklion authorities began the prosecution of Mr. Manoussakis and his associates for having "established and operated a place of worship for religious meetings and ceremonies of followers of . . . the Jehovah's Witnesses' denomination without authorization from the recognized ecclesiastical authorities and the Minister of Education and Religious Affairs, such authorization being required for the construction and operation of a church of any faith."[10]

---

[6] Manoussakis v. Greece, 23 EHRR 387 (1997) (ECtHR 1996-A, No. 59/1995/565/651, 26 September 1996).
[7] Ibid., paras. 7–9.
[8] Ibid., para. 10.
[9] Ibid., paras. 11, 51.
[10] Ibid., para. 12.

Greek laws required a valid application to come from at least fifty families "from more or less the same neighborhood and living in an area at a great distance from a temple of the same denomination, it being assumed that the distance makes it difficult for them to observe their religious duties."[11]

The law also required the Minister of Education and Religious Affairs to consider the non-binding "preliminary finding" of the local Orthodox Metropolitan as to whether "the true position regarding religious practice in the locality" warranted the construction of a temple.[12]

In convicting the defendants, the Heraklion Criminal Court found that they "had converted the room that they had rented into a place of worship, in other words a small temple . . . without the authorization of the recognized ecclesiastical authority and of the Ministry of Education and Religious Affairs."[13] The convictions were upheld by Greek appellate courts and the Heraklion police sealed the room rented by the Jehovah's Witnesses.

The European Court of Human Rights held that under article 9 of the European Convention on Human Rights, "the restrictions imposed on the Jehovah's Witnesses by the Greek Government effectively prevent them from exercising their right to freedom of religion."[14] Article 9 sets forth three tests for determining whether government action impermissibly interferes with the freedom of religion or belief; government action must not violate any of the tests in order to be legitimate. First, limitations must be "prescribed by law." This requirement "does not merely refer back to domestic law but also relates to the quality of law, requiring it to be compatible with the rule of law, which is expressly mentioned in the preamble to the Convention."[15] The "prescribed by law" requirement can therefore be considered a "rule of law constraint."[16] Second, limitations must have a "legitimate aim,"[17] specifically "in the interests of public safety, for the protection of public order, health or morals, or for the protection of the rights and freedoms of others."[18] Third, limitations must be "necessary in a democratic society."[19]

The "necessary in a democratic society" requirement was the basis for the Court's holding *Manoussakis*. The Court said that the Jehovah's Witnesses' conviction had been persecutory, unjustified and not necessary in a democratic society as it had been "manufactured" by the State. The State had compelled the applicants to commit an offence and to bear the consequences solely because of their religious beliefs. The apparently innocent requirement of an authorization to operate a place of worship had been transformed from a mere formality into a lethal weapon against the right to freedom of religion. The term "dilatory" used by the Commission to describe the conduct of the Minister of Education and Religious Affairs in relation to their application for an authorization was euphemistic. The struggle for survival by certain religious

---

[11] Ibid., para. 23.
[12] Ibid., para. 26.
[13] Ibid., para. 15.
[14] Ibid., para. 41.
[15] Malone v. United Kingdom (ECtHR 82-A, 2 August 1984), para. 67.
[16] W. Cole Durham, "Freedom of Religion or Belief: Laws Affecting the Structuring of Religious Communities," ODIHR Background Paper 1999/4, 30.
[17] Manoussakis v. Greece, para. 40.
[18] European Convention on Human Rights, Nov. 4, 1950, art. 9(2), 312 UNTS 221 art. 9, para. 2.
[19] Manoussakis v. Greece, para. 41.

communities . . . [including] Jehovah's Witnesses was carried on in a climate of interference and oppression by the State and the dominant church as a result of which article 9 of the Convention had become a dead letter.[20]

The Court noted particular practices in the *Manoussakis* case that were not justified: "a very wide discretion [in] the police, mayor or chairman of the district council";[21] "the possibility for the Minister of Education and Religious to defer his reply indefinitely. . . or to refuse his authorization without explanation or without giving a valid reason";[22] the government's power "to assess whether there is a 'real need' for the religious community in question to set up a church";[23] and the fact that in its judgment the Heraklion Criminal Court "relied expressly on the lack of the bishop's authorization as well as the lack of an authorization from the Minister of Education and Religious Affairs."[24]

III. Models of the Relationship between Church and State

The fundamental principles articulated in *Manoussakis* must be applied within a range of possible church-state systems. The position of religion in any given society depends on religion's relationship with the state and its role in state life. At one extreme, there are countries where ecclesiastical power is inseparably linked with state power and is foundational to its structure. This power is exercised through legislation and legal procedures, which are based on the norms of the dominant religious community. In these countries we commonly find prohibitions or limitations on the activities of "non-official" religious associations. Islamic countries provide vivid examples of this model. For example, in compliance with article 4 of the Islamic Republic Constitution of Iran, all civil, criminal, financial, economic, administrative, cultural, military, political and other laws and regulations must be based on Islamic criteria. By positioning this article prior to other articles, the founders of Iran's constitution symbolically emphasized that religion forms the basis for state action in Iran.[25]

At the other extreme, there are countries that do not recognize religion as an important part of social life and even have a negative attitude towards it. In this model, all religious associations are under strict supervision by the state; religious activity is essentially limited by law and, in some cases, it is presumed that religion will die out in the near future. Communist systems exemplify this model. As Darin W. Carlson writes, "[A]ccording to Chinese theorists, until the time when religion naturally dies out, it should be tolerated by the state in order to prevent its being driven underground. . . . [T]he policy of the [Chinese Communist Party] is to protect religious activity to the extent necessary to promote its extinction, with the caveat that religion must never be allowed to disrupt the harmony and progress of the state."[26]

---

[20] Ibid., para. 41.
[21] Ibid., para. 45.
[22] Ibid.
[23] Ibid.
[24] Ibid., para. 51.
[25] Islamic Republic of Iran Const (1979).
[26] Darin W. Carlson, "Understanding Chinese–U.S. Conflict Over Freedom of Religion: The Wolf-Specter Freedom From Religious Persecution Acts of 1997 and 1998," *Brigham Young University Law Review* (1998): 566–67.

Between these two poles are other models of church-state relationships. There are state churches that are granted special privileges and a large impact on state affairs. There are models of separation between church and state in which all religious associations are treated equally and both church and state avoid interference in each other's affairs. There are models in which states formally recognize the equality of churches, but where, in fact, the system favors one religion.[27]

We focus primarily on systems that fall between the two extremes, although the legal principles explored here have force wherever governments acknowledge the fundamental freedom of religion or belief and the necessity of the rule of law.

IV. Registration and Recognition Requirements

Many states exercise broad and far-reaching discretionary powers in the registration and official recognition of religious associations. These common registration requirements often force religious associations to contact the state in their infancy. The decisions of state bodies (courts, justice departments, internal affairs departments, ministries of education or specially formed departments on religious affairs) concerning registration or recognition of religion may decide the fate of an association. This begs the questions, why is it necessary either to register or to recognize religious associations? Can religious associations operate without being recognized? The answers to these questions will be different in each country. Because the answers vary, the consequences of registration, recognition or refusal are extremely important for religious associations in some countries and are unimportant in others.

In some countries, national legislation links the opportunity to satisfy demands for religious freedom with the necessity of registration or recognition of religious associations by state bodies. Such constraints, pursuant to which only registered bodies can assert religious freedoms, are problematic under international norms.[28]

In many countries, believers and their groups may freely operate without registration or official authorization from the state.[29]

In addition, religious associations may create or participate in voluntary associations or non-profit corporations without being distinguished in a legal sense from any other non-profit organizations.

Refusal to register a religious organization does not necessarily mean that the organization cannot continue to operate or that its foundation is contrary to law. (In this situation it is more correct to say that an organization is not recognized as a

---

[27] Several writers provide an insight into European models of ecclesiastical law systems and church-state systems in Gerhard Robbers, ed., *State and Church in the European Union* (Baden-Baden: European Consortium for State and Church Research, 1996), 60–61, 324–26. See also Durham, "Perspectives on Religious Liberty: A Comparative Framework," in Johan D. van der Vyver and John Witte, Jr., eds., *Religious Human Rights in Global Perspective: Legal Perspectives* (The Hague: Martinus Nijhoff Publishers, 1996) 1, 12–25.

[28] See, e.g., Vienna Concluding Document, principle 16(3).

[29] "[A]ny group with religious aims may be founded without the necessity of any authorization or prior registration and may operate within the Italian legal order" (Silvio Ferrari, "State and Church in Italy," in Robbers, *State and Church in the European Union,* 174). In Finland, "members of the group may decide to manifest their belief without forming a juridical person. In this case the Freedom of Religion Act affords their operation the protection of law" (Markku Heikkilä, Jyrki Knuutila, and Martin Scheinin, "State and Church in Finland," in Robbers, *State and Church in the European Union,* 286).

religious entity rather than that a religious organization is forbidden.) The believers can instead choose another form, but lack of official recognition as a religious organization may seriously affect the reputation of the organization and its property status.[30] Even more serious consequences occur, however, when, as a consequence of the refusal to register, the state considers it impossible to qualify the believers' activity as a religious organization and accordingly limits its activities.

At the same time, in accordance with the accepted practice in many countries,[31] official registration or recognition of an association as a religious one automatically brings official approval of the association,[32] which in turn rewards the association with certain property status, tax privileges, and state support. The "approved" organization may also receive access to schools, television, radio and other advantages.[33] The question of recognition is closely connected with granting a religious association the status of legal entity and legal capacity.[34] Nonetheless, in some countries, even registration cannot guard against state interference in the future. In Russia, the local authorities of one region tried to close a congregation of the Evangelical Lutheran Church under the false pretext that their charter documents were fraudulent.[35]

In a number of countries there is no registration of religious associations. However, a state may recognize and grant certain privileges to a religious organization through alternative methods such as by making agreements between state and religious associations or by passing distinct laws directed at specific religious associations.[36]

---

[30] See note 27 in this article.

[31] W. Cole Durham and Lauren B. Homer write, "it is true that many European countries afford differing levels of recognition to different religious organizations" (Durham and Lauren B. Homer, "Russia's 1997 Law On Freedom Of Conscience and Religious Associations: An Analytical Appraisal," *Emory International Law Review* 12 [1998]: 196).

[32] In addition, in some countries, the organizations are subdivided into public and private entities. Public Law or Public Corporations status is generally granted primarily to traditional religious associations or established churches. This means certain advantages as compared to those having the status of "private corporations" in the matters of public reputation, property status, state attitude, tax, and other privileges. For example, in Germany, this approach means that religious communities having the status of public corporations are part of public life. See Robbers, "State and Church in Germany," in Robbers, *State and Church in the European Union*, 62. In Finland, "the public law nature of two State Churches (Lutheran Church and the Orthodox Church) is manifested in the fact that both Churches have an internal court system" (Heikkilä, Knuutila, and Scheinin, "State and Church in Finland," in Robbers, *State and Church in the European Union*, 286).

[33] According to two American scholars, "[r]eligious organizations choose to adopt a civil law corporate form for many of the same reasons that businesses organized 'for profit' do: to limit liability, to own and control property in the name of organization, and to take advantage of benefits available to corporations under tax and other regulatory provisions of state and federal law" (Michael S. Ariens and Robert A. Destro, *Religious Liberty in a Pluralistic Society* [Durham, NC: Carolina Academic Press, 1996], 489).

[34] At the same time, in some countries not organizations but their bodies have legal capacity, or they are represented in legal actions by citizens. In Belgium, "[l]egal personality is attributed to the ecclesiastical administrations responsible for the temporal needs of the Church. The Church and Church structures themselves do not enjoy any legal personality" (Rik Torfs, "State and Church in Belgium," in Robbers, *State and Church in the European Union*, 19). In Ireland, "[c]hurch and religious groups do not automatically have legal personality; in general their legal status is that of unincorporated associations . . . . [C]hurch property is normally vested in trustees" (James Casey, "State and Church in Ireland," in Robbers, *State and Church in the European Union*, 153).

[35] See Durham and Homer, "Russia's 1997 Law," 230–31.

[36] In Denmark, for example, "[t]he special recognition would be normally be given as a decision made administratively by the Minister of Ecclesiastical Affairs, but in the form of a royal resolution" (Inger Dubeck, "State and Church in Denmark," Robbers, *State and Church in the European Union*, 43).

V. Problematic Modes of Exercising Discretion

In this section, we consider the types of problems that religious organizations may face in their efforts to gain discretionary approvals. The situation in *Manoussakis* typifies many of these problems. We will point out reasons why these obstacles are legally problematic and we will suggest legal arguments that may assist religious associations in demonstrating that such obstacles are inconsistent with appropriate standards of freedom of religion or belief.

A. Unreasonable Delay and Denial by Inaction

In the *Manoussakis* case, the European Court of Human Rights observed that the group of Jehovah's Witnesses had made five requests for a house of prayer permit in 1983 and 1984, and each time, in reply, the Minister of Education and Religious Affairs had told them that he was examining their file.[37] Up to the time of the Court's decision in 1995, the Minister still had not made an official decision on the requests.[38] "In these circumstances the Court considers that the Government cannot rely on the applicants' failure to comply with a legal formality to justify their conviction."[39] Given the government's unreasonable delay in responding to repeated lawful requests, there was nothing that the group of Jehovah's Witnesses could do to avoid criminal prosecution short of abandoning their right to practice their religion.

Lengthy delay in considering an application is one method of effectively shutting down disfavored religious organizations when direct legal means of doing so are not available. Indeed, in *Manoussakis*, the Court cited evidence that the Minister's delay in considering the applications may have been motivated by his "difficulty . . . in giving legally valid reasons for an express decision refusing the authorization or [by] his fear that he might provide the applicants with grounds for appealing to the Supreme Administrative Court to challenge an express administrative decision."[40]

The *Manoussakis* court considered this type of delay one reason for violation of article 9; the government's unreasonable delay created a limitation on religious freedom that is not necessary in a democratic society. At a minimum, statutory provisions setting forth governmental decision on approval procedures should be structured in ways that preclude inordinate delay. Reasonable and fixed periods for decisions should be established.

B. Discriminatory Exercise of Discretion

Precisely because many prohibitions and authorizations are discretionary, state officials often fail to apply them even-handedly to all religions and religious associations in the country. As Professor Nowak notes in his chapter, even if state action constraining religious freedom might otherwise be appropriate, such action is impermissible if

[37] Manoussakis v. Greece, 23 EHRR 387 (1997) (ECtHR 1996-A, No. 59/1995/565/651, 26 September 1996), para. 51.

[38] Ibid.

[39] Ibid., para. 52.

[40] Ibid., para. 51.

it is applied in a discriminatory manner.[41] Furthermore, where there is a confessional state structure, the differing roles and status of the various religions in the country increase the arbitrary nature of these discretionary decisions.

In addition, legislation in many countries directly secures advantages for some religious organizations over others. For example, according to article 2 of the Constitution of Argentina, "the Federal Government supports the Roman Catholic Apostolic Faith."[42] Similarly, the Evangelistic Lutheran Church of Iceland is the state religion in Iceland and enjoys state support and protection.[43] Also, in Mongolia, the law grants primary religious status to Buddhism.[44]

Even in countries where all citizens are considered equal before the law, some provisions appear to contradict this guarantee of equality by favoring certain religions over others. Though the Russian constitution guarantees religious equality, the preamble of the Federal Law of the Russian Federation 1997 "On Religious Freedom and Religious Associations" recognizes the special contribution of Orthodoxy to the history of Russia and to the establishment and development of Russia's spirituality and culture.[45] Of course, a preamble lacks operative legal effect, but it is problematic at least in the sense that it signals symbolic preferment.

In addition, several countries have reached agreements between church and state prohibiting state bodies from altering the status of religious associations at their discretion. However, such agreements often do not reach all religious associations, but benefit only those with established traditional ties. Thus, for example, in compliance with article 7 of the Constitution of the Italian Republic, the Catholic Church and the Italian state are independent and sovereign in their own spheres.[46] However, the Italian Constitution does not specifically address the independence of other, smaller religions.

Sometimes competing factions of registered associations are unable to operate because the state favors one faction over another. In Kazakhstan, where one of the major religious structures is the Russian Orthodox Church (Moscow Patriarchy), the government refused to recognize the Russian Orthodox Church functioning abroad (Karlovatsky Schism), which does not recognize the jurisdiction of the Moscow Patriarchy.

From these observations we can note that despite the formal equality granted believers and their associations, even in countries where there is no established church, some religions receive more favorable treatment by the state than others. Many researchers of church and state relationships recognize and emphasize this contradiction. For example, in Belgium, "[A]lthough all cults enjoy theoretically the same rights,

---

[41] See Manfred Nowak and Tanja Vospernik, "Permissible Restrictions on Freedom of Religion or Belief," in this volume.

[42] *Constitution of Argentina 1853* (Washington, DC: Pan American Union, 1968).

[43] Republic of Iceland Const, art. 62 (1944).

[44] Andrei Protopopov, "Mongoliia Zakon 'Ob otnosheniyakh mezdy tserkov'yu i gosydarstvom' [Mongolian Law 'On Relations Between Church and State'] 1993, art. 4.2" in *Religiya i Zakon* [Religion and Law] (Moscow: Institute of Religion and Law, 1996), 56.

[45] Federal'nyi Zakon O svobode sovesti i religioznykh ob'edineniyakh [Russian Federation Law On Freedom of Conscience and On Religious Associations] (1997), Sobranie zakonodatel'stva Rossiiskoi Federatsii, 1997, no. 39

[46] Italian Republic Const, art. 7 (1947). As Silvio Ferrari writes, "the Catholic Church and the six denominations which have reached an agreement with the State have the security that the legal status which they have at present will not be altered *in peius* against their will" (Ferrari, "State and Church in Italy," 177).

there is an important juridical difference between recognized and non-recognized cults."[47] In Portugal, despite the constitutional progress in matters of equality and autonomy, one scholar noted that the principle of equality has not yet been fully recognized.[48]

The state, in its discretion, can use its supervisory and regulatory authority over religion domestically to protect its traditional confessions. In doing so, it might also violate the rights and freedoms of believers who do not belong to traditional religions. The practice of utilizing discretionary power, in many aspects, depends on the role that state authorities perceive believers and their followers to play in society. It makes a difference whether authorities see religion, as a whole or as a particular denomination, as something to be prized and protected or whether they see it as a peril that must be limited. The treatment of religion also depends on whether it is considered an extremely private matter, in which case state interference would be prohibited, or whether religion is considered to be a public matter, in which case close cooperation between state and religious associations would be considered inevitable.

Certain minority or suspect religions may face even higher barriers from state actors. This problem arises in cases of the recognition and registration of non-traditional organizations, or, so-called innovative religious movements, which, for some reason, may be considered "undesirable" associations by the state or citizenry.[49]

Such special prohibitions on registration or recognition appear in other countries in regards to "unknown" and non-traditional religious associations. In order to comply with the registration legislation of Russia, the organization wishing to obtain registration must submit documentation confirming that it has been functioning for at least fifteen years in Russia.[50] Similarly, in Lithuania, an organization seeking status as a "traditional religion" must wait for a period of twenty-five years or longer.[51]

C. Substantive Review of Doctrinal Belief

At its most general level, impermissible substantive review can occur at the level of definition itself. There is always an element of subjectivity in discretionary processes, but the lack of consensus and predictability is especially obvious where there is no formal legal definition of religion and religious associations. "The French legal system has furnished no definition of a religion. . . . In practice it is the judge . . . which decides, case by case and avoiding giving a general definition which could be prayed in

[47] Torfs, "State and Church in Belgium," 35.

[48] Vitalino Canas, "State and Church in Portugal," in Robbers, *State and Church in the European Union,* 264. Further progress has no doubt been made in the new law on religious associations adopted in Portugal in June 2001. See the chapter written by Sousa e Brito in this volume.

[49] In many countries there is a mutual problem of registration or legal recognition for Jehovah's Witnesses, the Church of Scientology, and the Unification Church. The *Manoussakis* case is a good example of this type of obstacle. See also Kokkinakis v. Greece, 17 EHRR 397 (1994) (ECtHR 260-A, 25 May 1993).

[50] Federal'nyi Zakon O svobode sovesti i religioznykh ob'edineniyakh [Russian Federation Law on Freedom of Conscience and On Religious Associations] (1997), art. 11, para. 5, Sobranie zakonodatel'stva Rossiiskoi Federatsii, 1997, no. 39.

[51] Andrei O. Protopopov, "Zakon Litovskoy Respubliki 'O religioznykh obshchinakh i coobshchestvakh' [Law of Lithuanian Republic "On Religious Communities and Associations"], 1995," *Religiya i Zakon* [Religion and Law] (Moscow: Institute of Religion and Law, 1996), 54.

aid in other cases."[52] In the Netherlands, "[n]either the Civil Code nor any other piece of legislation provides a definition of a 'church.' . . . In concrete cases, the administration may have to decide on this issue, and, in case of conflict, the court may have to do so."[53] In Spain, "[t]he Organic Law of Religious Freedom does not provide a legal definition of what can be considered a church or denomination. Furthermore, the concept of 'religious purposes' is confusing because the law provides no legal definition."[54] American scholars Michael Ariens and Robert Destro note that even in the United States, "[d]espite half a century of intensive Supreme Court interpretation of the language of the First Amendment, the Court has not offered a constitutional definition of religion."[55]

Such vagueness often leads state actors to use their discretion in deciding whether this or that association has a religious basis during the process of registering religious associations. Professor Alberto de la Hera, Director of the Department of Religious Affairs in the Spanish Ministry of Justice, describing certain matters of inscription when registering religious organizations, explained that, "[a]s for whether the self-denominated groups actually have a religious basis or nature, the decision of the State in favor of or against the inscription in this case is discretionary; that is to say, it is the result of discretionary consideration by the State of a debatable reality."[56]

While definitional problems can be difficult, every effort should be made to insure that they are not invoked in ways that are discriminatory. As the UN Human Rights Committee has noted in its official interpretation of article 18 of the International Covenant on Civil and Political Rights,

> The terms belief and religion are to be broadly construed. Article 18 is not limited in its application to traditional religions or to religions and beliefs with institutional characteristics or practices analogous to those of traditional religions. The Committee therefore views with concern any tendency to discriminate against any religion or belief for any reasons, including the fact that they are newly established, or represent religious minorities that may be the subject of hostility by a predominant religious community.[57]

In some countries that do not directly prohibit the registration or recognition of religious associations, the granting of judicial recognition is indirectly restricted through the discretionary process of closely examining specific theology or religious doctrines.

---

[52] Brigitte Basdevant-Gaudemet, "State and Church in France," in Robbers, *State and Church in the European Union,* 123.

[53] Sophie C. van Bijsterveld, "State and Church in Netherlands," in Robbers, *State and Church in the European Union,* 217.

[54] Rosa María Martínez de Codes, "The Contemporary Form of Registering Religious Entities in Spain," *Brigham Young University Law Review* (1998): 379.

[55] Ariens and Destro, *Religious Liberty in a Pluralistic Society,* 947.

[56] Alberto de la Hera, "Relations with Religious Minorities: The Spanish Model," *Brigham Young University Law Review* (1998): 390. However, see Constitutional Tribunal of Spain, decision number 46/2001 of 15 February 2001, overruling the government's administrative decision to deny the Unification Church recognition in the official Register of Religious Entities and holding that the administrative body "should not arrogate to itself the function of judging the religious component of entities seeking recognition in the Register" (para. 10).

[57] Human Rights Committee General Comment 22 (48) on article 18, UN Doc. CCPR/C/21/Rev.1/Add.4 (1993), reprinted in UN Doc HRI/GEN/1/Rev.1 (1994), 35, para. 2.

Even a large following and a long history of operation in the country or the unquestionably religious nature of the organization will not prevent the state from exercising its discretionary authority in possibly denying registration or recognition. For example, "[t]he Jehovah's Witnesses have been in Austria since the 1920s and are 34,000 members strong. They have been trying for over twenty years to become recognized in Austria. . . . The question of whether or not they should be recognized bounced between the government and the Austrian courts for some years."[58] Austria only recently resolved the question when the Jehovah's Witnesses were finally refused recognition. According to the Austrian Minister of Education, this was due to their intolerant attitude towards government, their non-participation in blood transfusions (especially for children) and the fact that the church would be led from Brooklyn, New York.[59]

The laws of some countries require an investigation to determine whether a given organization is religious or not. As a result of such a requirement in Kazakhstan, the Church of the Last Testament was refused registration on the grounds that it was a philosophical rather than a religious trend. At the same time, however, the Church of the Last Testament was registered in Russia.

Because organizational patterns and practices are sometimes matters of belief, government review of religious belief also can occur when the state dictates organizational practices that a church must follow. Often this type of state intervention is unintentional. As Cole Durham observed,

> Laws designed with particular models of ecclesiastical polity in mind may force other religious organizations into Procrustean beds. In part this is a problem that what works for one faith community (e.g., a denomination with a hierarchial structure) does not work for another denomination (one with a congregational, or connectional, or representational structure). But it is also a problem of the complexity of religious organizations. Laws written with a Church in mind do not necessary apply neatly when the organization is a religious order. Wooden interpretations or insensitive rules can complicate the problem.[60]

In some cases, however, government intervention is dramatically more direct. For example, in the *Case of Hasan and Chaush v. Bulgaria*,[61] the Bulgarian government was held to have violated the European Convention's protection of freedom of religion or belief by intervening in the selection of the Chief Mufti of the Bulgarian Muslim community, twice dictating who would serve in that capacity.

International human rights documents place constraints on practices that allow the state to make substantive judgments about religious belief and practice. With reference to the European Convention on Human Rights, the *Manoussakis* decision announced, "The right to freedom of religion as guaranteed under the Convention excludes any discretion on the part of the State to determine whether religious beliefs or the means used to express such beliefs are legitimate."[62] Principle 16.3 of the Vienna

---

[58] Christopher J. Miner, "Losing My Religion: Austria's New Religion Law in Light of International and European Standards of Religious Freedom," *Brigham Young University Law Review* (1998): 614–15.
[59] Ibid., 615.
[60] Durham, "Freedom of Religion or Belief," 52.
[61] Hasan and Chaush v. Bulgaria, App. No. 30985/96 (ECtHR, 26 October 2000).
[62] Manoussakis v. Greece, 23 EHRR 387 (1997) (ECtHR 1996-A, No. 59/1995/565/651, 26 September 1996), para. 47.

Concluding Document provides that participating states will both "favourably consider applications" and that they "will . . . grant upon their request to communities of believers, practicing or prepared to practice their faith within the constitutional framework of their States, recognition of the status provided for them in their respective countries." Principle 16.4 of the Vienna Concluding Document protects the right of religious organizations to make their own decisions about the necessary practices of their faith. States will respect the right of these religious communities to

- establish and maintain freely accessible places of worship or assembly,
- organize themselves according to their own hierarchical and institutional structure,
- select, appoint and replace their personnel in accordance with their respective requirements and standards as well as with any freely accepted arrangement between them and their State,
- solicit and receive voluntary financial and other contributions.

Laws and administrative practices violate these principles when they treat different religions unequally,[63] or allow the state bureaucracy to approve the legitimacy of a particular religious belief, or allow the state to interfere in the structure of a religious community.

D. Impermissible Delegation of Authority

Because most countries are committed to the neutrality of the state, situations in which state authority is delegated to religious leaders are unusual. Nonetheless, such problems do tend to recur, particularly when they take non-obvious forms. A religious association that wishes to perform public worship must sometimes obtain permission from the official or state-recognized church, even when not otherwise required by law. For example, when the Seventh-Day Adventists, a registered and a very popular community in Russia, tried to obtain permission to hold meetings and conferences, the local government official required the Seventh-Day Adventists to first obtain consent from the local Orthodox clergy.[64] When the Jehovah's Witnesses in the *Manoussakis* case made application for a house of prayer permit, the government authorities took account of opinions from the local Orthodox clergy in considering the request.[65]

The *Manoussakis* court rejected this type of entanglement between the state and the official church, commenting that the authorities' actual practices went beyond even the degree of deference that Greek laws gave to the Orthodox Church.[66] Similarly, the United States Supreme Court invalidated a law that gave local churches the power to reject liquor license applications under certain circumstances, saying that even though "[s]ome limited and incidental entanglement between church and state authority is inevitable in a complex modern society," it is best to preserve religion as "a private matter for the individual, the family, and the institutions of private choice . . . for the preservation of civil liberty."[67]

---

[63] See section V(B) in this article.

[64] Lauren B. Homer and Lawrence A. Uzzell. "Federal and Provincial Religious Freedom Laws in Russia: A Struggle for and Against Federalism and the Rule Of Law," *Emory International Law Review* 12 (1998): 291.

[65] Manoussakis v. Greece, para. 51.

[66] Ibid.

[67] Larkin v. Grendel's Den, 459 US 116, 123, 126 (1982).

The hypothetical case in which a cleric may have informal private access to government decision-makers is also problematic. Even when government and religious leaders do not consciously intend to discriminate against minority religious associations, wherever the decision-making process lacks full transparency there may be a suggestion of unfairness.

E. Vague Standards and Unguided Discretion

Several reasons justify discretionary state actions, including the fact that relations within religious spheres cannot be regulated on a precise normative and objective basis. However, Italian professor Silvio Ferrari, while speaking about providing religious associations with ample opportunity to reach agreements with the state for favorable status in financing, religious foundation and pastoral care, mentions that "one of the aspects of Italian ecclesiastical law which attracts criticism concerns the excessive amount of discretion which public powers possess in deciding whether to accept or reject the proposal of a denomination to enter into negotiations on an agreement."[68]

In some cases, laws give so much discretionary power to the state that negotiation is hardly a question. In Russia, laws of different regions "ban religious groups, especially foreign ones, from using public buildings and fora, including schools, theaters, stadiums and radio and television stations—even if the groups have been accredited under local law."[69] Religious associations encounter exceptional hardships in those countries where they are not permitted to own property or are denied the opportunity to hold worship services in their own buildings. State bodies, as a rule, do not permit the heads of religious organizations to unofficially lease such buildings.

In countries where religious associations do not have the right of legal entity, other objects must be registered, which gives the state another opportunity to act on its discretion. Such a practice exists, for example, in Great Britain, where in compliance with the Places of Worship Registration Act of 1855,[70] places of worship can be registered. Although registration is not mandatory, an organization that does obtain registration receives certain advantages such as favorable tax benefits. And even when a religious organization does attempt to obtain this optional registration for tax purposes or otherwise, English officials have denied the requests in a seemingly arbitrary manner. For example, David McClean explained that "[t]he Church of Scientology wished to register a building as a place of worship, but the Court of Appeal held that this involved the assembly of persons to worship God or to do reverence to supreme being or deity; instruction in a secular philosophy was not sufficient. A humanist body, the South Place Ethical Society, was held for similar reasons not to be entitled to charitable status; it did not exist for the advancement of religion. The Mormon Church (the Church of Jesus Christ of Latter-Day Saints) would seem to qualify as a church, but its temple in England, which is only open to Mormons 'in good standing' especially recommended for the purpose, was held not to be a place of *public* religious

---

[68] Ferrari, "State and Church in Italy," in Robbers, *State and Church in the European Union*, 174.

[69] Homer and Uzzell, "Federal and Provincial Religious Freedom Laws in Russia," 268.

[70] *Places of Worship Registration Act*, 1855, 18 and 19 Vict., c. 49.

[71] David McClean, "State and Church in the United Kingdom," in Robbers, *State and Church in the European Union*, 313.

worship for rating (local tax) purposes."[71] While these problems arise in England, it is interesting to note that in many other countries both the Church of Scientology and the Church of Jesus Christ of Latter-day Saints have not faced such restrictions.

The wider the discretionary authority, the more it is possible for those who wield the authority to conceal the true reasons for their decisions. One interesting example is the case of *The Church of the Lukumi Babalu Aye, Inc. v. City of Hialeah*.[72]

In that case, followers of the Afro-Caribbean religion used some elements of animal slaughter and sacrifice. The court invalidated several city ordinances that prohibited ritual slaughter and sacrifice. The court held that despite the efforts of city officials to give plausible non-religious reasons for the ordinances, the laws were in fact aimed against religious ceremonies.[73] The court reached this decision despite extreme public indignation about the church's presence in the community. The court held that public indignation by itself was not sufficient justification to allow the government to prohibit the activity of the religious association.[74]

A most powerful argument against over-broad discretionary power was announced by the European Court of Human Rights in the *Case of Hasan and Chaush v. Bulgaria*.[75] In *Hasan*, the Bulgarian government was found to have improperly influenced the affairs of the Bulgarian Muslim community when the government effectively replaced the Chief Mufti of the Muslims and later reversed itself. The Court held that the government's actions were improper because they were based on impermissibly vague laws. The requirement that government actions must be "prescribed by law" and "in accordance with the law"[76] means that

> [t]he law should be both adequately accessible and foreseeable, that is formulated with sufficient precision to enable the individual—if need be with appropriate advice—to regulate his conduct. . . . For domestic law to meet these requirements it must afford a measure of legal protection against arbitrary interferences by public authorities with the rights safeguarded by the Convention. In matters affecting fundamental rights it would be contrary to the rule of law, one of the basic principles of a democratic society enshrined in the Convention, for a legal discretion granted to the executive to be expressed in terms of an unfettered power. Consequently, the law must indicate with sufficient clarity the scope of any such discretion conferred on the competent authorities and the manner of its exercise.[77]

Hasan represents the first time that the Court has found a violation of the freedom of religion or belief on the basis of the "prescribed by law" requirement of article 9. The Court's clear and forceful articulation of the rule-of-law principle in this case sets a precedent that may become crucial in future cases that turn on the exercise of discretionary powers.

---

[72] 508 US 520 (1993)

[73] Ibid., 547.

[74] The words of the First Amendment to the U.S. Constitution "have given legal protection to a wide range of faiths, even those originating abroad and deeply offensive to a majority of citizens" (Homer and Uzzell, "Federal and Provincial Religious Freedom Laws in Russia," 250).

[75] Hasan and Chaush v. Bulgaria, App. No. 30985/96 (ECtHR, 26 October 2000).

[76] European Convention on Human Rights, arts. 8–11.

[77] Hasan and Chaush v. Bulgaria, para. 84.

VI. Conclusion

In many countries, governments will continue using their discretionary authority to impede religious activities and to approve or disapprove various religions without a principled basis. Problems of discretionary state administration will no doubt exist for a long time in the practice of church-state relations. However, the existing international instruments on human rights and a growing body of international case law—and domestic case law, in many countries—emphasize the essential principles by which the law will protect the freedom of religion or belief from abusive discretionary decisions. In particular, the increasingly well-defined requirements that discretionary decisions must follow the rule of law provide strong prospects for norms that secure religious freedom in all countries.

Chapter 18

The Place of Religion in Public Life: The Lay Approach

Jean Baubérot

Laicism[1] signifies the absence of any official religion in a country, but also the absence of any official state atheism. If Scandinavian countries such as Denmark and Norway are not lay because they have a national religion, neither is the former Soviet Union because it favored atheism and, indeed, promoted religious persecution during certain periods of its history. What, therefore, is the place laicism grants to religion in the public sphere? Does religion share full rights of freedom of worship and expression, or does it face substantial limits? This chapter attempts to answer these questions, not in an abstract way but by taking the example of France, which is a typical lay country. As a first step, some of the historical traits of French laicism are indicated, for the present situation is not understandable once severed from its historical roots. Next, this chapter considers the present situation of religion in French lay society and the recent transformations that present new kinds of problems for laicism. In conclusion, some remarks of a more general nature are made.

I. The Historical Construction of Laicism

It is first necessary to analyze from a historical perspective one structural difference between France and countries of Protestant culture. Indeed, it is impossible to understand French laicism without taking into account one fundamental factor: in countries of Protestant culture—whether the United States or Northern European countries—religion has been integral to the emergence of modernity, whereas in France modernity erected itself against religion. To be sure, such a schematic view calls for nuance. Not all of the religious community has been active in the process of modernization

---

[1] Laicism is the English term used in this chapter to translate *laïcité*, the established French term that describes the French church-state system. *Laïcité* connotes a strong separation of church and state that has evolved over the past two centuries since the French Revolution. At its core, it represents a commitment that the state will be secular; that is, it will be "lay" rather than confessional, while still respecting freedom of religion or belief.

Tore Lindholm, W. Cole Durham, Jr., Bahia G. Tahzib-Lie (eds.), Facilitating Freedom of Religion or Belief: A Deskbook, *441–453.*

but rather certain religious reform movements: Puritanism in Anglo-Saxon countries, Pietism in Germanic and related countries. Yet it is not by chance that Puritanism and Pietism have been favorable toward education and have, for a long time, entertained positive relations with science (as the sociologist Robert K. Merton has shown).[2] A similar situation could have developed in France, as Jansenism and the Jesuit community represented paths to modernity. But starting in the seventeenth century and especially the eighteenth century, Jansenism found itself condemned by the Pope and suppressed by the French court. As for the Jesuits, they were expelled from France in 1762.[3] Things did not stop there: through the Enlightenment and the Revolution, French modernity developed in basic conflict with the Catholic Church.

Where as the British or German Enlightenment merely sought an "enlightened religion," the French Enlightenment proved more radical. Voltaire viciously attacked the Catholic Church ("Let us crush the vile one," he writes[4]). In 1762, Rousseau extolled a "civil religion," the dogmas of which "correspond to morality and to the duties that he who professes this religion must fulfill for others."[5] In addition to "positive dogmas" such as the existence of God, the immortality of the soul, the election of the righteous, and the punishment of the wicked, the French Enlightenment also embraced a "negative dogma," namely, the rejection of intolerance of the sort attributed to Catholicism following the revocation of the Edict of Nantes (1685), and which led to the persecution of Protestants. But was it possible to be tolerant without abiding the sole authorized Church whose influence so powerfully inflected daily life and ways of thinking? The French Revolution inherited this problem, one which it would not know how to resolve.

This explains the conceptual difference, in the area of basic rights, between the United States and France—the two nations in which declarations of rights were drawn up at the end of the eighteenth century. According to the American Declaration of Independence (1776), "[w]e hold these truths to be self-evident, that all men are created equal, that they are endowed by their Creator with certain inalienable Rights. . . ." God is thus the author of these rights. Unlike the American document, the French Declaration of the Rights of Man and Citizen written in 1789 proclaims "natural, inalienable and sacred rights." God is not the author of these rights, even when one cannot do without him; when the Assembly "sets forth" the rights of man "in the presence and under the auspices of the Supreme Being," God is a sort of honored but passive figure presiding over its work.[6]

What explains this difference? In the United States, the pluralism of Protestant denominations allowed for the invocation of a God for whom no Church is the guardian or exclusive interpreter of rights. It would be different in France where the Catholic Church—considered "intolerant" by many members of the Constituent Assembly (1789–1791)—would become the mediator of the rights of man.

Several events combined to make a rupture with the past: the Pope's condemnation of the Declaration of the Rights of Man and Citizen; the division of the Catholic Church in France into two parts—the "Civil Constitution of the Clergy" and the "refractory

---

[2] Robert King Merton, *Social Theory and Social Structure* (Glencoe, Ill.: The Free Press, 1957).

[3] Analogous measures were taken during the same period in other countries.

[4] Jacques Le Goff and René Rémond, eds., *Histoire de la France religieuse, tome 3: Du Roi très chrétien à la laïcité républicaine, XVIIIe - XIXe siècle* (Paris: Seuil, 2001), 150.

[5] Jean-Jacques Rousseau, *Du contrat social,* ed. B. de Jouvenel (Geneva: C. Bourquin, 1947), 369.

clergy" (the latter being the only legitimate one in the eyes of Rome); the emergence in 1793 of "revolutionary cults" (Cult of the Goddess Reason, of the Goddess Liberty, etc.); and the sacralization of the Revolution by itself. However short its duration in historical time, this rupture left a deep impression upon modern France, the symbolic foundations of which were situated outside of the existing religions.

From the start of the nineteenth century, under Napoleon Bonaparte, civil law no longer depended on religious dictates. New institutions, such as the school and medicine, were structured outside the constraints of religion. These institutions would produce new cultural perceptions independent of religion (for example, death perceived as the end of one's life and not as the passage into an afterlife), as they would also produce a new secular clergy (professionals such as teachers and physicians) entrusted with training the population and formulating meaningful social practices. This represents the first threshold of laicization.[7]

Certainly, the development of medicine, for example, was common to different countries of this period. Yet, as Claude Nicolet remarks, if in principle nothing apparently distinguishes most Western countries from one another in their recourse to medicine during the nineteenth century, "only in France would [medical science] become so clearly a moral obligation."[8] The reason for this is simple: the entire nineteenth century was witness to the "conflict of the two Frances." The conflict had nothing to do with "believers" and "nonbelievers" but with the opposition between two visions of France. Some wanted Catholicism to be the "soul" of France, the heart of its national identity; others insisted that modern France had to establish itself only upon the "principles of 1789" ("our Gospel," Jules Ferry would say[9]), to which religions would have to submit themselves. The clerical and anticlerical visions entailed competing conceptions of citizenship. The clerical view conceived of the individual as trained by secondary groups—principally by the Catholic Church. The anticlerical view privileged the face-to-face encounter of the individual with the State (and sometimes, in reality, the State with the individual). Despite periods of calm, this conflict resurfaced periodically and was a major factor in the instability of political regimes in nineteenth-century France. Indeed, these antagonistic visions were tied to political projects at war with each other and which triumphed in alternating fashion. In addition, each camp developed its own moral conceptions, and the physician emerged as the model of the devout scientist, the symbol of moral guidance that was effective because it was founded upon science.

Following the French defeat by Prussia in 1871, partisans of "Catholic France" attempted to restore the monarchy. Their failure, beginning near the end of the 1870s, left Republicans in power. But from the outset this power was problematic, and in order to govern with any degree of durability Republicans were forced to reduce the social influence of the Catholic Church, whose militant leaders and hardline wing were opposed to the Republic.

---

[6] On this problem, see Gilman Marston Ostrander, *The Rights of Man in America, 1606–1861,* 2d. ed. (Columbia, Mo.: University of Missouri Press, 1969); and Antoine de Baecque, Wolfgang Schmale, and Michel Vovelle, *L'an I des droits de l'homme* (Paris: Presse du CNRS, 1988).

[7] Jean Baubérot, "Two Thresholds of Laicization," in *Secularism and Its Critics,* ed. Rajeev Bhargava (New Delhi: Oxford University Press, 1999), 94–136; Baubérot, *Vers un nouveau pacte laïque?* (Paris: Seuil, 1990), 33–48.

[8] Claude Nicolet, *L'idée républicaine en France* (Paris: Gallimard, 1982), 310.

[9] J. M. Gaillard, *Jules Ferry* (Paris: Fayard, 1989), 437.

The erosion of the Church's influence occurred in two phases: the creation of the lay school (1880s); and the separation of church and state (1905). These developments mark the second threshold of laicization.[10]

The autonomy of schools in relation to religion had already been secured for high schools and universities but not for elementary schools. On the contrary, in the second half of the nineteenth century, religious congregations had acquired a significant influence, and ecclesiastical authorities supervised elementary teachers. But starting in the 1880s, supervision was abolished, public elementary teachers would gradually have to become lay, and courses in religious and moral instruction were replaced with a course in lay morality. Lay morality borrowed its elements from various traditions: antiquity, French moralists, the Enlightenment, Kantianism, positivism, diverse forms of Christianity, and Confucius. Lay morality revisited these various borrowings from the standpoint of two notions tied to the Republic: dignity and solidarity.[11] Thus, as an element of social relations, morality was considered a-religious, because it was neither founded upon religion nor was it hostile toward religion.

The separation of church and state occurred, in 1905, after renewed conflict motivated by the Dreyfus affair.[12] Once again, Republicans believed that the Republic was endangered by militant Catholicism.[13] The initial projects for separation placed numerous obstacles before freedom of religion;[14] the Catholic Church was the primary target, but in an effort to draft a law of more general value, Republicans also attacked the freedoms of Protestantism and Judaism. However, electoral realities, conjoined to Republicans' desire not to step outside of the frame of liberal democracy, led to an agreement that reversed course. This agreement promoted a law that was, according to cabinet minister Aristide Briand, "frank, loyal and honest" and capable of "ensuring the pacification of minds" because churches would not find "any serious reason to frown upon the new order" and would themselves sense "the possibility of living within this order."[15]

As a result, the 1905 law establishing separation of church and state appears liberal—as will become apparent in the second part of my argument—and a Catholic intellectual who initially opposed the separation willingly recognized the fact that "the law impedes us neither from believing what we wish, nor from practicing what we believe."[16] Nevertheless, the Pope rejected the law and ordered French Catholics not conform to its tenets. Would the conflict again resurface? Republicans continued their conciliatory politics by adopting two new laws in 1907 and 1908 that permitted Catholic clergy to inhabit churches as "occupants without legal title."[17] According to Briand, these laws were intended "to make it

[10] Baubérot, "Two Thresholds," 197; Baubérot, *Histoire de la laïcité française* (Paris: PUF, 2000), 93.

[11] Baubérot, *La morale laïque contre l'ordre moral* (Paris: Seuil, 1997), 117–278.

[12] Maurice Larkin, *Church and State after the Dreyfus Affair: The Separation Issue in France* (London: Macmillan, 1974), 102–206.

[13] Maurice Larkin, *Religion, Politics, and Preferment in France since 1890: La Belle Epoque and Its Legacy* (Cambridge: Cambridge University Press, 1995), 5–58.

[14] Concerning these projects and their refutation, see Baubérot, *Pacte laïque,* 49–80.

[15] Jean-Marie Mayeur, *La séparation des Eglises et de l'Etat* (Paris: Editions Ouvrières, 1991), 65a.

[16] Mayeur, "Les catholiques libéraux devant la loi de séperation," in *Religion et politique. Les deux guerres mondiales. Histoire de Lyon et du Sud-Est. Mélanges offerts à M. le doyen André Latreille* (Lyon: Audin, 1972), 207–24.

[17] Law of 2 January 1907 *concernant l'exercice public des cultes* C. ADM., Dalloz (1998) 542.

impossible for the Catholic Church, even when it might tenaciously desire so, to evade the law."[18] This is what we shall call a policy of the "lay pact,"[19] which allowed for an arrangement with the Papacy in 1923–24.

This appeasement led to the "lay" character of the French Republic being officially inscribed in the Constitutions of the Fourth (1946) and Fifth Republics (1958). Still, one conflict continued, revolving around the practical exercise of freedom of education. Laicist militants proclaimed, "Public funds for public schools. Private funds for private schools." But starting in the 1950s, and especially after the Debré law of 1959,[20] private schools with at least ninety-percent Catholic enrollment have received public funding, and this question contributes to the persistence of political stakes in religious problems. (It provoked a million Catholic sympathizers to demonstrate in 1984, and a million lay supporters to do the same in 1994.) If laicism ended the "conflict of the two Frances," as it had existed from the Revolution through the twentieth century, it has not entirely appeased the tensions over religion in France. Thus, since the end of the 1980s, other problems have emerged, notably those having to do with Islam and groups classified as "sects."

II. Laicism and the Public Sphere Today

Religion's current legal situation arises from the 1905 law of separation[21] and other laws that continue to build upon it, and from judicial decisions coming in their wake. The principal measures in the 1905 law include the following: "The Republic ensures the freedom of conscience. It guarantees the freedom of worship" (article 1). "[The Republic] neither recognizes, employs, nor subsidizes any religion," excepting those expenditures relative to chaplaincy (in hospitals, prisons, the army and the lycée[22]) (article 2). The absence of state atheism and of any official religion or any "recognized forms of religion" characterize the fundamental principles of these two articles. "Churches" (a generic term that in this sense signifies religious organizations) are no longer a matter for public law (***droit public***)—they may constitute themselves as official entities under the rule of private law (***droit privé***) (article 20). Churches must be self-sustaining financially,[23] but the vast rental stock of worship sites belonging to the state, to departments, and to communes[24] is placed at their disposal free of charge. This sort of initial subsidy is followed up by the possibility of using public funds for the maintenance of buildings (articles 12 and 13, completed by article 5 of the statute of April 13, 1908). At the time, one

---

[18] Mayeur, *La séparation des Eglises et de l'Etat,* 175.

[19] Baubérot, *Laïcité française,* 85–92.

[20] Law No. 59-1557 of 31 December 1959 *sur les rapports entre l'Etat et les établissements d'enseignement privés,* C. ADM., Dalloz (1998) 685.

[21] Law of 9 December 1905 *concernant la separation des Eglises et de l'Etat,* C. ADM., Dalloz (1998) 536.

[22] In order to guarantee the "free exercise of religion," there can be a quasi-official religious presence in public life. Today in France, this is particularly true where military chaplains have an official status in the army.

[23] Since 1987 it has been possible to deduct, within certain limits of its taxable revenue, gifts to churches. This constitutes a type of indirect subsidy.

[24] Departments and communes are units of administrative division in France. There are six levels of French administrative division, with units at each level normally divided into several units of the next lower level. The ninety-six departments comprise the third level, below the Republic and the regions. The more than 36,000 communes, including cities and towns, comprise the sixth level.

crucial element of the law heightened the conflict between lay camps but allowed Catholics, on the other side, to conceive of the 1905 separation as "sincerely liberal": property rightfully transferred by the State to churches for their use is guaranteed against schisms and internal divisions of the organization. In fact, in order to have at one's disposal "public worship establishments," it is necessary "to conform to the general regulations of worship the practice of which a religion proposes to follow" (article 4).[25] This means, for example, that Catholic parishes will have to respect the legal authority of their bishops, and that if the majority of adherents in a parish decide to do otherwise and attempt to question the hierarchical structure of its church, judicial recourse allows for granting the free use of the property to the minority which has remained loyal to the episcopate. During the interwar period, notably, judicial decisions upheld this clause. Today the clause is not always applied. The traditionalists who took control of the Church of Saint-Nicolas du Chardonnet in Paris answered no longer to the Bishop of Paris but had their own hierarchy, yet it appeared impossible to evict them by force. It seems rather logical that once a "fundamentalist" group of Catholics has assembled a sufficient number of adherents, it may occupy a church in order to hold religious observances according to its own dictates (e.g., mass according to the rites of Saint Pius V, etc.). This is so even when in their sermonizing these very fundamentalists contest certain laws (against, for example, the law concerning abortion or the possibility of a PACS union[26] for homosexual couples).[27] Nonetheless, the provisions of the 1905 law remain generally valid: a mayor may legally refuse the occupancy of a house of worship to a religious group that has not obtained the consent of its ecclesiastic authority. In case of conflict between several priests, pastors or rabbis over the use of a building, it is the authority appointed by the bishop, the synod or the consistory who resolves the situation.

Freedom of speech is guaranteed within houses of worship, though the law prohibits political organizing (concerts, variety shows, and lectures are authorized) and protects public servants from defamation (article 34). This provision is part of the limits placed on free expression within a democratic society. It is possible to say that the French Republic puts, free of charge, a vast public stock of real estate at the disposal of churches for their worship practices, not only in terms of practicing their rites but also conveying their message. This point must not be forgotten, for the social and ethical, and, indirectly, the political aspects of exhortations addressed to believers, are not without influence

---

[25] The formulation of article 4 of the 1905 law derives from legislation of the United States and from British legislation affecting the Free Church of Scotland. This produces an interesting paradox: French laicism in this case was able to establish itself in a relatively placatory manner by borrowing from Anglo-Saxon law.

[26] In 1999 the French Parliament passed a law creating formal recognition for gay partnerships. Known by its French acronym PACS (*pacte civil de solidarité*), the law does not provide all the benefits of marriage, but does allow registered couples, after a three-year waiting period, to file joint tax returns and to receive various government financial benefits (Law No. 99-944, 15 November 1999, J.O. 16.11.1999, S. 16959).

[27] "Direct provocation to resist the execution of laws" is forbidden (article 36), which is nothing out of the ordinary in democratic society. For example, it is possible to say in a sermon that abortion is an "abomination" and that those who take part in it "are excluded from salvation" and even that "the law should be changed." However, the sermon cannot incite to aggression against those caretakers who perform abortions, nor can it incite to cause damage to clinics or hospitals. Of course, in reality, the limits can be difficult to determine, but the law defines it as "direct provocation." All things considered, for religion, as for any belief, legal prosecution for beliefs is a borderline case. See P. Rolland, "Du délit d'opinion dans la démocratie française," in *Pouvoir et liberté: Études offertes à Jacques Mourgeon,* (Brussels: Bruylant, 1998), 645–70.

upon the public life of a nation and the place of religion in that nation. In this sense, a church established like the Church of England, which must maintain most of the buildings of worship in use on its own, is in fact in a less favorable financial situation than churches in France—at least those churches possessing buildings in 1905.[28]

What, then, is the situation of churches' activities outside of houses of worship? For "ceremonies, processions, and other exterior demonstrations of a religious group," the law of separation refers to general regulations governing communes (article 27). These regulations guarantee a rather large freedom to demonstrate on condition of following certain security regulations and not disrupting the public peace. Some mayors have used these same regulations as an excuse for imposing certain limits on funeral processions (such as the maximum number of choir children, the place of the clergy, the type of vehicle used), but those instances have been judged illegal; and if processions are less ostentatious today than in the past, it is because of a strong evolution in the role of death in modern societies and from changes internal to religions.

The same situation obtains in processions or marches on public byways by ministers and their faithful carrying religious emblems or symbols and praying or chanting openly. Before 1905, Catholic processions were forbidden by law from passing through quarters with significant populations of Protestants or Jews. This prohibition was eliminated in 1905 as some mayors made attempts to construe these processions, particularly in the case of large processions, as a disruption of the peace. The Council of State struck down these municipal decrees forbidding processions, and, as for other demonstrations on public byways, it became necessary to prove the real risk of trouble to the public peace in order to take repressive measures against them. Again, Catholic processions today are smaller and less ostentatious than in the past, though in the last few years a traditionalist current has revived ceremonies of this type.

The holding of collective assemblies raises another issue where the separation of church and state has increased the freedom of churches. Prior to the separation, bishops' assemblies were subject to governmental authorization which, between 1802 and 1905, never was granted. It was the same for Protestant synods—only a single assembly was permitted, in 1872, which amounted to a challenging handicap for this religion so dependent upon collective decision making. The law of separation changed this situation; after May 1906, for example, a group of bishops was able to assemble. Nevertheless, bishops have at times been very critical of the law. Thus, in 1925, they declared that the "so-called lay laws . . . are not laws" for they are "ungodly and unjust."[29] An attack of this kind would have been suppressed prior to 1905, according to what was called the "procedure for abuses." In time, declarations by bishops or other ecclesiastical authorities have become quite common. They often provoke debates within civil society, where, once again, we are within the normal exercise of democracy.

One question still remains: does public opinion in France consider declarations by religious authorities legitimate? In order to answer this question, we may turn to a study of European values completed in 1990.[30] Respondents were asked whether they looked

---

[28] This situation punishes Islam in particular. Nonetheless, several means are currently available for using public funds in the construction of mosques.

[29] It was only in 1945 that the bishops' assembly affirmed that laicism, as a "sovereign autonomy of the State," appeared acceptable.

[30] H. Riffaut, *Les valeurs des français* (Paris: PUF, 1994).

favorably upon stands taken by churches on various societal issues. In France, those answers indicated the following: the majority was favorable to stands taken vis-à-vis problems of the Third-World (70%) and racism (55%). If we take into account unanswered questions, half of the respondents were also favorable to stands taken regarding disarmament (48%) and euthanasia (47%). In a pattern of decreasing acceptance, other subjects included the environment (38%), unemployment (36%), abortion (35%), extramarital relations (34%), and homosexuality (26%). Finally, only a small minority (15%) declared themselves favorable to stands taken regarding government policy.

These findings are most instructive. The study showed that in all of these countries, the Third World and racism or disarmament headed the list of concerns. On the other hand, it also showed that in every country, church positions on government policy received the fewest positive responses. Although the French did not respond with any structural difference from the rest of the Europeans in the study, their responses were less positive than in most of the other countries. In comparison, 74% of the British responded positively to the Third World question (differential of 4% compared to France), 55% to disarmament (differential of 7%), 48% to extramarital relations (differential of 14%), and 34% to a stand taken vis-à-vis government policy (differential of 19%). It is interesting to note that, in general, when the number of French positive responses decreases, the gap between the two countries widens.[31] The explanation for this is that Third World aid is an ethical question without a political stake in the sense that, inasmuch as it does touch on politics, it is not subject to polemics and opposition between the left and the right. Neither side would officially declare itself against Third World aid, even though neither acts in more than in a limited fashion to support it. Public opinion does not consider it wrong for churches to make certain demands of justice, and churches are in their right to do so. But the more the items of the poll touch on political debate, the more French public opinion becomes reticent to concede that right, and it becomes frankly hostile to church stands if the item involves churches' having direct influence on the political debate. On the other hand, in Great Britain, where there are two established churches—the Church of England and the Scottish Presbyterian Church—and where Anglican Bishops are members of the House of Lords, reservations about these same items are less pronounced. On questions concerning sexuality, the French are also clearly more suspicious of church stands than the British, though the positions of the dominant churches are different in both countries. We should keep in mind that the Church of England has allowed for contraception since 1930, while the Catholic Church continues to prohibit its use, at least officially.[32]

To conclude this point, it seems undeniable that French lay culture contributes to making public opinion less favorable than in other European countries toward churches' taking stands on issues. But it could also be said that laicism took root in France, culturally

[31] The differentials set up as follows: Third World: 4%; racism: 10%; disarmament: 7%; euthanasia: 10%; environment: 22%; unemployment: 9%; abortion: 18%; extra-marital relations: 14%; homosexuality: 17%; government policy: 19%. The only real counterexample is the environment. Among the possible explanations for this are a belated awareness on the part of the French concerning the importance of this problem and a stronger politicization of this problem in France (where there is a notable ecological political party) than in Britain.

[32] It is not easy to determine to what extent this study's findings are intricately tied to whether the dominant church is Catholic or Protestant. The relationship to Catholicism is very different depending on the country; thus, for a majority of the items, it is two Catholic countries (Ireland and Belgium) whose responses are both the least and most favorable.

speaking, because many French had begun to distance themselves from the dominant church. Thus, just to consider the example of birth control, population growth slowed in France at the end of the eighteenth century, and it continued to decrease throughout the nineteenth. The fact that this demographic change was more extreme in France than elsewhere—the difference compared to Great Britain in particular is striking[33]—evidences a refusal, from this period on, to obey certain religious proscriptions. But this did not mean that people refused the benefits of official assistance to religion. Moreover, since the end of the seventeenth century, the British political scene has been stable, and, at least on that count, religion is not in any danger in Britain. This is not the case in France, where the potent nineteenth-century conjunction between the problem of the political regime and the "religious question" remains in the country's symbolic memory through the present.

We must point out that because of the historical conflict between religious institutions and political forces, the place of religion in public life is linked to the activity of associations.[34] There exist not only youth movements, but associations with widely varying goals, including socioprofessional, ethical, social, charitable, or other commitments and interests. Associations of a confessional type (or, at present, interconfessional ones such as Christian Action for the Abolition of Torture) serve as cultural mediators between religions and lay and secularized society. They represent, in fact, a cultural space where religion may acclimate itself to lay thought and secularization through the power of lay people (in the sense of nonclergy) within their own intimate physical space. But these associations are also a privileged space in which religions participate in the social debate and social action. They have a triple role: of socialization (at a time when the social role of institutions is declining); of experimentation (with values, with social conduct, with new modes of action, and of the ties among these three); and of decisional influence (at a time of crisis in representative democracy's search for new, more direct forms of democracy).

The last quarter of the twentieth century has witnessed profound socioreligious changes in France, and French lay culture has not always known how to deal with these changes. However, the situation is not necessarily so difficult. In the case of Buddhism, for example, we are witnessing the slow integration of an imported religion into the religious and cultural landscape of the country. The creation of the television program "Buddhist Voices" in the context of religious programming televised on a public station—programming beneficial also to Catholicism, Protestantism, Orthodox Christianity, Judaism, and Islam—is a powerful sign of this integration.[35]

In France, Buddhism counts some 600,000 followers; half of these have French citizenship, and close to a quarter of them are of French origin. The attraction of this religion goes far beyond its number of converts. According to a survey by CSA, a French opinion polling firm, 46% of young French people feel that Buddhism fosters

---

[33] In Britain, the decrease came about only progressively, and especially near the end of the nineteenth century. This points to a dissonance between people's contraceptive practices and the dominant church's stance on contraception, a stance that is strong in the French church but weaker in the English church.

[34] We could also say, sociologically speaking, that in a lay framework religion can function within the system as an institution, but it must assume socially a form analogous to the association.

[35] Public radio also transmits religious programming (intended also for the family of a-religious humanist thought).

personal fulfillment (29% say the same for Christianity) and is the most tolerant religion, not to mention the best adapted to modern life.[36] On another level, reincarnation represents a growing belief among Europeans (24% of French surveyed affirmed this according to a 1990 European study[37]); in a Western reinterpretation of Buddhist traditions, reincarnation is essentially viewed as offering a second chance for fulfillment to everyone.

Several levels of attachment to Buddhism exist in France. For some, this consists of little more than a vague sympathy. Others—in particular, social workers, doctors and paramedical workers—are participating in special training sessions. This sector of professional people who are faced with pain and suffering wonder whether the Buddhist emphasis on compassion could not contribute to improving their labors. Some go yet further by integrating elements of Buddhism into a personal religious identity which fuses different traditions. Finally, others want to become true Buddhists. In sum, Buddhism exemplifies the case of a religion recently imported into France, one capable of a certain degree of expression in the public sphere.

The situation of Islam is rather more complex. Approximately half of the more than three million Muslims in France have French citizenship, while two to four percent are of French extraction. Islam has long been a presence in France—the Mosque of Paris was built in the 1920s and was financed in part by public funds. But since 1975 an "Islam of families" is clearly claiming its place in the polis, having taken the place of an "Islam of celibate men" constituted by immigrant workers who would often return to their native countries. This legitimate claim to a place in the public arena has met with three obstacles: first, the after-effects of decolonization, particularly arising from the Algerian war; next, the social and economic crisis that, precisely at the same moment (and in conjunction with the Algerian crisis), struck immigrant and notably Muslim populations with full force; lastly, in the aftermath of the Iranian revolution, the rise of Islamism, amplified by the media, that gave a negative image of Islam.[38]

Thus, the Ayatollah Khomeyni's fatwa against the author of *The Satanic Verses*, Salman Rushdie, preceded what has been called "the veil affair." To summarize the facts: in the autumn of 1989 a school disciplinary problem attracted national attention. It centered on Muslim female junior high and high school students wearing the Islamic veil to cover their hair. In spite of a code that forbids wearing veils in the classroom, these young girls refused to remove them. In the face of such a refusal, is it necessary to exclude them from their school establishment?

A national debate ensued which lasted several years (more or less until 1994), because once it had been removed in one place, the Islamic veil appeared elsewhere. Is it necessary to forbid or to tolerate wearing the veil in school? The debate proved most disruptive along the usual fault lines. Partisans on both sides took their positions, on the left as on the right, including Christian and Jewish "faithful" as well as "agnostics" and "atheists." What is more, each claimed to be on the side of laicism.

From a judicial standpoint, the affair was decided by the Council of State,[39] which favored a case-by-case judgment. The Council of State determined that, in general, wearing religious insignia at school is not incompatible with laicism, although

[36] *La Vie,* 27 March 1997, 3.

[37] Riffaut, *Valeurs,* 316.

[38] Gilles Keppel, *Les banlieues de l'Islam* (Paris: Seuil, 1987), 225–312.

it may be so when it is ostentatious, or if it becomes a means of proselyting or a cause of disruption in the school, such as an excuse for not attending certain classes (for example, a biology class discussing the study of human anatomy or sexuality). This decision has afforded the possibility of dealing with specific situations, but by not giving a fixed rule, the Council of State has also allowed for a real battle of interpretations: for some teachers, merely wearing the veil appears, in and of itself, to be an "ostentatious" act which undermines the decisions of the Council of State.

Why does such an attitude arise? It may be that for certain lay-minded people, an ideological laicism exists alongside a more liberal judicial laicism concerned with respecting freedom of conscience. To be sure, this ideological laicism would also claim to respect freedom of conscience but would give it a narrower interpretation. Thus, in a school setting, "freedom of conscience" may lead to policies requiring strict neutrality toward religion but at the same time encouraging students to develop freedom of thought, meaning critical thinking in the face of any dogmatic system. This narrower view of freedom of conscience can imply a desire to resist special interest groups, and in fact Muslim, not to mention Islamist interest groups, have become vocal in certain places. At the same time there is a reaction, often tense, in the face of the evolution of schools. Schools have been the flagship lay institution and they have been undergoing a process of de-institutionalization. This process has resulted in the loss of social standing for teachers, the instrumentalization of the schools by parents and students, and calls for schools to democratize internally. This is how the "rights of students" were recognized only a matter of months prior to the beginning of the "veil affair." Thus, it was in context a general uneasiness about the place of schools in society that so intensified the debate surrounding this affair.

In parallel fashion, the construction of certain mosques has met with difficulties of two sorts. First, public opinion has been quite cool concerning the visibility of buildings proposed for construction, showing to what extent the public is not yet acclimated to religious pluralism. The public has been historically conscious of the political-religious conflict between a certain strain of Catholicism and modern ideas, and it has shown itself to be very sensitive to anything that might revive this opposition. Second, in the absence of an organized clergy or of a general organization of Islam in France, the construction of mosques has become an important cause within Islam, particularly for the various native countries of the majority of French Muslims (Morocco, Algeria, etc.) and for other countries such as Saudi Arabia. This has led the French government to intervene in order to initiate the self-organization of Islam in France. This intervention could have appeared antithetical to the separation of church and state, but it is no doubt guided by the circumstances. In time, elections will have to take place in order to establish Muslim spokespersons within the public sphere.

The tension is even higher regarding groups classified as "sects" and widely perceived—notably by the media—as a threat. They are attacked for issues of a financial nature (the Church of Scientology is often considered as having practices bordering on fraudulence) or a sexual nature (it is said that leaders qualified as "gurus" sometimes abuse their adherents), or when affiliation with a group involves a rupture with

[39] Advisory opinion (*avis*), 27 November 1989, RFSP (1991) 45; Decision (*arrêt*), 2 November 1992, Rec., 389.

an adherent's social milieu. One must add to these the reproach a religious group incurs by refusing certain medical practices, as in the case of blood transfusions for the Jehovah's Witnesses.

The Jehovah's Witness are not, however, a group of recent date, and social aggressiveness against them is on the rise just as they are in the process of evolving towards a less conflictual relationship with society.[40] But what causes most concern, perhaps, is their proselyting, which for several years now has gone beyond the popular classes to include members of the middle class. This is equally the case for more recent groups, like IVI,[41] which are nonconformist on religious and medical issues. Interestingly, doctors themselves are drawn to these groups. The medical establishment (like the educational establishment in the case of "the veil affair") finds itself relatively destabilized by these developments. Patients are less and less willing to accept an unequal relationship between the individual and the institution. They invoke the "rights of the sick." The doctor is losing his prestige while a process of de-institutionalization unfolds.

That such a situation holds risks is not in question; the incident involving the Order of the Solar Temple, which recruited in the higher echelons of society and ended with mass suicides, shows that the facts sometimes confirm the fears. The existence of a social problem with sects is not unique to France. But whereas in Great Britain there is an effort toward mediation and mutual understanding,[42] France has seen the rise of anti-sect associations that are largely subsidized by the government.[43] At the beginning of 1996, a Parliamentary Commission identified 173 "socially dangerous" organizations based on vague criteria (such as "antisocial activities") without revealing to these groups precisely what the commission held against them. As of September 2000, Parliament discussed a bill regarding "mental manipulation" that many jurists criticized on the grounds that it endangered liberties. If there is a tendency to stigmatize all cases of so-called "social deviance" rather than to examine each case on its own terms, this tendency undoubtedly arises from a sense of helplessness in the face of so many new sectarian movements that we do not yet understand.

III. Conclusion

Unlike countries that offer official recognition of certain religions, France and the United States have political orders characterized by the separation of church and state. However, the historical conditions in which this separation developed are vastly different in these two countries, and the particular circumstances of church–state separation in France play a significant part in public discussions of religion today. French laicism has taken the

---

[40] Régis Dericquebourg, "Les Témoins de Jéhovah: vers une sortie de la logique sectaire," in Françoise Champion and Martine Cohen, eds., *Sectes et démocratie,* (Paris: Seuil, 1999), 105–25. On the general subject of sects, see Jean Baubérot, "Laïcité, sectes, sociétés," in Champion, *Sectes,* 314–30.

[41] IVI (Invitation à la Vie Intense) originated in France during the 1980s, true to its founder's understanding of certain Roman Catholic traditions. Adherents of IVI observe, among other beliefs, the use of alternative medicine and prayer as treatments for illness (Jean Vernette, *Dictionnaire des groupes religieux aujourd'hui* [Paris: Presses Universitaires de France, 1995], 143).

[42] Consider, for example, the group INFORM directed by the sociologist Eileen Barker at the London School of Economics.

[43] Alain Garay, *L'activisme anti-secte de l'assistance à l'amalgame* (New York: Edwin Mellen, 1999).

historical role of pacifying the conflict of the two Frances. It successfully quelled this conflict and continues to ensure by judicial means the freedom of conscience and the free exercise of religious worship. For the most part, those freedoms are enjoyed peaceably and the "affairs" discussed in this Chapter must not overshadow the reality that each week millions of "believers" practice their religion without disruption and are free to express themselves publicly. Still, the long historical conflict over religion's place in French society has produced a particular sensitivity about religion. Religious demonstrations in the public space, understood as an effort to dictate social policy in the name of religious convictions, are repudiated by the majority public opinion among "believers" and "non-believers" alike. When a member of Parliament, Christine Boutin, brandished the Bible in a debate over the PACS (which permits a certain form of union for homosexual couples),[44] this blatant religious reference in the political sphere shocked the majority, even if some Catholics and Evangelical Protestants found the act courageous.

This said, in general, various public manifestations of traditional religions take place without incident. The problem for these religions has much less to do with laicization than with secularization. And this situation is ambivalent. On the one hand, hopes have been dashed for mutual progress in the development of science and morality, a hope which emerged simultaneously with laicism. By their very powerful advances, the sciences and technology pose nowadays the most challenging moral questions. Biomedicine, for example, leads to bioethical research in which, significantly, the authorities demand that people with religious sensibilities be a part of ethical consultation committees and participate in delineating what is appropriate and inappropriate to do to the human body. On the other hand, one can see emerging at present a new type of religious individualism in which each person invents (or believes he invents) a personal spiritual itinerary with sole reference to herself. But the individual does not realize that this spiritual itinerary is, in fact, substantially determined by the media. It is becoming more and more clear, from a sociological point of view, that it is precisely this media system that establishes the standards for what is legitimate and what is not, even in matters affecting public religious expression. Thus, in the pervasive influence of the media, we confront a new problem for freedom—a problem in which France is not alone.

[44] See n. 26 in this article.

Part IV

Women, Parents, and Children

Chapter 19

Dissenting Women, Religion or Belief, and the State: Contemporary Challenges that Require Attention*

*Bahia G. Tahzib-Lie***

> "States . . . must take measures to ensure that freedom of thought, conscience and religion . . . will be guaranteed and protected in law and in practice for both men and women, on the same terms and without discrimination . . . States . . . should . . . provide information on the status of women as regards their freedom of thought, conscience and religion, and indicate what steps they have taken or intend to take both to eliminate and prevent infringements of these freedoms in respect of women and to protect their rights against any discrimination."[1]

I. Introduction

Women and men suffer from violations of the right to freedom of religion or belief. Both sexes suffer from discrimination based on religion or belief. Women and men are harassed, oppressed, arrested, incarcerated, assaulted, and even killed for their beliefs. Considering the international community's growing emphasis on the application of a gender perspective on human rights violations,[2] one has to wonder whether women suffer abuses of their right to freedom of religion or belief due to the very fact that they are women or whether these abuses are unassociated with their gender. More specifically, one should ask to what extent and under which circumstances questions of gender are directly or indirectly relevant to the area of freedom of religion or belief.

---

* This chapter is a revised and expanded version of the author's articles that appeared as "Applying a Gender Perspective in the Area of the Right to Freedom of Religion or Belief," *BYU Law Review* (2000): 967, and as "The Advancement of Women's Equal Enjoyment of the Right to Freedom of Religion or Belief," *Freedom of Religion: A Precious Human Right*, ed. Jonneke M. M. Naber (Assen, The Netherlands: Van Gorkum, 2000), 54.

** The views expressed in this chapter are those of the author alone.

[1] Human Rights Committee General Comment 28 (2000) concerning equality of rights between men and women (ICCPR, art. 3), UN Doc. CCPR/C/21/Rev.1/Add.10, para. 21.

[2] Closer attention is also being paid to the application of a gender perspective in the area of freedom of religion or belief. See Committee on Human Rights Resolution 2001/42 (2001), para. 7.

Tore Lindholm, W. Cole Durham, Jr., Bahia G. Tahzib-Lie (eds.), Facilitating Freedom of Religion or Belief: A Deskbook, *455–495.*

Such queries prompt this chapter's examination of violations of women's right to freedom of religion or belief. This exercise requires questioning which violations are specifically directed against women and which women are particularly vulnerable. These issues are difficult to explore considering sensitivities and complexities surrounding matters relating to religion or belief,[3] and considering the public/private dichotomy that exists in various countries and cultures, where women are more or less constricted to the private sphere while men predominate in the public.

Potential female victims are dispersed across the world. They can be found among all societies, adhering to various religions or beliefs—including theistic, nontheistic, or atheistic beliefs,[4] and belonging to religious or belief minorities or majorities. Obviously, women belonging to religious or belief minorities are vulnerable because they do not—or no longer—belong to the majority religion or belief, nor do they subscribe to the religiously prescribed or religiously motivated practices of the majority of the population.[5] However, women belonging to a religious or belief majority can be vulnerable too. Religious or belief communities are not necessarily homogeneous nor are their teachings and precepts necessarily coherent and universally agreed upon. In a religion-based or religion-dominated state, women belonging to a religious majority can disagree with the state on a particular practice being religiously prescribed or religiously motivated and therefore mandatory. In a secular state, they can be prevented from exercising a religiously prescribed or religiously motivated practice. Due to their dissenting beliefs, this chapter refers to the vulnerable women in the three described situations jointly as "dissenting women."

The various situations in this chapter are analyzed on the basis of relevant international instruments relating to human rights, which clearly establish that a woman's gender should not be a reason to restrict her full and equal enjoyment of the right to freedom of religion or belief. These instruments determine two important matters. First, they provide that women and men are equally entitled to all human rights and fundamental freedoms,[6] which include the right to freedom of religion or belief.[7]

---

[3] It has, for instance, been stated that "Few issues are as capable of raising so much emotion as those relating to our religion or belief." See "Keynote Address by Hilde Johnson, Former Norwegian Minister for International Cooperation and Human Rights," *Seminar on Freedom of Religion or Belief in the OSCE Region; Challenges to Law and Practice,* ed. Chantal Grotens and Bahia Tahzib-Lie (The Hague: Dutch Ministry of Foreign Affairs, 2001), 27.

[4] The right to freedom of religion or belief embraces theistic, nontheistic, and atheistic beliefs. For a discussion, see Cornelis D. de Jong, *The Freedom of Thought: Conscience and Religion or Belief in the United Nations (1946–1992)* (Antwerp: Intersentia, 2000), 20–34. Human Rights Committee General Comment 22 (1993) (art. 18 ICCPR), UN Doc. A/48/40 (Pt. I), para. 2.

[5] The Human Rights Committee has observed that: "The fact that a religion is recognized as a state religion or that it is established as official or traditional or that its followers comprise the majority of the population shall not result in any impairment of the enjoyment of any of the rights under the [International] Covenant [on Civil and Political Rights], including articles 18 and 27, nor in any discrimination against adherents of other religions or non-believers" (General Comment 22, para. 9).

[6] See, e.g., *Beijing Declaration and Platform for Action of the Fourth World Conference on Women* (hereinafter "BDPA"), Annex I, paras. 8, 15, 32, 36; Annex II, paras. 5, 213; *Convention on the Elimination of All Forms of Discrimination Against Women,* art. 1 (hereinafter "CEDAW"); *United Nations Millennium Declaration,* UN Doc. A/RES/55/2, paras. 4, 6, 25 (2000) (hereinafter "United Nations Millennium Declaration"). See also *International Covenant on Economic, Social and Cultural Rights,* art. 3 (hereinafter "ICESCR"); ICCPR, art. 3. The latter should be read in conjunction with General Comment 28. It is furthermore noteworthy that various UN conferences have contributed to the understanding that women's

Second, they specifically prohibit discrimination on the basis of sex and the wider concept of gender,[8] which obviously also applies to the right to freedom of religion or belief. The right to freedom of religion or belief protected by numerous international instruments relating to human rights involves two distinct though interrelated and interdependent aspects, referred to as internal and external freedoms.[9]

First, internal freedom has been described as an individual's absolute freedom to have, maintain, adopt, and change a religion or belief.[10] It denotes the individual's alterable choice of religion or belief, made in the inner, private domain, which the individual may make known to others in private or public. An individual may, for

---

equality and nondiscrimination between women and men, as well as women's equal enjoyment of human rights and fundamental freedoms, do not occur automatically as a result of the overall protection and promotion of human rights. See report by the UN Secretary General, *Integrating the Gender Perspective into the Work of United Nations Human Rights Treaty Bodies,* UN Doc. HRI/MC/1998/6, para. 17 (1998) (hereinafter "Report by the UN Secretary General").

[7] Women's right to freedom of religion or belief has been specifically acknowledged in two global and one regional instrument specific to women, namely, the outcome document of the 23rd special session of the UN General Assembly entitled *Women 2000: Gender Equality, Development and Peace for the Twenty-First Century,* para. 98(c) (2000) (hereinafter "Beijing +5 document"); BDPA, Annex I, para. 12 and Annex II, paras. 24, 72, 80(f) and *Inter-American Convention on the Prevention, Punishment and Eradication of Violence against Women,* art. 4(i) (hereinafter "Convention of Belém do Pará").

[8] See, e.g., ICCPR, art. 2(1); CEDAW, art. 1; BDPA, paras. 214, 216; United Nations Millennium Declaration, para. 4. See also *Rome Statute of the International Criminal Court,* art. 21(3), UN Doc. A/CONF.183/9 (1998). See generally Douglas Cassel and Jull Guzman, "The Law and Reality of Discrimination Against Women," *Women and International Human Rights Law,* 3 vols., ed. Kelly D. Askin and Dorean M. Koenig (New York: Transnational Publishers, 1999), 1:287. Whereas "sex" refers to biological and physical differences between males and females, "gender" refers to socially defined or socially constructed differences, taking into account such factors as power imbalances, socioeconomic disparities and culturally reinforced stereotypes. See Report by the UN Secretary General, para. 16. Nevertheless, the concepts of "sex" and "gender" tend to be used inconsistently or interchangeably in international instruments in the areas of international human rights law, international humanitarian law, and international criminal law. See, e.g., Corinne Packer, "The Development of the Human Rights of Women," 14 June 1999, The Hague (a report submitted to the Royal Netherlands Ministry of Social Affairs and Employment, DCE), 26–27; Koenig and Askin, "International Criminal Law and the International Criminal Court Statute: Crimes against Women," in Askin and Koenig, *Women and International Human Rights Law,* 2:3.

[9] For compilations of international norms regarding freedom of religion or belief, see Bahiyyih G. Tahzib, *Freedom of Religion or Belief: Ensuring Effective International Legal Protection* (Boston: Martinus Nijhoff, 1996), Appendix B, 499–551; *Helsinki Monitor* 9, no. 3 (1998): 106–15; Tad Stahnke and J. Paul Martin, eds., *Religion and Human Rights: Basic Documents* (New York: Columbia University Press, 1998).

[10] See, e.g., *Universal Declaration of Human Rights,* art. 18 (hereinafter "UDHR"); ICCPR, art. 18(1); 1981 *Declaration on the Elimination of All Forms of Intolerance and of Discrimination Based on Religion or Belief,* art. 1(1) (hereinafter "1981 Declaration"); *European Convention on Human Rights,* art. 9(1) (hereinafter "ECHR"); American Convention on Human Rights, art. 12(1) (hereinafter "ACHR"); *Document of the Copenhagen Meeting of Representatives of the Participating States of the Conference on the Human Dimension of the Conference on Security and Co-operation in Europe,* principle 9(4) (1990) (hereinafter "Copenhagen OSCE Document"); *Charter of Fundamental Rights of the European Union,* art. 10(1). For a discussion on internal freedom, see de Jong, *Freedom of Thought,* 19–75. From the UDHR onward, the wording of internal freedom in global human rights instruments has, by and large, become more restrictive. The wording in later global instruments no longer explicitly guarantees free, ongoing choice for each individual in terms of religion or belief. At best it is alluded to. However, an interesting development is that the UN Commission on Human Rights has affirmed in recent years that the right to freedom of religion or belief also embraces the freedom to change. See, e.g., Committee on Human Rights Resolution 2001/42 (2001), para. 4(a); Committee on Human Rights Resolution 2000/33 (2000), para. 4(a). See also General Comment 22, para. 5 and General Comment 28, para. 21.

instance, inform her spouse that she decided to adopt a different religion, she may join as a member of this religious community and withdraw her membership from another religious community. People are not required to make a once-in-a-lifetime choice or resign themselves to follow the religion or belief of their parents, spouse, religious leaders, community, or society. Internal freedom allows people to be completely free, at any time, to explore other beliefs and to make their own choices as to religious commitment and membership, including taking up, abandoning, avoiding or openly rejecting a religion or belief if so inclined. Section II.A demonstrates the inviolable nature of internal freedom. States may not impose restrictions whatsoever on internal freedom, and may therefore not interfere with a person's choice of religion or belief.

Second, external freedom has been defined as an individual's "freedom, either alone or in community with others and in public or private, to manifest his religion or belief in teaching, practice, worship and observance."[11] It denotes the individual's manifestation of his or her beliefs in four specific areas of the external domain, i.e., teaching, practice, worship, and observance. External freedom is certainly not strictly a personal and intimate matter of the individual; it can be exercised in private or public, and alone or in community with others. Examples of this freedom are the building of places of worship, the display of religious symbols, the dissemination of religious publications and materials, the wearing of distinctive clothing and headcoverings, the observance of dietary restrictions, the teaching of a religion or belief, the establishment of communication with coreligionists, the election of religious leaders, and the observance of days of rest, religious holidays and ceremonies.[12] These examples indicate that external freedom is often intertwined with other human rights and fundamental freedoms—both civil and political rights (for example, freedom of expression, freedom of peaceful assembly, and freedom of association[13]) and economic, social, and cultural rights (for example, the right to the highest attainable standard of health, the right to education, and the right to work[14]).[15] Unlike internal freedom, states may impose restrictions on external freedom when three specific conditions are met. These conditions, which are often open to interpretation and abuse, are described in section II.B.

---

[11] UDHR, art. 18; ICCPR, art. 18(1). For a similar definition, see 1981 Declaration, art. 1(1); ECHR, art. 9(1); *Charter of Fundamental Rights of the European Union*, art. 10(1). For less elaborate definitions, see, e.g., *American Declaration of the Rights and Duties of Man*, art. 3; ACHR, art. 12(1); *Final Act of the Conference on Security and Co-operation in Europe*, principle 7, adopted 1 August 1975; *African Charter on Human and Peoples' Rights*, art. 8, adopted 27 June 1981. For a discussion on external freedom, see de Jong, *Freedom of Thought*, 77–168, 249–606.

[12] For a comprehensive list of examples of external freedom, see 1981 Declaration, art. 6; General Comment 22, para. 4; *Concluding Document of the Vienna Meeting of Representatives of the Participating States of the Conference on Security and Co-operation in Europe*, principle 16, 4 November 1986–17 January 1989 (hereinafter "Vienna Concluding Document").

[13] For a description of these human rights, see ICCPR, art. 19, 21, and 22.

[14] For a description of these human rights, see ICESCR, art. 12, 13, and 6.

[15] It has been pointed out that the right to freedom of religion or belief lies at the interface between civil and political rights and economic, social and cultural rights. Christine Chinkin, "Cultural Relativism and International Law," *Religious Fundamentalisms and the Human Rights of Women*, ed. Courtney W. Howland (New York: St. Martin's Press, 1999), 55, 56.

Section II highlights how both aspects of dissenting women's right to freedom of religion or belief can be violated. Section II.A discusses situations involving alleged violations of dissenting women's internal freedom, and section II.B situations involving alleged violations of dissenting women's external freedom. Although beyond the immediate focus of this chapter, section III draws attention to the fact that the international community's main concern about women and religion has been in terms of protecting women against discriminatory religious norms and practices that affect their human rights. Section III argues for expanding the international attention in this area to include women's right to freedom of religion or belief. Finally, section IV presents conclusions and recommendations, including a nine-point list of recommended actions, to combat violations of women's equal enjoyment of their right to freedom of religion or belief globally.

II. The Right of Dissenting Women to Freedom of Religion or Belief

A. Violations of Internal Freedom of Dissenting Women: Coercion, the Lack of Due Diligence, and Violence Against Women

Numerous international instruments relating to human rights prohibit state interference with the individual's inner, private beliefs on two fronts. First, internal freedom must be protected unconditionally, without any limitation and in all circumstances. Even in times of public emergency that threaten the life of the nation, such as internal or international disturbances or armed conflicts, states must refrain from imposing limitations.[16] Internal freedom is therefore inviolable and nonderogable. Second, "coercion" that would impair internal freedom must be barred.[17] This means that a person may not be forced to adopt particular beliefs. Although human rights instruments do not define coercion, it is widely accepted that the term should not be limited to the use or threat of physical force or penal sanctions to compel individuals to recant or convert.[18] For instance, some restrictive policies and practices have been condemned as "coercion," such as those that restrict access to education, medical care, employment, or the right to vote or participate in the conduct of public affairs.

---

[16] ICCPR, art. 4(2); ACHR, art. 27(2). See also *Fourth Geneva Convention Relative to the Protection of Civilian Persons in Time of War*, art. 27: "Protected persons are entitled, in all circumstances, to respect for . . . their religious convictions and practices" (hereinafter "Fourth Geneva Convention"). For an elaborate discussion on derogation clauses, see *Human Rights Quarterly* 7, no. 1 (1985): 1–14, 23–34, 89–131.

[17] ICCPR, art. 18(2); 1981 Declaration, art. 1(2). For the three possible meanings of coercion, see Peter Cumper, "Freedom of Thought, Conscience, and Religion," *The International Covenant on Civil and Political Rights and United Kingdom Law*, ed. David Harris and Sarah Joseph (Oxford: Clarendon Press, 1995), 355, 370–71.

[18] See General Comment 22, para. 5. Opinions are divided as to what constitutes indirect forms of impermissible pressure. For a framework of four interrelated variables designed to help disentangle the different factors that states have used to draw the line between "proper" and "improper" proselytism, see Tad Stahnke, "Proselytism and the Freedom to Change Religion in International Human Rights Law," *BYU Law Review* (2000): 251, 326–38.

The noncoercion clause is phrased in general terms and is not directed at any particular actor. This is significant since this means that coercion could even relate to situations in which a state or its agents have not perpetrated or condoned a particular act of coercion that impaired the woman's internal freedom. It raises, however, the question of the extent of state responsibility, in particular under which circumstances can the state be held responsible for the commission of acts of coercion by a private individual.[19] Although international norms regarding freedom of religion or belief do not shed light on this question, the concept of what is called "due diligence" has fairly recently emerged at the international human rights level and is still gaining international momentum.[20] The emerging international concept of due diligence in the area of human rights indicates "the threshold of effort which a state must undertake to fulfil its responsibility to protect individuals from abuses of their rights."[21] What due diligence essentially requires is that states take all reasonable and appropriate steps under the circumstances to prevent human rights violations. It is not an obligation to guarantee the nonoccurrence of a certain event. The Inter-American Court of Human Rights expounded on this concept: "[t]he State has a legal duty to take reasonable steps to prevent human rights violations and to use the means at its disposal to carry out a serious investigation of violations committed within its jurisdiction, to identify those responsible, to impose the appropriate punishment and to ensure the victim adequate compensation. This obligation implies the duty of state parties to organize the governmental apparatus and, in general, all the structures through which public power is exercised, so that they are capable of juridically ensuring the free and full enjoyment of human rights."[22] The concept of states exercising due diligence with

---

[19] The draft articles on responsibility of states for internationally wrongful acts (hereinafter "Draft Articles on State Responsibility"), adopted by the UN International Law Commission (hereinafter "ILC") on 3 August 2001, provides that: "There is an internationally wrongful act of a State when conduct consisting of an action or omission: (a) Is attributable to the State under international law; and (b) Constitutes a breach of an international obligation of the State" (art. 2). Article 3 sets forth that "[t]he characterization of an act of a State as internationally wrongful is governed by international law. Such characterization is not affected by the characterization of the same act as lawful by internal law." The Draft Articles on State Responsibility, art. 5, 7, 8, 9, also refer to the conduct of a person or group of persons. The final version of the articles (including some oral amendments made during the adoption of the commentaries) will be issued as part of the report of the ILC to UNGA and posted on the website of the ILC: <www.un.org/law/ilc/sessions/53/53sess.htm>. This chapter uses the last available version of the Draft Articles on State Responsibility, which does not incorporate oral amendments, contained in UN Doc. A/CN.4/L.602/Rev.1 (2001).

[20] The concept of due diligence emerged in some other areas of international law, such as international environmental law, international alien law, and international law concerning diplomatic immunity. However, the term due diligence has not always been explicitly utilized; it has been interchanged with "due care" and "all appropriate steps." In the area of the prevention of transfrontier water pollution, see, e.g., J. G. Lammers, *Pollution of International Watercourses: A Search for Substantive Rules and Principles of Law* (Dordrecht: Martinus Nijhoff, 1984), 348–56, 378–81, 597, 614–15, 632–33, and 661; *UN Convention on the Law of the Non-Navigational Uses of International Watercourses,* art. 7(1). In the area of the prevention of injuries to aliens, see, e.g., Richard B. Lillich and John M. Paxman, "State Responsibility for Injuries to Aliens Occasioned by Terrorist Activities," *American University Law Review* 26 (1977): 245–49. In the area of the protection of the premises of the mission, diplomats and their private residences, see, e.g., *Vienna Convention on Diplomatic Relations,* art. 22(2), 29(1), and 30(1); Case Concerning US Diplomatic and Consular Staff in Tehran (ICJ, 24 May 1980), particularly paras. 63, 67; Agbor v. Metropolitan Police Commissioner, 1 WLR 703 (1969) (CA).

[21] Amnesty International, *Broken Bodies, Shattered Minds: The Torture of Women Worldwide,* AI Index ACT 40/003/2001—News Service No. 26 (2001), 7.

regard to the prevention of human rights violations within its territory is becoming internationally more accepted and recognized as a mechanism of state responsibility in the area of human rights.

Hence, the concept of due diligence seems also applicable to prevention of acts of coercion impairing a person's internal freedom. The state's failure to take all reasonable steps, in accordance with the existing situation, to prevent, prosecute, and punish coercive acts would constitute an internal freedom violation. A state should therefore refrain from condoning or ignoring acts of coercion impairing a person's internal freedom, or from extending a form of impunity to the perpetrators by giving tacit, covert, or open support to these acts by, for example, failing to prosecute and punish the perpetrators.

Although the exact scope of internal freedom remains open to interpretation, there appears to be a variety of examples of alleged violations of internal freedom of dissenting women. Examples include cases of women being abducted and forcibly converted to a particular religion,[23] being forced to marry a man from a different religion and convert to his faith,[24] being harassed by expelling their children from school due to their mother's voluntary conversion to another religion,[25] being forced to secrecy due to their voluntary conversion to another religion,[26] being raped or murdered because of belonging to a certain religion or belief,[27] being arrested and subjected to intense physical and mental abuse in order to coerce them to recant their faith,[28] being executed because of refusal to recant their faith,[29] or finding themselves ostracized and rejected by society due to their voluntary conversion to another religion.[30]

---

[22] Velásquez Rodríguez Case, Series C: Decisions and Judgments, no. 4 (1988) (Inter-Am. CtHR, 29 July 1988), paras. 174, 177, *International Legal Materials* 28 (1989), 294. See generally Radhika Coomaraswamy, *Report of the Special Rapporteur on Violence Against Women, Its Causes and Consequences,* UN Doc. E/CN.4/1996/53, paras. 32–39 (1996). For a questionnaire to assess state adherence to the due diligence standard, see Coomaraswamy, *Violence against Women in the Family: Report of the Special Rapporteur on Violence against Women, Its Causes and Consequences,* UN Doc. E/CN.4/1999/68, para. 25 (1999).

[23] US Department of State, *Annual Report on International Religious Freedom 2000* (November 2000), 188, 434; Abdelfattah Amor, *Civil and Political Rights, Including Religious Intolerance,* report submitted by Special Rapporteur in accordance with Commission on Human Rights Resolution 1999/39, UN Doc. E/CN.4/2000/65, para. 50 (2000) (hereinafter Special Rapporteur's Report 2000); UN Secretary General, *Implementation of the Declaration on the Elimination of All Forms of Religious Intolerance and of Discrimination Based on Religion or Belief,* UN Doc. A/51/542/Add.2, para. 105 (1996) (hereinafter "Implementation Report of the Secretary General"); Amor, *Implementation of the Declaration on the Elimination of All Forms of Intolerance and of Discrimination Based on Religion or Belief,* UN Doc. E/CN.4/1996/95/Add.1, para. 66 (1996).

[24] Amor, *Implementation of the Declaration on the Elimination of All Forms of Intolerance and of Discrimination Based on Religion or Belief,* UN Doc. E/CN.4/1998/6, para. 62(e) (1998) (hereinafter "Special Rapporteur's Report 1998").

[25] Special Rapporteur's Report 2000, para. 79 (2000).

[26] Amor, *Civil and Political Rights, Including Religious Intolerance,* UN Doc. E/CN.4/1999/58, para. 72 (1999) (hereinafter "Special Rapporteur's Report 1999").

[27] Ibid., paras. 61 & 111; Special Rapporteur's Report 2000, para. 79 (2000).

[28] Bahá'í International Community, *The Bahá'ís: A Profile of the Bahá'í Faith and its Worldwide Community* (n.p., 1994), 58–59.

[29] Ibid.

[30] Secretary General, *Elimination of All Forms of Religious Intolerance,* UN Doc. A/54/386, para. 137 (1999) (hereinafter "Elimination of Religious Intolerance").

These examples suggest three characteristics of violations of dissenting women's internal freedom. First, the dissenting woman's choice of religion or belief must have become known to others. This could be voluntarily, at request, by force, through public or private records, through the grapevine, or by her public manifestations of her religion or belief—whether accurately so or by assumption.[31] Only with the knowledge of the woman's religious commitment and membership can a coercive act become apparent as a violation of her internal freedom. Typically, the intent of such an act is first and foremost directed at impairing the woman's choice of religion or belief, not at restricting a particular manifestation of her religion or belief.[32] This illustrates that the knowledge of a person's choice of religion or belief automatically extends it from the person's internal state of mind into the external domain. This indicates that there is a gray area between internal and external freedom.[33] It may therefore sometimes be difficult to make clear-cut distinctions between internal and external freedom, considering also that external freedom can be exercised within both the public and private spheres. The idea that internal freedom only lends itself to the internal, private domain is not tenable. Certainly, internal freedom falls first and foremost within the domain of the person's internal state of mind and conscience.[34] But the reach of internal freedom may also extend into the external domain.

Second, two groups of dissenting women appear to be particularly vulnerable to violations of women's internal freedom. Targets may be women who do not belong to the religion or belief of the majority of the population, but belong to a religious or belief minority. The fact that their religion or belief differs with that of the majority of the population makes them particularly vulnerable. It is therefore not surprising that international instruments relating to human rights have emphasized that every person belonging to a religious or belief minority has a right to freedom of religion or belief.[35]

---

[31] It has been argued that the state may not demand to know what belief a person holds. The obligation to reveal one's religion or belief in a census or other registration conflicts with internal freedom. It has been explained that perhaps the explanation for this very strong protection of internal freedom is "that there is no good reason why the state needs the information (though there are bad ones)" (D. J. Harris, M. O'Boyle, C. Warbrick, *Law of the European Convention on Human Rights* [London: Butterworths, 1995], 361). See also P. van Dijk and G. J. H. van Hoof, *Theory and Practice of the European Convention on Human Rights*, 3rd ed. (The Hague: Kluwer Law International, 1998), 542.

[32] Section II.B explains that a state may interfere under strict circumstances with a particular manifestation of a person's religion or belief.

[33] This grey area is often not acknowledged. For instance, it has been explained: "This absolute freedom to entertain any thought, moral conviction or religious view is not without practical importance. It is true that thoughts and views, as long as they have not been expressed, are intangible and that convictions are really valuable for the person concerned only if he can express them. This does not render the (inner) freedom of thought, conscience and religion useless. Its guarantee also implies that one cannot be subjected to a treatment intended to change the process of thinking, that any form of compulsion to express thoughts, to change an opinion, or to divulge a religious conviction is prohibited, and that no sanction may be imposed either on the holding of any view whatever or on the change of a religion or conviction: it protects against indoctrination by the State" (van Dijk and van Hoof, *Theory and Practice of the European Convention*, 541–42; footnotes 1392 and 1393 omitted).

[34] See, e.g., Arcot Krishnaswami, *Study of Discrimination in the Matter of Religious Rights and Practices*, UN Doc. E/CN.4/Sub.2/200/Rev.1, UN Sales No. 60.XIV.2 (1960), 16.

[35] See, e.g., ICCPR, art. 27; *Declaration on the Rights of Persons Belonging to National or Ethnic, Religious and Linguistic Minorities*, adopted by General Assembly Resolution 47/135 of 18 December 1992, art. 2(1); *Framework Convention for the Protection of National Minorities*, opened for signature 1 February 1995, ETS no. 157, art. 7; Copenhagen OSCE Document, principle 32.3.

Targets may also be women who belong to the religion or belief of the majority of the population of a secular state. They are usually not vulnerable to violations of internal freedom in a religion-based or religion-dominated state, because then they share the same religion as the state and the majority of the population. Sometimes, however, they can be vulnerable despite belonging to the majority, for instance, where rejection of the majority religion is assumed from one's writings or comments or where members of a religious community consider themselves as belonging to the majority but they are not considered as such.[36]

Third, violations of internal freedom of dissenting women could also qualify as acts of violence against women. The broad concept of "violence against women" has been defined as "any act of gender-based violence that results in, or is likely to result in, physical, sexual or psychological harm or suffering to women, including threats of such acts, coercion or arbitrary deprivation of liberty, whether occurring in public or private life."[37] The international community has expressly acknowledged in the area of violence against women that states have an obligation to exercise "due diligence" to prevent, investigate, and punish acts of violence against women, regardless whether those acts are perpetrated by government actors or by private persons, as well as an obligation to exercise due diligence to provide protection to potential victims.[38] Although the international community has explicitly accepted the due diligence obligation in the area of violence against women, international clarity regarding the scope and meaning of the obligation still has to be achieved. Perhaps this relates to the terminology "due diligence."[39] Phrases as "all appropriate steps" and "all reasonable steps" or even "due care" may be more clear.[40]

---

[36] For a further discussion of this issue, see Nazila Ghanea, "Apostasy and Freedom to Change Religion or Belief," in this volume.

[37] See Declaration on the Elimination of Violence against Women, art. 1 (hereinafter "DEVAW") and BDPA, para. 113. See also Convention of Belém do Pará, art. 1 and General Recommendation 19 concerning violence against women adopted by the *Committee on the Elimination of Discrimination against Women* (1992) (hereinafter "General Recommendation on Violence Against Women"). For examples of acts of violence against women, see DEVAW, art. 2; Convention of Belém do Pará, art. 2; BDPA, Section D.

[38] See, e.g., *Further Actions and Initiatives to Implement the Beijing Declaration and Platform for Action*, 10 June 2000, para. 13 of Resolution II , UN Doc. A/S-23/10/Rev.1 (2000); DEVAW, art. 4(c); BDPA, para. 124(b). See also General Recommendation on Violence Against Women, para. 9; Committee on Human Rights Resolution 2001/49 (2001), paras. 2, 10; Special Rapporteur's Report 1999, para. 101. It has further been argued that ICCPR, art. 2(1), imposes such an affirmative obligation on states. See Howland, "Safeguarding Women's Political Freedoms under the International Covenant on Civil and Political Rights in the Face of Religious Fundamentalism," in *Religious Fundamentalisms*, 93–103.

[39] It was apparent during the six-week negotiations on the Dutch-sponsored resolution "Working Towards the Elimination of Crimes Against Women Committed in the Name of Honor" (UNGA Resolution 55/66) in the Third Committee of the 55th session of the UN General Assembly in October/November 2000 that the scope and precise meaning of "due diligence" needs to be clarified. For instance, before asking for a vote on the draft resolution, the Permanent Representative of Jordan, HRH Prince Zeid Ra'ad Zeid Al-Hussein (in his oral statement in explanation of vote on 3 November 2000), critically commented: "How could states possibly exercise due diligence to prevent such crimes, if the crime in question is committed in a sudden state of rage? All states, wherein we find crimes of passion, would in due course leave themselves open to potential accusations of human rights violations for not having exercised 'enough' due diligence to prevent the commission of this crime." Due diligence does not impose impossible burdens on states; it merely requires them to take reasonable and appropriate steps where these may fairly be expected.

[40] The term due diligence has, for instance, not always been explicitly utilized in the areas of the prevention of transfrontier water pollution, the prevention of injuries to aliens, and the protection of the premises of

B. Violations of External Freedom of Dissenting Women: The Competing Interests of the State and the Woman

The relevant instruments relating to human rights establish that states may only impose restrictions on manifestations of religion or belief, and this only when three requirements are fully met. First, the restriction must be prescribed by law. Second, the restriction must be pursuant to one or more specified, public interest grounds—specifically, public safety, order, health or morals, or the fundamental rights and freedoms of others. Third, the restriction must be "necessary" to protect one or more of the aforementioned state interests.[41]

This strict three-prong test for permissible restrictions is applicable in all situations, even when a public emergency threatens the life of the nation.[42] The test may not be applied in a manner that would undermine a person's enjoyment of the right to freedom of religion or belief.[43] The onus is on the state to demonstrate that any restriction it imposes, satisfies the three-prong test. To determine the legitimacy of state interference with external freedom in a given case, its actions must therefore be assessed in terms of the above prongs. This has proved difficult, since the prongs are often interpreted in different ways. In particular, the state interests referred to in the second prong are often difficult to define and their necessity referred to in the third prong therefore implies a measure of relativity, in that they may change according to circumstance and country.

---

the mission, diplomats, and their private residences. It has been interchanged with phrases such as "due care," "special duty to take all appropriate steps," and "all appropriate steps." For references, see footnote 20. The Inter-American Court of Human Rights referred to "reasonable steps." See Velásquez Rodríguez Case.

[41] For the relevant limitation clauses, see, e.g., ICCPR, art. 18(3); ECHR, art. 9(2). Under these provisions, limitations are permissible only with respect to *manifestations* of religion or belief. The ECHR determines that the third condition should be necessary "in a democratic society." In the view of the European Court of Human Rights, democratic society necessarily presupposes religious pluralism. See Kokkinakis v. Greece, 17 EHRR 397 (1994) (ECtHR 260-A, 23 June 1993), para. 31; Manoussakis and Others v. Greece, 23 EHRR 387 (1997) (ECtHR 1996-IV, 26 September 1996), 1362–63. With this understanding, practice has shown that this addition is more a case of verbiage than of substance. Certainly, a human rights violation does not become more "necessary" just because it happens in a nondemocratic society. For a detailed discussion on limitation clauses, see *Human Rights Quarterly* 7, no. 1 (1985): 1–22, 35–88, 155. The European Court of Human Rights generally is reluctant to question a government's rationale for limiting manifestations of freedom of religion or belief. See T. Jeremy Gunn, "Adjudicating Rights of Conscience Under the European Convention on Human Rights" in *Religious Human Rights in Global Perspectives: Legal Perspectives,* ed. John Witte, Jr. and Johan D. van der Vyver (Boston: Martinus Nijhoff, 1996), 305. There have been, however, some exceptions to this general reluctance. See Darby v. Sweden, 13 EHRR 774 (1991) (EctHR 187-A, 23 October 1990), para. 34; Thlimmenos v. Greece, App. no. 34369/97 (ECtHR, 6 April 2000), para. 47.

[42] ICCPR, art. 4(2); ACHR, art. 27(2). See also Fourth Geneva Convention, art. 27.

[43] General Comment 22, para. 8; the UN Human Rights Committee also recommended that in "[i]nterpreting the scope of permissible limitation clauses, State's Parties should proceed from the need to protect the rights guaranteed under the Covenant, including the right to equality and nondiscrimination on all grounds specified in Articles 2, 3 and 26." This has also been emphasized by the UN Special Rapporteur on Freedom of Religion or Belief (formerly: Religious Intolerance). See, e.g., Amor, *Civil and Political Rights, Including the Question of Religious Intolerance,* UN Doc. E/CN.4/1999/58/Add.2, paras. 110(b), 122 (1998) (hereinafter "Report on Question of Religious Intolerance").

For the purpose of interpretation, international supervisory bodies generally allow a certain, though not unlimited, degree of deference to the judgement of state authorities—in view of their special knowledge and overall responsibility under domestic law—when they weigh competing public and individual interests and assess whether the contested restriction is necessary.[44] This room of maneuver is commonly referred to as the margin of appreciation.[45] The doctrine of the margin of appreciation serves as a mechanism, "as a lubricant at the interface between individual rights and public interest," by which "a tight or slack rein is kept on state conduct, depending on the context."[46] In each case a variety of factors may affect the actual scope of the margin of appreciation, for instance, the nature of the individual right protected, the nature of the duty incumbent on the state, the nature and context of the public interest pursued by the contested restriction, the nature of the applicant's activities regulated, the extent of the interference, the circumstances surrounding the case, and the existence or nonexistence of common ground among states parties in favor of the interference with the individual right.[47] For instance, a divergence in domestic law and practice may indicate that the nature and degree of importance of the individual interest is still in the process of being understood, recognized, and accepted. By contrast, when there is common ground, it is much harder for the departing state to make the case that the particular limitation is necessary. Strong international consensus therefore tends to indicate a narrow margin of appreciation and strict international scrutiny, while a lack of international consensus tends to signal a wide margin and more lenient scrutiny.[48] The interplay between the various factors makes it difficult to predict how the international supervisory body will decide the margin of appreciation question in any given case, especially where the variables point in different directions.[49] It should also be realized there may be more conformity in law and practice of states before a supervisory human rights body at regional level than before a supervisory body at global level.

---

[44] See, e.g., Oren Gross and Fionnuala Ní Aoláin, "From Discretion to Scrutiny: Revisiting the Application of the Margin of Appreciation Doctrine in the Context of Article 15 of the European Convention on Human Rights," *Human Rights Quarterly* 23 (2001): 627.

[45] The doctrine of a margin of appreciation was first explained by the European Court of Human Rights in Handyside v. U.K. (ECtHR 24-A, 7 December 1976), paras. 48–49. For a discussion, see Paul Mahoney et al., "The Doctrine of the Margin of Appreciation under the European Convention on Human Rights: Its Legitimacy in Theory and Application in Practice," *Human Rights Law Journal* 19, no. 1 (1998): 1–36; Howard Charles Yourow, *The Margin of Appreciation Doctrine in the Dynamics of the European Human Rights Jurisprudence* (The Hague: Kluwer Law International, 1996); Steven Greer, *The Margin of Appreciation: Interpretation and Discretion under the European Convention on Human Rights* (Strasbourg: Council of Europe, 2000); van Dijk and van Hoof, *Theory and Practice of the European Convention,* 82–95.

[46] Eloquently put by Harris, O'Boyle, and Warbrick in *Law of the European Convention on Human Rights,* 14.

[47] See also Paul Mahoney, "Marvellous Richness of Diversity or Invidious Cultural Relativism?" *Human Rights Law Journal* 19, no. 1 (1998): 5; Jeroen Schrokkenbroek, "The Basis, Nature and Application of the Margin-of-Appreciation Doctrine in the Case-Law of the European Court of Human Rights: General Report," *Human Rights Law Journal* 19, no. 1 (1998): 34–35. See also Rasmussen v. Denmark (ECtHR 87-A, 28 November 1984), para. 40.

[48] Noted in connection with the ECHR by van Dijk and van Hoof, *Theory and Practice of the European Convention on Human Rights,* 87.

[49] Ibid., 91.

This section addresses three situations in which state restrictions on external freedom appear to be specifically directed against women or to which women are particularly vulnerable. These cases are not only particularly illustrative, most recurring, and prominent, they appear to be the most immediate—if not only—examples of state interferences with the freedom to manifest religion or belief—as defined in international human rights instruments and interpreted by international human rights bodies—which are specifically directed against women or to which women are particularly vulnerable. Each situation involves sensitive, controversial, and complex issues in contemporary societies as well as a variety of beliefs.[50] Each case highlights a conflict—between what is in the interests of the state, which must be broadly construed to include the interests of society at large and the human rights and fundamental freedoms of others,[51] and the dissenting women's interest to manifest her religion or belief. The competing interests of the state and the dissenting woman need to be carefully balanced on a case-by-case basis. The outcome of the delicate balancing process must be based on the three-prong test and the facts surrounding the case.

The first case concerns women who wish to undergo female genital mutilation (FGM), a traditional, customary, or religious practice that is harmful to the health of women and girls.[52] Any state and any of the dissenting women discussed in section I may be involved in this case. The second case deals with women belonging to a particular religion who are required to remove their religious attire in the public workplace. Such women can belong both to a religious minority or the majority, and live in a secular country or in a country with an official or established religion that they do not subscribe to. The third case involves women in religion-based or religion-dominated societies who are required to wear dress prescribed by the religion of the majority of the population. They can be members of either a religious or belief minority or the religious majority.

Each case examines whether the state has satisfied the three-part test for permissible restrictions by debating the legal reasoning of different positions and counter-positions, as it unfolds. It is assumed in each case that the state in question has fulfilled the first

[50] No value judgement concerning the beliefs involved or the interpretations of the beliefs involved are intended. It has been critically noted that "[i]f one's religious beliefs dictate . . . the subjugation of women, they do not cease to do so merely because this is deemed incompatible with human rights protection. One might be required as a matter of public order or in the interests of preserving the rights of others to refrain from manifesting those rights, but is it the place of human rights law to attempt to influence and judge the validity of those beliefs themselves? . . . [I]t needs to be accepted that in recognizing the freedom of religion, the international system is recognizing the intrusion of systems of belief which are of fundamental importance to the believer and which may dictate patterns of behaviour which simply cannot be contained within the existing web of human rights thinking" (Malcolm D. Evans, "Religious Diversity and Religious Liberty as Human Right" [paper submitted for presentation at the *International Conference on Human Rights and Our Responsibilities Towards Future Generations: An Inter-Religious Perspective*, 6–8 May 1999, Valetta, Malta], 13 [endnotes 50 and 51 omitted]).

[51] This can be concluded from the second prong of the three-pronged test for permissible restrictions.

[52] FGM is a broad, collective term for "all procedures involving partial or total removal of the external female genitalia or other injury to the female genital organs whether for cultural or other non-therapeutic reasons." See *Female Genital Mutilation: A Joint WHO/UNICEF/UNFPA Statement* (Geneva: World Health Organization, 1997), 3. See generally Anika Rahman and Nahid Toubia, eds., *Female Genital Mutilation: A Guide to Laws and Policies Worldwide* (London: Zed Books, 2000); Isabelle R. Gunning, "Women and

prong of this test. This entails that the state has satisfied the two requirements of the "prescribed by law" test.[53] First, the limitation on a manifestation of religion or belief must have some basis in domestic law.[54] Second, the domestic law in question must be adequately accessible, foreseeable, and precise. In other words, in the three cases discussed below, the state has demonstrated that the domestic law in question was "accessible, unambiguous and narrowly and precisely drawn so as to enable individuals to predict with reasonable certainty in advance the legality or otherwise of a particular action."[55]

Furthermore, it is assumed that each case is successfully brought before an international supervisory human rights body, most notably the UN Human Rights Committee at global level or the European Court of Human Rights, the African Commission on Human and Peoples' Rights or the Inter-American Court of Human Rights at regional level.[56] In particular, all national remedies have been exhausted and the defendant state in question has recognized the competence of the supervisory body to examine the complaint.[57]

Traditional Practices: Female Genital Surgery," in Askin and Koenig, *Women and International Human Rights Law,* 1:651–82; *Report of the Working Group on Traditional Practices Affecting the Health of Women and Girls,* UN Doc. E/CN.4/1986/42, paras. 25–138 (1986) (hereinafter "Report of Working Group").

[53] See Hasan and Chaush v. Bulgaria, App. No. 30985/96 (ECtHR, 26 October 2000), para. 84. See also Larissis and Others v. Greece, 27 EHRR 329 (1999) (ECtHR 1998-I, 24 February 1998), 378, para. 40; *Report on the Question of Religious Intolerance,* paras. 107(d), 110(b); *Siracusa Principles on the Limitation and Derogation Provisions in the International Covenant on Civil and Political Rights,* UN Doc. E/CN.4/1985/4 (1984), annex, principles 15–18 (hereinafter "Siracusa Principles").

[54] It has been suggested that the "prescribed by law" test also extends to unwritten norms of common law which are clearly expressed. Manfred Nowak, *U.N. Covenant on Civil and Political Rights: CCPR Commentary* (Kehl: N. P. Engel, 1993), 324.

[55] "Principles on Freedom of Expression and Protection of Reputation," *Article 19, Defining Defamation* (London: Article 19, 2000), 4. See also *Johannesburg Principles on National Security, Freedom of Expression and Access to Information,* UN Doc. E/CN.4/1996/39 (1996), annex Principle 1.1(a). For examples of vague, imprecise, and so-called "catch-all" provisions, see Report on Question of Religious Intolerance, para. 107.

[56] *The Arab Human Rights Charter,* which has been presumably adopted by the Council of the Arab League on 15 September 1994 and which has not been ratified by a single Arab state since, is "weak on mechanisms for the implementation of the rights it recognizes, since the powers and competence of the committee of human rights experts it provides for are confined to examining reports submitted to it by states parties to the Charter, and reporting on them to the Permanent Commission of Human Rights of the Arab League" (Abdullahi A. An-Na'im, "Human Rights in the Arab World: A Regional Perspective," *Human Rights Quarterly* 23 [2001]: 701–32, 715 [footnote 25 omitted]).

[57] A wealth of literature is available on these international supervisory bodies, including a discussion on how to bring a case successfully before them. See, e.g., Sarah Joseph, Jenny Schultz, and Melissa Castan, *The International Covenant on Civil and Political Rights: Cases, Materials and Commentary* (Oxford: Oxford University Press, 2000); Martin Scheinin, "The Human Rights Committee," in this volume; Ineke Boerefijn, *The Reporting Procedure under the Covenant on Civil and Political Rights: Practice and Procedures of the Human Rights Committee* (Antwerp: Intersentia , 1999); Javier Martínez-Torrón and Rafael Navarro-Valls, "The Protection of Religious Freedom in the System of the Council of Europe", in this volume; van Dijk and van Hoof, *Theory and Practice of the European Convention*; Chidi Anselm Odinkalu and Camilla Christensen, "The African Commission on Human and Peoples' Rights: The Development of its Non-State Communication Procedures," *Human Rights Quarterly* 20 (1998): 235–80; Evelyn A. Ankumah, *The African Commission on Human and Peoples' Rights: Practice and Procedures* (Boston: Martinus Nijhoff, 1996); David Harris and Stephen Livingstone, *The Inter-American System of Human Rights* (Oxford: Clarendon Press, 1998).

Finally, it should be noted that the three cases discussed in this section do not necessarily only involve freedom of religion or belief. As discussed in section I, freedom to manifest religion or belief is often intertwined with a number of other human rights and fundamental freedoms. Depending on the specific circumstances of a case, the three cases could therefore involve a number of other human rights too. For instance, women may also invoke their right to freedom of expression when they are not free to dress the way they want and are subjected to clothing requirements that do not conform to their self-expression or when they desire to undergo FGM. Furthermore, women's freedom from torture or cruel, inhuman or degrading treatment or punishment is at stake when corporal punishment is imposed to enforce a certain dress code.[58] Depending on the particulars of a case, a dissenting woman may therefore rely not only on claiming her external freedom of religion or belief.

1. The Freedom to Undergo Female Genital Mutilation vs. the Protection of Public Health

FGM is practiced on females in different parts of the world, usually at an early age, for a variety of nontherapeutic reasons, including custom, tradition, religion, belief, and aesthetics.[59] It is known to be practiced among followers of different religions and beliefs, including Christians of many denominations, Sunni and Shiite Muslims, Ethiopian Jews (the Falasha), and adherents of indigenous African beliefs. FGM is generally accepted as having predated a variety of monotheistic religions, including Islam and Christianity. It is widely acknowledged that FGM is not encouraged or required by any major monotheistic religion and many therefore claim that FGM has erroneously been associated with religion.[60] Nevertheless, in some cultures women and girls consider this controversial practice to be associated with their religion or belief, including less wellknown, nonglobal, nontheistic or atheistic beliefs. They will argue that FGM is a religiously prescribed or religiously motivated ritual associated with certain stages of life.[61] On that basis they will demand protection of their external freedom of religion or belief.[62] Dissenting women who favor the practice will probably prefer to refer

---

[58] For other examples, see General Comment 28, para. 13.

[59] The World Health Organization estimates that 138 million women worldwide have undergone the procedure; Carol Midgley, "Why Must We Still Be Mutilated?" *The Times,* 24 August 2001, <http://www.thetimes.co.uk/article/0,,7-2001293129,00.html>.

[60] See, e.g., Rahman and Toubia, *Female Genital Mutilation: A Guide,* 6, 31, 34; Halima Embarek Warzazi, *Preliminary Special Rapporteur's Report on Traditional Practices Affecting the Health of Women and Children,* UN Doc. E/CN.4/Sub.2/1995/6, para. 40 (1995); Halima Embarek Warzazi, *Third Report on the Situation Regarding the Elimination of Traditional Practices Affecting the Health of Women and the Girl Child,* UN Doc. E/CN.4/Sub.2/1999/14, paras. 41, 47–50 (1999) (referring to a decision of the Egyptian Council of State and a symposium of twenty-six religious leaders and medical personnel from eleven African countries held in Banjul, Gambia, 20–24 July 1998, which emphasized that FGM is not prescribed by any religion); *Guidelines on the Prevention of Female Genital Mutilation,* 2d rev. ed. (Copenhagen: Danish Ministry of Foreign Affairs, 1986), 4, 19.

[61] General Comment 22, para. 4.

[62] Religion has been mentioned in nearly 19% of the cases and tradition in over 54% of the cases. Report of the Working Group, para. 59. Accordingly, it has been noted that since "religion or belief also includes indigenous beliefs, tradition will often coincide with religion or belief" (de Jong, *Freedom of Thought,* 152 n. 268). Furthermore, "if a woman holds a belief prescribing female circumcision, this practice should be

to it as "female circumcision," "female genital cutting," or "female genital surgery."[63] The term "female genital mutilation" is considered by them a derogatory value judgement by outsiders, which implies insensitivity and disrespect both toward women and girls who have undergone the practice and people involved in the practice.[64]

In a country that specifically bans any form of FGM in the interests of public health, the law of the state typically conflicts with dissenting women's outward manifestation of their religion or belief. This warrants an assessment of whether the state can justify the restriction of their external freedom on the grounds of public health. It has been established that a state may invoke the grounds of "public health" in order "to take measures dealing with a serious threat to the health of the population or individual members of the population. These measures must be specifically aimed at preventing disease or injury or providing care for the sick and injured."[65]

To justify in the present case a restriction based on the interests of "public health," a state must distinguish between situations involving dissenting adult women and those involving dissenting girls. In the case of dissenting women, the state must demonstrate that the health effects of FGM are serious. For instance, they can produce evidence of the immediate and long-term health risks FGM entails, which vary depending on the nature and extremity of the procedure followed.[66] The well-documented physical complications include hemorrhage, severe pain, damage to surrounding organs, urinary retention, keloids, recurrent infections, complications during childbirth, and in some cases death. Beyond physical injury, the health consequences may extend to severe shock, emotional stress, and various psychological, sexual, and reproductive disorders.[67] Furthermore, the state may demonstrate that the strong consensus of the

---

respected, or restricted, irrespective of the question of whether it constitutes the manifestation of a major religion or of a less well-known belief" (ibid., 153).

[63] For an explanation on the ramifications of the uses of the different terminologies, see Gunning, "Women and Traditional Practices," 651 n.1.

[64] It has been argued against approaching FGM as an "arrogant perceiver . . . [one who] sees himself as the center of the world" (Gunning, "Arrogant Perception, World-Travelling and Multicultural Feminism: The Case of Female Genital Surgeries," *Columbia Human Rights Law Review* 23 [1992], 229). See Coomaraswamy, "Different but Free: Cultural Relativism and Women's Rights as Human Rights," *Religious Fundamentalisms,* 83, 84, 86, 87, who rather speaks of "the communal arrogance of the international community." Although vehemently opposed to the practice, a circumcised Somali woman, born and brought up in the UK, explains that she is not angry with her mother: "People think 'Oh God, those mothers, how could they hurt their children?' but I know they did it for the love of us. In the old days a man wouldn't marry a woman who wasn't circumcised. To women in our culture, getting married and having children is everything and there is great shame on a woman who doesn't achieve that. Our mothers and grandmothers had had it done to them, yes, but they had forgotten the physical pain they went through. In fact, they had it worse. In the old days they used to use thorns to hold the skin together" (Midgley, "Why must we still be mutilated?" <http://www.thetimes.co.uk/article/0,,7-2001293129,00.html>).

[65] See Siracusa Principles, principle 25.

[66] See, e.g., *Traditional or Customary Practices Affecting the Health of Women: Report of the Secretary-General,* UN Doc. A/54/341 (1999); *Report of the Working Group,* part I .

[67] For instance, hemorrhage is a common and almost unavoidable immediate result. See "General Fact Sheet on Health Consequences," in the World Health Organisation's Information Kit on Female Genital Mutilation (WHO/FHE/94.4, 1994) (there are no pages given to the Fact Sheets). For more detail on the health effects, see, e.g., Rahman and Toubia, *Female Genital Mutilation: A Guide,* 8–9; Heidi Jones et al., "Female Genital Cutting Practices in Burkina Faso and Mali and Their Negative Health Outcomes," *Studies of Family Planning* 30 (1999): 220; Report Of Working Group, part I.

world community, as evidenced in numerous international forums and non-governmental organizations, has denounced FGM as a serious threat to the health of women and girls and specifically called upon states to legislate against it.[68] Moreover, the state may submit that the restriction is not arbitrary, unfair, or based on irrational considerations. The restriction is necessary in the interest of public health and warrants overriding external freedom. The public authorities will therefore argue that they have satisfied the second and third prongs too.

In the case of dissenting girls, the state can produce the same overwhelming evidence in revealing the harmful effects of FGM. In addition, it can refer to an internationally agreed prohibition on harmful practices such as FGM which establishes that "[p]ractices of a religion or belief in which a child is brought up must not be injurious to his physical or mental health or to his full development."[69] This prohibition demonstrates that the restriction of external freedom is justified to preserve the health or even the life choices of the girls in question. Furthermore, the state can point out that these girls are for the most part very young and in no position to give informed consent.[70] The life and health of the girl child must be protected.[71] In conjunction with the public health ground, the state can therefore also invoke the fundamental rights and freedoms of others ground, namely, the right of children to the enjoyment of the highest attainable standard of health. Especially given the vulnerability of children, it is unlikely that dissenting girls—or rather their dissenting parents or legal guardians—can successfully argue that the three-prong test for permissible restrictions has not been satisfied by the state.

---

[68] For a concise overview of action taken by the UN system, see *Traditional or Customary Practices Affecting the Health of Women: Report of the Secretary-General,* UN Doc. A/54/341 (1999). See also *Female Genital Mutilation: A Joint WHO/UNICEF/UNFPA Statement.* For a denunciation by the UN General Assembly, see UNGA Resolution 54/133 (1999), para. 3(d), UN Doc. A/RES/54/133 (2000). See also General Recommendation 24 on article 12 of the Convention on the Elimination of All Forms of Discrimination against Women—Women and Health, adopted by the Committee on the Elimination of Discrimination against Women, UN Doc. A/54/38/Rev.1, 3–7 (1999) (hereinafter "General Recommendation on art. 12 CEDAW") and the Beijing +5 document. For an overview of regional, national and international initiatives, see Warzazi , *Fifth Report on the Situation Regarding the Elimination of Traditional Practices Affecting the Health of Women and the Girl Child,* UN Doc. E/CN.4/Sub.2/2001/27 (2001), paras. 8–83.

[69] 1981 Declaration, art. 5(5). See also *Convention on the Rights of the Child,* art. 24(3) (hereinafter "CRC"); *African Charter on the Rights and Welfare of the Child,* art. 21(1); Committee on Economic, Social and Cultural Rights, General Comment 14 on the right to the highest attainable standard of health (art. 12 ICESCR), UN Doc. E/C.12/2000/4, para. 22 (2000) (hereinafter General Comment on art. 12 ICESCR). Although a specific reference to female genital mutilation was omitted in CRC, art. 24(3) (Brigit C.A. Toebes, *The Right to Health as a Human Right in International Law* [Antwerp: Intersentia , 1998], 57–58), the UN Committee on the Rights of the Child, in its evaluation of state reports, has consistently characterized FGM as a "harmful traditional practice" that governments must work to eliminate. See generally Rahman and Toubia, *Female Genital Mutilation: A Guide,* 48–49.

[70] Michael Freeman, *The Moral Status of Children: Essays on the Rights of the Child* (The Hague: Martinus Nijhoff, 1997), 145.

[71] This line of reasoning has been delineated in the context of refusals of a blood transfusion of children: "If . . . a Jehovah's Witness were to refuse a life-saving blood transfusion for his or her child, the State (doctor), in our opinion, not only has the right but also the duty to intervene with this manifestation of freedom of religion and exercise of parental rights in order to protect the life of the child" (Manfred Nowak and Tanja Vospernik, "Permissible Restrictions on Freedom of Religion or Belief," in Grotens and Tahzib-Lie, *Seminar on Freedom of Religion or Belief,* 65, see also 70). The authors doubt, however, whether the state may also prevent an adult from refusing a blood transfusion (ibid., 61–62, 65).

Dissenting women who make a cognizant, fully informed, and uncoerced choice to undergo FGM and give their informed consent[72] may nevertheless reject the claim that the restriction is necessary to protect public health, since only their health is at risk.[73] These women may argue that the state must distinguish between those manifestations of religion or belief that endanger the health of other persons and those that only affect the health of the participant. Only in the former case would it be justifiable for the state to invoke "public health" as a ground for imposing a restriction. As to the latter case, adults are allowed to make choices about their own bodies, including those that may adversely affect their health and impose a burden upon the public health system. In this connection, they can point out that the public health system is more burdened with the effects of excessive alcohol consumption and cigarette smoking than with the effects of FGM. According to this line of thinking, the adult's informed consent precludes a state from prohibiting persons to cut or carve their bodies and even injure themselves.[74]

The state may respond by providing numerous reasons why this line of reasoning is not tenable. First, the term "public health" includes both collective and individual health interests.[75] Second, if the woman has a sexual partner, the psychosexual and psychological effects of FGM could give rise to conflict with the partner and therefore affect his health and well-being too. Third, a sexually active woman who has contracted a blood borne disease, such as hepatitis B or human immunodeficiency virus/acquired immunodeficiency syndrome (HIV/AIDS), as a result of undergoing FGM, may transmit this disease to others and thereby put their health at

[72] Principle 11(2) of the *Principles for the Protection of Persons with Mental Illness and the Improvement of Mental Health Care* (UNGA Resolution 46/119 [1991]) defines "informed consent" to be "consent obtained freely, without threats or improper inducements." Prior to giving consent, the patient must be provided with "adequate and understandable information in a form and language understood by the patient" on such matters as alternative treatments and "possible pain or discomfort, risks and side effects of the proposed treatment." Informed consent thus requires that a woman be free from coercion and have adequate information in order to make her decision.

[73] It has been argued that public health should be interpreted in a restrictive way and that "it is difficult to see how public health at large can be affected by female circumcision" (de Jong, *Freedom of Thought,* 153).

[74] For an analogous case regarding the balancing of state and individual interests in cases of safety concerns relating to an adult, see K. Singh Bhinder v. Canada, Comm. No. 208/1986 (UN Human Rights Committee, 9 November 1989), UN Doc. A/45/40 (Vol. II), Annex IX, sec. E (1990). This case deals with a naturalized Canadian citizen and a Sikh by religion, whose labor contract as a maintenance electrician with the Canadian National Railway Company was terminated as a result of his refusal to wear safety headgear during his work, which would require him to relinquish his turban. From the views of the Human Rights Committee, it can be inferred that paternalistic safety legislation falls within the scope of legitimate restrictions. For a discussion, see Tahzib, *Freedom of Religion or Belief,* 294–300. See also Nowak and Vospernik, "Permissible Restrictions on Freedom of Religion or Belief," 57.

[75] See, e.g., Bert B. Lockwood et al., "Working Paper for the Committee of Experts on Limitation Provisions," *Human Rights Quarterly* 7, no. 1 (1985): 35, 64, 65. See also Siracusa Principles, principle 25; Alexandre Kiss, "Commentary by the Rapporteur on the Limitation Provisions," *Human Rights Quarterly* 7, no. 1 (1985): 15, 20. Doubts as to whether the state may invoke public health to protect individual health are expressed by Nowak and Vospernik, "Permissible Restrictions on Freedom of Religion or Belief," 61–62. At the same time, at 61, they argue that external freedom may be restricted "if the manifestation of a specific religion includes activities which as such are detrimental to the health of its members and possibly others. This applies, for instance, to the practice of female genital mutilation in certain African cultures and religions.

risk.[76] Fourth, FGM can lead to complications during pregnancy and childbirth, thereby endangering the health and life of the unborn child.[77] Fifth, it seems reasonable that states have an obligation to inform the public, most notably women and girls, of the risks of FGM and its detrimental effects on health.[78] Health information and education are crucial strategies for eliminating FGM and should not be seen as unusual.[79] For instance, states regularly inform the public of the harmful effects of excessive alcohol consumption and cigarette smoking as matters of public health.[80] Sixth, unlike excessive alcohol consumption and cigarette smoking, FGM is banned because it constitutes a physical intervention with immediate and long-term health risks. Any form of FGM involving partial or total removal of the external female genitalia is irreversible.[81] Seventh, the very nature of a public health system implies that the community as a whole will bear the costs of treating complications from FGM, which often occur frequently and in a variety of forms. The financial implications for the community are therefore another reason why it is in the "public" interest to ban the practice. Moreover, various African states have pointed out that FGM constitutes "a major public health problem for health services that are already overburdened and frequently deficient."[82] This last reason is, however, not or less relevant in some other parts of the world where, for example, the effects of over consumption of alcohol and nicotine is relatively a bigger burden to the public health system.

The state may bring to light that the second, third, and fourth reasons demonstrate that the health of others are at stake too. In addition to the public health ground, it could therefore also rely on the fundamental rights and freedoms of others ground to ban FGM, in particular by referring to the right of others to the enjoyment of the highest attainable standard of health.

---

76 World Health Organization, *Regional Plan of Action to Accelerate the Elimination of Female Genital Mutilation in Africa* (Brazzaville: WHO Regional Office for Africa, 1997), 4. See also the *Declaration of Commitment on HIV/AIDS*, para. 61; the agreed conclusions of the UN Commission on the Status of Women on Women, the girl child and human immunodeficiency virus/acquired immunodeficiency syndrome (HIV/AIDS), para. 3, UN Doc. E/2001/27 (2001), 9.

77 Logistic regression analyses have shown significant positive relationships between the severity of genital cutting and the probability that a woman would have gynecological and obstetric complications. See Jones et al., "Female Genital Cutting Practices," 219–28.

78 See CRC, art. 24(3). See also 1981 Declaration, art. 5(5); CEDAW, art. 10(h). Although not expressly mentioned in ICESCR, art. 12, and CEDAW, art. 12, this obligation can be inferred from these provisions. See Toebes, *Right to Health*, 57–58, 129, 148, 154, 258, 267–68, 332. See also General Comment on art. 12 ICESCR, para. 21; General Recommendation on art. 12 CEDAW.

79 Rahman and Toubia, *Female Genital Mutilation: A Guide*, 49–50. See also UN Sub-Commission on the Promotion and Protection of Human Rights, Resolution 2000/10 (2000), para. 2.

80 This line of reasoning has been used in regard to the state obligation to inform the public, including children, of the risks of contracting HIV/AIDS and other sexually transmitted diseases. See Corinne Packer, "Sex Education: Child's Rights, Parent's Choice or State's Obligation," in *Of Innocence and Autonomy: Children, Sex and Human Rights*, ed. Eric Heinze (Aldershot: Dartmouth, 2000), 163, 172; Rahman and Toubia, *Female Genital Mutilation: A Guide*, 49–50.

81 This fact must be emphasized when stating the possibility to undergo an operation to reverse FGM. This is, for instance, not clear in David Charter and Dominic Kennedy, "Doctors Put on Alert for Girl 'Butchery,'" *The Times*, 21 August 2001, <http://www.thetimes.co.uk/article/0,,2-2001290802,00.html>. When a female's external genitalia are removed with the remainder being stitched together leaving a matchstick-sized opening for the passage of urine or menstrual blood, an operation to widen the orifice is, however, possible.

82 World Health Organization, *Regional Plan of Action*, 4.

The foregoing demonstrates that there are compelling reasons to recognize the ban on FGM as necessary on the grounds of public health. From the interactive discussion above, it emerges that it is likely that the state can satisfy the second and the third prongs. Considering that the strong consensus of the international community has denounced FGM as a serious threat to the health of women and girls and specifically called upon states to legislate against it, the margin of appreciation of a state that is out of line appears to be reduced almost to vanishing point—and perhaps even absent—in this case, and the international supervisory body's scrutiny as to whether this state met the three-prong test more rigorous. In this case the defendant state is not out of line with international consensus, and the restriction of the woman's external freedom results in FGM being totally barred.

In this context, however, it is important to emphasize a broader governmental strategy to change individual behavior and social norms to deter people from practicing FGM. While not compromising the determination to prohibit FGM, states should be sensitive to affected women and girls and offer them assistance in finding non-harmful alternatives to the practice. For instance, in traditions in which FGM symbolizes the girl's passage to womanhood, the wearing of a special bracelet[83] or a symbolic gift-giving[84] may be encouraged. In this way the ceremonial traditions underlying the practice can continue without the harmful practice.

2. The Freedom to Wear Religious Clothing in the Workplace vs. the Protection of Public Safety, Order, Health or Morals, or the Fundamental Rights and Freedoms of Others

The wearing of "distinctive clothing or headcoverings" has long been practiced as part of the observance or practice of certain religions and beliefs. It is therefore not surprising that such garments have been explicitly recognized as falling within the ambit of external freedom by some human rights bodies.[85] This has meant that women have

[83] Naber, "Introduction," in Naber, *Freedom of Religion: A Precious Human Right*, 1, 5.

[84] Elaine Eliah, "Reaching for a Healthier Future," *Populi* 23, no. 1 (1996): 14; Rahman and Toubia, *Female Genital Mutilation: A Guide*, 77–78.

[85] Most notably, this has been recognized by the UN Human Rights Committee. See General Comment 22, para. 4. Incomprehensibly, however, the European Commission on Human Rights held that the wearing of religiously prescribed or religiously motivated headscarves is not embraced by external freedom. See Karaduman v. Turkey, 74 Decisions and Reports 93 (EComHR, 74 App. No. 16278/90, 3 May 1993), 93, 108–09; Bulut v. Turkey, App. No. 18783/91 (EComHR, 3 May 1993). Clearly, this indicates "a very restrictive view" of what counts as external freedom. Evans, *Religious Liberty and International Law in Europe* (Cambridge: Cambridge University Press, 1997), 312. See also Nowak and Vospernik, "Permissible Restrictions on Freedom of Religion or Belief," 58. However, the European Court of Human Rights does recognize the wearing of headscarf to be within the ambit of external freedom. See Dahlab v. Switzerland, App. No. 42393/98 (ECtHR, 15 February 2001). See also Case of Refah Partisi, Erbakan, Kazan, and Tekdal v. Turkey (ECtHR, 31 July 2001), para. 72, where the Court came fairly close to making a pronouncement. It should also be noted that the Court has found that "but for very exceptional cases, the right to freedom of religion as guaranteed under the Convention excludes any discretion on the part of the State to determine whether religious beliefs or the means used to express such beliefs are legitimate." See Hasan and Chaush v. Bulgaria, App. No. 30985/96 (ECtHR, 26 October 2000), para. 78. See also Manoussakis v. Greece, 23 EHRR 387 (1997) (ECtHR 1996-IV, 26 September 1996) (commented on by Willi Fuhrmann, "Perspectives on Religious Freedom from the Vantage Point of the European Court of Human Rights," *BYU Law Review* [2000]: 833).

the freedom, if they wish, to wear headscarves prescribed or motivated by their religion, or otherwise associated with it.[86] Nevertheless, in some states there have been several cases of protest against female teachers and students wearing headscarves in schools, universities, and other public settings.[87] There have also been cases of employers objecting to female employees wearing headscarves.[88] Such women are often forced to choose between relinquishing their headscarf and not being offered, or losing, a job.

The hypothetical case in this context concerns a public employer who does not permit a female employee to wear a religiously prescribed or religiously motivated headdress in the workplace. The hypothetical state in question is a secular state or a state with an official or established religion and a Muslim minority. The question discussed in this context is whether the state may legitimately prohibit a woman from making a cognizant, informed, and uncoerced decision to wear her headscarf in the workplace.[89] This question is analyzed under the three-prong test for permissible restrictions described above. As noted earlier, it is assumed that the first prong has been satisfied and that there is some basis in domestic law for the employer's refusal to allow the headscarf. According to the second prong of the test, it must be determined whether the state can invoke any of the five permissible compelling state interests to justify its ban on women in public office from wearing headscarves for religiously prescribed or religiously motivated reasons. Pursuant to the third prong, it must be determined whether the protection of the legitimate aim was necessary.

Depending on the relative facts surrounding the case, the state will obviously attempt to make a plausible case that it did have a good reason for interfering with the woman's external freedom by producing one or more legitimate aims. With regard to jobs that demand strict compliance with certain safety and health requirements, the state will likely invoke the public safety[90] or public health[91] ground. For instance, in

---

[86] For a detailed analysis and interpretation of the passages of the Koran relating to the hijab, the veil, see Fatima Mernissi, *The Veil and the Male Elite: A Feminist Interpretation of Women's Rights in Islam,* trans. Mary Jo Lakeland (Reading, Mass.: Perseus Books, 1991), 85–101. For the meaning and implications of wearing the veil for Muslim women who choose to do so, see, e.g., Fatheena Mubarak, "Muslim Women and Religious Identification: Women and the Veil," *Many Religions, All Australian: Religious Settlement, Identity and Cultural Diversity,* ed. Gary D. Bouma (Kew, Australia: The Christian Research Association, 1997), 123. It has been argued, however, that the function of the veil at the time of Muhammad was to protect women, and thus the veil's most appropriate modern equivalent is education and schooling which, in our times, gives the most protection to a woman. Soheib Bencheikh, *Mariane et le Prophète: L'islam dans la France Laïque* (Paris: Éditions Grasset & Fasquelle, 1998), 142–45.

[87] See, e.g., US Department of State, *Annual Report,* 295, 302, 341, 396; Elimination of All Forms of Religious Intolerance: note by the Secretary-General, UN Doc. A/55/280/Add.1, paras. 18–21, 48 (2000).

[88] See, e.g., US Department of State, *Annual Report,* 302, 341, 396; Amor, *Civil and Political Rights, Including Freedom of Expression,* UN Doc. E/CN.4/1999/58/Add.1, para. 37(a) (1998) . See also *Oral Statement on Freedom of Religion or Belief by the Finnish Presidency of the European Union to the OSCE Review Conference, Human Dimension,* 23 September 1999, Vienna, OSCE Doc. RC.DEL/103/99, para. 5.

[89] For a discussion of the variety of reasons advanced by Muslim women who make an informed choice to wear Muslim dress and a refutal of state justifications for a ban of such dress, see Barbara Roblin Mirza, "Selected Personal Rights and Freedoms: Rights to Wear Clothing of One's Choice, to Drive, and to Travel Unattended and Without Permission," in Askin and Koenig, *Women and International Human Rights Law,* 3:123.

[90] The "public safety" ground has been defined to mean "protection against danger to the safety of persons, to their life or physical integrity or serious damage to their property" (Siracusa Principles, principle 33. See also Nowak and Vospernik, "Permissible Restrictions on Freedom of Religion or Belief," 56–57).

the armed forces, specific safety conditions may preclude the wearing of certain kinds of headdress.[92] Another example may be found on an electrical facility where safety regulations require all employees to wear protective headgear.[93] Furthermore, a job involving close contact with hazardous materials or fire may preclude the wearing of certain loose, all-covering garments for religiously prescribed or religiously motivated reasons.

For other types of jobs, the state can consider presenting one or more of the other three grounds. For example, as regards a public school teacher post,[94] the state will likely refer to legislation that prescribes the secular nature and the religious and political neutrality of public schools or of all public services.[95] The state's line of reasoning could be that the headdress is a visible token of religion, ostentatious religiosity, a sign of extremism, or a symbol of female submission[96] and therefore not acceptable in public schools. Accordingly, the state will likely refer to the fundamental rights or freedoms of others,[97] most notably the rights and freedoms of the pupils and their

---

[91] The "public health" ground may be invoked "in order to allow a state to take measures dealing with a serious threat to the health of the population or individual members of the population. These measures must be specifically aimed at preventing disease or injury or providing care for the sick and injured" (see Siracusa Principles, principle 25. See also Nowak and Vospernik, "Permissible Restrictions on Freedom of Religion or Belief," 61–62).

[92] See, e.g., Goldman v. Weinberger, Secretary of Defense, et al., 475 US 503 (1986). Goldman involved an orthodox Jewish rabbi who served as a clinical psychologist in an US Air Force hospital. His religious obligation to wear a *yarmulke* conflicted with military regulation that required him to keep his head uncovered while on duty indoors. The US Supreme Court, in a narrow five-to-four decision, rejected his application for an exemption, emphasizing the military interest for uniformity in dress. Justice Brennan, in sharp dissent, lamented that the Court had abdicated "its role as principal protector of individual liberties in favor of credulous deference to unsupported assertions of military necessity." Critical questions have been asked in relation to this decision: "If wearing headcovering indoors were a Christian religious obligation rather than a Jewish one, one wonders if the result would have been the same. In fact, would the problem ever have arisen in the first place?" (Samuel Rabinove, *Religious Rights and Freedoms: What They Mean for Jews* [New York: The American Jewish Committee, 1988], 13). Congress subsequently passed legislation to exempt *yarmulkes* from the military dress code which the Court refused to craft judicially; see 10 USCA, sec. 774 (1988). By contrast, the British army has traditionally allowed Sikh soldiers to wear turbans. See Leon Shaskolsky-Sheleff, "Rabbi Captain Goldman's Yarmulke, Freedom of Religion and Conscience, and Civil (Military) Disobedience," *Israel Yearbook of Human Rights* 17 (1987): 206.

[93] For a case in which a practising Sikh working at an electrical facility had to remove his turban, see K. Singh Bhinder v. Canada, Comm. No. 208/1986 (UN Human Rights Committee, 9 November 1989), UN Doc. A/45/40 (Vol. II), Annex IX, sec. E, para. 6.2, (1990). For a discussion, see Tahzib, *Freedom of Religion or Belief*, 294–300.

[94] In this context, the reference to "public schools" is to be read as referring to schools maintained by public funds and supervised by municipal, county, or state authorities.

[95] Although this case deals with public employment, it should be emphasized that states should take all steps necessary to put an end to discriminatory actions both in the public and the private sector which impair the equal enjoyment by women of their right to freedom of religion or belief. See General Comment 28, para. 4.

[96] For instance, throughout much of the OSCE area, wearing the *hijab* in a particular way is interpreted as a sign of extremism. See Statement by Laila Al-Marayati, *US Delegation to the OSCE Implementation Review Meeting*, 27 October 1998, OSCE file IMP/98, no. 85, 7.

[97] The state in question can refer to European Court's holding in *Dahlab v. Switzerland*, where the Court declared that to wear the Islamic veil "seems to be imposed to women by a koranic prescription which . . . is difficult to reconcile with the principle of equality of sexes. To wear the Islamic veil is also difficult to reconcile with the message of tolerance, of respect for others, and above all of equality and nondiscrimination that every teacher must transmit to the students in a democracy" (unofficial translation; the text of the decision is available only in French in the website of the European Court: <http://www.echr.coe.int>).

parents or legal guardians.[98] In these circumstances the state considers the impact on young, vulnerable, impressionable pupils of a teacher wearing a headscarf or a garment covering her body and face in the classroom, the position of influence and trust that teachers assume over their pupils, the educational role of teachers, pupils' emulation of their teachers as role models, the liberty of parents or legal guardians to ensure that their children receive a religious and moral education in conformity with their own convictions, the likely interference with pupils' religious beliefs, and the principle of denominational neutrality within the school.[99]

For the position of judge, the state will most likely also rely on the fundamental rights and freedoms of others argument and emphasize the right of others to a neutral state, in particular to independent and impartial courts.[100] A neutral state should establish a framework of rules within which individuals can pursue their differing visions of the good life.[101] Within this framework, members of the judiciary must at all times maintain their independence and impartiality.[102] To offer sufficient guarantees to exclude any legitimate doubt in this respect, it has been argued that judges may not visibly affiliate themselves with a particular religion, belief, or political party while on duty.[103] This means that a judge wearing a headscarf during a court session may raise legitimate doubts as to the confidence and authority which the courts must inspire in the public.[104]

---

[98] For a description of the "fundamental rights and freedoms of others" ground, see Siracusa Principles, principles 35–37.

[99] For parental rights to direct child education, see, e.g., ICCPR, art. 18(4) and 24(1); ICESCR, art. 13(3); CRC, art. 14(2); 1981 Declaration, art. 5; Protocol No. 1 to the ECHR, art. 2; ACHR, art. 12(4); Vienna Concluding Document, principle 16(7); Convention Against Discrimination in Education, art. 5(1)(b); Charter of Fundamental Rights of the European Union, art. 14(3).

[100] This has, for instance, been argued by Paul B. Cliteur in a Dutch newspaper. See Cliteur, "Hoofddoekje past niet bij neutrale rechter [Headscarf does not suit a neutral judge]," *NRC Handelsblad,* 30 June 2001, 9.

[101] See Micheal Prowse, "Take a Peek Behind the Veil of Tolerance," *Financial Times,* 18–19 August 2001, xxiv.

[102] International human rights instruments refer to the independence and impartiality of the judiciary. See, e.g., ICCPR, art. 14(1); UDHR, art. 10; ECHR, art. 6(1). See also *Basic Principles on the Independence of the Judiciary,* adopted by the 7th UN Congress on the Prevention of Crime and the Treatment of Offenders held at Milan from 26 August to 6 September 1985 and endorsed by UNGA Resolutions 40/32 (1985) and 40/146 (1985) (hereinafter "Basic Principles on the Independence of the Judiciary"). The latter, principle 10, does state that "[i]n the selection of judges, there shall be no discrimination against a person on the grounds of race, color, sex, religion, political or other opinion, national or social origin, property, birth or status, except that a requirement, that a candidate for judicial office must be a national of the country concerned, shall not be considered discriminatory."

[103] In reply to questions of members of the Dutch Parliament regarding the permissibility of headscarves in the Dutch judiciary, the Dutch Minister of Justice, Albert Hendrik Korthals, has taken this position. For the Minister's reply, see his letter to the Chairperson of the Second Chamber of Dutch Parliament of 30 August 2001, reference 5109689/01/6, <http://www.minjust.nl/c_actual/persber/pb0809.htm> (only available in Dutch). In this letter reference is made to the following excerpt of a judgment of the European Court of Human Rights: "The existence of impartiality for the purposes of Article 6 para. 1 [ECHR] must be determined according to . . . an objective test, that is ascertaining whether the judge offered guarantees sufficient to exclude any legitimate doubt in this respect" (Fey v. Austria, App. No. 14396/88 [ECtHR 255-A, 24 February 1993], para. 28).

[104] The European Court of Human Rights has stated, in a different context, that "[un]der the objective test, it must be determined whether . . . there are ascertainable facts which may raise doubts as to his impartiality. In this respect even appearances may be of a certain importance. What is at stake is the confidence which the courts in a democratic society must inspire in the public. . . . What is determinant is whether this fear can be held to be objectively justified" (Fey v. Austria, para. 30).

Further to the fundamental rights and freedoms of others ground, especially when the particular employment situation makes this less relevant, an ostensibly secular state with a Muslim majority could consider referring to the protection of public order. Its line of reasoning would be that permitting such a visible token of religion in the workplace might result in non-Muslims being put under pressure, and order in the workplace or the smooth running of the public sector being disturbed. A state with a Muslim minority—this could be a secular state or a state with an official or established religion—could refer to the incompatibility with public order and morality norms of the general population.

The dissenting female employee can challenge the ground, or grounds, asserted by the state as being no more than rationalizations of limitations imposed for quite different and impermissible purposes. Her arguments obviously depend on the relative facts of her case, including the woman's professional duties and the state's claimed ground. Generally, in situations involving the fundamental rights of others, as discussed in the above examples, the dissenting woman can question why a person's headscarf would affect a person's professional duties, including any requirement of impartiality. What dress one may have may not necessarily constitute or imply partiality vis-à-vis any matter or person. A general assumption of partiality is not a necessary conclusion vis-à-vis a particular matter or person; it has to be established. Do the notions of the independence and impartiality of the judiciary and the religious and political neutrality of public schools mean that judges and school teachers cannot demonstrate any visible sign of possible predisposition, including their age, their gender, their race or origin, and their socioeconomic class? Is the state seeking androgynous, mechanical instruments to deliver judgements and education? Should all judges and school teachers be anonymous? Surely, society wishes to retain humans as its judges and schoolteachers. The dissenting woman can continue to argue that she fulfils her job requirements in an unbiased and professional manner—independent, impartial and neutral. Certainly, her appearance, her headscarf, does not change that fact vis-à-vis a matter or person. Indeed, except in contexts where the scarf is legally required, the fact that a woman is allowed to wear a headscarf may signal that the system is tolerant, pluralistic, and respecting of all. The absence of particular, visible signs of religion in the workplace may convey another sign, i.e., the state is promoting Judeo–Christian, agnostic, or atheistic values and excluding persons belonging to religious communities which require religiously prescribed or religiously motivated garments to be worn. The state also entirely ignores that religious signs are optional in some religions, while obligatory in other beliefs.[105] The state further overlooks that effective controls (e.g. professional codes of conduct) largely can constrain the possible fact of partiality in a particular case, while the appearance of partiality is a matter of public education.

[105] For instance, in connection with the above-mentioned case Goldman v. Weinberger, it has been pointed out that "there is a clear-cut differentiation between the Jew wearing a yarmulke (which is optional, as a military cap will serve just as well) and a Sikh, for whom wearing a turban is obligatory and exclusive." Leon Shaskolsky-Sheleff, "Rabbi Captain Goldman's Yarmulke, Freedom of Religion and Conscience, and Civil (Military) Disobedience," 201. Hence, "the difference between a turban or a dreadlock on the one hand, and a yarmulke on the other, is not merely a difference in 'appearance'—it is also the difference between a Sikh or a Rastafarian, on the one hand, and an Orthodox Jew on the other" (Justice Stevens in Goldman v. Weinberger, 1316).

The dissenting woman can also protest the state's reliance on public order. "Public order" should be narrowly construed to mean the prevention of public disorder.[106] It should not be confused with a similar sounding French legal expression used in civil and administrative law and private international law, *l'ordre public*, which relates to the fundamental public policies of a society.[107] The state's argument that an employee wearing a headscarf would disrupt order in the workplace or the smooth running of the public sector seems therefore rather untenable.[108]

In connection with the notion of "morals," the dissenting woman can bring to light that this notion is inherently vague and fluid, differing from time to time, from culture to culture, from society to society, and from one political system to another.[109] It is not derived from any single tradition, religion, or ideology, but from "many social, philosophical and religious traditions."[110] The fluid nature of morals therefore presumably creates "a significant obstacle" against restricting an individual's external freedom in the name of one particular religion or belief.[111] In this case the concept of morals appears to apply only to predominantly secular arguments. Certainly, the notion of neutrality appears to have resulted in the imposition of a nonreligious view and devaluation of religious convictions and manifestations in the public sector.[112]

---

[106] For instance, principle 22 of the Siracusa Principles incorrectly states: "The expression 'public order'(ordre public) as used in the Covenant may be defined as the sum of rules which ensure the functioning of society or the set of fundamental principles on which society is founded. Respect for human rights is part of public order (ordre public)."

[107] Unlike comparable limitation clauses in ICCPR, art. 18(3), lacks the parenthetical term *ordre public*. Furthermore, the French text of this provision refers to "la protection de l'ordre." This means that the expression "public order" may therefore only be used to "avoid disturbances to the order in the narrow sense" (Nowak, *CCPR Commentary*, 327; Nowak and Vospernik, "Permissible Restrictions on Freedom of Religion or Belief," 57), namely, "the prevention of public disorder" (UN Doc. E/CN.4/528, 59–62 [1951]) and not "to protect *ordre public* with its general connotations of national public policy" (Karl Josef Partsch, "Freedom of Conscience and Expression, and Political Freedoms," *The International Bill of Human Rights: The Covenant on Civil and Political Rights*, ed. Louis Henkin [New York: Columbia University Press, 1981], 212–13). It should be emphasized that "the protection of public order" in ECHR, art. 9(2), which deals with limitations on external freedom of religion or belief, should also be equated with the prevention of disorder. For an explanation, see Lockwood, *Working Paper*, 56–61. See also de Jong, *Freedom of Thought*, 696 n. 23. It has also been argued that "public order" in this provision refers only to the notion of "order in places accessible to everyone" (van Dijk and van Hoof, *Theory and Practice of the European Convention*, 554).

[108] Nowak and Vospernik, "Permissible Restrictions on Freedom of Religion or Belief," 58.

[109] It should be noted that even in a relatively homogeneous region such as Western Europe, the European Court of Human Rights has struggled to agree upon a common European concept of "morals" in the domestic law of European states. The Court concluded that notions of morals vary "from time to time and from place to place especially in our era which is characterised by a rapid and far-reaching evolutions of opinion on the subject" (Handyside v. U.K., 1 EHRR 737 [ECtHR 24-A, 7 December 1976], 22).

[110] General Comment 22, para. 8. In this context, it has been argued that "Since religions usually claim that their respective value systems constitute the most important moral guidelines, at least for those who adhere to this particular religion or belief, it seems difficult to conceive of a kind of higher and quasi universally accepted concept of morals which States could invoke to justify restrictions on religious manifestations. The only universally accepted value system one can think of is in fact human rights, which means that the protection of morals coincides with the protection of the fundamental rights and freedoms of others" (Nowak and Vospernik, "Permissible Restrictions on Freedom of Religion or Belief," 62).

[111] David Little, "Studying 'Religious Human Rights': Methodological Foundations," *Religious Human Rights in Global Perspective: Legal Perspectives*, 60.

The dissenting woman can point out in this connection that "state's failure to facilitate actual religious pluralism in society, and the corresponding external expressions of that pluralism, would be equivalent to support a certain belief (secularism, i.e., no-religion) over the others (religions)."[113] The female employee can therefore argue that it is hard to understand how the state can claim the protection of morals as a compelling state interest.

Assuming, however, that the state can demonstrate that its actions were in the interest of a legitimate aim and that it has satisfied the second prong, the issue remains as to whether the restriction was necessary. The question of necessity may be assessed on various fronts. First, one can question whether the restriction is proportional to the state interest pursued. This means that the least restrictive alternative must be adopted where several types of limitations are available or where the limitation could be implemented in a variety of ways.[114] Second, one can ask whether the state applied the restriction with a discriminatory purpose or in a discriminatory manner.

In determining these questions in this employment specific case, a number of conventions of the International Labor Organization ("ILO") give some guidance.[115] For instance, Convention No. 122 Concerning Employment Policy emphasizes that "there is freedom of choice of employment and the fullest possible opportunity for each worker to qualify for, and to use his skills and endowments in, a job for which he is well suited, irrespective of . . . sex, religion."[116] Furthermore, Convention No. 111 Concerning Discrimination in Respect of Employment and Occupation prohibits as a general rule "any distinction, exclusion or preference made on the basis of . . . sex, religion . . . , which has the effect of nullifying or impairing equality of opportunity or treatment in employment or occupation."[117] Exempt from this general rule on protection against employment discrimination is any distinction, exclusion or preference in respect of a particular job based on the inherent requirements of the job.[118] The objectives underlying such requirements of the job must be assessed in terms of whether they are truly necessary or arbitrary.[119] For instance, preference in employment for a person holding a particular religious or other belief may not amount to discrimination if that belief is a genuine qualification for the job.[120]

---

[112] For a discussion on liberals being nowhere near as tolerant as they seem, see *Religious Human Rights in Global Perspective: Legal Perspectives,* xxiv.

[113] Argued by Martínez-Torrón and Navarro-Valls, "The Protection of Religious Freedom in the System of the Council of Europe," in this volume.

[114] For a description of the concept of proportionality, see Nicholas Emiliou, *The Principle of Proportionality in European Law: A Comparative Study* (London: Kluwer International Law, 1996), 6.

[115] For a discussion on the relevance of the ILO conventions for female workers, see Anne Trebilcock, "ILO Conventions and Women Workers," in Askin and Koenig, *Women and International Human Rights Law,* 2:301–18.

[116] *ILO Convention No. 122 Concerning Employment Policy,* art. 1(2)(c) (hereinafter "ILO Convention No. 122"). CEDAW, art. 11 also prohibits discrimination in employment.

[117] ILO Convention No. 122, art. 1(1)(a).

[118] Ibid., art. 1(2).

[119] International Labor Office, *ILO Standards and Action for the Elimination of Discrimination and the Promotion of Equality of Opportunity in Employment,* UN Doc. HR/GENEVA/1984/WP.15, para. 32 (1984).

[120] Human Rights and Equal Opportunity Commission, *Article 18: Freedom of Religion and Belief* (Sydney: Commonwealth of Australia, 1998), 78 (in particular recommendations R4.1.1 and R4.1.2).

Numerous international human rights norms also specifically acknowledge that not all distinctions based on sex, gender, and religion or belief are discriminatory.[121] Furthermore, a well-developed corpus of international jurisprudence emphasizes that differences of treatment—situations in which similar situations are treated differently or significantly different situations are treated identical—are discriminatory when an objective and reasonable justification is lacking.[122] An objective and reasonable justification exists when there is a legitimate aim or a reasonable relationship of proportionality between the means employed and the aim sought to be realized. Without an objective and reasonable justification, a difference of treatment is discriminatory.

On the basis of these guiding norms, the dissenting woman can state that two forms of difference of treatment have taken place. First, she can contend that the purpose, or alternatively the effect or the result, of the restriction is discriminatory on the basis of religion or belief[123] because it virtually only affects members of religious denominations that oblige headcovering, although not all of them do.[124] Second, she can argue that the purpose,[125] or more likely the effect or the result,[126] of the state-imposed restriction is discriminatory on the grounds of sex or gender because the religious requirement to wear headscarves applies only to women.[127]

A dissenting woman belonging to a religious minority can further emphasize that, according to international standards on minority rights, persons belonging to religious minorities shall not be denied the right to practice their religion.[128] She can demand that their connection with one of the minority religions in the country should be respected. Persons belonging to religious minorities should be enabled to express their characteristics, which may include a right to use their traditional dress or attire.[129] In her situation, the headdress represents an overt expression of her religion.

---

[121] See, e.g., CEDAW, art. 1; 1981 Declaration, art. 2.

[122] See, e.g., General Comment 18 of the Human Rights Committee on Non-Discrimination, UN Doc. HRI/GEN/1/Rev.1, para. 13 (at 26–28) (1989); Case "Relating to Certain Aspects of the Laws on the Use of Languages in Education in Belgium" v. Belgium, App. Nos. 01474/62, 01677/62, 01691/62, 01769/63, 01994/63, 02126/64 (ECtHR 6-A, 23 July 1968), para. 10. See also Italy v. Commission, case 13/63 (ECJ, 17 July 1963), ECR 1963, para. 4 (at 375); Brown case, case C-394/96 (ECJ, 30 June 1998), ECR 1998, para. 29 (at I-4185). For a discussion, see Cassel and Guzman, *Law and Reality,* 309–12.

[123] For a definition of discrimination based on religion or belief, see 1981 Declaration, art. 2(2).

[124] This was the holding of the Dutch Equal Treatment Commission—an independent organization established by the Dutch Government to receive unequal treatment complaints by individuals—in a case where a female applicant was not offered the job of acting clerk at a Dutch court of law. For the Commission's decision, which is not legally binding, see <www.cgb.nl/oordelen_frameset.html> (only available in Dutch).

[125] Situations in which the purpose is discriminatory are commonly referred to as direct or intentional discrimination. See Titia Loenen, "Indirect discrimination: Oscillating Between Containment and Revolution," *Non-Discrimination Law: Comparative Perspectives,* ed. Loenen and Peter R. Rodrigues (The Hague: Martinus Nijhoff, 1999), 195–211.

[126] Situations in which the result or effect is discriminatory are commonly referred to as indirect or incidental discrimination (see ibid.). To establish indirect discrimination on the basis of, for instance, religion or belief, the result or effect of a certain measure or treatment on a particular religious or other belief group is determining, not the question whether the measure purports to treat all religious and belief groups in the same manner.

[127] See Dahlab v. Switzerland, App. No. 42393/98 (ECtHR, 15 February 2001), inadmissibility decision.

[128] See, e.g., ICCPR, art. 27; Framework Convention for the Protection of National Minorities, art. 8 (1995); Vienna Concluding Document, principles 16 and 19; *Declaration on the Rights of Persons Belonging to National or Ethnic, Religious and Linguistic Minorities,* art. 2(1) (1992) (hereinafter "Minorities Declaration"). See also General Comment 22, para. 9.

Furthermore, the dissenting woman can emphasize the need for equal access to public sector employment across the various religious communities.[130] Public employers would in this connection benefit from a recommendation to an Australian firm: "[w]ith employer goodwill, much may be done to ensure that such believers have just as good job prospects as anyone else. Allowing an employee to wear a . . . head-scarf in the firm's colours may seem, but is not, a trivial response, because through this action the employer indirectly acknowledges Australian religious diversity and respect for the individual."[131] An example of such a response is the introduction of a headscarf, with the distinctive police black and white check pattern, as a uniform option for interested Muslim female officers of London's Metropolitan Police.[132]

For these reasons and given the inescapable fact of pluralism, the dissenting female employee can argue that the state has neglected its obligation to take all appropriate measures, including the modification and rescission of existing laws, to prohibit discrimination on the basis of religion, belief, sex or gender.[133] The dissenting woman can further recall the state obligation to take all appropriate measures to combat intolerance on the grounds of religion or other beliefs.[134] Moreover, she can bring to light that the UN Special Rapporteur on Freedom of Religion or Belief[135] has urged, in another context, that "dress should not be the subject of political regulation" and that "flexible and tolerant attitudes" are called for in this regard, "so as to allow the variety and richness of . . . garments to manifest themselves without constraint."[136]

---

[129] See Minorities Declaration, art. 4(2), in conjunction with Asbjørn Eide, *Commentary to the Declaration on the Rights of Persons belonging to National or Ethnic, Religious and Linguistic Minorities*, UN Doc. E/CN.4/Sub.2/AC.5/2001/2, paras. 56–58 (2001).

[130] See Minorities Declaration, art. 2(3), in conjunction with Eide, *Commentary to the Declaration on the Rights of Persons belonging to National or Ethnic, Religious and Linguistic Minorities*, para. 49 (2001).

[131] Juliet Sheen, "Living within the Tensions of Plurality: Religious Discrimination and Human Rights Law and Policy," in Bouma, *Many Religions, All Australian*, 171–72.

[132] This decision was announced in combination with the Association of Muslim Police in Britain on 24 April 2001. The introduction of the optional headscarf follows a similar move by London's Metropolitan Police for Sikh officers who are allowed to wear a turban on duty. For more information, see Cindi John, "Police Hope for Muslim Head Start," BBC News, 24 April 2001, <http://news.bbc.co.uk/hi/english/uk/newsid_1294000/1294417.stm>; Hwaa Irfan, "Racism, Bigotry, and the Association of Muslim Police," in IslamOnline.Net, 29 May 2001), <http://www.muslims.net/English/Society/2001/05/article10.shtml>. By contrast, for instance, the Netherlands Police Institute has recently decided not to introduce religious headcovering, in distinctive police blue, as a uniform option. See Frits van Veen, "Plan voor keppeltjes, hoofddoeken en tulbanden blijkt stille dood gestorven: Alternatief politiepet van de baan" [Plan for yarmulkes, headscarves and turbans appears still-born: Alternative policeman's cap is off], *De Volkskrant*, 6 September 2001, 3 (in Dutch).

[133] See, e.g., 1981 Declaration, art. 4; CEDAW, art. 2.

[134] See 1981 Declaration, art. 4(2).

[135] At its 56th session in 2000 the UN Commission on Human Rights decided to change the title of the Special Rapporteur from Special Rapporteur on Religious Intolerance to Special Rapporteur on Freedom of Religion or Belief, to be implemented at the next extension of the Special Rapporteur's mandate in 2001. See Committee on Human Rights Resolution 2001/42 (2001), para. 11; Committee on Human Rights Resolution 2000/33 (2000), para. 11. This chapter uses the new title of the Rapporteur's mandate.

[136] Implementation Report of the Secretary General, para. 140. See also Amor, *Implementation of the Declaration on the Elimination of All Forms of Intolerance and of Discrimination Based on Religion or Belief*, UN Doc. E/CN.4/1996/95/Add.2, para. 97 (1996) (hereinafter "1996 Report of Special Rapporteur").

It seems reasonable to assume that some form of difference of treatment has taken place. The question of whether the state based the contested legislation on objective and reasonable criteria, in particular the question of whether the restriction is a legitimate occupational qualification, cannot be answered without carefully assessing the inherent requirements of the women's job and the employing institution's objectives.[137] For instance, if the woman is a teacher at a primary public school, the state could explain that the ban on the wearing of a Muslim headscarf while teaching had not been imposed because she was a woman but had pursued the legitimate aim of ensuring the neutrality of state primary education. A similar ban could be imposed on a man in the same context wearing clothes that identified him as a member of a particular religious denomination. This line of reasoning was used by the Swiss government in a case brought before the European Court of Human Rights.[138] The Swiss government argued that the ban on headscarves at a state primary school was justified by the likely interference with pupil's religious beliefs and with the principle of denominational neutrality (laïcité) within the school. The role of state-school teachers as representatives of both the education authorities and the state required them to tolerate proportionate restrictions on their freedom of religion or belief. The European Court endorsed this line of reasoning.[139]

Although these considerations are perhaps understandable, the dissenting woman can insist that the state must also consider whether the teacher embraces the same norms and values as the school, and whether she would be likely to proselytize in the classroom, for instance by persuading or forcing the pupils to adopt her religion or belief.[140] She can further note that "the evidence of religious pluralism seems to be more consistent with a neutral attitude of the state and . . . more educative for students than the fictional absence of religion on the part of school personnel."[141]

Moreover, the dissenting woman may further question whether the policy of the state is uniformly enforced. She may raise four questions in this regard. First, does the state also object on the same grounds to its employees wishing to wear other garments for religiously prescribed or religiously motivated reasons such as the Jewish skullcap (yarmulke, kippah), the Roman Catholic collar, soutane, and habit, the Sikh turban, and the Buddhist lama's robe? Second, does the state treat religiously prescribed or religiously motivated wearing of garments differently from religious ornaments and accessories, such as a necklace with a Christian crucifix, a Christmas tree, the Sikh ceremonial dagger (kirpan), steel wrist bracelet (kara) and beard, the Rastafarian dreadlocks or a Hindu mark on the forehead (bindi, tilak, kumkum, etc.)? Third, does the state countenance religious symbols such as an Islamic star and crescent, the Christian

---

[137] *Article 18: Freedom of Religion and Belief,* 78 (in particular recommendations R4.1.1 and R4.1.2).

[138] See Dahlab v. Switzerland. For a discussion of a dispute in Germany involving the place of Muslim dress in the public schools, see William Barbieri, "Group Rights and the Muslim Diaspora," *Human Rights Quarterly* 21 (1999): 921–25.

[139] For critical remarks regarding this case, see Martínez-Torrón and Navarro-Valls, "The Protection of Religious Freedom in the System of the Council of Europe," in this volume, n.78.

[140] For a case in which a teacher of religion and ethics was no longer allowed to teach at a public school, see Delgado Páez v. Colombia, Comm. No. 195/1985 (UN Human Rights Committee, 12 July 1990), UN Doc. A/45/40, vol. II, Annex IX, sect. D (1990), reprinted in *Human Rights Law Journal* 11 (1990): 313.

[141] Martínez-Torrón and Navarro-Valls, "The Protection of Religious Freedom in the System of the Council of Europe," in this volume, n.78.

cross, the Jewish Star of David or the Bahá'í nine-pointed star?[142] Fourth, does the state distinguish between ostentatious religious identifications and discrete signs? These questions are helpful in determining whether the state applies different rules to similar situations, whether and to what extent differences in otherwise comparable situations justify different treatments, and whether job requirements such as the religious and political neutrality or independence and impartiality are uniformly applied.

Concretely, to return to the school teacher scenario, the dissenting woman can, for instance, investigate whether the state would also apply the same criteria to a teacher at a state primary school who is a nun and wears a habit in the classroom. The inherent requirements of her job are the same, only the wearing of the religiously prescribed or religiously motivated dress is different. If there would be a different outcome, one may argue that the restriction is not a legitimate occupational qualification.

Unlike the FGM case described in section II.B.1, states will generally be more seriously challenged to show that the second and the third prongs have been satisfied. The outcome of the actual balancing between the interests of the state and of the woman very much depends on the nature and circumstances of her job, in particular the inherent requirements of the woman's job and the employing institution's objectives. Whether the state's curtailment of the dissenting woman's external freedom will be considered justified will therefore ultimately depend on the particulars of the individual case, including the extent of the state's margin of appreciation. Considering that globally the law and practice of states differ in this area, the state's margin of appreciation is likely to be wider than in the FGM case discussed in section II.B.1. Ultimately, in assessing the balance, it is important to remember that from the woman's perspective, a fundamental freedom of the first order is at stake, and the state must make a strong showing indeed before the woman's right can be overridden.

3. The Freedom Not to Wear Religious Garments in Public vs. the Protection of Public Safety, Public Order, or Morals

Section II.B.2 elucidated that women are in principle free, if they wish, to wear garments for religiously prescribed or religiously motivated reasons. Obviously, this would mean that they are also free, if they so wish, not to wear such garments.[143] Nevertheless,

---

142 It has been observed that "[w]hile wearing a scarf-like headcovering is relatively innocuous, full covering is clearly more obvious than the wearing of a cross or a yarmulke. Yet, minority religious rights are drained of much of their meaning if 'acceptable' religious practices are defined by reference to majority religious traditions" (Mirza, "Selected Personal Rights," 151 n.134).

143 de Jong, *Freedom of Thought*, 354. Such situations give rise to a variety of questions regarding the law to be applied to different religious or secular groups living within the same nonsecular country including: "Should the same law be applied to everyone or should it be so only as long as it is nonreligious or secular law? If only religious law governs, what of those persons who do not want to be governed by religious law? If the state only allows religious law, then is each religious community entitled to its own laws? Should a state have some persons governed under religious law and some under secular law? May an individual chose the system of law by which she wants to be governed?" (Howland, "Introduction," *Religious Fundamentalisms*, xviii). Religious fundamentalism and national laws are addressed by Ratna Kapur, "The Two Faces of Secularism and Women's Rights in India," *Religious Fundamentalisms*, 143; Frances Raday, "Religion and Patriarchal Politics: The Israeli Experience," ibid., 155; Marie-Claire S. F. G. Foblets, "Family Disputes Involving Muslim Women in Contemporary Europe: Immigrant Women Caught Between Islamic Family Law and Women's Rights," ibid., 167.

some religion-based or religion-dominated states with a religious majority require all women, regardless of their beliefs, to wear in public clothing prescribed or motivated by the religion of the majority of the population.[144]

The state-imposed dress requirement forces women belonging to a religious or belief minority to adopt a practice of the religious majority. However, women belonging to the religious majority can also suffer from the dress requirement. Such women may disagree with the state—often influenced by religious leaders and institutions—that the dress is religiously prescribed or religiously motivated and therefore mandatory.[145] Dissenting women have found it difficult to change the relevant laws or the attitudes of religious leaders, religious institutions, their government, and their society as a whole.[146] In a few nonsecular states with a religious majority, women who fail to comply in public with prescribed dress codes may risk sanctions, including the possibility of corporal punishment, popular vengeance, detention, and ill-treatment by officials.[147]

The following hypothetical case concerns a religion-based or religion-dominated state that obliges all women, regardless of their religion or belief and nationality, by law to wear in public a particular religious garment. The rationale behind the religion-based law is to accommodate the religiously prescribed or religiously motivated practice of the majority of the population, that women must wear concealing garments in public. Since such laws apply to the entire public sphere and not only to the area of public employment, it is apparent that a dissenting woman in this situation is far more restricted in her external freedom than the female state employee in section II.B.2 who can still wear her headscarf outside the workplace. The question under review is whether the state-imposed dress requirement is legitimate under such circumstances. As discussed in sections II.B.1 and II.B.2, this is only possible if the restriction serves a legitimate aim and proves to be necessary.

---

[144] See, e.g., United States Department of State, *Annual Report,* 494; Special Rapporteur's Report 2000, paras. 7, 8; Elimination of Religious Intolerance, paras. 41, 42; Special Rapporteur's Report 1998, para. 60(a); *Elimination of All Forms of Religious Intolerance: Note by the Secretary-General,* UN Doc. A/52/477, para. 31(a)(i) (1997) (hereinafter "1997 Religious Intolerance Note"); Implementation Report of the Secretary General, para. 51; 1996 Report of Special Rapporteur, para. 27; Amor, *Implementation of the Declaration on the Elimination of All Forms of Intolerance and of Discrimination Based on Religion or Belief,* UN Doc. E/CN.4/1995/91, 10 (1994). The UN Human Rights Committee has requested States Parties to the ICCPR to provide information on any specific regulation of clothing to be worn by women in public. See General Comment 28, para. 13.

[145] It has been argued that "The inclusion of group rights within a catalogue of human rights creates conceptual confusion, particularly in situations where assertions of individual liberty do not conform with those of the group to a collective identity, including a religious identity. For example, article 18 of the International Covenant on Civil and Political Rights provides individuals the right to manifest religious belief 'individually or in community with others,' but says nothing about an individual's right to be free from the imposition of the teachings and practices that a community might espouse as essential to religious conformity" (Chinkin, "Cultural Relativism and International Law," 56–57 [endnote 11 omitted]).

[146] For a discussion, see Bouthaina Shaaban, "The Muted Voices of Women Interpreters," *Faith & Freedom: Women's Human Rights in the Muslim World,* ed. Mahnaz Afkhami (Syracuse: Syracuse University Press, 1995), 61. For instance, in her book *al-Sufur wa'l-hijab,* published in 1928, Nazira Zin al-Din, a Muslim woman interpreter, set out to demonstrate that neither the text of the Koran nor the *hadith* require Muslim women to wear *hijab* and concluded that *hijab* is prohibited by the Islamic *Shari'a.*

[147] See, e.g., United States Department of State, *Annual Report,* 494; *Freedom of Religion and Belief: A World Report,* ed. Kevin Boyle and Juliet Sheen (London: Routledge, 1997), 78; *Saudi Arabia: A Secret State of Suffering* (London: Amnesty International, 2000), 2.

As to a legitimate aim, the conceivable interests that the state could invoke seems to be the protection of morals, public order, or public safety. The state could reason that the imposition of the prescribed strict dress code is an essential component of public morality, the morals of its society. Furthermore, it could argue the protection of public order and public safety by pointing out that the appearance of unveiled women in public "distract[s] men sexually leading to, on the one hand, inefficiency in the public sphere and, on the other, complete sexual anarchy and social chaos."[148] The legislation is geared towards avoiding popular vengeance and protection of the woman's safety, including her physical integrity and life.

The dissenting woman could first emphasize that norms relating to internal freedom also protect people from not being obliged to act in a way that entails the expression of the acceptance of a religion or belief that one does not share, and that no restrictions whatsoever may be imposed on internal freedom.[149]

Should it, however, be determined that this case rather involves external freedom,[150] the dissenting woman can protest that these grounds appear to be "a pretext for reintroducing unwarranted forms of interference."[151] By using similar arguments delineated in section II.B.2, she can question whether the restriction is legitimately aimed at the protection of "morals" or "public order." The dissenting woman can refer to the UN Human Rights Committee's concern over the official enforcement of prescribed dress requirements for women in public places "under the guise of public order and morality."[152] She can further argue that in order to prevent public disorder and to ensure public safety, the state is exactly required to facilitate the exercise of her external freedom in practice.[153] The dissenting woman can bring to light that the law in question most certainly does not encourage the population to be flexible towards other garments and tolerant towards persons belonging to other religions and beliefs, including theistic, nontheistic and atheistic beliefs. Refusal to observe the prescribed dress code in public may make the women concerned a likely target of violence. As the European Court of Human Rights has recognized in another context, "it is possible that tension is created in situations where a religious or any other community becomes divided, it considers that this is one of the unavoidable consequences of pluralism. The role of the authorities in such circumstances is not to remove the cause of tension by eliminating pluralism, but to ensure that the competing groups tolerate each other."[154] In this connection, the dissenting woman can also remind the state of its obligation to refrain from engaging in violence against women and to exercise due diligence to prevent, investigate and punish acts of violence against them, regardless of whether such acts are perpetrated by the state or by private persons.[155]

---

[148] Yasmeen Hassan, "Stove Burning, Acid Throwing, and Honor Killings," in Askin and Koenig, *Women and International Human Rights Law,* 2:589.

[149] See van Dijk and van Hoof, *Theory and Practice of the European Convention,* 547.

[150] It has been pointed out that it is not clear to what extent internal freedom also implies protection against the imposition of a particular conception of morals (ibid., 547–48).

[151] Little, "Studying 'Religious Human Rights,'" 143–55.

[152] *Report of the UN Human Rights Committee,* UN Doc. A/53/40, para. 133 (1998).

[153] In this connection, 1981 Declaration, art. 7, should be recalled, which reads: "The rights and freedoms set forth in the present Declaration shall be accorded in national legislation in such a manner that everyone shall be able to avail himself of such rights and freedoms in practice."

[154] Serif v. Greece, App. No. 38178/97 (ECtHR, 14 December, 1999), para. 53.

Assuming that the dress code would pursue one or more legitimate aims and that state has satisfied the second prong, the issue remains as to whether the restriction was necessary. In section II.B.2 it was pointed out that two questions need to be assessed. First, as to the question of whether the restriction is proportional to the compelling state interest pursued, the dissenting woman may bring to light that the imposition of strict dress codes on all women has rightly been described as one of "the most repressive governmental actions."[156] Without any consideration, all dissenting women are forced to wear clothing denoting a religiously prescribed or religiously motivated practice of the majority of the population. The state completely disregards women who believe and practice otherwise, which is an affront to their religion or belief.[157] It is also contrary to the 1981 Declaration which clearly states that: "The rights and freedoms set forth in the present Declaration shall be accorded in national legislation in such a manner that everyone shall be able to avail himself of such rights and freedoms in practice."[158] Dissenting women belonging to a religious minority may further emphasize that their connection with one of the minority religions in the country should be respected. The state should protect and create conditions for the promotion of the religious identity of minorities on their territory.[159] They should be enabled to express and preserve their own characteristics,[160] and therefore not be forced to express the characteristics of the religious majority. Like the veiled state employee in Section II.B.2, the dissenting woman can also emphasize that the UN Special Rapporteur on Freedom of Religion or Belief has urged that "dress should not be the subject of political regulation" and that "flexible and tolerant attitudes" are called for in this regard, "so as to allow the variety and richness of . . . garments to manifest themselves without constraint."[161]

---

[155] The obligations are referred to in note 22 of this article. It should furthermore be noted that "[s]tates should condemn violence against women and should not invoke any (...) religious consideration to avoid their obligations with respect to its elimination." See, e.g., DEVAW, art. 4; BDPA, para. 124(a). See also Committee on Human Rights Resolution 1999/42 (1999), paras. 3 & 12, UN Doc. E/CN.4/RES/1999/42 (1999).

[156] See T. Jeremy Gunn, "The Law of the Russian Federation on the Freedom of Conscience and Religious Associations from a Human Rights Perspective," in *Proselytism and Orthodoxy in Russia: The New War for Souls,* ed. John Witte Jr. and Michael Bourdeaux (Maryknoll: Orbis Books, 1999), 260.

[157] It must be realized that dress restrictions imposed by a religion-based or religion-dominated state on women in public may also affect policies of states that do not impose such restrictions on women. For instance, when American female military personnel leave their bases in Saudi Arabia, they are required by the Pentagon to abide by Saudi religious clothing restrictions for women. Major McSally, America's highest-ranking female top gun, has laid her career on the line in a crusade to oppose a US policy that requires female military personnel to wear Muslim robes in public in Saudi Arabia. While understanding that the Pentagon is reluctant to offend its host, McSally considers the rule an affront to her Christian faith: "It is a customary Muslim outfit for women, but I'm not Muslim and I'm not Saudi. I am a Christian. . . . Just as we don't want to make someone who is not Jewish wear a yarmulke on their head, why would we have our female troops being mandated to wear Muslim clothing?" (Laura Peek, "America's First Woman Combat Pilot Fights Cover-Up Order," *The Times,* 19 April 2001, <http://www.thetimes.co.uk/article/0,,3-116757,00.html>).

[158] 1981 Declaration, art. 7.

[159] Vienna Concluding Document, principle 19; Copenhagen OSCE Document, principles 32 and 33 (1990); *Charter of Paris for a New Europe,* para. 5 of the section on "A New Era of Democracy, Peace and Unity: Human Rights, Democracy and Rule of Law" (1990).

[160] See Minorities Declaration, art. 4(2).

[161] Implementation Report of the Secretary General, para. 140. See also 1996 Report of Special Rapporteur, para. 97.

Second, as to the question of whether the state applied the restriction with a discriminatory purpose or in a discriminatory manner, the dissenting woman can reason that the state interference is directly or indirectly discriminatory on the grounds of sex, gender, and religion or belief, and that it conveys disrespect for dissenting women.[162] The dissenting woman can remind the state of its obligation to take all appropriate measures, including the modification and rescission of existing laws, to prohibit discrimination on the basis of religion, belief, sex, or gender.[163] The state is also obliged to take all appropriate measures to combat intolerance on the grounds of religion or other beliefs.[164]

It is not certain whether the state's broad-sweeping curtailment of the external freedom of all dissenting women is permissible in such cases. There are reasons to believe that a dissenting woman's external freedom could weigh more heavily in the balance. The outcome of the balancing process ultimately depends on the particulars of the situation, including the extent of the state's margin of appreciation. Considering that globally the law and practice of states differ considerably, as in the case of the female state employee in section II.B.2, the state's margin of appreciation appears to be more wide than in the FGM case discussed in section II.B.1. The importance of the woman's fundamental freedom issues should not be forgotten in the process. It is significant that the Human Rights Committee has concluded that in situations in which women are subjected to clothing requirements that are not in keeping with their religion or belief a violation of article 18 of the ICCPR, on freedom of religion or belief, may be involved.[165]

Assuming that the third-prong would not been satisfied and that the woman would theoretically be free to refuse to wear the veil in public, she must then determine what price she is willing to pay to pursue this. Sometimes the pressure may force many girls and women to veil themselves, as explained by a dissenting woman: "None of us want to wear the veil. But fear is stronger than our convictions or our will to be free. Fear is all around us. Our parents, our brothers, are unanimous: Wear the veil and stay alive."[166] These words demonstrate the complexity of the subject matter and the vicious circle in which dissenting women may find themselves. It also indicates that the threats and difficulties faced by a dissenting woman in the above-described circumstances are of a different order than those of the female state employee in section II.B.2.

III. Conflicts between Gender-Discriminatory Religious Norms and the Human Rights of Women

Although the focus of this chapter is on the gender perspective in the area of the right to freedom of religion or belief, an area which has only relatively recently received international attention, the international community's repeated concern

[162] The UN Human Rights Committee has, for instance, stressed that regulations of clothing to be worn by women in public may involve a violation of ICCPR, art. 26, on nondiscrimination. See General Comment 28, para. 13.
[163] See 1981 Declaration, art. 4; CEDAW, art. 2.
[164] See 1981 Declaration, art. 4(2).
[165] General Comment 28, para. 13.
[166] Karima Bennoune, "S.O.S. Algeria: Women's Human Rights Under Siege," in *Faith & Freedom,* 187 n. 19.

about gender-discriminatory religious norms and practices that violate the human rights of women and discriminate against them deserves mention in this Section.[167] For instance, in 1993, the 171 states gathered at the Second World Conference on Human Rights called upon all governments to take all appropriate measures in compliance with their international obligations and with due regard to their respective legal systems to counter intolerance and related violence based on religion or belief, including practices of discrimination against women.[168] They further emphasized "the eradication of any conflicts which may arise between the rights of women and the harmful effects of . . . religious extremism."[169] From the World Conference onward, a variety of other international fora, including the UN General Assembly and the UN Commission on Human Rights, have made comparable statements.[170]

Without intending to discuss these particular issues in detail, which is beyond the focus of this chapter, this section illustrates some gender-discriminatory religious norms and practices that violate the human rights of women and discriminate against them. The purpose is to create awareness of the fact that, in the area of women and religion or belief, there is an incongruity between the international community's intense concern for a wide set of other human rights involving women and the lesser degree of concern manifested with respect to violations of women's right to freedom of religion or belief. Even the UN Special Rapporteur on Freedom of Religion or Belief has sometimes fallen into this pattern of giving priority to the former rights.

Part of the explanation for this may lie in the perception that the way religious authorities, or internal norms and doctrines of different religions and beliefs, address areas such as marriage, divorce, custody of children, abortion, contraception, property rights, inheritance, religious hierarchy, legal capacity, and participation in the conduct of public affairs can clash with a wide array of human rights norms.[171] It has, for instance, been pointed out that "it is not an exaggeration to say that, as in so many aspects of life, women, half the human race, have been invisible within churches and religions which have been dominated by men. Women's mode of practice and organization may be, as with other minorities, invisible and ignored. . . . Does it raise issues of human rights concern if women have to worship separately from men or are relegated to the back of the congregation during services? These are not easy issues to resolve."[172]

---

[167] This has, for instance, been pointed out by Ron Keller, Director-General for International Cooperation, Dutch Ministry of Foreign Affairs, in his keynote speech "Freedom of Religion or Belief and Cultural Development in the Context of Development Co-operation" (Speech to the International Conference on Muslim Women and Development, The Hague, 9–11 October 2000). See *Report of the International Conference on Muslim Women and Development*, ed. Harriëtte Mingoen (The Hague: Dutch Ministry of Foreign Affairs, 2001), 58.

[168] *Vienna Declaration and Programme of Action,* part II, para. 22, UN Doc. A/CONF.157/23, 32 ILM 1661 (1993).

[169] Ibid., part II, para. 38.

[170] Beijing +5 document, paras. 27 and 59; Committee on Human Rights Resolution 2001/42 (2001), para. 4(c).

[171] It has been noted that "Religion in itself is not the problem, but the ways in which religion has been practiced and used, or, in fact abused, throughout history. . . . I know that women are often severely disadvantaged in the name of religion" ("Keynote Address by Hilde Johnson, former Norwegian Minister for International Cooperation and Human Rights," in Grotens and Tahzib-Lie, *Seminar on Freedom of Religion or Belief,* 27).

[172] Boyle and Sheen, *A World Report,* 13 and 14.

One of the most controversial collisions between the human rights of women and religious norms and practices is in the area of women's sexuality and reproduction.[173] This was, for instance, apparent when these notions were defined at the UN International Conference on Population and Development in 1994, the Fourth UN Conference on Women in 1995, the twenty-first special session of the UN General Assembly for the review and appraisal of the implementation of the Programme of Action of the International Conference on Population and Development, and at the twenty-third special session of the UN General Assembly entitled "Women 2000: Gender Equality, Development and Peace for the Twenty-First Century."[174] From the perspective of human rights protection, it is understandable that international human rights fora have expressed concern about the potential contradiction between women's rights and religious norms and practices.[175] The policies and practices of the Taliban in Afghanistan provide the most egregious example.[176]

In response to requests of the Commission on Human Rights,[177] the Special Rapporteur on Freedom of Religion or Belief immediately included gender issues and the human rights of women among his priority issues.[178] His attention has especially been

---

[173] For a discusssion on this collision, see, e.g., Kari Elisabeth Børresen, "Religion Confronting Women's Human Rights: The Case of Roman Catholicism," in this volume; Rebecca J. Cook and Mahmoud F. Fathalla, "Advancing Reproductive Rights Beyond Cairo and Beijing," in Askin and Koenig, *Women and International Human Rights Law,* 3:73–90; Maja Kirilova Eriksson, "Abortion and Reproductive Health: Making International Law More Responsive to Women's Needs," in ibid., 3–71; Rebecca Cook, "Human Rights and Reproductive Self-Determination," *American University Law Review* 44 (1995): 975; Rhonda Copelon and Rosalind Petschesky, "Toward an Interdependent Approach to Reproductive and Sexual Rights as Human Rights: Reflections on the ICPD and Beyond," in *From Basic Needs to Basic Rights: Women's Claim to Human Rights,* ed. Margaret A. Schuler (Washington, DC: Institute for Women, Law, and Development, 1995), 343; Lynn P. Freedman, "Finding our Feet, Standing Our Ground: Reproductive Health Activism in an Era of Rising Fundamentalism and Economic Globalization," in *Religious Fundamentalisms,* 181; Frances Kissling, "Roman Catholic Fundamentalism: What's Sex (and Power) Got Do With It?," ibid., 193; Asma M. Abdel Halim, "Reconciling the Opposites: Equal But Subordinate," ibid., 203.

[174] For relevant pronouncements on reproductive rights by the international community, see in particular *Programme of Action of the International Conference on Population and Development,* adopted 13 September 1994, UN Doc. A/CONF.171/13 (1994), Chapter VII, in particular paras. 7.2–3; BDFA, paras. 94–97; *Key Actions for the Further Implementation of the Programme of Action of the International Conference on Population and Development,* Chap. IV; Beijing +5 document, paras. 55, 72(i)–(l), 72(o), 79(f). For a critical scrutiny of the definition of reproductive rights enshrined in such pronouncements, see Corinne Packer, "Defining and Delineating the Right to Reproductive Choice," *Nordic Journal of International Law* 67 (1998): 77–95.

[175] For a discussion on issues affecting the human rights of religious women, see, e.g., Ann Elizabeth Mayer, "Issues Affecting the Human Rights of Muslim Women," in Askin and Koenig, *Women and International Human Rights Law,* 3:367–77; Azizah al-Hibri, "Islam, Law, and Custom: Redefining Muslim Women's Rights," ibid., 3–71, 379–420; Janice Love, "Issues Affecting Christian Women," ibid., 443–59; Martha L. Schweitz, "Women's Rights in the Bahá'í Community: The Concept of Organic Equality in Principle, Law, and Experience," ibid., 3–71, 461–509; Jean Bethke Elshtain, "Thinking about Women, Christianity, and Rights," *Religious Human Rights in Global Perspectives: Religious Perspectives,* ed. John Witte, Jr. and Johan D. van der Vyver (Boston: Martinus Nijhoff, 1996), 143–55; Michael S. Berger and Deborah E. Lipstadt, Women in Judaism From the Perspective of Human Rights," ibid., 295–321; Riffat Hassan, "Rights of Women Within Islamic Communities," ibid., 361–86.

[176] Accordingly qualified in, for instance, the introductory statement on the draft resolution on the elimination of all forms of religious intolerance by Ambassador Richard Ryan, permanent representative of Ireland to the United Nations, 7 November 2000.

[177] Since 1996, the UN Commission on Human Rights has annually requested the Special Rapporteur "to apply a gender perspective, inter alia through the identification of gender-specific abuses, in the reporting

directed towards the status of women from the perspective of religion.[179] He expressed concern about conflicts between the human rights of women and gender-discriminatory religious norms and practices, including situations in which access to buses and public facilities is subject to sex segregation, women must be authorized by men to obtain a passport and to travel abroad, women may only study abroad when accompanied by a family member, women may not drive motor vehicles, and women may not marry a man from a different religion or belief. Clearly, the UN Special Rapporteur on Freedom of Religion or Belief has also given priority to this issue over women's right to freedom of religion or belief.

The Special Rapporteur has announced two initiatives to address collisions between the human rights of women and gender-discriminatory religious norms practices and to stimulate religious and belief communities to be more sensitive to gender. First, the Special Rapporteur is currently preparing a study on "freedom of religion or belief and the status of women in the light of religion and traditions."[180] This formulation suggests that the study would embrace a wide range of religions, beliefs, and traditions, and not address the status or position of women within one specific religion.[181] Second, the Special Rapporteur has recommended the holding of a broad-based seminar on this subject matter—although this seminar is not among the Rapporteur's immediate priorities.[182] With these activities, the Rapporteur envisages the elaboration and

process, including in information collection and in recommendations" (Committee on Human Rights Resolution 2001/42 (2001), para. 7).

[178] See, e.g., Special Rapporteur's Report 1999, para. 6 ; Special Rapporteur's Report 1998, para. 110.

[179] As announced in 1997 Religious Intolerance Note, para. 89 .

[180] Amor, *Civil and Political Rights, Including Religious Intolerance,* UN Doc. E/CN.4/2001/63, para. 194(b) (2001) para. 191(b) (hereinafter "Special Rapporteur's Report 2001"). See also Special Rapporteur's Report 1999, para. 6(a); Special Rapporteur's Report 2000, para. 113 (2000); Elimination of Religious Intolerance, para. 100; Special Rapporteur's Report 1998, para. 119. This topic first appeared in a 1986 study of the current dimensions of the problems of intolerance and of discrimination on the grounds of religion or belief, commissioned by the UN Sub-Commission on Prevention of Discrimination and Protection of Minorities (now called the Sub-Commission on the Promotion and Protection of Human Rights). Special Rapporteur's Report 1998, para. 119 (which incorrectly states that the study was first recommended by the 1984 UN Seminar on the encouragement of understanding, tolerance and respect in matters related to freedom of religion or belief). For the 1986 study, see Elizabeth Odio Benito, *Elimination of All Forms of Intolerance and Discrimination Based on Religion or Belief: Study of the Current Dimensions of the Problems of Intolerance and of Discrimination on Grounds of Religion or Belief,* UN Doc. E/CN.4/Sub.2/1987/26, para. 221(i) (1986).

[181] In 1987, the UN General Assembly rejected a recommendation from the UN Committee on the Elimination of All Forms of Discrimination Against Women that the UN and the specialized agencies "promote or undertake studies on the status of women under Islamic laws and customs and in particular on the status and equality of women in the family on issues such as marriage, divorce, custody and property rights and their participation in public life of the society, taking into consideration the principle of El Itjihad in Islam" (Siobhán Mullally, "Beliefs That Discriminate: A Rights-Based Solution?" *Understanding Human Rights,* ed. Conor Gearty and Adam Tomkins [London: Mansell, 1996], 484–85). See also UNGA Resolution 42/60 (1987), UN GAOR, 42d Sess., UN Doc. A/RES/42/60, 188 (1987); Andrew Byrnes, *Report on the Seventh Session of the Committee on the Elimination of Discrimination Against Women and the Fourth Meeting of States Parties to the Convention on the Elimination of All Forms of Discrimination Against Women,* 7th CEDAW/IWRAW report, 6–7 (1988).

[182] In November 2001, on the occasion of the twentieth anniversary of the 1981 Declaration, the Rapporteur convened in cooperation with the Spanish Government an international consultative conference on school education in relation to freedom of religion or belief. The aim of the conference was to discuss the

adoption by relevant UN bodies of a plan of action to combat discrimination and intolerance against women on the basis of religion and tradition.[183] In particular, the Rapporteur would like to develop closer cooperation with the UN Special Rapporteur on Violence Against Women, its Causes and Consequences and the Committee on the Elimination of Discrimination against Women.[184] It is hoped that the Rapporteur will also solicit the expertise and experience of experts, practitioners, and authorities in this area.[185]

In addition to conflicts between the human rights of women and gender-discriminatory religious norms and practices, dissenting women's enjoyment of the right to freedom of religion or belief needs to be moved further up the world's human rights agenda—or so, increasingly, it would seem. The change in the title of the UN Special Rapporteur's mandate—from religious intolerance to freedom of religion or belief—offered a fitting moment for the Special Rapporteur to encourage states to be more gender sensitive in the area of freedom of religion or belief, to examine more specifically alleged violations which are specifically directed against women and to which women are particularly vulnerable, and to recommend remedial measures for such situations. It is also an appropriate response to the request of the UN Commission on Human Rights to apply a gender perspective in the area of his mandate.[186] The UN Secretary-General's recommendation for more attention to the "relationship between freedom of religion and, in particular, the right to manifest religious beliefs, and women's right to equality"[187] is, for example, a particularly complex area that the Special Rapporteur can explore in more depth. In analyzing such matters, care must be taken not only to balance general gender-related rights against conflicting religious practices,

---

curricula and text books of primary or elementary and secondary schools which relate to tolerance, nondiscrimination, and freedom of religion or belief.

[183] Special Rapporteur's Report 2001, para. 194(b) (2001); Special Rapporteur's Report 1999, para. 125(b); Secretary-General, *Implementation of the Declaration on the Elimination of All Forms of Intolerance and of Discrimination Based on Religion or Belief*, UN Doc. A/53/279, para. 91 (1998).

[184] Special Rapporteur's Report 1998, para. 119. This proposal was made pursuant to Committee on Human Rights Resolution 1997/43 (1997) (*Cooperation with Representatives of United Nations Human Rights Bodies*, report of the Secretary-General Submitted in accordance with Commission on Human Rights Resolution 1996/70, UN Doc. E/CN.4/1997/50, para. 4 [1997]) which encouraged the strengthening of cooperation and coordination among all human rights treaty bodies in order to integrate a gender perspective in the UN system.

[185] See, e.g., Askin and Koenig, *Women and International Human Rights Law*, 3:367–512; Howland, "The Challenge of Religious Fundamentalism to the Liberty and Equality Rights of Women: An Analysis under the United Nations Charter," *Columbia Journal Of Transnational Law* 35 (1997): 271; *Muslim Women and Development Action Research Project: Presentation of Main Findings and Conclusions* (Amsterdam, Royal Tropical Institute, 2000); Mingoen, *Report of the International Conference on Muslim Women*; Ann Elizabeth Mayer, "A 'Benign' Apartheid: How Gender Apartheid Has Been Rationalized," *UCLA Journal of International Law and Foreign Affairs* 5 (2000): 237; Dinah Shelton,"Human Rights Within Churches: A Survey Concerning Discrimination Within Religious Organisations," *Human Rights Journal* 6 (1973): 526–57; Religious Fundamentalisms, *A World Report*, passim (especially the entries dealing with women); Donna J. Sullivan, "Gender Equality and Religious Freedom: Toward a Framework for Conflict Resolution," *NYU Journal of International Law and Policy* 24 (1991): 834–48; Theodor Meron, *Human Rights Law-Making in the United Nations: A Critique of Instruments and Process* (Oxford: Clarendon Press, 1986), 77–160.

[186] See Committee on Human Rights Resolution 2001/42 (2001), para. 7.

[187] Report by the UN Secretary-General, para. 70(h).

but also to take into account the rights of believing women to adhere to practices that outsiders may judge (contrary to the affected women themselves) to be against their interests. Paternalism among human rights advocates should not be allowed to violate the rights of or to discriminate on religious (or antireligious) grounds against the very women they ostensibly seek to protect.

IV. Conclusions and Recommendations

The examination of dissenting women's right to freedom of religion or belief in section II revealed a variety of possible violations which are specifically directed against women, or to which women are particularly vulnerable. It is hard to establish the exact scale on which violations occur in practice. This would require identifying and collecting, whenever possible, sex-disaggregated data pertaining to this right. Two dichotomies make this area particularly complex to explore. First, the effect of the public/private dichotomy on women's enjoyment of the right to freedom of religion or belief. Second, the broad-brush distinctions between internal and external freedom may at times get fuzzy. Despite these realities, it is significant that section II highlighted the fact that there may be a wider discrepancy between the protections afforded men and women with respect to their internal freedom than with respect to their external freedom. Certainly, this does not mean that violations of external freedom are less frequent or less widespread, but parity between the protections afforded men and women is much closer in the external than the internal domain.

Section II.A demonstrated that violations of internal freedom are usually not directed to women belonging to the religion or belief of the majority of a religion-based or religion-dominated state. Vulnerable women either belong to a religious or belief minority or to the religion or belief of the majority of the population of a secular state. Section II.B showed that any dissenting woman, described in section I, can suffer from violations of external freedom. From the three cases discussed in section II.B, it is apparent that the dilemma of retaining the values of the majority while respecting the rights of religious minorities is certainly not an easy one to resolve, regardless whether the laws of the country are defined as religious or not.[188]

Section II indicated that violations of women's right to freedom of religion or belief may amount to acts of violence against women. States have accepted an obligation to exercise due diligence to prevent, investigate, and punish acts of violence against women, regardless whether those acts are perpetrated by government actors or by private persons, as well as an obligation to exercise due diligence to provide protection to potential victims. Depending on the relevant circumstances surrounding a case, state interference with external freedom could also involve a number of other human rights of women, such as their right to freedom of expression.

Section III illustrated that, up to fairly recently, the question of dissenting women's right to freedom of religion or belief has received short shrift from international forums and that this matter merits more attention. In relation to women and religion or

[188] It has been noted that although this dilemma cannot be resolved permanently in an ever-changing society, "the basic rule of respect for the choice and the rights of the individual is actually easy to apply if there is a political will" ("Keynote Address by Hilde Johnson, former Norwegian Minister for International Cooperation and Human Rights," 27).

belief, international attention has been mostly geared toward the potential conflict between religious norms and practices and countervailing human rights norms, without fully taking into account situations where dissenting women may assert religious rights in *favor* of the religious norms and practices.

In terms of promotion and protection, governments, parliaments, courts, international organizations, non-governmental and community-based organizations, religious leaders and institutions, educators, public opinion leaders, academic and other experts, activists, and the media can each contribute in their own way to women's right to freedom of religion or belief. Legal and nonlegal methodologies should be pursued within national and international arenas. Concretely, the following nine subject areas are identified for further action—including consciousness-raising, political attention, activism, education, dialogue and study:

(1) the types of coercion that specifically impair women's internal freedom or to which they are particularly vulnerable;
(2) the types of restriction that specifically affect women's external freedom or to which they are particularly vulnerable;
(3) the permissibility of these gender-specific types of coercion and restriction;
(4) the nature and frequency of such coercion and restriction;
(5) the kinds of society in which violations take place and the actual role and status of women in such societies;
(6) the impact of violence against women on the enjoyment of their right to freedom of religion or belief;
(7) the adherence of states to the due diligence standard in the area concerning women's right to freedom of religion or belief;
(8) the reasons behind violations of women's right to freedom of religion or belief;
(9) the connection between violations of women's right to freedom of religion or belief and violations of their other human rights.

To illustrate how the above-mentioned actors can contribute to this nine-point list, five suggestions for action are made.

First, the fact that the title of the UN Special Rapporteur on Religious Intolerance has been changed and the fact that the Special Rapporteur is required to apply a gender perspective in the course of his work are reasons to suggest that alleged violations of dissenting women's right to freedom of religion or belief may receive more attention in the future.[189] The Special Rapporteur may accordingly wish to address one or more of the above-mentioned subject areas.

Second, international and national courts and human rights treaty bodies should become increasingly sensitive to the gender perspective when interpreting norms relating to the right to freedom of religion or belief and monitoring state compliance with such norms. A example of such an exercise is the Human Rights Committee's updated version of its General Comment on the equality of rights between men and

[189] This change has been implemented at the latest extension of the Special Rapporteur's mandate in 2001.

women, in which various aspects relating to the enjoyment by women of the right to freedom of religion or belief were addressed.[190] In this interpretative statement, the Committee specifically requested states parties to the International Covenant on Civil and Political Rights to take "measures to ensure that freedom of thought, conscience and religion, and the freedom to adopt the religion or belief of one's choice—including the freedom to change religion or belief and to express one's religion or belief—will be guaranteed and protected in law and in practice for both men and women, on the same terms and without discrimination."[191] States' parties are also required to provide "information on the status of women as regards their freedom of thought, conscience and religion, and indicate what steps they have taken or intend to take both to eliminate and prevent infringements of these freedoms in respect of women and to protect their rights against any discrimination."[192]

Third, the treaty bodies can provide more interpretative statements in this field. For instance, the Committee on the Elimination of Discrimination against Women and the Human Rights Committee might consider formulating a concrete general recommendation/comment on one or more of the above-mentioned subject areas. Since violence against women is a recurring issue before the Committee on the Elimination of Discrimination against Women and freedom of religion or belief before the Human Rights Committee, they may consider drafting a joint general recommendation/comment on the impact of violence against women on the enjoyment of their right to freedom of religion or belief. By way of interpretation and elaboration based on the experience gained through the supervisory activities of these treaty bodies, such statements would contribute to the development of the normative content of the relevant treaty provisions on freedom of religion or belief, the right to equality, and the prohibition of discrimination based on religion, belief, sex, and gender. Such statements would also promote more effective implementation of these treaty provisions.

Fourth, governments and non-governmental organizations could incorporate relevant information in reports they produce on the specific question of freedom of religion or belief or in the section dealing with this freedom in country-specific reports. Moreover, non-governmental and community-based organizations could pass on relevant information to the UN Special Rapporteur on Freedom of Religion or Belief, the Committee on the Elimination of Discrimination against Women, the Human Rights Committee, and other relevant international supervisory mechanisms.

Fifth, an international seminar, conference, or meeting of experts could be organized which would be wholly or partially devoted to women and their right to freedom of religion or belief. Like international events on a variety of areas relating to freedom of religion or belief, the initiative could come from governments,[193] the

---

[190] General Comment 28.

[191] Ibid., para. 21.

[192] Ibid. para. 21.

[193] For instance, the question of women and their right to freedom of religion or belief was raised a number of times at an international conference on "Muslim Women and Development," which was organized by the Dutch Ministry of Foreign Affairs in The Hague, from 9 to 11 October 2000. For the report on this conference, see Mingoen, *Report of the International Conference on Muslim Women*. The Netherlands further organized, in collaboration with the Romanian Chairman-in-Office of the OSCE, a seminar on "Freedom of Religion or Belief in the OSCE Region: Challenges to Law and Practice" in The Hague on 26 June

Special Rapporteur on freedom of religion or belief,[194] religious and belief communities and NGOs,[195] the academic world,[196] or an international organization such as the United Nations,[197] the Organization for Security and Cooperation in Europe (OSCE),[198] and the Council of Europe.[199]

2001. For the publication on this seminar, see Grotens and Tahzib-Lie, *Seminar on Freedom of Religion or Belief.*

[194] As noted in Section III of this chapter, the UN Special Rapporteur on Freedom of Religion or Belief, in cooperation with the Spanish Government, convened an international consultative conference on school education in relation to freedom of religion or belief in Madrid from 23 to 25 November 2001.

[195] For instance, sponsored by the Dutch Ministry of Foreign Affairs, the Dutch Justice and Peace Commission, the Dutch Missionary Council, and the Dutch Ecumenical Institute for Advocacy on International Cooperation organized an international expert meeting on religious freedom that took place in Soesterberg from 23 to 25 January 2000. Furthermore, the International Commission on Freedom of Conscience and the George Washington University Law School sponsored an international conference of experts on "The Role of Religious Pluralism in Contemporary Society" in Washington DC from 29 to 30 January 1999 and the Norwegian Council for Religious and Lifestance Communities, the Council on Ecumenical and International Relations of the Church of Norway, the Diakonhjemmet College Research Center, the Norwegian Centre for Human Rights, the Tandem Project, and the Roman Catholic Church of Norway held an international meeting of experts entitled "The Oslo Conference on Freedom of Religion or Belief" in Oslo from 11 to 15 August 1998.

[196] The area of women and their right to freedom of religion or belief has, for instance, been addressed at an academic conference on "Religious Fundamentalisms and the Human Rights of Women," organized by the International Rule of Law Center at the George Washington University Law School in Washington DC from 18 to 19 May 1998 and at the Sixth Annual Law and Religion Symposium on "Emerging Perspectives on Religion and Human Rights" held at Brigham Young University, Provo, Utah from 3 to 5 October 1999. For the book which grew out of the former conference, see Howland, *Religious Fundamentalisms,* and for the journal which grew out of the latter symposium, see *BYU Law Review* (2000).

[197] For instance, the UN Secretary-General convened an international seminar on "The Encouragement of Understanding, Tolerance and Respect in Matters Relating to Freedom of Religion or Belief" in Geneva, from 3 to 14 December 1984. Over one hundred representatives of UN Member States, the Holy See, UN organs and bodies, specialized agencies, regional intergovernmental organizations, national liberation movements, and NGOs attended the seminar.

[198] Such a seminar would be a follow-up to a number of special OSCE meetings earlier held on the subject of freedom of religion or belief. For instance, from 16 to 19 April 1996 a human dimension seminar on "Constitutional, Legal and Administrative Aspects of Freedom of Religion" took place in Warsaw and on 22 March 1999 a supplementary OSCE human dimension meeting on "Freedom of Religion and Belief" was convened in Vienna. At these meetings a variety of issues concerning freedom of religion or belief were raised in an open and unofficial setting. The meetings were well attended by states, international organizations, NGOs and media.

[199] For instance, the Secretariat General of the Council of Europe organized in cooperation with F. M. van Asbeck Centre for Human Rights Studies of the University of Leiden an international seminar on "Freedom of Conscience" in Leiden from 12 to 14 November 1992.

Chapter 20

Between Laicist State Ideology and Modern Public Religion: The Head-Cover Controversy in Contemporary Turkey

Özlem Denli

I. Introduction

This essay discusses the Islamic head-cover controversy in Turkey during the 1980s and the 1990s.[1] Turkey is a unique example of state-religion separation in the context of a predominantly Muslim society. The pursuit of secularization, mainly through official laicist policies implemented by Kemalist cadres, has engendered a wide spectrum of consequences affecting religious freedoms for both Muslims and members of minority religions. More than any other issue, however, the head-cover dispute has colored public debate on freedom of religion or belief during the last two decades.

Article 18 of the Universal Declaration of Human Rights (UDHR) establishes the right to freedom of religion or belief and lists the specific freedoms intrinsic to the enjoyment of that right.[2] The freedoms put forward in the UDHR are reiterated in the International Covenant on Civil and Political Rights (ICCPR) and further elaborated upon in the 1981 United Nations Declaration on the Elimination of all Forms of Intolerance and of Discrimination Based on Religion or Belief.[3] The internationally negotiated and accepted norms regarding freedom of religion or belief formulated in these key documents are designated to accommodate diverse cultural and religious contexts. They do not prescribe any particular juridical relationship between state and religion, and can, in principle, be implemented in different constitutional settings. Given this diversity, institutional arrangements substantiating freedom of religion or belief will, for the most part, be context dependent. For this reason, focusing on a

[1] Many thanks to Thomas W. Pogge and the editors of this volume for helpful comments. Research on this article is supported by a grant from the Ethics Program of the Norwegian Research Council.

[2] UDHR, art. 18 reads: "Everyone has the right to freedom of thought, conscience and religion; this right includes freedom to change his religion or belief, and freedom, either alone or in community with others and in public or private, to manifest his religion or belief in teaching, practice, worship and observance" (UDHR, UN GA Res. 217 A [III], UN Doc. A/810, at 71 [1948]).

[3] Both ICCPR, art. 18 and 1981 Declaration, art. 1 employ a slightly different expression from UDHR, art. 18 and do not explicitly mention the freedom to change one's religion or belief.

Tore Lindholm, W. Cole Durham, Jr., Bahia G. Tahzib-Lie (eds.), Facilitating Freedom of Religion or Belief: A Deskbook, *497–511.*

particular issue may be necessary for a critical assessment of a given array of domestic institutions as both the embodiment of certain values and principles as well as an outcome of historical contingencies and power struggles.

This chapter analyzes modern Turkey in the framework of its aspired model, namely a constitutional, democratic, secular polity. In broad terms, I contend that this model refers to a political regime that excludes interpenetration of the spheres of religion and public order. In contrast to states promoting a particular religious doctrine, the civic order of secular democracies does not depend directly upon an official religious doctrine, but rather is built upon the principle of equal citizenship and the establishment of a legal structure that guarantees the right of all citizens to pursue their conception of the good life. Furthermore, these secular democracies are distinct from the former Soviet-type regimes since they welcome the assumption that, for most members of the society, religion may be a significant part of a well-lived life. Based upon this assumption, these secular democracies do not suppress religion or belief. I shall take this approximate description as a point of reference for evaluating the individual characteristics of the Turkish example.

II. Modernity, Normative Plurality, and Freedom of Religion or Belief

The distinctive quality of modernity that sets it apart from all the other forms of social existence is a major topic of social theory. Developments brought about by this unique turn in human history are commonly labeled as the unsurpassable rise of a new social organization and a profound shift in moral values. In general terms, we can argue that modernity is built upon three interrelated principles. The first is a structural differentiation whereby sectors of society and culture are removed from the domination of religious institutions and symbols. The second is a plurality of symbolic universes, norms, and value/belief systems. The last is an institutionalization of social spheres outside the intervention of the state and of authoritative religious institutions.

The most significant aspect of modernity, pertaining to freedom of religion or belief, is the decline of religious consensus and the withdrawal of hegemonic religious worldviews as the cement of positive societal integration.[4] As José Casanova argues, the process of structural differentiation and the separation of value spheres amounted to the emergence of a new horizon towards which traditional religion was compelled to orient itself through a fundamental restructuring of its own premises.[5] In modern secular societies, religion has become a private affair of the individual, from which he or she is entitled to exclude the intervention and control of others.[6] In this context the individual realm of freedom of religion or belief comprises not only the individual affirmation of religion or belief,[7] but also the freedom to interpret and form one's own way of relating to religion. In

[4] José Casanova, *Public Religions in the Modern World* (Chicago: University of Chicago Press, 1994), 39.

[5] Ibid., 21, 22.

[6] Ibid., 40.

[7] Here it has to be clarified that the expression "to have" a religion or belief of one's choice does not imply that people have to choose their religion or beliefs by picking them from a series of possibilities. Rather, the right to private choice is meant to ensure the possibility of following one's own conscience or inner voice without prescribing that this choice be an outcome of profound reflection or a radical choice in the existentialist

this sense both free choice and individual interpretation of religion or belief are regarded as matters intimately related to the right to privacy, and are protected against state intrusion and religiously based infringements.

A. Manifestation of Religion or Belief

Freedom of religion or belief, as formulated in relevant provisions of international human rights instruments, is often interpreted as relying on a distinction between the internal and external forums. According to this distinction, the inner realm consists of the freedom to have or to adopt a religion or belief of one's choice, and the freedom to change one's religious conviction or belief. The outer realm incorporates the freedom to manifest in public or private one's religion or belief in worship, observance, teaching, and practice. Freedom of the inner realm is held to be absolute in the sense that it cannot be restricted in any way, even in times of public emergency,[8] whereas outward manifestations of the freedom of religion or belief may be subjected to certain limitations. The International Covenant on Civil and Political Rights defines permissible limitations as those that are "prescribed by law and are necessary to protect public safety, order, health, morals, or the rights and freedoms of others."[9]

The foremost explanation for this differentiation, inner freedom, is beyond the reach of political intervention, whereas outer freedom is commonly accepted as being within the appropriate exercise of civic authority. It seems, however, that the boundary between issues of conscience and social order is not as obvious as it may initially appear. Elaborating on this subject, Arcot Krishnaswami makes the point that "one would assume any outside intervention into the inner realm of conscience is not only illegitimate but impossible."[10] He, nonetheless, identifies certain "outward" aspects of the right to maintain and change one's religion. According to Krishnaswami, most of religious life is normally lived within a religious organization or a community of belief. In this respect, compelling an individual to join, or preventing her from leaving, an organization are infringements on the inner realm of conscience.[11]

In a similar vein, the differentiation between the freedoms of the internal forum and the external forum is far from being definitively settled. Several issues relevant to this distinction continue to be major topics of disagreement. For example, freedom to change one's religion or belief is one of the bitterly contested issues of international human rights. Consequently, one may argue that although the inner realm can be beyond the reach of external intervention, guaranteeing a realm of individual liberty as

---

fashion. See Helge Høibraaten, "Secular Society: An Attempt at Initiation," in *Islamic Law Reform and Human Rights: Challenges and Rejoinders,* ed.Tore Lindholm and Kari Vogt (Oslo: Nordic Human Rights Publications, 1993), 248.

[8] ICCPR, art. 18, which defines the right to freedom of religion or belief, belongs to the category of so-called "nonderogable" rights. The second paragraph of this article bars coercion that would impair the freedom to have or adopt a religion or belief of one's choice.

[9] ICCPR, art. 18.

[10] Arcot Krishnaswami, "Study of Discrimination in the Matter of Religious Rights and Practices," in *Religion and Human Rights: Basic Documents,* ed. Tad Stahnke and J. Paul Martin (New York: Columbia University, 1998), 15 (Krishnaswami's study was originally published in UN Doc. E/CN.4/Sub 2/200/Rev 1, UN Sales No. 60.XIV.2 [1960]).

[11] Ibid.

a right inherent in the individual necessarily requires certain institutional arrangements. This position demands that the basic structure[12] of society be designed to secure access of the individual to the objects of her religious rights.

When dealt with in the context of certain practical circumstances, human rights issues often involve conflicts and challenges of varying degrees. The first aspect of this challenge relates to the tension between the normative plurality characterizing most modern societies and the ensuing incompatibility of demands made in the name of different religions and belief systems.[13] The second aspect concerns the fact that, in a liberal constitutional democracy, it is not merely individuals that may legitimately demand immunity from state intervention, but also organizations. These diverging demands can, in turn, create an incongruity between the principles of the basic structure of the society on one hand, and those of religious organizations and communities on the other. More specifically, nonliberal tenets that may underlie a particular religious doctrine can generate conflict between its doctrinal and organizational integrity and the liberal principles embodied in the broader institutional structure of society.

These considerations suggest that in certain historical contexts different components of freedom of religion or belief have to be balanced against basic rights in general in order to fit into a coherent scheme. In this regard, John Rawls suggests that it is possible to distinguish between restricting basic liberties and regulating them in order to achieve a scheme that can be guaranteed for all.[14] On this view, the right to outwardly manifest one's religion or belief may be legitimately restricted when in conflict with compelling concerns spelled out in the international human rights instruments,[15] in ways which are consistent with the principle of nondiscrimination.[16] Alternatively, this right may be regulated so that it fits into a scheme of liberties that can be guaranteed for all members of society. Given the radical normative plurality characterizing modern societies, it is an arduous task to deal with these divergent claims equitably in specific instances. As repeatedly expressed in the Krishnaswami study: "Demands of religions vary radically and non-discrimination should be sensitive to these differences. Certain limitations imposed upon particular manifestations of religion or belief, although apparently conceived in general terms, may in fact tend to affect it more than others. This consideration cannot be ignored when deciding whether or not a particular limitation is legitimate."[17]

---

[12] John Rawls defines basic structure as a society's main political, social, and economic institutions, and how they fit together into one unified system of social cooperation from one generation to the next. Rawls also emphasizes basic institutions and the principles, standards, and precepts that apply to them. See John Rawls, *Political Liberalism* (New York: Columbia University Press, 1993), 11, 35.

[13] For example, regulation of days of rest in a multireligious society.

[14] Rawls, *Political Liberalism,* 333.

[15] UDHR, art. 29, para. 2, permits only those "limitations as are determined by law solely for the purpose of securing due recognition and respect for the rights and freedoms of others and of meeting the just requirements of morality, public order and the general welfare in a democratic society."

[16] The principle of equal dignity and rights is put forward in UDHR, art. 1. Article 2 protects the individuals against discrimination on the basis of religion or belief, and article 7 provides for equality before the law, also beyond the scope of freedom of religion or belief. Similarly, the general limitations applicable to the rights and freedoms incorporated in the UDHR allowed by articles 29 and 30 are themselves consistent with the principle of nondiscrimination. See Bahiyyih G. Tahzib, *Freedom of Religion or Belief: Ensuring Effective International Legal Protection* (Boston: Martinus Nijhoff, 1996), 77.

[17] Krishnaswami, "Study of Discrimination in the Matter of Religious Rights and Practices," 17.

Certain manifestations of religion or belief may require additional political and economic arrangements that are only indirectly relevant to the enjoyment of the freedom of religion or belief in question. For example, allowing individuals to perform their duty of pilgrimage requires the removal of obstacles against freely leaving their country and returning, as well as arrangements to make hard currency available. Yet these broad political and economic efforts are compatible with the principle of equal treatment, since these government actions would not support one religious sect over another, but rather would simply respond to the fact that religion may be significant for most members of the society.[18]

In addition to these considerations, an evenhanded protection of the freedom of religion or belief requires an examination of the direct and indirect effects of any given institutional arrangement in terms of discriminatory outcomes. Put in another way, in assessing the fairness of an institutional setting, one cannot disregard the question of whether under that particular constellation a certain group of individuals, who can be defined in terms of religion or belief, are avoidably put into a position of systematic disadvantage.

B. A Brief Note on the Use of Head Covers

Belonging to the external realm of manifestation, the freedom to wear a head cover in public life is not necessarily a nonderogable right. In a secular democratic society, the wearing of religious apparel in certain professional settings may be limited based on the circumstances of the occupation. For example, there may be uniform requirements due to workplace safety and similar concerns. In the general context of the freedom to choose one's occupation, not being able to be work in a particular occupation may not constitute a human rights violation. Similarly, it would be unreasonable for a religious individual to demand a remodeling of the occupation itself in line with the religious standards she sets for herself, if they are incompatible with the requirements of that particular job.[19]

In the case of contemporary Turkey, however, restrictions on the use of the head cover go beyond policies supporting valid regulatory laws. The next section will provide a brief background on the recent history and a delineation of present-day practices.

III. The Case of Turkey: An Overview of the Controversy

The "head-cover controversy" in Turkey is named by reference to the garb itself. Even so, this term should be understood in relation to the concept of "Islamic veiling," a term which better expresses the internal significance for Muslim women. In the tradition of Islam, veiling is an instrument of morality that illustrates a desire to hide femininity and to conceal the female body from the view of males. Veiling also demands modesty of

[18] This point is made by Richard Kraut, who argues that it would be appropriate for the state to insure that religious institutions or practices not be threatened or weakened due to the fact that they play an organizing role for many citizens in their efforts to lead meaningful lives (Richard Kraut "Politics, Neutrality, and the Good," *Social Philosophy and Policy* [Oxford: Blackwell, 1999], 16: 326 n. 1).

[19] For instance, a medical student's refusal to operate on cadavers on religious grounds would be qualified as unreasonable, provided that an equivalent training cannot be given by other means at reasonable costs.

behavior through the behavioral control that the woman must exercise to limit her appeal in public.[20] In present-day Turkey, Islamic veiling refers to the wearing of a head cover together with long, loose-fitting gowns. In contrast to the traditional head cover, which encloses the hair only partially and leaves the neck uncovered, the new veiling entails a usage that wraps the hair completely. To mark this difference the new use of head cover is labeled as *türban*[21] in the mass media and general public.

The *türban* controversy has primarily been an issue for institutions of higher education. The first instance of the veiling discord emerged in 1968 at the University of Ankara.[22] Nevertheless, the matter did not become the center of public debate until after the military coup of 1980. In 1982 a directive issued by the Council of Higher Education introduced the ban by prohibiting students from attending academic classes if they wore the veil. This event marked the collapse of a tacit agreement and women's dress at the institutions of higher education became the subject of formal regulation. A decade-long process of making and reversing decisions ensued.

In 1983 Kenan Evren, the former Chief of the General Staff and the key architect of the military coup, took over the Turkish presidency. The first general elections after the military coup were held the same year. The conservativly oriented Motherland Party emerged with a landslide victory in the elections and formed the government with a clear parliamentary majority. In addition to its general conservative stance, the Motherland Party included an Islamic wing that was particularly receptive to religious sentiments and to the grass roots dissatisfaction regarding the ban. After receiving prompting from the government, the Council of Higher Education issued a decree in 1984 redefining the *türban* as a modern garb and permitted its use at the universities. President Kenan Evren intervened to reverse the decision, referring to a ruling of the High Advisory Council. In 1987 the Disciplinary Manual issued by the Council of Higher Education was revised to reinstate the ban. This sequence of prohibitions caused a great wave of protest actions. The *türban* issue became a front line of contestation and mobilization for both its supporters and opponents. Muslim men and women organized street demonstrations, petition campaigns, and hunger strikes, while several laicist organizations expressed their commitment to the principle of laicism and their support for the ban.[23]

Motivated by the relentless grass roots mobilization of, and pressure from, the Islamic wing in the party, in 1989 the Motherland Party government passed a law lifting the ban. President Evren vetoed the new legislation and returned it to parliament for reevaluation. As a supplementary measure, the government modified the internal Manual of Higher Education to declare that the use of the *türban* did not

---

[20] It is interesting to note that Islamic arguments defending veiling of women are based on a concern for preserving social order. Accordingly, the sexuality and even the beauty of women are perceived as threats to order in the community.

[21] Türban, originally from Turkish "tül(i)bend" and Persian "dülband," refers to a headdress of Turkish origin, consisting of a long linen, cotton, or silk scarf. In modern Turkish, however, it is employed as a French word, one denoting a fashion of headdress, itself adopted from Ottoman Turkish. See Nilüfer Göle, *The Forbidden Modern: Civilization and Veiling* (Ann Arbor: The University of Michigan Press, 1996), 6.

[22] The case of theology faculty student Hatice Balaban (the reference is available from the author).

[23] Among these laicist associations were Cagdas Yasami Destekleme Dernegi (Association of Support for Modern Life), Türk Kadin Hukukcular Dernegi (Association of Turkish Female Jurists), and Istanbul Universitesi Kadin Sorunlari Arastirma ve Uygulama Merkezi (University of Istanbul, the Center of Research and Application on the Woman Question).

conflict with the requirements of modern dress. Later in 1989 the parliament passed the law lifting the prohibition, overriding the president. President Evren referred the decision to the Constitutional Court, which agreed with the president and declared the law unconstitutional. The Constitutional Court decision was followed by the annulment of the lenient manual article.

After Turgut Özal of the Motherland Party was elected president in 1989, the head-cover issue was reintroduced on the government agenda, only this time without the interference of a presidential veto. On 28 December 1989, a decree was issued that canceled the paragraph in the manual regulating dress code and left it to the rectors of the universities to decide whether to allow the wearing of headscarves.[24] Far from being a principled solution, the decision delegated the problem to the local level and to individual institutions. In the majority of cases, implementation of this decision meant a *de facto* lifting of the ban and many students committed to wearing head covers had the opportunity to complete their studies. Finally, in 1990, the disciplinary measures and any resulting consequences taken against these students were annulled.

The latest turning point in this controversy took place in 1997. Amidst the political atmosphere that lead to the resignation of the Islamic Welfare Party government and the initiation of procedures that lead to the permanent shutdown of the party, the head-cover ban was revived in an all-compassing form. Under the resulting regulations, which are currently still in effect, women wearing a head cover cannot attend universities or be employed in public offices. Women who consider veiling in public life to be a religious obligation are excluded from the entire public sector, which is rather sizeable in Turkey. Those women can, in principle, work in the private sector or be self-employed,[25] but under present regulations they are deprived of the opportunity of a university education, a prerequisite for many jobs.

Consequently, in present-day Turkey we witness the avoidable conflict between two elements central to veiled women's religious conceptions. Sociological research on the topic shows that the Muslim women consider learning and acquiring an education to be a religious duty prescribed by Islam.[26] In this sense, the ban engenders a conflict by forcing them to choose performance of one religious duty over the other. Furthermore, it creates avoidable incompatibility between veiled women's religious convictions and their desire to be productive members of society through education and employment.

IV. Justification Grounds

The official acceptance of the freedom to wear head cover would not require extensive institutional arrangements or the allocation of additional resources. Nor would it directly clash with the equal acceptance of rights and freedoms of others.[27] It is due to these characteristics that placing limitations on a woman's freedom to manifest her religion should require strong justification grounds.

---

[24] Erik J. Zürcher, *Turkey: A Modern History* (London: I. B. Tauris, 1993), 305.

[25] For example, there are private hospitals employing women with head covers.

[26] See Göle, *The Forbidden Modern,* 93–100. See also Aynur Ilyasoglu, *Örtülü Kimlik* (Istanbul: Metis Yayinlari, 1994), 96–99.

[27] An issue of concern might emerge, however, if the head cover began to function as a line of distinction by which women who do not wear head covers are harassed or discriminated against.

In their justification of the current ban, Turkish legislators and judges portray veiling as a politicized symbol of systemic rejection targeting the laicist organizing principle of the state. The fact that the use of head cover at the center of controversy is distinct from the traditional usage exacerbates these assumptions. A typical court ruling reads:

> We observe use of head cover among uneducated women who, without special reflection follow the customs and lived tradition in their immediate surroundings. We also observe that some women with higher education, so they no longer submit to custom or the influence of traditions, choose to wear head cover to demonstrate that they oppose the laicist foundations of the Republic and desire to establish a rule based on religion. For these individuals, use of head cover is no longer an innocent habit but symbolize their rejection of women's rights and a worldview antithetical to the foundations of our Republic.[28]

As this statement clearly demonstrates, the question of political legitimacy lies at the heart of the matter and invites an inquiry into the principles underlying basic institutions in contemporary Turkey, as well as the fundamental dynamics of the recent political history.

V. State and Religion in Turkey

The Ottoman legacy was characterized by state domination of the religious establishment. The Ottoman government established effective control over the *ulema*, the class of religious scholars, by turning them into state functionaries.[29] Jurists of Islamic law loosely organized themselves into schools of jurisprudence, but developed no hierarchy comparable to, for instance, the Catholic Church. Partially due to the fact that the Muslim community was not a political unit, the government had the capacity to control the religious community.[30] In turn, political power furnished the setting for application of Islamic law, and provided for the privileged status of Sunni Islam vis-à-vis other religions and interpretations of Islam practiced within the territories of the empire. In this sense the polity conferred as much legitimacy upon religion as religion did upon the polity. Sunni Islam relied on its position as the state religion to secure prevalence over the heterodox cults, sects, mystical orders, and the Shia.[31] Because of the primacy they accorded to the state, Ottoman bureaucrats reacted fiercely against any religious influence that could pose a challenge to the central authority. Religious heterodoxy was tolerated as long as it posed no threat to the political center. Every organization and institution was constrained by the duty to protect the state, which in turn acted in the name of the sacred.[32]

The most important turning point in the history of modernization and secularization of Ottoman-Turkish society was the founding of the Turkish Republic in 1923. The establishment of a new nation state led by a splinter fraction of the old

---

[28] *Resmi Gazete* (Official Journal), No. 20216, 5 July 1989, quoted in Dogan Duman, *Demokrasi Sürecinde Türkiye'de Islamcilik* (Izmir: Dokuz Eylül Yayinlari, 1997), 220.

[29] Serif Mardin, *Türkiye'de Toplum ve Siyaset* (Istanbul: Iletisim Yayinlari, 1995), 118.

[30] Niyazi Berkes, *Teokrasi ve Laiklik* (Istanbul: Adam Yayincilik, 1997), 17.

[31] Ilter Turan, "Religion and Political Culture in Turkey," in *Islam in Modern Turkey*, ed. Richard Tapper, (London: I. B. Tauris, 1991), 41.

[32] Berkes, *Teokrasi ve Laiklik*, 18.

ruling class required a rapid break from the old basis of legitimacy. Kemalist reformism concentrated its efforts on defining a political system free of religious and dynastic legitimacy, and constituted the republic on a laicist-nationalist basis.[33] Starting with the early years of the republic, the Kemalist cadres commenced a program of dislocating the institutional basis of religion in society. The Caliphate and Islamic courts were abolished and *tarikats* (mystical orders) were banned. The traditional institutions of religious education were closed down, and all education was brought under the supervision of the Ministry of National Education. In 1926 civil and penal codes were adopted. In 1928 Islam was disestablished as the state religion, and in 1937 the principle of laicism became an integral part of the Turkish Constitution.

The Republic of Turkey perpetuated the tradition of state domination of religion, and the incorporation of the Islamic religious establishment within state institutions continued. The Directorate of Religious Affairs was created as a body incorporated into the administrative apparatus, and as was the case in the Ottoman Empire, the concept of "religion" was limited to Sunni Islam. State policies of control and supervision continue to confer legitimacy upon the Sunni creed at the expense of other religions and Shia. Public resources are used to promote Sunni teaching through the establishment of special education institutions (*Imam Hatip Okullari*), Quran courses, emissions on state radio and TV, and ultimately compulsory religious education in the 1980s. The substantial Shia minorities, *Alevis*, and other Shia sects, are denied access to similar resources. While mosques are built with public resources, the building of *Alevi* prayer houses, *Cemevi*, is forbidden, or at least does not receive any public support. *Alevis* have even been coerced to build mosques in their own villages.[34]

The republican elite not only kept religious institutions under state control, but also dedicated a great deal of energy to regulating ordinary, day-to-day expressions of Islamic tradition and popular religiosity. The majority of the republican cadres viewed religion as something to be modernized and reformed rather than a mere anachronism.[35] In their characterization of the republic's model of laicism, Birtek and Toprak remark:

> It was radical enough to twist the separation of church and state into a full scale state domination and control of religious institutions. In that, republicanism tried to establish two things at once. On the one hand, it hoped to relegate religion to the private sphere—almost a Christianized form of Islam—by restricting it on a question of individual conscience, and on the other hand, it attempted to control the pulpit by trying to rewrite its language and subsume its organization under the heavy hand of state control.[36]

The civilian and military bureaucratic cadres not only regulated the institutions of religious life but also intervened to modify Islam's theological content and tradition. To a large extent religion was conceived as a policy instrument and a subject of social engineering. By the late 1980s, Turkey's political outlook was marked by paradoxical and unintended consequences of this official attitude.

---

[33] Caglar Keyder, *State and Class in Turkey: A Study in Capitalist Development* (London: Verso, 1987), 86.

[34] Bülent Tanör, *Türkiye'nin Insan Haklari Sorunu* (Ankara: BDS Yayinlari, 1994), 47.

[35] In its initial phase, the republic took steps to transform the theological content of Islam itself. See Ali Yasar Saribay, *Postmodernizm, Sivil Toplum ve Islam* (Istanbul: Iletisim Yayinlari, 1995), 59–61.

[36] Faruk Birtek and Binnaz Toprak, "The Conflictual Agendas of Neo-Liberal Reconstruction and the Rise of Islamic Politics in Turkey," *Praxis International* (Oxford: Blackwell) 13 (1993): 195 n. 2.

A. Dilemmas of the Official Ideology

Religiously inspired political ideologies in Turkey began to emerge as early as in the 1950s, although it was only in the 1980s that Islam became a central variable in the political equations. This new development was not simply the result of a global trend, but coincides with the 1980 military coup and the changing direction of official policies towards religion.

Alarmed by the heightened political polarization and the prevailing radical left-wing discourse, the high command of the—historically laicist—Armed Forces decided to pass laws that would promote a "religious culture." State investment in the promotion and control of religion increased substantially.[37] However, the aim of the military was clearly not to provoke extensive Islamization, since the Constitution of 1982 reiterated the constitutional provisions safeguarding the secular character of the state. Furthermore, the constitution accorded special protection to the eight "Principle Reform Laws" passed during the Ataturk era and embodying the principles of Kemalist laicism.[38] The military's policy entailed maintaining a rein on Islam and enhancing its social significance in a monitored and supervised fashion. The main intention underlying this change in official policy was to elicit the support of the Islamic loyalties of the population behind an authoritarian institutionalization.[39]

Nonetheless, in the 1980s Turkey became the scene of Islamic expressions that went far beyond the anticipated limits, both in terms of political significance and organizational strength. A fundamental consequence of this turning point was the politicization of state institutions and the increased permeability of the state apparatus to communally organized political networks. As a result of these activities, Islamic networks gained access to state resources, which, in turn, further enticed them to politicization.[40] In their analysis of the new political setting created by the Armed Forces and ensuing unintended consequences, Birtek and Toprak contend: "What they [the Armed Forces] failed to see is the most secular side of religious interests; that is, in Weberian terms, the organizational superiority an ideology acquires once it can offer systematic benefits to its members and thereby vest itself with political momentum." [41]

The efforts of Islamic groups to infiltrate educational institutions, civilian bureaucracy, the police force, and—with considerably less success—the Armed Forces, began in the 1970s, when the National Salvation Party participated in three coalition governments. These activities intensified after the military coup of 1980, particularly during

---

[37] The number of schools to train prayer leaders and preachers (the *Imam Hatip* schools) increased sharply from 258 to 350 during the three-year tenure of the armed forces. The number of students attending those schools rose dramatically to 270,000. Along with the *Imam Hatip* schools there has also been an expansion in the lower-grade Quranic schools. Before the coup of 1980 there were 2,610 such schools; by 1989 the number had grown to 4,715. See Feroz Ahmad, *The Making of Modern Turkey* (London: Routledge, 1994), 219–21.

[38] These are the laws establishing secular education and civil marriage, adopting the Turkish alphabet and the international numerals, introducing the hat, closing the dervish convents, abolishing certain titles, and prohibiting the wearing of certain garments. See Ergun Özbudun, "Constitutional Law," in *Introduction to Turkish Law*, ed. Tugrul Ansay and Don Wallace (Boston: Kluwer Law International, 1996), 31.

[39] Birtek and Toprak, "The Conflictual Agendas of Neo-Liberal Reconstruction," 193.

[40] Ibid., 197.

[41] Ibid.

the reign of the Motherland Party,[42] and reached a peak when the Welfare Party became the major partner in a coalition government in June 1996. Islamic efforts at infiltration of state institutions focus on manipulating and changing constitutional essentials to ensure the dominance of Islamic doctrines. In doing so, they attempt to insert an antagonistic principle of legitimacy into the heart of political institutions. Events such as systematic purges in the ranks of civilian and military bureaucracy are part of the official strategy of reimposing state-centered imperatives by shifting balances of political power.

The head-cover issue emerged in this political atmosphere of increased political significance and public visibility of Islam in the decade following the military coup of 1980. The entry of women wearing head covers into the institutions of higher education exemplified a new profile of Islam. Islam was no longer seen as being limited to a traditional periphery, but was now also embraced by educated and upwardly mobile social groups.[43] The presence of veiled women in institutions that had previously been the locus of modernist and progressive aspirations, came to be perceived on the same level as the aforementioned clandestine attempts, only this time on a symbolic level.

Muslim women transformed the head cover into a line of distinction between themselves and the progressive laicist elite, which effectively put the Turkish experience of modernization and Westernization back onto the public agenda. Today veiling portrays Islamic faith as a commitment to the totality of Islamic beliefs and obligations, including the scriptural basis for the veil, rather than a habitual participation without due reflection. The status of women as the core symbol of the civilized dimension of Islam is asserted as an alternative to the Kemalist cultural project.[44] The ***türban*** is presently an icon for a broad variety of Islamic agendas and the target of the most ardent laicist protests.

B. Women and Civilization

The central role of issues regarding women in the context of competing political ideologies is not a recent phenomenon. Starting in the nineteenth century, the social and legal status of women became a fault line separating the progressive nationalist elite and their traditionalist adversaries. Throughout the entire history of Ottoman-Turkish modernization, the symbolism associated with women has been at the core of controversy regarding the reach of modernization and discussions of identity. Both reformist and conservative stances have been positioned around this unique issue.[45]

The position of women in society was first discussed in the context of attempts during the Tanzimat period (1839–1876) to modernize and orient Turkey towards the Western social model. Ever since these early discussions women's issues have been at the center of political power struggles to determine how far attempts at modernization

---

[42] Turgut Özal gave members of the religious order ***Naqshibendi*** privileged positions in the Motherland Party, and the parliamentary groups were affiliated with various religious organizations.

[43] Birtek and Toprak, "The Conflictual Agendas of Neo-Liberal Reconstruction," 199; Göle, ***The Forbidden Modern***, 77–88; Ilyasoglu, ***Örtülü Kimlik***, 92, 93, 96–99.

[44] Göle, ***The Forbidden Modern***, 86, 87, 91.

[45] Ilyasoglu, ***Örtülü Kimlik***, 50.

should go.[46] As Kandiyoti notes: "Later debates would both reveal and create bitter cleavages among the Ottoman elite itself and the condition of women became more self-consciously identified as the touchstone of Ottoman cultural 'integrity' or 'backwardness,' as the case might be." [47]

Thus, the role of women is not defined merely by the social conditions in which women live, but also by broader issues of culture and civilization. This is the reason why the position of women in society is identified as the touchstone of Kemalist civilization:

> Although the most visible feature of the Turkish modernization movement is its transition from a patrimonial Islamic empire to a secular nation state, the increasing public visibility of women in social life and the principle of equality between men and women has helped to introduce the ideals of modernity into the collective imagination of a Muslim country. In contrast to the political transformation which targeted the state apparatus, the cultural renewals at the interpersonal level and between the sexes in fact have followed a slow, less striking, yet as I will demonstrate, concurrently more weighty course of action.[48]

The cultural renewal targeted by Kemalist reforms aimed at transforming lifestyles and clothing habits. Legal reform aimed at improving the status of women was accompanied by the discussion on the "new woman" and her outer appearance.[49] In the multiethnic and multireligious Ottoman Empire, differences in dress code indicated ethnicity, religious affiliation, status, or occupation.[50] In turn, the new outlook of women promoted by the republican cadres became the cornerstone for the project of "elevating the nation to the level of contemporary civilization."

In this respect the symbolic gravity of the matter cannot be overemphasized from the perspective of the guardians of the official state ideology as well as their Islamic opponents. The events of the last two decades, however, have resulted in an unprecedented level of sensitivity on the part of political elites. Historically, attempts to modify women's clothing habits have never taken the form of legally sanctioned interventions. The "hat laws" of 1925 and a law passed in 1934 forbidding the wearing of *kisve* outside religious ceremonies targeted men exclusively. In the early years of the republic, veiling was never legally banned, although a vigorous propaganda campaign led by Ataturk exhorted women to adopt modern styles of dress, and those spreading counter-propaganda were tried and given short prison sentences.[51] This lack of legislation and direct official regulation of women's dress code is in stark contrast to the otherwise fierce policies implemented during the foundational period of the Turkish Republic.[52]

---

[46] Göle, *The Forbidden Modern,* 30.

[47] Deniz Kandiyoti, "End of Empire: Islam, Nationalism and Women in Turkey," in *Women, Islam, and the State,* ed. Deniz Kandiyoti (Basingstoke: Macmillan Press, 1991), 26.

[48] Göle, *The Forbidden Modern,* 29.

[49] Ilyasoglu, *Örtülü Kimlik,* 54.

[50] Ibid., 50.

[51] Kandiyoti, "End of Empire: Islam, Nationalism and Women in Turkey," 23. Ilyasoglu contends that interventions in the clothing and veiling of women are expressed in oral history, but there exists no systematic study of the matter. See Ilyasoglu, *Örtülü Kimlik,* 56.

[52] For example, seventy men were hanged because of their opposition to the "hat laws," which banned a traditional male headdress. See Keyder, *State and Class in Turkey,* 84 n. 21.

C. The 1980s: Radicalization and Differentiation

As mentioned above, official efforts to limit Islam to the private sphere of individual conscience has largely been successful as regards popular religiosity, which more or less views religion as custom and ritual that has little relevance to the way individuals lead their public lives. In contrast, the more scripturally oriented segments of Islam view the religion as a comprehensive worldview with claims on all aspects of life. These Islamic expressions are rightly identified as different from traditional religiosity in terms of their public and political emphasis as well as their sociological characteristics.[53] Rather than understanding Islam as a religion of individual salvation, adherents of these modern interpretations insist on taking Islamic dictates as the normative perspective from which they evaluate the existing institutional framework.

These views, however, do not automatically imply that what are conceived to be dictates of Islam necessarily override the underlying principles of a constitutional democratic regime. Not every religiously based demand on the institutional structure of the society necessarily discriminates against freedom of religion or belief of those who do not share those convictions. In other words, public religious manifestations may very well be a legitimate exercise of rights that is compatible with the equal consideration and regard for all citizens.[54] A narrow conceptualization in terms of totalizing categories means simply glossing over these differences and the diversity of modern public religion.

Institutional rules established at the onset of the republic embodied an understanding of religion modeled on subjective forms. The arrangement was dismissive of the diversity of Islamic expressions and the demands that Islam places on the basic institutional structure. This largely exclusionist model was further tailored to fit the prescriptive vision of the official ideology. Far from being impartial, the official attitude towards religion resulted in a policy that privileged, and yet controlled, Sunni Islam, and which followed a substantive cultural outlook and civilized vision in which the status of women played a pivotal role.

Without a doubt, some reactions to secularism are largely due to negative sentiments regarding the state-centered orientation of the Turkish Republic and are often tainted by questions of political legitimacy. This fact requires sensitivity to the diversity of Islamic expressions, as opposed to the current generalizations. Such a policy could legitimately sanction attempts to manipulate public institutions and agencies in favor of a particular religious doctrine, to impose a comprehensive Islamic agenda, or to gradually take over of the current state apparatus. These activities bypass democratic mechanisms of modifying the legal framework, and are clear violations of the legal duty of government officials to act from and to follow constitutional principles and procedures.

---

[53] The newly emerging profile of Islam represents a move to the center from the periphery, mainly through the endorsement of upwardly mobile social groups.

[54] For an analysis of Islamic perspectives in Turkey on the framework developed by Rawls, see Özlem Denli Harvey, *Islam and the Freedom of Religion or Belief: Perspectives from Contemporary Turkey* (Oslo: Norwegian Institute of Human Rights, 2000), 1.

Significantly, when outward manifestations of Islam are more intimately related to the freedom of thought and expression, the question of whether these manifestations amount to infringements of human rights can be assessed independently of their distinctively religious content. Modifications of the Turkish Penal Code indicate a certain willingness to accommodate this line of reasoning. In March and April 1991 the cabinet introduced a package of constitutional amendments dealing in part with human rights. At the government's request, the assembly decided to approve the deletion of article 163 of the Penal Code, which banned religiously oriented politics and associations as well as public expression of ideas "against laicism."[55] The only exception was the use of terrorism to foster political ideals, which became illegal under the "anti-terrorism" law that was adopted at the same time.[56] Such developments indicate a willingness to negotiate the boundaries of religiously inspired political expression and a shift towards a more differentiated evaluation of their actual content.

Transitions like the one exemplified above have made some Islamic issues easier to address and have empowered a partially separate discourse. As a consequence, in the 1990s an Islamic public sphere of participation and deliberation flourished, finding expression in a large number of publishing houses, books, weekly and monthly journals, nationwide daily newspapers and TV channels, conferences, and panel discussions.

In contrast with these developments, current regulations seem to attach symbolic significance to the head-cover issue as a nonnegotiable boundary between laicism and Islamism. This topic of controversy is held by Kemalist military civilian bureaucracy and political elites to be an almost sacralized frontier beyond the reach of political mechanisms of making collectively binding decisions. The ban on the use of the head cover in public offices and universities stems from the transformation of a religious manifestation into a symbol of systemic political opposition. Advocates of the ban dismiss the idea that veiling may simply be a perfectly plausible interpretation of Quranic dictates without any hidden political agenda. Moreover, they have never assumed the burden of demonstrating organizational connection between the use of the head cover and illegal or subversive activity. The official treatment simply ideologizes the use of the head cover to the point of completely disregarding its significance as a tenet of individual religiosity.

VI. Towards a Conclusion

This chapter addresses the regulatory laws and administrative practices existing in present-day Turkey that seemingly define a neutral and nondenominational public space. It has assessed these institutional arrangements in relation to diverse religions—and particularly to certain modern Islamic viewpoints—in order to point out some of their discriminatory consequences. To this end the chapter has argued that laicist policies of the Turkish Republic are the expressions of a comprehensive doctrine that is systematically biased and exclusionist in its very makeup.

---

[55] The rationale of safeguarding laicism was used to censor, suppress, and punish a wide range of speeches and opinions. In some cases merely explaining Islamic principles or participating in public ritual or worship were regarded as punishable acts. See Tanör, *Türkiye'nin Insan Haklari Sorunu,* 6, 68.

[56] See Zürcher, *Turkey: A Modern History,* 305.

Moving away from the specifics of the Turkish case, it may still be possible to question laicism's abstract leveling of distinctions in public life. Laicism tends to endorse a definition of the freedom of religion or belief that is fashioned on subjective forms of religion that are confined to catering to individual souls. What we are in fact presented with is a normatively prescriptive model that favors certain forms of modern religion [57] at the expense of others that are equally legitimate. An adequate treatment of this more general question, however, should be the topic of another study.

[57] What Casanova calls the "Protestant privatized form" (Casanova, *Public Religions in the Modern World,* 39).

Chapter 21

Burdens on the Right of Women to Assert Their Freedom of Religion or Belief

Juliet Sheen

I. Women's Human Rights

Human rights are women's rights, and vice versa. The 1979 Convention on the Elimination of All Forms of Discrimination Against Women placed women's rights squarely on the international human rights agenda. The United Nations General Assembly set then the international standards, procedures, mechanisms, and monitoring of women's human rights and has since directed that women's human rights are not to be regarded as peripheral. Under resolution 1999/41 of the UN Commission on Human Rights, women's rights are to be integrated into every part of United Nations human rights organizations and mechanisms, there being a gender perspective to be realized in every rights violation.

This gender perspective is aided by a burgeoning body of feminist scholarly work that serves to monitor the human rights field. States' arguments that might have gone unchallenged twenty years ago are now regularly challenged by women's organizations, lawyers, and scholars contributing to the treaty-monitoring process.

Of particular interest are those rights violations that arise out of the human right to enjoyment and freedom of belief. Whilst that right has been set out in detail in the 1981 UN Declaration on the Elimination of All Forms of Intolerance and of Discrimination Based on Religion and Belief, there are violations that might go unnoticed even in our gender-sensitive environment. Religion is so heavily masculinized that the tenets and extensions of religious belief are sometimes, in and of themselves, violations of women's human rights.

The manifestations and practices which are protected under the freedom of religion and belief are deeply entwined with other rights and freedoms, directly or indirectly. These include the freedom to associate and to assemble peacefully, freedom of expression and communication, freedom of movement, freedom of political and other opinion, freedom from discrimination and access to effective remedies, freedom from arbitrary interference, freedom to marry and found a family, freedom to educate and be educated, and freedom to own property, among others. All

Tore Lindholm, W. Cole Durham, Jr., Bahia G. Tahzib-Lie (eds.), Facilitating Freedom of Religion or Belief: A Deskbook, *513–521.*

these rights and freedoms are crucial to the maintenance and continuity of religious and other belief systems and their organizations, as is recognized in articles 5 and 6 of the 1981 UN Declaration. Yet these are the very freedoms that are at issue for women when freedom of religion is played as a trump card to justify their subordination.

The 1981 UN Declaration does not limit acts of discrimination and intolerance to the circumstances stated in articles 5 and 6 but includes in those acts whatever may be held to arise, in broader terms, under articles 1 and 2. The Human Rights Committee has taken a wide view of what is pertinent to the operation of ICCPR article 18.[1] Howland notes that civil and political rights are envisaged by the ICCPR to be available to all under a democratic government to allow women and men the full development of human personality needed to function as politically effective citizens.[2] Chinkin also notes that freedom of religion and belief lies at the interface between civil and political rights, and economic, social, and cultural rights where freedom of religion and belief might be considered a group right as part of self-determination.[3] Infringement of women's human rights is thus also likely to entail infringement of their freedom of religion and belief rights.

This chapter will focus on the use of religious institutional power—both state-sponsored and culturally driven—that curtails the rights of women protected under both the 1979 CEDAW and 1981 DEAFI United Nations actions. In particular, this chapter will focus first on systemic and structural inequalities arising from a male-dominated religious theory and secondly on the female identity as constructed through visible/invisible external manifestations and religion-saturated cultural practices.

II. Human Rights Standards, State and Non-State Powers

State powers agreed on how power could be exercised legitimately when they delineated rights and freedoms in the international bill of human rights. They also agreed on what constitutes the illegitimate use of power: "might" is not "right." But state powers can only reach so far, even when deployed legitimately to their fullest extent. The international standards make it clear that the principles apply to more than just sovereign states even if nonstate actors are not directly subject to treaty-monitoring scrutiny. Nonstate actors include individuals, groups, collectivities, and organizations, being human institutions. People and their institutions are obliged to respect the rights and freedoms of others; there are reciprocal interests in doing so.

Confusion comes when rights are extorted by the powerful as rights due to might. Sovereign states are not the only ones to use religion as a trump card to protect continuing discrimination against women. Religious institutions legitimately claim

---

[1] See Human Rights Committee General Comment 22 (1993) (art. 18), general comment adopted by the Human Rights Committee under *International Covenant on Civil and Political Rights* (ICCPR), art. 40, para. 4, CCPR/C/21/Rev.1/Add.4.

[2] Courtney W. Howland, "Safeguarding Women's Political Freedoms under the International Covenant on Civil and Political Rights in the Face of Religious Extremism," in *Religious Fundamentalisms and the Religious Rights of Women*, ed. Courtney W. Howland (New York: St. Martin's Press, 1999), 96–97.

[3] Christine Chinkin, "Cultural Relativism and International Law," in Howland, *Religious Fundamentalisms*, 56.

religious freedom as a right based on the collective interests of a faith community, but religion may also be used by both state and nonstate institutions as a trump card to claim priority over other rights in the name of what Chinkin refers to as "imprecise and indefinite religious priorities."[4] The full force of religious rhetoric may be used politically to silence criticism and to promote, ostensibly in the name of all, a sectional agenda.

A state or a religious institution, or groups and individuals identified with religions and beliefs, cannot in a moral sense (and in the case of states, a legal sense) legitimately use the rights that they claim to protect their own identities in order to justify, protect, or carry out discrimination and intolerance towards women, as well as subordinating, restricting, excluding, secluding, or silencing them. To do so would be to infringe on women's legitimate right to have and to exercise their freedom of religion and belief.

III. Religious Institutional Power

Religion is essentially political and relational. In power relations, questions of boundaries, group identity, cohesiveness, and continuity are felt to be crucial, and male-dominated religious institutions have used their power to subordinate women to these ends. At a fundamental level, it is not possible to divorce the question of burdens for women and freedom of religion and belief from the status and position of women within institutions and organizations of religions and beliefs. Women, historically, have been excluded from positions of power, responsibility, and decision making. Because religious institutions have epitomized the structural and ideological suppression of women, those structures are slow to change to accommodate the religious needs and aspirations of their constituents, much depending on the politico-religious approach of their leaders.

Formal institutions of religion and belief are largely male creations. Men have talked to other men in terms considered universal, but these terms in fact reflect a male construction of the world divided into public and private concerns. An accepted presence in the public space is essential for building and maintaining institutions and organizations of belief. It might be argued that the extent of women's work in the home, in fields, and elsewhere has left little time for building—let alone maintaining—institutional structures concerned with religion and ideology, even though women are, in numbers, the major practitioners of belief. Women have been channeled towards only certain kinds of participation in religion and are less schooled in religion than they are in general education. The power of religion over the lives of women has had a formative influence on their roles in group and collective identity, in family and community. Women's lesser status in religion and family life compounds the effect of their gender status, as does the impact of caste, class, ethnicity, and belonging to a minority or majority group.

[4] Ibid., 58.

IV. Systemic and Structural Inequalities

Burdens on women have ancient origins in the major world religions. Threats to male dominance were posed by female sexuality and capacity to give birth; the blood of menstruation and afterbirth is still considered polluting in many cultures. Being a man, in short, meant not being a woman, and male control over women's sexuality was considered essential.[5]

Over centuries, this male control or dominance has led to systemic and structural inequalities and discrimination against women. This is seen in laws, policies, and practices which have derived from or are linked to religious law. As systems of religion and belief have been such a shaping force on believers' lives and the society in which they live, so their laws and practices have been reflected in sovereign states' laws, policies, and practices in past centuries and today. Links with religious systems do not have to be direct, as in religion-state identification. They may be indirect and dispersed, effecting the structures of the law and its application, its basic assumptions, its terms and procedures, and its capacity (or lack of it) to adapt to encompass the needs of a plural society. Furthermore, successive dominant powers in a country, displacing or accommodating indigenous law and custom over the centuries, may be followed by national liberation movements bringing further legal and policy development under some different secular or religious ideology. Complexities are legion, none more so than for women.

Laws for which states are responsible under the International Covenant on Civil and Political Rights may include family or personal status laws that effectively restrict women's civil and political expression, association, and participation.[6] In some states—such as Iran, Iraq, Saudi Arabia, and Sudan—the activities of all but a relatively few women (an elite) are removed from public space to private space. Under those conditions, women may not as fully exercise their freedom of religion and belief as the men in their societies do. In Afghanistan, under Taliban rule, conditions of gender apartheid have been internationally condemned, although some compromises and accommodations have reportedly appeared in the Taliban practice of gender segregation.[7]

Howland, in analyzing fundamentalist laws in states associated with five world faiths, reveals two norms burdening women's civil and political rights: obedience to the husband and modesty.[8] The enforcing of obedience can amount to condoning violence. The requirement for modesty in behavior and dress has wide ranging effects on the quality and scope of women's health, education, and employment. Such requirements may also restrict women's movement outside their home and their country without a male relative, prevent them from meeting other people in public

---

[5] See, for instance, Sidonie Smith, *A Poetics of Women's Autobiography: Marginality and the Fictions of Self-Representation* (Indianapolis: Indiana University Press, 1987), 38–39; Riffat Hassan, "Rights of Women within Islamic Communities," in *Religious Human Rights in Global Perspective: Religious Perspectives,* ed. John Witte Jr. and Johan D. van der Vyver (Boston: Martinus Nijhoff, 1996), 361–86.

[6] See Howland, "Safeguarding Women's Political Freedoms," n. 34.

[7] See a report by *Guardian* journalist Suzanne Goldenberg, "Women of Kabul learn to cope with Taliban," *Sydney Morning Herald,* 24 December 1999.

[8] Howland, "Safeguarding Women's Political Freedoms," 97–99.

or from raising their voices, and require them to wear in public a covering form of dress, which at its extreme stops women from facially communicating with other people. Everyday impediments accumulate in women's lives, restricting their participation in social interaction, education, and employment, thus hindering their participation in development. Women's poverty and illiteracy are closely linked throughout the world.

Structural and systemic discrimination has a detrimental impact on women through the terms of personal family law in marriage, divorce, custody, maintenance, and inheritance matters. Women may be limited in the way they take part as claimants or witnesses, and in the weight given to their evidence. For example, a Pakistani woman who cannot substantiate her claim of rape with four male witnesses to the act (as required by *sharia* law) may be charged with fornication or adultery.

In countries privileging communal and religious law systems, women are excluded from the administration of the very laws which directly affect their lives and those of their children. For instance, in Israel, a constitutional democracy, there is no civil divorce. No Jewish woman can adjudicate on matters of marriage and divorce in a rabbinical court, although the rabbinate now has a training program for women advocates who become expert in Jewish law and represent women in proceedings.[9] Personal law responsibilities were delegated to Jewish community authorities under Israeli law, a communal autonomy arrangement derived historically from the Ottoman Empire and the British Mandate. Raday is of the opinion that the autonomy of such a subgroup creates "havens of injustice" that threaten women's equality in Western constitutional democracies.[10]

V. Modernizing Personal Laws to Create Gender Equity

The process of modernization has presented challenges to sovereign states emerging from colonialism at varying times and experiencing the pressures of nationalism and fundamentalist religious revival. Modernization of personal laws is taking place in various Muslim countries, such as Tunisia, Egypt, and, now, Morocco. But change is indeed gradual. In Egypt, the sheikh of Al-Azhar University and other clerics and Egyptian women's organizations have supported legislation which now gives women a choice of law on divorce: proof (with witnesses) of marital mistreatment or a statement of incompatibility which a judge would have to grant if not able to reconcile the parties.[11] But inequalities still exist, such as a husband's instant *talaq* divorce, though he must then file a divorce paper, while the recognition of incompatibility leaves a woman with no maintenance and no right to her marital property.

Some changes beneficial to women come from political changes. In Morocco personal law traditionally has privileged the husband. In 1994 the UN Human Rights Committee had pressed for progress as, for instance, the three different personal law

---

[9] Blu Greenberg, "Feminism, Jewish Orthodoxy, Modernity, and Human Rights: Strange Bedfellows?" in *Religion and Human Rights: Competing Claims?* ed. Carrie Gustafson and Peter Juviler (Armonk, N.Y.: M. E. Sharpe, 1999), 145–73.

[10] Frances Raday, "Religion and Patriarchal Politics: The Israeli Experience," in Howland, *Religious Fundamentalisms,* 163–64.

codes (Muslim, Jewish, and Christian) had differing rules about intercommunal marriage and conversion which affected the inheritance rights of women.[12] Under Morocco's new king, changes to personal law have since been proposed.[13] Measures to encourage education for women, in order "to integrate them in development," include plans to raise girls' marriage age from fifteen to eighteen, to ban *talaq* divorce, and to share marital property equally in divorce. The changes were said "to guarantee Morocco a place in today's information society." The proposals, based on rural women's illiteracy rate, the number of violent attacks against women, and their low political participation rate, are to be debated by a special commission including religious scholars. Women's views quoted in the media, both for and against, sought legitimacy by appealing to the "real" Islam.

VI. Visibility and Invisibility in Religious Identity

External manifestations of belief are linked with the internal.[14] A visual signal of majority or minority identity, such as adopting (or removing) a religious head covering, has significance. Tensions between inner and outer arise because manifestation of religion and belief is embedded in a social dynamic, one which includes the potential for silence as well as speech, invisibility as well as visibility. Visibility incurs notice by others and makes change in the status of a person's belief more complex because of possible reactions. Because women have always been seen as markers for cultural identity, external signs of group identity tend to mask women's identities as individuals, thus inhibiting behavior that does not conform to orthodox expectations. But women can also use the power of religious dress to give their actions and utterances added force by deliberately confounding stereotypical expectations.

Women have become targets for intolerance because of visible identity and what may be held to imply in particular circumstances.[15] Girls and women in Algeria's climate of intolerance have been murdered for not wearing the head covering.[16] A Turkish feminist has been tortured and murdered for publicly advocating, among other things, that the message of Islam did not require women to wear head coverings.[17]

Girls and women may also experience hostility if they cover as a visible sign of their religious practice and community identity. In the secular democracies of Turkey and France, for instance, covering has been decried in places of political and ideological significance. Contrary to secular government policy, Merve Kavakci, newly elected

---

[11] Susan Sachs, "New divorce rights for women," *Sydney Morning Herald*, 29 January 2000.

[12] See entry on Morocco in Kevin Boyle and Juliet Sheen, eds., *Freedom of Religion and Belief: A World Report* (New York: Routledge, 1997), 48–50, and Ann Elizabeth Mayer, "Religious Reservations," in Howland, *Religious Fundamentalisms*, 107–08.

[13] "Islamic fury over plans for women," *Sydney Morning Herald*, 31 January 2000.

[14] See discussion on freedom of religion and belief's internal and external forays in Bahiyyih G. Tahzib, "Women's Equal Right to Freedom of Religion or Belief: An Important but Neglected Subject," in Howland, *Religious Fundamentalisms*, 119–23.

[15] See Donna E. Arzt, "The Treatment of Religious Dissidents under Classical and Contemporary Islamic Law," in *Religious Human Rights in Global Perspective: Religious Perspectives*, 387–453.

[16] See entry on Algeria in Boyle and Sheen, *Freedom of Religion and Belief*, 20–25.

[17] Stephen Kinzer, "Muslim feminist was torture victim," *Sydney Morning Herald*, 27 January 2000.

member of the Islamic Virtue Party, insisted on wearing the Islamic head covering at medical school and when she entered Parliament.[18] Her medical education was cut short by her refusal to remove her head scarf and her parliamentary career began with an outcry.

The wearing of the head covering in Turkish and French schools and universities has been so controversial that court challenges have resulted.[19] Turkey's Constitutional Court ruled that the head covering was a political symbol of opposition to freedom of women and the secular state. If headscarves and turbans made some students stand out as different from the rest of the student body, conflicts would prevent them from cooperating in the pursuit of scientific truth and rational enquiry. In France, the head covering was thought to bring the father's patriarchal dominance into the public space of education whose role was to free women as equal citizens of the republic. The Council of State eventually confirmed religious liberty, as long as pluralism and the freedoms of others were observed, while later directives from the Ministry of Education prohibited the wearing of unspecified "ostentatious political and religious symbols" in schools. Implementation of these policies varies within both countries.

VII. Cultural and Religious Practices

Religions, beliefs, traditions, and customs are intertwined. Many gender-specific human rights violations are grounded in cultural and religious practices.[20] In India, the interrelationship of cultural and religious identity and gender identity is dynamic and fraught with uncertainty and danger in the complex structural and politico-religious tensions of a secular state now ruled by a Hindu fundamentalist government. As "guardian of the rights of women," the state's cultural agenda combines nationalism and the role of the family, targeting the Muslim minority as having been given invalid "special treatment."[21]

Cultural practices may also be associated with religion without being sanctioned by religious law. Traditional practices harmful to women's lives and health and contrary to CEDAW include female genital mutilation, an ancient practice to control the threat of women's sexuality, which is used to ensure a girl's marriageability. The issues are very complex and the practice is not confined to areas dominated by one religion. Attempts by governments, Islamic leaders, and women's health activists to abolish or control the practice—almost all Egyptian girls have had the mildest form of the practice performed on them—have encountered resistance from families and communities. For instance, older women in Africa who perform the "operation" stand

[18] *Sydney Morning Herald*, 4 May 1999; *Guardian Weekly*, 16 May 1999.

[19] See the entries on France (296–300) and Turkey (395–97) in Boyle and Sheen, *Freedom of Religion and Belief*.

[20] See Donna J. Sullivan, "Gender Equality and Religious Freedom: Toward a Framework for Conflict Resolution," *NYU Journal of International Law and Politics* 24 (1992): 795; ICCPR, art. 40, para. 4; Human Rights Committee General Comment 22.

[21] Ratna Kapur thus finds government use of the language of equality suspect. See Kapur, "The Two Faces of Secularism and Women's Rights in India," in Howland, *Religious Fundamentalisms*, 147–48. See also discussion of the *Shah Bano* case in Sullivan, "Gender Equality and Religious Freedom," 849–52.

to lose both livelihood and community prestige. In Kenya, members of the Kikuyu who practice traditional Kenda Maiyuru (Nine Clans) also approve female genital mutilation to mark a return to traditional culture after colonialism and conversion to Christianity.[22] Legislative and education programs in various countries have been undertaken to counter the practice. South Africa, for instance, has passed discrimination legislation which includes provisions banning female circumcision among other traditional, customary, or religious practices undermining the dignity and well-being of the girl child.[23]

Sexual slavery is another practice as is its opposite, enforced renunciation. Some Ghanaian families appease the gods by donating a *trokosi* girl to the local shrine and its priest. In rural Pakistan, "marriage to the Qur'an" also occurs, where a family dedicates a daughter to spinsterhood in order to save expense of her marrying or to enlarge the wealth of her brothers.[24]

Religious practices and expectations may also indirectly and unintentionally place burdens on women. Thai culture, for instance, is male dominated and formal measures of equality have been slow to take hold. Peach has claimed that sex trafficking is indirectly related to the Buddhist belief in karma and the associated practice of merit-making, engaging young women in a vicious circle of obligations.[25] Whereas a man can make merit by temporarily entering a monastery as a novice, as many young Thais do, women are barred from the Buddhist *sangha*. Theravada tradition does not recognize the Buddha's establishment of an order of female renunciants.[26] As women are the major lay supporters of monks, young girls and women who feel obliged to support their parents may have few avenues for doing so except by earning money through the sex trade. Scriptural reinterpretation and practical strategies for women in development, to encourage women's education and varied avenues for work, have been advocated as the way forward.

VIII. Conclusion

The burdens women carry because of the development and influence of religiously based laws indicate infringements of the very rights and freedoms which are relied upon to assert those of religion and belief.

In the politics of religion, uses of power that appear to be illegitimate need to be inspected carefully and challenged in terms of violations of both CEDAW and ICCPR. As Chinkin says, "International response to the denial of women's human rights caused by fundamentalist demands must encompass all . . . options, from education and dialogue to sanctions and coercion."[27] In such responses, the assertion of women's right

---

[22] *Guardian Weekly*, 18–24 November 1999.

[23] *Guardian Weekly*, 3–9 February 2000.

[24] Boyle and Sheen, *Freedom of Religion and Belief*, 232.

[25] Lucinda Joy Peach, "Buddhism and Human Rights in the Thai Sex Trade," in Howland, *Religious Fundamentalisms*, 219.

[26] See Suwanna Satha-Anand, "Truth over Convention: Feminist Interpretations of Buddhism," in Howland, *Religious Fundamentalisms*, 281–91.

[27] Chinkin, "Cultural Relativism and International Law," 63.

to freedom of religion and belief, through reference to the 1981 UN Declaration, has its place. Further progress would thus be made if human rights lawyers and scholars working in the area of women's rights, including their rights to development, could become more informed about and make greater use of arguments based on the width of rights in freedom of religion and belief under the ICCPR and the 1981 UN Declaration.

The enjoyment of freedom of religion and belief—set out in detail in the 1981 UN Declaration on the Elimination of All Forms of Intolerance and of Discrimination Based on Religion or Belief—depends so fundamentally on the freedoms of movement, expression and communication, association, and assembly that we must suspect that any restriction of these rights for women also constitutes a burden on their freedom of religion and belief. These rights are protected for women, as for men, equally and without distinction, under the Universal Declaration of Human Rights and the International Covenant on Civil and Political Rights. But the extent to which laws, policies, and practices curb these rights for women suggests the misuse of male-dominated public and private power at many levels, state and nonstate. Arguments of religious liberty cannot legitimately be used to trump women's rights. Claims of an exclusive power to prevail in the name of liberty of belief disregard the right of people who believe and practice otherwise; their freedom of religion and belief is a fundamental right as well.[28]

[28] Sullivan, "Gender Equality and Religious Freedom," 856.

Chapter 22

Hinduism and Women: Uses and Abuses of Religious Freedom

Ursula King

> *"To all those women of India*
> *some known, but mostly unknown*
> *whose lives have been devoted*
> *to the struggle for freedom and dignity."*[1]

I. Understanding Religion and Women's Human Rights in India

The statement quoted above is the dedication in a book written by Indian feminists whose voices express the complex experience and problems of women in contemporary India. Their words succinctly convey the great struggle of Indian women in their search to live a life of human dignity and worth, a life that encompasses both the freedom of women and the freedom of religion in an ancient culture. Yet these two freedoms may well be in tension in present-day India—a vast country with more than a billion people consisting of numerous ethnic and religious groups surrounded by a dominant Hindu culture. Hinduism is one of the oldest religions of humankind, marked by an extraordinary heritage of religious rites, practices, symbols, and beliefs, and not easy for an outsider to grasp. This article will explore areas where the freedom of religion or belief in India is in tension, or even clashes, with the human rights of Indian women today.

This is not an easy issue to tackle. First of all, I am not Indian, but a European woman whose identity has been shaped by living in Germany, France, and England. But I have also lived in India for five years and have worked especially with Indian women. This experience initially stimulated my interest in the present topic, but I cannot write as an Indian feminist or a member of Indian society, although I have studied Hinduism for many years as an empathetic outsider who has found much to attract and repel me in this rich religious worldview. I have also been much concerned with women's issues in different world religions from both a scholarly and experiential

[1] See Madhu Kishwar and Ruth Vanita, eds., *In Search of Answers: Indian Women's Voices From Manushi* (New Delhi: Manohar, 1996), dedication.

Tore Lindholm, W. Cole Durham, Jr., Bahia G. Tahzib-Lie (eds.), Facilitating Freedom of Religion or Belief: A Deskbook, *523–543.*

perspective and have published widely on questions of religion and gender. I will discuss my topic mainly on the basis of existing literature, still relatively sparse, but I hope to present a brief survey of a complex situation that others may wish to investigate further.

In existing human rights literature, women's human rights are far less often discussed with regard to Hinduism than Islam or Christianity. There exists a great need for more detailed work on Hinduism and women's human rights. In one of the few existing articles on this topic, "Hinduism and Human Rights," Ved P. Nanda provides a helpful general survey, although only half a page deals with the status of women. The article concludes:

> Today, people of India claim and enjoy full civil and political rights under the prevailing legal framework of rights in the Republic of India, which is a federal, parliamentary democracy. The Constitution of India defines civil and political rights in its elaborate provisions on "Fundamental Rights," which enshrine the concept of equality under the law and protect rights in a fashion similar to the Anglo-American system . . . .
>
> . . . it is fair to conclude that Hinduism and the modern development of international human rights are not in conflict; instead, they reflect similar values and are aimed at promoting human dignity.[2]

Unfortunately, Nanda does not discuss how far Hinduism and the human rights of Indian women may sometimes be in tension or even clash. Legal writers often look at the universality of human rights in abstract, general terms without taking a gender perspective into account. Another author, Rachana Kaushal, has specifically examined *Women and Human Rights in India,*[3] providing a useful survey of women's human rights, crimes against women, and the exploitation of women in India, together with a documentation of the relevant Indian laws. However, the book only indirectly touches on the relation between abuses of women's human rights and traditional Hindu beliefs and practices.

In addition to the relative paucity of literature on Hinduism and women's human rights, the many layers of Indian society and its complex segmentation raise further difficulty. India is a very large continent with a multireligious society of great diversity, yet it forms one political entity that has both a secular constitution and many religion-based laws for its different religious communities. For many years there has been a lively debate to create a uniform civil code (UCC) for all groups of Indian society, but this has not happened yet. The influence of Hinduism, a prevalent and all-pervasive cultural factor in India, has been further strengthened over the last two decades through its narrow, exclusive redefinition for political purposes by the Hindu Right. This influence has important implications for women.

Neither Hinduism nor women are stable, unified categories with one specific meaning, for each comprises complex, sometimes even contradictory, realities. What is understood by Hinduism today, or at least what is claimed to be Hinduism by

[2] Ved P. Nanda, "Hinduism and Human Rights," in *Human Rights and Humanitarian Law: The Quest for Universality,* ed. Daniel Warner (Boston: Martinus Nijhoff, 1977), 29–41 (internal citations omitted); Leroy S. Rouner, ed., *Human Rights and World Religions* (Notre Dame: University of Notre Dame Press, 1988). Rouner's book contains a chapter on "Duties and Rights in Hindu Society" by John B. Carman (113–28), but it deals only with normative prescriptions, not with empirical social reality, nor is there any mention of women's rights.

[3] Rachana Kaushal, *Women and Human Rights in India* (New Delhi: Kaveri Books, 2000).

current Hindu political parties with strong right-wing, fundamentalist tendencies, is to some extent an idealized construction created during the colonial period of the nineteenth century and the postcolonial period of the twentieth century. Scholars prefer to speak of the many *Hinduisms* or to characterize Hinduism as a family of religions rather than one religion. The internal pluralism, so characteristic of Hinduism, applies to Indian women too. For, like women elsewhere, Indian women consist of many different groups, whether rural or urban women, educated or illiterate women, migrant women, women workers, housewives and mothers, or women professionals. The understanding of Hindu religious beliefs and the practice of Hindu customs will vary enormously between these different groups. It is, therefore, not easy to speak of Hinduism and women in general, as I do here.

Hinduism, as other religions, is a profoundly patriarchal, male-dominated religion in which women have been traditionally very subordinate, not enjoying the same rights and freedoms as men. On the other hand, the Hindu religious traditions also contain some rich symbolic and doctrinal resources for the affirmation, empowerment, and dignity of women. Many contemporary Indian women and men are fighting for greater gender justice in a society still marked by great gender disparities, where many violent crimes are committed against women and young girls.

The Indian state has provided constitutional and legal protection of both religious rights and women's rights. Article 14 of the Indian Constitution forbids all discrimination based on sex, and article 51 renounces "practices derogatory to the dignity of women." Moreover, the Indian state has ratified all major international human rights instruments, yet sadly still violates them. India possesses adequate legal resources to support and advance women's rights, but social practice lags far behind legal theory. Between 1971 and 1974, the Indian government set up a Committee on the Status of Women, whose report[4] recognized that the majority of women were still far from enjoying the rights and opportunities guaranteed to them by the constitution. According to Arati Rao,

> India has a long way to go in protecting and guaranteeing women's rights in many areas, particularly economic well-being, health and reproductive rights, education, domestic violence, and gender violence committed by authorities, such as rape and torture. . . . India today has one of the lowest female-male population ratios in the world: 927 women to 1,000 men in 1991 (the lowest since the statistics began to be compiled).[5]

However, the latest census taken in 2001 indicates an improvement in this ratio.

It is sometimes said that women are being denied dignity and fundamental human rights by traditional Hindu teachings, and that there is little they can relate positively to in the ancient myths and religious teachings of Hinduism. But this is far too simplistic. The real situation appears more complex and nuanced as Hinduism presents women

---

[4] National Committee on the Status of Women in India, ***Status of Women in India: A Synopsis of the Report of the National Committee on the Status of Women (1971–74)*** (New Delhi: Indian Council of Social Science Research, 1975).

[5] Arati Rao, "Speaking/Seeking a Common Language: Women, the Hindu Right, and Human Rights in India," in ***Religion and Human Rights: Competing Claims?*** ed. Carrie Gustafson and Peter Juviler (Armonk, N.Y.: M. E. Sharpe, 1999), 117–44.

with a profoundly ambivalent heritage, and it is this underlying ambivalence which modern interpreters use to their advantage in either promoting or obstructing women's equal rights and status in contemporary Indian society.

To help clarify these issues, I will discuss four interrelated topics: (1) images and roles of women in traditional Hinduism; (2) the Indian women's movement and the struggle for women's rights; (3) denial of and crimes against the human rights of Indian women; (4) the right to religious freedom and women's human rights in India: an insoluble conflict?

II. Images and Roles of Women in Traditional Hinduism

To understand the tension between Indian women's human rights and religious rights in India, it is necessary to look at the traditional understanding of women shaped by Hinduism, even though not all Indian women are Hindus. When some years ago incidents of *sati* (the burning of widowed wives) and "dowry murders" made headlines around the world, public attention became focused on women's issues in India. Tremendous discussion occurred in India itself, from which the idea emerged "that Indian women's problems are not only problems of Hindu women or problems caused by traditional Hinduism. It also became clear that within the long history of Hinduism itself, the story has many plots and subplots, and the narrative takes us down many different avenues."[6]

Hinduism is very different from Islam and Christianity in that is has no single founder, no centralized institution, no single authoritative text recognized by all Hindus. Thousands of religious texts were created during its long history of three thousand years or more. Hindu definitions of the nature of femaleness and roles of women are found both in sophisticated sacred texts and in many folk traditions across the continent. The nature of femaleness is premised on an important duality: woman is fertile and benevolent—the bestower, but she is also aggressive, malevolent—the destroyer. This duality is also reflected at the divine level among the goddesses and is related to the view that the female is both *sakti* (energy/power of the creative principle of the universe) and *prakriti* (nature or the undifferentiated matter of the universe). Anthropologist Susan Wadley, who has extensively studied Hindu women and their power, writes:

> The equation, Woman = Power + Nature = Danger, represents the essence of femaleness as it underlies Hindu religious belief and action about women. The equation summarizes a conception of the world order that explains the woman/goddess as the malevolent, aggressive destroyer.
>
> . . . however, the Hindu view of woman is not only one of danger—woman is also the benevolent, fertile bestower . . . woman is the necessary receptor of man's seed: she, like the closely conjoined images of cow and earth, represents growth, prosperity and fertility . . . good females—goddess or human—are controlled by males; that is Culture controls Nature.[7]

---

[6] See Klaus K. Klostermaier, *A Survey of Hinduism*, 2d ed. (Albany, N.Y.: SUNY Press, 1994). See especially chapter 23, "Stridharma: The Position of Women in Hinduism," a chapter that was added to the second edition after reviewers had pointed out that in surveying Hinduism the author had not included women, a position typical of much traditional scholarship on Hinduism where women remain largely invisible.

According to the male-dominated classical literature of brahmanical Hinduism, men must control women and their power. The traditional role of woman is circumscribed by her specific duties, her ***stridharma*** as wife and mother, which requires the performance of household and family tasks and, in conjunction with her husband, certain ritual duties. There exists a strong ambiguity in the brahmanical view of woman. On one hand, woman's eminent dignity in her role as mother is stressed, implying, however, an indirect homage to man. On the other hand, there is the contrasting image of woman's total subordination as the wife. A further complexity becomes apparent when one examines the image of woman at different levels. At the human level, the image of wife predominates, whereas at the divine level, the image of the mother goddess ranks higher than the goddess as divine consort or wife, which always implies subordination.

Traditional role models for Hindu women focus almost exclusively on women as wives. Mythology and Hindu law books—the *Dharmasastras* (of which the so-called *Laws of Manu*, written early in the Christian era, are the most important)—provide numerous examples of the good, faithful wife rather than the good mother. Yet it is the goddesses as mothers rather than as wives who are worshipped and feared. Paradoxically, the goddesses worshipped as "Mother" are usually not the ones who have children in Hindu mythology. *The Laws of Manu* stress the submission of women to male control as women's major duty. Often quoted are the famous passages:

> By a young girl, by a young woman, or even by an aged one, nothing must be done independently, even in her own house.
>
> In childhood a female must be subject to her father, in youth to her husband, when her lord is dead, to her sons; a woman must never be independent.
>
> Though destitute of virtue, or seeking pleasure (elsewhere), or devoid of good qualities, (yet) a husband must be constantly worshipped as a god by a faithful wife . . .
>
> By violating her duty towards her husband, a wife is disgraced in this world; (after death) she enters the womb of a jackal, and is tormented by diseases (the punishment) of her sin.[8]

Although the practical influence of sacred scriptures must not be overestimated, as many people will not know these texts directly, they nonetheless have provided a major formative matrix for social customs and traditions. Law books also devote sections to the impurity caused by women's menstruation, during which time women were supposed to withdraw "for three days to an outhouse, keep silent, not wear any ornaments, to sleep on the floor, not to show themselves to anyone." This and other customs severely restricted the freedom of women. From a traditional perspective of domesticity one can also interpret these practices as creating for women "a room of their own," "an area of competence and a sphere of authority, which guaranteed her considerable power in domestic concerns."[9]

---

[7] Susan Wadley, "Women and the Hindu Tradition," in *Women in Indian Society: A Reader,* ed. Rehana Ghadially (New Delhi: Sage Publications, 1988), 23–43.
[8] Ibid., 30.
[9] Klostermaier, *A Survey of Hinduism,* 364.

Classical Hindu literature emphasizes woman's devotion and dutifulness; her happiness, indeed her salvation, is primarily a function of her faithful devotion to her husband. The sacred texts, however, contain few injunctions for the behavior of the husband beyond the requirement that he must marry to procure the necessary sons for his salvation (a son is needed to perform the funeral rite). The greater value of sons is linked to the patrilineal and patrivirilocal kinship system of Hinduism. The continuity of the family depends on male offspring who alone, through the performance of certain religious rites, can ensure the welfare of ancestors and the salvation of parents.

Interestingly, the *Laws of Manu* also contain a passage that requires men to treat women well, or else women will destroy them:

> Women must be honored and adorned by their fathers, brothers, husbands, and brothers-in-law who desire (their own welfare). . . . The houses on which female relations, not being duly honored, pronounce a curse, perish completely, as if destroyed by magic. Hence, men who seek (their own) welfare should always honor women on holidays and festivals with (gifts of) ornaments, clothes and (dainty) food.[10]

After studying the references to women in the Hindu sacred scriptures—from the Vedas to the *Laws of Manu*, the medieval *Puranas*, the Epics and the *Bhagavadgita*—Mildred Worth Pinkham commented more than fifty years ago:

> Despite the many words of wisdom and high praise for women . . . there are to be found cases of extreme cruelty and insult. Too long in India, as well as in some literature of every country, woman often has been referred to as a sort of chattel. It would seem particularly shortsighted for religious leaders to uphold doctrines that encourage women to be helplessly dependent. Harmful prohibitions directed against women will turn out to be evils against society at large. The world sadly needs manhood and womanhood that result from full development of personality.[11]

In textually sanctioned Hinduism, women have little religious authority themselves, but, at the popular level, women are active religious practitioners, sometimes as exorcists and shamans, and especially in the performance of all kinds of *puja* (worship) that do not require the specialized services of a priest. This practice applies, above all, to regular family worship in the home, largely carried out by women.

At the ultimate philosophical level, sexual opposites do not exist in Hindu thought. The One that is Brahman is beyond all dualities and divisions, yet at the empirical level the Hindu tradition ranks women theologically with the lowest caste of the *Sudras* and the outcastes. All these groups share their exclusion from Vedic ritual, nor are they allowed to know the sacred literature of the Vedas, and sometimes are not permitted to listen to their recitation. In this respect, women as a group are not more disadvantaged than many Indian men, who were not admitted to primary religious authority and power either, predominantly held by the brahmanical elite. Through the *bhakti* movement of personal devotion, women, like low-caste men, gained access to the gods and salvation, a right well attested by the famous *Bhagavadgita* and other *bhakti* texts. In fact, women have always made an important contribution to Hindu religious life by handing down many aspects of the religious tradition within the family circle, and by

---

[10] Quoted in Wadley, "Women and the Hindu Tradition," 33.

[11] Mildred Worth Pinkham, *Woman in the Sacred Scriptures of Hinduism* (New York: AMS Press, 1967).

taking an active part in rituals connected with life cycle rites and calendrical festivals, all essential for the well-being of the individual, family, and community. This contribution reinforces the point that the normative models of Hindu women, the notion of ideal womanhood largely held by Brahmans, is really a "*wife* ideal" rather than that of an "ideal *woman*."[12] Susan Wadley sums up her discussion of "Hindu Ideology and Women":

> Norms for women in Hinduism derive from two separate, though related sources. First, the male-dominated literature prescribes control and subordination of the woman. Second, folk and oral traditions, often created and propagated by women, yield norms that are concerned with women's welfare and emphasize the behavior of crucial male kin (the husband as lover, the brother as protector, the son as security) as well as female kin (the mother-in-law, the husband's sister). In both these realms we find the mother—not merely as the bearer of children, but also as the mother of the devotee—given extreme importance. The wife is the woman under male control; the mother is the woman in control of herself and her "children". These two figures dominate Hindu thought about women.[13]

It is generally held today that women enjoyed a much higher position during the ancient Vedic period (more than 3,000 years ago)—and may have even held religious equality with men—than in the following periods of Hinduism which were marked by growing restrictions for women, eventually codified in the Hindu law books. During the Vedic period women were invested with the sacred thread, later restricted to high-caste males only, and were allowed to study the Vedas and teach sacred lore and ritual. However, while the position of women during the early period before the codification of classical Hinduism was no doubt quite different, the question arises whether the romantic idealization of an Aryan "golden age," largely reconstructed during the nineteenth-century Hindu Renaissance, did not also create a particularly idealized view of past Indian womanhood, in contrast to the actual position of Indian women during the modern colonial period. The interpretation of the Indian past and of the images and roles of women in traditional Hinduism has become a contested field of discourse ever since nineteenth-century reformers tried to improve the position of Indian women.

III. The Indian Women's Movement and the Struggle for Women's Rights

I cannot provide a history of the modern Indian women's movement here, but only sketch in the background to the contemporary situation. A full historical account is found in Radha Kumar's ***The History of Doing: An Ilustrated Account of Movements for Women's Rights and Feminism in India, 1800–1990.***[14] The women's movement's beginnings in the nineteenth century are linked to the debates among missionaries and Hindu reformers on providing education for women and abolishing what were considered evil social practices, such as *sati*, child marriage, polygamy, and the prohibition

[12] This point is made in Prabhati Mukherjee, *Hindu Women: Normative Models* (Andhra Pradesh, India: Orient Longman, 1978).

[13] Wadley, "Women and the Hindu Tradition," 34.

[14] Radha Kumar, *The History of Doing: An Illustrated Account of Movements for Women's Rights and Feminism in India 1800–1990* (London: Verso, 1993), 9.

of widow remarriage. In nineteenth-century Bengal, it was said India could not awake if Indian women did not awake first. However, women's status could not be improved without education, often opposed at that time by orthodox Hindus. As the British colonial administration pursued an official policy of noninterference with local customs, the administration did not promote education of women in the way it championed education of men. In early nineteenth-century Bengal, it was also believed that such education was against Hindu scriptures, and that a girl taught to read and write would soon after marriage become a widow and drive away the family's good fortune.

Female education was first started by Christian missionaries, especially their wives, but it was soon vigorously promoted by Hindu reformers. A lively debate developed between progressives and gradualists; the latter believed in the gradual education of women in preparation for being a good wife and mother, thus mainly reinforcing traditional ideals; whereas the former championed the same education for women as for men, including full access to western ideas. The advance of women's education in nineteenth-century Bengal was, first, largely due to progressive men of the urban middle class who had received western education. But soon orthodox Hindus also began to recognize the need for traditional education and Hindu religious instruction, gradually allowing women to learn Sanskrit, thereby enabling them to gain access to the Hindu scriptures, which had remained closed to them for so long. I mention these details to provide the contextual background for the rise of the modern Indian women's movement.

Following a generally accepted feminist typology, a distinction is made between the first wave of the Indian women's movement concerned with "women's uplift" and equal rights, lasting from the late nineteenth to the mid-twentieth century during the existence of imperial India, and the second wave, focusing on women's rights and empowerment, which emerged in independent India from the mid-twentieth century onwards. Thus the history of the Indian women's movement is closely interwoven with that of colonialism and postcolonialism. During the first wave, Hindu reformers and revivalists vigorously debated the "woman question," and the beginning of the Indian women's movement can be dated with the foundation of Ranade's Indian National Social Conference (1887). But soon pioneering women emerged who developed the Indian women's movement through creating numerous autonomous organizations formed by and for women. Some of the largest and most important were the Women's Indian Association (1917), the National Council of Women (1920), and the All India Women's Conference (1926). It is important to realize that these were inclusive, secular movements for *all* Indians, not only for Hindu women. Their members were drawn from an urban-based social elite which, through education, had gained access to professional positions. Their programs were largely devoted to social work and improvement of women's lives without planning any fundamental change for Indian society or the traditional areas of Hindu religious life.

The Indian women's movement brought together women from many different backgrounds: Hindus, Muslims, Parsis, and Western women. There also existed other religiously affiliated women's organizations, such as the Stree Zoroastrian Mandal (Zoroastrian Women's Circle), founded by Parsi women as early as 1903, and the All India Muslim Women's Conference, established in 1916. But the majority of women's work was carried out by inclusive, all-Indian women's associations, where Hindu references shaped the dominant discourse due to the all-pervasive presence and cultural dominance of Hinduism in the Indian subcontinent.

During the twentieth century, the single most important influence in improving the status of Indian women was their active participation in the Indian Independence Movement and the great encouragement and support women received from Mahatma Gandhi. In contrast to Gandhi's more widely based mass movement created during the mid- and late twentieth century, the Indian women's movement still remained by and large an elite, minority phenomenon with little effect on the downtrodden position of the vast majority of rural women. In fact, investigations by the Indian Social Science Research Council during the 1970s showed a trend of continued deterioration in the conditions of women since independence for the country as a whole, evidenced by higher mortality, low literacy, and an accelerated decline in women's participation in the labor force and decision-making bodies at the national level.

But it was also during the 1970s that the contemporary feminist movement emerged in India and more widely based women's action groups started. These movements were concerned with wider issues of women's health and labor, the increasing violence against women evident in wife beating, dowry deaths, the abortion of female fetuses based on prenatal sex selection, and many other concerns. These groups organized campaigns against women's oppression in areas of dowry and rape, and later against *sati*, religion-based personal laws, the abuse of alcohol, the use of religion to divide women, and a safe environment.[15]

The contemporary situation is marked by several tensions and paradoxes. There exists first the continuing contrast between the traditional ideal of the Indian Hindu woman, embodied in several epic heroines and goddess figures, and the western-derived image of the modern woman as a person in her own right with a sense of personal identity, subjectivity, and autonomy—a woman with full human rights. Modern women seek liberation from subordination and oppression, but this liberation often stands in stark contrast and tension to the ultimate Hindu ideal of religious liberation which is linked to the fulfillment of Hindu duties or ***dharma***.

A further tension exists regarding the understanding of what the Hindu tradition consists of. This tension is historically grounded in the nineteenth-century Hindu reformers' critical reappropriation of the Indian past, which made much use of the new construct of a "golden age" of ancient Indian civilization. This construct provided reformers with the model of an ideal ancient society, which could be recreated in modern India. In addition, Hindu sacred literature contained lofty ideals of womanhood, which could be equally applied to contemporary society. Different proponents of the equal rights of Indian women developed contrasting styles of reading the Hindu past, finding arguments for and against women's social and political rights.

Much of this debate continues in contemporary India. In his magisterial *Survey of Hinduism*, Klaus Klostermaier commented in 1994 at length on the relationship between Indian feminism and the Hindu tradition:

[15] See ibid., 115–90.

> Modern feminism everywhere had to struggle against political and religious establishments, which generally tended to be conservative, male dominated, and patriarchal. The story is no different in India. In spite of the worship of Sakti and the important role the "mother" plays in the extended family, the struggle for more adequate legal protection of women generally, and for their acceptance in public life, had to be waged against traditional religious prejudices, which stereotyped women as submissive wives and devoted mothers, with no rights to a development of their own. The large number of successful Indian businesswomen, women politicians, lawyers, professors, and other high-profile professionals is certainly proof of some success of feminism in India. Indian feminists are not satisfied with what has been accomplished so far; overall, Indian women are still disadvantaged, undereducated, overworked, and exploited. Like other patriarchal religions, Hinduism has a blind spot when it comes to questions of social justice, equality, and women's rights. Not surprisingly, prominent orthodox representatives of Hinduism have resisted every improvement of the lot of women, be it the abolition of *sati*, the ability to file for divorce, the freedom to choose their own careers, or the right to receive an education equal to that of men. . . .
>
> Traditional Hinduism is still strongly supported by women; women form the largest portion of temple-goers and festival attendants, and women keep traditional domestic rituals alive and pass on the familiar stories of gods and goddesses to their children. One can only hope that the representatives of traditional Hinduism reciprocate this faithfulness by developing within Hinduism regard for contemporary women's concerns and support the endeavors of those who are working toward full equality. There is much in the various strands of the Hindu tradition that would lend itself to a timely defense of women's rights and to the development of a contemporary *stridharma*, anchored in genuine spirituality and flexible to accommodate the changing concerns of today's society.[16]

The discussion shows that Hindu scriptures, like those of other religions, contain ambiguities and contradictions in relation to women and, therefore, are open to divergent interpretations sanctioning different customs. Here an important factor, influencing the implementation of women's rights today, is the work of the nineteenth-century British colonial administration in defining Hindu law by translating traditional texts to provide a basis for the decision making of colonial administrators. The extensive codification of Hindu law, which took place under British colonial rule, can be seen as a freezing of Hindu law in its nineteenth-century form, carrying a strong antiwoman bias. The Indian woman lawyer activist Flavia Agnes has pointed out that when the colonial legal codification took place, Hindu scriptural passages were not uniformly antiwomen and contained spaces for negotiating women's rights,[17] nor were sacred texts meant to be legal statutes. The English translation of the original Hindu texts subverted much of their context and meaning, especially as the antiwomen biases and orientalist approaches of the translators themselves colored much of the formulation of the Hindu Code Bills and the Anglo-Indian derived Muslim personal

---

[16] Klostermaier, *A Survey of Hinduism,* 375–76. A detailed analysis of the tensions and contradictions between the understanding of Hindu tradition and the liberation of women is found in Catherine A. Robinson, *Tradition and Liberation: The Hindu Tradition in the Indian Women's Movement* (Richmond, England: Curzon Press, 1999).

[17] See Flavia Agnes, *Law and Gender Inequality: The Politics of Women's Rights in India* (New Delhi: Oxford University Press, 1999).

laws. Many of the texts were also used to co-opt the antiwomen provisions of nineteenth-century English matrimonial statutes and women's economic rights in the family. The colonial lawmakers considered family property relationships as primarily legal matters to be governed by the colonial state's own versions of each group's religious laws. Thus they facilitated the construction of an Anglo-Indian amalgam that came to be known as each religious community's "personal law," which, in spite of the considerable personal law reforms of colonial statutes since independence, is still in force and much debated today. Hindus, Muslims, Parsis, and Christians were given their own distinct personal laws but for political reasons, Buddhists, Jains, Sikhs, and Jews were not.

A close scrutiny of Indian personal laws shows how gender discrimination prevails in their interpretation and application, despite constitutional guarantees of the equality of women. Women activists fight for an abolition of these personal laws and the creation of a uniform civil code for all Indian citizens. The Hindu Political Right also favors the abolition of personal laws, but for different reasons, as will be seen later.

If the freedom of religion or belief is a universal human right, the ***absolute, unconditional use of this right*** can be seen under certain circumstances to entail an ***abuse*** through the denial of the full human rights of women, especially their economic, social, and political equality. Such abuses occur when the antiwomen elements of traditional Hindu beliefs and practices, as well as of Hindu personal laws, are socially accepted, practiced, politically encouraged, and justified. This paradoxical dilemma of a clash between two differently articulated human rights—the right to religious freedom and the rights of women—characterizes much of the contemporary situation in India. Many crimes against women's human rights occur that are directly or indirectly related to traditional religious beliefs and deeply ingrained social practices rooted in Hindu religious culture.

IV. Denial of and Crimes against the Human Rights of Indian Women

The Committee on the Elimination of Discrimination Against Women (CEDAW), established under the convention of the same name, adopted by the United Nations in 1979, has issued "several general recommendations touching on conflicts between the obligations of the Convention and traditional religious and cultural practices." These recommendations include statements identifying "traditional attitudes that perpetuate such violent and coercive practices as forced marriage, dowry deaths, and female circumcision as contributing to discrimination against women."[18] India is a country where such conflicts between religious and cultural practices occur when women are submitted to coercive, violent practices. Similarly, the volume *Women International Human Rights Law*[19] carries a whole section on "Common Abuses of Women Around the World" which deals with violence against women, domestic violence, sexual harassment, discrimination, and trafficking in women. Examples of such common abuses can be found in contemporary India, where not only fundamental rights are often denied to women, but also many crimes are committed against women.

---

[18] See Tad Stahnke and J. Paul Martin, eds., *Religion and Human Rights: Basic Documents* (New York: Columbia University Press, 1998), 119.

[19] See Kelly D. Askin and Dorean M. Koenig, eds., *Women and International Human Rights Law*, vol. 1 (Ardsley, N.Y.: Transnational Publishers, 1999), section III.

Fundamental rights and civil liberties, guaranteed in the Indian Constitution, are denied many sections of the Indian population, but the most oppressed within each oppressed group are women. They are doubly oppressed—from the outside as member of an oppressed group and from the inside by male members of their own group as well as by men outside their own group. This is particularly true of Dalit women, formerly called "untouchables," on which Human Rights Watch produced a special report in 1999.[20] As untouchables outside the traditional Hindu caste system, Dalits are subject to numerous forms of discrimination. Women are subject to violence, especially sexual violence and rape by upper-caste men. As stated in the Human Rights Watch report:

> Rape is a common phenomenon in rural areas. Women are raped as part of caste custom or village tradition. According to Dalit activists, Dalit girls have been forced to have sex with the village landlord. In rural areas, "women are induced into prostitution (Devadasi system) . . . , which [is] forced on them in the name of religion." . . . Early marriage between the ages of ten years and sixteen years persists in large part because of Dalit girls' vulnerability to sexual assault by upper-caste men; once a girl is raped, she becomes unmarriageable . . . Dalit women are also raped as a form of retaliation. Women of scheduled castes and scheduled tribes are raped as part of an effort by upper-caste leaders to suppress movements to demand payment of minimum wages, to settle sharecropping disputes, or to reclaim lost land. . . . Attacks on Dalit women during massacres, police raids, and caste clashes are discussed throughout this report. Dalit women are easy targets for any perpetrator because upper castes consider them to be "sexually available" and because they are largely unprotected by the state machinery."[21]

Another Human Rights Watch report in 1995, entitled *Rape for Profit: Trafficking of Nepali Girls and Women to India's Brothels*,[22] states that there are probably more than a million women and children[23] employed in Indian brothels, and a large percentage of these are from Nepal. Research showed that

> trafficking victims in India are subjected to conditions tantamount to slavery, and to serious physical abuse. Besides being held in debt bondage for years at a time, women and girls in the brothels suffered rape and other forms of torture, severe beatings, exposure to AIDS, and arbitrary confinement. . . . Both the Indian and Nepali governments are complicit in the abuses against trafficking vicits. In India, police and local officials protect brothel owners from police raids and traffickers, and both policemen and civilian officials patronize the brothels.[24]

In an article in the early 1980s, Madhu Kishwar analyzed the denial of fundamental rights to Indian women. This denial makes for depressing reading and still reflects the current situation. Kishwar points out that the traditional Indian family structure provides little outside support for women and accounts for much of women's general lack of freedom and rights in the male-dominated family. While not denying that in many

---

[20] *Broken People: Caste Violence Against India's "Untouchables"* (New York: Human Rights Watch, 1999).

[21] Ibid., 30–32. See also Vimal Thorat, "Dalit Women and Human Rights: Some Neglected Issues," in *Human Rights of Dalits: Societal Violation,* ed. G. S. Bhargava and R. M. Pal (New Delhi: Gyan Publishing House, 1999), 163–68.

[22] Quoted in *The Human Rights Watch Global Report on Women's Human Rights* (New York: Human Rights Watch, 1995), 230.

[23] Estimates of the total number range from hundreds of thousands to over ten million nationwide.

[24] *Global Report on Women's Human Rights,* 231.

Indian homes women receive more than adequate love and care, she argues that the majority of women are kept in various types of bondage and "almost all the fundamental rights and civil liberties guaranteed in the Constitution are frequently snatched from women by powerful members of their own families. For too many women in India, their own fathers, brothers and husbands act like virtual prison guards, holding them captive and keeping them in a state of perpetual fear within the walls of their own homes, and denying them the right to make or even to take part in making the most fundamental decisions about their own lives."[25] Kishwar looks at some of the fundamental rights enshrined in the Indian Constitution and discusses how these rights are denied to Indian women: protection of life and personal liberty; freedom of movement; right to choose an occupation; right against exploitation; right to form associations and unions; right to property; and right to freedom of speech and expression.

According to Kishwar, in the still prevalent traditional Indian family system "women are mainly used as commodities, as vehicles for transfer of consumer forms of property from one family to another. Even control over women, as over slaves, is passed from one owner, the parents' family, to the other, the husband's family. By and for themselves, women can seldom acquire any real control over even what is customarily supposed to be theirs, such as jewelery and household goods" [given to them as dowry]. Thus she maintains "that the chains for women's bondage are first forged in the family" and "the silencing of women" begins there as well, but she also sees signs of hope in that "struggles are beginning to emerge all over the country in which women demand independent rights."[26]

These struggles have become publicly visible through the emergence and proliferation of autonomous women's groups in India during the 1970s and 1980s. Highly articulate women militants have formed organizations run by and for women, not by political parties. This rise of feminist activism among young Indian women from the middle classes, sometimes described as a "new awakening," is truly remarkable and includes organizations working for poor and oppressed women among peasant and tribal groups, and for women workers in cities.[27] Newsletters and feminist journals came to be published, and *Manushi*, a feminist journal founded in Delhi in 1979, produced through the collective efforts of feminists, came to be seen as a mouthpiece of the autonomous women's movement in India. These autonomous women's organizations also made an effort to make feminism acceptable to the masses of Indian people by using plays, songs, posters, and exhibitions; by forming special interest groups organizing antidowry, antirape, and other campaigns; and by challenging the personal laws of different religious communities.

Indian feminists are sometimes accused of imitating western women; of being colonialists, cultural imperialists, and supporters of capitalist ideology. But the wide response to the autonomous women's groups and their practical campaigns show that the demands for women's human rights have taken genuinely Indian roots. The women's movement now needs to align itself with other contemporary protest movements in

---

[25] Madhu Kishwar, "Denial of Fundamental Rights to Women," in Kishwar and Vanita, *In Search of Answers*, 191–203.

[26] Ibid., 200–202.

[27] See Vibhuti Patel, "Emergence and Proliferation of Autonomous Women's Groups in India: 1974–1984," in Ghadially, *Women in Indian Society*, 249–56.

order to combat the deeply ingrained sexism and discriminatory aspects of traditional Indian practices. These movements are also related to casteism and communalism, which shape so much of contemporary Indian politics. However, before discussing this, I will mention other violations and crimes against women's human rights in India.

I have already referred to the traditionally expected total subservience of women to their husbands or other male authority figures; the existence of female infanticide and feticide, due to the misuses of amniocentesis tests to determine the sex of the fetus in the womb caused by the religio-cultural preference for sons and resulting in an imbalanced sex-ratio; the high rate of prostitution; trafficking in women; and the problem of rape, including rape in marriage. The most notorious crimes, however, and the ones most closely associated with Hindu cultural norms, are the widespread dowry deaths, sometimes referred to as "dowry murders," and the continued existence of *sati* or the burning of widowed wives.

Since 1961, India has had a Dowry Prohibition Act, further amended in 1984, but it seems to exist only on paper. Only a tiny, vocal, nonconformist minority refuses to accept a dowry. For most Indians the traditional dowry system—the *stridhan* of jewelry, silks, gold, and household goods bestowed upon the bride by her parents and legally belonging to her or the *mehr*, the bride's portion for Muslim brides—is now connected with an increase in social status through the display of new wealth and the ever growing expansion of new horizons of consumption. Traditionally, the dowry was given to the bride as compensation for her being propertyless, as women could formerly not inherit land. Now the dowry is given to the husband's family according to the market value of their son, dependent on employment, financial expectations, education, looks, and his family's standing in the social hierarchy. Among affluent and status-conscious families, dowries can represent a considerable transfer of durable goods, real property, and cash. Dowry demands have become subject to inflation; they have created an "epidemic of greed," due in part to the influence of western consumer culture. There has even developed an upsurge of postnuptial demands for showy goods, such as television sets, motorcycles, and stereos. Young brides have been harassed and maltreated so as to put pressure on their parents to respond to these demands, and in extreme cases, such harassment can result in dowry deaths.

It is difficult to assess exactly all the factors in dowry-related violence, as violence can also be due to other crises in a marriage, and it is impossible to obtain precise statistics about dowry deaths from available census data. But commentators have described dowry deaths as

> . . . murders at the hands of husband and mother-in-law or self-murder following unbearable physical and psychological punishment. Observers in Delhi and Bombay who have studied emergency hospital admissions, police records, death certificates, and newspaper accounts of suspicious home accidents claim that as many as three dowry-related deaths take place each day in these metropolises. Most of these are deaths by fire: kerosene and matches are standard kitchen items, whose use is subject to "accident." In greater Bombay, of women in the fifteen-to-forty-four group who die "accidentally," one in five succumbs to burns.[28]

[28] Sara S. Mitter, *Dharma's Daughters: Contemporary Indian Women and Hindu Culture* (New Jersey: Rutgers University Press, 1991), 112.

Klostermaier quotes an article from 1988, which stated that "in Delhi alone, between 1979–1988, 2,055 young wives, aged 18 to 25, died in presumably prearranged kerosene stove burning accidents, victims of 'dowry murders.'"[29] Studies have shown that dowry-related problems usually arise out of three contexts: failure to pay the remaining part of the dowry, inability to meet the extra demands made by the bridegroom's family, and general dissatisfaction of the bridegroom's family with the gifts provided by the woman's parents.[30]

While economic factors seem to be the only reason for dowry murders, such motives play a much smaller role in the occurrence of *sati*, the burning of widowed wives on the funeral pyre of their husbands. *Sati* was originally a high caste *ksatriya* practice common in Northern India, especially among Rajputs, but the actual number of occurrences was never very large. Much has been written on *sati*, whose meaning is complex and difficult to explain. *Sati* is linked to traditional Hindu notions of religious perfection and devotion. It can be seen as a meritorious religious act, and also as a strategy for women to gain dignity and religious acclaim through their death when these are denied to them during their life.[31] Klostermaier summarizes the reasons for *sati*, indicating in his usage of the word that it was originally applied to the woman committing the immolation rather than the act of immolation itself:

> A wife, whose husband died young, was supposed to have been guilty of husband murder in one of her previous incarnations. She could atone for that crime by self-immolation. Also, widows were not allowed to remarry. Because after marriage they belonged to the family of their husbands, that family often saw them as an economic burden. Rules governing the lives of widows were so severe, that many may have considered voluntary death preferable to the miserable life they could look forward to. Especially so, because all kinds of celestial blessings were promised to those who became *satis*.[32]

Sati could occur in two forms, either as a concremation of the woman with her husband, or as separate immolation some time after the husband's cremation. Glorification, praise, and even deification of the *sati*, the immolated wife, occurred. She was called "a wife whose husband lives" and considered by some to have become a "goddess," deserving to be honored and worshipped. The practice of *sati* was officially made illegal by the British colonial administration as long ago as 1829, and the Hindu reformer Raja Rammohan Roy played an important role in its abolition.[33] Occasional incidents of *sati* continued to occur, but the contemporary interest and fascination with this phenomenon took off in an extraordinary way after a celebrated modern *sati* happened, that of the eighteen year old Roop Kanwar in 1987 in Rajasthan, Northern India. She was married for only eight months to a twenty-four-year-old Rajput man,

---

[29] Klostermaier, *A Survey of Hinduism*, 375.

[30] B. Devi Prasad, "Dowry Related Violence Toward Women: A Sociological Perspective," in *Violence Against Women*, ed. Sushma Sood (New Delhi: Arihant Publishers, 1990), 293–309.

[31] John Stratton Hawley, ed., *Sati, The Blessing and the Curse: The Burning of Wives in India* (New Delhi: Oxford University Press, 1994); Arvind Sharma, *Sati: Historical and Phenomenological Essays* (New Delhi: Motilal Barnasidass, 1988).

[32] Klostermaier, *A Survey of Hinduism*, 374.

[33] See the perceptive analysis of this in Lata Mani, "Contentious Traditions: The Debate on Sati in Colonial India," in *Recasting Women, Essays in Colonial History*, ed. Kumkum Sangari and Sudesh Vaid (New Delhi: Kali for Women, 1989), 88–126.

Mal Singh, who suddenly died. She mounted the funeral pyre with him; an event witnessed by thousands of people, many of whom disagreed over what happened. According to some, Roop willed her own death and carried it out with dignity and resolve:

> In the traditional fashion, it is said, she took her husband's head in her hands as she seated herself on the pyre and submitted calmly to the flames. The force of her inner truth (*sat*) ignited the pyre, making it plain to profane eyes that she had been transformed from a human being into a goddess, a *satimata*. Icons issued to commemorate the event . . . recall it just in this way. . . .
>
> Opponents of sati worship tell the story quite differently. According to them, villagers' reports indicate that Roop Kanwar was drugged into submission by her in-laws. Even so, she had the strength to try to escape from the pyre once—or as many as three times, some say, but she was pushed back on. . . . Other reports say that in her last moments she called out to her father for help or uttered cries that could not be understood because they were drowned out by the exuberant roar of the crowd.
>
> As for the other participants in the event, Roop Kanwar's in-laws are said to have acted primarily on economic motives . . . critics believe that Mal Singh's family expected large numbers of worshipful spectators to make offerings on the occasion of the sati itself, and to continue their generosity once a shrine (*sati sthal*) was established on the site of Roop Kanwar's death and transfiguration.[34]

Given the contradictions of this account, it comes as no surprise that the much-publicized event led to a heated public debate, and to many demonstrations for and against *sati*. However, this was not the first time the *sati* idea came to public notice. In 1983 an organization known as the *Rani Sati Sarva Sangh* (RSSS), funded by the Marwari community (India's most important group of merchants and industrialists), launched a campaign in Delhi to popularize *sati*. The RSSS, which already ran several *sati* temples in Rajasthan and Delhi, had been granted land by the Indian government on which to build another temple in Delhi. They organized a procession of men and women to celebrate this grant. Delhi feminists tried to organize a counter-demonstration, which, however, proved a failure as they were outnumbered and rather distressed by having to confront other women in a hostile situation. It turned out that the processionists had appropriated the language of rights, "stating that they should have the right, as Hindus and as women, to commit, worship and propagate sati. At the same time they also appropriated feminist slogans on women's militancy, for example . . . 'we the women of India, are not flowers, but fiery sparks.'"[35] This distressing experience determined Indian feminists to undertake research into the existence of *sati*; *sati* temples; the proponents of "*sati-dharma*," the religion of *sati*, created in India after independence. It is estimated that on average one *sati* occurs per year, and the campaign for *sati* and neofundamentalist Hinduism, with which Rajput identity is now fused, revealed the increasing opposition to feminism among a certain part of the Indian Hindu population and represented a setback for the feminist women's movement.

---

[34] Hawley, *Sati, The Blessing and the Curse*, 7 (Introduction).

[35] Kumar, *The History of Doing*, 172–81 (ch. 11, "The Agitation Against Sati 1987–88").

The question of *sati* is literally and metaphorically "a burning question." The pro-*sati* group defends the possibility of self-immolation as a voluntary act; whereas, the "opponents argue that it is not possible to speak about a 'free will' of women in traditional Hindu society because they have been taught not to make any decision in their life by themselves."[36] It is no real choice for a widowed woman, whose remarriage is out of the question in traditional Hindu society, when she can only choose between physical death or social death. The occurrence of *sati* has led to the erection of new and the reconstruction of old *sati* shrines where religious worship is conducted on a daily basis. The RSSS alone administers 105 *sati* shrines in India. The new Indian "Commission of *Sati* (Prevention) Act," promulgated in 1988, enabled the government to close or remove *sati* temples and shrines. But obstruction and nonenactment of Indian central government directives at the regional level have often prevented this and led to ongoing legal wrangles. Lourens van den Bosch has argued that the phenomenon of *sati* and *sati* shrines in recent Indian history

> . . . has produced a discussion on fundamental problems in the political arena of India, of which the end is not yet in sight. The first question is that of the relation between the freedom of religion as guaranteed in the Constitution and the *Commission of Sati (Prevention) Act*. . . . Within this context the definition of religion is a burning issue. Should the practice of *sati* be regarded as a highly meritorious religious act, in which divine reality expresses itself in a female form, or is it only a social evil and a crime, characteristic of a culture which is dominated by blameworthy "macho-values" presenting themselves disguised in a religious luster of holiness?[37]

The Indian women's movement fights against *sati* and the reconstruction of *sati* temples which some regard as a revival of traditional religion, often oppressive to women. According to van den Bosch, for Indian feminists there "is no place in a civilized country as India for institutions which promote an inhuman misogynous ideology under the disguise of religion." But with this standpoint the Indian women's rights activitists "make religion subordinate to more general human principles and restrict the freedom of religion."[38] This tension between two different kinds of rights—that of religion and that of women—is nowhere more visible than in Indian right-wing politics, where the right to religious freedom is used to defend and support abuses against women in the name of traditional religion and customs.

V. The Right to Religious Freedom and Women's Human Rights in India: An Insoluble Conflict?

Gabriele Dietrich has analyzed the tension between the constitutionally secular state of India and the freedom of religion and women's rights in her book *Reflections on the Women's Movement in India: Religion, Ecology, Development*.[39] She argues that many

---

[36] Lourens P. van den Bosch, "A Burning Question. Sati and Sati Temples as the Focus of Political Interest," in *Numen*, vol. 37, fasc. 2 (n.p., 1990), 174–94.

[37] Ibid., 185.

[38] Ibid., 187.

[39] Gabriele Dietrich, *Reflections on the Women's Movement in India: Religion, Ecology, Development* (New Delhi: Horizon India Books, 1992). See especially chap. 1, "The Secular State: Freedom of Religion and Women's Rights."

human rights violations are inflicted on Indian women by the different religion-based personal laws. Furthermore, women's rights are constantly violated in the name of the freedom of religion, and the increase of violence in family and public life is linked to the widespread assumption "that women are the property of their family and their husbands."[40] The demands for women's human rights are becoming ever more contradictory through the widespread appeal to tradition, linked to the rise of Hindu religious revivalism, communalism, and fundamentalism over recent years. These ideologies are closely tied up with Hindu nationalism and its reaffirmation of tradition against the perceived threat of secular and western influences.

The strains of modernity have led to a defense of tradition, but the content and contours of Hindu religious and cultural tradition are interpreted quite differently by different revivalist Hindu organizations, with the *Vishva Hindu Parishad* (VHP)[41] as the most prominent (speaking neither for nor against *sati*) and the *Hindu Mahasabha* (supporting the pro-*sati* Rajputs) also enjoying a large following. Political right-wing groups, such as the *Bharatiya Janata Party* (BJP) and the *Rashtriya Swayamsevak Sangh* (RSS), with their *Hindutva* (Hindu supremacy) ideology have appropriated women's rights and gender issues for their own purposes. "Woman" and "tradition" have again become highly contested fields of discourse. Emphasis has shifted from the earlier concerns of the twentieth century, when traditional ideals of Indian womanhood were claimed on behalf of the modernizing project of nationalism, to those of the twenty-first century, where the debate is now focused on the complex issues of the relationship between tradition and universal human rights, with women's human rights an even more contested area.

Indian nationalism and communalism are predominantly represented by the Hindu Right (although some Muslim and Sikh Right groups exist too), which, according to Arati Rao, is active through more than five hundred organizations in India today, many with paramilitary training of male and female cadets. Right-wing nationalists recognize a public role for women, although their ideal woman remains linked to the traditional roles of wife and mother even when dedicated to the nationalist cause. Unfortunately, members of the Hindu Right have aligned themselves with women's rights issues by hijacking the demands for a uniform civil code within a framework for equality and justice, but stated in terms of woman's "natural" roles and obligations in the family:

> Hindu Right organizations bring together women from the same background, class, and castes. Similarities of experience forge a sense of unity of identity alongside a unity of purpose, which encourages a heightened communal solidarity . . . Feminist groups, by contrast, bring together women from diverse backgrounds to work on issue-based projects that benefit themselves as well as others.[42]

Although Hindu nationalism is mainly a political phenomenon, it has appropriated certain aspects of traditional Hinduism that affect women in important ways. The Hindu Right's dream of a "Hindu India," rooted in the perceived superiority of the

[40] Ibid., 3.
[41] See Eva Hellman, "Political Hinduism: The Challenge of the Visva Hindu Parisad" (Ph.D. diss., Uppsala University, 1993).
[42] Rao, "Speaking/Seeking a Common Language," 132.

Hindu majority, can have frightening consequences for the status of Indian women. Even more frightening is the extraordinary violence adopted by some of the women activists in Hindu communal politics, especially as promoted by the women's organizations affiliated to the RSSS, VHP, and BJP.[43] The role of women in the militant Hindu Right has so far been little studied, especially their involvement in militant actions against Muslims and Sikhs.[44] For example, two of the most passionate speakers for the destruction of the Ayodhya mosque in 1992 were two militant right-wing women leaders, and another 5000 women right-wing activists took part in this violent event. The emergence of militant female leadership has been encouraged by the Hindu Right for whom women can assume an activist role without violating the traditional norms of Hindu womanhood. Here a link can be seen to the great goddesses, such as Durga and Kali, but also to the patriotic song "*Bande Mataram*," praising the mother goddess of the nation.

The politicization of Hinduism for the realization of traditional agendas can only mean that women's rights will remain aligned to traditional values, which often entail women's un-freedom. For some women activists, the liberation of women means only the liberation from atrocities, but not that women should be free from their traditional duties as wives and mothers. Whether the appropriation of women's rights language in the name of political fundamentalism will ultimately exacerbate women's oppression and bondage or open the way to greater freedom has yet to be seen. It remains unpredictable at present whether Hinduism will allow for constructive reinterpretations within a secular framework, thereby facilitating the development of a truly universalist, inclusive spirituality that alone can affirm and empower women in a true sense.

At times the tension and conflict between women's rights and traditional Hinduism seem insoluble; women's situation is often distressing and disheartening, but at other times it is also evident that there are many signs of hope in a country as vast and diverse as India. Like in many other countries of the world, there is still a long way to go before "human rights literacy"[45]—so recent a development in global human history—can be more fully developed through an advance in education and the consciencization of policymakers and people on a large scale. This will contribute to the crucial increase in awareness necessary for the full empowerment of women, and

---

[43] See Amrita Basu, "Hindu Women's Activism in India and the Questions It Raises," in *Appropriating Gender: Women's Activism and Politicized Religion in South Asia*, ed. Patricia Jeffery and Amrita Basu (London: Routledge, 1998), 167–84.

[44] Hindu fundamentalism in general is dealt with in a number of works, but there is little explicit reference to the role of women. This is true of Martin E. Marty and R. Scott Appleby, eds., *The Fundamentalism Project* (Chicago: University of Chicago Press, 1991), as well as a number of other studies. See John Stratton Hawley, ed., *Fundamentalism and Gender* (New York: Oxford University Press, 1994), especially his essay "Hinduism: Sati and Its Defenders," 79–110. Most helpful and unusual is Tanika Sarkar and Urvashi Butalia, eds., *Women and Right-Wing Movements: Indian Experiences* (London: Zed Books, 1995); see Amrita Basu, "Feminism Inverted: The Real Women and Gendered Imagery of Hindu Nationalism," *Bulletin of Concerned Asian Scholars* 25, no. 4 (1993): 158–80. Also very helpful is the wide-ranging survey by Courtney W. Howland, "Women and Religious Fundamentalism," in Askin and Koenig, *Women and International Human Rights Law*, 533–621.

[45] See Katrina Tomasevski, ed., *Women and Human Rights* (London: Zed Books, 1993).

much of this depends on education. As a former judge of the Indian Supreme Court so rightly said in "A Convocation Address on Gender Justice," given at an Indian women's university:

> the Constitution is a great instrument which frowns upon discrimination ***against*** women and sanctions affirmative discrimination ***in favor of women***. Nevertheless, the whole gamut of Indian jurisprudence in action has an unwritten estrangement against women . . . the tragedy is that despite all expectations and promises, home is the girl's prison and the woman's workhouse. This hostile climate results in frustration and denial of the enormous human potential latent in womanhood for society's advance. . . .
>
> The only way equal gender can be claimed as of right is through education. The potential for prosperity of a country or of the world depends not on the abundance of its revenues nor on the strength of its arsenals but on cultivated citizens, particularly its women, energized by education, enlightenment, character, determination and dynamism. No nation has a future with all the foreign investments, glamorous consumer goods, easy loans from abroad and the corruption that goes with these sources if its women are unfree. On the contrary, Operation Education is the surest process to make India great.[46]

However, education alone will not be able to resolve the current conflict between the right to religious freedom and the rights of women. Greater political openness and maturity; further legal changes; changes in traditional social practice in the distribution of economic power; a more flexible, dynamic, and pluralistic understanding of Hinduism; and the further growth of a truly collaborative, inclusive women's activist movement within a secular, all-India framework seem equally essential for achieving full human worth and dignity for all Indian women.

Radhika Coomaraswamy, the United Nations Special Rapporteur on Violence against Women, has eloquently argued that human rights have become universal in scope and application in today's global and pluralistic world, but that the articulation of women's human rights also produces new thinking and approaches to human rights at the international level while not resolving their collision with cultural movements at the national level. She comments:

> Human rights discourse is a powerful tool with which to criticize states. Nonetheless, insofar as it concerns a woman's private life, it is actually in many societies quite a weak discourse, particularly in the context of family and community relations . . . the reality in many societies is that women's rights are under challenge from alternative cultural expressions.
>
> This phenomenon is deeply troubling. Regardless of all the international standards and accompanying national legislation, unless there is resonance in national civil society, there is little scope for real transformation . . . at the national level, when it comes to family and community in many countries, civil society is far more conservative.

[46] V. R. Krishna Iyer, *Human Rights: A Judge's Miscellany* (Wilmington, N.C.: B. R. Publishing, 1995), 237.

> ... This national struggle is the difficult fight, not the international one. Unless human rights discourse finds legitimacy in these areas of a country's national life, women's rights and human rights will remain mere words on paper.[47]

In Coomaraswamy's view the next decade will have to show whether the tension between national and international understandings of women's human rights can be resolved. During that time it will also become clearer whether Indian political developments and the freedom of Hindus to practice their religion will include not only necessary protections against abuse, but also provide full support for Indian women and their human rights.

[47] Radhika Coomaraswamy, "Reinventing International Law: Women's Rights as Human Rights in the International Community," (The Edward A. Smith Visiting Lecturer, Harvard Law School Human Rights Program, 1997), 26f.

Chapter 23

Religion Confronting Women's Human Rights: The Case of Roman Catholicism

Kari Elisabeth Børresen

I. Introduction

This summary article is based on my research, undertaken since 1961, concerning formative Christian anthropology. Conflicts between normative religion and women's rights are already well analyzed concerning Islam,[1] but rather unexplored concerning traditional Christianity. Here the case of Roman Catholicism is highly significant, since the Catholic Church, according to 2001 Vatican statistics, is the world's largest branch of Christianity, comprising 17.3 % of the global population, or 1.050 billion human beings.

The Roman Catholic Church has a privileged status at the United Nations and wields a corresponding international influence. Since 1964, the nonterritorial administrative body of the Catholic Church, the Holy See, enjoys the status of a Non-Member State Permanent Observer.[2] Representing the pope's spiritual and temporal government

[1] Ann Elizabeth Mayer, *Islam and Human Rights: Tradition and Politics* (Boulder, Colo.: Westview Press, 1999); Shaheen Sardar Ali, *Gender and Human Rights in Islam and International Law: Equal Before Allah, Unequal Before Man?* (The Hague: Kluwer Law International, 2000); Jonas Svensson, *Women's Human Rights and Islam: A Study of Three Attempts at Accommodation* (Lund University, Sweden: Almqvist & Wiksell, 2000).

[2] The process of entry into the system of international organizations started in 1929 when the Vatican City joined the World Telegraph Union and the Universal Postal Union. Since 1957, the supreme organ of government of the Roman Catholic Church is uniformly termed the Holy See. As a legal entity, the Holy See obtained status as a Non-Member State Permanent Observer at the United Nations in 1964 when the Secretary General, U. Thant, accepted its self-designation as such. (Switzerland had obtained this status in 1948). See Josef Kunz, "The Status of the Holy See in International Law," *American Journal of International Law* 46 (1952): 308–14 (arguing the case for sending a US ambassador to the Holy See). The attribution of statehood to the Holy See appears somewhat anachronistic since the Papal State in central Italy, restored to the Roman pontiff at the Congress of Vienna in 1815, was finally conquered and annexed by Italy in 1870. In 1929 the Lateran treaty, signed by Il Duce Benito Mussolini and Cardinal Pietro Gasparri, recognized the papal sovereignty of the Vatican City (0.44 square kilometers or 108.7 acres) in compensation for the loss of the Papal State. See Anika Rahman, "Church or State? The Holy See at the United Nations," *Conscience* 20 (1999): 2–5; David Nolan, "The Catholic Church at the United Nations: Church or State?" *Conscience* 21 (2000): 4, 20–24.

Tore Lindholm, W. Cole Durham, Jr., Bahia G. Tahzib-Lie (eds.), Facilitating Freedom of Religion or Belief: A Deskbook, *545–559.*

through his Roman Curia, the Holy See participates in UN conferences with full voting rights, whereas other religious entities can only operate as nongovernmental organizations. In consequence, the Holy See has become a leading actor on the international stage in opposing women's human right to control their own fertility.[3]

Acting in accord with Muslim states against female reproductive autonomy at the UN conferences on Human Rights (Vienna 1993), Population (Cairo 1994), and Women (Beijing 1995), the Holy See has invoked a corresponding androcentric sexology, also advocated by so-called Evangelical Protestantism.[4] Reproductive autonomy is an indispensable condition for women's sociocultural equivalence with men and, therefore, a fundamental human right.[5] In order to clarify the rationale of this retrograde alliance, it is essential to analyze traditional Christian doctrine. Contemporary Catholic theology and anthropology are still based on androcentric paradigms, formulated from the Graeco-Roman Late Antiquity through the European Middle Ages. It follows that institutional Roman Catholicism refuses women's right to reproductive autonomy (*Humanae vitae* 1968) and negates women's cultic capability (*Ordinatio sacerdotalis* 1994).

II. The Gender of Religion

Following the collapse of Marxism and the enhanced visibility of Islam, the impact of religion as a fundamental sociocultural factor has become evident. In consequence, sociological gender roles are shaped by theological gender models and vice versa.[6] So-called higher religions define fully human status in terms of possessing a potential cultic capability, that is a capability to mediate between the Godhead and humanity.

---

[3] Female reproductive autonomy was established as a human right in international law by the *Convention on the Elimination of All Forms of Discrimination against Women* (CEDAW), in force since 1981, as of 16 July 2001 ratified by 168 states. Article 16, paragraph 1 reads: "States Parties shall take all appropriate measures to eliminate discrimination against women in all matters relating to marriage and family relations and in particular shall ensure, on a basis of equality of men and women . . . (e) The same rights to decide freely and responsibly on the number and spacing of their children and to have access to the information, education and means to enable them to exercise these rights." The Holy See, along with eight Muslim states, has not signed this Convention, nor the 1952 *Convention on the Political Rights of Women*. The US has signed but not ratified CEDAW, mainly because of political pressure from Protestant fundamentalism.

[4] Elissavet Stamatopolou, "Women's Rights and the United Nations," in *Women's Rights, Human Rights: International Feminist Perspectives,* ed. Julie Peters and Andrea Wolper (London: Routledge, 1995), 36–48; Rebecca J. Cook, "International Human Rights and Women's Reproductive Health," in *Women's Rights, Human Rights,* 256–75; Susan D. Rose, "Christian Fundamentalism: Patriarchy, Sexuality, and Human Rights," in *Religious Fundamentalisms and the Human Rights of Women,* ed. Courtney W. Howland (London: Macmillan, 1999), 9–20; Ann Elizabeth Mayer, "Religious Reservations to the Convention on the Elimination of All Forms of Discrimination Against Women: What Do They Really Mean," in *Religious Fundamentalisms and the Human Rights of Women,* 105–16.

[5] Margaret E. Galey, "International Enforcement of Women's Rights," *Human Rights Quarterly* 6 (1984): 463–90; Noreen Burrows, "International Law and Human Rights: the Case of Women's Rights," in *Human Rights: From Rhetoric to Reality,* ed. Tom Campbell et al. (London: Blackwell, 1986), 80–98; Kevin Boyle, "Stock taking on Human Rights: The World Conference on Human Rights, Vienna 1993," *Political Studies* 43 (1995): 79–95; Katerina Tomaševski, "Women's Rights," in *Human Rights: Concepts and Standards,* ed. Janusz Symonides (Paris: UNESCO Publishing, 2000), 231–58.

[6] Kari Elisabeth Børresen and Kari Vogt, *Women's Studies of the Christian and Islamic Traditions* (The Hague: Kluwer Academic Publishers, 1995).

This prerogative is mostly reserved for men and based on male religious experience. No historically known society has abolished women's subordinate status by way of recognizing goddesses and priestesses.[7] Female autonomy is, in fact, alien to all major religious systems. In Hinduism and Buddhism, women are placed between men and beasts through successive reincarnations and the wheel of rebirth. The same ontological gender hierarchy appears in the creation myth of Plato's *Timaeus* (41e–42d). Here, immortal souls are initially set in heavenly stars, to be incarnated as human beings in male bodies, and then reincarnated as women or animals according to the moral quality of previous existence.

III. One God and Two Sexes

In Judaism, Christianity, and Islam, the monotheistic Godhead is described as manlike or metasexual. Human godlikeness is correspondingly defined as male or asexual. Given the interaction between the concept of divinity and the definition of humanity, this fundamental incompatibility of Godhead and femaleness is negotiated by shifting inculturated exegesis of Biblical texts. Traditional Christian anthropology builds on two contrasting axioms: Female subordination is established by God's creative order and is, therefore, normative in this world. Human equivalence in the sense of women's parity with men results from Christ's redemption, to be fully realized only in the coming world.[8] During two millennia of church history, the resulting incoherence between creational gender hierarchy and eschatological gender equality is being gradually overcome by attributing fully human godlikeness to women as well.[9] This doctrinal process is elaborated in three main stages:

A. Based on literal exegesis of Biblical texts, early Christian anthropology excludes women from being created in God's image (Gen. 1:26–27a; 2:7; 1 Cor. 11:7). Nevertheless, women can achieve salvational equality with godlike men through incorporation into Christ's perfect maleness (Gal. 3:28; Col. 3:10–11; Eph. 4:13). Consequently, Christian women are "becoming male" by ascetic renunciation of female sexuality.[10]

B. Based on combined Stoic and Platonic anthropology, ancient Graeco-Roman Church Fathers redefine human godlikeness in terms of the sexless soul's rational capacity, which is also found in women. Initiated in the third century by Clement of Alexandria and further elaborated by Augustine (died 430), this new exegesis allows backdating women's *imago Dei* from redemption to creation, in spite of non-godlike femaleness (sexual differentiation in Gen. 1:27b disconnected from fertility blessing in Gen. 1:28 and linked to image-text in Gen. 1:26–27a). The second stage became normative in medieval theology, whereas the first stage persisted in medieval canon law.

---

[7] See Joan Bamberger, "The Myth of Matriarchy: Why Men Rule in Primitive Society," in *Women, Culture and Society*, ed. Michelle Z. Rosaldo and Louise Lamphère (Stanford: Stanford University Press, 1974), 263–80.

[8] Kari Elisabeth Børresen, *Subordination and Equivalence: The Nature and Role of Woman in Augustine and Thomas Aquinas* (Kampen, The Netherlands: Kok Pharos, 1995).

[9] Kari Elisabeth Børresen, ed., *The Image of God: Gender Models in Judaeo-Christian Tradition* (Minneapolis, Minn.: Fortress Press, 1995).

[10] Kari Vogt, "'Becoming Male': A Gnostic and Early Christian Metaphor," in Børresen, *The Image of God*, 170–86; Elizabeth A. Clark, *Ascetic Piety and Women's Faith* (New York: Edwin Mellen Press, 1986).

C. Anticipated by medieval Northern-European Church Mothers, like Hildegard von Bingen (died 1179) and Julian of Norwich (died after 1416), who used female metaphors describing God; the third doctrinal stage considers both women and men to be created in God's image qua female or male human beings.[11] This holistic definition was explicitly formulated by nineteenth-century feminist exegesis, first by the Norwegian Aasta Hansteen in 1878.[12] Superseding traditional concepts of male or sexless godlikeness, inclusive *imago Dei* became normative in twentieth century Western Christianity. Soon adopted by Protestant exegetes and endorsed in Catholic anthropology after the II Vatican Council (1962–65), it is of note that the second stage persists in Eastern Orthodox doctrine.

In conclusion, the recently inculturated concept of holistic godlikeness, now accepted by Catholic theology, provides the necessary doctrinal foundation for promoting the rights of women as fully autonomous human beings.

IV. Traditional Sexology

Despite the current updating of theological anthropology, institutional Roman Catholicism opposes women's reproductive autonomy. In order to explain the doctrinal rationale of this Vatican obstruction, it is necessary to outline the main themes of traditional sexology. In ancient Christianity, the two basic human drives of religiosity and sexuality are axiomatically considered to be antagonistic. In consequence, the perfect human prototype is defined as male or presexual, so that sexual differentiation, or more precisely femaleness, is interpreted as a cause or a consequence of primeval sin. This theme appears already in Hesiod's *Works and Days* (ca. 700 B.C.), where the female prototype Pandora is created as a curse for mankind by bringing sexuality and death into the world.

Therefore, ascetic Christian movements practiced sexual abstinence in order to restore humanity's pristine immortality. In this context of dualistic anthropology, where bodily death is caused by the original fall, the leading Greek Church Fathers Origen (died ca. 254) and Gregory of Nyssa (died ca. 395) elaborate a twofold scheme of creation: First, a purely spiritual human prototype is created in God's image. Second, God introduces male and female physicality in order to counteract death by sexual fertility.[13] The leading Latin Church Father, Augustine, contests this double creation, where gender differentiation is linked to humanity's loss of immortality. He strongly insists that female humanity is established by God's unique creation. Consequently, Augustine refutes the early Christian belief that women will resurrect in male or gender-free perfection, boldly stating that women will be restored as human females.[14]

---

[11] Kari Elisabeth Børresen, "Ancient and Medieval Church Mothers," in Børresen and Vogt, *Women's Studies of the Christian and Islamic Traditions*, 245–75; Kari Elisabeth Børresen, "Julian of Norwich: A Model of Feminist Theology," in Børresen and Vogt, *Women's Studies of the Christian and Islamic Traditions*, 295–314.

[12] Aasta Hansteen, *Kvinden skabt i Guds Billede* (Woman created in God's image) (Christiania: n.p., 1878; 2d expanded ed., Christiania: Steen, 1903).

[13] Giulia Sfameni Gasparro, "Image of God and Sexual Differentiation in the Tradition of Enkrateia," in Børresen, *The Image of God*, 134–69.

[14] Kari Elisabeth Børresen, "Patristic 'Feminism': The Case of Augustine," *Augustinian Studies* 25 (1994): 139–52.

It is important to note that liberal Church Fathers like Clement of Alexandria invoked Stoic sexology against extreme ascetic rejection of sexual activity for all Christians. Still praising virginity as a most godlike way of life for the Christian elite, they considered married sexuality to be legitimate for the common multitude, but only if practiced as a means of procreation.

Unfortunately, Augustine's androcentric explanation of original sin, where humanity's collective guilt is propagated from Adam via paternal seed, enforced the traditional connection of death and sexual activity. His ambivalent moral rule is succinctly expressed as "*bene uti malo,*" to neutralize bad orgasm by good fertility. Augustine also tolerated marital intercourse as a remedy for concupiscence, thereby mitigating the Stoic prohibition of coitus with pregnant, nursing, or menopausal women. Nevertheless, he condemned contraceptive avoidance of female fertile periods as a method used by Manichees to impede the imprisonment of divine sparks in material bodies. It is noteworthy that Augustine had embraced dualistic Manichaeism for at least ten years and that his concubine bore only one child during more than fifteen years of cohabitation.

As a converted Manichee, Augustine insists that fertility belongs to God's creation. In this perspective, Eve's formation from Adam's rib (Gen. 2:18, 21–23) is interpreted in terms of derived femaleness, created to serve as instrument for men's procreation. It follows that women's specific *raison d'être* is motherhood, defined according to androcentric biology, to receive and nourish the potential embryo contained in the male seed.[15] In fact, Augustine's sexology, reshaped by Thomas Aquinas's (died 1274) Aristotelian finality of male generative power, survives in the Vatican's current ban on contraception.[16]

V. Vatican Sexology

Efficient fertility control, introduced by twentieth-century medical technology, represents a revolution in human history. In premodern societies, population growth was mainly determined by extensive infant mortality. Contraceptive means were inefficient and provoked abortions were dangerous, so birth control was often practiced by *coitus interruptus*. Before the discovery of the female ovum in 1827 by Karl Ernst von Baer, dispersion of male seed was condemned as destroying potential embryos and, therefore, confused with abortion in traditional sexology.

It is significant that this biological shift was first negotiated in a Protestant context by approval of contraception as legitimate in marriage; cf. the 1930 Lambeth Conference of the Anglican Communion. Pius XI reacted against this novelty with a rehearsal of traditional doctrine in the encyclical *Casti connubii* (1930).

Challenged by the growing debate within the Catholic Church, John XXIII in 1963 nominated a pontifical commission of theologians and lay experts to examine the validity of current teaching. The global demographic explosion was taken into account, but without focus on female reproductive autonomy. Among progressive

[15] Erna Lesky, *Die Zeugung–und Vererbungslehren der Antike und ihr Nachwirken* (Mainz: Verlag der Wissenschaften und der Literatur, 1950); Aline Rousselle, *Porneia* (New York: Basil Blackwell, 1988).

[16] John T. Noonan Jr., *Contraception: A History of its Treatment by the Catholic Theologians and Canonists* (Cambridge, Mass.: Harvard University Press, 1986).

members were the leading moral theologians Bernhard Häring and Josef Fuchs, who in the 1950s had introduced a positive evaluation of sexual activity in marriage as expressing love.[17] This holistic approach represents a major reform of Christian anthropology. Traditional doctrine considers married intercourse and marital love to be antagonistic. In consequence, ancient Church Fathers regularly exhort pious married couples to actualize their loving union by sexual abstinence. Conservative members were afraid to endanger the church's authority by changing established doctrine. Their invocation of traditional sexology apparently ignored the fact that voluntary conception is a new option, resulting from the twentieth-century biological revolution and, therefore, not addressed in previous moral discourse. To Paul VI's consternation, the commission's final reports of 1966, leaked to an American Catholic newspaper in 1967, showed that a strong majority (sixty of sixty-seven members) recommended allowing contraception in marriage.[18]

It is important to know that the archbishop of Krakow, Karol Wojtyla, strongly supported the small minority, encouraging Paul VI to publish the contested encyclical *Humanae vitae* in 1968.[19] Based on a premodern concept of natural law, this document reaffirms that the biological finality of procreation is normative for each single conjugal act, thereby condemning so-called artificial contraception as intrinsically evil.[20] Insisting on the absolute inviolability of biological functions in every so-called use of marriage, the encyclical affirms that all acts of sexual intercourse must remain open to procreation, whether or not causally responsible at the given moment. In consequence, the only licit method of fertility control is conjugal abstinence during female fertile periods. (Previously condemned by Augustine!)

Intended to safeguard the pope's teaching authority concerning faith and morals, the encyclical proved counterproductive by provoking widespread dissent. In their comments on *Humanae Vitae*, leading Catholic theologians like Karl Rahner and Yves Congar pointed to the historical inculturation of Christian tradition, which has proved viable through reception by the faithful, not by pontifical *diktat*.[21] It is significant that only seventeen percent of episcopal responses to the encyclical expressed

---

[17] Ambrogio Valsecchi, *Controversy: The Birth Control Debate 1958–1968* (London: Geoffrey Chapman Ltd., 1968).

[18] "The Majority Papal Commission Report" is reprinted in *The Catholic Case for Contraception,* ed. Daniel Callahan (London: Macmillan, 1969), 149–73, where the core rationale is spelled out at page 161: "The reasons in favor of this affirmation are of several kinds: social changes in matrimony and the family, especially in the role of the woman; lowering of the infant mortality rate; new bodies of knowledge in biology, psychology, sexuality and demography; a changed estimation of the value and meaning of human sexuality and of conjugal relations; and most of all, a better grasp of the duty of man to humanize and to bring to greater perfection for the life of man what is given in nature." See ibid., 174–211; the Minority Report is a pathetic example of male celibate isolation from human reality.

[19] Jan Grootaers, "Humanae Vitae, encyclique de Paul VI," *Dictionnaire d'Histoire et de Géographie ecclésiastiques* 25 (1994): 328–34 (Wojtyla's conservative stance favored his papal election in 1978).

[20] Charles E. Curran, "Natural Law and Contemporary Moral Theology," in *Contraception: Authority and Dissent,* ed. Charles E. Curran (New York: Herder and Herder, 1969), 151–75; see Charles E. Curran and Richard A. McCormick, eds., *Dialogue about Catholic Sexual Teachings* (New York: Paulist Press, 1993); Charles E. Curran, *The Catholic Moral Tradition Today: A Synthesis* (Washington, D.C.: Georgetown University Press, 1999).

[21] Karl Rahner, "On the Encyclical 'Humanae Vitae,'" *Theological Investigations* 11 (1974): 263–87; Yves Congar, "Reception as an Ecclesiological Reality," *Concilium* 77 (1972): 43–68.

unmitigated acceptance. In developed countries, where women enjoy full civil rights and contraception is normal—like Scandinavia, France, The Netherlands, Belgium, Austria, and Canada—the bishops expediently referred to the moral judgment of individual conscience.[22]

Since Cardinal Wojtyla became John Paul II in 1978, he has used every opportunity to reinforce the doctrine of *Humanae Vitae*. Aptly co-opting the new inculturation of sexual union as an expression of conjugal love, he confirms the biological purposiveness of coitus by transforming procreative purpose into an essential part of love in marriage. The apostolic letter *Mulieris dignitatem* in 1988 condemns contraception as degrading women from their specific dignity of motherhood.[23] The encyclical *Veritatis splendor* in 1993 reiterates that every contraceptive act constitutes a violation of the God-given law of nature.[24]

VI. Pontifical Censure

The Roman Church's institutional blockage under John Paul II follows from his imposition of assent to Vatican sexology, including the opposition to women's priestly ordination, as the indispensable prerequisite to become a bishop. An oath of loyalty to the papal *magisterium* is imposed on teachers of theology at Catholic universities (*Professio fidei* 1989, *Ad tuendam fidem* 1998). By virtue of concordats, such Vatican control also extends to state universities, as in Germany and Austria. In fact, when the II Vatican Council approved religious freedom (*Declaratio de libertate religiosa* 1965), this new doctrine primarily envisaged corporate liberty for the Catholic Church in Communist societies. In consequence, the human right to religious freedom for individual Catholics within the institutional Church remains unresolved.[25]

Considered in the context of church history, the current ban on contraception has a privileged position among many fateful errors committed by the Roman papacy. Often concealed by contemporary apologetics and rarely known except by scholars, some mistakes are still operative, such as the excommunication of the Greek Orthodox patriarch in Byzantium in 1054 and the excommunication of Martin Luther in

---

[22] John Maloney, *The Making of Moral Theology: A Study of the Roman Catholic Tradition* (New York: Oxford University Press, 1987), 259–301; William H. Shannon, *The Lively Debate: Response to Humanae Vitae* (New York: Sheed and Ward, 1970), 117–46.

[23] See Kari Vogt, "Catholicisme et Islam: Une rhétorique apologétique commune à propos de la femme," in Børresen and Vogt, *Women's Studies of the Christian and Islamic Traditions,* 359–65. (The definition of motherhood as women's specific dignity corresponds to Islamic sexology.) See Kari Elisabeth Børresen, "Jean Paul II et les femmes," *Lumière et Vie* 257 (2003): 57–69.

[24] Joseph A. Selling and Jan Jans, eds., *The Splendor of Accuracy: An Examination of the Assertions Made by Veritatis Splendor* (Kampen, The Netherlands: Kok Pharos, 1995); see Charles E. Curran and Richard A. McCormick, eds., *John Paul II and Moral Theology* (New York: Paulist Press, 1998). For a pertinent critique of the papal concept of God as a superimpregnator, who creates new life through the biological finality of human sexual organs, contradicting human autonomy as being created in God's image, see Christian Duquoc, "Procréation et dogme de la création," *Lumière et Vie* 187 (1960): 51–65.

[25] James H. Provost, "Freedom of Conscience and Religion. Human Rights in the Church," in *Culture Chrétienne et Droits de l'Homme—du rejet à l'engagement,* ed. Michel J. Verwilghen (Rome: IFCU, 1991), 35–61; William Johnson Everett, "Human Rights in the Church," in *Religious Human Rights in Global Perspective: Religious Perspectives,* ed. John Witte Jr. and Johan D. van der Vyver (Boston: Martinus Nijhoff, 1996), 121–41.

1520. Commenting on John Paul II's retraction of the Holy Office's process against Galileo Galilei (1633), a noted Italian politician, Alberto Ronchey, succinctly states that if this condemnation could be rectified, even after centuries, the persistent Vatican obstruction of fertility control to solve the global demographic crisis, with growth from 3.5 billon in 1968 to 6 billion in 1998, cannot be exonerated.[26]

In conclusion, since the concept of female autonomy remains alien to all global religions, women's human right to control their own voluntary fertility represents a fundamental challenge to traditional gender models, and not only in Roman Catholicism. Recently forced to admit the socio-economic necessity of so-called responsible paternity (*paternitas conscia*), the Vatican advocates sexual abstinence or avoidance of female fertile periods as the only licit method of voluntary control of fertility. Biologically inefficient and harmful to the psychophysical equilibrium of couples, this clerical solution has proved to be impracticable. Invoking marital love and parental responsibility in order to restrict sexual intercourse, the traditional rejection of orgasmic coitus as sinful is here obfuscated by inverted apologetics. In fact, most Catholics in socially advanced societies no longer respect Vatican sexology, thereby producing a healthy criticism of ecclesiastical theocracy. Unfortunately, the Holy See's privileged status at the United Nations strengthens its political influence in underdeveloped countries.

VII. Androcentric Typology

The twentieth-century collapse of androcentrism represents a more fundamental challenge to traditional theology than the previous collapse of geocentrism (Kepler) and anthropocentrism (Darwin). Upheaval of gender hierarchy shakes the core of Catholic and Orthodox doctrinal symbolism, where androcentric gender models are transposed from God's creation to the order of redemption. Godlike Adam prefigures Christ, who as new Adam and divine Redeemer is incarnated in perfect maleness. Non-godlike Eve prefigures the Church/Mary, who as new Eve represents dependent and, therefore, womanlike humanity (Rom. 5:14; Eph. 5:32). Based on the early Christian concept of male godlikeness, this asymmetrical typology remains fundamental in Catholic and Orthodox Christology, ecclesiology, and Mariology. Thus excluding femaleness from a description of the Godhead, typological gender models serve as a prime obstacle to women's cultic capability in the non-Protestant majority of Christendom. According to Thomas Aquinas and Bonaventura (died 1274), Christlike maleness is an indispensable prerequisite for the sacramental signification of priestly eminence.[27] It is important to observe that this refusal to ordain women as priests and bishops issues from the preservation of a traditional incompatibility of Godhead and femaleness. In medieval canon law, women's cultic *impedimentum sexus* is explicitly justified by men's exclusive *imago Dei*, in accordance with the first stage of Christian anthropology. In line with women's legal incapacity in civil society, termed *infirmitas sexus* in Roman law, this cultic incapability remained unchallenged in all institutional churches until the

---

[26] Alberto Ronchey, "In sei milliardi stretti e caldi," (Six crammed and overheated billion) *Corriere della Sera*, 14 November 1998.

[27] Kari Elisabeth Børresen, "The Ordination of Women: To Nurture Tradition by Continuing Inculturation," *Studia Theologica* 46 (1992): 3–13.

twentieth century.[28] Previously, all mainstream Christian denominations were firmly opposed to women's civil rights, considered to violate God's order of creation. Enforced by the sociocultural consequences of new Western ideals like democracy and citizenship, female suffrage was first accepted in Protestant countries (New Zealand 1893, Australia 1902, Finland 1906, Norway 1913), and several years later in Catholic countries (France, Italy, Spain 1945). A similar Protestant precedence concerns women's cultic capability to be ordained as priests and bishops, (Lutheran Denmark respectively 1948/1995, Sweden 1958/1997, Norway 1961/1993, Anglican Great Britain 1994).

In Roman Catholicism, the recent acceptance of women's godlikeness qua female human beings entails a contradictory mixture of premises discarded and conclusions preserved. Simultaneously upholding the mutually exclusive doctrinal tenets of early androcentric typology and holistic godlikeness, the institutional church decrees that godlike women cannot be ordained as Christlike priests. The *Codex Iuris Canonici* of 1983 (canon 1024) repeats the formula from the *Codex* of 1917 (canon 968,1): "***Sacram ordinationem valide recipit solus vir baptizatus.***" ("Only a baptized male can receive valid ordination.")

At the initiative of the bishops' synod in 1971, Paul VI in 1973 nominated a pontifical commission to study the status of women in society and church, with twenty-five members, among them fifteen women.[29] It is significant that only one of these women, a female medical doctor, had professional expertise in theology, natural or social sciences; such expert knowledge was reserved for the male members. The question of ordaining women was deliberately excluded from their mandate and left to the papal Biblical commission, which included male theologians only. According to a secret report from 1975, published in 1976 by so-called indiscretion, this commission unanimously considered that referring to New Testament texts only could not solve the question of ordaining women. In fact, the Church's clerical hierarchy and monarchic episcopate were structured from the second/third centuries onwards. Hence, a majority of twelve exegetes (against five) found that the Church could ordain women without opposing Christ's initial intention.

Nevertheless Paul VI in 1977, overruling the majority of experts as he had done in 1968, sanctioned a doctrinal document against women's ordination: ***Inter insigniores***. The main argument is that the Church's constant tradition of excluding women from the priesthood is not based on socio-cultural androcentrism, but on the indispensable conformity between Christ's incarnate maleness and the priest's male sex. The courageous theologian Karl Rahner's critique of this Christological rationale is pertinent: "The mere fact that Jesus was of the male sex is no answer

[28] Haye van der Meer, ***Women Priests in the Catholic Church? A Theological Historical Investigation*** (Philadelphia: Temple University Press, 1973); Roger Gryson, ***The Ministry of Women in the Early Church*** (Collegeville, Minn.: Liturgical Press, 1976); Ida Raming, ***The Exclusion of Women from the Priesthood: Divine Law or Sex Discrimination?*** (New Jersey: Scarecrow Press, 1976). Ida Raming, ***Priesteramt der Frau—Geschenk Gottes für eine erneuerte Kirche*** (Münster, Hamburg: LIT Verlag, 2001).

[29] In 1974, five women members were refused to present their minority report that contested the commission's submissive final document. The women did not dare to publish this report until several years later. See Maria del Pilar Bellosillo et al., "Women Appeal to the Pastors of the Church," ***Pro Mundi Vita Bulletin*** 108 (1987): 1–36.

here, since it is not clear that a person acting with Christ's mandate and in that sense (but not otherwise) *in persona Christi* must at the same time represent Christ precisely in his maleness."[30]

Like *Humanae Vitae*, this declaration provoked a lively theological debate in the Church, giving rise to growing awareness among Catholic laypeople of the untenable arguments invoked to preserve the cultic impediment of femaleness.[31] Incidentally, Communist authorities in Czechoslovakia were conveniently duped by several women who were ordained to the Catholic priesthood before 1988, in spite of their canonical *impedimentum sexus*. This stratagem served them to perform forbidden pastoral work secretly, for instance, to administer the sacraments in prisons. [32]

VIII. Vatican Feminology

In Orthodox Christianity, the question of women priests is still marginal, debated only in Westernized context, as in France and the United States. In Protestant churches, priesthood is not defined in terms of androcentric typology, with axiomatic conformity between Christ's incarnate manhood and the priest's Christlike maleness. Christology does not, therefore, contravene women's ordination. Inversely, John Paul II invokes the typological gender models of Christ as new Adam, and Mary as new Eve, to justify the cultic incapability of femaleness. Combining women's Mariotypic motherhood with the new concept of female godlikeness in *Mulieris dignitatem*, he mixes the first and the third stage of Christian anthropology, that is, an androcentric typology and an updated *imago Dei*.[33] When Mary is proposed as the exemplary role model for women, this exhortation tends to obscure that Christ's mother as the new Eve has an instrumental and subordinate function vis-à-vis the Godhead, incarnated as the new Adam.[34]

In fact, the current incoherence between discarded male godlikeness and upheld female cultic impediment is manifest by John Paul II's apostolic letter *Ordinatio sacerdotalis* from 1994, where he refers to *Inter insigniores* and *Mulieris dignitatem*, concluding that the Church cannot ordain women because Christ called twelve male apostles and did not ordain his mother Mary. The traditional exclusion of women from the priesthood is, therefore, in accordance with God's plan for his Church ("*congruenter statuit mulierum exclusionem a sacerdotio convenire cum consilio Dei pro sua Ecclesia*"). Since this invocation of divine androcentrism did not silence the persistent demand for women priests in the Catholic Church, the pope's doctrinal chieftain, Cardinal Joseph Ratzinger, in 1995 issued a *Responsio*, certifying that the disputed apostolic letter pertains to the normative deposit of faith ("*ad fidei depositum pertinens*").

---

[30] Karl Rahner, *Theological Investigations XX: Concern for the Church* (New York: Crossroad, 1981), 35–47.

[31] Walter Gross, ed., *Frauenordination. Stand der Diskussion in der katholischen Kirche* (Munich: Erich Wewel Verlag, 1996).

[32] The Vatican prefers to keep these women priests underground, but they appear in Hansjacob Stehle, *Geheimdiplomatie im Vatikan. Die Päpste und die Kommunisten* (Düsseldorf: Benzinger Verlag, 1993), 320, 428.

[33] Kari Elisabeth Børresen, "Image ajustée, typologie arrêtée: Analyse critique de Mulieris dignitatem," in Børresen and Vogt, *Women's Studies of the Christian and Islamic Traditions*, 343–57.

[34] Kari Elisabeth Børresen, *Anthropologie mediévale et théologie mariale* (Oslo: Universitetsforlaget, 1971); Kari Elisabeth Børresen, "Mary in Catholic Theology," *Concilium* 188 (1983): 48–56.

In conclusion, it is certainly not a human right to be ordained a priest or a bishop in the Catholic Church. Nevertheless, it is a fundamental right for all human beings to be equally attributed a fully godlike humanity, being able to mediate between the Godhead and humankind. Preserving the canonical ***impedimentum sexus*** of femaleness, the institutional Church decrees that God is impeded from calling women to the priesthood because of their God-given cultic deficiency. Since the twentieth century, such an attribution of androcentric incapability to the Godhead has become perfectly unconvincing.

IX. Feminism and Christianity

The Vatican's efforts to counteract the current androcentric collapse have been succinctly described: "The Catholic Church . . . is writhing in knots around feminism like a worm impaled on a hook."[35] It is essential to observe that women's claim to bio-socio-cultural and religious autonomy results from the epistemological revolution of feminism, where women and men are defined as human beings of equal dignity: "Feminism is concerned with the shift in roles and the question of rights that have been unjustly denied women. But all of that, however important and essential, is secondary. The main event is epistemological. Changes in what we know are normal; changes in how we know are revolutionary. Feminism is a challenge to the way we have gone about knowing. The epistemological ***terra firma*** of the recent past is rocking, and as the event develops, it promises to change the face of the earth."[36]

From an historical perspective, the relationship between feminism and Christianity is radically ambivalent.[37] In Western civilization, the ideal of female autonomy is based on the Christian concept of women's equivalence with men in the order of salvation. The feminist revolution starts when redemptive inclusiveness is backdated as normative for the present world, thereby superseding creational gender hierarchy. In the European history of ideas, this process coincides with the transformation of human godlikeness from exclusively male to equal privilege for both sexes. Women's gradual achievement of autonomous humanity is realized through the stages of stratified communality in the Middle Ages, religious individualism in the Age of Reform, universal human rights for men in the Enlightenment, and the twentieth-century shift from ***droits de l'homme*** to inclusive ***droits humains***, when human rights are equally attributed to women.[38]

In consequence, this recent Western inculturation represents a fundamental challenge to traditional gender models in Roman Catholicism and Orthodox Christianity, where the core doctrine and symbolism are structured by androcentric typology. In conformity with Islam, traditional Christian discourse axiomatically connects creational

---

[35] Andrew Brown, "The Future of the Papacy," ***The Spectator*** (25 April 1998): 13–14.

[36] Daniel C. Maguire, ***The Moral Revolution: A Christian Humanist Vision*** (New York: Harper and Row, 1986), 122.

[37] Kari Elisabeth Børresen, "Christianisme et féminisme," in ***Maschio e femmina li creò***, ed. Fiorenza Taricone (Verona: Il Segno dei Gabrielli Editori, 1998), 83–99.

[38] See Jerome J. Shestack, "The Philosophical Foundations of Human Rights," in Symonides, ***Human Rights: Concepts and Standards***, 31–66; Arvonne S. Fraser, "Becoming Human: The Origins and Development of Women's Human Rights," ***Human Rights Quarterly*** 21 (1999): 853–906.

gender differentiation to the God-given division of male and female roles in church and society. In a European perspective, the eighteenth-century asymmetrical polarity of male and female functions (Rousseau and Kant) is in the nineteenth and twentieth centuries redefined in terms of complementarity of the sexes, where the subordinate character of female roles becomes strategically obscured. It is significant that the Northern-European partnership model—where women and men collaborate in all fields of society and church, precisely because of and not despite their sexual difference—proves to be alien in Mediterranean civilization.

The impact of Scandinavian state feminism and a Scandinavian welfare system, in which a strong participation of women in political government is correlated with a high voluntary birth rate, is striking.[39] In contrast, the lack of feminist welfare policy in Catholic countries, such as Spain and Italy, generates feeble participation of women in political government and a voluntarily reduced natality. It is of note that Norway did not join the European Union because of a significant gender gap in the referendum of 1994 in which sixty-two percent of the female electorate voted against membership, presumably in large measure to protect the feminist welfare system. From this point of view, it is regrettable that prospective new members from Eastern and Central Europe are not required to fulfil Western juridical norms for equality of the sexes and women's reproductive autonomy before entering the union. Enforcement of Canon law in civil society is especially problematic, as in the case of Malta's concordat with the Holy See from 1995.

X. Sex and Gender

Feminist epistemology presupposes a twentieth-century anthropology, where the human being is defined as a sexually differentiated psychophysical unity. It is essential to note that this holistic concept is completely different from the Platonized anthropology of Christian tradition, where the human being is defined as a sexless rational soul in a male or female body. This dualistic concept of humanity has shaped theology and philosophy from late antiquity until the nineteenth century. It is, therefore, paradoxically counterproductive when gender studies in the social sciences often persist in presupposing an anachronistic dichotomy of sex, as biologically programmed, and gender, as socially constructed. In fact, this division corresponds to traditional androcentric dualism, thereby inadvertently imitating the Church Fathers' promotion of women to godlike manhood in sexless intellect and virtue, despite bodily femaleness. The same strategy was repeated in seventeenth-century French salon feminism with the Cartesian adage: "*l'âme n'point de sexe*," and still echoed by Simone de Beauvoir: "*On ne naît pas femme, on le devient.*" Among the humanistic disciplines, gender studies in religion are at the scholarly forefront by applying human, that is, male or female "genderedness" as a main analytical category.[40] This holistic approach

[39] One indication is the differential total fertility rates 1995–1999 for Norway, Denmark, Finland, and Sweden compared to Italy and Spain: Norway 1.85, Denmark 1.72, Finland 1.73, Sweden 1.57, Italy 1.20, Spain 1.15. *The State of World Population 2000* is available online at <http://unfpa.org/swp/2000/english/indicators/indicators2.html>.

[40] Ursula King, "Gender and the Study of Religion," in *Religion and Gender*, ed. Ursula King (Oxford: Blackwell, 1995), 1–38.

highlights the connected interaction between psychophysical sex and sociocultural gender, which is equally fundamental for women and for men. Applied to the Christian tradition as in feminist theology, human God-language is consequently understood in terms of verbalized male or female experience.

The epistemological clash between God-given specific complementarity of the sexes and postmodernist deconstruction of gender was striking in the *dialogue des sourds* between the Vatican delegation and feminist activists at the 1995 United Nations conference in Beijing.[41] Both parties apparently ignored the historical construction of their respective agendas, in fact, equally resulting from millennia of androcentric socio-biology. Fervently fighting feminist efforts to strengthen women's human rights, the Holy See tactically abused less sophisticated variants of feminist constructionism. The demagogical confusion of abortion and contraception on both sides proved particularly counterproductive. The practical social reality that abortion of a healthy fetus generally presupposes involuntary conception makes the Vatican a causal agent of abortion in societies influenced by its ban on contraception. The Holy See's condemnation of condoms to protect against HIV and AIDS is a scandalous consequence of pontifical biotheology.[42]

When feminists advocate women's right to safe abortion in case of enforced pregnancy, their undisputed primary goal is to make the biological revolution of efficient contraceptive technology operative in underdeveloped areas. Female reproductive autonomy is first and foremost to be realized by voluntary conception in order to prevent subsequent abortion.[43] Inversely, the Holy See fiercely opposes women's control of fertility because the Vatican is fully aware that worldwide feminism presupposes reproductive choice and vice versa.

XI. Discourse and Reality

The argumentation of contemporary Vatican discourse on contraception and prevention of HIV/AIDS is clearly vicarious. My present summary of doctrinal construction shows that the historically shifting inculturation of traditional theology and anthropology has been logically coherent. The majority of Church Fathers and scholastic

[41] Doris E. Buss, "Robes, Relics and Rights: The Vatican and the Beijing Conference on Women," *Social & Legal Studies* 7 (1998): 339–63.

[42] See the statement of the Holy See concerning the *Declaration and Platform for Action* of the United Nations Conference on Women in Beijing, 1995: "The Holy See in no way endorses contraception or the use of condoms, either as a family planning measure or in HIV/AIDS prevention programmes," *Report of the Fourth World Conference on Women,* available online at <gopher://gopher.undp.org/00/unconfs/women/off/a—20.en>, chapter V, sec. 11. It is of note that faced with human disaster, the Vatican has now dissociated the medical use of condoms from its upheld ban on condoms as means of contraception. At the United Nations Special Session on HIV/AIDS, 25–27 June 2001, New York, the Holy See's Permanent Observer presented a statement after the adoption of the *Declaration of Commitment on HIV/AIDS,* 2 August 2001, with implicit reference to # 23 and # 52: "He emphazised that in accepting the language on the use of condoms as a method of prevention of the disease, the Holy See in no way changed its moral position." The full text of the 2 August 2001 UN Declaration is available online at: <http://www.unaids.org/whatsnew/others/un_special/Declaration020801_en.htm>.

[43] It is important to note that the widespread selective abortion of female fetuses in Asia mainly results from the axiomatic inferiority of femaleness. This discrimination in Hinduism and Buddhism is explained by the ontological hierarchy of reincarnation and rebirth, placing women between men and animals. The current

theologians were well-educated aristocrats; the socially mobile Augustine is a significant exception. This thorough knowledge of ancient and medieval learning made their articulation of the Christian tradition meaningful in a given sociocultural context and, therefore, viable. In fact, the current doctrinal incoherence between outdated premises and preserved conclusions, which affects the main themes of theological sexology, is a new phenomenon in the history of Christianity, resulting from the recent collapse of androcentric or dualistic axioms. In consequence, no longer able to control Catholics by condemning sexual activity as transmitting original sin, the pontifical castigation of "hedonism" insists on condemning contraception. Christianity's traditional conflict between love of God and sexual love is no longer axiomatic, but upheld by the obligation of cultic celibacy. Male priests must keep away from women and femaleness constitutes cultic incapability. According to Vatican statistics as of 2001, the number of nuns in the Catholic Church (801,185) doubles the number of priests (405,178) and nonordained monks (55,057). This peculiar situation helps explain why the Vatican invokes women's *impedimentum sexus* in order to exclude them from participation in the hierarchical government of the Church, reserved for the pope and his Roman Curia of male cardinals. During the theocratic pontificate of John Paul II, the collegial decision-making of bishops, envisaged by the Second Vatican Council, has been reduced to consultative status. In consequence, restoring episcopal collegiality on the model of the ancient Church, and recognizing women's cultic capability, will be urgent tasks for a third Vatican Council.[44] A decisive influence of male and female lay people has to be codified in concordance with recent norms of political democracy. The Catholic Church can no longer be governed on the model of the Roman Empire with a majority population of illiterate serfs.

As a Nordic Catholic feminist historian of theology, I find it paradoxical that Christian feminism has first been accepted in Protestantism, where the literal Bible is invested with a sacramental function as God's instrument of revelation, akin to the Islamic concept of the Koran as a divine revelatory medium. In this context, it is interesting to note that contemporary Islamic feminist theology emulates the strategy of previous Protestant feminist theology by criticizing the subsequent interpretations of sacred texts, not the androcentrism of revelatory scripture *ad litteram*.[45] Inversely, I argue that indispensable instruments for a feminist Reformation of Christianity are to be found in the Catholic and Orthodox traditions. A dynamic interpretation of incarnate scripture; that is, historically shaped revelation and an optimistic anthropology, in terms of Christ's redemptive divinisation of humanity, are essential means for this new

euphemism of blaming cultural relativism instead of androcentric religion is here especially fallacious; consider the widespread practice of direct or indirect female infanticide, well documented from classical antiquity to early modern Europe.

[44] It is noteworthy that a majority of leading feminist theologians are Catholics. Their contribution as experts will be important in a third Vatican Council. Some influential European scholars are as follows: Elisabeth Gössmann (Munich), Anne Jensen (Graz), Ursula King (Bristol), Cettina Militello (Rome), and Janet M. Soskice (Cambridge), and in the USA (significantly, all nuns): Anne E. Carr (Chicago), Margaret A. Farley (Yale), Elizabeth A. Johnson (New York), and Sandra M. Schneiders (Berkeley).

[45] Examples of similar approaches, with a significant time lag, are the following: Letty M. Russell, ed., *Feminist Interpretation of the Bible* (Philadelphia: Westminster Press, 1985) and Amina Wadud Muhsin, *Qur'an and Woman: Rereading the Sacred Text from a Woman's Perspective* (New York: Oxford University Press, 1999).

inculturation.[46] Divested of androcentric typology, the ancient Graeco–Roman Church Fathers' inculturation, emulated by the medieval Northern-European Church Mothers' holistic God-language, are exemplary models for reconstructing a viable Roman Catholicism.[47]

Vatican Documents published in *Acta Apostolicae Sedis*, Città del Vaticano:

Casti connubi—AAS 22, 1930, 539–592.

Humanae vitae—AAS 60, 1968, 481–503.

Inter insigniores—AAS 69, 1977, 98–116.

Mulieris dignitatem—AAS 80, 1988, 1653–1729.

Veritatis splendor—AAS 85, 1993, 1133–1228.

Ordinatio sacerdotalis—AAS 86, 1994, 545–548.

Responsio (Ordinatio sacerdotalis)—AAS 87, 1995, 1114.

[46] Kari Elisabeth Børresen, "Femmes et théologie depuis 1960—le parcours d'une protagoniste," in *Donne e Teologia. Bilancio di un secolo,* ed. Cettina Militello (Rome: Edizioni Dehoniane, 2003); see Christine Amadou, "An interview with Kari Elisabeth Børresen," in Børresen, *The Image of God,* xxii–xxix; Rosemary R. Ruether, *Women and Redemption: A Theological History* (Minneapolis, Minn.: Fortress Press, 1998), 190–93, 338.

[47] Kari Elisabeth Børresen, "Religious Feminism and Female God-language: From Hildegard von Bingen to Thérèse de Lisieux," in *Ab Aquilone: Nordic Studies in Honour and Memorv of Leonard E. Boyle. O.P., Suecoromana VI,* ed. Marie Louise Rodén (Marieberg, Sweden: Riksarkivet, 2000), 197–222.

Chapter 24

The Right to Be the Same, The Right to Be Different: Children and Religion

Geraldine Van Bueren

I. Introduction

Religion and international human rights law are like the two parallel lines of the railway track. One line traverses the terrain of reason; the other, of faith. So it is the ultimate conundrum: How does religion, a higher form of law, meet human rights, itself a higher form of law to which states must adhere? Which takes precedence, the divine or the secular? Perhaps, however, this is the wrong question.

Rather than deciding what trumps what—an approach more appropriate to the game of bridge than to life—it may be time for us to sit down and discuss what religion can learn from human rights and how human rights can in turn be enriched by religion in ways which will better protect the rights of children.

Religious belief can arouse concepts of self-worth and the recognition of the dignity of others. Children are a community's future, and sometimes they are caught between the ambiguities of recognizing their community's freedom of religion or belief, religion's centrality to the community's cultural identity, and their own pursuit of sincerely held beliefs.

The key issue is whether children have the right to be different—different from their respective community's majority belief and different from the religious beliefs of their individual families.

The right to be different is particularly complex in relation to religion, as religion has both an individual and a collective façade and many adults regard children as symbolizing continuity, affirmation, and the future. This is why the child's right to freedom of religion or belief was one of the most heatedly debated rights in the drafting of the Convention on the Rights of the Child (CRC).[1]

Yet, to regard children only as a community's future is to turn back the hands of time and reconceptualize children as passive vehicles of adults' desires. Children are not only the future; they are, more importantly, of the present. For many children,

---

[1] *The Convention on the Rights of the Child* (hereafter CRC), UN Doc. A/44/49 (1989), entered into force in 1990.

Tore Lindholm, W. Cole Durham, Jr., Bahia G. Tahzib-Lie (eds.), Facilitating Freedom of Religion or Belief: A Deskbook, *561–569.*

freedom of religion or belief means freedom from religious restrictions that impinge detrimentally on their lives. Children already face the risk of abuse of power by adults toward them, and the abuse of religious beliefs can lead to adult domination rather than a true exercise of responsibilities. Religion should not be abused as a shield to defend practices offensive to either the international or domestic human rights of the child. As a general rule, the more serious the impact of a practice on a right, the more compelling must be the justification.

II. Religion, Best Interests, and Community Duties

Holistic religions—such as Judaism and Islam—are organic systems of law with holy texts and high priests. Human rights is also an organic system of higher law; its ultimate values are autonomy and choice. The holy texts of human rights are found in international and regional treaties. Its high priests are the judges of international and regional human rights tribunals.[2] Both religion and international human rights law recognize the concept of the best interests of the child. It is a fundamental norm of international human rights law, and the idea of providing for the best interests of the child also echoes throughout the holy texts of the global religions.

The "best interests of the child" concept began essentially as a principle of compassion. It is a self-imposed limitation of adult power stemming from the recognition that an adult is only in a position to take a decision on behalf of a child because of the child's lack of experience and judgment. It is, however, rare for actions by adults not to be argued in the language of best interests. Deciding what is in the best interests of children "often poses a question no less ultimate than the purposes and values of life itself."[3] As has been frequently observed, though a question might be viewed from the perspective of a child's best interests, the answer is frequently given from an adult perspective.[4]

While the answer as to what constitutes the best interests of child is complex, very little guidance is found in human rights law regarding the weight that should be given to the various competing interests. What, for example, is the status of "the best interests of the child" in international law, and does it take second place to what may loosely be described as religious public policy? In reaching decisions, how do we assess the power relations between the relevant decision makers, religious as well as secular?

Many secular societies perceive that "the best interests of the child" is to be viewed from a more individualistic perspective: What is in the best interests of a particular child as an individual or as an individual member of a family? By contrast, many religious societies perceive "best interests" as both individual and collective, leading to the view that it is in the best interests of the child to adhere to the religion of the state.

In its broadest application, the principle is articulated in article 3(1) of the CRC, which provides that "[i]n all actions concerning children, whether undertaken by public or private social welfare institutions, courts of law, administrative

---

[2] I am grateful to my husband, James Michael, for this observation.

[3] Robert H. Mnookin, *In the Interests of Children* (New York: W. H. Freeman and Company, 1985), 18.

[4] See Geraldine Van Bueren, *The International Law on the Rights of the Child* (Boston: Martinus Nijhoff, 1995), 32.

authorities or legislative bodies, the best interests of the child shall be a primary consideration." By demoting the best interests from *the* primary consideration to *a* primary consideration, the CRC may allow states parties to balance the best interests of the child against other equally weighty "primary" considerations of the state party's own choosing, such as religious laws.[5] Such an approach is mitigated, to a degree, by articles 18(1) and 19 of the CRC, which provide that the best interests of the child is the parent's "basic concern" and protects the child against many forms of abuse and neglect. Thus, the CRC challenges the concept that parents are always capable of deciding what is in the best interests of children with regard to religious matters.[6]

This is reinforced both by the development of the concept of the evolving capacities of the child and the restrictions placed on parents by the CRC. The implication of placing a duty on states parties to respect the parents' rights and duties to provide direction to the child, in accordance with the child's evolving capacities, is that states parties are under a duty to recognize that parental power to provide direction to children decreases as the child matures.

The new approach to "best interests" requires states to scrutinize parental claims to control children's conduct on the basis of religion. In the United States, parents cannot claim freedom from compulsory vaccination on religious grounds, as "[t]he right to practice religion freely does not include liberty to expose the community or the child to communicable disease or the latter to ill health or death."[7] This new approach is "not putting religion on trial . . . but is merely examining the way in which the particular exercise of a given religion by a parent through his or her right of access affects the child's best interests."[8]

A contemporary approach to best interests has the potential to correct some of the past wrongs and to confront the complexities of children and choice of religion.

III. All Change, Perhaps? Children's Right to Choose Their Own Religion or Belief

A fundamental issue is whether children have the right to adopt a religion or belief of their own choice or to choose no religion or, on the other hand, whether religion superimposes communal duties above individual rights.

The right of children to have or adopt a religion or belief of their own raises two issues. The first is whether and at what stage of their childhood children can choose a religion or belief for themselves. The second issue involves which religion or belief children are to be brought up in when those responsible for the children cannot agree on the choice of religion or belief.

---

[5] Despite its clarion call, article 3 of the CRC must be contrasted with principle 2 of the Declaration of the Rights of the Child and with article 4 of the African Charter on the Rights and Welfare of the Child, both of which stress that the best interests of the child should be *the* primary consideration. There is technically a regrettable weakening of the primacy of the best interests of the child in the CRC, which has never been adequately explained.

[6] See Van Bueren, *The International Law on the Rights of the Child,* 32.

[7] See Prince v. Massachusetts, 321 US 158, 166–67 (1944) (Rutledge J.).

[8] P. v. S., 108 DLR (4th) 287, 317 (1994) (Supreme Court of Canada) (L. Heureux-Dube J.).

As for the second question, although individual religions legislate on the applicable religion for children, international law is silent as to choice of religion. Under international law, both spouses have equal rights and responsibilities in relation to the upbringing of children, including in religious matters, and international law does not offer much guidance where the spouses disagree.[9]

There are, however, international standards on the existence of a right of children to choose their own religion or belief, but the issue is not clear-cut and is surrounded by controversy. The Declaration on the Elimination of All Forms of Intolerance and of Discrimination Based on Religion or Belief incorporates, in article 5, specific provisions on the rights of the parents and the child, but viewed only from the parents' perspective. Consequently, the declaration fails to focus on the rights of the children themselves, even though such an omission was specifically highlighted during the drafting of the declaration.[10] The declaration merely proclaims that the parents or the legal guardians have the right to organize the life within the family in accordance with their religion or belief. The right of a child to choose his or her religion subsequently arose during the drafting of the CRC. Surprisingly, as the CRC concerns children's autonomy, the child's right to freedom of religion or belief, as formulated in article 14 of the CRC, incorporates less detail than is found in article 18 of the ICCPR, on which it is based.

Specifically, the CRC, in contrast to the ICCPR, omits any express reference to having or adopting a religion or belief of the child's choice. Consequently, it only implicitly prohibits any coercion that would impair the child's freedom to have or to adopt a religion or belief of his or her choice. In addition, unlike the ICCPR, the CRC does not expressly include the freedom of a child to manifest a religion or belief in worship, observance, practice, and teaching.

As the rationale behind any new treaty provision on human rights is the augmenting of human dignity and not its restriction, how did this limitation occur? The fundamental problem is that despite the proclaimed universality of international human rights law, such law must still be relevant and applicable to states representing all four different types of relationships existing between religious communities and the state: (1) religious states where the law is based upon and reflects religious beliefs; (2) states where there is a separation between the state and the religious community, but where one religion dominates the public philosophy; (3) states that are home to a diverse number of religions and where toleration of religion and freedom of religion or belief is a reality; and (4) states which adopt an official policy of atheism but where religion is more or less tolerated.[11] The approach of a state towards the child's right to freedom of religion or belief invariably reflects this relationship.

Islamic states in particular were not able to accept any provision granting children the freedom to choose and change their religion or belief. Morocco argued that, in accordance with Islamic law, the child does not have the right to choose his or her religion or belief, as it is regarded to be in the best interests of the child that he or she follows the religion of the father.[12]

---

[9] See CRC, art. 14.

[10] See Geraldine Van Bueren, ed., *International Documents on Children,* 2d ed. (Boston: Martinus Nijhoff, 1998).

[11] Karl Josef Partsch, "Freedom of Conscience and Expression and Political Freedoms," in *The International Bill of Rights: The Covenant on Civil and Political Rights,* ed. Louis Henkin, (New York: Columbia University Press, 1981), 210.

Other states, including Finland, Italy, and Sweden, stressed that the standards set by the CRC should not detract from those already established by the ICCPR and other basic human rights instruments. In particular, Sweden stated that it had only accepted the adoption of article 14 on the basis that the right to freedom of thought, conscience, and religion was adopted as laid down in article 18 of the ICCPR and included the freedom to have or adopt a religion or belief of the child's choice. Finland observed that the right of children to freedom of expression, including the right to have their views given due weight in accordance with their age and maturity, was also applicable in relation to religious matters. The Chair of the Working Group supported this approach and ruled that since the child's right to freedom of expression enshrined in article 12 of the CRC was "a general provision," it applied to all matters affecting the child, including religious matters.[13]

The right of individuals generally to have and to adopt a religion or belief of choice is not only enshrined in the ICCPR, but also in two regional human rights treaties: the European and American Conventions on Human Rights. For non-Islamic states that have not attached a reservation and that are party to either the CRC or to any of the other relevant treaties, the principle of being entitled to have or adopt a religion or belief of choice is equally applicable to both children and adults. In fact, there are a number of states in which children already possess such a right under their national law. In Iceland, children at the age of sixteen can decide whether to choose a particular religion or belief, but at the age of twelve their opinions must be taken into account.[14] In Norway, any child above the age of fifteen may choose to renounce a religion.[15]

For some Catholic and Islamic states that are party only to the CRC, it is clear from the drafting history that they do not acknowledge the right of children to adopt a religion or belief of their own choice. This is, for instance, evidenced by specific reservations to article 14 and by broad reservations made in relation to provisions of the CRC that are incompatible with Islamic law. These wide-ranging reservations by a number of Islamic states and the narrower reservations by a few Catholic states brings to the fore the public/private debate. It is here—where international human rights law conflicts with interpretations of divine law—that there will be the greatest support for the maintenance of the traditional public/private distinctions of public international law.

IV. Religion and Child-Centered Education

In the twenty-first century, children should be at the center of the school. Consequently, education ought to be child centered. However, consideration of the right of children to be educated in accordance with their religious beliefs is an unusual approach. The tradition in international law has been to place a duty on the state to educate the child in accordance with the parents' religious and philosophical convictions, regardless of the age and maturity of the child. Hence, article 18(4) of the ICCPR

[12] UN Doc. E/CN.4/1987/WG.1/WP.35.

[13] UN Doc. E/CN.4/1989/48.

[14] Religious Association of Iceland, *The Law Concerning the Official Recognition of Religious Associations*, Law 108, ch. 2, art. 8 (1999).

[15] Act Relating to Religious Communities (1969) (Norway).

only places a duty on states parties to have respect for the liberty of parents and, when applicable, legal guardians to ensure the religious and moral education of their children in conformity with their own convictions.

The issue arises because the state is in a position to influence the religious and other beliefs of children by teaching one religion or creed to the exclusion of others, or by indirectly supporting a religion or particular belief by favorable financial or administrative arrangements. The intent behind the international legislative framework on education was to establish the right of parents to protect children against the use of educational institutions by the state for ideological indoctrination.[16] Such an intent is laudable with children who are not sufficiently mature (and likely vulnerable to such influences), but with more mature children there ought to be a balancing of the rights of the child and the rights of other family members. One might assume that the omission was an oversight, not a deliberate attempt to exclude consideration of the child's religious educational wishes; after all, such an intent would have been plainly contrary to the best interests of the child.

A major attempt at reversing the trend of focusing exclusively on parental rights was made during the drafting of the CRC. The position for states parties to the CRC is that as the child becomes sufficiently mature, the child's wishes in relation to religious education should be taken into account. As the CRC still regrettably omits any type of individual petitioning mechanism, the majority of cases concerning violations of children's religious rights have been brought under the right to freedom of religion or belief and religious educational freedom enshrined in the ECHR. The focus is very different, as the ECHR was never designed to be a child-oriented human rights treaty and, consequently, only addresses the rights of parents to ensure such education and teaching in conformity with their own religious and philosophical convictions.

To what extent this undermines for children the right to freedom of religion or belief enshrined in article 9(1) of the ECHR has never been determined. Article 9(1) guarantees that:

> Everyone has the right to freedom of thought, conscience and religion; this right includes freedom to change his religion or belief and freedom, either alone or in community with others and in public or private, to manifest his religion or belief, in worship, teaching, practice and observance.

The majority of cases brought to the ECHR by parents regarding children's right to freedom of religion or belief have fallen under article 2 of Protocol No. 1. Applications, however, have been made jointly by parents and children alleging breaches both of article 2 of Protocol No. 1 to the ECHR and of article 9 of the ECHR. *Angelini v. Sweden* illustrates the approach developed by the Strasbourg organs, which have adopted a clear and consistent line of jurisprudence with regard to religious education.[17] A mother and daughter were atheists and were refused exemption by the Ministry of Education from participation by the daughter in the teaching of religious knowledge.

---

[16] ICCPR, art. 18(4), which was originally based on a Greek proposal, was introduced to prevent religious education from being imposed on children against the will of their parents. During its drafting, it was made clear that this provision only places a duty on states parties to respect the wishes of parents; it does not place a duty on states parties to provide instruction in the religion of the parents' choice.

[17] Angelini v. Sweden, 10 EHRR 123 (EComHR, 1988).

Arrangements, however, had been made on the initiative of the head of the school so that the daughter did not have to attend morning classes, which were of a religious nature and which involved the singing of hymns. In Sweden, exemption from the teaching of religious knowledge is only available to organized religions, including Roman Catholicism and Judaism, and atheists are obliged to participate in the instruction of religious knowledge.

The applicants alleged a breach of articles 9, 14, and 17 of the ECHR. They also alleged that a Swedish reservation to article 2 of Protocol No. 1 to the ECHR breached article 14 of the ECHR.[18] The European Commission of Human Rights had to determine whether the daughter had been subjected to indoctrination at school, which would have amounted to a breach of her right to respect for freedom of religion or belief as guaranteed by article 9(1) of the ECHR. The European Commission observed that article 9 affords protection against indoctrination of religion by the state, be it in education, at school, or in any other activity for which the state has assumed responsibility. Teaching that provides information only cannot be regarded as being in conflict with the ECHR or its Protocols. Education has to be about religion and not in religion. This reflects the underlying approach to children's religious education that it is factual information about religion generally and not of a particular faith.

The decision in *Angelini* is consistent with a ruling of the United Nations Human Rights Committee in *Hartikainen v. Finland*, which held that, provided instruction in the history of religions and ethics is given in a neutral and objective way, such teaching is in conformity with article 18(4) of the ICCPR and respects the convictions of parents or legal guardians who do not believe in any religion.[19]

Factual sexual education has also been the subject of complaint before the Strasbourg organs alleging a violation of parental Christian beliefs. In *Kjeldsen, Busk Madsen and Pedersen v. Denmark*, the applicants were parents who maintained that integrated and compulsory sex education, which had been introduced into Danish state schools, was contrary to their belief as Christian parents.[20] They alleged that the compulsory sex education amounted to a violation of their rights under article 2 of Protocol No. 1 to the ECHR.

The European Court of Human Rights ruled that article 2 of Protocol No. 1 to the ECHR applies to all of the state's functions in relation to education and teaching.[21] Under this provision, states parties are under a duty to respect the parents' religious convictions throughout the entire state education regime.[22]

The European Court also found that the sex education was aimed less at instilling knowledge which children do not have or cannot acquire by other means, than at giving them such knowledge "more correctly, precisely, objectively and scientifically."[23]

---

[18] Ibid.

[19] Hartikainen et al. v. Finland, Comm. No. 40/1978, UN Doc. A/36/40 (UN Human Rights Committee, 9 April 1981).

[20] Kjeldsen, Busk Madsen and Pedersen v. Denmark, 1 EHRR 711 (1979–80) (ECtHR 23, 7 December 1976), 724.

[21] Ibid., 729–30.

[22] Ibid., 729.

[23] Ibid., 731.

The sex education was not "an attempt at indoctrination . . . aimed at advocating a specific kind of sexual behavior."[24] Accordingly, the court found no breach of article 2 of Protocol No. 1 to the ECHR and the parents' claim failed.[25]

What has yet to be determined is the proper weight to be attached to the differing views of parents vis-à-vis the child as to religious education, bearing in mind that the child's rights under article 9 are broader than the parental responsibilities under the protocol. Guidance can be sought from two dissenting opinions. The point was initially raised at the European level in *Kjeldsen* in the separate concurring opinion of Kellberg, who stated that insufficient stress had been placed on the rights of the child. According to Kellberg, children of "a certain age" can demand that their views are respected. He cogently argued, "[i]t is hardly conceivable that the drafters would have intended to give parents something like dictatorial powers over the education of their children."[26]

The same approach was taken in the partially dissenting opinion of Justice Douglas in *Wisconsin v. Yoder*. In *Yoder*, a child, Frieda Yoder, had testified as to her own religious views. However, had she not so testified, Justice Douglas clearly stated that if an Amish child wished to attend high school and was sufficiently mature to have that desire respected, the state may well be able to override the parents' religiously motivated objections.[27]

Thus, the embryonic approach is to take into consideration the religious wishes of the child in relation to his or her religious education. As welcome as these dissents are, they must be understood in the context in which they were written in relation to states in which religion does not regulate all aspects of life.

V. Children, Religion, and Punishment

It appears universal that when national legislation abolishes physical punishment in schools, children do not initiate court cases seeking to have the ban lifted. Yet, for some adults, the imposition of corporal punishment on children by parents and the community is sincerely understood as a religious duty. Such viewpoints apparently rely both on the Bible and the Koran.

The religious duty of the community is captured in the following question: When national parliaments enact legislation to prohibit corporal punishment in schools, does it violate the religious rights of parents and children, when the parents may have consented to its use and delegated their responsibilities to the school?

The latest challenge to the abolition of school physical punishment on this basis was argued before the South African Constitutional Court in *Christian Education v. Minister of Education*.[28] Apart from constitutional provisions, the applicants relied upon Proverbs[29]

---

[24] Ibid., 732.
[25] Ibid., 729.
[26] Ibid., 23 ECtHR, 50.
[27] Wisconsin v. Yoder, 406 US 205, 242 (1972) (Douglas, J. dissenting).
[28] Christian Education South Africa v. Minister of Education, (10) BCLR 1051 (CC) (South Africa, 18 August 2000).
[29] Prov. 22:6; 22:15; 19:18; 23:13, 14.

and Deuteronomy,[30] arguing that the dignity of the child would be violated if misdeeds were left unpunished. Corporal punishment was important to the religious ethos and identity of the school.

Their arguments failed. The court held that freedom of religion or belief implies an absence of constraint and coercion, and that a respect for the dignity of the child which was to be interpreted within a constitutional order of reducing violence and increasing equality. [31]

The judgement of the court is in harmony with the Declaration on the Elimination of All Forms of Intolerance and of Discrimination Based on Religion or Belief, which states "[p]ractices of a religion or belief in which a child is brought up must not be injurious to his physical or mental health or to his full development."[32]

VI. Conclusion

In the English language, the word "religion" derives from the Latin *religare*, meaning "to bind together that which has once been broken." In this post CRC era, children may help bind society, but not without their consent and not at the expense of their individual rights. Ultimately, it is a question of balance, and the contribution of the CRC is that it has shifted the weight away from child sacrifice toward child autonomy.

---

[30] Deut. 6:4–7.

[31] See note 28. The unanimous judgment of the Court was delivered by Justice Sachs.

[32] Art. 5(5). It is also in accordance with article 19 of the CRC prohibiting child abuse.

MIX
Papier aus verantwortungsvollen Quellen
Paper from responsible sources
FSC® C105338

If you have any concerns about our products,
you can contact us on
ProductSafety@springernature.com

In case Publisher is established outside the EU,
the EU authorized representative is:
Springer Nature Customer Service Center GmbH
Europaplatz 3, 69115 Heidelberg, Germany

Printed by Libri Plureos GmbH
in Hamburg, Germany

Facilitating Freedom of Religion or Belief: A Deskbook

FACILITATING FREEDOM OF RELIGION OR BELIEF:
A DESKBOOK

Published by the Oslo Coalition on
Freedom of Religion or Belief
in celebration of the 20th anniversary of the Declaration
on the Elimination of All Forms of Intolerance
and of Discrimination Based on Religion or Belief

Editors: Tore Lindholm
W. Cole Durham, Jr.
Bahia G. Tahzib-Lie

Associate Editors: Elizabeth A. Sewell
Lena Larsen

BYU International Center for Law and Religion Studies
Provo, Utah, USA

The Norwegian Centre for Human Rights
University of Oslo
Norway

The Royal Norwegian Ministry of Foreign Affairs

Springer-Science+Business Media, B.V.

A C.I.P. Catalogue record for this book is available from the Library of Congress.

Printed on acid-free paper.

ISBN 978-90-04-13783-7 ISBN 978-94-017-5616-7 (eBook)
DOI 10.1007/978-94-017-5616-7

Originally published by Martinus Nijhoff Publishers in 2004
Softcover reprint of the hardcover 1st edition 2004

Koninklijke Brill NV incorporates the imprint Martinus Nijhoff Publishers.
http://www.brill.nl

Cover illustration: Pablo Picasso, "Dance of Youth"

To Defenders of Freedom of Religion or Belief
and
To Victims of Intolerance

"Is it not true, my friend, that the river has very many voices? Has it not the voice of a king, of a warrior, of a bull, of a nightbird, of a pregnant woman and a sighing man, and a thousand other voices?" "It is so," nodded Vasudeva, "the voices of all living creatures are in its voice."

–Hermann Hesse, *Siddhartha*

Any royalties of this book will be used to support the efforts of the Oslo Coalition on Freedom of Religion or Belief.

Contents

Part III: Freedom of Religion or Belief and the State

Part IV: Women, Parents, and Children

Part V: Changing Beliefs and the Tensions of Tolerance

Part VI: Contexts for Facilitating Freedom of Religion or Belief

Appendices

Foreword

By the Norwegian Minister of Foreign Affairs
March 2000–October 2001

Thorbjørn Jagland

Human rights know no borders. More than fifty years after the adoption of the Universal Declaration of Human Rights, we have only just begun to understand the true impact of recognizing the universality of human rights—"human rights for all." This means that the struggle for freedom of religion or belief for every individual is every government's struggle and every government's responsibility.

Religion is a powerful force. Freedom of religion or belief includes the freedom, either alone or in community with others, in public or in private, to practice one's religion or belief, whether through worship, observance of religious customs or teaching. Freedom of religion or belief also includes the right not to have a religion or belief, and to change one's religion.

Every society benefits from the full and unhindered practice of religion or belief. Full respect for this basic human right can be a powerful force for preventing, quelling and ending conflicts. Experience has shown that peaceful coexistence across religious, ethnic or national borders is only possible if the freedom to have different religious views is ensured, both formally and in practice.

This requires direct involvement on the part of religious leaders and communities, and also governments. Thus, dialogue between leaders and other trusted members of religious communities, NGOs, scholars and representatives of governments should be encouraged.

In order to be successful, such dialogues must be open and frank and they must address real issues. Exchanges like this help communities to see themselves through the eyes of others and to gain new insight into other religions or beliefs as well as their own. Discussing common concerns, listening to others and exchanging ideas promote tolerance and freedom of religion or belief. Such dialogues also give us an opportunity to analyze the obstacles to the unhindered practice of religion or belief. Since progress in the field of human rights is measured in terms of implementation, the objective of dialogue and discussion must be the fulfillment, safeguarding and defense of freedom of religion or belief.

Tore Lindholm, W. Cole Durham, Jr., Bahia G. Tahzib-Lie (eds.), Facilitating Freedom of Religion or Belief: A Deskbook, *xiii–xiv.*

I congratulate the Oslo Coalition on Freedom of Religion or Belief on producing this book, which will be a valuable tool for anyone desiring to understand and contribute to the promotion of such freedom. The book is a fruit of the Oslo Conference on Freedom of Religion and Belief, which was held in August 1998 and co-sponsored by the Norwegian Government. I hope the reader will find this collection of articles stimulating and challenging and that it will serve the cause of freedom of religion or belief everywhere.

Foreword

By the United Nations Special Rapporteur on Freedom of Religion or Belief

Abdelfattah Amor

The United Nations Commission on Human Rights continues to be alarmed that serious instances of intolerance and discrimination on the grounds of religion or belief, including acts of violence, intimidation and coercion motivated by religious intolerance, occur in many parts of the world and threaten the enjoyment of human rights and fundamental freedoms. For years the Commission has been reiterating its concern in its annual resolutions on the elimination of all forms of religious intolerance, most recently Resolution 2001/42.

The international community must, therefore, react by fighting against such acts and especially by preventing them. This book, published by the Oslo Coalition on Freedom of Religion or Belief on the occasion of the twentieth anniversary of the 1981 United Nations Declaration on the Elimination of All Forms of Intolerance and of Discrimination Based on Religion or Belief, is integral to this reaction. The great variety and the quality of contributions assembled here witness the necessity of greater recognition of violations of freedom of religion or belief and the importance and urgency that exist to combat every manifestation of intolerance and discrimination, and especially to prevent them. This publication contributes significantly to the reinforcement and the development of the right to freedom of religion or belief, a right underlying the establishment of the mandate on freedom of religion or belief, formerly referred to as the mandate on religious intolerance, and the evolution of action associated with it.

◆ ◆ ◆

By Resolution 1986/20 of 10 March 1986 the Commission on Human Rights decided to appoint a special rapporteur charged with examining incidents and governmental actions in all parts of the world which are inconsistent with the provisions of the 1981 Declaration on the Elimination of All Forms of Intolerance and of Discrimination Based on Religion or Belief, and recommending measures to remedy such situations. Fourteen years later, by Resolution 2000/33, the Commission on

Tore Lindholm, W. Cole Durham, Jr., Bahia G. Tahzib-Lie (eds.), Facilitating Freedom of Religion or Belief: A Deskbook, *xv–xviii. © 2004 Koninklijke Brill NV.*

Human Rights decided to change the title of the mandate of the Special Rapporteur on Religious Intolerance at the next extension of the Special Rapporteur's mandate, in 2001.

The new title of Special Rapporteur on Freedom of Religion and Belief came into effect at the 57th session of the Commission in March–April 2001.

The 1981 Declaration guarantees freedom of religion and belief, and elaborates the relevant norms enshrined in other international human rights instruments. These instruments include the International Covenant on Civil and Political Rights, in particular article 18, and the International Covenant on Economic, Social, and Cultural Rights, in particular article 13. From these instruments it can be inferred that the right to have, adopt or change freedom of religion or belief is absolute. It is also clear that manifestations of religion or belief may only be subject to certain specific limitations. The United Nations Committee on Human Rights has detailed in General Comment No. 22 of 20 July 1993 that restrictions on the freedom to manifest religion or belief are only permitted if limitations are prescribed by law and necessary to protect public safety, order, health or morals, or the fundamental rights and freedoms of others. The Committee has also pointed out that limitations imposed must not be applied in a manner that would vitiate the right to freedom of thought, conscience, and religion. The Committee has maintained that limitations may be applied only for those purposes for which they were prescribed and must be directly related and proportionate to the specific need on which they are predicated. Restrictions may not be imposed for discriminatory purposes or applied in a discriminatory manner.

• • •

Within the scope of the mandate on freedom of religion or belief, it has been noted for several years that manifestations of intolerance and discrimination based on religion or belief persist in countries that are in various stages of development and that have various political, social, and cultural systems—despite the multitude of established norms and the diversity of mechanisms in place to counteract them.

The identified infractions are diverse and concern violations of nondiscrimination and tolerance of religion and belief in the following areas: freedom of thought and conscience; freedom to practice one's religion or belief; freedom regarding the disposition of religious property; and, more generally, a person's right to life, bodily integrity, and health. Women, in the eyes of religion, or of considerations imputed to religion, continue to bear the brunt of violations.

The victims of such intolerance and discrimination are also diverse. Whether it involves believers or nonbelievers, religious communities, or society in general, those who are most affected are vulnerable groups. This implicates women on the one hand and minorities on the other. Minorities in this sense include new religious movements, for which freedom of religion or belief must be guaranteed. At the same time, it is necessary to guard against invoking the cloak of religious freedom as an alibi for purposes contrary to human rights.

Major challenges are emerging in the face of increasing manifestations of hatred, intolerance, and violence based upon extremism. Religious extremism may, in some cases, lead to situations that are difficult to control, even compromising the right to peace. Afghanistan was until recently the site of one of the most intolerable examples of extremism, but the challenge of religious extremism belongs to no particular society, state, or religion.

◆ ◆ ◆

In order to counter an alarming assessment regarding tolerance and nondiscrimination based on religion or belief, I suggest going beyond everyday management of these phenomena. Prevention by means of open communication, urgent calls for action addressed to states, and on-site visits are of vital importance to break the vicious circle of violations of freedom of religion or belief. This prevention depends primarily upon education and inter-religious dialogue. As the Preamble of UNESCO's Constitution states, "since wars begin in the minds of men, it is in the minds of men that the defenses of peace must be constructed."

◆ ◆ ◆

The teaching of tolerance and nondiscrimination must be oriented along various lines; including the family, society, religious communities, political parties, and the media. I have also been inclined to believe that training in school is especially suited to ensure that values supporting human rights are internalized and to foster a culture of tolerance and human rights.

This proposed education explains the initiative, taken within the framework of the mandate, to organize together with the Spanish Government an international consultative conference on school education in relation to freedom of religion or belief. This conference took place in Madrid in November 2001 to celebrate the twentieth anniversary of the adoption of the 1981 Declaration.

The conference developed an international, school-based strategy for students at elementary and secondary education levels. Additionally, the conference considered a set of recommendations to shed light on the establishment of programs and scholarly manuals, regarding education on tolerance and nondiscrimination in the areas of religion and belief.

◆ ◆ ◆

Inter-religious dialogue is essential for the prevention of misunderstandings, conflicts, and violations of freedom of religion or belief. As the United Nations High Commissioner for Human Rights so rightly pointed out in her 21 September 1999 address, marking the 950th anniversary of the City of Nuremberg and its conference on peace and human rights, "The full title of the conference, namely, 'Human Rights: Favored by Religions, Threatened by Religions,' illustrates the fact that religion's message of peace and love can be distorted to become an instrument of hatred and conflict. Religion can and should play an important role in conflict prevention and post-conflict reconciliation." At stake in the promotion and protection of freedom of religion or belief is not so much the search for one unique and exclusive truth, but rather a search to promote greater respect for the rights of individuals, groups, and communities. To this end, measures applied at national and international levels should overlap at the point of constructive dialogue among members of religious communities, and between different religious communities and public powers in a spirit of tolerance and respect.

There is good reason to celebrate initiatives that promote this dialogue, such as the Geneva Spiritual Appeal, which was delivered and signed by representatives of various religions and by the International Committee of the Red Cross (ICRC), the Office of the United Nations High Commissioner for Human Rights (OHCHR), the United Nations High Commissioner for Refugees (UNHCR), and the World Health Organization (WHO) during an interconfessional service held in Geneva on 24 October 1999 as part of United Nations Day. Furthermore, UNESCO has established the World Council on Inter-Religious Dialogue. Finally, hope is generated by the efforts of the United Nations Year of Dialogue between Civilizations, 2001.

In sum, education and inter-religious dialogue constitute two essential axes destined to prevent violations throughout the world. It must be remembered that the representation of one's own image hinges on the respect one bears toward the self-image of others. "The encounter with alterity is the encounter with ourselves," writes Federico Mayor, who adds, "the path that leads to the realization that 'others, they are us' is strewn with pitfalls."

Foreword

By the United Nations High Commissioner for Human Rights

September 1997–September 2002

Mary Robinson

The sense of shared purpose and commitment I witnessed at the Oslo Conference on Freedom of Religion or Belief, held 12–15 August 1998, was impressive. I welcome the initiative arising from the Oslo Conference to publish this book, *Facilitating Freedom of Religion or Belief*, growing out of papers submitted at the conference and based on the work of experts in the field.

The 1981 United Nations Declaration on the Elimination of All Forms of Intolerance and Discrimination Based on Religion or Belief elaborated on the basic rights and freedoms set out in article 18 of the Universal Declaration of Human Rights and other relevant provisions, and called on states to take all effective measures necessary to prevent and eliminate discrimination and appropriate measures to combat intolerance on the grounds of religion or other beliefs. The Declaration further expressed the conviction of the international community that freedom of religion or belief can contribute to the attainment of world peace, social justice and friendship among people.

The recent Millennium Peace Summit of Religions and Spiritual Leaders, which opened at the United Nations on 28 August 2000, affirmed the importance of dialogue and discussion between the world's religions in the pursuit of the fundamental purposes of the United Nations Charter.

It is evident that tolerance and respect for other religions and beliefs will make the world a more peaceful place. The opposite is also clear: that bigotry, prejudice and discrimination are a sure recipe for conflict and even war. There is an onus on all of us to defend the rights of all persons to follow their own religion or belief without hindrance. Religions themselves have responsibilities too. As I said at Oslo:

> The major religions, while concerned with ultimate questions, frequently present themselves as protectors and promoters of human dignity. They see themselves in particular as defenders of the deprived, the poor, the discriminated against. So their religious freedom is a freedom in society not merely to believe and to worship but also to uphold the cause of the deprived. In these circumstances they must ensure that their own internal practices are not discriminatory on grounds of gender or race or class. They have to learn from the good practice of wider society as well as teach it.

Tore Lindholm, W. Cole Durham, Jr., Bahia G. Tahzib-Lie (eds.), Facilitating Freedom of Religion or Belief: A Deskbook, *xix–xx.*

The Oslo Conference was noteworthy, not only because it brought together such a distinguished group of experts from academia, governments, international organizations, and NGOs, but because it forged an enduring coalition of interested parties to carry on the work of defending freedom of religion or belief. The launch of this book makes a significant contribution to that ongoing work by providing all of the actors involved with a valuable tool to help better understand the root causes of intolerance and discrimination and to learn more about how to combat these ills.

Acknowledgements

This volume would not have been possible without the dedicated efforts and assistance of many. The Royal Norwegian Ministry of Foreign Affairs has provided steadfast encouragement and generous financial support, making possible the wide distribution of the book to students, NGOs, and activists in developing countries. We are also indebted to the Norwegian Centre for Human Rights, the Oslo Coalition on Freedom of Religion or Belief, and the International Center for Law and Religion Studies at Brigham Young University for providing generous financial backing in the editorial process and for freeing up the time of Tore Lindholm, Cole Durham, and Elizabeth Sewell for their part of the work on the book. Many thanks are also in order to the Bahá'í community of the Netherlands for their hospitality during meetings held in The Hague.

The editors also gratefully acknowledge the research and editorial contributions of many talented students in both Oslo and Provo. Thanks to Christian Moe, Turid Smith Polfus, Lincoln T. Peterson, Patrick J. Thurston, Ann Elizabeth Gedicks, Hannah Clayson Smith, James and Jaimee Macanas Neel, Howard Baik, Gabe S. Clark, Claire Foley, Sarah and Carter Chow, Joshua D. Jewkes, Rana Lehr Lehnardt, Christopher R. Preston, Lance S. Lehnhof, Michael Monson, John Valentine, Natalie Peterson, Jonathon Tichy, Matthew Jarman, Jed K. Burton, Cory Talbot, David Garner, Eric Hunter, Erika Rowberry, Marc Porter, Michael Lopez, Nathan Jensen, Robert Roe, Tessa Santiago, Rod Andreason, Michele I. Cheney, Devaughn Fraser, and Richard Hawkins for their excellent assistance. We also are grateful to Professor Daryl Lee for his able English translations of the foreword by Special Rapporteur Abdelfattah Amor and the chapter by Doudou Diene. Most of all, we are thankful for the contributions of the various authors and for their patience through the editorial process.

The preproduction editing and formatting process would not have come together without the dedication, attention to detail, and hours of intensive labor of Kristen M. Bahlmann, Robert P. Schwartz, Rebecca S. Kellogg, Barbara Fuller, Peter Jasinki, and Christine Brown. Many thanks are also in order to the support and administrative team in Provo that helped push the book through to completion: Deborah Wright, Christine Scott, Kimberly Mantz, Marné Pieper, and Anthony Haws. We also appreciate

Tore Lindholm, W. Cole Durham, Jr., Bahia G. Tahzib-Lie (eds.), Facilitating Freedom of Religion or Belief: A Deskbook, *xxi–xxii.*

the support of Lindy Melman and Peter Buschman at Martinus Nijhoff/Brill. Finally, but certainly not least, we express appreciation for the great support, encouragement, and patience of our spouses and family members during the editorial and writing process.

We also would like to acknowledge the Artists Rights Society of New York, which granted us permission to use a copy of Picasso's *Dance of Youth* (© 2001 Estate of Pablo Picasso/Artists Rights Society [ARS], New York) on the cover of this book.

–The Editors

List of Abbreviations

1965 Convention	The United Nations Convention on the Elimination of All Forms of Racial Discrimination (1965)
1981 Declaration	Declaration on the Elimination of All Forms of Intolerance and of Discrimination Based on Religion or Belief (1981)
1990 Charter of Paris	Charter of Paris for a New Europe (1990)
ACHR	American Convention on Human Rights (1969)
African Charter	The African Charter on Human and Peoples' Rights (1981)
American Convention	American Convention on Human Rights (1969)
BCLR	Butterworths Constitutional Law Reports
BDPA	Beijing Declaration and Platform for Action of the Fourth World Conference on Women
Beijing +5 document	Report of the Ad Hoc Committee of the Whole of the 23rd special session of the UN General Assembly entitled Women 2000: Gender Equality, Development and Peace for the Twenty-First Century (2000)
BJP	Bharatiya Janata Party
BPA	Beijing Platform for Action of the Fourth World Conference on Women
CEC	Conference of European Churches
CEDAW	Convention on the Elimination of All Forms of Discrimination Against Women (1979)
CERD	Committee on the Elimination of Racial Discrimination
CESNUR	Centro Studi sulle Nuove Religioni (Center for Studies on New Religions)
CIS	Commonwealth of Independent States
COE	Council of Europe
Concluding Document of the Vienna Meeting	Concluding Document of the Vienna Meeting of Representatives of the Participating States of the Conference on Security and Co-operation in Europe (1986)

Convention of Belém do Pará Inter	American Convention on the Prevention, Punishment and Eradication of Violence against Women (1994)
Copenhagen Document	Document of the Copenhagen Meeting of Representatives of the Participating States of the Conference on the Human Dimension of the Conference on Security and Co-operation in Europe (1990)
CPCs	Countries of particular concern
CRC	Convention on the Rights of the Child
CSBMs	Confidence and Security Building Measures
CSCE	Conference for Security and Co-operation in Europe (now OSCE)
CTS	Consolidated Treaty Series
DEVAW	Declaration on the Elimination of Violence against Women (1993)
DRL	Bureau of Democracy, Human Rights and Labor in the US State Department
EC	European Communities
ECHR	European Convention on Human Rights (1950)
ECJ	European Court of Justice
EComHR	European Commission of Human Rights
ECOSOC	Economic and Social Council of the United Nations
ECR	European Court Reports
ECtHR	European Court of Human Rights
ETS	European Treaty Series
EU	European Union
European Convention	European Convention for the Protection of Human Rights and Fundamental Freedoms (1950)
FCRA	Foreign Contributions Regulation Act (1976)
FGM	female genital mutilation
FORB	freedom of religion or belief
Fourth Geneva Convention	Geneva Convention Relative to the Protection of Civilian Persons in Time of War (1949)
Framework Convention	Framework Convention for the Protection of National Minorities (1995)
FRY	Federal Republic of Yugoslavia
FSC	Forum for Security Co-operation
FYR Macedonia	Former Yugoslav Republic of Macedonia
GDR	German Democratic Republic
Geneva Convention I	Geneva Convention for the Amelioration of the Condition of the Wounded and Sick in Armed Forces in the Field (1949)
Geneva Convention II	Geneva Convention for the Amelioration of the Condition of Wounded, Sick and Shipwrecked Members of Armed Forces at Sea (1949)
Geneva Convention III	Geneva Convention Relative to the Treatment of Prisoners of War (1949)
Geneva Convention IV	Geneva Convention Relative to the Protection of Civilian Persons in Time of War (1949)

Genocide Convention	International Convention on the Prevention and Punishment of the Crime of Genocide (1948)
GONGO	governmental NGO
HCNM	High Commissioner on National Minorities
ICCPR	International Covenant on Civil and Political Rights (1966)
ICESCR	International Covenant on Economic, Social and Cultural Rights (1966)
ICJ	International Court of Justice
ICTR Statute	Statute of the International Criminal Tribunal for the Prosecution of Persons Responsible for Genocide and Other Serious Violations of International Humanitarian Law Committed in the Territory of Rwanda and Rwandan Citizens Responsible for Genocide and Other Such Violations Committed in the Territory of Neighboring States between 1 January 1994 and 31 December 1994 (1994)
ILC	International Law Commission of the United Nations
ILO	International Labor Organization
Implementation Report of the Secretary General	UN Secretary General, Implementation of the Declaration of on the Elimination of All Forms of Religious Intolerance and of Discrimination Based on Religion or Belief (1996)
INFORM	Information Network Focus on Religious Movements
Inter-American Commission	Inter-American Commission on Human Rights
Inter-Am Com HR	Inter-American Commission on Human Rights
IRF	Office of International Religious Freedom in the US State Department
IRFA	International Religious Freedom Act of 1998
ISKCON	International Society for Krishna Consciousness
LNTS	League of Nations Treaty Series
MILS	Mission interministérielle de lutte contre les sectes (French Interministerial Mission to Combat Sects)
Minorities Declaration	Declaration on the Rights of Persons Belonging to National or Ethnic, Religious, and Linguistic Minorities
NAACP	National Association for the Advancement of Colored People
NATO	North Atlantic Treaty Organization
NGO	Non-governmental organization
NIS	newly Independent States
NRM	new religious movement
OAS	Organization of American States
OAU	Organization of African Unity
ODIHR	Office for Democratic Institutions and Human Rights of the OSCE
OHR	Office of the High Representative of the International Community (in Bosnia)
OSCE	Organization for Security and Cooperation in Europe
QUANGO	quasi-NGO
RE	religious education

Rome Statute	Rome Statute of the International Criminal Court UN Doc. (2002)
SA	South Africa
SALR	South African Law Reports
SARA	State Administration of Religious Affairs
SFOR	Stabilisation Force in Bosnia and Herzegovina
Siracusa Principles	Siracusa Principles on the Limitation and Derogation Provisions in the International Covenant on Civil and Political Rights (1984)
The Hague Convention IV	The Hague Convention Respecting the Laws and Customs of War on Law (1907)
UDHR	Universal Declaration of Human Rights (1948)
UN Charter	United Nations Charter (1976)
UNDP	United Nations Development Programme
UNESCO	United Nations Educational, Scientific and Cultural Organization
UNFPA	United Nations Population Fund
UNHCHR	United Nations High Commissioner for Human Rights
UNHCR	United Nations High Commissioner for Refugees
UN HR Com	United Nations Human Rights Commission
UNICEF	United Nations International Children's Emergency Fund
UNIMIK	United Nations Interim Mission in Kosovo
Universal Declaration	Universal Declaration of Human Rights (1948)
USIP	United States Institute of Peace
WCC	World Council of Churches
WCRP	World Conference on Religion and Peace
WHO	World Health Organisation

Introduction

The Editors, with Nazila Ghanea

The Renewed Salience of Religion and Freedom of Religion or Belief

The challenge of freedom of religion or belief is as old as history, yet as current as today's headlines. It occupies some of humankind's most ancient narratives: Cain slew Abel following a dispute about the proper form of sacrifice;[1] Antigone buried Polyneices in a classic encounter of conscience with state power;[2] Prince Siddhartha Gautama had to turn from the allures of his father's court to follow the path of asceticism and ultimately enlightenment;[3] early in Islamic history exiled Muslims fleeing from persecution by the Quraysh tribe were given freedom to practice their religion under the protection of the Christian Emperor of Abyssinia.[4] But the challenge is more general. It arises wherever differences of fundamental beliefs create tensions in families or in communities, which seems to be virtually inescapable.

The underlying problems can take mild or acute forms, but they pervade human life, and the challenge has not receded with time. Contemporary struggles replicate ancient tragedies, too often on a far more massive scale. Witness the events of September 11, 2001 in the United States, March 11, 2004 in Spain, the litany of interreligious warfare in all too many countries, or recurrences of genocide that mock the post-holocaust motto, "never again." Other conflicts may be less life threatening, but if left to simmer too long, or under too much pressure, they also can explode.

As this volume was going to press, there were major public debates in several Western European countries about the acceptability of Muslim women (and girls) wearing the ***hijab***, or Islamic head scarf. In France major legislation prohibiting the wearing of ***hijab***, or comparable religious symbols, in public settings is in process. Taking just this one example, who can see all the ramifications of tensions and state

[1] Genesis 4:3–8.

[2] Sophocles, *Antigone*.

[3] E. H. Johnstone, *The Buddhacarita or Acts of the Buddha* (Calcutta, 1939).

[4] Muhammad Ibn Ishaq, *The Life of Muhammad*, trans. A. Guillaume (Islamabad: Oxford University Press, 1967).

Tore Lindholm, W. Cole Durham, Jr., Bahia G. Tahzib-Lie (eds.), Facilitating Freedom of Religion or Belief: A Deskbook, *xxvii–lxxiv. © 2004 Koninklijke Brill NV.*

action regarding the wearing of Muslim scarves that are currently arising in families, schools, employment, and countless other settings, in private and public, both in Europe and (by way of reaction and reverberation) throughout the Muslim world?

In the new millennium, the challenge seems at once greater and more urgent than ever before. It pervades the crucial sectors of modern life—from culture and civil society, to politics and identity, to security and conflict. Contrary to the prognostications of secularization theory, religion is not withering away. Rather, it is making a pronounced comeback in many parts of the world. But it is returning in many forms, and yielding a highly plural brew, particularly when viewed from a global perspective. Whatever one thinks of Huntington's "clash of civilizations" thesis, and the inevitability of conflict along religiously-based, civilizational lines,[5] the renewed prominence of religion has catapulted issues of freedom of religion or belief to center stage. From previously having been largely a specialist issue of interest to relatively few at the international level, its import can now scarcely be overestimated.

In the cultural sphere, the importance of this issue is evident in the tension between particularist claims and the view that human rights are genuinely universal. Some of the most contested problems in this context arise precisely in the field of freedom of religion or belief. These include issues of proselytism, the right to change one's religion, and the role of women as affected by religion. Impasse on these cultural issues helps to explain why the 1981 UN Declaration on the Elimination of All Forms of Intolerance and of Discrimination Based on Religion or Belief has been stalemated as a declaration and has not evolved into a legally binding covenant. Similarly, the 1993 Vienna World Conference on Human Rights did not succeed in crafting a new understanding on the universality or particularity of human rights. It merely acknowledged disagreement through its compromise language, giving continued recognition to the universality of human rights while accepting cultural and religious particularities as well.[6]

The significance of religion and belief and the freedom that protects them is also evident at the level of civil society. The associational rights that protect civil society organizations overlap with and reinforce the rights and freedoms that protect belief communities. The latter play a critical role in motivating, organizing, staffing, supporting, and partnering with civil society organizations to carry out countless projects that benefit society. Belief communities are a major repository of altruism and moral commitment. Civil society organizations, of course, reflect the full range of plurality of the societies in which they are found, and their interests may coincide with or diverge from those of religious organizations or the state. Sometimes this may lead to cooperation between public, religious, and governmental sectors. This is often the case in Europe and more recently has been evidenced in the United States by faith-based initiatives encouraged by United States President

[5] Samuel P. Huntington, *The Clash of Civilizations and the Remaking of World Order* (New York: Simon and Schuster, 1996).

[6] The Vienna Declaration and Programme of Action states in operative paragraph 5, "All human rights are universal, indivisible and interdependent and interrelated.... While the significance of national and regional particularities and various historical, cultural and religious backgrounds must be borne in mind, it is the duty of States, regardless of their political, economic and cultural systems, to promote and protect all human rights and fundamental freedoms."

George W. Bush.[7] Sometimes, however, alignments with religious communities can be divisive and can entrench conflicting cleavages. A potential remedy in this area is to encourage joint action that brings the efforts of different communities to bear on shared concerns. For example, the 2001 Cantle report on "Community Cohesion," commissioned by the Home Office in the United Kingdom, recommended that funds be allocated in such a way as to maximize contact, awareness, and activities *between* communities.[8]

The resurgence of religion is perhaps even more evident in politics. In this regard one thinks of the rise of the religious right and the significance of abortion politics in the United States, the rise of political Islam in many countries around the world, the significance of religion to the political movements that brought down communism in country after country in Eastern Europe, and so forth. In addition to these macro-political events, there is the constant flow of religion-related events that attract political interest and concern: the clergy sex abuse scandals in the United States are just one particularly sordid example.

Identity politics is yet another area implicating religion in major ways. Ethnicity and religion are often closely linked and have a long history of spawning conflict: Serb and Croat in Yugoslavia, Sunni and Shia in Iraq, Christian and Muslim in Indonesia. Identity politics is also in the emerging politics of sexual orientation. Issues of same-sex marriage have emerged as a major issue in United States presidential politics. Liberalization in this area is an emerging pattern in many parts of Europe. Sexual orientation has also become a significant issue in internal church politics in many denominations. To give only one example, the consecration of an openly active homosexual, Bishop Gene Robinson in New Hampshire, may yet split the worldwide Anglican Church.

Conflict and security have emerged as particularly urgent arenas in which religion has long been recognized as an important factor. Whether conflict is ***motivated*** by religion or ***aggravated*** by politicians who exploit religious identities is an ongoing discussion. However, the link itself is undeniable, and is illustrated by all too many recent episodes. Intercommunal violence led to the killing of twenty-one Copts in al-Kosheh in Upper Egypt in January 2000. Horrific bloodshed resulted from the violence between religious groups in Gujarat, India in spring 2002. In autumn 2002 sectarian violence left hundreds dead when violence was unleashed in Nigeria during the attempted hosting of the Miss World beauty contest. The decade of the 1990s witnessed interreligious conflicts in the former Yugoslavia, intercommunal killings in Northern Ireland, and slaughters in Algeria and the Sudan. The potential link between religion and

---

[7] January 2001 saw President George Bush expand government funding to faith-based organizations. He also set up a new White House Office of Faith-Based and Community Initiatives to give such organizations greater access to federal funds.

[8] The Home Office commissioned the Cantle report of December 2001 in response to the summer 2001 riots in the northern English towns that left hundreds injured and community relations in tatters. Cantle found that the towns where the riots occurred had been deeply polarized with segregated ethnic communities living "a series of parallel lives." It criticized the funding of separate and distinct community interests, as this tended to reinforce cultural differences. The report instead recommended that a government funding regime be set up to create an ethos "which constantly promotes joint work and collaboration" across communities. It recommended that funding bodies should require collaborative working and generally be provided both on a thematic basis and based on needs across communities.

violence has been evidenced in another way by suicides and attacks that have arisen from time to time in connection with unusual new religious movements in the United States, Japan, Switzerland, France, and Belgium.

While the dark side of religion and violence cannot be ignored, it is vital to remember that belief communities also play a potent role in conflict prevention, conflict resolution, post-conflict reconciliation, and general social stabilization. Religions have been guilty of contributing to tensions leading to war, but their fundamental message is peace. As Rüdiger Noll's chapter in this volume notes, religious leaders have often played particularly courageous roles in helping to find ways to resolve conflicts. They are often vital to achieving spiritual reconciliation, which is a necessary precondition to other more tangible forms of rebuilding after conflict. More generally, religion plays critical roles in inculcating habits of honesty, industry, loyalty, and numerous other traits without which societies would have difficulty functioning. The resurgence of religion around the world reflects most fundamentally the attractions of these positive sides of religion.

The tragic events of September 11, 2001 have prompted a tectonic shift in thinking about the relationship of religion, freedom, and security. These events provided a powerful reminder of the vulnerability of civilization—vulnerability that has been hammered home by bomb blasts in many other parts of the world, emphasizing that no homeland is secure. But in too many cases, this shared international experience has prompted overreaction. Human rights have been sacrificed to the supposed necessities of security. History's lesson, echoed in the key United Nations declaration on point, is too often forgotten: "the disregard and infringement of human rights and fundamental freedoms, in particular of the right to freedom of thought, conscience, religion or whatever belief, have brought, directly or indirectly, wars and great suffering to mankind. . . ."[9] What the rush to protect security forgets is that security purchased with the suppression of rights is only a stopgap. Temporary expedients may be necessary, but a solution that fails to protect rights is at best an illusion, and an illusion without a future. Injustice lacks long-term stability.

Far from withering away, then, religion has assumed new salience. But this has stirred new anxieties. The "ambivalence of the sacred"[10]—the fact that religion spawns both good and evil—has led on the one hand to a global resurgence of religion and on the other to global pressures to mitigate religious hazards. This in turn has given new urgency to questions of how to structure the freedom of religion or belief. In our pluralistic world, the alternatives are stark. Either we must find ways for groups with differing beliefs to live together (which appears to be possible only by respecting freedom of religion or belief, whether through state-enforced protections or through internalizing norms of respect for the dignity and religious choices of others), or we must face constant friction, all too frequent warfare, and the ultimate risk of nuclear Armageddon.

---

9 Preamble, United Nations Declaration on the Elimination of All Forms of Intolerance and of Discrimination Based on Religion or Belief (hereinafter "1981 Declaration").

10 See R. Scott Appleby, *The Ambivalence of the Sacred: Religion, Violence, and Reconciliation* (Oxford: Rowman & Littlefield Publishers, 2000).

Faced with these ineluctable alternatives, the right to freedom of religion or belief has the complex task of protecting religion and its potential for good while permitting certain limitations designed to filter out religion's negative hazards. In this sense, the right to freedom of religion or belief addresses both poles of the ambivalence of the sacred. It also bridges both universal and particular: it constitutes a ***universal*** call to respect ***particular*** world views and requires ***particular*** faiths to endorse ***universal*** religious freedom. But recognition that the right to freedom of religion or belief is designed to address these polarities—the ambivalence of the sacred and the tension of universal and particular—does not mean that translating it into practice is easy or automatic. Rather, it calls for continual striving to find sensitive ways to facilitate accommodation of religious and cultural differences within a broad framework of interpersonal and intercultural respect.

Facilitating Freedom of Religion or Belief

The present volume is the outgrowth of efforts to foster just such "continual striving" to facilitate freedom of religion or belief. The original impetus for the book came from the 1998 Oslo Conference on Freedom of Religion or Belief, a remarkable conference that was originally organized as part of efforts to celebrate the fiftieth anniversary of the Universal Declaration of Human Rights. This book is just one of many contributions that continue to flow from that seminal conference, and, indeed, the length of its gestation is attributable in no small part to the fact that its editors and authors have been at the forefront of a wide range of initiatives that exemplify the kind of "continual striving" that is needed. Some of these initiatives have followed as a direct result of the Oslo Conference; others have been part of broader efforts at the national and international level that the Oslo Conference hoped to support. Direct involvement of our authors in the unfolding course of events as noted in the following paragraphs has enriched the sense of engagement throughout the volume, sharpening awareness both of the issues that need to be addressed and of the measures that make a difference.

Funded by the Norwegian government and organized in association with the Council for Religious and Life Stance Communities in Norway, the Oslo Conference was a unique gathering of government officials, experts, intergovernmental actors, and representatives of various NGOs. The aim of the conference was to re-energize efforts aimed at effective enforcement of article 18 of the Universal Declaration of Human Rights. The conference used a networking methodology, reflected in the many differing voices and organizations it brought together, to focus on both the substance of the right and the modalities of its implementation.

The unique blend of deep understanding of the issues combined with commitment to finding practical ways forward among conference participants is reflected in the concluding document of the conference, the Oslo Declaration on Freedom of Religion or Belief (included as Appendix F to this volume). Framed by participants at the conference, the Oslo Declaration was also subsequently signed by representatives of twenty-five religious and life-stance communities in Norway on November 8, 2001. Even now, rereading this Declaration recalls the energy and commitment of the Oslo Conference. Beyond reassertion of the core values codified in international norms on freedom of religion or belief, the Oslo Declaration exudes commitment to make a difference. It identifies the key international norms as "a universal standard around which we wish to *rally.*" It recognizes practical needs for additional financial and personnel support for those in international institutions tasked with working on tolerance and freedom of religion or belief. At the same time, it calls for greater efficiency in use of resources that are available. It inventories the range of bodies that can make a difference, and challenges them to create educational and other programs that can contribute in practical ways to building a culture of tolerance. And so forth.

One of the most significant results of the Conference was that the participants, in the second recital of the Oslo Declaration, "accepted the challenge to build an international coalition and to develop a strategic plan of action to achieve substantial progress in and give practical support to the implementation of Article 18 . . . ." Responding to this challenge and the final paragraph of the Declaration, the organizers and sponsors of the Oslo Conference created the Oslo Coalition on Freedom of Religion or Belief. While based in Norway, the Coalition has maintained a broad outlook and international connections from the beginning. Among other things, it has a distinguished International Advisory Council; some of its members have authored chapters for this volume or have participated in other Oslo Coalition projects.

From the beginning, the Oslo Coalition has been committed to action, and in particular to practical action likely to have broad impact supportive of other international initiatives. It has aimed to facilitate freedom of religion or belief within a genuinely international framework—the level at which its activities are concentrated. The Oslo Coalition generally does not focus on the interests of particular individuals or religious groups, nor is it engaged in carrying out monitoring activities. While such activities are clearly vital, the Oslo Coalition has sought to avoid duplicating the work of other international organizations and NGOs that already carry out these tasks.

Rather, the Coalition has undertaken a number of projects with far broader impact. For example, the Coalition has played a significant role in supporting the UN's International Consultative Conference on School Education in Relation with Freedom of Religion and Belief, Tolerance and Non-discrimination held in Madrid from November 21–23, 2001. Prior to the conference, the Coalition took an active role in reviewing and commenting on documents. Also, in April 2001 it organized a side meeting in Geneva at the time of the UN Commission on Human Rights annual session entitled "Religious Education in Pluralistic Societies: Aims and Challenges." The objective was to help prepare and deepen thinking in advance of the November Conference. The Coalition has organized follow-up efforts aimed at acting on recommendations from the conference. Jolanta Ambrosewicz-Jacobs describes the recommendations of the conference in chapter 37, and Ingvill Plesner uses data from the conference as part of the basis for her analysis in chapter 36 of ways that tolerance can be promoted in the context of education. Coalition work in this area has now grown into an impressive ongoing program, including a major conference in September of 2004 and global networking efforts to identify appropriate models and best practices for teaching tolerance.[11]

[11] See the website of the Oslo Coalition, <http://www.oslocoalition.org/html/project_school_education/index.html> (last visited March 20, 2004), for an overview on current programs.

The Oslo Coalition has also been actively involved in conferences promoting improved implementation of freedom of religion or belief among religious leaders and government officials charged with making and administering public policy in Central Asia and the Caucasus. This initiative started with co-sponsorship of conferences with the Russian Academy of State Service in Moscow in 2000 and 2001. The Coalition's involvement made it possible to bring officials to Moscow from some of the outlying areas. Connections from these early conferences rapidly became the basis for projects in Azerbaijan (2000, 2002, 2003), the northern Caucasus (2002), and Central Asia (2003).

In addition to taking advantage of opportunities to work directly with key government officials and religious leaders in these projects, the Coalition has played a distinctive role by sharing the Norwegian experience with interfaith dialogue. This experience is described in considerable detail by Inge Eidsvåg, Tore Lindholm, and Barbro Sveen in chapter 35. In particular, in the various regional conferences, Coalition representatives laid recurrent emphasis on the fact that finding common projects that different religious groups can work on jointly is often much more effective in building trust and understanding than formal dialogues on theological themes. Significantly, that experience was being applied in practice in various settings in the former Soviet Union at the same time the chapter describing the Norwegian experience was being written, resulting in valuable synergies. In retrospect, the Oslo Conference itself can be seen as an application of this methodology—bringing numerous groups together to work on the common project of promoting freedom of religion or belief for all—and the initial methodological insight is having a significant impact in other areas.

The Coalition has also undertaken major projects in China and Indonesia, which have added both geographic and substantive scope to its efforts. The China initiative has involved a series of exchanges with Chinese experts aimed at promoting dialogue on freedom of religion and belief issues. The Coalition is acutely aware of some of the areas and religions of China that have suffered most from violations of freedom of religion or belief. The Coalition's work in China has demonstrated its ability to build constructive channels for sensitive dialogue on human rights performance. In Indonesia, against the background of tragic violence associated with interreligious tensions, similar exchanges have focused on establishing relationships between faith groups and academics with the aim of adding conflict resolution efforts to the Coalition's repertoire of promoting interfaith dialogue and human rights compliance. These efforts have sought to apply in practice many of the ideas highlighted by Rüdiger Noll in chapter 33, on "The Role of Religion and Religious Freedom in Contemporary Conflict Situations."

In 2002 the Coalition added another major initiative of tremendous potential significance: the Project on New Directions in Islamic Thought and Practice. Here efforts are aimed at "creating a forum where Muslim reform thinkers may present and discuss ideas and develop strategies for further action."[12] As in so many other areas, this initiative couples academic expertise, networking, and a strong interest in allowing groups to

[12] Oslo Coalition website, <http://www.oslocoalition.org/html/project_new_horizons/index.html> (last visited March 20, 2004).

think through their own issues in dialogue within a religious tradition and across traditional divides. One important sub-theme for this project is Islam, Women, and Religious Freedom. Islam is sometimes used as an argument for practices that flout standards of human rights. Conflicts and tensions with respect to CEDAW provisions are well known. Not so widely known is the fact that Muslim women's issues raise questions of freedom of religion or belief. Several major challenges regarding Muslim women hinge on contestable interpretations of Islam. Solutions may be sought by way of new readings and interpretation, as proposed by Shirin Ebadi, Nobel Peace Prize Laureate for 2003.

In 2004 the Coalition initiated a project on Proselytism and Human Rights. This has become an urgent religious freedom topic, in a time of post-colonialism, post-communism, and religious resurgence. The project addresses questions about human rights as well as broader concerns about appropriate behavior and ethical standards for the conduct of missionary activity.

Of course, it is not only the activities of the Oslo Coalition itself that have absorbed the energies of our authors. The years since the Oslo Conference have witnessed a number of significant developments affecting freedom of religion or belief, and these have engaged our authors in countless ways. Many have vast experience in United Nations settings. Professor Theo van Boven, author of chapter 7 on the UN Commission on Human Rights, for example, has vast experience, having served for many years on various United Nations human rights bodies, including his current appointment for the Commission as Special Rapporteur on the question of torture and other cruel, inhuman or degrading treatment or punishment. Martin Scheinin, author of chapter 8 on the UN Human Rights Committee, currently serves as a member of that Committee. Manfred Nowak, co-author of chapter 6 on limitations clauses, has also served in many positions dealing with human rights in the UN system. Doudou Diene, author of chapter 9 on "UNESCO's Facilitation of Freedom of Religion or Belief," has worked in various capacities at UNESCO ever since his days as Senegal's representative to UNESCO in the 1970s. In particular, he has had many high-level assignments involving him in UNESCO dialogue projects. Many of the other authors, such as Natan Lerner and Johan van der Vyver, are well-known experts on human rights norms, both in the United Nations and other settings.

Other authors have had significant experience in other emerging institutional settings. For example, the Organization for Security and Cooperation in Europe (OSCE) has been an important energy center for freedom of religion or belief over the past five years. Norway assumed the Chairmanship of the OSCE in 1999, shortly after the Oslo Conference, allowing many of the ideas from the conference to have direct influence. Janne Haaland Matlary was State Secretary for Foreign Affairs of Norway during this period and was thus in a particularly good position to write chapter 12, in which she gives an account of how implementation of religious freedom norms could best be advanced from within the Chairmanship. Bahia Tahzib-Lie also had an insider's perspective while working at the Human Rights Division of the Human Rights and Peacebuilding Department of the Dutch Ministry of Foreign Affairs. She played a major role in organizing a seminar on "Freedom of Religion or Belief in the OSCE Region: Challenges to Law and Practice" that was sponsored by the Foreign Ministry of the Netherlands in The Hague in June 2001 in cooperation with the Romanian Chair-in-Office of the OSCE.

Another significant development over the last five years has been the work of the Advisory Panel on Freedom of Religion or Belief, created under the auspices of the OSCE's Office of Democratic Institutions and Human Rights. The Advisory Panel has emerged as a significant resource for strengthening religious freedom commitments in OSCE participating states. Several of our authors have played significant roles in this regard. Rüdiger Noll has served as overall chair for the Panel and has co-chaired the working group on conflict resolution with Bahia Tahzib-Lie. Cole Durham has served as a co-chair on legislative matters, with Karen Lord, Jeremy Gunn, and Roman Podoprigora serving with his working group. Jolanta Ambrosewicz-Jacobs has been a co-chair regarding educational issues, with Urban Gibson serving as one of the members of the working group on education.

Still another significant institutional development over the past five years was the passage of the International Religious Freedom Act in the United States. Passed just a few weeks after the Oslo Conference in 1998, this led to the creation of an office in the US State Department headed by an Ambassador-at-Large charged with responsibility for religious freedom matters, establishment of the United States Commission on International Religious Freedom, and new requirements for annual reports by the US State Department on the compliance of nations around the world with international standards governing freedom of religion or belief. This development has been controversial both within the United States and abroad, but at a minimum it has helped focus attention on religious freedom issues and, since US embassies around the world are charged with collecting information for these reports, has provided an impetus for dialogue on current issues in every country. Jeremy Gunn, who served as a principal adviser to the first Ambassador-at-Large and also as the first director of research for the Commission on International Religious Freedom, was uniquely placed to write chapter 32, which gives a more detailed picture of how the new United States institutions emerged and what they were designed to do. Tad Stahnke, author of chapter 27 on "The Right to Engage in Religious Persuasion," also has significant background with the Commission, serving as Deputy Director for Policy for the Commission as this volume goes to press.

Of course, it is not only institutions but also particular issues that have attracted the engagement of our authors. This will be described in due course. The point is that the book has benefited immeasurably from the immersion of its authors in the practical realities of building more effective mechanisms for implementing this fundamental freedom. Moreover, in large part because of direct engagement with developments in the field, the book has evolved in significant ways since it was first envisioned.

The original intention had been just to publish a selection of the conference papers presented in 1998. However, as the project developed the editors realized the need for a work with more comprehensive coverage that could serve as a consolidated reference to all aspects of freedom of religion or belief. About a year after the original conference, the idea of publishing a "deskbook" emerged. This entailed totally revamping the organization of the volume to be published and recruiting busy scholars already immersed in activities such as those described above. Active engagement continued to suggest new topics that led to expanding the scope of the volume. One of the inevitable results has been that different chapters have been completed at very different times. Between the crush of pressures on the editors and the complexity of managing a volume with so many authors from so many countries, it has simply not been possible to assure that every article could take into account all events up to a uniform cutoff date. Our sense, however, is that this is not a critical problem. Our aim has not been to provide an up-to-the-minute report on developments, but rather to provide a comprehensive picture of the full complex of ideas, applicable norms, institutional leverage points, key emerging issues, and contexts relevant to facilitating freedom of religion or belief. This the various chapters amply provide. If the lives of those working on the book had been less busy and less intensively engaged in furthering the aims of the book in practical settings, the book would no doubt have appeared earlier. We hope there will be understanding for the trade-offs we have been forced to make.

It goes without saying that the authors in this volume each have their own views, and disagree with each other on many points. In this sense, the deskbook itself has been an example of the kind of dialogue that the Oslo Coalition fosters. It is important to emphasis that the views of each of the authors are theirs alone and do not necessarily represent the views of the Oslo Coalition, the editors, or other authors. The deskbook is a collaborative project aimed at identifying core notions of freedom of religion or belief and ideas for better implementing its ideals. The deskbook responds itself to this ideal recognizing the importance of respecting the range of views held by the different authors in the volume, coming as they do from many different countries and belief traditions.

One shortcoming of the volume of which we are acutely conscious is that despite strenuous efforts, the overwhelming majority of the chapters are written by experts from the West. No one working on the project had any doubt that understanding of the issues would be deepened by interaction with experts from other parts of the world. While it has not been possible to satisfactorily address this concern within the actual pages of the book, it is anticipated that the Oslo Coalition, working with partners from other regions, will sponsor conferences and other activities designed to stimulate the kind of trans-cultural dialogue on freedom of religion or belief that has not been adequately captured in the book. Our hope, then, is that the book will be viewed as a starting point for deepened dialogue on the relevant issues, and not as an incomplete endpoint of discussion.

The Normative Core of Freedom of Religion or Belief

Before turning to a more detailed overview of the contents of this volume, it seems appropriate to identify briefly what we have come to regard as the normative core of the right to freedom of religion or belief. As we have worked with the range of issues covered by this volume, we have come to a fuller understanding of the complexity of the values involved. We understand that the issues involved arise in a host of different historical and cultural contexts, and that the institutional arrangements in any particular society will inevitably vary in many ways. But there are certain core values that will be protected and features that a regime will exhibit if freedom of religion or belief is respected. These constitute a set of minimum standards; obviously, many systems go much further in building genuine cultures of tolerance and mutual respect.

Freedom of religion or belief, in its current historical form,[13] is a universally applicable *human right* codified in international human rights instruments. At the normative level, it has been clear from the beginning of the modern human rights era that freedom of religion or belief is a *fundamental* right,[14] and indeed one of the preeminent fundamental rights. Emerging from the ashes of the Second World War, the right has been articulated most authoritatively in article 18 of both the Universal Declaration of Human Rights and the International Covenant on Civil and Political Rights. Individuals—all human beings everywhere in the world—are the primary holders and beneficiaries of this freedom; states—ideally under continual critical scrutiny by informed citizens—are the primary addressees and thus the primary holders of the correlative obligations. Beyond the religious freedom provisions of the Universal Declaration and the ICCPR, key elaborations and specifications of the human right to freedom of religion or belief are provided by, inter alia, the 1981 Declaration, the European Convention for the Protection of Human Rights and Fundamental Freedoms, the American Convention on Human Rights, the Concluding Document of the Vienna Meeting of Representatives of the Participating States of the CSCE (particularly its principles 16 and 17). The United Nations Human Rights Committee General Comment No. 22 (48) provides normative substance to article 18 of the ICCPR.

The normative core of the human right to freedom of religion or belief may be condensed to eight components:[15]

1. *Internal freedom:* Everyone has the right to freedom of thought, conscience and religion; this right includes freedom for all to have, adopt, maintain or change[16] religion or belief.[17]

---

[13] See Evans, chapter 1 of this volume.

[14] One clear sign of this is the fact that religious freedom protections are nonderogable.

[15] The key provisions drawn on are article 18 of the Universal Declaration; article 18.1 to 18.4, article 2.2 and article 4.2 of the ICCPR and article 14 of the CRC. See also the 1981 Declaration; article 9 of the ECHR; article 12 of the ACHR; article 8 of the ACHPR; and Principles 16 and 17 of the Concluding Document of the Vienna Meeting of Representatives of the Participating States of the CSCE. Component 6 differs from the other eight, in that it is implied from rather than directly stated in the express language of the relevant treaties. See note 21 below.

[16] While the notion that freedom of religion or belief includes the right to "have or adopt" a religion is undisputed, there has been considerable controversy about whether it includes the right to "change." The Universal Declaration (article 18) and major regional treaties (ECHR, art. 9[1]; ACHR, art 12[1]), as well as leading commentaries recognize that this is an integral part of freedom of religion or belief. See, e.g., John P. Humphrey, "Political and Related Rights," in *Human Rights in International Law: Legal and Policy Issues*, ed. Theodor Meron (Oxford: Clarendon Press, 1984), 171, 179; Richard B. Lillich, "Civil Rights," in *Human Rights in International Law: Legal and Policy Issues,* ed. Theodor Meron (Oxford: Clarendon Press, 1984), 115, 159; Manfred Nowak, *U.N. Covenant on Civil and Political Rights, CCPR Commentary* (Kehl/Strasbourg/Arlington: N.P. Engel, 1993), 316; Karl Josef Partsch, "Freedom of Conscience and Expression, and Political Freedoms," *The International Bill of Rights: The Covenant on Civil and Political Rights*, ed. Louis Henkin (New York: Columbia University Press, 1981), 209, 211. Commenting on the "have or adopt" locution that was settled upon in the ICCPR in an effort to avoid controversy with Muslim countries over the word "change." The UN Human Rights Committee has observed that "the freedom to "have or to adopt" a religion or belief necessarily entails the freedom to choose a religion or belief, including, inter alia, the right to replace one's current religion or belief with another or to adopt atheistic views, as well as the right to retain one's religion or belief." General Comment 22 (48), para. 5; see also Ghanea, chapter 29, 670–75. In our view, this is tantamount to saying that freedom of religion implicitly includes the

2. *External freedom:* Everyone has the freedom, either alone or in community with others, in public or private, to manifest his or her religion or belief in teaching, practice, worship and observance.[18]
3. *Noncoercion:* No one shall be subject to coercion that would impair his or her freedom to have or to adopt a religion or belief of his or her choice.[19]
4. *Nondiscrimination:* States are obliged to respect and to ensure to all individuals within their territory and subject to their jurisdiction the right to freedom of religion or belief without distinction of any kind, such as race, color, sex, language, religion or belief, political or other opinion, national or other origin, property, birth or other status.[20]
5. *Rights of parents and guardians:* States are obliged to respect the liberty of parents, and, when applicable, legal guardians to ensure the religious and moral education of their children in conformity with their own convictions, subject to providing protection for the rights of each child to freedom of religion or belief consistent with the evolving capacities of the child.[21]
6. *Corporate freedom and legal status:* A vital aspect of freedom of religion or belief, particularly in contemporary settings, is for religious communities to have standing and institutional rights to represent their rights and interests as communities. That is, religious communities themselves have freedom of religion or belief, including a right to autonomy in their own affairs. While religious communities may not wish to avail themselves of formal legal entity status, it is now widely recognized that they have a right

freedom to change without using the word. Thus, while we understand that there may be disagreement, we believe that freedom of religion or belief in the present-day world necessarily includes the right to change religion or life stance. At the same time, we note that a particular religion or religious community is free to take the position that a person who has changed religion and departed from the faith may be excluded from the religious community and be the subject of religious discipline, but the individual's civil and political rights should not be reduced as a result.

[17] The HRC General Comment to article 18 of the ICCPR clarifies that, "Article 18 protects theistic, non-theistic and atheistic beliefs, as well as the right not to profess any religion or belief." The human right to freedom of religion or belief is therefore intended to equally protect believers and nonbelievers, religions and beliefs.

[18] ICCPR, art. 18(1); ECHR, art. 9(1).

[19] ICCPR, art. 18(2).

[20] Antidiscrimination norms, and in particular, norms that bar discrimination on the basis of freedom of religion or belief, pervade the key international instruments. See, e.g., UDHR, art. 2; ICCPR, art. 2(1); ECHR, art. 14 ("the rights and freedoms set forth in this Convention shall be secured without discrimination on any ground such as . . . religion"); ACHR, art. 1(1)(States Parties undertake to ensure "free and full exercise of those rights and freedoms, without any discrimination for reasons of . . . religion"). Moreover, as the UN Human Rights Committee has noted, restrictions on religious freedom "may not be imposed for discriminatory purposes or applied in a discriminatory manner." UN Human Rights Committee, General Comment No. 22(48), para. 8. Thus, the nondiscrimination norm is built into the requirement that limitations on religious freedom be "necessary" in order to be permissible under article 18 of the ICCPR. Similarly, articles 2 and 3 of the 1981 Declaration make it clear that discrimination is inconsistent with freedom of religion or belief. In general, the emphasis on nondiscrimination is so pervasive that one might almost conclude not only that non-discrimination is central to the normative core of freedom of religion or belief, but that the norm in question is *only* an equality norm. In our view, however, as emphasized by listing nondiscrimination along with the other elements of the normative core, it is vital not to forget the *freedom* dimension of the right, acknowledging of course that this is a freedom all are equally entitled to claim.

[21] ICCPR, art. 18(4); CRC, art. 14. See also chapter 24 in this volume.

to acquire legal entity status as part of their right to freedom of religion or belief and in particular as an aspect of the freedom to manifest religious beliefs not only individually, but in community with others.[22]

7. *Limits of permissible restrictions on external freedom:* Freedom to manifest one's religion or belief may be subject only to such limitations as are prescribed by law and are necessary to protect public safety, order, health, or morals or the fundamental rights of others.[23]
8. *Nonderogability:* States may make no derogation from the right to freedom of religion or belief, not even in times of public emergency.[24]

These eight components of the human right to freedom of religion or belief can be identified from amongst the complex body of mutually supporting, internationally codified, human rights norms. When applied to particular contexts and for practical

---

[22] The corporate dimension of freedom of religion or belief is analyzed in much greater depth in chapters 14 (Roland Minnerath's treatment of religious autonomy) and 15 (Cole Durham's analysis of religious association laws). See, especially, Minnerath, chapter 14, 291–93; Durham, chapter 15, 321–25, 356–57, 365–66, 370–77. The key treaty language from the ICCPR states that the right to "freedom of thought conscience and religion . . . shall include . . . freedom, either individually *or in community with others* and in public or private, to manifest his religion . . . ." ICCPR, art. 18 (emphasis added). We believe that the binding status of the corporate freedom component of the normative core is implicitly recognized in article 18, and can be deduced from existing standards, the factual necessities of protecting individual rights, and the jurisprudence that has emerged. See, e.g., Metropolitan Church of Bessarabia v. Moldova, ECtHR, App. No. 45701/99, 13 December 2001. There has been disagreement over the years as to whether freedom of religion or belief has the corporate, "group rights" dimension identified in this sixth component of the normative core. The alternative was to hold that the international instruments created only individual rights, and that to the extent religious groups were granted standing to represent rights of religious communities, they were doing so only in a derivative capacity. In many respects, this is merely a metaphysical dispute, because as a functional matter, the rights of religious communities have been consistently recognized and protected. In fact, freedom of religion or belief has collective dimensions that cannot be fully protected without an institutional rights bearer (typically with some type of corporate form or legal entity status) that can stand for and express the rights of the community. See generally chapters 16 and 17. Accordingly, we have concluded that there is a corporate dimension that belongs to the normative core of freedom of religion or belief. Even if there is a disagreement on the point whether collectivities can themselves be right bearers, there can be no doubt that there is a collective dimension to the religious freedom rights held in common by the many members of religious communities.

[23] ICCPR, art. 18(3); ECHR, art. 9(2); UN Human Rights Committee, General Comment No. 22 (48), adopted by the UN Human Rights Committee on July 20, 1993, UN Doc. CCPR/C/21/Rev.1/Add.4 (1993), reprinted in UN Doc. HRI/GEN/1/Rev.1 at 35 (1994). It is important to emphasize that while some limitations on the scope of freedom of religion or belief are necessary, they are to be construed very narrowly in order to maximize the scope of the freedom. The strictness of the constraints on limitations is analyzed in depth by Manfred Nowak and Tanja Vospernik in chapter 6 of this volume. Failure to understand the strictly limited nature of the limitations can itself pose a hazard to the freedom.

[24] ICCPR, art. 4(2). The right to freedom of religion or belief was not listed among the nonderogable rights under the ECHR, but all parties to the ECHR have subsequently ratified the ICCPR, and are thereby obligated to recognize the nonderogable character of the right to freedom of religion or belief. ECHR, art. 15(1) provides that derogations are permissible "under this Convention [only] to the extent strictly required by the exigencies of the situation, provided that such measures are not inconsistent with its other obligations under international law." Thus, freedom of religion or belief would now appear, at least indirectly, to be a nonderogable right under the ECHR. Of course, the fact that the right to freedom of religion or belief is nonderogable does not mean that limitations may not be imposed on manifestations in that limited range of circumstances where the limitations clauses of international instruments permit.

purposes, these norms may need further interpretation and elaboration. For example, early doubts about whether freedom of religion or belief necessarily implied that religious communities could be rights bearers and that these rights could have a corporate dimension have now been largely resolved in favor of the existence of such institutional rights. Within the Council of Europe and the OSCE, for example, it is now recognized with particular clarity that the right to freedom of religion and the right to freedom of association entail the right of religious communities to acquire legal entity status in order to carry out their affairs.[25] Similarly, it is clear that religious communities are to enjoy broad autonomy.[26] In addition to receiving additional elaboration, the elements of the normative core receive independent reinforcement from other human rights norms that often have vital significance for the exercise and enjoyment of religious freedom,[27] notably freedom of expression, freedom of assembly, freedom of association, and freedom of movement.[28]

While freedom of religion or belief applies to ***individual human beings,*** it also includes protection of ***community activities*** (component 2 above) and ***intergenerational relations*** (component 5 above). Religion or belief ***communities*** benefit from the protection granted community activities. States are burdened with the correlative obligation to safeguard collective as well as institutional religious group rights.[29]

As the enumeration of the core elements of freedom of religion or belief makes clear, this is a complex right, containing sub-elements that overlap with a variety of values protected by other human rights. This has led to tendencies to interpret freedom of religion or belief through the conceptual filter of other norms to which the various sub-elements of religious freedom are linked, such as equality or freedom of expression or the rule of law. Some have gone even further, recommending that freedom of religion be reduced to or supplanted by one of these other norms. These tendencies impoverish our understanding of freedom of religion or belief and fail to understand the extent to which the differing values constitute a seamless web crucial as a whole to protecting the fragile yet vital interactions of belief, action, and community that constitute belief systems.

Clearly facilitating the human right to freedom of religion or belief is not limited exclusively to providing legal protection for the eight core components identified above. Furthermore, there is more to freedom of religion or belief than human rights protection. Many countries provide additional, more concrete protections in

---

[25] See Sidiropoulos v. Greece, ECtHR, App. No. 26695/95, 10 July 1998; Hasan and Chaush v. Bulgaria, ECtHR, Application No. 30985/96, 26 October 2000; Canea Catholic Church v. Greece, ECtHR, App. No. 25528/94, 16 December 1997; Freedom and Democracy Party v. Turkey, ECtHR, App. No. 23885/94, 8 December 1999.

[26] See principle 16, Vienna Concluding Document; Hasan and Chaush v. Bulgaria, ECtHR, Application No. 30985/96, 26 October 2000; Serif v. Greece, ECtHR, App. No. 38178/97, 14 December 1999; Bessarabian Metropolitan Church v. Moldova, ECtHR, App. No. 45701/99, 13 December 2001.

[27] Most chapters in the present volume are devoted to the study of specific aspects of freedom of religion or belief, examining issues of international law, domestic legislation, administrative structures and functions, as well as particular historical, social, and cultural contexts.

[28] ICCPR articles 19, 21, 22, and 12 respectively.

[29] For the distinction between individual, collective, and institutional group rights, see chapter 4 of this volume. The rights of religious groups are spelled out in article 6 of the 1981 Declaration and in articles 16 and 17 of the Vienna Concluding Document.

their constitutional or legal orders. Such national elaborations are largely shaped by the religion-state structure, which stretches from various forms of "separation" through to establishment of religion and identification of the state with a particular religion. Countries that provide for "separation" of religion and state do so in different formats and to different effects. This can range from the benign neutrality in the United States, through various types of *laïcité* or secularism, to the harsh separation that existed in former socialist bloc regimes. Countries that allow for various degrees of "establishment" of religion may make legal provision for significant cooperation with, and financial support of, religious institutions.

The institutional configuration of religion-state relations reflects diverse histories, cultures, and political compromises. The core values protected under the auspices of freedom of religion or belief allow for a broad range of options in the ways that different states structure the relationship with religion, belief communities, and individual believers.[30] However, there is a core set of values, including at least the eight identified above, that constitute the ***minimum*** requirements for a just society and for protection of the universal right to freedom of religion or belief.

The large majority of the world's nations, including those containing the overwhelming majority of the world's population, have ratified the key international instruments affirming this right. Even if this were not the case, however, the right to freedom of religion or belief is so fundamental and so widely accepted that it is generally held to be protected as part of customary international law.[31]

---

[30] See UN Human Rights Committee, General Comment 22 (48), para. 9.

[31] See, e.g., Philip Alston, "The Universal Declaration at 35: Western and Passé or Alive and Universal," *The Review of the International Commission of Jurists* 31 (1983): 60, 69 (arguing that the Universal Declaration is customary law); Richard Bilder, "The Status of International Human Rights Law: An Overview," in *International Human Rights Law and Practice,* ed. James Tuttle (Chicago: American Bar Association, 1978), 1, 8 (arguing that the Universal Declaration is customary law); Derek Davis, "The Evolution of Religious Freedom as a Universal Human Right: Examining the Role of the 1981 United Nations Declaration on the Elimination of all Forms of Intolerance and of Discrimination Based on Religion or Belief," *BYU Law Review* (2002): 217, 230 (arguing that the 1981 Declaration is customary law); Louis Henkin, *The Age of Rights* (New York: Columbia University Press, 1990), 19 (arguing that the Universal Declaration is customary law); John Humphrey, *No Distant Millennium: The International Law of Human Rights* (Paris: UNESCO, 1989), 155 (arguing that the Universal Declaration is customary law); John Humphrey, "The International Bill of Rights: Scope and Implementation," *William and Mary Law Review* 17 (1976): 527, 529 (arguing that the Universal Declaration is customary law); Richard B. Lillich, "Civil Rights," in *Human Rights in International Law: Legal and Policy Issues,* ed. Theodor Meron (Oxford: Clarendon Press, 1984), 115, 116 (arguing that the Universal Declaration is customary law); A. H. Robertson and J. G. Merrills, *Human Rights in the World,* 3d ed. (Manchester: Manchester University Press, 1989), 96 (arguing that the Universal Declaration is customary law); Louis B. Sohn, "The Human Rights Law of the Charter," *Texas International Law Journal* 12 (1977): 129, 133 (arguing that the Universal Declaration is customary law); Bahiyyih G. Tahzib, *Freedom of Religion or Belief: Ensuring Effective International Legal Protection* (Boston: Martinus Nijhoff, 1996), 184–85 (arguing that the 1981 Declaration is customary law); Patrick Thornberry, *International Law and the Rights of Minorities* (Oxford: Clarendon Press, 1991), 237–38 (arguing that the Universal Declaration is customary law); Humphrey Waldock, "Human Rights in Contemporary International Law and the Significance of the European Convention," *The European Convention of Human Rights* (Brit. Inst. Int'l & Comp. L.) (Ser. No. 5, 1965): 1, 15 (arguing that the Universal Declaration is customary law). See also Hurst Hannum, "The Status of the Universal Declaration of Human Rights in National and International Law," *Georgia Journal of International and Comparative Law* 25 (1995/1996): 287, 317–52 (summarizing statements of constituents of several states and international bodies as well as influential authors holding that the Universal Declaration of Human Rights is customary law).

Despite broad acceptance of international norms affirming freedom of religion or belief, experience at the level of implementation has born sad testament to the challenges of effectively protecting this right. Egregious violations remain all too common:

- the genocide of religious groups
- the incarceration and punishment of individuals primarily for reasons of religion and conscience
- the abuse of antiterrorism and national security laws to suppress religious minorities across the continents
- discrimination and attacks on new religious movements
- the incitement of hatred along religious lines—particularly Islamophobia and anti-Semitism

Of course, not all recurrent denials of this freedom are of the order of those endangering life or other extreme violations. The spectrum of discrimination and intolerance in the field of religion or belief is vast. Stringent registration laws, for example, can severely restrict the activities of groups, as can unwarranted interference in the internal organization of communities by government officials. Barriers to the religious education of children hinder the conveyance of the belief to the next generation and may continue the wider public's ignorance about the particular group involved. Discrimination can severely impact all areas of life for individual believers as well as the group as a whole, and may reveal itself in a variety of avenues such as political life, employment, and legal access. Whereas such denials may not seem to "qualify" as being particularly severe human rights violations, as compared with torture, disappearances, and the like, they can lead to longstanding grievances, simmering under the surface, and possibly later erupt into violence. It is of critical importance that such issues are dealt with effectively and early by governments acting in good faith towards their human rights obligations. Of course, different levels of violation deserve different levels of response. Dealing with other rights violations can sometimes take higher priority. But care must be taken to assure that in prioritizing other urgent matters, religious freedom issues are not allowed to slip off the list altogether. While protection of religious rights sometimes appears to be a back-burner item, it is one that we neglect at our peril, because of the high risk that simmering tensions today may boil over tomorrow.

Overview of the Book

We turn now to the task of providing an introduction to the structure and contents of the book. As noted above, this volume was reconceived early in its history as a "deskbook." That is, the aim was to produce a work that could serve as a comprehensive resource for anyone seriously engaged in the task of facilitating freedom of religion or belief. With this in mind, our objective here is to provide a guide to the contents of the book, and to suggest some of the ways it might most effectively be used.

Before proceeding to a chapter-by-chapter analysis, a few words on the broad structure of the volume may be helpful. The book brings together many voices, coming from different religious, national, and cultural backgrounds, each speaking for themselves and often disagreeing with others in the book. It goes without saying that each author is responsible solely for his or her own contribution.

The "deskbook" vision has shaped the book in several ways that are reflected in the broad divisions of the book. In the first place, it meant that we wanted the book to be useful as a practical matter for human rights workers. That meant that our aim was not so much to unravel new theoretical reflections on this subject as to provide a sound understanding of the ideas, institutions, and issues that shape the field. At the same time, this objective required some introduction to the historical and philosophical issues involved. Our solution was to call on two individuals with strong activist credentials—Malcolm Evans and Tore Lindholm—who could describe the "Origins and Grounds of Freedom of Religion or Belief" in part I of the book in a way that connects directly with practical issues.

The second key element of the deskbook is a thorough exposition of the relevant "International Norms and Institutions." The idea behind this part of the book was that serious human rights workers need access to high-level commentaries on the array of relevant norms and on the international institutions charged with implementing these norms. Thus, part II aspires to guide the reader through the complex web of norms, institutions, and procedures set up to protect freedom of religion or belief. The volume of relevant international legal materials is expanding to the point of being unmanageable. From this perspective, Natan Lerner's chapter provides an immensely useful overview of the entire body of relevant norms. This is supplemented by Johan van der Vyver's analysis of the relationship of religious freedom norms to other human rights and by Llewellyn and Condé's chapter addressing the often-overlooked implications of religious freedom rights for international humanitarian law and the emerging field of international criminal law. These contributions are then rounded out by the chapter by Nowak and Vospernik on permissible limitations. In many ways this is one of the most crucial chapters in the volume, because for the most part, encroachments on religious freedom occur not because government officials question the existence of the right to freedom of religion or belief, but because they (erroneously) believe that the particular limitation they impose is justified.

Discussion of the substantive norms is then augmented by a series of chapters describing the array of institutions charged with implementing freedom of religion or belief. Accordingly, there are chapters written by leading experts on the United Nations Commission on Human Rights (van Boven), the UN Human Rights Committee (Scheinin), UNESCO (Diene), the Council of Europe, including the European Court of Human Rights, (Martínez-Torron and Navarro-Valls), and the Organization for Security and Cooperation in Europe (Gibson, Lord, and Matlary). A major objective in this part is to provide background on the institutional and procedural levers available at the international level to help facilitate better protection of freedom of religion or belief.

Part III of the book turns to a series of key issues concerning the relationship of religion and the state. This section opens with José de Sousa e Brito's analysis of the importance of protecting conscientious objection not only in military, but also in a variety of other contexts in which conscience confronts the state. This is followed by a general essay on the importance of religious autonomy by Archbishop Roland Minnerath, and a more detailed chapter by Cole Durham analyzing the implications of religious freedom norms for religious association laws. These two chapters are particularly significant for the legal issues faced by religious institutions in their interactions with the state. Lee Boothby then addresses the unique issues that arise in state-controlled environments such as prisons, hospitals, and the military. This is followed by Roman Podoprigora's analysis of the constraints religious freedom norms impose on exercise of official discretion in granting or denying approvals for various types of religious activity. Finally, Jean Baubérot describes one of the major models of the place of religion in public life: the French laicist approach. Each of these chapters explores crucial dimensions of the interface between religion and the state. Each national order invariably has its own institutional arrangements; the deskbook is designed to illuminate the key problem areas, noting where international human rights norms leave flexibility and drawing attention to areas where they set minimum standards.

Part IV recognizes that changing attitudes toward gender, family, and children are raising a host of new issues for freedom of religion and belief. While our treatment of these questions cannot hope to be exhaustive, the authors of chapters 19–24 provide an impressive opening to dialogue in this area. Bahia Tahzib-Lie sketches the range of issues that "dissenting women" face. Özlem Denli's essay on the Islamic scarf controversy, while focused on Turkey, raises broader issues relevant to similar controversies in other parts of the world. Juliet Sheen, who helped identify a range of women's issues in her work as co-editor with Kevin Boyle of the world report on freedom of religion or belief,[32] analyzes burdens that women face in asserting their rights to freedom of religion or belief. Ursula King brings years of academic experience to her study of "Hinduism and Women." Similarly, Kari Elisabeth Børresen brings distinguished academic credentials to her critique of the normative status of women within her own (Roman Catholic) tradition. Finally, Geraldine van Bueren, writing as both an academic and as an active participant in the framing of children's rights instruments, provides a particularly helpful view of the belief rights of children.

No set of chapters can be fully representative of the range of issues percolating in this area. Our hope was that we could raise some of the salient issues, remembering that while women and children have sometimes suffered most at the hands of religion, in many settings they are also its largest class of devotees, its greatest beneficiaries, and in the case of women, its most ardent defenders. Here, perhaps more than in any other area, there is an urgent need for religious freedom to succeed in its above-noted task of protecting religion and its potential for good while filtering out religion's negative hazards and finding sensitive ways to facilitate accommodation of religious and cultural differences within a broad framework of interpersonal and intercultural respect.

Part V deals with two major areas of particular sensitivity for freedom of religion or belief: issues concerning religious "sects" or "cults," and issues regarding religious persuasion. Each of the chapters in this part of the book is connected more or less directly to questions concerning the right to "have or adopt" or to "change" religion. The chapters on "sects" and "cults" are ultimately about the protections that accrue to those who "have or adopt" a religion that may appear unfamiliar or strange. In recent years, there has been a substantial volume of legislation prompted by fears based on stereotypical images of new religious movements. This trend has been paralleled in many ways by legislation prompted by fears of "religious extremists" from

[32] Kevin Boyle and Juliet Sheen, eds., *Freedom of Religion or Belief: A World Report* (London: Routledge, 1997).

various traditions. While events of recent years leave no doubt that genuine problems exist, legal reactions are often overbroad, imposing constraints on legitimate groups that are inconsistent with religious freedom norms. Eileen Barker, an internationally acclaimed sociologist and one of the world's leading experts on these phenomena, helps to dispel some of the myths and stereotypes. For their part, Fautré, Garay, and Nidegger provide a case study in the French-speaking countries of Europe. These chapters are vital because the real test of religious freedom always comes down to how the unfamiliar and unpopular groups are treated. Tolerance for the popular is no challenge.

The remaining chapters in part V focus on long-running debates on the right to engage in religious persuasion on the one hand and issues of protecting religious and cultural identity on the other. Tad Stahnke's chapter provides a helpful analytic framework for sorting out the differences between protected witnessing of one's faith and "improper proselytism," arguing in the end for broad protections for religious persuasion. Makau Mutua, on the other hand, is sharply critical of most traditional missionary efforts, viewing them as inappropriate assertions of cultural power that undermine traditional cultural identities. Nazila Ghanea focuses on the Muslim doctrine proscribing apostasy from Islam. These issues are vital to an understanding of current international religious freedom norms, because they constitute one of the critical areas of disagreement concerning the scope of religious freedom norms: whether religious freedom includes the right to "change [one's] religion or belief," as many in the Christian world believe and as stated in the Universal Declaration of Human Rights and the European and American Conventions, or whether it would constitute impermissible apostasy (at least in the case of conversion from Islam). It may be possible to reach greater consensus on this point once political loyalty and religious affiliation are clearly differentiated, since within contemporary Muslim discourse, new approaches to religious freedom are being discussed that recognize that apostasy is primarily a religious issue that triggers religious but not necessarily civil and political sanctions. Such approaches leave choice of religion to the individual where change of religion is not taken as entailing disloyalty to the state.

Part VI focuses on a variety of "Contexts for Facilitating Freedom of Religion or Belief." What ties the chapters in this section together is that each addresses practical settings and practical methodologies that are important for ameliorating implementation of religious freedom norms. Several of the chapters focus on bridge building and dialogue between religious communities (i.e., those of Archbishop Anastasios, Leonard Swidler, and the Norwegian coauthors Inge Eidsvåg, Tore Lindholm, and Barbro Sveen). Rüdiger Noll addresses the increasingly significant positive role that religion can play in conflict situations. Babu Gogineni and Lars Gule, as leaders of humanist organizations, draw attention to the "or belief" half of "freedom of religion or belief," emphasizing the rights of nonreligious belief and life-stance groups. Chapters discussed earlier dealing with education (by Jolanta Ambrosewicz-Jacobs and Ingvill Plesner) and the mechanisms associated with the United States International Religious Freedom Act (by Jeremy Gunn) also belong to this "Contexts" section. Finally, Elizabeth Sewell's chapter provides useful insights into ways that NGOs can facilitate freedom of religion or belief.

The conclusion and the appendices constitute an important final element of the "deskbook" plan. The conclusion draws together many of the practical recommendations made throughout the volume. We hope it will stand as an open-ended agenda for continued action. Key documents and provisions are provided in Appendices A and B, along with a list of relevant treaties in Appendix C. The book would be impossibly long if the full texts of all relevant documents were included, but sufficient information is provided to make it easy to access relevant texts online at websites such as www.religlaw.org. Relevant General Comments of the UN Human Rights Committee are included in Appendices D and E, followed by the text of the Oslo Declaration on Freedom of Religion or Belief in Appendix F. Finally, we hope that the list of NGOs working in the field provided by Appendix G (including contact information) will make a contribution to networking among those working to facilitate freedom of religion or belief.

In what follows a more detailed guide to the contents of the various chapters is provided. This follows the structure of the book's table of contents. We highlight contents of the various chapters not so much to summarize them as to suggest reasons why someone working in the field might find each chapter helpful.

Part I: Origins and Grounds of Freedom of Religion or Belief

The historical overview provided in the opening chapter by ***Malcolm Evans*** helps to place all the other chapters in the book in historical perspective. The timescale considered in his chapter stretches from the Roman Empire to the present. But the real focus is on identifying different major phases in the international law of freedom of religion or belief. Evans shows that concern by political authorities for religious freedom is much older than the modern state system. For the most part, religious freedom has not been promoted as an end in itself, but as a technique for preserving stability, limiting conflict, or as a pretext for intervention. Through much of history, granting religious freedom has been used as means of avoiding conflict, whereas limiting its enjoyment has been a source of conflict. In general, there has been a shift away from the practice of attempting to ensure civil harmony by keeping people of different religions apart towards providing a common institutional framework for facilitating peaceful coexistence. This is most evident in the modern regime of internationally codified universal human rights.

After tracing some of the failures of premodern experience, such as the role reversal that transformed Christianity from a victim of persecution into a source of state intolerance, Evans identifies three major configurations in the modern evolution of freedom of religion: (1) the "*cuius regio, eius religio*" model, in which the prince determined the religion of his people; (2) the minority protection model, in which international treaties provided protection for religious minorities; and (3) the contemporary human rights model. Each of these fundamental approaches to religious freedom is portrayed in significant detail.

Somewhat surprisingly, in light of the fact that the historical progression associated with the historical succession of the three approaches is toward strengthening of individual religious freedom protections, Evans argues that the past fifty years have witnessed a diminution of the political importance attached to achieving freedom of religion or belief. His point is that in contrast to the early days during and immediately after World War II, when the foundational role of religious freedom was clearly recognized, freedom of religion or belief tends now to be seen simply as one of many protections tucked away in the panoply of human rights. Moreover, its strength is further weakened by the fact that its protections are balanced against a welter of other social values. The claim that religious freedom values are eroding is surely a controversial point, and no doubt intended as such, but it is the kind of question that historical perspective entitles an author to ask. Has the right to freedom of religion or belief been subject to steady attrition, or to overshadowing as other rights have been built up? Has there been a "relativizing" political approach to religion? Are these trends a reflection of secularization and of shifting perceptions of the role of religion in society that could be reversed as religion becomes more salient? What do the long-term trends mean for the ability of freedom of religion or belief to meet the challenges of an increasingly pluralized world?

Tore Lindholm's chapter on *Philosophical and Religious Justifications of Freedom of Religion or Belief* attempts to answer at least one of the questions left by Evans' historical chapter: is religious freedom relegated to playing an essentially passive role in acknowledging and perhaps sanctifying the relativizing of values that pervades our age? Or can it provide social structures within which deeply divided worldviews can live together? In order for the latter option to be a possibility, it is vital to be able to elucidate public justification(s) of the universally applicable human right to freedom of religion or belief in a religiously, philosophically, and culturally division-prone world. A solution to this problem needs to go beyond being intellectually well-grounded and socially stable. It must facilitate *both* mutual respect and solidarity across religious and life-stance divides *and* the unflinching integrity of each normative tradition. For Lindholm, the task of philosophy in approaching this challenge is "meta-facilitation" of freedom of religion carried out by assuming the role of a Lockean "under-labourer" tasked with clearing conceptual ground rather than that of the Platonic "philosopher-king." In Lindholm's view, the major contemporary approaches to the dilemmas of religious plurality, difference, and conflict—traditional half-hearted toleration, religious relativism or skepticism, salvific pluralism, privatization or marginalization of religious commitment, and exclusion of religion from the public square (whether by strident laicist politics or by a hegemonic secularist culture)—are all found wanting. Lindholm's alternative is to draw on the emerging worldwide public commitment to human dignity as a shared focus for overlapping justification of freedom of religion or belief. Arguing the case for an expressly pluralist approach, he contends that the challenge is for every life stance (whether religious or secular) to generate and publicize espousals of the human right to freedom of religion or belief by embracing the doctrine of inherent dignity while remaining well-grounded in the heartland of their particular normative traditions. Once our differing, perhaps even incompatible, *justificatory platforms* are publicly recognized to converge in stable and internally legitimate support of this *justificandum*, prudentially based toleration will no longer be seen to suffice, and the inadequate halfway houses posed by relativism, skepticism, salvific pluralism, privatization, or exclusivist secularism will no longer be compelling ways out of the dilemmas of religious and life-stance difference. The dynamics of *overlapping justification* (as opposed to mere overlapping consensus) make it possible for one group to come to understand and trust another group's commitment to freedom of religion or belief and mutual respect, even if the premises of the justification are not totally shared. This in turn makes it possible to achieve "mutual respect with uncompromised integrity."

Lindholm's argument in this short form sounds abstract, but in fact it is enlivened with historical, sociological, and theological considerations, drawing on many of the great pioneers in articulating particular religious groundings for the universal value of religious freedom, from Emperor Ashoka to Pope John XXIII. In the spirit of contributing to the practical aims of the deskbook, the chapter concludes with a section advocating the priority of cooperation across religious divides as a means for the realization of a common commitment to—and enjoyment of—the human right to freedom of religion or belief.

Part II: Freedom of Religion or Belief: International Norms and Institutions

Natan Lerner's chapter offers a comprehensive overview of *The Nature and Minimum Standards of Freedom of Religion or Belief* in international law. He traces the evolution of this freedom in the array of international instruments that have been adopted, from the Universal Declaration in 1948 to the end of the twentieth century. Of the three aspects of freedom of religion or belief encapsulated in article 18 of the Universal Declaration ([i] the *forum internum*, [ii] conversion and proselytizing and [iii] the *forum externum*), Lerner focuses most of his attention on the latter, for the obvious reason that manifestations of religion are most likely to face limitations in practice. The ICCPR is highlighted as the only binding treaty applicable worldwide that specifically and coherently protects religious rights. For this reason, Lerner devotes particular attention to article 18 and emphasizes the need to pay close attention to the UN Human Rights Committee's General Comment 22, which interprets this key provision on freedom of religion or belief. He also provides a valuable analysis of the 1981 Declaration, which he describes as being ambitious in its achievement, imprecise in a number of respects, but "reasonably good" in its text, and amounting to "a very positive step" overall. The balance of the chapter surveys regional and other international documents bearing on freedom of religion or belief. As a practical matter, Lerner's chapter is particularly useful in providing an overview of the proliferating set of documents that codify international religious freedom norms. Despite the seeming abundance of international instruments, Lerner contends that there is still a strong need to *better* protect religious groups from discrimination, persecution, and other violations of freedom of religion or belief.

Johan van der Vyver's chapter undertakes the complex task of analyzing *The Relationship of Freedom of Religion or Belief Norms to Other Human Rights.* This includes examining both areas where religious freedom and other human rights are mutually supportive and overlap, and areas where they can come into conflict. The overlaps pose few problems: freedom of expression and association, for example, provide "double protection" in areas such as religious persuasion and the right to acquire legal entity status. The areas of conflict are more controversial. Van der Vyver explores a rich range of examples from around the world illustrating the different types of conflicts with other rights. The chapter repays reading simply for the plenitude of situations it addresses. But the chapter goes further in putting forward a number of principles that are pertinent to the resolution of such conflicts.

At the outset van der Vyver addresses the potential conflicts that arise from internal disputes within a religious community. Among other things, he notes the significance of institutional group rights to freedom of religion vesting in religious institutions themselves, as opposed to collective group rights, which vest in the individual members of a group.[33] This has significant implications for the rights of religious institutions to religious autonomy and to legal entity status, as described in more detail in chapters 14 and 15 (by Minnerath and Durham, respectively). In this domain, he invokes principles drawn from the general analytic structure of "sphere sovereignty," which recognizes the exclusive competence of religious institutions to determine their own organization structure, dogma, procedures, activities, and internal disciplinary measures. To this he adds the state responsibility to respect the self-determination of religious communities. Whereas the principle of sphere sovereignty is described as an "institutional group right," which vests in a social institution, the right to self-determination is described as a "collective group right," which is afforded to individual persons belonging to that category and can be exercised separately and jointly with others of that group.

The distinction between collective and institutional rights is important and enlightening. However, couching that discussion in terms highly reminiscent of the right of peoples to self-determination might cause misunderstanding. The right of peoples to self-determination, addressed in the parallel articles 1 of the ICCPR and the ICESCR, addresses rather different matters: its *holders* are peoples and the *goods* protected by the peoples' rights to self-determination are external independence and internal democratic self-rule. Of course, van der Vyver does not intend to elevate religious communities to political peoples, nor to accord them the right to political independence (i.e., secession), nor to impose internal democratic self-rule on religious organizations that have other modes of internal ordering. The basic principle is surely sound; it may be helpful to use the language of religious autonomy to avoid confusion, but van der Vyver may believe this sounds too much like an institutional right, when it is the partially overlapping collective dimension of an associational right that he wants to bring out.

Another area van der Vyver focuses on is the interaction of equality norms with religious freedom. Often, of course, equality norms reinforce religious freedom protections. Indeed, as noted above, nondiscrimination norms are part of the normative core of freedom of religion or belief. Van der Vyver takes a strong position in this regard against privileged relationships of particular religious communities with the state, contending that such privileging discriminates against the religions and beliefs that are thereby disadvantaged, condescends towards those it "tolerates," and interferes in the internal affairs of the supposedly privileged religion.[34] This position will clearly be controversial in the many countries that continue to have official state churches or other strong forms of cooperation with particular religious denominations. Benefited groups are likely to be critical of the position; smaller and less popular groups are likely to concur. The significant point is that the strength of the equality norm in contemporary society imposes a burden of justification where privileging occurs.

---

[33] Van der Vyver, chapter 4, 91.

[34] Ibid., 106–07

Yet there are other situations in which religious freedom protections may collide with equality norms. Examples cited by van der Vyver include discrimination by some religions against women and against gays and lesbians.[35] Van der Vyver appears to assume that sphere sovereignty will protect doctrinally based internal practices,[36] but absent that, he appears to endorse placing equality ahead of liberty: "countries founded on libertarian principles which permit freedom of religion or belief to trump individual rights founded on human dignity and equality are at odds with the international standards of human rights protection."[37] The tension between liberty and equality is well known, and can have particularly significant ramifications for freedom of religion. Not everyone will accept van der Vyver's position on these issues, but his chapter is a significant starting point for discussion.

A final section of van der Vyver's chapter deals with permissible limitations on freedom of religion or belief. Here his analysis is conceptual, focusing on (1) "inherent limitations," (2) limitations determined by the rights and freedoms of others, and (3) limitations "in the general interest." What van der Vyver provides in this section is analysis of the type that is more typical at the level of the constitutional law of a state, in contrast to Nowak and Vospernik's discussion in chapter 6 of limitation clause issues at the level of international norms.

The next chapter, by *David Llewellyn* and *Victor Condé* considers an area which has received little scholarly attention thus far—that of *Freedom of Religion or Belief under International Humanitarian Law and International Criminal Law*. The authors argue for the fundamental importance of this matter, because not only does religious need and interest escalate during times of war or armed conflict, but religion may be deeply implicated in the violence, and solutions may be impossible without respecting religious rights. To make their point, the authors compare human rights norms regarding freedom of religion or belief with corresponding norms under international humanitarian and international criminal law. Despite the very different origins and purposes of these three areas of international law, the relevant norms reveal a close degree of correlation and resemblance. As a practical matter, the chapter underscores an idea that is often expressed, but that seldom finds more compelling vindication: freedom of religion or belief is nonderogable under all circumstances, from peace time to war to armed conflicts to post-war situations.

It is through the interplay of the principle of freedom of religion or belief and its restrictions that the *actual* scope of freedom of religion or belief is determined. Thus, the chapter on *Permissible Restrictions on Freedom of Religion or Belief* by *Manfred Nowak* and *Tanja Vospernik* is particularly critical for the volume. The authors undertake a rigorous analysis of the typical limitation clauses found in international instruments. Focusing on issues of "brainwashing" and religious persuasion, they raise questions about the borders of the *forum internum*, which is supposed to be totally exempt from limitations. They then work through the various legitimating grounds for imposing constraints on manifestations of religion listed in article 18 of the ICCPR: protection of "public safety, order, health, or morals or the fundamental rights and freedoms of others."

---

[35] Ibid., 114.
[36] Ibid., 115.
[37] Ibid., 120.

Particularly noteworthy is the treatment of "public order." This is often taken to be the most expansive justification for imposing limitations on freedom of religion, since many assume that what is intended is the broad notion of "*ordre public*" in French law used to describe a generalized sense of prevailing public policies. The authors point out that both the English and French versions of the ICCPR make it clear that in context, the phrase "public order" is intended to justify incursions on religious freedom only in the narrow sense of preventing public disturbances.[38] "Morals" as a ground of limitation is considered to be the least clear and most controversial of the grounds, because of the risk that one religion-based moral principle may be invoked to override another religious belief.

Moving beyond the formal legitimating factors, Nowak and Vospernik focus attention on nondiscrimination as an additional factor that is vital if a limitation is to be justified. As noted by the UN Human Rights Committee, discriminatory treatment invalidates a finding that a particular limitation is necessary, even if it falls within an otherwise legitimate category. Unfortunately, genuine neutrality is all too rare a commodity and the "differential" treatment meted out often amounts to outright discrimination.

A final practical critique of the handling of limitations clauses is that international and regional human rights bodies are often too deferential in assessing state limitations. The European Court, for example, has sometimes afforded governments an unnecessarily broad margin of appreciation. More could no doubt have been said about the fact that even if one of the permissible grounds for legislation is present, it is still necessary to demonstrate that the limitation in question is strictly necessary and proportionate. But in general the authors do an excellent job of stressing the narrowness of the grounds for permissible limitations, thereby facilitating protection of a broader sphere of freedom of religion or belief.

The next chapter, *Theo van Boven's* essay on *The United Nations Commission on Human Rights and Freedom of Religion or Belief*, launches the set of six chapters in the deskbook addressing the institutional mechanisms available to foster protection of the right. The author identifies three phases in the work of the Commission with respect to freedom of religion or belief: (i) standard setting from 1946–55, (ii) the (painstaking) elaboration of these standards from 1960–81, and (iii) the implementation phase from 1986 to the present. Van Boven describes in detail the evolving and growing role of the Commission's Special Rapporteur on Religious Intolerance, since 2001 referred to as the Special Rapporteur on Freedom of Religion or Belief. In van Boven's view, the Special Rapporteur has been "the main actor" in the recent contribution of the Commission to this field. The means at the Rapporteur's disposal have included the preparation of annual and interim reports to the UN regarding the state of freedom of religion or belief, the setting up of an urgent appeals procedure to respond to more serious violations, the carrying out of *in-situ* visits to observe the phenomenon of intolerance more closely and to pursue dialogue with relevant parties, and a visit follow-up procedure to pursue the matters arising from the *in-situ* visits. In the attempt to contribute to the elimination of intolerance in this field, the Rapporteur has identified particular priority issues (most notably, education for tolerance), identified categories of violations, and also undertaken the initiative of visiting major religious communities and institutions.

[38] Nowak and Vospernik, chapter 6, 152.

While van Boven is positive about the efficacy of the activities of the Special Rapporteur, he is critical of the Commission as a whole. Despite being "the central human rights policy organ of the United Nations," the Commission fails to deliberate constructively on freedom of religion or belief. Its annual resolution on religious intolerance tends to be repetitive. Insufficient time is given to the presentation of the Special Rapporteur's report and scant attention is paid to it in subsequent discussion under the relevant religious intolerance item on the Commission's agenda. To van Boven it is clear that the Special Rapporteur makes a more "substantial and coherent contribution to the cause of freedom of religion" than the Commission itself. The Special Rapporteur is therefore described as being "the investigative, intellectual, and operational arm of the Commission." Van Boven urges the Commission to make a more substantial and coherent contribution to the area of freedom of religion or belief, to more seriously consider the reports of the Special Rapporteur, and to further strengthen his mandate. Despite limitations on the Special Rapporteur's resources, his position remains one of the most significant channels as a practical matter to bring religious freedom problems to the attention of the United Nations.

In the next chapter, *The Human Rights Committee and Freedom of Religion or Belief, Martin Scheinin* tackles the second key international human rights body in the United Nations system. Scheinin reminds us that article 18 is not the only relevant provision of the ICCPR regarding freedom of religion or belief. Articles 2(1), 4(2), 24(1), 26, and 27 are also relevant in offering further protection and clarifying nonderogation and nondiscrimination. Scheinin looks at the three primary functions of the Human Rights Committee in turn, describing how each of these has been used to advance freedom of religion or belief. First, he analyzes the impact of the Committee in considering periodic state reports. Second, he notes that the Committee has had significant influence through its General Comments. The most significant of these in the field of freedom of religion or belief has unquestionably been its General Comment 22, providing what amounts to an official interpretation and elaboration of the meaning of article 18 of the ICCPR. Thirdly and finally, he assesses the case law emerging from individual complaints alleging violation of freedom or religion or belief. Although this case law remains sparse and underdeveloped in Scheinin's view, the resources in this area may be richer than appears at first blush, since related issues have been explored in connection with other provisions of the ICCPR. Overall, the Committee has special significance in relation to freedom of religion or belief because its jurisdiction is universal and its procedures are sufficiently flexible for it to be able to deal with the entire range of religious freedom issues.

Doudou Diene's chapter, *UNESCO's Facilitation of Freedom of Religion or Belief*, considers an institution that contributes in significant ways to real-world cultivation of tolerance, but is sometimes overlooked because its role is less legalistic and less focused on the vindication of rights. UNESCO's emphasis has been on intercultural dialogue and, more particularly, on interreligious dialogue. This is a reflection of the renewed recognition of the importance that religions and spiritual traditions have in addressing the essential questions of our time. The recent reemphasis of such matters signals a return to the most fundamental impetus behind the founding of UNESCO—that it is "in the minds of men that the defenses of peace must be constructed." Against this background, Diene outlines the relevant UNESCO declarations, activities, and projects that help foster effective implementation of the ideals of religious freedom. Through these initiatives, UNESCO has tried to reinforce the value of interaction, the experience of cultural and spiritual proximity, and the acknowledgement of pluralism, each of which contribute to the overall facilitation of freedom of religion or belief.

Turning from the United Nations to the most effective of the regional human rights systems, we have the chapter of ***Javier Martínez-Torrón*** and ***Rafael Navarro-Valls*** on ***The Protection of Religious Freedom in the System of the Council of Europe.*** The central focus is on the European Convention for the Protection of Human Rights and Fundamental Freedoms, and the associated European Court of Human Rights, located in Strasbourg. The Court, which now has jurisdiction over roughly 800,000,000 people, has become the premier human rights tribunal in the world. In contrast with so many other human rights institutions, which are essentially "soft law" institutions, the Court is in the relatively unique position among international bodies of being able to issue binding and enforceable decisions. With this in mind, it is surprising and perhaps a little disappointing that no cases were decided by the Court squarely under the religion provision of the European Convention (article 9) until 1993. A number of cases were decided by the European Commission of Human Rights, pursuant to the older procedure whereby the Commission filtered cases going to the Court, but none were decided by the Court itself. Particularly since 1998, however, when the new court structure and procedures went into effect,[39] the volume of case law on religion issues has been steadily increasing. This is important not only for those within the jurisdiction of the Court, but for the world at large, because the provision the Court is interpreting (article 9 of the ECHR) is almost exactly parallel to the key provisions of article 18 of the ICCPR, and the Court's decisions are an extremely credible source of persuasive authority on human rights issues.

The chapter on the Council of Europe is thus extremely important because of the overview it provides of the Court's burgeoning article 9 jurisprudence. While the primary focus of the chapter is on this case law, the authors do include a section on initiatives of the Council of Europe's Parliamentary Assembly and Committee of Ministers,[40] the most interesting of which relate to new religious movements. The ultimate outcome of these deliberations was a recommendation that called for the establishment of "information centers on 'groups of a religious, esoteric or spiritual nature,'" but at the same time urged governments "to use the normal procedures of criminal and civil law against illegal practices carried out in the name" of such groups.[41]

After a brief description of the structure and procedure of the Court, the authors turn to an exposition of its case law (as well as that of earlier Commission decisions). This goes into much greater depth and detail than can be repeated here, but a few of the particularly vital issues and potential problems the authors identify deserve mention.

A first major feature of the Court's jurisprudence is its implicit recognition that there is a "margin of appreciation" that defers to historically established structures of the relationship between religion and the state.[42] This is a practical recognition of the

---

[39] Martínez-Torrón and Navarro-Valls, chapter 10, 214.

[40] Ibid., 211–14.

[41] Ibid., 213–14.

[42] Ibid., 215.

diverse structures—ranging from states with established churches, to states with strong cooperationist regimes, to those with a strong laicist separation of church and state. As the authors state the apparent principle:

> Equality (article 14 of the European Convention) must be applied rigorously in many contexts to preserve religious freedom, but some flexibility is permissible in structuring cooperation with religious communities, particularly where failure to do so would disrupt long-established patterns and expectations. . . . In other words, article 9 of the European Convention is aimed at providing an adequate guarantee of the right to freedom of religion and belief. Its purpose, however, is not to establish certain uniform criteria for church-state relations in the Council of Europe members states nor—even less—to impose a compulsory secularism (*laïcité*).[43]

Established churches are permissible so long as membership in the official church is not mandatory. The Court has also made it clear that the sensitivities of dominant religious communities deserve respect.[44]

Turning from treatment of dominant to minority religious groups, the authors address cases interpreting the equality principle, worship, proselytism, and internal autonomy. They note a certain irony in the fact that while the wording of the European Convention tends to focus primarily on the rights of individuals, the European system has disregarded the individual dimension of freedom of religion or belief more often than its corporate dimension.[45] In part, this is the result of a much narrower interpretation of the notion of protected religious "practice" under the Convention, derived from earlier Commission decisions, than the interpretation that the UN Human Rights Committee has recommended with respect to the parallel language of the ICCPR.[46] Specifically, the Commission construed the notion of practice narrowly so that it covered only actions *manifesting* religion in the strict sense, as opposed to conduct *motivated* by religion.[47]

A second major concern with European Court case law has to do with ostensibly neutral laws that impose indirect restrictions on religious freedom.[48] The tendency to assume that neutral laws necessarily override conscience was more pronounced in the decisions of the Commission, but is a discernible trend (if not a confirmed position) in some of the decisions of the Court. In the view of the authors, the better position is that "freedom to practice one's religion or belief must be understood as protecting, in principle, every act of the individual when he obeys the dictates of his own conscience"[49]—thus offering the maximum presumptive protection under article 9(1). To the extent that limitations of this right are necessary, they must be justified under article 9(2), with the state having the burden of proof regarding the legitimacy and the necessity of any limitations. The authors find that the restrictions permitted to

---

[43] Ibid., 216.
[44] Ibid., 217.
[45] Ibid., 228.
[46] Ibid.
[47] Ibid., 229–30.
[48] The issue here is parallel to that raised by the much-criticized decision of the United States Supreme Court in Employment Division v. Smith, 494 US 872 (1990), which held that any neutral and general law that does not directly target a particular religious group (or groups) can override religious freedom claims.
[49] Martínez-Torrón and Navarro-Valls, chapter 10, 233.

date are much more skewed toward state initiatives, and that this has the effect of restricting manifestation of religion or belief and freedom of conscience. In their view, this may lead to a kind of secular fundamentalism or indoctrination, which can be as dangerous to pluralism and to minorities in particular as more blatant forms of religious fundamentalism.[50] They conclude that in the effort to eliminate intolerance, it is as important to avoid the dangers of "secularism-oriented intolerance" as it is to prevent "religion-oriented intolerance."[51]

The next two chapters consider the work of the Organization for Security and Cooperation in Europe ("OSCE"). Originally known as the Conference for Security and Cooperation, or the "Helsinki Process" because of its establishment pursuant to the 1975 Helsinki Final Act, the OSCE is currently the largest regional security and human rights organization in the world, with fifty-five member states in North America, Europe, and Central Asia. With respect to the OSCE, ***Urban Gibson*** and ***Karen Lord*** look at ***Advancements in Standard Setting: Religious Liberty and OSCE Commitments. Janne Haaland Matlary*** focuses more specifically on ***Implementing Freedom of Religion in the OSCE: Experiences from the Norwegian Chairmanship***. Both chapters discuss the history, emergence, institutional structure, norms, and influence of the OSCE. OSCE standards in the field of freedom of religion or belief are particularly advanced, detailed, instructive, and precise. Gibson and Lord describe these commitments to be "by far the clearest delineation of religious liberty commitments in the international arena"[52] and argue that they serve as a universal example as they "represent the aspirations of millions who seek to worship and live freely as their conscience dictates."[53] They pay particular attention to the 1989 Vienna Concluding Document[54] and note a series of OSCE seminars and the creation of the Advisory Panel on Freedom of Religion or Belief, on which both authors have served.[55]

Acknowledging that OSCE commitments are "politically" rather than "legally binding," Matlary's chapter provides both practical insight into the internal workings of OSCE institutions and theoretical insight into the significance of the "soft power" instruments utilized in the OSCE. Her chapter is an important reminder to those working in the field of religious human rights that instruments of "soft power" can often be as effective and sometimes even more so than "hard law."[56] These instruments include persuasion, legal and political aid, as well as both open and discreet criticism. Among other things, precisely because they are not legally binding, OSCE commitments can be considerably more detailed and comprehensive than legally binding commitments, and this has substantially augmented their force. They link human rights more clearly to democracy and the rule of law and provide policy prescriptions that can help guide practical realization of religious freedom ideals.

Matlary also discusses how OSCE missions and various monitoring mechanisms come together to ensure the implementation of commitments. During the Norwegian Chairmanship of the organization in 1999, the goals of mainstreaming consideration of

---

[50] Ibid., 235–36.
[51] Ibid., 236
[52] Gibson and Lord, chapter 11, 254.
[53] Ibid.
[54] Ibid., 248–51.
[55] Ibid., 252–54.
[56] Matlary, chapter 12, 259–61.

religious freedom into OSCE missions and highlighting the importance of freedom of religion in conflict resolution were uppermost. Matlary reports setbacks and some persistent failures in the field of religious freedom. Even so, the experience from the Norwegian Chairmanship of the OSCE bears out the case for political promotion of religious freedom through work with an array of soft power mechanisms and initiatives, and in close cooperation with religious communities, with NGOs, and with academia. In this respect, Matlary's chapter complements in interesting ways that of Elizabeth Sewell (chapter 38) on facilitating freedom of religion or belief through NGOs. The examples of how religious dialogue was used as a strategy in conflict prevention or resolution should also be of particular interest.

Part III: Freedom of Religion or Belief and the State

The next part of the deskbook addresses various key aspects of the interface between religion and the state. *Conscientious Objection*, the topic of the chapter by *José de Sousa e Brito*, has always been one of the most dramatic and crucial of these interaction points. Too often the subject of conscientious objection has been assumed to arise only in the context of objection to military service, but it can also include objection to performing abortions,[57] participating in flag ceremonies,[58] or taking oaths in the name of God.[59] Conscientious objection refers to the refusal to obey a legal duty in the name of individual conscience. Its acceptance, therefore, requires upholding the inviolability of conscience over the application of the law, thereby, in Sousa e Brito's words, transforming "the principle of tolerance, which is prior to and a social precondition of the constitutional state, into a human right."[60] While freedom of conscience is intimately related to freedom of religion or belief, the two freedoms differ according to Sousa e Brito in that only individuals can claim conscientious objection. Conscientious objection to military service is recognized as a constitutional right in some countries, whereas in others it is covered only at the statutory level, as a part of laws stipulating conditions upon which exemption from military service will be granted. Even where recognized in principle, its extension to conscientious objection based on secular ethical convictions or to selective opposition to particular wars or weaponry remains controversial. In general, a balance obviously needs to be struck between the claims of conscience and the interests of the state. But Sousa e Brito is critical of what he refers to as an "unfortunate American retrogression" that has reverted to nineteenth-century precedent and rejected intervening developments which had insisted that ordinary laws could override religious freedom only where there was a compelling state interest that could not be advanced in some less burdensome way.[61]

Archbishop *Roland Minnerath*'s chapter on *The Right to Autonomy in Religious Affairs* addresses the general right of religious communities and institutions to autonomy in structuring their own affairs. It thus elaborates one of the ideas belonging

---

[57] Sousa e Brito, chapter 13, 284.
[58] Ibid, 285–86.
[59] Ibid., 286. The general point that conscientious objection extends beyond military contexts is also addressed by Martínez-Torrón and Navarro-Valls, chapter 10, 232 & n. 83.
[60] Sousa e Brito, chapter 13, 274.
[61] See ibid., 289.

to the normative core of freedom of religion or belief as described earlier in this introduction. It also correlates in significant ways with the idea of sphere sovereignty elaborated in the chapter by van der Vyver.[62] Not surprisingly, then, Minnerath finds the autonomy of religious or belief communities to structure their own affairs to be "one of the crucial features of any system of freedom of religion or belief."[63] This is because the ecclesiastical or social structures of such communities are often "themselves the focus of deeply held beliefs."[64] Without this right, therefore, religious authenticity would be compromised and communal autonomy impaired. Because the religious life of individuals is generally interwoven with the broader life of a religious community, breaches of religious autonomy will violate not only collective and institutional rights, but individual rights as well.

Minnerath maintains that the boundary of religious autonomy goes "beyond matters that are strictly internal to the life of a religious community"[65] to include a broader range of the community's "own affairs"—i.e., the realm over which the state has no competence. Minnerath traces the grounds for the right to religious autonomy in the classic human rights instruments, and shows how these guarantee the corporate right of religious organizations to exist and to be protected in their internal autonomy. Through a detailed historical analysis of various models of autonomy, including a careful analysis of developments in the United States,[66] Europe,[67] and the European Court of Human Rights[68] dealing with disputes within religious communities, the author shows how autonomy has emerged as a right in both constitutional and international law. Minnerath then demonstrates how the right to autonomy applies with respect to matters of doctrine and teaching; faith and order; freedom in appointing, disciplining, and dismissing religious personnel; and the operation of charitable and educational organizations.

Cole Durham's chapter on *Facilitating Freedom of Religion or Belief through Religious Association Laws* contains an extensive analysis of the bearing of human rights norms on laws that govern the process of acquiring legal entity status. Because these laws are such a routine feature of the legal landscape of most countries, their significance from a human rights standpoint is often overlooked. But in fact, this turns out to be one of the most significant areas for facilitating freedom of religion or belief, both because difficulties at the stage of acquiring entity status through incorporation or registration can have such profound impact on the ability to exercise religious beliefs, and because this is an area in which reform is relatively easy.

One of the difficulties in this area is that while virtually all states have laws governing acquisition of legal entity status, these laws can be applied in very different ways. Countries with strong human rights records characteristically view such laws primarily as vehicles for facilitating religious freedom. The laws provide readily accessible legal forms that religious communities can use to structure their own affairs. In other countries,

---

62 Van der Vyver, chapter 4, 94–99.
63 Minnerath, chapter 14, 291.
64 Ibid.
65 Ibid., 292.
66 Ibid., 296–300.
67 Ibid., 305–09.
68 Ibid., 309–14.

however, a "control" mentality continues to lead to restrictive applications of religious association laws. The contrast of "facilitation" and "control" orientations is a thread running through the entire chapter.

The chapter provides a comparative overview of the types of legal entities available within and across legal systems.[69] It then turns to an analysis of the implications of key international human rights norms for various features of religious association laws.[70] In effect, the chapter shows how analysis from many of the other chapters in the book is relevant to recurrent problems that emerge in the formulation and application of the basic laws governing the creation of legal entities for religious communities. The main focus in this area is on the requirements of substantive religious freedom norms.[71] However, particularly in light of the emerging recognition that freedom of association entails a right to acquire legal entity status, attention is paid to the implications of freedom of association for religious association law.[72] The relevance of several other human rights norms, including nondiscrimination, freedom from arbitrary decision making, and the right to effective remedies, is also noted.[73] The chapter then identifies a number of recurrent practical problems that arise in connection with religious association laws and need to be avoided.[74] In the overall design of the deskbook, this chapter is intended to provide a comprehensive guide to analyzing the practical problems that arise when religious association laws are being adopted or revised.

Lee Boothby looks at *Protecting Freedom of Religion or Belief in Restricted or Institutional Settings*—such as prisons, the military, and state-operated medical facilities. The focus is on the US experience of the past forty years, but the discussion is clearly of wider interest. The rights that may be compromised are most often those of manifestation of religion or belief through dress, headgear, diet, compulsion to work on holy days, or being denied the facilities for prayer or other religious practices. Boothby highlights the importance of upholding this freedom in institutional settings, as the persons concerned have a particularly acute need for the support of their beliefs, and such protection can help reinforce the objectives these various institutions strive to attain. The tensions in US case law relating to the extent to which individual beliefs should be accommodated in prison settings have largely been clarified with recent legislation. The Bureau of Prisons insists on the religious neutrality of the Bureau itself and on providing inmates of all faiths with opportunities to participate in their religious beliefs and practices (within the budgetary and security constraints of the prison system). The Congressional Religious Land Use and Institutionalized Persons Act of 2000 goes further and insists that no substantial burden be placed on religious exercise even if the burden results from a general rule, unless the government demonstrates a compelling interest and it is the least restrictive means of furthering that compelling governmental interest. To Boothby this demonstrates that toleration of religious diversity and neutrality is possible in such settings, even in a separationist system such as that of the United States.

---

[69] Durham, chapter 15, 337–47.
[70] Ibid., 347–84.
[71] Ibid., 350–66.
[72] Ibid., 366–77.
[73] Ibid., 378–84.
[74] Ibid., 384–400.

Roman Podoprigora focuses on a key interaction between religion and the state that is characteristic of (but not limited to) administrative law: *Freedom of Religion and Belief and Discretionary State Approval of Religious Activity.* Discretionary approvals can result in restrictions on registration, juristic personality, worship facilities, tax status, visas, or approval to run schools—to name just a few possibilities. Whereas these approvals may come from different bodies, often at relatively low levels, and may reflect the burdens of overworked bureaucracies rather than intentional discrimination, abuse of discretion in these areas can seriously curtail religious freedom. This is particularly true with respect to the activities of smaller and less popular communities. The author addresses a range of different types of problems: unreasonable delay, denial by inaction, and outright refusals stemming from either express or more frequently undisclosed bias. When such abuse of discretion occurs, it violates not only freedom of religion and belief, but fundamental rule of law values as well. Podoprigora argues it is essential that the discretionary authority of governments that can impede religious activities be wielded on a well-defined and principled basis. This is the only way that freedom of religion and belief can be fully assured.

In *The Place of Religion in Public Life: The Lay Approach, Jean Baubérot* explores one of the major models of the appropriate nature of the relationship between religion and the state. He explains in detail the French lay approach to the place of religion in public life. Drawing on a historical account of *laïcité* (French-style separation of church and state) over the two centuries since the French Revolution, Baubérot's chapter illustrates how deeply this historical background has molded the current place religion holds in the public sphere within France. In contrast to the United States and northern Europe, where "religion has been integral to the emergence of modernity," in France "modernity erected itself against religion."[75] The historical conflict over religion's place in French society has produced an acute sensitivity verging on allergic reaction to any reference to religion in the public sphere. Though some manifestations of traditional religion manage to avoid this reaction, the general picture in France is one in which society remains leery of religion in public space. In effect, the nineteenth-century restructuring of public institutions outside the control of religion produced a new "secular clergy" of professionals in fields such as education and medicine. While Baubérot's chapter was completed before the latest round of public debate on the Islamic scarf in France, his chapter helps contextualize French disquiet over "the veil affair." It also helps to explain attitudes toward Jehovah's Witnesses and other smaller groups. Without condoning some of the more prejudiced reactions, Baubérot indicates that these can be understood at least in part by the loss of prestige within the ranks of the "secular clergy" in areas such as education and medicine. Other aspects of the French reaction, including the rise of government subsidized anti-sect associations and the concomitant stigmatization of numerous smaller groups, no doubt stem from fear of the unknown—from "a sense of helplessness in the face of so many new sectarian movements that we do not yet understand."[76] In the end, these issues are taking on new forms as a result of new social pressures coming from increased pluralization and the heightened role of the media. These are obviously forces that are exerting a transformative influence on relations of religion, state, and society not only in France, but around the globe.

---

[75] Baubérot, chapter 18, 441.

[76] Ibid., 452.

Part IV: Women, Parents, and Children

The fourth part of the deskbook deals with a range of issues of extraordinary importance and profound controversy: the encounter of religious rights and religious vision (including all-too-human failures of vision) with the rights of women and children and the politics of gender. Some feminists, such as Juliet Sheen, believe that "[r]eligion is so heavily masculinized that the tenets and extensions of religious belief are sometimes, in and of themselves, violations of women's human rights."[77] In her view, "[a]rguments of religious liberty cannot legitimately be used to trump women's rights."[78] Others are less inclined to assume that women's rights automatically override religious freedom claims. Thus, though Kari Børresen is deeply critical of her own (Catholic) tradition on an array of sensitive issues, including ordination of women, she acknowledges that "it is certainly not a human right to be ordained a priest or a bishop. . . ."[79] This appears to imply that though the doctrinal foundation for the religious position is "perfectly unconvincing,"[80] and though she would work intensely to bring about change within her tradition, it does not automatically follow that international or national norms should be allowed to coerce change. On the other hand, there are positions such as that of Özlem Denli, who is troubled by a secularist state that disallows the wearing of religious symbols.[81] Still others are troubled by the fact that (typically secularist) concerns about religion-sourced discrimination seem so much more prevalent than (religiously based) concerns for incursions on women's right to freedom of religion or belief. Bahia Tahzib-Lie illustrates the multiple contexts in which women may respond to the call of conscience and examines which violations are specifically directed against women and which women are particularly vulnerable.[82] Because of the range of views in this area and the intensity with which such views are held, it is inevitable that various positions taken by our authors will attract sharp and differing disagreements from people holding a wide range of views. But we are convinced that the chapters in this part contribute more light than heat.

Three of the chapters look at the conflict between religion, religious rights, and women's rights in the context of major world religions: Hinduism (Ursula King), Catholicism (Kari Elisabeth Børresen), and Islam (Özlem Denli). Nazila Ghanea's chapter on apostasy belongs substantively to part V with its focus on changing beliefs, but sociologically it has much to say about problems that Muslim women in particular face in changing religion. The other chapters take a more general human rights approach: Bahia Tahzib-Lie focuses on the extent to which and circumstances under which questions of gender are directly or indirectly relevant to the area of freedom of religion or belief; Juliet Sheen talks about conflicts of women's and religious rights; and Geraldine Van Bueren discusses children's rights.

By focusing on the connecting thread of dissent, *Bahia Tahzib-Lie* is able to distill out many of the distinctive types of violations of freedom of religion or belief that women suffer, whether as dissenters within dominant religious traditions, dissenters

[77] Sheen, chapter 21, 513.
[78] Ibid., 521.
[79] Børresen, chapter 23, 555.
[80] Ibid.
[81] Denli, 510.
[82] Tahzib-Lie, chapter 19, 493.

from majority traditions who are affiliated with smaller religious communities, dissenters within or against minority traditions, believers in any tradition who dissent from the secularity of the state, dissenters from belief in general (i.e., nonbelievers), or female dissenters from male beliefs in the family context. Tahzib-Lie's chapter stands at the beginning of this part of the book, because in many ways it is the most general of the chapters dealing with women's issues, but the focus on the many settings of dissent helps contextualize all that follows. Among other things, this approach helps to bring out that international attention to women and religion thus far has been concerned almost exclusively with the protection of women against *discriminatory* religious norms and practices to the detriment of protecting their *freedom*.

The author analyzes a variety of violations of freedom of religion or belief, drawn from both the "internal" and the "external" forum, and shows in case after case how a dissenting woman's right to freedom of religion or belief is violated through coercion and violence in both types of settings. One of the somewhat unexpected results is that "there may be a wider discrepancy between the protections afforded men and women with respect to their internal freedom than with respect to their external freedom."[83] Another important contribution is the chapter's recognition that the emerging international obligation to exert due diligence to protect individuals from violations of their human rights may have significant applications in the context of preventing coercion and violence against the religious freedom rights of dissenting women.[84] The due diligence principle is especially important in this context, because it affirms that certain governmental obligations may apply even when violations are perpetrated by non-state actors. In the "external forum" setting, the author provides detailed analysis of three very sensitive current issues in which state actions are directed specifically against women: female genital mutilation,[85] wearing religious garb in the workplace,[86] and the freedom not to wear religious clothing.[87] In addition, while the principle focus of the chapter is on religious freedom concerns, the author looks with some care at a number of situations in which gender-discriminatory religious norms and practices violate the human rights of women. While acknowledging the seriousness of such problems, however, she draws attention to the fact that, "in the area of women and religion or belief, there is an incongruity between the international community's intense concern for a wide set of other human rights involving women and the lesser degree of concern manifested with respect to violations of women's right to freedom of religion or belief."[88] Not content to identify a number of sensitive issues, Tahzib-Lie concludes with concrete proposals for further action by a variety of actors in the promotion of the freedom of religion or belief of "dissenting women."[89]

Özlem Denli provides an overview of the head-cover controversy in contemporary Turkey, a secular country with a Muslim majority. The state-imposed head-cover ban has far-reaching consequences for women who consider veiling in public life to be a religious obligation. Such women are excluded from the entire public sector, which

[83] Ibid., 492.
[84] Ibid., 460–61.
[85] Ibid., 466–73.
[86] Ibid., 473–83.
[87] Ibid., 483–87.
[88] Ibid., 488.
[89] Ibid., 492–95.

is rather sizeable in Turkey. Among other things, they are deprived of the opportunity of a university education. This in turn blocks access to employment and other forms of engagement in public life. For the last two decades, this controversy has set the tone for public debate on freedom of religion or belief. More than just giving an account of the problem, however, Denli uses the concrete religious headdress issue in Turkey to provide an insightful sociological account of the tensions between laicist ideology and the resurgence of public religion in Turkey. She demonstrates how the head-cover issue has become a "nonnegotiable boundary between laicism and Islamism," and concludes that the "laicist policies of the Turkish Republic are expressions of a comprehensive doctrine that is systematically biased and exclusionist in its very makeup."[90]

Juliet Sheen is particularly dubious about claims that religious freedom can override women's rights. In her view, male dominance in the religious sphere has led to such pervasive systemic and structural inequalities that the only effect of allowing religious freedom claims to prevail over women's rights is to reinforce discrimination. Particularly suspect in her view are situations where freedom of religion is played by states and religious institutions as a trump card to justify the subordination and exclusion of women. Whereas the link between the causes of the inequalities and discrimination against women and religion may be indirect and dispersed, the results are felt in many contexts: family or personal status laws; modesty norms; expectations of obedience to husband; and so forth. These religious causes of discrimination against women are further reinforced by cultural practices that "may also be associated with religion without being sanctioned by religious law."[91] The author appeals to multifaceted strategies to reverse the denial of women's human rights due to fundamentalist demands, from education and dialogue, to sanctions and coercion against offending states.[92]

From Sheen's general critique of religious pressures to violate women's rights, we move to a highly particularized case study of India in *Ursula King's* chapter on *Hinduism and Women: Uses and Abuses of Religious Freedom*. King focuses on areas where freedom of religion or belief is in tension, or even clashes, with the human rights of Indian women. Modern interpreters use the rich but profoundly ambivalent Hindu traditions and images about the role of women to promote, as well as to obstruct, women's equal rights and status in contemporary Indian society. Whereas there have been long-standing attempts to abolish social practices such as sati, child marriage, polygamy, and the prohibition of widow remarriage, the repression of women continues. All too often, systematic and severe violations of women's rights are perpetrated in the name of religion and its free exercise, and then amplified by caste. These patterns were not helped by the colonialist's codification of Hindu law in the nineteenth century, which stripped it of ambiguities running in favor of women, translated it into the male-dominated idiom of Victorian English, and effectively locked it into a rigid anti-woman form. Nor were they assisted by the development of personal laws within which gender discrimination was prevalent. Despite these problems, King remains

[90] Denli, chapter 20, 510.
[91] Sheen, chapter 21, 519.
[92] Ibid., 520.

optimistic about the proliferation of autonomous women's groups in India since the 1970s that have helped to cultivate "genuinely Indian roots" for women's rights. However, the challenge remains enormous. Especially in light of the politicization of Hinduism in recent years, King remains deeply uncertain "whether Hinduism will allow for constructive reinterpretations within a secular framework, thereby facilitating the development of a truly universalist, inclusive spirituality that alone can affirm and empower women in a true sense." [93]

In chapter 23, *Kari Elisabeth Børresen* tackles the theme of conflicts between women's rights and normative religion in the Roman Catholic tradition. Her acerbic approach will no doubt be controversial in Catholic circles. She submits that the present-day Vatican, acting in alliance with many Muslim states and supported by vociferous fundamentalist Protestants, has launched a major campaign opposing women's human rights to control their own fertility. To explain this "retrograde alliance," she turns to an analysis of traditional Christian doctrines about the gender of the Godhead, the ensuing androcentric interpretation of preferred status for men, the denial of women's sociocultural equivalence with men, the instrumental understanding of sex as geared solely to the purpose of reproduction, and the denial of eligibility for the priesthood to women. In sum, she traces the exclusion of women from partaking in "Christ's redemptive divinisation of humanity" on equal footing with men to what she views as discredited theology. She lambasts what she calls "the current doctrinal incoherence between outdated premises and preserved conclusions."[94] Børresen finds it paradoxical that Christian feminism has first been accepted in a Protestantism that sees God's instrument of revelation primarily in the literal Bible. To the contrary, she argues, the indispensable instruments for a feminist Reformation of Christianity are still to be found in the Catholic and Orthodox traditions, when divested of androcentric distortions.

Most fascinating in Børresen's condensed and well-documented contribution is her analysis of the abiding impact of historical theological doctrines on contemporary human rights issues. This entails the need to exercise our religious freedom to probe such doctrines critically. Børresen does not call on the authority of human rights to buttress her theological agenda. As already noted, she recognizes that "it is certainly not a human right to be ordained a priest or a bishop in the Catholic Church."[95] She marshals theological and historical arguments in support of the position that all human beings are entitled to be attributed a fully Godlike humanity—and hence not be denied equal dignity, neither before God nor before humans. On her analysis, present-day Vatican doctrines simultaneously embrace freedom of religion of belief and exploit this human right to uphold anthropological and sexological tenets detrimental to women. She argues that this denial has burdened underdeveloped countries most heavily, as Catholics in most "socially advanced societies no longer respect Vatican sexology."[96]

The final chapter in this section is *Geraldine Van Bueren's The Right to be the Same, The Right to be Different: Children and Religion*. Recognizing the potential for conflict in the triangle of children's rights, parental rights and duties, and the interests

---

[93] King, chapter 22, 541.
[94] Børresen, chapter 23, 558.
[95] Ibid., 555.
[96] Ibid., 552.

of the state, Van Bueren contends that we need to get beyond asking what trumps what. We need to "sit down and discuss what religion can learn from human rights and how human rights can in turn be enriched by religion in ways which will better protect the rights of children."[97] Her essay is an eloquent appeal for balance: balance in understanding the best interests of the child, balance in assessing whether children have the right to be different from dominant views in their states or even in their families, balance in weighing the importance of parental authority against the autonomy of the child, balance in resolving how a child should be raised when its parents disagree on religion, balance in determining when children should be seen "as symbolizing continuity, affirmation, and the future"[98] and when the focus should be on their present.

In addressing the scope of a child's right to freedom of religion or belief, Van Bueren discloses some of the ways in which vague general norms paper over deep cultural divides. Thus, she notes that "the CRC, in contrast to the ICCPR, omits any express reference to having or adopting a religion or belief of the child's choice. . . . In addition, unlike the ICCPR, the CRC does not expressly include the freedom of a child to manifest a religion or belief in worship, observance, practice, and teaching."[99] For those who assume that the CRC simply builds on the ICCPR, the assumption is that the CRC implicitly incorporates the omitted ICCPR notions and that both children and adults have the right to "have or adopt a religion." But a number of Islamic and Catholic states "were not able to accept any provision granting children the freedom to choose and change their religion or belief."[100] Similarly, the CRC waffles to some extent on the strength of parental authority. In these areas Van Bueren believes better balancing is needed.

The chapter addresses a number of the sensitive issues concerning religion and education—religious instruction, controversial secular instruction (e.g., "factual sex education")—and how the sometimes conflicting interest of the state in educating its future citizenry is to be weighed against parental authority to control what instruction is received. Again there is a call for balance, a plea that education be "child-centered" and the implicit suggestion that it not be disrupted by religious tug-of-wars between parents (and sets of parents). Recent case law concerning corporal punishment of children is also addressed.[101]

Ultimately, Van Bueren concludes, "it is a question of balance, and the contribution of the CRC is that it has shifted the weight away from child sacrifice toward child autonomy."[102] Unstated, perhaps, is one last recognition: that the balance is shifted ***toward*** child autonomy, but not all the way. Children are not adults; they have "evolving capacities."[103] There are still profound reasons why adults need to judge just how much autonomy children can be given, and why (most) parents are better judges of their children's capacities and best interests than the state. Children

---

[97] Van Bueren, chapter 24, 561.
[98] Ibid.
[99] Ibid., 564.
[100] Ibid,, 564–65.
[101] Ibid., 568–69.
[102] Ibid., 569.
[103] CRC, art. 14.

mature; parents err and disagree. The state is left with the delicate task of balancing all these balances, and of doing so without undue interference in the lives children and their families.

Part V: Changing beliefs and the Tensions of Tolerance

Part V addresses the notion of changing beliefs in two senses: the change registered by the emergence of new religious movements and the inner individual change marked by conversion. Both lie within or near the boundary of the absolutely unregulable domain of inner belief. Yet both for a variety of reasons continue to stir controversy. This reflects the inner residuum of intolerance and the tensions it creates, even in the central stronghold of freedom of religion or belief.

Chapters 25 and 26 focus on freedom of religion or belief as relating to "New Religious Movements," or "NRMs"—a preferred way to refer to smaller religious groups without engaging in the discrimination of disparagement by referring to them as "sects" or "cults." The first chapter is a general introduction to new religious movements by *Eileen Barker*, one of the premier sociological experts in the world on these groups. The second, by *Willy Fautré*, *Alain Garay*, and *Yves Nidegger*, is a case study of the problematic treatment of new religious movements that has been occurring in Francophone Europe over the past several years.

Barker explores what it is about NRMs that attracts discrimination, persecution, and in general, violation of freedom of religion or belief. While noting the extraordinary diversity of NRMs, Barker outlines certain recurring characteristics of NRMs: the preponderance of first-generation members, often composed of an atypical segment of the population (young, middle class, good education); clear-cut beliefs; charismatic authority; and a tendency to create sharp social boundaries around a group, often resulting in a group's cutting itself off from the rest of society. In addition, NRMs change and evolve over time. Perhaps, Barker suggests, it is the "enthusiastic commitment, inexperience, unpredictability, and novelty"[104] that appears to pose a threat to society and lead to NRMs being treated with such suspicion and fear.

Instead of engaging in the complex process of coming to a scientifically responsible understanding of NRMs, governmental organizations and anticult groups tend to construct their perception of the reality of NRMs by relying on stereotypical images drawn from the media and other sources that often (not always) exaggerate the danger of NRMs. The images thus constructed, the reports, lists, and laws that are predicated on such stereotypes often lack credible basis in reality, and have led to extensive discrimination, and sometimes even to attacks, against the concerned groups. One of the most tenacious stereotypes is that NRMs brainwash their converts. There is now extensive research on this issue, and what it shows is that the typical groups do not use techniques that have the irresistible and irreversible impact that the idea of brainwashing conjures up.[105] Barker acknowledges that such groups often do exert pressure and sometimes impose constraints on their members, but the levels of pressure would be difficult to distinguish from legitimate groups.[106]

---

[104] Barker, chapter 25, 578.
[105] Ibid., 583–84.
[106] Ibid., 584.

In line with recurrent recommendations from the Council of Europe,[107] the authors of both chapters believe that it is counter-productive and inappropriate to adopt specialized laws that target NRMs and punish entire groups on the basis of preconceived notions about cults or on the basis of wrongful conduct perpetrated by particular members. Instead, they argue, normal criminal and civil laws equally applicable to all should be used to take effective action against *any* individuals convicted of illegal activities.

The study of Francophone Europe stresses the importance of this proposal as a counter to recent anticult initiatives in recent years in France, Belgium and Switzerland. These activities have "triggered an unprecedented wave of discrimination and intolerance" against such groups and violated international standards in the field of freedom of religion or belief. The authors are critical of the confrontational mentality used in these "Crusades" against "foreign sects," and particularly concerned about the "sect observatories" set up to study this phenomenon. Such observatories need to exert great care both to utilize scholarly methods for their activities and to avoid actions that will themselves violate international norms on freedom of religion or belief.

The next three chapters explore various dimensions of one of the more sensitive areas in the field of freedom of religion or belief—that of the right to have, adopt, or change one's religion, and the related rights to engage in persuasion, missionary work, and proselytism. *Tad Stahnke* provides a thorough and balanced overview of the scope and limits of religious persuasion. He defines proselytism as "expressive conduct undertaken with the purpose of trying to change the religious beliefs, affiliation, or identity of another."[108] It is therefore intimately linked with change in religion or belief, which is explored by *Nazila Ghanea* in her chapter on *Apostasy and Freedom to Change Religion or Belief.* The attempt to persuade covered by Stahnke's definition, if successful, results in a change of belief, and if this is a change from another belief, it will appear as apostasy to those who continue to hold the convert's original belief.

Stahnke reminds us that convictions about obligations to engage in religious persuasion and missionary work are themselves religious in nature, deserving religious freedom protection as surely as other doctrines that a missionary might teach. Stahnke also reminds us of something that, surprisingly, is often overlooked: namely, that efforts to engage in religious persuasion are covered both by freedom of religion and by freedom of expression.[109] It thus has "double" human rights protection. States restrict proselytism both directly and indirectly, intentionally and unintentionally, through their various regulations on registration and manifestation of expression and of religion or belief. Though such restrictions may be neutral in construction, they often lead to impermissible discrimination and may violate religious freedom norms in other ways.

Possible criteria for "improper proselytism" are explored by Stahnke; the touchstone he identifies in this area is the notion of coercion. This is where the emphases of Stahnke and *Makau Mutua* diverge. The former believes that the "preservation of a particular religious tradition, the official ideology of a state, or the religious character of a state's institutions—divorced from any of the other limitations expressly provided

---

[107] See discussion of this issue in Martínez-Torrón and Navarro-Valls, chapter 10, 211–14.
[108] Stahnke, chapter 27, 620.
[109] Ibid., 627.

for in international instruments—cannot support limitations on the freedom to manifest religion or belief."[110] Such one-sided protectionisms and penalties, Stahnke argues, are biased and can lead to the abuse of minorities.

Mutua's perspective on the situation is quite different. He views proselytism as a form of cultural imperialism whereby (typically) foreign missionaries demonize and deliberately destroy an indigenous belief system. This, Mutua believes, can compromise other rights and result in cultural warfare and even cultural genocide. Is there a right to be left alone, and allow the continuation of diversity of cultures? Is there a right to cultural self-preservation? If freedom of religion or belief should be protected, doesn't that mean that the religion of the "target" group should be protected as well? The example Mutua focuses on is the historical one of the spread of Islam and Christianity in Africa and the decimation of indigenous African religion where proselytizing was coupled with force and power, and therefore illegitimate. In a sense, both Stahnke and Mutua agree: proselytism that involves inappropriate levels of coercion is impermissible. The difficulty is how to define what is inappropriate. Disagreements will no doubt continue in this area, and indeed, the Oslo Coalition has undertaken a project to pursue further dialogue on this particular issue.

Whereas coercion can be coupled with proselytism, it can also be coupled with the threat against change of religion or belief. Ghanea examines international and regional standards, and finds that only the Universal Declaration, the ECHR, the American Convention on Human Rights, and various OSCE Documents explicitly protect freedom to change religion or belief. Primarily because of Muslim sensitivities, the term "change" was dropped in the ICCPR and the 1981 Declaration. Nevertheless, numerous experts, the Special Rapporteur on Freedom of Religion or Belief, and the Human Rights Committee have all found freedom to change religion or belief to constitute a legally essential component of freedom of religion or belief. Unfortunately, violence, coercion, and even death can still result from change of religion or belief. Numerous Islamic countries, for example, legally uphold penalties for apostasy. The author contends that such penalties for apostasy are not sanctioned in the Qur'an, and that the main barrier to allowing for change of religion or belief in such societies is in fact political rather than religious.

All three of the "change of religion" chapters highlight an area where delicate balancing may be required between the converter, converted, proselytizer, seeker, and those not seeking. As Ghanea argues, a more cosmopolitan and tolerant attitude needs to be nurtured, but one that is also cognizant of both the power relationships between the actors and any coercion that may be implicated.

Part VI: Contexts for Facilitating Freedom of Religion or Belief

The final section of the deskbook examines a series of contexts that are particularly important for freedom of religion or belief. It opens on the hopeful note suggested by the essay of ***Archbishop Anastasios*** of Tirana and all Albania on ***Developing Shared Values and Common Citizenship in a Secular and Pluralist Society: How Religious Communities Can Contribute***. The focus is on Christians and Muslims in a modern Europe. One of

[110] Ibid., 637.

the first duties facing Europe's Christians and Muslims is to emphasize to secular society, through their actions, that religion has a vital place in human life. This, to Archbishop Anastasios, requires them to be self-critical, admit past mistakes, reject any violence in the name of religion, and then to articulate common values and spiritual norms. The values and norms promoted by religion are eternal. It is for this reason that religious leaders should not allow religion to be politicized and manipulated for egotistical short-term motives at the expense of others. Respect for human rights, especially for freedom of conscience, can serve as the foundation for such harmonious coexistence between religious groups. However, human rights should not just be a rallying call for aggrieved minorities, quickly forgotten when majority status is achieved. In order for Europe's Christians and Muslims to progress toward serving as models of peaceful coexistence, Archbishop Anastasios promotes the need for "a dialogue of life": a dialogue focused on the most practical issues for creative interreligious understanding, such as ecology, globalization, poverty, and ethnic reconciliation. Dialogue is obviously a particularly significant context for facilitating freedom of religion or belief, as attested in several other chapters—especially 9, 33, 34, and 35.

The next chapter is an important reminder that religion is not the only context that needs to be considered: the "belief" half of "religion or belief" needs to be remembered. That is an important element in the essay on ***Humanism and Freedom from Religion*** by ***Rajaji Ramanadha Babu Gogineni*** and ***Lars Gule***. There are many world views that are not necessarily religious and yet come within the ambit of the right to "thought, conscience, and religion." The authors describe one such outlook, Humanism, as a "modern life stance rooted in rational thinking, providing a way of understanding our universe and our place in it in naturalistic terms"[111] and upholding "an open-ended and continuous interrogation about our life and the universe."[112] For Humanists, therefore, the highest priority should be given to the realization of tolerant environments conducive to free enquiry. Such environments would allow all life stances to flourish in "peaceful competition" and this, to the Humanists, crucially requires freedom *from* state-supported religion in the public sphere. Despite international standards on freedom of religion simultaneously protecting beliefs, many legal systems have not translated this into an equal protection of life stances such as Humanism. Humanists particularly face barriers in terms of their interest in the public school system, lack of media attention, and lack of toleration from the general public. Genuine state neutrality towards all religion and belief communities would mean, for example, the state not imputing religious meaning to public holidays, not making reference to religion or belief in public documents such as constitutions, not imposing religious education on children in schools, and eliminating blasphemy laws. Overall, the authors call for a strict separation of law and religion, church and state, private religion and public politics. At one point the authors state,

> It might seem like a contradiction that Humanists demand, on the one hand, recognition and even financial support from the authorities, and, on the other, freedom from religion in the public domain. However, the contradiction is only apparent, and the demands are coherent.[113]

---

[111] Gogineni and Gule, chapter 31, 699.
[112] Ibid.
[113] Ibid., 705.

The resolution of the contradiction comes in recognizing that Humanists and other nonbelievers should be treated equally. One can easily understand why unbelievers should not suffer discrimination due to their life stance, but it is not clear why the "realization of tolerant environments . . . crucially requires freedom *from* religion," if that means total exclusion of religion from the public square. To some, that would appear to be more like remaking public space in the humanist image along the lines of what Tore Lindholm calls "strident laicism," and contrasts with what he views as the preferred position of "universal (or nonexclusive) religious freedom."[114] In fact, however, Gogineni and Gule's approach can be given a much less strident reading. They do indeed call for "recognition and even financial support," but only to the extent this grants nonbelievers equal treatment. Ultimately, they conclude that it is "impossible to demand freedom from religion in the public space. Freedom of organization and expression as well as the freedom of religion or belief make people's right to present their religious views publicly a self-evident matter."[115] What they object to at core is state-backed support of a particular religion. They do not insist on a "strident laicist" approach calling literally for total freedom from religion. The tension between "strident laicism" and "universal (nonexclusive) religious freedom is representative of larger societal debates which are unlikely to be resolved any time soon.

The next chapter, *Jeremy Gunn's* treatment of *The United States and the Promotion of Freedom of Religion and Belief*, focuses on a rather different "context" for facilitating freedom of religion or belief: that opened up by the passage of the International Religious Freedom Act (IRFA) in the United States in October 1998. In many ways this chapter has an emphasis that parallels earlier chapters (7–12) dealing with institutions responsible for facilitating freedom of religion or belief. We have concluded that it should be treated separately, however, because it represents the initiative of one particular country (albeit an influential one) to support international religious freedom standards. In this respect the chapter is significant not only for the information it provides on the important new initiatives of the United States, but also as a reminder of the increasing importance of national initiatives in promoting freedom of religion or belief in the contemporary international human rights system. Foreign ministries around the world are constantly called upon to address religious freedom concerns, both as they deal with countries where violations occur and as they respond to concerns about their own country's practices (no one is perfect). Both Norway and the Netherlands have been particularly active in this regard. As a practical matter, those striving to improve implementation of religious freedom norms at the international level should not overlook the influence foreign ministries can have.

Having recognized that the case of the United States is just one example of the more general importance of foreign policy establishments to international religious freedom, it remains the case that the recent initiatives of the United States have been particularly significant. The passage of IRFA has made the United States "the state that most visibly promotes the rhetoric of freedom of religion in the international arena,"[116] and immediate and positive benefits from this can already be noted.

---

[114] Lindholm, chapter 2, 43–46.
[115] Gogineni and Gule, chapter 31, 718.
[116] Gunn, chapter 32, 722.

Whereas the US has a long history of contributing to the development of international norms in the field of freedom of religion or belief and of cognizance of this freedom in its foreign policy, that position has now been strengthened. The Act has required the US State Department to promote international religious freedom as part of its foreign policy, issue annual reports on the status of religious freedom in all other countries, establish an office in the State Department to oversee implementation of the law, and take actions in response to each country that violates international standards of religious freedom. Moreover, IRFA established an independent body, the US Commission on International Religious Freedom, which is charged with monitoring State Department activity in this area and making recommendations both to the president and the State Department regarding ways that US foreign policy can more effectively foster support for international religious freedom standards. All this means that religious freedom is not allowed to slip out of sight behind other priorities on human rights agendas, and as a result, the US regularly raises issues related to religious freedom in both bilateral and multilateral fora. Victims and human rights workers worldwide may do well to note that since 1998 US Embassies abroad have been instructed to pay added attention to issues of religious freedom, and are required to file an annual report on these issues. As a practical matter, one of the most significant impacts of IRFA has been that the reporting process itself opens high-profile channels in which violations of religious freedom rights can be heard and brought to the attention of domestic government leaders. This often results in quiet, back-channel diplomacy that resolves a significant volume of problems. Gunn's chapter is significant not only in describing how the various aspects of the new IRFA mechanisms work, but also in defusing misunderstandings about the motivations behind passage of IRFA. Most fundamentally, the Act is not about imposing an American agenda, but about making certain that US foreign policy is responsive to the goal of supporting *international* standards of freedom of religion or belief.

Rüdiger Noll addresses another vital context in his chapter on *The Role of Religion and Religious Freedom in Contemporary Conflict Situations.* The hope that religious leaders and communities can contribute to conflict avoidance and resolution runs through several chapters in the book, including chapter 12 on the Norwegian experience in the OSCE and chapter 38 dealing with NGOs. Rüdiger Noll brings extensive practical experience to his treatment of this theme. Anyone working with religious groups at peacemaking activities can benefit from his insights. Acknowledging that religion has too often played a negative role in violent conflict situations, Noll nonetheless challenges the view that the best means forward is to eliminate religion from politics and public life. Rather, he advances a number of reasons for thinking that religions and religious leaders can play a more positive role in preventing and resolving conflict and contributing to peace and reconciliation: their commitment to values, their competence as mediators, their structures at the local and national levels, and their long-standing presence in the field. However, in order to be able to play such a role, religions themselves need to be allowed sufficient space by states. Ensuring full implementation of freedom of religion or belief is vital to this objective. Without it there can be a dangerous escalation from discrimination to other tensions, and this can induce the negative cycle of violence rather than opening the positive potential of peacemaking.

Closely linked to the context of conflict avoidance is the theme of dialogue. This too is an idea that has emerged in several chapters in the volume (2, 9, and 30, to name just a few), but this methodology receives more specialized treatment in Leonard Swidler's chapter on *Freedom of Religion and Dialogue* and in the case study of *The Emergence of Interfaith Dialogue in Norway* submitted by *Inge Eidsvåg*, *Tore Lindholm* and *Barbro Sveen*. Swidler refers to religious freedom and dialogue as constituting "two of the most powerful transformative concepts in the history of humanity."[117] He particularly welcomes the historical emergence of neutral states committed to recognition of freedom of religion or belief. He believes that this development has been central to the "awesome, unparalleled achievements" of western civilization and its globalization.[118] In his view, uncoupling religion from the power of the state has been essential to unleashing the creative capabilities of both religion and the state. Similarly, the transformative power of dialogue constitutes a further condition for the flourishing of humanity—especially where there is "deep dialogue" where one individual or group seeks to learn from another. For effective dialogue Swidler has identified ten ground rules (the "Dialogue Decalogue"), which are detailed in his chapter.[119] He also identifies three levels at which interreligious or interideological dialogue operate: the practical, the spiritual, and the cognitive. There are, of course, voices in other parts of the world that would be more critical of Swidler's account of western civilization and globalization and the way that religious freedom has figured the rise of the West. Makau Mutua's chapter (28) with its critique of western proselytism comes to mind in this regard. But Swidler would have a ready answer on this point: more, better, and deeper dialogue.

It is at Swidler's practical level that the interreligious dialogue in Norway has concentrated its efforts, as described in the Norwegian case study. The authors of this chapter provide a detailed account of the experience of interfaith dialogue and cooperation over the past twenty years in Norway—a country where dialogue has been complicated by the fact that there is a state church that retains a number of privileges. The focus has been first on elaborating a communal ethic shared by nine Norwegian religions and life-stance communities and then on identifying foreseeable conflicts and finding constructive ways to handle them. This has involved the Norwegian Council for Religious and Life Stance Communities in dialogue and action on moral, educational, legislative, social and interethnic issues. One secret to the success of this council may have been their reliance on consensus decision making in all matters—a measure that has been key to sustaining trust and upholding a sense of equality among participating groups. This experience provides a positive example of the possibility of realizing the vision elaborated in chapters 30 and 33, that religion and belief can indeed "serve as a basis for eliminating animosities and strengthening understanding and cooperation across ethnic, ideological, and religious divides."[120]

Education is another key context for freedom of religion or belief. It is both an area where some of the major recurrent issues arise, and also a context of extraordinary importance for cultivating tolerance and mutual respect. The next two chapters

[117] Swidler, chapter 34, 761–62.
[118] Ibid., 765.
[119] Ibid., 772–75.
[120] Eidsvåg, Lindholm, and Sveen, chapter 35, 789.

turn to this area of endeavor. Both chapters ground their analysis in the educational initiatives of the UN Special Rapporteur on Freedom of Religion or Belief, whose activities also received attention in chapter 7. *Ingvill Thorson Plesner* considers *Promoting Tolerance through Religious Education* in general, and *Jolanta Ambrosewicz-Jacobs* concentrates on *Religious Tolerance, Freedom of Religion or Belief, and Education: Results of the 2001 UN Conference.* The question both chapters address is how religious education can be successfully delivered in our pluralistic times in ways that foster tolerance and mutual respect, without limiting the freedom of religion or belief of others. While Plesner focuses on the experience of various European countries, Ambrosewicz-Jacobs examines the findings of the 2001 UN International Consultative Conference.

Like Van Bueren's chapter (24) dealing with religion and the rights of the child, these chapters recognize the various tensions that may arise between the three-way considerations of the duty of the state to promote tolerance, the best interests of the child, and respect for the rights of parents or guardians to bring up their children in line with their religious and moral convictions. For example, the Special Rapporteur has criticized the "separation" or "ghetto" approach to religious education, which separates pupils in accordance with religious affiliation in the religious education provided by public schools. Instead he supports the "integration" approach. However, the preference of some parents is precisely to have separate denominationally-aligned religious instruction for their children. Furthermore, as Plesner suggests, the child's self-conception may also be changed by the encounter with the other, leading to further challenges by some parents or guardians. A broad dialogue about the content of religious education across religions and beliefs may be an important prerequisite to gaining support within society that can reduce opposition to the integration approach.

Both authors concur with the Special Rapporteur that schools are one of the most important arenas for fostering tolerance and laying the long-term societal foundation for freedom of religion or belief. The International Consultative Conference on School Education in Relation with Freedom of Religion and Belief, Tolerance and Non-discrimination held in Madrid in 2001, the results of which are described in the chapter by Ambrosewicz-Jacobs, focused on developing strategies towards this end. The Final Document of the conference reiterated the importance of education as a means to ensure respect for religion and belief, nondiscrimination, and tolerance. The effective implementation of its findings not only requires the cooperation of various actors such as states, NGOs, parents, and religious or belief communities, but also a range of further follow-up activities and studies. As noted earlier, the Oslo Coalition is actively engaged in implementing a number of the recommendations emerging from the Madrid conference.

The final chapter by *Elizabeth Sewell* looks at *Facilitating Freedom of Religion or Belief through NGOs.* The chapter, taken together with the list of NGOs compiled in Appendix G, is designed to extend effective NGO work on freedom of religion or belief in three ways. First, it draws on theoretical work on the role of international human rights NGOs to develop models of NGO influence. In particular, it provides an analysis of the processes whereby NGOs develop and become more (or less) effective in shaping social reality.[121] Second, it aims at highlighting the vast potential that

[121] Sewell, chapter 38, 820–26.

NGOs have to promote and further establish the right to freedom of religion or belief and the diverse array of NGOs that are contributing to this undertaking in many different ways. The NGOs may be domestic, regional, or international in scope; they may promote this freedom exclusively or as part of its larger defense of human rights in general; they may be religious organizations themselves, or academic institutions; and they could be consortia bringing together a variety of actors. Their methods vary widely, and may be colored by the above characteristics. Their key roles include "standard setting, violation reporting, providing technical advice, and lobbying and agenda setting."[122] Sewell examines each of these roles in detail, bringing examples from a variety of actors to bear on this study. Third, by sharing knowledge about what various NGOs are doing, the chapter aims to encourage cooperation and to avoid duplicative efforts. Sewell's analysis of the important roles of NGOs in facilitating freedom of religion or belief underscores the power of networking, reasonable argument, and mutually respectful dialogue in the advancement of religious liberty.

The Path Forward

Unfortunately, the need for continued facilitation of freedom of religion is not likely to diminish any time soon. Intolerance, discrimination, and persecution continue—reduced by the impact of religious freedom norms, but not abated. Most states strive to implement international standards of freedom of religion or belief, but many continue to fall short, and none are perfect. Government officials rotate in office; most are constantly learning and relearning the lessons of how to be more sensitive in respecting differing beliefs. But some are not interested in learning, and,unfortunately, some have contrary agendas. Against this often discouraging backdrop, the concluding comment about Professor Sewell's chapter deserves reiteration with respect to the contents of the deskbook and more generally with respect to its objective of facilitating freedom of religion or belief: there is great power in networking, reasonable argument, and mutually respectful dialogue.

The deskbook itself is a venture in all three. As noted earlier, its authors were brought together initially by networking through the 1998 Oslo Conference, and subsequently through additional networking as the project evolved in response to argument and dialogue. It is important to stress again that this process took time, with different chapters being finished at very different times. The result is that many of the chapters have not been able to include every late-breaking event of relevance. But the fundamental issues are amply covered. It is also important to reiterate once again that different authors come from very different backgrounds and take very different positions for which they alone are responsible. This is part of the reasonable argument and mutually respectful dialogue that is so much needed. There is much to disagree about, and yet at the same time, much to learn. Good friends disagree, and yet join again and again together to move forward.

There is much left to be done. This is not the place to go into detailed recommendations. These can be found in many of the chapters, and in addition, we have tried to collect suggestions and ideas for future effort in what we call not a conclusion,

---

122 Ibid, 828.

but more appropriately, a "Conclusion and Agenda for the Future." There we identify additional types of support that are needed at the level of international institutions, issues that need to be addressed, monitoring that needs to be done, minimum standards that need better and more concrete formulations, websites that need to be built, literature that needs to be written, and beyond everything else, an extensive research agenda that can enable further progress. Despite the size of this volume, it provides at best a basic tool. We hope, however, that it will be a useful resource, and that it will serve as a launching pad for additional dialogue, expanded networks, and high-level reasoning that will in turn provide a powerful impetus to facilitating freedom of religion or belief.

Beyond all the tasks that demand action, there is a need for each generation to rekindle the fundamental vision of freedom of religion or belief. Sometimes the spark comes in reaction to oppression; sometimes in gratitude for the experience of freedom and respect; sometimes in the process of defending rights that are imperiled. Whatever the source of the spark, the resulting flame needs to be sustained and facilitated in the countless ways suggested in this volume. If we succeed in nurturing this flame, even in imperfect measure, we contribute to what the American founder, James Madison, once called "the lustre of our country."[123] He was writing at a time when the idea of religious freedom was young, fragile, and very much at risk, not only in his own country, but everywhere. The world has come far in the intervening centuries, though not far enough. Today the challenge is to work for this luster in all our countries, and thereby to enhance the luster of our world.

[123] James Madison, "A Memorial and Remonstrance," (1785) in *The Papers of James Madison*, ed. Robert A. Rutland et al., vol. 8 (Chicago: University of Chicago Press, 1973), 299, para. 9. This phrase has been brought to our attention by John T. Noonan's wonderful book, *The Lustre of Our Country: The American Experience of Religious Freedom* (Berkeley: University of California Press, 1998).

Part V

Changing Beliefs and the Tensions of Tolerance

Chapter 25

Why the Cults? New Religious Movements and Freedom of Religion or Belief

Eileen Barker

All religions can both inflict and suffer from abuses of human rights. This chapter asks what it might be about new religious movements (NRMs), "cults," or "sects" that could make them peculiarly susceptible to such discrimination. Is it that there is something intrinsic to an NRM that invites others to feel the need to treat them as deserving of a special kind of control? And/or is it that there is something about societies that encourages them to restrict the freedom of new religions?

In order to address these questions, we need to consider a few more questions, such as what *is* an NRM? How do they differ from established religions? To what extent do they cross the boundaries of acceptable behavior? Under what conditions are they most likely to be picked out for discriminatory treatment? Finally, we might ask: What, if anything, might be done about it?

I. What is an NRM?

In the course of my research, I have tended to define the current wave of new religions as consisting of groups that (a) have become visible in their present form since World War II and which (b) are religious in the sense that they offer answers to some of the ultimate questions that have traditionally been addressed by mainstream religions: *Who am I? Is there a God? Is there life after death? What is the meaning/purpose of life?* For the purposes of this chapter, however, I shall be using the concept to include any group or movement that is referred to as an NRM, a cult, or a sect in popular parlance. This is both broader and narrower than the above definition as, for example, it can include nineteenth-century sects such as the Jehovah's Witnesses or the Bahá'í but it excludes a number of groups not normally distinguished for purposes of discrimination with such labels.

To decide what is meant by terms such as NRM, cult, and sect and, thus, to which groups the label can be applied is not merely an academic exercise. There can be very real consequences for those involved, depending on whether or not they find themselves falling under the rubric of NRM, cult, or sect or are classified as a proper and/or

Tore Lindholm, W. Cole Durham, Jr., Bahia G. Tahzib-Lie (eds.), Facilitating Freedom of Religion or Belief: A Deskbook, *571–593.*

genuine religion. The application of one label can, without any further clarification or information, bestow respectability and privileges such as status and tax exemption; the application of the other label can give a society permission to damn an organization and to treat its members as lesser citizens, or even as noncitizens, denied what would otherwise be considered their basic rights.

While it is *necessary* for the existence of society that we know what we are talking about when we use the concepts with which we communicate with each other, exactly how we construct our definitions will always be to some extent *arbitrary*. Definitions are not more or less true; they are more or less useful—and their boundaries are more or less open to manipulation. We can make a distinction between two kinds of definitions: the stipulative and the popular. For purposes such as scientific research and legislation, definitions are explicitly stipulated, their construction being such that, in theory at least, it is comparatively easy to decide whether or not a particular phenomenon does, as a question of fact, fit inside, lie outside, or overlap the boundaries laid down by the definition. Popular definitions are more fluid and more open to manipulation by a subtle (or, quite often, crude) sleight of hand—thereby resulting in a phenomenon, purportedly displaying the characteristics necessary to qualify it for inclusion in a particular category, finding itself excluded.[1]

It is usually claimed in a modern democracy that a stipulative definition is based on recognizable, nonevaluative criteria; a popular definition can, however, be more or less imbued with positive or negative evaluation—although those using it might well be claiming, and themselves believe, that it is comprised of objective criteria. Thus, although there are technical uses of such concepts as church, denomination, cult, sect, and NRM in the literature of religious studies and the social sciences,[2] the terms cult and sect are popularly used in the media and everyday parlance as terms of disapproval, with the explicit or implicit suggestion that they are inherently bad and dangerous, rather than denoting any empirically recognizable features. For this reason, scholars prefer to use the more neutral term "NRM" when talking about those groups that are popularly called cults or sects. This is not without its own problems, however, as not all NRMs are new and not all are recognizably religious—at least according to several commonly accepted definitions of religion.[3] But so long as it is clear what scholars are talking about when they are describing or explaining different religious groupings, there should not be any consequences for human rights merely because a stipulative definition is being used one way rather than another.[4]

---

[1] A university chaplain once told me that he could not call the International Society of Krishna Consciousness a religion because (despite the fact that it would fit all the criteria he would normally use in defining "religion") there were "not enough rooms"—and the university had a rule that each religion should have a room. When I asked whether it might not be more honest to change the rule, he replied in a shocked voice that to do that could be seen as religious discrimination.

[2] Meredith B. McGuire, *Religion: The Social Context,* 4th ed. (Belmont, Calif.: Wadsworth, 1997), chap. 5.

[3] No attempt is going to be made here to explore all the problems to which attempts to define religion have given rise. I have, however, discussed the general dilemma in Eileen Barker, "But Is It a Genuine Religion?" in *Between Sacred and Secular: Research and Theory on Quasi Religion,* ed. Arthur Greil and Thomas Robbins (Greenwich, Conn.: JAI Press, 1994).

[4] Unfortunately, social scientists have on occasion succumbed to the request to draw on their expertise to say what a "real" religion is, as though there were some Platonic truth that they have divined. In fact, it should be recognized that their expertise can lie only in making a hypothetical statement (*if* by religion/cult you mean . . . *then* . . . is/is not a religion/cult), or in *reporting* what a popular definition or usage of the term is

This is not, however, the case so far as the law is concerned. Nearly all legislative bodies have recognized the very real difficulty of finding any satisfactory criterion (or criteria) with which they could define NRMs or "cults"—by satisfactory I mean criteria that would include those movements that they would like to include for the purposes of their constitution or law, while excluding others which they would not wish to include. A number of governmental organizations and some cult-watching groups have attempted to get round this problem by defining (or, more likely, listing) as a cult or sect those movements that are perceived (by someone) to be in some (unspecified) way dangerous.[5] To do this is, of course, to prejudge the outcome of any investigation into the actual characteristics of any particular movement, for if something is *defined* as dangerous one cannot *demonstrate* or *question* whether it is or is not; it *must* be—by definition or because it is included in the list.

For these reasons, if for none other, the chances of at least some unwarranted discrimination might be allayed if government and other officially sponsored reports do not produce lists that imply, even if they do not explicitly state, that those religions, spiritual communities, or groups on the list are dangerous or undesirable in a way that other religions, spiritual communities, or groups are not. If, however, subdivisions or categories of religion are to be drawn, this should be done on the basis of empirically identifiable—and testable—characteristics. In other words, by starting from a more neutral definition of the type of groups to be selected, questions can be asked as to whether or not any particular group, at that stage in its history, poses an actual or potential threat that might lead a society to want to treat it differently from other groups. Then if, for example, reference is made to criminal organizations, the decision as to whether or not particular religions are criminal should depend not on a label or on their being included in a list, but on whether the movements (or their members) have been convicted in a court of law of some criminal activity. At the same time, it should be recognized that other, possibly mainstream, religions would also be included if they (or their members) have ever committed similar offences.

II. What Are NRMs Like?

A. The Impossibility of Generalizing

The most important generalization that one can make about NRMs is that one *cannot* generalize about them. They differ according to tradition and within traditions. While most of the earlier waves of new religions in the West have, for hundreds of years, had their origins within the Judaeo-Christian tradition, the current wave that became visible during the past century owes its origins to almost all the traditions of the world, as well as to a few novel ideologies and philosophies. There are, of course, plenty which

---

by a specified group of persons (such as the media) at a particular time and place. For the distinction between characterizing and appraising value judgements, see Ernest Nagel, *The Structure of Science: Problems in the Logic of Scientific Explanation* (London: Routledge, 1961); and for a discussion on the use of definitions in social science, see Eileen Barker, "The Scientific Study of Religion? You Must Be Joking!" *Journal for the Scientific Study of Religion* 34, no. 3 (1995): 287–310.

[5] Eileen Barker, "Watching for Violence: A Comparative Analysis of the Roles of Five Cult-Watching Groups," in *Cults, Religion and Violence*, ed. David G. Bromley (Cambridge: Cambridge University Press, 2002).

are based on Judaic-Christian tenets (such as The Family, The International Churches of Christ, the Unification Church, the Messianic Community, Jews for Jesus, the New Jerusalem, the Branch Davidians, and the Peoples Temple)—although more orthodox Christians might well consider some, if not all, to be heresies. But there are also NRMs owing their roots to Hinduism (ISKCON, the Brahma Kumaris, Sahaja Yoga), to Buddhism (Soka Gakkai, Friends of the Western Buddhist Order), to Islam (the Nation of Islam, Hizb ut Tahrir), to Sufism (Murabitun), and to Shinto (Ōmoto), as well as to various offshoots of other religions such as those of the Jains, the Sikhs, and the Zoroastrians.

Then one can find Pagans and Neo-Pagans, Wicca and Witchcraft, the New Age, and a whole variety of Human Potential groups (such as the Church of Scientology, the Institute of Self Actualization, MSIA, and Insight) which, while not always calling themselves religious or even spiritual movements, do tend to follow a philosophy that celebrates "the god within," "the temple of the body" and, perhaps, the Cosmic Christ. Further movements include the so-called UFO-cults (such as the Raëlians and the Aetherius Society) and all manner of esoteric and occult groups, syncretistic philosophies, and spiritual communities which draw from a variety of traditions, each adding its own particular flavour to the wisdoms of yesteryear and/or tomorrow. And then, on the darker side, one may stumble across the occasional Satanist group such as Anton LaVey's Church of Satan or Michael Aquino's Temple of Set.

Turning to lifestyles, we can find members of NRMs living in communes, communities, detached houses, or high-rise apartment blocks. They may work full time for their movement, or they may lead normal lives apart from attending gatherings for worship or some kind of ritual practice. Such practices may include praying, chanting, various kinds of yoga and meditation, dance, or the sacrifice of chickens. An NRM's organization may be authoritarian, totalitarian, hierarchical, anarchical, democratic, theocratic, or various combinations of these or other styles. The group may expect celibacy or promote promiscuity, or its members may enjoy an "ordinary family life." Women may be considered equal, subordinate, or complementary to men. Homosexuality may be celebrated or it may be seen as one of the most evil of sins. Children may be welcomed and lovingly cared for, or avoided, ignored, or abused. Education may be by home schooling, in special schools run by the NRM, or in regular state schools. The movement may devote many of its resources to actively proselytising for new members, or it may be secretive and relatively difficult to join. Money may be gained through businesses, tithing, donations, selling flowers or literature in public places, or by offering courses to reach spiritual enlightenment or to improve one's relationship with God or one's partner. The proceeds may be distributed internally and used for the benefit of the NRM or its members, or it may be used to help the needy, or to promote the movement's goals—be these religious, political, social, or artistic. Some NRMs are rich, others are poor; leaders may accumulate wealth while their followers live in poverty. Attitudes towards outsiders may be friendly and open, or hostile and guarded.

New religions, like old religions, differ also in the effects that they have on their own members and on the rest of society. Some NRMs are undoubtedly benign and others clearly malevolent. Some bring benefits to some of their members but result in harm for others. Furthermore, in so far as NRMs are potentially or actually dangerous, they are so in different ways. One movement might be as safe as (or even safer than) traditional religions so far as illegal sex is concerned, but may be more effective in pressurising its members to part with inordinate amounts of money; another may be no more or less interested in money than an older religion, but impose a very demanding schedule on its members, which might jeopardize their health and/or cut them off from their families.

The catalogue of differences could be expanded indefinitely, but I hope enough has been said to underscore the point that it is a practice fraught with danger to lump NRMs or "cults" under one umbrella and then assume the label is sufficient to tell us what the movement is like. About the only thing the NRMs share is that they are new and religious (using a wide definition of the term) and that they have at some point been called an NRM, a cult, or a sect.

B. Some Characteristics of New Religions

That said, there are, however, some characteristics that are common to many NRMs merely because they *are* new religions—and an awareness of such characteristics might alert us to some of the reasons why they could be considered actually or potentially dangerous (or undesirable), and thus deserving of special treatment.

1. First-Generation Membership

First, being new, it follows that NRMs consist of a first-generation membership. It has frequently been noted that converts to *any* religion tend to be far more convinced than those who have been born into their religion that they, the converts, are right—that they have discovered The Truth. This fact alone can account for much of the enthusiasm, even fanaticism, that one can often find within NRMs and which can appear unnerving to those who take their religion for granted as part of an often-unnoticed backdrop to their daily life. Furthermore, converts are often desperately anxious to convince their friends and relations (and anyone else whom they can persuade to listen to them) about the importance of their new Truth and to be infuriatingly infuriated if those whom they seek to save or enlighten reject their evangelizing advances.

2. Atypical Membership

Second, NRMs tend to attract an atypical segment, rather than a random sample, of the whole population. The present wave has appealed disproportionately to young adults (in their twenties or thirties) who have come from the middle classes and have enjoyed a better-than-average education. There are rarely dependents in the form of either children or the elderly to look after, and the young, largely unattached converts have little in the way of financial or other responsibilities such as keeping up mortgage payments. They are eager and free to travel wherever their mission calls them or their Master sends them. Such a demographic profile would lead one to expect, moreover, that the vast majority of members will have had experience of life or of leadership with which to match their enthusiasms.

3. Clarity

Third, the beliefs and practices of NRMs tend to be far more clear-cut, precise, and absolute than those of older religions, which will have typically accommodated to the views and influences of successive generations of believers. It is usually pretty clear exactly what one is expected to believe and to do in an NRM, and the membership tends to have a relatively homogeneous understanding of the belief system, rather than, say, some being more fundamentalist and literal, with others being more liberal and interpretive. There may, nonetheless, be differences in the depth of knowledge between the different levels of members, with novitiates not yet initiated into the inner gnosis of the ideology or the secret practices of the inner core.[6] This, however, is by no means peculiar to NRMs except that in older traditions it is usually easier to find out what the hidden truths might be, though not necessarily what the leadership is thinking or doing.

4. Charismatic Authority

Fourth, NRMs are often founded or quickly taken over by a charismatic leader who, his (or, occasionally, her) followers believe, has a special gift of grace, and who may be understood to have a hotline to God—or even to *be* a god. Charismatic authority is, by definition, exercised in accord with the dictates of the charismatic person and is, thereby, unbound by rules or tradition. It is an authority that can be extended over all aspects of the followers' lives—what they wear, where they live, what kind of work they do, whom they marry, with whom they sleep, and, perhaps, whether they live or die. In other words, charismatic leaders are not accountable to any other human being, and, given that they can change their minds at a moment's notice, their movement's actions will be far less predictable than those that follow an established tradition or a bureaucratically administered set of rules.

5. Dichotomies

Fifth, insofar as NRMs espouse beliefs and follow practices that offer an alternative to the beliefs and practices of the wider society, they will frequently protect their new belief and practices by cutting themselves off from the rest of society; sometimes physically, but more frequently socially. This is understandable if they are to secure and preserve a different way of looking at the world from that of their members' families and others who might challenge their new commitments. This too is by no means peculiar to the present wave of new religions. Jesus is reported to have announced that he came to break up families (Matthew 10:35–37), and told potential followers that if they did not hate their parents (and even their own life) they could not expect to become his disciple (Luke 14:25–26).

This need for protection from the rest of the world, and the demand for loyalty to the group and/or leader, can result in a more or less sharp boundary being drawn between followers and nonfollowers—in fact, it is not uncommon (though by no means universal) for NRMs (or new ideologies of any kind) to entertain a generally dichotomous worldview, with clear-cut distinctions being drawn not only between the

---

[6] The "lower" or "outer" levels of Aum Shinrikyo and the Solar Temple were unaware of the atrocities planned by the inner core of their leadership.

social "them" and "us," the theological "godly" and "satanic," and the morally "good" and "bad," but also between the temporal "then" and "now" or "before" and "after," be this referring to a conversion in the past or some eschatological expectation for the future. In such instances boundaries tend to be drawn unambiguously, with relatively little room for grays or negotiability. This, curiously enough, may also be the case among *some* of the new age and human potential groups that avowedly stress the holistic oneness and unity of all things.[7]

6. Change

A sixth characteristic is obvious enough, but surprisingly often forgotten. This is that new religions do not stay new indefinitely, and, thus, the salience of those features that predispose them to behave in the ways outlined above are liable to diminish with the passage of time. Indeed, several of the most significant changes that NRMs undergo are related to little more than inevitable demographic factors.[8] The arrival of a second generation means that first-generation members have new responsibilities; scarce resources such as time and energy have to be diverted towards the nurturing and socialization of children. Then, as the children grow up, they are quite likely to question their parents' beliefs and possibly revolt against the practices they see imposed upon them. Unlike recalcitrant converts, however, they cannot be excommunicated or expelled. Often an NRM will respond to the children's intransigent rebellion by watering down some of its more extreme beliefs and/or practices, and gradually, as the second and subsequent generations grow into leadership positions, more "ordinary," or at least less fanatic, beliefs and lifestyles are introduced. At the same time as the children are growing, the original converts are maturing, gaining more experience of life and how to deal with its contingencies. They may also witness the disconfirmation of empirical claims, such as the imminent arrival of Jesus on earth.

Furthermore, before or after his/her death, the charismatic founder is typically replaced by a more bureaucratic authority; rules become established, traditions develop, and the leadership becomes more accountable and more predictable. In these and other ways, qualifications and accommodations gradually erode the more uncompromising and dichotomous worldviews, and the NRM, although it may keep some of its distinctive features, can begin to merge with less stridency into the rest of a pluralistic society—if it is allowed to do so; for while the movements may change relatively rapidly, their image is likely to change far more slowly. We can still hear NRMs described and treated as though they were exactly the same as they were more than a generation ago, in the late 1960s or early 1970s.

7. Suspicion and Discrimination

This leads us on to a further characteristic of NRMs: they tend to be treated with fear and suspicion and are frequently reviled by the rest of society. This is not altogether surprising given that, at both the family and societal level, NRMs are challenging the

---

[7] Eileen Barker, "The Cage of Freedom and the Freedom of the Cage," *Society* 33, no. 3 (1995): 53–59.

[8] Eileen Barker and Jean-François Mayer, eds., *Twenty Years On: Changes in New Religious Movements* (London: Sage, 1995).

status quo and can, consequently, be seen to be rejecting the normal and the "natural" by offering ideas and ways of life that are new (or new to their members' parents or their particular society). And while none of the characteristics mentioned above will, of themselves, necessarily result in NRMs posing severe problems, it is understandable how enthusiastic commitment, inexperience, unpredictability, and novelty can appear to pose a threat to both the NRMs' members and the rest of society, and why it is frequently felt that "something ought to be done"—a sentiment that has resulted in persecution and a denial of customary freedoms.

Discrimination against new religions is hardly anything new; throughout history there have been untold numbers of atrocities committed against them. The early Christians were thrown to the lions; the Cathars were denounced by the Inquisition and burned at the stake; and countless others have been killed in bloody battles by those who believed—or at least used the justification—that the newcomers were a blasphemy against God, a danger to the individual and/or undermining the very fabric of society.

Today's persecutions may be less dramatic than those of early Christian or medieval times, but they continue nonetheless. There have been numerous physical injuries and some deaths meted out to members of NRMs for no reason other than that they are members of a new or a foreign religion.[9] The Unification Church has, for example, had its members murdered in the Dominican Republic; executed in Ethiopia; beaten up in Bulgaria; imprisoned in Thailand, Czechoslovakia, Laos, and elsewhere; and scores of its centers were burned in Brazil in the 1980s.

Since the late 1990s, the Chinese government, on the grounds that the teachings of Falun Gong are harmful both to the individual and to the body politic,[10] has felt the need to detain thousands of practitioners in prison, where, the movement claims, its members have been raped, tortured, and murdered.[11] The storming by law-enforcement agencies of the Branch Davidians at Waco is seen by many as an unnecessary tragedy that could have been avoided had the authorities understood better the content and fervor of the religious beliefs held by Koresh's followers.[12] Other movements, as intimated above, have been the subject of discrimination merely as a result of their having appeared on an official or semiofficial list of sects.[13]

As is well known, all religions were discriminated against under the atheistic regimes of communism; Krishna devotees were but a few of the many who died in Soviet jails. But, although the situation has undoubtedly improved since the collapse

---

[9] Information listing some of these acts of discrimination can be found in reports published by the International Helsinki Federation for Human Rights <www.ihf-hr.org>; Amnesty International <www.amnesty.org>; the OSCE <www.osce.org/docs/>; the Keston Institute <www.keston.org>; Human Rights Without Frontiers <www.hrwf.net>; and the US State Department <http://www.state.gov/g/drl/hr/index.cfm?id=1470>. See also Alfonse D'Amato, ed., ***Religious Intolerance in Europe Today*** (Washington, D.C.: US Government Printing Office, 1997).

[10] People's Republic of China, ***Li Hongzhi and His "Falun Gong": Deceiving the Public and Ruining Lives*** (Beijing: New Star, 1999); Danny Schechter, ***Falun Gong's Challenge to China: Spiritual Practice or "Evil Cult"?*** (New York: Akashuc, 2000).

[11] See the Falun Dafa Information Center website <http://www.faluninfo.net/>.

[12] Catherine Wessinger, *How the Millennium Comes Violently: From Jonestown to Heaven's Gate* (Chappaqua, N.Y.: Seven Bridges Press, 2000); Stuart Wright, ed., ***Armageddon in Waco: Critical Perspectives on the Branch Davidian Conflict*** (Chicago: University of Chicago Press, 1995).

[13] N. L. Lheureux et al., ***Report on Discrimination against Spiritual and Therapeutical Minorities in France*** (Paris: Coordination des Associations et Particuliers Pour la Liberté de Conscience, 2000).

of the Berlin Wall, there are still numerous instances of physical attacks being perpetrated on unorthodox religions—sometimes by not merely the members but also ordained clergy of the Orthodox Churches. To take but one example from the Caucasus; in June 2001 the Jehovah's Witnesses asked the European Court of Human Rights to investigate the situation in Georgia, where officials have ignored recorded complaints of at least seventy-seven criminal attacks on their members since October 1999.[14]

There have been violent incidents in Western Europe and the Americas, too. Returning to the example of the Unification Church: in 1975 a missionary was beaten up to the screams of "Moonie! Moonie!" in front of Madison Square Garden, New York;[15] in 1976 the French Headquarters of the Unification Church was firebombed; a young Norwegian member was hospitalized for six months and remains severely disabled to this day. Ten years later, following the Report of the French Parliamentary Commission (which includes the "Moon sect" on its list) a series of articles appeared in the French media declaring that "something must be done,"[16] and at 4 A.M. on 29 January 1996, the Paris center was again bombed. This resulted, according to Unificationists, in about $60,000 of damage, although, by luck (there was no prior warning), no one was injured on this occasion. A few months later a similar bomb was delivered to the headquarters of the New Acropolis (another NRM on the French report's list) in the same area of Paris, again at 4 A.M.[17]

More frequently today, however, NRMs face discriminatory curtailment of their freedoms in the guise of legal and other forms of harassment, the denial of civil rights, and/or the creation of insurmountable obstacles to manifesting their religion. The discrimination can involve denying an NRM the right to build a church or to hire a hall in which worshippers could meet, or last-minute cancellation of bookings when it has been pointed out to the owners of the building that the group to which they were hiring their premises is on a list of dangerous cults. Raëlians have lost their jobs in France; the children of Scientologists have been excluded from schools in Germany; in England and elsewhere parents have been denied custody of their children merely on the grounds that they are members of an NRM.[18]

Although the practice does not occur in the West as often today as it did a decade or so ago, literally hundreds of members of NRMs have been kidnapped and held against their will for deprogramming.[19] Drawing on the brainwashing metaphor, deprogrammers have persuaded converts' parents that if they wanted to see their (adult) child again they should pay them (the deprogrammers) thousands of

---

[14] Rosalind Russell, "Jehovah Witnesses take Georgia case to Europe court [*sic*]" *Reuters,* 5 July 2001.

[15] Antonio Benanatcourt, "Unification Church," in ***Religious Freedom and the New Millennium,*** ed. Dan Fefferman (Falls Church, Va.: International Coalition for Religious Freedom, 2000), 460–61.

[16] See, for example, Michel Richard, "Sectes: la chasse est ouverte," [Sects: The Hunt is On] *Le Point,* 13 January 1996, 1217.

[17] AP Paris, "Bomb Hits Paris Cult Bookstore," *Los Angeles Times,* 14 August 1996; see <burn.ucsd.edu/archives/ats-l/1996.Aug/0022.html>.

[18] It might be added that there are antagonists on "both sides" who appear to revel in what have been called "atrocity tales," recounting with something akin to glee how the other side has hounded "their side" by carrying out acts of discrimination or persecution.

[19] For a remarkably frank account by a deprogrammer of his (often violent) participation in this illegal practice, see Ted Patrick and Tom Dulack, *Let Our Children Go* (New York: Ballantine, 1976).

dollars or pounds to "rescue" the "victim."[20] The practice continues in Japan, where Unificationists are frequently targeted, with Lutheran pastors being among the chief instigators,[21] and it does still occasionally occur in western Europe. In 1996 several relatives and an imported American deprogrammer were given suspended prison sentences after being found guilty of grievous bodily harm and unlawful detention in a case in the Netherlands involving a twenty-seven-year-old woman who had joined a Yoruba splinter group.[22] In the USA, exit counseling has become more popular as it does not involve the criminal use of force and is now considered more effective than the earlier, more violent, methods; an even less aggressive practice is "thought-reform consultation."[23] Another not-infrequent practice has been the "medicalization" of converts, which has involved hospitalization and the administration of drugs and electric shock therapy in order to "cure the patients" of their crazy beliefs.[24] This too has become less frequent in the West.

Examples of discrimination could fill many pages, and have indeed taken up many pages elsewhere,[25] but let us now approach the phenomenon from a somewhat different angle by examining in a bit more depth some of the external processes that contribute to the extraordinarily wide-spread suspicion and dislike of NRMs. The aim is to try to understand better how perfectly sincere and well-meaning individuals and governments come to feel they *ought* to discriminate against the NRMs—not only in the best interests of the host society, but also for the sake of the members of the movements themselves.

C. Images of NRMs

One clue can be found in the ways that images of social reality are constructed.[26] There are numerous different images of NRMs available in the cultural milieu, and it is by no means obvious that the most reliable images are those most likely to be

[20] Eileen Barker, *New Religious Movements: A Practical Introduction* (London: HMSO, 1989), Appendix III; Thomas S. Brandon, *New Religions, Conversions and Deprogramming: New Frontiers of Religious Liberty* (Oak Park, Ill.: The Center for Law & Religious Freedom, 1982); David G. Bromley and James T. Richardson, eds., *The Brainwashing/Deprogramming Controversy* (New York: Edwin Mellen Press, 1983); James T. Richardson et al., "Leaving and Labeling: Voluntary and Coerced Disaffiliation from Religious Social Movements," *Research in Social Movements, Conflicts and Change* 9 (1986): 97–126; Anson D. Shupe and David G. Bromley, *The New Vigilantes: Deprogrammers, Anti-Cultists, and the New Religions* (Beverly Hills: Sage, 1980).

[21] Manabu Watanabe, "Reactions to the Aum Affair: The Rise of the 'Anti-Cult' Movement in Japan," *Bulletin of the Nanzan Institute for Religion & Culture* 21 (1997): 43.

[22] Wim Haan, "The Oracle of Ifa and the Verdict of the Court: A Failed Attempt to Deprogram from the African 'Ifa' Religion," <www.bezinningscentrum.nl/tecksten/wim_eng/oracle.htm> (1997).

[23] Livia Bardin, *Coping with Cult Involvement: A Handbook for Families and Friends* (Bonita Springs, Fla.: American Family Foundation, 2000); Carol Giambalvo, *Exit Counselling: A Family Intervention: How to Respond to Cult-Affected Loved Ones* (Bonita Springs, Fla.: American Family Foundation, 1992).

[24] Lee Coleman, *Psychiatry the Faithbreaker: How Psychiatry Is Promoting Bigotry in America* (Sacramento: Center for the Study of Psychiatric Testimony, 1982); James T. Richardson, "Sociology and the New Religions: 'Brainwashing,' the Courts, and Religious Freedom," in *Witnessing for Sociology: Sociologists in Court*, ed. Pamela J. Jenkins and Steve Kroll-Smith (Westport, Conn.: Praeger, 1996), 115–34; Thomas Robbins and Dick Anthony, "Deprogramming, Brainwashing and the Medicalization of New Religious Movements," *Social Problems* 29 (1982): 283–97.

[25] Eileen Barker, "The British Right to Discriminate," in *Church-State Relations: Tensions and Transitions*, ed. Thomas Robbins and Roland Robertson (London: Transaction, 1987), 269–80; Alain Garay, *L'activisme*

selected for use by the general public. People perceive things differently because they are observing from different geographical, temporal, and cultural positions, and they have different interests in what is happening.[27] While there is always some agreement between the different images (such as the fact that the movement was founded by a certain person in a certain place at a certain time), there is also considerable disagreement. If we want to understand why there is discrimination against NRMs, one of our tasks must be to discriminate between the images that are "out there."

It is, of course, impossible for anyone to construct a complete description of any social phenomenon, but some constructions are significantly more accurate and balanced than others. Apart from deception and downright lies (which are by no means unknown), there are a number of methodological tactics or approaches that can account for some of the systematic differences between images. For the purposes of this chapter, I would like to draw attention to four such approaches. First, there is ***defining and labelling***, the use of which has already been discussed. Second, people will ***select*** what to include and exclude in their accounts according to their interests. Third, there is the practice of drawing ***generalizations*** from specific instances. And, fourth, there is the ***comparative*** method, which is used in all the sciences in their attempts to understand whether and how different phenomena are related to each other. Let me now elaborate briefly some of the ways in which these last three practices can make a difference to our image of NRMs.

1. NRMs and Cult-Awareness Groups

It is not surprising that new religions (like older religions and most other individuals and organizations) present themselves in the best possible light, keeping any skeletons firmly locked in closets. Nor is it surprising that their opponents (frequently referred to generically as the anticult or cult-awareness movement)[28] will concentrate on prizing open such closets and exposing their contents to the glaring light of day; and, in their attempts to depict the cults as pernicious groups that need to be controlled and/or

---

Anti-Sectes: De L'assistance á L'amalgame (Lampeter: Edwin Mellen Press, 1999); Drew Youngman, *Double Standards: An Independent View of Religious Discrimination in Australia* (Australia: n.p., 1995).

26 Peter L. Berger and Thomas Luckmann, *The Social Construction of Reality: Everything That Passes for Knowledge in Society* (London: Allen Lane, 1967).

27 Eileen Barker, "Will the Real Cult Please Stand Up? A Comparative Analysis of Social Constructions of New Religious Movements," in *The Handbook of Cults and Sects in America*, ed. David G. Bromley and Jeffrey Hadden (Greenwich, Conn.: JAI Press, 1993); Barker, "The Scientific Study of Religion? You Must Be Joking!" 287–310.

28 For descriptions of the rise of organized opposition to NRMs in the United States, Europe, and Japan, see, for example, James Beckford, *Cult Controversies: The Societal Response to the New Religious Movements* (London: Tavistock, 1985); Garay, *L'activisme Anti-Sectes;* Marat Shterin and James T. Richardson, "Effects of the Western Anti-Cult Movement on Development of Laws Concerning Religion in Post-Communist Russia," *Journal of Church and State* 42, no. 2 (2000): 247–71; Anson Shupe and David G. Bromley, *Anti-Cult Movements in Cross-Cultural Perspective* (New York: Garland, 1994); Shupe and Bromley, *The New Vigilantes: Deprogrammers, Anti-Cultists, and the New Religions;* Watanabe, "Reactions to the Aum Affair," 32–48. For examples of publications by members of these groups, see Ronald Enroth, *The Lure of the Cults* (New York: Christian Herald, 1979); Steven Hassan, *Combatting Cult Mind Control: Protection, Rescue and Recovery from Destructive Cults* (Wellingborough: Aquarian Press, 1988); Margaret Singer and Janja Lalich, *Cults in Our Midst: The Hidden Menace in Our Everyday Lives* (San Francisco: Jossey-Bass, 1995).

eradicated, they tend to select only the negative aspects of NRMs and to generalize from the particulars that they select.[29] How successful the two sides are in disseminating their image of the movements will depend on a number of factors, such as their relative access to resources (such as funding), their status within the wider community, and the attractiveness their particular image has for the media.

2. The Media

In modern society, it has frequently been observed that the media play a far more important role in defining our pictures of reality than they have in the past. It is also the case that, in order to attract readers, listeners, and viewers, the media tend to focus on the newsworthy—the novel, the sensational, the sexy, and the wicked are far more attractive to most audiences than the passé, the commonplace, or the worthy. For the media, bad news is, generally speaking, good news. The four-letter word "cult" imparts the thrills and tingles of the exotic, the sinister, the weird, and the depraved. A story about a cult member committing suicide is a far better story than one about an Anglican or Lutheran doing so (the latter would not be "news"), thereby giving rise to a popular perception that killing oneself is typical of cults and atypical of other groups.

Furthermore, the use of evaluative nouns (cult, zombie, maniac) and adjectives (bizarre, ominous, menacing), rather than informative descriptions, and the employment of passive grammar ("the brainwashed victim had to be rescued") reinforce an image of robotic recruits, ruthlessly exploited by a psychopathic leader, presenting an intrinsic danger to themselves and the rest of society. Such images give permission not only to the general public, but also to those in positions of authority, to treat NRMs and their members as something different—clearly not "one of us."[30]

3. Social Science

A somewhat different picture tends to be constructed by scholars who have studied NRMs using the methods of social science. Not only will both "good" and "bad" and normal and unusual elements of behavior be included, but an attempt is also made to present as balanced a view as possible by drawing on information about the group as a whole, or at least from a *randomly selected* sample, to ensure that the eventual image does not rely on a generalization from a few, possibly atypical, examples. The social scientist will also *compare* the NRM with other groups in order to elicit the extent to which observed characteristics are related to the movement, it being part of the social scientists' job to ensure that visibility is not mistaken for factuality. Thus, while the media might quite accurately report the occurrence of suicides (or some criminal act such as child abuse) among members of NRMs, the social scientist would

---

[29] Barker, "Watching for Violence."

[30] For reasons of space, the role of the Internet cannot be explored here, but it ought to be at least mentioned that it is playing an increasingly important role in shaping our images of reality. One commentator has, indeed, coined the phrase "Internet terrorism" to describe some of the "dirty tricks" that are entered into through this particular medium: Massimo Introvigne, "'So Many Evil Things': Anti-Cult Terrorism via the Internet," in *Religion on the Internet: Research Prospects and Promises*, ed. Jeffrey K. Hadden (New York: Elsevier Science, 2000), 281.

also investigate the suicide rate for other religions (or the population as a whole) as it may well turn out that the rate of suicide (or child abuse) is greater among members of a traditional religion or the general population of a similar age and social background. This might lead to questioning the assumption that cult members are particularly likely to indulge in, say, child abuse, and asking why is it that members of NRMs are *less* likely than normal to commit the felony.

III. Brainwashing, Mind Control, and Mental Manipulation

One of the most tenacious images associated with NRMs is that they brainwash their members, and one of the most popular reasons given for discriminating against them stands on its head our question ("Are the cults having their freedoms restricted?") by insisting that it is the NRMs that have taken away the freedom, human rights, or civil liberties of their members by using manipulative techniques to recruit them in the first place, and then to ensure that they do whatever they are told to do, even when it is patently against their best interests.[31] This sometimes appears to bewildered relatives to be the only account that could explain why intelligent people accept incredible beliefs and spend their lives doing abnormal and unnatural things. The prevalence of this belief suggests it is worth briefly considering the evidence.

Let us begin by agreeing that some NRMs put potential converts under considerable pressure in trying to persuade them to join—though probably no more than committed members of some evangelical Protestant churches. It has been argued that mainstream religions use a far more subtle method of inculcating a particular set of beliefs and practices into their children as they bring them up within the fold—the adage popularly, and probably inaccurately, attributed to Ignatius of Loyola, "Give me a child up to the age of seven and I shall make a Catholic of him for life," is not without some substance.

Be that as it may, research has shown over and over that the techniques which the NRMs use have not been nearly as efficient as they would doubtless wish, or their opponents have insisted is the case. I myself conducted a study in the late 1970s into the success of the methods employed by the Unification Church, which was at that time accused of employing irresistible and irreversible techniques. What I found was that ninety percent of those whom the Unificationists persuaded to attend the residential seminars (at which the so-called brainwashing techniques were administered) were perfectly capable of deciding that they did not wish to join the movement. Furthermore, the majority of those who joined did so only for a short time, leaving of their own free will within a couple of years at the most.[32] In the light of this and similar results from other scholars, it has been argued that it has been the deprogrammers, kidnapping individuals from their movements under the pretext of liberating them, who could more aptly be accused of removing the freedom of converts to NRMs. In 1990, as the result of several academics and professional bodies objecting to the claims

---

[31] The deprogrammer, Ted Patrick, is quoted as having said "What I do is not kidnapping. What I do is rescuing. When I deprogram a person he has already been unlawfully imprisoned. His mind has been unlawfully imprisoned by a cult" ("*Playboy* Interview with Ted Patrick," *Playboy*, March 1979, 53, 58, 77, 120).

[32] Eileen Barker, *The Making of a Moonie: Brainwashing or Choice?* (Oxford: Blackwell, 1984).

made by some of the opponents of NRMs, it was ruled in an American court that expert testimony purporting to prove that brainwashing or other similar practices had been carried out on a victim was inadmissible as evidence since there was no agreement in the scientific community about the meaning or applicability of such a concept.[33]

To repeat, this is not to say that NRMs do not put both pressures and constraints on their members—they undoubtedly do.[34] But it is to suggest that a law, such as that enacted by France in 2001, which introduces the crime of making people alter their judgement,[35] is likely to make the lawyers rich, for there exists no noncontentious way of deciding that a person has been forced to believe something against his or her better judgement—and those criteria that might be used could threaten the freedoms of some old religions as readily as they threaten those of the new religions that the law is intended to control.

IV. Action at the State Level

Let us consider what has been happening recently at the state level.

A. Reports

First of all, several governments have felt the need to set up official inquiries, resulting in a number of reports about the movements in general,[36] and on particular NRMs.[37] There have also been reports commissioned by the European Parliament and the Council

---

[33] Dick Anthony, "Religious Movements and Brainwashing Litigation," in *In Gods We Trust: New Patterns of Religious Pluralism in America*, 2d ed., ed. Thomas Robbins (New Brunswick: Transaction, 1990), 295–344; Richardson, "Sociology and the New Religions."

[34] Eileen Barker, "Authority and Dependence in New Religious Movements," in *Religion: Contemporary Issues*, ed. Bryan R. Wilson (London: Bellew, 1992), 237–55. It has been remarked more than once that it would be difficult to find many organizations that are as efficient in instilling obedience and a particular outlook on the world as the US Marines. See Coleman, *Psychiatry the Faithbreaker*, 24.

[35] On 30 May 2001, the French Senate adopted the following passages as an amendment to the Law for the Prevention and Repression of Sectarian Movements: "Sect. 223-15-2.—The fraudulent abuse of the state of ignorance or the condition of weakness of either a minor . . . or of a person in a state of psychological or physical subjection resulting from serious pressures exercised or repeated or from techniques likely to alter his judgment, leading this minor or this person to an act or an abstention which are seriously harmful to him, is sentenced to three years in prison and a 2,500,000 Francs fine. When the offence is committed by the legitimate or *de facto* leader of a group which is pursuing activities with the purpose or effect to create, maintain or exploit the psychological or physical subjection of persons taking part in these activities, the sentences are extended to five years in prison and a 5,000,000 Francs fine" (Sénat session ordinaire no. 83, 2000–2001).

[36] Daniel G. Hill, *A Study of Mind Development Groups, Sects and Cults in Ontario* (Ontario: The Queen's Printer, 1980); Tobias A. M. Witteveen, *Overheid En Nieuwe Religeuze Bewegingen* (The Hague: Tweede Kamer, 1984); Alain Vivien, *Les Sectes En France: Expression De La Liberté* (Paris: La Documentation Française, 1985); A. Kulikov, *Inquiry on the Activities of Certain Foreign Religious Organizations* (Moscow: Ministry of Internal Affairs of the Russian Federation, 1996); Duquesne and Luc Willems, *Enquete Parlementaire Visant À Élaborer Une Politique En Vue De Lutter Contre Les Practiques Illégales Des Sectes Et Le Danger Qu 'elles Représentent Pour La Société Et Pour Les Personnes, Particulièrement Les Mineurs D'âge* (Brussels: Belgian House of Representatives, 1997); Ortrun Schätzle, *New Religious and Ideological Communities and Psychogroups in the Federal Republic of Germany: Final Report of the Enquete Commission on "So-Called Sects and Psychogroups"* (Bonn: German Bundestag, 1998); Margó Ingvardsson, Sonja Wallbom, and Lars Grip, *I God Tro: Samhället Och Nyandligheten* (Stockholm: Statens offentliga utredningar, Socialdepartementet, 1998).

of Europe.[38] Some of these reports (e.g., Ontario, the Netherlands, Sweden) concluded that the existing law seemed to be sufficient to deal with the movements; others (e.g., Russia, France, Belgium) concluded that special measures should be introduced to control them.[39]

B. Lists, Methodology, and Example

Within Western Europe and North America, the French and Belgian Reports have been criticized on a number of counts,[40] one of which has been the lists of "sects": 172 in France and 189 in the case of Belgium, including the Quakers, Mormons, Seventh-Day Adventists, Opus Dei, a small Jesuit community, the Young Women's Christian Association (though, curiously, not the YMCA), and some other religions not normally considered sects elsewhere. It is, perhaps, a reflection of the extent to which sects are accepted as being bad and deserving of discrimination that some of the religions that have found themselves on such a list have been extremely vocal in their complaints about the injustice of *their* presence on the list, while apparently indifferent to the possible injustice of the very existence of such a list.[41] A similar insistence that "we are part of us, not them" can be observed in a variety of ways in large parts of Europe.[42]

It should be noted that both French and Belgian spokespersons have repeatedly pointed out that the lists are not official in the sense that they are incorporated in any law (but that, in the case of the Belgian Report, it was nothing more than an index of groups that were considered by the Parliamentary Commission). But the damage has been done and, as mentioned previously, the very fact that the lists appeared in a report commissioned by the government has already led to numerous acts of discrimination.

---

[37] John G. Foster, ***Enquiry into the Practice and Effects of Scientology*** (London: Her Majesty's Stationery Office, 1971); Donald M. Fraser, ***Investigation of Korean-American Relations*** (Washington, D.C.: US House of Representatives, 1978); Franz-Josef Kniola, ***Zur Frage Der Beobachtung der scientology-Organisation Durch die Verfassungsschutzbehörden*** (Düsseldorf: Innenministerium des Landes Nordrhein-Westfalen, 1997).

[38] Richard Cottrell, ***The Activity of Certain New Religions within the European Community*** (Strasbourg: European Parliament, 1984); John Hunt, ***Report on Sects and New Religious Movements*** (Strasbourg: Council of Europe Parliamentary Assembly, 1991); Maria Berger, ***Draft Report on Cults in the European Union*** (Strasbourg: European Parliament, 1997); Adrian Nastase, ***Illegal Activities of Sects*** (Strasbourg: Council of Europe Parliamentary Assembly, 1998).

[39] The differences between the Reports and their recommendations are compared in some detail in James T. Richardson and Massimo Introvigne, "'Brainwashing' Theories in European Parliamentary and Administrative Reports on 'Cults' and 'Sects,'" *Journal for the Scientific Study of Religion* 40, no. 2 (June 2001): 143–68. Another useful overview can be found in the European Consortium for Church and State Research, ***New Religious Movements and the Law in the European Union***, vol. 15 (Milan: Università degli Studi di Milano, 1997).

[40] Willy Fautré, ed., ***The Belgian State and the Sects: A Close Look at the Work of the Parliamentary Commission of Inquiry on Sects' Recommendations to Strengthen the Rule of Law***, vol. 10, 1/2 (Brussels: Human Rights Without Frontiers, 1998); Massimo Introvigne and J. Gordon Melton, eds., *Pour En Finir Avec Les Sectes: Le Débat Sur Le Rapport De La Commission Parlementaire* (Paris: CESNUR, 1996). See also the chapter by Fautré et al. in this volume.

[41] Interestingly, the US State Department has a subheading in its ***Annual Report on International Religious Freedom*** that reads: "Stigmatization of Certain Religions by Wrongfully Associating them with Dangerous 'Cults' or 'Sects'" (***Annual Report on International Religious Freedom***, 5 September 2000, xxiv).

[42] Eileen Barker, "But Who's Going to Win? National and Minority Religions in Post-Communist Society," in ***New Religions in Central and Eastern Europe***, ed. Irena Borowik (Kraków: Nomos, 1997), 7–44.

It might also be noted that the Swedish Report did include a list of religions in Sweden—but this was of *all* the known religions, including both what was then the state church and five satanic groups.[43]

Another criticism of the French and Belgian Reports is the methodology that they employed, relying on anticult groups[44] and former members, rather than scholars who had studied NRMs, or giving the movements themselves an opportunity to refute some of the more extreme inaccuracies. Further grounds for concern have lain in the fact that, while both France and Belgium can be trusted not to go beyond certain limits in legal discrimination, other countries with more dubious track records, in particular China and Chile, have been pointing to the French government's stance against sects to vindicate their own, more draconian, restrictions on "dangerous cults."[45]

C. Introduction of Laws

It is already clear that it is not only repressive regimes, but also those that are intrinsically bound to the fight for liberty, equality, and fraternity which are experiencing a need to legislate against NRMs. In France, Alain Vivien, President of the Interministerial Commission to Combat Sects (MILS) is quoted as saying, "Legislation against cults cannot be prohibited in the name of human rights. It is absurd when it is known to what point these movements can violate the more elemental rights";[46] and Catherine Picard, co-architect of the 2001 Law for Prevention and Repression of Sectarian Movements, is quoted as saying, "We need to give judges repressive tools. The law is a response to the evolution of society and the growing importance that sects have in it."[47]

There are contentious issues that could be disproportionately associated with some NRMs—issues ranging from conscientious objection to home schooling to proselytism;[48] and from alternative medicine to the accumulation of money.[49] But while few would have any disagreement whatsoever with the position that there should be legal means of controlling movements that violate basic human rights, some might question the wisdom of translating such a position into one that would appear to assume *all* sects and *only* sects are responsible for such violations. Surely we have to look at what any particular group or its members *actually do*, rather than discriminating *a priori* on the basis of an ill-defined and question-begging classification?

---

[43] Ingvardsson, Wallbom, and Grip, "I God Tro: Samhället Och Nyandligheten," 52–67.

[44] Mainly branches of the Association for the Defense of the Family and the Individual (ADFI).

[45] Joseph A. Bosco, "China's French Connection," *Washington Post,* 10 July 2001, editorial; O. Santa Maria and H. Cossio, "Members of Parliament seek to cancel the legal status of these organizations: 20 cults under investigation," *Mercurio de Valparaiso,* 5 April 2001; Jorge Pizarro, "Sectas y Estado de Derecho," *Mercurio de Valparaiso,* 12 April 2001; for the Parliamentary Commission's profile of destructive cults, see *El Mercurio de Valparaiso,* 15 April 2001.

[46] Andrea Desormeaux, "A Law was Approved by Parliament: The French are Determined to put an end to Cults," *El Mercurio de Valparaiso,* 16 June 2001.

[47] Bosco, "China's French Connection."

[48] John Witte, ed., *Soul Wars: The Problems of Proselytism in Russia. Special Edition of Emory International Law Review,* 3 vols. (Atlanta, Ga.: Emory University School of Law, 1998).

[49] Gerhard Robbers, "Religious Freedom in Germany," in *La libertad religiosa y de conciencia ante la justicia constitucional: Actas del VIII Congreso Internacional de Derecho Eclesiástico del Estado,* ed. Javier Martínez-Torrón (Granada: Comares, 1998), 201–6.

Given the increasing number of democratic societies that are signatories to international human rights documents yet have introduced, or are currently in the process of introducing, laws that differentiate between what for them are traditional or established religions and what they call cults or sects or pseudo religions, it might be helpful to remind ourselves that this is neither a universal nor a necessary practice in a democracy. The First Amendment of the United States Constitution explicitly forbids any such interference between church and state; while both England and Scotland have Established Churches,[50] there is no British law distinguishing cults, sects, or NRMs from older, more mainstream religions; roughly the same situation exists in the Nordic countries.

The Dutch Equal Treatment Act distinguishes between and embraces both direct and indirect discrimination.[51] Direct discrimination is defined as "discrimination between persons on the grounds of religion, belief, political opinion, race, sex, nationality, heterosexual or homosexual orientation, or civil status" (ch.1, sect.1b), while indirect discrimination is "on the grounds of other characteristics or behavior, resulting in direct discrimination" (sect.1c). There are some situations in which indirect discrimination is not prohibited, one being when it is "objectively justified" (sect. 2.1). To take possible examples from England: it has been ruled that a Sikh male working in an ice cream factory could be reasonably required to remain clean-shaven for health reasons (*Singh v. Lyons Maid Ltd.)*, but that it is difficult to justify ordering a Rastafarian to cut his dreadlocks if he wants to hold down a job as a van driver (*Dawkins v. Crown Suppliers (PSA) Ltd.)*.[52]

Sometimes distinctions are enacted at a rather crude level; at other times they are more subtle or sophisticated. There are both implicit and explicit reasons why governments are implementing new laws. Clearly the title of the French Law for the Prevention and Repression of Sectarian Movements (2001) indicates that direct discrimination is involved, but other countries employ more indirect discrimination. One of the puzzles in such instances is teasing out both *why* the criteria that are introduced in such legislation are in fact there, and what the consequences of employing such criteria are—especially when the preamble affirms equality of religious belief for all.[53] Let us now take a brief look at some of the criteria that are used to distinguish between different religions in contemporary legislation, particularly in determining whether or not a religion can be registered or recognized so as to qualify for certain rights.

D. Numbers

Laws that include the requirement of a minimum number of members as a criterion for registration are likely to benefit older, more established religions rather than those that are either indigenous NRMs or religions that are new to the country concerned. Only a handful of first-generation movements have as many as fifty members in any

[50] This is no longer the case in Wales or Northern Ireland.

[51] The full text of the *Equal Treatment Act* (AWGB 1994) is available in English at <http://www.cgb.nl/engels/act.html>.

[52] For a discussion of these and other cases related to new religions in Britain, see Peter Cumper, "Religious Human Rights in the United Kingdom," *Emory International Law Review* 10, no. 1 (1996): 115–26.

[53] At a meeting held in the Hungarian Parliament to discuss the introduction of a new law that would indirectly discriminate against minority groups, I asked why the law was considered necessary at all, Hungary being one of the most religiously liberal post-communist countries. The question seemed to confuse both lawyers and politicians, and I was unable to elicit an answer—the proposed law was eventually dropped.

one country at any one time. One argument that is sometimes given for not registering small groups is that they might be transitory and/or just not worth the administrative effort. This is reasonable enough when the limit is a dozen or so members (as in Estonia). Another reason one can hear voiced in Hungary (where the limit is one hundred) is that small groups would demand equal rights including such benefits as the same time on television or radio as mainstream religions that cater to a congregation a thousand times, even a million times, the size of the NRM.[54]

But a law requiring even a relatively small number of members for registration can operate to the detriment of new and/or fledgling movements, possibly preventing them from being able to manifest their religion because they cannot meet for community worship or perform various other functions that would help them to develop their membership. This has been a complaint frequently made by small religions in Armenia where, in 1997, the minimum number of members required for registration as a religious organization was raised from fifty to two-hundred adult believers. The amendment was explicitly described by one of its authors as clarifying "which of the religious groups are engaged in schismatic, and which of them in serious religion." He is further reported to have said that the tightening of the law would enable authorities to detect "malignant sects."[55]

E. Length of Time in the Country

Another criterion frequently used for purposes of registration is the length of time that a religion has been in a country. It does not take much imagination to realize that, by definition, the newer the religion, the less time it will have been around. Lithuania does not have a state church, but it does recognize nine traditional faiths,[56] and, although this is not officially spelled out in any law, the acknowledged criterion employed by the Ministry of Justice is that they have passed the test of time with a history of 300–400 years on Lithuanian soil. In July 2001 the Seimas (parliament) decided that the Union of Evangelical Baptist Churches in Lithuania could be a second-tier recognized religion, entitled to some of the privileges granted to the traditional faiths—largely, it seems, because it has a one-hundred-and-ten-year heritage in the country.[57] Other religious associations may apply for state recognition no less than twenty-five years after their initial recognition in Lithuania, and, should the request be denied, reapplication is permitted only after a further ten years.[58]

Another country that has been accused of considerably more discrimination than Lithuania (where religions are able to exist relatively freely even when they are not officially recognized) is Russia, where one of the requirements for registration

[54] A strictly proportional representation would be equally ridiculous—simple mathematics shows that a relatively popular new religion (say ISKCON in the UK) could "be entitled" to something like one second's broadcast time for every thirty hours of a traditional religion's broadcast time.

[55] *International Helsinki Federation for Human Rights Annual Report,* 1988, 12.

[56] The Roman Catholic, Greek Catholic, Lutheran, Reformed, Russian Orthodox, Old Believer, Jewish, Sunni Muslim, and Karaite faiths.

[57] Keston News Service, <keston.institute@keston.org>, 13 July 2001.

[58] Rūta Ziliukaitė and Donatas Glodenis, "Law and Religion in Lithuania" (paper presented at CESNUR annual conference, Riga, Latvia, 29–30 August 2000); Felix Corely, "Lithuania: Controversy Surrounds Four-Tier Religious Status" (Keston News Service, 25 May 2001; see also 22 June 2001).

according to the 1997 Law is documental proof that the organization has existed over the course of no less than fifteen years on the relevant territory (art. 11.5).[59] Those religions that do not succeed in getting registered may be "liquidated,"[60] and at the time of writing several new and not-so-new foreign religions (such as the Salvation Army and Jehovah's Witnesses) are fighting in the courts in their attempts to avoid liquidation.[61]

F. Post-Communism

The fear and suspicion of the new that is felt in societies which are undergoing rapid economic, political, social, and cultural changes with, perhaps, large numbers of immigrants and foreign missionaries apparently flooding their territory, is not too difficult to understand. In post-communist societies, traditional churches are struggling against all manner of difficulties, and citizens are still trying to establish an identity that is not undermined by the confusions of collapsed economies, political upheavals, escalating pluralism, and ever-increasing globalization. National churches, as the historical transmitters of cultural heritage, and wielders of political power in periods such as the Ottoman millet system, offer some sort of focus for identification with a golden age of the past in the face of unwelcome and uncontrollable change of an insecure future. Uncertainty about who one is and where society is going can, for many, be experienced as even more terrifying than Soviet control. The honeymoon with freedoms anticipated with the collapse of the Berlin Wall is over: "Freedom of conscience was being confused with anarchy," Catholicos Karekin II is reported to have said when discussing the restrictive amendments to Armenia's 1997 Law on Freedom of Conscience and Religion Organizations.[62]

Frustrations and feelings of helplessness have, throughout history, led to a search for a scapegoat, and the new and the foreign perennially find themselves cast in such a role. A quest for national pride can become exclusivist and aggressive nationalism—even indigenous NRMs can be labeled as traitors rather than heretics, for to leave the group for individual salvation is treachery at such times.[63] And, although the situation is patently different in different societies, it is possible to observe a perceived threat to past securities and cultural identity at least contributing to discriminations against multinational NRMs that are seen as trespassing across, and breaking down, cherished boundaries throughout the world.

G. Privileges and Controls

It can be argued with some cogency that laws discriminating between religions in order to compensate for wrongs done in the past, or good works done in the present, differ radically from those laws that take away basic human rights and/or freedoms

[59] An English translation by Lawrence Uzzell of the 1997 *Russian Federation Federal Law on Freedom of Conscience and on Religious Associations* can be found as Appendix A of *Emory International Law Review* 12, no.1 (1998): 657–80.

[60] Article 14 describes the grounds for "liquidating" a religious organization.

[61] On 10 July 2001, the Salvation Army filed an application with the European Court of Human Rights requesting an intervention to prevent their imminent liquidation by the Russian judicial authorities.

[62] Stephen Brown, "Armenian Church Faces Up to Post-Communist Challenges" *Christianity Today,* 5 March 2001.

[63] This argument is elaborated in Barker, "But Who's Going to Win?"

normally extended to all citizens. For example, most religions had property confiscated during the Soviet period: churches were turned into swimming pools, potato stores, or old people's homes. Some have been restored to their erstwhile owners, compensation has been offered in other cases. It is not unreasonable to accept that religions not around at the time should not receive compensation for what they did not lose. Nevertheless, insensitive wording of a law offering financial privileges to all religions *except* for a few named NRMs, can, at least on the face of it, be taken as unfair discrimination.[64] It could be preferable to decree explicitly that compensation will be offered to those who can show they are entitled to recompense—if that is the underlying intention of the law.

Another privilege that is frequently available for registered religions is some kind of tax concession. Although in British law there is no distinction between religions apart from the Established Church, the Charity Commissioners have had the task of deciding whether a particular organization is a religion and thus eligible for tax exemption and this has given rise to claims both that those who do not deserve exemption have been granted it and that those who ought to be entitled have not. For example, an abortive attempt was made to remove the charitable status of Unification organizations in the 1980s;[65] and the Church of Scientology has been refused charitable status on the grounds that it is not a "real" religion.[66] The refusal to recognize new religions as "real religions" is historically tied to the assumption that a "real religion" is good, and should, thus, be distinguishable from "bad" groups by the label of, say, sect or cult.

Once again the Netherlands offers a solution by circumventing the need to evoke an irrelevant and potentially discriminatory definition of religion. For the Dutch, being a religion will not in itself grant an organization special tax exemption, but being a nonprofit foundation (*Stichting*) does. In other words, tax concessions rest on a legal status that is related to the *financial,* not the religious status of the organization.

H. Crime

One of the most frequent justifications used for discriminating against NRMs is that they are criminal organizations. It is undoubtedly true that some members of some NRMs have committed serious crimes such as murder and child abuse, and the media have done an excellent job in the popularization (if such a word can be used) of macabre tragedies such as the murders and suicides of the Peoples Temple in Jonestown, Guyana in 1978; of the Solar Temple in Canada, Switzerland, and France in 1994 and

[64] In March 1993 it was proposed in the Hungarian Parliament that all religions except four "destructive cults" (the Krishna movement, Scientology, the Unification Church, and Jehovah's Witnesses) would get government support, and a motion was tabled to the effect that the requirements to qualify as a church were (a) 10,000 Hungarian members or (b) a one-hundred-year history in Hungary—this was eventually overruled. See István Kamaras, "Devotees of Krishna in Hungary," *ISKCON Communications Journal* 7, no. 2 (1999), 14.

[65] Eileen Barker, "General Overview of the 'Cult Scene' in Britain," *Nova Religio* 4, no. 2 (2001): 237.

[66] Scientology has, however, managed to be defined as a religion by the IRS in the US and is recognised as a religion in a number of other countries.

1995; and the Movement for the Restoration of the Ten Commandments of God in Uganda in 2000; as well as the gross iniquity of Aum Shinrikyo's depositing sarin gas in the Tokyo underground in 1995.

A number of points need to be stressed here. First, as already intimated, criminal behavior is not peculiar to new religions—old religions too have been guilty of murder and child abuse. Second, there are literally thousands of NRMs around the world and, depending on the precise definition used, probably two thousand identifiable movements in the West; yet members of the vast majority of these lead perfectly law-abiding lives. Third, all societies have a criminal law, and, according to all democratic constitutions, all citizens are to be considered equal before the law. If members of NRMs are convicted of a crime after a fair trial in a court of law, then they should be as liable as any other citizen to the appropriate penalty—and neither more nor less so.[67]

It may, quite plausibly, be argued that the arrival of NRMs has led to antisocial behavior that has not previously been covered by the criminal law, so new legislation needs to be introduced. This is a perfectly justifiable position—new laws are being introduced all the time—but if they are introduced then international law requires that they should be applicable to everyone, as well as being interpreted in the same way, and administered equally to all citizens, irrespective of their belief.

I. Wrong Beliefs

Individuals, organizations, and societies frequently refer to what they perceive to be heretical beliefs as a justification for discrimination, including violence. It is less common, but not uncommon, for a court to accept arguments based on theological matters. In a current court case in which it is being decided whether the Jehovah's Witness community in Moscow should be liquidated, the expert evidence includes arguments that the Witnesses' interpretation of the Bible is incorrect.[68] The judge in an English court has suggested that no reasonable man could believe that Sun Myung Moon was the Messiah, and the jury had, therefore, to decide whether the appellant was either a dupe or a fraud.[69] In Slovakia, the Christian Democratic Movement (KDH), part of the ruling coalition, has threatened to leave the cabinet, declaring a plan to introduce yoga (for relaxation purposes) into schools to be the "continuation of liquidation of Slovak Christianity" similar to the communist fight against the church.[70] In many a brainwashing debate, one can detect that it is the *content* of the belief, rather than the method by which it came to be believed, which is the real basis of the argument; that is, it is "what" rather than "how" that is being condemned.

---

[67] A case in the ECHR concerned a Jehovah's Witness in Greece who was refused employment as an accountant because he had a criminal record. The criminal record was as a result of his stand as a conscientious objector. The ECHR ruling removed his criminal record and awarded him 9,000,000 Greek drachmas for damages and costs (Thlimmenos v. Greece, App. No. 34369/97 [ECtHR, 6 April 2000]).

[68] V. P. Belyanin, et al, *Combined Expert Conclusion for the Civil Case 2-452/99*, 4 October 2000, Golovinsky Intermunicipal Court NAD of the city of Moscow.

[69] Transcript of summation given in the High Court of Justice, Queen's Bench Division, by Mr. Justice Comyn in Orme v. Associated Newspapers Group Ltd., 30 March 1981, 232.

[70] Marius Kopcsay, "The Ghost of Yoga," trans. Shawn Landres, *Novy Cas*, 13 July 2001, 2.

V. Utilizing a Social Science Model

Around the mid-1980s I became increasingly convinced that it would be helpful if more use could be made of a social scientific perspective. By then I had been researching the "cult scene" for nearly twenty years, and had found myself observing what seemed to be a great deal of unnecessary suffering as the result of people acting inappropriately because of either ignorance or misinformation. With the support of the British government and mainstream religions, I founded INFORM, a charity whose main objective is to provide information that is as accurate, balanced, and up-to-date as possible.

INFORM collects, assesses, and disseminates information gathered from a variety of sources, and makes copious use of an international network of scholars, and other experts such as legal, counseling, and medical specialists. It also draws on the help of former members, the friends and families of members, and, indeed, the NRMs themselves. This does not mean that INFORM necessarily agrees with any of its sources, but it does start from the premise that all interested parties have, minimally, the right to be heard and that any information is data—even when what it illustrates is deception or ignorance. Those making use of INFORM's now considerable resources include relatives of members, the media, governments, religions, educational establishments, researchers, law enforcement agencies, and a variety of other individuals and organizations from around the world.

As well as responding to individual or organizational enquiries, INFORM organizes day-long seminars twice a year that deal with particular aspects of the new religions (such as NRMs and education, the family, the media, the law, health, violence, etc.), and has also organized two international four-day conferences with literally hundreds of participants (most of whom are scholars interested in the NRMs) from over thirty different countries.

Of course, INFORM has no magic wand; it has no expertise to pass judgement on nonempirical beliefs, nor does it presume to tell enquirers what they should do. Reliable information is not easy to secure and even the most accurate information is not sufficient as a means of combating discrimination and prejudice, but it is clearly necessary, and so long as inaccurate and biased information goes unchallenged, individuals and societies will find it easy not only to excuse, but also to fan the flames of prejudice.

VI. Conclusion

This chapter has purposely not focused on countries where there is general religious discrimination, but on democracies where "cults" or "sects" have been singled out for special treatment. Some examples of discrimination have been illustrated, and there has been an attempt to understand their occurrence in terms both of characteristics associated with new religions and of features and processes to be found within the host societies. It has also been stressed that not all movements fit the stereotype that is part of present-day conventional wisdom, and that not all societies feel the need to make discriminatory distinctions between religions.

It has not been denied that NRMs can give cause for concern but, it has been argued, rather than introducing special laws that directly or indirectly discriminate between religions, the most appropriate way for a democracy to deal with such concerns is through obtaining reliable information and applying the criminal law. Though neither is perfect, the methods of the social sciences can facilitate the former, and the law of the Netherlands can provide an example for the latter.

Chapter 26

The Sect Issue in the European Francophone Sphere

Willy Fautré, Alain Garay, and Yves Nidegger

I. Introduction

In the first half of the 1990s, the world was shaken up and horrified by a series of collective suicides, homicides, and attacks perpetrated in America, Europe, and Asia at the initiative of leaders of religious movements or movements claiming to be religious.

On 19 April 1993, eighty-eight Davidians died from confrontations with the police in Waco, Texas. On 4 October 1994, a mass suicide-homicide cost the lives of fifty-three members of the Order of the Solar Temple in Switzerland and Canada. On 5 March 1995, about five thousand people were injured and eleven killed in a gas attack perpetrated by Aum Shinrikyo in Tokyo's subway. In December 1995, another suicide-homicide of sixteen members of the Order of the Solar Temple took place in the Vercors in France. Since then, one more homicide/suicide claiming almost a thousand lives took place in the African state of Uganda in March 2000.

The European Union,[1] the Council of Europe,[2] and a number of member states[3] have expressed their concern about those phenomena in various ways. The issue is whether a specific policy should be designed and carried out with regard to unconventional religions in order to prevent the repetition of such tragedies. The responses have been varied.

---

[1] In 1997 the Committee on Civil Liberties and Internal Affairs appointed a rapporteur, Mrs. Maria Berger (Austria, Socialist Party), to draft the *Report on cults in the European Union* (11 December 1997, A4-0408/97). A majority could never be found in the European Parliament to adopt the draft report. On 14 July 1998 it was finally sent back to the committee, where it died a natural death.

[2] Parliamentary Assembly Recommendation 1412 (1999), "Illegal activities of sects," published in the *Official Gazette* of the Council of Europe, assembly debate on 22 June 1999 (18th sitting) (see Doc. 8373, *Report of the Committee on Legal Affairs and Human Rights,* rapporteur Mr. Nastase; Doc. 8379, *Opinion of Social, Health and Family Affairs Committee,* rapporteur Mr. Hegyi; and Doc. 8383, *Opinion of the Committee on Culture and Education,* rapporteur Mr. de Puig). Text adopted by the assembly on 22 June 1999 (18th sitting).

[3] For France: See *Rapport fait au nom de la commission d'enquête sur les sectes, Assemblée nationale, Commission d'enquête, Rapport n° 2468* (Report drafted on behalf of the enquiry commission on sects, National Assembly, Enquiry Commission, Report No. 2468), 20 December 1995. For Belgium: See

Tore Lindholm, W. Cole Durham, Jr., Bahia G. Tahzib-Lie (eds.), Facilitating Freedom of Religion or Belief: A Deskbook, *595–618.*

The position of eleven member states of the European Union was that "sects" do not harm the individual, the family, society, or their democratic institutions to the point that new institutions or organizations are needed to combat them.[4]

In the Netherlands, the 1996 Annual Report of the Internal Security Service published in 1997 says in sec. 2.8.3, under the heading "Religious sects": "Because of incidents in foreign countries where religious sects were involved, it has been looked into how far these sects in The Netherlands are a serious threat. So far, it has not appeared that in The Netherlands religious movements are a serious threat for the security of the state, the democratic order or other important interests of the state." This was only a confirmation of the stand taken by the Dutch government in 1984 (Dutch Government Report on New Religious Movements): "In general, new religious movements are no real threat to mental public health." In Sweden, a similar conclusion was reached in 1998.[5]

In their view, just as in past years, problems posed by certain religious movements could be resolved using the existing legislative arsenal or, where necessary, by resorting to normal legal methods. Consequently, they did not take any political or legal measures that might have encroached on international human rights norms pertaining to freedom of religion or belief, such as the provisions of ICCPR art. 18.3 (specifying the extent and ground of permissible limitations) and ICCPR art. 4.2 (making freedom of religion or belief a nonderogable right).

However, four EU member states decided to take a new course of action: two German-speaking countries (Austria and Germany), a French-speaking country (France), and a linguistically and culturally mixed country (Belgium).

Austria created an information and documentation center about sects, placing it under the authority of the Federal Ministry of the Environment, Youth and the Family. A brochure containing information about sects was also widely distributed.[6] This prevention campaign warned principally against eleven guru-led movements of oriental origin, three psychological groups, two groups claiming to spring from new revelations, three religions of Christian origin, and four other groups under the category "Various."

Enquête parlementaire visant à élaborer une politique en vue de lutter contre les pratiques illégales des sectes et le danger qu'elles représentent pour la société et pour les personnes, particulièrement les mineurs d'âge. Rapport fait au nom de la commission d'enquête par MM Duquesne et Willems (Parliamentary enquiry commission aiming at working out a policy in order to fight against the illegal practices of sects and the danger that they pose to society, persons and particularly to minors. Report drafted on behalf of the enquiry commission by Mssrs. Duquesne and Willems), 28 April 1997. For Germany: See *Endbericht der Enquete-Kommission "Sogenannte Sekten und Psychogruppen"* (Final Report of the Enquete Commission on "So-Called Sects and Psychogroups"), 9 June 1998.

[4] In the Netherlands, the 1996 Annual Report of the Internal Security Service published in 1997 says in sec. 2(8)(3), under the heading "Religious sects": "Because of incidents in foreign countries where religious sects were involved, it has been looked into how far these sects in The Netherlands are a serious threat. So far, it has not appeared that in The Netherlands religious movements are a serious threat for the security of the state, the democratic order or other important interests of the state." This was only a confirmation of the stand taken by the Dutch government in 1984: "In general, new religious movements are no real threat to mental public health" (Dutch Government Report on New Religious Movements). See also for Sweden, *In Good Faith: Society and the New Religious Movements* (Stockholm: SOU, 1998), <http://social.regeringen.se/propositionermm/sou/pdf/sou98_113eng.pdf>.

[5] See *In Good Faith,* 113.

[6] *Sekten: Wissen schützt. Eine Information des Bundesministeriums für Umwelt, Jugend und Familie,* 1996 (Sects: Knowledge protects. Information from the Federal Ministry of the Environment, Youth, and the Family, 1996).

Germany set up a parliamentary commission and published a report. Scientology was placed under surveillance but no legal action is currently being taken against the movement. Various *Länder* published and distributed information brochures warning against sects.

The choice of the French-speaking European countries as an area for examination is motivated by the fact that several Order of the Solar Temple massacres took place in Switzerland and France, and that Belgian citizens were also implicated and lost their life during these tragedies. These three European states are also linked in part by linguistic, cultural, and historical characteristics that explain the common traits rapidly displayed by each country in their perception and analysis of these tragedies. However, the multilinguistic and multicultural nature of Belgium and Switzerland has influenced and softened to various degrees the tone set by France. The varying palette of political choices and strategies implemented by these countries is of great interest to those researching the problems posed or potentially posed by certain "sects."[7]

This chapter, which has been drafted by three observers of the sect issue in France, Belgium, and Switzerland, analyzes and assesses the developments, the consequences, and the results of the anti-sect policies implemented by these states, as well as how they conform to international human rights standards. The authors also draw conclusions from the political, ideological, and strategic choices made by their own countries and make some recommendations.

II. Development of State Anti-Sect Policies

A. France

As early as 1985, following a request by the prime minister, former member of Parliament and minister, Alain Vivien, wrote a report entitled *Sects in France: Expression of Moral Freedom or Sources of Manipulation?* This report described the sect phenomenon and made certain recommendations (maintain appropriate surveillance of the sect phenomenon by means of an interministerial structure, warn and inform the public in an impartial way, etc.).

On 29 June 1995, the National Assembly unanimously adopted a resolution creating an inquiry commission "to study the sect phenomenon." The commission, chaired by the National Assembly representative Alain Gest, carried out its work in strict secrecy (conducting twenty interviews over a total of twenty-one hours) and published the Gest-Guyard report on *Sects in France*.[8] By listing 173 movements as constituting potentially harmful sects, the commission gave legitimacy to the investigations carried out by the

---

[7] The English distinction between "sect" (a generally more neutral term) and "cult" (a more pejorative term) is reversed in French. The word *secte* is used in parliamentary documents on this issue, by the media, and in society in general in the European Francophone sphere. Scholars prefer to use the term "new religious movement" rather than *secte* (or "cult" in English) because of the latter's pejorative connotation. Political personages involved in anti-sect state policies have tried to reach a consensus on an operational definition of the concept of "sect" but have failed in their attempt, whether the approach is etymological, sociological, legal, or based on the perceived dangers posed by sects. (See Eileen Barker's chapter in this volume.) France, Belgium, and Switzerland have circumvented the definition problem in their own way, as can be seen further in this chapter.

[8] *Sects in France,* National Assembly Report No. 2648 (rapporteur Jacques Guyard).

Renseignements Généraux[9] (R.G.). In its report, the Commission advocated increasing information about such groups and administrative repression of sects,[10] including small evangelical churches.

The Republic's courts have taken care not to draw a legal dividing line between religions and sects on the grounds of ideological considerations.[11] According to the Administrative Tribunal of Strasbourg, "the fact that a movement has been listed in the Gest-Guyard Report on 'sects' does not relieve the administrative authority of the responsibility to establish, through specific and concurring facts, that an association comprising individuals who belong to such a movement is in fact pursuing an activity that poses a threat to public policy."[12]

Notwithstanding these precautions, anti-sect activists have encouraged not only increased administrative and legal repression, but also, since 1996, the consensual and unanimous adoption of a series of political measures against sects.[13]

1. The very first measure adopted in the aftermath of the Gest Report to the National Assembly was a circular from the Ministry of Justice dated 29 February 1996, concerning the fight against attacks on persons or private property committed by sectarian movements.[14] The Ministry of Justice asked all state prosecutors for stricter application of the existing law respecting the "risks incurred by the existence and activity of the organizations in question according to the conclusions of the National Assembly Commission of Inquiry." The annex to the circular officially lists the 173 movements.

2. Following the recommendations of the Gest Report, Prime Minister Alain Juppé decided, by means of a decree on 9 May 1996, to create an Interministerial Observatory on Sects. Commissioned to analyze the phenomenon of sects, to inform the Prime Minister of its work, and to make recommendations so as to provide better tools to fight sects, the observatory did not survive the publication of its first report of activities in 1998. It seems that some members, notably member of Parliament Jean Pierre Brard, wanted to go further than simply studying and "observing" the sect phenomenon. From

---

[9] France's Intelligence Service, the security branch of the police force.

[10] Academics took a position only in 1999 and proposed a group to act as a mediator between the National Assembly and the anti-sect movement.

[11] See Conseil d'État, *Association internationale pour la conscience de Krishna* (Paris: Dalloz, 1982), 516–20.

[12] Judgement of 7 July 1997, Ass. La Ritournelle, No. 97810. "Public policy" stands for the French term *ordre public*. In recent case law from the European Union courts, the term is translated this way (cf. European court decision on the free movement of capital between countries where one of the parties was a member of the Church of Scientology). Public policy is a broader term and includes what may be considered the highest form of the public interest. It refers to the principles and standards regarded by the legislature as being of fundamental concern to the state and the whole of society. This is really the best match for *ordre public*, which is the prevailing policy of the law in matters of public interest and the fundamental principles of French civilization. On the other hand, in English "order" is usually associated with the maintenance of law and order to allow the proper and orderly functioning of society and relates to such things as offenses against the public peace, public nuisances, and civil disturbances. Of course, maintaining law and order is also a matter of public policy, so it may not always be clear which term is the best translation in a given context, but law and order is certainly the more restrictive term of the two.

[13] On the militancy and success of so-called anti-sect associations, see Alain Garay, *L'activisme anti-secte: de l'assistance à l'amalgame* (New York: The Edwin Mellen Press, 1999).

[14] *Journal Officiel*, 5 March 1996; Alain Garay, "La circulaire du 29 février 1996," *JCP*, no. 15 (10 April 1996).

1996 to 1998, training and awareness programs for the police, state prosecutors, judges,[15] and teachers were initiated with the goal of reinforcing control of sects by government agencies and the state. Academics were not involved in the process.

3. On 7 November 1997, Minister of the Interior Chevènement, whose responsibilities include supervision of the police, sent a circular to the police chiefs concerning the "combat against reprehensible actions of sectarian movements." Minister Chevènement appealed to the nongovernmental organizations UNADFI[16] and CCMM[17] (two different associations for the protection of "victims of sects") for help in heightening public awareness. However, the government created no mechanism for checking the accuracy of the statements made about sects by these groups, nor was a mechanism provided that would ensure open debate on the information, interpretations, and assessments presented. Additionally, the circular called for the mobilization of all state officials against the reprehensible actions of "sects," including exchanging information, heightening vigilance, and work, school, and health inspections. The circular repeated, "this fight comes within the framework of an activity of national priority."

4. Spurred on by certain representatives of the Study Group on Sects at the National Assembly and by the effective militancy of UNADFI and CCMM leaders, at the end of 1998, the authorities accelerated their pace. From October through December 1998 a three-step battle plan was created, culminating in new legislation in 1999 specifically targeting sects.

1. The Interministerial Mission to Combat Sects (MILS)

By a decree presented to the cabinet and signed by both the president of the Republic and the prime minister on 7 October 1998, the *Mission interministérielle de lutte contre les sectes* (MILS—Interministerial Mission to Combat Sects) was set up. It is headquartered at the prime minister's offices at the Hotel Matignon. Article 1 of the decree reads:

> Art. 1. An Interministerial Mission to Combat Sects under the auspices of the Prime Minister is being created. Its role is:
>
> 1. To analyze the phenomenon of sects. To this end, the various government agencies concerned should forward any information in their possession on schemes by sects. It can also request these agencies to carry out studies or conduct research into sects.
> 2. To spur public services, while respecting public liberties, to take any appropriate measures to anticipate and counter the actions of sects that undermine human dignity or that pose a threat to public policy. The Mission will

[15] "State prosecutors" and "judges" stand for the French term *magistrats,* which is not the equivalent of the English term "magistrate." In the French system, *magistrat* refers to representatives of the state empowered to require the administration of justice and to administer justice and have their decisions enforced; this definition includes state prosecutors as well as the members of the bench, whereas the English term "magistrate" refers strictly to judges. In French the distinction between state prosecutors and judges is conveyed by the use of *debout* and *assis,* i.e., the prosecutor is a *magistrat debout* and the judge a *magistrat assis.*

[16] Union Nationale des Associations pour la Défense de la Famille et de l'Individu.

[17] Centre Contre les Manipulations Mentales.

accordingly inform the appropriate administrations of schemes brought to its attention that it feels call for an initiative to be taken. It will report acts that are likely to be described as criminal to the prosecutors of the Republic.

3. To share in informing and training civil servants on the methods for combating sects.
4. To inform the public about the dangers of the sect phenomenon.
5. To participate in studies and projects undertaken by international bodies on matters in which it is specialized.[18]

2. The Ministry of Justice Circular

Sent to the staff of the public prosecutor's office on 1 December 1998, this circular was the next step in the attempt to "combat attacks on persons or private property committed by groups of a sectarian nature."[19]

The circular asked prosecutors and judges to maintain institutional contacts with "associations that can be taken seriously, such as the UNADFI and the CCMM, that combat sects. Only good can result from state prosecutors' establishment of ties with these associations, in order to discuss the schemes of sect-like movements that fall within their competence." One purpose of this initiative was apparently to increase the number of complaints filed.

3. The Parliamentary Commission of Inquiry into the Finances, Property, and Fiscal Standing of Sects, as well as Their Economic Activities and Their Relations with Economic and Financial Circles

The momentum created by the anti-sect lobby drew the authorities and politicians into its wake, prompting the creation of another commission on 15 December 1998, this time to look into the finances of the groups targeted. This commission had six months to broadly investigate and report on the financial dealings, resources, and assets of groups it had classified as sects. The commission's report[20] was seized upon by the media and the courts despite the fact that parliamentary commission reports do not have any legal status and are not binding, except on their authors.[21] Furthermore, since such detailed financial information is not necessarily made public even by legitimate groups, this political and administrative attempt to attack groups deemed undesirable by spotlighting their financial resources was not certain to reach criminal and pathological movements.

---

[18] Decree No. 98.890 of 7 October 1998, <http://www.hrwf.net/English/france01.html> (visited 29 October 1999).

[19] See *Circulaire contre les sectes du Ministre de la Justice français*, <http://www.cesnur.org/testi/guigou.htm> (republishing the full text of the 1998 circular) (visited 29 October 1999).

[20] See the text of the report on the Center for Studies on New Religions (CESNUR) website, <http://www.cesnur.org/testi/fr99/fr_summary.htm>. For an excellent analysis of the law (as it was constituted in a similar earlier draft), see Hannah Clayson Smith, "Liberté, Egalité, et Fraternité at Risk for New Religious Movements in France," *BYU Law Review* (2000): 3, 1099–1151.

[21] For the first time, a parliamentary commission has listed individuals as "notorious cultists," although they have not been personally accused of any wrongdoing. This is a clear intrusion on their privacy.

4. A Law Providing for the Dissolution of Sects

On 30 May 2001, all parliamentary groups of the French National Assembly unanimously adopted on second reading the About and Picard draft law meant "to strengthen prevention and repression of sectarian groups liable to undermine human rights and fundamental freedoms." This draft legislation had been adopted on first reading by the Senate on 16 December 1999 and then by the French National Assembly on 22 June 2000 before being referred to the Senate, where it was amended and approved on 3 May 2001.[22]

This law allows courts to dissolve associations when they or one of their leaders has been convicted of causing harm to individuals, the illegal practice of medicine or pharmaceuticals, or misleading publicity or fraud.[23] It also stipulates that banned groups which re-form under a different name can face prosecution.[24]

A controversial clause making a crime of "mental manipulation," a first in the world, sparked an outcry from several minority religious groups, Catholic and Protestant leaders, and academics when it first went before the National Assembly in June 2000.[25] It was eventually dropped after an official consultative human rights body as well as then-Minister of Justice Elisabeth Guigou found it questionable. However, it was replaced by a similar provision that extends an existing crime in the criminal code.[26] Despite a change in the legal basis of the law, its philosophy remained the same, as well as the result. The crime of "abuse of a person's state of weakness," as it is now termed, is applicable to activities of so-called cults and can be punished by a possible sentence of up to three years in jail and a maximum fine of up to USD $350,000. A convicted leader or "guru" can be sentenced to five years in jail and a fine of approximately USD $700,000.[27] The law also allows anticult groups, which are recognized by the state as having public utility, to be civil parties on behalf of the victims.[28]

A number of personalities in European institutions raised their voices against the law. On 6 October 2000, Mr. McNamara, a British socialist, submitted a proposal signed by fourteen members of the Parliamentary Assembly of the Council of Europe, of which eleven were socialists, to express their concern as regards this law. The proposal regrets that the About-Picard law qualifies 173 religious groups as "sects," which is a term of negative connotation rejected by the Council of Europe Nastase Report.[29] On 26 April

---

[22] For full English text of the law, see <http://www.cesnur.org/2001/fr_law_en.htm>.
[23] Ch. I, sec. 1.
[24] Ibid.; ch. II, sec. 2(14).
[25] See *Religious Liberty in Western Europe: Deterioration of Religious Liberty in Europe Briefing Before the Comm'n on Sec. and Cooperation in Europe of the United States Congress,* 105th Cong. (1998) (statement of Dr. Massimo Introvigne, Managing Director, Center for Studies of New Religions); Rev. Jean-Arnold de Clermont, *La Croix,* 22 June 2000 (President of the French Protestant Federation); *Le Figaro,* 23 June 2000, editorial (quoting the French National Consultative Commission on Human Rights and religious leaders). See also Garay, *L'activisme anti-secte: de l'assistance à l'amalgame,* 107–29 (arguing against the legal validity of mental manipulation claims); James T. Richardson, "'Brainwashing' Claims and Minority Religions Outside the United States: Cultural Diffusion of a Questionable Concept in the Legal Arena," *BYU Law Review* (1996): 873.
[26] Ch. V, sec. 6*bis* (codified as Criminal Code secs. 223-15-2 and -3).
[27] Ch. V, sec. 6*bis* (codified as Criminal Code secs. 223-15-2 and -4).
[28] Ch. VI, sec. 8 (codified as Code of Criminal Procedure sec. 2-17).
[29] Committee on Legal Affairs and Human Rights, *Illegal Activities of Sects,* Council of Europe, Doc. No. 8373 (1999), <http://stars.coe.fr/doc/doc99/edoc8373.htm> (visited 25 July 2001).

2001, 50 members of the Parliamentary Assembly of the Council of Europe signed Declaration no. 321, whereby they expressed their concern as regards this law and demanded the vote be suspended until the appointed rapporteur of the Parliamentary Assembly of the Council of Europe submitted an assessment of the law.[30]

B. Belgium

On 10 January 1996, the Justice Commission of the House of Representatives started examining a proposal from Antoine Duquesne and several of his colleagues[31] who wished to set up a parliamentary enquiry commission[32] which would work out a policy against sects[33] and the dangers they pose to people, particularly to minors.[34]

This enquiry commission, which comprised eleven members, was created on 28 March 1996. It started its work on 25 April 1996, held fifty-eight meetings, and heard 136 witnesses, making no distinction between public and private spheres. Among those duly invited to take part in the public hearings were three members of the government, four magistrates, three police or intelligence officers, three administration officers, six academics, six journalists and writers, six representatives of associations defending victims of sects, eight former members of sects, and relatives of former members. All the other witnesses were heard behind closed doors, sometimes by only a few members of the commission and without the others' knowledge. Sociologists of religion were not consulted. Associations suspected of being dangerous or harmful sects, including some small evangelical churches, were not invited to participate in the hearings, but the commission sent a letter to seventy-one of the associations mentioned by various state

---

[30] *Religious Freedom and Religious Minorities in France,* Council of Europe Parliamentary Assembly, Doc. No. 9064 (2001), <http://stars.coe.fr/doc/doc01/edoc9064.htm > (visited 25 July 2001).

[31] Mr. Duquesne (Liberal Party PRL) was then in the opposition. After the June 1999 parliamentary elections, he was appointed Minister of the Interior. The sect issue partly falls under his responsibility.

[32] The first title of the proposal was *Commission d'enquête parlementaire chargée d'élaborer une politique en vue de lutter contre les sectes et les dangers que représentent ces sectes pour les personnes et particulièrement les mineurs d'âge* (Parliamentary enquiry commission in charge of working out a policy in order to combat sects and the dangers that these sects pose to persons and particularly to minors). At the final stage, the Justice Commission renamed the proposal as follows: *Commission d'enquête parlementaire visant à élaborer une politique en vue de lutter contre les pratiques illégales des sectes et le danger qu'elles représentent pour la société et pour les personnes, particulièrement les mineurs d'âge* (Parliamentary enquiry commission aiming at working out a policy in order to combat the illegal practices of sects and the danger that they pose to society, to persons and particularly to minors).

[33] Belgian definition of "sect": At the 55th session of the UN Commission on Human Rights, Mr. Abdelfattah Amor, Special Rapporteur on Religious Intolerance and Discrimination, submitted a report entitled *Civil and Political Rights, Including Religious Tolerance,* 11 January 1999, E/CN.4/1999/58, (hereafter *1999 Amor Report*), in which he summed up as follows Belgium's reply to a communication he had previously sent to Belgian authorities:

> The Parliamentary Commission provided definitions of the terms '*secte*' ('organized group of individuals espousing the same doctrine within a religion'—the Commission considers sects in this sense to be respectable and to reflect the normal exercise of the freedom of religion and assembly guaranteed by fundamental rights) and '*organisation sectaire nuisible*' [harmful sectarian organization] ('group having or claiming to have a philosophical or religious purpose whose organization or practice involves illegal or injurious activities, harms individuals or society or impairs human dignity').

[34] Sexual abuses of children, denial of medical treatments by parents, isolation from society, sectarian religious education under cover of homeschooling, and so on.

agencies as potentially harmful to society or to the individual. The letter[35] asked the groups to describe their objectives and to refute their possibly sectarian character, but they were not informed of the accusations raised against them during the public and nonpublic hearings. They could therefore not defend themselves. The other 118 movements that were listed did not get such an invitation and were consequently not able to present a summary of their activities or to contest any accusations.

On 28 April 1997, the parliamentary commission issued its 670-page report.[36] A list of 189 movements was attached. In the introduction to the list, the drafters admitted that they had not been able to control the collected data. Nevertheless, unilateral accusations made against the movements were reproduced in the report without any further investigation or cross-examination, and sometimes despite strong evidence presented by the incriminated movements (e.g., the Anthroposophic Society) that criticisms voiced under oath were false. The Parliament failed to adopt the report as such and only voted to accept the conclusions and recommendations (19 pages). This reluctance, mainly expressed by the ruling Catholic political parties CVP and PSC, was certainly due to the fact that some Catholic movements such as the Opus Dei, The Work, the Opstal Community, and the Charismatic Renewal were included on the list. Despite this disavowal, the government did not find it inappropriate to publish the whole report, including the controversial list.[37]

In the aftermath of this report, a draft law was introduced that proposed the creation of a Federal Observatory of Sects under the authority of the Ministry of Justice.[38] Amendments were proposed. At the 15 April 1998 ordinary session of the House of

---

[35] Translation into English of such a letter dated 29 July 1996 and addressed in Dutch to the Anthroposophic Society:

> *Concerns*: Parliamentary commission of enquiry in charge of the policy of fight against the illegal practices of sects and against the dangers they pose to society and to the individual, especially to minors.
>
> In the framework of the activities of the commission of enquiry, some official agencies stated that your association (on the basis of the conclusions of the French commission of investigation) could be considered as a sect that carries out some activities that are dangerous to society or to the individual.
>
> If you wish, you can send us a memorandum (maximum 2 pages) in which you expose the goals of your organization and, in case, refute its so-called sectarian and dangerous nature.
>
> Yours faithfully
>
> Mr Serge Moureaux, chairman of the enquiry commission

[36] The official title of the report is *Enquête parlementaire visant à élaborer une politique en vue de lutter contre les pratiques illégales des sectes et le danger qu'elles représentent pour la société et pour les personnes, particulièrement les mineurs d'âge. Rapport fait au nom de la Commission d'enquête par MM Duquesne et Willems* (Parliamentary enquiry commission aiming at working out a policy in order to fight against the illegal practices of sects and the danger that they pose to society, persons and particularly to minors. Report drafted on behalf of the enquiry commission by Mssrs. Duquesne and Willems).

[37] The strongest opposition to the report came from the Christian Democratic parties CVP and PSC. See Alain Lallemand, "Sectes: Va-t-on réactiver la 'cellule Bulthé'?" (Sects: Will the 'Bulthé cell' be revived?), *Le Soir*, 6 May 1997, 23. In a letter dated 21 May 1997 and addressed to the Anthroposophic Society, Dr. Jan Van Erps, a CVP member of the House of Representatives, wrote: "I have read your letter about the Sect Report very carefully. The Commission has indeed been very negligent and biased in its work. That is why I and a substantial majority of my colleagues at the CVP have refused to adopt the report of activities, have rejected the famous list and have only adopted the general lines of the recommendations. . . . As you certainly know, the report was not even put to a vote."

[38] The proposed law was presented by Mr. Antoine Duquesne on 22 September 1997 under the name *Proposition de loi créant un Observatoire fédéral des sectes* (Proposed law for the creation of a federal observatory on sects).

Representatives, two important changes were brought to the draft law: the Federal Observatory of Sects was renamed Information and Advice Center on Harmful Sectarian Organizations, and a chapter called "Administrative agency coordinating the fight against harmful sectarian organizations" was added to it. Both changes expressed a will to dissociate the independent examination of the phenomenon from the interministerial agency created to combat it. The law, however, provided for the close collaboration of both agencies.[39]

On 2 June 1998, the Parliament adopted the Law Regarding the Establishment of an Information and Advice Center and an Administrative Coordination Agency. This law was published in the *Moniteur Belge* (the Official Gazette) on 25 November 1998. On 6 March 1999, the Council of Ministers drew up the list of candidates and deputy candidates for the Information and Advice Center. On 16 March 1999, this list was presented to the House of Representatives.

On 29 April 1999, at its last session before its dissolution, the House of Representatives appointed the twelve members and the twelve deputy members of the Information and Advice Center for a period of four years. The members were chosen "from eminent personalities that are known for their knowledge, experience, and interest in the problems of the harmful sectarian movements."[40]

On 12 October 1999, five months after the parliamentary elections, the new House of Representatives adopted the "Internal Regulation" of the Information and Advice Center.

As to the Administrative Coordination Agency for the Fight against Harmful Sectarian Organizations, a royal decree dated 8 November 1998 determines its composition, its operation, and its structure.[41] The members of this agency were appointed by the Ministry of Justice on 3 May 2000.[42]

The two agencies only became operational in fall 2000.[43]

C. Switzerland

On 14 December 1988, Swiss Parliament member Gilles Petitpierre asked the Swiss government (the Swiss Federal Council) to take a stand regarding the dangers threatening individuals joining religious sects.[44] He claimed that young adults had joined such groups in the United States during the 1980s causing their concerned families to appeal to the public

---

[39] See law of 2 June 1998, art. 6, sec. 1(5).

[40] Law of 2 June 1998, art.4.

[41] According to that royal decree, published in the *Moniteur Belge* on 9 December 1998, the Administrative Coordination Agency is composed of fourteen members: a representative of the College of Public Prosecutors, a magistrate and representatives of the Gendarmerie, the Criminal Investigation Department, the police of the Ministry of the Interior, the State Security, the Ministry of Public Service, the General Directorate of the Ministry of Justice for Civil Legislation and Religions, the General Directorate of the Ministry of Justice for Criminal Legislation and Human Rights, the Criminal Police Service of the Ministry of Justice, the Ministry of Interior, the Ministry of Finances, the Ministry of Employment. Fourteen deputy representatives were also appointed. Both categories of representatives were nominated by their respective ministers and appointed by the Minister of Justice.

[42] Publication in the *Moniteur Belge* on 30 May 2000.

[43] The first report of the Information and Advice Center on Harmful Sectarian Organizations is expected in the first half of 2001. The Administrative Coordination Agency meets at least once every two months and reports to the Center every six months. The meetings are chaired by the Minister of Justice or his representative.

authorities for help.[45] The government's response to Petitpierre was that a sect policy was not necessary at the federal level and that it would exceed the authority of the federal government.[46] Ten years later, the same question was raised again, in a much more detailed way and in an insistent tone, this time by the powerful parliamentary *"Commission de gestion"*[47] (administration commission), which called for a nationwide policy against "cults and indoctrinating movements" and the creation of a state-sponsored national database on "cults."

On 29 June 2000 the Swiss Federal Council rejected all propositions included in the report of 1 July 1999.[48] The government did not consider it necessary to draw up a "specific policy as regards sects," as it had followed a clear and coherent policy as to sects and/or indoctrinating movements for many years. The report on sects prepared by the parliamentary administration commission raised important questions, but in its response, the government indicated that it gave precedence to the protection of fundamental rights, in particular freedom of conscience and belief. The government therefore made the following replies to the questions from the commission:

- In the field of the authority bestowed upon the Confederation, the adoption and enforcement of legislation on protection of children, consumers, and health are sufficient and satisfactory.
- The co-ordination and exchange of information within the federal administration could be improved, but the government rejects the idea of setting up a federal information and advice centre.
- The information targeted to the various institutions concerned (schools, youth organisations, consultation centres, legal authorities and the police, etc.) outlining the legal situation and aimed at promoting the necessary sensitivity in dealing with concerned individuals merits being examined. The government considers however that informing public opinion is not the primary responsibility of the Confedertion.
- The government considers it desirable to reinforce interdisciplinary research activity. This having been said, universities and other research institutes have the primary responsibility of initiating and financing these activities. If it appears in the middle term that an area of research important to society has not been taken into consideration, the government will give it the necessary attention during the planning of the next national research programmes.

In short, no matter how traumatizing the Solar Temple tragedy has been to the Swiss people, it has failed to increase the government's authority beyond constitutional limits: religion is still a matter of cantonal authority.

Switzerland, which has been a federal state since 1848, comprises twenty-four cantons, each of which has a unique religious history. In this political and historical framework, the church-state relationship remains a prerogative of the cantons; the federal constitution only guarantees freedom of religion.[49] The canton of Geneva, which

---

44 Swiss National Council, winter session, 1988, question 88.1068.

45 Südafrikanisch-Deutsche Kulturvereinigung (SADK) report, June 1989.

46 Answer to question 88.1068 released on 6 March 1989.

47 "'Sects' or indoctrinating movements in Switzerland. Necessity for State action or towards a Federal 'sect' policy," in *Report of the Administration Commission of the National Council*, 1 July 1999.

48 "'Sects' or indoctrinating movements in Switzerland. Necessity for State action or towards a Federal 'sect' policy," response of the Federal Council to the *Report of the Administration Commission of the National Council*, June 2000.

49 Switzerland Const, art. 15.

historically has been the one most influenced by France, has taken the lead in the area of state-sponsored anti-sect campaigns. Even though Basel was the first canton to pass new restrictive legislation,[50] Geneva has certainly developed the most creative, although pragmatic, approach to the issue.

"Our citizens are just tired of hearing that the State has no competency or no legal base to act against sects," explained Geneva Minister of Justice Gérard Ramseyer to an audience of opinion leaders on 25 November 1999.[51] "Let us rather do something *somewhat right* today, rather than something *completely right* tomorrow," he continued, defending his bold, yet hazardous, full-scale anticult legislation project, which was subsequently rejected by the canton's Parliament in November 1999.[52]

The Geneva anti-sect campaign started in 1997 with the publication of an analysis of the existing law and of the perspective of new legislation on this matter. Misleadingly entitled "Audit on sectarian deviations,"[53] the survey is a legal opinion issued by four legal scholars at the Justice Department's request. It provides no case of "sectarian misconduct," no definition of the terms, and no positive conclusion regarding the need for new legislation, yet does include a number of recommendations to the authorities such as the following:

> Civil servants, even part-time, having an activity with a group of religious, spiritual or esoteric nature find themselves in a conflict of interest: they should therefore choose between their religious activity and their job as civil servants.[54]

> Effective prevention is only possible with a State-sponsored data base, collecting the sectarian affiliations of the State employees. Police services should systematically inform the authorities when State employees are discovered to be in relationship with a sectarian movement.[55]

> As far as service providers are concerned, a list of the ones to be avoided should be kept up to date and circulated to all Departments. Witch hunting, though, should be avoided.[56]

The audit also suggested the enforcement of the still existing anti-Catholic legislation of 1872, which allows the banning and dissolution of congregations if they are established in Geneva without official permission by the canton's government (p. 126).

Following these recommendations, no less than six projects for new legislation were drafted by the government and presented to the Geneva Parliament during 1999:

---

[50] On 19 September 1998, Basel passed a piece of legislation banning "deceitful proselytism" from the streets.

[51] *L'Etat face aux dérives sectaires,* Colloque de la Faculté de Droit de l'Université de Genève, 25 November 1999.

[52] "Genève a raté son projet de loi contre les sectes" (Geneva misses out on its anti-sect bill), *Le Courrier de Genève,* 20 November 1999.

[53] *Audit sur les dérives sectaires,* report from the Geneva expert group to the Department of Justice, Geneva, February 1997.

[54] Ibid., 171.

[55] Ibid., 173.

[56] Ibid., 174.

1. A revision of the Swiss civil law regarding the creation of associations (R373). According to the government, access by the "sects" to a very liberal status is too easy under current law. The proposed concept, however, was alien to Swiss tradition. The project was unanimously rejected in a single session of the Geneva Parliament.

2. A law about the proper use of the word "church" (PL7872). Intending to ban religious associations from doing business as well as to ban business for religious purposes, the proposed law allowed exemptions for the National Protestant Church and the Catholic Church. Understandably, this outraged the Jewish community, not to mention numerous other religions that are part of the multicultural international community of Geneva. Even the Catholics and the Protestants did not really like the idea of making the word "church" a protected trademark. Frozen for six months in order to be completely reformulated, the project has not been heard of since.

3. A law on the illegal practice of medicine aimed at preventing alternative medical treatments by members of "sects" in the medical and paramedical profession (PL7941). Unable to distinguish between natural medicine and personal development, the law appeared to be applicable to a limitless number of associations and individuals. After it aroused the opposition of the Naturopathic Association, the government retreated. This project is also said to be in the process of being rewritten.

4. A revision of the Geneva law of judicial procedure, offering supplementary protection to sect victims (PL7881). The law is supposed to distinguish between ordinary victims and victims of "sectarian misconduct." Its objective is to strengthen the position of the latter in lawsuits and to grant anti-sect associations access to criminal courts, whether in support of a party or in their own capacity. The Parliament basically accepted this idea. However, another approach to reach the same goal was preferred and is supposed to be presently under discussion.

5. The only project to be accepted by the Geneva Parliament has been the creation of an intercantonal observatory of beliefs. The project has been put at a disadvantage by its approach, however; it was conceived in effect as similar to a police file, and was supposed to gather information on existing beliefs and their possibly dangerous nature. To date, the Genevan politicians behind the project have not been able to mobilize a single university which specializes in this field. Besides this, the financial participation of the other cantons has been compromised by differences of opinions or competing approaches.

6. Last but not least, the Geneva government has published a report on mind control[57] and has prepared a proposal on antibrainwashing legislation to be presented to the Federal Parliament. According to this project, a new article 182 would be introduced into the Swiss criminal code, reading as follows: "Whoever has carried out physical or psychological actions in a repeated and systematic way, aimed at impairing the capacity of another person to make autonomous judgment, or at placing this other person in a state of dependency, will be punished with a jail term and a fine." Before the idea can be submitted to the Federal Parliament for discussion, it must first be endorsed by the Geneva Parliament. The debate between the government and its intellectual opponents is already in the media.[58]

---

[57] Report of the Criminal Commission on Sectarian Misconduct about mind control.

[58] Charles Poncet, "'Pour une liberté des sectes' vs Gérard Ramseyer 'Et les enfants morts du Temple Solaire?'" *Le Temps,* 3 November 2001.

The neighboring French-speaking Canton of Vaud has launched its own "Observatory of religions in Switzerland," inaugurated on 14 December 1999 during the symposium "State regulation of religion: new perspectives?" held at the University of Lausanne, where the observatory has since been based.[59] Unlike the Genevan project, the canton's observatory has managed to create a network of specialists in the field from French-speaking Swiss universities.[60]

As regards concrete relations between authorities and minority religious groups, the city of Lausanne in the Canton of Vaud is famous for an astonishing practice in its dealings with the Church of Scientology. Rather than risking the possibility of uncertain legal innovations after 2000, as did Geneva, and without relying on any legal basis, Lausanne simply took over from the canton authorities the decision of whether to authorize the presence of Scientologists, even to the degree of their circulating leaflets individually on the streets of the town. Since then, such activity has been allowed by the police only on Tuesdays, to the exclusion of every other day of the week. Fines have already been imposed on one woman contravening this decision, which she opposed. The outcome of the pending court case, however, is quite clear, in that the federal jurisprudence has ruled on the matter for decades, providing that "distribution of tracts by an individual cannot be submitted to authorization without illicitly undermining freedom of expression and freedom of the press."[61]

As already mentioned, the Parliament of Basel was the first to pass new legislation. A new cantonal criminal law was adopted in September 1998, banning the "deceitful recruiting" of converts from the streets. Even though the law, in force since 1 November 1998, avoids defining its terms, the parliamentary discussion has made it perfectly clear: "deceitful recruiting" means recruiting by the Scientology Church. Understandably enough, the Scientologists attacked the new law in the Federal Tribunal (Supreme Court), claiming it violates their constitutional right to exercise their religious freedom. On 30 June 1999, the Federal Tribunal conceded that the Basel law does infringe upon religious freedom, yet asserted that it does so in the public interest,[62] namely in order to protect the religious liberty of passersby, i.e., their right not to believe in a particular creed. Thus, concluded the Swiss Supreme Court, the Basel law is constitutionally valid.

III. Deviations of State Anti-Sect Policies from International Human Rights Norms for Freedom of Religion and Belief

A. Relevant Human Rights Norms

As members of the United Nations, the Organization for Security and Cooperation in Europe, and the Council of Europe, France, Belgium, and Switzerland have committed themselves to numerous international and European treaties and covenants that protect religious freedom.

---

[59] Université de Lausanne, "Observatoire des religions en Suisse," *Bulletin I,* October 2000.

[60] "La vie religieuse sera mise sous observation à l'université" (Religious life to be brought under observation at universities, an interview with the historian Jean-François Mayer), *Le Courrier,* 10 December 1999.

[61] ATF 96 I 586.

[62] Verein "Scientology Kirche Basel" v. Regierungsrat des Kantons Basel-Stadt und Grosser Rat des Kantons Basel-Stadt (Swiss Federal Tribunal, 30 June 1999).

The two most relevant international instruments are the International Covenant on Civil and Political Rights (ICCPR), to which the three countries are parties, and the Declaration on the Elimination of All Forms of Intolerance and of Discrimination Based on Religion or Belief (the 1981 Declaration).

Article sections 18.1 and 18.3 of the ICCPR read:

> 18.1: Everyone shall have the right to freedom of thought, conscience and religion. This right shall include freedom to have or to adopt a religion or belief of his choice, and freedom, either individually or in community with others and in public or private, to manifest his religion or belief in worship, observance, practice and teaching.
>
> 18.3: Freedom to manifest one's religion or beliefs may be subject only to such limitations as are prescribed by law and are necessary to protect public safety, order, health, or morals or the fundamental rights and freedoms of others.

Articles 2 and 26 of the ICCPR prohibit any form of discrimination based on religion, and state that all persons shall be guaranteed the "equal and effective" protection of the law. This is particularly important for members of new or newly established religious movements, to which governments often deny the same guarantees as the so-called historical religions. Addressing this precise issue, the United Nations Human Rights Committee interpreted article 18 in its General Comments No. 22(48) by stating:

> The terms belief and religion are to be broadly construed. Article 18 is not limited in its application to traditional religions or to religions and beliefs with institutional characteristics or practices analogous to those of traditional religions. The Committee therefore views with concern any tendency to discriminate against any religion or belief for any reasons, including the fact that they are newly established, or represent religious minorities that may be the subject of hostility on the part of a predominant religious community.[63]

The 1981 Declaration on the Elimination of All Forms of Intolerance and of Discrimination Based on Religion or Belief is one of the most complete statements of international religious freedoms. Article 2 reads:

> 1. No one shall be subject to discrimination by any State, institution, group of persons, or person on the grounds of religion or other belief.
>
> 2. For the purpose of the present Declaration, the expression "intolerance and discrimination based on religion or belief" means any distinction, exclusion, restriction or preference based on religion or belief and having as its purpose or as its effect nullification or impairment of the recognition, enjoyment or exercise of human rights and fundamental freedoms on an equal basis.

Further, according to Article 4:

> 1. All States shall take effective measures to prevent and eliminate discrimination on the grounds of religion or belief in the recognition, exercise and enjoyment of human rights and fundamental freedoms in all fields of civil, economic, political, social and cultural life.

---

[63] UN Human Rights Committee, General Comment No. 22 (1993). See Martin Scheinin's chapter in this volume.

> 2. All States shall make all efforts to enact or rescind legislation where necessary to prohibit any such discrimination, and to take all appropriate measures to combat intolerance on the grounds of religion or other beliefs in this matter.

Two major European human rights instruments also protect religious freedom: the European Convention for the Protection of Human Rights and Fundamental Freedoms and OSCE commitments, particularly the Concluding Document of the Vienna Meeting of Representatives of the Participating States of the OSCE (1989).[64]

Article 9 of the European Convention explicitly protects freedom of religion and belief. Article 11 ensures the rights to assemble peacefully and to form minority associations. Article 14 prevents discrimination based on religion.[65]

The Vienna Concluding Document elaborates specific principles regarding the freedom to profess and to practice religion or belief (excerpts, emphases added):

> 16. In order to ensure the freedom of the individual to profess and practice religion or belief, the participating States will, *inter alia*,
>
> 16.1 – take effective measures to *prevent and eliminate discrimination* against individuals or communities on the grounds of religion or belief in the recognition, exercise and enjoyment of human rights and fundamental freedoms in all fields of civil, political, economic, social and cultural life and *ensure the effective equality* between believers and non-believers;
>
> 16.2 – *foster a climate of mutual tolerance and respect* between believers of different communities as well as between believers and non-believers;
>
> 17. The participating States recognize that the exercise of the above-mentioned rights relating to the freedom of religion or belief *may be subject only to such limitations as are provided by law and consistent with their obligations under international law and with their international commitments.* They will ensure in their laws and regulations and in their application the full and effective implementation of the freedom of thought, conscience, religion or belief.

The developments of the state anti-sect policies in France, Belgium, and Switzerland, as described at the beginning of the chapter, must be read in the light of the provisions of these international instruments to which the three countries are committed.

The numerous abuses created by parliamentary inquiry commissions and reports on sects, lists of sects, and sect observatories must also be analyzed in the same perspective.

B. Parliamentary Reports and Lists of Groups

A number of leading academics, especially sociologists of religion,[66] have decried the methodology and results of the French and Belgian parliamentary commission reports. However, such analyses were easily overlooked in the nearly unanimous call by politicians and the media for even stronger measures to fight sects.

---

[64] For a more complete discussion of the OSCE commitments on freedom of religion or belief and the OSCE process, see the chapter in this volume by Urban Gibson and Karen Lord.

[65] For a thorough discussion of the European Convention on Human Rights' protection of freedom of religion, see the chapter by Rafael Navarro-Valls and Javier Martínez-Torrón in this volume.

Criticism has mainly focused on the lack of rigorous studies by qualified scholars in the pertinent fields, the refusal to take into account the expertise of sociologists of religion, the biased, unrepresentative choice of witnesses heard by the commissions, the nonconsultation of representatives of the groups under consideration, the inclusion of accusations unsupported by evidence from other sources, the indiscriminate lumping together of groups across the spectrum of belief and practice, numerous errors of fact, and the publication of lists labeling sects—real or apparent—as dangerous.[67] For example, as part of the Swedish government's report on sects issued in 1998, it examined prior sect reports and heavily criticized their methodology.[68]

The criticism on the merits was well summarized by Professor Johan Goethals, an expert called by the Belgian commission: "My limited experience showed me clearly that a parliamentary inquiry commission was not fit to conduct scientific research successfully because it does not have the academic training to do so, because deontological and ethical principles were too often made to serve political or personal goals, and because a number of other requirements were not fulfilled, such as compliance with copyright restrictions over the material collected, publication as scheduled, clear distribution of the tasks and clear definition of the mission of the experts."[69] His analysis applies with equal validity to the French parliamentary commission.

Following publication of the parliamentary reports and the "lists of sects," many cases of intolerance and discrimination in the public and private sectors were reported in France,[70] Belgium,[71] and Switzerland.[72] Complaints from French and Belgian individuals

---

[66] For a critique of the French report, see Massimo Introvigne and J. Gordon Melton, eds., *Pour en finir avec les sectes. Le débat sur le rapport de commissions parlementaires* (Paris: Cesnur-Di Giovanni, 1996). See also Françoise Champion and Martine Cohen, eds., *Sectes et démocratie* (Paris: Seuil, 1993). For a detailed analysis of the failings of the Gest-Guyard report, see Jean Baubérot, "Le rapport de la commission parlementaire sur les sectes: entre neutralité et dangerosité sociale" in Introvigne and Melton, *Pour en finir avec les sectes,* 63–72.

[67] See, e.g., *Illegal Activities of Sects,* Eur. Consult. Ass., Doc. No. 8373 (1999), sec. II(C)(5), <http://stars.coe.fr/doc/doc99/edoc8373.htm> (noting the danger of "the temptation to lump harmless and dangerous groupings together," which "would be manifestly . . . disproportionate in the context of freedom of belief.") (visited 25 July 2001); *Illegal Activities of Sects,* Eur. Consult. Ass., Doc. No. 8373 (1999), sec. II(C)(1), 6–14 (criticizing the tendency of state authorities to make distinctions between sects and religions). In Belgium, the opposition to the list mainly came from the movements listed therein, but also from the Christian Democrat parties CVP and PSC, which were in power at that time. See Alain Lallemand, "Sectes: Va-t-on réactiver la 'cellule Bulthé'?" (Sects: Will the 'Bulthé cell' be revived?), *Le Soir,* 6 May 1997, 23.

[68] See *In Good Faith* (SOU, September 1998), 113.

[69] Johan Goethals, *De sektencommissie. Het verhaal van een expert* (The sect commission. The story of an expert) (Leuven: Uitgeverij van Halewijck, 1998), 161.

[70] In France, prisoners were denied the reception of magazines published by Jehovah's Witnesses. In a letter dated 15 November 1999 to Mr. René Schneerberger, a JW minister, the director of the Bapaume prison, D. Laurent, stated that he had decided to have the magazine delivery suspended "because of the sectarian character of the congregation, recognized by the parliamentary commission." See Alain Garay, "Discrimination and Violations of Freedom of Conscience of Prisoners in France," in *Religion-Staat-Gesellschaft, Journal for the Study of Beliefs and Worldviews,* ed. Gerhard Besier and Hubert Seiwert (Berlin: Duncker & Humblot, 2000), Heft 2.

[71] In Belgium, the tax department denied the group Sukhyo Mahikari an exemption from property taxes on its place of worship on the grounds that it is on the so-called list of sects. This group is officially registered as a religious association in Spain (unpublished material collected during an interview of the leader of Sukyo Mahikari by Human Rights Without Frontiers in 2001).

belonging to one of the blacklisted sects have steadily increased: libel[73] and slander;[74] victimization in the neighborhood, at the workplace, and at school;[75] damage to individuals' reputation;[76] loss of jobs or promotions;[77] dismissals;[78] loss of visitation rights or child custody in divorce settlements;[79] inability to rent facilities for religious ceremonies or for meetings;[80] unilateral and unfounded closure of bank accounts of "sects" or of individuals affiliated with them;[81] humanitarian agencies' refusal to accept donations from "sects";[82] denial of access to public display boards;[83] and police surveillance.[84]

It was reported that "Some Belgian municipalities have made it a requirement for candidates for positions as civil servants to swear an oath that they do not belong to a 'harmful sectarian organization'" (Louis-Léon Christians, "Liberté d'opinion en droit européen: observations belges [II]—Les limitations," *Conscience et Liberté* 58 [1999]: 10 n. 1.).

In March 1999, the French Community of Belgium (one of the federated entities of the Belgian state) launched a campaign against "sects." This consisted of fliers, radio and TV spots warning people against sects and gurus and promoting the thirty-eight-page, richly illustrated brochure *Gourou gare à toi !* (Guru, you'd better watch out!), and directing people to anti-sect groups. About thirty religious movements from the synoptic table of 189 groups listed in the Belgian Parliamentary Commission's Report were targeted as dangerous sects. This campaign was unanimously supported by the Francophone media. The brochure was and is still widely used in schools. Several belief groups complain that they and their members were and are still victimized because of that campaign, especially children in schools. On 24 April 1999, the Court of First Instance at Brussels ordered, in an emergency procedure, the French Community of Belgium to stop distributing the sixty thousand copies of its brochure. The temporary injunction had been entered on a complaint filed several weeks before by the Anthroposophic Society. On appeal the French Community was allowed to resume the distribution of the brochure, but they had run out of it.

72 Wrongly "denounced" as Scientologist, a high-ranking official of the Geneva Department of Public Education, Mrs. Perrin, was heavily targeted by the press. Although this case is not isolated to Switzerland, it is an excellent example of the collateral damages caused by the anti-sect war.

73 Brussels judge Damien Vandermeersch was accused of being a member of the Opus Dei, listed in the Belgian parliamentary report. See his denial in Frédéric Delepierre, "Je ne suis pas membre de l'Opus Dei," *Le Soir,* 31 October 1998.

74 Since 1998, Baptist pastor Louis Demeo, who is also the director of the Institut Théologique de Nîmes (ITN), has been accused in the media of being a guru. See "L'ITN, une inquiétante organisation tentaculaire" (The ITN, a disturbing tentacular organization), *Le Midi Libre,* 28 October 1998.

75 In October 1998, the principal of a school in Chomerac (Ardèche, France) came under fire because he was a member of the Mandarom, a blacklisted sect. The rumor of sect involvement was sufficient for a number of parents to withdraw their children from his school and to draw the attention of anti-sect movements and of the Ministry of Education to this "danger." There was an official inquiry, but no professional negligence or proselytism could be established. It was sufficient that he was perceived as a potential danger. (French TV Channel FR3, Evening News, 28 October 1998.)

76 See the reply to a reader by journalist Eddy Daniëls, *Intermediaire,* 22 September 1998, 2: "Even a prominent sociologist of religions such as Karel Dobbelaere, Professor at the Catholic University of Leuven, was accused of colluding with dangerous sects because he spoke with members of sects to learn what they were doing and what motivated them."

See also the case of psychotherapist Bernard Lempert in "L'honneur perdu du psy de Landerneau" (The lost honor of the psychotherapist of Landerneau), *Libération,* 1 April 1996; "Deux ans pour éteindre le bûcher. La justice a blanchi Bernard Lempert, accusé d'être un gourou" (Two years to put out the fire. A court clears Bernard Lempert accused to be a guru), *Libération,* 25 October 1998. In 1996, a small association called *L'arbre du milieu,* which was helping physically and sexually abused children, was included in the Gest-Guyard list of 173 sects published by the French parliamentary commission on sects. The commission relied on information from the French Intelligence Service. However, the source of the accusation against this group was an influential, former patient of Bernard Lempert (the founder of *L'arbre du milieu*) who used an anti-sect group to help settle a personal score. Bernard Lempert, a well-known psychologist, lost his reputation, his patients, and his sources of financing. Yet in October 1998,

C. State "Observatories" and Agencies to Fight against Sects

In France, Prime Minister Alain Juppé created an Interministerial Observatory in 1996. Its mission was to analyze the phenomenon of sects and to make recommendations so as to improve the means to combat sects. The observatory did not survive the publication of

the Court of Rennes found Mr. Lempert "not guilty" of the charge of being the guru of a sect. Jacques Guyard acknowledged that the movement *L'arbre du milieu* should not have been included in the list of sects, but there is no procedure for removing a group from that list.

[77] In mid-December 1998, an engineer working in a nuclear plant for the French national electricity company was refused a key position and was transferred to another non-nuclear department because of belonging to the Church of Scientology. Although the engineer had not committed any professional mistake nor had ever tried to disseminate his beliefs, he was suspected of being used by the Church of Scientology to infiltrate the nuclear plant. The engineer had been denounced by several anonymous letters just when he was about to be given responsibility over a dozen workers. See "Gravelines: Malaise à la centrale nucléaire. Un scientologue devait piloter deux réacteurs. Il sera muté" (Disquiet at the nuclear power plant. A scientologist was to pilot two reactors. He will be transferred), *Le Journal du Dimanche,* 31 December 1998; "Le spécialiste du nucléaire était scientologue. Il devait s'occuper des réacteurs de la centrale de Gravelines" (The specialist in nuclear power was a Scientologist. He was to have been in charge of the reactors at the power plant in Gravelines), *Le Parisien,* 14 December 1998.

[78] See *Rapport sur la discrimination à l'encontre des minorités spirituelles et thérapeutiques en France,* published by Omnium des Libertés, October 2000, 14.

[79] There are numerous such cases for all religious groups in France and Belgium listed in the parliamentary reports. In Belgium, Lieve Van Roy's case has received regular coverage in the media. See "Ik wil en mijn kind en mijn geloof behouden" (I want to keep both my child and my faith), *De Standaard,* 14–16 August 1998, 31.

[80] Human Rights Without Frontiers press release, 2 November 2000:

> Three hours after it had begun, a public meeting of the new religious movement Sahaja Yoga was banned by order of the mayor. A dozen police officers accompanied by a bailiff turned up to make sure the ban was respected.
>
> On Thursday October 26, 2000 at 4:30 P.M., the organisers of the meeting, scheduled for later that evening, were informed that it had been banned, following orders from state security. The auditorium of the cultural center in Woluwe St Pierre (Brussels) had been hired several months in advance for a presentation of the Sahaja Yoga movement, and the meeting had been advertised by radio, posters, and leaflets.
>
> At 6:30 P.M. barricades were erected in front of the entrance to the cultural center and a dozen uniformed and plainclothes policemen were in attendance. Some stated that they belonged to the public relations department of the gendarmerie, others that they were part of the state security services and others to the Belgian Brigade of Surveillance and Research (BSR). An affidavit was also presented by a bailiff. The organisers were informed that all meetings of any kind were forbidden and that any discussion of Sahaja Yoga would result in arrest.
>
> The individual responsible for hiring out the hall claimed that the sect's dangerous nature had only been discovered at the last minute. He added that the presence of the gendarmerie and the state security services was justified by the sect's attempt to infiltrate the town's dance center. Allegedly, the group had hired the hall to stage a dance display, but in reality it turned out they wanted to talk about their 'guru', Shri mataji NIRMALA DEVI. He claimed also that this sect was extremely dangerous because it kidnapped children.

[81] Unpublished material collected during interviews with members of the Raelian religion by Human Rights Without Frontiers in 1999.

[82] Ibid.

[83] Unpublished material collected during interviews with members of Sahaja Yoga by Human Rights Without Frontiers in 1999.

[84] In 1999, the Surveillance and Research Brigade visited parents of former students of the only Steiner School in French-speaking Belgium (in the Flemish-speaking part there are about fifteen, all financed by the Flemish parliament), collecting statements and value judgements about the school. The Steiner

its first report of activities in 1998 and was replaced by a supposedly more "effective" tool, the Interministerial Mission to Fight Sects (MILS). This change of policy marked a turning point at which the government undertook efforts to penalize and repress the 173 groups listed in the Gest-Guyard Parliamentary Report. To make the MILS truly "operational," a ministerial order on 23 November 1998 officially assigned senior civil servants responsible for financial inspections, tax audits, social and labor law inspections, and customs inspections to the MILS. Unlike the observatory, the MILS then had real power to implement administrative verification procedures and apply penalties. Thus, based only on the list drawn up unilaterally by the internal intelligence and police force and published in the Gest-Guyard parliamentary report, the MILS can now take the initiative to implement official and legal action against the 173 groups listed. In early 2001, that is how things stood.

Simply by virtue of being listed in the parliamentary report, the "sects" affected now face coercive measures without having had the opportunity to argue their case and contest the merits of the Gest-Guyard report. The MILS investigates the case for the prosecution relating to all these groups and relies on information forwarded by the associations who act as intermediates, namely the powerful anti-sect associations who receive state subsidies. The lack of any forum for an adversarial proceeding and the refusal of any dialogue because of an institutionalized policy "to combat sects" clearly constitute a repressive model of civil service management of the issue and have generated numerous lawsuits before the French courts. In France, the courts have now become the arbitrator in the application of a repressive policy advocated by a limited number of members of Parliament and institutionalized by the government.

The entire tissue of judicial and administrative provisions arising from the efforts of some parliamentarians clearly deviates from international norms that proclaim and protect freedom of belief and guarantee the right to a fair hearing. The annual reports of the MILS virtually thrash "sects" for their attitude when the latter indicate their intention to avail themselves of the international legal instruments guaranteeing their right to freedom of religion and belief (notably, the 1948 Universal Declaration of Human Rights, the 1950 European Convention on Human Rights, and the 1966 International Covenant on Civil and Political Rights). The MILS holds that these groups cannot claim protection under these treaties, because the groups' practices are deemed by the MILS to be in inherent contradiction with the rights the groups seek. The MILS tends to deny "sects" any legitimate recourse to the law, that is, the benefit of national and international legislation. Any reliance on the laws or recourse to the legal system and the courts is perceived *a priori* as excessive and inappropriate. Any efforts by such groups to appeal to the courts and mount a legal defense are seized upon as evidence for the theory that we are dealing with a "legal nit-picking sect." Thus, in France, any reference to international legal instruments is seen as objectionable and criticized.

Schools are linked to the Anthroposophic Society, which is on the French and Belgian parliamentary report lists of sects (unpublished material collected during interviews with members of the Anthroposophic Society by Human Rights Without Frontiers in 1999).

In spring 1999, a Flemish family practicing Sahaja Yoga received a visit from the BSR, who had heard that the child was with his grandmother at an ashram in Rome. At the time of the visit the child was on his way back home. The parents made and signed a positive statement about the movement. A member of Sahaja Yoga in Mechelen, who had advertised courses, was visited by BSR officers from Leuven (unpublished material collected during interviews with members of Sahaja Yoga by Human Rights Without Frontiers in 1999).

Consequently, to some degree, in the various measures taken against sects, the principle of the right to a fair hearing has been flouted. Article 6 of the European Convention on Human Rights states that "in the determination of his civil rights and obligations or of any criminal charge against him, everyone is entitled to a fair and public hearing within a reasonable time by an independent and impartial tribunal established by law." In this connection, in 1999 the *Fédération chrétienne des Témoins de Jéhovah de France* (the Federation of Jehovah's Witnesses of France) filed an application at the European Court of Human Rights (Application 53430/99). The group claims that article 6 of the European Convention has been contravened by France making it a "victim" of two parliamentary reports on "sects." The case will undoubtedly be worth watching.

In Belgium, the Sect Observatory was named the Information and Advice Center. Its tasks are described as follows in article 6 of the 2 June 1998 Law:

> Section 1. The Center is charged with the following tasks:
>
> 1. to study the phenomenon of harmful sectarian organizations in Belgium and their international relations;
> 2. to organize a documentation center which is accessible to the public;
> 3. to ensure that members of the public may visit the center and receive answers to their questions and to inform all those who submit a request to the Center about their rights and obligations and how they can ensure that their rights are respected;
> 4. to publish, whether on its own initiative or at the request of any public authority, advice and recommendations about the phenomenon of harmful sectarian organizations and especially on the policy regarding the fight against these organizations;
>
> Section 2. In order to fulfill its tasks the Center is empowered to:
>
> 1. collect all relevant information;
> 2. conduct any studies or scientific research required to be able to perform its tasks in practice;
> 3. have access to files in any archive or documentation foundation whose subject corresponds to that of its tasks;
> 4. give support and guidance to institutions, organizations and legal consultants;
> 5. consult or invite professionals and associations to its meetings if their participation is useful.
>
> In the performance of its tasks, the Center will work together with the Administrative Coordination Agency.

When this chapter was written, the center had not yet published its first report. However, during a meeting between one of the coauthors of this chapter, Willy Fautré, and the president of the center, Professor Adelbert Denaux, and his coworkers, clarification of the following points related to article 6 was requested: the center's degree of political independence, the nature of the center's relationship with the Administrative Coordination Agency for the Fight against Harmful Sectarian Organizations, the drafting and the distribution of advice on such organizations, and the structure and the functioning of the center's information service.

The following information was obtained at the meeting: The center states that it operates with full independence and is not subject to any political interference.[85] It does not have capacity to bring proceedings before the courts. While cooperating with the coordinating administrative agency, the center will not share personal information it has obtained.[86] The advice issued by the center on the dangerous nature or the illegal activities of harmful sectarian organizations will be forwarded only to the public authorities (the executive branch) following a request by the authorities or on the center's own initiative. Opinions on specific religious groups will not be shared with other organizations, journalists, reporters, lawyers, private individuals, and so forth. The center is currently in the process of setting up a specialized library. It will have several clearly identified sections: academic reference works, publications by religious movements, those by anti-sect groups and individuals, and those by the media. A video library is also planned. The center will also respond to requests for information made by letter[87] or telephone. The center will not publish any "list of sects."[88] Like the Belgian House of Representatives, it will not publish the transcripts or stenographer's minutes of public hearings held by the parliamentary commission of inquiry into sects.

IV. Conclusions and Recommendations

Anti-sect policies in France, Belgium, and Switzerland have triggered an unprecedented wave of discrimination and intolerance against nonconventional religious and belief groups. They also contravene the obligations regarding freedom of religion and belief that are enshrined in international and European treaties and covenants to which these countries are committed.

France's choice to combat sects stands in contrast to that of the majority of the member states of the European Union. Part of the explanation for this is certainly to be found in its history, the Age of Enlightenment, and the philosophical movements that have shaped the French mentality through the centuries. But the stance taken by France also reveals a political will to stand out and to affirm its cultural identity, difference, and leadership within its zone of influence. The "sect issue" has moved out of the sphere of a social phenomenon scrutinized by sociologists of religions and has become a public, political, and diplomatic issue.

---

[85] The center's operating budget comes from the Ministry of Justice and amounts to 640,000 Euros (about USD $640,000) for the year 2001. Staff is provided by the Ministry of Justice after consultation with the center (law of 2 June 1998, art. 12).

[86] See law of 2 June 1998, art. 6, sec. 3: "For the tasks mentioned in sec. 1 pts. 1 and 3 the Center is empowered to deal with data of a personal nature relating to opinions and religious and philosophical activities as mentioned in article 6 of the law of 8 December 1992 for the protection of privacy in relation to the treatment of personal data. The King determines, by order, which is deliberated in the Council of Ministers, the guarantees concerning confidentiality and security of personal data, the status and duties of an appointee for the protection of data within the Center and the way in which the Center must report to the Commission for the protection of privacy concerning processing of personal data."

[87] On 22 February 2001, the president of Sahaja Yoga, Mr. Bernard Cuvelier, sent a protest letter to the director of the center in which he complained that only negative reports on his movements had been sent on 5 January 2001 and 12 February 2001 to people who had asked the center for information about Sahaja Yoga.

[88] See law of 2 June 1998, art. 6, sec. 4: "The information which the Center supplies at the request of the public is based on the information which the Center has available and may not be presented in the form of lists or systematic statements about harmful sectarian organizations."

In the escalating war against "sects," France has certainly taken the most initiatives and has been the most ingenious. Neighboring French-speaking territories, for their part, have to various degrees followed French policies in this matter. With its "Law aimed at reinforcing the prevention and repression of groups with a sectarian character," also known as the About-Picard law, France has opted for a unique solution to concerns raised by the phenomenon of unpopular or minority new religious movements, a solution that has attracted worldwide criticism.

A number of human rights organizations and states have criticized the French government's position, especially at the Implementation Meetings on Human Dimension Issues of the OSCE in 1998, 1999, and 2000. Up to now, French political decision makers have failed to take those criticisms into account and to adapt their policy to international human rights standards. For example, during the debates on the About-Picard law proposal, French Socialist Senator Dynah Dericke praised France's determination in its fight against "sects." Last summer, France denounced the United States' "attempts at intimidation." This was in response to some widely publicized American reports on religious freedom around the world that had targeted France because of its war against "sects."

Moreover, the Interministerial Mission to Fight Sects has been trying to export the French anti-sect model to other countries, especially in central and eastern Europe, and to make common cause with states and mainstream churches which have chosen to combat sects. If effective, this will likely exacerbate the types of human rights abuses that minority religions have experienced in France, because many other countries currently considering the possibility of following the French model have weaker judiciaries and thus less effective judicial protections of freedom of religion or belief.

Belgium and Switzerland are now being stigmatized in the international community because they have made the same choice as France: to fight against sects instead of opening a dialogue. The confrontation policy practiced in the European francophone sphere also raises some basic questions: Are France, Belgium, and the Swiss francophone canton of Geneva different from other western European states when it comes to their relations with nonmainstream religious movements? Do they have specific characteristics that must be taken into account in their dealings with such movements? Although these questions remain unsettled and require further investigation, there does seem to be a strong cultural convergence in French-speaking Europe around France, which has taken the lead in the fight against "sects." The rest of Europe has generally followed the Report of the Council of Europe's Committee on Legal Affairs and Human Rights, which determined that it would be sufficient for member states "to use the normal procedures of criminal and civil law against illegal practices carried out in the name of groups of a religious, esoteric, or spiritual nature."[89]

In the "sect issue," France may be said to practice cultural protectionism to preserve its domestic policy, just as it fights to protect its position in areas such as the film industry, or agriculture and food products, from the uniform standards it perceives as being imposed on it by other entities or phenomena (the European Union, the United States, or "globalization"). Its crusade against a federal European Union or European homogenization appears to be one and the same war as that against "foreign sects." In this respect, the attitude of the French secular republic is in the end no different from

---

[89] *Illegal Activities of Sects,* Eur. Consult. Ass., Doc. No. 8373 (1999), sec. I(5), <http://stars.coe.fr/doc/doc99/edoc8373.htm> (visited 25 July 2001).

dominant Orthodox and Catholic Churches in central and eastern Europe. They all tend to act as watchdogs over their own sphere of influence and serve as a bulwark against the invasion of cultural and ideological pluralism.[90]

As the economies and politics of countries become increasingly interwoven, it is probably time to create a forum for discussion, study, proposals, and decision making on a continental level to ensure the public and scholarly scrutiny of the information about such groups. Currently, each country develops its own response with its own historical and cultural background, but without considering the international dimension of the phenomenon.

Given the scope of activities by groups deemed to be "sects" or "cults," Adrian Nastase and nine other delegates to the Parliamentary Assembly of the Council of Europe have proposed acting at this level by creating an "observatory of activities by sects at European level."[91] This recommendation was also included in Nastase's report, "Illegal Activities of Sects."[92] Inasmuch as governments follow this recommendation, it is important to stress that observatories should be forums for expert opinion and study that could guide countries in their action by reliance on scholarly methods and international norms of religious freedom. Their purpose should be to study and provide expert opinion on the documented activities of philosophical, ideological, and religious groups across Europe, and not to make broad generalizations about "sects" or new religious movements. The drafting of documented reports based on research by a multidisciplinary, multicultural scholarly group could help promote the emergence of a common approach to the realities of the situation.[93]

A European observatory for research and study of beliefs, under the auspices of the Council of Europe, for example, which now has forty-three member states, could constitute a practical, functional, and adequate tool for the democratic aspirations of European countries and public opinion, if it is run in a scholarly manner consistent with principles of freedom of religion or belief.

---

[90] See the strange alliance between Alain Vivien and the Cypriot Orthodox Church in their fight against "sects," <http://www.hrwf.net/france99e.html>.

[91] See the *Proposal for a recommendation,* Parliamentary Assembly of the Council of Europe, 2 May 1997, Doc. 7826, <http://stars.coe.fr/doc/doc97/edoc7826.htm>.

[92] *Illegal Activities of Sects*, Eur. Consult. Ass., Doc. No. 8373 (1999), sec. I(5), <http://stars.coe.fr/doc/doc99/edoc8373.htm> (visited 25 July 2001).

[93] On the need for an intermediate authority providing a forum for debate and dialogue, see Alain Garay, "La liberté religieuse en Europe—restriction et protection," *Conscience et Liberté,* no. 59 (2000): 81–99.

Chapter 27

The Right to Engage in Religious Persuasion

Tad Stahnke

I. Introduction

Justice Frankfurter of the United States Supreme Court once wrote, "Adjustment of the inevitable conflict between free speech and other interests is a problem as persistent as it is perplexing."[1] Proselytism is one form of expression that has resulted in inevitable, and sometimes fierce, conflict. But on Justice Frankfurter's terms, proselytism—whether it is viewed as an exercise of free expression or a manifestation of religious belief—is not in itself the problem. The problem lies in finding the proper balance between the freedom to proselytize and the multitude of rights, duties, and interests of religious groups, individuals, and the state that may conflict with that freedom.

The difficulty of this "adjustment" is deepened by a number of factors. Persons who proselytize, whether as a matter of conscience or religious belief, may adhere to their entitlement to do so with great strength. Likewise, the targets of proselytism may hold their religious beliefs (or their sense of privacy in those beliefs) with equal strength; attempts to persuade them in matters of religious belief may lead to injury to religious feelings. Finally, religious groups, desiring to preserve or expand their numbers, may have strong views as to the terms on which persons may change their religious identity or affiliation. This may influence the groups' views on proselytism.

Within the framework of international human rights law, states are responsible for sorting out these and other competing interests in formulating policies that adequately protect the rights of all involved. But states themselves exhibit different views on the necessity of regulating, or the wisdom of influencing, religious choices of their people. In some societies a change in religious beliefs may have far-reaching social ramifications, whereas in others, such a change will have only a private impact. Inevitably, different state practices will be a reflection of more general societal considerations. It appears that the extent to which other rights and interests give way to the freedom to proselytize is indicative

---

[1] Niemotko v. Maryland, 340 US 268, 275 (1951) (Frankfurter, J, concurring).

Tore Lindholm, W. Cole Durham, Jr., Bahia G. Tahzib-Lie (eds.), Facilitating Freedom of Religion or Belief: A Deskbook, *619–649.*

of the extent to which a society views itself as hospitable to change in the religious beliefs of its members, and considers an open (and consequently confrontational) exchange of different religious viewpoints to be acceptable, or even desirable.

The goal of this chapter is to set out the different rights and interests at issue when conflict arises over proselytism. States must consider these rights and interests in order to establish a decision-making framework consistent with international human rights law. This chapter concludes that state action which restricts proselytism by employing discriminatory methods or by furthering interests not recognized in international instruments is inconsistent with international human rights standards. The validity of other restrictions will depend upon a variety of circumstantial variables primarily relating to the potential for coercion. These variables cannot be sorted out in any consistent way without resorting to the particulars of each case.

II. Preliminary Issues

A. The Definition of Proselytism

The term "proselytism" has been used so far without definition. In many contexts, it has had a decidedly negative connotation.[2] As used in this chapter, "proselytism" means expressive conduct undertaken with the purpose of trying to change the religious beliefs, affiliation, or identity of another. The person initiating the conduct is the "source," and the person on the receiving end is the "target."

This definition of proselytism encompasses several important concepts. First, it avoids the notion of *per se* improper conduct; whether proselytism is improper ultimately depends on a variety of factors to be discussed below. The definition also stresses that proselytism is intentional conduct, undertaken with a particular goal in view. For this reason, the term "proselytization" is avoided, as that term can suggest a process, rather than a purposeful human action. Finally, this definition implies that the source need not have religious beliefs of her own. Thus, proselytism includes attempts to persuade the targets to abandon their current religious beliefs or affiliation without necessarily replacing them with those of the source.

B. Religious Views on Proselytism

Religions hold a wide variety of views on the propriety of proselytism. While one religion may require its adherents to attempt to bring others to the faith, such activity may be prohibited or even impossible for another. The views of various other religions span the entire range of possibilities in between. Furthermore, a religion may have a different view on being the source of proselytism, as opposed to being the target.[3]

---

[2] See "Common Witness and Proselytism," *The Ecumenical Review* 23, no. 1 (January 1971): 9–20 (prepared by the Joint Theological Commission of World Council of Churches and the Catholic Church); "Proselytism embraces whatever violates the right of the human person, Christian or non-Christian, to be free from external coercion in religious matters, or whatever, in the proclamation of the Gospel, does not conform to the ways God draws free men to himself in response to his calls to serve in spirit and in truth" (ibid., 9).

Likewise, views on proselytism may vary depending upon the religious identity of the target. For instance, a distinction may be drawn between targeting those of a different denomination within the same religion, and those of a different religion altogether. Given these divergent views, proselytism can raise problems of an intra-religious nature, as well as problems of interreligious relations and unity.[4]

Proselytism within a religion can precipitate conflict as intense as that between religions. For example, if a Christian church refuses to recognize that "other churches also . . . provide access to salvation in Christ,"[5] then that church will make no distinction between its proselytism directed at other Christians and proselytism directed at non-Christians. However, if a church considers that at least some other churches provide access to salvation, a distinction may be made between proselytism towards these Christians and proselytism directed at non-Christians.

It is this latter distinction that underlies the standards on proselytism expressed by the World Council of Churches and the Catholic Church in *Common Witness and Proselytism.*[6] In that document, Christians are reminded that "[t]he Lord has called all his disciples to be witnesses to him and his Gospel, to the ends of the earth."[7] This witness, whether directed at other Christians or non-Christians, "should be completely . . . conformed to the spirit of the Gospel, especially by respecting the other's right to religious freedom."[8] A number of requirements are stated in this regard, including the avoidance of "physical coercion, moral constraint or psychological pressure,"[9] the "offer of temporal or material benefits,"[10] the "exploitation of . . . need [and] weakness,"[11] and "unjust or uncharitable reference to the beliefs or practices of other religious communities."[12] Additional considerations apply to witness by members of one Christian church to those of another. Under these circumstances, witness "should be completely concerned to do nothing which could compromise the progress of ecumenical dialogue and action,"[13] and should "be concerned in fostering whatever can restore or strengthen between [Christians] the bonds of true brotherhood."[14]

---

[3] This position may be directly related to a religion's view on conversion:

> [W]hile many religions or beliefs welcome—and in some cases even encourage—the conversion of individuals belonging to other faiths, they are reluctant to admit the conversion of individuals of their own faith; apostasy is viewed with disfavour by them and often is prohibited by their religious law or discouraged by social ostracism (Tad Stahnke and J. Paul Martin, eds., *Religion And Human Rights: Basic Documents* [New York: Columbia University, 1998], 2, 22).

The above quote was originally found in Arcot Krishnaswami, *Study of Discrimination in the Matter of Religious Rights and Practices,* UN Doc. E/CN.4/Sub 2/200/Rev 1, UN Sales No. 60.XIV.2 (1960) (reprinted in Stahnke and Martin, *Religion and Human Rights: Basic Documents*).

[4] For a good review of views on proselytism as articulated in documents issued by Catholic, Protestant, and Orthodox Christian church bodies and associations, see Joel A. Nichols, "Mission, Evangelism, and Proselytism in Christianity: Mainline Conceptions as Reflected in Church Documents," *Emory International Law Review* 12 (1998): 563.

[5] "Common Witness and Proselytism," para. 11.

[6] Ibid.

[7] Ibid., para. 1.

[8] Ibid., para. 25.

[9] Ibid., para. 27(a).

[10] Ibid., para. 27(b).

[11] Ibid., para. 27(c).

[12] Ibid.

[13] Ibid.

[14] Ibid., para. 28.

As important as religious beliefs are to the individuals that hold them and to the societies of which they are a part, considerations beyond those of a strictly religious character must guide a state's approach to proselytism. While international human rights instruments recognize the right to have religious beliefs and the freedom to act on them, these instruments also confirm that states can limit this freedom to act in order to ensure other specified interests.[15] Therefore, even the strongest religious imperative to engage in proselytism, such as a requirement to bring as many to the "true" religion as possible, cannot prevail over a valid limitation. This is the case even though those who believe they are entitled to engage in proselytism may be burdened, perhaps severely, in the manifestation of their religious beliefs.

Conversely, a strictly religious basis for restricting proselytism is not by itself a valid limitation on the activity. Thus, a religious group's assessment of "the quality of the Christian message"[16] of a church, or a determination that proselytism weakens "the bonds of true [Christian] brotherhood"[17] would not give rise to a valid limitation on proselytism. As a result of this principle, members of some religions may be frustrated in the attempt to enforce what they believe to be appropriate standards of behavior. But by employing these principles, international human rights standards are directed at achieving a peaceful balance between the interests of those holding different religious views on proselytism, as well as the interests of those holding no religious beliefs.

C. Restrictions on Proselytism

States can restrict proselytism in a variety of ways: directly or indirectly; intentionally or unintentionally. Such restrictions may—again intentionally or unintentionally—fall heavier on some religions than others, thereby raising the possibility of discrimination.

1. Indirect Restrictions

In addition to laws that directly regulate proselytism, there are a myriad of laws, rules, and regulations that indirectly restrict proselytism. For instance, the failure of a religious group to be registered with or be recognized by the state as a prerequisite to functioning as an organizational entity can result in a restriction on proselytism. Moreover, activity that can be characterized as proselytism may take different forms, such as religious discussions; preaching; teaching; the publication, distribution, or sale of printed and electronic works; broadcasting; solicitation of funds; or provision of humanitarian or social services. All of these actions can be proselytism depending upon the intent with which they are undertaken. Therefore, regulation of any of these activities may intentionally or unintentionally restrict proselytism.

---

[15] These interests are the protection of "public safety, order, health, or morals or the fundamental rights and freedoms of others" (*International Covenant on Civil and Political Rights* [ICCPR], 19 December 1966, art. 18[3], 999 UNTS 171, reprinted in 6 ILM 368, 383). See also *The European Convention for the Protection of Human Rights and Fundamental Freedoms,* 4 November 1950, art. 9(2), 312 UNTS 221 (hereafter "European Convention"); reprinted in Barry E. Carter and Phillip R. Trimble, eds., *International Law: Selected Documents* (Boston: Little, Brown & Co., 1995), 467–68.

[16] "Common Witness and Proselytism," para. 28(b).

[17] Ibid., para. 28.

Further, laws that do not have as their apparent purpose the prohibition of proselytism can nevertheless be employed in furtherance of that goal. For example, government officials may determine which religious views can be disseminated through the discretionary grant or denial of permits required for activities related to proselytism (such as distributing literature); or, officials can suppress such activity through means such as a tax or fee.[18]

2. Discrimination in Restrictions on Proselytism

Restrictions on proselytism can also give rise to a number of issues regarding discrimination on the basis of religion or belief. A restriction may, on its face, make distinctions on the basis of religion or belief (either that of the source or that of the target). Even in the absence of a facial distinction, a restriction may have a differential effect on religious groups due to differences between those groups (either in terms of belief or otherwise). Further, a restriction may be applied or enforced by the relevant authorities in a differential manner. All of these differentiations are potentially discriminatory. The danger of discrimination is particularly high where underlying the distinctions are tensions between the dominant religious group and minority groups, coupled with the ability of the dominant group to effect public policy, the law, and its application.

Facially neutral restrictions on proselytism more heavily impact religious groups that encourage, mandate, or frequently engage in proselytism than those groups that discourage, prohibit, or otherwise do not engage in proselytism. Similarly, facially neutral restrictions of proselytism may affect majority and minority religious groups in different ways. To the extent that a control on proselytism is intended to preserve a certain pattern of religious affiliation by limiting the opportunities for conversion, such a provision will naturally favor the majority religious group, particularly if the majority is not aggressively seeking converts of its own.

Regulations that are vague or that leave official decision makers broad discretion are susceptible to discriminatory abuse in their application. Furthermore, even restrictions that are framed in more precise, neutral terms can be enforced in a differential manner. In *Kokkinakis v. Greece*,[19] an applicant to the European Court of Human Rights described such a situation. Although the Greek statute in question prohibited proselytism by members of all religious groups,[20] the applicant asserted that Greece did not uniformly enforce the prohibition:

> [I]t would surpass "even the wildest academic hypothesis" to imagine, for example, the possibility of a complaint being made by a Catholic priest or by a Protestant clergyman against an Orthodox Christian who had attempted to entice one of his flock away from him. It was even less likely that an Orthodox Christian would be prosecuted for proselytizing on behalf of the "dominant religion."[21]

---

[18] Tad Stahnke, "Proselytism and the Freedom to Change Religion in International Human Rights Law," *BYU Law Review*, no. 1 (1999): 251, 262–66.

[19] Kokkinakis v. Greece, 17 EHRR 397 (1994) (ECtHR 260-A, 25 May 1993).

[20] See note 55 and accompanying text.

[21] Kokkinakis v. Greece, 16–17.

Regardless of whether or not this is, or was, an accurate portrayal of the enforcement of the Greek restrictions, it sufficiently illustrates the type of problem that can arise. Differential application or enforcement of nondiscriminatory rules can bring about the same results as discriminatory ones.

III. Proselytism and International Human Rights Law

All major international human rights instruments recognize the right to freedom of religion or belief, which includes not only the freedom to hold religious beliefs, but also the freedom to manifest those beliefs.[22] While the freedom to hold beliefs is considered to be absolute—i.e., not subject to limitation by the state—the freedom to manifest beliefs is subject to valid limitations that "are prescribed by law and are necessary to protect public safety, order, health or morals, or the fundamental rights and freedoms of others."[23] Such limitations "may be applied only for those purposes for which they were prescribed and must be directly related and proportionate to the specific need on which they are predicated."[24] In addition, both the Human Rights Committee and the European Court have clearly stated that those provisions guaranteeing the right to freedom of religion or belief protect not only religious beliefs, but also other beliefs of a similar fundamental character, including atheism and agnosticism.[25]

Along with the right to freedom of religion or belief, international human rights instruments recognize the principles of equality and nondiscrimination on the basis of religion or belief. The ICCPR and the European Convention both contain obligations to secure the rights specified in those instruments without "distinction of any kind" (in the words of article 2(1) of the ICCPR) or "discrimination on any ground" (in the words of article 14 of the European Convention).

Furthermore, both instruments recognize that the principle of nondiscrimination extends beyond the assurance of the specific rights articulated in the instruments. Article 26 of the ICCPR obligates states to provide for the equal protection of the law and "equal and effective protection against discrimination on any ground." This protection extends to "any field regulated and protected by public authorities."[26] Although the obligation to prevent discrimination contained in article 14 of the European Convention

[22] See ICCPR, art. 18; European Convention, art. 9; *American Convention on Human Rights,* art. 1, 9 ILM 99 (1969) (hereafter "American Convention"); *Declaration on the Elimination of All Forms of Religious Intolerance and of Discrimination Based on Religion or Belief,* art. 1(1), GA Res. 36-55, UN GAOR, 36th Sess., Agenda Item 75, Supp. No. 51, UN Doc. A/36/55 (1981) (hereafter "1981 Declaration"); *Concluding Document of the Vienna Meeting: Conference on Security and Cooperation in Europe,* principle 16, reprinted in 28 ILM 53 (hereafter "Concluding Document of the Vienna Meeting").

[23] ICCPR, art. 18, para. 8.

[24] Ibid. According to the European Court, an interference with the freedom to manifest religion or belief "is contrary to Article 9 unless it is prescribed by law, directed at one or more of the legitimate aims in paragraph 2 [of Article 9] and necessary in a democratic society for achieving them" (Kokkinakis v. Greece, 18 [citations omitted]). For an interference to be "necessary in a democratic society," it must be both "justified in principle and proportionate" to the aim to be achieved (ibid., 21).

[25] See Human Rights Committee General Comment 22 (1993), art. 18, UN GAOR, 48th Sess., para. 2, UN Doc. CCPR/C/21/Rev 1/Add 1 (1989), reprinted in UN Doc. HR1/GEN/1/Rev 1 at 26 (1994); Kokkinakis v. Greece, 17.

[26] S.W.M. Broeks v. The Netherlands, Comm. No. 172/1984 (UN Human Rights Committee, 9 April 1987), para. 12.3; General Comment 22, para. 12.

does not have the same reach as article 26 of the ICCPR, an independent violation of another right specified in the European Convention is not necessary to support a claim of discrimination under article 14. To raise a valid claim of discrimination, it is enough to show that the subject matter of the claim falls within the scope of an article protecting a specified right. This relationship is established when a state enacts measures that go beyond the minimum requirements of specified rights,[27] or when the state seeks to justify limitation on specified rights.[28]

Finally, it should be mentioned that not every case of differential or unequal treatment is considered to be discrimination.[29] Under both the ICCPR and the European Convention, unequal treatment is not discrimination if it is made in pursuit of a legitimate aim and is based on reasonable and objective criteria.[30] The right to freedom of religion or belief is also explicitly recognized in those provisions of international human rights documents that concern the rights of minorities. Specifically, article 27 of the ICCPR provides, "In those States in which ethnic, religious or linguistic minorities exist, persons belonging to such minorities shall not be denied the right, in community with the other members of their group, to enjoy their own culture, to profess and practice their own religion, or to use their own language."[31] Although it has been expressed by the Human Rights Committee that article 27 provides for distinct, and additional, protection of the right of persons belonging to religious minorities to profess and practice their religion, it is not entirely clear how these provisions provide any additional protection in this regard than that provided to all persons under the general provisions covering the rights to freedom of religion or belief and to equal protection of the laws. One possible exception to this general statement is the obligation of the state to take measures to protect the identity, including the religious identity, of those belonging to a minority group.[32] However, such measures must be constructed and applied in a manner consistent with a state's obligations to prevent discrimination; in other words, they must be in pursuit of the aim of correcting conditions that prevent the exercise of rights protected under article 27 and be based on reasonable and objective criteria.[33] The key factor here is some condition that truly threatens the existence or way of life of the minority, or the ability to exercise their rights.

---

[27] See, e.g., Case "Relating to Certain Aspects of the Laws on the Use of Languages in Education in Belgium" v. Belgium, App. Nos. 01474/62, 01677/62, 01691/62, 01769/63, 01994/63, 02126/64 (ECtHR 6-A, 23 July 1968) (hereafter "Belgian Linguistics Case").

[28] See, e.g., Grandrath v. Federal Republic of Germany, App. No. 2299/64 (ECHR 626, 1967).

[29] For the definition of discrimination employed by the Human Rights Committee, see Human Rights Committee General Comment 18 (1989), 37, para. 7; UN Doc. CCPR/C/21/Rev 1/Add 2.

[30] See S.W.M. Broeks v. The Netherlands, para. 13; General Comment 18, para. 13; Belgian Linguistics Case, ECtHR 6-A, 34 (1968).

[31] See also *Declaration on the Rights of Persons Belonging to National or Ethnic, Religious, and Linguistic Minorities,* UNGA Res. 47/135, art. 1(1) (hereafter "Minorities Declaration"); *Framework Convention for the Protection of National Minorities,* art. 8 (hereafter "Framework Convention"); *Document of the Copenhagen Meeting of the Conference on the Human Dimension of the Conference on Security and Cooperation in Europe,* para. 32 (hereafter "Document of the Copenhagen Meeting").

[32] See Human Rights Committee General Comment 23 (1994), art. 27, UN GAOR 50th Sess., paras. 6.2, 8; UN Doc. CCPR/C/21/Rev 1/Add 5 (1994); Framework Convention, paras. 4(2), 4(3); Document of the Copenhagen Meeting, para. 33.

[33] See General Comment 23, para. 6.2; Minorities Declaration, art. 8.3; Document of the Copenhagen Meeting, para. 33.

IV. The Rights and Interests Implicated by Restrictions on Proselytism

In conflicts involving proselytism, the rights and interests of the source, the target, and the state can be arrayed against one another. The task of determining whether proselytism can be restricted consistent with international human rights standards will necessarily involve an analysis of these rights and interests. This section explores the rights and interests of each of these parties.

A. The Rights of the Source

1. The Freedom to Manifest Religion or Belief

Is proselytism a manifestation of religion or belief, and therefore encompassed within the concept of the right to freedom of religion or belief? There is no definitive consensus in international human rights instruments. With the exception of the American Convention, which explicitly states in article 12(1) that the right to freedom of religion or belief includes the freedom to "disseminate one's religion or beliefs," neither proselytism nor the freedom to disseminate a religion or belief is mentioned in international instruments.[34] The lack of any direct recognition of proselytism may be an indication of the sensitivity of states to the issues it raises and the difficulty of delineating agreeable standards.

Given that proclaiming religious experience and belief is important to many of the major religions of the world, it is logical that the freedom to manifest religion or belief would include the attempt to persuade another to adopt new religious beliefs or affiliation.[35] As Arcot Krishnaswami has said:

> While some faiths do not attempt to win new converts, many of them make it mandatory for their followers to spread their message to all, and to attempt to convert others. For the latter, dissemination is an important aspect of the right to manifest their religion or belief.[36]

International recognition of the freedom to change religion or belief further supports this view. The European Court has held that proselytism is a component of the freedom of religion or belief guaranteed by article 9 of the European Convention:

> While religious freedom is primarily a matter of individual conscience, it also implies, *inter alia,* freedom to manifest [one's] religion. Bearing witness in words and deeds is bound up with the existence of religious convictions.

---

[34] Some activities that are closely associated with proselytism are mentioned in these international documents. See, e.g., General Comment 18, 35 ("freedom to prepare and distribute religious texts or publications" is part of teaching and practice of religion); 1981 Declaration, arts. 6(d) (freedom to "write, issue and disseminate relevant publications") and 6(f) (freedom "[t]o solicit and receive voluntary financial . . . contributions"); Concluding Document of the Vienna Meeting, principles 16(d) (solicit financial contributions) and 16(j) (disseminate religious publications).

[35] Not all states are in agreement. The Malaysian government has argued that laws prohibiting proselytism directed at Muslims do not impact the right to religious freedom of non-Muslims. See *Implementation of the Declaration on the Elimination of All Forms of Intolerance and of Discrimination Based on Religion or Belief,* UN ESCOR, 46th Sess., Capital Provisional Agenda Item 24, Committee on Human Rights, para. 58, UN Doc. E/CN.4/1990/46 (1990) (hereafter "Special Rapporteur's Report 1990").

> According to Article 9, freedom to manifest [one's] religion . . . includes in principle the right to try to convince one's neighbour, for example through teaching, failing which, moreover, freedom to change [one's] religion or belief, enshrined in Article 9, would be likely to remain a dead letter.[37]

As proselytism falls within the ambit of the manifestation of religion or belief, it does so regardless of the form that it may take. A particular problem arises where the proselytizing activity is in a form that is unusual in comparison to other religious groups, or where it includes practices that are disfavored by those groups. However, in the words of the Human Rights Committee, the scope of the right to freedom of religion or belief "is not limited [to] . . . practices analogous to those of traditional religions."[38]

2. The Right to Freedom of Expression

As proselytism is here defined as expressive activity, it is encompassed by the right to freedom of expression protected under international human rights instruments. Although the distinction between proselytism as the manifestation of religion or belief and proselytism as expression may seem formal, there can be practical ramifications to the designation as one or the other. First, that branch of proselytism where the source is motivated by a desire to convince the target to change her religious beliefs, but not adopt new ones, does not fall easily within the notion of the manifestation of religion or belief because the source does not necessarily have religious beliefs of her own. Second, categorizing proselytism as expression relieves the examiner from the task of determining whether or not the beliefs asserted by the source are "religious," or whether proselytism falls within the scope of freedom of religion or belief. Third, different results might be reached concerning the same conduct if the legal principles and standards employed to review the manifestation of religion or belief differ from those governing expression. Although this requires a close examination of the particulars in any given legal system, an example can be found in international human rights instruments. While these instruments recognize that the protection of national security is a valid interest that may support a limitation on the right to freedom of expression,[39] they do not list national security as a justification for limitations on the freedom to manifest religion or belief.[40]

3. Conclusion

Determining that proselytism is encompassed within either the freedom to manifest religion or belief or the right to freedom of expression does not mean that it cannot be restricted. However, such a determination establishes a presumption in favor of

---

[36] Krishnaswami, *Study of Discrimination in the Matter of Religious Rights and Practices,* 34.

[37] Kokkinakis v. Greece, 17 EHRR 397 (1994) (ECtHR 260-A, 17, 25 May 1993). The Inter-American Commission on Human Rights has apparently reached a similar conclusion, although in a case that did not directly concern proselytism. See Dianna Ortiz v. Guatemala, Case 10.526, Report No. 31/96, Inter-Am. ComHR, OEA/Ser.L/V/II.95 Doc. 7, rev. at 332 (1997).

[38] General Comment 22, para. 2. See Murdock v. Pennsylvania, 319 US 105, 108–09 (1943).

[39] See ICCPR, art. 19(3)(b); European Convention, art. 10(2); American Convention, art. 13(2)(b); 1981 *African Charter on Human and Peoples' Rights,* 27 June 1981, art. 27(2), reprinted in 21 ILM 59 (hereafter "1981 African Charter").

[40] See General Comment 22, para. 8.

permitting proselytism, and any restriction must meet the requirements laid down in international instruments. Therefore, the validity of limitations on proselytism turns on the existence of overriding interests, articulated on behalf of the state, either in the protection of society in general or in the protection of the rights of others. Equally important, the limitations must sufficiently further those interests.[41] These rights and interests are discussed in the following sections.

B. The Rights of the Target

The protection of the rights and freedoms of others is a recognized ground for limiting the freedom to manifest religion or belief or the freedom of expression. Thus, the source may be limited in order to protect the rights of the target to maintain a religion or belief and be free from injury or offense to religious feelings. However, limiting the source may also restrict the target as the target is entitled to the freedom to change religion or belief and the freedom to receive information. These considerations can move a state in contradictory directions.

1. The Freedom to Change Religion or Belief

There is some controversy in the international community over the question of whether or not the right to freedom of religion or belief encompasses the freedom to change religion or belief.[42] Although this freedom is explicitly guaranteed in the Universal Declaration, the European Convention, and the American Convention,[43] the ICCPR adopted a related, but different, formulation: "No one shall be subject to coercion which would impair his freedom to have or to adopt a religion or belief of his choice."[44] The Human Rights Committee's comment on the scope of this provision states that

> The Committee observes that the freedom to "have or to adopt" a religion or belief necessarily entails the freedom to choose a religion or belief, including the right to replace one's current religion or belief with another or to adopt atheistic views, as well as the right to retain one's religion or belief.[45]

In certain countries, the treatment of apostasy overshadows and determines that of proselytism. For example, certain Islamic states have laws prohibiting apostasy from Islam based on purported requirements of the Shari'a.[46] If apostasy, i.e., the abandonment or renunciation of one's religious beliefs, is considered an offense, it naturally follows that proselytism, as the attempt by another to change one's beliefs, will be prohibited.

---

[41] See ibid.; Human Rights Committee General Comment 10 (1994), art. 19, UN GAOR, 19th Sess., para. 4, UN Doc. HRI/GEN/1/Rev 1 at 11.

[42] See Malcolm D. Evans, *Religious Liberty and International Law in Europe* (Cambridge: Cambridge University Press, 1997), 238.

[43] See *Universal Declaration of Human Rights*, GA Res. 217, UN GAOR, art. 18 (1948) (hereafter "Universal Declaration"); European Convention, art. 9(1); American Convention, art. 12(1).

[44] ICCPR, art. 18(2). Over time, reaching a consensus on this point seems to be even more elusive. The 1981 Declaration, art. 1(2), adopted the same wording as article 18(2) of the ICCPR, but deleted the important phrase "or to adopt." See 1981 Declaration, art. 1(2).

[45] General Comment 22, para. 5.

[46] See Special Rapporteur's Report 1990, para. 60 (Mauritania); *Implementation of the Declaration on the Elimination of All Forms of Intolerance and of Discrimination Based on Religion or Belief*, UN ESCOR,

Nonetheless, laws penalizing apostasy are inconsistent with international human rights standards. In those instruments that explicitly recognize the freedom to change religion or belief, at the very least, penal sanctions on apostasy impermissibly restrict that freedom. In addition, the Human Rights Committee has clearly stated that:

> Article 18.2 [of the ICCPR] bars coercion that would impair the right to have or adopt a religion or belief, including the use of threat of physical force or penal sanctions to compel believers . . . to adhere to their religious beliefs.[47]

It does not necessarily follow that the freedom to change religion or belief, the freedom to abandon religious belief, or the "right to replace one's current religion or belief with another or to adopt atheistic views,"[48] supports the freedom of others to proselytize. In other words, does restricting the ability to proselyte impair the rights of those who have not expressed a desire to receive such information? There is no international consensus on the answer to this question. For example, the Malaysian government has argued that a prohibition on proselytism of Muslims by non-Muslims does not interfere with the ability of Muslims to change their religion:

> If any Muslim desires to seek knowledge about another religion or even to possess another religion of his own free will and on his own initiative, [laws prohibiting proselytism] are not capable of deterring him. Those laws are merely aimed at protecting Muslims from being subjected to attempts to convert them to another religion.[49]

However, as noted above, the European Court has adopted a different view, stating that the freedom to change religion or belief would likely be "a dead letter" if the freedom to manifest religion or belief did not include "the right to try to convince one's neighbour."[50]

The distinction between these two views lies in the conditions necessary to ensure a person's freedom to change her religion or belief. Under one view, the absence of any hindrance or penalty on the part of the state is considered sufficient. The other view holds that, in order to truly ensure a person's right to change her religion or belief, the state may not overly restrict the source from seeking out targets and attempting to deliver information relevant to exercising that freedom. This conflict of views is taken up again in the following section.

47th Sess., Provisional Agenda Item 22, Commission on Human Rights, para. 76, UN Doc. E/CN.4/1991/56 (1991); ***Implementation of the Declaration on the Elimination of All Forms of Intolerance and of Discrimination Based on Religion or Belief***, UN ESCOR, 49th Sess., Provisional Agenda Item 22, Commission on Human Rights, para. 56, UN Doc. E/CN.4/1993/62 (1993) (hereafter "Special Rapporteur's Report 1993"). Islamic States are not the only ones that have, or have had, punishments for apostasy. According to Blackstone's commentary on the laws of England, apostasy was at one time apparently punished by death (William Blackstone, ***Commentaries on the Laws of England: A Facsimile of the First Edition of 1765–1769*** [Chicago: University of Chicago Press, 1979], 44). Nepal apparently had, until recently, a prohibition on apostasy that applied to all religions (Nepal Const, art. 19[1]; reprinted in Albert P. Blaustein and Gisbert H. Flanz, eds., ***Constitutions of the Countries of the World*** [Dobbs Ferry, N.Y.: Oceana, 1971]).

[47] General Comment 22, para. 5.

[48] Ibid.

[49] Special Rapporteur's Report 1990, para. 58.

[50] Kokkinakis v. Greece, 17 EHRR 397 (1994) (ECtHR 260-A, 17, 25 May 1993).

2. The Freedom to Receive Information

The freedom to receive information has been expressed in international human rights instruments as a corollary to the right to freedom of expression.[51] As stated in article 19(2) of the ICCPR, the right to freedom of expression "shall include freedom to seek ... [and] receive ... information and ideas of all kinds."[52] The European Court has noted that the right of a person to "take cognisance" of certain views is implied in the right to impart those views.[53]

As with the freedom to change religion or belief, an important question here is whether the person exercising the freedom to receive information must seek it out themselves, or whether that person has some right to be confronted with views that others would like to put before him, which could then be accepted or declined. If the former is the case, the state may place significant restrictions on the mechanisms used to deliver information, and consequently will determine the information with which people will be confronted. Under the latter viewpoint, the state cannot usurp from potential receivers of information the power to determine the information with which they will be confronted; thus the state will be limited in its ability to restrict the delivery of information, even to those who have not expressed a desire to receive it.[54]

International human rights standards do not provide a simple solution to this problem. The presumption is on the side of expression, and the state seeking to restrict expression must justify the limitation. However, restrictions on expression must be viewed in light of the circumstances in which they arise, including the extent to which information of all kinds flows freely within a society. For instance, if people are continually confronted with information designed to influence their political opinions, their moral values, and even their consumer choices, it might be inconsistent to otherwise overly restrict information designed to influence their religious choices. Such may be the case in European and American democracies. On the other hand, in societies where information is generally restricted and people must seek it out rather than be confronted by it, it may be more problematic to allow information on religion or belief to flow freely. Although generally restrictive policies on free expression cannot, in themselves, support further restrictions, it should be left open to states to articulate the specific harm that could result from the confrontation occasioned by unsolicited expression.

3. The Freedom to Have or Maintain a Religion or Belief

While the freedoms to change religion or belief and to receive information may conflict with limitations on proselytism, other rights and freedoms support restrictions on proselytism. In *Kokkinakis v. Greece*,[55] Greece successfully argued to the European Court that a restriction on proselytism can, in theory, be sustained as an effort to protect the right of the target to the peaceful enjoyment of their freedom of religion

[51] See ICCPR, art. 19(2); European Convention, art. 10(1); American Convention, art. 13(1); 1981 African Charter, art. 9.
[52] ICCPR, art. 19(2).
[53] See Otto-Preminger-Institut v. Austria, 19 EHRR 34 (1995) (ECtHR 295-A, 20, 20 September 1994).
[54] See Martin v. City of Struthers, 319 US 141 (1943).
[55] Kokkinakis v. Greece , 17 EHRR 397 (1994) (ECtHR 260-A, 25 May 1993).

or belief. However, the court ruled that, for such a restriction to be a valid limitation on the right of the source to manifest his religion or belief, particular circumstances must be present that render the proselytism "improper."

In the *Kokkinakis* case, the European Court examined the conviction of a Jehovah's Witness, Minos Kokkinakis, for a violation of a Greek law criminalizing proselytism. The Greek government argued to the European Court that "[t]he sole aim of [the prohibition on proselytism] was to protect the beliefs of others from activities which undermined their dignity and personality,"[56] and that such a prohibition was necessary "to protect a person's religious beliefs and dignity from attempts to influence them by immoral and deceitful means."[57] Although not explicitly adopting these arguments, the court ruled that the conviction of Mr. Kokkinakis was in pursuit of the legitimate aim of protecting the rights of others.[58] Furthermore, the court went on to approve of the attempt in the Greek legislation to develop criteria that would separate what it termed "Christian witness" from "improper proselytism."

> First of all, a distinction has to be made between bearing Christian witness and improper proselytism. The former corresponds to true evangelism, [which has been] describe[d] as an essential mission and a responsibility of every Christian and every Church. The latter represents a corruption or deformation of it. It may . . . take the form of activities offering material or social advantages with a view to gaining new members for a Church or exerting improper pressure on people in distress or in need; it may even entail the use of violence or brainwashing; more generally, it is not compatible with respect for the freedom of thought, conscience and religion of others.
>
> Scrutiny of [the Greek statute] shows that the relevant criteria adopted by the Greek legislature are reconcilable with the foregoing if and in so far as they are designed only to punish improper proselytism, which the Court does not have to define in the abstract in the present case.[59]

Noting, however, that it had not been shown in the Greek courts that Mr. Kokkinakis had done anything improper, the court determined that his conviction was a violation of article 9 of the European Convention.[60] Although it is open to other interpretations, "improper proselytism" in this case seems to correspond to the notion of coercion that would impair the freedom to have—or more precisely—to maintain, a religion or belief. The important question that follows is at what point can expression by one person work a coercion on another to relinquish their religious beliefs? This question is taken up further in part V below.

4. Freedom from Injury to Religious Feelings

Proselytism may fall within the ambit of laws prohibiting blasphemy or the injury to religious feelings where the expression by the source includes criticism or a negative portrayal of the doctrine, scriptures, or founder of a particular religious tradition.

---

[56] Ibid., 18.
[57] Ibid., 20.
[58] Ibid., 20.
[59] Ibid., 21.
[60] See ibid., 50.

The precise scope of these laws raises sensitive issues, as an attempt to change a person's religious beliefs will at times include some argument as to what is incorrect or undesirable about those beliefs. These types of laws can be used to suppress the expression of religious beliefs or opinions on religious issues that are perceived to be incorrect by, or are unpopular with, adherents of other religious groups—particularly the dominant group.

Because proselytism can include criticism of the religious beliefs of a target, the unsuccessful attempt to change those beliefs is likely to cause injury to religious feelings. While states may legitimately seek to curtail such injury by limiting proselytism, these restrictions must be carefully structured. Legal provisions protecting religious feelings, either denominated as prohibitions of blasphemy or cast in more general terms, can sweep into their purview almost any act of proselytism if states define the offense too broadly. Specifically, states must carefully consider the level of intent necessary to commit the offense and the perspective from which the offensive acts must be viewed. As to the former, if any attempt to convince someone that her religious beliefs are worthy of replacement satisfies the intent requirement of a statute prohibiting injury to religious feelings, the application of the law to proselytism will be quite broad. As to the latter, if the offense is viewed from the subjective perspective of the actual target or from the point of view of a "typical" adherent to the beliefs of either the source or the target, the application of the law may be biased and subject to abuse.[61]

The European Court has on two occasions addressed whether laws prohibiting blasphemy and the injury to religious feelings were consistent with article 10 of the European Convention protecting free expression. Although these cases did not involve proselytism, they do articulate general principles that would pertain to the application of these laws to proselytism.[62]

---

[61] A 1960 case from Pakistan illustrates these problems. See Punjab Religious Book Society v. State, PLD 629 (WP) Lahore 631 (Pakistan) (1960) wherein the High Court of Pakistan stated:

> It is clear that in the attempt to show that a particular religion is better than the others, things may be said or written which will outrage the religious feelings of followers of other religions. When a person does that, the law will presume that he intended to insult religious beliefs of the followers of other religions. But even so the ingredients of section 295-A of the Pakistan Penal Code will not have been satisfied because they can be satisfied only if it is established that the intention to insult the religious beliefs was deliberate and malicious. When the thing objected to on the ground that it outrages the religious feelings of others is extremely offensive and has no reliable source to justify its acceptance as correct, the Court will presume that it was done with the deliberate and malicious intention of insulting the religious beliefs of the followers of the religion to which or the founder of which the thing relates. The same presumption will be raised when the thing objected to indicates that the argument in favour of one religion has sunk to the level of abuse of another (ibid., 637–38).

Furthermore, the Court cautioned that the perspective from which the action was to be judged was that of a neutral person of normal susceptibilities: "a person who is neither connected with the religion of the person who is alleged to have outraged the religious feelings of someone nor with that of the person or persons whose religious feelings are stated to have been outraged" (ibid., 638).

[62] The European Commission has indicated that prohibitions on blasphemy could be applied to manifestations of religious belief; see Gay News v. United Kingdom, 5 EHRR 123 (1983), para. 13 (EComHR, 1982): "Even assuming that there had in fact been an interference with the applicants' rights under Art. 9, it would have been justified under Article 9(2) on the same grounds as the restriction of the applicants' freedom of expression under Article 10(2)."

In *Wingrove v. United Kingdom*,[63] the European Court considered the English common law of blasphemy as it was applied by the British authorities to prohibit the distribution of an original video work entitled *Visions of Ecstasy*.[64]

In the view of the European Court, the interference with free expression resulting from the law of blasphemy was in furtherance of "the protection of 'the rights of others'. . . . It is also fully consonant with the aim of the protections afforded by Article 9 to freedom of religion or belief."[65]

In determining that there had been no violation of article 10 resulting from the restrictions on the video, the court found that because the English law of blasphemy "does not prohibit the expression, in any [possible] form, of views hostile to the Christian religion," or necessarily "opinions which are offensive to Christians,"[66] "the reasons given to justify the measures taken can be considered as both relevant and sufficient for the purposes of Article 10(2)."[67]

In the case of *Otto-Preminger-Institut v. Austria*,[68] the European Court addressed an Austrian law prohibiting conduct that

> disparages or insults a person who, or an object which, is an object of veneration of a church or religious community established within the country, or a dogma, a lawful custom or a lawful institution of such a church or religious community.[69]

The law was applied to seize a film entitled *Das Liebeskonzil* ("Council in Heaven").[70] In the course of its decision, the court recognized that persons of all religions

> must tolerate and accept the denial by others of their religious beliefs and even the propagation by others of doctrines hostile to their faith. However, the manner in which religious beliefs and doctrines are opposed or denied is a matter which may engage the responsibility of the State, . . . guaranteed under Article 9 to the holders of those beliefs and doctrines. Indeed, in extreme cases the effect of particular methods of opposing or denying religious beliefs can be such as to inhibit those who hold such beliefs from exercising their freedom to hold and express them.
>
> . . . The respect for the religious feelings of believers as guaranteed in Article 9 can legitimately be thought to have been violated by provocative portrayals of objects of religious veneration; and such portrayals can be regarded as malicious violation of the spirit of tolerance, which must also be a feature of democratic society.[71]

---

[63] Wingrove v. United Kingdom, 24 EHRR 1 (1997) (ECtHR 1996-V, 25 November 1996).

[64] The English courts had defined blasphemy as follows:

> Every publication is said to be blasphemous which contains any contemptuous, reviling, scurrilous or ludicrous matter relating to God, Jesus Christ or the Bible, or the formularies of the Church of England as by law established. It is not blasphemous to speak or publish opinions hostile to the Christian religion, or to deny the existence of God, if the publication is couched in decent and temperate language. *The test to be applied is as to the manner in which the doctrines are advocated and not to the substance of the doctrines themselves* (ibid., 24 EHRR 14, emphasis added).

[65] Ibid., 24 EHRR 28.

[66] Ibid., 24 EHRR 31.

[67] Ibid.

[68] Otto-Preminger-Institut v. Austria, 19 EHRR 34 (1995) (ECtHR 295-A, 20, 20 September 1994).

[69] *Austrian Penal Code,* sec. 188, reprinted in Otto-Preminger-Institut v. Austria, 12.

[70] See Otto-Preminger-Institut v. Austria, 8–9.

[71] Ibid., 17–18. The dissenting judges opposed the idea that the right to freedom of religion encompassed the protection of religious feelings from injury. See ibid., 24 (Palm, Pekkanen and Makarczyk, JJ, dissenting).

The court determined that the seizure of the film did not violate article 10 of the European Convention because the Austrian courts could reasonably determine that seizure was necessary to protect the religious peace in the district in which it was going to be shown.[72]

In both *Wingrove* and *Otto-Preminger-Institut,* it was the manner in which the message was delivered, and not the content of the message, that implicated a restriction on the freedom to deliver it. Any harm resulting from the substance of a message must generally be tolerated in respect of the different views that make up a pluralistic society.[73] Harm resulting from the method of its delivery, however, may be limited through restrictions when the manner of expression is extreme enough.[74]

5. The Right of Persons Belonging to Religious Minorities to Maintain their Religious Traditions and Identity

As related above, one of the purposes of the protection of the rights of persons belonging to religious minorities is to ensure the "survival and continued development" of their particular religious identity.[75] States may take "positive measures" necessary to further this goal.[76] This raises the question of whether proselytism targeted at a minority group in danger of losing its religious identity may be justifiably restricted.

The loss of identity through successful conversion efforts cannot, without more, render proselytism a violation of the rights of persons belonging to a religious minority. Success in proselyting may only be indicative of the free choice of the target. It is the individual's desire to maintain an identity that triggers protection for that identity.[77] This issue has arisen in connection with the rights of indigenous peoples, and the protection of those who continue to adhere to their native religious beliefs. However, to more fully appreciate the situation of indigenous peoples, it is necessary to take a step back and consider briefly the process of religious change that attended the colonial experience.

Religious change has historically gone hand in hand with international exploration, conquest, and colonization, and the resulting political realignments. The attempt to spread European Christianity was a feature of the colonial enterprise in Africa and

---

[72] See ibid., 20–21.

[73] An exception to this principle may be found in the obligation to prohibit "[a]ny advocacy of national, racial or religious hatred that constitutes incitement to discrimination, hostility or violence" as provided in ICCPR, art. 20(2) and similar provisions of other international instruments. Where the content of proselytism includes expression that falls within the ambit of these provisions, the state may be obligated to act to prohibit such expression. See General Comment 22, para. 7.

[74] In contrast, the United States Supreme Court has taken the view that the state may not legitimately prohibit "attacks upon a particular religious doctrine," because of the inherent difficulty in administering such a prohibition without favoring certain groups over others (Joseph Burstyn, Inc. v. Wilson, 343 US 495, 505 [1952]).

[75] General Comment 23, para. 9.

[76] Ibid., para. 6.2.

[77] In this regard, there can be significant conflict between individual members of minority groups and the group as a collective body or its leadership. See Francesco Capotorti, Special Rapporteur of the Sub-Commission on Prevention of Discrimination and Protection of Minorities, *Study on the Rights of Persons Belonging to Ethnic, Religious and Linguistic Minorities,* UN ESCOR, 32d Sess., para. 250, UN Doc. E/CN.4/Sub 2/384/Rev 1, UN Sales No. E 78.XIV.1 (1979).

Asia, although policies and practices varied from imperial power to imperial power and according to local conditions. The propagation of Christianity among the native inhabitants was an attendant purpose to the exploration, conquest and settlement of the lands of the Western hemisphere. Likewise conversion to Islam accompanied the expansion of Arab empires into North Africa, the Middle East, and Persia.

To some subsequently independent peoples, this experience has left an ambivalent legacy.[78] On the one hand, there is a measure of acceptance of the beliefs of the newcomer—as "adopted" by the native inhabitants and as an important part of the culture of the now independent nation. On the other hand, there is a sometimes bitter or painful awareness of the elements of suppression and coercion that led to their adoption. The religious policies of certain independent states reflect this ambivalence, which has led in some cases to heightened concern with proselytism and the activities of foreign missionaries.[79]

One concern in this regard is official policy based on the notion that a change in religious beliefs and practices, i.e., the adoption of the dominant or another recognized religion, is in the best interests of the indigenous peoples because it will assist them in becoming more fully integrated or assimilated into society at large.[80] Regardless of the considerable debate over whether or not such efforts at assimilation have been successful, these policies substitute the choice of the state for the choice of the individual. In this regard, the Draft United Nations Declaration on the Rights of Indigenous Peoples provides that:

> Indigenous peoples have the collective and individual right not to be subjected to ethnocide and cultural genocide, including prevention of and redress for:
>
> (a) Any action which has the aim or effect of depriving them of their integrity as distinct peoples, or of their cultural values or ethnic identities. . . . (d) Any form of assimilation or integration by other cultures or ways of life imposed on them by legislative, administrative or other measures.[81]

C. The Interests of the State

As with the protection of the rights and freedoms of the target, a consideration of other interests of the state may support both the freedom to proselytize and its restriction. As already noted, the primary interest supporting the freedom to proselytize is the protection of the rights of the source. In addition, states may be motivated to

[78] See José R. Martinez Cobo, *Study of the Problem of Discrimination Against Indigenous Populations,* UN Doc. E/CN.4/Sub.2/1982/2/Add.7, para. 48 (1982).

[79] See Zimbabwe Const, art. 19(5)(b) (permitting limitations on the freedom of religion "for the purposes of protecting the rights and freedoms of other persons, including the right to observe and practise any religion or belief without the unsolicited intervention of persons professing any other religion or belief"), reprinted in Blaustein and Flanz, *Constitutions of the Countries of the World.*

[80] For an example of a restriction on proselytism in the face of this concern, see *State Party Report of Brazil to the Human Rights Committee,* UN Doc. CCPR/C/81/Add.6, para. 235 (1997): "All churches and denominations are free to establish places of worship and religious education, though the Government controls access of missionaries to indigenous areas so as to avoid forced acculturation."

[81] *Draft United Nations Declaration of the Rights of Indigenous Peoples,* Sub-Commission on Prevention of Discrimination and Protection of Minorities, Res. 1994/1995, 26 August 1994, art. 7, UN Doc. E/

grant and protect that freedom if they perceive that benefits from freedom of religion or belief, generally, are maximized by free choice and a self-directed population in matters of religion or belief. A state may also hold the view that the religious pluralism resulting from vigorous competition in matters of religious belief is an important addition to the overall cultural diversity of its people. This section, however, will focus primarily on those state interests commonly asserted to restrict proselytism. These include the protection of a particular dominant religious tradition or dominant political ideology, the preservation of public order, and the regulation of the religious "marketplace" in order to ensure fairness and to encourage informed religious choices.

1. Protection of a Dominant Religious Tradition or Political Ideology

Restrictions on proselytism can exist within an integrated system of laws, regulations, policies, and practices designed to (1) inhibit conversions from or otherwise protect the position of the dominant religious group or (2) encourage adherence to the dominant political ideology. Examples of the first type are generally found among the Islamic states, where there may exist some or all of the following: prohibitions on apostasy, expansive application of laws against blasphemy and the injury to religious feelings, and prohibitions on proselytism. Closely related to these restrictions are civil and social disabilities that may result from adherence to a religious community other than the dominant one.

Examples of the second type of restrictions are primarily found among those states that espouse a communist or socialist ideology. Here, the restrictions serve to establish and preserve the primacy of atheism or beliefs of a similar antireligious character that form a part of the officially sanctioned political ideology. Prohibitions on blasphemy or injury to religious feelings may be replaced or supplemented by expansive rules limiting expression that criticizes the policies of the ruling political party or the state. Civil or social disabilities are placed on those who adhere to any religious belief.

A hallmark of both of these situations is that, for the most part, the prohibitions and penalties run in a single direction. One scholar of Islamic society has characterized the situation in those states in this way: "[N]on-Muslim missionary efforts to convert Muslims are generally curtailed when not absolutely prohibited. . . . Missionary work to convert non-Muslims to Islam is, on the other hand, officially encouraged and even publicly funded in some countries."[82] Penalties for apostasy only apply to Muslims. Restrictions on blasphemy are framed or enforced to suppress only expression critical of Islam. The same bias can be found in the efforts to protect official ideologies in communist states.

Three examples of restrictions on proselytism imposed for the purpose of protecting the dominant religious group or official political ideology are Malaysia, The People's Republic of China, and the Ukraine. In Malaysia, laws prohibiting proselytism targeted at Muslims are specifically sanctioned by the constitution. The government has defended this provision as necessary to protect Islam and Islamic institutions in a multi-religious

---

CN.4/1995/2, E/CN.4/Sub.2/1994/56, reprinted in Stahnke and Martin, *Religion and Human Rights: Basic Documents*, 133, 134.

[82] Ann Elizabeth Mayer, "Law and Religion in the Muslim Middle East," *American Journal of Comparative Law* 35 (1987): 127, 149.

state.[83] In the People's Republic of China, religious activities, including proselytism, are restricted in order to properly guide society in its development as a socialist state.[84] Finally, Ukrainian statutes on proselytism and religious freedom which restrict the right to freedom of religion or belief to citizens alone illustrate one of the reactions to proselytism and growing religious pluralism in the states of eastern Europe and the former Soviet Union following the collapse of communism.[85]

The preservation of a particular religious tradition, the official ideology of a state, or the religious character of a state's institutions—divorced from any of the other limitations expressly provided for in international instruments—cannot support limitations on the freedom to manifest religion or belief. The Human Rights Committee has addressed this problem from at least three angles, all of which lend support to the assertion that the preservation and promotion of a dominant religious tradition or political ideology cannot support a limitation on the freedom to manifest religion or belief. First, the existence of a dominant religion, in and of itself, must not result in an impairment of the rights of those belonging to a different religious group.[86] In this regard, "measures . . . imposing special restrictions on the practice of other faiths" are specifically singled out as being "not in accordance with the prohibition of discrimination based on religion or belief and the guarantee of equal protection."[87] The Human Rights Committee expressed the same concerns with respect to the existence of an official ideology.[88] Second, states are prohibited from restricting the manifestation of religious beliefs by adopting an overly narrow conception of public morality:

> The Committee observes that the concept of morals derives from many social, philosophical and religious traditions; consequently, limitations on the freedom to manifest a religion or belief for the purpose of protecting morals must be based on principles not deriving exclusively from a single tradition.[89]

In other words, what furthers public morality is not necessarily coextensive with what furthers the dominant religion in a society. Finally, any limitations on the right to manifest religion or belief should not be "imposed for discriminatory purposes or applied in a discriminatory manner."[90] Any distinction based on religion or belief should be supported by reasonable and objective criteria in pursuit of a legitimate aim under the ICCPR.[91]

---

[83] See ***Implementation of the Declaration on the Elimination of All Forms of Intolerance and of Discrimination Based on Religion or Belief,*** UN ESCOR, 45th Sess., Provisional Agenda Item 22, Commission on Human Rights, paras. 51–52, UN Doc. E/CN.4/1989/44 (1988); Special Rapporteur's Report 1990, para. 58. See also Minister for Home Affairs v. Othman, 1 MLJ 418, 420 (Supreme Court, 1989): "The freedom to profess and practice one's religion must be given effect unless the actions of a person go well beyond what can normally be regarded as professing and practising one's religion."

[84] See Stahnke, "Proselytism and the Freedom to Change Religion," 310–12.

[85] Howard L. Biddulph, "Religious Liberty and the Ukrainian State: Nationalism Versus Equal Protection," *BYU Law Review* (1995): 321.

[86] See General Comment 22, para. 9. For an example of this from the European Court, see Darby v. Sweden, App. No. 11581/85 (ECtHR 187-A, 23 October 1990), where the European Court determined that a state cannot force an individual to contribute to a state church if they are not a member of that church.

[87] General Comment 22, para. 9.

[88] Ibid., para. 10.

[89] Ibid., para. 8.

[90] Ibid.

[91] See General Comment 18, para. 13.

2. The Preservation of Public Order

State laws in India regulating conversion and proselytism with respect to all religions have been supported by the asserted goal of protecting public order. The Indian Supreme Court has upheld the laws of two Indian states, Orissa and Madhya Pradesh, that criminalize the conversion of persons to another religion under certain circumstances. For the purposes of this discussion, the two acts are essentially the same. The relevant section of the Orissa Freedom of Religion Act 2 of 1968 provides: "No person shall convert or attempt to convert, either directly or otherwise, any person from one religious faith to another by the use of force or by inducement or by any fraudulent means nor shall any person abet any such conversion."[92]

The terms used in this provision are defined as follows:

> (a) 'conversion' means renouncing one religion and adopting another;
> (b) 'force' shall include a show of force or a threat of injury of any kind including threat of divine displeasure or social ex-communication;
> (c) 'fraud' shall include misrepresentation or any other fraudulent contrivance;
> (d) 'inducement' shall include the offer of any gift or gratification either in cash or in kind, and shall also include the grant of any benefit, either pecuniary or otherwise.[93]

The statutes in question were challenged in the high courts of the respective states as being invalid restrictions on religious freedom in violation of article 25 of the constitution.[94] Both courts upheld the prohibition against conversions by means of force or fraud.[95] In addition, the High Court of Madhya Pradesh upheld the prohibition of conversion by means of "allurement" (defined in practically identical terms as "inducement" in the Orissa Act).[96] The Orissa High Court, however, held that the definition of "inducement" was too broad to be justified under the permissible limitations of article 25.[97]

On other grounds than those relied on by the state high courts, the Indian Supreme Court, hearing both cases together, affirmed the decision of the Madhya Pradesh court and reversed that portion of the Orissa court's decision that invalidated the "inducement" section of the statute.[98] The Supreme Court determined that the right to freedom of religion or belief guaranteed by article 25 did not encompass the right to attempt to convert another person to one's religion or belief.[99]

---

[92] Yulitha Hyde v. State, AIR 116 (Ori) 120 (India, 1973).

[93] Ibid.

[94] See ibid.; Stainislaus v. State, AIR 163 (MP) (India, 1975). Indian Const, art. 25(1) provides: "[S]ubject to public order, morality and health and to the other provisions of this Part [of the Constitution], all persons are equally entitled to freedom of conscience and the right freely to profess, practice and propagate religion."

[95] See Yulitha Hyde v. State, AIR 116 (Ori) 121; Stainislaus v. State, AIR 163 (MP) 168.

[96] See Stainislaus v. State, AIR 163 (MP) 168.

[97] Yulitha Hyde v. State, AIR 116 (Ori) 121.

[98] See Stainislaus v. Madhya Pradesh & Ors, 2 SCR 611 (1977).

[99] Ibid., 616. The court noted that the term "propagation" as used in art. 25 meant "to transmit or spread one's religion by an exposition of its tenets" (ibid.).

The Supreme Court did not consider proselytism, as it is defined here, to fall within the protection of article 25. Even if it had, it would probably have sustained the acts as valid limitations on the right to religious freedom in furtherance of public order. On a separate legal issue, the Supreme Court held that the restrictions were valid efforts to maintain public order:

> [T]he right of freedom of religion guaranteed by Articles 25 and 26 of the Constitution is expressly made subject to public order, morality and health, and that "it cannot be predicted that freedom of religion can have no bearing whatever on the maintenance of public order or that a law creating an offence relating to religion cannot under any circumstances be said to have been enacted in the interests of public order." . . . [I]f a thing disturbs the current life of the community, and does not merely affect an individual, it would amount to disturbance of the public order. Thus if an attempt is made to raise communal passions, *e.g.* on the ground that some one has been "forcibly" converted to another religion, it would, in all probability, give rise to an apprehension of a breach of the public order, affecting the community at large. The impunged Acts . . . are meant to avoid disturbances to the public order by prohibiting conversion from one religion to another in a manner reprehensible to the conscience of the community.[100]

Given the sometimes violent relations between religious groups, international standards cannot be indifferent to the relationship between public order and those acts perceived to be attacks on another religion, particularly the dominant religion. But such a connection must be carefully scrutinized, as the argument can be subject to abuse. For instance, limitations on the rights of members of minority religious groups or persons holding atheistic or agnostic views should not be based solely on the unpopularity of their message. Furthermore, any limitations on rights in this regard should be viewed in light of the state's fulfillment of its own obligation to promote tolerance, mutual understanding, and peaceful relations between groups.[101] In other words, it should be difficult for a state to support a limitation on rights in furtherance of public order where the danger, in part, stems from the state's own actions in respect to relations between religious groups. If the threat to public order stems solely from the intolerance of others to the otherwise peaceful exercise of rights, a state may be less able to justify a limitation than if the threat derives directly from the violent or disorderly nature of the exercise itself.[102]

---

[100] Ibid., 617–18.

[101] See Universal Declaration, art. 26(2); *International Covenant on Economic, Social and Cultural Rights,* 16 December 1966, art. 13(1), 993 UNTS 3; *International Convention on the Elimination of All Forms of Racial Discrimination,* opened for signature 7 March 1966, 660 UNTS 195, reprinted in 5 ILM 352; 1981 African Charter, arts. 28, 29(7); Concluding Document of the Vienna Meeting, principle 16b.

[102] For discussion of these issues in the context of racial discrimination in the United States, see Palmore v. Sidoti, 466 US 429, 433 (1984): "The question, however, is whether the reality of private biases and the possible injury they might inflict are permissible considerations for removal of an infant child from the custody of its natural mother. We have little difficulty concluding that they are not. The Constitution cannot control such prejudices but neither can it tolerate them. Private biases may be outside the reach of the law, but the law cannot, directly or indirectly, give them effect." Watson v. City of Memphis, 373 US 526, 535 (1963): "Constitutional rights may not be denied simply because of hostility to their assertion or exercise." Buchanan v. Warley, 245 US 60, 81 (1917): "[P]reservation of the public peace cannot be accomplished by laws or ordinances which deny rights created or protected by the Federal Constitution."

3. Protection of Consumers in the Religious Marketplace

Given the existence in many societies of a multitude of religious choices, some states have articulated an interest in protecting the choices of its people from the influence of ignorance, misrepresentation, and fraud. This interest—which might be termed the protection of consumers in the modern marketplace of religion—has been advanced in favor of regulating groups such as those termed "cults," "sects," or "new religious movements" that engage heavily in proselytism. It has also engendered programs designed to provide information to the public on those groups.[103]

This is a particularly sensitive area for a number of reasons. First, regulation of a particular group because of its alleged activities is a significantly more drastic, and perhaps less effective, step than regulating the offending activities themselves, regardless of their source. Second, determining the existence of fraud or misrepresentation may place the state in the position of determining the truth or falsity of religious beliefs. Third, the desire to provide persons with information in order to make "informed" choices can mask an effort to prevent people from making the "wrong" choices. If the latter were the case, the state would be in the position of arbiter of the proper choice of religion for its people. Thus, the objectivity of the information and the neutrality of its presentation are extremely important. For example, a state taking an interventionist attitude towards the information available to its people when making religious choices may refuse to do so with regard to *all* religious choices. Sometimes what is new, different, or unusual is considered for that reason alone to be harmful. A state may therefore provide information on groups of this nature but not on established religious groups, even in areas where there exists substantial ignorance (either of adherents or non-adherents) about established groups or where significant harm would be found in an objective assessment of the practices of those established groups. In this case, the state may be attempting to dissuade people from making particular religious choices based on a view of the propriety of those choices, rather than on neutral criteria applicable to all religious groups.[104]

---

[103] A number of governmental entities in western Europe have begun investigations into the activities of religious groups considered to be "dangerous" to its members or others, with a view towards the necessity or desirability of legal reforms or educational programs. The work of the Council of Europe is discussed below. The European Parliament's investigation culminated in the *Rapporteur's Report on Behalf of the Committee on Youth, Culture, Education, Information and Sport on the Activity of Certain New Religious Movements Within the European Community,* European Parliament Doc. 1-47/84 (1984), which called for member states to set up their own study commissions. Reports have recently been issued by such commissions in France, Belgium, Germany, Italy, Switzerland, and Sweden.

[104] For the recommendation of the European Parliamentary Assembly of the Council of Europe on this question, see Parliamentary Assembly Recommendation 1178 (1992) on sects and new religious movements, para. 7(i)–(ii). See also *Opinion of the Commission on Culture and Education,* Eurpean Parliamentary Assembly, 43d Sess., Doc. No. 6546, 3 (1992): "The solution of the problem of sects does not lie in legislation. The problem of sects which commit offences exists, but so do the laws which punish these offences. What is needed is a greater awareness, preventive measures, and the collective responsibility of society. Greater vigilance will of course be necessary, but the most effective action, in the medium term and long term, is education in this field, general information, creative and free association between young people, friendships between the people and groups concerned, and cultural growth with an enhanced capacity for thought and critical analysis."

With respect to fraud, a particular problem may arise concerning the "truth" of religious beliefs asserted by the source. If fraud is to be shown—either as an element of a direct prohibition of proselytism or as a general fraud provision applied to proselytism—then, in the usual circumstance, falsity or misrepresentation must be proved or, in the alternative, "truth" would be a successful defense. This could leave a court or a jury in the position of determining whether or not assertions in the nature of religious doctrines or beliefs are true or false. Such a situation might lead to conviction of those persons with beliefs that, although sincerely held, were unbelievable or fantastic to the minds of the majority of others.[105]

V. Important Factors in Drawing the Line between Proper and Improper Proselytism

The mere assertion of certain interests by the proponent of proselytism, or by the state in defense of the restriction of proselytism, does not clarify what factors lead to the conclusion that proselytism in a particular case is proper or improper. Indeed, in his partly concurring opinion in the *Kokkinakis* case, Judge Pettiti chastised the European Court for not attempting to clarify the meaning of "improper proselytism." He thought that it was possible to "define impropriety, coercion and duress more clearly and to describe more satisfactorily, in the abstract, the full scope of religious freedom and bearing witness."[106] The remainder of this chapter takes up that task, but by no means completes it.

In considering state practices regarding restrictions on proselytism, the outline of a framework emerges that helps to disentangle the factors that have been used to draw the line between proper and improper proselytism. The framework involves consideration of four variables, corresponding to certain relevant factual circumstances. The variables are all interrelated, and should be considered in combination, as appropriate. They are (1) the attributes of the source, (2) the attributes of the target, (3) where the action alleged to be improper proselytism takes place, and (4) the nature of the action. Each of these variables is laid out on a scale, and using the scales together one can see where the various states and other bodies that have considered the question have sought to draw the line between proper and improper action. As will be apparent, the framework is an incomplete one and does not generate any answers of its own as to where the line should be drawn. However, it is hoped that the proffered framework will provide a starting point for a more focused discussion on the range of choices available to states consistent with international human rights standards. The array of scales are presented in the accompanying chart, and brief descriptions are presented in the following sections.

---

[105] The United States Supreme Court has held that the First Amendment precludes courts from deciding the truth or falsity of religious doctrines and beliefs. See United States v. Ballard, 322 US 78, 86 (1944): "Men may believe what they cannot prove. They may not be put to the proof of their religious doctrines or beliefs. Religious experiences which are as real as life to some may be incomprehensible to others. Yet the fact that they may be beyond the ken of mortals does not mean that they can be made suspect before the law." For a different view regarding consumer fraud, see Church of Scientology and Another v. Sweden, App. No. 7805/77, 16 Decisions and Reports 70 (EComHR 511, 5 May 1979).

[106] Kokkinakis v. Greece, 17 EHRR 397 (1994) (ECtHR 260-A, 28, 25 May 1993) (Pettiti, J, partly concurring).

The touchstone of the framework is the notion of coercion. It is a basic assumption that an individual should be able to make a considered and unrestrained choice in matters of religious belief and affiliation. Thus, the more that proselytism interferes with that ability to freely choose, the more the regulatory power of the state may be attracted. Coercion exists in a variety of forms. Sources may exert different forms of coercive authority and control over others. Targets may be more or less susceptible to certain types of action or certain sources. The location of the action can contribute to coercion where the freedom of the target to freely move in and out of that place is restricted. Finally, the nature of the proselytism, in particular the nature of any proposed exchange between source and target, may be more or less coercive.

A. The Characteristics of the Source

1. Coercive Sources

Attributes of the source, in particular as they pertain to the relationship between the source and the target, can be a determining factor in defining improper proselytism. Concern arises where the relationship is such that the target may not be able to exercise free choice in accepting or resisting the change in beliefs proffered by the source. Action that may be perfectly appropriate between two persons who are strangers, (i.e., at "arms-length" from one another) may not be appropriate where there exists some physical, legal, or economic advantage that the source has over the target. Examples of potentially coercive sources include the state and its official representatives, private persons acting with state authority or endorsement,[107] providers of important health or social services, and employers or employment superiors.[108]

2. Foreign Sources

A related concern over the attributes of the source is the problem of foreign sources. In this regard, does the "foreignness" of the source raise any concerns that cannot be adequately addressed by regulation of all sources, without distinction between native and foreign? Some of the resentment of foreign religious personnel stems from the confluence of the religious intolerance they espoused and the civil power they once possessed. Another concern, as in the case of China, may be foreign interference, through religious groups, with the internal political affairs of a state. Imbedded in the concern over foreigners may also be the notion of economic advantage. Given the vast discrepancies in wealth among many societies, foreigners operating in poor and developing countries may have far greater economic means than the local inhabitants and their native institutions.

Regulation of the foreign source necessarily implicates the protection of the rights of noncitizens. As to this point, the state's obligation to protect human rights generally runs to anyone subject to its jurisdiction regardless of their citizenship

---

[107] See, e.g., Lee v. Weisman, 505 US 577 (1992).

[108] See Larissis and Others v. Greece, 27 EHRR 329 (1999) (ECtHR 1998-I, 24 February 1998).

status.[109] With very few exceptions, aliens present within a state should have the same rights as citizens. It is recognized, however, that foreigners do not have the right to enter any particular state.[110] On the other hand, once a state has opened its doors to foreigners, it must do so without discrimination. To the extent that the foreign source may not even be present in the territory of the state, as, for example, where contacts and communications are made across borders, it should be noted that the right to freedom of expression includes the freedom to receive information "regardless of frontiers."[111]

Restrictions that are targeted specifically at foreigners, such as those of China and Ukraine, or restrictions intended by their terms to fall most heavily on foreigners, must be carefully scrutinized to ensure that they are based on a legitimate aim and that they set out reasonable and objective criteria in pursuit of that aim. In particular, in the case of restrictions on foreign sources it is important to identify policies based on such subjective interests as (1) the disapproval of the religious message that foreigners seek to spread (either because it is new to the native territory or may conflict with the message of native religious groups) or (2) the desire to maintain a particular pattern of religious adherence. These considerations, divorced from any of the specifically mentioned grounds for limitations on rights to freedom of religion, belief, or expression, impermissibly favor some religions over others.

As a final matter, it is important to carefully distinguish between economic advantage as between religious groups "competing" for adherents, and an economic advantage that the source may have over the target. Economic advantage in the former case must fall under the rubric of protection of certain religions and should be subject to the constraints discussed above. In the later case, the economic advantage of the foreign source may weigh directly on the ability of the target to act without coercion. Because the harm in this regard, discussed below, occurs regardless of the foreign or native identity of the source, there does not appear on this point to be a need to regulate foreign sources in a distinctive manner.

B. The Characteristics of the Target

The primary concern with the attributes of the proselytism target relates to the perceived susceptibility of the target to the types of persuasion (and, potentially, coercion) that may be employed by different sources. In essence, the greater the perceived "vulnerability" of the target, the more likely that proselytism directed towards it will be restricted. This principle is manifested in a variety of ways. For instance, some of the target's vulnerability may result directly from its relationship to the source. This was discussed above in relation to hospital patients, prisoners, employees, etc.

Another type of vulnerability stems from the nature of the target, and may raise concern regardless of the identity or the tactics of the source. Certain people may be susceptible to a change in religious beliefs, as they might be susceptible to persuasion

---

[109] See Human Rights Committee General Comment 15 (1986) on the position of aliens under the covenant, UN GAOR, 28th Sess., 22 July 1986, paras. 2, 7, UN Doc. CCPR/C/21/Add.5/Rev.1.

[110] See ibid., para. 5.

[111] See Universal Declaration, art. 19; ICCPR, art. 19(2); European Convention, art. 10(1); American Convention, art. 13(1); Document of the Copenhagen Meeting, paras. 9.1, 32.4. In the context of minorities, see 1981 Declaration, art. 6(i); Minorities Declaration, art. 2(5); Framework Convention, art. 17(1).

in any matter. Children fall in this category along with targets that are uneducated, naïve, or generally weak or unsure of themselves. It is apparently on this basis that the Greek proselytism statute prohibits "taking advantage of [the] inexperience, low intellect and naivety" of the target.[112]

Another example is that portion of the Orissa statute that includes the use of a "threat of divine displeasure" within the definition of conversion by force.[113] This provision was sustained by the Orissa High Court based on the need to protect those with "undeveloped mind[s]" from the "numb[ing of] the mental faculty" that such threats create.[114] A distinction may be drawn here between those persons who are suffering from some form of physical or mental incapacity and those persons whose decision-making capacity may be affected by certain social or cultural factors. In the case of the former, the law will frequently provide protection against others taking advantage of such incapacity by not acting in their best interests. In the case of the latter, the underlying factors can be addressed—particularly in the form of education and exposure to the beliefs of others—in order to enhance the target's decision-making capacity.

Other important attributes of the target are more explicitly tied to types of action that are considered to be improper. For example, a person who is needy may be more susceptible to financial inducement than one who is not; a person who is dependent on a particular facility for health care or food assistance may be more susceptible to its proselytism than those who are not, and so on. These types of vulnerable targets include persons in distress or in need as mentioned by the European Court in *Kokkinakis.*[115]

A further example comes from Nepal. The Nepalese government has argued that legal provisions against conversion and proselytism in that country are necessary to guarantee the rights of "weak person[s]," and "reflect . . . the intent to discourage the anomaly in a socio-economically weak society where instances of involuntary religious conversion are found to have taken place by means of financial enticement and other temptations."[116] This example illustrates the important point that the means used to address concern over the vulnerability of the target should correspond to the type and extent of the activity of the source. In this instance, can a blanket prohibition on all conversions resulting from proselytism be supported by a concern with the weakness of certain targets to financial and other inducements? A rule directed at that specific behavior may serve the same function and not unduly restrict the freedom of others, including those who may not be subject to the same form of persuasion.

C. Where the Action Takes Place

Where the proselytism takes place may have some impact on the necessity of its restriction in accordance with the likelihood that the target is in that place by choice and is free to leave. A state's determination to respect the privacy of the home may lead to a

---

[112] Kokkinakis v. Greece, ECtHR 260-A, 12.

[113] Yulitha Hyde v. State, AIR 116 (Ori) 121 (India, 1973).

[114] Ibid.

[115] See Kokkinakis v. Greece, 17 EHRR 397 (1994) (ECtHR 260-A, 12, 25 May 1993).

[116] *Implementation of the Declaration on the Elimination of All Forms of Intolerance and of Discrimination Based on Religion or Belief,* UN ESCOR, 50th Sess., Provisional Agenda Item 20, Commission on Human Rights, para. 66, UN Doc. E/CN.4/1994/79 (1994).

restricted ability to regulate proselytism that takes place in the home of the source or of a willing target. On the other hand, proselytism in the home of an unwilling target may be subject to greater restriction. A similar dichotomy exists with respect to places of worship or religious education. Proselytism is an expected manifestation of religious belief when it takes place at the place of worship or in the religious classroom of the source, at least as long as the targets are at these places voluntarily. It can be considered to be an unwarranted intrusion when it takes place at the place of worship or in the classroom of the target. It is to this situation, among others, that laws protecting religious worship from disturbance are directed. Other distinctions can be drawn with respect to places open to the public. For instance, preaching or leading worship in a church or synagogue is different than doing the same activity on the street or in a public park. The difference lies in the listeners; in the former case they are likely to be there voluntarily, while in the latter the speaker also reaches those who may have chosen not to listen.[117]

On the other hand, while practically all persons use the public streets and other public places, they are also likely to be free to move to other places if occasionally confronted with unwanted proselytism. For this reason, proselytism may be permitted (subject to safety considerations) in certain public places like streets or parks to a greater extent than in others. The same freedom to leave cannot be said of other public places where persons may be, for the most part, required to be present, such as government offices, courtrooms, schools, and other public facilities.[118]

D. The Nature of the Action

The most significant factor in the separation of improper from proper proselytism is the nature of the action, in the sense of its tendency to create coercive pressures on the target. In a loose way, the potential for coercion lies in the nature of the exchange, whether proposed or actually realized, between the source and target. At one end of the scale lies the bare communication of religious beliefs, which, with some significant exceptions, is generally not considered to be improper. At the other end lies a conversion or change in beliefs through violence or threat of violence. This method appears to be universally denounced not only as a violation of the rights of the target, but also as contrary to current religious views regarding the appropriate means of bringing people to the faith. Between these two extremes lies a broad range of actions, and it is within this area that many states have sought to draw the dividing line between proper and improper proselytism.

The exchange of religious ideas or the communication of religious beliefs where the target is merely listening does not raise significant concerns about coercion. These are the underlying facts of the *Kokkinakis* case, where Mr. Kokkinakis was found by the Greek courts to have engaged in religious discussions using skillful explanations and "in a pressing manner."[119]

---

[117] See Kunz v. New York, 340 US 290, 298 (1951) (Jackson, J, dissenting); Niemotko v. Maryland, 340 US 268, 282–83 (1951) (Frankfurter, J, concurring).

[118] An additional attribute considered by the United States Supreme Court in the regulation of speech, including proselytism, in public places is the degree to which the place is historically "devoted to assembly and debate" or has been opened by the state "for use by the public as a place for expressive activity" (Perry Education Association v. Perry Local Educators' Association, 460 US 37, 45, 46 n.7 [1983]).

The European Court determined that a criminal conviction on this basis was a violation of article 9 of the European Convention. The facts of the *Othman* case also fall into this category, where the petitioner had allegedly participated in religious meetings and seminars; the Supreme Court of Malaysia determined that this activity, without more, did not prejudice the security of the state.[120]

There are, however, some significant exceptions to this principle. One example is that of Sudan, where the law criminalizing apostasy encompasses anyone who "propagates for the renunciation of the Creed of Islam."[121] Laws prohibiting blasphemy or injury to religious feelings that penalize statements solely because they are not in conformity with another religion make up a further exception to this principle. Other significant exceptions relate to the exchange of religious ideas in conjunction with one of the other factors discussed above. Examples of this include the prohibition in the United States of the discussion of religious ideas or the exchange of religious views by the state or those acting in an official capacity or with official endorsement.[122] The same may hold true for the discussion of religious subjects by persons working in state facilities in whose care others have been placed, such as prisons or hospitals. The *Larissis* case extends this principle to discussion by a hierarchical superior or employer, at least in certain settings.[123] In these situations, even the most basic exchange may be tainted by the coercive nature of the relationship within which it takes place.

A further species of religious discussion that is generally thought not to be coercive is that which includes a denial of the truth of the beliefs of others or is otherwise critical of those beliefs. The case law of the Greek courts, as related in the *Kokkinakis* case, has held that spiritual teaching that "demonstrates the errors of other religions" is not prohibited proselytism.[124] Likewise, in *Punjab Book Society*, the Lahore High Court determined that attempts "to show that [one's] religion is the best in the world" did not evidence a "deliberate and malicious" intent to insult the religious feelings of another.[125] Furthermore, the European Court determined that the English law of blasphemy and the Austrian law prohibiting injury to religious feelings did not violate the right to freedom of expression, in part, because they did not penalize the denial of the existence of God or other religious beliefs or all expression of opinions that are hostile or offensive to the Christian religion.[126]

However, when these expressions are delivered in a certain manner, states may feel compelled to prevent them. The Pakistani Court, for example, determined that "extremely offensive" or abusive views, or those with "no reliable source to justify its acceptance as correct" may fall within the statute prohibiting injury to religious feelings.[127] Austria places "gratuitously offensive"[128] expressions that "insult[] . . . an object

---

[119] See Kokkinakis v. Greece, ECtHR 260-A, 21, 50.

[120] See Minister for Home Affairs v. Othman, 1 MLJ 418 (Supreme Court, 1989).

[121] See Special Rapporteur's Report 1993, para. 56.

[122] See Lee v. Weisman, 505 US at 577, 587, 589 (1992).

[123] See Larissis and Others v. Greece, 27 EHRR 329 (1999) (ECtHR 1998-I, 24 February 1998), Case No. 140/1996/759/958-60.

[124] Kokkinakis v. Greece, 13.

[125] See Punjab Religious Book Society v. State, PLD 629 (WP) Lahore 637 (Pakistan) (1960).

[126] See Otto-Preminger-Institut v. Austria, 19 EHRR 34 (1995) (ECtHR 295-A, 20, 20 September 1994); Wingrove v. United Kingdom, 24 EHRR 1 (1997) (ECtHR 1996-V, 25 November 1996).

[127] See Punjab Religious Book Society v. State, PLD 629 (WP) Lahore 637.

of veneration,"[129] in this category of prohibited religious expressions, and English blasphemy law similarly places "contemptuous, reviling, scurrilous, or ludicrous matter" in this category.[130] It is here that the United States parts company with the European Court and others. In several United States cases involving Jehovah's Witnesses, for example, proselytism was protected regardless of its hostile, abusive, and offensive nature.[131]

The next category of activity includes promises or offers of something of value to the target in exchange for their change in beliefs or affiliation. A division may be made here between, for lack of more precise terms, "tangible" and "intangible" benefits. An example of an intangible benefit arose in the Orissa proselytism statute, where the term "inducement" was defined to include the "grant of any benefit." The High Court of Orissa invalidated this provision of the statute because it believed that "inducement" as therein defined could include purely spiritual benefits such as the promise of an eternity in the hereafter.[132] Spiritual benefits are, of course, one of the primary reasons for holding religious beliefs, and it is difficult to imagine making a principled division between proper and improper in this area. The Greek provision that penalizes offers of "moral support" as improper proselytism may be subject to similar difficulties.[133]

The offer or granting of tangible benefits, such as money, "material assistance," and "social advantages," in exchange for a change in religious beliefs or affiliation is prohibited by a number of proselytism statutes, including those of India, Israel, and Greece.[134] Likewise, the European Court in the ***Kokkinakis*** case identified the "offering [of] material or social advantages" as a possible example of improper proselytism.[135]

On the reverse side of the offer of benefits is the injury of or the threat to withhold, injure, or destroy something of value. Again, there arises the question of intangible versus tangible value. The injury to religious feelings in a gratuitously offensive manner may fall into the category of injury to something of an intangible nature. Likewise, the "threat of divine displeasure" prohibited by the Orrisa proselytism statute may also fall into this category.[136]

Threats of a more tangible nature include that of "social ex-communication," as found in the Orissa statute.[137] In this category should also fall policies and practices such as "those restricting access to education, medical care, employment, [political rights] or the rights guaranteed by . . . other provisions of the [ICCPR]" that are

---

[128] See Otto-Preminger-Institut v. Austria, ECtHR 295-A, 19.

[129] Ibid., at 12.

[130] Wingrove v. United Kingdom, 24 EHRR 14.

[131] Murdock v. Pennsylvania, 319 US 105, 115–16 (1943) (citations omitted); Martin v. City of Struthers, 319 US 141, 157 (1943); see also Heffron v. Int'l Society for Krishna Consciousness, Inc., 482 US 569 (1987); Board of Airport Commissioners v. Jews for Jesus, Inc., 482 US 569 (1987); Jimmy Swaggart Ministries v. Board of Equalization, 493 US 378 (1989); International Society for Krishna Consciousness v. Lee, 505 US 672 (1992); Lee v. International Society for Krishna Consciousness, 505 US 830 (1992).

[132] See Yulitha Hyde v. State, AIR 116, 120, (Ori) 120 (India, 1973).

[133] See Kokkinakis v. Greece, 17 EHRR 397 (1994) (ECtHR 260-A, 12, 25 May 1993); see also note 67 and accompanying text.

[134] See ibid.; see also notes 59 and 93 and accompanying text; *Penal Law Amendment (Enticement to Change Religion) Law,* 5738-1977, reprinted in 32 *Laws of the State of Israel* 62 (1977/78).

[135] Kokkinakis v. Greece, ECtHR 260-A, 21.

[136] See text accompanying notes 92 and 93.

[137] See ibid.

identified by the Human Rights Committee as tantamount to coercion employed to compel conversion.[138] Finally, on the far end of the scale, are actions such as the threat or use of physical violence that are mentioned as improper practices by both the Human Rights Committee and the European Court.[139] The nature of the exchange in these latter circumstances is such that the targets relinquish their religious beliefs or affiliation in order to preserve their rights, health, safety, and even their lives.

VI. Conclusion

Proselytism frequently results in controversy between sources and targets, and between religious or political communities that may become identified with either. In many cases, the rights of religious minorities conflict with the interests of the dominant religious or political group. Conflicts arise between religions and between denominations within religions. A state may wish to take sides or may feel compelled to join in these controversies. The dynamics of state involvement under these circumstances depends upon the relationship that exists between the state and particular religious groups. Such a mix of forces creates a situation in which the rights of religious dissenters, minorities, or nonbelievers are particularly at risk. Because international instruments are generally silent on the issue of proselytism, the effect of international human rights obligations on conflicts engendered by proselytism has been minimal. International bodies have either not dealt extensively with the problem or have not been particularly aggressive in defining the parameters of the freedom to engage in proselytism. This silence, or reluctance to deal with proselytism issues, may be the result of the widely divergent practices of states, ranging from severe limitations on the activity in all of its forms to broad freedom to engage in the activity regardless of the effect it may have on the target.

Developing international standards to govern proselytism within this range of state practices is no easy task. However, a careful review of international and state practice yields a number of important principles that can guide states in their efforts to address proselytism conflicts consistent with their international obligations.

First, the purposeful attempt to change another's religious beliefs or affiliation is a manifestation of religion or belief and falls within the scope of the freedom to engage in such activity recognized in international instruments.

Second, the freedom to engage in proselytism must be protected irrespective of the content of the views asserted by the source, the manner in which those views are asserted, and whether the interference stems from state or private action.

Third, as with all freedoms, the freedom to engage in proselytism is not unlimited. However, restrictions on proselytism must further a secular interest (i.e., restrictions cannot further purely religious or ideological goals), and the restrictions must be proportionate to the realization of those interests. In practice, the interests asserted by states to support restrictions on proselytism are typically (a) the protection of public order or (b) the right to have or to maintain a religion or belief without coercion. The two interests can be interrelated, in that coercive methods of proselytism may provoke sharp responses.

---

[138] General Comment 22, para. 5.

[139] See ibid.; Kokkinakis v. Greece, ECtHR 260-A, 21.

Fourth, with respect to the protection of public order, the state's response to proselytism must be directly proportionate to the disorderly nature of the activity itself, and only in extreme circumstances (and for temporary periods) can it be related to the responses of others to the activity. In other words, significant resistance to the expression of noncoercive methods of proselytism is indicative of a need for the state to address its obligation to promote peace, tolerance, and mutual understanding between communities, rather than a need to restrict proselytism.

Fifth, with respect to improper coercion, whether an act of proselytism is improperly coercive will depend upon the characteristics of the source, the characteristics of the target, the place where the act occurs and the nature of the act itself. The combination of circumstances in each case is important. The location of an act, or a particular relationship between source and target can introduce an element of coercion to an act that might not be coercive in other circumstances.

Sixth, unwanted, annoying or offensive acts of proselytism—even though they may result in social disruption—are not necessarily improperly coercive. Indeed, these conditions reflect circumstances under which a person can make a free and informed choice regarding religious beliefs.

Finally, states must walk an admittedly fine line between securing minimum conditions for a free choice of religion or belief and protecting against the erosion of the ability to maintain the religion or belief that has been chosen. In this regard, states should be guided, in the words of Arcot Krishnaswami, by the need "to ensure a greater measure of freedom for society as a whole" according to the circumstances of each case and keeping in mind the necessity of protecting the freedom of minority communities.[140]

---

140 Krishnaswami, *Study of Discrimination in the Matter of Religious Rights and Practices*, 16.

CHAPTER 28

PROSELYTISM AND CULTURAL INTEGRITY

Makau Mutua

Yet Christians have often denied the Gospel;
yielding to a mentality of power,
they have violated the rights of ethnic groups and peoples,
and shown contempt for their cultures and religious traditions:
be patient and merciful towards us, and grant us your forgiveness!
We ask this through Christ our Lord.[1]

I. INTRODUCTION

On 12 March 2000, Pope John Paul II issued a historic statement in which the Catholic Church publicly acknowledged for the first time some of the gross human rights violations that it has committed, perpetrated, condoned, or tolerated over its two-thousand-year history. Using the euphemism "sins" to describe such atrocities, Pope John Paul II bluntly stated that the church had violated the rights of ethnic groups and peoples, and in particular, shown contempt for their cultures and religions. He asked for forgiveness and called for the authentic purification of memory. While a step in the right direction, the confession and plea for forgiveness failed to address the basic contradictions between proselytizing, universalist faiths and indigenous religions and cultures, and the underlying arrogant and inflexible assumption of the moral, ethical, and racial superiority of the former over the latter. It is this vexed relationship between imperial faiths and the indigenous beliefs and moral universes of non-white, non-European, and non-Arabic peoples of Africa, Asia, the Pacific, and the Americas that is the subject of this inquiry.

This chapter explores the historical experiences of religious penetration and advocacy and demonstrates the possibilities of conflict between proselytism and some human rights norms. Using Africa as an illustration, this chapter deconstructs the meaning of freedom of religion or belief at the point of conflict between the universalist

[1] Alessandra Stanley, "Pope Asks for Forgiveness for Errors of the Church Over 2,000 Years," *New York Times,* 13 March 2000.

Tore Lindholm, W. Cole Durham, Jr., Bahia G. Tahzib-Lie (eds.), Facilitating Freedom of Religion or Belief: A Deskbook, *651–668.*

faiths and African religions. It argues that the meeting of the two universes resulted in cultural genocide. The chapter problematizes the concept of the right to the free exercise of proselytizing faiths, which includes the right to proselytize in the presumed marketplace of religions. Since religion is woven into virtually every aspect of life, its delegitimization can easily lead to the collapse of social norms and cultural identities. The result, as has been the case in most of Africa, is a culturally disconnected people, neither African nor European or Arab. I argue that imperial religions have necessarily violated the individual conscience and the communal expressions of Africans and their communities by subverting African religions. In so doing, they have robbed Africans of essential elements of their humanity. Inasmuch as this chapter is a protest, it is also a plea for the better understanding of African religions, their freedom from imperial faiths, and the necessity for the rights regime to devise norms and mechanisms for protecting them.

Since the right to freedom of religion or belief includes the right to be left alone—to choose freely whether and what to believe—the rights regime incorrectly assumes a level playing field by requiring that African religions compete in the marketplace of ideas. The rights corpus not only forcibly imposes on African religions the obligation to compete—a task for which as nonproselytizing, noncompetitive creeds they are not historically fashioned—but also protects evangelizing religions in their march towards universalization. In the context of freedom of religion or belief, the privileging by the rights regime of the competition of ideas over the right against cultural invasion, in a skewed contest, amounts to condoning the dismantling of African religions. I also argue that the playing field, the one crucial and necessary ingredient in a fair fight, is heavily weighted against Africans. Universalist religions were either forcibly imposed or introduced as part of the colonial cultural package. Missionaries did not simply offer Jesus Christ as the savior of "benighted" souls; his "salvation" was frequently a precondition for services in education and health, which were quite often the exclusive domain of the church and the colonial state.[2] It makes little sense to argue that Africans could avoid acculturation by opting out of the colonial order; in most cases the embrace of indigenous societies by the European imperial powers was so violent and total that conformity was the only immediate option. In making this argument, I rely on notions of human rights law which, as I show, suggest that indigenous beliefs have a right to be respected and left alone by more dominant external traditions.

This reasoning poses serious questions that go to the root of the rights regime. Some difficulties are obvious. A key ideal of the human rights movement, and indeed of liberalism, is the commitment to the open society in which the freedom to advance, receive, and disseminate ideas is assumed necessary for the greater social good. Though not absolute—permissible limitations can be placed on what ideas and under what circumstances advocacy is allowed by the law—this commitment creates a rights regime conundrum in conversations about the universality of human rights norms. Questions arise about the validity of the advocacy of certain norms beyond the borders of their origin. The right of advocacy itself and its centrality in the human rights corpus becomes an issue. Is it possible, for instance, to question advocacy in connection with other creeds, ideologies, and institutions? Should advocacy by the industrial

[2] For the Akamba of Kenya, for instance, formal European education was inextricably linked to conversion to Christianity (J. Forbes Munro, *Colonial Rule Among the Kamba: Social Change in the Kenya Highlands 1889–1939* [New York: Oxford University Press, 1975], 147–48).

West to spread free markets and democracy to non-democratic, non-Western cultures, complete with their power to transform and fundamentally change economic, social, and political systems, be protected under the human rights regime? Could theocratic states, for example, seek protection for their political orders and social systems under the rights corpus? Other examples come to mind: Should human rights law invade cultures that subordinate women and seek to eradicate gender bias through advocacy? Are these acceptable forms of advocacy, which the human rights movement should protect? Ultimately, one must ask, who decides what is good for the universe and what should be advocated transnationally?

First, I briefly sketch the history of the human rights movement and outline those ideals within it that are relevant for my purposes. Second, I discuss the view of the universalist religions on human rights and other religious traditions, particularly indigenous religions. My goal here is to indicate some of the bases for demonizing the "other" and draw attention to possible contradictions between the human rights corpus and some of the positions taken by proselytizing religions. Third, I explore the forms of proselytization preferred by both Islam and Christianity in Africa and the use of coercion, both physical and cultural, as a tool in that process. I then briefly review the human rights, constitutional, and other legal bases for freedom of religion or belief and the protection of indigenous religions in Africa. The last section addresses the tension inherent in the rights regime and the dilemmas posed to the human rights movement by the practical and historical experience of evangelization in Africa.

This inquiry, which seeks to limit the reach of imperial faiths, appears to frustrate some of the major ideals of the human rights movement. It raises the question about the tension between the restriction of the right to evangelize or advocate a point of view and one of the central ideals of the human rights movement: the promotion of diversity and the right to advocate ideas or creeds. An exploration of the manner in which the human rights corpus ought to view religious rights—whether further to limit or to expand the protections religions currently enjoy—raises this fundamental tension: How does a body of principles that promotes diversity and difference protect the establishment and manifestation of religious ordering that seeks to destroy difference and forcibly impose an orthodoxy, as both Christianity and Islam, the two major proselytizing religions, attempted, and in many cases successfully did in Africa? Precisely because of the ethos of universalization common to both, these faiths sought to eradicate, with the help of the state, all other forms of religious expression and belief and close off any avenues through which other competing faiths could be introduced or sustained. This coerced imposition of a religious orthodoxy implies a desire and a social philosophy to seek the forcible destruction of that which is different. Yet, it seems inconceivable that the human rights movement would have intended to protect the right of certain religions to destroy others. In this chapter, I explore this tension—between protecting the right to proselytize in Africa and limiting the circumstances in which that right can be exercised—within the confines of the human rights corpus.

II. A Sketch of the Development of the Human Rights Movement

To situate my discussion and provide a context for my views on religious rights in the African setting, I shall briefly sketch the history of the development of the human rights movement. The human rights movement—that collection of norms, processes, and institutions—is largely a product of the horrors of World War II. Its rise, development, and elaboration cannot be understood without resort to the abominations committed by European states and their agents during that war. Drawing on the Western liberal tradition, the movement arose primarily to control and contain state action against the individual. Two principal instruments on which it is based—the 1948 Universal Declaration of Human Rights (UDHR) and the 1966 International Covenant on Civil and Political Rights (ICCPR)—establish negative rights that either limit or prohibit altogether governmental reach into the private and individual realms. Primarily, the movement has been restrictive of state power. In the recent past, however, as the traditional human rights movement has grown in strength and effect, its language has been appropriated by other causes, which recognize its legitimizing power. Women's groups, gay and lesbian organizations, environmentalists, and advocates of economic, social, and cultural rights, all seek recognition by the official human rights movement.

There is a growing realization internationally that the struggle for human rights is a quest for the reduction of conditions that engender weakness; in effect, it is a push against the denial of certain fundamental rights by any individual or institution regardless of its relationship to the state. Certain institutions, such as the family, which traditionally have been part of the private realm, are now coming under increasing scrutiny to comply with international human rights standards. The state—the political instrument that gives legal personality and protection to private institutions—is being pressed to intervene to secure basic rights for individuals under the control or influence of entities in the private realm. Advocates base their claims on the influence or control that the state ought to exercise over such entities. The challenge for the human rights movement is to move beyond the singular obsession with wrongs committed directly by the state—although it remains the most important obligor of the discourse—and regulate nonstate actors in order to contain and control human rights violations in the private sphere. To do so, the movement has to take on powerful institutions in the private realm, including established religion.

Although religious human rights must be defined, secured, and protected, there is a correlative duty on the part of religions to respect the human rights of nonbelievers and adherents of other religions or faiths and not to seek their coerced conversion either directly or through the manipulation and destruction of other cultures. Although article 18 of the ICCPR guarantees the right to freedom of thought, conscience, and religion and provides for certain limitations, it does not spell out the duties that must be borne by proselytizing religions. I attempt in this chapter to balance the interests of these religions with those of African societies, both individual and collective, and to explore ways in which the respectful coexistence between these radically different spiritualities could be imagined and worked out.

III. The Demonization of Difference

The two most geographically widespread religions—Christianity and Islam—are also the most imperial: they are proselytizing and universalist; that is, they seek to convert into their faith the entire human race.[3] Although these religions are generally not

[3] The designation of nonbelievers—individuals who do not profess Judaism, Islam, or Christianity—by both Muslims and Christians as either pagans or infidels is one manifestation of belief in their own superiority

spread through physical violence today, they have historically been forcibly introduced. They have also been negatively competitive against each other as well as other creeds as they have fought over the souls of third groups and individuals.[4] But central to them is the belief in the racial superiority of the proselytizers; the other is quite often depicted as inferior. Arab Muslims, for example, have historically viewed black Africans as racially inferior; Islamized Africans are regarded as having taken an important step towards overcoming that inferiority. The capture and enslavement of millions of Africans by Arab Muslims over the centuries bore the trademarks of this theological and racial justification. It does not require a profound knowledge of history to show that both Arab and European perceptions of Africa have been decidedly racist over the centuries. Asserting that the "Bantu mind" was inferior to that of the "civilized man," a leading European missionary described Africans thus:

> It is suggested that the mere possession on the part of the Bantu of nothing but an oral tradition and culture creates a chasm of difference between the Native "mind" and that of civilized man, and of itself would account for a lack of balance and proportion in the triple psychological function of feeling, thinking and acting, implying that thinking is the weakest of the three and that feeling is the most dominant. The Native seeks not truth nor works, but power—the dynamical tool.[5]

Writing about the importance of evangelization in Africa, another European missionary asserted that the "Mission to Africa was the least that we [Europeans] can do to strive to raise him [the African] in the scale of mankind."[6] The catalog of writing by pioneer missionaries in Africa is inexhaustible and strikingly similar. Paternalistic at best, European missionaries left no doubt of their belief in the superiority of their race, religion, and culture, and the necessity of freeing the African from his heathen and subhuman belief and status.

---

over other religions. Christian missionaries and Muslim clerics evidence this zeal and drive to universalize through the conversion or salvation of unbelievers from what they regard as eternal damnation. Abdullahi Ahmed An-Na'im, "Human Rights in the Muslim World: Socio-Political Conditions and Scriptural Imperatives," *Harvard Human Rights Journal* 3 (1990): 13.

[4] The wars between the Christian Portuguese and Muslim North Africans are well documented. In the fifteenth century the Portuguese, under the command of Prince Henry, carried the crusades to Africa as part of the campaign to win back the continent from Muslims. An admiring portrait of Prince Henry said that the "flame that lit the Soldier of the Cross was kindled in his heart in early youth, and to win back Morocco from the Moors was the ambition of his life. He never drew his sword in any other cause" (Hans Debrunner, *A History of Christianity in Ghana* [Accra: Waterville, 1967], 15). Elsewhere he is called the "commander of the Portuguese Crusaders' Order of the Knight of Christ" (ibid.). Even among different Christian denominations, competition for souls often turned violent, as evidenced by the conflict in 1637 between the Dutch and the Catholic Portuguese at historic Elmina, part of what is today Ghana. A Catholic account of the conflict said that the "new conquerors, the Dutch, were then bitter enemies of Catholicism. Wherever they came, they burnt and destroyed the churches and would not allow a Catholic priest to preach to the people" (H. Pfann, *A Short History of the Catholic Church in Ghana* [Cape Coast, 1965]).

[5] Denys W. T. Shropshire, *The Church and Primitive Peoples* (London: SPCK, 1938), xix. The author goes on to write:

> Though he [the Native] relies a good deal on what he has observed, he will always seek the true cause in the world of unseen powers above and beyond what we call "Nature"—in the metaphysical realm in the literal sense, and his peculiar mental activity is largely due to his lack of distinction between what is actually present to sense and what is beyond (ibid.).

[6] Alfred Henry Barrow, *Fifty Years in West Africa* (London, 1900), 29.

Such attempts, often quite successful, at the universalization of the proselytizing imperial faiths have resulted in untold suffering throughout history. The religious crusades and jihads waged by both Muslims and Christians, in which millions were killed and enslaved, are just one example of the destruction that accompanied or was the excuse for proselytization. In strange symbolism, the cross, with its linear structure, becomes a sword once turned on its side.[7] The causal link, historically, between evangelization and war appears to be indisputable.[8] The philosophy and practice of remaking the "other" appears therefore to be based on contempt for that which is different and belief in the superiority of the aggressive creed. Major bodies of both Christian and Islamic jurisprudence directly assert the inferiority of and disrespect for nonbelievers. Although some scholars argue that Shari'a, for example, is just one particular interpretation of the Qur'an and the Sunna, it is the only coherent, unified body of law for Muslims.[9] Other, more liberal interpretations of Islam have been of little consequence to the lives of Muslims. Yet Shari'a itself contradicts basic human rights standards by discriminating against non-Muslims. Abdullahi An-Na'im, a leading advocate for reform of Islamic jurisprudence to bring it into conformity with international human rights standards, has written:

> The claim that Shari'a is fully consistent with and has always protected human rights is problematic both as a theoretical and a practical matter. As a theoretical matter, the concept of human rights as rights to which every human being is entitled by virtue of being human was unknown to Islamic jurisprudence or social philosophy until the last few decades and does not exist in Shari'a. ***Many rights are given under Shari'a in accordance with a strict classification based on faith and gender and are not given to human beings as such.*** As a practical matter, fundamental inconsistencies exist between Shari'a as practiced in Muslim countries and current standards of human rights.[10]

A number of theoretical and scriptural examples illustrate this point. Unbelievers, defined by Shari'a as those who do not believe in the revealed heavenly scriptures[11]—that is, non-Muslims except Jews and Christians—are not regarded as fully human and could be legally enslaved. Shari'a only discusses the manner in which slaves ought to be treated; it does not prohibit the enslavement of nonbelievers.[12] In addition, according

---

[7] Matthew Fox, *A Spirituality Named Compassion* (San Francisco: Harper and Row, 1990), 112:

> Crusades, inquisitions, witch burnings—which invariably meant the burnings of heretics and gay people, of fellow Christians and of infidels—all in the name of the cross. It is almost as if Constantine, and his empire's conversion to Christianity in the fourth century, uttered a well-fulfilled prophecy when he declared: 'in the name of this cross we shall conquer.' The cross has played the role of weapon time and time again in Christian history and empire building.

[8] Ibid. Christian armies, much in the same way that Muslim crusaders saw themselves, considered it an honor to die for Christianity. According to many:

> The supreme sacrifice was to die fighting under the Christian emperor. The supreme self immolation was to fall in battle under the standard of the cross. . . . But by the time Christianity was ready to meet Asia and the New World, the Cross and the sword were so identified with one another that the sword itself was a cross. It was the only kind of cross some conquistadors understood (ibid.).

[9] Shari'a, the legal and ethical code of Islam, is derived from both the Qur'an and the Sunna, the Prophet's elaboration of the Qur'an through his statements and actions.

[10] An-Na'im, "Human Rights in the Muslim World," 22; emphasis added.

[11] Not surprisingly, the revealed scriptures are only the Bible, the Qu'ran, and the Torah or Old Testament, the holy books of Christianity, Islam, and Judaism respectively. It is inexplicable that Shari'a would disregard all other religious persuasions, such as Hinduism and indigenous African or native American religions, among others, as illegitimate.

to Shari'a, only Muslims can fully enjoy the benefits of citizenship in an Islamic state. Even members of other revealed faiths such as Jews or Christians are only entitled to the lesser status of *dhimma* under which their security of person and property is guaranteed with some freedom to practice their own religion. In return, they have to pay taxes and submit to Islamic rules in all public matters.[13] Shari'a also punishes by execution Muslims who repudiate their faith. The assumption of the right to Islamicize and then prevent others from converting—or countering the penetration of other faiths—is at the very least a manifestation of intolerance for difference and diversity.

Racist clerics, from South Africa to the United States, have used scriptures to buttress the subhumanity of Africans to justify apartheid, slavery, and other violations of basic freedoms based solely on race and skin color. In the United States and the European colonies and possessions in Africa, law and religion were often synthesized to create an oppressive social philosophy in order to justify the institutionalization of slavery, colonialism, and the ubiquity of white or European power over blacks and other nonwhite peoples. Many settled on the story of the curse of Noah's son Ham in Genesis 9 as the divine curse on all people of African descent. Religion and pseudoscience were often handwoven to prove the bestial, subhuman characteristics of Africans. These philosophies and practices allowed good Christians brutally to subjugate or to acquiesce with a clear conscience in the subjugation of Africans, their cultures, and their religious traditions.

IV. Proselytization as Cultural War

In this section, I explore the views of the evangelizer and the processes of evangelization in black Africa and the human rights issues implied by their penetration of the continent. I attempt to highlight the tension between proselytization, coupled with force and power, and respect for difference and cultural identity. The Arabs introduced Islam to Africa through military conquest. Thereafter, the processes of Arabization (in North Africa and the Nile Delta) and Islamicization (in East and West Africa) proceeded simultaneously through force, the slave trade, and general commerce. The entry of Christianity into the continent was no less violent, coming as it did in partnership with the colonial imperial powers.[14] Most European missionaries saw their duty in the image painted by Rudyard Kipling in 1899:

---

[12] An-Na'im, "Human Rights in the Muslim World," 22–23.

[13] Ibid., 24. An-Na'im adds:

> Non-Muslim subjects of an Islamic state can aspire only to the status of *dhimma* under which they would suffer serious violations of their human rights. *Dhimmis* are not entitled to equality with Muslims. Their lives are evaluated as inferior in monetary terms as well: they are not entitled to the same amount of *diya* or financial compensation for homicide or bodily harm as Muslims (ibid.).

[14] Many African communities did not see any functional distinctions between the colonial administrators and the missionaries:

> The political factor [colonialism] worked to the disadvantage of the missionaries in that the Kamba [an ethnic community in Kenya] like all other Africans, viewed the newcomers in terms of their local political situation. They identified the missionaries, arriving with the colonial power which gave them its support and approval, as part of the colonial authority system, barely distinguishable from administrative officers. In 1913, for example, elders in Mwala [area of Kenya inhabited by the Akamba] went to the mission at Kabaa to obtain licenses for sugar mills (Munro, *Colonial Rule Among the Kamba*, 104).

> Take up the White Man's burden, send forth the beast ye breed.
> Go bind your sons to exile to serve your captives' need.
> To wait in heavy harness on fluttered folk and wild
> *your new-caught, sullen peoples, half-devil, half-child.*[15]

A missionary who worked among Zimbabweans early in the twentieth century exemplified these beliefs; to him, "unlettered Natives" were in the "technically barbaric and pre-literacy stage of cultural and social development."[16] In a book written for those "responsible for the development of a primitive people or are concerned for their progress—missionary and administrator, government official and teacher, employer and civilian,"[17] the missionary stated starkly:

> Indeed, primitive people all over the world who have not yet acknowledged a sovereignty of reason arm themselves with similar weapons against their physical and spiritual foes and have the same elemental passions, emotions and instincts. Institutions and beliefs such as initiation ceremonies, the medicine-man, witchcraft, and all the magico-religious assumptions are part and parcel of the lives of such peoples.[18]

In contrast, Christianity, which has undergone "centuries of theological learning . . . labour of intellect, and subtlety of reasoning throughout its whole history, stands for a literary type of religion giving prominence to beliefs that can be put into ideas as dogma and doctrine."[19] That is why, according to the missionary, he was "amazed at my own impertinence in desiring to impose a new and strange religion and culture upon a primitive people with whose cultural inheritance I was quite unacquainted."[20] Hence he advises, "Before sowing, know your ground."[21] He emphasizes that the purpose of the evangelist is not "merely to civilize but to Christianize, not merely to convey the 'Gifts of Civilization.'"[22]

European missionaries, sociologists, and anthropologists have historically treated African religions as bizarre and primitive phenomena completely different from and inferior to the universalist faiths. Part of this process of demonization betrays the prejudice, ignorance, and cultural vantage point of the outsider. Hence the description of Africans as heathens and pagans. Many of the writers and missionaries describe African religions as superstitious, unscientific, and without reason.[23] Missionaries therefore sought to discredit and dismantle those African religions and cultural expressions that

---

[15] Quoted in Kamuti Kiteme, *We, The Pan-Africans: Essays on the Global Black Experience* (New York, 1992), 94.
[16] Shropshire, *The Church and the Primitive Peoples,* xiii.
[17] Ibid. The author develops a methodology for evangelization in "primitive" cultures and pleads for the "careful discrimination, preservation, transmutation and transformation of the religious and cultural institutions and beliefs of the Southern Bantu [the African peoples of southern Africa], by and within a full-orbed presentation of the Christian religion" (ibid., xix).
[18] Ibid., xiii–xiv.
[19] Ibid., xxiv.
[20] Ibid., xiii.
[21] Ibid.
[22] Ibid., 425.
[23] Ibid. Eric O. Ayisi, *An Introduction to the Study of African Culture* (London: Heinemann, 1972), 57:

> It has been said that they [African religions] lack any theological ideas and all the elements which make Judaism, Islam or Christianity sublime are lacking in African religion. People who should have known better, especially missionaries, were completely misguided about African religion, and by their muddled thinking propagated erroneous ideas about African religious beliefs.

they deemed un-Christian or resistant to Christianization and Westernization. Some missionaries, however, did not advocate the full destruction of "false religions" but rather a process of assimilation:

> It is becoming increasingly clear, and governors and missionaries alike are coming to realize, that the method of the destruction of religion and culture of primitive races, as happened in the cases of the Tasmanians, Australians, . . . and American Indians, is both scandalous and futile. For such a method destroys all the values that give meaning and zest to their lives, rendering them impotent and ill-equipped to face the future, cutting them loose from all their moorings on a vast and uncharted sea where they drift to despair and finally to destruction.[24]

This paternalistic approach, which sought to "secure, at whatever cost, the fullness of the development of the personality of the African," would not simply target African religions but would be a "concerted attempt" in the "spheres of religion, law, medicine, politics and economics for the simple reason that the life of those we are seeking to transform is all of a piece."[25] In this process of reeducation, missionaries ended up denouncing as satanic African ceremonies and actions of worship for the spirit world. African dances, marriage ceremonies, female circumcision, and polygamy were deemed pagan or heathen practices incompatible with Christianity. Among the Agikuyu and Akamba of Kenya, for example, parents who permitted female circumcision were not allowed access to churches and schools, although the practice was deeply bound up with other cultural norms.

The deliberate destruction of African values was epitomized by the introduction of a "white" god and Jesus Christ and a black devil or Satan. The visual images displayed and popularized by missionaries to date—drawings and other impressions of Jesus Christ, the Virgin Mary, and God—are those of whites with blue eyes and long, usually blond, hair. Verbal and written descriptions of these figures also gave the impression that they were European. Growing up in Africa as a young boy—and my experience was typical—I thought that God was a silver-haired, white sage resident somewhere in the deep blue sky. The system of formal education introduced by the missionaries and the colonial authorities emphasized the superiority of Europe over the rest of the world. This educational and religious orientation did what it was meant to do, namely to disembowel African traditional outlooks and replace them with Western, Judeo-Christian conceptions of life.

The alliance between, and in many cases the practical fusion of, the church and the colonial flag, even where naked force was not applied, served to quash African values. As a reaction to the Eurocentric and racist curricula of the mission schools, together with their opposition to African and religious practices such as female circumcision, Africans in Kenya started in the late 1920s to establish independent schools under the leadership of Jomo Kenyatta, later the first president of Kenya. The frontal

---

[24] Shropshire, *The Church and Primitive Peoples*, 425.

[25] A more forceful method was favored by others, as this description of Henry the Navigator reveals:

> The heathen lands were kingdoms to be won for Christ, and the guidance of their backward races was a duty that must not be shirked. Henry shouldered this responsibility. If he had the spirit of a crusader, he had that of a missionary as well. Wherever he explored, his aim was to evangelise, to civilise, and to educate the simple natives. . . . He sent out teachers and preachers to the black men on the Senegal river (Debrunner, *A History of Christianity in Ghana*, 15).

attack on religious values and practices and ethnic and racial identities developed over hundreds of years was particularly damaging because religion was an integral part of being African.[26] African religious beliefs centered on individual and group existence; their subversion overthrew ethnic identities. The devaluation of their culture dehumanized Africans and created a self-hatred that continues to devour the continent today.

Predictably, different denominations of Christianity, primarily the Protestant and Roman Catholic, introduced bitter rivalries between African communities. The rivalry engendered by the competition for converts created deep political antagonisms between ethnic groups and introduced one more cleavage in societies already destabilized by colonization. In countries like Uganda, these sectarian rivalries have periodically erupted into ethno-political violence. In countries such as the Sudan or Nigeria, the primary source of violence has been interreligious: between Muslims and Christians.

It is not the purpose of this section to document the destruction of African religions and cultural values through the agencies of the proselytizing religions and colonialism. My purpose is to explore the views of the missionaries and the methods employed in their work. There is little doubt that the coupling of Islam with force and Christianity with the colonial state—with a technologically superior base—virtually assured the decimation of indigenous religions or, at the very least, the imposition of alien religions. The material and military resources available to the colonial administrators enabled them to crush resistance and establish political hegemony. From their privileged vantage points, the missionaries—utilizing equally sophisticated means of pacification and communication—were able to force and pressure whole communities to abandon their indigenous faiths if they hoped to benefit from the new order. In all probability, the dismantling of African religions and cultures—even under colonialism—would have been much more difficult without the combination of proselytization with racism. According to Basil Davidson, the Africanist, none of this was an accident or a mistake:

> By racism I mean the conscious and systematic weapon of domination, of exploitation, which first saw its demonic rise with the onset of the trans-Atlantic trade in African captives sold into slavery, and which, later, led on to the imperialist colonialism of our yesterdays.
>
> This racism was not a mistake, a misunderstanding or a grievous deviation from the proper norms of behavior. It was not an accident of human error. It was not an unthinking reversion to barbarism. On the contrary, this racism was conceived as the moral justification—the necessary justification, as it was seen by those in the white man's world who were neither thieves or moral monsters—***for doing to black people what church and state no longer thought it permissible to do to white people: the justification for enslaving black people.***[27]

---

[26] According to a leading African scholar, religion is an essential element of African culture. "Africans are notoriously religious, and each people has its own religious system with a set of beliefs and practices. Religion permeates into all the departments of life so fully that it is not easy to isolate it" (John S. Mbiti, *African Religions and Philosophy* [Garden City, N.Y.: Doubleday, 1970], 1).

[27] Basil Davidson, *African Civilization Revisited* (Trenton, N.J.: Africa World Press, 1991), 3–4; emphasis added.

V. Indigenous Religions: The Absence of Legal Protection

The subject of indigenous religions is one of the most underdeveloped areas of inquiry in human rights. Indeed, it remains a question whether the view adopted by the human rights corpus on the freedom of religion, belief, and conscience—in article 18 of both the UDHR and ICCPR—took into account indigenous religions and their historical relationship with universalist faiths. In this section, I briefly examine what protections, if any, are afforded indigenous religions in the human rights regime and in several African countries. For the purposes of my argument, I do not attempt to define the complex and contentious term "indigenous peoples." Instead, I focus my attention on indigenous religions which I define as nonimperial faiths but excluding dominant and politically established religions such as Judaism, Buddhism, and Hinduism. The key to the inclusion of a religion as indigenous is its history of attack and domination by the imperial faiths and colonialism and its status as the cultural inheritance and spiritual expression of the original, non-white, non-Arabic peoples of Africa.[28] I also examine United Nations documents regarding the cultural rights of indigenous peoples to indicate how the human rights regime might consider thinking about the protection of indigenous religions.

The UDHR and the ICCPR do not specially recognize indigenous religions in relation to dominant faiths or cultures; they do not even refer to them. Article 18 simply provides the right of everyone to freedom of thought, conscience, and religion and prohibits the use of coercion to impair the freedom of others to have or to adopt a religion or a belief of their choice. The freedom to manifest one's religion or belief may be subject to such limitations as are prescribed by law and are necessary to protect public safety, order, health, morals, or the fundamental rights and freedoms of others.[29] This provision prohibits the use of force to make converts as was the case in early European crusades in Africa and the conquest of parts of the continent by Arab Muslims. It would also appear to disallow using state resources—such as educational, health, and other services—to disadvantage particular faiths. Missionaries who worked against other religions with the help of colonial regimes would seem to be in violation of this provision.

While no authoritative human rights body has issued a definitive interpretation with such a construction, the Human Rights Committee[30] has adopted a General Comment[31] on article 27 of the ICCPR,[32] providing that states are under an obligation to protect the cultural, linguistic, and religious rights of minorities. It said, in part:

---

[28] Simply put, I define as indigenous all African religions that predated Islamization and Christianization. Similarly, the term could also be used to denote the religious beliefs of native, nonsettler peoples in the Americas and parts of Asia.

[29] *International Covenant on Civil and Political Rights* (ICCPR), 16 December 1966, GA Res. 2200 (XXI), UN GAOR, 21st Sess., Supp. No. 16, at 52, UN Doc. A/6316 (1966), 999 UNTS 171, art. 18 (entered into force 23 March 1976).

[30] The ICCPR, the principal civil and political human rights treaty, establishes the Human Rights Committee, the body responsible for the elaboration, interpretation, and encouragement of the implementation of the treaty (ICCPR, art. 28).

[31] Article 40(4) of the ICCPR directs the Human Rights Committee to "study" state reports and to "transmit its reports, and such general comments as it may consider appropriate." The general comments are meant to be authoritative interpretations of the ICCPR's provisions.

[32] Article 27 of the ICCPR provides that "in those States in which ethnic, religious or linguistic minorities exist, persons belonging to such minorities shall not be denied the right, in community with others members of the group, to enjoy their own culture, to profess and practice their own religion, or to use their language."

> Although the rights protected under Article 27 are individual rights, they depend in turn on the ability of the minority group to maintain its culture, language or religion. Accordingly positive measures by States may also be necessary to protect the identity of a minority and the rights of its members to enjoy and develop their culture and language and to practice their relig-ion, in community with other members of the group.[33]

In its 1981 Declaration on the Elimination of all Forms of Intolerance and of Discrimination Based on Religion or Belief,[34] the United Nations did not address the subject of indigenous religions. The Declaration is basically an elaboration of article 18 of the ICCPR.

Some more recent developments, however, indicate a willingness to recognize indigenous religions within the ambit of the United Nations. Due to the relentless and focused advocacy of indigenous peoples and their supporters, the General Assembly in 1992 instructed the Working Group on Indigenous Populations to draft a Declaration on the Rights of Indigenous Peoples for consideration by the Commission on Human Rights.[35] The Draft Declaration, which now awaits action by the Commission on Human Rights, explicitly recognizes indigenous religions and goes further than any other United Nations document in recognizing the rights of indigenous peoples and protecting their indigenous religions.

The Draft Declaration, in dramatic and definitive language, affirms in the preamble that: "all doctrines, policies and practices based on or advocating superiority of peoples or individuals on the basis of national origin, racial, religious, ethnic or cultural differences are racist, scientifically false, legally invalid, morally condemnable and socially unjust."[36]

The Draft Declaration would find unacceptable the philosophical and theological assumptions propagated by missionaries in Africa; the demonization of African religions as backward and inferior would violate the letter and spirit of the document. Elsewhere, the Draft Declaration protects indigenous peoples from any "adverse discrimination, in particular based on their indigenous origin and identity."[37] More importantly, the Draft Declaration prohibits "cultural genocide" and disallows "any form of assimilation or integration by other cultures or ways of life imposed on them."[38] In a sweeping assertion of sovereignty, the Draft Declaration appears to prohibit all forms of advocacy or proselytization by agents external to the indigenous culture when it calls for the "prevention of and redress for," among other things, "any form of propaganda directed at them [indigenous peoples]."[39] The objective of this reasoning is to create space in which indigenous peoples and their cultures are left alone by external

---

[33] General Comment No. 23, UN Doc. ICCPR/C/21/Rev.I/Add.5 (1994), para. 6.2.

[34] Proclaimed by General Assembly Resolution 36/55, 25 November 1981. *United Nations, Human Rights: A Compilation of International Instruments* (New York, 1993), 122–25.

[35] The Working Group on Indigenous Populations was established in 1982 by the United Nations as a subsidiary body of the UN Sub-Commission on Prevention of Discrimination and Protection of Minorities (now the UN Sub-Commission on the Promotion and Protection of Human Rights).

[36] UN Commission on Human Rights, Sub-Commission on Prevention of Discrimination and Protection of Minorities, *Draft Declaration on the Rights of Indigenous Peoples,* 46th Sess., Agenda Item 15, UN Doc. E/CN.4/Sub.2/1994/Add.1 (1994) (hereafter "Draft Declaration").

[37] Draft Declaration, art. 2.

[38] Ibid., art. 7(d).

[39] Ibid., art. 7(e).

agents including imperial religions. If adopted, the Draft Declaration would provide guidance for the human rights movement in understanding indigenous religions and creating processes to protect them.

While the protection of indigenous cultures appears to be gaining international currency, African states remain uninterested in reclaiming the precolonial past and restoring those aspects of traditional norms and values, including elements of spirituality, which were discredited during the colonial era. The lack of interest in the past is partially due to its thorough demonization and the shame and backwardness with which the Westernized and Christianized or Islamized ruling African elites associate it. Good culture in Africa today is defined by its distance from traditional cultures and proximity to Western values. In many instances, African states continue to carry out modernization campaigns against "backward peoples" such as the Masai of Kenya and Tanzania. So-called African customary laws, for example, are ordinarily overridden by received colonial laws in most legal systems and jurisdictions in Africa. In many African countries, there have been no national debates to evaluate and contextualize African customs and laws within the modern state. Many traditional practices, from polygamy to traditional healing and worship, which were discredited by the colonial state, are actively prohibited and punished by the new African-led governments. In this process of continued acculturation, African religions have been one of the major casualties of the culture of imitation.

A rare exception to the general disregard of the African past is the African Charter on Human and Peoples' Rights, the continental human rights instrument adopted by the Organization of African Unity in 1981.[40] In its preamble, the African Charter recognizes the "virtues" of Africa's traditions and its civilization. Elsewhere, it imposes upon individual Africans the "duty to preserve and strengthen positive African values," although it neither spells out those values nor mentions African religions.[41] But its use of the word "positive" betrays a Eurocentric bias and implies that there is much that is negative in African culture. The only reference to religion is a boilerplate provision, taken mainly from the ICCPR, that protects freedom of religion or belief.[42]

The most impressive effort at reclaiming, developing, and protecting the African religious and cultural heritage has taken place in Benin. In January 1996, Benin became the first African postcolonial state to officially recognize an African religion when it declared a National Voodoo Day.[43] In a departure from the practices of other states, the 1990 constitution of the Republic of Benin creates a secular state but protects the "right to culture" and places a duty on the state to "safeguard and promote the national values of civilization, as much material as spiritual, as well as the cultural

---

[40] *African Charter on Human and Peoples' Rights,* 26 June 1981, OAU Doc. A/CAB/LEG/67/3, Rev. 5 (entered into force 12 October 1986), reprinted in 21 ILM 58 (1982) (hereafter "African Charter"). The charter establishes a continental human rights system by creating the African Commission on Human and Peoples' Rights, its implementing body. Although widely criticized as lacking in effectiveness, the commission remains the only continent-wide human rights body.

[41] Ibid., art. 29(7).

[42] Ibid., art. 8.

[43] Makau Mutua, "Returning to My Roots: African Religions and the State," in *Proselytization and Communal Self-Determination in Africa,* ed. Abdullahi Ahmed An-Na'im (New York: Orbis Books, 1999), 169–90.

traditions."[44] The example of Benin blazes an important trail because if African states expect African values to be respected by outsiders—and by imperial faiths—it is incumbent upon them to demonstrate their own commitment to the African spiritual, moral, and cultural universes first.

Since independence from colonial rule, however, most African constitutions and laws have regrettably shown no inclination towards restoring the humanity of African religions and morality. A survey of the constitutions of several African states show that they make no mention of indigenous religions, choosing instead to provide the generic protection of freedom of religion or belief contained in international human rights instruments.[45] The wording of several other constitutions suggests that some forms of evangelization may be restricted.[46] The constitution of Zambia, for example, guarantees freedom of religion except that limitations could be placed to "ensure that the enjoyment of the said rights and freedoms of any one individual does not prejudice the rights and freedoms of others."[47] The constitution of Mauritius seems to limit attempts at proselytization by protecting "the right to observe and practice any religion or belief without the unsolicited intervention of persons professing any other religion or belief."[48] Although the legislation respecting indigenous religions is quite thin if not lacking, the general orientation of the policies of most African states has been hostile to precolonial, pre-Islamic, or pre-Christian values but very protective of one or both of the proselytizing faiths. In many cases, states actively pursue campaigns to root out "unenlightened" customs and traditions.

VI. The Paradox of Liberalism and Human Rights

Two basic human rights documents—the UDHR and the ICCPR—seek to entrench and encourage the free exchange of ideas[49] and the respect for difference and diversity. The emphasis placed on the importance of creating and maintaining a diverse society is one of the most striking characteristics of human rights law. Diversity is encouraged, though not required, by the rights corpus in cultural, religious, political, and other endeavors and pursuits. Through this emphasis, human rights law "evidences throughout its hostility to imposed uniformity."[50] According to Henry Steiner:

> The ideal of encouraging and protecting diversity informs many human rights provisions. No other norm in the human rights corpus plays as vital a role in the struggle to realize that ideal as the principle of equal protection, perhaps the preeminent human rights norm. *Its premise of the equal worth of individuals and their right to equal respect*

---

[44] Republic of Benin Const, 1990, art. 10, Law No. 90–32.

[45] Republic of Ghana Const, 1979, sec. 27(l); Mozambique Const, 1975, art. 33; Mali Const, 1977, sec. 11.

[46] Mauritius Const, 1971, sec. 11 5(b); Zimbabwe Const, 1980, sec. 19 5(b).

[47] Zambia Const, 1974, sec. 13.

[48] Mauritius Const, 1971, sec. 11(b). The Constitution of Zimbabwe, 1980, section 19 5(b), repeats almost verbatim the corresponding section of the Constitution of Mauritius.

[49] Article 19 of the UDHR provides that "everyone has the right to freedom of opinion and expression; this right includes the freedom to hold opinions without interference and to seek, receive and impart information and ideas through any media and regardless of frontiers." Article 19 of the ICCPR is the equivalent provision, although it warns that these rights carry "special duties and responsibilities" and are therefore subject to "certain restrictions" for the "respect of the rights . . . of others and for the protection of national security or of public order (*ordre public*), or public health and morals."

> ***necessarily applies to the ethnic groups with which individuals are associated, for discrimination has the same systemic character whether it is directed against a group or selectively against a member.***[51]

Indeed, article 26 of the ICCPR prohibits discrimination on the basis of race, color, sex, language, religion, political or other opinion, national or social origin, property, birth, or other status. Article 27 affirms the same philosophy by requiring states to make sure that minorities shall not be denied the right to enjoy their own culture and to profess and practice their own religion.[52] Elsewhere, the ICCPR repeatedly confirms its adherence to difference by protecting the rights of persons to assemble peacefully[53] and to associate freely with others.[54] Lawful restrictions, however, could be imposed on the basis of national security, the protection of public health or morals, or the protection of the rights and freedoms of others.[55] Although it is clear that human rights law is obsessed with the creation, protection, and preservation of diversity, it is also clear that rights advancing this ideal—which is central to the movement—could also be curtailed to protect the rights of others.

This propagation of diversity through the freedom to exchange ideas and to associate across divides and traditional cleavages such as race, religion, culture, national origin, and gender by human rights law assumes—an assumption that is still being tested—that there is inherent benefit in cross-fertilization or contact with "otherness." When the ICCPR declares, for example, the "freedom to seek, receive, and impart information and ideas of all kinds, regardless of frontiers,"[56] it presupposes, without final proof, an ultimate good in the exercise of that right. There are presumed "goods"—growth, vitality, search for truth, and new challenges—that would benefit humanity from interaction, difference, and diversity. Ethnic separation—whether voluntary or enforced—is not preferred; instead, openness and transparency towards "the other" might nurture respect for difference and reduce bigotry and demonization.

With regard to the right to freedom of religion or belief, the ICCPR grants wide latitude:

> Everyone shall have the right to freedom of thought, conscience and religion. This right shall include freedom to have or to adopt a religion or belief of his choice, and freedom, either individually or in community with others and in public or private, to manifest his religion or belief in worship, observance, practice and teaching.[57]

Significantly, the ICCPR also provides that no one shall be "subject to coercion which would impair his freedom to have or to adopt a religion or belief of his choice."[58] Additionally, the freedom to manifest one's religion or belief "could be lawfully limited

[50] Henry J. Steiner, "Ideals and Counter-Ideals in the Struggle for Autonomy Regimes for Minorities," *Notre Dame Law Review* 66 (1991): 1548.
[51] Ibid.; emphasis added.
[52] ICCPR, art. 27.
[53] Ibid., art. 21.
[54] Ibid., art. 22.
[55] Ibid., art. 22(2).
[56] Ibid., art. 19(2).
[57] Ibid., art. 18(1).
[58] Ibid., art. 18(2).

on the grounds of public safety, order, health, or morals or the fundamental rights and freedoms of others."[59] Article 18 of the UDHR also provides for the "right to freedom of thought, conscience and religion."

Taken together, the provisions advocating difference and diversity and those providing explicitly for religious rights, would seem to allow proselytization by the universalist religions, although they also provide for certain limitations which might be read as possibly excluding certain modes of evangelization. For example, proselytization through force or coercion, or in the context of colonization, would appear to be excluded.

Although human rights law amply protects the right to proselytize through the principles of free speech, assembly, and association, the pecking order of rights problematizes the right to evangelize where the result is the destruction of other cultures or the closure of avenues for other religions. It is my argument that the most fundamental of all human rights is that of self-determination[60] and that no other right should override it. Without this fundamental group or individual right, no other human right could be secured, since the group would be unable to determine for its individual members under what political, social, cultural, economic, and legal order they would live. Any right which directly conflicts with this right ought to be void to the extent of that conflict. Traditionally, the self-determination principle has been employed to advance the cause of decolonization or to overcome other forms of external occupation. The principle was indispensable to the decolonization process. This usage of the principle—as a tool for advancing demands for external/internal self-determination—could be expanded to disallow cultural and religious imperialism or imposition by external agencies through acculturation, especially where the express intent of the invading culture or religion, as was the case in Africa, is to destroy its indigenous counterparts and seal off the entry or growth of other traditions. Furthermore, the principle could also be read to empower internal self-determination, that is, the right of a people to cultural survival.[61] This usage of self-determination is advanced by the Draft Declaration on the Rights of Indigenous Peoples. It is also an argument against cultural genocide. It is one of the ideas advanced by advocates of autonomy regimes for minorities: unless groups are given protection against invasion and control by others, their cultural and ethnic identities could be quashed by more powerful cultures and political systems. The violent advocacy of proselytizing religions in Africa could be seen as a negation of this right particularly because religion is often the first point of attack in the process of acculturation.

Christianity and Islam forcibly entered Africa not as guests but as masters.[62] The two traditions came either as conquerors or on the backs of conquerors. As they had done elsewhere, they were driven by the belief and conviction of their own innate

---

[59] Ibid., art. 18(3).

[60] ICCPR, art. 1: "All peoples have the right of self determination. By virtue of that right they freely determine their political status and freely pursue their economic, social and cultural development." Article 1 of the *International Covenant on Economic, Social and Cultural Rights,* the other treaty that together with the ICCPR and the UDHR makes the so-called International Bill of Human Rights, is identically worded.

[61] Steiner, "Ideals and Counter-Ideals," 1545–47.

[62] Christians and Muslims came to Africa to wage holy war, as it were, and to subjugate and eradicate indigenous religions and cultures. They did not come to persuade; they came to conquer and did indeed conquer. This is a contradiction of the right to self-determination.

superiority—and conversely what they saw as barbaric African religions and cultures. This belief was not a function of an objective assessment and reflection about African religions and cultures. It was born of the contempt and ignorance of that which was different and the exaggerated importance of the universalist faiths. The evangelizing, universalist religions—Christianity to be precise—came to Africa at a time of great technological and scientific imbalance between the West and the continent. Already the beneficiaries of the industrial revolution, the colonial church and state commanded superior resources in the areas of the military, economic organization and finance, the media, and other social and political spheres. Africa was no match, and the successful imposition of colonialism is proof of that fact. The West was able through coercion, intimidation, trickery, and force to impose a new political, social, cultural, and—thanks to the missionaries—religious order in Africa. African political, social, and religious traditions were delegitimized virtually overnight.

Thus began the process of de-Africanization through large-scale, cash crop farming for European industries, industrialization, urbanization, and the wholesale subversion of traditional values and structures. Africa—from top to bottom—was remade in the image of Europe, complete with modern states on the European model. Christianity played a crucial role in this process: weaning Africans from their roots and pacifying them for the new order. Utilizing superior resources, it occupied most political space and practically killed local religious traditions, and then closed off society from other influences. It is in this sense that the practice of colonial Christian advocacy constituted a violation of the fundamental freedoms of Africans. Islam, which had invaded Africa at an earlier date, was equally insidious and destructive of local religions. Its forceful conversions and wars of conquest, together with its ban on the repudiation of the faith violated the rights of Africans as well.

VII. Conclusions

The existence of individuals does not square with the atomized language prevalent in the human rights movement. Usually, individuals, even in the industrial democracies of the West, are members of an ethnic, social, religious, or political group. Quite often, a single individual will fall under several classifications. Although many of the rights enumerated in human rights law attach to individuals, they only make sense in a collective, social perspective. This is the case because the creation or development of a culture or a religion are societal, not individual, endeavors. I make this point to underline the importance of culture or religion to individuals and groups. An individual's morals, attitudes towards life and death, and identity come from this collective construction of reality through history.

No one culture or religion is sovereign in relationship to any other culture or religion. All cultures must be viewed as being equal. This view rejects the notion that there is a hierarchy of cultures or religions; that some cultures are superior to others even though technologically they may be more advanced. Belief to the contrary has led to military invasions to civilize, colonize, and enslave, as was the case with Christianity in Africa. Cultures, however, have always interacted throughout history; there are no pure cultures, as such, although many traditions retain their distinctive personality. In many cases, the voluntary, unforced commingling of cultures has led to a more vital and creative existence. Several lessons can be drawn from this premise.

The human rights movement should encourage the cross-breeding of cultures and tolerance for diversity. But it should also frown upon homogenization and the imposition of uniformity.

As I mentioned at the beginning, the human rights movement is premised on societies being open to new ideas and challenges; even when a creed seeks homogenization, it must be open to persuasion from other traditions. Although I agree with and share this basic ideal of the human rights corpus, I am deeply concerned that the movement's central tenets may support forms of advocacy that negate certain rights and give legitimacy to abusive conduct. In the case of Africa, the arrival of Christianity, for example, was so violent towards indigenous traditions that the possibility of the free exchange of values and a voluntary commingling was nonexistent. The missionaries and the colonial authorities defined local cultures as demonic; one had to choose between the old and the new. The new ways were promoted as the salvation from a satanic past. Progress, culture, and humanity were identified entirely in Islamic or Christian terms, never with reference to indigenous traditions. But the new converts could not become fully Christian or European; many, to this day, remain suspended between a dim African past and a distorted, Westernized existence. Many have been robbed of their humanity.

I share with other scholars and activists in the human rights movement a sense of the importance of protecting religious human rights and enjoining governments from unduly burdening or prohibiting the free exercise of religion or belief. But I am concerned by those dimensions of proselytizing religions that claim a right not merely to persuade individuals or groups of peoples of the truth as they see it but rather actively demonize, systematically discredit, and forcibly destroy and eventually replace nonuniversalist, noncompetitive, indigenous religions. Quite often, indigenous religions, like all religions, anchor a total worldview, and their destruction usually entails a fundamental distortion of ethnic identities and history.

Perhaps there is not much that can be done today to reverse the negative effects of forced or coerced religious proselytization during the era of colonialism in Africa. Nor is it possible to reclaim wholly the African past as though history has stood still. This does not mean, however, that we should simply forget the past and go on as if nothing happened. The anguish and deprivation caused by that historical experience is with me and millions of other Africans today. We bear the marks of that terrible period. For those Africans who choose not to be Christians or Muslims, the past is not really an option: it was so effectively destroyed and delegitimized that it is practically impossible to retrieve. It is this loss that I mourn and for which I blame Christianity and Islam. The human rights corpus should outlaw those forms of proselytization used in Africa, because their purpose and effect have been the dehumanization of an entire race of people. It could do so by elaborating a treaty that addresses religious human rights, but protects indigenous religion and provides mechanisms of redress for forms of proselytization that seek to unfairly assimilate or impose dominant cultures on indigenous religion. The recent papal apology for violations committed by, and in the name of, the Catholic Church ought to spur action for such a treaty.

Chapter 29

Apostasy and Freedom to Change Religion or Belief

Nazila Ghanea

I. Apostasy: Definition and Parameters

The *Catholic Encyclopedia* defines apostasy as "the desertion of a post, the giving up of a state of life."[1] Furthermore, it distinguishes apostasy from heresy, stating, "The heretic differs from the apostate in that he only denies one or more of the doctrines of revealed religion, whereas the apostate denies the religion itself, a sin which has always been looked upon as one of the most grievous."[2] The gravity of the sin seems to be due to the enormity of concern with a one-time believer knowingly turning away from the truth. Hence, it is considered to be of a much greater order than mere unbelief.

Though particular religions or beliefs may wish to label apostasy as "sin," the question for the human rights regime is the issue of the pressure that may be brought to bear on the so-called apostate in this world. If it is merely left to the afterlife to settle accounts for the change of heart then clearly this does not concern human rights. There has been a long and unfortunate tradition stretching to the present day of denial of civil rights, dissolution of marriage, denial of inheritance rights, excommunication, and even imposition of the sentence of death on the apostate. For example, the Spanish Inquisition was directed chiefly at apostates, the *Catholic Encyclopedia* explains.[3] However, it softens this admission by noting that it was directed against "new Christians, Jews converted by force rather than by conviction."[4] The process and means of proselytism are, therefore, intimately linked here with the question of apostasy.[5]

Some groups are so opposed to the risk of apostasy that they become intolerant of any kind of proselytizing effort. For example, the mere teaching of a belief can come to be considered a political activity that can "excite or make trouble among the

---

[1] A. Van Hove, *The Catholic Encyclopedia* (New York: Robert Appleton Company, 1907), s.v. "apostasy." Available online at <http://www.newadvent.org/cathen/01624b.htm>.

[2] Ibid.

[3] Ibid.

[4] Ibid.

[5] The issue of proselytism and religious persuasion is addressed in depth by Tad Stahnke's chapter in this volume.

Tore Lindholm, W. Cole Durham, Jr., Bahia G. Tahzib-Lie (eds.), Facilitating Freedom of Religion or Belief: A Deskbook, *669–688.* *© 2004 Koninklijke Brill NV.*

people."[6] The previous statement continues, "Egyptians don't want people to shift from one religion to another to gain some personal benefit."[7] Indeed, in discussing the adoption of the Universal Declaration of Human Rights in 1948, the Egyptian representative similarly argued regarding the right to change religion. "The Egyptian delegation was not entirely in agreement with that 'right.' Religious beliefs could not be cast aside lightly. When a man changed his religion it was often due to outside influences or for purposes which were not very commendable, such as divorce."[8]

It is clear however, that the previous three references come from the position of those who welcome conversion *into* a particular tradition, in the latter case Islam, but not conversion *out of* that tradition to adopting another religion or belief. They are not solely concerned with aggressive proselytism.[9] In commenting on this perspective in his seminal study on discrimination in the matter of religious rights and practices, UN Sub-Commission Special Rapporteur Arcot Krishnaswami noted in 1959 "while many religions or beliefs welcome—and in some cases even encourage—the conversion of individuals belonging to other faiths, they are reluctant to admit the conversion of individuals of their own faith; apostasy is viewed with dis-favour by them."[10] Indeed, there is a significant body of opinion that is explicitly opposed to freedom to change religion or belief, holding the understanding that one is culture-bound to retain the religion or belief into which one happens to be born. They consider that, if one does not genuinely hold this belief, at least one should not be so discourteous as to adopt another.

The imposition of penalties for apostasy in this world requires a certain degree of affinity between spiritual and temporal power. The *Catholic Encyclopedia* acknowledges that temporal penalties are no longer imposed today, but notes that spiritual penalties remain. Although heresy is clearly categorized as a lesser sin, it is explained that "[t]he present-day legislation against heresy has lost nothing of its ancient severity; but the penalties on heretics are now only of the spiritual order; all the punishments which require the intervention of the secular arm have fallen into abeyance."[11] A certain level of disassociation between the two sources of power, therefore, seems to lead to a lapse in temporal penalties for apostasy, and herein lies the key to threats of apostasy that remain to the present day.[12] Such temporal penalties for apostasy cover a broad

---

[6] Statement by Egypt's Minister Mahjub, quoted in Pedro C. Moreno, ed., *Handbook on Religious Liberty Around the World* (Charlottesville: The Rutherford Institute, 1996), 269.

[7] Ibid., 268.

[8] Mr. Raafat of Egypt, UN GAOR, 3d session, part 1, Plenary Meetings V2, 913, UN Doc. A/C.6/SR.72 (1948).

[9] If these apprehensions were purely concerned with the extension of improper inducements toward conversion, then it would seem that it may have been adequately catered for under article 18(2) of the *International Covenant on Civil and Political Rights* (ICCPR), which states: "No one shall be subject to coercion which would impair his freedom to have or to adopt a religion or belief of his choice."

[10] Arcot Krishnaswami, *Study of Discrimination in the Matter of Religious Rights and Practices* (New York: United Nations, 1960), 25; UN Doc. E/CN.4/Sub.2/200/Rev. 1, UN Sales No. 60.XIV.2 (1960).

[11] *The Catholic Encyclopedia*, s.v. "heresy." Available online at <http://www.newadvent.org/cathen/07256b.htm>.

[12] For example, after mentioning a range of Jewish penalties for dissenters, Broyde writes, "Despite these classical formulations, Jewish law has not had the judicial authority to inflict any of these punishments for nearly two thousand years" (Michael J. Broyde, "Forming Religious Communities and Respecting Dissenter's Rights," in *Religious Human Rights in Global Perspective, Religious Perspectives*, ed. Johan D. van der Vyver and John Witte Jr. [Boston: Martinus Nijhoff, 1996], 205).

scope and can impinge the civil, political, economic, social, and cultural rights of the accused. Although not often resorted to, the penalty for apostasy resembles either a fundamental impediment to the enjoyment of human rights or a symbolic threat designed to instill loyalty through fear—therefore constituting coercion.

II. Human Rights and Regulations on Apostasy

A. General Considerations

An interesting aspect of the problem of apostasy, in human rights terms, is that it both spans the individual and the collective dimension of human rights, and traverses the neat divide lawyers may imagine to exist between freedom to "have" and freedom to "manifest" religion or belief. Although apostasy initially stems from the individual conscience and decision to change religion or belief, assuming it has not been undertaken under duress and as the result of aggressive proselytism, community consequences are often deemed to result from it. This makes it more congruous to the collective dimensions of human rights. After all, this "holding" of a belief is not usually kept private, though it may be. More often, it encompasses the holding of the belief in association with others, and the collective sense of worship and belonging that this confers. In many societies, therefore, holding a religion or belief is much associated with issues of identity, status, and collective belonging, rather than merely limiting itself to a matter of private personal conscience.

Apostasy, therefore, cannot solely be located either within the right to "have" freedom of thought, conscience, and religion, or within the freedom to "manifest" religion and belief. Although many living in secular societies would locate it in the former realm, it may be worthwhile to consider the opinion of those who would locate it definitively within the latter. This may stem from the perspective that in closely knit communities and strongly religious localities, change of religion may be considered a disruption to the status quo, a source of tension, and reprehensible as the outcome of aggressive proselytism. In this manner, an overlap may also be asserted between apostasy and perceived incitement to hatred, as it may be considered an aggressive show of defiance intended to provoke a community response.

Article 4 of the International Convention on the Elimination of All Forms of Racial Discrimination refers to the illegality of "all dissemination of ideas based on racial superiority or hatred, incitement to racial discrimination, as well as all acts of violence or incitement to such acts against any race or group of persons" and "all other propaganda activities which promote and incite racial discrimination." The call for the enactment of anti-incitement legislation is clearly made in this convention, and is echoed in article 20 of the International Covenant on Civil and Political Rights, which will be discussed below. Article 2 of the 1981 Declaration on the Elimination of All Forms of Intolerance and Discrimination Based on Religion or Belief is notable for its clear definition of discrimination based on religion or belief. Such discrimination is said to include "distinction, exclusion, restriction or preference" and "nullification or impairment of the recognition, enjoyment or exercise of human rights and fundamental freedoms on an equal basis." Its exercise is forbidden, whether practiced by states, institutions, groups, or individuals. Article 4 places the responsibility on states to take "effective measures" to prevent and eliminate such discrimination.

Although these articles are clearly of importance with regard to the illegality of incitement toward religious hatred, it is unlikely that individual acts of apostasy could possibly be subsumed under this heading. A particularly public and aggressive show of apostasy resulting from an overt hatred and prejudice towards one's former belief may conceivably be considered "incitement" to religious hatred, as may large numbers of conversions that result from particularly aggressive proselytism. However, this would seem to be very much the exception to the rule.

B. Norms of Freedom to Change Religion or Belief

In the following, attention will be given to the place of freedom to change religion or belief within international norms, such as the texts of the United Nations and the CSCE/OSCE.

(1948) The Universal Declaration of Human Rights

The main provision for the freedom of religion or belief is contained in article 18 of the declaration: "Everyone has the right to freedom of thought, conscience and religion; this right includes freedom to change his religion or belief, and freedom, either alone or in community with others and in public or private, to manifest his religion or belief in teaching, practice, worship and observance."

It is interesting to note that the article mentions thought, conscience, and religion. By implication, this means that a person should be free to give up his or her religious belief entirely and adopt a belief such as atheism.

The explicit stance of article 18, unfortunately, was not reflected in all subsequent formulations, particularly its explicit inclusion of freedom to "change" religion or belief. The freedom to change one's religion or belief may be described as the most controversial and divisive element in article 18.[13] Representatives of Muslim countries exerted pressure to omit the phrase. The chairman of the Third Committee had to put the phrase itself to the vote by roll call. With twenty-seven in favor, five (Islamic states) against, and twelve abstentions the phrase was adopted. The overall text of the UDHR was adopted with forty-eight states in favor, although Saudi Arabia abstained from voting because of the inclusion of change of religion or belief within article 18.[14] The freedom to change one's religion or belief has, in fact, not been expressed with such clarity in any UN instrument since.

---

[13] For an outline of the drafting history of article 18 of the *Universal Declaration of Human Rights,* see Johannes Morsink, *The Universal Declaration of Human Rights: Origins, Drafting, and Intent* (Philadelphia: University of Pennsylvania Press, 1999), 260–63.

[14] As Morsink explains: "After much struggle the Third Committee voted to keep the right to change one's religious convictions in the Declaration. This was done over the strong objections of Muslim delegations and led Saudi Arabia to abstain in the final vote on the Declaration" (ibid., 2–3). However, Martin Scheinin's reading of the *travaux préparatoires* is somewhat different. He argues that "A group of Moslem States supported a Saudi Arabian amendment deleting the words 'freedom to change his religion or belief.' According to Mr. Baroody of Saudi Arabia, the amendment was meant to prevent abuse of the right by missionaries who in fact were often forerunners of political intervention. He did not, however, contest the individual's right to change religion" (Martin Scheinin, "Article 18," in *The Universal Declaration of Human Rights: A Common Standard of Achievement,* ed. Gudmundur Alfredsson and Asbjørn Eide [Boston:

(1953) European Convention for the Protection of Human Rights and Fundamental Freedoms

Article 9 of this convention also explicitly includes the right to change religion or belief. It states:

> 1. Everyone has the right to freedom of thought, conscience and religion; this right includes freedom to change his religion or belief and freedom, either alone or in community with others and in public or private, to manifest his religion or belief, in worship, teaching, practice and observance.
>
> 2. Freedom to manifest one's religion or beliefs shall be subject only to such limitations as are prescribed by law and are necessary in a democratic society in the interests of public safety, for the protection of public order, health or morals, or for the protection of the rights and freedoms of others.

(1966) International Covenant on Civil and Political Rights

Article 18 is the most relevant provision of the ICCPR. It is renowned for being one of the most substantial in international law in outlining the right to freedom of religion and belief, except with regard to change of religion or belief. Article 18 states:

> 1. Everyone shall have the right to freedom of thought, conscience and religion. This right shall include freedom to have or to adopt a religion or belief of his choice, and freedom, either individually or in community with others and in public or private, to manifest his religion or belief in worship, observance, practice and teaching.
>
> 2. No one shall be subject to coercion which would impair his freedom to have or to adopt a religion or belief of his choice.
>
> 3. Freedom to manifest one's religion or beliefs may be subject only to such limitations as are prescribed by law and are necessary to protect public safety, order, health, or morals or the fundamental rights and freedoms of others.
>
> 4. The States Parties to the present Covenant undertake to have respect for the liberty of parents and, when applicable, legal guardians to ensure the religious and moral education of their children in conformity with their own convictions.

The first paragraph refers to both the individual and the collective. It initially echoes the language of article 18 of the Universal Declaration of Human Rights. However, it replaces the UDHR's controversial statement on freedom to change one's religion or belief with "freedom to have or to adopt a religion or belief of his choice." The logic of the terms "have" and "adopt" is not entirely evident. "Have" connotes greater continuity (providing the choice of whether or not to continue to have) than "adopt"

Martinus Nijhoff, 1999], 381; with reference to November 1948, General Assembly Official Records III, part I, 391, 404).

(in popular usage you do not continue to adopt something), which suggests a once-and-for-all choice. Both words imply more fixed notions than that of "freedom to change."[15]

The ICCPR provision is clearly not as extensive as that provided under the UDHR. It was diminished as a concession to objections voiced by Muslim countries. The logic it purportedly enshrines is seriously problematic. Is it that the individual only has the freedom to choose his belief once? Does it resign itself to the understanding that one's freedom of choice, conscience, and religion may be circumscribed according to one's place of residence and interpretations of the clergy? The phrase is obviously a debacle for human rights, but perhaps a necessary compromise necessitated by the political circumstances surrounding its adoption. Nevertheless, it is disappointing that a standard of human rights should be diminished in such a core covenant, just two decades after agreement on the issue had already been struck.

These difficulties, however, do not call into question the freedom to change religion or belief, and there have been few attempts to claim otherwise. For example, An-Na'im emphasizes that both article 18 of the UDHR and article 18 of the ICCPR include the freedom to change one's religion, "in their formal definition of religious freedom."[16] As the Special Rapporteur has asserted, "It is now established that religious freedom cannot be dissociated from the freedom to change religion,"[17] and that "the right to change religion is a legally essential aspect of religious freedom."[18] He also points to the affirmation of Elisabeth Odio Bénito, that regardless of varying formulations, everyone has the right to leave his or her religion or belief, and that freedom to change religion or belief "was implicit in the concept of the right to freedom of thought, conscience, religion and belief, regardless of how the concept was presented."[19] The Human Rights Committee itself, in its General Comment 22, puts forward the same assertion: "The Committee observes that the freedom to 'have or to adopt' a religion or belief necessarily entails the freedom to choose a religion or belief, including the right to replace one's current religion or belief with another or to adopt atheistic views, as well as the right to retain one's religion or belief."[20]

Nevertheless, the ICCPR article reflects a significant surrender to the forces of inherited orthodoxy and bears witness to intransigent conservative elements.

The second paragraph of article 18 of the ICCPR forbids coercion in the individual's choice in matters of religion or belief. Clearly the overwhelming threat of being charged with apostasy could be considered a factor in such coercion—both in terms of the death penalty as well as the provisions of the "civil death" consequences threatening apostates.

---

[15] At the time of the adoption of the UDHR, the Egyptian delegation commented on freedom to change, and linked it to proselytism: "His delegation feared that by proclaiming man's freedom to change his religion or belief the declaration would be encouraging, even though it might not be intentional, the machinations of certain missions, well known in the Orient, which relentlessly pursued their efforts to convert to their own beliefs the masses of the population of the Orient" (Mr. Raafat of Egypt, UN GAOR, 3rd session part 1, Plenary Meetings V2, 913, UN Doc. A/C.6/SR.72 [1948]).

[16] Abdullahi Ahmed An-Na'im, "Religious Freedom in Egypt: Under the Shadow of the Islamic *Dhimma* System," ***Religious Liberty and Human Rights in Nations and in Religions,*** ed. Leonard Swidler (Philadelphia: Ecumenical Press, 1986), 49.

[17] UN Doc. E/CN.4/1997/91, sec. A, para. 77.

[18] Ibid., para. 80.

[19] Ibid., sec. A, para. 78.

Although article 2 does not define "coercion,"' the 1993 General Comment of the Human Rights Committee does. Coercion is defined as "the use or threat of physical force or penal sanctions to compel believers or nonbelievers to adhere to their religious beliefs and congregations, to recant their religion or belief or to convert."[21] It is clear that penalizing apostasy *does* constitute such coercion, and is, therefore, in violation of article 18(2).

Article 3 outlines restrictions on the manifestation of freedom of religion or belief. However, it clearly does not address restrictions with regard to change of religion or belief. In fact, the Human Rights Committee specifically stresses in its General Comment that "[t]he freedom from coercion to have or adopt a religion or belief . . . cannot be restricted."[22] The committee also adds that less-established religions or beliefs cannot be targeted for particularly harsh treatment: "The Committee therefore stresses that the terms 'beliefs' and 'religion' are to be broadly construed," and "views with concern any tendency to discriminate against any religion or belief for any reasons, including the fact that they are newly established, or represent religious minorities that may be the subject of hostility by a predominant religious community."[23]

Article 20 of the International Covenant on Civil and Political Rights also raises the issue of religion, this time in the important context of incitement of violence and hatred. Paragraph 2 states, "Any advocacy of national, racial or religious hatred that constitutes incitement to discrimination, hostility or violence shall be prohibited by law." Contrary to the definition of genocide, such incitement does not require intent. In the *traveaux préparatoires* it becomes evident that this, together with the fact that preventative action in the form of anti-incitement legislation[24] is implied, caused much controversy. However, in its General Comment 11 on article 20 of the ICCPR (Prohibition of propaganda for war and inciting national, racial or religious hatred), the Human Rights Committee stated "In view of the nature of article 20, States parties are obliged to adopt the necessary legislative measures prohibiting the actions referred to therein."[25] This is clearly an issue which needs to be respected alongside compatibility with article 19 and the right to freedom of expression. Its relationship with apostasy has already been discussed above.

(1975) Conference on Security and Co-operation in Europe, Final Act, 1 (A)

Section VII includes the following statement: "Within this framework the participating States will recognize and respect the freedom of the individual to profess and practice, alone or in community with others, religion or belief acting in accordance with the

---

[20] Human Rights Committee General Comment 22 (1993) on ICCPR, article 18, *The Right to Freedom of Thought, Conscience, and Religion,* 30 July 1993, 48th Sess., para. 5; UN Doc. HRI\GEN\1\Rev.1 at 35 (1994).

[21] Ibid.

[22] Ibid., para. 8.

[23] Ibid., para. 2.

[24] Article 4 of the *Convention on Racial Discrimination* also imposes on governments the obligation to enact anti-incitement legislation.

[25] Human Rights Committee General Comment 11 (1983) on ICCPR, article 20, 29 July 1983, 19th Sess., para. 1; UN Doc. HRI\GEN\1\Rev.1 at 12 (1994).

dictates of his own conscience." This formulation is interesting in that it pointedly emphasizes the role of states in ensuring freedom of religion or belief for individuals. However, it is unfortunate, once again, that explicit reference is not made to the freedom to change religion or belief.

(1978) American Convention on Human Rights

Article 12, addressing freedom of conscience and religion, includes the following:

> 1. Everyone has the right to freedom of conscience and of religion. This right includes freedom to maintain or to change one's religion or beliefs, and freedom to profess or disseminate one's religion or beliefs, either individually or together with others, in public or in private.
>
> 2. No one shall be subject to restrictions that might impair his freedom to maintain or to change his religion or beliefs.
>
> 3. Freedom to manifest one's religion and beliefs may be subject only to the limitations prescribed by law that are necessary to protect public safety, order, health, or morals, or the rights or freedoms of others.

The only possible "escape clause" here may be the assertion that the freedom to manifest one's apostasy may be subject to laws for the protection of the public "safety, order, . . . or morals . . . of others." However, such an understanding could only be reached by reading the article out of context, which emphasizes respect for an individual's freedom to change.

(1981) Declaration on the Elimination of All Forms of Intolerance and Discrimination Based on Religion or Belief

This Declaration is clearly the most comprehensive international instrument in the field of freedom of religion or belief.

Article 1 states:

> 1. Everyone shall have the right to freedom of thought, conscience and religion. This right shall include freedom to have a religion or whatever belief of his choice, and freedom, either individually or in community with others and in public or private, to manifest his religion or belief in worship, observance, practice and teaching.
>
> 2. No one shall be subject to coercion which would impair his freedom to have a religion or belief of his choice.
>
> 3. Freedom to manifest one's religion or beliefs may be subject only to such limitations as are prescribed by law and are necessary to protect public safety, order, health or morals or the fundamental rights and freedoms of others.

The marked omission is, therefore, that of the absence of the term change of religion or belief. In fact, the phrase, "including the right to choose, manifest and change one's religion or belief" was deleted from the end of the second draft preambular paragraph of the 1981 Declaration at the insistence of delegates from Islamic states. However, article 8 of the declaration does state: "Nothing in the present Declaration shall be construed as restricting or derogating from any right defined in the Universal Declaration of Human Rights and the International Covenants on Human Rights." This statement offers something of a reassurance that the absence of an explicit guarantee cannot be taken as an official legal affirmation of the dilution of this right[26] and saves the declaration from regress. Politically, however, it is indeed a witness to backsliding on the issue of freedom to change religion or belief. However, the Special Rapporteur is insistent that "the omission cannot be interpreted as betokening an intention to dilute the provisions of the 1948 Declaration."[27]

(1986) The African Charter on Human and Peoples' Rights

The freedom to change is not explicit in the African Charter. The relevant article, article 8, merely states, "Freedom of conscience, the profession and free practice of religion shall be guaranteed. No one may, subject to law and order, be submitted to measures restricting the exercise of these freedoms."

(1989) Concluding Document of the Vienna Meeting of Representatives of the Participating States of the Conference on Security and Co-operation in Europe

Principle 16(a) states that participating states will "take effective measures to prevent and eliminate discrimination against individuals or communities, on the grounds of religion or belief in the recognition, exercise and enjoyment of human rights and fundamental freedoms in all fields of civil, political, economic, social and cultural life, and ensure the effective equality between believers and non-believers." The right to change religion or belief is not explicit, but may be inferred from the reference to discrimination on the grounds of religion or belief.

(1990) Document of the Copenhagen Meeting of the Conference on the Human Dimension of the CSCE

Part 5.9 of this document states, "All persons are equal before the law and are entitled without any discrimination to the equal protection of the law. In this respect, the law will prohibit any discrimination and guarantee to all persons equal and effective protection against discrimination on any ground."

Part 9.4 is more explicit on change of religion or belief: "Everyone will have the right to freedom of thought, conscience and religion. This right includes freedom to change one's religion or belief and freedom to manifest one's religion or belief, either alone or in community with others, in public or in private, through worship, teaching, practice and observance. The exercise of these rights may be subject only to such restrictions as are prescribed by law and are consistent with international standards."

---

[26] For a discussion of the impact of article 8, see Bahiyyih G. Tahzib, *Freedom of Religion or Belief, Ensuring Effective International Legal Protection* (Boston: Martinus Nijhoff, 1995), 184–85.
[27] UN Doc. E/CN.4/1997/91, sec. A, para. 73.

(1989) Convention on the Rights of the Child

Delegates from Islamic states succeeded in eliminating any mention of a child's right to change his or her religion or belief in the Convention on the Rights of the Child,[28] leaving only article 14's recognition of the child's right to freedom of "thought, conscience and religion" together with that of the parents or legal guardians to "provide direction to the child in the exercise of [this] right in a manner consistent with the evolving capacities of the child."[29]

(1999) Commission on Human Rights, Resolution on the Implementation of the Declaration on the Elimination of All Forms of Intolerance and of Discrimination Based on Religion or Belief

Resolution E/CN.4/RES/1999/39 was groundbreaking in that, unlike previous years, it explicitly included freedom to change religion or belief. Operative paragraph 4[30] urges states

> (a) To ensure that their constitutional and legislative systems provide adequate and effective guarantees of freedom of thought, conscience, religion and belief to all without discrimination, *inter alia* by the provision of effective remedies in cases where the right to freedom of religion or belief, including the freedom to change one's religion or belief, is violated;
>
> (b) To ensure, in particular, that no one within their jurisdiction is deprived of the right to life or the right to liberty and security of person because of religion or belief, or is subjected to torture or arbitrary arrest or detention on that account.

The limitations on this freedom are set out in the commission's 1997 resolution, in which the commission

> *Emphasizes* that, as underlined by the Human Rights Committee, restrictions on the freedom to manifest religion or belief are permitted only if limitations are prescribed by law, are necessary to protect public safety, order, health or morals, or the fundamental rights and freedoms of others, and are applied in a manner that does not vitiate the right to freedom of thought, conscience and religion.[31]

---

[28] For a discussion see Tahzib, *Freedom of Religion or Belief*, 100–102.

[29] However, Krishnaswami describes particular problem areas pertaining to the change of religion or belief and the upbringing of children: antenuptial agreements between parents, marriage between members of different faiths, upbringing of children removed or torn from their family environment, methods of propagation of a religion or belief and improper inducements, educational activities (e.g., orphanages and schools) or humanitarian activities, and change of religion. Regardless of such problematic dimensions, Krishnaswami asserts that as a general rule everyone should be free to adhere, or not to adhere, to a religion or belief in accordance with his conscience and should not be subjected to coercion or improper inducements that impair this freedom (Krishnaswami, *Study of Discrimination*, 26–28).

[30] Commission on Human Rights Resolution 1999/39 (1999), UN Doc. E/CN.4/RES/1999/39, adopted without a vote at the 55th meeting on 26 April 1999.

[31] Commission on Human Rights Resolution 1997/18 (1997), UN Doc. E/CN.4/RES/1997/18, para. 4, adopted without a vote at the 56th meeting on 11 April 1997.

Overview

Clearly, the most comprehensive expression of the right to hold or manifest a religion or belief is that of article 18 of the Universal Declaration of Human Rights, article 9 of the European Convention on Human Rights and article 12 of the American Convention on Human Rights. All three overtly recognize the right to change one's religion or belief, as well as the individual and community dimensions of that right and its manifestation in teaching, practice, worship, and observance. It is unfortunate that the positive tone and clarity expressed in the UDHR on freedom to change religion was somewhat clouded within subsequent international texts on freedom of religion or belief. Reference to change of religion clearly diminished with time, and the fragile consensus reached at the time of the adoption of the UDHR was not to be repeated in subsequent UN texts registering intergovernmental consensus on the issue.[32] The decline in the political consensus is evident, for example, in the weaker article 18 of the ICCPR and article 1(1) of the 1981 Declaration. However, it is argued that agreed standards cannot be subsequently diminished or derogated despite omission, and hope can also be invested in the widely accepted perception that much if not all of the UDHR constitutes customary international law.

III. Apostasy and Current State Practice

De Jong has argued that whilst violations directly relating to enforced recantation and prohibiting change of religion or belief do occur, more cases arise in relation to the punishment and discrimination of apostates.[33] Furthermore, infringements on "freedom from coercion" include both physical violence and other indirect forms of coercion resulting in discrimination on the basis of religion or belief. He explains that most of the examples "refer to governmental policies: either through the imposition of dubious legal obligations or through persecutory or discriminatory measures States allegedly tried to bring about the recantation of certain religions or beliefs. Although some of the State policies mentioned may not even consist of directly discriminatory measures, they would certainly constitute incitement to discrimination. . . . Such policies could also be condemned on the basis of the prohibition of coercion."[34]

In order to better understand the extent of the challenge posed by apostasy to freedom of religion or belief world wide, it may be valuable to consider the countries described as infringing the freedom to change religion or belief in 1994–1998 reports of the United Nations Special Rapporteur on Religious Intolerance.[35] These include[36] the following:

[32] Although the mentioned 1999 resolution by the UN Commission on Human Rights is notable, its significance is purely political, and its language is not as positive as that of the UDHR.

[33] Cornelis D. de Jong, *The Freedom of Thought, Conscience and Religion or Belief in the United Nations (1946-1992)* (Antwerpen: Intersentia, 2000), 62.

[34] Ibid., 67.

[35] The title of the Special Rapporteur has been changed from "Special Rapporteur on Religious Intolerance" to "Special Rapporteur on Freedom of Religion or Belief." Commission on Human Rights, *Implementation of the Declaration on the Elimination of All Forms of Intolerance and of Discrimination Based on Religion or Belief,* 20 April 2000, 56th Sess., UN Doc. E/CN.4/RES/2000/33, para. 11 (2000).

[36] This list results from an exhaustive analysis of the 1994–1998 reports of the Special Rapporteur on Freedom of Religion or Belief, though the Rapporteur's reports on country visits have intentionally been excluded.

- Bangladesh: Accusations of apostasy against the writer Taslima Nasrin.[37]
- Bhutan: Prohibitions on change of religion.[38]
- Egypt: A number of incidents in the case of Muslim converts to Christianity;[39] the arrest and interrogation of a Muslim convert to Christianity;[40] obstacles to conversion, under threat of arrest;[41] and the declaration by a court that Professor Nasr Abu Zeid was an apostate and required to divorce his wife, due to his writings being considered anti-Islamic.[42] The allegation of apostasy was also made against Professor Hassan Hanafi by Al-Azhar scholars, due to his interpretations of Islam. The authorities did not recognize this declaration as carrying any legal weight, so no action was taken against him. The decision ordering Mr. and Mrs. Abu Zeid to separate was also later suspended.[43]
- India: The attack on a Hindu convert to Christianity by Hindu extremists[44] and the drafting of legislation that would ban conversion.[45]
- Indonesia: Forced conversions.[46]
- The Islamic Republic of Iran: The sentencing of four Bahá'ís (Talibi, Mahrami, Mithaqui, and Khalajabadi) to death on the grounds of apostasy.[47] Reported threats against Christians who had converted from Islam. The disappearance and murder of Reverend Dibaj,[48] and uncertain circumstances surrounding the murder of the Christian priest Yusefi. Both had been converts from Islam.[49] Threats against churches to ensure they did not attempt to convert Muslims.[50]
- Iraq: The forcible conversion and marriage of a Christian woman to a Muslim.[51]
- Israel: The drafting of legislation that would ban conversion.[52]
- Kuwait: The strict prohibition of the conversion of a Muslim to another religion[53] and the liability to prosecution for Muslims converting to another religion.[54]

---

[37] Commission on Human Rights, *Implementation of the Declaration on the Elimination of all Forms of Intolerance and of Discrimination Based on Religion or Belief,* 22 December 1994, 51st Sess., UN Doc. E/CN.4/1995/91 (report submitted by Mr. Abdelfattah Amor), sec. II (1995).

[38] UN General Assembly, *Implementation of the Declaration on the Elimination of All Forms of Intolerance and of Discrimination Based on Religion or Belief,* 23 October 1996, 51st Sess., UN Doc. A/51/542 (report submitted by Mr. Abdelfattah Amor), para. 34 (1996).

[39] UN Doc. E/CN.4/1995/91, sec. II.

[40] Commission on Human Rights, *Implementation of the Declaration on the Elimination of All Forms of Intolerance and of Discrimination Based on Religion or Belief,* 22 January 1998, 54th Sess., UN Doc. E/CN.4/1998/6 (report submitted by Mr. Abdelfattah Amor), para. 62c (1998).

[41] Ibid., 15 December 1995, 52d Sess., UN Doc. E/CN.4/1996/95 (report submitted by Mr. Abdelfattah Amor), sec. VI, para. 46 (1996).

[42] UN Doc. E/CN.4/1996/95, sec. VI, para. 39. Further information on the Abu Zaid case can also be found at the following website: <http://msanews.mynet.net/Scholars/NasrAbu/>.

[43] Commission on Human Rights, *Civil and Political Rights, Including Religious Intolerance,* 11 January 1999, 55th Sess., UN Doc. E/CN.4/1999/58 (report submitted by Mr. Abdelfattah Amor), paras. 50–51 (1999).

[44] UN Doc. E/CN.4/1998/6, para. 62(d). Also noted in UN Doc. A/52/477, para. 33(b)(iv).

[45] Ibid., para. 62(b). Also noted in UN Doc. A/52/477, para. 33(b)(ii).

[46] UN Doc. E/CN.4/1996/95, sec. VI, para. 46.

[47] UN Doc. E/CN.4/1997/91, para. 11.

[48] UN Doc. E/CN.4/1995/91, sec. II, Islamic Republic of Iran.

[49] UN Doc. E/CN.4/1997/91, para. 11.

[50] UN Doc. E/CN.4/1995/91, sec. II.

- Lao People's Democratic Republic: An official campaign to force believers to renounce their faith.[55]
- Malaysia: Obstacles to conversion, particularly legislative.[56]
- Maldives: Prohibitions against converting to another religion[57] and against change of religion.[58]
- Mexico: Allegations of ill-treatment by communities against converted persons.[59]
- Morocco: The detention and subsequent hospitalization of a Muslim who had converted to Christianity and was found guilty of evangelism,[60] obstacles to conversion, under threat of arrest[61] and expulsion.[62]
- Myanmar: Forced conversions.[63]
- Nepal: Obstacles to conversion, under threat of arrest.[64]
- Qatar: The conversion of a Muslim to another religion was punishable by death.[65]
- Saudi Arabia: Cases of legal opinions declaring Shi'is apostates.[66]
- Sudan: Forced conversions[67] and prohibitions against converting to another religion.[68]

Since the majority of the above mentioned examples are from the Muslim world,[69] and since Muslim countries, as indicated above, have objected strongly to including the freedom to change religion and belief in international norms, attention will now be given to the issue of apostasy under Islam.

IV. Apostasy Under Islam

A. The Traditional View

As in Catholicism, apostasy under Islam is clearly distinguished from lesser sins: a person who "denies Allah or who merely commits a great sin is a kafir [unbeliever]. A Muslim who reverts to polytheism or adopts another religion is murtadd [apostate]."[70] As to the punishment for such people, Khadduri continues,

---

[51] Not so much an example of freedom to change, but of coercion to change. UN Doc. E/CN.4/1998/6, para. 62(e).

[52] UN Doc. E/CN.4/1998/6, para. 62(b). Also noted in UN Doc. A/52/477, para. 33(b)(ii).

[53] UN Doc. E/CN.4/1998/6, para. 62(a). Also noted in UN Doc. A/52/477, para. 33(b)(i).

[54] UN Doc. E/CN.4/1997/91, para. 21(c)(ii).

[55] UN Doc. A/51/542, para. 34.

[56] UN Doc. E/CN.4/1996/95, sec. VI, para. 46. See also UN Doc. E/CN.4/1995/91, sec. II, Malaysia.

[57] UN Doc. E/CN.4/1996/95, sec. VI, para. 46. Also UN Doc. A/51/542, para. 34.

[58] UN Doc. E/CN.4/1997/91, para. 21(c)(i).

[59] UN Doc. E/CN.4/1997/91, para. 21(c)(iii). Also UN Doc. A/51/542, para. 34.

[60] UN Doc. E/CN.4/1997/91, para. 35.

[61] UN Doc. E/CN.4/1996/95, sec. VI, para. 46.

[62] Ibid.

[63] Ibid. Also noted in UN Doc. A/52/477, para. 33(b)(vi).

[64] Ibid.

[65] UN Doc. E/CN.4/1998/6, para. 62(a). Also noted in UN Doc. A/52/477, para. 33(b)(i).

[66] UN Doc. E/CN.4/1995/91, sec. II.

[67] UN Doc. E/CN.4/1996/95, sec. VI, para. 46.

[68] Ibid. See also UN Doc. E/CN.4/1995/91, sec. II, Sudan.

> both jurists and theologians agree that apostasy constitutes a violation of the law punishable both in this world and the next. Not only is the person denied salvation in the next world, but he is also liable to capital punishment by the state. . . . [A]ll the commentators agree that a believer who turns back from his religion (irtadda), openly or secretly, must be killed if he persists in disbelief. The traditions are more explicit in providing the death penalty for everyone who apostatizes from Islam.[71]

Even if the unconditional applicability of the death penalty for apostasy *is* accepted, questions still arise as to how it is to be enforced. Some emphasize the possibility of forgiveness for the repentant apostate. If this period of grace for the consideration of repentance is unlimited, then the death sentence cannot be carried out.[72] Khadduri, however, contends that the apostate should be given just three days to make the choice between "Islam and death."[73]

However, many Muslims reject Khadduri's standing on this issue. One writer even suggests that such a stance originates from "an interpretive error of early Muslim jurisprudence" and that the position is "in fact, based on medieval Christianity."[74]

An-Na'im explains the "civil death" consequences for those who are not killed for their apostasy, "Besides losing the capacity to conclude any contract, whether in disposition of property or in relation to personal status such as a contract of marriage, an apostate loses all his or her property to the state. If married to a Muslim, his or her marriage is immediately dissolved."[75] Furthermore, although Doi asserts that "[t]he punishment by death in the case of apostasy has been unanimously agreed upon by all the four schools of Islamic jurisprudence,"[76] Ben Cheikh[77] has categorically stated that "he could not accept that the Prophet, peace be upon him, could have imposed such a cruel punishment as death that directly prejudiced religious freedom."[78] The discussion about apostasy under Islam, therefore, must be understood in the context of vast divergences of opinion and interpretations.

Such discussion stems primarily from the fact that the punishment is *not* based on Qur'anic text but on the Hadith of Islam. The Hadith are the codified records of the practice of the Prophet, his teachings and conduct. This forms the traditional backdrop to the interpretation of the Qur'anic text, and it is resorted to regarding issues on which the Qur'an is silent. The Qur'an does speak of the gravity of this sin in terms of a spiritual condemnation "the curse of Allah, of His Angels and of all mankind."[79]

---

[69] De Jong also argues that most of the cases that arise in relation to the infringement of this right to change religion or belief relate to Islamic and Hindu countries. See de Jong, *The Freedom of Thought, Conscience and Religion*, 62.

[70] Majid Khadduri, *War and Peace in the Law of Islam* (Baltimore: Johns Hopkins University Press, 1955), 149.

[71] Ibid., 149–51.

[72] For a further discussion of this issue see Amir Arjomand, "Religious Human Rights and the Principle of Legal Pluralism," in *Religious Human Rights in Global Perspective*, 345.

[73] Khadduri, *War and Peace in the Law of Islam*, 149–51.

[74] Hazrat Mirza Tahir Ahmad, *Murder in the Name of Allah* (Cambridge: Lutterworth Press, 1990), 49.

[75] An-Na'im, "Religious Freedom in Egypt," 55.

[76] 'Abdur Rahman I. Doi, *Shari'ah: The Islamic Law* (London: Ta Ha Publishers, 1984), 266.

[77] Souheib Ben Cheikh, Mufti of Marseille.

[78] *Enriching the Universality of Human Rights: Islamic Perspectives on the Universal Declaration of Human Rights*, 9–10 November 1998, UN Doc. HR/IP/SEM/1999/I, Part I, 54 (1999).

[79] The Qur'an 3:86–89 (quoted in Doi, *Shari'ah: The Islamic Law*, 266).

However, this has to be placed in the context of other Qur'anic texts such as "There is no compulsion in religion"[80] and "Your religion for you, and mine for me."[81] Despite such Qur'anic texts, it has still been asserted that apostasy "is definitely, if ambiguously, proscribed in the Qur'an."[82] Nevertheless, it is clear that the punishment of death for apostasy is not spelled out and enshrined in the Qur'an, and hence the lively debate about the authenticity of Hadith sources, the context of its possible relevance in the past, and its political rather than religious utility today would appear absolutely legitimate.

B. Contextualizing the Apostasy Ban

Those who wish to reform or restrict the punishment for apostasy use several lines of argument. Many of those who reject Khadduri's stance do so by distinguishing between the early practice of the Prophet Muhammad and later custom. Since this practice became less lenient, some have described the early practice as a reflection of the relative weakness of the Muslim community and practical realities dictating appeasement, rather than action from the position of strength. Traditionalists argue that such early, tolerant traditions were abrogated by the later, harsher ones. However, others suggest that the earlier traditions, with their emphasis of justice and dignity, were more in line with the guidance of the Prophet. For some, such a distinction even needs to be made between the verses of the Qur'an revealed during the Makkan and Madinan period of the life of the Prophet. This concept is controversial,[83] as it challenges the integrity of all Qur'anic verses being on an equal basis. However, as the punishment for apostasy is not stated in the Qur'an, this controversy is not directly relevant to a discussion of apostasy. This therefore brings into question the Hadith in which Muhammad is reported to have stated "Whoever changes his religion, kill him," the contrast of this statement with other Hadith, and its even sharper contrast with the verse of the Qur'an regarding no compulsion in religion.

A number of observers[84] have linked the punishment assigned in the Hadith for apostasy with the punishment for desertion and treason—particularly during jihad or from battles for the cause of Islam. A clear linkage can historically be deduced between the punishment for apostasy and other "crimes" such as counterrebellion, betrayal,

---

[80] Ibid. 2:256.

[81] Ibid. 109:6.

[82] Donna E. Arzt, "The Treatment of Religious Dissidents Under Islamic Law," in *Religious Human Rights in Global Perspective,* 408.

[83] See Mahgoub el-Tigani Mahmoud, "Islamic Law, Human Rights and International Law, A Critique of Mahmoud Taha and An-Na'im, Part I," *Islamic, The Journal of the Islamic Society of the London School of Economics* 2, no. 3 (summer 1996): 31–42.

[84] Kurdi is one such writer who compares the crime of apostasy to that of treason. See Abdulrahman Abdulkadir Kurdi, *The Islamic State: A Study based on the Islamic Holy Constitution* (London: Mansell, 1984), 57–61. Another writer who equates apostasy to treason is Muhammad Zafrullah Khan—the Ahmadiyya who was formerly Foreign Minister of Pakistan, member of the Pakistan Delegation to the UN General Assembly, and member of the International Court of Justice. He makes a direct linkage between the punishment of the death penalty and treason during a state of war: "If in that state [the state of war] a Muslim went over to the enemy and took up arms against the Muslims he would be guilty of treason whether a change of faith was or was not involved" (Muhammad Zafrullah Khan, *Islam and Human Rights* [Tilford: Islam International Publishers, 1989], 117).

breach of contract, and sedition. Such positions therefore attempt a more sensitive understanding of the historical and social context in which this punishment may be understood. By giving adequate emphasis to context, the weight of historical circumstance and specificities are brought to the fore. The Qur'an states that such retreat from the field of battle in the cause of Islam will draw to the deserter "the wrath of Allah, and his abode is hell, an evil refuge indeed."[85] Doi claims, "The *hadd* punishment for this grave and dangerous crime of fleeing the battlefield is death according to the consensus of opinions of the Muslim jurists of all the schools."[86] It is clear that the lives of numerous others may well be endangered by such action, and the punishment can be seen in the light of penalties imposed by military courts for desertion from the battlefield. It is in this context that a number of distinctions emerge.

Such formulations contextualize the death penalty for apostasy as a requirement at a time when the Muslim community was under siege and under risk of extermination. It is also asserted that this context certainly does not hold when Islam is established and enjoys majority status. For example, Anderson suggests that this punishment should be regarded as the punishment for an act "which could be equated with political treason when the very survival of the infant Muslim community was at stake, but as no longer applicable in days in which no such danger exists."[87] Such exceptional circumstances surrounding the necessity of self-defense for a fledging community have long since ceased to apply. Furthermore, some believe that it is the coupling of apostasy with desertion from military duties that threatens the community, not just an individual's change of religion or belief. Mere change of religion needs to be squared with the Qur'anic injunction of "no compulsion in religion,"[88] a principle clearly at odds with a practice of imposing the death penalty for apostasy.

C. Abolishing the Death Penalty for Apostasy?

There are, therefore, many reasons supporting the conclusion that the punishment of the death penalty is no longer justified for apostasy; namely, because it no longer poses a threat to the Muslim community, it is no longer an implicit declaration of war, and it no longer implies the joining of the enemy. Conclusions such as these lead many to the belief that the law of apostasy in Islam should be dropped, by restricting the Shari'a sanction to such an extent that it would become inoperable.

An-Na'im claims that "The cultural challenge posed by Shari'a in Islamic countries is certainly serious, but by no means insurmountable."[89] He explains, "Though it may not be possible to abolish, as a matter of Islamic law, the punishments specified by the Qur'an, the practical application of these punishments can be restricted almost indefinitely. The real difficulty is political rather than jurisprudential."[90] This argument comments on punishments which have been specified in the Qur'an. Since the apostasy

[85] The Qur'an 8:15–16 (quoted in Doi, *Shari'ah: The Islamic Law*, 267).
[86] Doi, *Shari'ah: The Islamic Law*, 267.
[87] Nicholas Anderson, *Law Reform in the Muslim World* (London: The Athlone Press, 1976), 196.
[88] The Qur'an 2:256.
[89] Abdullahi Ahmed An-Na'im, "The right to reparation for human rights violations and Islamic culture(s)," in *Seminar on the Right to Restitution, Compensation and Rehabilitation for Victims of Gross Violation of Human Rights and Fundamental Freedoms*, ed. Theo van Boven et al. (Maastricht: University of Limburg, 1992), 180–81.

punishment is of a lower order, since it stems only from the Hadith, its reversibility is all the more possible. The authentic Islamic resources, methodologies, and principles that are available to those who call on the abolishment of current punishments are those of ***ijtihad*** and ***maslaha***.

Ijtihad is the principle of independent reasoning and judgement in legal matters. Its utility in this context stems from the fact that, "because ijtihad has been redefined through human reason in the past, rather than being the direct function of divine revelation as such, it can be re-regulated through human reason today and in future."[91] The argument would be that, "since socio-economic and cultural contexts within which Qur'anic verses were first presented have substantially changed, the legal grounds on which such laws were based are no longer valid."[92] Ijtihad could, therefore, come into play in the reformulation of the reasoning surrounding the issue of apostasy. This would certainly not be an initiative without precedent in the Muslim world. In fact, there is much evidence of "the frequent adoption of pragmatism in the Muslim world."[93]

The Shariah regulations in this regard may also be deemed to be subject to abrogation or ***naskh***. An-Na'im argues that a process of abrogation has, in fact, already come into play—allowing the early Muslim jurists to determine which verses and traditions are operative and which are not, and to repeal the Qur'anic verses advocating freedom of religion or belief in favor of the current position of the Shariah. Early jurists decided that

> Chapter 18, verse 29 of the Qur'an, which instructs the Prophet to tell people that he is bringing forth the truth as he received it from the Lord and that they are free to believe or disbelieve does not mean that one can remain an unbeliever in Islam without suffering adverse consequences or that a Muslim is free to repudiate his or her faith in Islam.[94]

Now An-Na'im proposes that abrogation should be utilized once again, this time in favor of the original Qur'anic texts. The purpose of such abrogation would be to bring about a body of law suited to the needs of the Islamic community at a different stage of its development. A number of Islamic scholars argue that this tool of abrogation is highly necessary today with regard to outmoded apostasy penalties. The controversy surrounding the abrogation of Qur'anic verses themselves is discussed above. However, the proposal of abrogating Hadith in favor of Qur'anic texts is of a less controversial nature, and does not undermine the Qur'an itself in any way. The aim would be to rationalize and develop laws that would foster the interests of the Islamic community—known as ***maslaha***.

V. Public Order, Governments, and Apostasy

Even with the acceptance of the legal and cultural possibility of change to the laws of apostasy under Islam, a further, more daunting challenge remains: the political challenge of bringing about such change.

---

[90] Ibid., 180.

[91] Mahmood Monshipouri, "The Muslim World Half a Century after the Universal Declaration of Human Rights: Progress and Obstacles," *Netherlands Quarterly of Human Rights* 16, no. 3 (September 1998): 287–314.

[92] Ibid., 301.

[93] Ibid., 294.

[94] An-Na'im, "Religious Freedom in Egypt," 57.

Present formulations of apostasy law, after all, can provide governments ruling over Muslim communities with ample latitude for maneuver. It provides them with cultural and apparent religious sanction for legitimately infringing on the rights of the populace by denying the individual both freedom of religion and freedom of belief in the interpretation and application of his or her beliefs.

The apostasy problem encapsulates three major dilemmas; namely, that Muslims do not have the right to change their religion, that Muslims are not entitled to interpreting the Holy Texts in a manner that diverges from the "standard" interpretations of any purported Islamic states, and that rights derive from one's "status," not simply from one's humanity. Apostasy can be inferred from a person's views or actions, which may be "deemed . . . to contravene the basic tenets of Islam and therefore be tantamount to apostasy, regardless of the accused's personal belief that he or she is a Muslim."[95] The more recent political manipulations of the death penalty have been highlighted by those who present the penalty as a threat that potentially hangs over *every* individual living within a given government's sphere of influence. "The ban [on apostasy] can also affect Muslims who adhere to doctrines that are out of keeping with whatever standard of orthodoxy is currently being espoused by a government pursuing Islamization. . . . Thus the ban on apostasy has become a curb on the religious freedom of Muslims—not only on their freedom to convert from Islam, but also on their freedom to follow their consciences in selecting what Islamic teachings to follow."[96] These arguments undermine the claim that apostasy is an internal issue of concern only to Muslims. In this vein, Al-Marzouqi has argued that the "restriction" preventing Muslims from change of religion "may be considered as a sort of internal or domestic affair which only concerns Muslims . . . all religions, moral and legal systems stipulate certain conditions which are applicable only to their adherents or to people under their jurisdictions."[97] In fact, since the penalty for apostasy is only applied to those who have either chosen to leave Islam or who are accused of having left Islam, it cannot merely be dismissed as a domestic issue within the private sphere.

To the same extent that the ban on apostasy provides the grounds for the infringement of the right of individuals, it is "power" in the hands of the leadership. It is, therefore, not surprising that some governments are reluctant to see any changes brought about to it, and that many tend toward the most conservative interpretations of this issue. One such statement on the necessity of the punishment of apostasy stemmed from a response from the Sudanese government to the Special Rapporteur "Apostasy from Islam is classified as a crime for which *ta'zir* punishment may be applied (*ta'zir* is a 'disciplinary, reformative and deterrent punishment'). . . . The punishment is inflicted in cases in which the apostasy is a cause of harm to the society, while in those cases in which an individual simply changes his religion the punishment is not to be applied. But it must be remembered that unthreatening apostasy is an exceptional

---

95 Abdullahi Ahmed An-Na'im, "Human Rights in the Muslim World: Socio-Political Conditions and Scriptural Imperatives," in *International Human Rights in Context; Law, Politics, Morals: Text and Materials*, ed. Henry J. Steiner and Philip Alston (Oxford: Clarendon Press, 1996), 213 (originally in *Harvard Human Rights Journal* 3 [1990]: 13).

96 Ann Elizabeth Mayer, *Islam and Human Rights, Tradition and Politics*, 2d ed. (Boulder: Westview Press, 1995), 143.

97 Ibrahim Abdulla Al-Marzouqi, *Human Rights in Islamic Law* (Abu Dhabi: n.p., 2000), 442–43

case, and the common thing is that apostasy is accompanied by some harmful actions against the society or State."[98] What is of most concern in this statement is the association of apostasy with crimes against the state. Schirazi's interpretation of the scope of apostasy laws in the Islamic Republic of Iran is that "apostates . . . are threatened with the harshest of punishments, namely the death penalty, a threat which may be carried out suddenly at any moment that suits the interests of the hierocracy."[99] Here the punishment can clearly be seen not only as having deterrence value, but also as being manipulated by governments in order to enforce conformity. Arzt has no doubt about the motivation behind governmental support for retaining such penalties. She argues that "much of the persecution of alleged apostates, heretics, and infidels has been politically motivated, designed to benefit hegemonic, orthodox groups who have resorted to religious justifications to legitimize their abusive power."[100]

All this leads to the understanding that the "interpretation of Islam depends on factors other than its supposed inherent nature,"[101] that "Islam, as such, is not 'something' independent of the societies which gave expression to it,"[102] and that there are emerging multiple Muslim perspectives on apostasy. The tools, mechanisms, and resources exist for the apostasy discussion debate to go in a variety of directions within the Muslim world, including that of the eventual unfettered acceptance of the freedom to change religion or belief. In fact, the danger of not combating the challenges posed by apostasy is dire. Monshipouri argues that "Failure to overcome obstacles to modern human rights standards will result in tensions not only between the Muslim world and the West but also within the Muslim world itself by pitting forces of the status quo against reform."[103]

Due to these remaining divergences within the Muslim world about apostasy, it is not surprising that a number of Muslim states have strongly objected to the norm of freedom to change religion or belief, as we have seen in the context of the emerging international norms regarding freedom to change religion and belief.

VI. Conclusion

Some of the problematical, and perhaps subtle, features of the apostasy ban are that it acts as the strongest threat against proselytism; discriminates against minorities who have converts from Islam amongst their ranks; rests on shaky foundations as to when, on whom, and how it can be imposed; inhibits projects for interreligious dialogue and respect; and often stigmatizes the family and offspring of the apostate, leading to a kind of inherited guilt.

---

[98] Commission on Human Rights, *Implementation of the Declaration on the Elimination of all Forms of Intolerance and of Discrimination Based on Religion or Belief*, 6 January 1993, 49th Sess., UN Doc. E/CN.4/1993/62 (report submitted by Mr. Angelo Vidal d'Almeida Ribeiro), para. 56 (1993).

[99] Asghar Schirazi, *The Constitution of Iran: Politics and the State in the Islamic Republic* (London: I. B. Tauris 1997), 139.

[100] Donna E. Arzt, "The Treatment of Religious Dissidents Under Islamic Law" in *Religious Human Rights in Global Perspective*, 452.

[101] Katerina Dalacoura, *Islam, Liberalism and Human Rights* (London: I. B. Tauris, 1998), 2.

[102] Ibid., 42.

[103] Monshipouri, "The Muslim World Half a Century after the Universal Declaration of Human Rights," 314.

The discussions between those who support the temporal punishments for apostasy and those advocating international human rights legal standards seem startlingly polarized. This continuing gap between the theory and the practice of human rights, at the international as well as other levels, clearly constitutes a dilemma of the human rights project that is nowhere more apparent than in the case of apostasy.

The increase in the resort to legal sanctions against apostasy is alarming, and may be the consequence of a number of trends. One is the polarization in debates over the universality of human rights versus cultural relativity, or at least the extent to which religious and cultural particularities may be accepted to trump international human rights standards.[104] While all countries agreed to the principle of the universality of human rights at the 1993 Vienna World Conference on Human Rights, it was compromised with reference to "national and regional peculiarities" and "religious backgrounds."[105] A second reason is the retreat of nation states to more conservative interpretations of religion as the presumed basis of ensuring solidarity and loyalty in their realm. Resorting to punishing apostasy may, therefore, be more a signal of the sense of being politically and ideologically under siege than an indicator of religious loyalty and orthodoxy. The subject of apostasy could, therefore, be fruitfully examined in the context of identity, and the penalties, threats, and intimidation that can be extended to ensure continued loyalty. Communities cannot rely on maintaining strength through imposing such extreme measures on this kind of dissent. Clearly, a more cosmopolitan and tolerant attitude needs to be nurtured to ensure that loyalty based on threats is not accorded such high political value, and that solidarity not be assumed to depend on affiliation with a particular religion or belief.

---

[104] For a more extensive discussion of this issue see Nazila Ghanea-Hercock, "Faith in Human Rights, Human Rights in Faith," in *Religion, Law and Freedom: A Global Perspective,* ed. Joel Thierstein and Yahya R. Kamalipour (Westport: Praeger Publishing, 2000).

[105] See *Vienna Declaration and Programme for Action,* sec. I, operative paragraph 5. It states: "All human rights are universal, indivisible and interdependent and interrelated. The international community must treat human rights globally in a fair and equal manner, on the same footing, and with the same emphasis. While the significance of national and regional particularities and various historical, cultural and religious backgrounds must be borne in mind, it is the duty of States, regardless of their political, economic and cultural systems, to promote and protect all human rights and fundamental freedoms."

Part VI

Contexts for Facilitating Freedom of Religion or Belief

CHAPTER 30

DEVELOPING SHARED VALUES AND COMMON CITIZENSHIP IN A SECULAR AND PLURALIST SOCIETY: HOW RELIGIOUS COMMUNITIES CAN CONTRIBUTE

Archbishop Anastasios

I. CHRISTIANS AND MUSLIMS LIVING TOGETHER IN MODERN EUROPE[1]

A. RELIGIOUS VALUES IN MODERN EUROPE

Living in a secular, pluralistic society, one of the first duties of Christians and Muslims in Europe alike is to emphasize that religion has a vital place in human life. Religion is not a by-product of the moral, rational, or emotional life of a society but is an independent and primary phenomenon relating to a special category: the Sacred, the Holy. It continuously expands the human consciousness beyond earthly limits. It opens the heart to the Ultimate. Religion is an essential experience of all human societies, and thus it cannot be repressed, as it was in atheistic regimes, nor fully neglected, as in some secular states.

Simultaneously, Christians and Muslims must be self-critical and admit our mistakes. Too often—not only in the past but also today—religion has divided people and promoted animosities and conflicts, including ethnic cleansing. Members of both religions should consciously reject any aggressive policy and overcome all types of violence performed in the name of religion. Intensive and continuous efforts are needed on many levels of personal and social life to realize such a vision.

Secularism and practical atheism in the capitalistic societies of modern Europe have created new norms in the life of the common person. We see not only a mere indifference to religious values in Europe but also a completely new orientation. Money is the norm and priority, influencing the rhythm of our entire lives. The temples of today's culture are the banks, which have become the most impressive buildings in many towns. They represent the "cathedrals" of modern secular society. Money means power, luxury, sex, and social influence. Instead of acting as a means of serving humankind,

---

[1] This chapter is an edited version of a presentation made at the conference "Christians and Muslims in Europe: Responsibility and Religious Commitment in the Pluralistic Society" held in Sarajevo, 12–16 September 2001.

Tore Lindholm, W. Cole Durham, Jr., Bahia G. Tahzib-Lie (eds.), Facilitating Freedom of Religion or Belief: A Deskbook, *689–697.*

money has become a false god, an idol. Unfortunately this worship of money tempts even many religious people. Of course, this is not a new phenomenon, since both the Bible and the Qur'an condemn this temptation. Collaborating with this new idolatry is the emphasis on individualism and self-deification. Still, many people in these secular societies feel the need for an ultimate meaning to life. They long for spiritual identity, for forgiveness, for community, for perfection; in other words, they need a religious dimension to their lives.

Both Christianity and Islam reject the dangerous secular orientation that leads people to confusion, anxiety, slavery, and loneliness. Religious experience opens the human mind and heart to the Infinite, revealing the spiritual potential of the human being and facilitating communion with God through faith, prayer, worship, and obedience to the divine commandments. Religious understanding helps people cultivate a communion of respect and sympathy for every human being, even the stranger and the enemy. It guides, inspires, and empowers us to overcome captivity and slavery to our own ego. It inspires a positive attitude to life, creating responsible people who often become the protagonists for new initiatives of peace and resistance to social injustice.

Christians and Muslims in Europe can and must work to articulate and promote common values and spiritual norms, the certainty that man is not independent in the universe and that human interest alone cannot be the final criterion for humankind. The faithful are persuaded that God created all from one and feel His presence and providence in their everyday lives. Relation to and dependence upon God help the human person to be honest with God and peaceful within himself, giving him a strong hope and confidence in God during the trials of life.

Many European societies have marginalized religion. This marginalization creates anxiety in some religious people who focus on statistics regarding majority and minority religions. We must free ourselves from such insecurity. "Fear not, little flock" (Luke 12:32), said Jesus Christ. The final criterion of truth does not depend on the vote of the majority. We see in science and art, as well as throughout the progress of humanity, that truth does not emerge through voting.

Religion has another vocation, as we have indicated above. The essential issue is not how few our numbers are, but whether we are authentic and sincere in our quest for God and in our obedience to His will, conforming our lives to what we confess and believe.

Every generation must purify its religious life from within. Our main priority, speaking from the Christian perspective, is whether we are ready to live the entire Gospel and arrange our lives according to the Beatitudes, the message of the parable of the Good Samaritan, the text of the Last Judgment, St. Paul's hymn of love, etc., and the examples of love, humility, justice, and self-sacrifice in our saints.

B. Harmonious Coexistence and Mutual Respect among Different Religious Communities: The Importance of Human Rights

The peaceful coexistence of Christians and Muslims in Europe is an ideal that has to be sincerely fostered. This type of coexistence among religious communities can derive from two opposite starting points: one, an indifference to the religious experience, or a conscious experience of the innermost essence of religion, as represented in the lives of many distinguished personalities of all religions. On the other hand, intolerance between coexisting religious communities can grow from either religious seeds (i.e., extreme fundamentalism) or nonreligious roots (i.e., political, nationalistic, psychological, or selfish factors). All of these have played powerful roles in the past, and continue unabated in Europe.

In today's Europe, the foundation for a harmonious coexistence between religious groups, as well as with nonreligious ones, can be based on the sincere acceptance of and respect for human rights, especially for the freedom of conscience. Even though many Muslims may consider the Universal Declaration of Human Rights and ensuing international human rights instruments too Western, they offer, nevertheless, a basis for further discussion and improvement. Christians, as well, have some hesitations and have produced some serious proposals for improving the documents concerned. The religious composition of each European country is complex. In many countries, one religion is traditionally connected to the identity, culture, endurance, and expectations of the people.

In order to cultivate a positive climate between Christians and Muslims, a careful study and emphasis on relevant anthropological principles from both religions must be offered. I will mention a few of these.

1. Islam

The idea that man forms a divine "sign" (*aya*) remains an axiom for Islam. Man's dignity springs forth from his own nature; it is on this point that all further thoughts about human rights are based. In his last pilgrimage to Mecca, Mohammed accentuated: "O mankind! We created you from a single (pair) of a male and a female, and made you into nations and tribes, that ye may know each other (not that ye may despise each other). Verily the most honoured of you in the sight of Allah is (he who is) the most righteous of you" (Qur'an 49:13).[2] At the same time, however, Islam emphasizes the sociability of man and his interrelations with politics, economics, and culture as a whole. It also underscores man's immediate link with and dependence upon God, denoting the relativity of the human will and submission to the divine will (Islam). Nevertheless, it makes a real criticism: since every man is essentially a slave of God, autonomous human value does not exist. Humanism is inconceivable for Islam if it is cut off from the eternal and deprived of any spiritual dimension; such a direction may lead to the deification of man, some Muslim thinkers underline.

Islam accepts the human dignity of followers of other monotheistic religions as well. It respects and protects the rights of the *dhimmis*—the non-Muslim protected ones. In certain cases, the Qur'an refers generally to non-Muslims, and in other instances, specifically to the followers of Jesus. In these Qur'anic verses, there appears at times a sympathy, while at other times a clear opposition (e.g., Qur'an 5:85). Elsewhere, it bitterly attacks both groups (Qur'an 5:56). Throughout the centuries, Muslim authorities were permitted to interpret each case according to their immediate interests and, therefore, had the possibility to act in accord with their own decision each time.

---

[2] All Qur'anic quotations are taken from The Presidency of Islamic Researches, IFTA, Call and Guidance, ed., *The Holy Qur'an: English Translation of the Meanings and Commentary* (Al-Madinah, Saudi Arabia: King Fahd Holy Qur'an Printing Complex, 1411 AH).

Islamic attitudes become severe and intolerant with polytheists and atheists (Qur'an 9). How will Islam deal with people outside any religious faith in Europe today? This remains a critical question for Muslim theological-legal thought. Nevertheless, Islam defines itself as "the religion of logic" and will surely look for a logical proposal corresponding to the modern situations in the world.

2. Christianity

As far as Christianity is concerned, official ecclesiastical circles in western Europe initially opposed the Declarations of Human Rights, mainly because they considered such efforts a fruit of humanist philosophy and antireligious tendencies. At the same time, though, many Christians tried to theologically justify these rights. The foundation of Christian anthropology originates, first, from the Old Testament verse, "He made him (the human being) in the likeness of God" (Gen. 5:1), and second, from the dogma of the Incarnation of the Divine Word, where Christ assumed the entire humanity. Here rests firmly the conception of, and the certainty for, the dignity of each human person. Throughout history, the church, with her dogma and worship, has preached and lived the biblical revelation that man is created in the image of God and ought to move towards His likeness; and that all humankind originated from a couple who was created by God (Acts 18:16). Therefore, all human beings, independent of race, color, language, and education, are endowed with the dignity of their divine origin.

While Western Christian religious thought gave emphasis to the mind, intellect, and will, Eastern Christian theology gave special emphasis to the elements of freedom and love, putting as its center of reference the love and communion of the three persons of the Holy Trinity. By taking on human nature, Christ, the second person of the Holy Trinity, bestowed upon every human being inestimable value, and secured personal freedom and dignity.

Love is the focal point from which Christians must see their responsibility at the local and universal levels. The freedom of love is not bound by the conviction of others. "Blessed is he who can love every man the same" (Maximos the Confessor). Christian love, by definition, has worldwide dimensions. No obstacle can suspend it, whether it be national or religious. When we accept the other human being and the other community respecting their freedom, and not forcing them to accept our own views, then we can feel at ease with the followers of different religious views, showing a deep respect for their human rights and a readiness to cooperate with them on the basis of mutual acceptance and support.

C. Responsible Citizens

European countries accept the Universal Declaration of Human Rights, the European Convention of Human Rights, and, in particular, the "Charter of Fundamental Rights of the European Union," the first one in the twenty-first century, which was proclaimed at Nice on 7 December 2000. Christians and Muslims in Europe enjoy many privileges as citizens, but they ought also to fulfill a concrete role and obligation to the countries where they live. Religious communities must be open to the society, offering the best that they can. The temptation to become ingrown clubs, focused on our own interest, remains a danger. What we receive from God, we must share with others, respecting their freedom.

In a pluralistic society, religious communities maintain a certain power, but they must be careful to avoid the temptation to identify religion with a particular political party. This can prompt them in a dangerous direction. Political parties are mixed with many other interests, and the rules of politics are quite different from the rules of religion. Religion must promote eternal values and not allow political programs and persons to use it for egotistical interests at the expenses of others. We must focus on how to make religious values instruments for a better society. Religion should promote freedom, justice, care for the creation, and respect for the freedom of conscience—for all, not only for those who belong to our religious group.

With our creative critiques and proposals, we can improve the formulation of various points in the International Documents on Human Rights, stressing social rights, special care for the poor, and respect for every human being, irrespective of what he/she believes or does not believe, and irrespective of racial or ethnic identity. The Universal Declaration of Human Rights and ensuing instruments are about important principles that we accept in general and reiterate, but which we are very far from implementing.

II. Basic Priorities for Today's Situation

A. Overcoming Every Form of Violence

The need to overcome violence in Europe as well as in the whole world is imperative. The World Council of Churches felt the necessity to declare the first decade of the new millennium as the "Decade to Overcome Violence" (2001–2010). This can become a priority for all Christian and Muslims, particularly in Europe.

Usually, those most prone to the temptation of violence are those who have power—whether it be political, financial, military, or administrative power. This is because they have the possibility to impose their intentions through various forms of manipulation, misinformation, electronic and human brainwashing, as well as through threats or attempts to buy off consciences.

Violence, however, is not only found where the mass media turns our attention. It also settles on smaller cities and communities—those thought to be safe. Violence often surprises us by its various forms of crime. It frightens us by destroying the human person through drugs, xenophobia, and racism. And, tragically, some people do not hesitate to bring religious slogans and arguments into this wild dance of violence. An essential thing to recognize, however, is that this virus of violence lurks within each one of us, and in critical moments, infects our relations with others. Let us take care not to minimize the aggression that hides within every human heart.

In the struggle to overcome violence, the religious communities can offer an essential contribution, such as principles of eternal value, a vision of peace and reconciliation, living examples, and the power of continuous self-criticism and renewal.

Please allow me to refer specifically to two cases from our own situation in Albania. In the first case, the church responded with a prophetic attitude. In the second case, she offered sincere love to the victims of violence. In 1997, when a horrifying anarchy engulfed the country, many Albanian families had the opportunity to acquire a Kalashnikov and use it to resist, or even to exert, violence. In those dramatic hours of statewide chaos and internal lawlessness, uncontrolled dark powers burst out from the hearts of countless people, including even the simplest people. As soon as an opportunity opened, those people did not hesitate to plunder hospitals, orphanages, and religious institutions, making victims of the sick, the elderly, and even innocent children. The church, newly raised after decades of violent persecution, raised her voice prophetically: "No more blood! No to the fighting! No to the arms! No to the hatred! . . . It is only with self-control, repentance, truth, forgiveness and reconciliation that substantial peace can be secured" (Public Appeal, 6 March 1997). And people of different convictions heard the church's voice with attention and respect.

We had not had time to recover, when in 1999, hundreds of thousands of victims of violence from Kosovo overran the country. The Orthodox Church rallied to embrace as many people as she could with practical love, never asking about their religious identity; knowing, in fact, that the majority of the refugees were Muslim. The church mobilized all her members, especially the youth and women. She motivated friends from all over the world, collecting more than twelve million dollars, and developed a very wide outreach of affectionate care that relieved the suffering of more than 30,000 refugees. While voices from several circles tried to add religious tones to the war in Kosovo, we protested strongly, saying repeatedly that, "No one has the right to use the holy oil of religion to intensify the flame of armed conflicts, but instead should use it as a divine gift to soothe the hearts, heal the wounds, and bring individuals and peoples together in peace" (13 March 1998).

B. Striving for Authentic Reconciliation and Sustainable Peace

Religion has been used in the past, during critical times, to strengthen national identity and resistance. Today, religious leaders and people should fulfil another high calling—to work, with enthusiasm and perseverance, for reconciliation among nations and peoples, and to establish a sustainable peace in Europe and in the entire world. The great common enemy is hatred, and it is this that we must face. Only through an intense and common effort can we hope to diminish and even heal this great disease. Like a serpent's venom, suspicion and hatred have poisoned the hearts of thousands of people. Authentic religious teaching and example can cultivate the only antidote to this danger—the antidote of forgiveness and love within the hearts of people. Sustainable peace cannot be established only with diplomatic and political negotiations, but will come mainly through the hard work of inspired people of faith, people who believe in the God of love and dedicate their lives to the struggle of creative initiatives for reconciliation and peace.

As we stressed in a meeting in Morges, Switzerland, in June 2001, when nineteen leaders from all the religious communities of the Former Yugoslav Republic of Macedonia gathered,

> peace is too important to leave only to the politicians. Peace is also a responsibility of the churches and of the religious communities. We strongly believe that answers to problems should always be sought with an open, constant dialogue, based on a complete, mutual respect for the differences and values of the other religious traditions and communities.

In a public appeal (24 June 1999), the Orthodox Church of Albania insisted that

> the different religious communities must draw from the deepest and most genuine layers of their teachings and traditions, becoming inspired workers of reconciliation and peace. We should take the initiative to build a free and just society that respects the religious freedom and particularity of the other. We must build a society where the other does not cease to be God's creation, and our own brother and sister, regardless of what he or she believes.

The people of faith in God are obliged to be peacemakers and agents of reconciliation within society. We have to give voice to those who have lost it through fear. We must protect the unprotected, fight for the peace and justice of God, and celebrate the "ministry of reconciliation." We must accentuate to all: No to hatred; no to misinformation; no to the persistence of old enmities. The borderline between good and evil cannot be found among persons, social groups or peoples. It is located within the heart of every human being. Therefore, it is necessary that the light of love penetrate the innermost folds of our conscience and thought.

C. Encouraging a Sincere Religious Dialogue

Christians and Muslims have been in various types of theological dialogue for centuries, starting from the Byzantine period.[3] During the last few decades, the need for a new, more objective dialogue among the followers of monotheistic religions has become more evident, and serious steps have already been realized. Interreligious dialogue can help to overcome misunderstandings and misinterpretations of the others' religious views and facilitate a better understanding of the serious points in the religious experience of other cultures and peoples. Concrete interreligious dialogue is not an abstract encounter between religious systems, but rather a meeting between human persons who share a common nature.

A dialogue that respects the religious principles and views of others does not imply syncretism and discoloration of our faith. To the contrary, genuine and fruitful interaction demands substantial knowledge of our faith, together with a continual living out of it in repentance, humility, and genuine love. "Perfect love casts out fear," (1 John 4:18) every kind of fear, and fills us with hope. The power of God's truth and love creates unexpected openings in the impasse. We are obliged to share with others the certainties and deepest spiritual experiences that God has freely given us. We should, however, not proceed in a pompous manner, but in simplicity and peace, with gratitude and knowledge, respecting all people and their freedom.

In our time, the process of globalization is creating new and urgent problems for humankind. It is imperative, therefore, that people of faith in God search together for reliable answers. From this perspective, the most practical issues for creative interreligious dialogue are those confronting humanity through the process of globalization—ecology, poverty, ethnic reconciliation, international justice, peace, etc.

---

[3] Anastasios Yannoulatos, "Der Dialog mit dem Islam aus orthodoxer Sicht," in *XLVI. Ökumenisches Symposion, 16. Oktober 1986 in Wien: Ein Laboratorium für die Einheit,* Pro Oriente no. 13, ed. R. Kirschläger and A. Stiernemann (Innsbruck: Tyrolia Verlag, 1991), 210–22.

Besides scholarly dialogue, we can also discern various important opportunities for a "dialogue of life" within the framework of multireligious societies. This last dialogue does not demand common agreement, but focuses on the acceptance of and respect for the religious freedom of others, and their right to choose their own ultimate visions and goals.

To abandon interreligious dialogue is to give new impetus to the formation of ghettos, the horror of religious cleansing, and the development of new expressions of religious fanaticism that ultimately lead to another terrible "dialogue"—the "dialogue" between terrorists' bombs and the rockets of the powerful. We all are obliged to live with one another in our own countries, as well as in this complex "global village" called Planet Earth.

D. Promoting a Constructive Religious Education

We, Christians and Muslims, have to promote these principles with a new style of religious education. Neglect of religious education creates deeper crises in the system of values. For instance, in many eastern European countries, slogans of utopian collectivism that prevailed in past years have been replaced by today's messages of egocentric capitalism. A particular reticence dominates, sometimes expressing itself as apathy and indifference, while at other times as escapism. Within this spiritual vacuum, the religious communities should strive to cultivate a faith in God and to open new spiritual horizons which will strengthen moral ideas and inner discipline, as well as to invigorate the endurance and creativity of the people.

We must work for a basic religious education curriculum in public schools. An argument often heard against this is that in a civic society with many religious communities, religion can divide the people. This is a pretext, however, from people who want to promote a style of social life that is indifferent to religion or belief, and therefore insist in pushing religion into the private sector. We have to resist this attitude which prevails in some postcommunist, eastern European countries. The religious commitment in a pluralistic society is not a threat, but can make a very positive contribution to stability and sustainable peace.

There is also an urgent need to rewrite many of our religious books, with an open mind about the past, and without the spirit of aggression and polemics. It should be possible to study certain themes together, and decide which cultural values and norms we can emphasize. This type of education has to be continued in the churches and mosques, as well as in the press and electronic media.

The special responsibility of religious leaders in a pluralistic society is to guide our people with this spirit of brotherly coexistence, not permitting various fundamentalist and extreme ideas to mislead our communities. If religion cultivates hatred, racism and xenophobia, it can be a terrible danger. Religion has a vital role in every society in that it can offer love and respect for the other.

This does not mean, of course, that we will be silent about the particularities of our religious beliefs and betray our own identity. To expose our own beliefs and the truths on which our lives are based is quite different from being aggressive toward others, distorting their views.

E. A Worldwide Responsibility

Christians and Muslims in Europe do not live in isolation apart from people of other continents. In our century, the process of globalization is bringing all the nations and peoples into economic and cultural interdependence. From the beginning both our religions have had a worldwide perspective, often thinking about globalization in terms of imposing our views on others. Today, this vision has radically changed. We are obliged to accept religious pluralism and proceed toward creative interreligious dialogue on many themes that confront us from new challenges coming from technology and science. Overcoming past misunderstandings and spending time together, we have to cultivate personal relations, contacts, and even friendships, among religious leaders.

People of faith in God in Europe can give to the whole world a model of peaceful coexistence. But too often we underscore human rights as long as we are minorities. But when we become majorities, we suddenly take on a different attitude—forgetting about the equal rights of people, the other faith, or life stance. Being responsible citizens of Europe, we are obliged to have a concern and care not only for our continent, but also for the global international reality, offering creative contribution and right judgement.

III. Conclusion

In summary, for a peaceful coexistence among the religious communities in Europe and a creative contribution to our pluralistic society, we Christians and Muslims have to search for and promote the principles of a healthy anthropology, drawing on the depths of the teachings of our religions and the best pages of our traditions, stressing the sincere respect for each human being, and the duty to overcome violence and work for reconciliation. Simultaneously, we are obliged to struggle for the development and prevalence of these principles through the ethos of the leadership and the education of the members of our communities.

In this way, we can contribute to a wider commonwealth of peace and solidarity in Europe that will secure justice and human dignity for every person, for every people, for every minority, and will lead to a deeper and more humane culture.

Chapter 31

Humanism and Freedom from Religion

Rajaji Ramanadha Babu Gogineni and Lars Gule

I. Humanist Beliefs and Religious Freedom

For Humanists, Humanism refers to a modern life stance rooted in rational thinking, providing a way of understanding our universe and our place in it in naturalistic terms, rather than in supernatural or theistic terms. As a philosophy of life, Humanism offers its adherents, both as individuals and as members of society, a secular ethic grounded in human values and in the human experience. As Humanists we are conscious of our common humanity and are impelled by a sense of the moral worth of *all* human beings. We want our actions to be guided by compassionate reason and the realization of humankind's common destiny. As Humanists we reject absolute authorities and revealed wisdoms; we promote free inquiry; we refuse to let custom replace conscience and reason; and we defend intellectual integrity. We are committed to responsible freedom of thought and action and to civilized law. Asserting the centrality of the human being, the Humanist proposes that the purpose of life is that which each of us gives to it.

As a philosophy for the human being, Humanism tries to help answer, as best as possible, the great questions of life: Who are we? What are we? How did the universe come about? What is the good life? And so on. Are these questions religious? Do Humanists become religious when they try to answer them? And is Humanism a religion because it helps answer these questions?

No doubt Humanists are trying to answer some of the questions that traditionally religion has attempted to answer. But philosophy is not theology, and Humanism is not religion. While Humanists might be engaged in the same questions as religion, our interest is in the eternal questions rather than in the alleged eternal answers traditional religion offers. Humanism is nothing if it is not an open-ended and continuous interrogation about our life and the universe. As an enterprise of questions rather than of answers, it is the pursuit of truth that is important for Humanism, not its possession.

These Humanist beliefs and approaches to life raise particular problems with respect to Humanists' right to religious freedom or freedom of belief. Because of their emphasis on the questions rather than the answers, Humanists find that an environment conducive

Tore Lindholm, W. Cole Durham, Jr., Bahia G. Tahzib-Lie (eds.), Facilitating Freedom of Religion or Belief: A Deskbook, *699–719.*

to the continuous asking of questions is important, something they find is not encouraged by organized and traditional religions. As the Humanists' beliefs and attitudes often contradict the dogmatic and absolute answers provided by the various religions, this sets them in opposition to traditional religious attitudes.

Nevertheless, Humanists, like religious people, are interested in Truth, and in knowing the ultimate nature of reality. But we understand that "Truth is the content of Knowledge,"[1] and we look upon science as the means to obtain such knowledge. As science is the extension of free thought to the domain of knowledge, Humanists are convinced that science's self-correcting approach is the best way of getting closer to Truth. We therefore insist that any account of nature must pass the tests of scientific evidence. Science empowers us by explaining and by demonstrating our capability to fathom the depths of the universe, and thereby adds to the dignity and self-worth of humankind. Knowledge is directly connected to freedom—unless we understand our position and place in the universe, we will not understand our limitations or the scope of our freedom. Human freedom is best advanced and defended within a democratic system, which alone recognizes the equal worth of all human beings. These ideas, then, sum up the Humanist worldview or the Humanist life stance.

Broadly, in the field of freedom of religion or belief (FORB), the challenge in the modern world as Humanists see it is to establish a tolerant environment for free inquiry where all life stances, whether secular or religious, can find room to flourish in peaceful competition. However, in a world dominated by competing religious worldviews, for Humanists to preserve the equal freedoms and liberties they are entitled to along with the religious, freedom *from* religion in the public sphere is crucial for living their own ideals.

How can this be achieved in practice? The challenge is related to several more specific issues that again are linked to how the state in different countries recognizes, protects, and supports various religious organizations in general and (organized) Humanism in particular. And it is also related to how civil society is ordered and the degree of tolerance that exists in this sphere of society.

In the following we seek further to describe Humanism's relationship with various religions and what kind of protection international norms on freedom of religion or belief offer Humanists. However, the main part of the analysis will be on the observed lack of equality between religious and secular life stances and the lack of recognition of the right to freedom *from* religion. Impediments to the free practice of Humanism will be described and discussed with the view of overcoming them.

II. Humanism and Religion

"I am pleased to see that Humanists stand for something positive, and to discover that they do not merely oppose religion," a participant at a conference organized by the International Humanist and Ethical Union (IHEU) said to one of the authors in Oslo in 2001. The conference theme was "Towards a Secular Society," and apart from distinguished Humanists, human rights activists, and academics from over a dozen countries, representatives from the Norwegian Lutheran State Church and from other faiths, as well

[1] M. N. Roy, *New Humanism: A Manifesto* (Calcutta: Renaissance, 1953).

as homosexual communities, participated in the deliberations. Indeed, the friend who made the comment was a female leader of the Islamic community in one of the Scandinavian countries.

In times past, such a cordial dialogue in a human rights context among religious representatives and Humanists was impossible, and the presence of a woman at an important meeting like this unthinkable. After all, Hinduism as well as the three Abrahamic religions of Judaism, Christianity, and Islam considered women inferior to men: physically, morally, and intellectually. Nor was the concept of equality—in relation to gender, race, and social status—a familiar one to traditional religions. It may be recalled that in 1829, a bishop warned Britain's House of Lords of divine retribution if it granted civic rights to Jews.[2] In Norway, Jews were only granted access to the realm with the change of the constitution in 1851, and Jesuits were barred from establishing themselves in the country until another change of the constitution in 1956. In the 1840s, American Methodism split, north against south, in an argument about whether God's word condemned slavery or justified it. And still, in spite of official attempts to eradicate the practice of untouchability and to reform the caste system, Hinduism in many ways continues to be based on the strictly hierarchical caste system, and the contemporary resurgence of Islam in many places has reduced the historically achieved rights and social status of women, and eliminated them in countries like Afghanistan and the Sudan. It may also be recalled that in Europe it took several centuries after the Protestant Reformation before a modicum of toleration and peaceful coexistence among religions was agreed upon by Christian churches.

We believe the historical record shows that Humanists and Rationalists of the Age of Enlightenment were pivotal in laying the foundation of modern human rights, and we believe that most of the recent gains in human rights and freedoms can be traced directly to the liberating power of Humanist ideas and principles.[3] Indeed, the dark ages in human history were the periods when religion was at its height. As the iron grip of religion was loosened, rationality and critical intelligence advanced, and human freedom progressed. There is a clear link between knowledge, rationalism, morality, and human liberty. "The concept of liberty comprises the values of freedom as well as of rationalism. A person cannot have liberty unless he is self-reliant, and he cannot be self-reliant unless he has faith in his own reason. Thus liberty is not possible except on the basis of rationalism. Self-sustained morality is also essential if a person is to be free and moral at the same time."[4]

However, we would like to clarify that while Humanists have always been in opposition to all forms of tyranny and bigotry, and have consistently defended the dignity of the human being against all attempts to control minds, bodies, and societies, Humanism is not just a reaction to regressive religion or primitive social structures and hierarchies: it is about creating a positive philosophy of life for human beings, and about trying to make freedom a reality for all human beings.

---

[2] In England, it was not until 1858 that Parliament was freely opened to the Jews by the suppression of the clause "On the true faith of a Christian" from the oath of office, and not until 1870 that all restrictions for every position (except that of sovereign) in the British Empire were abolished.

[3] For somewhat different historical assessments, see the chapters by Evans and by Swidler in this volume.

[4] V. M. Tarkunde, ***Radical Humanism: The Philosophy of Freedom and Democracy*** (Delhi: Ajanta Publishers, 1983).

Since human liberties are an undivided whole, a threat to one form of liberty implies a danger to other liberties as well. As defenders and promoters of *all* human freedoms and rights, on a global level, Humanists will continue their work in the domain of religion as well as the other sectors of human life. If we confine ourselves to freedom of religion or belief, which is the subject we are addressing here, despite obvious and welcome progress, the situation in many parts of the world is still depressing. Humanity undergoes uneven progress and in several parts of the world the protection of universal standards of human rights is severely underdeveloped. For example, there is the glaring insanity of Islamic fundamentalists in Afghanistan, the barbaric blasphemy laws in Pakistan, the newly resurgent Hindu cultural nationalism, the religio-tribal conflicts in Africa and in eastern Europe, the sectarian divisiveness of Northern Ireland, and the present Roman Catholic pope (as well as other Christian, Jewish, Muslim, and Hindu religious leaders) who cannot accept homosexuals on an equal footing with other human beings. All these examples represent clear dangers for the future of human freedoms.

III. International Human Rights Instruments

Are Humanists, then, entitled to the protection of their beliefs and life stance on an equal footing with traditional religions? In many national legal systems the answer is no. This unequal footing is clear from both the law and the practice of various countries, but what does international law and human rights say about this?

International declarations and conventions establish the same rights for theistic and nontheistic life stances. The rights of Humanists are clearly covered under article 18 of the Universal Declaration of Human Rights (UDHR). These rights have been followed up in article 18 of the UN Covenant on Civil and Political Rights. Furthermore, the UN Human Rights Committee has elaborated on this in its comments:

> 1. The right to freedom of thought, conscience and religion (which includes the freedom to hold beliefs) in article 18.1 is far-reaching and profound; it encompasses freedom of thought on all matters, personal conviction and the commitment to religion or belief, whether manifested individually or in community with others. The Committee draws the attention of States parties to the fact that the freedom of thought and the freedom of conscience are protected equally with the freedom of religion and belief. The fundamental character of these freedoms is also reflected in the fact that this provision cannot be derogated from, even in time of public emergency, as stated in article 4.2 of the Covenant.
>
> 2. Article 18 protects theistic, non-theistic and atheistic beliefs, as well as the right not to profess any religion or belief. The terms "belief" and "religion" are to be broadly construed. Article 18 is not limited in its application to traditional religions or to religions and beliefs with institutional characteristics or practices analogous to those of traditional religions. The Committee therefore views with concern any tendency to discriminate against any religion or belief for any reason, including the fact that they are newly established, or represent religious minorities that may be the subject of hostility on the part of a predominant religious community.[5]

[5] UN Human Rights Committee General Comment 22 (1993) to ICCPR art. 18, in *Religion and Human Rights: Basic Documents*, Tad Stahnke and J. Paul Martin, eds. (New York: Columbia University, 1998), 92–95.

Thus it seems clear that secular beliefs are protected in the same way as religious beliefs. This is an important insight not yet recognized by some governments that only nominally recognize the human right to freedom of religion or belief. However, this does not mean that the recognition of secular life stances on a par with religious ones would solve all problems. There is also a potential for conflict between freedom of religion and freedom from religion. For example, as Dr. Victor Gunasekara, Australia, points out,

> Articles 5 and 6 of the UN Declaration on Elimination of All Forms of Intolerance and Discrimination Based on Religion or Belief (1981) specify the freedoms given to religions: therein Art. 6(b) gives the freedom to maintain charitable and humanitarian institutions. As such, institutions can be maintained by anyone—so they should not be regarded as a religious freedom. "Charitable" institutions could be used as a means of proselytizing. Art 6(e) allows teaching in "suitable" places, leaving the religion to decide where it is suitable. Religions can abuse this and make a public nuisance as when sermons are broadcast over public address systems. Art 6(f) allows "voluntary" contributions, but it is known that many contributions are solicited which are less than voluntary. These freedoms cannot be denied to any group calling itself a religion, but the word religion is not defined anywhere. Art 5 gives parents the unfettered right to impose their religious views on the child. The child's own views, or even the capability of the child to form a view of its own, is not considered.[6]

Dr. Gunasekara also mentions female genital mutilation and male genital mutilation as not having received adequate attention in FORB instruments, and points out that the explicit reference to "the freedom to change his religion or belief" in the UDHR is absent in subsequent declarations, presumably because of pressure from Islamic states. Article 1 of the 1981 Declaration of course recognizes everyone's "freedom to have a religion or whatever belief of his choice" and this implies the right to change one's religion; nevertheless, the omission of the explicit wording is curious to say the least.[7]

IV. Impediments to the Free Practice of Humanism

Impediments to the free practice of Humanism fall into roughly three categories:

- Lack of freedom of religion or belief in general
- Lack of freedom of secular belief on an equal footing with religious beliefs
- Lack of freedom from religion in the public domain

Humanists share the first, and the most serious, category of problems with other beliefs and life stances. This is the general topic of the present book and therefore we do not need to make a special analysis in this chapter; suffice it to say that this is the most important and acute impediment to the free exercise of Humanism, as can be seen in a number of cases, from Saudi Arabia to Pakistan, from China to Cuba, and from Poland to Israel. Organized Humanists will be a part of the international efforts to strengthen the freedoms of religion or belief in general.

---

6 *Queensland Humanist* 34, no. 1 (January 2000), available online at <http://www.uq.net.au/slsoc/manussa/qh_jan00.htm#art2>. For more on children and FORB see the chapter by Sheen in this volume.

7 The gradual weakening of language in international provisions on the right to change one's religion or belief is reported and discussed in section II.B of the chapter by Ghanea in this volume.

The second and third categories of problems are more unique to Humanists. There are many examples of the second category of problems: the official Indonesian requirement to believe in a god,[8] the rejection in many Muslim countries of non-Abrahamic beliefs, and the lack of official recognition of and support for Humanist groups and organizations on an equal footing with religious groups as seen in Sweden and Slovakia. The third category of problems is found, on the one hand, in countries that do not recognize secular life stances, and on the other hand, in countries that do recognize such life stances but maintain, for example, a state church and/or religious education in the public schools. These two sets of problems need further discussion.

A. Lack of Freedom of Secular Belief on an Equal Footing with Religious Belief

The lack of recognition of Humanism as a life-stance on an equal footing with religious worldviews can have various consequences depending on the situation in the individual state. In some instances it is an expression of a fundamental lack of freedom of religion or belief as when only certain religions are recognized. This is the case in many Muslim countries where Islam is the state religion and only the other Abrahamic religions are tolerated. But this is also the case in China where the authorities have accepted and registered only five religions with the State Administration for Religious Associations (SARA). In these cases, the establishment of a new religious grouping has been met with persecution, as is the case of the Falun Gong, which has experienced much harassment and harsh persecution from the Chinese authorities.

The lack of recognition of Humanism as an organized life-stance can also have consequences, though less dramatic. This is the case in Sweden where organized Humanists are not recognized on an equal footing with the various religious denominations. In Sweden, discrimination results in a lack of the same kind of financial support that is allotted to the religious communities. However, the state does not prevent the Humanists from maintaining an organization and publishing their own journal (or otherwise participating in public life). But the lack of recognition results in an unacceptable discrimination of a life-stance that has the same right to protection as religious beliefs, according to the international human rights standards (cf. section III above).

The case of Sweden is lamentable because it seems to be the result of an oversight more than a deliberate policy. According to information obtained by one of this chapter's authors during a "fact-finding mission" to Stockholm,[9] Swedish authorities did not even consider secular life-stances when they established their current system of support for religious communities in the 1990s. The most important reason for this "oversight" is probably the fact that organized Humanists in Sweden are few. However, the whole point of human rights and nondiscrimination provisions is that they oblige authorities to consider the interests of even the smallest of minorities. Furthermore, while the organized Humanists in Sweden are a small minority, a vast number of people in the country are in fact quite secular. Nevertheless, while several adults abandon religion,

[8] For recent modifications, see section IV.B of the chapter by Swidler in this volume.
[9] In April 2001.

the fact that they were baptized as infants leads the church to claim these adults as their own, in some instances making financial claims on the state in the name of these nonpracticing persons who still figure on their register.

The situation in Sweden is not unique. Especially in the newly emerging democracies of eastern Europe there is a lack of understanding of how broadly the freedom of religion or belief is to be interpreted. In many instances it seems that a secular life-stance is seen as synonymous with the ideology of the former communist regimes. With no love lost for the former regimes' once canonized beliefs, Humanism is also penalized. Both the international Humanist movement and the governments of these countries have a responsibility to clarify this misunderstanding.[10] In addition, the governments will have the obligation to ensure both the protection and equal recognition of Humanism on a par with religious beliefs.

Lack of state recognition of Humanism is often followed by a lack of understanding of Humanism's legitimate interests in the public school system. With no recognition (and protection where this is required), Humanism is overlooked with regards to religious education in public schools. This "oversight" can take two forms, which may coexist. The first form is deficient presentation in religious education curriculums of Humanism as a possible life stance. The second form is a lack of understanding for Humanists' demand for freedom from religion in the school system (cf. below).

Such lack of government recognition of Humanism can easily spill over to other spheres of society. One consequence can be a lack of media attention to Humanism and Humanist ideals and positions, and a further consequence can be the lack of necessary toleration for Humanism among the general public.

B. Lack of Freedom from Religion in the Public Domain

It might seem like a contradiction that Humanists demand, on the one hand, recognition and even financial support from the authorities, and, on the other, freedom from religion in the public domain. However, the contradiction is only apparent, and the demands are coherent.

For a state to fulfil its obligation under international law to secure freedom of religion or belief for all citizens, the state should be neutral towards, and treat equally, all religious and belief communities. Furthermore, beliefs that cannot flourish on the strength of their inherent appeal are not worth preserving; values that are upheld by state-imposed coercion rather than by personal conviction forfeit their ethical quality as pointed out by Dr. Johan van der Vyver.[11] Life-stance communities must therefore take

[10] And a misunderstanding it is as the International Humanist and Ethical Union (IHEU) was itself established as a post–WW II reaction with the specific purpose of counteracting all totalitarian ideologies including Fascism, Nazism, and Communism. The founding document describes Humanism as "dedication to and responsibility for human life by maintenance, furtherance and development of human values, cultivation of science, loyalty to democratic principles and repudiation of authoritarian principles in all social relations, and practice of good faith, without reliance upon authority or dogma." The statement is repeated in the first paragraph of IHEU bylaws (as amended by the General Assembly on 3–4 May 2000, Los Angeles, USA); available online at <http://www.iheu.org/IHEU_bylaws.htm>.

[11] Johan van der Vyver, "Religious Freedom and Proselytism: Ethical, Political and Legal Dimensions," paper presented at the Oslo Conference on Freedom of Religion or Belief, August 1998.

the lead in renouncing any privileges of their own: they must stop looking at themselves as merely subjects of the right to religion or belief and rise to be "the wardens of such freedoms." A nonreligious state does not promote nonbelief; it assures neutrality. Accordingly, Humanists do not seek to establish Humanism as a new official creed in any state.

It is beyond a state's competence to judge the truth claims of any religion, and states are morally and legally obliged to protect the free exercise of the freedom of conscience. This freedom includes the right to express oneself freely without hindrance and to persuade others to one's own point of view through proper, peaceable means.[12] Though states have no business passing judgements on the competing truth claims of religions or belief systems they do, however, have the moral duty to foster common values, as for example, those expressed in international human rights, which may sometimes call for an interventionist role in reforming certain societies and practices. For example, in the hierarchical Hindu society or in other societies where religiously legitimated exploitation might occur, mere neutrality will not suffice—the state must play a constructive role, offer positive discrimination to the disadvantaged, and remedy the wrongs. While some might see this as an example of state intervention based on Humanist values, it is actually based on human rights values, which is the closest the world has come to common values. Humanists wholeheartedly endorse these values but do not claim any monopoly on human rights or on the human values that are the foundation of these rights.

For this reason Humanists seek to move states with a historically rooted, religious bias in the direction of life-stance neutrality. As stated earlier, this does not in our eyes have to be a value-neutral state. We hold human rights and similar norms embodied in international law to be binding on every state in the contemporary world and see no need for deriving their compelling moral status from other sources. No state, and no individual, can escape this global, universal obligation.

When state neutrality is lacking one, and most often a religious,[13] life stance will predominate in the public sphere to the detriment of other worldviews. Not only will it favor the employment prospects of persons belonging to the privileged denomination, but it can also prevent citizens' access to important services left by the state to the dominant religion to administer, such as arranging marriages, which determine the civil status of the citizens (cf. below). Therefore, the lack of freedom from religion in the public domain can become a serious problem not only for Humanists but for other life stances.

Of course, any state's public display of adherence to a religious dogma, as for example the religious motto "In God we trust" printed on US currency notes, violates a right to freedom from religion.[14] In this case the problem may easily be remedied, in

[12] See the chapter by Stahnke in this volume.

[13] This is not overlooking the secular ideologies of so-called communist states.

[14] Originally the New Jersey cent of 1786, as well as the 1795 coins struck at the United States Mint, bore the motto "E Pluribus Unum," which was first proposed in a design for the great seal of the United States that Thomas Jefferson first presented unsuccessfully to the US Congress in 1776. But the post–Civil War religious fanaticism saw the ascendance of President Lincoln's handpicked appointee James Pollock, who became director of the US Mint. Pollock believed that the United States must become an official theocracy, and he was crucial in the attempt to Christianize American coins. "In God We Trust" was first

theory, by designing new currency bills. But litigation in American courts of law has thus far brought no change. Other particular traditions penetrate the social fabric of a given society, such as religious holidays that are protected by law in many countries. Can they be de-secularized? Do Humanists demand a new French Revolution with a new and nonreligious way of counting days and holidays?

We do not see a need for such radical "solutions." It is possible to live well with a reinterpretation of traditions. Christmas for example is based on pre-Christian solstice festivals and ceremonies and can be celebrated without a religious content if one so wishes by going back to the original traditions from which Christianity borrowed. The important thing is that the state in its laws and regulations does not impute a religious meaning to the holidays.

When religions that are new to a country become established, they might raise the demand for new holidays for religious purposes. An example could be a demand for Friday as a day off for prayer and religious ceremonies for Muslims in the Christian-dominated Europe. It might seem that such a demand would be just, in view of Sunday being a Christian holiday. However, such questions can probably not be settled in a fully just way, i.e., with full regard for the equality of all beliefs, because of the practical and nonreligious issues related to days of work and days of rest. Thus, in practical life history, tradition and majority opinion (as well as laws and labor market agreements) are relevant factors to consider. Nevertheless, the state as well as civil society (especially industry and the business community) should be flexible in their response to such demands.

Humanists have no special demands in this respect and can enjoy the consequences of expanded leisure time regardless of whether this expansion follows religious demands or the success of organized labor.

Many constitutions make reference to general or specific religious dogmas. Sometimes this is followed up in laws regulating specific institutions. In Norway the law establishes a religious purpose for a number of public institutions, such as public schools. For practical purposes, children of Muslims, Buddhists, Jews, Catholics, Humanists, etc., are forced into an educational system geared to giving children "a Christian and moral education" of Evangelical-Lutheran proclivity.[15]

The issue of freedom from religion might be said to be most important with respect to children. When there is religious instruction in schools, even when it is neutral with respect to the various religious denominations, the basis is most often the religious paradigm as such, i.e., the presumption that there is a god or a divine realm. Thus, the fundamental religious dogma, even if in a generalized and "neutral" form, as the pedagogical basis for instruction about religions, still represents an infringement of Humanists' rights to raise their children in the spirit of free inquiry. Again, this leads to the state-sanctioned imposition of a life stance on young citizens, albeit a general one.

---

used on the bronze two-cent piece issued from 1864 to 1873. In 1908, under Theodore Roosevelt, Congress passed a bill that ensured that the motto "In God We Trust" would be present on all gold and silver coins. With Lyndon B. Johnson's 1955 bill, that became law without much discussion, and the motto was used on paper currency as well. In 1956, in the midst of the McCarthy era, a law was passed by Congress that made "In God We Trust" the national motto as well.

[15] See section III.B in the chapter by Plesner in this volume.

V. State and Civil Society Impediments to the Free Practice of Humanism

The general problems related to the lack of freedom of secular belief not being recognized and protected on an equal footing with religious beliefs, and the lack of freedom from religion in the public domain, deserve a more detailed analysis. In the subsequent paragraphs we will look closer at the following areas:

- Religious states
- Unjust laws
- Taxes
- State schools
- Children's rights
- Ceremonies and counseling
- Media
- Civil society

The sections that follow do not represent a comprehensive analysis of the problems but afford a number of illustrative examples and a discussion of possible approaches and solutions.

A. Religious States

Several constitutions mention, or appeal to, God in their preambles. This is of course not surprising with regards to explicitly religious states like the Islamic Republic of Iran. However, such references are found in the constitutions and laws of a number of modern and seemingly secular states. In 1994, triggered by the proposed inclusion of God in the preamble to the German constitution, the IHEU issued the following statement:

> In the view of IHEU the proposed reference to God in the constitution, like every other religious connection in the constitution, is contrary to articles 2 and 3 in the [1981] Declaration. . . . By linking state legislation to an exclusively religious belief, the superiority of religious beliefs over non-religious beliefs is implied . . . it is essential for society that the state treats all its citizens as equal before the law and that it respects the principles of freedom of conscience and toleration of dissenting viewpoints. If it is to fulfil these functions the constitution must not favour the ideology, religion or worldview of some of the state's citizens over the worldview of others. Nor should it seek to establish a religion, thus violating the separation of church and state. . . . Making the state independent of any particular religion or ideology has been an important step in the democratic progress of many countries. . . . The IHEU cautions against putting this progress in jeopardy by giving in to the pressure from religious groups.[16]

In many cases the reason for the mention or invocation of God in the preambles of constitutions is historical. Out of respect for tradition these references are not changed. However, Humanists find that appeal to tradition is a bad argument and often invocation is not only nominal. Too frequently they still have practical consequences in spite of

[16] This and other Resolutions of the IHEU General Assembly and Board, 1952–1993, are available online at <http://www.iheu.org/resolutions/iheu_resolutions.htm>.

constitutional amendments or special laws that guarantee the freedom of religion for all citizens. In England the Queen, the Head of State, also continues to be Head of the Church of England. In Norway the favored position of the Evangelical-Lutheran State Church includes a constitutional requirement that 50% of cabinet ministers must be members of that church! In Poland and some other eastern European countries the influence of the church, also on state affairs, is so great that the real separation of church and state seems to be a distant goal.

This paradoxical and contradictory situation is clearly seen in the situation in Greece. The current constitution established in 1975, in article 13, paragraphs 1 and 2, guarantees religious freedom as an individual right, and also guarantees religious tolerance. Furthermore, article 4 of the constitution guarantees the legal equality of all Greeks. Thus the state should be obliged to offer every religious community full autonomy with regard to its practices as far as these do not contravene public law. This freedom, however, needs to be viewed relative to the constitution's article 3, which recognizes the Christian Eastern Orthodox Church as Greece's "dominant" religion and hails "Our Lord Jesus Christ" as "its head."[17] In this way, intentionally or unintentionally, the state and the law maker in Greece is identified with the dominant religion, without regard for the fact that within the Greek populace there are individuals of other faiths or religions as well as atheists and the irreligious.[18] This creates difficulties for other religious groups as well as for Humanists who will have great problems in obtaining the necessary recognition by the state. This state of affairs has however, until recently, also created more serious problems. In keeping with the dominant religion's position in state and society, Greek citizens have been required to have their religious affiliation inscribed on the official identity cards. In this way the individual's right to privacy has been violated.[19]

The State of Israel is more often than not seen as secular state. However, over the last two to three decades, religious influences have increased markedly and have exposed the religious basis of the state. Israel was established as a Jewish state in 1948, albeit by a secular nationalist movement (Zionism). The state has no constitution but only a number of fundamental laws that has resulted in a patchwork of laws and practices, which can be difficult to grasp.

> There is a division of labour between the civil and the religious courts of law in Israel. The religious courts of law governed by each religious community have jurisdiction in cases concerning personal status, such as marriage and divorce. For the Jewish population the Rabbinical Courts have the responsibility for these cases. Similarly, Muslims and Christians have their religious courts. What is not adequately provided for is secular people's right to have a civil judicial system to which they can turn in matters concerning personal status. The inhabitants are therefore forced to identify and register according to one of the religious communities in Israel, and there is no non-religious alternative in matters of personal status.[20]

---

[17] See Forum 18, *Freedom of Religion: A Report With Special Emphasis on the Right to Choose Religion and Registration Systems* (Oslo: n.p., 2001), 63. (Forum 18 is a Norwegian network of representatives from different NGOs devoted to the promotion of freedom of religion or belief.)

[18] Ibid.

[19] Ibid., 64. The situation has changed, despite protests from the Orthodox Church, because of EU requirements.

[20] Ibid., 69.

The situation in Israel has been characterized as a mixture of "non-intervention in religious affairs" and "interpenetration of religion and Government."[21] The UN Human Rights Committee has expressed concern about the "preference given to the Jewish religion in the allocation of funding for religious bodies."[22] Equality between the different religious communities in this respect is not practiced to a satisfying degree, and a 1995 plan to improve the situation has not yet been implemented.[23] Thus, the religious bias of the state is borne out in everyday practice, creating a situation in which it is more than difficult to be a secular or Humanist citizen. In addition to the institutional preference for Jews, there is a lack of protection for the non-Jewish or secular citizen from the harassment instigated by Jewish religious leaders and groups.

In the Israeli election campaign in the fall of 2000, Ehud Barak, then Prime Minister, attempted to launch a secular revolution to diminish the influence of religion on the state and Israeli society. Humanists viewed this initiative with favor. However, the outcome of the 2001 election prevented the implementation of the secular reforms proposed by Barak. Thus, because of the state's religious character, the situation for the nonreligious and Humanists in Israel remains difficult.

The situation is not much better in the emerging Palestinian state, currently known as the Palestinian Authority (PA). The area under Palestinian self-rule is regulated by a number of laws, ranging from Ottoman and Mandate times to current Jordanian and Egyptian laws. The Palestinian Legislative Council passed a Palestinian Basic Law in 1997, but it was not signed by President Arafat and has therefore not come into force. The Basic Law proposes that Islam be recognized as the official religion but will also guarantee freedom of worship to adherents of other faiths.[24] While this is not an indication that the Palestinians, under the leadership of Yassir Arafat, are moving in a more Islamist direction, it is a clear expression of traditional religious influences. While the suggestion that Islam be the official religion of a future state does not represent a violation of religious freedom (in a narrow legalistic sense), as long as the law provides equality and nondiscrimination for all religious and nonreligious groups, Humanists see this as a regrettable lack of state neutrality in life-stance matters. Furthermore, the PA has failed to address the *millet* system which requires that citizens be affiliated with some religion. A person's religious affiliation must be declared on identification papers and constitutes a condition for his or her entering into marriage and other civil arrangements. Hence, a Humanist identity is not a viable option for the individual. Moreover, it is generally unacceptable to declare atheism in public, and the Palestinian police have little experience in or training for protecting the human rights of individuals. The mandatory declaration of one's religious affiliation is certainly an infringement of the right to privacy. But the matter is more serious as the political system in the Palestinian areas is based on quotas for different religious communities. The majority of seats in the legislative council are reserved for Sunni Muslims, and there is no opportunity to seek public office for declared Humanists—again because of the religious "foundations" of the emerging state. There is no reason to think that this situation will improve in the short run, in view of the increasing influence of fundamentalist Islamist groups, especially Hamas.

---

[21] Ibid.

[22] UN Human Rights Committee Concluding Observations: Israel, 8 August 1998, UN Doc. CCPR/C/79/Add.93, para. 28; as quoted in Forum 18, *Freedom of Religion*, 72.

[23] Ibid.

[24] Legal documents pertaining to the Palestinian Authority may be found online at <www.lawsociety.org>.

While a country like Sweden began the process of disestablishing the State Church in the 1990s, in a large number of states in several parts of the world where religion is made, or maintained as, the foundation of the polity the situation is still clearly unacceptable. With the exception of those of the privileged faith, religiously based or influenced states are prone to violate the rights of all other citizens. Therefore, Humanists ought to find allies among all religions in our struggle against religious states.

B. Unjust Laws

Even though Australia has no State Church (but God is mentioned in the constitution), it has a blasphemy law on the statute book just as the UK does. In mainland Europe, blasphemy laws are in force in Germany, Austria, and in the Scandinavian countries. In countries like India and Bangladesh there are regulations relating to "disrespecting religious sentiments." Relic of the colonial law, such legislation has often been deployed to infringe on the right to legitimate criticism, free inquiry, or artistic expression. In Indonesia, belief in God is constitutionally required. More unjust and barbaric are the blasphemy laws in Saudi Arabia or Pakistan (and some other Islamic countries), where the "offence" is punishable by death.[25] The IHEU has vigorously campaigned for Humanist Taslima Nasrin, who had to flee Bangladesh when charged with blasphemy, for the reform of blasphemy laws in Pakistan and for the liberation of Dr. Shaikh, a Humanist sentenced to death on the grounds that he "blasphemed" merely by saying that the Prophet Muhammad and his parents could not have been Muslims before the revelation of the Koran.

Humanists hold blasphemy laws to be undesirable and redundant relics of unjust religious privilege, having no legitimate entitlement under modern human rights regimes. Normally, laws against obscenity, slander, defamation, etc., already exist, and these can be applied without explicit reference to religion. Blasphemy laws are also discriminatory when referring only to one religion. In the UK, for example, they apply only to blasphemy of Christianity. Such laws can also easily be used to prohibit legitimate and rational criticism of religious beliefs and practices, as well as to limit artistic freedom. This is a serious impediment to the growth of human knowledge. Humanists desire both free inquiry and the free dissemination of knowledge, regardless of the implied criticism of religious dogmas; hence they are at special risk of being persecuted by blasphemy laws.

On the other hand, in many Islamic countries, the right to change religion is not accepted as a necessary corollary of freedom of religion or belief—while it is easy to opt into Islam, repudiation of faith by a Muslim may be punished by death. Similar treatment is reserved for heretics.[26]

In a number of countries a contradictory situation has emerged. For example, in the 1973 Constitution of Pakistan freedom of religion is guaranteed as a fundamental right under article 20: "every citizen shall have the right to profess, practice and propagate his religion." Pakistan was early a staunch supporter of the Universal Declaration of Human Rights where article 18 gives the right to change religion, and in the earlier

---

[25] The 1860 Blasphemy Law was modified in 1926 before Pakistan was born, and again in independent Pakistan in 1986 and in 1991 when criminal law was Islamicized.

[26] See the chapter by Ghanea in this volume.

decades of Pakistan's history the law and the bureaucracy generally upheld this right.[27] In two earlier constitutions the freedom to change religion was, if not explicitly, at least implicitly granted. In the 1956 constitution, part II 18 (a) states: "every citizen has the right to profess, practice and propagate any religion." The 1962 constitution kept the same wording. Now, if every citizen has the right to profess, practice and propagate any religion he would also have the right to change his religion. In the present constitution of Pakistan, however, the wording "his religion" does not imply the right to convert from Islam to another religion, since that is explicitly prohibited in the Shari'ah. Thus, the religious influences on law and practice in Pakistan seriously violate the freedom of religion or belief.

Laws that protect religious beliefs and sentiments can easily lend themselves to be used against Humanists. For many believers any nonreligious position is blasphemous and unacceptable. In order to change this culture of intolerance, governments should repeal unjust laws and provide equal protection for Humanists and other nonbelievers.

C. Taxes

The Australian Humanist Association submitted to their government the suggestion that although a sound case can be made for all charities and nonprofit organizations to receive special tax allowances, these allowances should not be extended to cover religions—just because they are "religious." Religions that are organized as nonprofit organizations or charities would automatically qualify anyway. At present, religions benefit from special tax arrangements even when they conduct profitable businesses. This situation is both unethical and anticompetitive. For these reasons special benefits determined solely on the basis of religion should cease.

In many countries "church taxes" are collected even from nonmembers. This is a grossly unfair situation. In some countries, like Norway, this situation is compensated by public financial support, on a proportional basis, for the "unofficial" religions and the secular life stance of Humanism. However, in order to benefit from such reallocation schemes, it is usually necessary to be a member of a registered religious community. Therefore, without a system of refunding for nonorganized people, even the Norwegian system represents an "injustice" to nonorganized Humanists or irreligious people.

A different situation occurs in Sweden, where, as explained earlier, organized Humanists are not recognized on an equal footing with the various religious denominations. Therefore, they are currently not eligible for public financial support. The result is an unacceptable discrimination against a life stance community that has the right to equal protection and treatment.

In matters of taxation, it would seem impossible to establish a 100% fair system of redistribution and public support for life stance organizations. Thus, governments, religious organizations, and organized Humanists will have to enter into a continuous dialogue that takes historical precedents into consideration, in order to establish and develop a system of taxes and refunds that is as fair as possible. What has to be avoided, of course, is a system that flagrantly favors one specific religious community.

---

[27] Forum 18, *Freedom of Religion,* 56.

D. State Schools

Another area of contention is the public school, where battles concerning the freedom of religion or belief have been fought with much emotion and controversy. Education is preparation for life in society, and the school education system must prepare children for their complex responsibilities in a multicultural and pluralistic world. Apart from instruction in the sciences and the arts, children should also receive moral education that sensitizes them to issues in society. But, should schools take up the task of teaching religion as well, or should that be the private task of parents? If schools were to teach religion, which religion should it be? In India, Indonesia, and Bangladesh, religiously oriented policy makers are introducing biased curricula in schools that are weighted in favor of one religion. What rights will parents who do not wish their children to receive any religious education have? What of religious minorities who do not want their children to be taught the religion of the majority? Are they allowed to withdraw their children from these classes? Should the state always decide what is in the best interests of children? Do children have a choice or say in this?

Norway and Argentina have been particular violators of the liberties of nonreligious children and parents. In 1884 Argentina passed the most modern and secular education law in South America, the famous Law 1420. It promoted the integration of millions of immigrants and their children into a new nation. Nevertheless, since 1943, during a fascist regime, religion was sometimes imposed in public education, and during the last dictatorship (1976–83), religion was considered a sort of "vaccine" against socialism, and imposed again as a subject in several states. Even though the situation of religious subjects as a part of the curricula changed in most of the country after the restoration of democracy, the continued pressure exercised by the Catholic Church moved back the situation in several provinces, where prayers in school are officially promoted or tolerated. This is a violation of federal law, but there has only been one official declaration condemning this practice. Moreover, public schools are used as centers of religious indoctrination for children, as these schools offer facilities for First Communion courses. In almost every classroom Catholic crosses and images of the Virgin Mary or some saints are placed. Religious celebrations take place at public schools, and moral pressure is exercised on teachers, pupils, or parents who dissent.[28]

In 1997 Norway introduced a new compulsory syllabus for primary and secondary schools in which the centerpiece is Christianity, predominantly in its Evangelical-Lutheran variety. Non-Christian minorities have challenged this situation, maintaining that public schools are meant for commonly accepted educational goals, including education about religions and life-stances, but not for "indoctrination" in the majority culture. Norwegian Humanists have maintained that both parents and children have the right to nondenominational, alternative education. In fact, the Norwegian Humanist Association has taken the matter to court and, having lost in the two first instances, brought the case to the Supreme Court, where the association lost for the third time in August 2001.[29]

---

[28] See Hugo Daniel Estrella, *Religious Intolerance in Argentina*, an IHEU Report presented to the UN Special Rapporteur on Freedom of Religion or Belief in 2001.

[29] At the time of this writing, the Norwegian Humanist Association is in the process of assessing whether or not to bring the case to the Human Rights Court in Strasbourg.

In the UK the current government's policy is to give more public funds to finance church schools, which can deny admission to nonreligious and non-Christian pupils! Humanists would like to see these resources used in common public schools that are in dire need of more funds, rather than strengthen religious privilege.

An even more dangerous development in the school system has been the one already referred to in the Unites States of America. Teaching biological evolution has been downgraded in many state school curricula, and so-called "creation science"—a literal interpretation of Genesis disguised in language and argument to appear as a contending theory of the origin of life and its forms—is being taught in science classes. Thus, seventy-five years after the *Scopes* trial, in 1999 there was renewed outrage when the Kansas School Board decided by a majority vote to make the teaching of evolution optional, and removed many evolutionary topics and explanations of the role of natural selection from the curriculum in that state's public schools. In a 21 August 1999 editorial, *The New Scientist* wrote:

> We have said it before, but it appears we must say it again: there can be no such thing as 'creation science'. The business of science is not to claim any absolute knowledge. As Richard Feynman once put it: 'Scientific knowledge is a body of statements of varying degrees of certainty—some most unsure, some nearly sure, none absolutely sure'. Those who begin with an absolute, religious certainty about the origins of the Earth and life cannot study these events as scientists. Creation scientists are nothing but wolves in sheep's clothing, adopting the guise of open-minded science to disguise their narrow-minded dogma. And unfortunately for the school children of Kansas, the wolves have been at the school curriculum.

Creationism is rooted in religious doctrine, and, in a sense, immune to change when confronted with opposing evidence. Humanists are not the only ones who hold the position that the state is obliged to present, in adequate pedagogical form, the most solidly based, i.e., scientific, knowledge to the pupils. Of course, as part of their training in the scientific method, pupils should also be made aware of the fallibility, revisability, and nondogmatic character of scientific knowledge. Nevertheless, whatever it may be, creationism is not a science and should never be taught in a science classroom.

In 1992, the International Humanist and Ethical Union issued a declaration condemning the new Common Syllabus for Religious Education in Northern Ireland because it was exclusive and was bound to deepen the division among the people.

The only religion studied in the compulsory core is Christianity. This is offensive to Muslims, Hindus, Jews, and members of other faiths, as well as the twelve percent who, according to a recent poll, declare that they have no religion. It is against the interest of the children, who have a right to a broad education and the opportunity to learn understanding and tolerance towards those of differing beliefs.

> Humanists have in general preferred joint public schools to private sectarian schools. Both parents and the state, and therefore the schools, have a clear duty to provide education on morals and values, but this does not mean that schools have to teach religion. A multitraditional and open approach that contributes to a culture of tolerance implies that schools evolve nonconfessional and impartial educational syllabi, and teach about religion, providing children with objective information and thus empower them to make their own choices. The (minimal) value system that binds all states today is the international human rights regime. Children should also receive instruction about International Declarations that protect their own rights.[30]

Humanists feel that it should be possible to find ways of informing and educating children about religions and values while at the same time respecting the right to freedom from religion.

E. Children's Rights

Empowerment of children is important for they are more than the objects of the religious rights of parents. Children are often the victims of religious abuse. Parents have rights, but these rights are intended to neutralize the intrusive power of the state and to preserve the family; they are not intended to work against the child. The views of the child must also be respected, her identity preserved, her education assured, and she must receive parental guidance. Children have the right to appropriate information, to be protected from indoctrination and brainwashing (from the state, or from sects or from their own parents), and to grow up into mature and responsible adults. The right of children to adopt a religion of their choice is explicit in article 14 of the Convention on the Rights of the Child (ratified by all countries except the USA and Somalia). However, fearing proselytizing by missionaries, many Muslims looked upon this article as an infringement upon the standard practice of child rearing in the religion of his parents.[31] Moroccan legislation stipulates that the child shall follow the father's religion, and the child cannot choose his religion since the state religion is Islam. These are clear infringements of the child's freedom of religion or belief and do not help the child to be an agent of tolerance when he grows up.

However, in both international law and most national legal systems, it is presumed that parents are best suited to protect the interests of their children. Humanists agree that the requirements for the state to intervene in the family have to be strict. Thus, the *legality* of an upbringing that is religiously narrow and intolerant cannot be contested. Therefore the state should not intervene in a direct way in such situations. What Humanists challenge is the *legitimacy* of such a religiously narrow and intolerant education. We find it morally reprehensible and want the state to use its resources to create an environment conducive to a broadminded and tolerant education. This is what is best in keeping with children's rights.

Humanists have also worked hard to highlight the much-neglected issue of abuse of children's rights in the name of religion. A resolution passed unanimously by the General Assembly of the IHEU (June 1997, London) stated

> Whereas children's rights have gained official recognition ever since 1990 when the United Nations hosted the World Summit on Children where 71 countries adopted goals to improve children's lives by 2000;
>
> Whereas the Convention on the Rights of the Child has been ratified by 187 nations, making it the most widely accepted human rights treaty ever;

---

[30] *IHEU Policy and Resolutions Documents,* online at <http://www.iheu.org/resolutions/iheu_resolutions.htm>.

[31] This sentiment is reflected in reservations made by Muslims to the Convention on the Rights of the Child.

> Whereas the idea behind the Convention was to turn children, seen as powerless property of their parents, into people with their own rights—civil, economic, cultural, social and political, with countries agreeing that children face unique circumstances and need special protection;
>
> Whereas much progress has been achieved since 1990 in diverse areas such as school enrolment, immunisation, poverty, hunger and child labour (and the UNICEF itself now enters its 51st year), there still exists one form of enduring and pervasive child abuse that has gone on for centuries but has been ignored and deliberately neglected: child abuse perpetrated in the name of religion;
>
> The IHEU resolves that countries that are tackling issues of child-protection must seriously examine the issue of all abuse of children including in particular in the name of religion and God. World bodies like the UN cannot remain silent on such issues in the name of religious correctness and must take a principled and unambiguous stand against such abuse.[32]

Humanist children's rights are also infringed in many other ways: a 1998 ruling by a California court found that as the Boy Scouts were a private organization, they were immune to antidiscrimination law and therefore could keep away those youths who would not take the mandatory religious oath. This excluded thousands of young Humanist children from participating in an activity that does indeed receive support from the state.[33]

F. Ceremonies and Counseling

Humanists in many countries seek to fulfil an essential service to those who do not wish to affiliate with a religious belief by offering them nonreligious celebration of their rites of passage. Humanists also offer terminally ill patients counseling in hospitals and advise and counsel nonreligious prisoners in jails. In several countries a ceremony like a wedding that is performed by a Humanist still needs to be registered at the local town hall; whereas a ceremony performed at a religious place of worship automatically has the sanction of law. In this area Humanists are demanding equal treatment under the law. It is unacceptable that in many countries ceremonies with great consequences for the individuals' civil status are left to the various religious communities. When such religious ceremonies have a legally binding character, and when there are no official secular or (private) Humanist alternatives, it can often make it impossible (or very difficult) for

---

[32] *IHEU Policy and Resolutions Documents,* online at <http://www.iheu.org/resolutions/iheu_resolutions.htm>.

[33] The American Anti-Discrimination Network and the American Atheists point out that the Boy Scouts of America were formally incorporated on 8 February 1910 and were "Chartered by Congress" in 1916. It is one of several dozen "Patriotic Societies and Observances" listed under the United States Code, title 36. Other groups include The American Legion; Daughters of the American Revolution; Navy Club of the United States of America; Civil Air Patrol; Little League Baseball, Inc.; Gold Star Wives of America; and Former Members of Congress. It is this special status—acting under a Congressional Charter—that critics of Scout discrimination say should qualify the BSA and its programs for coverage under antidiscrimination statutes. In addition, the President of the United States is considered the honorary head or "commander-in-chief" of the Boy Scouts of America organization.

nonbelievers to change their legal status, for example get married. It will also make interreligious marriages impossible or very difficult. In this area it is of paramount importance that the state allows for freedom from religion and accepts nonreligious ceremonies on an equal footing with religious ones. Furthermore, it has been an old Humanist demand that the state provides nonreligious ceremonies for those who would like to have freedom from ***all*** life stances.

Many institutions, like hospitals and jails, allow religious counselors of the official creed access. Often the government or the organs of the state religion pay these counselors. This represents an unacceptable limitation on the counseling spectrum and an unacceptable discrimination of nonofficial and/or secular alternatives. On the one hand Humanists must demand state help—financial and legislative—to gain access to institutions where counseling could be required. On the other hand, it is also important that the various religious offers are not imposed on patients or prisoners. Again, it is important for Humanists to stress the right to freedom, even for prisoners, from religion.[34] Such rights are clearly recognized in the Benelux countries.

G. Media

In the media, it would be impossible to demand freedom from religion. Religious as well as secular life stances have the right to freedom of expression. Therefore there must always be room for religion in the media.

However, while Humanism is legally accepted in many countries as a life stance that is an alternative to religion, state sponsored organizations like the BBC in the UK refuse to give Humanism access to participation in the "Thought for the Day" program. This is in sharp contrast to the airtime allocated to Humanists in the Netherlands and in Belgium. In Slovakia, persistent attempts by the Prometheus Society of Slovakia to obtain parity of treatment were rebuffed by broadcasting authorities that welcome church input to their programs.

Again, it is the state's duty to establish equal opportunities for various belief systems. Therefore it has a special obligation to ensure equal participation or airtime in government controlled media. The presentation of Humanist beliefs on equal footing with religious beliefs is the closest we can get to freedom from religion in the (state controlled or sponsored) media.

H. Civil Society

Civil society can be defined as the social sphere between the state and the family. Accordingly, civil society, including production and distribution, represents the largest social sphere. Therefore the position of religion and secular life stances within this sphere is of the greatest importance. Historically this sphere has been dominated not by the state but by religion. In the West it has been the church, an organized entity with great powers. In the Muslim world the religious institution has been less rigorously organized but its influence seems not to have been any less. The situation has been similar in most cultures.

---

[34] See the chapter by Condé and Llewellyn in this volume.

However, in modern societies the state is the most pervasive and powerful influence. A competing influence can only be found in modern market economic factors and relations. In many ways this is also an expression of the more secular character of modern societies. Nevertheless, religions are still an important influence on societies in formal and organized versions as well as in informal varieties. Modern societies are also characterized by pluralism in social roles and values as well as life stances.

Within this framework all religions and secular life stances will have to find their place without support from the state. This requires a culture of tolerance and mutual respect as the common basis for social interaction. In many ways the logical consequence of respect for human rights is toleration towards others ***and their right to hold and manifest their own beliefs***. Thus, it will be impossible to demand freedom from religion in the public space. Freedom of organization and expression as well as the freedom of religion or belief make people's right to present their religious views publicly a self-evident matter. This should not prevent the proselytizer from showing the common courtesy of respecting the reservations of those who wish to avoid religious propaganda. No life stance should be imposed on others against their will and wishes. It is for this reason that the proselytizer has to find the balance between "spreading the word" and tolerating others' rights to freedom from (religious or secular) propaganda or information.

The demand for respect for freedom from religion that Humanists raise in this way can never be absolute. Not only are religious expressions in the public sphere unavoidable in a life-stance-pluralistic society, but a totally religion-free public sphere would represent an unacceptable limitation of the religious freedom of various religious denominations. For this reason the Humanist demand for freedom from religion does not imply the prohibition of religious symbols worn by individuals in various public places—like schools or hospitals. For example a Christian nurse or teacher must be allowed to carry a crucifix, a (male) Jew the kipper, a (male) Sikh the turban, or a (female) Muslim the headscarf at work, if they so wish. The wearing of such symbols can be connected to the innermost convictions of the individual and—as long as no harm is done to others—the individual's right to wear them has to be respected. Accordingly, the Humanist demand for freedom from religion does not mean that Humanists condone the discrimination in the public or private work place of people because of their choice of apparel and symbols.

It is unacceptable that Muslim women are refused work as cleaning staff of hotels because they wear a headscarf or that pupils or students are expelled from schools and universities for the same reason. However, the authors do need to record their sense of bewilderment as to how in the United States several towns allow erection of prominently displayed religious symbols of specific denominations, like crosses, in several publicly owned places.

VI. Freedom of Religion and Belief in the Emerging Global Society

All societies need moral principles for their survival, as does the emerging global society. Nations, ethnic groupings, and religions are responding to the immense strains of globalization by a retreat into the apparent certainties of their roots and fundamentals. The encounter between different religious or nonreligious belief systems, thanks to increased access to mass media, large-scale migration of peoples, growing free trade, etc., raises questions and problems relating to freedom of religion or belief that need to be addressed.

Despite the seeming contradictions between religious and nonreligious traditions, there are many recurrent themes that appear in nearly all cultural traditions; together with the relatively new concepts of human rights, these common traditions can serve as an inspiration for a new global ethics where the rights of all shall be guaranteed. Universalism should be the fundamental principle of this new global ethics and its moral minimum would consist of human rights and responsibilities, democracy (embodying the idea of political autonomy and human empowerment), protection of minorities (10,000 distinct identities in 200 states), equity between and within generations, peaceful conflict resolution, and fair negotiation as indicated by the UN Document "Our Creative Diversity" produced under the supervision of UN Secretary General Xavier Perez de Cueillar. Such a global arrangement should ensure that there is no mixing of the functions and role of law and religion, church and state, private religion and public politics.

One might remark that this optimism is actually utopian. To such a reaction, the authors would like to respond that the only freedoms denied in Thomas Moore's *Utopia* were the freedom to be an atheist and the freedom to deny the immortality of the human soul. This means that even in Utopia the Humanist has to diligently fight for the preservation of the hard earned freedoms of the last few centuries. And not just for the sake of Humanists, but for the sake of all Humanity.

Yes, Humanists are prepared to keep that vigil.

Chapter 32

The United States and the Promotion of Freedom of Religion and Belief

T. Jeremy Gunn[1]

From the point of view of Europeans and Asians, Muslims, Africans, and Latin Americans, the United States seems at once too mighty to ignore, too magnanimous to mock, too arrogant to admire, too erratic to trust, and too befuddled to explain.

—Walter A. McDougall[2]

The inconstancy of American foreign policy is not an accident but an expression of two distinct sides of the American character. Both are characterized by a kind of moralism, but one is the morality of decent instincts tempered by the knowledge of human imperfection and the other is the morality of absolute self-assurance fired by the crusading spirit.

—Senator J. William Fulbright[3]

Introduction

On 27 October 1998, President Clinton signed into law the International Religious Freedom Act of 1998 (IRFA), which had recently been adopted unanimously by both the Senate and the House of Representatives.[4] IRFA now requires the US State

---

[1] The author wishes to express his appreciation for the valuable assistance provided by Ms. Rana Lehr Lehnardt. He also wishes to acknowledge the helpful advice and suggestions provided by Professor Cole Durham, Dr. Rosalind Hackett, Dr. David Little, Ambassador Robert Seiple, Ms. Laura Bryant Hanford, Dr. Thomas Farr, Ms. Alexandra Arriaga, Ms. Melinda Reingold, and others. He also deeply appreciates the willingness of a number of persons who were involved in the Wolf-Specter/IRFA events to share their recollections, interpretations, and copies of many of the documents cited herein. Nevertheless, the author accepts full responsibility for all statements, interpretations, and analyses.

[2] Walter A. McDougall, *Promised Land, Crusader State: The American Encounter with the World Since 1776* (Boston: Houghton Mifflin Company, 1997), 9.

[3] J. William Fulbright, *The Arrogance of Power* (New York: Random House, 1966), 245–46.

[4] *The International Religious Freedom Act of 1998,* 22 USC 6401 (Public Law No. 105–292, 112 Stat. 2787, as amended by Public Law No. 106–55, 113 Stat. 401 and Public Law No. 107–228, 116 Stat.

Tore Lindholm, W. Cole Durham, Jr., Bahia G. Tahzib-Lie (eds.), Facilitating Freedom of Religion or Belief: A Deskbook, *721–746.*

Department to promote "international religious freedom" as a part of the foreign policy of the United States, to issue an annual report on the status of religious freedom in all countries of the world (except the United States), and to establish an office in the State Department, headed by an Ambassador at Large, to oversee implementation of the law. The law also requires the president to take actions in response to each state that violates standards of international religious freedom. IRFA further established a quasi-independent US Commission on International Religious Freedom to make recommendations to the US government on religious freedom issues and to review State Department activities. With the adoption and implementation of IRFA, the United States has become the state that most visibly promotes the rhetoric of freedom of religion in the international arena.

By enacting a law to promote international religious freedom, the United States understandably raises the suspicions of observers, both at home and abroad, as to its motives and its actions. It is commonly, but incorrectly, believed that IRFA was enacted in response to an effective lobbying effort by fundamentalist and evangelical Christians whose ultimate goal was to protect and promote Christianity. In the words of an informed journalist of religion and public affairs, IRFA was "perceived as a bill that came out of the religious right and was for the protection of Christians."[5] Others believe that IRFA is another heavy-handed attempt by the United States to use unilateral economic sanctions to promote its foreign policy objectives. Still others complain that IRFA exemplifies American unilateralism by its single-minded advocacy of one right—"religious freedom"—while ignoring not only international standards that protect "freedom of religion *and* belief," but by emphasizing this particular right while failing to ratify widely accepted human rights treaties such as the Convention on the Elimination of All Forms of Discrimination Against Women; the Convention on the Rights of the Child; the Covenant on Economic, Social and Cultural Rights; and the American Convention on Human Rights. Critics can thus portray the adoption of IRFA as an example of the United States pandering to conservative Christians, acting

1408). The year 1998 witnessed one of the most contentious partisan struggles in the history of the US Congress and government. In 1998, the dominant political issue was the pending impeachment of President Clinton, and it was a year of bitter political fighting in the United States. That IRFA was adopted unanimously signals its rise above the partisan fray that marked the year. There has as of yet been no comprehensive study of IRFA, though some studies have appeared. See, e.g., Christy Cutbill McCormick, "Exporting the First Amendment: America's Response to Religious Persecution Abroad," *Journal of International Legal Studies* 4 (1998): 283–334; Kristin N. Wuerffel, "Discrimination Among Rights?: A Nation's Legislating a Hierarchy of Human Rights in the Context of International Human Rights Customary Law," *Valparaiso University Law Review* 33 (1998): 369–412; T. Jeremy Gunn, "A Preliminary Response to Criticisms of the International Religious Freedom Act of 1998," *Brigham Young University Law Review* (2000): 841–65. Peter G. Danchin, "U.S. Unilateralism and the International Protection of Religious Freedom: The Multilateral Alternative," *Columbia Journal of Transnational Law* 41 (2002): 33–135 (harshly critical of IRFA), and T. Jeremy Gunn, "American Exceptionalism and Globalist Double Standards: A More Balanced Alternative," *Columbia Journal of Transnational Law* 41 (2002): 137–52 (critique of Danchin).

[5] Rosalind I. J. Hackett, Mark Silk, and Dennis Hoover, eds., *Religious Persecution as a U.S. Policy Issue* (Hartford: Center for the Study of Religion in Public Life, 2000), 57 (Ira Rifkin). This publication is a revised transcript of the proceedings of a conference held at Trinity College in Hartford, Connecticut, on 26–27 September 1999—one year after IRFA was enacted. (The name following the page number in the citation refers to the speaker who is being cited.)

unilaterally, ignoring the greater human rights discussion, foisting its own ideology of church and state, and using sanctions to force others to adopt its peculiar priorities in the human rights agenda.

Before addressing these understandable apprehensions, it is important to recognize that there have been immediate and positive benefits from the adoption of IRFA. This author has heard members of persecuted religious groups, in many parts of the world, say "you have no idea how important it is for us to know that representatives of the most powerful government in the world are willing to listen to us—especially when our own governments refuse to talk with us." Religious prisoners of conscience have been released as a result of US diplomatic efforts. Draft laws that would restrict freedom of religion and belief have been revised or withdrawn following discussions with US State Department officials. These positive benefits have followed neither from explicit nor implicit threats from the United States; rather, they have been the result of serious and engaged discussions between governments.

In order to have a more complete understanding about the role the United States plays in regard to the promotion of international religious freedom—and sometimes freedom of religion *and* belief—it is important first to place IRFA in the broader context of prior US activities to promote freedom of religion and belief, which will be the subject of part I. Part II will summarize the debates that ultimately led to the adoption of IRFA. There it will be seen that although the "Christian rhetoric" and the demands for "sanctions" against persecuting regimes were highly salient features that motivated early supporters of legislation, IRFA—as finally adopted—rejected the ideological and aggressive approach of some early draft bills and substituted a much more balanced and reasonable approach. Finally, part III will summarize the implementation of IRFA.

I. United States Efforts to Promote Freedom of Religion and Belief Prior to 1998

Prior to the 1990s, Americans had already taken a number of modest steps to promote freedom of religion and belief. In the years immediately following World War II, American diplomats were involved in the drafting of the Universal Declaration of Human Rights (Universal Declaration). Former First Lady Eleanor Roosevelt is generally credited with being the principal force in the UN Human Rights Commission to promote the adoption of the Universal Declaration of Human Rights, including articles 1 and 7 on equality and nondiscrimination as well as article 18, which has since become the source text for all international instruments on freedom of religion and belief.[6] American diplomats, non-governmental organizations (NGOs), and individuals also were involved in the drafting of other major human rights instruments of the postwar era, including the Genocide Convention, the International Covenant on Civil and Political Rights (ICCPR), the American Declaration on Human Rights, the American Convention on Human Rights, and the International Covenant on Economic, Social

[6] See Mary Ann Glendon, *A World Made New: Eleanor Roosevelt and the Universal Declaration of Human Rights* (New York: Random House, 2001).

and Cultural Rights.[7] The single most important effort to draft an international instrument devoted specifically to freedom of religion or belief was, of course, the 1981 United Nations Declaration on the Elimination of All Forms of Intolerance and of Discrimination Based on Religion or Belief. The United States, again with many other states, was an active participant in this effort.[8] In 1986, the United States introduced and cosponsored the United Nations resolution that created the position of a Special Rapporteur on intolerance based upon religion or belief and has since repeatedly supported the mandate of the rapporteur. Until 2001, the United States was an active participant on the UN Human Rights Commission and a regular cosponsor of resolutions critical of religious discrimination and intolerance and a supporter of a number of resolutions making country-specific allegations of violations of religious freedom. The United States also supported, on a number of occasions, resolutions in the UN General Assembly on topics related to religious freedom.[9]

During the Cold War, the United States engaged in a number of diplomatic and political efforts to draw attention to the needs of religious communities behind the Iron Curtain. In the early 1970s, Congress enacted a law known as the Jackson-Vanik amendment to the Trade Act of 1974.[10] The Jackson-Vanik amendment was designed to respond principally to Soviet efforts to restrict the emigration of Jews. Although targeting the Soviet Union, the law applied to any nonmarket economy that restricted free emigration. It prohibited the United States from granting such countries most-favored-nation trade status. It is generally believed that Jackson-Vanik, which targeted only one human rights practice (free emigration), and which focused principally on one group (Jews), led to the lifting more generally of restrictions against those who had been prohibited from leaving the Soviet Union. For an extended period in the 1970s, several Russian Pentecostals seeking religious asylum were sheltered by the US Embassy in Moscow, much to the annoyance of the Soviet government.

Beginning in Helsinki in 1973, in a process leading to what has now become the Organization for Security and Cooperation in Europe (OSCE), American diplomats worked actively to include language on religious freedom in the Helsinki Final Act (1975), the Vienna Concluding Document (1989), and other OSCE documents.[11]

---

[7] For the involvement of the United States and its citizens in such activities, see Paul Gordon Lauren, *The Evolution of International Human Rights* (Philadelphia: University of Pennsylvania Press, 1998), 172–240. Unfortunately, as is frequently the case with the United States, its active involvement with the drafting of international agreements is followed either by a delay in ratification, a failure to ratify altogether, or a ratification with reservations, understandings, and declarations. It took the US Senate almost twenty years to ratify the ICCPR, and it has never ratified the American Convention on Human Rights or a number of other major international human rights conventions. The ambivalent approach by the United States to international relations generally—sometimes highly activist and multilateral and sometimes highly autonomous and unilateral—is exemplified by its approach to human rights.

[8] See Donna J. Sullivan, "Advancing the Freedom of Religion or Belief through the UN Declaration on the Elimination of Religious Intolerance and Discrimination," *American Journal of International Law* 82 (1988): 487–520.

[9] See Department of State, *United States Policies in Support of Religious Freedom: Focus on Christians* (undated, released 22 July 1997), 11–12. The report was released in photocopy format; see <www.state.gov/www/global/human_rights/970722_relig_rpt_christian.html>.

[10] *Trade Act of 1974*, sec. 402(c), 19 USC 2432.

[11] For publications on the OSCE and religion, see T. Jeremy Gunn, "The Organization for Security and Co-Operation in Europe and the Rights of Religion or Belief," in Peter G. Danchin and Elizabeth A. Cole, eds.,

The United States also took the lead during the early years of the Helsinki process to raise particular cases about abridgement of religious freedom in Warsaw pact countries, particularly regarding Christian minorities and Jews. The State Department and its human rights bureau, now the Bureau of Democracy, Human Rights and Labor, also raised issues of religious freedom along with many other issues over the years.

During the 1970s, a predominantly Democratic Congress became critical of the perceived inattention of Republican presidents to the issue of human rights. In 1976, Congress adopted, over the initial objection of President Gerald Ford and Secretary of State Henry Kissinger, a law creating a semi-independent US Commission on Security and Cooperation in Europe, now commonly known as the "US Helsinki Commission." Since 1976, the Helsinki Commission, largely in a bipartisan way, has been perhaps the most persistent and vehement entity within the US government to criticize both foreign governments' human rights records and to promote policies of the US government in favor of human rights.

In 1977, following the election of President Jimmy Carter, Congress enacted legislation that required the State Department to issue, on an annual basis, reports on human rights practices of foreign countries. The first report, released on 8 February 1979, was short and sketchy. Although religion was one of the topics treated, it was unusual for any of that year's country reports to offer more than one sentence about freedom of religion. The single sentence specifically concerning religious freedom in Saudi Arabia, for example, states briefly "Islam is the established religion of Saudi Arabia and Saudis are not permitted to practice other religions, although non-Muslim foreigners have been able to hold private and discreet religious services."[12] Since that time, the reports have expanded significantly both in the depth and quality of their coverage.

In 1983, several members of Congress, led by Democrat Tom Lantos of California and Republican John Edward Porter of Illinois, joined together to form the Congressional Human Rights Caucus, which subsequently became very active in a broad range of human rights issues and participated in projects directly related to religious freedom.[13] From the mid-1980s, it played an active role by holding hearings, encouraging members to travel for on-site visits, promoting a religious prisoner adoption program, and conducting letter-writing campaigns related to religious persecution and discrimination in China, Tibet, Indonesia (particularly East Timor), Pakistan, Sudan, Saudi Arabia, Burma, Syria, Cuba, Vietnam, Egypt, Iran, Iraq, Turkey, Ethiopia, the former Soviet Union (and then Russia), Serbia, Romania, Bosnia, Slovakia, Ukraine, Northern Ireland, and Hungary. In 1992–93, it conducted a series of hearings on the topic of religious intolerance.

Protecting the Human Rights of Religious Minorities in Eastern Europe (New York: Columbia University Press, 2002), 222–50; Harm J. Hazewinkel, "Religious Freedom in the OSCE/CSCE process," *Helsinki Monitor* 9, no. 3 (1998): 9–16; T. Jeremy Gunn, "Majorities, minorities, and the rights of religion or belief," *Helsinki Monitor* 9, no. 3 (1998): 38–44; Malcolm D. Evans, *Religious Liberty and International Law in Europe* (Cambridge: Cambridge University Press, 1997), 366–70. For the role of the United States in the Helsinki process, see William Korey, *The Promises We Keep: Human Rights, the Helsinki Process, and American Foreign Policy* (New York: St. Martin's Press, 1993).

[12] Department of State, *Report on Human Rights Practices in Countries Receiving U.S. Aid* (8 February 1979), 624.

[13] For the current website, see <www.house.gov/lantos/caucus/caucuswebpage.htm>.

Although not formally a part of the US government, the United States Institute of Peace (USIP) was created by Congress and is funded by the US government to provide both intellectual and practical advice for the promotion of peace. In 1988, USIP launched a special initiative entitled Religion, Ethics and Human Rights, headed by Dr. David Little, later a professor at Harvard University. USIP sponsored conferences and seminars on the interrelationship of religion, intolerance, and human rights. Among the many contributions to emerge from this initiative were detailed studies and proposals on religion and human rights issues in Ukraine, Sri Lanka, Lebanon, Nigeria, Tibet, the former Yugoslavia, and Sudan.[14] The work of Dr. Little and USIP has proved valuable in helping to focus the attention of policy makers on the complexity of issues of religion and human rights, where nationalism, identity, and religious traditions complicate efforts to promote peace and religious freedom.[15]

Beginning in the 1990s, the issue of freedom of religion and belief became a more prominent issue in the international arena. A flood of academic studies began to appear, including, perhaps most importantly, a major international conference at Emory University in 1994 and the publication of the major two-volume work of papers emerging from that conference.[16] The OSCE began to act as well. The OSCE, which now includes fifty-five participating states from Europe, North America, and Central Asia, has been one of the trend-setters in the international human rights movement. In 1996 it convened a seminar in Warsaw entitled "Constitutional, Legal and Administrative Aspects of Freedom of Religion," and has since created an Advisory Panel of Experts on Freedom of Religion or Belief. In 1999, the OSCE Permanent Council in Vienna held a supplementary meeting on freedom of religion, and in June 2001, the Dutch and Romanian governments sponsored a seminar in The Hague for OSCE participating states to explore how state laws can harm or improve freedom of religion or belief.[17]

Governmental and political institutions within the United States also had become more interested in the issue of international religious freedom by the mid-1990s. The US Helsinki Commission, like the Congressional Human Rights Caucus, had long shown an interest in religious freedom. In 1995, the Helsinki Commission retained a

---

[14] See, e.g., David Little, *Ukraine: The Legacy of Intolerance* (Washington, D.C.: United States Institute of Peace Press, 1991); David Little, *Sri Lanka: The Invention of Enmity* (Washington, D.C.: United States Institute of Peace Press, 1994). See also <www.usip.org/research/rehr.html>.

[15] Stressing the complexity of Sudan, for example, the report on Sudan cautioned against simplifying issues in that problem-strewn country by stating: "Thus, the north-south conflict is exacerbated by considerable tensions in the north as well as military engagement between parties in the south. . . . Thus, the Sudan conflict is more complex than the usual references to a north-south split suggest" (Report of United States Institute of Peace Seminar, "Sudan: Ending the War, Moving Talks Forward" [1994], <www.usip.org/oc/sr/sudan.html>).

[16] Johan D. van der Vyver and John Witte Jr., eds., *Religious Human Rights in Global Perspective*, 2 vols. (The Hague: Martinus Nijhoff, 1996). Among the other leading publications were Kevin Boyle and Juliet Sheen, eds., *Freedom of Religion and Belief: A World Report* (London: Routledge, 1997) (the culmination of an effort that began in the early 1990s); Bahiyyih G. Tahzib, *Freedom of Religion or Belief: Ensuring Effective International Legal Protection* (The Hague: Martinus Nijhoff, 1996); Evans, *Religious Liberty and International Law in Europe*.

[17] There are several plausible reasons for the developing interest. These include the collapse of the Soviet bloc and the opening of that region both to foreign missionary activity and to older antagonisms, as well as to the rise of what has loosely been described as "fundamentalisms." The Internet enables religious communities to make better contact with their coreligionists and to better publicize their plights. Thus, during the 1990s, religion became more salient, while suffering on the account of belief became more visible.

full-time staff member to work on the issue of religious freedom.[18] Shortly thereafter, in mid-1995, the Helsinki Commission organized briefings on the issue of religious freedom in the OSCE region and invited experts on the region to testify.[19] The briefings identified emerging problems in Europe on the issue of religious intolerance, discrimination against minority religions, and noted the emerging trend toward discriminatory legislation.

In January 1996, following this emerging international, academic, and congressional interest in the broader issue of freedom of religion and belief, a group of activists decided to publicize what they identified as the specific problem of the persecution of Christians. Under the auspices of Freedom House, these activists organized a conference entitled "Global Persecution of Christians."[20] This conference, attended by individuals prominently associated with the religious right in the United States, launched a campaign, principally by religious conservatives, to pressure the US government and the Clinton administration to respond vigorously to allegations of persecution of Christians abroad. In conjunction with this conference, the National Association of Evangelicals issued a document entitled the "Statement of Conscience of the National Association of Evangelicals Concerning Worldwide Religious Persecution," which alleged that persecution of Christians is increasing in the world.[21] Following these successful efforts to publicize the problem of the persecution of Christians, the US Congress became increasingly sensitive not only to the problem of religious persecution, but to public pressure generated by the activists and it adopted resolutions on the topic.[22]

By the end of 1996, the mounting congressional and public interest in religious persecution prompted the US Department of State to take steps to address international religious freedom as a distinct issue. Secretary of State Madeleine Albright began to make public statements on the topic and issued a cable to US embassies worldwide in

---

[18] In 1995, Karen S. Lord became the Counsel for Freedom of Religion to the Helsinki Commission, and she later became the first person employed by the US government to work full-time on the issue of international religious freedom.

[19] [US] Commission on Security and Cooperation in Europe, ***Religious Liberty in the OSCE: Present and Future*** and ***Religious Liberty: The State Church and Minority Faiths*** (27 September 1995 and 28 November 1995).

[20] It should be recognized, of course, that NGOs in the United States had been involved in concerns regarding religious freedom long before January 1996. One close observer asserts that "Human rights organizations have reported on religious persecution extensively for decades, and their international grassroots membership has campaigned on behalf of countless religious prisoners of conscience" (Stephen Rickard, "Repression and Response," *SAIS Review* 18 [Summer-Fall 1998]: 56–57). Paul Marshall acknowledged, despite their shortcomings, that Amnesty International and Human Rights Watch "have done more than almost any other organizations to bring religious persecution to our attention" (Paul Marshall, *Their Blood Cries Out: The Worldwide Tragedy of Modern Christians Who Are Dying for Their Faith* [Dallas: Word Publishing, 1997], 147). Among specialized NGOs that have been concerned about religious freedom are the International Religious Liberty Association (established in 1893), the Jacob Blaustein Institute, Project Tandem, and, more recently, the International Academy for Freedom of Religion and Belief.

[21] *Statement of Conscience of the National Association of Evangelicals Concerning Worldwide Religious Persecution,* 23 January 1996, <www.nae.net/sig_doc12.html>.

[22] For congressional hearings, see House Subcommittee on International Operations and Human Rights, *Persecution of Christians Worldwide,* 104th Cong., 2d sess. (15 February 1996) and House Subcommittee on International Operations and Human Rights, *Worldwide Persecution of Jews,* 104th Cong., 2d sess. (27 February 1996). For congressional resolutions, see H.R. 102, 104th Cong. (1996) (Bahá'ís); S. Con. Res. 71, 104th Cong. (1996) (Christians); and H.R. 515, 104th Cong. (1996) (Christians).

December 1996, instructing foreign service officers to pay added attention to issues of religious freedom.[23] The State Department, in response to a congressional request, issued a report on 22 July 1997, entitled *United States Policies in Support of Religious Freedom: Focus on Christians*.[24] The eighty-two-page report consisted of thirteen introductory pages describing US government efforts to promote religious freedom and a lengthy annex describing the religious situation in several countries. The Saudi section began, for example, by pointedly stating that "Freedom of religion does not exist in Saudi Arabia."[25] The report commented critically on the religion bill that the Russian Duma had recently adopted, and would later be signed (in revised form) by President Yeltsin. This report was cited frequently in the ensuing congressional debates about the advisability of adopting legislation on international religious freedom. In early 1997, President Clinton and Secretary of State Albright appointed and met with the twenty-member "Secretary of State's Advisory Committee on Religious Freedom Abroad." The committee, which included participants from a wide range of religious, political, and professional backgrounds, worked over a two-year period making inquiries into a range of issues involving religion and foreign policy. It issued an interim report in 1998 and a final report the following year.[26]

Among its early recommendations, the Advisory Committee urged that the State Department appoint a high-level official to coordinate a new office in the State Department on issues related to religious freedom. Despite the diversity of religious and political beliefs of its members, the committee's final report was issued without dissent. Indeed, the Advisory Committee noted that it was *because* of its diversity that its work was a success.[27] It stressed that the United States should emphasize the application of international standards of freedom of religion and belief and strongly urged that the United States act multilaterally and make use of international institutions.[28] It recognized that underlying religious persecution and violations of religious freedom is the problem of intolerance, and that the United States should make use not only of punitive tools, but should make positive efforts to promote understanding of religious freedom and to provide positive incentives. It made recommendations to revise US government practices with regard to its foreign policy activities and treatment of refugees. It was recommended that all branches of the government that have programs affecting freedom of religion revise their programs so as to take better account of the needs of those who suffer for their beliefs.

II. The Adoption of the International Religious Freedom Act of 1998

The legislative process that ultimately culminated in the adoption of IRFA began on 20 May 1997, when Republican Congressman Frank Wolf of Virginia introduced a bill in the US House of Representatives entitled the Freedom from Religious Persecution

---

23 See Department of State, *United States Policies in Support of Religious Freedom*, 8.

24 See note 9 in this chapter.

25 Department of State, *United States Policies in Support of Religious Freedom*, 69.

26 The Secretary of State's Advisory Committee on Religious Freedom Abroad, *Interim Report to the Secretary of State and to the President of the United States* (23 January 1998); *Final Report of the Advisory Committee on Religious Freedom Abroad* (17 May 1999).

27 *Final Report of the Advisory Committee on Religious Freedom Abroad* (17 May 1999), 4.

Act of 1997 (the Wolf-Specter bill).[29] Between 1997, and the final vote in May 1998, the Wolf-Specter bill was studied and revised by five House committees, including International Relations, Ways and Means, Banking, Rules, and Judiciary. The amended version of the Wolf-Specter bill passed the House of Representatives on 14 May 1998, by an overwhelming vote of 375–41.

Unbeknownst to the Wolf-Specter supporters in the House of Representatives, four staff members of the Senate and House, working behind the scenes, had drafted a strikingly different bill to promote religious freedom, a bill that ultimately would become IRFA.[30] These four staff members accurately anticipated that, despite the substantial support for Wolf-Specter in the House of Representatives, it had no chance of adoption by the Senate. Their prediction was confirmed immediately after passage of Wolf-Specter in the House, when no Senator agreed to sponsor the final Wolf-Specter bill.

This back-room draft first became known publicly at a hearing ("mark-up session") on the Wolf-Specter bill in the House International Relations Committee on 25 March 1998, where it was briefly introduced and then withdrawn under the name of the "Brady amendment."[31] On the following day, March 26, Senator Don Nickles of Oklahoma, finally introduced the alternative draft as "S. 1868, the International Religious Freedom Act of 1998" (hereafter the "Nickles bill"). It was the Nickles bill, as amended, that ultimately became IRFA. According to one Senate staffer, following the introduction of the Nickles bill, "we were immediately bombarded by every interest group that you can possibly imagine that has an office in Washington. . . . It took us most of the summer [of 1998] to work through constant negotiation of those changes—up until probably a couple hours before the bill passed."[32] The unanimous final vote on IRFA, despite the words of harmony and congratulations spoken on the Senate floor on October 9, did not reflect what had transpired behind closed doors. The forces that had supported legislation in the House desperately, but unsuccessfully, attempted to convince senators to adopt a variation on the Wolf-Specter bill rather than the Nickles bill. Their attempts to convince senators were often acrimonious. "The 98-to-nothing vote in the Senate and a [unanimous] voice vote in the House is not an accurate picture of what actually happened. This was a very contentious debate."[33] But, as will be

---

[28] Ibid., 11–20, 51–52.

[29] 105th Cong., 1st sess., H.R. 1685. The bill was simultaneously introduced in the Senate as S. 772 by Republican Senator Arlen Specter of Pennsylvania. This paper only summarizes the complicated history of the transformation of the original Wolf-Specter bill into IRFA as it was finally adopted. The author is preparing a more lengthy study of these events.

[30] The congressional staff members who are generally credited with drafting and championing the alternative bill were Laura Bryant (now Laura Bryant Hanford) in the office of Democratic Congressman Bob Clement of Tennessee, John Hanford in the office of Republican Senator Richard Lugar of Indiana, William Inboden in the office of Republican Congressman Tom DeLay of Texas, and Steve Moffitt in the office of Republican Senator Don Nickles of Oklahoma. These four later participated in an open discussion on the drafting of IRFA. See Hackett, Silk, and Hoover, eds., *Religious Persecution as a U.S. Policy Issue*. For praise of these staff members by Senators and Representatives see *Congressional Record* (8 October 1998), S11943, S11945, S12099. John Hanford later became the second US Ambassador at Large for International Religious Freedom.

[31] For the full text of the Brady amendment, see House Committee on International Relations, *H.R. 2431: Freedom From Religious Persecution Act,* 105th Cong., 2d sess., 25 March 1998, 167–230.

[32] Hackett, Silk, and Hoover, eds., *Religious Persecution as a U.S. Policy Issue,* 9 (Steve Moffitt). Laura Bryant described them as "furious, hectic last hours leading up to IRFA's passage" (ibid., 10 [Bryant]).

[33] Ibid., 9–10 (Steve Moffitt).

shown, the debate related not to the importance of the principle of protecting freedom of religion as such. The disagreement was over whether there should be a broad and international approach to a genuine problem, or whether the approach should be one of narrowly and punitively reacting to offending regimes. Although the debate behind the scenes was indeed contentious, the contentiousness was caused principally by the tactics and rhetoric of some Wolf-Specter supporters whose backgrounds principally were in domestic US politics rather than diplomacy and international relations. Congress ultimately and overwhelmingly adopted the much broader and internationalist approach of the Nickles bill.

The striking difference of viewpoints between the original Wolf-Specter supporters and those who supported Nickles-IRFA will be contrasted below.[34]

A. The Wolf-Specter Bill and Its Supporters

1. The Wolf-Specter Rhetoric

There are two individuals who properly may be cited as having launched the ideological and lobbying effort behind the original Wolf-Specter bill: Michael Horowitz of the Hudson Institute and Nina Shea of Freedom House.[35] Horowitz, a Jew, proved adept at prodding many Christian leaders associated with the religious right in the United States to protest worldwide persecution of Christians. Many believe the reason that Horowitz was so successful in galvanizing the Christian right was that he, as a Jew, was able to emphasize persecution of Christians without appearing to be engaged in special pleading for his own religion.

By the end of 1995, Horowitz and Shea had begun to build an energetic, grassroots campaign to pressure Congress to take an active role in publicizing and combating persecution of Christians in communist and Islamic countries. In January 1996, Shea organized the conference, mentioned above, entitled "Global Persecution of Christians." At the conference, several dozen participants heard horror stories about the torture, persecution, enslavement, and martyrdom of Christians around the world. In conjunction with this event, Horowitz drafted what was to become a manifesto, the "Statement of Conscience of the National Association of Evangelicals Concerning Worldwide Religious Persecution." The document recited the suffering of Christians and urged Americans to demand that the United States government respond to

---

[34] There were others who eschewed all legislation designed to promote rights related to religion. The Clinton administration, concerned about constraints on the ability of the Executive Branch to conduct foreign policy, originally opposed all legislation, though it finally agreed to a revised IRFA version. Parts of the business community also opposed all human rights legislation that would have imposed sanctions on countries.

[35] Michael Horowitz was the general counsel at the Office of Management and Budget in the Reagan administration. At the Hudson Institute, Horowitz engaged in advocacy work to bring about changes in civil tort law in the United States. Nina Shea is a lawyer who founded the Puebla Institute, a religious-rights NGO that has since been folded into the Center for Religious Freedom at Freedom House. Shea published a thinly researched and highly polemical book that captured the imagination of many conservative political activists who were previously unaware of the problem of religious persecution (Nina Shea, *In the Lion's Den* [Nashville: Broadman & Holman Publishers, 1997]). She took a much less active role in promoting the Wolf-Specter legislation than did Horowitz, though her book was cited frequently by proponents of the legislation.

persecution around the world. The conference and the Statement of Conscience galvanized the leaders of several important groups associated with the Christian right and prompted them to begin communicating with their memberships about the worldwide persecution of Christians. Seizing the momentum from the conference and the Statement of Conscience, Horowitz subsequently drafted what became the original Wolf-Specter bill and convinced Congressman Wolf to sponsor it in the House of Representatives.

With regard to their efforts to promote popular interest in religious persecution—particularly persecution of Christians—Horowitz and Shea have been widely and extravagantly praised.[36] It should be noted, however, that others have not been so complimentary and have questioned their tactics and factual accuracy.[37] There were others, less visible than Shea and Horowitz, who also can be identified as speaking in favor of the Wolf-Specter legislation.[38] Although not everyone in this coalition was affiliated with the Christian right—some Jewish groups were involved—the Christian right nevertheless was its backbone as represented by the Christian Coalition and the National Association of Evangelicals.

Perhaps the single most provocative demand of many Wolf-Specter supporters was that the United States government should move the problem of persecution of Christians toward the top of its human rights and foreign policy agenda. Although

---

[36] Horowitz was described as the "mastermind of a crusade," the "prime mover," the "spearhead," and the "spark of [the] budding movement" (Paul Blustein, "Crusader for a Religious Right," *The Washington Post,* 30 September 1997, E01). Congressman Frank Wolf described Horowitz as the person who "has probably done more than anyone else in the country to sensitize the religious community" to religious persecution (ibid., E01). Senator Joseph Lieberman, who cosponsored the Nickles bill, and others similarly credit Horowitz and Shea for their efforts. "I want to join Senator Nickles in paying tribute to the band of believers and battlers who have in recent years brought this problem to the forefront of our attention—Michael Horowitz, Nina Shea, the host of leaders in the religious communities, and our colleagues here in Congress, Senator Specter and Congressman Wolf" (Senate Committee on Foreign Relations, *S. 1868: The International Religious Freedom Act of 1998,* 105th Cong., 2d sess. [12 May and 17 June 1998] [hereafter "Senate Committee Hearings"], 6 [Senator Lieberman]).

[37] For example, one official associated with the National Association of Evangelicals has been quoted as follows: "'By force of personality, intimidation or moral suasion, he usually gets his way,' says Richard Cizik who admits that Horowitz's bare-knuckle tactics often disturb him. 'I know people who disagree with Mike who feel that they're persecuted'" (Blustein, "Crusader for a Religious Right," E01). Kenneth Roth of Human Rights Watch is quoted as saying about Horowitz, "Under the guise of religious tolerance, he spreads divisiveness wherever he goes" (ibid). Stephen Rosenfeld called Horowitz "a terror as an advocate" (Stephen S. Rosenfeld, "Human Rights for Christians," *The Washington Post,* 9 February 1996, A21). Another reporter concluded, after interviewing a number of participants involved in the legislative efforts, that "a number of religious groups, including the mainstream National Council of Churches, oppose his confrontational approach as counterproductive and likely to endanger missionaries" (Blustein, "Crusader for a Religious Right," E01). Horowitz himself acknowledges that "I may be a pretty tough guy to be in partnership with because I still pound tables and want things to happen yesterday" (Michael Cromartie, "The Jew Who Is Saving Christians," *Christianity Today* (1 March 1999): 55.

[38] See, e.g., House hearings on the Wolf-Specter bill: House Committee on International Relations, *Freedom from Religious Persecution Act of 1997, Part II—Private Witnesses,* 105th Cong., 1st sess., 10 September 1997 (hereafter "House Committee Hearings"), testimonies of Dr. Richard D. Land (President, Ethics and Religious Liberty Commission, Southern Baptist Convention), Dr. Donald Argue (President, National Association of Evangelicals), Mr. Donald Hodel (President, Christian Coalition), Mr. William J. Bennett (President, Empower America and former Secretary of Energy). See also the testimony of Richard Land on the Nickles bill, Senate Committee Hearings, 40 (Richard Land).

supporters of Wolf-Specter sometimes referred to other persecuted faiths, notably the Tibetan Buddhists and the Bahá'ís, a principal goal was to draw attention to the persecution of Christians. Richard Land of the Southern Baptists stated that the bill should "focus on anti-Christian persecution because that is what is the most widespread at the moment in the world. It is the one that has been most ignored."[39] Nina Shea repeatedly asserted that Christians are the "most persecuted" of any religious faith and that there have been more Christian martyrs in the twentieth century than all previous centuries combined.[40] Her allegations have been often repeated and widely accepted as true by many of those who joined in advocating something more be done. However gripping these assertions might sound, those who made these allegations did not document them with any meaningful specificity and such unquantifiable assertions can be not only misleading, but inflammatory.

Wolf-Specter supporters argued that Christians are specifically targeted for persecution because of their specific religious beliefs. In the first sentence of her book, Shea asserts that "Christians in many parts of the world suffer brutal torture, arrest, imprisonment, and even death—their homes and communities laid waste—for *no other reason than that they are Christians.*"[41] She later asserted that the "most egregious human rights atrocities are being committed against Christians living in communist and militant Islamic societies *solely because of their religious beliefs and activities.*"[42] Others repeat this belief that Christians are singled out because of their particular beliefs.[43] Thus the Wolf-Specter supporters argued that attacks are directed at Christians because they are Christians—rather than because abusive governments are intolerant of dissent generally, or because they are opposed to human rights generally, or because Christians appear to be foreign or to represent outside influences. By implying that Christians *qua* Christians are uniquely targeted by persecuting regimes, the Wolf-Specter advocates aroused Christians in the United States who were incensed at the persecution of their coreligionists and antagonized foreign observers who believed that not only was it false, but that it was intentionally made in order to fan the flames of the culture war predicted by Samuel Huntington.

The Wolf-Specter approach assumed that once a country had been identified as a persecuting country, the United States should undertake two actions. First, the United States should apply verbal pressure denouncing the persecuting country, particularly in bold and pointed speeches by the president. "We are urging the President to condemn the slaughter of Christians in Sudan, to speak out against the torture and imprisonment of Christians in China, and to address the problem of global intolerance toward Christians in Muslim countries."[44] Horowitz's continuing belief in the unilateral power of

---

[39] House Committee Hearings, 45 (Richard Land).

[40] See, e.g., "Christians today are the most persecuted group in the world. At the time of the Jewish Holocaust, we said 'never again' and it's happening again" (Linda Lawson, "Christians labeled 'most persecuted,'" *Reporter Interactive News,* 26 December 1996, <www.umr.org/HTpersec.htm> [quoting Nina Shea]). "Christians are the chief victims of this religious persecution around the world today" (Shea, *In the Lion's Den,* 4).

[41] Ibid., 1 (emphasis added).

[42] Ibid., 1–2 (emphasis added). Christians are "facing ferocious campaigns against them because of their religious beliefs" (ibid., 4).

[43] Ibid., iii (citing Don Argue).

[44] Steven L. Snyder, Open Letter, 28 August 1996, <www.persecution.org/letters/ltr-1996-08-28.html>.

denunciations was articulated shortly after the enactment of IRFA: "If, as I expect, the commission established under [IRFA] does its job, world press attention to religious persecution will significantly increase—and with it, massive pressure on persecuting regimes."[45]

Second, the United States should employ sanctions against offending governments. A striking omission from the Wolf-Specter supporters is any substantial analysis of the *actual effect* of denunciations and sanctions on the persecuted people whom they ostensibly wish to help. Indeed, throughout the testimonies and writings, there appears to be an *assumption* that denunciations and sanctions would change the persecutors' bad behavior and that, with the use of force and pressure by the United States, these regimes would alter their behavior toward persecuted minorities. Some advocates even believed that simply by passing a law in the United States, the US Congress would enhance people's lives all over the world. "When this bill passes, in small villages in southern Sudan, people with their little crystal radio sets, people in villages in China with their crystal sets, when they hear that the United States Congress, the people's House, the House of Representatives, has voted for this legislation, it will send a message to the people who are being persecuted around the world that this Congress and this country stands with them."[46]

2. The Wolf-Specter Bill

The Wolf-Specter bill, as originally introduced, consisted of thirteen sections. Certainly the most significant provision of the Wolf-Specter bill was its creation of a powerful "Office of Religious Persecution Monitoring" in the White House (the executive office of the president). The director would be a presidential appointee, subject to confirmation by the Senate, who would have the unchecked authority to make the "determination whether a particular country is engaged in . . . religious persecution" (sec. 5[e][4]). If the director determined that a country engaged in religious persecution as defined in the bill, then sanctions against that country would be imposed automatically (sec. 7). The president, under certain circumstances and after following certain procedures, might waive the imposition of sanctions for up to twelve months (sec. 8). Only the director has the power to terminate the sanctions (sec. 11). This would have given an unprecedented amount of power to a single individual.[47] The two other significant provisions of the original draft of the Wolf-Specter bill were important amendments to immigration laws that would effectively have given asylum priority to persons claiming religious persecution from countries that had been designated by the Director of the Office of Religious Persecution Monitoring (sec. 9). The other significant provision was the language of the imposition of sanctions against Sudan was taken virtually verbatim from the sanctions that had been imposed on South Africa during apartheid (sec. 12).

---

[45] Cromartie, "The Jew Who Is Saving Christians," 54 (quoting Michael Horowitz). Horowitz's prediction has not proved true. Though the commission did condemn the persecuting regimes, there has, unfortunately, been an absence of "massive public pressure" on the regimes.

[46] Congressman Frank Wolf, *Congressional Record*, 11 May 1998, H3019.

[47] Though the president could demand the resignation of the director, neither the president nor Congress, short of enacting a new law, would have been able to terminate the sanctions.

There are five salient features of this draft legislation:

First, as discussed above, Wolf-Specter relied exclusively on the unilateral threat and imposition of sanctions by the United States as the means for combating religious persecution. These sanctions were to be imposed without regard to whether they harm the people of a country as a whole or whether they harm the people whose persecution brought about the sanctions. It was a bill that was designed to punish states identified as persecutors.

Second, and relatedly, it envisioned no additional role for the US Department of State to promote religious freedom or to attack religious persecution. Although the State Department was instructed to enhance its reporting of religious-freedom violations and to improve training of foreign service officers (sec. 10), the State Department was given no additional diplomatic tools or responsibilities for dealing with problems. Even the Office of Religious Persecution Monitoring was to be located outside the State Department.

Third, the original Wolf-Specter bill envisioned no multilateral approach to the problem of persecution. Even the provision on sanctions that referred to "Multilateral assistance," (sec. 7[c]), simply instructed US representatives in selected international bodies how to vote on measures pertaining to countries identified as persecutors. These first three thematic features suggest an attitude of disrespect (or perhaps even hostility) toward the State Department and the international system, and a remarkable degree of optimism about the power of the United States, acting alone, to change the world by imposing punishments on others.

Fourth, the Wolf-Specter bill defined "persecuted community"—the subject of its solicitude—in a peculiar way.[48] Rather than defining these communities in neutral terms that would include all religious persons and groups that suffer on the basis of their religion, it identified specific religious communities in specific regions that would be protected by the law, including: Roman Catholics, evangelical Protestant Christians, and Tibetan Buddhists (in communist countries); Bahá'ís, Christians, and other religious minorities (in Islamic countries); and "moderate Muslims" in Sudan. Falling outside the ambit of Wolf-Specter's "definition" of "persecuted community" were Jews, Orthodox Christians, Muslims (other than "moderate" Muslims in Sudan), Hindus, Sikhs, or nativist religions. Although the director was empowered to supplement this list by adding additional persecuted communities in the future, the bill did not approach the problem conceptually and neutrally, but offered its list of favored communities.[49]

Finally, the Wolf-Specter bill targeted two types of perpetrator of religious persecution: "Communist countries" and "Islamic countries."[50] Although the bill does not assert that these are the only types of persecutor, it does specifically name them and it identifies no other type of country that persecutes on the basis of religion. The named targets are, clearly, communist and Islamic countries.

---

[48] Rather than providing a straightforward definition of "persecuted community," the bill requires cross-referencing sections that identify some specific groups that have suffered.

[49] It was later stated that Congressman Wolf had always wished that his bill would offer protection for all religious communities, and not certain specified groups (Congressman Chris Smith, *Congressional Record*, 14 May 1998, H3270). That may well be, but it would have been much easier to write such a provision than the one that actually appeared in the Wolf-Specter bill.

[50] The bill does not identify what it means by "Islamic countries," and we can only guess whether it means that the government purports to follow *Shariah*, whether there are clerics in the government, or whether a

B. IRFA and its Supporters

1. The Nickles-IRFA Rhetoric

Other than the senators themselves, there were no supporters of the Nickles bill and IRFA whose visible roles were as prominent as those of Horowitz and Shea. Among the persons who can be identified with the approach taken by the Nickles bill and IRFA were several congressional witnesses and, above all, the congressional staff members, identified above, who drafted the original Nickles bill and who enlisted a number of senators to sponsor and support the alternative bill.[51] The legacy of these staff members is not in public statements or press releases, but in the text of the bill that ultimately became IRFA. When the legislation moved from the Senate to the House, the Episcopal Church also became an influential supporter of the Nickles bill and helped encourage other religious groups to support it.

In congressional hearings, several witnesses suggested that the Wolf-Specter legislation needed to be broadened beyond its emphasis on Christians, Tibetan Buddhists, and Bahá'ís. Father Drew Christiansen, a Catholic, testified that the Wolf-Specter "coverage should be expanded to cover all persecuted religions in all countries. The world's persecutors must be clear that the United States will not tolerate persecution of Muslims, Hindus or Jews any more than it does persecuted Christians."[52] Another witness, applauding a later version of Wolf-Specter that had become broader in its coverage, acknowledged that it "is of great import that this body has established a mandate that is inclusive and would apply to all faiths. Where Christians of all denominations, or Muslims, Hindus, Baha'i [sic], Jews, and yes Zoroastrians, are persecuted for their beliefs and practices, this nation must demonstrate that it cares for their security."[53] Felice Gaer testified that "the freedoms we seek to promote abroad are the same that have shaped our own nation: religious tolerance, pluralism, and a belief in fairness, equality, and liberty for all persons, including men and women, Jews, Christians, Moslems, Buddhists, Hindus, Baha'is, and others."[54]

---

majority (or even plurality) of the population is Muslim. The Wolf-Specter bill might well be read as being anticommunist and anti-Islam.

[51] Representatives of this broader viewpoint also appeared in the House International Relations Committee hearings on the Wolf-Specter bill, including Father Drew Christiansen, Jerry Goodman, Stephen Rickard, and Lauren Homer. Several Senate Foreign Relations Committee witnesses can also be identified with this viewpoint, including John Akers (Chairman of the Board, East Gate Ministries International), Felice Gaer (Director, Jacob Blaustein Institute for the Advancement of Human Rights, American Jewish Committee), Bishop Munawar Kenneth Rumalshah ("Bishop Mano") (Anglican Bishop of Peshawar Pakistan), and Dr. William R. O'Brien (Director, Global Center, Samford University). For the congressional staff members, see note 30 above.

[52] House Committee Hearings, 26 (Drew Christiansen).

[53] House Committee Hearings, 55 (Jerry Goodman).

[54] Senate Committee Hearings, 102 (Felice Gaer). (Gaer later became chair of the US Commission on International Religious Freedom.) More directly, Joan Brown Campbell of the National Council of Churches, which ultimately did not endorse any version of the legislation, observed that the persecution viewpoint's "emphasis on persecuted Christians . . . is theologically arrogant. 'We are equally concerned about persecution of any faith'" (Jeffrey Goldberg, "Washington Discovers Christian Persecution," *The New York Times Magazine* (21 December 1992): 60.

Others believed that the scope of coverage should not be limited to extreme cases of "persecution" (a term that is not included in the major international human texts), but for all violations of religious freedom. Bishop Mano, from Pakistan, testified that a "severe limitation of [the Wolf-Specter bill] is that it only responds to the most extreme cases of religious persecution, ignoring the vast majority of restrictions on religious liberty that occur around the world."[55] Thus it is not just torture that is at issue, but restrictions on registration of religious communities, suppression of religious literature, and restrictions on travel, speech, and public religious meetings. For those approaching the issue from the broader perspective, these violations are easier to remedy than the more egregious violations and responding to them in their earlier forms may help prevent them from becoming much worse.

Those who rejected the Wolf-Specter approach, on the other hand, identified the suffering of Christians as part of a much more complex interaction of identity, ethnicity, culture, and history. According to William R. O'Brien, who worked as a Baptist missionary in Indonesia and who has been involved in overseas missionary work for more than thirty years:

> In attempting to define religious persecution so that the perpetrators can be exposed and dealt with, we discover a multi-complex braid of culture, ethnicity, economics, politics, and religion. Any legislation that calls for concrete and pejorative steps must be wisely crafted in order to avoid deeper problems on the ground where the conflict exists, as well as a negative boomerang effect on the United States.[56]

Another clear statement of this second viewpoint was made by John Ackers, who is the Chairman of the Board for the Billy Graham ministries. Although he is an evangelical Christian and, like William O'Brien, has devoted much of his life to missionary work outside the United States, his viewpoint is strikingly different from that of the Wolf-Specter perspective. He asks, rhetorically, "Why are people persecuted for their faith?" "There are many answers to that question, of course. At the root of most persecution, however, is the perception that a minority religious group is different, and that they are therefore a threat to the established social or political order."[57]

Bishop Mano, in his Senate testimony, similarly observed that the Nickles bill, unlike the Wolf-Specter bill, "will address the concerns that we would have concerning the complexity of religious persecution in various parts of the world."[58] When Congressman Alcee Hastings made an amendment to the Wolf-Specter bill on the floor of the House, he said, "One of my key concerns is that this bill takes a negative approach to trying to solve a very, very complex issue. That is why I offer this amendment, which would institute positive incentives to promote religious freedom."[59] From this perspective, the fact that problems are complex means that responses must be more sophisticated. Supporters of Wolf-Specter, on the other hand, would sometimes express contempt for those who found complexity in the problem of religious freedom.

---

[55] Senate Committee Hearings, 101 (Bishop Mano).
[56] Ibid., 114 (William R. O'Brien).
[57] Ibid., 113 (John Akers).
[58] Ibid., 58–59 (Bishop Mano).
[59] *Congressional Record,* 14 May 1998, H3290.

Although Nickles supporters acknowledged that in some limited cases sanctions can be effective, they argued that they should be considered as only part of a broad range of possible actions that might be taken and should be the last measures imposed rather than the first. "[T]he experience we have had with sanctions in recent years leads us to be cautious and deliberate in invoking them as a remedy in public affairs."[60] Felice Gaer particularly emphasized that the use of sanctions should be a part of an integrated policy and not simply an automatic punishment to wrongful behavior by a government. "Sanctions," she said,

> are a key tool of US foreign policy, but they should not be the sole substitute for a broader and focused policy response. In the 1990s, sanctions have been employed with increasing frequency; one study reminds us that the US has employed sanctions more since 1993 than in all the prior years of this century. It is our view that US sanctions should be designed to fit the specific policy objectives of specific cases. They are most effective when they are part of a policy response, not an alternative to one.[61]

She praised the Nickles bill for having a "sophisticated and calibrated menu of sanctions."[62] Bishop Mano complimented the Nickles bill, in contrast to the "high-handed" Wolf-Specter bill, as not being a law to "persecute the persecutors. This [Nickles] bill is there to rectify the situation."[63] As stated above, supporters of the IRFA viewpoint also urged that, whenever possible, actions be taken on a multilateral basis rather than unilaterally by the United States.

Perhaps even more important, the Nickles-IRFA viewpoint stressed, unlike Wolf-Specter, that careful attention must be paid to the potential effect that sanctions, denunciations, or any other action will have on the people of the country and on those whom the actions are designed to help. "In my experience, unilateral and uniform sanctions applied to all countries who violate a particular set of rules are seldom effective and may be counterproductive."[64] This viewpoint was particularly concerned that sanctions in support of a religious minority could prove to be counterproductive by further isolating the minority and perhaps even lead to reprisals by the government or individuals. Renewing the concern about the "complexity" of the problem, John Ackers observed that in

> some societies, stringent and thoughtless measures by the United States could actually make the situation worse for believers, rather than better. Religious persecution is usually a far more complex issue than we are willing to admit. As a church leader from

[60] House Committee Hearings, 26 (Drew Christiansen). Sanctions, if "used wisely and sparingly," Jerry Goodman testified, "are likely to be most effective if placed in the context of other strategies and, above all in the context of other tactics. . . . [Q]uiet diplomacy is necessary and useful" (ibid., 54 [Jerry Goodman]).

[61] Senate Committee Hearings, 105 (Felice Gaer).

[62] Ibid., 106.

[63] Ibid., 57 ("high handed"), 61 ("persecute the persecutors") (Bishop Mano). Not surprisingly, Senator Nickles also recognized the downside of imposing sanctions (ibid., 3, 9 [statements of Senator Nickles]). An article published in October 1998 reported that "Nickles believed that the Wolf-Specter bill's provisions for automatic sanctions against the worst persecuting countries would lead to fruitless confrontations, negative fallout on indigenous Christians and missionaries, and an America isolated from it allies" (Tony Carnes, "Religious Persecution Bill Encounters Stiff Resistance" [*Christianity Today*, 5 October 1998, 26]).

[64] House Committee Hearings, 59–60 (Lauren Homer).

> one Asian country said to me, 'If my government concludes we Christians are the cause of bad relations between our two countries, it will only make life more difficult for us.'[65]

Accordingly, IRFA supporters favored consultations with local religious communities that might feel the negative effects of US actions, rather than the automatic imposition of sanctions under Wolf-Specter.

2. IRFA as Enacted

The final version of IRFA, as adopted unanimously by the Senate and House, is a complex piece of legislation, consisting of seven titles, and twelve-thousand words. IRFA has as its professed aim to "condemn violations of religious freedom, and to promote, and to assist other governments in the promotion of, the fundamental right to freedom of religion" (sec. 2[b][1]). According to one of its drafters, "Really the cornerstone of our bill, however, is that action is required in response to violations of religious liberty."[66] The complex means for accomplishing this simple goal was through creating new governmental offices and positions, requiring several new reports, requiring the president to take targeted actions against states found to be violating international religious freedom standards, requiring improvements in training for officials at the Department of State and the Immigration and Naturalization Service, and providing for actions to be taken to promote religious freedom. Although there are reasonable grounds for different opinions as to the relative priority of the different provisions of IRFA, the following certainly are among the most important.

First, creating an Office of International Religious Freedom at the US Department of State, headed by an Ambassador at Large for International Religious Freedom. The office was to become the principal locus in the US government for coordinating activities to promote international religious freedom and to report on violators. [67]

Second, requiring the State Department to issue an Annual Report on International Religious Freedom. In coordination with the ambassador, the Department of State is required to issue an annual report on all foreign countries and make findings regarding violations of religious freedom and to report on actions taken by the United States to promote religious freedom in those countries (sec. 102[b]).

Third, requiring "presidential actions" be taken regarding countries found to be violating international religious freedom or engaging in "particularly severe" violations of international religious freedom. Under Title IV of IRFA, the president, in response to findings of violations of international religious freedom, is provided a list of fifteen possible responses, at least one of which must be made toward the country.[68] The president is required to apply at least one of the measures (1) through (15) (or a commensurate action) for the violation of religious freedom, and one of the measures (9) through (15) (or a commensurate action) for a particularly severe violation of

[65] Senate Committee Hearings, 112–13 (John Akers).

[66] Hackett, Silk, and Hoover, eds., *Religious Persecution as a U.S. Policy Issue,* 11 (Laura Bryant).

[67] "The primary responsibility of the Ambassador at Large shall be to advance the right to freedom of religion abroad, to denounce the violation of that right, and to recommend appropriate responses by the United States Government when this right is violated" (IRFA, sec. 101[c][1]).

[68] The fifteen possible presidential actions are found at IRFA, sec. 405(a).

religious freedom. Before taking any of the more serious actions, the president should take steps to minimize any adverse impact on the people of the country that is targeted or on humanitarian relief operations (sec. 401[c][2][A]). The words "sanction" and "sanctions" are used a total of eight times in IRFA, and always refer either to sanctions that pre-existed the enactment of IRFA (sec. 402[c][4][D]) or to the commission's possible recommendation of new sanctions (sec. 202[b]).

Fourth, creating the US Commission on International Religious Freedom and the position of a Special Adviser for International Religious Freedom at the National Security Council. Title II, sections 201 to 206, creates a commission, which is to be composed of nine members, appointed by the president and the leadership of the Senate and House, as well as the ambassador who serves in an *ex officio* capacity. The quasi-independent commission is given the responsibility for providing an "annual and ongoing review of the facts and circumstances of violations of religious freedom" and making policy recommendations (sec. 202[a]). Specifically, the commission is charged to make recommendations "with respect to each foreign country the government of which has engaged in or tolerated violations of religious freedom, including particularly severe violations of religious freedom" (sec. 202[b]). IRFA recommends the appointment of a Special Adviser for International Religious Freedom at the National Security Council who is to compile information and coordinate activities within the White House (sec. 301).

Fifth, providing for several activities to promote international religious freedom. IRFA provides that the US government shall undertake positive measures, including improving training for Foreign Service Officers and the Immigration and Naturalization Service (secs. 104, 602, 603), encouraging the United States to promote religious freedom by meeting with NGOs and religious prisoners (sec. 105), providing financial assistance to groups supporting freedom of religion (sec. 106), providing religious groups access to embassy facilities equal to that granted to nonreligious groups (sec. 107), creating prisoner lists (sec. 108), and promoting international exchanges (Sec. 503), and providing merit awards for Foreign Service Officers (sec. 504).

Finally, requiring modifications of refugee and asylum procedures. One of the original motivating efforts for the Wolf-Specter bill had been to revise significantly rules and procedures of the INS and to give priority to religious asylum claims. Although IRFA ultimately did not adopt that approach, it did provide for additional training for officials involved with potential asylum claims (secs. 602, 603), and required the issuance of new guidelines through the Attorney General and Secretary of State to ensure that religious asylum claims are not disadvantaged due to prejudice or bias.

C. Conclusion

The early and vigorous promoters of the Wolf-Specter bill, sometimes simplistically characterized as "the Christian right," should be credited for creating the momentum that ultimately led to the adoption of IRFA. But there was, as should now be clear, a significant difference of perspectives between the promoters of the Wolf-Specter bill and the promoters of IRFA.

The unsuccessful Wolf-Specter bill and the successful Nickles-IRFA bill reveal two strikingly different approaches to the goal of promoting religious freedom. The Wolf-Specter approach was characterized by its focusing on the more egregious cases of "religious persecution" (as it would be defined in US law), its emphasizing persecution of Christians, its suspicion of the Clinton administration and the diplomacy of the US State Department, and its choice of automatic sanctions as the best means to force offending regimes to alter their behavior. The Nickles-IRFA approach emphasized, to the contrary, support for all people who suffer from violations of religious liberty as defined by international standards, diplomacy rather than sanctions, and providing better information on the status of religious freedom worldwide.[69]

By comparing the first version of Wolf-Specter and the arguments that were used to support it to IRFA, it is possible to see the dramatic transformation and maturing process that took place. Indeed, the original Wolf-Specter approach exemplified "the morality of absolute self-assurance fired by the crusading spirit" identified years ago by Senator Fulbright.[70] IRFA, on the other hand, exemplified "the morality of decent instincts tempered by the knowledge of human imperfection." Both are characteristics—perhaps peculiar characteristics—of Americans, but in this case the decent instincts ultimately prevailed and sensible rather than extremist legislation ultimately succeeded. But one of the deeply unfortunate legacies of the rhetoric employed to support the Wolf-Specter bill is that it has left the inaccurate impression that IRFA embodies the Wolf-Specter vision. It continues to be believed, inaccurately, that IRFA reflects the narrow viewpoint of the Christian right and that it is a law whose principal enforcement mechanism is the unilateral imposition of sanctions by the United States. The fact that such inaccurate assumptions are widely believed reveals the potency and the damage caused by the Wolf-Specter rhetoric, thereby making the legitimate effort of US diplomacy to promote freedom of religion all the more difficult.

III. Activities of the United States to Promote Religious Freedom under IRFA: The Statute and Its Implementation

A. Diplomatic activities of the State Department and the Office of International Religious Freedom

At the time IRFA was enacted, the State Department had already created an office of International Religious Freedom ("IRF" in its State Department acronym) that was headed by Robert A. Seiple, who had become the secretary's special adviser for

[69] It is interesting to note one significant difference between many of the original supporters of Nickles and IRFA and those who supported Wolf-Specter. This difference was not one of political viewpoint (left versus right), but of one viewpoint that arose out of ***substantial international experience dealing with religious freedom and religious persecution*** (Nickles-IRFA), while the other arose out of domestic US experience in lobbying and pressuring Congress and the United States government. In examining the backgrounds of supporters of Wolf-Specter, it can be noted that the vast majority had very little, if any, experience in foreign policy and had not spent a significant amount of time living outside of the United States. The perspective of most Wolf-Specter supporters, who had little international experience, may be contrasted with that of Mr. Sam Ericsson, who is well regarded by many Wolf-Specter supporters, but who has had a significant amount of international experience. In a letter to his friend, Congressman Wolf, Ericsson criticized the Wolf-Specter legislation: "First the philosophical cornerstone of the Act is retaliatory—'an eye for an eye, tooth for a tooth.' This troubles me. . . . Second, I expressed concern about the list of countries identified as being particularly troublesome. . . . Third, the way I read the thrust and possible application of the Bill, it ignores any progress that may have been made in any given country.

international religious freedom in August 1998. In signing IRFA, on October 27, President Clinton announced his intention to appoint Seiple to be the new ambassador at large for international religious freedom, an appointment that was subsequently confirmed by the Senate. During the first few months of its existence, IRF had only two full-time employees, Seiple himself and his secretary, though the State Department also had allotted the part-time services of two other persons and the US Institute of Peace sent a Senior Fellow to work for the office. The State Department chose not to emphasize Seiple's statutory authority of "principal adviser" to the president and secretary of state on issues relating to religious freedom, but placed his office bureaucratically within the Bureau of Democracy, Human Rights and Labor ("DRL"), and required that contacts from him to the secretary of state go through the assistant secretary of state for human rights.

During his two-year tenure (he resigned shortly after issuing the second religious freedom report), Seiple became responsible for raising the profile of religious freedom both within the State Department and internationally. Much of his time was devoted to explaining the functions of his office to officials within the US government. He and his office traveled on more than two-dozen trips outside the United States to express American concern about violations of religious freedom and to offer assistance if requested. A description of these efforts are contained in the *Religious Freedom Reports* issued in September 1999 and 2000.[71] The State Department has also taken steps, as required by IRFA, to enhance the training of Foreign Service Officers on religious issues.[72] Although outside the jurisdiction of the State Department, the Immigration and Naturalization Service also has implemented changes to correspond with its own obligations under IRFA.[73]

The United States government, as part of its bilateral relations with the countries of the world, now regularly includes issues related to religious freedom as a part of the discussion. With Greece there is a discussion about minority Muslims as well as Jehovah's Witnesses. With Turkey there is a discussion not only about the treatment of Orthodox Christians, but about Muslims. With China there have been discussions about Falun Gong and the House Church movement. With countries in Central Asia there are discussions about how attempts to crack down on extremists are alienating large segments of the population and are harming small Christian groups. Countries of the world now expect, for better or worse, that the United States will be placing such issues on their bilateral agenda.

The United States has also, albeit in a much less pronounced way, continued to place the issue of international religious freedom in multilateral fora. This is particularly apparent in the OSCE, where the United States makes at least one major presentation

---

After spending eight years and over 20,000 hours on the international side of the issue, I conclude that it is very difficult to take accurate 'snapshots' of conditions within some countries" (Samuel E. Ericsson, Letter to Congressman Frank R. Wolf, 9 March 1998, 1–2). Ericsson cautiously endorsed the Wolf-Specter bill. However, after the introduction of the Nickles bill, Ericsson wrote an enthusiastic letter to Senator Nickles praising the approach that resulted in IRFA (Samuel E. Ericsson, Letter to Senator Don Nickles, 2 May 1998).

[70] See the epigraph at footnote 3 in this chapter.

[71] Department of State, *Annual Report: International Religious Freedom* (1999 and following years). The reports are available at the State Department website, <www.state.gov>.

[72] Department of State, *Annual Report on International Religious Freedom 2000*, 551–53.

[73] Ibid., 555–62 (Appendix D).

each year at the implementation meetings in Warsaw or the review meetings in Vienna. The United States uses OSCE meetings as an opportunity to engage both bilaterally and multilaterally with other countries. Until 2001, when the United States failed to be re-elected to the UN Human Rights Commission, it continued to raise issues of religious freedom in country-specific resolutions regarding China, Cuba, Iran, and Iraq—though there was little difference between the practices of the United States in this regard before and after the enactment of IRFA.

While it is understandable how some may characterize this as American arrogance and interference with the internal affairs of foreign countries, such objections ignore two fundamental facts: first, by agreeing to international human rights conventions, the countries of the world have acknowledged that human rights are not a matter solely of internal affairs, but are a legitimate international issue. Second, all states of the world are completely free to comment on the actions of other states—and they do so. The United States is often criticized for many of its domestic practices: the death penalty, racism, insufficient attention to the plight of the poor, a health care system that favors the rich, its energy consumption, and environmental pollution.[74] The use of words to criticize countries is a traditional part of both public and private diplomacy. This author is aware of no decision of any international court, the opinion of no recognized international legal scholar, or the existence of any international convention that suggests that commenting or reporting on another state's actions is an interference with the internal affairs of that state. The assertion that a verbal denunciation is "an interference in internal affairs" is simply a rhetorical device to deflect attention from the underlying denunciation. Indeed, the suggestion that a state and its citizens should be precluded from commenting on the religious situation in other countries is itself anathema to the freedom of expression. If a country asserts that the United States is interfering with its internal affairs when it comments on freedom of religion, then that country is itself engaged in the very act of doing what it insists that the other has no right to do. The assertion that states should be precluded from commenting on the human rights practices of other states is without any moral or legal merit whatsoever.

It is possible that the two most enduring legacies of the Seiple office will be the integration of religious freedom as part of US foreign policy and the launching of the *Religious Freedom Reports*.[75] Although the reports have understandable shortcomings, as any such enormous endeavor must have, it nevertheless is fair to say that they are well on their way to becoming the standard international reference on the state of religious freedom.[76] By comparing the 1996 and 2000 *Country Reports on Human*

---

[74] For an example of the Chinese government's criticism of the human rights record of the United States, see, e.g., *US Human Rights Record in 2000,* <http://www.humanrights-china.org/en/eindex.html>.

[75] People have reached different conclusions about whether the United States should exempt itself from this review. On the one hand such an exemption suggests—however unintentionally—that the United States does not need to be evaluated with regard to its own policies on religious freedom. On the other, a self-evaluation by the United States might not be taken as being fair or objective. Whatever the conclusion reached on this issue, other states and NGOs are fully free to issue reports on the United States, and they do so.

[76] For critiques of the *Annual Reports,* see *Report of the United States Commission on International Religious Freedom,* 1 May 2000, 59–66, and Rosalind I.J. Hackett (unpublished paper delivered at Harvard University, May 2001).

Rights Practices (*Country Reports*) and the 2000 *Annual Report on International Religious Freedom* (*Religious Freedom Report*), we see that not only has the amount of reporting increased substantially, so has the quality of the reporting.

Although there is much overlap between the *Country Reports* and the *Religious Freedom Reports*, the quality of religious rights reporting in the *Religious Freedom Reports* is superior to that of the *Country Reports.* Whereas the *Country Reports* are unable to delve into substantial detail and explanations of the ramifications of the religious discrimination, the annual *Religious Freedom Reports* add to the *Country Reports* with additional detail, anecdotes, discussion of law and the ramifications of these laws, government involvement, and societal pressures. The distinction between the reporting prior and post IRFA is the completeness. By including sections on religious demography, government actions, and societal attitudes, the reader is better able to understand the situations in these countries.

Despite the continuing improvements in country reporting, there nevertheless is a need for more and better information. One of the significant services that could be performed by people around the world is to provide information to US embassies on problems of discrimination on the basis of religion and belief. This is particularly important where the reports have failed to include credible reports of discrimination and persecution.

B. "Presidential Actions"

The sanctions and "presidential actions" provisions of Wolf-Specter and IRFA were among their most contentious and contested provisions. The rhetoric of the Wolf-Specter supporters stressed that the president must be held accountable for failing to impose sanctions on persecuting regimes. Unlike the automatic sanctions provisions of Wolf-Specter that applied uniformly to all persecuting countries, IRFA identified two categories of violation: first, "violations of religious freedom,"[77] and second, "particularly severe violations of religious freedom."[78] Under IRFA, countries that engaged in "particularly severe violations of religious freedom" were designated "countries of particular concern" (CPCs). For violations of religious freedom, the president was required to respond with "presidential actions" within a range of fifteen enumerated "targeted responses" that were to be invoked in a manner proportionate to the violation.[79]

With regard to the lesser category, "violations of religious freedom," the sole responsive actions of the US government thus far have been to issue public and private démarches and to make public condemnations in multilateral fora. In other words, with respect to almost 190 countries, the US response has not gone beyond issuing words. No sanctions have been imposed.

With regard to the more serious category, the CPCs, the State Department has thus far identified only six countries as satisfying the statutory criteria: Burma, China, Iran, Iraq, North Korea, and Sudan. In addition, the State Department previously designated the Taliban in Afghanistan and the Milosevic regime in Serbia as falling

---

[77] IRFA, secs. 3(13), 401.

[78] IRFA, secs. 3(11), 402.

[79] See note 68 in this chapter.

under this general rubric, although these two were not considered "countries."[80] Although the designations were published in the *Federal Register*, the identifications of the responsive "presidential actions" for the CPCs were not published, though they were transmitted to the congressional leadership.[81] In its first report to Congress, the State Department identified the severity of the violations of five states (and two entities), described public condemnations that the United States has made, but reported that actions that had previously been taken by the US government for other purposes also satisfied the requirements of IRFA.

Thus, under the presidential actions provisions of IRFA, *the United States has not taken any additional actions other than making public or private criticisms.* Anyone who believes that IRFA has led to the United States imposing new sanctions on any country is simply misinformed.

C. The US Commission on International Religious Freedom

IRFA, as amended in 2002, created a nine-member commission to exist until the year 2011.[82] This commission, whose role is advisory, has received an annual appropriation between two and three million dollars, which has enabled it to secure office space and hire a staff of approximately twenty people. (This contrasts markedly with the small staff of the Office of International Religious Freedom in the State Department, which is actually charged with administering and implementing IRFA.)

As required by sections 202 and 203 of IRFA, the commission has issued its annual reports on May 1 of each year on the "facts and circumstances" surrounding violations of religious freedom and made policy recommendations.[83] The commission's reports included chapters that described, in varying degrees of detail, the situations in countries of the world and made a number of recommendations. The commission also held hearings, issued press releases, and sent letters to the president urging that certain actions be taken.[84]

Although IRFA specifically requires the commission to report on "*each* foreign country" whose government violates freedom of religion,[85] the commission has ignored this statutory requirement and has emphasized instead—like the Wolf-Specter bill—identifying the worst violators and arguing for imposing sanctions on those

---

80 Serbia has since been removed from the list.

81 Although Congress has apparently not released it publically, the author obtained a copy of the first "presidential actions" report, which was dated 22 October 1999. The 1999 report consists of a three-page cover letter and a ten-page Memorandum of Justification. The report is not classified.

82 As originally conceived, the commission would have ceased to exist in 2003. Amendments in the year 2002, however, prolonged the life of the commission until the year 2011 and altered the duration of commission membership. Public Law 107–228, 116 Stat. 1409.

83 *Report of the United States Commission on International Religious Freedom* (1 May 2000); *Report of the United States Commission on International Religious Freedom* (1 May 2001) (hereafter "Commission 2001 Report"). The Commission 2001 Report was supplemented by an addendum on 14 May 2001, which also contains an individual opinion by Commissioner al-Marayati that dissents from the commission's decision not to include a statement on Israel and the Occupied Territories. The commission continues to issue annual reports.

84 The commission's activities are reported at its website, <www.uscirf.gov>.

85 IRFA, sec. 202(b) (emphasis added).

countries. The commission's second report, for example, repeatedly criticized the State Department for not having designated several additional states as "CPCs."[86] Although the principal statutory reason for designating a state as a CPC would be to trigger the imposition of the more serious of the defined "presidential actions," the commission curiously does not identify which of such presidential actions it would recommend be imposed against the countries that it sought to add to the list. For example, in 2001 the commission insisted that Saudi Arabia should be labeled a "CPC" and criticized the State Department for not making this designation and for not imposing sanctions, but the commission itself identified no sanctions that it would have imposed on Saudi Arabia. This policy of criticizing the State Department for not imposing sanctions on Saudi Arabia while failing to recommend any of its own continued through 2003. By emphasizing the worst offenders and by using the term "sanctions" rather than "presidential actions," the commission seems to be reverting to some of the rhetoric and themes of the original Wolf-Specter bill and to have departed from IRFA as ultimately enacted.[87] The commission does discuss a number of countries that are not among the worst offenders, and during its first years did not even mention many issues of religious freedom that were the subject of congressional hearings and State Department actions, such as the increasingly harsh treatment of religious minorities in some European countries.[88] It is curious that a commission created for the *exclusive* purpose of advising on religious freedom in all countries of the world, that has a staff of twenty people and an annual budget of two to three million dollars, was not able to devote any analysis toward such topics and that it continues to address only a small portion of the countries included in the State Department's annual report.

Perhaps the most interesting work of the commission has been its recommendations regarding access to US capital markets for governments and companies whose actions may either cause or be complicit with violations of freedom of religion.[89] The commission assumes, reasonably enough, that if a government is abusing the rights of its citizens and that companies operating in those countries are contributing to those abuses, the US government should consider taking steps to limit the ability of those

---

[86] Commission 2001 Report, 17, 20, 155–56, 171, 173–74, Addendum, 6.

[87] Some commission members were affiliated, directly or indirectly, with the Wolf-Specter bill, including the first two chairmen, Rabbi David Saperstein (who endorsed, with reservations, the first version of Wolf-Specter) and Elliott Abrams (whose Center for Ethics and Public Policy endorsed Wolf-Specter), Nina Shea, Richard Land and Archbishop (now Cardinal) McCarrick, who wrote a letter endorsing Wolf-Specter. The first executive director of the commission, Steven McFarland, worked closely with the Wolf-Specter lobbying coalition and, at least initially, opposed the Brady amendment and the Nickles bill. It should be stressed, however, that the various supporters of Wolf-Specter had different reasons for doing so and that they did not share uniform opinions about the merits of particular provisions of the bill. Rabbi David Saperstein, for example, although endorsing the bill on the day it was first introduced in the House, later said that "As committed as we are to combating religious persecution, the legislation as it was originally introduced was problematic for some of us. However, the bill coming to the House floor is substantially different from when it was introduced. . . . The current version of the bill now addresses some of our most pressing concerns by: broadening the coverage of the bill to include all religious groups in all countries; moving the monitoring office from the White House to the State Department [and by making other important changes]" (quoted by Congressman Frank Wolf, *Congressional Record,* 14 May 1998, H3269).

[88] See House Committee on International Relations, *The Treatment of Religious Minorities in Western Europe,* 106th Cong., 2d sess. (14 June 2000).

[89] See, e.g., Commission 2001 Report, 26, 126–27, 155–63.

companies to raise funds through securities offerings in the United States. Whereas on some issues the commission has interpreted its mandate (religious freedom) narrowly, with regard to the capital markets it has interpreted its mandate quite broadly.[90]

Conclusion

As can be seen from the discussion above, the debate over religion and human rights brought forth two different attitudes and responses on the part of Americans who seek to have the United States more fully engaged in the process of promoting a fundamental human right. One attitude stresses the unilateral role that the United States should take to respond to certain of the most serious abuses of religious freedom. It emphasizes forceful denunciations and strong responses by the United States. It suggests that the principal reason for religious persecution is because of ideologies that are hostile either toward religion generally or to Christianity in particular. Those who share this attitude typically believe that the best method for changing the behavior of the persecutors is to denounce them publicly and to put economic and political pressure on them to change. The emphasis is on employing forceful words and meaningful sanctions to change behavior, while believing that a failure to impose sanctions signifies indifference or callousness to human rights abuses.

The other attitude views violations of religious freedom as part of complex and interrelated problems that typically include hostility to all rights of expression and association. In this view, violations of religious freedom typically are part of deep historical and cultural beliefs that will not easily be shed in response to pressure from the United States. Denunciations and accusations by the United States may indeed have counterproductive results by increasing prejudice against beleaguered minorities and thereby make regimes even more intransigent. When trying to make improvements, this second attitude believes, it is critical to understand the situation from the perspective of the country that is abusing human rights. This does not mean agreeing with the persecutors; it means trying to understand why the persecution is taking place and to address it in an effective way.

These contrasting viewpoints perhaps exemplify something more than Americans' contradictory attitudes about freedom of religion or even human rights generally. They perhaps exemplify two different strands in American thinking about the role of the United States in the world. Both strands understand the need for American engagement in the world, but the terms of that engagement are quite different. The first believes that the United States and its government know best what should be done, and the question is whether the government has the courage and fortitude to push, pull, cajole, and sanction other countries until the American objective is accomplished.[91] The second viewpoint, although fully wishing to engage the United States in an effort to improve the lives of those who suffer for their religious beliefs, nevertheless understands that the United States leads best when it leads by a genuine, informed, and sincere commitment to promoting all human rights.

---

[90] For example, the commission recommends significant new disclosure requirements on all companies ("issuers") that do business in countries that have been designated as "CPCs" (ibid., 161–62).

[91] The text of this paragraph was originally written prior to the United States-led military invasion of Iraq in 2003. The impulse for that invasion similarly typifies this strand of American foreign-policy behavior.

Chapter 33

The Role of Religion and Religious Freedom in Contemporary Conflict Situations

Rüdiger Noll

I. Introduction

Religion in connection with violent conflict situations seems to have hit the front pages of international newspapers more than ever before in recent weeks and months. The "marching season" in Northern Ireland resulted in violent incidents between Roman Catholics and Protestants, which threaten the peace process; Jews and Palestinians fight over holy places in Jerusalem; laying the foundation stone for the reconstruction of the mosque in Banja Luka (Bosnia and Herzegovina) led to riots of Orthodox Serbs against Muslims; two Roman Catholic nuns were convicted by a Belgian court for their role in the Rwandan genocide; Russia and the Central Asian states feel threatened by the progress of the radical Islamic Taliban from Afghanistan; the destruction of places of worship of Christians and Muslims is repeatedly reported from India, Indonesia, the Philippines, and Sri Lanka. All of the headlines refer only to the most recent manifestations of long, ongoing conflicts, and the list of headlines and countries involved could easily be prolonged.

Religious communities feel threatened and governments as well as international organizations are becoming increasingly worried. More and more violent incidents are recorded in the reports of the UN Special Rapporteur on Freedom of Religion or Belief (formerly on Religious Intolerance).[1] The Organization of Security and Cooperation in Europe (OSCE) held a special seminar in March 1999, which emphasized the role of religion in conflict situations.[2] It also established an Advisory Panel of Experts on Freedom of Religion or Belief, which among other things deals with dialogue, tolerance, and nondiscrimination and serves as an early warning instrument.[3]

---

[1] For the reports of the UN Special Rapporteur on Freedom of Religion or Belief, see <www.unhchr.ch>.

[2] For the report of this seminar held in Vienna on March 22, 1999, see <www.osce.org>.

[3] For general information on the Advisory Panel, see Office for Democratic Institutions and Human Rights, *Annual Report 2000* (Warsaw: OSCE, 2000), 34; or the OSCE websites: <www.osce.org>, <www.religlaw.org>.

Tore Lindholm, W. Cole Durham, Jr., Bahia G. Tahzib-Lie (eds.), Facilitating Freedom of Religion or Belief: A Deskbook, *747–760.*

The Norwegian OSCE Chairmanship-in-Office organized a roundtable conference on religion and conflict prevention in Oslo in June 1999.[4] Furthermore, the commissioner for human rights of the Council of Europe convened an experts' meeting on the role of religion in armed conflicts.[5]

Religion becomes increasingly associated with violent conflicts. Religious communities and governments appear to lack ways and means to stop the trend. In the light of this, one might argue—and some people do—that the sphere of influence of religion should be limited, religion should be banned from politics and public life, and international standards regarding freedom of religion or belief should be limited to traditional, well-established religions. This chapter will argue in the opposite direction: infringing on the right to freedom of religion or belief will increase and fuel conflict situations. Attempts to expel religion from society and politics will create violence and not reduce it.

Much less public attention is paid to the positive role of religion in conflict prevention, nonviolent conflict management, and community building in post-conflict situations. But both are equally true as the then Norwegian minister for development and human rights, Hilde F. Johnson, said before the UN Commission on Human Rights in 1999: "Religion is often described as a source of radical prejudice, the germ of conflict. Although this judgment is often misplaced, it points to the fact that religion or belief can also be a powerful source for the resolution of conflict."[6] Emphasizing the positive role of religion for peace and reconciliation, some authors go as far as to speak of "Religion, the Missing Dimension of Statecraft."[7] In order to fulfill that positive role, religions need the space protected by international standards regarding freedom of religion or belief.

The issue to be addressed is not whether or not religion should play a role in society and politics. The issue is strengthening the positive role of religion. The full implementation of the right to freedom of religion or belief appears as a precondition to conflict prevention, peaceful settlement of conflicts, and post-conflict stability.

Before looking at how the implementation of freedom of religion or belief affects conflict situations, I want to take a closer look at the role of religion itself in contemporary conflicts and religion as a potential promoter of peace and reconciliation. As the Carnegie Commission on Preventing Deadly Conflict rightly stated, "[R]eligion can be part of the solution to the problem of ethnic and religious conflict—no one doubted it has been part of the problem."[8]

II. Religion as an Element in Contemporary Conflicts

The 1998 Oslo Declaration on the Freedom of Religion or Belief,[9] the founding document of the Oslo Coalition for Freedom of Religion or Belief, stated that: "religions and beliefs teach peace and good will."[10] Peace and reconciliation as well as the care for

[4] For the rapporteur's report of this roundtable conference, see *Helsinki Monitor* 10, no. 4 (1999): 87–90.

[5] The conclusions of the meeting can be found on the website of the commissioner: <www.commissioner.coe.int>.

[6] Mentioned by Hilde F. Johnson, the Norwegian Minister for Development and Human Rights, in her statement to the 55th session of the *UN Commission on Human Rights*, 26 March 1999, Geneva, 6.

[7] See Douglas Johnston and Cynthia Sampson, eds., *Religion, the Missing Dimension of Statecraft* (New York: Oxford University Press, 1994).

one's neighbor are an integral part of all religions' doctrine and value orientation. How can it be then that we witness today an increased involvement of religions in conflict situations? Did religions themselves become a force of violence or were they misused by other forces?

Indeed, history has shown, that the expansion of one religion onto the territory of another often went along with violence. Incidents continue to occur today. In general, however, issues such as aggressive mission activities and proselytism are discussed in international, ecumenical, and interreligious fora in order to avoid violence.[11] It is also true that every period in history has been faced with the issue of whether or not the struggle for religious values such as freedom, justice, equality, and human rights justifies the use of violence. In this connection reference can be, for instance, made to the just war developed by Christianity and jihad developed by Islam. More recently the discussion centered on the issue of whether or not the Special Fund of the World Council of Churches' Program to Combat Racism could also support liberation movements in Southern Africa, which also used violence, if no other means brought about change of the apartheid system. Situations such as in the Sudan or in Milosovic's Yugoslavia ensued a debate on the legitimacy of military intervention for humanitarian purposes. In January 2001, the member churches of the World Council of Churches launched a Decade to Overcome Violence and adopted a statement on "The Protection of Endangered Populations in Situations of Armed Violence,"[12] which reflects the diverging opinions among various religions on this issue.

The incidents where religious beliefs were the recent cause of armed conflicts are, however, rather few compared to those situations in which religion was misused for other purposes. It is the misuse of religion that is on the increase.

Two important trends must be considered in this regard. A first trend is that the nature of armed conflicts in general has changed since the end of the Cold War.[13] While the number of armed conflicts remains fairly constant, the 1990s saw a remarkable increase of armed conflicts in eastern Europe (particularly in the former Soviet Union) and in Asia, while there was a decline in major conflicts in Latin America. A second trend shows that most of the current wars are intrastate conflicts, which center around issues of autonomy or self-government. As religion and ethnicity often become the framework for expressing one's own identity, analysts speak of an increase of religious and ethnic conflicts. Religion and ethnicity, however, are seldom the root cause of such

---

[8] R. Scott Appleby, *The Ambivalence of the Sacred: Religion, Violence, and Reconciliation* (New York: Rowman and Littlefield, 2000), xi.

[9] The Oslo Declaration was accepted by acclamation at the conclusion of the August 1998 Oslo Conference on Freedom of Religion or Belief. For its text, see Appendix E of this book.

[10] See Hans Küng and Karl-Josef Kuschel, eds., *A Global Ethic: The Declaration of the Parliament of the World's Religions* (London: SCM Press, 1993), 8–24.

[11] On 14–16 October 1999, Muslim and Christian representatives met in the US upon invitation of the World Council of Churches and affirmed "the importance of distinguishing between proselytism and witness, as the WCC has done within the Christian context, and emphasize the necessity to express an ethics of mission and do work to which both Christians and Muslims can agree" (n.p., n.d.).

[12] See World Council of Churches, Central Committee Minutes, 51st Meeting, *The Protection of Endangered Populations in Situations of Armed Violence: Toward an Ecumenical Ethnical Approach,* 28 January–6 February 2001, Potsdam, Germany, 62–67, 219–42.

[13] See John Paul Lederach, *Building Peace: Sustainable Reconciliation in Divided Societies* (Washington, D.C.: United States Institute of Peace Press, 1999), 7–10.

conflicts. Therefore, John Paul Lederach and Ernie Regehr prefer to speak of "identity conflicts," because "it is often the failure of governing structures to address fundamental needs, provide space for participation in decisions, and ensure an equitable distribution of resources and benefits that makes identification with a group so attractive and salient in a given setting."[14]

Some features of modern-type identity conflicts are worth mentioning here. People seek for identity in increasingly smaller and narrower identity groups, which leads to a growing fractionalization and a diffusion of power. Most conflicts are lodged in long-standing relationships, and the enemy is not half way around the globe but in close geographic proximity. These features explain why previous governmental and international mechanisms for dealing with contemporary conflicts are limited. They were mainly established for interstate conflicts. In consequence, John Paul Lederach argues for a shift of paradigm in peace building—an approach worth remembering as we will look on the positive contribution of religions in peace building: "[P]eace building must be rooted in and responsible to the experiential and subjective realities shaping peoples' perspective and needs. . . . I believe this paradigmatic shift is articulated in the movement away from a concern with the resolution of issues and towards a frame of reference that focuses on the restoration and re-building of relationships."[15]

The process of globalization increases the search for identity and poses a new challenge in this regard. At a time when decision making moves ever further away from the people, when people feel powerless vis-à-vis "these actors who are financially strong and those who are less concerned about ethical or other environmental concerns, that feel free to do as they like,"[16] the issue of identity and solidarity in peer groups becomes more pressing.

Problems arise when the issue of identity leads increasingly to fundamentalism or extremism as a counter-force to resist "modern trends" of secularization. Appleby refers to fundamentalism as "a specifiable pattern of religious militance by which self-styled true believers attempt to arrest the erosion of religious identity, fortify the borders of the religious communities, and create viable alternatives to secular structures and processes. The fundamentalist pattern of militance begins as a reaction to the penetration of the religious community by secular or religious outsiders."[17]

I do not want to engage at this stage in a debate on whether or not Appleby's explanation proves to be a sufficient rationale for religious fundamentalism or religious extremism. The point I want to argue, however, is that today we witness a growing fundamentalism, which is a source of conflict. The need to combat Islamic extremists (terrorists) served as an argument in the Chechen war. Attacks by the Hizbollah movement hit the news every other day and acts of violent extremism are repeatedly reported from countries such as Indonesia, India, Pakistan, and Sri Lanka.

The difficulty is, as Roger Williamson has shown, that in combating fundamentalism,

> [p]rescriptions of dialogue and tolerance do not necessarily help—since the protagonists are the non-dialoguing monotheists. It therefore follows that dialogue and compromise are out. The fundamentalist does not refuse to talk. It is often very

[14] Ibid., 8.
[15] Ibid., 24.
[16] Eskil Johnson, "New Routes for Life and Peace," *New Routes* 6, no. 1 (2001): 35.

> difficult to stop them talking—but the talk is not with a view to finding a common position, understanding better the fears and persepective of the other side in order to find a way forward, it is to assert the non-negotiable position and to achcieve its implementation.[18]

The response to fundamentalism cannot be sought in banning religion altogether from the public sphere or from being involved in politics. Religion as an advocate for the marginalized, also in its modest and humble form in which it is open for dialogue, will always want to play an advocacy role in public. The way to tackle religious fundamentalism is to address its root causes and to involve not only religious leaders, but also ordinary believers in dialogue and the promotion of tolerance. This is also an element to be remembered when asking for the role of religion in preventing violent conflict.

According to Samuel P. Huntington and his theory of a "clash of civilizations," we have only seen the tip of the iceberg as far as growing fundamentalism and an increasing number of identity conflicts are concerned.[19] According to him, these will not be limited to low-scale, intrastate conflicts. In the age of globalization, religion as a main feature of civilizations will become the major factor in a global clash, in particular between Islam and the western culture (characterized by western Christianity). It is especially Islam and the West that will engage in a civilization conflict, because of their expanding nature and their different if not contradictory value systems.

In the meantime, Huntington's theory is met with considerable criticism. Opponents suspect that Huntington's intention was to build up a new enemy picture and target group for US foreign policy after communism. Huntington may be right in speaking about an increasing number of conflicts with a religious or cultural component. He does not, however, recognize the differentiation within the cultures, which are in no way monolithic blocs. And as noted above, cultural differences are seldom the root cause of contemporary conflicts. "The underlying causes are to be found in the expansion of an economic system, which reduces human reality to its own rationality and which makes these left behind use traditional forms of conflict, which in reality are a result of the (economic) system."[20] Huntington's theory may serve as a warning. Any attempts to create new enemy pictures and to divide the world or continents such as Europe according to cultural or religious lines may fuel conflicts, rather than reduce them.[21] The UN Commission on Human Rights has expressed "deep concern at negative stereotyping of religions" and "that Islam is frequently and wrongly associated with human rights violations and with terrorism."[22]

---

[17] Appleby, *Ambivalence of the Sacred*, 86–87.

[18] Roger Williamson, "Religious Fundamentalism as a Threat to Peace: Two Studies" (LPI working paper, October 1992), 18.

[19] See Samuel P. Huntington, "The Clash of Civilizations," *Foreign Affairs* 72 (1993): 22–49; Samuel P. Huntington, *The Clash of Civilizations* (New York: Simon and Schuster, 1996); see also Bassam Tibi, *Krieg der Zivilisationene: Politik und Religion zwischen Vernunft und Fundamentalismus* (Hamburg: Hoffman und Campe, 1995); Harald Müller, *Das Zusammenleben der Kulturen: Ein Gegenentwurf zu Huntington* (Frankfurt: Fischer Taschenbuch Verlag, 1998).

[20] François Houtart, "Gewalt im Namen der Religion," *Concilium* 33 (1997): 447.

[21] See, for instance, Johan Galtung, "The Role of Communication in Rethinking European Identity in Media Development," *Journal of the World Association for Christian Communication* 40, no. 4 (1993): 3–7. A similar division of Europe underlies the statement of the former Austrian Minister for Economic Affairs, "Europe ends where orthodoxy begins!"

[22] Commission on Human Rights Resolution 2000/84 (2000), paras. 1, 2.

According to the above analysis, which tries to make a connection between root causes and the effects of conflicts, it comes as no surprise that religious communities as well as international analysts most often refuse to speak of "religious conflicts," as contemporary examples show.

All the way through the Kosovo crisis, religious leaders from the region as well as international visitors emphasized: "This is not a religious war!"[23] Ger Duijzings showed in several studies that "Kosovo also has a history of co-existence with considerable movements across its ethnic and religious frontiers, through trade, cultural diffusion, religious exchange and conversion; most people are not great believers and do not comply with religious precepts."[24] The community building across religious border lines came to a sudden and radical end though, when gross human rights violations and the war divided the country according to ethnic entities: "Religious identification has been made subordinate to ethnic identification. . . . Ethnic lines of division have become more important then religious ones, in spite of the fact that the latter continue to play a crucial role in defining the former."[25]

Another example often referred to as a "religious war" took place in Sudan, where the former British colonial power linked up with the cultural and intellectual Muslim elite and contributed thereby to a split between the Muslim community in the North and the Christian community in the South of what we know today as Sudan. A first war between the North and the South began under British rule in 1955 and lasted until 1972. The World Council of Churches and the All Africa Conference of Churches played an important role in negotiating the 1972 peace agreement of Addis Ababa. Key to the peace agreement was the guarantee for the black African minority in the South to practice their religion and to be treated equally, free of the oppressive policies of the Arab-Islamic majority in the North. One result of the peace agreement was that the Southerners were promised a far-reaching autonomy under the "Southern Provinces Regional Self-Government Act." But when in 1983 President Numeiri declared the Islamic Sharia to be the law of the entire country, this lead the Southerners to start the war again, which goes on even today. Contrary to the situation in Kosovo, most Sudanese are very religious. But despite the fact that the divisions in the Sudanese war are so clearly along religious lines, Susanne Thurfjell from the Swedish Life and Peace Institute comes to the conclusion that "[i]n fact this war—as most 'religious wars'—is not primarily over religious faith or dogma, but over equal access to political, economic and social development, benefits and power."[26]

Northern Ireland may serve as a third example. The "troubles," often reduced to a conflict between Protestants and Catholics date back to the early seventeenth century, when the English Crown wanted loyal English and Scottish settlers to replace the native Irish population. Every year, the Protestant Orange Order commemorates the defeat of the Catholic King James II in 1691, by marching through many quarters of Northern Irish cities—an offence to Roman Catholics. Several times the marching season led to riots threatening the peace process, which created new hopes since the

---

[23] See World Council of Churches, "The Churches and the Kosovo Crisis: Background Information," Press Update, 28 May 1999, Geneva.

[24] Ger Duijzings, *Religion and the Politics of Identity in Kosovo* (London: Hurst and Company, 2000), 1.

[25] Ibid., 29–30.

[26] Susanne Thurfjell, "Sermons of Sudan," *New Routes: A Journal of Peace Research and Action* 4, no. 4, (1993): 13.

signing of the "Good Friday Agreement" in 1998. In contrast to the commonly held opinion that the troubles are basically a conflict between Protestants and Roman Catholics, John D. Brewer, a Roman Catholic, explained to a meeting of the Protestant Leuenberg Church Fellowship:

> It is easy to see how some people, especially outsiders to Ireland, can mistakenly perceive the conflict as a religious one, caused by religion, fought to defend religious principles, and contested by people for whom religious affiliation is the primary identity. For most people however, their religious affiliation has no substance in the conflict, such that "Protestant" and "Catholic" are merely labels representing contrasting positions on the legitimacy of the State.[27]

The distinction whether religion is at the core of a conflict or whether it is just misused for other purposes is often hard to make. But it has to be made. If religion is not the root cause of a conflict, other root causes have to be addressed and prospects for engaging the religious community in solving a conflict are likely to be better. The question has to be raised, however: if religion is not at the core of a conflict, how is it that religion is misused as an element to accelerate and label conflict?

T. K. Oommen, François Houtart, and R. Scott Appleby have tried to respond to this question.[28] T. K. Oommen goes as far as to say that "religion as religion cannot in and of itself be an independent source of conflict."[29] In view of history, in which religions often used violence in order to expand their sphere of influence, this statement might well be disputed. But as the above-mentioned examples show, as well as others that could be mentioned, religion is much more prone to become a source of violence if it is identified with a state, a nation, or an ethnicity. Consequently, international human rights standards, which encourage the separation between the state and religious communities, or a minimum neutrality of the state toward religion, need to be highlighted and implemented. But while the separation of state and religious communities might be an accepted concept in Western Christianity, it is not in Islam and Sikhism. The most recent statement of the Russian Orthodox Church on their social concepts recognizes both a close connection between the Orthodox Church and a nation or an ethnicity as well as the dangers involved in this:

> When a nation, civil or ethnic, represents fully or predominantly a macro-confessional Orthodox community, it can in a certain sense be regarded as the one community of faith—an Orthodox nation. At the same time, national sentiments can cause such sinful phenomena as aggressive nationalism, xenophobia, national exclusiveness and inter-ethnic enmity. At their extremes, these phenomena often lead to the restriction of the rights of individuals and nations, wars and other manifestations of violence. . . . Thus, in inter-ethnic conflicts, she (the Orthodox Church) does not identify herself with any side, except for cases when one of the sides commits evident aggression or injustice.[30]

---

[27] John D. Brewer, "A History of Northern Ireland's Conflict," *epd-Dokumentation* 32 (2001): 44.

[28] Tharaileth Koshy Oommen, "Religion as a Source of Violence: A Sociological Perspective," *Ecumenical Review* 53 (2001), 168–79; Houtart, "Gewalt im Namen der Religion," 447; Appleby, *Ambivalence of the Sacred*, xi.

[29] Oommen, "Religion as a Source of Violence," 178.

[30] Russian Orthodox Church, Jubilee Bishops' Council, "Basis of the Social Concept of the Russian Orthodox Church," 13–16 August 2000, <www.russian-orthodox-church.org.ru/sd00e.htm>.

III. Religion as an Agent for Peace and Reconciliation

Despite the fact that religion is increasingly referred to as an element in violent conflicts, it "can and should play a significant role in conflict prevention and post-conflict resolution."[31] The potential of religious communities to contribute to peace and reconciliation is frequently recognized, but much less emphasized and even less used in actual conflict situations.

There are several good reasons why religions are well-placed to play a positive role. All religions are committed to values of freedom, justice, peace, and reconciliation. Initiatives such as the Parliament of the World's Religions try to bring religious leaders together around these values. A key passage of the 1993 Declaration of the Parliament reads, "We commit ourselves to a culture of nonviolence, respect, justice and peace. We shall not oppress, injure, torture or kill other human beings, forsaking violence as a means of settling differences."[32] It is important to realize that these initiatives do not remain just on an abstract level. The competence of religious communities to act as mediators in conflict situations has developed considerably over the last decade. Training courses for nonviolent mediation exist in almost every context and, as a result, many participants are already involved in peace and community building in divided societies. Several specialized institutes such as the Life and Peace Institute in Uppsala and Nairobi have been founded and play an important role.

Another important aspect, perhaps the most important, was highlighted by Kumar Rupesinghe of International Alert: "Religious organizations can be effective on all levels of society. While the work of the local church and religious leaders can complement the peace process at the grass-roots level, international religious establishments such as the Quakers or the Catholic Church can bring pressure and influence on a wider spectrum."[33] That religions have structures in place on a local, national, and international level is an important factor, often underestimated. From their context, religious communities understand themselves as part of a broader international community that transcends national or ethnic borders. Today, there are numerous international structures in place, mono-religious, ecumenical, as well as interreligious, which are known for their third-party interventions as well as their mediating role in many conflict situations, whether they have a religious component or not. Besides the Quakers and the Roman Catholic Church, mentioned by Kumar Rupesinghe, one might think of organizations such as the World Council of Churches (WCC), the World Conference on Religion and Peace (WCRP), the Orthodox Peace Fellowship and the Appeal of Conscience Foundation. As contemporary conflicts take place mostly in local or national contexts and international political instruments, which were established mainly for interstate confrontations, have limited effects, the positive contribution of local communities becomes increasingly important. It is through them and the interplay with international religious organizations that resolution of conflicts can be launched more effectively.

---

[31] *Civil and Political Rights, Including Religious Intolerance,* report submitted by Abdelfattah Amor, Special Rapporteur, in accordance with Commission on Human Rights Resolution 1999/39, UN Doc. E/CN.4/2000/65, para. 179 (2000).

[32] Küng and Kuschel, *A Global Ethic,* 8.

[33] Kumar Rupesinghe, "Multi-Track Solutions to Armed Conflicts," *Prevention and Management of Conflicts,* ed. The Dutch Center for Conflict Prevention (Amsterdam: NCDO, 1996), 15.

Finally, in most cases establishing peace is a long process. One of the strategic advantages of religions is that they have a long-standing presence in conflict situations, which enables them to accompany projects and initiatives for long duration. In contrast to politicians, religious communities and their leaders do not depend on short-term successes and solutions, which are often not sustainable. Religions have not only the potential to promote peace and reconciliation; there are many examples where religions have made important contributions to the resolution of contemporary conflict situations.

A. Religion and Conflict Prevention

Conflict prevention is the much more human and cost-effective alternative to reconstruction after a military intervention. But generally speaking, too little attention is paid to the prevention of conflicts. Governments still invest more resources in military operations and post-conflict reconstruction—as recent history in southeast Europe shows.

As the UN Special Rapporteur on Freedom of Religion or Belief rightly points out, even the international human rights system tends to have rather retroactive effects: "The Special Rapporteur considers it essential that special attention should continue to be paid to 'traditional mandate fulfillment' activities, namely in most cases, *a posteriori* action on human rights violations. At the same time, however, a strategy to prevent intolerance and discrimination must be devised."[34]

In order to react to emergency conflicts before they turn into violent confrontations "early warning" mechanisms are essential. Intolerance, discrimination, and human rights violations, and in particular infringements on minority rights and the right to freedom of religion or belief, are often indicators of emerging violence. Due to the extensive networks that religious communities have, their representatives often bring early warning signals to the attention of international political organizations. They are, however, much more seldom approached by the international organizations as they collect their data.

At the time when conflicts attract public attention, the international community often calls for a dialogue of the conflicting parties—in cases that a religious component is involved, also for a dialogue between the religious communities. In most cases, however, it will be too late for a genuine dialogue and the international organizations will need to exercise economic, political, or military pressure to gather the conflicting parties around one table and to be rather an element of conflict prevention than of conflict mediation. It needs platforms for dialogue, which are in place before conflicts turn violent, in order for potential conflicting partners to gain trust and confidence in each other and in order to promote tolerance. As Wesley Ariarajah rightly notes: "Dialogue is not an ambulance service; it is a public health program. . . . Dialogue is not so much about attempting to resolve immediate conflicts, but about building a 'community of conversation,' a 'community of heart and mind' across racial, ethnic, and religious barriers where people learn to see differences among them not as threatening but as 'natural' and 'normal!'

[34] *Civil and Political Rights, Including Religious Intolerance,* report submitted by Abdelfattah Amor, Special Rapporteur, in accordance with Commission on Human Rights Resolution 1998/18, UN Doc. E/CN.4/1999/58 72, para. 7 (1999).

Thus dialogue is an attempt to help people to understand and accept the others in their 'otherness!'"[35] In many countries, religious communities have established structures for dialogue and encounter, which do play an important role in building trust among the religious communities and are an instrument in conflict situations. Almost all over the world national and regional councils of churches, and sometimes even interreligious councils, exist. As mentioned already, it was, for instance, the WCC together with the Africa Council of Churches (ACC), which had the credibility to mediate between the conflicting parties in Sudan in 1972. As demonstrated by the example of the interreligious council in Bosnia and Herzegovina, which was established with the support of WCRP, it is very difficult to turn an instrument like this into an effective mediating tool once a conflict has started.[36] It should not be the task of governments to establish councils of churches or interreligious councils. Government involvement might even turn out to be counter-productive, as examples from communist times have proven. But governments have to protect the space in which religions can meet across national, ethnic, and religious borders.

B. Religion and Conflict Mediation

Once conflicts have reached the stage of violence, dialogue structures, whether religious or secular, which did not develop sufficient trust between the dialoguing parties, tend to break down. As recent conflicts have shown, religious communities are often highjacked and misused by other forces. Nevertheless, religious organizations and structures can play an important role. Once a conflict starts, it is often the international religious organizations that are instrumental in bringing the local communities together. In the case of the wars in Bosnia and Herzegovina and the Kosovo crisis, it was organizations like the WCC, the Conference of European Churches, and the Appeal of Conscience Foundation that organized roundtable meetings for the religious communities in the former Yugoslavia. Those meetings brought the religions closer together and gave a clear signal to the nonreligious world. The round tables refused that religion be exploited for national purposes, and they defined common policies with regard to relief operations, refugee concerns, and their approach to the media. In Bosnia and Herzegovina and in Kosovo such round tables came into being rather late during the conflict.[37] More timely was the recent joint declaration[38] of the religious communities in the Former Yugoslavian Republic of Macedonia from 13 June 2001, which states,

> Led by the principles of our faith and bound to live and work together as brothers and sisters . . . we condemn the violence and conflict which, instead of bringing a solution, will only leave chaos. The recent violence and conflicts are not based on religion or religious differences, and we reject attempts to label them as acts of religious

[35] S. Wesley Ariarajah, *Not Without My Neighbor: Issues in Interfaith Relations* (Geneva: WCC Publications, 1999), 12–14.

[36] See Appleby, *Ambivalence of the Sacred,* 641.

[37] For more information on the roundtable statements and other initiatives see Duijzings, *Religion and the Politics of Identity in Kosovo;* Syndesmus, the World Fellowship of Orthodox Youth, ed., *For the Peace from Above: An Orthodox Resource Book on War, Peace and Nationalism* (Bialystok, Poland: Orthodox Printing House, 1999), 133–46.

[38] The full text of the declaration can be found on the World Council of Churches website: <www.wcc-coe.org>.

> intolerance. . . . We strongly reject any tendency to allow ourselves to be involved and manipulated, as well as any misuse of religious symbols and language for purposes of violence.[39]

The declaration came just at the right time as attempts had been started to draw religious communities into the conflict. As important as the role of the WCC and the Conference of European Churches might have been in providing a platform for the religious representatives to meet, the agreement could not have been reached with the long-standing mediating role of a local NGO, the Macedonian Center for International Cooperation.

Even in conflicts without a religious component, it is often the religious organizations or religious personalities that have the credibility from the people to mediate. An outstanding example is the mediation of the Communio St. Egidio in Mozambique.[40] The success of the Truth and Reconciliation Commission in South Africa could not have been imagined without the involvement of a personality such as the Anglican Bishop Tutu. The churches in the former GDR played an important role in ensuring that the revolution against the communist government and the transition to democracy remained nonviolent. In South Africa, as well as in the states of the former GDR, many religious personalities who were involved in the transition process were later elected to leading positions in their government and in civil society organizations in order to contribute to the post-conflict peace building.

Third-party interventions in conflict situations do not, however, need to come from outside or from top structures. In Northern Ireland, for instance, local communities such as the Corrymeela community bring grass-roots people together beyond their religious and national loyalties in order to develop a common peace witness. The Irish School of Ecumenic engages people from conflicting parties in processes on the healing of memories. During the wars in Bosnia and Herzegovina, it was the "women in black" who demonstrated publicly against the use of violence. In Croatia the Osijeh Center of Peace, Non-Violence, and Human Rights trained people in nonviolent conflict mediation and sent them in bicommunal villages once international mediators had left. The more locally these initiatives are organized and the more they involve the local community the more promising they are. "Virtually all of the recent transitions towards peace . . . were driven largely from the grass roots."[41]

C. Religion and Postwar Community Building

In after-war situations, civil society has usually ceased to exist. Often it is the religious communities which are the only survivors of such societal structures. They are often instrumental in expressing the voice of the people and in supporting the redevelopment of civil society.

In the case of the former Yugoslavia, numerous religion-based aid agencies have pooled their resources in a Southeast Europe Partnership Program under the auspices of the WCC. After a period of relief and emergency aid, the agencies are now embarking

---

[39] The complete mediation process is documented in Roberto Morozzo della Rocca, *Vom Krieg zum Frieden. Mosambik: Geschichte einer Ungewöhnlichen Vermittlung* (Hamburg: Verlag Dienste in Übersee, 1997).
[40] Lederach, *Building Peace*, 56.
[41] For full details consult <www.wcc.seeep.org>.

on long-term development involving the local communities and civil society organizations. The program emphasizes three crucial issues: peace and reconciliation, capacity building for local NGOs, and the repatriation and integration of refugees and internally displaced people.[42]

An extraordinary example of postwar community building can be seen in the activities of the Life and Peace Institute in Somalia. For many years, Somalia had no central government. Therefore, the Life and Peace Institute aimed at empowering local communities and strengthening their institutions and structures in order to counteract the unduly heavy emphasis given to faction leaders by the international community. This objective is based on the conviction that peace cannot be achieved in Somalia through outside intervention but by the efforts of the people themselves.[43] The program of the Life and Peace Institute in Somalia includes a Women's Peace and Development Program, support for locally initiated and community-based reconciliation conferences and dialogues, as well as an advocacy program to spread accurate and balanced information on Somalia. The Somalians' trust in the Institute stems from long-term positive involvement in the region.

These are just a few examples of how religion in its various organizational structures contributes to conflict prevention, mediation, and post-conflict community building. The list of projects, countries concerned, and organizations involved could be endlessly prolonged.

IV. The Implementation of Freedom of Religion or Belief as a Pre-Condition for Religions' Contribution to Peace and Reconciliation

It should be evident from the above that banning religion from politics and public life cannot be an adequate response to the involvement of religion in conflict situations. "The best way to counter religious extremism or manipulation of religion . . . is with strengthened, more authentic religion, not weakened religion."[44] Consequently, the full implementation of the right to freedom of religion or belief as stipulated in article 18 of the International Covenant on Civil and Political Rights (hereinafter referred to as the ICCRP), and elaborated in the 1981 UN Declaration on the Elimination of All Forms of Intolerance and of Discrimination Based on Religion or Belief (hereinafter referred to as the 1981 Declaration), constitutes a precondition for religions to fulfill their role in conflict prevention, mediation, and post-conflict community building. Other global and regional standards relating to human rights, including the politically binding OSCE commitments, regarding freedom of religion or belief are obviously significant too. Some of these standards are particularly important with regard to the involvement of religion in conflict situations. Effective implementation of these standards, by affirmatively showing respect for groups that otherwise feel threatened, can contribute to eliminating distrust and can help remove the possibility that religious intolerance and discrimination can feed or be exploited in conflict situations.

---

[42] "LPI in Somalia: 7 Years Later," *New Routes* 4 (1999): 21.

[43] Appleby, *Ambivalence of the Sacred*, 76.

[44] *Implementation of the Declaration on the Elimination of All Forms of Intolerance and of Discrimination Based on Religion or Belief*, report submitted by Abdelfattah Amor, Special Rapporteur, in accordance with Commission on Human Rights Resolution 1995/23, UN Doc. E/CN.4/1996/95/Add.1, para. 82 (1996).

In order to be able to fulfill their role in peace building and reconciliation, it is of utmost importance that religious communities have a secure status vis-à-vis their governments[45] and a protected space to express themselves. According to the UN Human Rights Committee, the principle of equality of all religions vis-à-vis the state does not necessarily mean that all religious communities in a given state must have the same status, but "[t]he fact that a religion is recognized as a state religion or that it is established as official or traditional or that its followers comprise the majority of the population shall not result in any impairment of the enjoyment of any of the rights under the [International] Covenant [on Civil and Political Rights], including articles 18 and 27, nor in any discrimination against adherents of other religions or non-believers."[46] International human rights standards have defined discrimination based on religion or belief as: "any distinction, exclusion, restriction or preference based on religion or belief and having as its purpose or as its effect the nullification or impairment of the recognition, enjoyment or exercise of human rights and fundamental freedom on an equal basis."[47] As this chapter has tried to show, it is often the discrimination by governments or the fact that governments do not protect minority communities from discrimination by others, that give rise to tensions, conflicts, and religious extremism. In contrast, in countries where all religious communities are recognized and enjoy the right to freedom of religion or belief, the misuse of religion for national and ethnic purposes is unlikely to happen.

The suppression of minorities, as referred to in almost all of the above case studies, as well as the search of the offices of the Women in Black under the Milosevic regime in Yugoslavia, serve as examples of clear acts of discrimination. Conflict mediation in cases with a religious component therefore often means to first and foremost reenforce the right to freedom of religion or belief.

Dialogue is indispensable for conflict prevention, and the interplay between local and national religious communities and their international structures is indispensable for conflict mediation. To enable this dialogue to take place, the 1981 Declaration stipulates that the right to freedom of religion or belief includes, *inter alia*, the freedom "to establish and maintain communications with individuals and communities in matters of religion and belief at the national and international levels."[48] National legislation on freedom of religion or belief that attempts to prohibit close international ties of minority religions and of new forms of religion constitute a violation of this right. As stated above, it is not the task of governments to establish structures for intrareligions or intrareligious dialogue, but it is their task to ensure that the dialogue and communication can take place in a climate of tolerance and nondiscrimination.

According to international human rights norms, restrictions on the freedom to manifest religion or belief must be prescribed by law and be necessary to protect public safety, order, health or morals, or the fundamental rights and freedoms of others.[49] The fact that a religious community in its advocacy role is critical towards the government or

---

[45] See, e.g., *Concluding Document of the Vienna Meeting of Representatives of the Participating States of the Conference on Security and Co-operation in Europe,* principle 16(c), 4 November 1986–17 January 1989.

[46] Human Rights Committee General Comment No. 22 (1993) (ICCPR, art. 18), UN Doc. A/48/40 (Pt. I), para. 9.

[47] 1981 Declaration, art. 2(2).

[48] 1981 Declaration, art. 6(i).

[49] For the relevant limitation clauses, see, e.g., ICCPR, art. 18(3); ECHR, art. 9(2).

that a religious community represents a minority not favored by a government do not constitute legitimate reasons to infringe on their right to freedom of religion or belief. To the contrary, the OSCE Participating States committed themselves to "favourably consider the interest of religious communities to participate in public dialogue,"[50] regardless of whether they constitute a majority or a minority, or whether they are critical to or compliant with governmental policies.

Following the UN Special Rapporteur's on-site visits to and his written communications with countries known for their violent incidents involving religions, such as Pakistan and India, it seems evident that the nonimplementation of tolerance and discrimination that constitutes the major threat to religious minorities. In countries such as Pakistan, it is legal norms themselves that are "likely to favor or foster intolerance in society."[51] In India, for instance, the failure to implement the right to freedom of religion or belief in connection with the implementation of democracy causes difficulties.[52]

The international community is therefore particularly challenged to monitor whether national legislation and state practice comply with internationally recognized standards regarding freedom of religion or belief. In light of the fact that contemporary conflicts arise most frequently in intrastate conflicts, whereas international human rights instruments and supervisory mechanisms were established for interstate conflicts, the question needs to be raised, whether such instruments and mechanisms are adequate for effective interventions at an early stage. Clearly, human rights can no more be regarded as exclusively the domestic affairs of a state.[53]

---

[50] Vienna Concluding Document, principle 16(11).

[51] *Implementation of the Declaration on the Elimination of All Forms of Intolerance and of Discrimination Based on Religion or Belief,* report submitted by Abdelfattah Amor, Special Rapporteur, in accordance with *Commission on Human Rights Resolution 1996/23,* UN Doc. E/CN.4/1997/91/Add.1, para. 81 (1997).

[52] Ibid., para. 81.

[53] For a broad analysis of the transformation of international human rights law that has changed it from a body of rules that governed only relations between nations into a set of norms that are increasingly given direct effect in a variety of ways within national legal systems, see Henry J. Steiner and Philip Alston, *International Human Rights in Context: Law, Politics, Morals,* 2d ed. (Oxford: Oxford University Press, 2000), 56–135, 987–1081.

Chapter 34

Freedom of Religion and Dialogue

Leonard Swidler

I. Something New under the Sun

Religious freedom is a relatively new phenomenon in human history. It was a goal of Christian thinkers and writers before Constantine in the early fourth century A.D.—but not afterwards, when Christianity became the state religion. It was not a desideratum even in the main branches of sixteenth-century Protestant Reformation. Despite a more benign attitude at times and places in the history of the other large monotheistic religion, Islam, the now largely Muslim world from Dakar to Mindinao did not become so without Muslim armies.

Religious freedom as a human right and a social reality did not appear on the human stage until the latter part of the eighteenth century, most clearly in the inception of the United States of America and in the French Revolution. It was one of the core human rights—if not the most fundamental—that was declared simultaneously in 1789 in the French *Declaration des droits des hommes et citoyens* and the American *Bill of Rights.*[1]

Dialogue among religions is an even newer idea to rise in prominence in the story of humankind. Dialogue, as we use the term today—meaning to talk, in the broadest sense, with those who think differently from us so *we* can learn—is a new consciousness born slowly in the twentieth century. One can see its beginning in the 1893 Chicago *World Parliament of Religions,* followed by the launching in 1910 and 1912 of the *Ecumenical Movement* among Protestants and Orthodox Christians, and joined by Catholics at the *Second Vatican Council* (1962–65), and then gradually by other religions and ideologies as well.

Freedom of religion or belief—or even more specifically, disconnecting religion (or ideology) from the power of the state, for that is the essence of religious freedom—and dialogue are two of the most powerful transformative concepts in the history of

[1] For details see Leonard Swidler, "Human Rights and Religious Liberty: From the Past to the Future," in *Religious Liberty and Human Rights,* ed. Leonard Swidler (New York: Hippocrene Books, 1986), vii–xvi.

Tore Lindholm, W. Cole Durham, Jr., Bahia G. Tahzib-Lie (eds.), Facilitating Freedom of Religion or Belief: A Deskbook, *761–776.*

humanity, matching in magnitude the influence of the invention of writing millennia before. I would like to reflect a little on each of these key insights separately and then on their relationship to each other.

II. Disconnecting Religion from the *Power* of the State

A. Union of Religion and State All-Pervading

In all past civilizations, religion has been an integral, constitutive element. Among other things, religion supplied the ethical basis on which the authority of the state and law was built. As a result, in all past civilizations there has been a very intimate relationship between religion and state. Very often that relationship was so close that one could speak of the union of religion and state. In that close relationship, religion at times tended to dominate the state, and at other times the state tended to dominate religion. We have seen it both in recent times and even still today. The Soviet state's domination of Orthodox Christianity was an example of the former, and the Ayatollahs' and Mullahs' domination of the state in Iran is an example of the latter. The emergence of a neutral state committed to the recognition of freedom of religion or belief is a unique phenomenon in human history that occurred first in the modern West—more about that below.

In the early centuries of Christianity in the Greco-Roman world, Christian writers were strongly in favor of religious liberty. After the Constantinian embrace of the Christian religion in the fourth century, however, they quickly switched to the position that the state had the responsibility of seeing that the truth was protected and favored—and of course Christianity had the truth.[2] In theory, of course, no one was to be forced to accept Christianity, but the theory was not frequently translated into practice. With the development of medieval Christendom in the western half of the former Roman Empire, almost everyone became Christian, with the exception of the Jews, who for the most part were allowed to continue a separate existence, often in ghettos.

The history of Islam was not very different: in theory no individual or community was to be forced to embrace Islam. But in practice the *jihad*, in the sense of a holy war against non-Muslim states, was in fact frequently launched aggressively. Although the *millet* system allowed non-Muslims, *dhimmis*, within a Muslim-conquered state to practice their religion, the non-Muslims were clearly second-class citizens—which fact doubtless encouraged conversion to Islam, and surely not the contrary.

---

[2] In the second or third century, the North African Christian Tertullian wrote: "It is a fundamental human right, a privilege of nature, that all human beings should worship according to their own convictions; one human person's religion neither harms nor helps another. It is not proper to force religion. It must be undertaken freely, not under pressure" (Tertullian, "Ad scapulam," in *Patrologia Latina*, vol. 1, ed. Jacques-Paul Migne [Paris: n.p., 1844], 699).

In a way, a high point of religious liberty, and thus much of the basis of human rights, was reached publicly with the universal declaration for the whole Roman Empire in the Edict of Milan (A.D. 313) by Emperor Constantine: "We should therefore give both to Christianity and to all others free facility to follow the religion which they may desire" (from the Edict of Milan as contained in "De mortibus persecutorum," in Migne, *Patrologia Latina*, vol. 7, 267). This moment of freedom was, however, short lived, for in A.D. 380 the Edict of Thessalonica was issued by Emperor Theodosius, stating that "It is our will that all the peoples who are ruled by the administration of Our Clemency shall practice that religion which the divine Peter the

At various times during the intertwined history of Christianity and Islam, one side or the other pointed, usually with justification, an accusing finger at the other as a brutal aggressor. In fact, neither Christianity nor Islam can claim to have been predominantly the victim and the other the aggressor; the acid of history dissolves any such claim from either side. *Jihad* and the crusades easily match each other in gratuitous aggressiveness.

B. Development of the Disconnection of Religion from the *Power* of the State

Something unique in human history, however, began to take place in western Christianity, in Christendom: the gradual, painful move toward disconnecting religion from the power of the state. Some might trace its beginnings to the Gregorian Reforms when Pope Gregory VII (1021–1085 A.D.) attempted dramatically and substantially to separate the Catholic Church from the power of the Holy Roman Empire and other civil powers. Of course no one at the time promoted the notion of the separation of church and state. Rather, each side attempted to wrest power to their side; witness the thirteenth-century "imperial interregnum" manipulated by the popes (when for fifty years the popes effectively prevented the election of a Holy Roman Emperor), followed soon by the imprisonment of that most authoritarian of all popes, Boniface VIII, by the king of France, Phillip the Fair, at the beginning of the fourteenth century.

But it was precisely this mammoth power struggle that encouraged a weariness with the unquestioned assumption of the union of church and state. The Renaissance, with its shifting of interest from the divine to the human, provided a further basis for the gradual questioning of the wisdom of the union of church and state. This questioning manifested itself visibly in the so-called left wing of the sixteenth-century Reformation: the Anabaptists and related sects clearly and vigorously rejected the idea of the union of church and state, for which, of course, they were viciously persecuted by Catholics and mainline Protestants.

In the end it was the pitting of Catholics and Protestants against each other that magnified the incipient weariness with the consequences of the union of church and state—induced by the earlier struggle between the pope and civil rulers—to the point of the full embrace of the principle of the disconnection of religion from the power of the state during the eighteenth-century Enlightenment. Antecedents began to emerge in the Netherlands and Britain, but it was the 1789 US Constitution that for the first time raised religious freedom to constitutional rank. From that time it spread throughout the West in various juridical expressions, and from there increasingly around the globe.

C. Developments in Islam

Like all previous civilizations, Islam (speaking now of Islam as a civilization that has the religion Islam as its vital source) initially grew vigorously, sustained a level of dominance for a time, and then, as many Muslim scholars themselves have descried, began

Apostle transmitted to the Romans" ("Codex Theodosianus" [XVI, I, 2], in *Readings in Church History*, vol. 1, ed. Coleman J. Barry [Westminster, Md.: Newman Press, 1960], 142).

losing its dominance. The loss of dominance became increasingly apparent from the eighteenth century onwards. In the nineteenth and twentieth centuries, much of the Islamic world fell under western colonialism and was increasingly dominated by Christendom, now largely become "the West."

The observation of the decline of the dominance of Islamic countries vis-à-vis Christian ones cannot be a warrant for Christian arrogance. Doubtless many Christians attribute the unprecedented advances of western civilization mainly to Christianity, but that is because they do not recognize that it is more the *dis*-engaging of Christianity (and all religions and ideologies) from the power of the state that is the main source of those ongoing advances.

In fact, Muslim scholars have increasingly been articulate about the depressed state of Islamic countries. For example, in Dr. Seyed Othman Alhabshi's book[3] explaining the background of the newly founded Institute of Islamic Understanding in Malaysia, we find the following strong statement: "The Muslim world is currently plagued with almost nothing but negative attributes of a civilization." He then went on to list some of the "plagues": "underdevelopment, backwardness, poverty, inequitable income and wealth distribution, high inflation, acute illiteracy and serious unemployment, economic and political instability." If possible, even clearer was the comment, "Although eight hundred years was long enough to accumulate a wealth of experience to ward off various human ills, the Muslims declined almost without any rebound till this day."[4]

Several Muslim nations, e.g., Iran and Sudan, have tried to regain their former Islamic glory by reuniting religion and state through the embrace of "Islamism"[5] (the term Muslim scholars use rather than the less accurate western term "fundamentalism"); the same goal is being sought by radical Islamists within other Muslim countries, e.g., Egypt and Algeria. Unfortunately, rather than regaining former "Islamic Glory," the Islamists are thereby insuring that their nations will remain backward societies. That fact seems to be dawning slowly even on that bastion of Muslim religious conservatism, Saudi Arabia—judging from some tentative moves to suppress Islamism and start down the path toward democracy.

D. The Unique Quality of Western Civilization

When historians like Arnold J. Toynbee survey the total history of humankind, they find that there have been a number of civilizations that have come into existence, flourished, and then declined (Toynbee discerns twenty-six civilizations in human history).

---

[3] Syed Othman Alhabshi, *An Inspiration for the Future of Islam* (Kuala Lumpur: Institute of Islamic Understanding, 1994), 8.

[4] Ibid., 12. One finds not only an acknowledgment of the present stagnation of Islamic nations, but also a determination to do something positive about it in certain leading Muslim circles, for example in Malaysia: "None of the Muslim countries are considered to be developed or advanced, despite about ten are among the rich nations of the world. . . . Muslim countries are so weak politically, economically, socially and even educationally. . . . Muslims have become so weak and dependent on others in almost every field."

[5] See the excellent volume by the Moroccan-Spanish Muslim Khalid Duran, *The Children of Abraham: An Introduction to Islam for Jews* (Hoboken, N.J.: Ktav, 2001). Duran provides a sympathetic and realistic presentation of Islam, including present-day Islamism and Jihadism. This latter earned him a death contract *(fatwa)* from an Islamist extremist in Jordan, as well as innumerable letters of support and laudatory reviews.

Many of them achieved admirable accomplishments, the Greco-Roman Civilization being the one best known to westerners. Its achievements were indeed great—so much so that during the late Renaissance there was a lively debate about whether the Ancients (meaning the Greeks and Romans) or the then moderns had attained greater cultural heights. But doubtless the Greco-Roman accomplishments were in many regards matched, and in some surpassed, by the Chinese and Islamic Civilizations.

However, it is no cultural hubris to be aware that the rising arc of western civilization (which is largely a synthesis of [1] the Judeo-Christian tradition, [2] the Greco-Roman tradition, [3] the Germanic tradition, [4] with a significant influence of medieval Islam, and [5] modern science and thought) has reached far beyond where any of Toynbee's other twenty-five civilizations have gone, whether in culture, science, politics, economic prosperity, technology, etc. Moreover, western civilization, together with the rest of the world's existing civilizations, is now being transmorphed into global civilization in a way that had never occurred before, and this process of globalization appears to be intensifying in exponential fashion. This is not to discount "western-cum-other-now-becoming-global civilization's" defects, blind spots, and seething problems—some of the most critical of which are largely a result of its very accomplishments, e.g., the population explosion (because of, *inter alia*, medical and agricultural advances) or the ecological crisis (because of, *inter alia*, technological advances and the population explosion). But even that illustrates the main point: western civilization-transforming-into-global civilization's greatest problems flow not from its weaknesses, but from its even more awesome, unparalleled achievements.

E. The Disconnection of Religion from the Power of the State: A Vital Key

One of the essential elements in the advances of western civilization in culture, science, politics, economic prosperity, and technology, the likes of which—for all of its problems, which are correspondingly massive—were never before experienced in human history, is the disconnection of religion from the *power* of the state. And religion here includes any "ideology" that functions like a religion—Atheistic Marxism for example(it is clear to see today in Eastern Europe and the former USSR what disaster the union of state and the "religion" of Marxism led to).

Christendom in the late Middle Ages began reaching the cultural level of the earlier Greek and Roman and the then contemporary Islamic civilizations. All historical data strongly suggest that Christendom would have plateaued at approximately that level for a longer or shorter period of time, and then slipped from dominance—*as had all other civilizations before then*, and as eventually the Chinese, Greco-Roman, Islamic civilizations, etc. did as well.

That did not happen, however. Why? One very fundamental reason was that starting with the Gregorian Reforms, through the Renaissance, the Reformation, and on into the Enlightenment and beyond, religion and the power of the state slowly and very painfully began to be disconnected. This disconnection broke the forced quality of religion/ideology and, consequently, freed the human spirit and mind to pursue their limitless urge to know ever more, to solve every problem they confront. This resulted in a series of what historians call revolutions in the West: the Commercial Revolution (sixteenth–seventeenth centuries), Scientific Revolution (seventeenth century), Industrial Revolution (eighteenth century), Political Revolution (epitomized in the eighteenth-century American and French Revolutions), and on into the nineteenth and twentieth centuries with myriads of revolutions of all sorts occurring at geometrically increasing speed and magnitude.

As Christianity became less and less the religion of the state in the West, so too the West became less and less *Christendom* and was transformed into what is today usually called *western civilization*.

With the "exponential" advances in capabilities in the West, of course, the possibilities of destructiveness increased correspondingly—as the medieval philosophers said: The corruption of the best becomes the worst, *corruptio optimae pessima*. Nevertheless, because freedom is of the *essence* of being human, even though we may well destroy ourselves if we do not learn wisdom and live virtuously, we can never turn back to an unfree stage of human development any more than an individual can roll back the transforming effects of puberty.

Hence, those societies that try to reunite religion/ideology with the power of the state prevent themselves from harnessing the almost unlimited energy that liberty releases. New problems and challenges will always arise in human societies. Humans, however, have a virtually limitless capability of intellect, imagination, and spirit (which is another way of saying what the book of Genesis in the Bible meant by recording that God made humans in God's image, the *imago Dei*) with which to address and overcome those problems and challenges ever anew. Unfortunately, when that innate human creative spirit is imprisoned in a doctrinal straitjacket ("ortho-doxy," or "straight-doctrine," becomes in fact "strait-doctrine") imposed from above by the power of the state, it will die or be severely weakened from spiritual strangulation. And then that society will fall behind, and perhaps even succumb to, those societies that retain their creativity.

That is why, for example, in India the present attempt of resurgent Hindu "fundamentalists," brandishing their *Hindutva* ("Hinduization"), seems so fraught with dangers for the progress and development of the second largest country of the world. The path to recovery lies not in trying to impose a narrow dogmatism by coercion, but by finding ways to promote more open exploration of ways that core Hindu values can contribute to meaningful life in contemporary settings.

Of course, the same disastrous consequences would also result, e.g., if the efforts of Islamists to reestablish the Muslim law, the *shar'ia*, in the Muslim world succeeds, China, North Korea, and Vietnam will likewise always remain relatively "backward" as long as they maintain a union of ideology and state.

Extremist Jewish and Islamist apologists argue that Judaism or Islam is different from the West and its major religion, Christianity, because, unlike Christianity, Judaism and Islam are holistic religions that include politics as well as all other aspects of life. In this, unfortunately, they are forgetting that Christendom was exactly the same for well over a millennium—the Constantinian Era. It was only when Christendom became "the West" and began to break out of that mischievous marriage of religion/ideology and state (only allegedly virtuously "holistic") that it embarked on the path of human freedom with its limitless possibilities of creativity (and destruction).

As we know, however, at its best the separation of religion and state did not, and does not, mean hostility between religion and state. Rather, it frees each, religion and state, to fulfill its respective function untrammeled by, but closely related to, the other.

For the state that function can be briefly described as the responsibility "to organize society so as to protect the rights of all, and promote the common good," and for religion, "to provide an explanation of the ultimate meaning of life, and how to live accordingly."

Clearly the West does not have the perfect solution to the question of the relation between religion and the state; it has many different imperfect solutions. The quite "anaemic" condition of a Christianity not completely disconnected from the power of the state in Germany, Scandinavia, England, and other European countries, vis-à-vis its turbulent but comparatively vital condition in the US with its quite complete disconnection of any particular religion, or of religion as such, from the *power* of the state, further bears out the thesis of this essay that the separate but creative relationship of religion and state is good for both religion and state, and hence, for humankind.

The "perfect" solution of the relationship of religion and state lies only in an "infinite" future, toward which humans are always striving. But clearly the West—and countries such as Japan, South Korea, etc., inspired by the principles of democracy and religious liberty—has shown that the disconnection of religion (or ideology) from the *power* of the state is *essential* to the true, full functioning of both religion and state and to human progress to "infinity." Said in other words: The disconnection of religion from the *power* of the state is a *necessary*, though not *sufficient*, cause of the unending creative development of humanity.

III. Dialogue, a Whole New Way of Thinking

A. A New Consciousness for Humanity

Another concept essential to the full flourishing of humanity is *dialogue*, not in any pedestrian sense, but in the sense of a deep dialogue, a transformative kind of consciousness that seeks to primarily *learn* from rather than teach those who think differently from us.

The world is becoming ever more interdependent on all levels. Democratization and globalization are increasing at an exponential rate. Therefore, in order to become full citizens of our nation and the globe, espousing democratic and ethical values, we humans must develop to the fullest our core competencies of knowing and deciding/loving, utilizing all our faculties (rational, emotional, physical). That means: (1) to intelligently hold a position, while being open to the other; and (2) to think clearly and critically and decide/love with care—so the differing worldviews we humans build can be creatively related in a dialogic, critically reflective, and caring manner.

These core human competencies, which my Global Dialogue Institute (GDI) and I have named Deep-Dialogue/Critical-Thinking (one may, of course, use other names for the fundamental realities), must be developed as the new basic mentality—and consequent practice—on which all education, cradle to the grave, indeed, all thought and action, is built. Deep-Dialogue/Critical-Thinking embodies democratic and ethical values, and thus ought to be both the all-embracing matrix of human thinking and being in the world, within which all thought, action, and education needs to take place, as well as the *mindset*, the *consciousness* (and consequent practice) that all education, cradle to the grave, should seek to develop as its fundamental goal.

B. Why Dialogue Arose

One can, of course, justifiably point to a number of recent developments that have contributed to the rise of dialogue—e.g., growth in mass education, communications, and travel; a world economy; and threatening global destruction. Nevertheless, a major underlying cause is a paradigm shift in the West in how we perceive and describe the world. A paradigm is simply the model, the cluster of assumptions, on whose basis phenomena are perceived and explained. An example is the geocentric paradigm for explaining the movements of the planets; a shift to another paradigm—as from the geocentric to the heliocentric—will have a major impact. Such a paradigm shift has occurred, and is still occurring, in the western understanding of truth statements; it has made dialogue not only possible, but even necessary.

Whereas the understanding of truth in the West was largely absolute, static, monologic, or exclusive up to the nineteenth century, it has subsequently become deabsolutized, dynamic, and dialogic—in a word: relational. This relatively "new" view of truth came about in at least six different but closely related ways.

Until the nineteenth century in Europe, *truth*, that is, *a statement about reality*, was conceived in an absolute, static, exclusivistic manner. It was believed that if a statement was true at one time, it was always true, and not only in the sense of statements about empirical facts, but also in the sense of statements about the meaning of things. Such is a *classicist* or *absolutist* view of truth.

1. Then, in the nineteenth century scholars came to perceive all statements about the truth of the meaning of something as being partially products of their historical circumstances; only by placing truth statements in their historical situations, their historical *Sitz im Leben*, could they be properly understood. A text could be understood only in context. Therefore, all statements about the meaning of things were seen to be deabsolutized in terms of time. Such is a *historical* view of truth.
2. Later on it was noted that we ask questions so as to obtain knowledge, or truth, according to which we want to live; this is a *praxis* or *intentional* view of truth, that is, a statement has to be understood in relationship to the action-oriented intention of the thinker.
3. Early in the twentieth century, Karl Mannheim developed what he called the sociology of knowledge, which points out that every statement about the truth of the meaning of something is perspectival. All reality is perceived and spoken of from the cultural, class, sexual, and so forth perspective of the perceiver. Such is a *perspectival* view of truth.
4. A number of thinkers, most especially Ludwig Wittgenstein, have discovered something of the limitations of human language: Every description of reality is necessarily only partial, for although reality can be seen from an almost limitless number of perspectives, human language can express things from only one perspective at once. This partial and limited quality of all language is necessarily greatly intensified when one attempts to speak of the transcendent, which by definition "goes beyond." Such is a *language-limited* view of truth.
5. The contemporary discipline of hermeneutics stresses that all knowledge is interpreted knowledge. This means that in all knowledge I come to know something; the object comes into me in a certain way, namely, through the

lens that I use to perceive it. As Thomas Aquinas wrote, "Things known are in the knower according to the mode of the knower" (*Summa Theologiae*, II/II, Q. 1, a. 2). Such is an *interpretative* view of truth.

6. Further yet, reality can "speak" to me only with the language that I give it; the "answers" that I receive back from reality will always be in the language, the thought categories, of the questions I put to it. If and when the answers I receive are sometimes confused and unsatisfying, then I probably need to learn to speak a more appropriate language when I put questions to reality. For example, if I ask the question, "How heavy is green?" of course I will receive a nonsense answer. Or if I ask questions about living things in mechanical categories, I will receive confusing and unsatisfying answers. I will likewise receive confusing and unsatisfying answers to questions about human sexuality if I use categories that are solely physical biological: Witness the absurdity of the answer that birth control is forbidden by the natural law—the question falsely assumes that the nature of humanity is merely physical biological. Such an understanding of truth is a *dialogic* understanding.

C. Meaning of *Deep-Dialogue* and *Critical-Thinking*

In brief, our understanding of truth and reality has been undergoing a radical shift. The new paradigm that is being born understands all statements about reality, especially about the meaning of things, to be historical, praxial or intentional, perspectival, language-limited or partial, interpretative, or dialogic. Our understanding of truth statements, in short, has become "deabsolutized." It has become "relational" in the sense that all statements about reality are now seen to be *related* to the historical context, praxis intentionality, perspective, etc. of the speaker, and in that sense are no longer "absolute." Therefore, my perception and description of the world is true only in a limited sense, that is, only as seen from my place in the world. It follows that if I wish to expand my grasp of reality, I need to learn from others what they know of reality and what they can perceive from their place in the world that I cannot see from mine. That, however, can happen only through dialogue.

Thus, dialogue, in this sense of Deep-Dialogue, very simply means to:

1. Reach out in openness to the other in the search for truth and goodness.
2. Be open to the other primarily so we can learn and find truth and goodness.
3. Perceive that for us to learn, to find the good, the other must teach and open themselves—and vice versa.
4. Recognize that because dialogue is a two-way project, we then *both* learn—and share the good.
5. Learn there are other ways of understanding, of embracing the world, than our own.
6. Learn to recognize our commonalities and differences—and value both.
7. Learn to move between different worlds and integrate them in care.
8. Learn that Deep-Dialogue thus gradually transforms our inner selves—and our shared lives.

Further, the converse, or the flip side of the single coin of authentic humanity, is Critical-Thinking, which very simply means to:

1. Raise our *un*-conscious *pre*-suppositions to the conscious level.
2. Make a reasoned judgment ("critical," Greek *krinein*, to judge) about them after analysis.
3. Recognize that *our* view of reality is *one* view, shaped by *our* experience.
4. Become aware of multiple worldviews.
5. Understand all statements/texts in *their con*-texts.
6. Only then apply them to *our* contexts.
7. See that each worldview is a new meaning network.
8. Again, only then can we reasonably critique them.
9. Understand and use very *precisely* each word and phrase so that our deliberations and decisions are informed with clarity and grounded in reality.

Thus, the relationship between Deep-Dialogue and Critical-Thinking means:

1. Deep-Dialogue and Critical-Thinking are two sides of the one human reality.
2. Deep-Dialogue entails at its root clear, reflective, critical thought.
3. Critical-Thinking entails a dialogue within our own minds and lives—and hence, at its root is dialogic.
4. Deep-Dialogue and Critical-Thinking are thus two sides of the coin of humanity.
5. Deep-Dialogue/Critical-Thinking must eventually become a habit of mind and spirit, traditionally known as a virtue—a new basic mentality and consequent practice.

IV. Dialogue and Religious Freedom in Practice

There are, of course, myriads of interreligious dialogues going on in the world today. As a small sample, let me briefly mention a few that I have been personally involved in. At the end of this section I include a set of basic *Ground Rules* for dialogue that I have found exceptionally helpful in practical dialogue settings since I first published them in 1984. I include them here with the hope that they may benefit those working on facilitating freedom of religion or belief through dialogue.

A. Standing Up for Dialogue and Freedom: Morocco

The Muslim world today is under pressure from the radical Islamist states such as Afghanistan, Sudan, and Iran (and increasingly Pakistan[6]) to reject positive relations with other religions and modernity. Both religious liberty and dialogue are anathema to them. In the face of this and internal pressure from Islamists, the new King of Morocco, Mohammed VI, made a bold move as one of his first public profile acts. Through his Personal Advisor Andre Azoulay (who is Jewish!), the king cosponsored with the Spanish "Foundation for the Three Cultures of the Mediterranean" (Jewish-Christian-Muslim) a Jewish-Christian-Muslim Dialogue on "Religion, Tolerance and Modernity" at Al-Akawayn University, Ifrane, Morocco, 14–16 October 1999.

[6] See the dozens of articles by the brilliant, irenic, Indian-Muslim scholar Asghar Ali Engineer, founder and director of the Institute of Islamic Studies and Centre for Study of Society and Secularism. They are

Though the organizers of the dialogue, and indeed most of the participants, were clearly new at dialogue, the very fact that the conference was held was an extraordinary event in itself. In effect, the new king publicly rejected the extremists' three rejections: (1) dialogue with other religions, especially Judaism and Christianity, (2) dialogue with "the West," and (3) dialogue with "modernity," and did so in the name of religious freedom and tolerance!

B. Interreligious Dialogue Efforts at Peace and Freedom: South Asia and Indonesia

There are doubtless many organized efforts at promoting interreligious dialogue among persons of various religions in South Asia. I will mention only one, which is easily accessible around the world through its website—I recommend regularly visiting it. It is entitled the *Association for Communal Harmony in Asia* (ACHA). It was begun by a Hindu in Oregon, USA in 1993, but includes members from most of the world's religions.[7]

Indonesia is the largest Muslim country in the world, having more Muslims than all the Arab countries together. It is, despite the recent outbreaks of interreligious and interethnic violence (mainly fomented by corrupt power brokers of the former regime who fear losing their power if democracy succeeds), recognized as one of the most dialogue-oriented, free-spirited living versions of Islam. There are a number of organizations that have been promoting dialogue among the religions of Indonesia for years. The latest integration of these manifold efforts is MADIA *(Masyarakat Dialog Antar Agama)* SIDA *(Society for Interreligious Dialogue)*, which works on the adult education and activist levels.[8]

Under the dictator Suharto, there was already a general freedom of religion, though not of belief, in the form of Marxism or of Confucianism. Hence there developed the series of interreligious activities referred to above. Under the presidency of Abdurrahman Wahid (a widely revered Muslim scholar and "Holy Man" who headed the forty-million-strong Muslim organization *Nadalul Ulama*), freedom of both religion and belief was promoted, as well as interreligious dialogue. For him the two went together. He was able to reinstate the official recognition of Confucianism and was attempting to do something similar about communism when he lost power. President Wahid also vigorously promoted interreligious dialogue, most prominently by hosting in the Presidential Palace in Jakarta the festive opening of the Jewish-Christian-Muslim Dialogue sponsored by GDI in February 2000.

Perhaps the potentially most far-reaching and interesting project in Indonesia at the present time is the education project undertaken by GDI in conjunction with UNICEF, the Ministry of Education, and the Ministry of Religious Affairs of Indonesia—the *Whole Child Education* Project. This is a project designed to fundamentally change the teaching

---

collected at <http://ecumene.org/IIS/csss.htm>, a website designed and maintained by Global Dialogue Institute web editor, Professor Ingrid Shafer.

[7] See <http://asiapeace.org/acha.htm>, designed and maintained by Global Dialogue Institute web editor, Professor Ingrid Shafer.

[8] See <http://ecumene.org/MADIA/MADIA.htm>, designed and maintained by *Global Dialogue Institute* web editor, Professor Ingrid Shafer.

method from one that is authoritarian and student-passive to one that fosters a dialogic and critical-thinking ***mentality***. It was substantively launched in the July 2001 with the initial training of the first batch of Indonesian school teachers and teacher trainers. Happily, the response of the teachers and trainers was extremely positive, and the commitment to making the project successful on the part of the leadership within the two ministries and the UNICEF staff is enthusiastic.

C. Ground Rules for Effective Dialogue

Several years ago, in an effort to help identify practical rules that contribute to effective interreligious dialogue, I developed a set of rules that I refer to as "The Dialogue Decalogue: Ground Rules for Interreligious, Interideological Dialogue."[9] Based on extensive experience in practical religious dialogue, I continue to endorse these principles. I include them here with the hope that they may contribute to efforts on the part of those seeking to facilitate freedom of religion or belief through interreligious dialogue.

THE DIALOGUE DECALOGUE

Ground Rules for Interreligious, Interideological Dialogue

Dialogue is a conversation on a common subject between two or more persons with differing views, the primary purpose of which is for each participant to learn from the other so that he or she can change and grow. This very definition of dialogue embodies the first commandment of dialogue.

In the religious-ideological sphere in the past, we came together to discuss with those differing with us, for example, Catholics with Protestants, either to defeat an opponent, or to learn about an opponent so as to deal more effectively with her or him, or at best to negotiate with him or her. If we faced each other at all, it was in confrontation; sometimes more openly polemically, sometimes more subtly so, but always with the ultimate goal of defeating the other, because we were convinced that we alone had the absolute truth.

But dialogue is ***not*** debate. In dialogue each partner must listen to the other as openly and sympathetically as he or she can in an attempt to understand the other's position as precisely and, as it were, as much from within, as possible. Such an attitude automatically includes the assumption that at any point we might find the partner's position so persuasive that, if we would act with integrity, we would have to change, and change can be disturbing.

---

[9] Leonard Swidler, "Dialogue Decalogue: Ground Rules for Interreligious Dialogue," *Journal of Ecumenical Studies* 20, no. 1 (winter 1983): 1–4.

We are here, of course, speaking of a specific kind of dialogue, an interreligious, interideological dialogue. To have such, it is not sufficient that the dialogue partners discuss a religious-ideological subject, that is, the meaning of life and how to live accordingly. Rather, they must come to the dialogue as persons somehow significantly identified with a religious or ideological community. If I were neither a Christian nor a Marxist, for example, I could not participate as a "partner" in Christian-Marxist dialogue, though I might listen in, ask some questions for information, and make some helpful comments.

It is obvious that interreligious, interideological dialogue is something new under the sun. We could not conceive of it, let alone do it in the past. How, then, can we effectively engage in this new thing? The following are some basic ground rules, or "commandments," of interreligious, interideological dialogue that must be observed if dialogue is actually to take place. These are not theoretical rules, or commandments given from "on high," but ones that have been learned from hard experience.

FIRST COMMANDMENT: ***The primary purpose of dialogue is to learn, that is, to change and grow in the perception and understanding of reality, and then to act accordingly.*** Minimally, the very fact that I learn that my dialogue partner believes "this" rather than "that" proportionally changes my attitude toward her; and a change in my attitude is a significant change in me. We enter into dialogue so that *we* can learn, change, and grow, not so we can force change on the *other*, as one hopes to do in debate, a hope realized in inverse proportion to the frequency and ferocity with which debate is entered into. On the other hand, because in dialogue *each* partner comes with the intention of learning and changing herself, one's partner in fact will also change. Thus the goal of debate, and much more, is accomplished far more effectively by dialogue.

SECOND COMMANDMENT: ***Interreligious, interideological dialogue must be a two-sided project within each religious or ideological community and between religious or ideological communities.*** Because of the "corporate" nature of interreligious dialogue, and since the primary goal of dialogue is that each partner learn and change himself, it is also necessary that each participant enter into dialogue not only with his partner across the faith line, the Lutheran with the Anglican, for example, but also with his coreligionists, with his fellow Lutherans, to share with them the fruits of the interreligious dialogue. Only thus can the whole community eventually learn and change, moving toward an ever more perceptive insight into reality.

THIRD COMMANDMENT: ***Each participant must come to the dialogue with complete honesty and sincerity.*** It should be made clear in what direction the major and minor thrusts of the tradition move, what the future shifts might be, and, if necessary, where the participant has difficulties with her own tradition. No false fronts have any place in dialogue.

Conversely, each participant must assume a similar complete honesty and sincerity in the other partners. Not only will the absence of sincerity prevent dialogue from happening, but the absence of the assumption of the partner's sincerity will do so as well. In brief: no trust, no dialogue.

FOURTH COMMANDMENT: *In interreligious, interideological dialogue we must not compare our ideals with our partner's practice,* but rather our ideals with our partner's ideals, our practice with our partner's practice.

FIFTH COMMANDMENT: *Each participant must define himself.* Only the Jew, for example, can define what it means to be a Jew. The rest can only describe what it looks like from the outside. Moreover, because dialogue is a dynamic medium, as each participant learns, he will change and hence continually deepen, expand, and modify his self-definition as a Jew, being careful to remain in constant dialogue with fellow Jews. Thus it is mandatory that each dialogue partner define what it means to be an authentic member of his own tradition.

Conversely, the one interpreted must be able to recognize herself in the interpretation. This is the golden rule of interreligious hermeneutics, as has been often reiterated by the "apostle of interreligious dialogue" Raimundo Panikkar. For the sake of understanding, each dialogue participant will naturally attempt to express for herself what she thinks is the meaning of the partner's statement; the partner must be able to recognize herself in that expression. The advocate of "a world theology," Wilfred Cantwell Smith, would add that the expression must also be verifiable by critical observers who are not involved.

SIXTH COMMANDMENT: *Each participant must come to the dialogue with no hard-and-fast assumptions as to where the points of disagreement are.* Rather, each partner should not only listen to the other partner with openness and sympathy but also attempt to agree with the dialogue partner as far as is possible while still maintaining integrity with his own tradition; where he absolutely can agree no further without violating his own integrity, precisely there is the real point of disagreement, which most often turns out to be different from the point of disagreement that was falsely assumed ahead of time.

SEVENTH COMMANDMENT: *Dialogue can take place only between equals,* or *par cum pari* as Vatican II put it. Both must come to learn from each other. Therefore, if, for example, the Muslim views Hinduism as inferior, or if the Hindu views Islam as inferior, there will be no dialogue. If authentic interreligious, interideological dialogue between Muslims and Hindus is to occur, then both the Muslim and the Hindu must come mainly to learn from each other; only then will it be "equal with equal," *par cum pari.* This rule also indicates that there can be no such thing as a one-way dialogue. For example, Jewish-Christian discussions begun in the 1960s were mainly only prolegomena to interreligious dialogue. Understandably and properly, the Jews came to these exchanges only to teach Christians, although the Christians came mainly to learn. But, if authentic interreligious dialogue between Christians and Jews is to occur, then the Jews must also come mainly to learn; only then will it too be *par cum pari.*

EIGHTH COMMANDMENT: *Dialogue can take place only on the basis of mutual trust.* Although interreligious, interideological dialogue must occur with some kind of "corporate" dimension, that is, the participants must be involved as members of a religious or ideological community, for instance, as Marxists or Taoists, it is also fundamentally true that it is only *persons* who can enter into dialogue. But a dialogue among persons can be built only on personal trust. Hence it is wise not to tackle the most difficult problems in the beginning, but rather to approach first those issues most likely to provide some common ground, thereby establishing the basis of human trust. Then, gradually, as this personal trust deepens and expands, the more thorny matters can be undertaken. Thus, as in learning we move from the known to the unknown, so in dialogue we proceed from commonly held matters, which, given our mutual ignorance resulting from centuries of hostility, will take us quite some time to discover fully, to discuss matters of disagreement.

NINTH COMMANDMENT: ***Persons entering into interreligious, interideological dialogue must be at least minimally self-critical of both themselves and their own religious or ideological traditions.*** A lack of such self-criticism implies that one's own tradition already has all the correct answers. Such an attitude makes dialogue not only unnecessary, but even impossible, since we enter into dialogue primarily so *we* can learn, which obviously is impossible if our tradition has never made a misstep, if it has all the right answers. To be sure, in interreligious, interideological dialogue one must stand within a religious or ideological tradition with integrity and conviction, but such integrity and conviction must include, not exclude, a healthy self-criticism. Without it there can be no dialogue, and, indeed, no integrity.

TENTH COMMANDMENT: ***Each participant eventually must attempt to experience the partner's religion or ideology "from within";*** for a religion or ideology is not merely something of the head, but also of the spirit, heart, and "whole being," individual and communal. John Dunne here speaks of "passing over" into another's religious or ideological experience and then coming back enlightened, broadened, and deepened. As Raimundo Panikkar notes, "To know what a religion says, we must understand what it says, but for this we must somehow believe in what it says": for example, "A Christian will never fully understand Hinduism if he is not, in one way or another, converted to Hinduism. Nor will a Hindu ever fully understand Christianity unless he, in one way or another, becomes Christian."

◆ ◆ ◆

Interreligious, interideological dialogue operates in *three areas*: the *practical*, where we collaborate to help humanity; the ***depth or spiritual dimension***, where we attempt to experience the partner's religion or ideology "from within"; the *cognitive*, where we seek understanding and truth. Interreligious, interideological dialogue also has three phases. In the first phase, we unlearn misinformation about each other and begin to know each other as we truly are. In phase two, we begin to discern values in the partner's tradition and wish to appropriate them into our own tradition. For example, in the Buddhist-Christian dialogue, Christians might learn a greater appreciation of the meditative tradition, and Buddhists might learn a greater appreciation of the prophetic, social justice tradition; both values are traditionally strong, though not exclusively associated with the other's community. If we are serious, persistent, and sensitive enough in the dialogue, we may at times enter into phase three. Here we together begin to explore new areas of reality, of meaning, and of truth, of which neither of us had even been aware before. We are brought face to face with this new, as-yet-unknown-to-us dimension of reality only because of questions, insights, probings produced in the dialogue. We may thus dare to say that patiently pursued dialogue can become an instrument of new "re-velation," a further "un-veiling" of reality on which we must then act.

There is something radically different about phase one on the one hand and phases two and three on the other. In the latter, we do not simply add on quantitatively another "truth" or value from the partner's tradition. Instead, as we assimilate it within our own religious self-understanding, it will proportionately transform our self-understanding. Since our dialogue partner will be in a similar position, we will then be able to witness authentically to those elements of deep value in our own tradition that our partner's tradition may well be able to assimilate with self-transforming profit. All this, of course, will have to be done with complete integrity on each side, each partner remaining authentically true to the vital core of his or her own religious tradition. However, in significant ways that vital core will be perceived and experienced differently under the influence of the dialogue; but if the dialogue is carried on with both integrity and openness, the result will be that, for example, the Jew will be authentically Jewish and the Christian will be authentically Christian, not despite the fact that Judaism and/or Christianity have been profoundly "Buddhized," but because of it. And the same is true of a Judaized and/or Christianized Buddhism. There can be no talk of a syncretism here, for syncretism means amalgamating various elements of different religions into some kind of a (con)fused whole without concern for the integrity of the religions involved, which is not the case with authentic dialogue.

V. Dialogue and Religious Freedom in the Future

A. The Relationship between Dialogue and Religious Freedom

Religious liberty can become a reality only to the degree that religion, or ideology, is disconnected from the *power* of the state. Also, to the extent that a dialogic mentality spreads, it will become apparent that no single religion or ideology is *absolute*, that is, can encapsulate all knowledge and goodness. Hence, the expansion of a dialogic consciousness will automatically promote religious liberty, for it will be seen to everyone's advantage for all religions and ideologies to be free so all can learn ever more from each other.

B. Religion in Dialogue: The Core of the Global Civilization

Since the beginning of history, there has been at the heart of every civilization a religion that both reflected the core meaning of that civilization and foundationally shaped it: The Egyptian religion was at the core of Egyptian civilization for millennia, Chinese religion was at the center of Chinese civilization, Christianity at the heart of Christendom, Islam of Islamic civilization, and Marxism at the core of Communist civilization.

But now the world is entering a new stage, the like of which was never seen before—the emergence of global civilization. While it is true that western civilization has been the precipitator of this emerging global civilization and has played a major role in shaping it, the latter will not simply be western civilization "writ large," but will be a pluralistic civilization with multiple centers. It will, indeed, be an *Unum e pluribus*, a unity made out of many.

But then, if this is really an emerging *civilization*—not just a congeries of disparate cultural elements, but a true civilization with an essential kind of unity (*not* uniformity)—what will be its heart? The present author believes that the answer is at hand: the core of the emerging global civilization is *Religion-in-Dialogue*.

Chapter 35

The Emergence of Interfaith Dialogue: The Norwegian Experience

Inge Eidsvåg, Tore Lindholm, and Barbro Sveen

I. Introduction

Norway, a small country of 4.5 million inhabitants in the northernmost corner of Europe, has enjoyed constitutional, democratic government since 1814, except for five years of Nazi-German rule from 1940 to 1945. But only during the last thirty-five years or so has Norway also become a wealthy country, thanks in large part to the discovery and exploitation of oil and gas in the North Sea.

During the same period, Norway has received an unprecedented flow of immigrants from many countries, continents, and cultural backgrounds. Norway has become manifestly multicultural and multireligious. The new challenges and uncertainties have given rise to difficulties and conflicts, but have also inspired new ideas, generated cross-cultural solidarities, and, in particular, triggered interreligious dialogue and understanding.

The authors of the present chapter know from personal and "institutional" dialogue experience that representatives from different belief communities can engage in constructive conversation and sustained cooperation about matters of common concern, for example about moral, educational, legislative, social, and interethnic issues in the larger society. We consider communication, interaction, and partnership between differing confessions to be an increasingly important dimension of the exercise of our freedom of religion or belief.

This chapter gives an account of Norwegian experience with interfaith dialogue and interfaith cooperation during the last fifteen years. It reports on a number of serious and extensive dialogue projects, as well as other cooperative undertakings, across the barriers that separate different religious and "life stance" (or "worldview") communities in Norway.

For background, we begin with a sketch of Norway's long tradition as a culturally homogeneous and a religiously monolithic Christian state.

Tore Lindholm, W. Cole Durham, Jr., Bahia G. Tahzib-Lie (eds.), Facilitating Freedom of Religion or Belief: A Deskbook, *777–789.*

II. The Historical Background

For a period of one thousand years Norway has been a kingdom with a Christian "state church." When Christianity was introduced, rather violently, a thousand years ago, the law of the land soon laid down that "every man shall be a Christian in the Realm of Norway" (The Frostating Code). Being a Norwegian *implied* being also a Christian. Royal power and church power were always intimately related, though the balance of power would shift back and forth between royal and church dominance.

When the Lutheran Reformation was introduced in Norway, by royal decree of our then Danish king in 1536, the bond between state and church was further intensified. During the eighteenth century political control of religion and religious life became absolutist. Appointments and dismissals of bishops and priests, control of church doctrine and church property, the development of church liturgy, and the organization of popular religious education were all matters decided by the sovereign—and more or less benign—king and his administration. Two cases in point:

1739: Elementary schooling for all Norwegian children became mandatory, so that all Norwegians should be able to read the Bible and the Lutheran Catechism firsthand. For more than one hundred years, knowledge of catechism plus Bible and basic literacy were the only mandatory school subjects for all the king's subjects.

1741: A law was passed proscribing any religious gathering of people that was not permitted by officials of the Church of Norway and was not conducted in line with Church of Norway doctrine and liturgical rules ("Konventikkelplakaten"). Two generations later this law was to become infamous when it was applied, with cruelty and devastating effects, to curb and imprison for ten years the greatest Christian teacher and preacher in the history of Norway, Hans Nielsen Hauge.

In 1814 Norway got a short lease of national independence, as a side effect of the Napoleonic Wars. Before being forced to form a union with Sweden, Norwegians made use of the window of opportunity to create their own constitution, which is by now the oldest constitution in Europe. In 1814 it was also the most liberal, the most egalitarian, and the most democratic constitution in all of Europe. But, with respect to freedom of religion and interreligious understanding, Norwegians did admittedly establish what was religiously a near-totalitarian state. It appeared self-evident to Norway's constitutional Founding Fathers that in independent Norway the Evangelical-Lutheran Church should carry on as the public religion of the state, just as earlier under the Danish-Norwegian king. At Norway's constitutional convention in 1814 a weak provision of religious freedom was proposed, only to be dropped—or forgotten. Instead, paragraph 2 of Norway's new 1814 Constitution was given this wording:

> The Evangelical-Lutheran religion shall remain the public religion of the state. Inhabitants belonging to it have the duty to raise their children in it. Jesuits and monastic orders are not to be tolerated. Jews are still to be excluded from access to the Realm.

So, independent Norway got started on a footing of candid religious intolerance. And, after 1814, Norway has only slowly evolved toward a modern, multicultural, pluralist, and religiously tolerant society. Here are a few main steps in this slow process:

1845: Lutheran Religious Monopoly Partly Lifted. Only in 1845 was legislation passed that lifted the ban on religious dissidents, a ban barring any religious affiliation other than that of the Church of Norway, i.e., the Evangelical-Lutheran state church. The new 1845 Act on Religious Dissidents recognized the right of a limited set of Protestant denominations to exist in Norway.

1851, 1897, and 1956: Constitutionally Mandated Intolerance Repealed. After intense public debates and against much resistance, liberal forces succeeded in 1851 in having the constitutional provision excluding Jews from access to Norway reversed. Similarly, the constitutional ban on monastic orders was lifted in 1897, and the ban on Jesuits was finally dropped in 1956. (The banning of Jesuits from Norway was incompatible with Norwegian compliance with the European Convention on Human Rights, which Norway had already helped draft, and had ratified.)

1878: Civil Service Careers Opened to Non-Lutherans. The Constitution originally required that all public servants belong to the Church of Norway. This rule was revoked in 1878, and civil service careers also became open to people who were not members of the state church.

1919: End to Exclusion of Non-Lutherans from Ministerial Posts in the Government of Norway. The constitution originally required that all cabinet ministers belong to the Church of Norway. In 1919 this rule was modified to the effect that at least fifty percent of government ministers must belong to the Church of Norway.

1964: Breakthroughs for Religious Nondiscrimination. In 1964 freedom of religion became guaranteed by the constitution by insertion of the following provision into the text of paragraph 2 (quoted above; as reported, the three original provisions of religious intolerance in paragraph 2 had already been deleted): *"All inhabitants of the Realm shall enjoy free exercise of religion."*

1969: Breakthroughs for Religious Nondiscrimination. Then, in 1969, new legislation regulating the legal status and the public support of *all* religious communities was passed. A new Act on Communities of Belief provides that any *religious community* outside the Church of Norway (and, as amended in 1981, also any nonreligious "*life-stance" community*) is entitled to receive annually from the Norwegian state and municipalities the same financial support per member as is received per member by the Church of Norway. (All costs of running the Church of Norway are covered by the government and financed from ordinary taxes.) This new arrangement means that the Norwegian state has taken on a *general legal obligation* to support all religious communities *and* all nonreligious life-stance communities in Norway *without any discrimination*. As a consequence, dissident belief communities of all descriptions receive more generous financial support from the public purse in Norway than in any other European country. Incidentally, in Norway legal registration of new religious communities or of nonreligious belief communities is relatively easy: To become recognized and registered you need a written statement of a creed (or a worldview, or a life stance), a list of members who adhere to this doctrine, plus written statutes and a responsible associational leadership. Once a belief community meets such conditions, it is eligible for public support without being subjected to any additional governmental "quality control."[1]

1999: Major International Human Rights Treaties Incorporated into Norwegian Law. In 1999 Stortinget (Norway's legislature) passed the Norwegian Human Rights Act, making the European Convention on Human Rights with its several Protocols, the International Covenant on Civil and Political Rights, and the International Covenant on Economic, Social and Cultural Rights directly applicable by Norwegian courts, and with legal priority over conflicting provisions in other Norwegian laws. Henceforth the major international human rights provisions on freedom of religion or belief may be enforced by Norwegian courts.

Especially in light of the last two points, one might think that all is now well for freedom of religion or belief in the social-democratic petroleum kingdom of Norway. But not so—at least not in the eyes of many discerning Norwegians, inside as well as outside the Church of Norway. Why? A number of peculiar privileges, and peculiar liabilities, pertaining to the Church of Norway still remain:

- The Church of Norway is, in spite of everything, a fully intact, and still somewhat privileged, state church, with eighty-three percent of the country's population *automatically* enrolled as members;
- On the other hand, secular state officials still control some of the internal affairs of the Church of Norway;
- Norway's public kindergartens and schools still have the legal obligation to provide *all* pupils with "a moral and Christian education";
- The Church of Norway administers all public graveyards;
- First and foremost, priests from the Church of Norway are employed in the Norwegian military, in Norwegian state hospitals, and in Norwegian prisons;
- And by and large only priests from the Church of Norway are called on to speak in situations of public emergencies, or at public festive occasions, in Norway.

These, then, are among the remaining controversial matters that have been addressed in the sequence of noteworthy interfaith dialogues and interconfessional cooperation projects that have been conducted in Norway after 1985.

---

[1] Unfortunately, a discriminating rider has been added to the administrative regulation of annual financial support from the government to religious and life-stance communities in Norway. Whereas belief communities recognized as "religious" are eligible for state and municipal support according to the number of their members *without further qualification,* a belief community that does not seek—or is denied—state recognition as a "religious community" ("trudomssamfunn") is routinely recognized as a "life-stance community" ("livssynssamfunn"). But life-stance communities are eligible for governmental financial support *only if they have five hundred members or more.*

III. 1985 to Present: Interfaith Dialogue Emerges in Norway

Having indicated the historical background, we can now report on seven major events in the emerging interfaith dialogue in Norway during the last fifteen years of the twentieth century.

A. 1985: Christians and Humanists Start Interfaith Dialogue at Lillehammer

Norway's Humanist Association is the largest national Humanist Association in any country and by the end of 2000 had more than 70,000 members. Founded in 1956, the Humanist Association has been the standard antagonist of the Church of Norway, both criticizing the Christian religion and combating the existence of a state church and its predominance in Norwegian schools and in many other arenas of public life. In 1984 in the town of Lillehammer, regional chapters of the Humanist Association and of the Church of Norway Association, cooperating with the Nansen Academy, opened Norway's first organized interfaith dialogue on the theme: "Humanists and Christians: What Separates Us—What Unites Us?"

At the 1985 Lillehammer dialogue, participants were very candid, giving free outlet to many years of pent-up mutual aggression and prejudice—and ignorance. But, the air was cleared. Certainly, old grievances were expressed and important divides between Christian believers and Humanist nonbelievers were underlined, but by engaging in serious discussion, participants were also profoundly surprised to discover large and significant areas *of common moral concern*, e.g., about abuse of drugs, treatment of the elderly, how to combat xenophobia, and the moral education of the young. And many participants not only learned to know, but also learned to like, persons on the other side of the confessional fence. Personal and institutional bonds were established across confessional divides, and a tradition of annual interfaith dialogues at the Lillehammer Nansen Academy was initiated. In this way boundaries have become less rigid, and black-and-white images of one another have become modified. Through dialogue based on mutual respect, old disagreements have become better understood, to some extent even appreciated, and supplemented with a widening area of publicly significant normative agreement and common causes.

B. 1988: Muslims and Christians Begin Serious Dialogue in Oslo

The presence in Norway of a sizable number of Muslims is a very recent phenomenon, predominantly due to immigration of workers during the last forty years, mainly from Pakistan, Turkey, and other Muslim countries. Muslims in Norway now number about sixty thousand people.

Organized dialogue between Muslims and Christians in Norway started in September 1988 at the invitation of Vestre Aker congregation (Church of Norway) in Oslo. The topic for this first public Christian-Muslim dialogue was "Norway as a multicultural society." This dialogue was to initiate a series of Christian-Muslim conferences and projects in the Oslo region, addressing both spiritual questions and secular issues of concern to both parties. The foremost Church of Norway personality in this process has been, and still is, Oddbjørn Leirvik, a priest and a scholar whose deep knowledge of Islam and practical grasp of dialogue is widely recognized. An important feature of the Oslo dialogue between Muslims and Christians has been the unobtrusive emphasis on equality and mutual respect between the two parties. As a follow-up, the Islamic Council Norway and the Church of Norway Council on Ecumenical and International Relations institutionalized a permanent link in 1992, thus launching a publicly formalized co-operation between the largest religious minority and the majority religion in Norway.

C. 1991: Nansen Academy Dialogue "Communal Ethic in Multicultural Norway"

Before the arrival in Norway of guest workers from abroad in the beginning of the 1970s, only the Humanist Association (1956), the Mosaic Community of Faith (1892), and the Bahá'í community (1948) represented organized alternatives to Christian majority society.

Around 1970 several of the great world religions arrived in Norway and gradually established organizations of their own. The number of organized Muslims has grown steadily from about one thousand in 1980 to about sixty thousand today. Also, Buddhists, Hindus, and Sikhs have formed organizations and so have new religious movements. Religious and life stance pluralism have gained momentum and become a challenge to the state church and the majority religion.

Against this background the Nansen Academy, having obtained financial support from the Norway Ministry of Church and Education, initiated a dialogue project in 1991 called "Communal Ethics in Multicultural Norway." Its purpose was to:

- establish personal bonds between people from different religious and life stance backgrounds,
- impart knowledge about the religion or life stance of other parties,
- make an attempt at establishing a basic communal ethic in a multicultural Norway,
- seek solutions for practical conflicts that arise once people with differing religions and life stances meet and are bound to live together.

On the part of Christians, the Church of Norway, the Catholic Church, and the Methodist Church were represented; beyond that, representatives of Islam, Humanism, Judaism, Hinduism, Sikhism, Buddhism, and the Bahá'í community were participants. This group of sixteen people undertook something hitherto untried in Norway: they sought by way of dialogue to seek out a maximally extensive set of shared value commitments, to identify foreseeable conflicts, and to find constructive ways of handling these conflicts.

The dialogue was founded on a number of core values: a considered ***toleration*** that may be grounded in various normative traditions, an aptitude for empathy across border lines, a readiness to appreciate and learn from others, and the ability to put up with what one is critical of. Fidelity to partly diverging fundamental values implies readiness to be clear also about ***disagreements*** and about ***limits to toleration***. Therefore candid interfaith conversation includes conflicts and confrontations.

The dialogue group agreed that conversations had to be conducted in a spirit of unimpeded *truthfulness* where one is ready to recognize destructive features of one's own traditions. Religions have been deployed in the service of good and evil, destructively as well as constructively. Here the concept of *truth* is crucial. The group agreed that peaceful coexistence is possible, provided each party permits the other party to testify to the truth it has found—and simultaneously recognizes that the whole and perfect truth belongs to no party.

Open and candid dialogue is predicated on *equal dignity*. No party must have reason to think it is overruled due to basic inequalities of power and life circumstances. To establish such equality within the group, conversations started with each participant telling her or his life story. The group did not begin with doctrines but with human beings, who are always more than their opinions and positions. The upshot was that getting to know others as human beings also made it is easier to relate constructively to the opinions of others.

Once initial procedures and principles were settled, the group started its conversation about questions related to the course of human life, from conception to death. On each theme "shared positions" as well as "peculiar or conflicting positions" were expressed and noted. Among the themes addressed were: biotechnology, abortion, naming of persons, circumcision, children and youth, freedom and limits to freedom, marriage and divorce, equal rights and equal dignity, polygamy, homosexuality, old age, euthanasia, autopsy, funerals, the value basis of public schools, same public schools for all/private schools, education in religion and life stance, celebration of public or religious holidays and feasts, economic support of religious or life stance communities, and access to Norway for religious leaders.

The purpose of these first discussions among participants of all major religious and life stance communities in Norway was *not* to discover a *shared ethic*, but to elaborate a *communal ethic*. A shared ethic, in the intended sense, would only touch on themes about which consensus was available, and also grind down diverging views to generally acceptable minimum standards. A communal ethic, on the other hand, addresses all themes of importance to a decent community and examines basic values about which binding agreement can be achieved (on diverging grounds)—including how competing values must frequently be weighed. It deals with how a multicultural and multireligious people may live with their differences in institutions that can accommodate differences in mutually acceptable ways.

In their dialogue about a communal ethic in multicultural Norway, participants were forced to attend both to the beauty of a good compromise and the voice of individual conscience. After six two-day discussions spanning one year, the dialogue group expressed what really separated them in the following terms:

> Our dialogue group has conducted several discussions of whether basic differences in ethical thinking separate "religious" from "secular" worldviews, or whether we are in crucial questions confronted with alliances that transgress against "spiritual" and "this-worldly" positions and also against the divides between religions. It seems that differences within religions and life stances are often as great as differences between them.

The above statement is borrowed from the 108-page report on the "Communal Ethic in a Multicultural Norway" dialogue project published by the Norwegian University Press in 1993.[2] The report contains a wealth of specific and more general proposals, recommendations, and analyses, and has functioned as a fount of ideas for interfaith dialogue work in Norway.

D. 1996: Nansen Academy Dialogue "Religions, Life Stances, and Human Rights in Norway"

One of the crucial themes addressed by the 1991 dialogue group was the challenge both to religions and ideologies stemming from universally binding human rights: "How does each community of faith or belief accommodate, support, and justify a commitment on internally credible grounds for the endorsement and observance of human rights?" But human rights is also a challenge to the state and the larger society: "How well are all human rights pertaining to the recognition, unimpeded exercise, and enjoyment of freedom of religion or belief catered for by the Norwegian state or by our society?"

In 1996 the Nansen Academy obtained governmental financial support for its second interfaith dialogue and cooperation project devoted exclusively to the theme "Religions, Life Stances, and Human Rights in Norway." The purpose was to:

- elucidate the potential grounding of, and the traditions pertaining to, human rights in the various religions and life stances present in Norway,
- reflect upon and systematize the interrelations of human rights ideals and realities practiced in Norway,
- make proposals for the strengthening of human rights within different religious and life stance groups—and in Norway generally.

It would lead too far to report, even in outline, on the ramified discussions about these matters during more than one year between Muslims, Sikhs, Jews, Catholics, Pentecostals, Buddhists, Bahá'ís, Humanists, New Age people, Greek Orthodox, and Lutherans. The matters addressed by the dialogue group include: lofty issues of high principles, as well as practical realities of public administration; thorny issues of past failures in each tradition and recent reinterpretations of scriptures and principles in support of equal dignity and human rights; and the testing of minority demands on state and society in Norway against the practice of coreligionists in majority positions in other countries. Many issues of principle and a host of practical proposals can be found in the dialogue report (250 pages), again published by the Norwegian University Press.[3] To a very large extent interfaith agreement was reached—without compromising specificity.

This dialogue report became more controversial than the earlier one (on communal ethics in Norway) since some of its recommendations, especially on public education in religion, life stance, and ethics in Norwegian schools, went against political majority compromises reached by the legislature (Stortinget). We cannot spell out details here

---

[2] Oddbjørn Leirvik, ed., *Fellesskapsetikk i et flerkulturelt Norge* (Common ethics in a multicultural Norway) (Oslo: Universitetsforlaget, 1993).

and shall turn to another interconfessional undertaking that further demonstrates that such enterprises, though peaceful and orderly, may also indicate deep conflicts of value and interests—but can hopefully facilitate their long-term resolution.

E. 1994 to Present: Interfaith "Campaign for Freedom of Belief in Norwegian Schools"

Norway has few private schools. Eighty-nine percent of all children attend public schools. For more than 150 years, there has been some possibility for pupils not belonging to the state church to be exempted from the school subject "Knowledge of Christianity." Since 1974 such pupils have had the option to attend the subject "Education in Alternative Worldviews."

In 1995 the Norwegian government presented plans to replace "Knowledge of Christianity" and "Education in Alternative Worldviews" with an integrated, and mandatory, school subject: "Knowledge of Christianity and Information about Other Religions and Life Stances."

Minorities perceived that their parental rights to freedom of belief were jeopardized. Their protest against the mandatory new school subject gave birth to a broadly based "Campaign for Freedom of Belief in Norwegian Schools." Leaders of minority religious communities and life stance organizations came together. Jews and Muslims, Humanists and Buddhists worked side by side, along with some members of the Church of Norway. Several political youth organizations, some trade unions, and some student organizations also joined this interfaith campaign for religious freedom and equality in Norwegian schools.

In the course of working together for campaign targets, minority representatives became aware of several additional matters of common concern—issues that it would be fruitful to discuss and try to tackle cooperatively. Gradually the idea matured that what was needed was a national forum for interfaith dialogue and cooperation that would embrace as many religious and life stance communities as possible. The attempt was made to include all major religious and belief groups in Norway including the Church of Norway. In this way the experience of divisive struggle about freedom of belief in Norwegian schools gave rise to the founding of a common interfaith institution that now enjoys wide political support. The aims of the Campaign for Freedom of Belief in Norwegian Schools have not been achieved. The struggle is still being waged against majority political decisions, and cases filed by minority communities (Humanists and Muslims respectively) are still pending before Norwegian courts. In the case of Humanist parents against the Norwegian state, a Supreme Court decision was reached 22 August 2001. Five judges unanimously found against the Humanist parents' right to have their children exempted from mandatory participation in "Knowledge of Christianity, Religions, and Life Stances" classes (as the new Norwegian religious education curriculum is now called). The Humanists are likely to bring their case to the European Human Rights Court in Strasbourg. Norway's Muslims will surely follow suit.

---

[3] Inge Eidsvåg and Lena Larsen, eds., *Religion, livssyn og menneskerettigheter i Norge* (Religions, life stances, and human rights in Norway) (Oslo: Universitetsforlaget, 1997).

F. 1996: The Council for Religious and Life Stance Communities in Norway is Founded

The Council for Religious and Life Stance Communities in Norway was established 30 May 1996. Representatives from eight major belief communities came together in the quarters of a Muslim congregation. It was a very special occasion when, one by one, their leaders rose and affirmed their intent to be part of the proposed interfaith council in Norway.

The Council for Religious and Life Stance Communities is unique because of the broad scope of member communities, because members work together on a platform devised entirely by themselves, and because they operate independently of government interference. Member communities today include: the Alternative Network (a New Age group), the Bahá'í Community of Norway, the Buddhist Community of Norway, the Jewish Communities in Norway, the Norwegian Humanist Association (which organizes nonbelievers, agnostics, and atheists), the Islamic Council of Norway, the Council of Free Churches in Norway (Protestants), Sanatan Mandir Sabha Norway (Hindus), and the Church of Norway.

The only major group still not participating as a full member is the Catholic Church, but it has observer status and participates in all meetings. The first elected leader of the Council was a Pentecostal pastor. The present leader is a Buddhist.

The goals of the Council for Religious and Life Stance Communities are defined in the statutes as follows:

- to promote mutual understanding and respect between different religious and life stance communities through dialogue,
- to work towards equality between various religious and life stance communities in Norway based on the United Nations Covenants on Human Rights and on the European Convention on Human Rights,
- to work, internally and externally, with social and ethical issues from the perspective of religions and life stances.

From the beginning, the Norwegian government took a great interest in the Council for Religious and Life Stance Communities in Norway. A quotation from a 1996 parliamentary document is a case in point (Stortingsmelding nr. 17, 1996/1997):

> Information exchange and dialogue between religious and humanist communities, public authorities, and the general public are important in order to avoid regarding other people as enemies and to prevent conflict. The Council can be a useful partner in a dialogue with the authorities. The relevant public authorities should encourage this type of dialogue and assure that the Council is heard in issues that arise.

The Council for Religious and Life Stance Communities in Norway never practices majority voting. Everyone must agree before the Council goes public with a position. This does imply quite a bit of work, but it is absolutely necessary to sustain trust among member communities.

A key word, then, is serious and well-informed dialogue—and dialogue with no hidden agenda. The agenda of such dialogues does not include proselytizing, it does not aim for a comprehensive consensus between differing religious or life stance communities, and it does not strive for agreement in theological matters. In Norway the state church has enjoyed a near monopoly in public theological and moral discourse; hence minorities will never trust a decision taken by the religious majority on their behalf. Mutual trust is grounded on cooperation and in the possibility of making oneself heard.

Each member organization is expected to put in an equal amount of work and an equal financial contribution. Each member organization has two members on the board of the Council. It is strange that the majority religion, covering about 83 percent of the people, has the same formal influence as have the Bahá'ís with only few members in Norway. But this arrangement enhances the sense of equality.

Since 1999 the Council has received an annual grant from the government, enabling it to have a small administration and making it possible for the Council to keep up its interreligious dialogue work. The Council has to apply for a grant each year, and the government may approve or deny the application. As a consequence the Council also has to submit an annual report and a financial account of its operations.

All issues where religious faith and humanism have significant social repercussions are discussed by the Council, including questions about human rights, genetic research, euthanasia, educational policies, the role of media in society, contested court and administrative decisions, etc. The Council hosts interfaith seminars and, hopefully, it will inspire scholarly research.

So far the Council has hardly conducted theological dialogues, but it has discussed how to make authors of school textbooks give a better and more correct presentation of each religion or belief. The Council has also addressed a host of issues of particular concern to religious communities; e.g., it has advised against modernization of the spelling of religious terms, protested against a proposal from a political party to forbid circumcising baby boys, and requested that political parties not use religions or beliefs as tools in their electoral campaigns. The Council has also pointed out that it is unsatisfactory that Norway gives only a four-year residence permit to most Muslim, Jewish, Hindu, or Buddhist clergy coming from abroad, whereas Christian priests who can document a higher education have no problem getting residence permits lasting more than four years.

Of course, the Council for Religious and Life Stance Communities in Norway is still very much occupied with the mandatory school subject "Knowledge of Christianity, Religions, and Life Stances." The subject was reassessed by parliament (Stortinget) in early summer 2001. The outcome, beyond the revised *name*, brought little significant change. Minority religion/life-stance parents are still not allowed to withdraw their children entirely from this subject. And Norwegian public schools are still by law obliged to provide all pupils with a "moral and Christian education." The struggle for unfettered freedom of religion or belief in Norwegian schools continues.[4] But there is an irony at work here: The political forces in Norway that persistently uphold a modicum of restrictions on freedom of religion or belief are probably oblivious to the service they thereby render to interfaith solidarity and cooperation! The Council for Religious and Life-Stance Communities in Norway surely "remains apprised of the matter."

[4] See also the chapter by Plesner in this volume.

G. The Oslo Coalition on Freedom of Religion or Belief

In 1997 the Council for Religious and Life Stance Communities in Norway was approached by a group of academics, as well as by some prominent religious leaders who wanted to organize a large international conference in support of freedom of religion or belief. The Council for Religious and Life Stance Communities was invited to host what became the Oslo Conference on Freedom of Religion or Belief.

The plans were ambitious. Supported by the Ministry of Foreign Affairs in Norway, and also later by the European Communities, the Oslo Conference took place in August 1998. More than two hundred religious leaders, academics, experts, and resource persons participated. At the conclusion of the conference the Oslo Declaration on Freedom of Religion or Belief [5] was unanimously adopted, identifying directions for future action. In accordance with the Declaration, the Oslo Coalition on Freedom of Religion or Belief has been established as a non-governmental and internationally responsive organization.

The Oslo Coalition on Freedom of Religion or Belief is a new international network consisting of experts and representatives from religious and life stance communities worldwide. Academics are one important group, and so are representatives from NGOs, other international organizations, and civil society. The Council for Religious and Life Stance Communities in Norway is the national underpinning of the Oslo Coalition and presently has three board members.

The activity of the Oslo Coalition is based on the Oslo Declaration on Freedom of Religion or Belief. As a follow-up of the Oslo Declaration, the Coalition has worked out a strategic plan for development and practical support for article 18 of the Universal Declaration of Human Rights.

The work of the Oslo Coalition addresses the United Nations System, prodding for an increase in resources, financial and otherwise, in support of freedom of religion or belief. It endorses the implementation of the work and recommendations of the United Nations Special Rapporteur on Freedom of Religion or Belief, and encourages the High Commissioner for Human Rights to develop a plan for coordination of resources for freedom of religion or belief within the UN.

High priority tasks of the Oslo Coalition are: promotion of interfaith dialogue and practical cooperation projects, reconciliation, and education. The Oslo Coalition is prepared to work with academic institutions, the media, and political institutions at different levels and in various countries, as well as with different religious or belief communities, NGOs, and international organizations.

The Oslo Coalition has an International Advisory Council consisting of distinguished persons from all over the world. Its president is the Church of Norway Bishop of Oslo, Gunnar Stålsett. The small coalition administration is at the Norwegian Centre for Human Rights, University of Oslo. A board of seven members and a coordinator have the responsibility for running the administration.

In 1999 and 2000 the Oslo Coalition cosponsored and participated in several international conferences devoted to the scholarly study and/or practical advance of freedom of religion or belief, in Russia, Ukraine, each of the Baltic countries, Azerbaijan, the United States, and western Europe.

---

[5] Reprinted in this volume, Appendix F.

In 2000 a delegation from the Coalition visited China and conducted extensive conversations with administrative and religious leaders about the situation for different faith communities in China. The visit was the beginning of an extensive cooperative process of dialogues and mutual visits between the two countries dealing with freedom of religion or belief. A Chinese delegation visited Norwegian religious and life stance communities and administrative bodies in September 2001.

As of summer 2001, Oslo Coalition plans for the immediate future include:

- to participate in and contribute to a United Nations project on screening and reform of school curriculums in religious and ethical education (The Madrid Conference in November 2001);
- to publish and distribute worldwide, with generous support from the Royal Norwegian Ministry of Foreign Affairs, the volume in which this essay is published: *Facilitating Freedom of Religion or Belief: A Deskbook*. The purpose of this publication is to analyze, elucidate, and inform competently about important issues and problems in the field of freedom of religion or belief worldwide, and to facilitate the implementation of international conventions and declarations in this field;
- to help organize a long-term dialogue and cooperation project between Muslims and Christians in Indonesia;
- to explore the basis for Norwegian support of interreligious dialogues and cooperation projects locally in the Russian Federation, tentatively in the Orenburg and/or Kazan regions.

IV. Conclusion

Religion and belief is a powerful tool, and in the wrong hands it may lead to bitter and bloody conflicts and even prolonged wars: not necessarily because of the religious belief or ideology itself, but because some persons or some groups use religion (or atheist ideology, for that matter) as a tool to gain power or to maintain special interests. Norwegians have been spared such calamities, but Norwegian history exhibits ample evidence of another troublesome aspect of religion and belief: Intrinsic in religions and other comprehensive normative traditions is the temptation of excluding outsiders from equal public status and from equal respect, as persons or as communities.

Our recent experience in Norway is that religion and belief can also serve as a basis for eliminating animosities and strengthening understanding and cooperation across ethnic, ideological, and religious divides. Here interfaith dialogue, as described in this chapter, is a commendable option, also from the vantage point of the society at large.

Our experience also indicates that the modern state may play a significant and constructive role, if our goal is to nurture the potentials of religions and life stances for dialogue, reconciliation, mutual understanding, and solidarity in society at large.

The state is responsible for the space between and around the communities of faith, for protecting their exercise of confessional freedom, and for safeguarding the rights of individual human beings to exercise and enjoy real freedom of religion or belief.

Exercising these freedoms, leaders and individual members of confessional communities should, in an increasingly plural and multireligious world, be ready to engage in serious interfaith dialogue and sustained interreligious cooperation.

Chapter 36

Promoting Tolerance through Religious Education

Ingvill Thorson Plesner

Freedom of thought, conscience and religion is one of the foundations of a "democratic society" within the meaning of the Convention. It is, in its religious dimension, one of the most vital elements that is to make up the identity of believers and their conception of life, but also a precious asset for atheists, agnostics, skeptics and the unconcerned. The pluralism indissociable from a democratic society, which has been dearly won over the centuries, depends on it.

European Court of Human Rights 1993:
Kokkanakis v. Greece

I. Introduction

A. Preconditions for Pluralism

In the statement quoted above, the European Court of Human Rights points to a precondition for peaceful coexistence in pluralistic societies. As a human right, freedom of religion or belief not only makes pluralism possible, but the right to have and to manifest a religious, or nonreligious, conviction is also closely related to the equal and inherent dignity of all human beings.

At the state level, toleration of different religious and nonreligious opinions and manifestations can be seen as one dimension of freedom of religion or belief.[1] The state is obliged to accept (tolerate) the existence of a diversity of opinions among its

[1] Sophie van Bijsterveld distinguishes the negative dimension from the positive dimension of freedom of religion or belief. Toleration, as defined in the following, refers mainly to the negative dimension of this basic human right. Sophie C. van Bijsterveld, "Religion and Law: Legal Structures in an International and Comparative Context," in *Church and State Consultation: Conference of European Churches, 13–16 March 1997, Czech Republic* (Geneva: Conference of European Churches, 1998).

Tore Lindholm, W. Cole Durham, Jr., Bahia G. Tahzib-Lie (eds.), Facilitating Freedom of Religion or Belief: A Deskbook, *791–812.*

citizens. Also, it is obliged to respect the freedom of its inhabitants to change their religion or belief, as well as their freedom—either alone or in community with others and in public or private—to manifest their religion or belief in teaching, practice, worship and observance.[2] But the responsibilities of the state in relation to freedom of religion or belief extend beyond the "negative" dimension of this human right. States have also committed themselves to the promotion of awareness of and respect for human rights among citizens, in order to minimize the possibilities of human rights violations resulting from the actions of "third parties" ("Drittwirkungen").[3] This awareness should also include respect for the right to freedom of religion or belief of all individuals, so that discrimination based on religious intolerance can be prevented. The fostering of tolerance—defined as an attitude among inhabitants towards people who hold differing convictions or who lead their lives in deviating ways—can be seen as one measure by which the state might contribute to the prevention of human rights violations caused by "third parties" in the field of freedom of religion or belief.

With respect to the promotion of freedom of religion or belief, we might distinguish between "toleration" at the state level, and "tolerance" at the individual or group levels.[4] Whereas state toleration of different beliefs and practices may or may not be based on the values or worldview of a certain religion or tradition, tolerance as an individual attitude or conviction will always have some particular worldview and value system as its foundation. At the individual level, tolerance—by the very meaning of the word—presupposes that you have a basic conviction that differs from the convictions of the person or the practice that you tolerate. In liberal states, state toleration of different religions or belief systems, and hence the protection of freedom of religion or belief, will follow from the principles of equal human rights and equality before the law. In some "confessional" states the toleration may be motivated by the values of the belief system that the state has given priority to, values that also may include or give support to the liberal principles of human rights and freedom of religion or belief.

At the state level, freedom of religion or belief puts clear limits on the degree of state affiliation with a specific, comprehensive belief system. At the individual level, on the other hand, freedom of religion or belief safeguards the right of all persons to choose their (degree of) affiliation with any belief system.

---

[2] Cf. *1966 UN Covenant on Civil and Political Rights* (CCPR), article 18; *1981 Declaration; 1950 European Convention on Human Rights,* article 9. Whereas the state may never interfere with the individual's conviction or belief (the "forum internum"), there may be limitations to the right to express or manifest one's conviction (the "forum externum"), when necessary in order to protect public safety, order, health, morals or the fundamental freedom of others (cf. CCPR, art. 18[3]). One might say that the limitations to the right to freedom of religion or belief based on the criteria just mentioned also express limits to prescribed state *toleration* of different expressions of religion or belief.

[3] "Drittwirkungen" are human rights effects caused by the actions of other individuals or groups in civil society ("third parties").

[4] A similar distinction is made by Howard L. Biddulph in a paper presented at the Conference on Religious Freedom in Kiev, 2001. Biddulph makes a fruitful distinction between the term "toleration" and the term "tolerance" that might be used, respectively, for the level of state and the level of individuals and groups. Biddulph's definition of these terms will be used as a point of departure in this article. Cf. my paper to the 1998 *Oslo Conference on Freedom of Religion or Belief,* "The Relevance of Tolerance to Freedom of Religion or Belief," in which I argue that relevance of tolerance to freedom of religion or belief differs for these two domains.

The distinction between "toleration" and "tolerance" may be studied further by examining its relevance in the field of religious education. In several countries of the world, religious education is taught in public schools either as an independent subject or as a part of other subjects. In the field of religious education, a state's toleration of and attitude towards different religious or philosophical traditions becomes manifest, and, hence, freedom of religion or belief and the principle of nondiscrimination may be challenged. Also, in this part of school curriculums, different religious and moral convictions may be presented and discussed, and hence the pupils' conceptions of their own as well as of other traditions may be influenced and challenged. This makes religious education vital for addressing the challenge of fostering tolerance at the individual level.

If the state is to be credible in its use of the education system to promote tolerance among people of different confessions, state toleration of different groups and opinions must be articulated and freedom of religion or belief must be accommodated by the content of textbooks and curricula, as well as in the choice of teaching methods.

B. Main Question and Approach

Bearing in mind the great significance of toleration and tolerance to freedom of religion in the field of religious education, the main aim of this article is to study criteria for successful religious education[5] in pluralistic societies. By "successful" religious education, I refer to religious education that can be assumed to:

- contribute effectively to the fostering of tolerance, and
- respect the equal rights to freedom of religion or belief of all individuals affected.

A main question therefore will be:

> *What approaches to religious education in pluralistic societies can contribute* effectively *to the fostering of tolerance and at the same time respect the* equal *right of all inhabitants to freedom of religion or belief?*

My discussion of this question is a combination of normative and empirical elements. It will be based on results of different comparative surveys on religious education. The main empirical focus will be on experiences of different European countries. A regional focus is chosen mainly because of limited access to studies in the field conducted in other parts of the world. Nevertheless, some results from the global survey of the Special Rapporteur on Freedom of Religion or Belief will be presented, based on summaries of the survey, in documents made available for the International Consultative Conference on Tolerance, Non-Discrimination and Freedom of Religion or Belief in Relation with School Education, in Madrid, 23–25 November 2001.[6]

---

[5] By "religious education" I shall refer to education about both religions and secular worldviews or life stances.

[6] The conference was initiated by the Special Rapporteur, Mr. Abdelfattah Amor, in cooperation with the Spanish government. An aim of the conference was to discuss the possibilities for developing an international strategy for the fostering of tolerance through education. Documents from the conference are available online, including "Introductory Note" by Abdelfattah Amor at <http://www.unhchr.ch/html/menu2/7/b/cfedy-home.html>. The Madrid Final Document is available online at <http://www.oslocoalition.org/html/project_school_education/index.html>.

In examining different approaches to religious education, the human rights norms on freedom of religion or belief constitute the main standard of evaluation. Also, my normative discussion will draw on the recommendations for the promotion of tolerance through religious education presented by the UN Special Rapporteur in the documents for the 2001 Madrid Consultative Conference and in the final document of the Madrid Conference.

I shall first address the relevant human rights standards and then present some results of a survey conducted by the Special Rapporteur. Subsequently I shall have a closer look at the experiences of some European countries in the field of religious education. Finally, I shall draw on these experiences in a concluding discussion of the main question raised in this article.

II. Models for Religious Education: Aims and Challenges

A. Freedom of Religion or Belief and the Fostering of Tolerance through Education

The UN human rights standards on freedom of religion or belief include, much like other fundamental human rights norms, a strong emphasis on the principle of nondiscrimination. The equal right of all inhabitants to freedom of religion or belief is stated in several human rights documents,[7] i.e., in the 1981 UN Declaration on the Elimination on All Forms of Intolerance and of Discrimination Based on Religion or Belief.[8] The Declaration underlines the close relation between promotion of tolerance and freedom of religion or belief. It states:

> The child shall be protected from any form of discrimination on the grounds of religion or belief. He shall be brought up in the spirit of understanding, tolerance, friendship among peoples, peace and universal brotherhood, respect for freedom of religion or belief of others, and in full consciousness that his energy and talents should be devoted to the service of his fellow men (art. 5, para. 3).[9]

Further, it states that

> every child shall enjoy the right to have access to education in the matter of religion or belief in accordance with the wishes of his parents or, as the case may be, legal guardians, and shall not be compelled to receive teaching on religion or belief against the wishes of his parents or legal guardians, the best interest of the child being the guiding principle (art. 5, para. 2).[10]

---

[7] Cf. *The Universal Declaration of Human Rights* (UDHR), article 2.

[8] General Assembly Resolution 35/55 (November 25, 1981).

[9] These aims and principles have later on been included in the *UN Convention on the Rights of the Child of 1989* (CRC). Article 3 of CRC further underlines a basic principle that must also be heeded by the state in the field of education: In all actions concerning the child, "the best interests of the child shall be a primary consideration" (art. 3[1]). Article 29 of the CRC outlines aims and principles for the education of the child: It shall be directed to the development of the child's personality and talents to their fullest potential (29.1a). Further, it shall ensure respect for the child's parents and his or her own cultural identity, language, and values, as well as respect for the national values of the country in which the child is living and for civilizations different from his or her own (29.1c). The education also shall prepare the child for "responsible life in a free society, in the spirit of understanding, peace, tolerance, equality of sexes, and friendship among all peoples, ethnic, national and religious groups" (29.1d).

According to the two statements from the 1981 Declaration, several concerns must be taken into account in defining the content of religious education: on the one hand, the public educational aim of promoting tolerance and mutual understanding, on the other hand, the rights of the parents to have a last say in the religious and moral education of their children. By examining the experiences of different countries, we shall see how dilemmas deriving from these competing concerns may be met in ways that can effectively serve the fostering of tolerance as well as respect the equal right to freedom of religion of all inhabitants.

B. The Global Survey of the Special Rapporteur

Another tension among human rights norms in this field is between, on the one hand, the rights of the parents to decide the religious and moral education of their children, and, on the other hand, the rights of the child to freedom of religion or belief, expanding with increasing age, and the right of the child to receive pluralistic information and in other ways an education that meets with the aims set out in the 1989 Convention on the Rights of the Child, the best interests of the child being the guiding principle.[11] This strain is again closely related to that between the state and parents, because a discussion of what religious education is in the best interest of the child will normally be conducted between the state and parents or their organizations.

Since the early 1990s, the Special Rapporteur has worked on developing preventive strategies in the field of religious freedom, tolerance and nondiscrimination. Such strategies may supplement the traditional monitoring strategy focusing on human rights violations. Education—and in particular religious education—has been emphasized as one of the most effective means for fostering tolerance and mutual understanding across borders of faith and culture in pluralistic societies.[12]

In 1994 the Commission on Human Rights encouraged the Special Rapporteur to examine the role of education in the promotion of tolerance of different religious views and traditions, and to study how education might contribute to the fostering of tolerance in a more effective way.[13] The Special Rapporteur conducted a survey that was to explore if and how the curricula on religious education at the primary and secondary school levels of different countries contributes to the protection of human rights in general and to the protection of religious freedom and a climate of tolerance and nondiscrimination in particular. A questionnaire was sent to the UN member states, and responses were received from seventy-seven states. The

[10] The right of parents (or guardians) to decide upon the religious and moral education of their children is also stated in several other human rights treaties, e.g., the 1948 UN *Universal Declaration on Human Rights* (art. 26[3]), the 1950 *European Convention on Human Rights* (art. 2 of Protocol No. 1 to the Convention), the 1966 *International Covenant on Civil and Political Rights* (arts. 18, 4), the 1966 *International Covenant on Economic, Social and Cultural Rights* (art. 13[3]), the 1969 *UNESCO Declaration on the Elimination of Discrimination in Education* (art. 5[1]), and the 1989 *Convention on the Rights of the Child* (arts. 14, 28, and 29).

[11] CRC, arts. 3, 12, and 29.

[12] Commission on Human Rights Resolution 1994/18 (February 25, 1994) and Resolution 1998/18 (April 9, 1998).

[13] Commission on Human Rights Resolution 1994/18 (February 25, 1994).

answers were analyzed and summarized, and the Special Rapporteur presented the results in his report to the Commission on Human Rights at its 2001 Assembly in Geneva.[14]

The material collected in the Special Rapporteur's survey provides a rich basis for discussions both of the challenges to religious freedom and tolerance in the field of religious education and of possible strategies to meet these challenges. The Special Rapporteur concludes that there is a "considerable variety in the approaches taken with regard to education in the field of religion and conviction. What emerges clearly is that beside a consistent number of interesting experiences there are just as many situations nurturing a 'ghetto approach' based on exclusion."[15] In his report the Special Rapporteur warns against the kind of "ghetto mentality" that might be created by a religious education that does not provide knowledge about religions other than one's own, and that does not serve the aim of tolerance, nondiscrimination, and respect for human rights.

The two approaches to religious education discussed by the Special Rapporteur might be called a "separation" or "ghetto" approach and an "integration" approach. The Special Rapporteur argues for the latter approach to religious education, according to which all pupils are kept together as much as possible, rather than being separated into groups, and learn not only about their own tradition but also about that of the others.

The Special Rapporteur points out the differences in the status given to religious education in the school systems of various countries. In some countries religious education is a compulsory subject but still does not "affect the passage from a level to the subsequent one," the Special Rapporteur notes.[16] The Special Rapporteur underlines that where religious education is a subject on line with other parts of the curriculum, this may express a conviction that this subject can foster "understanding of the others, of cultural and moral differences, and contribute to the creation of a culture of peace, human rights and tolerance."[17] The Special Rapporteur points out the importance of and need for training teachers and educators in the field of human rights and religion so that they are able to deliver their teaching in a credible way. His main emphasis is, however, on the aims of religious education. The focus should be both on developing the child's self-understanding and on the child's understanding of "the other," by providing knowledge about and respect for the different religions and traditions. These two aims should be connected by the universalist dimension of education, expressed in universal human rights and the principles of equal human dignity, tolerance and nondiscrimination. By recognizing these values, the Special Rapporteur argues, we learn to see the unity of mankind ("mankind is One") and hence to see that "the others are indeed us."[18] In these statements, the Special Rapporteur hence expresses the view that religious education, and education in general, should not only contribute to increased knowledge, but also to identity building and internalization of values, as well as a certain image of man or mankind.

---

[14] Cf. Amor, "Introductory Note."

[15] See ibid., para. 14.

[16] Amor, "Introductory Note," para. 38.

[17] Ibid.

[18] Ibid., paras. 17, 22.

Human rights standards imply that education should provide knowledge and respect for other groups, as well as the national culture in which the child is living. However, they also make it clear that the cultural, religious, or philosophical identity of the child should be respected in accordance with the convictions and wishes of the parents.[19] An encounter with different religious and philosophical traditions might lead to changes in the self-conception of the individual child, including his or her religious identity. Therefore, if one important aim of religious education is to help the pupils to "see themselves as the other," as the Special Rapporteur puts it, schools will have to deal with the challenges that follow from parents' rights to decide about the religious and moral education of their children.

C. Regional Surveys of Approaches to Religious Education

The broad, global approach of the survey of the Special Rapporteur has provided useful materials both for the development of educational strategies and for further research in this field. It might be interesting to compare some of his empirical findings with results of regional comparative studies. A focus on only a small number of cases may still give information of broad relevance and general interest.

During the last years some comparative and systematic studies on different models and dimensions of religious education in European countries have been undertaken.[20] The studies show that it is possible, for instance, to distinguish between two main types of religious education (RE)—a "confessional approach" on the one hand, and a "non-confessional approach" on the other:[21]

- The "confessional approach" indicates that a religious community or a church is responsible for the curriculum, for the qualifications and acknowledgment of RE teachers, and sometimes also for schoolbooks. As a rule, this type of RE is organized for the children of a specific faith community, but in some countries pupils can choose the subject without being an affiliated member (e.g., in Belgium and Protestant RE in Germany). In all cases the pupils and their parents have the right to opt out and/or to choose other alternative subjects like ethics or philosophy, in line with freedom of religion. The main aim of this type of RE is to facilitate the identity formation of pupils concerning religious questions, e.g., about the meaning of life, death and sorrow, love and happiness, to give orientation and knowledge.
- RE based on a "non-confessional approach" often has the aim to inform about religion(s) and other world views. Learning *about* religion is combined with

[19] Cf. *Convention on the Rights of the Child.*

[20] Cf. Peter Schreiner, *Religious Education in Europe: A Collection of Basic Information about RE in European Countries* (Münster: Comenius Institut/Intereuropean Commission on Church and School, 2000); Ingvill T. Plesner, "Religion-political models and models for religious and moral education," *Panorama: International Journal of Comparative Religious Education and Values,* ed. Peter Schreiner, vol. 14, no. 2 (winter 2002): 111–22; Ingvill T. Plesner, "Hvordan definere fellesskapets grunnlag? Om pluraliseringens betydning for offentlig religionsundervisning" (How to Define the Basis of Community? On the Impact of Pluralisation on Religious Education in Public Schools), in *Identitet og pluralitet* (Identity and Plurality), ed. Jan-Olav Henriksen (Oslo: Gyldendal akademiske, 2001).

[21] Schreiner, *Religious Education in Europe.*

learning *from* religion to help the pupils make their own choices. It can focus mainly on one religion, or, as is the case in England and Wales, on a number of religions.[22]

The confessional/non-confessional distinction above has similarities to the distinction between an "integration approach" and a "separation approach" drawn from statements of the Special Rapporteur. Peter Schreiner's distinction is based both on differences in responsibility for developing the curriculum and on differences in content and aims of religious education.[23] A supplementary approach might be one that distinguishes between several dimensions of religious education:[24]

(a) different ways of cooperating about RE based on who has overall responsibility for the content of religious education: public schools, faith communities, or both;

(b) different ways of organizing the teaching of RE: either one or several alternative RE subject(s); compulsory or noncompulsory RE; RE taking place only outside school hours or included in school curriculums;

(c) different approaches to RE based on the pedagogical profile of the subject in terms of content, aims, and guiding principles (a focus on one or on several confessions/religions, aiming mainly to provide knowledge, or also emphasizing religious experience and religious or existential identity building); and last but not least;

(d) different ways of defining the value basis of RE and of school education in general, focusing on moral and other values of the "cultural heritage" of the country, linking it to specific religious tradition(s); and/or focusing on values that are taken to be "common" for different religions, by reference either to national legislation and constitutional principles or to universal human rights standards.

Using a multidimensional approach, we may analyze the religious education of different countries in more detail. Summarizing our findings, it is useful to sort the approaches of different countries into main categories. If we combine two of the four dimensions presented above, and then sort findings of empirical studies of religious education in Europe and the USA, we may—at a very general level—group the different main approaches as follows:

---

[22] Ibid., 8.

[23] We see that this dichotomy has some similarities with the distinction that Amor made between the "ghetto" or "separation" approach and the "integration" approach.

[24] Plesner, "Et komparativt utblikk" and "Hvordan definere."

Models for Religious Education

Dimension 1: The *profile* of Religious Education curriculums and aims*
Dimension 2: The institutional *arena* and responsibility for Religious Education**

Dimension 1:	Confessional (Segregated)	Pluralistic (Integrated)	Ethics (Integrated)
Dimension 2: School		Sweden Norway Iceland	(Brandenburg)
Cooperation school/church (in school)	Finland Germany Italy Austria	England	
Church (in school)	(Berlin)		
Church (outside school)	France USA		

* Dimension 1 indicates different *profiles* of religious education in terms of curriculum contents and teaching goals: focusing on the teachings of one particular confession ("Confessional"), on different religions or life stances ("Pluralistic"), or on ethics and philosophical thinking ("Ethics"). Dimension 1 also maps the ***organizational*** separation of pupils and/or students of religious education along confessional divides ("Segregated") or, alternatively, the organizational integration of all pupils/students in shared religious education classes ("Integrated").
** Dimension 2 maps different institutional arenas for religious education: whether provided for in public school venues and as a part of regular school hours; or as a shared responsibility between school authorities and faith communities for curriculum, text books, and teacher training and qualification; or as provided for outside public school premises and managed by religious or life-stance communities.

This overview of different models of religious education is based on studies of curricula and legal provisions regarding religious education in the countries named, supplemented by presentations of the country's approach to religious education in public documents, reports, and scholarly articles.[25] In some cases sorting religious education practices of different countries into these categories may prove difficult. For instance, there are differences in the profiles of the so-called "pluralistic" and "integrated" approaches of different countries. The English—often called the

[25] Ibid.

"multifaith approach"—as well as the Swedish models have a more comparative and multireligious profile than the Norwegian and Danish ones (especially at the lowest levels). In Norway and Denmark a main emphasis is still on the Christian tradition, even though knowledge about other religions and philosophical traditions is a part of the curriculum.[26] It would, however, be misleading to group them with countries that still provide "confessional" education in the traditional sense. Loyalty to the doctrines of a particular denomination is no longer required for teaching RE in Norwegian and Danish public schools. Also, some interesting variations can be found at regional and local levels of the countries surveyed here. In parts of England, many schools strongly emphasize the pluralistic approach, both in the content of their RE and in their development of RE didactic principles.[27] A main focus is on religions present in the local community; hence children can meet different traditions through the life and convictions of their representatives. This principle of "local differentiation" has also been implemented in the new Norwegian RE subject and has led to differences in the profile of RE at the local level. As shown in the table, the main model in Germany is confessional education in segregated groups, but some German states (Bundesländer) have chosen other models, for instance Berlin and Brandenburg. In France there is no national curriculum for religious education, but in Alsace-Lorraine (the province of Alsace-Moselle), religious education is an ordinary school subject. Here the development of the curriculum and the recruitment of teachers is carried out in cooperation between churches and public school authorities.

To some extent, different approaches to religious education are correlated to the different religio-political systems of countries.[28] For instance, in the Nordic countries (with the exception of Finland), church and state still maintain close relations, and the state has the general responsibility for the content as well as the teaching of RE. In Germany, where there is a separation of church and state but close cooperation between the state and the majority churches at the level of the Bundersländer, we find close local level cooperation agreements in the field of religious education. In France and the USA, the separation between church and state is much stricter than in Germany, and religious education is left as a responsibility for faith or belief communities and is not a part of public school curricula.

Despite variations in analytical categories and differences in empirical materials, the findings of the European survey point in the same direction as the findings of the global survey of the Special Rapporteur, based on answers to questionnaires to state parties and

---

[26] In Norway the parliament has recently reiterated that at least fifty percent of the time in the RE classes in total shall be spent on the Christian traditions. In Denmark knowledge about religions other than Christianity is not to be taught before the second level of primary school (about the age of eleven).

[27] The multireligious approach in the English school system is also expressed by the fact that the schools are obliged to organize "collective worship," where all pupils shall gather in a veneration of a divine creature or force. As a main rule, the collective worship (CW) shall have a "mainly Christian" character, though "without being distinctive of any particular denomination" (Department of Education Circular, 1994). The schools might also choose to have a CW of a mainly non-Christian character if this seems more natural with regard to the religious diversity of the pupils (ibid).

[28] Cf. Ingvill T. Plesner, "Religion-political models and models for religious and moral education," *Panorama: International Journal of Comparative Religious Education and Values,* ed. Peter Schreiner, vol. 14, no. 2 (winter 2002).

curricula and textbook materials attached to their answers. The distinction of the Special Rapporteur between the "integration logic" and the "ghetto approach," and Schreiner's distinction between the "non-confessional" and the "confessional" approach, leads to broadly similar groupings, as do the alternative distinctions between different kinds of models for organizing the religious education as well as different pedagogical profiles of the subject(s).

The differences that are revealed through comparative studies of religious education must not cover the fact that there are also some common characteristics and some general tendencies of development, at least on the European scene of religious education. The dominant feature is that most European countries have some kind of religious education as a part of the school curricula, or at least as a part of the education given during the school time and on the premises of public schools. France is the most obvious exception from this, despite the province of Alsace–Lorraine where RE is taught in the public schools. Another general characteristic is that religious education in public schools in almost all the countries is either noncompulsory or pupils have a choice between different RE subjects with different confessional or non-confessional profiles. Exceptions are Norway and Sweden where the parents and children, since 1997 and 1998 respectively, can only be exempted from specific parts of a RE subject that is compulsory and common for all pupils. In Norway this limited right to exemption from the RE subject has caused severe conflicts between school authorities and some groups of parents. Secular Humanists and Muslims have sued the Norwegian state for violations of international human rights obligations. We shall have a closer look at this conflict in our discussion of dilemmas related to different models of religious education in section III.

When surveying approaches to religious education of various countries, another similarity found is the focus on "common values" across religious borders. Often these are values that are also supposed to be part of the normative foundation of public school education in general. The definition of "common values" differs from country to country, and sometimes also between regions within a country. In most of the Nordic countries (Norway, Denmark, Iceland, and Sweden), as well as in some of the German Bundesländer, there is a particular emphasis on the "Christian tradition" as a normative foundation for some of the core values like human dignity, even though the importance of a cross-religious consensus about some basic values is also stressed. In some countries the value foundation of the national educational system is rather defined by the universal principles of human rights or by similar principles enshrined in national constitutions (France and Germany). In England a "Charter on Values in Education and Community" has been developed by different groups of civil society taking part in a national dialogue, initiated by the school authorities. This charter emphasizes respect for human rights and the rule of law, but also describes a number of other values that are assumed to be common for all.

These attempts to define some kind of common value foundation for public school education in general, or for religious education in particular, can be seen as expressions of different definitions of what is—or should be—the basis for a common identity in pluralistic societies. If one shall succeed in defining the basis of such a common "we" that transcends differences of faiths, it is important not to define the basis for identification too narrowly.

The basis for common identification in a pluralistic society can be approached in different ways. For instance, one might distinguish between the "cultural heritage" approach and the "meeting point" approach to the issue of collective identification.[29] Focusing on a country's cultural heritage as a basis of identification for all in a pluralistic society may exclude rather than serve as a means of social integration. This unintended consequence might be avoided if the cultural heritage view is combined with a more pluralistic and dynamic approach to common identification, focusing on contact and communication between people with different cultural and religious backgrounds as a basis of identification and solidarity formation.

D. Changes in Models of Religious Education: A Process of Secularization?

I shall now discuss how recent changes in the aims for religious education of different countries might be interpreted, to what extent they are attempts to meet the challenges of growing religious diversity, and how successful these changes have been when assessed in terms of the criteria for success presented in the introduction.

Studies undertaken in 1990 and 2000 by the Inter-European Commission on Church and School[30] show that in several European countries the traditional models of religious education have been changed during the last years or are now being evaluated.[31] In some countries where the religious education has so far been "confessional," in the sense that it has mainly focused on knowledge about one denomination or tradition, or where pupils have had the possibility of choosing between different subjects emphasizing different confessions or philosophical traditions and ethics, there are now tendencies towards a more ecumenical approach or even a multireligious approach.[32] For instance, in England a "multifaith approach" was introduced in order to replace the former religious instruction with a predominantly Christian focus. In Norway a new compulsory RE subject that permits only partial exemptions was introduced in 1997, replacing the former model of one "confessional" and one alternative "non-confessional" subject, to use Schreiner's terms. Also, in other countries with long traditions of "confessionally" based or divided RE classes, curricula reforms in the late 1980s and in the 1990s have led to a stronger emphasis on knowledge about different religions, e.g., in Iceland and Denmark. Parallel to these changes in the content of religious education, state school authorities have taken over most of the formal responsibility for developing curricula in Norway, Sweden, Denmark and Iceland, a responsibility formerly shared by school and church.[33] In England, however, the

---

[29] Terms translated from Norwegian, see Geir Skeie's article in Heid Leganger-Krogstad and Elisabeth Haakedal, eds., *Religiøse og pedagogiske idealer* (Religious and Pedagogical Ideals) (Oslo: Norges forskningsråds skriftserie KULT nr. 42, 1995); and Thomas Hylland-Eriksen, ed., *Flerkulturell forståelse* (Multicultural Understanding) (Oslo: Tano Aschehoug, 1997).

[30] Schreiner, *Religious Education in Europe.*

[31] These processes of change in most cases cause public debates involving scholars, politicians, and members of different faith communities. In some cases the debates end up as open conflicts, and in a few countries—for instance in Norway and Germany—there are even trials taking place at the moment because of the regards that are at stake. In section III below I shall discuss dilemmas related to different models of religious education.

[32] Schreiner, *Religious Education in Europe.*

responsibility for development of the RE curriculum is still shared by local school authorities and local faith communities. Also in England, more faith communities are invited to take part in this process than before, and they are represented in the "Local Education Authority" bodies.

In most European countries, the changes in the content and organization of religious education have taken place in a process parallel to the changes in the definition of value foundations and aims for public schools in general and for religious education in particular.[34] For instance, there is now a stronger emphasis on "common values," "values shared by different religions," or "human rights" in the general curricula as well as in religious education curricula in all Nordic countries and in England. Recently a stronger emphasis on the "cultural heritage" of the respective countries has been introduced in Norway, Denmark, and Sweden. Also, in England the new multireligious approach is combined with a focus on Christianity as an important part of the "cultural heritage" of the country. Further, by comparing the present general curriculum and legally binding aims of schools with the situation only one decade ago, we find that the individual's right to choose his or her conviction both in religious and moral questions has been reinforced. There is also a stronger emphasis on the development of critical thinking as a general educational aim. This is very clearly expressed in the present curriculum of religious education in Denmark, Sweden, and Norway.[35]

These parallel processes in some European countries give reason to ask if the changes in content, aims, and organization of religious education, as well as changes in the definition of the value foundation of the schools, are signs of "secularization," or if we are rather witnessing tendencies of "resacralization" or "compensation."

The term "secularization" used in theories of secularization describes the process of ***differentiation*** of the larger society, its institutional spheres becoming functionally separated, without the benefit of an overarching religious value system. Hence the relations between state and faith communities, and their respective spheres of authority and responsibility, are redefined.[36] Increasing cultural and religious ***diversity*** manifested by the arrival and voice of several religious groups, along with enhancing the focus on individual freedom and integrity in the development of a religious and moral identity, are also components of the modernization process referred to by the term secularization. Also, understanding secularization as a process of ***privatization*** of religion goes well with the position in social theory that no longer sees a need for religious legitimization of political institutions of the national community.[37]

---

[33] Göran Gustafsson, ed., ***Religiös förändring i Norden 1930–1980*** (Religious Change in the Nordic Countries 1930–1980) (Malmø: Liber, 1985); Plesner "Religio-Political Models and New Models of Religious Education."

[34] Plesner, "Religion-political models and models for religious and moral education."

[35] Ibid, cf. notes 20 and 28.

[36] Niklas Luhmann, "The Paradox of System Differentiation and the Evolution of Society," in ***Differentiation Theory and Social Change: Comparative and Historical Perspectives,*** ed. Jeffrey C. Alexander and Paul Colomy (New York: Columbia University Press, 1990); Karel Dobbelaere, "Church Involvement and Secularization: Making Sense of the European Case," in ***Secularization, Rationalism and Sectarianism,*** ed. Eileen Barker, James A. Beckford, and Karel Dobbelaere (Oxford: Clarendon, 1993); Malcolm Waters, ***Modern Sociological Theory*** (London: Sage, 1994).

[37] Jürgen Habermas and Norbert Elias, ***Nasjonalisme og nasjonal identitet*** (Nationalism and National Identity) (Oslo: Cappelen akademiske forlag AS, 1994); John Rawls, ***Political Liberalism*** (New York: Columbia University Press, 1993).

Theories of compensation, on the other hand, presume that functional equivalents to religion—or other compensating mechanisms—will develop where religions and religious explanations lose their former importance for the individual and for the community as a source of national identification and political legitimization.[38] The "vacuum" that is created will lead to counterreactions where religion in its functional sense reinforces its role and place both in the life of the individual and in society. The theories that presume that secularization as described above will be followed by compensational processes, for instance in the development of some kind of "civil religion,"[39] can be connected with the position in social theory that believes that common sources of national identifications, based on a common cultural or religious tradition, are necessary to secure social cohesion and political legitimization.[40]

Taking "secularization" to include the different dimensions presented above (differentiation, pluralization, individualization, privatization), the changes in religious education in several European countries over the last years can certainly be seen as signs of secularization. The content of religious education has increasingly become a responsibility of secular school authorities in the Nordic countries ("differentiation" of the sphere of public education from that of churches), whereas in England a variety of religious groups have gained more influence through representatives in Local Education Authority bodies ("pluralization"). Pluralization of general educational curriculums and aims during the last ten years is also manifest in the increasing weight on different religions and on values that are "common" for different religions. Further, we have discovered a tendency to upgrade the right and responsibility of the individual to choose his or her way in the existential questions that are addressed in religious education and to develop his or her ability of critical thinking. These are clearly tendencies toward individualization and secularization, as defined above.

On the other hand, in the countries studied there are no clear signs of "privatization" in the field of religious and moral education in public schools. Rather, in several European countries the public role and importance of religious education has been clearly expressed in curriculums, and also by politicians and scholars in public debates about changes in models of religious education. Also, the focus on religion as an important part of the "cultural heritage" of a country, and on the importance of values that receive support from different normative traditions, points in the direction of what I have called "compensation" strategies.

Can ongoing developments—at least in some northern European countries that have been studied here—be understood as tendencies both of secularization and of compensation? I cannot answer this question, but I want to stress the importance of further analysis, from the perspective of social theory, of the changes in models of religious and moral education of different countries. It would be interesting if the

---

[38] See article by Rodney Stark and William Sims Bainbridge in Malcolm B. Hamilton, ed., *The Sociology of Religion: Theoretical and Comparative Perspectives* (London: Routledge, 1995).

[39] Robert N. Bellah, *The Broken Covenant: American Civil Religion in Time of Trial* (New York: Seabury, 1975); Inger Furseth, *Samfunnsreligion i Norge? En analyse av nasjonal legitimering 1905–1980* (Civil Religion in Norway? An Analysis of National Legitimation 1905–1980) (Oslo: University of Oslo, 1986).

[40] Anthony D. Smith, *National Identity* (London: Penguin Books, 1991); Ernst Gellner, *Nations and Nationalism* (Oxford: Blackwell, 1993); Kåre Lunden, *Nasjon eller union?* (Nation or Union?) (Oslo: Det norske samlaget, 1993).

global, comparative survey of the Special Rapporteur could be followed up by a similar survey some years into the future, in order to understand these processes on a broader basis.

More important in our context is to find out if certain dimensions or models of religious education are more likely than others to cause tensions or even conflicts with the human rights standards of freedom of religion or belief, and with the principles of tolerance and nondiscrimination. The normative dilemmas related to different approaches of religious education makes a continuous and open discussion of alternative models of religious education—their weaknesses and possibilities—important also in the human rights discourse.

III. Dilemmas Related to Different Approaches to Religious Education

A. Some Main Dilemmas

Looking at human rights standards, we found an inherent tension between, on the one hand, the rights of parents to have the last say about the religious and moral education of their children and, on the other hand, the state's obligation to see that all children receive an education in conformity with the aims spelled out in human rights instruments. This tension derives from the fact that it is hard to find support for a value-based RE that will be regarded as "neutral" in relation to different conceptions of truth and differing considered views of what is important knowledge. I shall elaborate on this dilemma by looking at experiences with different models of religious education in some European countries.

Two main approaches to religious education—as defined by Schreiner as well as by the Special Rapporteur—are, respectively, to include children of all faiths ("integration approach") and to separate them into groups divided by confessional belongings ("segregation approach"). Taking my initial definition of "successful religious education" as a starting point (an education that contributes effectively to the fostering of tolerance and heeds freedom of religion or belief), and taking the experiences of different countries into account, I shall argue that there are dilemmas related to both main approaches.

The dilemmas related to segregated RE and to RE that does not include knowledge about different confessions have been pointed out by the Special Rapporteur:

- If the pupils do not get any common religious education or knowledge about each other's beliefs and traditions, education may fail to secure a foundation for tolerance and the development of a global and interreligious solidarity.

In the presentation of a regional survey of approaches to religious education in Europe, we have seen how a number of countries have tried to find models that meet the challenges of increasing religious diversity and the dilemma connected to the "segregation approach." In most of the Nordic countries and in England, they use an "integration approach," bringing together pupils of different confessions. But there is also a dilemma with the integration approach:

- If a controversial common religious education is introduced without sufficient rights to exemptions, freedom of religion or belief of the pupils and their parents may not be properly respected.

In order to see how this latter dilemma arises, I shall now have a closer look at the experiences of countries that have tried an "integration" approach to religious or moral education.

B. Some Examples

In the German state (Bundesland) of Brandenburg, until 1989 a part of GDR, the new subject "Lebensgestaltung, Ethik und Religionskunde" (Life Formation, Ethics and Religious Knowledge, LER) was first introduced in 1992 as a pilot project.[41] It was incorporated into the school curriculum for the whole state of Brandenburg in 1996. The subject is supposed to give young people knowledge and help them develop skills necessary in a pluralistic society, but it emphasizes dialogue and ethical questions more than religious belief systems and traditions and differs from RE subjects of most European countries and of most German states. This profile has made some of the religious groups in Brandenburg, Protestant as well as Catholic communities, claim the right to full exemption from the new RE subject (which they have been granted), because they do not see it as neutral but as promoting a particular belief—the secular humanistic one. They also claim the right to religious education as an "ordinary subject" ("Ordentliches Lehrfach"), which is the general model for religious education in Germany according to the German Constitution of 1949 (arts. 7, 3). The state of Brandenburg refuses to replace or supplement the LER subject with religious education as an ordinary school subject, and it refers to the possibility in the Constitution (art. 141) for exemptions from the general rule. The case was taken up by the Constitutional Court of Germany in 1996. The German Constitutional Court has reached a decision on this case that might be seen as a compromise and a quest for dialogue and practical conflict resolution at the regional level. The German conflict about the LER subject shows that attempts to develop "neutral" approaches to religious and ethical instruction can lead to tensions with the parental right to decide the religious and moral instruction of their children.

Just like the LER subject, the present Norwegian model for RE, introduced in 1997, aims at providing tolerance and understanding between religions by providing knowledge about different traditions and facilitating dialogue about common values in multireligious societies. This aim of the new Norwegian RE subject therefore at first glance fits well with the principles for RE that are presented in the reports of the Special Rapporteur. This aim is also given as a reason for the subject being compulsory for children of all faiths, with only a limited right to exemption from certain parts of it (for instance activities that may be seen as exercise of religion). Even though the subject provides knowledge about other religions as well as about nonreligious worldviews (life stances), more than half of the curriculum is knowledge about Christianity or the Christian cultural heritage of Norway. The combination of a main focus on Christianity and a limited right to exemption has made the subject controversial among parents of different minority groups. Also, the Norwegian law on public schools provides that Christian morality is a foundation of school education in general, in conjunction with the values of tolerance and freedom of thought. This has made groups of parents

[41] Guri Jørstad, *Gemeinsam Leben Lernen* (master's thesis in pedagogics, University of Oslo, 1995) (Oslo: Norges forskningsråds KULT-serie, 1995).

fear the possible effects of the role of Christianity and Christian values in the new RE subject. Proposals for having "Christian and humanistic values" as a normative foundation for public education and for the new RE subject have been rejected by minority groups.

Criticism voiced by different minority groups when the subject was first introduced led to some changes in Norway's new RE curriculum. Different religious traditions will henceforth also be presented in lower grades, and school authorities have underlined that knowledge about Christianity and about other religions or life stances shall be taught applying the same pedagogical principles, not presenting any of them as superior to others. However, several minority groups reject that such evenhandedness is possible, taking the present content of the new RE subject into consideration. They claim that the subject leads to discrimination, referring, for instance, to the fact that more than half of the time shall be spent learning about Christianity. Two legal cases raised by secular Humanist and by Muslim parents have, since 1998, been pending before Norwegian Courts, assisted by the Norwegian Humanist Association and by the Islamic Council Norway. These parents claimed that the denial of full exemption from RE for their children contravenes Norway's international human rights obligations and is therefore invalid. The case of the Humanists against the Norwegian state was decided by the Supreme Court of Norway on 22 August 2001. The five judges unanimously found against the claim of Humanist parents. Hence, this case may be finally decided by the European Court of Human Rights in Strasbourg. Humanists and Muslims have voiced the fear that the dominant place of Christianity in the new RE subject may influence, or even indoctrinate, their children to see the Christian faith as better or more true than others. On the other hand, the majority of the parents, belonging mostly to the Evangelical-Lutheran Church of Norway, are for the most part satisfied with the new subject. The school authorities are reluctant to make the subject optional, as they see it as an important arena for providing knowledge necessary for dialogue and interreligious understanding in an increasingly multireligious society. The authorities argue that the dominant role of Christianity in the subject is reasonable because of the role of Christianity in the Norwegian history and the fact that eighty-five percent of the Norwegian population belongs to the Evangelical-Lutheran State Church.

A less controversial approach to pluralistic religious education seems to be the one in England. Here the parents hold the right to full exemption for their children from the subject, but only a limited number of parents exercise this right to exemption. Trust seems to have been built up over the years, not at least through the cooperation between the school authorities and representatives of different confessions at the local level where the general curricula is developed into syllabuses for the religious education. Because of this way of organizing the subject, there are, however, great variations between schools and between regions when it comes to content of RE and the weight of the different parts of the curriculum (knowledge about Christianity and about other traditions). Also, the quest for consensus on the syllabus among the different groups represented at the local committees makes the process a challenge to all parties. The result, however, can be said to have a broader legitimacy than in countries where school authorities have the last word and where parents do not have the right to ask for exemption if they cannot accept the content and aims of the RE syllabus.

Schools in countries that attempt integration approaches to RE look for models that respect religious freedom and yet bring together children of all faiths in order to create an arena for dialogue and mutual understanding. As we have seen, the countries have so far chosen different models. In Germany there are also different models in the different "Bundesländer." The main challenge is to devise a RE subject that may be common for all pupils and thereby contribute to the fostering of tolerance, without interfering with the rights of parents to decide upon the moral, philosophical, and religious education of their children. Also, in some countries there are disputes about the content of the RE subject, some groups finding that the current model is not "neutral" or "nondiscriminatory" with regard to the different religious or philosophical traditions.

IV. Religious Education in Pluralistic Societies: What Are the Criteria of Success?

The main objective of this article is to discuss what approaches to religious education can contribute to the fostering of tolerance and at the same time respect the right of all inhabitants to freedom of religion or belief. This should serve as a contribution to the definition of certain criteria of success for religious education in pluralistic societies. In the concluding discussion the experiences of different countries, pertinent human rights norms and the aims and strategies for religious education presented by the Special Rapporteur are taken into account.

A. Legitimate and Illegitimate Aims for Religious Education in Pluralistic Societies

One important question: What are legitimate aims for a common religious education in pluralistic societies? First of all, shared religious education programs must endeavor to foster tolerance, without encroaching on the right to freedom of religion or belief. Secondly, they must be designed to promote respect for universal human rights and equal human dignity.

As we have seen in the introduction, the 1981 Declaration, as well as other international human rights instruments, outlines certain aims for public education. Human rights norms also restrict the discretion of public authorities in their development of the content of education in general and of compulsory religious education in particular. According to pronouncements by the UN Human Rights Committee and the European Court of Human Rights, public schools may provide knowledge about different religions provided this is done in a "neutral" and "pluralistic" way. Such a pluralistic approach may focus on the history of religion and comparative studies of religion and ethics. However, instruction that aims at or is likely to influence pupils in the direction of embracing a particular religious belief is incompatible with human rights to freedom of religion or belief unless provisions are made for nondiscriminatory exemptions or for educational alternatives that would accommodate the wishes of parents or guardians.[42] The European case law in this field does not require that

[42] Cf. Human Rights Committee General Comment 22 (1993) on CCPR, art. 18.

there be no quantitative differences in the presentation of different religions or philosophical views. Any differential treatment should, however, be "reasonable" and not result in violation of the demand for a pluralistic approach (e.g., that knowledge about different religions or normative traditions should be presented).[43]

The Special Rapporteur rightly points to the importance of understanding and identifying with the other as an aim for the public school education. Education should help in seeing that "the others are indeed us," he writes. Knowledge about other religions is an important precondition for the development of such an understanding, and hence also of a culture of tolerance.[44]

Support of the idea of human dignity and human rights is another foundation for solidarity and identification across religious and cultural divides. The universality of human rights calls for support both of the idea of equal human dignity and for equal human rights for all people. But human rights and human dignity also include the right to be different—to preserve and develop one's own identity. The importance of having in mind the distinction between the conceptions of equality and of similarity should, however, be emphasized. When discussing possible foundations for a conception of an inclusive "we," for a common identity in pluralistic societies or for the whole of humankind, the recognition of an equal human dignity and of other shared values must never challenge the basic right to distinguish oneself from others by holding, for instance, different religious or philosophical views that do not recognize other doctrines and positions as equally true.

The exclusiveness of particular religious or philosophical views and beliefs must not, however, be understood as a negation of the principle of tolerance. On the contrary, tolerance presupposes that you have a basic conviction that differs from the convictions of the person that you tolerate. Nevertheless, fostering tolerance demands a dialogue on the limits of tolerance. The Special Rapporteur underlines that freedom of religion—including the freedom to search for truth—should never lead to the undermining of the universality of human rights. One might add that human rights also circumscribe the outer limits of tolerance. Sometimes we do not tolerate doctrines and ideologies that imperil support for equal human dignity and universal human rights. The same conception of equal human dignity demands a respect for the dignity of persons who hold these views, even when we may not tolerate their views.

These dilemmas related to the fostering of tolerance and the respect for freedom of religion or belief are also relevant for the practice of religious dialogue as part of RE. Dialogue between pupils and students as representatives of different faith and life-stance communities might be one important measure in the search for common values in religious education. At least two approaches to religious dialogue must be distinguished. Interreligious dialogue can be seen as either:

- a search for the minimum common denominator (for instance a cross-cultural consensus about the universality of human rights)

[43] Relevant decisions in this field are presented in Erik Møse, "Fritak fra undervisning i faget Kristendomskunnskap med religions- og livssynsorientering: Forholdet til Norges internasjonale forpliktelser" (Exemption from Participation in the Subject Christian Knowledge with Orientation about Religion and Life Stance) in Ot. Prp. nr. 39 1996/97 (Oslo: Kirke-, utdannings- og forskningsdepartementet, 1997).

[44] Just as the right to freedom of religion or belief also includes the freedom not to hold a religious view, it is important to stress the fact that an inclusive RE should also teach about life stance and philosophical convictions.

- or a search for the maximum common denominator (understood as a broader sense of "common values").

These approaches to the aims of religious dialogue can also be seen as two conceptions of what is the necessary value foundation of a pluralistic society (cf. section II.C).[45] The more ambitious the aims of identity formation of pupils through religious education, the higher the risk of causing conflicts with the norms of religious freedom. This dilemma should be taken into account when developing and discussing the roles of dialogue and the search for common values in religious education. It should not, however, result in a weaker emphasis on the need for using school education as an arena for the fostering of tolerance. As long as the individual identities of the pupils are respected, the aim of finding a basis for identification that transcends particular identities is legitimate, also from the perspective of freedom of religion or belief. Both experience with dialogue projects and scholarly studies indicate that most religions and life stances (philosophical convictions) have the requisite resources, in their view of man and in their basic value foundations, to embrace the ideas of equal human dignity and universal human rights.[46] RE in public schools, therefore, can play an important role both in the teaching of human rights and in the search for common, cross-cultural values in a broader sense.

The persistent conflict, both in Norway and in the German state of Brandenburg, about RE subjects that are supposed to be common for all pupils, clearly indicates the dilemmas we have pointed out: on the one hand, the wish to provide religious education for children of all faiths, and, on the other hand, the concern for the rights of parents to decide about the religious, moral, and philosophical upbringing of their children. The case of Norway also shows that this tension may be amplified if a RE subject for all includes special emphasis on one particular religious tradition because of its historical and present role in society, and even more so if the common RE subject is made mandatory.

Further, we have learned that the success of "RE for all" presupposes that the subject is truly inclusive in the sense that it has broad support from both the majority and different minority communities. The English approach seems to be the most constructive response to these challenges so far. In England the conflict is considerably more muted than in Norway, probably as a consequence of the fact that the subject is noncompulsory. The right to full exemption from RE, however, makes it more difficult to secure a common religious education for all pupils.

The experiences reported certainly give support to the notion that no model of religious education is spared normative dilemmas, though some approaches are more promising than others. I submit that any approach to religious education should be assessed in light of the admittedly demanding normative standards outlined at the outset of the present subsection.

---

[45] Incidentally, some vitally important interreligious dialogues may address neither minimum common denominators nor maximum common denominators, in the senses spelled out above. Interreligious dialogue and cooperation projects may circumvent doctrinal questions and address shared practical concerns at local, regional, national, or global levels. Undertaking practical dialogues are of course both feasible and sometimes morally necessary options, and this may also be reflected in RE curriculums.

[46] Cf. Hans Küng, *Etikk for verdens fremtid* (Norwegian translation of the book *Towards a Global Ethic*) (Oslo: Gyldendal, 1991); Inge Eidsvåg and Lena Larsen, eds., *Religion, livssyn og menneskerettigheter i Norge* (Religion, Life Stance and Human Rights in Norway) (Oslo: Universitetsforlaget, 1998).

B. The Need for Dialogue *About* Religious Education

By looking at the experiences of a number of countries, we can also learn something about the need for a broad dialogue about the content of religious education.

In many countries there is broad consensus among the different groups about the need for (at least some) common education about religions and life stances. In Norway there is so far no corresponding consensus about what should be the content and aims for an integrated and inclusive RE model. But there is an ongoing dialogue both among different religious and life-stance communities and between these groups and school authorities about what changes are required in order to find a model that pupils from all groups may attend. Both before the introduction of the new Norwegian RE subject in 1997 and as a result of the new subject, extensive dialogues have been conducted between different faith and life-stance communities. As a result of the controversies about the new RE curriculum, there has now been a breakthrough in the contact between different minority groups and Norwegian school authorities. When the basic premises for the new RE subject were formed five years ago, there was hardly any dialogue between school authorities and different minority groups. It is my conviction that such a dialogue, at an early stage before political prestige is invested in particular models, constitutes a most important precondition for successful development of a RE model that may find broad consensual support in the civil society.

The religious and religio-political dialogues during the last years in Norway have been institutionalized through the development of two permanent network structures, bringing together representatives of a broad variety religions and life stances. In 1996 the Council for Religious and Life Stance Communities in Norway was established. The Council has provided an arena for dialogue between the different faith communities about religio-political challenges, for instance in regard to the new and controversial subject of religious education. Then the Oslo Coalition on Freedom of Religion or Belief was established at the conclusion of the 1998 Oslo Conference on Freedom of Religion or Belief, which was co-hosted by the Council. The establishment of the Council, with a domestic agenda, and the Oslo Coalition, with and international agenda, are positive unintended effects of the difficult religio-political process in Norway during recent years, in good part related to struggles and debates over the new RE subject.

In England local committees of school authorities and representatives of different faith communities, entrusted with the task of developing local curricula for the RE,[47] appear to be constructive arenas for dialogue in this field. There is a need for dialogue between the authorities and representatives of different faith communities about curriculum, textbooks, and didactic principles for the religious education, in order to secure broad participation without violating the right to freedom of religion or belief. And this dialogue is necessary both at the national and the local level. The establishment of permanent structures for dialogue between faith and life-stance communities and between these and school authorities may prove to be an important step towards devising successful religious education programs in pluralistic societies.

---

[47] So-called "Local Education Authority Agreed Syllabus."

V. Concluding Remarks

In the draft documents for the Madrid Consultative Conference, the Special Rapporteur warned against the "ghetto" or "segregation" approach, keeping pupils separated according to their religious affiliation in the religious education provided by public schools. Concurring with the Special Rapporteur, I am also convinced that school classrooms are the most important potential arenas for the fostering of tolerance and understanding across borders of faith. Public schools may in this way become platforms for peaceful coexistence in pluralistic societies. Surely some shared religious education can provide young people with opportunities to learn about other confessions and to take part in dialogues about differences and similarities between religions and life stances, and hence is a vehicle for the fostering of tolerance. By looking at the experiences of a number of European countries, however, I have also tried to show that the "integration approach" (common RE for all pupils) is caught up with dilemmas in combining the quests for equal treatment of all, respect for the religious freedom of all, and the fostering of tolerance. In my view the need for dialogue, involving representatives of the different faith communities in developing and evaluating the curriculum and textbooks for the RE, is a most important precondition for the "integration approach" to succeed. Further, I have argued that dialogue about "common values" such as equal human dignity and universal human rights should be an important part of the curriculum and aims for the RE, in order to outline limits to tolerance for differences in belief and traditions.

Representatives of different faith and life-stance communities should take part in the discussion about possible strategies for fostering tolerance and nondiscrimination through public religious education. The experiences of different countries in the field of religious education should be evaluated both from the point of view of the school authorities and that of faith communities (parents), as well as by independent scholars and experts. The survey of the Special Rapporteur gives an overview of the experiences and models of different countries in the world. There is, however, a need for more detailed studies and analyses of the models and experiences of different countries in order to disclose and better understand specific advantages and dilemmas related to different approaches and contexts. Such studies are still much-needed inputs in future discussions—both at the national and international level—about strategies for public religious education that may effectively foster tolerance and respect for freedom of religion or belief as well as for other human rights.

Chapter 37

Religious Tolerance, Freedom of Religion or Belief, and Education: Results of the 2001 UN Conference

Jolanta Ambrosewicz-Jacobs

The International Consultative Conference on School Education in Relation with Freedom of Religion and Belief, Tolerance and Non-discrimination was held in Madrid from 23 to 25 November 2001. It was organized by the United Nations Special Rapporteur[1] on Freedom of Religion and Belief, Prof. Abdelfattah Amor, in cooperation with the Spanish government.[2] The Conference, as pointed out in the opening statement by the Special Rapporteur, was not intended as a theological or pedagogical meeting, but was convened to design an international educational strategy focused on the right to freedom of religion and belief among students. As stated in the message of United Nations Secretary General Kofi Anan, delivered at the Opening Ceremony by Mrs. Mary Robinson, UN High Commissioner for Human Rights, the Conference aim was "to break new ground" through a "discussion about how education about religions and belief can contribute to building global tolerance." The conference also served to commemorate the twentieth anniversary of the adoption by the General Assembly of the UN Declaration on the Elimination of All Forms of Intolerance and of Discrimination Based on Religion and Belief on 25 November 1981.

I. Conference background

In order to combat intolerance and discrimination based on religion and belief which continue to be manifested in various parts of the world, the Special Rapporteur has been monitoring the situation in the field of freedom of religion and belief and has been alerting the international community concerning problems.[3] For the most part, his attention has been directed to the manifestations of intolerance and discrimination,

---

[1] For a further discussion of the role of the Special Rapporteur, see the chapter in this volume on the United Nations Commission on Human Rights by Theo van Boven.

[2] General information on the conference is available on the UN High Commissioner for Human Rights' website at <www.unhchr.ch/>.

[3] See the Special Rapporteur's website at <http://www.unhchr.ch/huridocda/huridoca.nsf/FramePage/intolerance%20En?OpenDocument&Start=1&Count=15&Expand=2>.

Tore Lindholm, W. Cole Durham, Jr., Bahia G. Tahzib-Lie (eds.), Facilitating Freedom of Religion or Belief: A Deskbook, *813–818.*

not to their prevention. A survey conducted by the Special Rapporteur in 1994 by means of a questionnaire addressed to States, on problems relating to freedom of religion and belief in schools, revealed that elaboration of prevention strategies is an issue of great importance.[4] Altogether, replies were received from 77 States, providing issues for further debate and helping to shape the framework of the Conference.[5]

The Conference was preceded by consultations and discussions, based on analysis and interpretation of the data gathered during the survey (comments to replies were available on the website before the Madrid Conference started). Recommendations were submitted by representatives of States, intergovernmental organizations, religious communities, NGOs and experts. Much preliminary work was done prior to the conference. For example, the Spanish government, in collaboration with the International Religious Liberty Association, invited a group of experts to respond to a questionnaire on this topic and brought them together to discuss their responses. The questionnaires and responses and resulting reports were collected into a volume published prior to the conference, *Religious Freedom, Tolerance, and Non-Discrimination in Education*.[6]

II. Conference Goals and objectives

Taking into account the UN Charter, the Universal Declaration on Human Rights, the International Covenant on Civil and Political Rights, the provisions of the 1981 Declaration on the Elimination of All Forms of Intolerance and of Discrimination based on Religion or Belief, the call of the Vienna World Conference on Human Rights, the Convention on the Rights of the Child, and the UNESCO Convention Against Discrimination in Education and its recommendations on education for international understanding, peace and co-operation, the Madrid Conference aimed to examine the draft of a document defining a set of recommendations in support of principles outlined for the development of textbooks and curricula related to tolerance and non-discrimination in the field of freedom of religion and belief. Special attention was paid to redesigning the role that school education should play to contribute to the promotion and protection of human rights.

In order to pursue the Conference objective, a Preparatory Committee consisting of the Special Rapporteur and experts was established to oversee the preparation of the Conference, to make the list of participants other than States, and to prepare a draft document submitted to States and the other participants prior to the Conference (also available on the website), so that they could put forward their views, proposals and comments.

The general debate on the promotion of tolerance in school education (with the participation of around 50 speakers) was accompanied by drafting group sessions that examined objections to the draft document.

---

[4] A copy of the questionnaire is available on-line at <http://www.unhchr.ch/html/menu2/7/b/mrei_quest.htm>.

[5] A report containing the replies is available on-line at <http://www.unhchr.ch/html/menu2/7/b/cfedu-basicdoc.htm>.

[6] Rosa M. Martínez de Codes and Jaime Rossell, eds., *Religious Freedom, Tolerance, and Non-Discrimination in Education* (Caceres: Universidad de Extremadura, 2001).

III. Conference Debate

As many speakers noted, in the aftermath of September 11, questions related to violence based on religion or belief had to be re-evaluated. The Conference goal to call upon States to fulfill their responsibility to promote, through education, respect for human rights and fundamental freedoms, became therefore increasingly urgent. Another issue that arose in the presentations was whether religious education can contribute to the promotion of human rights. Some State representatives responded by describing their States' problem of lack of access to any education, not only religious education or education about religions.

The preventive strategy proposed by the Special Rapporteur met with understanding and the full support of the participants. The need for textbook analysis and revision so that religious groups can recognize descriptions of themselves as accurate was raised.

Some governments, NGO representatives and experts provided examples of good practice in international projects monitoring freedom of religion and belief (i.e., the Tandem Project group from Minnesota, U.S.A., which brought to Madrid a draft of a secondary school curriculum to be discussed)[7] and projects on the national level fostering understanding among different religious groups in their countries. The Teaching Tolerance Institute of the Southern Poverty Law Center from Montgomery, Alabama, U.S.A., was not present at the forum with their presentation, but samples of their materials available for free to teachers across the U.S.A. were displayed.[8] Models of publicly funded schools offering options for confessional religious education were presented (e.g., the proposal of the British Humanist Association[9]). The U.S. First Amendment Center has also prepared relevant material, including a book on religious liberty in U.S. public schools that includes guides for teachers and parents, which have been endorsed by national educational and religious organizations, including the National Education Association, Christian Legal Society, Council on Islamic Education, American Jewish Congress, and National School Boards Association.[10]

The most interesting presentations underlined that what is crucial in education is the development of values and attitudes among students so they can appreciate the diversity and richness of different ethnic, religious, social and cultural groups as a source of positive contributions to the whole society. Speakers reiterated that the eradication of stereotypes, biases and myths from textbooks, which lead to misunderstanding and possible discrimination, is the first step of a preventive educational strategy.

The teaching of comparative religion versus education in one religious tradition was raised by numerous speakers during the debate as valuable approaches and tools in preventing prejudice and hatred toward other groups. The debate also included the

---

[7] See The Tandem Project and the University of Minnesota Human Rights Resource Center, "Lifting the Spirit: Human Rights and Freedom of Religion or Belief: A Secondary School Curriculum to Promote Tolerance and Prevent Discrimination Based on Religion or Belief" (forthcoming, 2002).

[8] They also maintain a website with materials on tolerance for teachers, parents, and children at <http://www.tolerance.org>.

[9] See their website at <http://www.humanism.org.uk>.

[10] More information on their materials and projects is available at their website, <www.freedomforum.org>. The reference book referred to in the text is Charles C. Haynes and Oliver Thomas, *Finding Common Ground: A Guide to Religious Liberty in Public Schools* (Nashville: First Amendment Center, 2001).

question of whether religious education should be a specific subject in schools or rather be incorporated within the framework of other subjects such as history, philosophy and ethics. A further topic was the need for appropriate teacher training, including internships abroad and the designing of international educational programs providing bilateral school exchanges. The presentations did not bring up the conditions required for such contacts and exchanges to be successful, but such specific information is a matter for specifically pedagogical seminars, rather than the Madrid Conference, which was designed to be a human rights conference focused on freedom of religion and belief.

Most States' declarations contained a general approach to the topic of the Conference, and did not contain an answer to the concrete question of whether the existing curricula on religious education contribute to the protection of human rights and fundamental freedoms, particularly freedom of religion and belief, or whether they enable the child to have a balanced outlook on religion. It seems that the need for evaluation of school instruction in relation to the development of children's identity vis-à-vis others has become crucial, and that this is lacking in many school systems in various countries.

IV. Conference Outcome

The Conference's Final Document,[11] highlighting the importance of education as a means to ensure respect for religion and belief, was reached by consensus in the drafting group by the end of the second day of debate. The commitment and effort of the drafting group to accommodate all objectives and recommendations in the draft of the Final Document drew great applause.

Stressing the need for awareness of the interdependence between nations, the Final Document states that efforts aimed at promoting freedom of religion and belief through education require "cooperation among States, concerned organizations and institutions, and that parents, groups and communities based on religion or belief have an important role to play in this regard."[12] In this connection, the Final Document recognized "the right of parents, families, legal guardians and other legally recognized care givers to choose schools for their children, and to ensure their religious and/or moral education in conformity with their own convictions," with minimum educational standards as established by State authorities.[13] This confirms the right of parents "to

[11] A complete copy of the Final Document is available on-line at <http://www.unhchr.ch/html/menu2/7/b/cfedu-home.html>.

[12] Office of the High Commissioner for Human Rights, *Final Document of the International Consultative Conference on School Education in Relation with Freedom of Religion and Belief, Tolerance and Non-Discrimination,* sec. (t) (hereinafter "Final Document"). See also sec. 14: "Encourages all parts of society, both individually and collectively, to contribute to an education based on human dignity and to respect freedom of religion or belief, tolerance and non-discrimination"; and 15: "Encourages States at the appropriate level of government, non-governmental organizations and all members of civil society to join their efforts."

[13] Ibid., sec. (n). See also sec. 9: "Deems that the role of parents, families, legal guardians and other legally recognized care givers is an essential factor in the education of children in the field of religion or belief; and that special attention should be paid to encouraging positive attitudes and, in view of the best interest of the child to supporting parents to exercise their rights and fully play their role in education in the field of tolerance and non-discrimination."

ensure the religious and moral education of their children in conformity with their own convictions" as established in the International Covenant on Civil and Political Rights[14] and other international documents.[15]

Expressing concern about continuing discrimination against women, the Final Document considers gender equality in education in relation with freedom of religion and belief and deems that each State should protect the right of girls to education.[16] The Document includes the understanding that freedom of religion and belief comprehends theistic, non-theistic and atheistic beliefs, and recognizes the right not to profess any religion or belief,[17] consistent with international documents that protect the freedom of religion and belief.[18]

The strategy reflected in the Madrid Declaration does not deal specifically with the content of religious education and education about religion, but emphasizes that teaching should familiarize children with the concept of religious pluralism. It stresses that education about others should be objective and positive, built around learning about international human rights norms. Considering favorably "[t]he encouragement of those engaged in teaching to cultivate respect for religions or beliefs, thereby promoting mutual understanding and tolerance,"[19] the Final Document calls on States to "promote and respect educational policies aimed at strengthening the promotion and protection of human rights, eradicating prejudices and conceptions incompatible with freedom of religion or belief, and ensuring respect for and acceptance of pluralism and diversity in the field of religion or belief as well as the right not to receive religious instruction inconsistent with his or her conviction."[20] The Final Document also asks States to encourage the principles of non-discrimination and tolerance "both in school education and out-of-school activities organized by educational institutions of any nature."[21]

The Final Document also includes a set of encouragements and recommendations to States, organizations, institutions such as museums and libraries, and organs such as the UNESCO system of schools,[22] proposing ways to improve the quality of

---

[14] ICCPR, art. 18(4).

[15] See, e.g., *Convention on the Rights of the Child,* art. 14(1)–(2): "States Parties shall respect the right of the child to freedom of thought, conscience and religion. States Parties shall respect the rights and duties of the parents and, when applicable, legal guardians, to provide direction to the child in the exercise of his or her right in a manner consistent with the evolving capacities of the child."; *First Protocol to the Convention for the Protection of Human Rights and Fundamental Freedoms,* art. 2: "No person shall be denied the rights to education. In the exercise of any functions which it assumes in relation to education as to teaching, the State shall respect the right of parents to ensure such education and teaching in conformity with their own religious and philosophical convictions."

[16] See Final Document, sec. (o): "conscious of the need to consider the equality of gender in school education in relation with freedom of religion or belief, tolerance and non discrimination"; sec. 5: "Deems also that each State should take appropriate measures to ensure equal rights to women and men in the field of education and freedom of religion or belief, and in particular reinforce the protection of the right of girls to education, especially for those coming from vulnerable groups"; and sec. 7(d): "The awareness of gender aspects, with a view to promoting equal chances for men and women."

[17] Ibid., Conclusion: "With understanding that freedom of religion or belief includes theistic, non-theistic and atheistic beliefs, as well as the right not to profess any religion or belief."

[18] See, e.g., 1981 *United Nations Declaration on the Elimination of All Forms of Intolerance and Discrimination Based on Religion or Belief,* UNGA Res. 36/55, art. 1 (25 November 1981).

[19] Final Document, sec. 7(b).

[20] Ibid., sec. 4.

[21] Ibid., sec. 8.

teaching and materials on tolerance and non-discrimination.[23] Among other things, the Final Document suggests State support of academic research on freedom of religion and belief,[24] development of teachers' motivation to take action,[25] studies on and dissemination of innovative educational experiments,[26] provision of opportunities for student and teacher exchanges,[27] exchanges of "best practices,"[28] and the use of media and other means including new educational technology to provide knowledge relevant to freedom of religion and belief.[29]

Finally, the Document invites all States, civil society, and the international community to promote its principles, objectives and recommendations, and to contribute to the protection of freedom of religion and belief by creating a culture of nondiscrimination.[30]

V. Conclusion

As was stated in the background paper prepared by the Office of the High Commissioner for Human Rights,[31] there is a lack of knowledge of the content of religious educational curriculum and a lack of evaluation of school policy related to curriculum change, teacher trainings or textbook writing. Although much remains to be done, the principles of educational objectives in reference to freedom of religion and belief set out at the Madrid Conference should be able to serve as a basis for further in-depth studies of educational progress and of the various educational tools used in different countries.

---

[22] See, e.g., ibid., sec. 15: "Encourages States at the appropriate level of government, non-governmental organizations and all members of civil society to join their efforts with a view to taking advantage of the media and other means for self and mutual teaching as well as cultural institutions such as museums and libraries, to provide the individual with relevant knowledge in the field of freedom of religion or belief."

[23] See ibid., secs. 10, 11.

[24] Ibid., sec. 10(f): Encouraging States to consider "Encouraging, at the appropriate level, general knowledge and academic research in relation to freedom of religion or belief."

[25] Ibid., sec. 10(a): Encouraging States to consider "Developing the motivation of teachers for their action by supporting and encouraging commitment to the human rights values and in particular tolerance and non-discrimination in the field of religion or belief."

[26] Ibid., sec. 10(c): Encouraging States to consider "Encouraging the study and the dissemination of different experiences in education in relation with freedom of religion or belief, especially innovative experiments carried out all over the world."

[27] Ibid., secs. 10(f): Encouraging States to consider "Encouraging, at the appropriate level, general knowledge and academic research in relation to freedom of religion or belief"; and 13: "Recommends that States should consider promoting international cultural exchanges in the field of education, notably by concluding and implementing agreements relating to the freedom of religion or belief, non-discrimination and tolerance and respect for human rights."

[28] Ibid., sec. 12: "Recommends that States as well as concerned institutions and organizations should consider studying, taking advantage of and disseminating best practices on education in relation to freedom of religion or belief, which attach particular importance to tolerance and non-discrimination."

[29] Ibid., sec. 11(a): Recommending that "Appropriate and constructive use should be made of the entire range of equipment available, from traditional means to the new educational technology, including Internet, as relevant to the field of freedom of religion or belief."

[30] See, e.g., ibid., secs. 18: "Encourages also States, at the appropriate level of government, non-governmental organizations and other members of civil society to take advantage of relevant social and cultural activities of all kinds to promote the objectives of this document"; and 19: "Invites all States, civil society and the international community to promote the principles, objectives and recommendations in the present document on school education in relation with freedom of religion or belief, tolerance and non-discrimination."

[31] Copy in the author's possession.

Chapter 38

Facilitating Freedom of Religion or Belief through NGOs

Elizabeth A. Sewell[1]

The renaissance of interest in civil society has added recent emphasis to the role of non-governmental organizations (NGOs).[2] NGOs and other voluntary associations, which make up the fabric of civil society, play a key role in ensuring a stable and democratic social order. The practical effect and relevance of NGOs has also been increasingly recognized in the international political and diplomatic community. For example, the 1993 UN World Conference on Human Rights noted in its Vienna Declaration and Programme of Action "the important role of non-governmental organizations in the promotion of all human rights. . . . The World Conference on Human Rights appreciates their contribution to increasing public awareness of human rights issues, to the conduct of education, training and research in this field, and to the promotion and protection of all human rights and fundamental freedoms."[3]

The United Nations General Assembly has also recognized the role of NGOs and civil society in promoting human rights through the Declaration on the Right and Responsibility of Individuals, Groups, and Organs of Society to Promote and Protect Universally Recognized Human Rights and Fundamental Freedoms.[4] The Declaration recognizes the rights of individuals and groups to promote human rights through

---

[1] The author is grateful to Tore Lindholm and W. Cole Durham Jr. for their helpful comments and appreciates the support of Wade Sewell and the research assistance of Justin Elswick, Michael Monson, Devaughn Fraser, and Aaron Brogdon.

[2] See., e.g., Don E. Eberly, ed., *The Essential Civil Society Reader* (Oxford: Rowman & Littlefield, 2000); Adam Seligman, *The Idea of Civil Society* (New York: Free Press, 1992); Charles Taylor, "Modes of Civil Society," *Public Culture,* vol. 3, no.1 (fall 1990): 95–118; Edward Shils, "The Virtues of Civil Society," *Government and Opposition*, vol. 26, no.2 (winter 1991): 3–20; Michael Waltzer, "The Idea of Civil Society," *Dissent* (spring 1991): 293–304; Daniel Bell, "American Exceptionalism Revisited: The Role of Civil Society," *The Public Interest,* no. 95 (1989): 38–56.

[3] *Vienna Declaration and Programme of Action,* UN Doc A/CONF.157/23 (12 July 1993), para. 38, reprinted in 32 ILM 1661 (see also paras. 13, 18); see generally Manfred Nowak, ed., *World Conference on Human Rights: The Contributions of NGOs: Reports and Documents* (Wien: Manz, 1994).

[4] *Declaration on the Right and Responsibility of Individuals, Groups, and Organs of Society to Promote and Protect Universally Recognized Human Rights and Fundamental Freedoms,* General Assembly Resolution 53/144, UN Doc. A/RES/53/144, adopted 8 March 1999, arts. 5, 6, 8, 9.

Tore Lindholm, W. Cole Durham, Jr., Bahia G. Tahzib-Lie (eds.), Facilitating Freedom of Religion or Belief: A Deskbook, *819–842.*

associating, disseminating information, advocacy, submitting criticism and proposals to state bodies, having complaints reviewed under law, having access to international bodies, and other means. It also specifically recognizes that non-governmental organizations "have an important role to play in contributing to making the public more aware of questions relating to all human rights and fundamental freedoms through activities such as education, training and research" and that they, along with governments and other civil society actors, "have an important role to play and a responsibility in safeguarding democracy, promoting human rights and fundamental freedoms and contributing to the promotion and advancement of democratic societies, institutions and processes."[5]

This chapter attempts to trace the workings of NGOs in promoting and establishing the fundamental right of freedom of religion and belief. In addition to offering a taxonomy of NGOs working in this field, the chapter also offers explanations of ways in which they can be most effective. Building on political theories of the roles of NGOs, the chapter examines some of the internal debates among human rights NGOs on how best to promote political and practical change and attempts to put these debates in perspective. This chapter uses current political theories of transnational relations and norm socialization to suggest that while multiple avenues can be productive, their effectiveness in a particular situation depends primarily on the extent that the target country has socialized norms of freedom of religion and belief.

I. Models of NGOs' Influence

A. NGOs in Political Theory

In the late twentieth century international NGOs have grown rapidly. According to the Union of International Organizations, international NGOs grew from 973 in 1956 to 5,471 in 1996.[6] Theories of the role and influence of international human rights NGOs have struggled to keep up with the tremendous growth in the field. State-centered approaches to the theory of international relations have gradually given way to sophisticated theories of transnational relations that offer useful explanations of the unique position of international NGOs[7] and their powerful effects in promoting human rights.[8]

---

[5] Ibid., arts. 16, 18.

[6] Claude E. Welch Jr., ed., *NGOs and Human Rights: Promise and Performance* (Philadelphia: University of Pennsylvania Press, 2001), 1. See also Thomas Risse-Kappen, ed., *Bringing Transnational Relations Back In: Non-state Actors, Domestic Structures, International Institutions* (Cambridge: Cambridge University Press, 1995), 10–11 (citing figures).

[7] The term "transnational relations" was coined by Karl Kaiser in "Transnationale Politik," *Die anachronistische Souveränität,* ed. Ernst-Otto Czempiel (Cologne-Opladen: Westdeutscher Verlag, 1969), 80–109. See generally Robert O. Keohane and Joseph S. Nye Jr., eds., *Transnational Relations and World Politics* (Cambridge, Mass.: Harvard University Press, 1971); Risse-Kappen, *Bringing Transnational Relations Back In,* 3–33. Risse-Kappen defines "transnational relations" as "regular interactions across national boundaries when at least one actor is a non-state agent or does not operate on behalf of a national government or an intergovernmental organization" (Risse-Kappen, *Bringing Transnational Relations Back In,* 3).

[8] See, e.g., Rein Müllerson, *Human Rights Diplomacy* (New York: Routledge, 1997), 144: "It is difficult to overestimate the role of the non-governmental (both national and international) organizations (NGOs) in the promotion of human rights." See also Welch, *NGOs and Human Rights,* 261–80 (evaluating NGOs' roles in promoting human rights).

Theoretical attention to the role of international NGOs has been gathering momentum comparatively recently. For many years scholars looking at international political interactions relied heavily on regime theory. Regime theory focused scholarly emphasis on the role of identifiable legal and practical regimes—"principles, norms, rules and decision-making procedures around which actor expectations converge in a given issue-area."[9] International regime theory identified areas of international interactions where international cooperation, whether formal or informal, had established a basic set of principles or rules. These "regimes" could deal with anything from the width of railway tracks to international banking procedures, but generally dealt with economic and political cooperation among nations and international norm-setting bodies.[10] Regime theorists did not typically look at human rights NGOs, although the theory did open room for discussion of the role of human rights NGOs in international norm creation and maintenance.[11] Theories of transnational relations, which flourished in the 1970s, also initially provided limited theoretical understanding of the role of international NGOs in influencing states. Transnational relations theorists set up a dichotomy between "state-centered" and "society-centered" views of international politics, but paid less attention to the interactions between national and international actors.[12]

A major thinker in the emerging discussion of the relationship between international systems and domestic politics was Robert Putnam. In a landmark 1988 article, Putnam expressed the relationship between national and international politics through the idea of "two-level games."[13] Putnam's metaphor places political leaders as participants in one or many games. Each nation has its own game board, attended by the national leaders. In addition, one game board is surrounded by international leaders. Moves rational at one board may be less sensible at the others. Although the international board and national boards are largely independent of each other, at times movements on one board will trigger realignments on the others.[14] Putnam's

---

[9] Stephen D. Krasner, "Structural Causes and Regime Consequences: Regimes as Intervening Variables," *International Organizations* 36 (spring 1982): 185.

[10] See, e.g., Friedrich Kratochwil and John Gerard Ruggie, "International Organization: A State of the Art on the Art of the State," *International Organization* 40, no. 4 (autumn 1986): 759 ("Regimes are broadly defined as governing arrangements constructed by states to coordinate their expectations and organize aspects of international behavior in various issue-areas. They thus comprise a normative element, state practice, and organizational roles.").

[11] A few authors did deal with issues of human rights and international organizations. See, e.g., Jack Donnelly, "International Human Rights: A Regime Analysis," *International Organization* 40 (summer 1986): 599–642; John Gerard Ruggie, "Human Rights and the Future International Community," *Daedalus* 112 (fall 1983): 93–110; Nicholas G. Onuf and V. Spike Peterson, "Human Rights from an International Regimes Perspective," *Journal of International Affairs* 38 (winter 1984): 329–42.

[12] The theories, of course, had more nuances than can be explored in this chapter. Some major contributions to the debate in the 1970s include: Walter Bühl, *Transnationale Politik* (Stuttgart: Klett-Cotta, 1978); Czempiel, *Die anachronistische Souveränität;* Keohane and Nye, *Transnational Relations and World Politics;* Harold Jacobson, *Networks of Interdependence: International Organizations and the Global Political System* (New York: A. A. Knopf, 1979); Keohane and Nye, "Transgovernmental Relations and International Organizations," *World Politics* 27 (October 1974).

[13] Robert D. Putnam, "Diplomacy and Domestic Politics: The Logic of Two-Level Games," *International Organization* 42 (summer 1988): 433–35.

[14] Ibid.

exploration of the role of international actors in domestic politics laid the groundwork for the serious study of international NGOs and their influence in preventing abuses of human rights at the national level.

Discussions of NGOs have not only arisen in works building on Putnam's articulation of the relationship of international actors and domestic politics. Transnational relations theory has regained some popularity as recent writers have attempted to broaden international relations theory to accommodate the increased role of NGOs and other multinational actors. For example, Jessica Matthews and others have argued that the growth of NGOs and "people power" reflects the end of a system of territorial states.[15] While recognizing the clout of international NGOs, these discussions often ignore NGOs' interaction with state governments—a theoretical link that cannot be ignored since, at least in the field of religious freedom, many if not most NGOs focus on effecting change in individual countries' governmental practices and laws.[16]

B. Models of NGOs' Influence on States

A few authors have recently focused on the effect NGOs can have on states, rejecting the common separation in the discipline between international relations and comparative politics. Building on Putnam's work, they analyze the complex interactions between states and transnational relations.[17] One extremely valuable result of scholarly attention to the interactions of states and transnational actors such as NGOs is an emerging model of how NGOs have been able to promote change most effectively.[18] At its simplest version, this has been referred to as the "boomerang" pattern:[19] individual states violate their citizens' human rights and limit recourse through internal political or judicial channels. Facing limited recourse at the national level, domestic NGOs bypass the state and seek out international NGOs that can provide leverage and pressure from outside. Based on the information gained from domestic NGOs, these

---

[15] Jessica T. Matthews, "Power Shift," *Foreign Affairs* 76, no. 1 (1997), reprinted in *Is Global Capitalism Working? A Foreign Affairs Reader* (Washington, D.C.: Council on Foreign Relations, 1998), 55–71.

[16] This is less true in discussions of NGOs dealing with environmental or economic justice issues, where NGOs often focus more on multinational corporations and other international economic actors. Human rights NGOs have been criticized for paying excessive attention to state atrocities and failing to address the sources of atrocities in the structure of the state and civil society. See, e.g., Rajni Kothari, "Human Rights—A Movement in Search of a Theory," in Smitu Kothari and H. Sethni, eds., *Rethinking Human Rights: Challenges for Theory and Action* (New York: New Horizons Press, 1989), 19.

[17] See, e.g., Margaret E. Keck and Kathryn Sikkink, *Activists Beyond Borders: Advocacy Networks in International Politics* (Ithaca: Cornell University Press, 1998); Thomas Risse-Kappen, ed., *Bringing Transnational Relations Back In;* Susan Burgerman, *Moral Victories: How Activists Provoke Multilateral Action* (Ithaca: Cornell University Press, 2001).

[18] The most complete of these models are explored in the text, but a number of other thinkers have proposed similar individual elements of successful NGO activities. For example, Burgerman identifies some key preconditions for state change: the development of international human rights norms and their use in foreign policy; an activist transnational human rights network; a state government that becomes concerned about its reputation; and domestic NGOs to provide information and keep the state's violations on the international agenda (Burgerman, *Moral Victories,* 4–5).

[19] Keck and Sikkink, *Activists Beyond Borders,* 12; Morton E. Winston, "Assessing the Effectiveness of International Human Rights NGOs: Amnesty International," in Welch, *NGOs and Human Rights,* 39–40 (adopting Keck and Sikkink's boomerang model).

international NGOs mobilize their own states and international organizations to pressure the rights-violating government to change.[20] In this way pressure "boomerangs" back against the violating state, encouraging change.

Risse and Sikkink (one of the developers of the "boomerang pattern") provide a sophisticated description of the interaction of domestic and international NGOs, international norms, and states that violate human rights.[21] Their "spiral model" further elaborates on the "boomerang pattern," describing five phases in the process of states' human rights socialization. Risse and Sikkink recognize that governments may regress or remain static for a lengthy period of time,[22] but persuasively argue that the "spiral pattern" accurately models the stages through which governments progress from norm violation to rule-consistent behavior.

An in-depth examination of this model is valuable because it highlights the differing roles NGOs, both domestic and international, play at various stages in the process of promoting governmental change. Reflecting on this model provides a response to the debate that often rages among human rights NGOs over how they can be most effective. Heated disputes among NGOs often center on whether they, and the governments or international organizations that they can influence, should focus on "finger-pointing," or identifying, publicizing, and/or sanctioning violations, or "lighting a candle" through quiet diplomacy, dialogue, providing expert advice, and/or negotiating with violating states. The spiral model suggests that there is a place for both types of activities and that each will be most successful at different stages in a violator state's norm socialization.

The spiral model is also particularly significant because the model provides support for and development of the idea of norm socialization—the belief that actors can influence government through articulating principled norms and identifying violations of those norms, as well as through instrumental power politics.[23] The spiral model highlights the important role of argument and persuasion in promoting norm institutionalization and change, incorporating social constructivism theories with some elements of rational choice theory.[24]

At the first stage in the spiral model, "repression,"[25] individual states engage in human rights violations. Extremely repressive states may remain at this stage for a lengthy period of time by eliminating internal opposition and preventing the spread of information of their violations to the international community. When a transnational

[20] Winston has elaborated on this model by adding lines of information from sources other than local human rights NGOs to international human rights NGOs and adding lines of *influence* from international NGOs and transnational corporations directly to the target state (Winston, "Assessing the Effectiveness of International Human Rights NGOs," 39).

[21] Thomas Risse and Kathryn Sikkink, "The Socialization of International Human Rights Norms Into Domestic Practices: Introduction," in *The Power of Human Rights: International Norms and Domestic Change,* ed. Thomas Risse et al. (Cambridge: Cambridge University Press, 1999), 1–38.

[22] Thomas Risse and Stephen Ropp argue, however, that the power of global human rights norms and transnational advocacy networks has increased from the 1960s to the 1990s; the rate of movement through the spiral model has itself increased during this time—which they call the "world time" phenomenon (Risse and Stephen C. Ropp, "International Human Rights Norms and Domestic Change: Conclusions," in Risse, *The Power of Human Rights,* 264–65).

[23] Risse and Ropp, "International Human Rights Norms and Domestic Change: Conclusions," 270.

[24] Ibid., 272–3.

[25] Risse and Sikkink, "The Socialization of International Human Rights Norms," 20.

advocacy network—a loose connection of international and domestic NGOs, foundations, and some governmental and intergovernmental officials with a common support of human rights norms[26]—gains information on the violations and places them on the international agenda, the situation moves to phase two.

In phase two of the spiral model, or the "denial stage," the transnational advocacy network publicizes the human rights violations and engages in pressure and moral persuasion of the violator state and international organizations and states that have traditionally supported human rights. The target state, in turn, generally responds with denials, typically not only rejecting the specific charges, but also denying the validity of the norms and the right of international bodies and other states to concern themselves in the internal affairs of the target country. At times the norm-violating state can even use the external criticism to feed national sentiment opposing foreign involvement and criticism. As Risse and Sikkink note, "the initial 'boomerang throw' often appears to be counterproductive because it allows the state to solidify domestic support."[27] The denial stage can nevertheless be considered part of the socialization process, because denial means at least implicit awareness that the country's international reputation may be at stake. Yet, as Risse and Sikkink recognize, some governments care little for their reputations and prefer to squelch protest by killing or buying off internal opposition.

The primary challenge for transnational human rights networks under the spiral model is the transition to phase three, the "tactical concessions" stage. The effectiveness of the transition depends on a combination of the strength and mobility of the network and the vulnerability of the target government to international pressure.[28] In phase three, continuous combined pressure from above and below forces the norm-violating government to appease international critics through cosmetic changes. By making tactical concessions, the government accepts the legitimacy of external criticism on human rights grounds and becomes vulnerable to a normative process of "shaming." Government leaders, becoming entrapped in their own rhetoric, are increasingly forced by the weight of opposing arguments to respond with specificity to criticism. "In other words," argue Risse and Sikkink, "a process which began for instrumental reasons, with arguments being used merely rhetorically, increasingly becomes a true dialogue over specific human rights allegations in the 'target state.'"[29]

The international attention and connections strengthen domestic NGOs, positioning them to be able to promote further changes. Of course, as Risse and Sikkink note, the process is not inevitable; norm-violating governments can head off domestic opposition through arresting or killing key leaders. If target governments allow domestic NGO networks to develop, they become confronted with the choice between "controlled liberalization"[30] and increased repression. Increased repression at this late stage strengthens domestic opposition and eliminates any international support for the target state, often leading to an overthrow of the regime.

---

[26] Ibid., 21. NGOs play a "core role" in any transnational advocacy network. See Keck and Sikkink, *Activists Beyond Borders*, 8–9.

[27] Risse and Sikkink, "The Socialization of International Human Rights Norms," 23.

[28] Ibid., 25; see also Burgerman, *Moral Victories*, 5: "A violator state will comply with human rights norms only if a key element of its domestic political elite, one capable of exercising its authority over armed elements, perceives itself to be vulnerable to human rights condemnation or has concern for its country's international reputation as a violator state."

[29] Risse and Sikkink, "The Socialization of International Human Rights Norms," 28.

Through either controlled liberalization in the government or a more dramatic change in government, previously norm-violating states enter the fourth stage, in which human rights norms are elevated to "prescriptive status."[31] In this phase government acceptance of the validity of international norms can be seen not only in their use of the norms in dialogue over accusations of violations, but also in their institutionalization of practices consistent with the norms. Acceptance of norms at this stage does not guarantee implementation of norms; it is important that domestic and transnational networks maintain international scrutiny and pressure in order to ensure improved compliance with international human rights norms.

The fifth and final phase, "rule-consistent behavior," comes as governments bring their actions into full compliance with the previously accepted norms. At this point Putnam's two-level game may come into play as domestic pro-human rights leaders take power and use international influence and leverage to implement changes. Socialization of norms takes place as continued external and internal pressure makes norm compliance habitual and institutionalized.

As is readily apparent from a brief examination of Risse and Sikkink's spiral pattern, NGOs play a key role in promoting government compliance with human rights norms, including freedom of religion or belief. The model highlights some of the varied roles of NGOs, such as providing information of norm violations or influencing governments or international organizations to put pressure on violating states. As the model presupposes the existence of international norms, it would be helpful to add an additional preliminary stage in the model—the formation of international norms, in which NGOs also play a part.[32]

The spiral model is significant because it illuminates the need for both domestic and international NGOs, as well as for strong transnational networks that tie them together. Domestic NGOs are especially needed in the "repression" phase to provide information[33] and in the final two stages ("prescriptive status" and "rule-consistent behavior") to oversee continued compliance with norms and to influence the creation and operation of domestic institutions designed to protect human rights. International NGOs play a particularly significant role in the first three stages ("repression," "denial," and "tactical concessions"), as they report on violations of rights and mobilize other international actors to condemn and pressure rights-violating governments. The effectiveness of both domestic and international NGOs, however, depends on the networks they develop with other NGOs and governments, intergovernmental organizations, and media leaders.

The stages also shed light on conflicts among international NGOs on their proper role—whether they should attack violations or foster facilitating institutions. The simple answer is that both are needed, but their effectiveness depends greatly on the norm socialization stage of the violator state. At the "repression" stage and the beginning of the "denial" stage, states respond most to sanctions, "shaming," threats, and other forms of instrumental sticks and carrots. To be most effective at these stages, NGOs

---

[30] Ibid.

[31] Ibid., 20.

[32] See section II.B.1.

[33] See also Bergerman, *Moral Victories,* 5: "Organized local members of the human rights network are necessary to keep their issues on the international agenda and to provide information to international allies."

can provide information on violations and pressure violator states, either directly or through other states or international organizations. When violator states begin to enter into a meaningful dialogue at the end of the "denial" phase, and then as they transition into the "prescriptive status" stage, NGOs will find that promoting dialogue, technical assistance, and quiet diplomacy are increasingly effective. The instrumental techniques that were most effective at the earliest two stages will become increasingly less effective in the norm-socialization efforts of the final "prescriptive status" and "rule-consistent behavior" stages.

In summary, NGOs can play vastly different roles that may all serve to foster norm socialization. A wide variety of seemingly contradictory approaches are needed over the lifespan of the norm-socialization process. Undermining the mutual criticism that NGOs with differing approaches often engage in, the spiral model instead suggests that their efforts, if used judiciously and appropriately, complement one another and are all necessary to move a violator state through the norm-socialization process.

II. Natures of NGOs Promoting Freedom of Religion or Belief

The analytical models of change presented in part I of this chapter suggest that effective human rights NGOs exist in a multiplicity of forms and play a wide variety of roles. NGOs promoting freedom of religion or belief are similarly varied. In this section I will attempt to give a more concrete feel for the various forms these NGOs take, their sponsors, and their missions. During the discussion of various missions of NGOs, I will flesh out aspects of the theoretical model established in part I by providing more specifics on how NGOs promoting freedom of religion and belief work to pressure or otherwise influence states that violate freedom of religion or belief.

A. What Kind of NGOs Are Promoting Freedom of Religion or Belief?

Early international human rights NGOs, though not focused on promoting freedom of religion or belief, were often motivated by religious ideals and sometimes coalesced around churches or missionary programs.[34] Some goals of these early NGOs included the abolition of slavery, the promotion of women's suffrage, and the elimination of female circumcision and footbinding.[35]

---

[34] Keck and Sikkink, "Historical Precursors to Modern Transnational Advocacy Networks," *Activists Beyond Borders,* 39–78 (arguing at 75 that "[a]ll of these campaigns emerged from religious organizations"); J. D. Armstrong, "Non-Governmental Organizations," *Foreign Policy and Human Rights: Issues and Responses,* ed. R. J. Vincent (Cambridge: Cambridge University Press, 1986), 247–48. Klaus Hüfner provides the following list of early NGOs: "the British and Foreign Anti-Slavery Society (1823), and the World's Evangelical Alliance (1846), the World Alliance of YMCA's (1855), the International Workers' Associations (1864), the International Law Association (1873), the Inter-Parliamentary Union (1888), the Second International (1889), the Young Women's Christian Association (1894) and the Union of International Associations (1907)" (Klaus Hüfner, "The Role of NGOs vis-à-vis International Organizations and National Governments," in *The Role of Non-Governmental Organizations in the New European Order,* ed. Jürgen Schramm [Baden-Baden: Nomos Verlaggesellschaft, 1995], 15).

[35] Keck and Sikkink, "Historical Precursors to Modern Transnational Advocacy Networks," *Activists Beyond Borders: Advocacy Networks in International Politics,* 39–78.

A survey of contemporary NGOs that seek to facilitate freedom of religion or belief reveals more variety than continuity, which would be expected under the spiral model. Some NGOs are purely domestic, others have an international scope, and still others are regionally focused. Some NGOs, such as the International Helsinki Foundation for Human Rights,[36] promote freedom of religion or belief as one among many human rights. Others focus exclusively on religious freedom issues, such as the International Association for Religious Freedom.[37] Still others are human rights groups with well-established subdivisions focusing on religious liberty issues, such as Freedom House's Center for Religious Freedom.[38]

NGOs promoting freedom of religion or belief are typically established as nonprofit organizations and receive funding from membership dues, grants from foundations, and private donations from individuals, corporations, churches, governments, or intergovernmental or interchurch organizations.[39] A broad membership base can spread awareness of and commitment to an NGO, but often involves high fundraising costs. While Amnesty International is a classic example of a member-supported human rights NGO, it is also one of the few that have made a success of this method.[40] Government funding may be seen as reducing the impartiality of an NGO, but some governmental programs attempt to mitigate this by establishing intermediate bodies without political accountability to administer the funds.

It is also important to recognize the important roles played by nontypical NGOs. For example, religious organizations are themselves non-governmental organizations and often promote religious freedom directly, through loose coalitions, through organizations of religious associations, or through organizations sponsored by faith groups. For example, many churches work through the World Council of Churches, the Council of European Churches, or through councils of religious organizations at national or local levels that focus on religious freedom issues. In addition, some religious organizations have established their own or affiliated organizations to promote religious freedom. One example of this sort would be the International Religious Liberty Association, founded and energized by Seventh-Day Adventists, which promotes freedom of religion for all religious organizations and involves members of many faiths.[41]

Religious freedom is an issue that can bring together numerous, extremely diverse religious organizations and civil libertarian groups. For example, in the United States representatives of a broad range of religious organizations and civil liberty groups participate in a joint Religious Liberty Committee, which tracks issues relating to religious freedom. Similarly broad interreligious coalitions have also been created to work together on specific legislation or court cases that raise religious liberty concerns.[42] Broad ranges of groups can also be brought together through

---

[36] See their website at <www.ihf-hr.org>.

[37] See their website at <www.iarf-religiousfreedom.net>.

[38] See their website at <http://www.freedomhouse.org/religion/>.

[39] See discussion in section III.

[40] Winston, "Assessing the Effectiveness of International Human Rights NGOs," 36–43.

[41] See their website at <http://www.irla.org/welcome.html>. In a similar vein, the International Coalition for Religious Freedom is affiliated with the Unification Church; see their website at <www.religiousfreedom.com>.

[42] For example, several hundred religious and civil libertarian groups cooperated in promoting broader governmental protection of religious freedom in the *Religious Freedom Restoration Act of 1993* (see

NGOs created to reflect interfaith religious liberty concerns, such as the Oslo Coalition on Freedom of Religion or Belief,[43] the International Academy for Freedom of Religion and Belief, and the Dutch Platform for Freedom of Religion or Belief.

Other nonstereotypical, non-government actors include academic centers or consortia involved in religion and law issues. These types of institutions and groups, often referred to as "knowledge-based" or "epistemic" communities,[44] can draw on the expertise and institutional resources of universities and make unique contributions to a transnational advocacy network.[45]

While governments and intergovernmental organizations by definition are not non-governmental organizations, they play an important role in transnational advocacy networks and should not be overlooked in a discussion of NGOs.[46] Many governments or intergovernmental organizations have established official human rights foundations or have offices in departments of foreign affairs that deal with religious freedom or human rights. As described further in the following section, NGOs can have extremely fruitful interactions with these governmental and intergovernmental players.

B. What Roles Do NGOs Play in Promoting Freedom of Religion or Belief?

As is suggested in the preceding sections, NGOs facilitate freedom of religion or belief through multiple overlapping methods. Some NGOs choose to focus on one approach, while others use various combinations. Some key roles of NGOs include standard setting, violation reporting, providing technical advice, and lobbying and agenda setting. I will address these roles in turn. Conflict resolution, networking, facilitating interfaith cooperation, and education are also important functions performed by some NGOs, but I will not discuss them here, as they have been addressed in depth in other chapters of this volume.[47]

<http://hydra.gsa.gov/pbs/pt/call-in/pl103141.htm>) and in supporting its constitutionality in the case *City of Boerne v. Flores* (see <http://supct.law.cornell.edu/supct/html/95-2074.ZS.html>).

[43] See their website, <www.hri.ca/partners/forob>.

[44] Peter Haas, "Introduction: Epistemic Communities and International Policy Coordination," *International Organization* 46, no.1 (winter 1992): 1–36.

[45] See, e.g., the European Consortium for Church and State Research (bringing together scholars and academic centers from EU countries) (online at <http://www.uni-trier.de/uni/fb5/robbers/eng/Welcome.HTML>); the J. M. Dawson Institute for Church–State Studies at Baylor University (online at <http://www.baylor.edu/Church_State/>); Emory University's Law and Religion Program (online at <http://www.law.emory.edu/LAW/REL/law-rel1.html>); Columbia's Center for the Study of Human Rights (online at http://www.columbia.edu/cu/humanrights/); DePaul's Center for Church–State Studies (online at http://www.depaul.edu/about_DP/centers.asp#Church/State>); the University of Essex's Human Rights Centre (online at http://www2.essex.ac.uk/human_rights_centre/); and the Brigham Young University International Center for Law and Religion Studies (online at <http://www.law2.byu.edu/Law&Religion/>). Many others could be named as well.

[46] See, e.g., chapters on the Human Rights Committee, the Organization for Security and Co-Operation in Europe, and the Council of Europe in this volume. Some individual countries are also heavily involved in promoting freedom of religion or belief. See, e.g., Dutch Ministry of Foreign Affairs, 2001 Memorandum on Human Rights Policy (May 2001) (describing Dutch support for initiatives promoting freedom of religion or belief).

[47] See chapters by Noll, Plessner, Swidler, Ambrosewicz-Jacobs, the chapter by Eidsvåg, Lindholm, and Sveen, and the Conclusion and Agenda for the Future.

1. Standard Setting and Cooperation with International Organizations

Implicit in the spiral pattern is the existence of international norms accepted by an international community of states and non-governmental actors. The creation of norms could be seen as a preliminary step before the spiral pattern of change can happen, and the adoption of these norms by violator states plays significant part in the "prescriptive status" step. NGOs can play an important role in both establishing the international norms and promoting common understanding and acceptance of them. The technical expertise in drafting and articulating proposals for norms may come from epistemic communities, while other NGOs may play a greater role in influencing international organizations to accept these proposals.

NGOs have been instrumental in setting international standards on freedom of religion and belief.[48] NGOs have also been instrumental in the equally difficult process of encouraging countries to ratify international agreements. Jeremy Gunn's chapter in this volume, which focuses on how individuals and groups influenced key religious freedom legislation in the United States, provides an important example of the pre-eminent role NGOs can play in promoting religious freedom in domestic legislation and in states' foreign policies.

Involvement in standard setting can be approached through different avenues, and varying types of NGOs may be best suited for various aspects of standard setting. International NGOs that have consultative status or lobbying access at international organizations may effectively participate in the drafting discussions directly, but even so, they may rely on epistemic communities or NGOs with technical expertise for information or advice. Other NGOs can also exert influence over drafting processes through state representatives in a drafting body.[49]

NGOs seeking to be involved in the standard-setting process should evaluate their strengths to see where they can play a significant role in the drafting process. One commentator described the fluid character of a multilateral negotiation: the negotiation "usually changes drastically from its initiation to the conclusion of a final agreement that terminates the process. For example, the need for new knowledge and information is much more limited at the end of the negotiation, when concessions are exchanged and deals are made, than when the agenda is set and issues are clarified in the earlier stages of the process."[50] Clearly different types of NGOs are needed at different stages of the process of formulating norms.

---

[48] See Bahiyyih G. Tahzib, *Freedom of Religion and Belief: Ensuring Effective International Legal Protection* (The Hague: Martinus Nijhoff, 1996) (describing NGO influence on, *inter alia*, the UN's 1981 Declaration). William Korey also details NGO involvement in the formation of numerous international human rights norms, such as the human rights provisions in the UN Charter to the Universal Declaration of Human Rights and OSCE Commitments. See generally William Korey, *NGOs and the Universal Declaration of Human Rights: "A Curious Grapevine"* (New York: St. Martin's Press, 1998).

[49] See Nigel Rodley, "The Work of Non-Governmental Organizations in the World-Wide Promotion and Protection of Human Rights," *UN Bulletin of Human Rights* 90, no. 1 (1991): 85.

[50] Gunnar Sjöstedt et al. as quoted in Henry J. Steiner and Philip Alston, *International Human Rights in Context: Law, Politics, Morals* (Oxford: Oxford University Press, 1996), 498.

NGO interactions with international organizations are not limited to norm setting. NGOs can also influence international organizations to condemn violator states or impose sanctions, which are particularly effective at the "repression" and "denial" stages, and can use international organizations as a means to facilitate dialogue and expert consultations, emphasize international norms, and support domestic rights-protection institutions, which are valuable as the target state moves through the "tactical concessions" to the "prescriptive status" and "rule-consistent behavior" stages.

International organizations each have varying policies on cooperation with NGOs. Some international organizations, such as the United Nations, have established formal and informal observer or consultative relationships with NGOs.[51] While achieving observer or consultative status grants certain formal privileges to NGOs, it is not generally a precondition for cooperation with or informal lobbying of most international organizations.[52] Often NGOs are also granted opportunities to present written and oral statements at committee meetings and conferences of international organizations. Of these, institutions associated with UN bodies, the OSCE, and the Council of Europe have been most active on freedom of religion issues. All of the organizations here described, however, have a scope that includes protection of freedom of religion and belief.

The United Nations has established a procedure under Resolution 1296 (XLIV), updated in Resolution 1996/31 of the UN Economic and Social Council (ECOSOC), whereby international NGOs can obtain one of three levels of consultative status.[53] The levels correspond with the number of fields of ECOSOC in which NGOs are involved, and grant correspondingly varied privileges. General consultative status is granted to NGOs dealings with most of ECOSOC's activities. These are the only NGOs permitted to propose items for ECOSOC's agenda. Obtaining special consultative status, granted to NGOs with special interest in a few of the fields covered by ECOSOC (such as human rights NGOs), allows NGO representatives to attend meetings, speak, and submit written statements for circulation. NGOs in the third category, or the Roster, are those with the most specialized interests. In practice, the distinctions between the categories blur.[54]

To obtain ECOSOC consultative status, NGOs must apply to the UN Committee on NGOs and submit reports on their activities every four years.[55] The grant of some level of consultative status or placement on the Roster also allows NGOs to

---

[51] See generally Martin A. Olz, "Non-Governmental Organizations in Regional Human Rights Systems," *Columbia Human Rights Law Review* 28 (winter 1997): 307; Arie Bloed et al., *Monitoring Human Rights in Europe: Comparing International Procedures and Mechanisms,* vol. 30, *International Studies in Human Rights* (Dordrecht: Martinus Nijhoff, 1993).

[52] See, e.g., Council of Europe Resolution (93) 38, appendix A, para. 12: "The procedures [relating to consultative status] described above shall not restrict the right of the Committee of Ministers, or of the Parliamentary Assembly, or of the Standing Conference of Regional and Local Authorities to initiate any action concerning other non-governmental organisations in pursuance of their respective rules of procedures. It should also not prevent the Secretariat of the Council of Europe from considering practical cooperation on an ad hoc basis with other international and national non-governmental organisations in any field of mutual interest."

[53] UN Resolution 1996/31, adopted by the UN Economic and Social Council, 25 July 1996 (available online at <gopher://gopher.un.org:70/00/esc/recs/1996/E-RES96.31>); see also UN Resolution 1296 (XLIV), 23 May 1968; for a broad range of information on NGOs and ECOSOC, see generally <http://www.un.org/partners/civil_society/ngo/n-ecosoc.htm#top>.

[54] See Bloed, *Monitoring Human Rights in Europe,* 126–27.

participate in UN conferences on request; other NGOs may only participate through individual application. Even without formal consultative status, NGOs can still be apprised of and involved in UN activities. NGOs may join mailing lists of the UN Office of the High Commissioner for Human Rights,[56] the UN Department of Public Information,[57] and the United Nations Children's Fund.

Gaining consultative status with ECOSOC or joining a mailing list, however, are not the only ways for NGOs to become involved in UN activities. NGOs dealing with human rights and freedom of religion or belief issues at the UN can work with and testify before the Commission on Human Rights and submit information to its Special Rapporteur on Freedom of Religion or Belief (formerly called the UN Special Rapporteur on Religious Intolerance), both discussed in depth elsewhere in this volume.[58] UNESCO also has its own types of consultative status for NGOs, and allows organizations with consultative status to send representatives to sessions of UNESCO's General Conference and take part in UNESCO-sponsored Conferences of International Non-Governmental Organizations.[59] UNESCO also cooperates with unaccredited NGOs for information distribution and contracting purposes. In addition to UN charter bodies, the Human Rights Committee, which was created under the International Covenant on Civil and Political Rights, and is also discussed elsewhere in this volume, is an important forum for international NGO involvement, and has its own rules for NGO involvement.[60]

International NGOs can also obtain consultative status with the Council of Europe.[61] To obtain consultative status, NGOs must file an application with the Council of Europe's Secretary General. The application must contain the NGO's statute, a report of recent activities, and a formal declaration that the organization accepts the principles of the Council of Europe as set forth in the preamble and article 1 of the Council's statute.[62] The Secretary General determines whether consultative status will be granted; in the absence of objections by the Committee of Ministers and the

---

[55] See ECOSOC Rule 80; UN-NGLS Factsheet for Applying for Consultative Status with the UN Economic and Social Council (ECOSOC), available online at <http://www.unsystem.org/ngls/english/factsheets/ecosoc.htm>.

[56] See their website at <www.unhchr.ch>.

[57] The Department of Public Information has an NGO section that organizes briefings, conferences, and workshops for NGOs, and maintains and distributes information on the UN and a directory of NGOs registered with its office. See <http://www.un.org/MoreInfo/ngolink/dpingo.htm>. For information on application for associated status with the DPI, see <http://www.un.org/MoreInfo/ngolink/brochure.htm>.

[58] General information and links for human rights NGO interactions, directories, and committees associated with these and other UN bodies are available at <http://www.un.org/partners/civil_society/ngo/n-hr.htm>. For additional information on the UN Commission on Human Rights, see the chapter in this volume by Theo van Boven and the Commission's website, <http://www.unhchr.ch/html/menu2/2/chr.htm>.

[59] For more information on UNESCO's activities promoting freedom of religion or belief, see the chapter in this volume by Doudou Diene. UNESCO has an NGO-UNESCO Liaison Committee (online at <http://www.unesco.org/ext/ngo/comite/>). For a useful evaluation of UNESCO's cooperation with NGOs done by the Union of International Organizations, see <http://www.uia.org/organiz/unesa.htm>.

[60] For additional information on the Human Rights Committee's role in promoting freedom of religion or belief and NGO interactions with the Committee, see the chapter in this volume by Martin Scheinen. See also their website, <http://www.unhchr.ch/html/menu2/6/hrc.htm>.

[61] For general information on the Council of Europe, see their webpage at <http://www.coe.int> and the chapter in this volume by Javier Martínez-Torrón and Rafael Navarro-Valls.

[62] Council of Europe Resolution (93) 38, appendix A (outlining "Rules for Consultative Status").

Parliamentary Assembly, he or she will grant consultative status after three months.[63] The Council of Europe also grants observer status for individual committees created by the Committee of Ministers.[64]

The European Court of Human Rights (European Court)[65] also allows for NGO involvement. NGOs can apply to the European Court on their own behalf or in behalf of a victim of human rights abuse if they serve as legal counsel for the victim.[66] The European Court has also accepted ***amicus curiae*** briefs from NGOs.[67]

The Organization for Security and Co-Operation in Europe encourages NGO participation, but has no formal consultative status for NGOs. NGO involvement is usually coordinated through individual field offices or through the Office for Democratic Institutions and Human Rights (ODIHR), particularly its NGO Unit.[68] NGOs regularly participate at OSCE meetings and seminars and at the ODIHR Human Dimension Implementation Meetings. Among other capacity-building projects, the NGO Unit currently has a fund to facilitate Central and East European NGO participation in OSCE Human Dimension events.[69] NGOs may also communicate with ODIHR's Advisory Panel of Experts on Freedom of Religion or Belief through its responsible advisors and officers.[70]

The Organization of American States has no formal procedure for NGOs to obtain observer status, but has formal agreements of cooperation with some NGOs and informally cooperates with many more. The OAS General Assembly has also accredited NGOs as observers on an ad hoc basis, and NGOs have been allowed to address the Meeting of Consultation of Foreign Ministers as well as the Permanent Council, which proposes actions to the General Assembly.[71]

The Inter-American Commission on Human Rights (Inter-American Commission) and the Inter-American Court of Human Rights, both established under the American Convention on Human Rights, have created additional opportunities for

---

[63] Ibid.

[64] Council of Europe Resolution (76) 3; see also Resolution (93) 38 (referring to "Rules of Procedures" of Council of Europe committees).

[65] The European Commission for Human Rights was disbanded in 1998 under Protocol 11. For a discussion of the Commission, the European Court of Human Rights, and the Court's case law on freedom of religion or belief, see the chapter in this volume by Javier Martínez-Torrón and Rafael Navarro-Valls. See also the website of the European Court at <http://www.echr.coe.int/>.

[66] See ***European Convention for the Protection of Human Rights and Fundamental Freedoms,*** art. 34 (recognizing the right of the European Court to receive applications "from any person, non-governmental organisation or group of individuals claiming to be a victim of a violation" of rights protected under the European Convention) (available online at <http://conventions.coe.int/Treaty/EN/CadreListeTraites.htm>).

[67] See Arie Bloed, ***Monitoring Human Rights in Europe,*** 136–67. See generally Rules of Court (available online at <http://www.echr.coe.int/Eng/EDocs/RulesOfCourt.html>). The European Court also maintains a database of human rights cases at <http://www.echr.coe.int/Hudoc.htm>.

[68] See Secretariat of the Organization for Security and Co-Operation in Europe, ***OSCE Handbook,*** 160–61 (available online in English and Russian at <http://www.osce.org/publications/handbook/handbook.pdf>). The website for the NGO Unit is <http://www.osce.org/odihr/democratization/ngo/>.

[69] See <http://www.osce.org/odihr/projects/prj2001_ngo.pdf>. Contact information for the NGO Unit is available at its website, <http://www.osce.org/odihr/democratization/ngo/ >.

[70] See their website at <http://www.osce.org/odihr/democratization/religion/ >.

[71] Olz, "Non-Governmental Organizations in Regional Human Rights Systems," 355.

NGO cooperation. The Inter-American Commission, which performs fact-finding and advisory functions,[72] allows NGOs to help arrange in-country Commission visits,[73] to be involved in standard setting, to file petitions denouncing or complaining of state action on behalf of themselves or others, and to participate in hearings or settlement negotiations to resolve petitions. [74] Most human rights petitions filed before the Inter-American Commission are filed by NGOs.[75] The Inter-American Court of Human Rights[76] also provides many opportunities for NGO involvement. NGO officials can serve as legal advisors to the court, represent victims before the court, and file briefs as *amicus curiae* in both advisory and contended cases.[77]

NGOs also have opportunities to work with the Organization of African Unity (the OAU) and the African Commission of Human and Peoples' Rights.[78] The OAU has granted observer status to a few Africa-oriented international NGOs,[79] but most human rights issues involve the African Commission of Human and Peoples' Rights (the African Commission), where NGOs have more influence.[80] NGOs can not only submit communications to the African Commission,[81] but can also work informally with the African Commission[82] and obtain formal observer status. To obtain formal

[72] For more information on the Inter-American Commission, see their website, <http://www.cidh.oas.org>.

[73] See David Padilla, "The Inter-American Commission on Human Rights of the Organization of American States: A Case Study," *American University Journal of International Law and Policy* 9 (1993): 104; *American Convention on Human Rights* (ACHR), art. 48 (available online at <http://www.cidh.oas.org/B%C3%A1sicos/basic3.htm>); *Statute of the Inter-American Commission on Human Rights,* art. 18(g) (allowing on-site observations with the consent or at the invitation of a Party State) (available online at <http://www.cidh.oas.org/Básicos/basic15.htm>).

[74] American Convention on Human Rights, arts. 43, 44, 48 (available online at <http://www.cidh.oas.org/B%C3%A1sicos/basic3.htm>); see also Regulations of the Inter-American Commission on Human Rights (8 April 1980), art. 26 (as modified on 27 June 1987) (providing that "any nongovernmental entity legally recognized in one or more member states of the Organization, may lodge petitions with the Commission containing denunciations or complaints of violations of this Convention by a State Party"). Information on petitioning and an online petition form are available at <http://www.cidh.oas.org/esemail9.asp> (Spanish) and <http://www.cidh.oas.org/email9.asp> (English).

[75] Olz, "Non-Governmental Organizations in Regional Human Rights Systems," 357.

[76] For more information on the Inter-American Court of Human Rights, see their website at <http://www.corteidh.or.cr>.

[77] Rules of Procedure of the Inter-American Court of Human Rights, arts. 22, 23, 26 (available online at <http://www.cidh.oas.org/Básicos/basic18.htm>); see also Dinah Shelton, "The Jurisprudence of the Inter-American Court of Human Rights," *American University Journal of International Law and Policy* 10 (fall 1994): 348–51; Olz, "Non-Governmental Organizations in Regional Human Rights Systems," 358–59.

[78] As this volume was going to press, the Organization of African Unity was replaced by the African Union.

[79] Olz, "Non-Governmental Organizations in Regional Human Rights Systems," 360–70; see generally <http://www.oau-oua.org/> (OAU website).

[80] Olz, "Non-Governmental Organizations in Regional Human Rights Systems," 361. See generally Rachel Murray and Malcolm Evans, eds., *Documents of the African Commission on Human and Peoples' Rights* (Oxford: Oxford, 2001).

[81] See *African Charter of Human and Peoples' Rights,* art. 45 (available online at <http://www.oau-oua.org/oau_info/rights.htm>).

[82] For example, the African Commission's mandate requires that it "co-operate with other African and international institutions concerned with the promotion and protection of human and peoples' rights" (*African Charter of Human and Peoples' Rights,* art. 45.1[c], available online at <http://www.oau-oua.org/oau_info/rights.htm>).

observer status, NGOs must submit written applications with the Commission's secretariat, listing the organization's statute and rules of procedure, a list of the names of its officials, a report on its activities, and a financial disclosure.[83]

Obtaining observer status or being involved with international organizations not only allows NGOs to influence norm creation, but also provides an excellent opportunity for NGOs to build networks with other NGOs. These ties may be unofficial or may be officially promoted through the international organizations. For example, the Council of Europe has established a partially funded Liaison Committee and Plenary Conference, established under the responsibility of NGOs with consultative status.[84] These allow NGO representatives to meet together regularly and to coordinate with the Committee of Ministers' working group on NGO relations. Similarly, the UN Non-Governmental Organizations Committee on Freedom of Religion or Belief, part of the UN's Conference on Non-Governmental Organizations, organizes activities for NGOs and UN representatives on issues relating to freedom of religion or belief.[85]

2. Compliance Monitoring

NGOs also play a critical role in monitoring and spreading information on violations of international norms. It has been argued that "NGOs have significantly supplemented states, and to a large extent supplanted them, in human rights monitoring."[86] As the spiral pattern would suggest, compliance monitoring is a key element in all stages of norm socialization. Reporting of violations to the international community, for example, is key to moving a state from the initial "repression" stage to the "denial" stage. Accurate reporting also provides a base of information with which governments and NGOs can bring violator states into a true dialogue about specific abuses during the "tactical concessions" and "prescriptive status" phases. At the "rule-consistent behavior" stage, continued stable and effective compliance monitoring at the domestic level becomes critical.

Violation monitoring is done particularly effectively by networks of NGOs, as they have more flexibility and less institutional reserve than governments. Claude E. Welch suggests that the convention-based human rights system "would be almost totally ineffective if it were based on reports submitted by governments. NGOs' goal of providing information about abuses remains central to the reporting systems."[87]

The effectiveness of NGOs at compliance monitoring, however, depends heavily upon their reliability and ability to spread information quickly. NGOs need to be able to provide both technical information and dramatic testimony to policy makers, other NGOs, and the media in order to effectively place local problems on the international

---

[83] See Olz, "Non-Governmental Organizations in Regional Human Rights Systems," 367; see generally *Rules of Procedures of the African Commission,* ch. 13 (available online at <http://www.oau-oua.org/oau_info/rules.htm>); Gino J. Naldi, *Documents of the Organizations of African Unity* (New York: Mansell, 1992).

[84] See Liaison Committee of NGOs enjoying consultative status with the Council of Europe, Representative bodies of the NGOs having consultative status with the Council of Europe and the conduct of their business, ONG.CL (93) 2 (1993).

[85] See their website at <http://www.conferenceofngos.org/ngosubs/freedrel.htm>.

[86] Welch, *NGOs and Human Rights,* 275.

[87] Ibid., 265.

agenda.[88] NGOs that focus on reporting should be aware of potential problems in their coverage, such as biased or limited sources and the tendency to report on particular governmental practices and ignore overall conditions.[89] To be effective, NGOs need credibility, accurate and dramatic information, and strong links with the media.[90]

NGOs monitor religious freedom at national, regional, and international levels, and spread information by internet postings, emails, newsletters, or periodic reports. Important academically based reports with broad international scope are Kevin Boyle and Juliet Sheen's *Freedom of Religion and Belief: A World Report*[91] and Freedom House's *Religious Freedom in the World: A Global Report on Freedom and Persecution.*[92] Other groups involved in significant religious freedom violation reporting at the international level include the Center for Studies on New Religions/Centro Studi sulle Nuove Religioni (through its website, www.cesnur.org), Human Rights Without Frontiers (through its website, www.hrwf.net, and an email service), and Aiuto alla Chiesa che Soffre (Aid to the Church in Need).[93] Annual or periodic reports by many human rights organizations include some reporting on religious freedom issues.[94] At a regional level, Keston News Service has long been recognized as a reliable and important source for information on violations of religious freedom in the former Eastern Bloc nations.[95] Keston publishes a periodic journal, distributes a newsletter, and provides an email news service.

NGOs can also contribute to monitoring efforts through contributing information to official state or interstate bodies that issue reports. Particularly significant in this context are reports of the Human Rights Committee and the UN Special Rapporteur on Freedom of Religion and Belief, as well as the annual international religious freedom reports of the United States State Department[96] and the US Commission on International Religious Freedom.[97] These rely heavily on reporting from domestic

---

[88] See Keck and Sikkink, *Activists Beyond Borders,* 16.

[89] See Henry Steiner, *Diverse Partners: Non-Governmental Organizations in the Human Rights Movement* (report from a retreat for human rights NGO activists in Crete, 1991), 19, quoted in Steiner and Alston, *International Human Rights in Context,* 462–63; David L. Cingranelli and David L. Richards, "Measuring the Impact of Human Rights Violations," in Welch, *NGOs and Human Rights,* 230–32.

[90] See discussion in Keck and Sikkink, *Activists Beyond Borders,* 18–22.

[91] Kevin Boyle and Juliet Sheen, eds., *Freedom of Religion and Belief: A World Report* (London: Routledge, 1997).

[92] Paul Marshall, ed., *Religious Freedom in the World: A Global Report on Freedom and Persecution* (Nashville: Broadman & Holman, 2000).

[93] See, e.g., *Report on Religious Freedom in the World 2000,* available in Italian online at <http://www.alleanzacattolica.org/acs/index.htm>, and available in English by sending an email to info@alleanzacattolica.org with the subject line: "Please send me the 2000 Report."

[94] Reports of this sort include the annual Human Rights Watch Report (2002 report available online at <http://www.hrw.org/wr2k1/index.html>) and reports by the International Helsinki Foundation for Human Rights (see especially their Report on Religious Intolerance in Selected OSCE Countries in 2000 <http://www.ihf-hr.org/reports/osce01/Religious%20Intolerance/ReligiousFreedom%20ReportJune01.pdf>; for more general information and other reports see <http://www.ihf-hr.org/index.htm>).

[95] See their website at <www.keston.org>.

[96] Available online at the US State Department's website, <www.state.gov>. The 2001 report is located at <http://www.state.gov/g/drl/rls/irf/2001/>. Annual reports are generally published in October.

[97] Available online at the Commission's website, <http://www.uscirf.gov/index.php3>. The 2001 report is located at <http://www.uscirf.gov/reports/01May01Report_Index.php3>, with an addendum at <http://www.uscirf.gov/reports/14May01report_Addendum.php3>. The Commission's reports are published annually at the beginning of May.

and international NGOs. The US State Department, for example, designates one person in each US embassy to collect information on religious freedom violations in that country for the annual report. This official often relies on information submitted by domestic and international NGOs and religious organizations, in addition to in-country government sources, to put together a complete report.[98]

As explained in greater depth in Theo van Boven's chapter in this volume, NGOs have many opportunities to contribute to reports and country reviews of the UN Special Rapporteur and the Human Rights Committee. NGOs, as one member of the Human Rights Committee explained, are "absolutely indispensable" to the Committee, as without them there would be "virtually no sources of information" to question official government reports.[99]

3. Research and Technical Advice

An additional role of NGOs in promoting religious freedom is to provide scholarly and technical advice to governments and governmental critics. Largely provided by epistemic communities, scholarly research and technical advice can benefit all other functions of NGOs—standard setting, reporting of violations, and lobbying of policy-makers.[100] In terms of the spiral model of change, technical advice is valuable in different ways at various stages. Initially, research and technical advice can help policy-makers understand the depth of the problems in target states and develop effective means of both instrumental leverage and moral persuasion. At later stages, particularly the crucial "tactical concessions" stage, technical experts can serve as neutral brokers in dialogue with the target country over specific violations. Finally, academic experts can offer support, guidance, and training for emerging domestic rights-protecting institutions. This becomes particularly crucial in ensuring a successful transition to the final, "rule-consistent behavior" stage.

Academic communities' strengths in research and technical advice most obviously lend themselves to roles in the research and technical sides of drafting and analyzing legislation and international norms. Numerous academic centers have gathered and analyzed national laws affecting religious organizations, which in turn allows them to provide concrete analyses of draft laws or proposed international norms.[101] An international consortium of universities and academic centers, in connection with the OSCE's Advisory Panel of Experts on Freedom of Religion or Belief,[102] has developed an online

---

[98] See, e.g., Preface to 2001 International Religious Freedom Report, available online at <http://www.state.gov/g/drl/rls/irf/2001/index.cfm?docid=5529>.

[99] Thomas Buergenthal, as quoted in Korey, *NGOs and the Universal Declaration of Human Rights*, 269.

[100] See generally Peter Haas, "Introduction: Epistemic Communities and International Policy Coordination," *Knowledge, Power and International Policy Coordination*, special issue, *International Organization* 46 (winter 1992): 1–36; Keck and Sikkink, *Activists Beyond Borders*, 30.

[101] A representative sample of such books and commentaries on norms affecting religious freedom could include Inge Gampl et al., *Österreichisches Staatskirchenrecht*, 2 vols. (Vienna: Orac, 1990); Joseph Listl and Dietrich Pirson, *Handbuch des Staatskirchenrechts der Bundesrepublik Deutschland*, 2d ed., 2 vols. (Berlin: Duncker &Humblot, 1994). Similar volumes have also been published by government offices or NGOs. See, e.g., Alberto de la Hera and Rosa María Martínez de Codes, *Spanish Legislation on Religious Affairs* (Madrid: Ministerio de Justicia Centro de publicaciones, 1998); Institut religii i prava, *Religioznye ob'edineniia svoboda sovesti i veroispovedaniia: Normativnye akti sudebnaia prakitka* (Moscow: Yurisprudentsiia, 2001).

database of constitutional provisions, laws affecting religious organizations and rights, and key international reports on religious freedom in OSCE member states, located at www.religlaw.org.

Scholarly research and conferences can also help to provide depth and background into situations in norm-violating states, which can serve as a healthy corrective to some of the otherwise possible weaknesses in NGO violation monitoring.[103] NGO violation reporting, in the nature of things, is uneven, depending on the NGO involved. As a result, there are criticisms that NGO monitoring sometimes manifests excessive bias, a lack of depth, limited sources, and a tendency to focus on individual government practices instead of an overall situation. While traditional NGOs are often more effective at quickly obtaining and publicizing information, scholarly research from epistemic communities can help provide the correctives and balance that come with distance and in-depth research.

Many international journals focus on questions of freedom of religion or belief. A sampling of some significant ones includes *The European Journal for Church-State Research*, published by the European Consortium for Church-State Research; the *Anuario de Derecho Eclesiástico del Estado*, published by Complutense University of Madrid; *The Journal of Church and State*, published by the J. M. Dawson Institute for Church-State Studies at Baylor University; *Religion, State, and Society*, published by the Keston Institute; *Fides et Libertas*, published by the International Religious Liberty Association; and *Conscience et Liberté*, published by the International Association for the Defense of Religious Liberty. Some significant scholarly journals also focus on national or topical issues, including *Islam and Muslim-Christian Relations*, *Österreichisches Archiv für Recht und Religion* (Austria), *Gosudarstvo, religia, tserkov* (Russia), and *Religiina panorama* (Ukraine).

4. Policy Formation and Agenda Setting

A key role of NGOs promoting freedom of religion is to educate and influence policymakers. As suggested by the spiral model described previously, human rights NGOs, to have maximum effect, need to influence not only norm-violating governments, but also countries and international bodies with influence over the norm-violating governments. All of these types of influence exist both through formal and less formal channels. NGOs should carefully examine domestic laws before engaging in formal lobbying, since in some countries extensive formal lobbying may affect the tax-exempt status of NGOs.

What has been referred to as "leverage politics," or "the ability to call upon powerful actors to affect a situation where weaker members of a network are unlikely to have influence,"[104] is one of the core roles of NGOs in the boomerang model or the spiral model. In trying to assert leverage, NGOs bring pressure to bear on organizations or states that have some leverage—be it material or moral—over the violator

---

[102] See the chapter by Urban Gibson and Karen Lord in this volume.

[103] See text accompanying note 88.

[104] Keck and Sikkink, *Activists Beyond Borders*, 16; see also Morton E. Winston, "Assessing the Effectiveness of International Human Rights NGOs: Amnesty International," in Welch, *NGOs and Human Rights*, 36–43 (adopting Keck and Sikkink's typology).

state.[105] Efforts by US human rights advocates to link the Peoples' Republic of China's human rights record to a US Congressional grant of most-favored-nation trading status or the possibility of holding the Olympics in Beijing are clear examples of leverage politics. Keck and Sikkink suggest other forms of perhaps less obvious leverage, such as influence over public opinion (and votes) in a democracy.[106] The spiral model also suggests that public criticism has an effect akin to traditional forms of leverage. Success in leverage politics of any sort often, but not always, depends on links to media or powerful decision makers and the ability to link human rights practices with something else of value.

A final important element of policy formation attempts is what Keck and Sikkink call "accountability politics,"[107] or what Risse and Sikkink refer to as the normative practice of shaming.[108] Essentially, this tactic focuses on forcing governments to publicly articulate human rights principles and then publicizing cases in which governments violate articulated principles. The spiral model suggests that, far from being mere "talk," government recognition of the applicability of human rights norms is an integral part of the socialization of international norms. This approach should be particularly effective in the transition to phase three, where governments accept the rhetoric of international norms, and in the fourth stage, where governments need to be held accountable to their newly adopted reliance on international norms.[109] As Keck and Sikkink point out, this can be done effectively in the United States through litigation (*amicus curiae* briefs as well as group and individual representation), which explains the large number of US NGOs that focus on litigation.[110] Similar shaming roles are played elsewhere by the Council of Europe and the European Court of Human Rights, the Inter-American Commission on Human Rights, the African Commission on Human and Peoples' Rights, and other regional and international organizations.[111] Individual complaints may also be filed with the UN Office of the High Commissioner on Human Rights[112] of the Human Rights Committee.[113] Shaming can also be achieved through successful media campaigns or through public statements made by religious leaders or international organizations.[114]

While it makes sense to separate the various roles of NGOs for analytical purposes, in practice the roles blur. To give only a few examples, research and scholarly work can form the basis of norm-setting or lobbying efforts. Violation reporting can also be used as a form of influencing policy, since effective NGOs have the "ability

---

[105]See discussion in Keck and Sikkink, *Activists Beyond Borders,* 23-24.

[106] See discussion in ibid.

[107] See discussion in ibid., 24–25.

[108] Risse and Sikkink, "The Socialization of International Human Rights Norms," 15.

[109] Risse and Ropp provide a useful reminder that "[e]xternal actors need to be aware that different modes of socialization are at work during different phases of the 'spiral model'" (Risse and Ropp, "International Human Rights Norms and Domestic Change," 276).

[110] Keck and Sikkink, *Activists Beyond Borders,* 25.

[111] See discussion of NGO relations with these and other international bodies in section II.B.1.

[112] For information and instruction on filing complaints, see <http://www.unhchr.ch/html/menu2/8/ex_conv.htm>.

[113] Information on filing complaints with the Human Rights Committee is available at <http://www.unhchr.ch/html/menu2/8/oppro.htm>.

[114] See, e.g., the attempts to prevent passage of the French antisect law as described by Fautre, Garay, and Niedigger in their chapter in this volume.

to quickly and credibly generate politically usable information and move it to where it will have the most impact."[115] Effective policy formation depends not only on accurate and timely information of violations, but also clear articulation of domestic and international standards and relevant technical advice. Attempts to remedy individual injustices through courts or petitions may also have shaming and norm-creation effects.

Individual NGOs may choose to focus on a particular type of activity, but it becomes clear that work by differing NGOs can be mutually reinforcing. Indeed, to create effective transnational networks, NGOs depend on other NGOs, governments, international organizations, epistemic communities, and the media. As a close examination of the spiral pattern might suggest, NGOs and other transnational actors can work effectively together and reinforce each other's efforts even without agreement or close cooperation. An NGO or government with ties to a rights-violating state may dislike and disapprove of the public rhetoric and criticism voiced by other states, NGOs, and intergovernmental actors against the rights-violating state, feeling that quiet diplomacy is more effective. Nevertheless, the leverage of public criticism at the other end of the "boomerang" may place the issue on the international agenda and increase the willingness of a rights-violating state to engage in just such quiet diplomacy. In a similar vein, actors that engage in high-profile shaming or threats may not themselves be able to negotiate with rights violators or enter into discussion of specific abuses with them, but are clearly the beneficiary of NGOs and other actors who help persuade rights-violating states to make tactical concessions or liberalize.

Reference to the spiral model would also suggest, however, that not all approaches are effective at all stages. Leverage politics may be the only way to force the worst rights-violating countries to change, but it may be too blunt an instrument for countries at the later stages of the spiral.

III. How Do NGOs Promoting Freedom of Religion or Belief Operate?

Information on the practical side of running a religious freedom NGO could itself fill many chapters. Of necessity this chapter will only give a brief overview of a vital issue in running NGOs: developing the material resources to maintain an NGO.

Funding, along with volunteerism, is the lifeblood of NGOs. Before examining potential sources of funding, however, a cautionary note is worthwhile. NGO funding is primarily a result, not a cause, of successful programs: "Although the greater access to funding for their work undeniably helps such groups to be effective and have greater impact, few would deny that superior organisational capacities and successful execution of their programmes are the starting point. The finances come as a result."[116] Obtaining any outside resources depends on the NGO's having a clear mission, strong organization, and demonstrable effectiveness. With a clear identity and purpose, NGOs

[115] Keck and Sikkink, *Activists Beyond Borders*, 16.

[116] S. Bruce Schearer et al., "A Strategic Guide to Resource Enhancement," in *Sustaining Civil Society: Strategies for Resource Mobilisation*, ed. Leslie M. Fox and S. Bruce Schearer (Washington, D.C.: CIVICUS, 1997), 15.

promoting freedom of religion or belief have the potential to draw on a variety of resources: foundation grants, private donations, corporate donations, and government or multigovernment grants.

Foundations, including the Ford Foundation, the Rockefeller Foundation, the Rockefeller Brothers Fund, the Pew Charitable Trusts, George Soros's Open Society Institute, and many others, have become a major source of funding for human rights NGOs.[117] From 1977 to 1993, grants from US foundations for international human rights work rose from less than one million dollars per year to nearly twenty-three million dollars per year.[118] Larger, more established NGOs may also provide grants, internships, partnerships, and other forms of capacity-building opportunities to NGOs in developing countries and countries in transition.[119] Funding is also often available from official human rights foundations, international organizations, and other governmental or semipublic organizations.[120] Some NGOs avoid directly receiving funds from governmental sources or limit government grants and contracts to specific projects in an attempt to avoid charges of partiality.[121] Similar issues may arise in receiving funding from religious organizations or coalitions or associations of religious organizations.

Resource contributions from individuals or foundations can take many forms: volunteered labor, counsel, or goods; one-time monetary gifts; endowments; or regular donations to name a few. By partnering with other NGOs, individual NGOs can leverage their resources and increase their effectiveness. A high level of volunteerism is particularly vital for the success of new NGOs. Challenges involved in all forms of fundraising and resource development include providing up-to-date and honest information to donors and limiting overhead fundraising costs (one author suggests a rule of thumb that fundraising costs should never exceed twenty percent of generated revenue).[122] Grass-roots fundraising, or fundraising of small amounts from a large number of individuals, is extremely costly—aside from Amnesty International, few if any human rights NGOs depend on membership dues or small contributions; most continue to rely on volunteer efforts, large private donations, and grants.[123]

---

[117] See, e.g., Makau Mutua, "Human Rights International NGOs: A Critical Evaluation," in Welch, *NGOs and Human Rights,* 154; William D. Carmichael, "The Role of the Ford Foundation," in Welch, *NGOs and Human Rights,* 248–60.

[118] Keck and Sikkink, *Activists Beyond Borders*, 99.

[119] For example, Freedom House has various grant and training programs for NGOs, particularly those in the former Communist countries of Central and Eastern Europe and the NIS. See Freedom House's website at <www.freedomhouse.org>. Freedom House also runs a newsletter for NGOs, *NGO News,* that contains information on other grants and training programs (see <www.ngonet.org>). Two websites designed to help provide information on European partnerships and grants for NGOs in the former Eastern Bloc are <www.visegrad.ngo.pl> and <www.eupraxis.com>.

[120] Keck and Sikkink, *Activists Beyond Borders*, 98. Despite the oxymoron, these groups are often referred to as "GONGOs" (governmental NGOs), or "QUANGOs" (quasi-NGOs). For example, information on NGO funding from the EU is available at <www.europa.eu.int/comm/secretariat_general/sgc/ong/en>. See also Open Society Institute's *Guide to Funding and Participation in European Union Programmes* (2001) (available from the Open Society Institute at <www.osi.hu>), and Euro Citizen Action Service's *A Guide to EU Funding Sources in the Candidate Countries* (2001) (available from Euro Citizen Action Service at <www.ecas.org>).

[121] Welch, *NGOs and Human Rights,* 270–71.

[122] Alan Fowler, *The Virtuous Spiral: A Guide to Sustainability for NGOs in International Development* (London: Earthscan Publications, 2000), 114.

Many NGOs face a crisis as they attempt to move from project-based funding to financial autonomy. Financial self-sufficiency requires a strategic plan, the development of reserves, and resources or methods of ensuring dependable independent income. Such permanent self-sufficiency may be obtained through, for example, the creation of an endowment, or an invested capital reserve fund, sufficient to allow core budgetary functions to be covered by the interest.[124]

Another form of economic self-sufficiency is reflected in the current trend for NGOs, particularly development NGOs, to be involved in "development enterprise" or "social entrepreneurship."[125] Under these models, NGOs become hybrid public–private entities that both raise outside money and independently generate revenue. This model is similar to that used by many hospitals in the United States or churches in various parts of the world.[126] In the freedom of religion or belief sphere, this might be reflected in an NGO simultaneously representing religious clients for profit and being involved in not-for-profit activities such as violation reporting, conflict prevention, or policy formation. While a model of this sort has the advantage of generating independently controlled funds for NGO activities, a hybrid entity may encounter legal, accounting, and managerial pitfalls and damage the NGO's public image.[127] Specific advantages and difficulties will depend on the cultural and legal requirements of individual countries. One option that might work in some countries would be to have separate legal entities for for-profit and not-for-profit activities, and use the profit stream from the for-profit entity to finance the NGO.

IV. Conclusion

NGOs have vast potential to promote freedom of religious belief. This chapter has only touched on some significant ways in which they can assist in establishing this significant right. While this chapter's focus has been on NGO influence on violator states and recent developments in the social sciences that provide additional support and understanding for the unique roles that NGOs can play in this arena, this is certainly not the only the area in which NGOs can promote religious freedom. As is well illustrated by other chapters in this volume, NGOs can have significant influence in

---

[123] See Welch, *NGOs and Human Rights*, 271.

[124] See the discussion in Fernand Vincent and Piers Campbell, *Towards Greater Financial Autonomy: A Manual on Financing Strategies and Techniques for Development NGOs and Community Organizations* (Geneva: NGO Management Network, 1989), 41–55.

[125] See, e.g., Horacio R. Morales Jr., "Earning Income Through Trade and Exchange," in Fox and Shearer, *Sustaining Civil Society*, 21–41.

[126] See, e.g., Fowler, *The Virtuous Spiral*, 80–98.

[127] See discussion in Fowler, *The Virtual Spiral*, 81–98. Vincent and Campbell give the following suggestions for NGOs with profit-making centers: "The [for-profit] enterprise must be managed separately, i.e., the directors must be free to take decisions, to hire people, to build up reserves . . . the NGO should retain policy-making control, particularly over major financial decisions; very competent managers should be hired, with the relevant entrepreneurial experience; there must be sufficient capital reserves to ensure that the enterprise can expand, invest in new equipment, allow for depreciation, survive in 'low' periods. . . . This means that the profits from such activities must initially be re-invested in the enterprise and hence that the surplus for the NGO will be relatively small, if not negligible, during the first few years" (Vincent and Campbell, *Towards Greater Financial Autonomy*, 69).

promoting education, dialogue, interfaith cooperation, and other important ventures. One important idea flowing from the spiral model, however, applies to these groups as well. Simply put, NGOs need each other and need each other to fill different roles. Success in promoting socialization of human rights norms requires a combination of compliance monitoring, shaming, moral persuasion, use of leverage, academic research, policy-making efforts, and many other activities. While a view of the spectrum of human rights NGOs seems to reveal a multiplicity of organizations and perhaps mere chaos, I would suggest that the natural disorderliness inherent in the independent ordering of NGOs can prove to be extremely effective when they work together along the lines suggested by the spiral pattern.

Conclusion and Agenda for the Future

The Editors, with Michael M. Roan

At the end of this thoughtful and incisive collection, we as editors would like to gather together some of the key recommendations made by authors in this volume and add some of our own. The quality of the thought and recommendations contained in this volume deserve additional attention and should not be lost amidst the scope and breadth of the volume. While we cannot reiterate all the valuable suggestions made throughout this book, by highlighting some significant points raised by the authors, we hope to encourage and suggest courses for further action in this field. Freedom of religion or belief is too crucial a right to be neglected. To the extent that we as individuals, religious and belief communities, countries, NGOs, and international organizations are not actively engaged in promoting and protecting this right, we are allowing religious tensions, oppression, and conflict to increase and are in part responsible for violations of freedom of religion or belief throughout the world.

First, we would like to at least briefly acknowledge the many achievements in promoting tolerance and preventing discrimination based on religion or belief. All of the following have made significant positive contributions: the growing number of websites and NGOs; the UNESCO year of dialogue conferences; governments' publications, including the US State Department country reports on freedom of religion; a published corpus from a growing number of universities; OSCE regional initiatives in Europe; human rights courts for redress of grievances; the UN meeting of spiritual and religious leaders; The Hague Seminar on Freedom of Religion or Belief in the OSCE; the Madrid conference on education for tolerance; and local and national councils on freedom of religion or belief. We offer here a range of additional suggestions for improvement. Clearly different players in the field have different priorities and abilities, but we hope that by presenting a wide-ranging agenda for the future we can stimulate additional avenues for thought and action in numerous different quarters.

As Hilde Frafjord Johnson, at that time the Norwegian Minister of International Development and Human Rights, indicated in her closing remarks at the Oslo Conference on Freedom of Religion or Belief in 1998, a "key point of departure" in recommendations "must be the UN Special Rapporteur on Freedom of Religion or

Tore Lindholm, W. Cole Durham, Jr., Bahia G. Tahzib-Lie (eds.), Facilitating Freedom of Religion or Belief: A Deskbook, *843–851. © 2004 Koninklijke Brill NV.*

Belief" because of its significant worldwide scope. The office of the Special Rapporteur needs greater funding and support to be able to continue monitoring trends worldwide at a country level, disseminating information to the public, making direct calls on governments, mediating in cases of conflict, and coordinating with other UN mechanisms, especially the Commission on Human Rights. Given the limited resources of the Special Rapporteur's office, the work done has been exemplary. But a limit has been reached on what can be done by the UN Special Rapporteur to protect freedom of religion or belief without increased funding and staff support. Only a small fraction of the member states of the UN have ever been monitored for compliance with the articles of the 1981 Declaration. Yet the Special Rapporteur has been charged by the UN Commission on Human Rights with performing this task in a fair and impartial way. As Theo van Boven suggests, the Special Rapporteur's effectiveness would also be enhanced if the Commission engaged in substantive debate with the Special Rapporteur on his annual reports.

The former High Commissioner for Human Rights and her successor are also to be congratulated for developing a number of initiatives to establish more effective working methods and coordination between their office and the UN Human Rights Committee, UN Commission on Human Rights, UN Special Rapporteurs, Working Groups, and other UN organs and bodies. But a coordinated management plan, with a commitment targeted at support for Article 18 of the International Covenant on Civil and Political Rights and the 1981 UN Declaration has not been written by the United Nations. This is necessary to raise outside funds for the UN to promote freedom of religion or belief and help others who wish to cooperate with the UN in a wide variety of programs to promote the Declaration. As indicated in the Oslo Declaration, a coordinated plan is also needed to focus the resources of the UN and all its specialized agencies and bodies on problems involving freedom of religion and belief.

The Office of the High Commissioner on Human Rights and the Special Rapporteur have made great strides in using the internet and creating databases to facilitate gathering, analysis, synthesis, and sharing of data, which needs to continue. These offices have done important work in raising the profile of violations of freedom of religion and belief, but they need additional resources and staff to be able to effectively address their broad mandates.

The work of the Special Rapporteur and the UN not only needs greater support from governments and the UN, but also from religious and belief organizations, NGOs, and the academic community. Faith communities and NGOs can provide monitoring of violations and information on best practices of governments. They can also make greater use of existing UN mechanisms, both at the level of the Human Rights Committee and other treaty bodies, as well as through the work of the Special Rapporteur.

Academic partners and research institutes are also needed to provide the research and collection of documents and information. For example, there is a growing body of religious, philosophical, and scientific research into the root causes of intolerance and discrimination, but very little of this research has been made available in simplified form for analysis by the UN The 2001 Madrid conference was a positive step forward and should lead to efforts to fund an international strategy for school education. A 1989 UN Sub-Commission report stated a need for "solid preparatory work on the basis of sound research and careful analysis."

Another proposal to give greater research support to the UN is the suggestion to set up a research institute in Geneva, roughly modeled on the US Commission on International Religious Freedom, with a staff of ten to fifteen experts and a yearly budget of around $3 million USD. Funding would come from governments and private donors interested in supporting freedom of religion and belief. The institute would be independent of the UN, but it would give support to the Office of the High Commissioner for Human Rights and the Special Rapporteur and would launch a truly international effort to promote tolerance and prevent discrimination based on religion or belief. It could be set up as a three-year pilot program to help carry out the mandate of the 1981 Declaration and work with initiatives on freedom of religion or belief throughout the world. This is one approach to addressing the core problem that the Special Rapporteur needs mechanisms for reliable support, both academic and financial. We recognize the biases and problems that arise when support comes from any particular group of states or institutions. Additional thought should be given to other ways to support the Special Rapporteur without compromising the work of his office.

Other academic studies, discussed later in this chapter, could also benefit the UN, but they need financial support from governments, religions, and private foundations to be realized. For example, the Human Rights Committee's General Comment on Article 18 of the ICCPR, which has made a significant contribution to the interpretation and application of this provision, is relatively accessible (and contained in an appendix to this volume). But, as Martin Scheinin noted during the Oslo Conference, the Human Rights Committee's Concluding Observations under reporting procedures are emerging as a kind of case law that needs to be made more accessible in printed and electronic form. Professor Scheinin's chapter provides an excellent introduction to the work and case law of the Human Rights Committee, and provides examples of Concluding Observations relevant to freedom of religion or belief, but additional work remains to be done.

Professor Scheinin has also recommended the use of external academic support for the work of the Committee. In general, he noted that the Human Rights Committee (as well as other treaty bodies) is inadequately resourced, which endangers the quality of the Committee's work and creates a backlog of reports and complaints to be considered. He emphasized that urgent action is needed to secure permanent secretariat assistance, in particular to secure a coherent approach to cases under the Optional Protocol.

There has been no multilateral government cooperation on the 1981 Declaration since the 1984 UN Geneva Seminar, with the exception of the annual Special Rapporteur reports to the Human Rights Commission. At the Oslo Conference, Hilde Frafjord Johnson suggested that "the idea of a Working Group in a UN context should be considered seriously. Consultations, probably informal ones, should be held on the subject with governments, religious groups, and humanist communities." In 1986 the study by Odio Benito, currently second-vice president of Costa Rica, proposed a working group within the Commission to engage in the elaboration of a draft convention on freedom of religion or belief, but no action was taken. Actions that have been taken by governments, while positive steps forward, have been regional or bilateral in character, such as those by the European Commission, Council of Europe, and OSCE, or have been the efforts of one government, such as the US bodies created under

IRFA. This would lead some to argue for an international convention on freedom of religion or belief. While positivization of norms can be helpful by giving a locus for efforts for change, we feel that at this point international work on behalf of freedom of religion or belief would be more effectively spent elsewhere. Certainly this is a complex question, but other ways and means of enhancing international legal protection of religion or belief can be more fruitfully pursued using existing bodies and agreements. Some such current needs include the adoption of additional general comments, general recommendations, or suggestions by supervisory human rights treaty bodies.

UNESCO has also played an important role in promoting dialogue on issues of religious tolerance, peace, and interreligious understanding. As Doudou Diene, Director of the United Nation's Division of Intercultural Dialogue, indicated in his chapter, UNESCO should continue and expand its series of conferences and professorships dedicated to these issues and find ways to work with national governments, NGOs, and religious communities to raise these issues. The Oslo Declaration likewise calls on UNESCO "to expand work for peace through religious and cultural dialogue and encourage intensified co-operation with UNESCO in this field."

The UN has been a valuable tool and can accomplish much more in the field of religious tolerance and freedom, but active protection of freedom of religion and belief cannot be limited to the UN level. Important initiatives at regional and national levels have been introduced in recent years and should continue. For example, regional human rights treaty bodies, particularly the European Court of Human Rights, have been playing an important role in increasing awareness of religious freedom violations and enforcing and raising regional standards. As additional countries continue to join the Council of Europe system, these bodies must continue to keep standards high and assist countries in transition in developing a respect for rule of law and understanding the ramifications of guaranteeing freedom of religion or belief. Other regional treaty bodies similarly need to increase their effectiveness in implementing the protections of freedom of religion and belief contained in regional treaties.

The Organization for Security and Co-operation in Europe's Office for Democratic Institutions and Human Rights has also played an increasingly important role in providing technical support and consultations with member states on freedom of religion or belief, particularly through its Advisory Panel of Experts on Freedom of Religion or Belief. OSCE participating states should continue to give support and funding to this body.

The OSCE, under the Romanian chair-in-office and together with the Dutch Foreign Ministry, has also made a major contribution through organizing a very successful conference in The Hague on freedom of religion and belief in the OSCE region in June 2001. This seminar focused attention on the issues of registration and recognition of religion and belief communities and restrictions on the activities of religion and belief communities. The papers from the conference, together with reports by the Dutch Advisory Council on International Affairs and a compilation of OSCE standards regarding freedom of religion or belief, were published and provide a very useful resource.

The greatest changes, however, do not need to come at the level of the UN or international organizations, but in the laws and actions of governments. As Hilde Frafjord Johnson indicated, "[g]overnments are clearly the entities that most urgently need to change their behaviour. . . . The direct responsibility for human rights violations will always lie with governments. It is also an important task for governments to address violations of freedom of religion or belief when they take place in other states."

This volume raises a number of challenges for states—for example, charging them to respect conscientious objection, the right to engage in religious persuasion, the rights of persons in restricted settings, and the autonomy of religious organizations. Conscientious objection is a complex issue overlapping with the limits of religious freedom, but states must be encouraged to allow as much conscientious objection as permitted by international law. While religious persuasion should be culturally sensitive, states should carefully limit direct or indirect regulations of proselyting by following international instruments. It is significant in this regard to remember that the rationale of preserving historical religious traditions cannot itself be used to support limitations on manifestations of freedom of religion and belief under international norms. In this volume governments are likewise warned to avoid granting excessive discretion or using restrictive registration laws to restrict religious freedom. Harsh registration laws can be particularly problematic, because they are often used to deny basic religious freedoms to religious communities, as highlighted in the 2001 OSCE The Hague Seminar.

Finally, numerous thoughtful chapters demonstrate the obligations of governments to respect the rights of humanist groups, women, children, and new religious movements. International norms give special attention to women and children and extend protection to belief systems as well as to religions. States should avoid infringing on the religious freedom of new religious movements by using existing criminal law to regulate harmful actions rather than stigmatizing or categorizing groups as "sects" or "cults."

We urge government leaders and all people with influence on governmental policy to highlight these issues, as detailed in chapters in this book, and to push for change and improvement.

While governments are the key actors affecting the freedom of religion or belief of their citizens, and this book has done much to point out areas of needed improvement, this conclusion focuses primarily on inter-governmental and non-governmental bodies, which can often effectively force change on governments. The chapters by Janne Haaland Matlary and Jeremy Gunn illustrate some ways that intergovernmental bodies or NGOs can promote change in governmental actions and legislation. The Oslo Conference, which led to this book, also serves as an example of the effectiveness of building international networks to promote freedom of religion or belief. Transnational networks of NGOs, faith and belief communities, academics, and concerned individuals can have a tremendous power to promote change, and we strongly support efforts to build and strengthen such coalitions and networks.

Academics and NGOs also need to increase violation monitoring and research in relevant fields. As important as the right to freedom of religion or belief is, it is clear that much research needs to be done if the persistent problems in this area are to be addressed in a sensitive, competent, credible, and effective manner. Issues of freedom of religion or belief are imbedded in differing national histories and interact with a broad range of political, cultural, ethnic, and economic issues, as well as with a variety of other fundamental rights, such as freedom of speech, freedom of association, and equality rights, to name a few. Unlike other areas of human rights, there is often not the same degree of consensus on exactly what constitutes a violation of the right to freedom of religion or belief, and the outer limits of protection are less certain. Moreover, empirical data on acknowledged violations is sadly lacking. In addition, comparative legal materials that would facilitate understanding the legal setting in various countries is surprisingly difficult to obtain. This creates informational shortfalls for everyone working in the field. This volume is intended to bring together significant work by prominent thinkers in this area, but serves more as a thoughtful introduction to many of the key issues rather than as an exhaustive commentary.

We suggest some areas where additional research and dissemination of information is needed, along with specific research needs, below:

Legal Research Needs

- Copies of relevant international norms, international case law, general comments, national constitutional provisions, applicable laws, court and administrative decisions. The ideal would be to have these available in electronic form in original language and in English translation and translation into other major languages where feasible.[1]
- Bibliography of relevant research from countries around the world that can help expand comparative research on issues of freedom of religion or belief.
- Information on concrete resolutions of key issues of freedom of religion or belief.
- An up-to-date list of state parties to all applicable international treaties and reservations attached to provisions regarding freedom of religion or belief.

Minimum Standards

- Research and analysis are needed to further clarify minimum standards for compliance with international norms governing freedom of religion or belief. Such analysis needs to be as concrete as possible in order to develop clear standards for reporting violations. The research should take into account information and experience gained from international bodies; indeed the United Nations Human Rights Centre could undertake the research, provided adequate specialized staff is available.
- It is also helpful to identify what indicators manifest the presence or absence of freedom of religion or belief.
- Collection of information on actual cases is vital. Different persons or groups may assess the gravity of various situations differently, but it is vital to have the information collected in a reliable and credible way.

[1] A project to collect and post these on the internet is underway thanks to a consortium of universities and the OSCE's Advisory Panel of Experts on Freedom of Religion and Belief. The material is posted at <www.religlaw.org>.

Major Issues Needing Research

- Strategies that have proven successful in resolving tensions and implementing norms governing freedom of religion or belief.
- Ways that education can contribute to the development of a culture of tolerance.
- The connection of ecological issues and religion, particularly for indigenous peoples.
- Research that can provide background understanding and understanding of the context in which violations of freedom of religion or belief occur.
- Causes for erosion or disintegration of belief communities.
- Implications of globalization for freedom of religion or belief (e.g., whether increased tourism breeds disrespect for sacred places, objects, and rituals).
- Freedom to change one's religion (apostasy), and the effects of civil punishments for apostasy on community solidarity and loyalty.
- Coercion (including fraudulent or manipulative practices) in the conversion process.
- Tensions between women's issues and freedom of religion or belief and the need for a gender perspective in the application of this freedom.
- Legitimate limitations to manifesting freedom of religion or belief.
- Types of legal entities available to religious organizations for carrying out their affairs.

Practical Information Needed to Address Religious Freedom Issues Effectively

- Access to information on the nature and extent of violations of religious freedom for specific religious communities, and in general.
- Quantitative information on gross violations, including deaths, disappearances, torture, and other violations that are religion related.
- Networking information—sources of strategic information on lawyers, government officials, and others that can be helpful in addressing and redressing violations.

Dissemination of Information

- Urgent action networks should be developed.
- A database of useful websites on religious freedom issues or a webpage with helpful cross-links should be developed.
- A database of violations for human rights NGOs should be developed. Ideally this should have a form-based complaints submission procedure and gather information from NGOs for NGO reports and responses to the country reports of the Special Rapporteur and other reports. This should maintain links to other organizations and host electronic mailing lists.
- A website for human rights journalists with resource information and contacts on issues of current importance should be developed.

In addition to providing research and dissemination of information relating to freedom of religion or belief, NGOs, academic organizations, and governments can play a significant role through education. One form education can take is exchanges of students and other experts through training programs, conferences, consultations, and other such programs. This is significant not only for the collection and dissemination of information, but also for building the personal links that are crucial for effective networking. It is also vital for developing personnel with the competence and credibility necessary to effectively remedy infringement of freedom of religion or belief.

On another front, formal education programs constitute a key arena, as the Special Rapporteur has recognized, for creating a culture of tolerance. More information is needed on effective programs and curricular offerings that can promote tolerance and understanding. Follow-up from the Madrid Conference should lead to an effort to fund an international strategy for school education. Religion and belief communities can also play an important role in conflict resolution, as several of our authors note. We feel that such efforts, to be most effective, should be focused on cooperative social ventures rather than theological dialogue. Members and leaders of faith communities, by working together on practical issues affecting the community at large, such as child care, educational curricula, drugs, prison reform, etc., can form levels of trust, solidarity, and understanding that prevent deep conflict and misunderstanding from arising. The Oslo Coalition is hoping to encourage and promote dialogue and patterns of collaboration and cooperation across religious and life-stance divides in partner countries, working on the ground with representatives of belief communities, academics and students, NGOs and other activists, and government officials and students. The agenda for interreligious dialogue and cooperation is, of course, up to the needs and interests of the parties involved, at local or regional levels. Possible issues to be addressed are local or regional blockages in the implementation of national and international standards of freedom of religion or belief, spiritual and moral questions of principle, and—very important—pressing social issues in the wider society that cry for action by morally concerned groups and activists. Such practical cooperation also has the favorable indirect effect of facilitating mutual trust, solidarity, and friendships across traditional religious divides. The practice and theory of this is dealt with in several chapters in the book, and we have also experienced this as a multifaith editorial group.

For respect for freedom of religion and belief to be truly ingrained in society, however, an understanding of the importance of this right needs to be developed from within various faith and belief traditions, as suggested by Tore Lindholm in his chapter. Religious leaders, members, and academics can effectively promote freedom of religion by examining their respective belief communities' track record in dealing with the religious freedom of others and by looking carefully at their own belief systems and articulating and teaching principles supporting freedom of religion and belief from their own traditions.

As we all seek to develop and implement a deep understanding and commitment to religious freedom across our range of faiths and belief systems, we will establish a broad base of support that will carry the right to freedom of religion or belief through the turbulent times in which we live.

In conclusion, we quote a story related by Hilde Frafjord Johnson:

> On Christmas Day 1914, the British and German soldiers left their trenches in Flanders and sang Christmas carols for each other in no-man's land. This was a brave and moving gesture, a great example of 'cultural exchange,' even in time of war. It was an expression of humanity in the midst of appalling inhumanity. However, that terrible war was to go on for another four years. The gesture changed nothing—except, perhaps, in the hearts of those who made it. And that is the point about culture and about religion or belief. In the darkest hour it can be an expression of ideals, strength of character, hope and our common aspirations. It can be an expression of human dignity. And it can, when the circumstances are right, be the spark that sets off change, and the driving force that makes the difference.

Religion and belief have transformative power in the lives of individuals and communities. May the expression of belief in all our lives give us the strength and resources to respect and protect others' similar rights and thus transform our world.

Epilogue

By the President of the International Advisory Council, The Oslo Coalition on Freedom of Religion or Belief

Bishop Gunnar Stålsett

Freedom of religion or belief belongs to the fundamental freedoms of every human being, as has been abundantly documented and analyzed in this important book. It is a right of individuals, which, at the same time, safeguards religious communities and life stance associations, and it is a matter of great consequence for any society.

This fundamental right is sometimes ignored or even violated by religious institutions and organizations, as well as in the name of secular ideologies. The history of religious oppression and persecution is long and painful, for religions and states alike. Many "unholy alliances" have been built in order to keep things holy in their circumscribed place and out of the public square. The twentieth century, which in so many ways boasted tolerance, witnessed some of the harshest violations of religious liberty in human history.

The German philosopher Friedrich Nietzsche, who died at the dawn of the twentieth century, is credited, or criticized, for two basic assumptions that are indelibly imprinted on at least the western and northern hemisphere. The notion of the "Ubermensch" and the proclamation of "the death of God", were both echoed in one of the bloodiest centuries in human history. However, neither socialist experiments nor relentless capitalist expansion satisfied people's transcendent aspirations. They promoted, instead, gross materialistic orientations.

Towards the end of the twentieth century a new awareness of the spiritual dimension of human existence began to challenge atheistic and agnostic views. Religion began again to be seen as relevant both to the individual and to society. In Europe this did not necessarily mean an invigoration of established religion. Individually tailor-made faiths, cults and pseudo-religious movements filled a void, and became challengers of traditional faiths and beliefs.

One notable change has been the recent resurgence of religion in the public arena. Social movements and political reforms have been pushed with new vigor by lay-people in many religions. Religion is gradually gaining a place in the academic discourse, in areas of philosophy, ethics, psychology and medicine. Religion is no longer

Tore Lindholm, W. Cole Durham, Jr., Bahia G. Tahzib-Lie (eds.), Facilitating Freedom of Religion or Belief: A Deskbook, *853–854.*

the (totally) lost dimension of statecraft. Diplomats, politicians, military leaders, all have had to reorient themselves to relate to religion not only as a reality in national and international conflicts, but also as a possible contribution to their solution.

Religion-based peace groups have always existed, but now such groups are beginning to be an integral part of political and diplomatic efforts of peace-making.

The slogan "no peace without peace between religions" (Hans Küng) has a message to many conflict areas, such as Northern Ireland, the Middle East, Kosovo and the Sudan. In the Middle East the three monotheistic religions of Judaism, Islam and Christianity are put to a test. Holy land and holy sites are notions that carry deep emotion with believers. And conflicts about the same land and the same holy city seem to be the most difficult to address.

Freedom of religion may become one of the major victims of the terror attack of 11 September 2001, against the USA. In the wake of these acts of extreme violence, in which innocent men, women and children were targets, we may hear a new cry of freedom from religion. We may soon be faced with arguments like this: Religion is tantamount to hate, violence and terror, and in order to overcome this threat against humanity freedom of religion must be curbed!

It is in this perspective that work for freedom of religion or belief assumes new importance. The great challenge is to use that freedom to begin to tap the reservoir of religions and secular life-stances for reconciliation and justice. The truth claim of any faith is tested in its contribution to promote human dignity and to sustain life for future generations. Every religious community and every life-stance association must learn to speak clearly and consistently in defense of the equal freedom of adherents of all faiths and beliefs. Therefore freedom of religion is experienced in dialogue between equals, without compromising the integrity of each participant. In an age of globalization and interdependence the universal claim of religions and beliefs can only be addressed in the spirit of dialogue and cooperation across religious divides. Any other approach would be to the detriment of all.

It is my firm conviction that more attention needs to be devoted to the role and place of religion in the shaping of a more peaceful world with deeper respect for human rights and the requirements of nature. To that end higher priority need to be granted to the study and promotion of freedom of religion and belief both in religious teaching, secular ideologies, academic institutions and in national and international bodies, such as the United Nations. This book documents that there is a great number of issues yet to be resolved and legislated, but also that there is an abundance of competent and dedicated people who are committed to the cause of freedom of religion and belief.

The language of faith is prayer, so I offer my prayers for the cause of freedom of every human being as a reflection of its inherent worth and dignity.

Oslo November 1st 2001

Gunnar Stålsett
Bishop of Oslo, Church of Norway
President of the International Advisory Council,
The Oslo Coalition on Freedom of Religion or Belief

Contributors

JOLANTA AMBROSEWICZ-JACOBS is a researcher and lecturer at the Centre for European Studies of the Jagiellonian University in Cracow. A native of Vilnius, she holds an M.A. and Ph.D. from the Jagiellonian University. She was a Fellow at the Center for the Study of Human Rights at Columbia University (1996), at the Simon Wiesenthal Center in New York (1997), and at the Carnegie Council on Ethics and International Affairs (2000–2001). Ms. Ambrosewicz-Jacobs is currently co-chair of the working group "Education for Tolerance" of the OSCE/ODIHR Advisory Panel of Experts on Freedom of Religion or Belief. She is a member of the European Consortium for Political Research's Standing Group on Extremism & Democracy and is involved in numerous educational projects that focus on social, ethnic, and religious prejudices, intercultural education, and politics of reconciliation. Her areas of research and publications focus on the evaluation of effects of education on attitudes, mechanisms of xenophobia, and intolerance.

ABDELFATTAH AMOR is Chair of the United Nations Human Rights Committee. He was appointed United Nations Special Rapporteur on Freedom of Religion or Belief in 1993. Mr. Amor is currently based at the faculty of juridical, political, and social science at the University of Tunis and has worked as a higher education lecturer since 1979.

ARCHBISHOP DR. ANASTASIOS (YANNOULATOS) OF TIRANA AND ALL ALBANIA is Professor emeritus of the University of Athens and a Corresp. Member of the Academy of Athens. He studied Theology at the University of Athens and History of Religions at the Universities of Hamburg and Marburg, Germany, with the Alexander von Humbold scholarship. Archbishop Anastasios received a B.D. from the University of Athens, highest distinction, a Th.D. from the University of Athens, summa cum laude, a Th.D. (honoris causa) from three Theological Faculties, a Ph.D. (honoris causa) from seven universities, and an M.D. (honoris causa) from the University of Patras. Archbishop Anastasios is an Honorary Member of the Theological Academy of Moscow. He was a full Professor of History of Religions at the University of Athens (1976–1992) and Dean of the Theological Faculty (1983–1986). He was ordained Bishop of Androussa in 1972 for the position of the General Director of Apostoliki Diakonia of the Church of Greece (until 1991) and was acting Archbishop of East Africa from 1981–1990. He is Patriarchal Exarch of the Ecumenical Patriarchate in Albania (1991) and Archbishop of

Tore Lindholm, W. Cole Durham, Jr., Bahia G. Tahzib-Lie (eds.), Facilitating Freedom of Religion or Belief: A Deskbook, *855–870.*

Albania (since June 1992). He was Moderator of the Commission of World Mission and Evangelism of the World Council of Churches (1984–1991). Archbishop Anastasios is the author of eleven books, including *Islam: A General Survey* (1976, 11th ed. 2002) and *Universality and Orthodoxy* (2000, 2002). He has published more than 230 essays and articles in various languages. He has been honored with many international awards, such as the Grand Cross of the Order of Honour of the Hellenic Republic (1997) and the Athenagoras Human Rights Award (2001). Archbishop Anastasios is a leading Orthodox scholar in the field of interreligious dialogue and has struggled as a peacemaker within Albania and the Balkans.

EILEEN BARKER is Professor of Sociology with Special Reference to the Study of Religion at the London School of Economics. For over thirty years Prof. Barker has focused her research on "cults," "sects," new religious movements, and the social reactions such movements create. Additionally, since 1989 she has spent much of her time investigating changes in the religious situation of post-communist countries. Prof. Barker has produced over 200 publications, including her award-winning books, *The Making of a Moonie: Choice or Brainwashing?* (Oxford: Blackwell, 1984) and *New Religious Movements: A Practical Introduction* (London: HMSO, 1989). In the late 1980s, with support from the British Government and mainstream churches, Prof. Barker founded INFORM, a charity that provides accurate, objective, and up-to-date information on new religions. Prof. Barker is the only non-American to have been elected President of the Society for the Scientific Study of Religion.

JEAN BAUBÉROT is Professor of History and Sociology of Laïcity and directs the Group of Sociology and Religions and Laïcity. Additionally, Prof. Baubérot is the president of the Ecole Pratique de Hautes Etudes, Sorbonne, where he teaches. Recently the Académie Française awarded Prof. Baubérot a prize for his publication *"Une haine oubliée", l'antiprotestantisme avant le pacte laïque*, (avec Valentine Zuber) (Paris: Albin Michel, 2000). Prof. Baubérot is a Doctor of History and a Doctor of Literature and Social Sciences.

LEE BOOTHBY is a Senior Partner at the law firm Boothby & Yingst and is President of the International Commission on Freedom of Conscience. Mr. Boothby also serves as Vice President for the Council on Religious Freedom and is Vice President for the International Academy for Freedom of Religion and Belief. Mr. Boothby has been lead counsel in trials throughout the United States and has argued before the United States Supreme Court on important First Amendment issues. He has consulted with numerous governments in Eastern and Central Europe about church-state relations and international religious rights and is the author of numerous law review and magazine articles.

KARI ELISABETH BØRRESEN is Professor of Historical Theology/Gender Studies in the Department of Church History at Oslo University. Prof. Børresen has worked as a Research Fellow for the Norwegian Research Council and the Department of Systematic Theology at Arhus University and as a Research Professor for the Royal Norwegian Ministry of Culture. Prof. Børresen was a consultant for the World Council of Churches in Genève, she is a member of the Conseil de l'association internationale d'études patristiques, a member of several advisory boards for university research projects, and the Co-Director of a research project at Upsala University. In 1992 she received a Doctor Theologiae Honoris Causa from Uppsala University. Since 1995 she has been a member of the Norwegian Academy of Science and Letters. Prof. Børresen has published eleven books and numerous articles. She received her Doctor Philosophiae from the University of Oslo, and she has studied abroad in Paris, Poitiers, Heidelberg, Mainz, Oxford, and Rome.

H. VICTOR CONDÉ is Adjunct Professor of International Human Rights and Humanitarian Law and Professor in Residence at the Strasbourg Human Rights Program of Trinity Law School, California. He received an L.L.M. in International Human Rights Law at the University of Essex, England and a J.D. from the University of California at Davis. Prof. Condé fulfilled a United Nations legal internship and received an M.A. in International Human Rights at Simon Greenleaf University, California. He has a *Diplome* in International and Comparative Human Rights Law from the International Institute of Human Rights in Strasbourg, France. His specializations include religious freedom and international law, the convergence of international human rights, humanitarian law, and international criminal law, and human rights education. Prof. Condé is author of *Human Rights in the United States: A Dictionary and Documents* (Santa Barbara, Ca.: ABC-CLIO, 2000) and *A Handbook of International Human Rights Terminology* (Lincoln, Nebr.: Univ. of Nebraska Press, 1999). He is also a member of Amnesty International USA, the Human Rights Education Committee (western U.S.), and the Legal Support Network. He is a practicing lawyer admitted in California and Hawaii.

ÖZLEM DENLI works as a Research Fellow of the Norwegian University of Science and Technology, Trondheim. Her doctoral project at the intersection of politics and philosophy is titled "Islam and Human Rights: The Public Significance of Liberal Islamism in Turkey." Ms. Denli was born in Istanbul, Turkey in 1966. She majored in Political Science and Sociology at Bosphorus University in Istanbul, Turkey. Ms. Denli did postgraduate studies at the University of Oslo and received a Cand. Polit. degree in the Department of Political Science of the University of Oslo. Her thesis was titled "Islam and the Freedom of Religion or Belief: Perspectives from Contemporary Turkey."

DOUDOU DIENE directs the United Nations' Division of Intercultural Dialogue. Mr. Diene worked as Senegal's representative to UNESCO until 1977, when he joined the UNESCO Secretariat as Director of the United Nations' Educational, Scientific, and Cultural Organization Office. From 1985 until 1987, Mr. Diene worked as Deputy Assistant Director-General in the External Relations Sector, as Spokesman for the Director-General, and as Action Director of the Office of Public Information. Mr. Diene directed the task force for the Silk Roads Project until December 1988, at which time he was appointed Director of a project entitled "Integral Study of the Silk Roads: Roads of Dialogue." Within the framework of these Silk Roads projects, Mr. Diene organized several international expeditions to retrace the ancient silk roads in China, Mongolia, and Nepal. He has published a number of articles and has coauthored a book. Mr. Diene graduated both from the Institut d'Etudes Politiques de Paris (Sciences-Po) and from the University of Caen Law School. He also holds a

Ph.D. in Law from the University of Paris. Since his retirement from UNESCO in December 2001, Mr. Diene has been elected by the United Nations Commission on Human Rights as "United Nations Special Rapporteur on Contemporary Forms of Racism, Racial Discrimination, Xenophobia and Related Intolerance."

W. COLE DURHAM, JR. is Gates University Professor of Law at Brigham Young University. He also serves as Co-Chair of the OSCE/ODIHR Advisory Panel of Experts on Freedom of Religion or Belief and as Vice-President of the International Academy for Freedom of Religion and Belief. A graduate of Harvard College and Harvard Law School, Prof. Durham has been heavily involved in comparative law scholarship, with a special emphasis on comparative constitutional law and church-state relations. Prof. Durham has served as the Secretary of the American Society of Comparative Law and is an associate member of the prestigious International Academy of Comparative Law in Paris. He currently serves on the boards of the DePaul Center for Church-State Studies, the J.M. Dawson Institute for Church-State Studies, the Oslo Coalition on Freedom of Religion or Belief, and the International Center for Not-for-Profit Law, and has also served as Chair of both the Comparative Law Section and the Law and Religion Section of the American Association of Law Schools. He has published widely on comparative church-state themes and has testified in Congress, at the state level, and in various foreign countries on religious freedom issues.

INGE EIDSVÅG directed the Fridtjof Nansen Academy in Lillehammer from 1986 to 1998. Mr. Eidsvåg now holds the Academy's Free Speech Grant. As a writer and lecturer, Mr. Eidsvåg has initiated and participated in several dialogue projects, has edited six books, and has authored five books. In 1992 he was awarded the Bridgebuilder Prize.

MALCOLM D. EVANS is Professor of Public International Law at the University of Bristol. Prof. Evans researches the international protection of human rights with particular emphasis on freedom of religion; he also researches torture prevention and maritime law. His principal publications include *Relevant Circumstances and Maritime Delimitation* (Oxford: Oxford University Press, 1989); *Religious Liberty and International Law in Europe* (Cambridge: Cambridge University Press, 1997); with Professor Rod Morgan, *Preventing Torture* (Oxford: Oxford University Press, 1998); and *Protecting Prisoners* (Oxford: Oxford University Press, 1999). Additionally, he has contributed chapters concerning religion and human rights to a number of edited collections, including most recently Edge, ed., *Law and Religion in Contemporary Society* (Aldershot: Ashgate, 2000); Adhar, ed., *Law and Religion* (Aldershot: Ashgate, 2000); Lewis and O'Dair, eds., *Current Legal Issues: Law and Religion* (Oxford: Oxford University Press, 2001). Prof. Evans is a member of the International Law Association Committee on International Human Rights Law and Practice and is a board member of the Association for the Prevention of Torture. He has also acted as a consultant to the Council of Europe on religious liberty issues.

WILLY FAUTRÉ is Director of the Brussels-based group Human Rights Without Frontiers and is a member of the Association of Religious Journalists in Belgium. Mr. Fautré is also the press correspondent for the American religious news agency Compass Direct. In 1978 Mr. Fautré founded EGLISI, a press agency in French and Dutch for freedom of religion and belief. Mr. Fautré worked as the Editor-in-Chief of EGLISI from 1978 to 1996. He was also the Project Manager of a Phare Democracy Programme on Religious Minorities in Albania, Bulgaria, and Romania from 1995 to 1996. Mr. Fautré was the former Chargé de Mission at the Cabinet of the Ministry of Education for linguistic exchanges between French- and Dutch-speaking students in Belgium. Mr. Fautré authored a book titled *Nos Prisonniers du Goulag* (S.N., 1980) and has participated in human rights missions in Albania, Armenia, Azerbaijan, Bulgaria, Czech Republic, Georgia, Greece, Hungary, Latvia, Nicaragua, Panama, and Russia.

ALAIN GARAY is a practicing attorney in the Court of Appeals in Paris, France. Additionally, Mr. Garay has defended several individuals on freedom of conscience and religion issues before the European Court of Human Rights. His past cases before the European Court have included human rights disputes with Austria, Greece, Bulgaria, France, Romania, and Russia. Mr. Garay has authored numerous legal articles on civil liberties, including a study on anti-sect activism in 1999 that was published in French under the title "L'activisme anti-sectes—de l'assistance à l'amalgame" (New York: The Edwin Mellen Press, 1999). Mr. Garay traveled to Latvia for the Council of Europe to provide an expert opinion on matters involving religious freedom and has also acted as an advisor on freedom of religion in Cuba and Vietnam. Mr. Garay is a member of the Council of Presidents of the World Association on Medical Law and is the cofounder of a Latin American medical law association, Associación Latinoamericana de Derecho Médico in San José, Costa Rica. Mr. Garay has a degree in political science.

NAZILA GHANEA lectures on international law, human rights, and is the Course Convenor for the M.A. in Understanding and Securing Human Rights at the University of London, Institute of Commonwealth Studies. She has participated in a number of United Nations events such as the Commission on Human Rights, the Sub-Commission Working Group on Minorities, the Beijing World Conference on Women, and the Copenhagen Plus Five Review. Prof. Ghanea has also worked with a number of international NGOs in the United Kingdom and in Geneva. Prof. Ghanea's doctoral research and publications deal with religious minorities in Iran and under Islam, human rights and religious liberty, and the U.N. human rights machinery. She has authored the recent monograph, *Human Rights, the United Nations and the Bahá'ís in Iran* (The Hague: Kluwer Law International, 2003), and has edited the forthcoming collection *The Challenge of Religious Discrimination at the Dawn of the New Millennium* (The Hague: Martinus Nijhoff, forthcoming 2003).

URBAN GIBSON is the Chairman of a network of OSCE-interested organizations in Sweden. He is also a member of the OSCE/ODIHR Advisory Panel of Experts on Freedom of Religion or Belief, Working Group III: Education/Awareness for Tolerance, and is a member of the Council and the Executive Board of the International Peace Bureau (IPB) in Geneva. Mr. Gibson has been invited to speak on OSCE regulations of Freedom of Religion and Belief at several conferences arranged by the International Academy for Freedom of Religion and Belief, the OSCE Advisory Panel of Freedom of Religion, and governments in Latvia, Estonia, Ukraine, and Lithuania. Mr. Gibson has worked to strengthen the role of freedom of religion in the Organization for Security and Co-operation in Europe and especially in the Office for Democratic Institutions and

Human Rights. Since 1975 Mr. Gibson has been a member of the Church of Sweden Assembly. For some years he has also been a member of the Church of Sweden Board and the Board of the Nordic Ecumenical Council. He is Senior Advisor to the Swedish Fellowship of Reconciliation. Mr. Gibson has been a teacher, director of a Swedish headmaster organization, Mayor of Sollentuna (a suburb of Stockholm), and President of the Church of Sweden Fund Stock Company.

RAJAJI RAMANADHA BABU GOGINENI is the Executive Director of the International Humanist and Ethical Union and Editor of *International Humanist News.* Additionally, Mr. Gogineni is a member of the International Advisory Board of the Oslo Coalition on Freedom of Religion or Belief and is Secretary to both the IHEU Committee on Universal Values and the IHEU Committee on Religious Abuse of Children. Originally from India, Mr. Gogineni was Joint-Secretary of the Indian Radical Humanist Association, General Secretary of the Rationalist Association of India, and Trustee of the Indian Renaissance Institute. Before moving to London for his IHEU appointment, he taught French at the Alliance Francaise of Hyderabad in India (1987–1996), where he was in charge of the Alliance Francaise's Cultural Centre as well as the Scientific Resource Centre and its scientific and commercial translation wing. Mr. Gogineni has coedited two books: *Rationalist Essays* and *The Humanist Way*, published by the Rationalist Association of India, and he regularly publishes articles in various newspapers, magazines, and journals in Europe, North America, and India—in English and in French. His articles have been translated into German, Polish, Finnish, Norwegian, Swedish, Telugu, and Hindi. He has lectured in Mexico, the Netherlands, Belgium, Sweden, Finland, Israel, Italy, France, India, the UK, and Norway. Babu Gogineni has a degree in Microbiology (Nizam College, 1988) and a Postgraduate Diploma in International Trade (1991).

LARS GULE is Secretary General of the Norwegian Humanist Association. Before becoming Secretary General, he worked as a researcher and research administrator at the Chr. Michelsen Institute and the University of Bergen. Mr. Gule researches political philosophy and specializes in Arab and Islamic political thinking, human rights, and religion. Mr. Gule defended his dissertation, "Social Development and Political Progress in Two Traditions—A Conceptual and Comparative Analysis of Western and Arab-Islamic Ideas of Social and Political Change and Improvement" in 2001. Mr. Gule has an M.A. in Philosophy from the University of Bergen.

T. JEREMY GUNN is Executive Fellow and Guest Scholar for the United States Institute of Peace in Washington, D.C. and has served as the Principle Adviser to the Ambassador-at-Large for International Religious Freedom at the U.S. Department of State, Bureau of Democracy, Human Rights, and Labor. He practiced international law, appellate law, and church and state litigation with the law firm Covington & Burling in Washington, D.C. and was a law clerk for the United States District Court in Boston, Massachusetts. Mr. Gunn has served as a member of several advisory panels on religion, including the International Advisory Board for the World Report on Freedom of Conscience and Belief. Additionally, he was General Counsel for the National Committee for Public Education and Religious Liberty. Mr. Gunn authored a book titled *A Standard for Repair: The Establishment Clause, Equality, and Natural Rights* (New York: Garland,

1992) and has published numerous articles. Mr. Gunn received a B.A. from Brigham Young University, an A.M. from the University of Chicago, a J.D. from Boston University School of Law, and a Ph.D. from Harvard University.

THORBJØRN JAGLAND has been Leader of the Norwegian Labor Party since 1992, was Prime Minister of Norway from October 1996 to October 1997, and was Minister of Foreign Affairs from March 2000 to October 2001. Mr. Jagland has been Chairman of the Committee on Foreign Affairs in Stortinget (Norway's Parliament) since October 2000.

URSULA KING is Professor Emerita, Senior Research Fellow, and Associate Member of the Institute for Advanced Studies, University of Bristol, England, and Professorial Research Associate at the Centre for Gender and Religions Research, School of Oriental and African Studies, University of London. From 1989–1997 she chaired the Department of Theology and Religious Studies at the University of Bristol, where she also directed the Centre for Comparative Studies in Religion and Gender (CCSRG) for several years. From 1998–2001 she held a visiting Chair in Feminist Theology at the University of Oslo. Prof. King has published several books on religion and gender, including the forthcoming volume, coedited with Tina Beattie, on *Religion, Gender and Diversity: Cross-Cultural Perspectives* (Continuum, 2004). She has also published extensively on the French thinker Pierre Teilhard de Chardin, and on contemporary spirituality. Currently Prof. King is researching comparative gender perspectives in world religions and is acting as consultant on gender and religion entries for the second edition of *The Encyclopedia of Religion* (1st ed., M. Eliade, 1987). Prof. King has received several degrees, including an STL (Paris), M.A. (Delhi), Ph.D. (London), FRSA, and honorary doctorates from the universities of Edinburgh (1996), Oslo (2000), and Dayton (2003).

LENA LARSEN is Coordinator of the Oslo Coalition on Freedom of Religion or Belief (since March 1999). Since March 2000 Ms. Larsen has been President of the Islamic Council of Norway. She is a member of the Committee for Revision of the Mandatory Religious Education Curriculum taught in Norwegian Schools, appointed by the Ministry of Education, Research, and Church Affairs, and she has served as a consultant for quality control of the presentation of Islam in textbooks from 1996 to 1998. Her publications include *Religion, livssyn, og menneskerettigheter i Norge* (Religion, Life Stance, and Human Rights in Norway), ed. Eidsvåg and Larsen (Oslo: Universitetsforlaget, 1997); *Dialog med og uten slør* (Dialogue with and without the veil), Grung and Larsen (Oslo: Pax, 2000). Ms. Larsen is also Associate Editor of the present volume. She received a Master's degree in Religious Studies (Cand. Philol.) from the University of Oslo in 1995. Her M.A. thesis deals with conversions to Islam in Norway: "Velkommen til en stor familie: islam og konversjon i norsk kontekst" (Welcome to a Vast Family: Islam and Conversion in the Norwegian Context).

NATAN LERNER is Professor of International Law at the Interdisciplinary Center in Herzliya, Israel and also teaches International Human Rights at Tel Aviv University. Prof. Lerner practiced law in Buenos Aires for several years. Later he worked at the International Affairs Department of the World Jewish Congress in New York. In addition, he has served as the Director of the World Jewish Congress Branch in Israel.

Prof. Lerner has lectured at Universities in Mexico, Venezuela, Spain, the United States, Japan, and Australia. He has also published legal articles in English, Spanish, and Hebrew on international law, human rights, minority rights, and religious freedom. Prof. Lerner's more recent publications include *Religion, Beliefs and International Human Rights* (New York: Orbis, 2000); *Group Rights and Discrimination in International Law* (Dordrecht: Martinus Nijhoff, 1991); and *The U.N. Convention on the Elimination of All Forms of Racial Discrimination* (Alphen aan den Rijn, 1980). Prof. Lerner graduated from the Buenos Aires University School of Law.

TORE LINDHOLM is Associate Professor at the University of Oslo's Norwegian Centre for Human Rights (NCHR), Head of its Research Committee, and Coordinator of its Research Program on Human Rights and Normative Traditions. His academic field is philosophy, originally working in the philosophy of science, social theory, and ethics. He has done extensive critical work on the social theory of Karl Marx, including a study of Marx's critique of human rights (1989, in Norwegian). Working at the NCHR since 1989, he has authored a number of publications, including: "Prospects for Research on the Cultural Legitimacy of Human Rights: The Cases of Liberalism and Marxism" in *Human Rights in Cross-Cultural Perspectives*, ed. An-Na'im (Philadelphia: University of Pennsylvania Press, 1992); "Article 1: A New Beginning?" in *The Universal Declaration of Human Rights: A Common Standard of Achievement*, ed. Alfredsson and Eide (The Hague: Martinus Nijhoff, 1999); *The Emergence and Development of Human Rights. An Interpretation with a View to Cross-Cultural and Inter-Religious Dialogue* (Oslo: NIHR, 1997; in Turkish, 1998); and "Ethical justification of universal rights across normative divides," in *Universal Ethics: Perspectives and Proposals from Scandinavian Scholars*, ed. Bexell and Andersson (The Hague: Kluwer, 2002); and coedited with Kari Vogt a book on An-Na'im's reform thinking: *Islamic Law Reform and Human Rights: Challenges and Rejoinders* (Oslo: Nordic Human Rights Publishers, 1993). Prof. Lindholm co-initiated and sat on the steering committee of the Norwegian Research Council Ethics Program from 1990 to 2001 and is a board member of the Oslo Coalition on Freedom of Religion or Belief. His ongoing research addresses conditions and strategies for constructive and critical collaboration, cooperation, and dialogue across religious and cultural divides, on further elaboration, entrenchment, and plural justification of human rights norms and mechanisms.

DAVID LLEWELLYN is Professor of Law and former Dean, Trinity Law School, California. His principal subjects are U.S. constitutional law, jurisprudence, international human rights, and religious liberty. Prof. Llewellyn received a Juris Doctor from the University of California at Los Angeles, School of Law; a *Diplome* of International and Comparative Human Rights Law from the International Institute of Human Rights, Strasbourg, France; and a M.A. in English Literature from the University of Tennessee at Knoxville. He also did graduate study in Theology at Dallas Theological Seminary. Prof. Llewellyn is former President and legal counsel for the Western Center for Law and Religious Freedom, a public interest law firm. He is now a practicing civil rights attorney and CEO of a Christian economic development NGO. He is also author of "America's Constitutional Covenant," in *The Christian Vision: Man and State*, ed. Brown (Hillsdale, Mich.: Hillsdale College Press, 1989); and "Licensed To Kill: The Death With Dignity Initiative," *Criminal Law Journal*, Western State University School of Law, San Diego.

KAREN S. LORD spent the last six years of her life working as the Counsel for Religious Freedom at the U.S. Commission on Security and Cooperation in Europe. Ms. Lord also served as a member of the United States Delegation to the OSCE/ODIHR Human Dimension Seminar on Constitutional, Legal, and Administrative Aspects of the Freedom of Religion held in Warsaw in April 1996, where she served as the rapporteur for the working group on Law, Church, and Religious Communities. She was one of the initial members of the Advisory Panel of Experts on Freedom of Religion or Belief for the OSCE's Office for Democratic Institutions and Human Rights. Ms. Lord received her Bachelor's degree in Political Science from Wheaton College in 1989, where she served as class Vice-President. She attended the American University School of Law in Washington, D.C., where she received her J.D. in 1992. She was a member of the Maryland Bar, the District of Columbia Bar, and the Latvian Bar. Ms. Lord died on Monday, January 29, 2001 at the age of thirty-three after a long and courageous struggle against cancer.

JAVIER MARTÍNEZ-TORRÓN has been a Professor of Law (*Catedrático*) since 1993. He obtained his first chair at the University of Granada and later moved to Complutense University in Madrid. Prof. Martínez-Torrón is the founder and Director of the Seminar of Comparative Law at the University of Granada and is a visiting professor and researcher at universities in Europe, North America, and Latin America. He is a member of the International Academy for Freedom of Religion and Belief and is also a member of the International Advisory Council of the Oslo Coalition on Freedom of Religion or Belief. In 1995 he helped found the first Spanish legal periodical specifically focused on religious and legal issues of the State (*Anuario de Derecho Eclesiástico del Estado*, 1995). The results of his research on religion have been published in Spanish, English, Italian, French, and Russian.

JANNE HAALAND MATLARY is Professor of International Politics in the Department of Political Science at Oslo University. Dr. Matlary focuses her study on the European Union as a political system, the European Union's foreign and security policy, European security at large, human rights, "soft law," and public diplomacy. From 1997 to 2000 Dr. Matlary was State Secretary for Foreign Affairs of Norway, representing the Christian Democratic Party in the Bondevik government. Apart from her daily leadership functions, she was responsible for the security policy (especially the Norwegian OSCE chairmanship in 1999 and the Balkans), the Norwegian campaign for membership in the U.N. Security Council, international human rights negotiations, and internationalization of Norwegian fishing and energy. Dr. Matlary also does political risk analysis for the international communications company CGI Monsen and is a member of the Pontifical Council for Justice and Peace and for the Family in the Vatican.

ROLAND MINNERATH is Professor at the Catholic Theological Faculty of the University of Strasbourg, France, teaching history of Christianity and Church-State relationships. His main publications are *Les chrétiens et le monde, 1er-2e siècle* (Paris: Gabalda, 1973); *Le droit de l'Église à la liberté. Du Syllabus à Vatican II* (Paris: Beauchesne, 1982); *L'Église et les États concordataires, 1846-1965* (Paris: Cerf, 1983); *Jésus et le pouvoir* (Paris: Beauchesne, 1987); *De Jérusalem à Rome. Pierre et l'unité de l'Église apostolique* (Paris: Beauchesne, 1995); *Histoire des conciles* (Paris: PUF, 1996); *Apologie A Diognète – Exhortation aux Grecs*

(Paris: Migne, 2002). Professor Minnerath also serves as a consultant to the Secretariate of State (Vatican) and is a member both of the Pontifical Academy for Social Sciences and the International Theological Commission. He is a member of the Board of the International Religious Liberty Association. He was ordained Archbishop of Dijon, France in March 2004.

MAKAU MUTUA is Professor of Law and Director of the Human Rights Center at the State University of New York, Buffalo School of Law. Prof. Mutua has been a visiting professor at Harvard Law School, the University of Iowa College of Law, and the University of Puerto Rico School of Law. Prof. Mutua has worked as the Associate Director at the Harvard Law School Human Rights Program and has directed the Africa Project at the Lawyers Committee for Human Rights. He serves as the Chairman of the Kenya Human Rights Commission and sits on the boards of several international organizations and academic journals. Prof. Mutua has conducted numerous human rights, diplomatic, and rule of law missions to countries in Africa, Latin America, and Europe and has spoken at public fora in many parts of the world, including Japan, Brazil, France, and Ethiopia. Prof. Mutua has written numerous scholarly articles exploring topical subjects in international law, human rights, and religion. He has also written human rights reports for the United Nations and leading NGOs and has authored dozens of articles for popular publications such as *The New York Times* and *The Washington Post*. Prof. Mutua was educated at the University of Nairobi, the University of Dar-es-Salaam, and at Harvard Law School, where he obtained a Doctorate of Juridical Science in 1987.

RAFAEL NAVARRO-VALLS is both a Professor of Law and Secretary General at Complutense University in Madrid. From 1983 to 1995 he directed the Department of Church-State Relations (*Derecho Eclesiástico del Estado*) at Complutense University. Prof. Navarro-Valls is a member of the Advisory Commission on Religious Freedom at the Spanish Ministry of Justice and is a member of the Board of Directors of the International Association of Canon Lawyers. He is also a founding member of the Spanish Society of Sciences of Religions, which is part of the International Association for the History of Religions. He has lectured widely at Spanish, European, and Latin-American Universities. He is a founding member of the first Spanish legal periodical specifically focused on the State's law on religious issues (*Anuario de Derecho Eclesiástico del Estado*, 1995) and is also a member of the advisory boards for the Italian periodicals *Il diritto eclesiástico* and *Revista de la Facultad de Derecho de la Universidad Complutense*. Prof. Navarro-Valls has published almost one hundred legal essays, especially in the areas of marriage and family, religious freedom, and conscientious objection.

YVES NIDEGGER is an Attorney at Law in Geneva, Switzerland. Mr. Nidegger worked as a journalist in the 1980s and as a Professor of Accounting in the 1990s. Mr. Nidegger has published a number of articles in reviews and journals. He is the legal adviser for CLIMS, a Geneva-based Center of Information on Religious Minorities, and he is an expert for Human Rights Without Borders, a Brussels-based NGO. Mr. Nidegger earned his BBA from the Ecole Supérieure de Commerce in Geneva in 1977 and later studied general History and the History of Christianity at Geneva University. Mr. Nidegger earned a law degree from Geneva Law School.

RÜDIGER NOLL is the Executive Secretary for Church and Society of the Conference of European Churches with an emphasis on Human Rights, Security, and Environment. He is the Chairperson of the OSCE Advisory Panel on Freedom of Religion and Belief and has represented the Conference of European Churches at various intergovernmental conferences, including UNCED and the World Conference on Human Rights. From 1990 to 1994 Mr. Noll was a Consultant for Justice, Peace, and the Integrity of Creation at the Conference on European Churches. From 1995 to 1997 he was the Organizing Secretary for the Second European Economical Assembly in Graz. In addition, Mr. Noll has served as the Parish Pastor of the United Church of Westphalia, Germany. His publications include nearly fifty titles on various themes related to church and society issues such as civil society, human rights, religious freedom, environment and development, and minority issues. Mr. Noll focuses his educational studies on Theology, Philosophy, and Political Sciences at the Universities and Institutes of Bochum, Wuppertal, Bossey, and Geneva.

MANFRED NOWAK is the Chairman of the European Master's Degree in Human Rights and Democratization. He has served as the Director of the Ludwig-Boltzmann Institute of Human Rights in Vienna and was elected by the Committee of Ministers of the Council of Europe as Vice-President of the Human Rights Chamber for Bosnia-Hercegovina, which was established under the Dayton Peace Agreement. Since October 1989 Prof. Nowak has been a Professor of Law at the Austrian Federal Academy of Public Administration in Vienna. From 1973 to 1987 he was an Assistant and later an Associate Professor at the Institute of Constitutional and Administrative Law at Vienna University, and from 1987 to 1989 he was the Director of the Netherlands Institute of Human Rights (SIM) at the University of Utrecht. In 1994 Prof. Nowak received the UNESCO Prize for the Teaching of Human Rights. He received a Dr. iuris from the University of Vienna in 1973, an LLM from Columbia in 1975, and a Dr. habil of constitutional law from the University of Vienna in1986. Prof. Nowak has participated in several human rights fact-finding missions, including missions to Brazil, Suriname, and Tibet.

INGVILL THORSON PLESNER has been a Research Fellow at the Norwegian Centre for Human Rights since April 2003, with a doctoral project on the concepts of "neutrality" and "tolerance" in relation to freedom of religion or belief. Until April 2003 Ms. Plesner was an Advisor for the Norwegian Ministry for Education, Research, and Church Affairs. Ms. Plesner has focused her work on state relations to religion and freedom of religion or belief. She helped evaluate a religious education project financed by the Norwegian Research Council and also helped evaluate a research project on "Religious and Moral Plurality" financed by the Nordic Council of Ministers. From 1999 to 2000 Ms. Plesner received grants from the Deutsche Akademische Austauschdienst (DAAD) and was affiliated with the Berlin Freie Universität in conducting research on a project called "Religio-Political Models." She has published several articles and reports on freedom of religion or belief, models of religious education, and state relations to religion. Ms. Plesner received a Master's Degree in Sociology (Cand. Polit.) from the University of Oslo in 1998. In her Master's Thesis Ms. Plesner analyzed the public debate about the new model for religious education in Norway that was introduced in Norwegian primary schools in 1997.

ROMAN PODOPRIGORA is Professor of Administrative Law and Legal Status of Non-Profit and Religious Associations and is Chair of the Administrative Law Department of Adilet Law School in Almaty, Kazakhstan. He is also a legal consultant for numerous religious associations in Kazakhstan and has authored many publications on religious freedom. Prof. Podoprigora is a member of the Advisory Panel of Experts on Freedom of Religion or Belief at the OSCE Office for Democratic Institutions and Human Rights (ODIHR). In 1993 he received a Ph.D. from Kazakh State University. He titled his dissertation "Legal Status of Religious Organizations in Kazakhstan."

MICHAEL M. ROAN has worked to help implement freedom of religion or belief since 1984. He was the representative of the World Federation of United Nations Associations (WFUNA) at a two-week United Nations Seminar in 1984 on ways to implement the 1981 Declaration on the Elimination of All Forms of Intolerance and of Discrimination Based on Religion or Belief. In 1985 he founded The Tandem Project, a non-governmental organization formed to help implement the 1981 Declaration. His publications include a paper written with Leonard Swidler of Temple University titled, "Attitudes of Religions and Ideologies Toward the Outsider." Mr. Roan, together with John Witte, Jr. of Emory University, contributed a chapter to the two-volume publication *Religious Human Rights in Global Perspective* (Boston: Martinus Nijhoff, 1996). Mr. Roan was on the Preparatory Committee for the "International Consultative Conference on School Education in Relation with Freedom of Religion and Belief, Tolerance and Non-discrimination ," a conference organized in Madrid in 2001. He received an undergraduate degree in Political Science from the University of Minnesota and a Master's degree from Luther Theological Seminary in St. Paul, Minnesota.

MARY ROBINSON was President of Ireland from 1990–97 and United Nations High Commissioner for Human Rights from 1997–2002. She was educated at Trinity College and holds law degrees from the King's Inns in Dublin and Harvard University.

MARTIN SCHEININ is the Armfelt Professor of Constitutional and International Law. He also directs the Institute for Human Rights at Åbo Akademi University in Finland. He has taught Human Rights Law at several universities in different parts of the world, including the University of Toronto, Canada; Cardozo Law School and St. Thomas University, USA; Kaliningrad University and Petrozavodsk University, Russia; the University of Latvia; the University of Tartu, Estonia; the University of Troms, Norway; and the African and European Master's Programmes in Human Rights and Democratization. Prof. Scheinin is a member of the Human Rights Committee acting under the International Covenant on Civil and Political Rights. His publications range from articles on the domestic implementation of international human rights norms and the nature of economic and social rights to articles on specific legal issues such as nondiscrimination, indigenous people's rights, social and economic rights, freedom of movement, and freedom of religion or belief. Prof. Scheinin received a Master of Laws in 1982 from the University of Turku, Finland, and a Dr. iuris in 1991 from the University of Helsinki.

ELIZABETH A. SEWELL is Associate Director of the Brigham Young University International Center for Law and Religion Studies. Prior to joining the Center, Prof. Sewell was an associate in the Washington, D.C. office of Mayer, Brown & Platt, where she was a member of the Appellate and Supreme Court Litigation Group. She has briefed a variety of constitutional issues in federal and state courts of appeal and in the U.S. Supreme Court. Prof. Sewell also clerked for Judge J. Clifford Wallace of the U.S. Court of Appeals for the Ninth Circuit. Drawing on her multilingual talents in Russian, Czech, German, and French, she has been active in writing and lecturing on church-state and comparative law topics and has testified before the U.S. Congress on religious freedom issues. Prof. Sewell graduated ***summa cum laude*** from the J. Reuben Clark Law School at Brigham Young University, where she was Editor-in-Chief of the *BYU Law Review*.

JULIET SHEEN has been a fellow of the Human Rights Centre, University of Essex, United Kingdom, since 1994. She is based in Australia and New Zealand. She compiled with coeditor Professor Kevin Boyle, the HRC director, the book ***Freedom of Religion and Belief: A World Report*** (Routledge, London & New York, 1997). From 1977 to retirement in 1994, she pursued research, policy, and law reform proposals for the NSW Anti-Discrimination Board, for which she compiled the Board's report ***Discrimination and Religious Conviction*** (ADB, Sydney, 1984). She represented Australia at the U.N. Seminar on the 1981 Declaration held in Geneva in 1984, and took part in subsequent NGO international conferences on DEAFI. She has written widely on freedom of religion or belief, human rights, minority issues, women's rights, and discrimination. Ms. Sheen received a Doctor of Philosophy from the University of Sydney in 1979 and a Master of Arts in English Language and Literature from Victoria University of Wellington, New Zealand in 1962.

JOSÉ DE SOUSA E BRITO has been judge of the Constitutional Court in Lisbon since 1989 and is a Professor at the Universidade Moderna in Lisbon. He has been President of the European Consortium of Church and State Research and of the Committee for the Reform of the Law of Religious Liberty of Portugal. Since 1977 he has been the Portuguese expert at the Committee of Experts for the Development of Human Rights of the Council of Europe. Mr. Brito was a visiting professor at the University of Munich. He holds a law degree from Lisbon University, and he also studied at the Universities of Vienna, Freiburg im Breisgau, Heidelberg, and Oxford.

TAD STAHNKE joined the staff of the U.S. Commission on International Religious Freedom in February 2000 and currently serves as the Deputy Director for Policy. Prior to joining the Commission, Mr. Stahnke spent three years with Cleary, Gottlieb, Steen & Hamilton, a law firm in New York City. He also worked as a judicial clerk for the Hon. Wilfred Feinberg in the United States Court of Appeals. From 1996 to 1998 Mr. Stahnke helped lead a program on "Religion, Human Rights, and Religious Freedom" at Columbia University Law School, where for several years he taught a seminar on religious freedom and international human rights law. Mr. Stahnke's published works include "Proselytism and the Freedom to Change Religion in International Human Rights Law," ***BYU Law Review*** (1999): 251–350; ***Religion and Human Rights: Basic Documents,*** ed. Stahnke and Martin (New York: Columbia Univ. Press, 1997); and "Equality and Religious Preferences: Theoretical, International, and Religious Approaches" in ***Protecting the Human Rights of Religious Minorities in Eastern Europe,*** ed. Danchin and Cole (New York: Columbia Univ. Press, 2002). Mr. Stahnke received his J.D. from Columbia University Law School, and his Master's in Urban Planning and his B.A. from New York University.

GUNNAR STÅLSETT is Church of Norway Bishop of Oslo (since 1998), President of the International Advisory Council of The Oslo Coalition on Freedom of Religion or Belief, President of the World Conference on Religion and Peace, President of the International Religious Liberty Association, as well as a member of several international and national boards and councils, including the Norwegian Nobel Committee (since 1984). His career has included service as minister in the Church of Norway, Leader of the Norwegian Center Party (1977–1979), Secretary General of the Lutheran World Federation (1985–1994), and Director of Practical-Theological Seminary at the University of Oslo (1994–1998). He has published and edited several books, including Bible translations, theological studies, and sermons. He has received several prizes, including the Albert Schweitzer Humanitarian Award, The Wittenberg Award, and the Grand Order of Quetzal of the Republic of Guatemala (for constructive involvement in the peace process, 1998), and he is Commander of the Royal Order of St. Olav.

BARBRO SVEEN is today employed as the first Administrative Leader of the Council for Religious and Life Stance Communities in Norway and was one of the persons behind its establishment in May 1996. The members are the ten most important and numerous religious and life-stance communities in Norway, from the Norwegian state church to the Norwegian Humanist Association. Barbro Sveen has a diploma as a journalist from the Department of Journalism and Mass Communication, Gothenburg University, Sweden and has a Master's degree in Sociology, Oslo University, Norway. She has also taken some courses at the Technische Hochschule in Berlin, Germany and in San Francisco, USA. Barbro Sveen has been working as an editor for different periodicals in Norway for nearly twenty-five years, among them the Norwegian Humanist Association's "Fri tanke" (Free Thought). She was born in Sweden.

LEONARD SWIDLER is Professor with tenure at Temple University in the Religion Department. Additionally, he has been an exchange and visiting professor at universities in several different countries around the world and has organized and led several interfaith dialogues. In 1972 Prof. Swidler won the "Outstanding Teacher of America" award, and in 1977 he was the recipient of an Honorary Doctorate, L.L.D. from La Salle University. Prof. Swidler has authored numerous books and well over one hundred articles in several different languages. He received a B.A. in Philosophy from St. Norbert's College, an M.A. in History with minors in Philosophy and Literature from Marquette University, a Ph.D. in History from the University of Wisconsin, and has studied extensively at universities in Germany.

BAHIA G. TAHZIB-LIE is a Human Rights Advisor to the Human Rights and Peacebuilding Department of the Dutch Ministry of Foreign Affairs in The Hague. Dr. Tahzib-Lie currently serves as the Co-Chair of the Working Group on Conflict Prevention/Dialogue of the OSCE ODIHR Advisory Panel of Experts on Freedom of Religion or Belief and is a member of the International Advisory Council of the Oslo Coalition on Freedom of Religion or Belief. She has served as a legal staff member at the Council of State, Legislation Department in The Hague and the Dutch Refugee Council in Amsterdam. She has been an associate lecturer in the fields of international law and international organizations at Utrecht University. Her career started as a volunteer human rights advisor to the U.N. office of the Bahá'í International Community in Geneva.

She has published various works in the field of human rights and in the area of freedom of religion or belief, including her Doctorate on "Freedom of Religion or Belief: Ensuring Effective International Legal Protection." Dr. Tahzib-Lie received an LL.B. in 1988, a Ph.D. in 1995 from Utrecht University, and an additional LL.M. in 1989 from the University of Michigan.

THEO VAN BOVEN is Professor of International Law at the University of Maastricht in the Netherlands. He is a member of the International Commission of Jurists, Geneva and a Vice-President of the International Institute of Human Rights, Strasbourg. He was the Director of Human Rights for the United Nations from 1977 to 1982 and served for many years on various United Nations human rights bodies, including the Commission on Human Rights, the Sub-Commission on the Promotion and Protection of Human Rights, and the Committee on the Elimination of All Forms of Racial Discrimination. At present he is Special Rapporteur on Torture for the Commission on Human Rights. Prof. van Boven received a Doctor of Law degree from the University of Leiden, Netherlands and holds Doctoral degrees *honoris causa* from the Catholic University of Louvain-la-Nueve, Belgium, the Erasmus University of Rotterdam, Netherlands, and the University of New York at Buffalo, USA. He wrote his doctoral thesis on the international protection of religious liberty and has authored a series of articles on freedom of religion or belief.

GERALDINE VAN BUEREN is Professor of International Human Rights Law and Director of the Programme on International Rights of the Child at Queen Mary College, University of London. Additionally, she is the inaugural Wates Visiting Fellow and is a visiting professor at the University of Cape Town. She helped draft the U.N. Convention Policy on the Rights of the Child as well as other international laws. She has been a consultant to the Commonwealth Secretariat on children's rights and advised the Law Commission in Uganda on revising their law on children. Prof. Van Bueren represented the United Nations before the Law Commission in South Africa. She is on the Legal Advisory Board of the Redress Trust, the Human Rights Watch (Children's Rights Project), and is the author of *The International Law on the Rights of the Child* (Boston: Martinus Nijhoff, 1998) and *Childhood Abused* (Dartmouth: Dartmouth Pub. Co., 1998).

JOHAN D. VAN DER VYVER is the I.T. Cohen Professor of International Law and Human Rights at Emory University Law School in Atlanta, Georgia. Prof. van der Vyver has also worked as a Professor of Law at the Potchefstroom University for Christian Higher Education and at the University of the Witwatersrand in Johannesburg, South Africa. He has authored over 250 published works, including books, monographs, chapters in books, law-review articles, lectures, popular articles, and book reviews. Prof. van der Vyver coedited the two-volume treatise on "Religious Human Rights in Global Perspective" (Boston: Martinus Nijhoff, 1996) and edited a special edition of the Emory International Law Review on "Problems of Proselytization in South Africa" (2000). Prof. van der Vyver received his Bachelor of Laws degree from the Potchefstroom University for Christian Higher Education (1956), the degree of Doctor Legum from the University of Pretoria (1974), the degree Doctor Legum (honoris causa) from the University of Zululand (1993), and another Doctor Legum (honoris causa) from the Potchefstroom University for Christian Higher Education, South Africa (2003).

TANJA VOSPERNIK is a legal researcher at the Ludwig Boltzmann Institute of Human Rights in Vienna, Austria. Since January 2000 she has been working on an editorial collaboration with the journal *Die Union* (Representation of the European Commission in Austria). Since 1999 Ms. Vospernik has been an honorary legal guardian, and in 1999 she was legal advisor at the Refugee Organization "Helping Hands" in Vienna. In 1998 she completed her legal studies at the University of Vienna.

Introduction to the Appendices

Most states have undertaken extensive and detailed commitments and obligations in the area of freedom of religion or belief. Within the UN system, there are a variety of documents containing provisions relating to freedom of religion or belief, and of course, many significant standards have been established by regional organizations such as the Council of Europe, the European Union, the Organization of American States, the Organization of African Unity and the Organization for Security and Cooperation in Europe. The Appendices contain a collection of the most important documents articulating these standards that those working in the field need to have at hand. Appendix A contains selections from the most important international human rights documents regarding freedom of religion or belief at global and regional levels. Provisions in Appendix A are arranged by organization and then chronologically by document. The UN's 1981 Declaration on the Elimination of All Forms of Intolerance and of Discrimination Based on Religion or Belief is set forth in Appendix B. Appendix C provides a more exhaustive list of treaties that address freedom of religion or belief. Appendix D contains the text of the UN Human Rights Committee's General Comment which provides the authoritative interpretation of Article 18 of the International Covenant on Civil and Political Rights. It provides an excellent concise statement of the meaning of international human rights standards with respect to freedom of religion or belief. Since religious and minority rights issues are often intertwined, the UN Human Rights Committee's General Comment No. 23 (50), included here as Appendix E, is also very helpful. Finally, Appendix F contains the Oslo Declaration on Freedom of Religion or Belief. Many states have also taken on obligations and commitments relating to freedom of religion or belief at the regional level.

In preparing the Appendices, we have been conscious that many additional human rights norms beyond those that deal directly with freedom of religion or belief provide supplemental or overlapping coverage for the rights of believers. For example, many of the rights of believers are also covered by freedom of expression and freedom of association. Equality and nondiscrimination norms provide protection for believers. Conscience and religion are central aspects of human dignity and are also properly shielded by privacy norms. Claims relating to cultural rights and property can also be very significant for religions. General protection of minorities may benefit religious groups. Moreover, the scope of religious protections cannot be fully understood without clarity about other state interests, the nature and weight of sometimes conflicting rights, and the extent to which issues of security, health, safety, and morality can be taken into account in limiting manifestations of religion.

Tore Lindholm, W. Cole Durham, Jr., Bahia G. Tahzib-Lie (eds.), Facilitating Freedom of Religion or Belief: A Deskbook, *871–872.*

In light of these considerations, it comes as no surprise that it is not possible within a single volume to include the full range of international norms that are relevant to protecting religious believers and institutions in the broadest sense. Our aim has been to include the major provisions that ought to be at hand in a "deskbook." We have been forced due to space constraints to focus here on the major norms that relate most directly to freedom of religion or belief itself, and those that play a particularly important role in protecting the rights of believers.

Of course, in today's internet world, full texts of the various documents are increasingly accessible online. Full texts of all the documents cited in the Appendices, together with relevant citations to original sources, are available in the online library of the Religion and Law Research Consortium at www.religlaw.org. This site has the advantage of that it collects sources that are particularly relevant to freedom of religion or belief issues. Each of the major international and regional organizations generating standards in the field of freedom of religion or belief has its own webpage. For convenience, we are listing the relevant websites here:

United Nations	
General	http://www.un.org/
High Commissioner for Human Rights	http://www.unhchr.ch/
Council of Europe	
General	http://www.coe.fr/
European Court of Human Rights	http://www.echr.coe.int/
European Union	
General	http://europa.eu.int/
Eur-Lex / European Union Law	http://europa.eu.int/eur-lex/en/index.html
Organization of American States	
General	http://www.oas.org/
African Union (Organization of African Unity)	http://www.africa-union.org/en/home.asp
Organization for Security and Cooperation in Europe (OSCE)	
General	http://www.osce.org
Office of Democratic Institutions and Human Rights (ODIHR)	http://www.osce.org/odihr/
Oslo Coalition on Freedom of Religion or Belief	http://www.oslocoalition.org
For references to other sources, see:	http://www.religlaw.org

Appendix A

Major International Provisions on Freedom of Religion or Belief

I. United Nations

A. Universal Declaration of Human Rights (1948)[1]

Article 1

All human beings are born free and equal in dignity and rights. They are endowed with reason and conscience and should act towards one another in a spirit of brotherhood.

Article 2

Everyone is entitled to all the rights and freedoms set forth in this Declaration, without distinction of any kind, such as race, color, sex, language, religion, political or other opinion, national or social origin, property, birth or other status.

(...)

Article 7

All are equal before the law and are entitled without any discrimination to equal protection of the law. All are entitled to equal protection against any discrimination in violation of this Declaration and against any incitement to such discrimination.

Article 8

Everyone has the right to an effective remedy by the competent national tribunals for acts violating the fundamental rights granted him by the constitution or by law.

---

[1] Adopted and Proclaimed by United Nations General Assembly Resolution on 10 December 1948, GA Res. 217A (III), UN Doc A/810 at 71 (1948).

ARTICLE 12

No one shall be subjected to arbitrary interference with his privacy, family, home or correspondence, nor to attacks upon his honour and reputation. Everyone has the right to the protection of the law against such interference or attacks.

ARTICLE 13

1. Everyone has the right to freedom of movement and residence within the borders of each State.
2. Everyone has the right to leave any country, including his own, and to return to his country.

ARTICLE 14

1. Everyone has the right to seek and to enjoy in other countries asylum from persecution.
2. This right may not be invoked in the case of prosecutions genuinely arising from nonpolitical crimes or from acts contrary to the purposes and principles of the United Nations.

ARTICLE 16

1. Men and women of full age, without any limitation due to race, nationality or religion, have the right to marry and to found a family. They are entitled to equal rights as to marriage, during marriage and at its dissolution.

(...)

ARTICLE 17

1. Everyone has the right to own property alone as well as in association with others.
2. No one shall be arbitrarily deprived of his property.

ARTICLE 18

Everyone has the right to freedom of thought, conscience and religion; this right includes freedom to change his religion or belief, and freedom, either alone or in community with others and in public or private, to manifest his religion or belief in teaching, practice, worship and observance.

ARTICLE 19

Everyone has the right to freedom of opinion and expression; this right includes freedom to hold opinions without interference and to seek, receive and impart information and ideas through any media and regardless of frontiers.

ARTICLE 20

1. Everyone has the right to freedom of peaceful assembly and association.
2. No one may be compelled to belong to an association.

ARTICLE 26

(...)

2. Education shall be directed to the full development of the human personality and to the strengthening of respect for human rights and fundamental freedoms. It shall promote understanding, tolerance and friendship among all nations, racial or religious groups, and shall further the activities of the United Nations for the maintenance of peace.

(...)

ARTICLE 29

(...)

2. In the exercise of his rights and freedoms, everyone shall be subject only to such limitations as are determined by law solely for the purpose of securing due recognition and respect for the rights and freedoms of others and of meeting the just requirements of morality, public order and the general welfare in a democratic society.

3. These rights and freedoms may in no case be exercised contrary to the purposes and principles of the United Nations.

B. CONVENTION ON THE PREVENTION AND PUNISHMENT OF THE CRIME OF GENOCIDE (1948) [2]

ARTICLE II

In the present Convention, genocide means any of the following acts committed with intent to destroy, in whole or in part, a national, ethnical, racial or religious group, as such:

(a) Killing members of the group;
(b) Causing serious bodily or mental harm to members of the group;
(c) Deliberately inflicting on the group conditions of life calculated to bring about its physical destruction in whole or in part;
(d) Imposing measures intended to prevent births within the group;
(e) Forcibly transferring children of the group to another group.

[2] Adopted and Opened for Signature by the United Nations General Assembly on 9 December 1948. GA Res. 260A (III) (1948), 102 Stat. 3045, 78 UNTS 277, entered into force January 12, 1951.

C. International Covenant on Civil and Political Rights (1966)[3]

Article 2

1. Each State Party to the present Covenant undertakes to respect and to ensure to all individuals within its territory and subject to its jurisdiction the rights recognized in the present Covenant, without distinction of any kind, such as race, colour, sex, language, religion, political or other opinion, national or social origin, property, birth or other status.

(...)

Article 3

The States Parties to the present Covenant undertake to ensure the equal right of men and women to the enjoyment of all civil and political rights set forth in the present Covenant.

Article 4

1. In time of public emergency which threatens the life of the nation and the existence of which is officially proclaimed, the States Parties to the present Covenant may take measures derogating from their obligations under the present Covenant to the extent strictly required by the exigencies of the situation, provided that such measures are not inconsistent with their other obligations under international law and do not involve discrimination solely on the ground of race, colour, sex, language, religion or social origin.
2. No derogation from Articles 6, 7, 8 (paragraphs 1 and 2), 11, 15, 16 and 18 may be made under this provision.

(...)

Article 8

(...)

3. (a) No one shall be required to perform forced or compulsory labour;

(...)

(c) For the purpose of this paragraph the term "forced or compulsory labour" shall not include:

(...)

(ii) Any service of a military character and, in countries where conscientious objection is recognized, any national service required by law of conscientious objectors;

(...)

---

[3] Adopted and Opened for Signature by the United Nations General Assembly on 16 December 1966. GA Res. 2200A (XXI), 21 UN GAOR Supp. (No. 16) at 52, UN Doc. A/6316 (1966), 999 UNTS 171, entered into force March 23, 1976.

ARTICLE 18

1. Everyone shall have the right to freedom of thought, conscience and religion. This right shall include freedom to have or to adopt a religion or belief of his choice, and freedom, either individually or in community with others and in public or private, to manifest his religion or belief in worship, observance, practice and teaching.

2. No one shall be subject to coercion which would impair his freedom to have or to adopt a religion or belief of his choice.

3. Freedom to manifest one's religion or beliefs may be subject only to such limitations as are prescribed by law and are necessary to protect public safety, order, health, or morals or the fundamental rights and freedoms of others.

4. The States Parties to the present Covenant undertake to have respect for the liberty of parents and, when applicable, legal guardians to ensure the religious and moral education of their children in conformity with their own convictions.

ARTICLE 19

1. Everyone shall have the right to hold opinions without interference.

2. Everyone shall have the right to freedom of expression; this right shall include freedom to seek, receive and impart information and ideas of all kinds, regardless of frontiers, either orally, in writing or in print, in the form of art, or through any other media of his choice.

3. The exercise of the rights provided for in paragraph 2 of this article carries with it special duties and responsibilities. It may therefore be subject to certain restrictions, but these shall only be such as are provided by law and are necessary:

(a) For respect of the rights or reputations of others;

(b) For the protection of national security or of public ordre (order public), or of public health or morals.

ARTICLE 20

(...)

2. Any advocacy of national, racial or religious hatred that constitutes incitement to discrimination, hostility or violence shall be prohibited by law.

ARTICLE 21

The right of peaceful assembly shall be recognized. No restrictions may be placed on the exercise of this right other than those imposed in conformity with the law and which are necessary in a democratic society in the interests of national security or public safety, public order (ordre public), the protection of public health or morals or the protection of the rights and freedoms of others.

ARTICLE 22

1. Everyone shall have the right to freedom of association with others, including the right to form and join trade unions for the protection of his interests.

2. No restrictions may be placed on the exercise of this right other than those which are prescribed by law and which are necessary in a democratic society in the interests of national security or public safety, public order (ordre public), the protection of public health or morals or the protection of the rights and freedoms of others. This article shall not prevent the imposition of lawful restrictions on members of the armed forces and of the police in their exercise of this right.

(...)

ARTICLE 24

1. Every child shall have, without any discrimination as to race, colour, sex, language, religion, national or social origin, property or birth, the right to such measures of protection as are required by his status as a minor, on the part of his family, society and the State.

(...)

ARTICLE 26

All persons are equal before the law and are entitled without any discrimination to the equal protection of the law. In this respect, the law shall prohibit any discrimination and guarantee to all persons equal and effective protection against discrimination on any ground such as race, colour, sex, language, religion, political or other opinion, national or social origin, property, birth or other status.

ARTICLE 27

In those States in which ethnic, religious or linguistic minorities exist, persons belonging to such minorities shall not be denied the right, in community with the other members of their group, to enjoy their own culture, to profess and practice their own religion, or to use their own language.

D. INTERNATIONAL COVENANT ON ECONOMIC, SOCIAL AND CULTURAL RIGHTS (1966)[4]

ARTICLE 2

(...)

2. The States Parties to the present Covenant undertake to guarantee that the rights enunciated in the present Covenant will be exercised without discrimination of any kind as to race, colour, sex, language, religion, political or other opinion, national or social origin, property, birth or other status.

(...)

[4] Adopted and Opened for Signature by the United Nations General Assembly on 16 December 1966. GA Res. 2200A (XXI), 21 UN GAOR Supp. (No. 16) at 49, UN Doc. A/6316 (1966), 993 UNTS 3, entered into force January 3, 1976.

ARTICLE 13

1. The States Parties to the present Covenant recognize the right of everyone to education. They agree that education shall be directed to the full development of the human personality and the sense of its dignity, and shall strengthen the respect for human rights and fundamental freedoms. They further agree that education shall enable all persons to participate effectively in a free society, promote understanding, tolerance and friendship among all nations and all racial, ethnic or religious groups, and further the activities of the United Nations for the maintenance of peace.

(...)

3. The States Parties to the present Covenant undertake to have respect for the liberty of parents and, when applicable, legal guardians to choose for their children schools, other than those established by the public authorities, which conform to such minimum educational standards as may be laid down or approved by the State and to ensure the religious and moral education of their children in conformity with their own convictions.

(...)

E. CONVENTION ON THE ELIMINATION OF ALL FORMS OF DISCRIMINATION AGAINST WOMEN (1979)[5]

ARTICLE 5

States parties shall take all appropriate measures:

(a) To modify the social and cultural patterns of conduct of men and women, with a view to achieving the elimination of prejudices and customary and all other practices which are based on the idea of the inferiority or the superiority of either of the sexes or on stereotyped roles for men and women;

(...)

ARTICLE 16

1. States Parties shall take all appropriate measures to eliminate discrimination against women in all matters relating to marriage and family relations. . . .

F. CONVENTION ON THE RIGHTS OF THE CHILD (1989)[6]

ARTICLE 2

1. States Parties shall respect and ensure the rights set forth in the present Convention to each child within their jurisdiction without discrimination of any kind,

---

[5] Adopted and Opened for Signature by the United Nations General Assembly Resolution on 18 December 1979. GA Res. 34/180, 1249 UNTS 13, entered into force September 3, 1981.

[6] Adopted and Opened for Signature by the United Nations General Assembly on 20 Nov. 1989, GA Res. 44/25, UN GAOR, 44th Sess., Supp. No. 49, art. 32(1), UN Doc. A/44/49 (1989), entered into force September 2, 1990.

irrespective of the child's or his or her parent's or legal guardian's race, colour, sex, language, religion, political or other opinion, national, ethnic or social origin, property, disability, birth or other status.

2. States Parties shall take all appropriate measures to ensure that the child is protected against all forms of discrimination or punishment on the basis of the status, activities, expressed opinions, or beliefs of the child's parents, legal guardians, or family members.

Article 14

1. States Parties shall respect the right of the child to freedom of thought, conscience and religion.

2. States Parties shall respect the rights and duties of the parents and, when applicable, legal guardians, to provide direction to the child in the exercise of his or her right in a manner consistent with the evolving capacities of the child.

3. Freedom to manifest one's religion or beliefs may be subject only to such limitations as are prescribed by law and are necessary to protect public safety, order, health or morals, or the fundamental rights and freedoms of others.

Article 20

1. A child temporarily or permanently deprived of his or her family environment, or in whose own best interests cannot be allowed to remain in that environment, shall be entitled to special protection and assistance provided by the State.

2. States Parties shall in accordance with their national laws ensure alternative care for such a child.

3. Such care could include, *inter alia,* foster placement, *Kafalah* of Islamic law, adoption or if necessary placement in suitable institutions for the care of children. When considering solutions, due regard shall be paid to the desirability of continuity in a child's upbringing and to the child's ethnic, religious, cultural and linguistic background.

Article 29

1. States Parties agree that the education of the child shall be directed to:

(...)

(d) The preparation of the child for responsible life in a free society, in the spirit of understanding, peace, tolerance, equality of sexes, and friendship among all peoples, ethnic, national and religious groups and persons of indigenous origin;

(...)

Article 30

In those States in which ethnic, religious or linguistic minorities or persons of indigenous origin exist, a child belonging to such a minority or who is indigenous shall not be denied the right, in community with other members of his or her group, to enjoy his or her own culture, to profess and practice his or her own religion, or to use his or her own language.

II. Council of Europe

A. European Convention for the Protection of Human Rights and Fundamental Freedoms (1950)[7]

Article 8

1. Everyone has the right to respect for his private and family life, his home and his correspondence.

2. There shall be no interference by a public authority with the exercise of this right except such as is in accordance with the law and is necessary in a democratic society in the interests of national security, public safety or the economic well-being of the country, for the prevention of disorder or crime, for the protection of health or morals, or for the protection of the rights and freedoms of others.

Article 9

1. Everyone has the right to freedom of thought, conscience and religion; this right includes freedom to change his religion or belief and freedom, either alone or in community with others and in public or private, to manifest his religion or belief, in worship, teaching, practice and observance.

2. Freedom to manifest one's religion or beliefs shall be subject only to such limitations as are prescribed by law and are necessary in a democratic society in the interests of public safety, for the protection of public order, health or morals, or for the protection of the rights and freedoms of others.

Article 10

1. Everyone has the right to freedom of expression. This right shall include freedom to hold opinions and to receive and impart information and ideas without interference by public authority and regardless of frontiers. This article shall not prevent States from requiring the licensing of broadcasting, television or cinema enterprises.

2. The exercise of these freedoms, since it carries with it duties and responsibilities, may be subject to such formalities, conditions, restrictions or penalties as are prescribed by law and are necessary in a democratic society, in the interests of national security, territorial integrity or public safety, for the prevention of disorder or crime, for the protection of health or morals, for the protection of the reputation or rights of others, for preventing the disclosure of information received in confidence, or for maintaining the authority and impartiality of the judiciary.

Article 11

1. Everyone has the right to freedom of peaceful assembly and to freedom of association with others, including the right to form and to join trade unions for the protection of his interests.

---

[7] Opened for Signature by the Council of Europe on 4 November 1950. E.T.S. No. 5, entered into force September 3, 1953.

2. No restrictions shall be placed on the exercise of these rights other than such as are prescribed by law and are necessary in a democratic society in the interests of national security or public safety, for the prevention of disorder or crime, for the protection of health or morals or for the protection of the rights and freedoms of others. This Article shall not prevent the imposition of lawful restrictions on the exercise of these rights by members of the armed forces, of the police or of the administration of the State.

ARTICLE 14

The enjoyment of the rights and freedoms set forth in this Convention shall be secured without discrimination on any ground such as sex, race, colour, language, religion, political or other opinion, national or social origin, association with a national minority, property, birth or other status.

B. PROTOCOL NO. 1 TO THE EUROPEAN CONVENTION FOR THE PROTECTION OF HUMAN RIGHTS AND FUNDAMENTAL FREEDOMS (1952)[8]

ARTICLE 2

No person shall be denied the right to education. In the exercise of any functions which it assumes in relation to education and to teaching, the State shall respect the right of parents to ensure such education and teaching in conformity with their own religious and philosophical convictions.

C. EUROPEAN SOCIAL CHARTER (1961)[9]

PREAMBLE

(...)
Considering that the enjoyment of social rights should be secured without discrimination on grounds of race, colour, sex, religion, political opinion, national extraction or social origin;
(...)

D. FRAMEWORK CONVENTION FOR THE PROTECTION OF NATIONAL MINORITIES (1995)[10]

ARTICLE 5

1. The Parties undertake to promote the conditions necessary for persons belonging to national minorities to maintain and develop their culture, and to preserve the essential elements of their identity, namely their religion, language, traditions and cultural heritage.
(...)

[8] Opened for Signature by the Council of Europe on November 4, 1950. E.T.S. No. 9, entered into force 3 September 3, 1953.

ARTICLE 6

1. The Parties shall encourage a spirit of tolerance and intercultural dialogue and take effective measures to promote mutual respect and understanding and co-operation among all persons living on their territory, irrespective of those persons' ethnic, cultural, linguistic or religious identity, in particular in the fields of education, culture and the media.

2. The Parties undertake to take appropriate measures to protect persons who may be subject to threats or acts of discrimination, hostility or violence as a result of their ethnic, cultural, linguistic or religious identity.

ARTICLE 7

The Parties shall ensure respect for the right of every person belonging to a national minority to freedom of peaceful assembly, freedom of association, freedom of expression, and freedom of thought, conscience and religion.

ARTICLE 8

The Parties undertake to recognise that every person belonging to a national minority has the right to manifest his or her religion or belief and to establish religious institutions, organizations and associations.

ARTICLE 17

1. The Parties undertake not to interfere with the right of persons belonging to national minorities to establish and maintain free and peaceful contacts across frontiers with persons lawfully staying in other States, in particular those with whom they share an ethnic, cultural, linguistic or religious identity, or a common cultural heritage.

2. The Parties undertake not to interfere with the right of persons belonging to national minorities to participate in the activities of non-governmental organizations, both at the national and international levels.

III. EUROPEAN UNION

A. TREATY ON EUROPEAN UNION (1992, CONSOLIDATED VERSION 1997)[11]

ARTICLE 6

(...)

2 The Union shall respect fundamental rights, as guaranteed by the European Convention for the Protection of Human Rights and Fundamental Freedoms signed

[9] Signed Oct. 18, 1961, Eur. Consult Assembly, E.T.S. No. 035.

[10] Opened for Signature by the Council of Europe on February 1, 1995. E. T. S. No. 157, entered into force February 1, 1998.

in Rome on 4 November 1950 and as they result from the constitutional traditions common to the Member States, as general principles of Community law.

B. Treaty Establishing the European Community (1997)[12]

Article 13

Without prejudice to the other provisions of this Treaty and within the limits of the powers conferred upon it by the Community, the Council, acting unanimously on a proposal from the Commission and after consulting the European Parliament, may take appropriate action to combat discrimination based on sex, racial or ethnic origin, religion or belief, disability, age or sexual orientation.

(...)

C. Protocol 33 on Protection and Welfare of Animals (annexed to the Treaty of the European Community) (2 Oct. 1997)[13]

The Protocol on protection and welfare of animals annexed to the Treaty requires that in formulating and implementing the Community's agriculture policy, the Community and the Member States shall pay full regard to the welfare requirements of animals, while respecting the legislative or administrative provisions and customs of the Member States relating in particular to religious rites, cultural traditions and regional heritage.

D. Declaration on the Status of Churches and Non-Confessional Organizations (1997, Declaration No. 11 to the Last Act of the Treaty of Amsterdam)[14]

The European Union respects and does not prejudice the status under national law of churches and religious associations or communities in the Member States.

The European Union equally respects the status of philosophical and non-confessional organizations.

---

[11] TEU, adopted 7 February 1992, OJ 1992 C191, p.1 (Treaty of Maastricht), as amended by the Treaty of Amsterdam, OJ 1997 C 340, p. 0145-0172 (10 Nov. 1997).

[12] Treaty of Rome of 25 March 1957, as amended by the Treaty of Amsterdam of 2 Nov. 1997, OJ 1997 C 340 p. 0185 (10 Nov. 1997).

[13] Protocol 33 annexed to the Treaty of the European Community of 2 Oct. 1997, OJ 1997 C 340, p. 0110 (10 Nov. 1997).

[14] Declaration No. 11 to the Last Act of the Treaty of Amsterdam (Declarations adopted by the Conference), OJ 1997 C 340, p. 0133 (10 Nov. 1997).

E. Declaration by Greece Concerning the Declaration on the Status of Churches and Non-Confessional Organizations (1997, Declaration No. 59 to the Last Act of the Treaty of Amsterdam)[15]

With reference to the Declaration on the status of churches and non-confessional organizations, Greece recalls the Joint Declaration on Mount Athos annexed to the Final Act of the Treaty of Accession of Greece to the European Communities.

F. Charter of Fundamental Rights of the European Union (2000)[16]

Preamble

The peoples of Europe, in creating an ever closer union among them, are resolved to share a peaceful future based on common values.

Conscious of its spiritual and moral heritage, the Union is founded on the indivisible, universal values of human dignity, freedom, equality and solidarity; it is based on the principles of democracy and the rule of law. It places the individual at the heart of its activities, by establishing the citizenship of the Union and by creating an area of freedom, security and justice.

Article 10 – Freedom of thought, conscience and religion

1. Everyone has the right to freedom of thought, conscience and religion. This right includes freedom to change religion or belief and freedom, either alone or in community with others and in public or in private, to manifest religion or belief, in worship, teaching, practice and observance.

2. The right to conscientious objection is recognized, in accordance with the national laws governing the exercise of this right.

Article 14 – Right to education

(...)

1. The freedom to found educational establishments with due respect for democratic principles and the right of parents to ensure the education and teaching of their children in conformity with their religious, philosophical and pedagogical convictions shall be respected, in accordance with the national laws governing the exercise of such freedom and right.

---

[15] Declaration No. 8 to the Last Act of the Treaty of Amsterdam (Declarations of which the Conference took note), OJ 1997 C 340, p. 0144 (10 Nov. 1997).

[16] OJ 2000 C 364, p. 1-22 (18 Dec. 2000).

Article 21 – Non-discrimination

1. Any discrimination based on any ground such as sex, race, colour, ethnic or social origin, genetic features, language, religion or belief, political or any other opinion, membership of a national minority, property, birth, disability, age or sexual orientation shall be prohibited.

(...)

Article 22 – Cultural, religious and linguistic diversity

The Union shall respect cultural, religious and linguistic diversity.

IV. Organization of American States

A. American Declaration of the Rights and Duties of Man (1948)[17]

Article II – Right to equality before law

All persons are equal before the law and have the rights and duties established in this Declaration, without distinction as to race, sex, language, creed or any other factor.

Article III – Right to religious freedom and worship

Every person has the right freely to profess a religious faith, and to manifest and practice it both in public and in private.

Article XXII – Right of association

Every person has the right to associate with others to promote, exercise and protect his legitimate interests of a political, economic, religious, social, cultural, professional, labor union or other nature.

B. American Convention on Human Rights (1969)[18]

Article 1 – Obligation to Respect Rights

1. The States Parties to this Convention undertake to respect the rights and freedoms recognized herein and to ensure to all persons subject to their jurisdiction the free and full exercise of those rights and freedoms, without any discrimination for

[17] OAS Resolution XXX, Final Act of the Ninth International Conference of American States, 48 (March 30–May 2, 1948).

[18] Signed by the Organization of American States on 22 November 1969. Entered into Force July 18, 1978.

reasons of race, color, sex, language, religion, political or other opinion, national or social origin, economic status, birth, or any other social condition.

(...)

Article 12 – Freedom of Conscience and Religion

1. Everyone has the right to freedom of conscience and of religion. This right includes freedom to maintain or to change one's religion or beliefs, and freedom to profess or disseminate one's religion or beliefs, either individually or together with others, in public or in private.

2. No one shall be subject to restrictions that might impair his freedom to maintain or to change his religion or beliefs.

3. Freedom to manifest one's religion and beliefs may be subject only to the limitations prescribed by law that are necessary to protect public safety, order, health, or morals, or the rights or freedoms of others.

4. Parents or guardians, as the case may be, have the right to provide for the religious and moral education of their children or wards that is in accord with their own convictions.

Article 13 – Freedom of Thought and Expression

(...)

5. Any propaganda for war and any advocacy of national, racial, or religious hatred that constitute incitements to lawless violence or any other similar illegal action against any person or group of persons on any grounds including those of race, color, religion, language, or national origin shall be considered as offenses punishable by law.

Article 16 – Freedom of Association

1. Everyone has the right to associate freely for ideological, religious, political, economic, labor, social, cultural, sports or other purposes.

(...)

Article 27 – Suspension of Guarantees

1. In time of war, public danger, or other emergency that threatens the independence or security of a State Party, it may take measures derogating from its obligations under the present Convention to the extent and for the period of time strictly required by the exigencies of the situation, provided that such measures are not inconsistent with its other obligations under international law and do not involve discrimination on the ground of race, color, sex, language, religion, or social origin.

2. The foregoing provision does not authorize any suspension of the following articles: Article 3 (Right to Juridical Personality), Article 4 (Right to Life), Article 5 (Right to Humane Treatment), Article 6 (Freedom from Slavery), Article 9 (Freedom

from Ex Post Facto Laws), Article 12 (Freedom of Conscience and Religion), Article 17 (Rights of the Family), Article 18 (Right to a Name), Article 19 (Rights of the Child), Article 20 (Right to Nationality), and Article 23 (Right to Participate in Government), or of the judicial guarantees essential for the protection of such rights.

C. Additional Protocol to the American Convention on Human Rights in the Area of Economic, Social and Cultural Rights (1988)[19]

Article 3 – Obligation of Non-Discrimination

The States Parties to this Protocol undertake to guarantee the exercise of the rights set forth herein without discrimination of any kind for reasons related to race, color, sex, language, religion, political or other opinions, national or social origin, economic status, birth or any other social condition.

Article 13 – Right to Education

(…)

2. The States Parties to this Protocol agree that education should be directed towards the full development of the human personality and human dignity and should strengthen respect for human rights, ideological pluralism, fundamental freedoms, justice and peace. They further agree that education ought to enable everyone to participate effectively in a democratic and pluralistic society and achieve a decent existence and should foster understanding, tolerance and friendship among all nations and all racial, ethnic or religious groups and promote activities for the maintenance of peace.

Article 15 – Right to the Formation and the Protection of Families

1. The family is the natural and fundamental element of society and ought to be protected by the State, which should see to the improvement of its spiritual and material conditions.

(…)

3. The States Parties hereby undertake to accord adequate protection to the family unit and in particular:

(…)

(c) To adopt special measures for the protection of adolescents in order to ensure the full development of their physical, intellectual and moral capacities;

(…)

[19] Adopted at San Salvador, El Salvador, OAS General Assembly, 18th Regular Sess., November 17, 1988, OAS Treaty Series No. 69 (Protocol of San Salvador).

V. Organization of African Unity

A. OAU Convention Governing the Specific Aspects of Refugee Problems in Africa (1969)[20]

Article I – Definition of the term "Refugee"

1. For the purposes of this Convention, the term "refugee" shall mean every person who, owing to well-founded fear of being persecuted for reasons of race, religion, nationality, membership of a particular social group or political opinion, is outside the country of his nationality and is unable or, owing to such fear, is unwilling to avail himself of the protection of that country, or who, not having a nationality and being outside the country of his former habitual residence as a result of such events is unable or, owing to such fear, is unwilling to return to it.

Article IV – Non-Discrimination

Member States undertake to apply the provisions of this Convention to all refugees without discrimination as to race, religion, nationality, membership of a particular social group or political opinions.

B. African Charter on Human and Peoples' Rights (1981)[21]

Article 2

Every individual shall be entitled to the enjoyment of the rights and freedoms recognized and guaranteed in the present Charter without distinction of any kind such as race, ethnic group, colour, sex, language, religion, political or any other opinion, national and social origin, fortune, birth or other status.

Article 8

Freedom of conscience, the profession and free practice of religion shall be guaranteed. No one may, subject to law and order, be submitted to measures restricting the exercise of these freedoms.

Article 12

(...)

5. The mass expulsion of non-nationals shall be prohibited. Mass expulsion shall be that which is aimed at national, racial, ethnic or religious groups.

---

[20] Organization Of African Unity, Convention Governing Specific Aspects Of The Problem Of Refugees In Africa, 1001 UNTS 45 (Sept. 10, 1969), entered into force June 20, 1974.

[21] Adopted by the Organization of African Unity on June 17, 1981. O.A.U. Doc. CAB/LEG/67/3 Rev. 5 (1981), entered into force 21 October 1986.

C. Constitutive Act of the African Union (2000)[22]

(...)

3(h) Promote and protect human and peoples' rights in accordance with the African Charter on Human and Peoples' Rights and other relevant human rights instruments;

(...)

4(m) Respect for democratic principles, human rights, the rule of law and good governance;

(...)

VI. CSCE/OSCE[23]

A. Final Act of the Conference on Security and Co-operation in Europe (Helsinki, 1975)

Questions Relating to Security in Europe
Chapter 1(a) – Declaration on Principles Guiding Relations Between Participating States
Principle VII – Respect for Human Rights and Fundamental Freedoms, Including the Freedom of Thought, Conscience, Religion or Belief

The participating States will respect human rights and fundamental freedoms, including the freedom of thought, conscience, religion or belief, for all without distinction as to race, sex, language or religion.

(...)

Within this framework the participating States will recognize and respect the freedom of the individual to profess and practise, alone or in community with others, religion or belief acting in accordance with the dictates of his own conscience.

(...)

Co-operation in Humanitarian and Other Fields
Chapter 1 – Human Contacts
Section D – Travel for Personal or Professional Reasons

(...)

They [the participating States] confirm that religious faiths, institutions and organizations, practising within the constitutional framework of the participating States, and their representatives can, in the field of their activities, have contacts and meetings among themselves and exchange information.

---

[22] Entered into force May 26, 2001.

[23] CSCE and OSCE documents can be found at the OSCE website, <www.osce.org>.

B. Concluding Document of the Madrid Meeting of Representatives of the Participating States of the Conference on Security and Co-operation in Europe (1983)

Questions Relating to Security in Europe

The participating States reaffirm that they will recognize, respect and furthermore agree to take the action necessary to ensure the freedom of the individual to profess and practise, alone or in community with others, religion or belief acting in accordance with the dictates of his own conscience.

In this context, they [the participating States] will consult, whenever necessary, the religious faiths, institutions and organizations, which act within the constitutional framework of their respective countries.

They [the participating States] will favorably consider applications by religious communities of believers practicing or prepared to practice their faith within the constitutional framework of their States, to be granted the status provided for in their respective countries for religious faiths, institutions and organizations.

Co-operation in Humanitarian and Other Fields Human Contacts

They [the participating States] will further implement the relevant provisions of the Final Act, so that religious faiths, institutions, organizations and their representatives can, in the field of their activity, develop contacts and meetings among themselves and exchange information.

C. Concluding Document of the Vienna Meeting of Representatives of the Participating States of the Conference on Security and Co-operation in Europe (1989)[24]

Questions Relating to Security in Europe – Principle 11

11. They [the participating States] confirm that they will respect human rights and fundamental freedoms, including the freedom of thought, conscience, religion or belief, for all without distinction as to race, sex, language or religion. They also confirm the universal significance of human rights and fundamental freedoms, respect for which is an essential factor for the peace, justice and security necessary to ensure the development of friendly relations and co-operation among themselves, as among all States.

Questions Relating to Security in Europe – Principle 13

13. In this context they [the participating States] will

(...)

13g. ensure human rights and fundamental freedoms to everyone within their territory and subject to their jurisdiction, without distinction of any kind

[24] Adopted in Vienna on January 17, 1989.

such as race, color, sex, language, religion, political or other opinion, national or social origin, property, birth or other status;

(...)

QUESTIONS RELATING TO SECURITY IN EUROPE – PRINCIPLE 16

16. In order to ensure the freedom of the individual to profess and practice religion or belief the participating States will, *inter alia*,

16a. take effective measures to prevent and eliminate discrimination against individuals or communities on the grounds of religion or belief in the recognition, exercise and enjoyment of human rights and fundamental freedoms in all fields of civil, political, economic, social and cultural life, and ensure the effective equality between believers and non-believers;

16b. foster a climate of mutual tolerance and respect between believers of different communities as well as between believers and non-believers;

16c. grant upon their request to communities of believers, practising or prepared to practise their faith within the constitutional framework of their states, recognition of the status provided for them in their respective countries;

16d. respect the right of religious communities to

- establish and maintain freely accessible places of worship or assembly,
- organize themselves according to their own hierarchical and institutional structure,
- select, appoint and replace their personnel in accordance with their respective requirements and standards as well as with any freely accepted arrangement between them and their State,
- solicit and receive voluntary financial and other contributions;

16e. engage in consultations with religions faiths, institutions and organizations in order to achieve a better understanding of the requirements of religious freedom;

16f. respect the right of everyone to give and receive religious education in the language of his choice, individually or in association with others;

16g. in this context respect, *inter alia*, the liberty of parents to ensure the religious and moral education of their children in conformity with their own convictions;

16h. allow the training of religious personnel in appropriate institutions;

16i. respect the right of individual believers and communities of believers to acquire, posses, and use sacred books, religious publications in the language of their choice and other articles and materials related to the practice of religion or belief;

16j. allow religious faiths, institutions and organizations to produce and import and disseminate religious publications and materials;

16k. favorably consider the interest of religious communities in participating in public dialogue, *inter alia*, through the mass media.

QUESTIONS RELATING TO SECURITY IN EUROPE – PRINCIPLE 17

17. The participating States recognize that the exercise of the above-mentioned rights relating to the freedom of religion or belief may be subject only to such limitations

as are provided by law and consistent with their obligations under international law and with their international commitments. They will ensure in their laws and regulations and in their application the full and effective exercise of the freedom of thought, conscience, religion or belief.

Questions Relating to Security in Europe – Principle 19

19. They [the participating States] will protect and create conditions for the promotion of the ethnic, cultural, linguistic and religious identity of national minorities on their territory. They will respect the free exercise of rights by persons belonging to such minorities and ensure their full equality with others.

Questions Relating to Security in Europe – Principle 21

21. The participating States will ensure that the exercise of the above-mentioned rights will not be subject to any restrictions except those which are provided by law and are consistent with their obligations under international law, in particular the International Covenant on Civil and Political Rights, and with their international commitments, in particular the Universal Declaration of Human Rights. These restrictions have the character of exceptions. The participating States will ensure that these restrictions are not abused and are not applied in an arbitrary manner, but in such a way that the effective exercise of these rights is ensured.

Co-operation in Humanitarian and Other Fields
Human Contacts – Paragraph 32

They [the participating States] will allow believers, religious faiths and their representatives, in groups or on an individual basis, to establish and maintain direct personal contacts and communication with each other, in their own and other countries, *inter alia* through travel, pilgrimages and participation in assemblies and other religious events. In this context and commensurate with such contacts and events, those concerned will be allowed to acquire, receive and carry with them religious publications and objects related to the practice of their religion or belief.

Co-operation in Humanitarian and Other Fields
Co-operation and Exchanges in the Field of Education – Paragraph 68

They [the participating States] will ensure that persons belonging to national minorities or regional cultures on their territories can give and receive instruction on their own culture, including instruction through parental transmission of language, religion and cultural identity to their children.

D. Document of the Copenhagen Meeting of Representatives of the Participating States of the Conference on the Human Dimension of the Conference on Security and Co-operation in Europe (1990)[25]

Chapter II – Principle 9

(9) The participating States reaffirm that

(9.1) everyone will have the right to freedom of expression including the right to communication. This right will include freedom to hold opinions and to receive and impart information and ideas without interference by public authority and regardless of frontiers. The exercise of this right may be subject only to such restrictions as are prescribed by law and are consistent with international standards. In particular, no limitation will be imposed on access to, and use of, means of reproducing documents of any kind, while respecting, however, rights relating to intellectual property, including copyright;

(9.2) everyone will have the right of peaceful assembly and demonstration. Any restrictions which may be placed on the exercise of these rights will be prescribed by law and consistent with international standards;

(9.3) the right of association will be guaranteed. The right to form and—subject to the general right of a trade union to determine its own membership—freely to join a trade union will be guaranteed. These rights will exclude any prior control. Freedom of association for workers, including the freedom to strike, will be guaranteed, subject to limitations prescribed by law and consistent with international standards.

(9.4) everyone will have the right to freedom of thought, conscience and religion. This right includes freedom to change one's religion or belief and freedom to manifest one's religion or belief, either alone or in community with others, in public or in private, through worship, teaching, practice and observance. The exercise of these rights may be subject only to such restrictions as are prescribed by law and are consistent with international standards;

(...)

Chapter II – Principle 18

(18) The participating States

(18.1) note that the United Nations Commission on Human Rights has recognized the right of everyone to have conscientious objections to military service;

(18.2) note recent measures taken by a number of participating States to permit exemption from compulsory military service on the basis of conscientious objections;

(18.3) note the activities of several non-governmental organizations on the question of conscientious objections to compulsory military service;

(18.4) agree to consider introducing, where this has not yet been done, various forms of alternative service, which are compatible with the reasons for conscientious

[25] Adopted in Copenhagen on June 29, 1990.

objection, such forms of alternative service being in principle of a non-combatant or civilian nature, in the public interest and of a non-punitive nature;

(18.5) will make available to the public information on this issue;

(18.6) will keep under consideration, within the framework of the Conference on the Human Dimension, the relevant questions related to the exemption from compulsory military service, where it exists, of individuals on the basis of conscientious objections to armed service, and will exchange information on these questions.

CHAPTER II – PRINCIPLE 24

(24) The participating States will ensure that the exercise of all human rights and fundamental freedoms set out above will not be subject to any restrictions except those which are provided by law and are consistent with their obligations under international law, in particular the International Covenant on Civil and Political Rights, and with their international commitments, in particular the Universal Declaration of Human Rights. These restrictions have the character of exceptions. The participating States will ensure that these restrictions are not abused and are not applied in an arbitrary manner, but in such a way that the effective exercise of these rights is ensured.

Any restriction on rights and freedoms must, in a democratic society, relate to one of the objectives of the applicable law and be strictly proportionate to the aim of that law.

CHAPTER II – PRINCIPLE 25

(25) The participating States confirm that any derogations from obligations relating to human rights and fundamental freedoms during a state of public emergency must remain strictly within the limits provided for by international law, in particular the relevant international instruments by which they are bound, especially with respect to rights from which there can be no derogation. They also reaffirm that

(25.1) measures derogating from such obligations must be taken in strict conformity with the procedural requirements laid down in those instruments;

(25.2) the imposition of a state of public emergency must be proclaimed officially, publicly, and in accordance with the provisions laid down by law;

(25.3) measures derogating from obligations will be limited to the extent strictly required by the exigencies of the situation;

(25.4) such measures will not discriminate solely on the grounds of race, colour, sex, language, religion, social origin or of belonging to a minority.

CHAPTER IV – PRINCIPLE 30

(...)

(30) They also recognize the important role of non-governmental organizations, including political parties, trade unions, human rights organizations and religious groups, in the promotion of tolerance, cultural diversity and the resolution of questions relating to national minorities.

(...)

CHAPTER IV – PRINCIPLE 32

(32) To belong to a national minority is a matter of a person's individual choice and no disadvantage may arise from the exercise of such choice.

Persons belonging to national minorities have the right freely to express, preserve and develop their ethnic, cultural, linguistic or religious identity and to maintain and develop their culture in all its aspects, free of any attempts at assimilation against their will. In particular, they have the right.

(...)

(32.2) to establish and maintain their own educational, cultural and religious institutions, organizations or associations, which can seek voluntary financial and other contributions as well as public assistance, in conformity with national legislation;

(32.3) to profess and practice their religion, including the acquisition, possession and use of religious materials, and to conduct religious educational activities in their mother tongue;

(32.4) to establish and maintain unimpeded contacts among themselves within their country as well as contacts across frontiers with citizens of other States with whom they share a common ethnic or national origin, cultural heritage or religious beliefs;

(...)

(32.6) to establish and maintain organizations or associations within their country and to participate in international non-governmental organizations.

Persons belonging to national minorities can exercise and enjoy their rights individually as well as in community with other members of their group. No disadvantage may arise for a person belonging to a national minority on account of the exercise or non-exercise of any such rights.

Chapter IV – Principle 33

(33) The participating States will protect the ethnic, cultural, linguistic and religious identity of national minorities on their territory and create conditions for the promotion of that identity. They will take the necessary measures to that effect after due consultations, including contacts with organizations or associations of such minorities, in accordance with the decision-making procedures of each State.

Any such measures will be in conformity with the principles of equality and non-discrimination with respect to the other citizens of the participating State concerned.

CHAPTER IV - PRINCIPLE 35

(35) The participating States will respect the right of persons belonging to national minorities to effective participation in public affairs, including participation in the affairs relating to the protection and promotion of the identity of such minorities.

The participating States note the efforts undertaken to protect and create conditions for the promotion of the ethnic, cultural, linguistic and religious identity of certain national minorities by establishing, as one of the possible means to achieve these aims, appropriate local or autonomous administrations corresponding to the specific historical and territorial circumstances of such minorities and in accordance with the policies of the State concerned.

CHAPTER IV - PRINCIPLE 36

(36) The participating States recognize the particular importance of increasing constructive co-operation among themselves on questions relating to national minorities. Such co-operation seeks to promote mutual understanding and confidence, friendly and good-neighborly relations, international peace, security and justice.

Every participating State will promote a climate of mutual respect, understanding, co-operation and solidarity among all persons living on its territory, without distinction as to ethnic or national origin or religion, and will encourage the solution of problems through dialogue based on the principles of the rule of law.

CHAPTER IV - PRINCIPLE 40

(40) The participating States clearly and unequivocally condemn totalitarianism, racial and ethnic hatred, anti-semitism, xenophobia and discrimination against anyone as well as persecution on religious and ideological grounds. In this context, they also recognize the particular problems of Roma (gypsies).

They declare their firm intention to intensify the efforts to combat these phenomena in all their forms and therefore will

(40.1) take effective measures, including the adoption, in conformity with their constitutional systems and their international obligations, of such laws as may be necessary, to provide protection against any acts that constitute incitement to violence against persons or groups based on national, racial, ethnic or religious discrimination, hostility or hatred, including anti-semitism;

(40.2) commit themselves to take appropriate and proportionate measures to protect persons or groups who may be subject to threats or acts of discrimination, hostility or violence as a result of their racial, ethnic, cultural, linguistic or religious identity, and to protect their property;

(...)

E. CHARTER OF PARIS FOR A NEW EUROPE (1990)

A NEW ERA OF DEMOCRACY, PEACE AND UNITY
HUMAN RIGHTS, DEMOCRACY AND RULE OF LAW – PARAGRAPH 6

We [the participating states] affirm that, without discrimination, every individual has the right to:

freedom of thought, conscience and religion or belief,

(...)

A New Era of Democracy, Peace and Unity
Human Rights, Democracy and Rule of Law – Paragraph 7

We affirm that the ethnic, cultural, linguistic and religious identity of national minorities will be protected and that persons belonging to national minorities have the right freely to express, preserve and develop that identity without any discrimination and in full equality before the law.

Guidelines for the future
Human Dimension – Paragraph 3

Determined to foster the rich contribution of national minorities to the life of our societies, we undertake further to improve their situation. We reaffirm our deep conviction that friendly relations among our peoples, as well as peace, justice, stability and democracy, require that the ethnic, cultural, linguistic and religious identity of national minorities be protected and conditions for the promotion of that identity be created. We declare that questions related to national minorities can only be satisfactorily resolved in a democratic political framework. We further acknowledge that the rights of persons belonging to national minorities must be fully respected as part of universal human rights. Being aware of the urgent need for increased co-operation on, as well as better protection of, national minorities, we decide to convene a meeting of experts on national minorities to be held in Geneva from 1 to 19 July 1991.

Guidelines for the Future
Human Dimension – Paragraph 4

We express our determination to combat all forms of racial and ethnic hatred, anti-semitism, xenophobia and discrimination against anyone as well as persecution on religious and ideological grounds.

F. Document of the Moscow Meeting of the Conference on the Human Dimension of the Conference on Security and Co-operation in Europe (1991)

Chapter II – Paragraph 28

(28) The participating States consider it important to protect human rights and fundamental freedoms during a state of public emergency, to take into account the relevant provisions of the Document of the Copenhagen Meeting, and to observe the international conventions to which they are parties.

(...)

(28.6) The participating States confirm that any derogation from obligations relating to human rights and fundamental freedoms during a state of public emergency must remain strictly within the limits provided for by international law, in particular the relevant international instruments by which they are bound, especially with respect to rights from which there can be no derogation.

(28.7) The participating States will endeavor to refrain from making derogations from those obligations from which, according to international conventions to which they are parties, derogation is possible under a state of public emergency. Measures derogating from such obligations must be taken in strict conformity with the procedural requirements laid down in those instruments. Such measures will neither go further nor remain in force longer than strictly required by the exigencies of the situation; they are by nature exceptional and should be interpreted and applied with restraint. Such measures will not discriminate solely on the grounds of race, color, sex, language, religion, social origin or of belonging to a minority.

(...)

CHAPTER III – PARAGRAPH 38

(38) The participating States recognize the need to ensure that the rights of migrant workers and their families lawfully residing in the participating States are respected and underline their right to express freely their ethnic, cultural, religious and linguistic characteristics. The exercise of such rights may be subject to such restrictions as are prescribed by law and are consistent with international standards.

(38.1) They condemn all acts of discrimination on the ground of race, color and ethnic origin, intolerance and xenophobia against migrant workers. They will, in conformity with domestic law and international obligations, take effective measures to promote tolerance, understanding, equality of opportunity and respect for the fundamental human rights of migrant workers and adopt, if they have not already done so, measures that would prohibit acts that constitute incitement to violence based on national, racial, ethnic or religious discrimination, hostility or hatred.

(...)

CHAPTER III – PARAGRAPH 42

(42) The participating States

(42.1) affirm that human rights education is fundamental and that it is therefore essential that their citizens are educated on human rights and fundamental freedoms and the commitment to respect such rights and freedoms in domestic legislation and international instruments to which they may be parties;

(42.2) recognize that effective human rights education contributes to combating intolerance, religious, racial and ethnic prejudice and hatred, including against Roma, xenophobia and anti-semitism;

(42.3) will encourage their competent authorities responsible for education programmes to design effective human rights relates curricula and courses for students at all levels, particularly students of law, administration and social sciences as well as those attending military, police and public service schools;

(42.4) will make information on all CSCE human dimension provisions available to their educators;

(42.5) will encourage organizations and educational establishments to co-operate in drawing up and exchanging human rights programmes at the national as well as the international level;

(42.6) will seek to ensure that activities undertaken with a view to promoting human rights education in the broader sense take into account experience, programmes and forms of co-operation within existing international governmental and non-governmental bodies, such as the United Nations and the Council of Europe.

G. Budapest Document Toward a Genuine Partnership in a New Era (1994)

Chapter IV. Code of Conduct on Politico-Military Aspects of Security
Section VIII – Paragraph 37

37. The participating States will not use armed forces to limit the peaceful and lawful exercise of their human and civil rights by persons as individuals or as representatives of groups nor to deprive them of their national, religious, cultural, linguistic or ethnic identity.

Chapter VIII. The Human Dimension
Commitments and Co-operation
Tolerance and Non-Discrimination – Paragraph 27

27. Reaffirming their commitment to ensure freedom of conscience and religion and to foster a climate of mutual tolerance and respect between believers of different communities as well as between believers and non-believers, they expressed their concern about the exploitation of religion for aggressive nationalist ends.

Chapter VIII. The Human Dimension
Commitments and Co-operation
Migrant Workers – Paragraph 28

28. The participating States reconfirm that human rights are universal and indivisible. They recognized that the protection and promotion of the rights of migrant workers have their human dimension. They underline the right of migrant workers to express freely their ethnic, cultural, religious and linguistic characteristics. The exercise of such rights may be subject to such restrictions as are prescribed by law and consistent with international standards.

H. Charter for European Security (Istanbul, 1999)

Chapter III. Our Common Response
The Human Dimension – Paragraph 19

19. We [the participating States] reaffirm that respect for human rights and fundamental freedoms, democracy and the rule of law is at the core of the OSCE's comprehensive concept of security. We commit ourselves to counter such threats to

security as violations of human rights and fundamental freedoms, including the freedom of thought, conscience, religion or belief and manifestations of intolerance, aggressive nationalism, racism, chauvinism, xenophobia and anti-semitism.

The protection and promotion of the rights of persons belonging to national minorities are essential factors for democracy, peace, justice and stability within, and between, participating States. In this respect we reaffirm our commitments, in particular under the relevant provisions of the Copenhagen 1990 Human Dimension Document, and recall the Report of the Geneva 1991 Meeting of Experts on National Minorities. Full respect for human rights, including the rights of persons belonging to national minorities, besides being an end in itself, may not undermine, but strengthen territorial integrity and sovereignty. Various concepts of autonomy as well as other approaches outlined in the above-mentioned documents, which are in line with OSCE principles, constitute ways to preserve and promote the ethnic, cultural, linguistic and religious identity of national minorities within an existing State. We condemn violence against any minority. We pledge to take measures to promote tolerance and to build pluralistic societies where all, regardless of their ethnic origin, enjoy full equality of opportunity. We emphasize that questions relating to national minorities can only be satisfactorily resolved in a democratic political framework based on the rule of law.

Chapter IV. Our Common Instruments
Operation Center – Paragraph 44

44. We will work to enhance the OSCE's role in civilian police-related activities as an integral part of the Organization's efforts in conflict prevention, crisis management and post-conflict rehabilitation. Such activities may comprise:

- Police monitoring, including with the aim of preventing police from carrying out such activities as discrimination based on religious and ethnic identity;
- Police training, which could, *inter alia*, include the following tasks:

  (...)
- Creating a police service with a multi-ethnic and/or multi-religious composition that can enjoy the confidence of the entire population;

  (...)

Appendix B

Declaration on the Elimination of All Forms of Intolerance and Discrimination Based on Religion or Belief*

The General Assembly,

Considering that one of the basic principles of the Charter of the United Nations is that of the dignity and equality inherent in all human beings, and that all Member States have pledged themselves to take joint and separate action in co-operation with the Organization to promote and encourage universal respect for and observance of human rights and fundamental freedoms for all, without distinction as to race, sex, language or religion,

Considering that the Universal Declaration of Human Rights and the International Covenants on Human Rights proclaim the principles of nondiscrimination and equality before the law and the right to freedom of thought, conscience, religion and belief,

Considering that the disregard and infringement of human rights and fundamental freedoms, in particular of the right to freedom of thought, conscience, religion or whatever belief, have brought, directly or indirectly, wars and great suffering to mankind, especially where they serve as a means of foreign interference in the internal affairs of other States and amount to kindling hatred between peoples and nations,

Considering that religion or belief, for anyone who professes either, is one of the fundamental elements in his conception of life and that freedom of religion or belief should be fully respected and guaranteed,

Considering that it is essential to promote understanding, tolerance and respect in matters relating to freedom of religion and belief and to ensure that the use of religion or belief for ends inconsistent with the Charter of the United Nations, other relevant instruments of the United Nations and the purposes and principles of the present Declaration is inadmissible,

---

* Proclaimed by United Nations the General Assembly on 25 November 1981. GA Res. 36/55, UN GAOR, 36th Sess. (1981).

Convinced that freedom of religion and belief should also contribute to the attainment of the goals of world peace, social justice and friendship among peoples and to the elimination of ideologies or practices of colonialism and racial discrimination,

Noting with satisfaction the adoption of several, and the coming into force of some, conventions, under the aegis of the United Nations and of the specialized agencies, for the elimination of various forms of discrimination,

Concerned by manifestations of intolerance and by the existence of discrimination in matters of religion or belief still in evidence in some areas of the world,

Resolved to adopt all necessary measures for the speedy elimination of such intolerance in all its forms and manifestations and to prevent and combat discrimination on the ground of religion or belief,

Proclaims this Declaration on the Elimination of All Forms of Intolerance and of Discrimination Based on Religion or Belief:

Article 1

1. Everyone shall have the right to freedom of thought, conscience and religion. This right shall include freedom to have a religion or whatever belief of his choice, and freedom, either individually or in community with others and in public or private, to manifest his religion or belief in worship, observance, practice and teaching.

2. No one shall be subject to coercion which would impair his freedom to have a religion or belief of his choice.

3. Freedom to manifest one's religion or belief may be subject only to such limitations as are prescribed by law and are necessary to protect public safety, order, health or morals or the fundamental rights and freedoms of others.

Article 2

1. No one shall be subject to discrimination by any State, institution, group of persons, or person on the grounds of religion or other belief.

2. For the purposes of the present Declaration, the expression "intolerance and discrimination based on religion or belief" means any distinction, exclusion, restriction or preference based on religion or belief and having as its purpose or as its effect nullification or impairment of the recognition, enjoyment or exercise of human rights and fundamental freedoms on an equal basis.

Article 3

Discrimination between human being on the grounds of religion or belief constitutes an affront to human dignity and a disavowal of the principles of the Charter of the United Nations, and shall be condemned as a violation of the human rights and fundamental freedoms proclaimed in the Universal Declaration of Human Rights and enunciated in detail in the International Covenants on Human Rights, and as an obstacle to friendly and peaceful relations between nations.

Article 4

1. All States shall take effective measures to prevent and eliminate discrimination on the grounds of religion or belief in the recognition, exercise and enjoyment of human rights and fundamental freedoms in all fields of civil, economic, political, social and cultural life.

2. All States shall make all efforts to enact or rescind legislation where necessary to prohibit any such discrimination, and to take all appropriate measures to combat intolerance on the grounds of religion or other beliefs in this matter.

Article 5

1. The parents or, as the case may be, the legal guardians of the child have the right to organize the life within the family in accordance with their religion or belief and bearing in mind the moral education in which they believe the child should be brought up.

2. Every child shall enjoy the right to have access to education in the matter of religion or belief in accordance with the wishes of his parents or, as the case may be, legal guardians, and shall not be compelled to receive teaching on religion or belief against the wishes of his parents or legal guardians, the best interests of the child being the guiding principle.

3. The child shall be protected from any form of discrimination on the ground of religion or belief. He shall be brought up in a spirit of understanding, tolerance, friendship among peoples, peace and universal brotherhood, respect for freedom of religion or belief of others, and in full consciousness that his energy and talents should be devoted to the service of his fellow men.

4. In the case of a child who is not under the care either of his parents or of legal guardians, due account shall be taken of their expressed wishes or of any other proof of their wishes in the matter of religion or belief, the best interests of the child being the guiding principle.

5. Practices of a religion or belief in which a child is brought up must not be injurious to his physical or mental health or to his full development, taking into account article 1, paragraph 3, of the present Declaration.

Article 6

In accordance with article I of the present Declaration, and subject to the provisions of article 1, paragraph 3, the right to freedom of thought, conscience, religion or belief shall include, *inter alia*, the following freedoms:

(a) To worship or assemble in connection with a religion or belief, and to establish and maintain places for these purposes;

(b) To establish and maintain appropriate charitable or humanitarian institutions;

(c) To make, acquire and use to an adequate extent the necessary articles and materials related to the rites or customs of a religion or belief;

(d) To write, issue and disseminate relevant publications in these areas;

(e) To teach a religion or belief in places suitable for these purposes;

(f) To solicit and receive voluntary financial and other contributions from individuals and institutions;

(g) To train, appoint, elect or designate by succession appropriate leaders called for by the requirements and standards of any religion or belief;

(h) To observe days of rest and to celebrate holidays and ceremonies in accordance with the precepts of one's religion or belief;

(i) To establish and maintain communications with individuals and communities in matters of religion and belief at the national and international levels.

Article 7

The rights and freedoms set forth in the present Declaration shall be accorded in national legislation in such a manner that everyone shall be able to avail himself of such rights and freedoms in practice.

Article 8

Nothing in the present Declaration shall be construed as restricting or derogating from any right defined in the Universal Declaration of Human Rights and the International Covenants on Human Rights.

Appendix C

List of Relevant International Treaties

Prepared by Bahia Tahzib-Lie

The list below gives the titles of all relevant global and regional treaties as well as the references to the provisions governing freedom of religion or belief. The treaties are presented in chronological order of their adoption. Note that the focus on treaties results in exclusion of a number of key documents dealing with freedom of religion or belief, either because they are "declarations" or because they are "politically binding" rather than "legally binding," as in the case of OSCE commitments. Key documents and provisions in these categories are included in other appendices.

1945 Charter of the United Nations:
Articles 1(3), 13(1)(b), 55(c) and 76(c).

1947 ILO Convention No. 82 concerning Social Policy in Non-Metropolitan Territories:
Article 18(1) and (2).

1948 Convention on the Prevention and Punishment of the Crime of Genocide:
Article II.

1949 ILO Convention No. 97 concerning Migration for Employment (Revised):
Article 6(1).

1950 European Convention for the Protection of Human Rights and Fundamental Freedoms:
Articles 9 and 14.

1951 Convention relating to the Status of Refugees:
Articles 1(A)(2), 3, 4 and 33(1).

1952 Protocol No. 1 to the European Convention for the Protection of Human Rights and Fundamental Freedoms:
Article 2.

1954 Convention relating to the Status of Stateless Persons:
Articles 3 and 4.

1957 ILO Convention No. 105 concerning the Abolition of Forced Labor:
Article 1(e).

ILO Convention No. 106 concerning Weekly Rest in Commerce and Offices:
Article 6(4).

ILO Convention No. 107 concerning the Protection and Integration of Indigenous and Other Tribal and Semi-Tribal Populations in Independent Countries:
Article 4(a).

European Convention on Extradition:
Article 3(2).

1958 ILO Convention No. 110 concerning Conditions of Employment of Plantation Workers:
Article 2.

ILO Convention No. 111 concerning Discrimination in Respect of Employment and Occupation:
Article 1(1)(a).

1960 UNESCO Convention against Discrimination in Education:
Articles 1(1), 2(b) and 5(1)(a) and (b).

1961 Convention on the Reduction of Statelessness:
Article 9.

1962 ILO Convention No. 117 concerning Basic Aims and Standards of Social Policy:
Article 14(1) and (2).

1964 ILO Convention No. 122 concerning Employment Policy:
Article 1(2)(c).

1965 International Convention on the Elimination of All Forms of Racial Discrimination:
Article 5(d)(vii).

1966 International Covenant on Civil and Political Rights:
Articles 2(1), 4, 18, 20(2), 24(1), 26 and 27.

1966 International Covenant on Economic, Social and Cultural Rights:
Articles 2(2), and 13(1) and (3).

1969 OAU Convention Governing the Specific Aspects of Refugee Problems in Africa:
Articles I(1) and IV.

American Convention on Human Rights:
Articles 1(1), 12, 13(5), 16(1) and 27.

1970 ILO Convention No. 133 concerning Crew Accommodation on Board Ship (Supplementary Provisions):
Article 12.

1974 ILO Convention No. 140 concerning Paid Educational Leave:
Article 8.

1977 European Convention on the Legal Status of Migrant Workers:
Articles 6(1) and 10(3).

1979 Convention on the Elimination of All Forms of Discrimination against Women:
Articles 2, 5 and 16.

1981 African Charter on Human Rights and Peoples' Rights:
Articles 2, 8 and 12(5).

European Convention for the Protection of Individuals with regard to Automatic Processing of Personal Data:
Article 6.

1982 ILO Convention No. 158 concerning Termination of Employment at the Initiative of the Employer:
Article 5(d).

1985 International Convention against Apartheid in Sports:
Article 1(c).

1987 ILO Convention No. 163 concerning Seafarers' Welfare at Sea and in Port:
Article 3(1).

1988 ILO Convention No. 168 concerning Employment Promotion and Protection against Unemployment:
Article 6(1).

Additional Protocol to the American Convention on Human Rights in the Area of Economic, Social and Cultural Rights:
Articles 3 and 13(2).

1989 Convention No. 169 concerning Indigenous and Tribal Peoples in Independent Countries:
Articles 5(a), 7(1) and 32.

Convention on the Rights of the Child:
Articles 2, 14, 20(3), 29(1)(d), and 30.

1990 African Charter on the Rights and Welfare of the Child:
Articles 1(3), 3, 9, 11(2)(d) and (4), 25(3) and 26(2).

International Convention on the Protection of the Rights of All Migrant Workers and Members of Their Families:
Articles 1(1), 7, 12 and 13(3)(d).

1992 Treaty on European Union:
Article 6(2).

1994 Inter-American Convention on the Prevention, Punishment and Eradication of Violence against Women "Convention of Belem do Para":
Article 4(i).

1995 European Framework Convention for the Protection of National Minorities:
Articles 5(1), 6, 7, 8, 12(1) and 17(1).

1996 European Social Charter (revised):
Article E (part V).

1997 ILO Convention No. 181 Concerning Private Employment Agencies:
Article 5.

Treaty Establishing the European Community:
Article 13.

2000 Constitutive Act of the African Union:
Articles 3(h) and 4(m).

Charter of Fundamental Rights of the European Union:
Articles 10, 14, 21 and 22.

Appendix D

United Nations Human Rights Committee General Comment No. 22 (48)*

The Right to Freedom of Thought, Conscience and Religion
(Article 18)
(Forty-Eighth Session, 1993)

1. The right to freedom of thought, conscience and religion (which includes the freedom to hold beliefs) in article 18(1) is far-reaching and profound; it encompasses freedom of thought on all matters, personal conviction and the commitment to religion or belief, whether manifested individually or in community with others. The Committee draws the attention of States parties to the fact that the freedom of thought and the freedom of conscience are protected equally with the freedom of religion and belief. The fundamental character of these freedoms is also reflected in the fact that this provision cannot be derogated from, even in time of public emergency, as stated in article 4(2) of the Covenant.

2. Article 18 protects theistic, non-theistic and atheistic beliefs, as well as the right not to profess any religion or belief. The terms "belief" and "religion" are to be broadly construed. Article 18 is not limited in its application to traditional religions or to religions and beliefs with institutional characteristics or practices analogous to those of traditional religions. The Committee therefore views with concern any tendency to discriminate against any religion or belief for any reason, including the fact that they are newly established, or represent religious minorities that may be the subject of hostility on the part of a predominant religious community.

3. Article 18 distinguishes the freedom of thought, conscience, religion or belief from the freedom to manifest religion or belief. It does not permit any limitations whatsoever on the freedom of thought and conscience or on the freedom to have or adopt a religion or belief of one's choice. These freedoms are protected unconditionally, as is the right of everyone to hold opinions without interference in article 19(1). In accordance with articles 18(2) and 17, no one can be compelled to reveal his thoughts or adherence to a religion or belief.

* Adopted by the UN Human Rights Committee on 20 July 1993. UN Doc. CCPR/C/21/Rev.1/Add.4 (1993), reprinted in UN Doc. HRI/GEN/1/Rev.1 at 35 (1994).

4. The freedom to manifest religion or belief may be exercised "either individually or in community with others and in public or private." The freedom to manifest religion or belief in worship, observance, practice and teaching encompasses a broad range of acts. The concept of worship extends to ritual and ceremonial acts giving direct expression to belief, as well as various practices integral to such acts, including the building of places of worship, the use of ritual formulae and objects, the display of symbols, and the observance of holidays and days of rest. The observance and practice of religion or belief may include not only ceremonial acts but also such customs as the observance of dietary regulations, the wearing of distinctive clothing or headcoverings, participation in rituals associated with certain stages of life, and the use of a particular language customarily spoken by a group. In addition, the practice and teaching of religion or belief includes acts integral to the conduct by religious groups of their basic affairs, such as the freedom to choose their religious leaders, priests and teachers, the freedom to establish seminaries or religious schools and the freedom to prepare and distribute religious texts or publications.

5. The Committee observes that the freedom to "have or to adopt" a religion or belief necessarily entails the freedom to choose a religion or belief, including the right to replace one's current religion or belief with another or to adopt atheistic views, as well as the right to retain one's religion or belief. Article 18(2) bars coercion that would impair the right to have or adopt a religion or belief, including the use of threat of physical force or penal sanctions to compel believers or non-believers to adhere to their religious beliefs and congregations, to recant their religion or belief or to convert. Policies or practices having the same intention or effect, such as, for example, those restricting access to education, medical care, employment or the rights guaranteed by article 25 and other provisions of the Covenant, are similarly inconsistent with article 18(2). The same protection is enjoyed by holders of all beliefs of a non-religious nature.

6. The Committee is of the view that article 18(4) permits public school instruction in subjects such as the general history of religions and ethics if it is given in a neutral and objective way. The liberty of parents or legal guardians to ensure that their children receive a religious and moral education in conformity with their own convictions, set forth in article 18(4), is related to the guarantees of the freedom to teach a religion or belief stated in article 18(1). The Committee notes that public education that includes instruction in a particular religion or belief is inconsistent with article 18.4 unless provision is made for non-discriminatory exemptions or alternatives that would accommodate the wishes of parents and guardians.

7. In accordance with article 20, no manifestation of religion or belief may amount to propaganda for war or advocacy of national, racial or religious hatred that constitutes incitement to discrimination, hostility or violence. As stated by the Committee in its General Comment 11 [19], States parties are under the obligation to enact laws to prohibit such acts.

8. Article 18(3) permits restrictions on the freedom to manifest religion or belief only if limitations are prescribed by law and are necessary to protect public safety, order, health or morals, or the fundamental rights and freedoms of others. The freedom from coercion to have or to adopt a religion or belief and the liberty of parents and guardians to ensure religious and moral education cannot be restricted. In interpreting the scope of permissible limitation clauses, States parties should proceed from the need to protect the rights guaranteed under the Covenant, including the right to equality and non-discrimination on all grounds specified in articles 2, 3 and 26. Limitations imposed must be established by law and must not be applied in a manner that would vitiate the rights guaranteed in article 18. The Committee observes that paragraph 3 of article 18 is to be strictly interpreted: restrictions are not allowed on grounds not specified there, even if they would be allowed as restrictions to other rights protected in the Covenant, such as national security. Limitations may be applied only for those purposes for which they were prescribed and must be directly related and proportionate to the specific need on which they are predicated. Restrictions may not be imposed for discriminatory purposes or applied in a discriminatory manner. The Committee observes that the concept of morals derives from many social, philosophical and religious traditions; consequently, limitations on the freedom to manifest a religion or belief for the purpose of protecting morals must be based on principles not deriving exclusively from a single tradition. Persons already subject to certain legitimate constraints, such as prisoners, continue to enjoy their rights to manifest their religion or belief to the fullest extent compatible with the specific nature of the constraint. States parties' reports should provide information on the full scope and effects of limitations under article 18(3), both as a matter of law and of their application in specific circumstances.

9. The fact that a religion is recognized as a state religion or that it is established as official or traditional or that its followers comprise the majority of the population, shall not result in any impairment of the enjoyment of any of the rights under the Covenant, including articles 18 and 27, nor in any discrimination against adherents to other religions or non-believers. In particular, certain measures discriminating against the latter, such as measures restricting eligibility for government service to members of the predominant religion or giving economic privileges to them or imposing special restrictions on the practice of other faiths, are not in accordance with the prohibition of discrimination based on religion or belief and the guarantee of equal protection under article 26. The measures contemplated by article 20, paragraph 2 of the Covenant constitute important safeguards against infringement of the rights of religious minorities and of other religious groups to exercise the rights guaranteed by articles 18 and 27, and against acts of violence or persecution directed towards those groups. The Committee wishes to be informed of measures taken by States parties concerned to protect the practices of all religions or beliefs from infringement and to protect their followers from discrimination. Similarly, information as to respect for the rights of religious minorities under article 27 is necessary for the Committee to assess the extent to which the right to freedom of thought, conscience,

religion and belief has been implemented by States parties. States parties concerned should also include in their reports information relating to practices considered by their laws and jurisprudence to be punishable as blasphemous.

10. If a set of beliefs is treated as official ideology in constitutions, statutes, proclamations of ruling parties, etc., or in actual practice, this shall not result in any impairment of the freedoms under article 18 or any other rights recognized under the Covenant nor in any discrimination against persons who do not accept the official ideology or who oppose it.

11. Many individuals have claimed the right to refuse to perform military service (conscientious objection) on the basis that such right derives from their freedoms under article 18. In response to such claims, a growing number of States have in their laws exempted from compulsory military service citizens who genuinely hold religious or other beliefs that forbid the performance of military service and replaced it with alternative national service. The Covenant does not explicitly refer to a right to conscientious objection, but the Committee believes that such a right can be derived from article 18, inasmuch as the obligation to use lethal force may seriously conflict with the freedom of conscience and the right to manifest one's religion or belief. When this right is recognized by law or practice, there shall be no differentiation among conscientious objectors on the basis of the nature of their particular beliefs; likewise, there shall be no discrimination against conscientious objectors because they have failed to perform military service. The Committee invites States parties to report on the conditions under which persons can be exempted from military service on the basis of their rights under article 18 and on the nature and length of alternative national service.

Appendix E

United Nations Human Rights Committee General Comment No. 23 (50)*

The Rights of Minorities
(Article 27)
(Fiftieth Session, 1994)

1. Article 27 of the Covenant provides that, in those States in which ethnic, religious or linguistic minorities exist, persons belonging to these minorities shall not be denied the right, in community with the other members of their group, to enjoy their own culture, to profess and practise their own religion, or to use their own language. The Committee observes that this article establishes and recognizes a right which is conferred on individuals belonging to minority groups and which is distinct from, and additional to, all the other rights which, as individuals in common with everyone else, they are already entitled to enjoy under the Covenant.

2. In some communications submitted to the Committee under the Optional Protocol, the right protected under article 27 has been confused with the right of peoples to self-determination proclaimed in article 1 of the Covenant. Further, in reports submitted by States parties under article 40 of the Covenant, the obligations placed upon States parties under article 27 have sometimes been confused with their duty under article 2.1 to ensure the enjoyment of the rights guaranteed under the Covenant without discrimination and also with equality before the law and equal protection of the law under article 26.

3.1. The Covenant draws a distinction between the right to self-determination and the rights protected under article 27. The former is expressed to be a right belonging to peoples and is dealt with in a separate part (Part I) of the Covenant. Self-determination is not a right cognizable under the Optional Protocol. Article 27, on the other hand, relates to rights conferred on individuals as such and is included, like the articles relating to other personal rights conferred on individuals, in Part III of the Covenant and is cognizable under the Optional Protocol. 1/

*Adopted by the UN Human Rights Committee on 6 April 1994. UN Doc. CCPR/C/21/Rev.1/Add.5 (1994), reprinted in UN Doc. HRI/GEN/1/Rev.1 at 38 (1994).

3.2. The enjoyment of the rights to which article 27 relates does not prejudice the sovereignty and territorial integrity of a State party. At the same time, one or other aspect of the rights of individuals protected under that article - for example, to enjoy a particular culture - may consist in a way of life which is closely associated with territory and use of its resources. 2/ This may particularly be true of members of indigenous communities constituting a minority.

4. The Covenant also distinguishes the rights protected under article 27 from the guarantees under articles 2.1 and 26. The entitlement, under article 2.1, to enjoy the rights under the Covenant without discrimination applies to all individuals within the territory or under the jurisdiction of the State whether or not those persons belong to a minority. In addition, there is a distinct right provided under article 26 for equality before the law, equal protection of the law, and non-discrimination in respect of rights granted and obligations imposed by the States. It governs the exercise of all rights, whether protected under the Covenant or not, which the State party confers by law on individuals within its territory or under its jurisdiction, irrespective of whether they belong to the minorities specified in article 27 or not. 3/ Some States parties who claim that they do not discriminate on grounds of ethnicity, language or religion, wrongly contend, on that basis alone, that they have no minorities.

5.1. The terms used in article 27 indicate that the persons designed to be protected are those who belong to a group and who share in common a culture, a religion and/or a language. Those terms also indicate that the individuals designed to be protected need not be citizens of the State party. In this regard, the obligations deriving from article 2.1 are also relevant, since a State party is required under that article to ensure that the rights protected under the Covenant are available to all individuals within its territory and subject to its jurisdiction, except rights which are expressly made to apply to citizens, for example, political rights under article 25. A State party may not, therefore, restrict the rights under article 27 to its citizens alone.

5.2. Article 27 confers rights on persons belonging to minorities which "exist" in a State party. Given the nature and scope of the rights envisaged under that article, it is not relevant to determine the degree of permanence that the term "exist" connotes. Those rights simply are that individuals belonging to those minorities should not be denied the right, in community with members of their group, to enjoy their own culture, to practise their religion and speak their language. Just as they need not be nationals or citizens, they need not be permanent residents. Thus, migrant workers or even visitors in a State party constituting such minorities are entitled not to be denied the exercise of those rights. As any other individual in the territory of the State party, they would, also for this purpose, have the general rights, for example, to freedom of association, of assembly, and of expression. The existence of an ethnic, religious or linguistic minority in a given State party does not depend upon a decision by that State party but requires to be established by objective criteria.

5.3. The right of individuals belonging to a linguistic minority to use their language among themselves, in private or in public, is distinct from other language rights protected under the Covenant. In particular, it should be distinguished from the general right to freedom of expression protected under article 19. The latter right is available to all persons, irrespective of whether they belong to minorities or not. Further, the right protected under article 27 should be distinguished from the particular right which article 14.3 (f) of the Covenant confers on accused persons to interpretation where they cannot understand or speak the language used in the courts. Article 14.3 (f) does not, in any other circumstances, confer on accused persons the right to use or speak the language of their choice in court proceedings. 4/

6.1. Although article 27 is expressed in negative terms, that article, nevertheless, does recognize the existence of a "right" and requires that it shall not be denied. Consequently, a State party is under an obligation to ensure that the existence and the exercise of this right are protected against their denial or violation. Positive measures of protection are, therefore, required not only against the acts of the State party itself, whether through its legislative, judicial or administrative authorities, but also against the acts of other persons within the State party.

6.2. Although the rights protected under article 27 are individual rights, they depend in turn on the ability of the minority group to maintain its culture, language or religion. Accordingly, positive measures by States may also be necessary to protect the identity of a minority and the rights of its members to enjoy and develop their culture and language and to practise their religion, in community with the other members of the group. In this connection, it has to be observed that such positive measures must respect the provisions of articles 2.1 and 26 of the Covenant both as regards the treatment between different minorities and the treatment between the persons belonging to them and the remaining part of the population. However, as long as those measures are aimed at correcting conditions which prevent or impair the enjoyment of the rights guaranteed under article 27, they may constitute a legitimate differentiation under the Covenant, provided that they are based on reasonable and objective criteria.

7. With regard to the exercise of the cultural rights protected under article 27, the Committee observes that culture manifests itself in many forms, including a particular way of life associated with the use of land resources, especially in the case of indigenous peoples. That right may include such traditional activities as fishing or hunting and the right to live in reserves protected by law. 5/ The enjoyment of those rights may require positive legal measures of protection and measures to ensure the effective participation of members of minority communities in decisions which affect them.

8. The Committee observes that none of the rights protected under article 27 of the Covenant may be legitimately exercised in a manner or to an extent inconsistent with the other provisions of the Covenant.

9. The Committee concludes that article 27 relates to rights whose protection imposes specific obligations on States parties. The protection of these rights is directed towards ensuring the survival and continued development of the cultural, religious and social identity of the minorities concerned, thus enriching the fabric of society as a whole. Accordingly, the Committee observes that these rights must be

protected as such and should not be confused with other personal rights conferred on one and all under the Covenant. States parties, therefore, have an obligation to ensure that the exercise of these rights is fully protected and they should indicate in their reports the measures they have adopted to this end.

Notes

1/ See *Official Records of the General Assembly, Thirty-ninth Session, Supplement No. 40* (A/39/40), annex VI, General Comment No. 12 (21) (article 1), also issued in document CCPR/C/21/Rev.1; ibid., *Forty-fifth Session, Supplement No. 40*, (A/45/40), vol. II, annex IX, sect. A, Communication No. 167/1984 (*Bernard Ominayak, Chief of the Lubicon Lake Band v. Canada*), views adopted on 26 March 1990.

2/ See ibid., *Forty-third Session, Supplement No. 40* (A/43/40), annex VII, sect. G, Communication No. 197/1985 (*Kitok v. Sweden*), views adopted on 27 July 1988.

3/ See ibid., *Forty-second Session, Supplement No. 40* (A/42/40), annex VIII, sect. D, Communication No. 182/1984 (*F.H. Zwaan-de Vries v. the Netherlands*), views adopted on 9 April 1987; ibid., sect. C, Communication No. 180/1984 (*L.G. Danning v. the Netherlands*), views adopted on 9 April 1987.

4/ See ibid., *Forty-fifth Session, Supplement No. 40*, (A/45/40), vol. II, annex X, sect. A, Communication No. 220/1987 (*T.K. v. France*), decision of 8 November 1989; ibid., sect. B, Communication No. 222/1987 (*M.K. v. France*), decision of 8 November 1989.

5/ See notes 1 and 2 above, Communication No. 167/1984 (*Bernard Ominayak, Chief of the Lubicon Lake Band v. Canada*), views adopted on 26 March 1990, and Communication No. 197/1985 (*Kitok v. Sweden*), views adopted on 27 July 1988.

Appendix F

The Oslo Declaration on Freedom of Religion or Belief

Whereas the Oslo Conference on Freedom of Religion or Belief, meeting in celebration of the fiftieth anniversary of the Universal Declaration of Human Rights, reaffirms that every person has the right to freedom of religion or belief;

And whereas participants in the Oslo Conference have accepted the challenge to build an international coalition and to develop a strategic plan of action to achieve substantial progress in and give practical support to the implementation of Article 18 of the Universal Declaration of Human Rights, Article 18 of the International Covenant on Civil and Political Rights, and the 1981 United Nations Declaration on the Elimination of All Forms of Intolerance and of Discrimination Based on Religion or Belief;

Therefore, we the participants in the Oslo Conference:

Recognise that religions and beliefs teach peace and good will;

Recognise that religions and beliefs may be misused to cause intolerance, discrimination and prejudice, and have all to often been used to deny the rights and freedoms of others;

Affirm that every human being has a responsibility to condemn discrimination and intolerance based on religions and belief, and to apply religion or belief in support of human dignity and peace;

Consider the founding of the United Nations and the adoption of the Universal Declaration of Human Rights to be watershed events, in which the world community recognised for the first time that the existence of human rights transcends the laws of sovereign states;

Confirm that Article 18 of both of the Universal Declaration of Human Rights and the International Covenant on Civil and Political Rights together with other instruments create both a mandate for freedom of religion or belief and a universal standard around which we wish to rally;

Recognise that the U.N. has made significant accomplishments in strengthening this universal standard by passage of the 1981 U.N. Declaration on the Elimination of All Forms of Intolerance and of Discrimination Based on Religion or Belief, by the appointment of a Special Rapporteur to monitor its implementation, and by further defining freedom of religion or belief in the General Comment on Article 18 of the International Covenant on Civil and Political Rights;

Recommend that the U.N. Commission on Human Rights change the title of the Rapporteur to Special Rapporteur on Freedom of Religion or Belief;

Urge increased financial and personnel support to the U.N. to implement the work of the Special Rapporteur and his recommendations;

Request the U.N. High Commissioner for Human Rights to develop a co-ordinated plan to focus resources of the United Nations, including all specialised agencies and bodies such as UNESCO, ILO, UNDP, and UNHCR on problem involving freedom of religion or belief;

Call for UNESCO to expand its work for peace through religion and cultural dialogue and encourage intensified co-operation with UNESCO in this field;

Urge scholars and teachers to study and apply the Universal Declaration of Human Rights, the International Covenant on Civil and Political Rights and the 1981 Declaration as universal standards on freedom of religion or belief and as a way to solve problems of intolerance and discrimination caused by competing beliefs;

Challenge governments, religious bodies, interfaith associations, humanist communities, non-governmental organisations and academic institutions to create educational programs using the 1981 Declaration as a universal standard to build a culture of tolerance and understanding and respect between people of diverse beliefs;

Further urge U.N. member states to use the 1981 Declaration and other relevant instruments to mediate, negotiate, and resolve intolerance, discrimination, injustice and violence in conflicts where religion or belief plays a role;

Support research and development of other informational resources and methodologies for collecting information, monitoring compliance and initiating comparative country studies to strengthen the work of the United Nations and protect freedom of religion or belief;

Urge the organisers and sponsors of the Oslo Conference, in consultation with Conference participants: to review the discussions and recommendations of the Conference with the purpose of creating an "Oslo Coalition on Freedom of Religion or Belief", inviting support and participation by governments, religious or belief communities, academic institutions and non-governmental organisations; and to develop a strategic plan of action and seek funding to carry out programs and projects based on its recommendations, in co-operation with the United Nations system.

Appendix G
List of NGOs

Organization	Address	City	Country	Telephone	Fax	E-mail	Website
Action of Christians for Abolition of Torture (ACAT NEDERLAND)	1018 VE	Amsterdam	The Netherlands	020 420 2891	31 74 376 27 86	acatnederland@ hotmail.com	http://acat.nfg.nl
Administrative Center for Jehovah's Witnesses in Russia	Srednyaya 6, Solnechnoye	189649 St. Petersburg	Russian Federation	7 902 680 63 25	7 812 437 09 70	john.burns@wtbts.org.ru	
African American Islamic Institute	PO Box 411	Medina Kaolack	Senegal	011 221 941 2353	011 221 941 1786	halimcisse@earthlink.net	www.home.earthlink.net/ ~halimcisse/aaii-2.html
Agudath Israel World Organization	84 William St	New York, NY 10038	United States of America	1 212 797 9000	1 212 269 2843		
Alianza Espiritualista Internacional	Calle Sazie 2078	Santiago	Chile	56 2 695 1170	56 2 695 1170	luisat@entelchile.net	http://web.jet.es/ planetagaia/pla14.htm
Almaty Helsinki Committee	Koktem-1, 29/17	480090 Almaty	Kazakhstan	7 3272 499555	7 3272 496331	office-ahc@nursat.kz	www.humanrights.kz
American Baptist Churches - USA National Ministries	PO Box 851	Valley Forge, PA 19482-0851	United States of America	1 610 768 2000	1 610 768 2453	webmaster@abc-usa.org	www.abc-usa.org
American Civil Liberties Union	125 Broad St	New York, NY 10004-2400	United States of America	1 212 549 2500		aclu@aclu.org	www.aclu.org

Organization	Address	City	Country	Telephone	Fax	E-mail	Website
American Humanist Association	1777 T St, NW	Washington, DC 20009-7125	United States of America	1 202 238 9088 Toll Free: 1 800 837 3792	1 202 238 9003	aha@ americanhumanist.org humanism@juno.com	www.americanhumanist .org
American Jewish Committee	Institute of Human Relations 165 East 56th St	New York, NY 10150	United States of America	1 212 751 4000	1 212 891 1492	PR@ajc.org	www.ajc.org
Amnesty International, International Secretariat	Peter Benenson House, 1 Easton St	London WC1X 0DW	United Kingdom	44 20 7814 6200	44 20 7833 1510	amnestyis@amnesty.org	www.amnesty.org
Andrei Sakharov Foundation	65 Park Ave	New York, NY 10128	United States of America	1 212 369 1226	1 212 722 0557	anls@mail.wdn.com	http://asf.wdn.com
Association of American Buddhists	301 West 45th St	New York, NY 10036	United States of America	1 212 489 1075	1 212 489 1075	oneil@mail.com	
Association of Christian Churches in Russia	PO Box 275	St. Petersburg 196105	Russian Federation	7 812 110 1500	7 812 110 1079	accr@mail.rcom.ru	www.accr.ru
Association Internationale pour la Defense de la Liberte Religieuse	Schosshalden-strasse 17	3006-Berne	Switzerland	031 359 1527 /28	031 359 1566		
Bahá'í Community of the Netherlands	Riouwstraat 27	2585 GR, The Hague	The Netherlands	31 70 355 40 17		nsa@bahai.nl	www.bahai.nl

Organization	Address	City	Country	Telephone	Fax	E-mail	Website
Beckett Fund	1350 Connecticut Ave, NW Suite 605	Washington, DC 20036	United States of America	1 202 955 0095 or 1 800 BECKET 5	1 202 955 0900	mail@becketfund.org	www.becketfund.org
Belief Order of St. Augustine	Curia Generalizia Agostiniana, Via Paolo VI, 25	Rome 00193	Italy	815 485 8049	312 368 1090		
Bible League	PO Box 567	3800 AN Amersfoort	The Netherlands	31 33 4725800	31 33 4724950		www.bibleleague.nl
Bulgarian Helsinki Committee	7 Varbitsa St	Sofia BG-1504	Bulgaria	359 2 943 4876	359 2 943 4876	bhc@bghelsinki.org	www.bghelsinki.org
BYU International Center for Law and Religion Studies	Brigham Young University, PO Box 28000, 419 JRCB	Provo, UT 84602	United States of America	1 801 422 6842	1 801 422 0390	law_religion@byu.edu	www.law2.byu.edu/ Law&Religion
Cairo Institute for Human Rights Studies	9 Rustern St, Apt 35	Borden City, Cairo	Egypt	202 354 3715, 202 795 1112	202 355 4200, 202 795 4700	cihrs@idsc.gov.eg	www.cihrs.org
Calamus Foundation	18j Eaton Square	London SW1W 9D0	United Kingdom	44 171 235 03 02	44 171 245 68 21		
Canadian Civil Liberties Association (CCLA)	394 Bloor St West, Suite 200	Toronto M5S 1X4	Canada	1 416 363 0321	1 416 861 1291	ccla@ilap.com	www.ccla.org

Organization	Address	City	Country	Telephone	Fax	E-mail	Website
Center for Human Rights/ Romanian Helsinki Committee	Str Nicolae Tonitza 8, Sector 3	704012 Bucharest	Romania	40 1 312 45 28	40 1 312 37 11	apador@dnt.ro	www.apador.org
Center for Religious Dialogue (CRD) Sarajevo	Kosevsko BRDO 25	71000 Sarajevo	Bosnia and Herzegovina	387 71 66 65 16	387 71 66 65 18		
Center for the Study of Religious Freedom (Virginia Wesleyan College)	1584 Wesleyan Dr	Norfolk, VA 23502-5599	United States of America	1 757 455 3129	1 757 455 2110	csrf@vwc.edu	www.vwc.edu/academic/csrf
CESNUR (Center for Studies on New Religions)	Via Confienza 19	10121 Torino	Italy	39 011 541950	39 011 541905	cesnurto@tin.it	www.cesnur.org
Christian Solidarity Worldwide	PO Box 99	Surrey KT3 3YF	United Kingdom	44 20 8942 8810 (UK 0208 942 8810)	44 20 8942 8821 (UK 0208 942 8821)	admin@csw.org.uk	www.csw.org.uk
Christians Associated for Relationships with Eastern Europe (CAREE)	c/o Dr. Jim Payton Redeemer College, 777 Garner Rd East	Ancaster, Ontario L9K 1J4	Canada	905 648 2131 x4287	905 648 2134	caree@redeemer.on.ca	
Christians in Crisis	1111 Fairgrounds Rd	Grand Rapids, MN 55744	United States of America	1 218 326 2688 Toll free: 1 800 286 5115		reiners@northernnet.com	www.members.aol.com/biblprof/crisis.htm
The Christophers	12 East 48th St	New York, NY 10017	United States of America	1 212 759 4050	1 212 838 5073	mail@christophers.org tci@idt.net	www.christophers.org

Organization	Address	City	Country	Telephone	Fax	E-mail	Website
Church of Scientology, European Human Rights Office	9, rue General Macarthur	B-1180 Brussels	Belgium	32 2 347 16 48	32 2 347 42 90	101540.51@ compuserve.com	www.scientology.org
Church Women United	475 Riverside Dr, Suite 1626	New York, NY 10115	United States of America	1 212 870 2347	1 212 870 2338	cwu@churchwomen.org	www.churchwomen.org
Church World Service	475 Riverside Dr, Room 678	New York, NY 10115	United States of America	1 212 870 2061	1 212 870 3523		www.churchworldservice.org
Churches Human Rights Programme	Ecumenical Centre c/o Ruediger Noll rue Joseph II, 174	B-1000 Brussels	Belgium	32 2 230 17 32	32 2 230 14 13	rno@cec-kek.be	
Colloquium of European Parishes	Wienbergstrasse 36/11	A-1120 Vienna	Austria	43 1 817 66 63	43 1 817 66 63		www. cep-eu.com
Commission of the Bishops' Conferences of the EC (COMECE)	42 rue Stévin	B-1000 Brussels	Belgium	32 2 235 05 10	32 2 230 33 34	comece@comece.org	www.comece.org
Commission for Justice and Peace Netherlands/Dutch Platform for International Freedom of Religion or Belief	PO Box 16334	2500 BH The Hague	The Netherlands	31 70 313 68 00	31 70 313 68 01	info@justitiaetpax.nl	www.justitiaetpax.nl
Committee for the Protection of Personal Rights - Uzbek Section of the International Society for Human Rights	Pr. Rashidov 40-141	700029 Tashkent	Uzbekistan	7 371 184 43 23	7 371 256 14 23		

Organization	Address	City	Country	Telephone	Fax	E-mail	Website
Community of Saint Egidio	Piazza S. Egidio 3/a	00153 Rome	Italy	39 06 585 661	39 06 580 0197	info@santegidio.org	www.santegidio.org
Conference of European Churches - Church and Society Commission	Ecumenical Centre rue Joseph II, 174	BE-1000 Brussels	Belgium	32 2 230 17 32	32 2 231 14 13	csc.bru@cec-kek.be	www.cec-kek.org
Congregation of the Mission	Via dei Capasso, 30	00164 Rome	Italy	39 6 666 3730	39 6 666 3831	MDO801@mclink.it	www.famvin.org
Congrégation de Notre-Dame	2330 Rue Sherbrooke Ouest	Montreal, QC H3H 1G8	Canada	514 931 5891 x223	514 931 2915	cnd@cnd-m.com	www.cnd-m.com
Congress of Jewish Religious Organizations and Associations in Russia	10 Bolshoi Spasoglisischevsky per.	101000 Moscow	Russian Federation	7 095 728 40 79			
Consistoire National des Temoins de Jehovah	2, Avenue des Abattoirs		France	33 2 32 25 55 55	33 2 32 25 56 56		
Cooperative Baptist Fellowship, United States of America (CBF)	PO Box 450329, 3001 Mercer, University Dr	Atlanta, GA 31145-0329	United States of America	1 770 220 1600	1 770 220 1685	contact@ thefellowship.info	www.cbfonline.org
Council on American-Islamic Relations	453 New Jersey Ave, SE	Washington, DC 20003	United States of America	1 202 488 8787	1 202 488 0833	cair@cair-net.org	www.cair-net.org

Organization	Address	City	Country	Telephone	Fax	E-mail	Website
Council for America's First Freedom	Nations Bank Center, 1111 East Main St, Suite 200	Richmond, VA 23219-4117	United States of America	1 804 643 1786	1 804 644 5024	caff@firstfreedom.org	www.firstfreedom.org
Council for Human Rights and Religious Freedom (Int'l)	6 rue Moncrabeau	B-5000 Namur	Belgium		32 81 22 06 76		
Czech Helsinki Committee	Jeleni 5, PO Box 4	118 00 Prague	Czech Republic	420 2 24 37 23 34	420 2 24 37 23 35	sekr@helcom.cz	www.helcom.cz
Derechos Human Rights	Apartado de Correo 156037	156037 Madrid	Spain	34 91 526 7502	34 91 526 7515	hr@derechos.org	www.derechos.org
Diocese of the Armenian Church of America	630 Second Ave	New York, NY 10016	United States of America	1 212 686 0710	1 212 779 3558		www.armenianchurch.org
Dominican Leadership Conference (DLC)	7200 West Division St	River Forest, IL 60305	United States of America	1 708 771 0909	1 708 771 4510	op7200@theramp.net	www.op.org/dlc
Dutch Platform on International Freedom of Religion and Belief	Mr. J. M. M. Naber, Secretary PO Box 16334	2500 BH The Hague	The Netherlands	31 6 28 64 13 59		nzr@antenna.nl	www.zendingsraad.nl
Ecumenical Council of Denmark/Dan Church Aid	Dag Hammerskjolds Alle	21000 Kopenhagen 0	Denmark		45 33 15 41 56	eh@hslaw.dk	

Organization	Address	City	Country	Telephone	Fax	E-mail	Website
Educational and Charitable Society "Orthodoxy"	Allika 5-10	68204 Valga	Estonia	372 510 34 76		oleg.tesla@neti.ee	
Emory University School of Law, Center for the Interdisciplinary Study of Religion	310 Gambrell Hall 1301 Clifton Rd	Atlanta, GA 30322	United States of America	1 404 712 8710	1 404 712 8605	cisr@law.emory.edu	http://law.emory.edu/cisr
Episcopal Church, Executive Council of the	815 Second Ave	New York, NY 10017	United States of America	1 212 922 5385	1 212 557 5827	pmordecai@dfms.org	www.episcopalchurch.org
Estonian Orthodox Church of Moscow Patriarchy	Laane tee-20	13111 Tallinn	Estonia	372 623 23 38	372 641 13 02		
European Association of Jehovah's Witnesses for the Protection of Religious Freedom	Rue d'Argile 60	B-1950 Kraainem-Brussels	Belgium	32 2 782 00 15	32 2 782 05 92	pgillies@wtbts.org.uk	
European Center, Albania		Qendra Noli	Albania	355 4 25 03 02		gjsinani@yahoo.com	
European Centre for Law and Justice	4, quai Koch	67000 Strasbourg	France	33 3 88 24 94 40	33 3 88 24 94 47	c.wharton@wanadoo.fr	www.eclj.org
European Party for Democracy and Diversity	PO Box 23529	3001 KM Rotterdam	The Netherlands	31 10 414 05 34	31 10 414 15 01		

Organization	Address	City	Country	Telephone	Fax	E-mail	Website
Evangelical Covenant Church	5101 North Francisco Ave	Chicago, IL 60625	United States of America	1 773 784 3000	1 773 784 4366	webster@covchurch.org	www.covchurch.org/cov
The Family	Family Info Dept, Maxet House, Liverpool Rd	Luton LU1 1RS	United Kingdom	44 7740 64 50 03		info@ thefamilyeurope.org	
Fédération Internationale des Droits de l'Homme	17 Passage de la main d'or	Paris F-75011	France	33 1 43 55 25 18	33 1 43 55 18 80	fidh@fidh.org	www.fidh.org
Federation of Jewish Men's Clubs, Inc.	475 Riverside Dr, Suite 832	New York, NY 10115	United States of America	1 212 749 8100	1 212 316 4271	international@fjmc.org	www.fjmc.org
Federation for World Peace and Unification			The Netherlands	31 346 57 29 89	31 703 83 59 38	info@fwu.nl	www.fwu.nl
Forum 18	PO Box 6663 Rodeløkka	N-0502 Oslo	Norway			f18news.editor@ forum18.org	www.forum18.org
Freedom Forum	1101 Wilson Blvd	Arlington, VA 22209	United States of America	1 703 528 0800	1 703 284 3770	news@ freedomforum.org	www.freedomforum.org
Freedom House (Center for Religious Freedom)	1319 18th St, NW	Washington, DC 20036	United States of America	1 202 296 5101	1 202 296 5078	religion@ freedomhouse.org	www.freedomhouse.org

Organization	Address	City	Country	Telephone	Fax	E-mail	Website
Fundación Mundial Hastinapura	Venezuela 818	Buenos Aires, 1095	Argentina	54 11 4342 4250	54 11 4342 4250	edithasti@sion.com central@ hastinapura.org.ar	www.hastinapura.org.ar
General Conference of Seventh-day Adventists	12501 Old Columbia Pike	Silver Spring, MD 20904	United States of America	1 301 680 6000	1 301 680 6695	jongallagher@ compuserve.com	www.adventist.org
Glasnost Defence Foundation	4 Zubovsky Bul. Room 432	119021 Moscow	Russian Federation	7 095 201 4974	7 095 4947	fond@gdf.ru	www.gdf.ru
Global Ethic Foundation	Stiftung Weltethos, Waldhäuser Strasse 23	D-72076 Tübingen	Germany	0 70 71 64 26 46	0 70 71 61 01 40	office@weltethos.org	www.weltethos.org
Global Forum of Spiritual and Parliamentary Leaders on Human Survival	336 East 45th St 10th Floor	New York, NY 10017	United States of America	1 212 953 7947	1 212 557 2061	globalforum@ worldnet.att.net	www.oneworld.org/ globalforum
Greek Helsinki Monitor	PO Box 51393	GR-14510 Kifisia	Greece	30 1 620 01 20	30 1 807 57 67	office@greekhelsinki.gr	www.greekhelsinki.gr
Greek Orthodox Archdiocese of America	8 East 79th St	New York, NY 10021	United States of America	1 212 570 3500	1 212 570 3569	archdiocese@goarch.org	www.goarch.org
Helsinki Foundation for Human Rights (Poland)	Zgoda str. 11	00-026 Warsaw	Poland	48 22 828 10 08	48 22 828 69 96	hfhr@hfhrpol.waw.pl	www.hfhrpol.waw.pl

Organization	Address	City	Country	Telephone	Fax	E-mail	Website
Human Rights Center of Azerbaijan	165-3 Bashir Safaroglu Str.	Baku 370000	Azerbaijan	994 12 077 026	994 12 942 471	hrca@mail.ru aihmm@lycos.de	www.mitglied.lycos.de/ hrca
Human Rights Centre	University of Essex Wivenhoe Park	Colchester, Essex, CO4 3SQ	United Kingdom	44 1206 87 25 58	44 1206 87 36 27	hrc@essex.ac.uk	www2.essex.ac.uk/ human_rights_centre
Human Rights in China	350 Fifth Ave, Suite 3309	New York, NY 10118	United States of America	1 212 239 4495	1 212 239 2561	hrichina@hrichina.org	http://iso.hrichina.org/ iso
Human Rights Watch	350 Fifth Ave, 34th Floor	New York, NY 10118-3299	United States of America	1 212 290 4700	1 212 736 1300	hrwnyc@hrw.org	www.hrw.org
Human Rights Without Frontiers	Avenue Winston Churchill 11/33	B-1180 Brussels	Belgium	32 2 345 61 45	32 2 343 74 91	info@hrwf.net	www.hrwf.net
Human Rights Without Frontiers International	Avenue Winston Churchill 11/33	B-1180 Brussels	Belgium	32 2 345 61 45	32 2 343 74 91	info@hwrf.net	www.hrwf.net
Humanitarian Legal Centre	M. Gafur st. 18	705011 Bukhara City	Uzbekistan	998 65 224 30 27	998 65 224 30 27		
Index on Censorship	Lancaster House, 33 Islington High St	London N1 9LH	United Kingdom	44 20 72 78 23 13	44 20 72 78 18 78	contact@ indexoncensorship.org	www.indexonline.org

Organization	Address	City	Country	Telephone	Fax	E-mail	Website
Information Network Focus on Religious Movements (INFORM)	INFORM Houghton St	London WC2A 2AE	United Kingdom	44 20 7955 7654	44 20 7955 7679	inform@lse.ac.uk	www.inform.ac/ infmain.html
Institute for Public Affairs of the Orthodox Union	800 Eighth Street, NW	Washington, DC 20001	United States of America	1 202 513 6484	1 202 289 8936	info@ou.org	www.ou.org
Institute for War and Peace Reporting (IWPR)	Lancaster House, 33 Islington High St	London N1 9LH	United Kingdom	44 20 77 13 71 30	44 20 77 13 71 40	tony@iwpr.net	www.iwpr.net
International Academy for Freedom of Religion and Belief	4545 42nd St, NW, Suite 2	Washington, DC 20016	United States of America	1 202 363 1754	1 202 363 1773		
International Association for Religious Freedom (IARF)	2 Market St	Oxford OX1 3EF	United Kingdom	44 (0) 1865 202 744	44 (0) 1865 202 746	iarf@interfaith-center.org hq@iarf.net	www.iarf.net
International Association of Sufism	14 Commercial Blvd #101	Novato, CA 94949	United States of America	1 415 472 6959 1 415 382 7834		ias@ias.org	www.ias.org
International Center for Non-for-Profit Law	1126 16th St, NW, Suite 400	Washington, DC 20036	United States of America	1 202 452 8600	1 202 452 8555	infoicnl@icnl.org	www.icnl.org
International Christian Concern (ICC)	2020 Pennsylvania Ave, NW, #941	Washington, DC 20006	United States of America	1 301 989 1708 (Toll free in USA 1 800 ICC 5441)	1 301 989 1709	icc@persecution.org	www.persecution.org

Organization	Address	City	Country	Telephone	Fax	E-mail	Website
International Coalition for Religious Freedom (ICRF)	7777 Leesburg Pike, Suite 404 N-A	Falls Church, VA 22043	United States of America	1 703 790 1500	1 703 790 5562	ICRF@aol.com	www.religiousfreedom.com
International Commission on Freedom of Conscience	4545 42nd St, Suite 201	Washington, DC 20016	United States of America	1 202 363 1773	1 202 363 0304	leeboothby@aol.com	
International Federation of Journalists (IFJ)	IPC-Residence Palace, Bloc C Rue de la Loi 155	B-1040 Brussels	Belgium	32 2 235 22 00	32 2 235 22 19	ifj@ifj.org	www.ifj.org
International Helsinki Federation for Human Rights (Austria)	Wickenburggasse 14/7	A-1080 Vienna	Austria	43 1 408 88 22	43 1 408 88 22-50	office@ihf-hr.org	www.ihf-hr.org
International Humanist and Ethical Union	1 Gower St	London WC1E 6HD	United Kingdom	44 20 7631 3170	44 20 7631 3171	humanism@iheu.org	www.iheu.org
International Institute for the Study of Islam in the Modern World (ISIM)	Rapenburg 71, PO Box 11089	2301 EB Leiden	The Netherlands	31 71 527 79 05	31 71 527 79 06	info@isim.nl	www.isim.nl
International Kolping Society	Kolpingplatz 5-11, PO Box 10 08 41	D-50448 Köln	Germany	49 221 207 0148	49 221 207 0146	ikw@kolping.de	www.kolping.net
International League for Human Rights	228 E 45th St, 5th floor	New York, NY 10017	United States of America	1 212 661 0480	1 212 661 0416	info@ilhr.org	www.ilhr.org

Organization	Address	City	Country	Telephone	Fax	E-mail	Website
International Network of Engaged Buddhists	PO Box 19 Mahadthai Post Office	Bangkok, 10206	Thailand	662 433 7169	662 433 7169	ineb@ipied.tu.ac.th ineb@loxinfo.co.th	www.sulak-sivaraksa.org
International Religious Foundation	4 West 43rd St	New York, NY 10036	United States of America	1 212 869 6023	1 212 869 6424		
International Religious Liberty Association (IRLA)	12501 Old Columbia Pike	Silver Spring, MD 20904	United States of America	1 301 680 6686	1 301 680 6695	ViHughes@compuserve.com	www.irla.org
International Religious Liberty Association (IRLA) Euro-Asia Chapter	Krasnoyarskaya street 3	107589 Moscow	Russian Federation	7 095 786 8150	7 095 786 8155	vpkrushnitsky@esd-sda.ru	
International Scientific Conference Minorities for Europe of Tomorrow (ISCOMET)	H. Tomsica 4	Si-2000 Maribor	Slovenia	386 2 235 53 70	386 2 235 53 72	iscomet@siol.net	
International Shinto Foundation	Hirai 5-22-9, Edogawa-ku	Tokyo, 132-0035	Japan	81 3 3610 3975	81 3 3610 3975	shinto@mx1.alpha-web.ne.jp hdqrs@shinto.org	www.shinto.org
International Young Christian Workers	11, rue Plantin	Brussels, 1070	Belgium			info@jociycw.net	www.jociycw.net
Internews International	14 cité Griset	F-75011 Paris	France	33 1 53 36 06 06	33 1 53 36 83 41	johnson@internews.fr	www.internews.fr

Organization	Address	City	Country	Telephone	Fax	E-mail	Website
Islamic Human Rights Commission	PO Box 598	Wembley HA9 7XH	United Kingdom	44 20 8902 0888	44 20 8902 8889	info@ihrc.org	www.ihrc.org
J. M. Dawson Institute of Church-State Studies (Baylor University)	Baylor University PO Box 97308	Waco, TX 76798-7308	United States of America	1 254 710 1510	1 254 710 1571	Derek_Davis@ baylor.edu	www3.baylor.edu/ Church_State
Jagiellonian University; Center on Jewish History and Culture	1010 Wisconsin Ave, NW, Suite 345	Washington, DC 20007	United States of America	1 202 554 3600	1 202 338 4393	info@Judaica.org	www.judaica.org/ otherprojects/other5.html
Jordanian Society for Citizen Rights (JSCR)		Amman	Jordan	962 7 95877000 962 6 4776147	962 6 4776147	citizenrightssociety@ yahoo.com	
Jubilee Campaign NL	PO Box 21	3970 AA Driebergen	The Netherlands	31 343 510 159	31 343 510 395	info@ jubileecampaign.nl	www.jubileecampaign.nl
JUST International	PO Box 288 Jalan Sultan	45730 Petaling Jaya, Selangor SE	Malaysia	603 7727 7389	603 7727 7389	muza@po.jaring.my	www.just-international.org
Keston Institute	38 St Aldates	Oxford OX1 1BN	United Kingdom	44 (0) 1865 792929	44 (0) 1865 240042	keston.institute@ keston.org	www.keston.org
Knights of Columbus	1 Columbus Plaza	New Haven, CT 06510-3326	United States of America	1 203 752 4000	1 203 865 2310	info@kofc.org	www.kofc.org

Organization	Address	City	Country	Telephone	Fax	E-mail	Website
Liberty Counsel	PO Box 540774	Orlando, FL 32854	United States of America	1 407 875 2100	1 407 875 0770	liberty@lc.org	www.lc.org
Liga Espanola Pro-Derechos Humanos	C/Hermosilla 114, bajo A	28009 Madrid	Spain	34 91 401 96 95	34 91 401 96 95	lepddhh@lander.es	
Lutheran World Federation	150, route de Ferney PO Box 2100	CH-1211 Geneva 2	Switzerland	41 22 791 61 11	41 22 791 66 30 41 22 798 86 16	info@lutheranworld.org	www.lutheranworld.org
Messianic Jewish Alliance of America	PO Box 274	Springfield, PA 19153	United States of America	1 800 225 6522	1 610 338 0471	info@mjaa.org	www.mjaa.org
Minority Rights Group	54 Commercial St	London E1 6LT	United Kingdom	44 020 7422 4200	44 020 422 4201	minority.rights@ mrgmail.org	www.minorityrights.org
Montenegrin Helsinki Committee for Human Rights	K. Ivanovica 3	85310 Budva	FR Yugoslavia	381 81 23 42 05	381 81 23 42 05	montheco@cg.yu	
Moscow Partriarchate; Department for External Church Relations	44/28-3 Studencheskaya St	Moscow	Russian Federation	7 095 230 20 28	7 095 230 26 19		
Muslim World League (MWL)	PO Box 537	Makkah Al-Mukarramah	Saudi Arabia	542 2733			

Organization	Address	City	Country	Telephone	Fax	E-mail	Website
National Baptist Convention of the United States of America, Inc.	1700 Baptist World Center Dr	Nashville, TN 37207	United States of America	1 866 531 3054		info.nbcusa@ verizon.net	www.nationalbaptist.com
National Council of the Churches of Christ in the United States of America	475 Riverside Dr, #880	New York, NY 10115	United States of America	1 212 870 2227	1 212 870 2030	news@ncccusa.org	www.ncccusa.org
National Council on Islamic Affairs	764 Lincoln Blvd, PO Box 1028	Long Beach, NY 11561	United States of America	1 516 889 0005	1 516 889 0005		
Netherlands Helsinki Committee	PO Box 93132	2509 AC The Hague	The Netherlands	31 070 392 6700	31 070 392 6550	office@nhc.nl	www.nhc.nl
Netherlands Institute of Human Rights (SIM)	Janskerkhof 3	3512 BK Utrecht	The Netherlands	31 30 253 80 33	31 30 253 71 68	sim@law.uu.nl	www.law.uu.nl/ english/sim
North American Mission Board, Southern Baptist Convention	4200 North Point Pkwy	Alpharetta, GA 30022-4176	United States of America	1 770 410 6000	1 770 410 6018	proberts@namb.net	www.namb.net
Norwegian Centre for Human Rights/Program for Human Rights and Normative Traditions	PO Box 6706 St. Olavs plass	NO-0130 Oslo	Norway	47 22 84 20 01	47 22 84 20 02	tore.lindholm@ nchr.uio.no	www.humanrights.uio.no/ english
Norwegian Forum for Freedom of Expression	Menneskerettig-hetshuset Urtegata 50	N-0187 Oslo	Norway	47 22 67 79 64	47 22 57 00 88	nffe@online.no	

Organization	Address	City	Country	Telephone	Fax	E-mail	Website
Norwegian Mission to the East	PO Box 6663 Rodelokka	N-0502 Oslo	Norway	47 22 38 05 13	47 22 38 24 06	mail@normis.no	www.normis.no
Open Doors	Lijsterlaan 16	3853 TC Ermelo	The Netherlands	31 341 41 95 02	31 341 42 55 54	ron@solcon.nl	www.opendoors.nl
Open Society Institute - Brussels	Rue des Minimes 26	Brussels B-1000	Belgium	32 2 505 46 46	32 2 502 46 46	osi@osi-brussels.be	
Order of Saint Augustine	Curia Generalizia Agostiniana Via Paolo VI, 25	Rome, 193	Italy	773 684 6510 815 485 8049	312 368 1090	jpsosa@msn.com	
Organization of Jewish Communities in the Netherlands - NIK	PO Box 7967	1008 AD Amsterdam	The Netherlands	31 20 644 99 68	31 20 644 26 06	info@nik.nl	
Organization for the Protection of Human Rights and Social Guarantees of Lithuania	kestucio 54-2	LT-3000 Kaunus	Lithuania	370 37 206 233	370 61 619 520	info@zmogausteises.lt	www.zmogausteises.lt
OSCE Network in Sweden	Polhemsvagen 43	S-19134 Sollentuna	Sweden	46 8 35 58 33	46 8 92 78 55	urban.gibson@swipnet.se	
Oslo Coalition on Freedom of Religion and Belief	PO Box 6706 St. Olavs plass	NO-0130 Oslo	Norway	47 22 84 20 45	47 22 84 20 02	lena.larsen@nchr.uio.no	www.oslocoalition.org

Organization	Address	City	Country	Telephone	Fax	E-mail	Website
Pax Christi Nederland	PO Box 19318	3501 DH Utrecht	The Netherlands	31 30 233 33 46	31 30 236 81 99	reactie@paxchristi.nl	www.paxchristi.nl
Peace and Justice Center, Shkoder Albania	Boreelstraat 31-c	3039 WH Rotterdam	The Netherlands	355 38 203 40 79	355 22 43 001	kosterw@albnet.net	
Radio Free Europe - Radio Liberty	1201 Connecticut Ave, NW	Washington, DC 20036	United States of America	1 202 457 6947	1 202 457 6992	jensend@rferl.org	www.rferl.org
Radio Free Europe - Radio Liberty	Vinohradska 1	110 00 Prague 1	Czech Republic	420 2 21 12 24 07	420 2 21 12 36 30	lukaso@rferl.org	www.rferl.org
Religious Freedom Page							http://religiousfreedom.lib.virginia.edu
Reporters sans frontières (RSF)	5, rue Geoffroy Marie	Paris F-75009	France	33 1 44 83 84 84	33 1 45 23 11 51	rsf@rsf.org	www.rsf.fr
Russian Orthodox Church (Moscow Patriarchate)	DECR 22 Danilovsky val	113191 Moscow	Russian Federation	7 095 955 6756	7 095 954 7567		
Salvation Army, Inc., Philippine Territory	1414 Leon Guinto Sr. St, PO Box 3830	Ermita, Manila, 2800	Philippines				

Organization	Address	City	Country	Telephone	Fax	E-mail	Website
Sisters in Islam	PO Box 8334	Kelana Jaya Post Office 46787 Selangor	Malaysia	603 2142 6121 603 2148 3705	603 2148 3601	sistersinislam@pd.jaring.my basmah@basmah.com	www.sistersinislam.net
Slavic Center for Law and Justice, European Center for Law and Justice	4 quai Kock	67000 Strousbourg	France	33 03 88 24 94 40	33 03 88 24 94 47	contact@eclj.org	http://sclj.org
Stichting 3xM	Nijverheidsweg Noord 133	3812 PL Amersfoort	The Netherlands	31 33 286 41 03	31 33 286 17 57	info@3xm.nl	www.3xm.nl
Stichting De Ondergrondse Kerk (SDOK)	PO Box 705	4200 AS Gorinchem	The Netherlands	31 183 56 11 86	31 183 56 12 29	info@sdok.org	www.sdok.org
Stichting Fundament	PO Box 28068	3828 ZH Hoogland	The Netherlands	31 38 444 04 25	31 38 444 01 78	info@stichting-fundament.nl	www.stichting-fundament.nl
Stichting Hulp Oost-Europa	PO Box 455	3770 AL Barneveld	The Netherlands	31 342 420554	31 342 420553	info@hulpoosteuropa.nl	www.hulpoosteuropa.nl
Stichting Kom Over En Help	PO Box 138	3860 AC Nijkerk	The Netherlands	31 33 246 32 08	31 33 246 28 07	info@koeh.nl	www.koeh.nl
Stichting Open Doors	PO Box 47	3850 AA Ermelo	The Netherlands	31 341 417844	31 341 412622		www.opendoors.nl

Organization	Address	City	Country	Telephone	Fax	E-mail	Website
Stichting Roemenië Beraad Nederland	p/a Meidoornlaan 3	8024 AW Zwolle	The Netherlands	31 38 452 77 07	31 38 452 77 07	coördinator@ roemenieberaad.nl	www.roemenieberaad.nl
Syrian Orthodox Church in America	2295 Victory Blvd	Staten Island, NY 10314	United States of America	1 718 698 0700	1 718 727 8639	socus@undp.org	
Thanks-Giving Foundation, Thanks-Giving Square	1627 Pacific Ave	Dallas, TX 75201	United States of America	1 214 363 3141 1 214 969 1977	1 214 754 0152	info4@thanksgiving.org	www.thanksgiving.org
Union of Spiritual Communities of Christ, Doukhobor	Box 760	Grand Forks, B.C. VOH 1HO	Canada	250 442 8252	250 442 3433		www.doukhobor-homepage .com
Unitarian Universalist Association	25 Beacon Street	Boston, MA 02108	United States of America	1 617 742 2100		twongmo@uua.org	www.uua.org
United Church Board for World Ministries	700 Prospect Ave East, 6th Floor	Cleveland, OH 44115-1100	United States of America	1 216 736 3200	1 216 736 3259	bishopd@ucc.org	
United Church of Christ/Office for Church in Society	700 Prospect Ave	Cleveland, OH 44115	United States of America	1 216 736 2172	1 216 736 2176	ryankurw@ucc.org	
United Churches in the Netherlands	Global Ministries Postbus 8506	3503 RM Utrecht	The Netherlands	31 30 880 18 35		l.hogebrink@ sowkerken.nl	

Organization	Address	City	Country	Telephone	Fax	E-mail	Website
United Religions Initiative (URI)	PO Box 29242	San Francisco, CA 34129	United States of America	1 415 561 2300	1 415 561 2313	office@uri.org	www.uri.org
United Synagogue of Conservative Judaism	155 Fifth Ave	New York, NY 10010	United States of America	1 212 533 7800	1 212 353 9439	info@uscj.org	www.uscj.org
Vaishnava Communications Institute	65, Divinity Rd	Oxford OX4 1LH	United Kingdom	44 1865 30 43 11	44 1865 30 43 01	mo@pamho.net	
Watch Tower Bible & Tract Society of Pennsylvania	25 Columbia Heights	Brooklyn, NY 11201	United States of America	1 718 560 5000	1 845 306 0709	generalcounsel@ wtbts.org	
Werkgroep AGNI	Postbus 61646	2506 AP The Hague	The Netherlands	31 65 140 80 18	31 70 362 24 34	werkgroepagni@ hotmail.com	
Women's Federation for World Peace International	Catharinaland 149	2591 CH The Hague	The Netherlands	31 70 383 59 38	31 70 383 59 38	WFWPIntl1@aol.com	www.wfwp.org
Women's League for Conservative Judaism	475 Riverside Dr, Suite 820	New York, NY 10115	United States of America	1 212 870 1260	1 212 870 1261	womensleague@wlcj.org	www.wlcj.org
WON Buddhism	344-2 Shinyong-Dong	Iksan-City, Chunbuk-Do 570-754	Rep. of Korea	82 653 50 3190	82 653 857 8856	web@ won.wonbuddhism.or.kr	www.wonbuddhism.or.kr

Organization	Address	City	Country	Telephone	Fax	E-mail	Website
World Christian Life Community	Borgo Santo Spirito 8, C.P. 6139	Rome, 00195	Italy	39 06 686 8079	39 06 686 8079	r.cooper@agora.stm.it mcvx@sclc@agora.stm.it	
World Conference of Religions for Peace (WCRP)	777 United Nations Plaza	New York, NY 10017	United States of America	1 212 687 2163	1 212 983 0566	info@wcrp.org	www.wcrp.org
World Council of Churches	PO Box 2100	1211 Geneva 2	Switzerland	41 22 791 6111	41 22 791 0361	info@wcc-coe.org	www.wcc-coe.org
World Council of Conservative Synagogues	155 Fifth Ave	New York, NY 10010	United States of America	1 212 533 7800 x2014	1 212 353 9439	worldcouncil@ compuserve.com	
World Islamic Call Society	PO Box 2549, Sawani Rd	Tripoli	Libya	218 2148 08461	218 2148 00295	cipac@iprimus.ca	www.islamic-call.org
World Vision	Amsterdamseweg 16-1	3812 RS Amersfoort	The Netherlands	31 33 46 43 444	31 33 46 43 445	info@worldvision.nl	http://meero.worldvision.org www.worldvision.nl
Zionist Organization of America	4 East 34th St	New York, NY 10016	United States of America	1 212 481 1500	1 212 481 1515	info@zoa.org	www.zoa.org

Bibliography
Books and Articles

Abuza, Zachary. *Renovating Politics in Contemporary Vietnam*. Boulder, Colo.: Lynne Rienner, 2001.

Adhar, Rex, ed. *Law and Religion*. Aldershot, England: Ashgate, 2000.

Afkhami, Mahnaz, ed. *Faith and Freedom: Women's Human Rights in the Muslim World*. Syracuse, N.Y.: Syracuse University Press, 1995.

Agnes, Flavia. *Law and Gender Inequality. The Politics of Women's Rights in India*. India: Oxford University Press, 1999.

Ahmad, Feroz. *The Making of Modern Turkey*. London: Routledge, 1994.

Ahmad, Hazrat Mirza Tahir. *Murder in the Name of Allah*. Cambridge: Lutterworth Press, 1989.

Alexander, Jeffrey C. and Paul Colomy, eds. *Differentiation Theory and Social Change: Comparative and Historical Perspectives*. New York: Columbia University Press, 1990.

Alfredsson, Gudmundur and Asbjørn Eide, eds. *The Universal Declaration of Human Rights: A Common Standard of Achievement*. The Hague: Martinus Nijhoff Publishers, 1999.

Alhabshi, Syed Othman. *An Inspiration for the Future of Islam*. Kuala Lumpur: Institute of Islamic Understanding, 1994.

Ali, Shaheen Sardar. *Gender and Human Rights in Islam and International Law. Equal Before Allah, Unequal Before Man?* The Hague: Kluwer Law International, 2000.

Al-Marzouqi, Ibrahim Abdulla. *Human Rights in Islamic Law*. Abu Dhabi: n.p., 2000.

Alston, Philip. "The Universal Declaration at 35: Western and Passé or Alive and Universal." *The Review of the International Commission of Jurists* 31 (1983): 60–70.

Alston, Philip, ed. *The United Nations and Human Rights*. New York: Oxford University Press, 1992.

Althusius, Johannes. *Politica Methodice Digesta*. 3d ed. Herborn: Scientia Aalen, 1614.

Anderson, Nicholas. *Law Reform in the Muslim World*. London: The Athlone Press, 1976.

Ankumah, Evelyn A. *The African Commission on Human and Peoples' Rights: Practices and Procedures*. Boston: Martinus Nijhoff Publishers, 1996.

An-Na'im, Abdullahi Ahmed. "Human Rights in the Arab World: A Regional Perspective." *Human Rights Quarterly* 23 (2001): 701–32.

Tore Lindholm, W. Cole Durham, Jr., Bahia G. Tahzib-Lie (eds.), Facilitating Freedom of Religion or Belief: A Deskbook, *947–976.*

An-Na'im, Abdullahi Ahmed. "Human Rights in the Muslim World: Socio-Political Conditions and Scriptural Imperatives." *Harvard Human Rights Journal* 3 (1990): 13–52.
———. "Synergy and Interdependence of Religion, Human Rights and Secularism." *Polylog: Forum for Intercultural Philosophy* 2 (2001): 1–43.
———, ed. *Human Rights in Cross-Cultural Perspectives: A Quest for Consensus.* Philadelphia: University of Pennsylvania Press, 1992.
———, ed. *Proselytization and Communal Self-Determination in Africa.* New York: Orbis Books, 1999.
Ansay, Tugrul and Don Wallace, eds. *Introduction to Turkish Law.* Boston: Kluwer Law International, 1996.
Appleby, R. Scott. *The Ambivalence of the Sacred: Religion, Violence, and Reconciliation.* New York: Rowman and Littlefield, 2000.
Ariarajah, S. Wesley. *Not Without My Neighbor: Issues in Interfaith Relations.* Geneva: WCC Publications, 1999.
Ariens, Michael S. and Robert A. Destro. *Religious Liberty in a Pluralistic Society.* Durham, N.C.: Carolina Academic Press, 1996.
Armstrong, Karen. *Holy War. The Crusades and Their Impact on Today's World.* New York: Doubleday/Anchor Books, 1992.
Askin, Kelly D. and Dorean M. Koenig, eds. *Women and International Human Rights Law.* 3 vols. New York: Transnational Publishers, 1999.
Assaad, Marie Bassili. "Female Circumcision in Egypt: Social Implications, Current Research, and Prospects for Change." *Studies in Family Planning* 11, no. 1 (1980): 3–16.
Ayisi, Eric O. *An Introduction to the Study of African Culture.* London: Heinemann, 1972.
Balim, Cigdem, et al., eds. *Turkey: Political, Social and Economic Challenges in the 1990s.* London: E. J. Brill, 1995.
Barbieri, William. "Group Rights and the Muslim Diaspora." *Human Rights Quarterly* 21 (1999): 907–26.
Bardin, Livia. *Coping with Cult Involvement: A Handbook for Families and Friends.* Bonita Springs, Fla.: American Family Foundation, 2000.
Barker, Eileen. "The Cage of Freedom and the Freedom of the Cage." *Society* 33, no. 3 (1996): 53–59.
———. "A General Overview of the 'Cult Scene' in Britain." *Nova Religio* 4, no. 2 (2001): 235–41.
———. *The Making of a Moonie: Choice or Brainwashing?* Oxford: Blackwell, 1984.
———. *New Religious Movements: A Practical Introduction.* London: HMSO, 1989.
———. "The Scientific Study of Religion? You Must Be Joking!" *Journal for the Scientific Study of Religion* 34, no. 3 (1995): 287–310.
Barker, Eileen, James A. Beckford, and Karel Dobbelaere, eds. *Secularization, Rationalism and Sectarianism.* Oxford: Clarendon Press, 1993.
Barker, Eileen and Jean-François Mayer, eds. *Twenty Years On: Changes in New Religious Movements.* London: Sage, 1995.
Barragan, Javier Moctezuma and Alvaro Castro Estrada, eds. *Foro Internacional Sobre Libertad Religiosa: Memoria.* 2003.
Barrow, Alfred Henry. *Fifty Years in West Africa.* London, 1900.

Basova, Irina G. "Freedom Under Fire: The New Russian Religious Law." *Temple International & Comparative Law Journal* 14, no. 1 (2000): 181–208.
Bassett, William W. *Religious Organizations and the Law.* 2 vols. Eagan, Minn.: Thomson/ West, 2003.
Baubérot, Jean. *Histoire de la laïcité française.* Paris: PUF, 2000.
———. *La morale laïque contre l'ordre moral.* Paris: Seuil, 1997.
———. *Vers un nouveau pacte laïque?* Paris: Seuil, 1990.
Bauer, Joanne R. and Daniel A. Bell, eds. *East Asian Challenge for Human Rights.* Cambridge: Cambridge University Press, 1999.
Bayer, Klaus Dieter. *Das Grundrecht der Religions- und Gewissensfreiheit unter besonderer Berücksichtigung des Minderheitenschutzes.* Baden: Nomos Universitätsschriften, 1997.
Beardsley, James E. "The Constitutional Council and Constitutional Liberties in France." *American Journal of Comparative Law* 20 (1972): 431––52.
Beckford, James. *Cult Controversies: The Societal Response to the New Religious Movements.* London: Tavistock, 1985.
Bell, Daniel. "American Exceptionalism Revisited: The Role of Civil Society." *The Public Interest,* no. 95 (1989): 38–56.
Bell, John. *French Constitutional Law.* Oxford: Clarendon Press, 1992.
Bellah, Robert N. *The Broken Covenant: American Civil Religion in Time of Trial.* New York: Seabury, 1975.
Bencheikh, Soheib. *Mariane et le Prophète: L'islam dans la France Laïque.* Paris: Éditions Grasset & Fasquelle, 1998.
Benecke, Gerhard. *Germany in the Thirty Years War.* London: Edwin Arnold, 1978.
Berger, Maria. *Draft Report on Cults in the European Union.* Strasbourg: European Parliament, 1997.
Berger, Peter L. and Richard J. Neuhaus. *To Empower People: The Role of Mediating Institutions in Public Policy.* Washington, D.C.: American Enterprise Institute for Public Policy Research, 1977.
Berger, Peter L. and Thomas Luckmann. *The Social Construction of Reality: Everything That Passes for Knowledge in Society.* London: Allen Lane, 1967.
Berger, Peter L., ed. *The Desecularization of the World. Resurgent Religion and World Politics.* Washington, D.C.: Ethics and Public Policy Center, 1999.
Berka, Walter. *Die Grundrechte: Grundfreiheiten und Menschenrechte in Österreich.* Vienna: Springer Verlag, 1999.
Berkes, Niyazi. *Teokrasi ve Laiklik.* Istanbul: Adam Yayincilik, 1997.
Berry, Brian. *Culture and Equality: An Egalitarian Critique of Multiculturalism.* Cambridge: Harvard University Press, 2001.
Besier, Gerhard and Hubert Seiwert, eds. *Religion-Staat-Gesellschaft, Journal for the Study of Beliefs and Worldviews.* 1. Jahrgang 2000, Heft 2. Berlin: Duncker & Humblot, 2000.
Bettenson, Henry and Chris Maunder, eds. *Documents of the Christian Church.* 3d ed. Oxford: Oxford University Press, 1999.
Bexell, Göran and Dan-Erik Andersson, eds. *Universal Ethics. Perspectives and Proposals from Scandinavian Scholars.* The Hague: Kluwer Law International, 2002.
Bhargava, Rajeev, ed. *Secularism and Its Critics.* New Delhi: Oxford University Press, 1999.

Biddulph, Howard L. "Religious Liberty and the Ukrainian State: Nationalism Versus Equal Protection." *Brigham Young University Law Review* (1995): 321–46.

Blackstone, William. *Commentaries on the Laws of England: A Facsimile of the First Edition of 1765–1769.* Chicago: University of Chicago Press, 1979.

Blaustein, Albert P. and Gisbert H. Flanz, eds. *Constitutions of the Countries of the World.* Dobbs Ferry, N.Y.: Oceana, 1971.

Bloed, Arie, ed. *The Conference on Security and Co-operation in Europe: Analysis and Basic Documents, 1972–1993.* Boston: Kluwer Academic Publishers, 1993.

———, ed. *The Conference on Security and Co-operation in Europe: Analysis and Basic Documents, 1993–1995.* Boston: Kluwer Academic Publishers, 1997.

———, ed. *From Helsinki to Vienna: Basic Documents of the Helsinki Process.* Boston: Martinus Nijhoff Publishers, 1990.

Bloed, Arie, et al., eds. *Monitoring Human Rights in Europe: Comparing International Procedures and Mechanisms.* Dordrecht: Martinus Nijhoff Publishers, 1993.

Blum, Nikolaus. *Die Gedanken-, Gewissens- und Religionsfreiheit nach Art.9 der Europäischen Menschenrechtskon-vention.* Berlin: Duncker & Humblot, 1990.

Boerefijn, Ineke. *The Reporting Procedure under the Covenant on Civil and Political Rights: Practice and Procedures of the Human Rights Committee.* Antwerp: Intersentia, 1999.

Borowik, Irena, ed. *New Religions in Central and Eastern Europe.* Kraków: Nomos, 1997.

Børresen, Kari Elisabeth. *Anthropologie mediévale et théologie mariale.* Oslo: Universitetsforlaget, 1971.

———. "The Ordination of Women: To Nurture Tradition by Continuing Inculturation." *Studia Theologica* 46 (1992): 3–13.

———. "Patristic 'Feminism': The Case of Augustine." *Augustinian Studies* 25 (1994): 139–152.

———. *Subordination and Equivalence. The Nature and Role of Woman in Augustine and Thomas Aquinas. A Reprint of a Pioneering Classic.* Kampen: Kok Pharos Publishing House, 1995.

Børresen, Kari Elisabeth and Kari Vogt. *Women's Studies of the Christian and Islamic Traditions.* Dordrecht: Kluwer Academic Publishers, 1993.

Børresen, Kari Elisabeth, ed. *The Image of God. Gender Models in Judaeo-Christian Tradition.* Minneapolis, Minn.: Fortress Press, 1995. Italian edition: *A Immagine di Dio.* Carroci Editiore, 2001.

Bossuyt, Marc J. *Guide to the Travaux Préparatoires of the International Covenant on Civil and Political Rights.* Boston: Martinus Nijhoff Publishers, 1987.

Bouma, Gary D., ed. *Many Religions, All Australian: Religious Settlement, Identity and Cultural Diversity.* Kew, Australia: The Christian Research Association, 1997.

Boyer, William J., Jr. "Property Rights of Religious Institutions in Wisconsin." *Marquette Law Review* 36 (1953): 329–70.

Boyle, Kevin. "Stock-taking on Human Rights: The World Conference on Human Rights, Vienna 1993." *Political Studies* 43 (1995): 79–95.

Boyle, Kevin and Juliet Sheen, eds. *Freedom of Religion and Belief: A World Report.* London: Routledge, 1997.

Brandon, Thomas S. *New Religions, Conversions and Deprogramming: New Frontiers of Religious Liberty.* Oak Park, Ill.: The Center for Law & Religious Freedom, 1982.

Brekke, Torkel. *Gud i norsk politikk. Religion og politisk makt* (God in Norwegian politics. Religion and political power). Oslo: Pax Forlag, 2002.
Brewer, John D. "A History of Northern Ireland's Conflict." *epd-Dokumentation* 32 (2001): 44.
Britsch, R. Lanier. "The Current Legal Status of Christianity in China." *Brigham Young University Law Review* (1995): 347–99.
Brölmann, Catherine, René Lefeber, and Marjoleine Zieck, eds. *Peoples and Minorities in International Law.* Boston: Martinus Nijhoff Publishers, 1993.
Bromley, David G. and J. Gordon Melton, eds. *Cults, Religion and Violence.* Cambridge: Cambridge University Press, 2002.
Bromley, David G. and James T. Richardson, eds. *The Brainwashing/Deprogramming Controversy.* New York: Edwin Mellen Press, 1983.
Bromley, David G. and Jeffrey Hadden, eds. *The Handbook of Cults and Sects in America.* Greenwich, Conn.: JAI Press, 1993.
Brown, Stephen. "Armenian Church Faces Up to Post-Communist Challenges." *Christianity Today* (5 March 2001).
Brownlie, Ian. *International Law and the Use of Force By States.* Oxford: Clarendon Press, 1963.
———. *Principles of Public International Law.* 4th ed. New York: Oxford University Press, 1990.
———. *The Rule of Law in International Affairs.* The Hague: Martinus Nijhoff Publishers, 1998.
Bruce, Steve. *Politics and Religion.* Cambridge: Polity, 2003.
Buergenthal, Thomas. "Copenhagen: A Democratic Manifesto." *World Affairs* 153, no. 1 (summer 1990): 5–8.
———. "The CSCE Rights System." *George Washington Journal of International Law and Economics* 25, no. 2 (1991): 333–86.
Buergenthal, Thomas and Dinah Shelton. *Protecting Human Rights in the Americas: Cases and Materials.* 4th ed. Arlington: N. P. Engel, 1995.
Bühl, Walter. *Transnationale Politik.* Stuttgart: Klett-Cotta, 1978.
Burgerman, Susan. *Moral Victories: How Activists Provoke Multilateral Action.* Ithaca, N.Y.: Cornell University Press, 2001.
Burkholder, Mark A. and Lyman L. Johnson. *Colonial Latin America.* 2d ed. New York: Oxford University Press, 1994.
Buss, Doris E. "Robes, Relics and Rights: The Vatican and the Beijing Conference on Women." *Social & Legal Studies* (Sage Publications) 7 (1998): 339–363.
Campbell, Tom, et al., eds. *Human Rights. From Rhetoric to Reality.* Oxford: Blackwell, 1986.
Capotorti, Francesco. *Study on the Rights of Persons Belonging to Ethnic, Religious and Linguistic Minorities.* New York: United Nations, 1991.
Cappelletti, Mauro, John Henry Merryman, and Joseph M. Perillo. *The Italian Legal System: An Introduction.* Stanford: Stanford University Press, 1967.
Carlson, Darin W. "Understanding Chinese-U.S. Conflict Over Freedom of Religion: The Wolf-Specter Freedom From Religious Persecution Acts of 1997 and 1998." *Brigham Young University Law Review* (1998): 563–606.
Carnes, Tony. "Religious Persecution Bill Encounters Stiff Resistance." *Christianity Today* 42, no. 11 (5 October 1998).

Carter, Barry E. and Phillip R. Trimble, eds. *International Law: Selected Documents.* Boston: Little, Brown & Co., 1995.

Casanova, José. *Public Religions in the Modern World.* Chicago: University of Chicago Press, 1994.

Castellan, Georges. *History of the Balkans from Mohammed the Conqueror to Stalin.* New York: Columbia University Press, 1992.

Champion, Françoise and Martine Cohen, eds. *Sectes et démocratie.* Paris: Seuil, 1999.

Chan, Kim-Kwong and Eric Carlson. *Religious Freedom in China: Policy, Administration, and Regulation.* Forthcoming, 2004.

Chaskalson, Matthew, et al., eds. *Constitutional Law of South Africa.* Cape Town: Juta & Co., 1996.

Chessler, Abbie J. "Justifying the Unjustifiable: Rite v. Wrong." *Buffalo Law Review* 45 (1997): 555–613.

Christians, Louis-Léon. "Liberté d'opinion en droit européen: observations belges (II)—Les limitations." *Conscience et Liberté* 58 (1999): 8–32.

Church and State Consultation, 13–16 March 1997, Czech Republic. Geneva: Conference of European Churches, 1998.

Clark, Elizabeth A. *Ascetic Piety and Women's Faith.* Lewiston, N.Y.: Edwin Mellen Press, 1986.

Clark, Ian and Iver B. Neumann, eds. *Classical Theories of International Relations.* Basingstoke: Macmillan, 1996.

Claude, Richard and Burns H. Weston, eds. *Human Rights in the World Community.* 2d ed. Philadelphia: University of Philadelphia Press, 1992.

Cohen-Almagor, Raphael. "Harm Principle, Offence Principle, and the Skokie Affair." *Political Studies* 41 (1993): 453–70.

Coleman, Lee. *Psychiatry the Faithbreaker: How Psychiatry Is Promoting Bigotry in America.* Sacramento: Center for the Study of Psychiatric Testimony, 1982.

"Common Witness and Proselytism." *The Ecumenical Review* 23, no. 1 (January 1971): 9–20 (prepared by Joint Theological Commission of World Council of Churches and Catholic Church).

Condé, H. Victor. "Protection of Religious Freedoms under International Humanitarian Law and International Human Rights Law in Times of Armed Conflict." *UC Davis Journal of International Law and Policy* 5 (winter 1999): 95–110.

Congar, Yves. "Reception as an Ecclesiological Reality." *Concilium* 77 (1972): 43–68.

Cook, Rebecca. "Human Rights and Reproductive Self-Determination." *American University Law Review* 44 (1995): 975–1016.

Cottrell, Richard. *The Activity of Certain New Religions within the European Community.* Strasbourg: European Parliament, 1984.

Cromartie, Michael. "The Jew Who Is Saving Christians." *Christianity Today* 43, no. 3 (1 March 1999): 50–55.

Cumper, Peter. "Religious Human Rights in the United Kingdom." *Emory International Law Review* 10, no. 1 (1996): 115–26.

Curran, Charles E. *The Catholic Moral Tradition Today. A Synthesis.* Washington, D.C.: Georgetown University Press, 1999.

Curran, Charles E., ed. *Contraception. Authority and Dissent.* New York: Herder and Herder, 1969.

Curran, Charles E. and Richard A. McCormick, eds. *Dialogue about Catholic Sexual Teachings*. New York: Paulist Press, 1993.

———. *John Paul II and Moral Theology*. New York: Paulist Press, 1998.

Czempiel, Ernst-Otto, ed. *Die anachronistische Souveränität*. Cologne-Opladen: Westdeutscher Verlag, 1969.

Dalacoura, Katerina. *Islam, Liberalism and Human Rights*. London: I. B. Tauris, 1998.

D'Amato, Alfonse, ed. *Religious Intolerance in Europe Today*. Washington, D.C.: U.S. Government Printing Office, 1997.

Danchin, Peter G. "U.S. Unilateralism and the International Protection of Religious Freedom: The Multilateral Alternative." *Columbia Journal of Transnational Law* 41 (2002): 33–135.

Danchin, Peter G. and Elizabeth A. Cole, eds. *Protecting the Human Rights of Religious Minorities in Eastern Europe*. New York: Columbia University Press, 2002.

Davidson, Basil. *African Civilization Revisited*. Trenton, N.J.: Africa World Press, 1991.

Davidson, Scott. *The Inter-American Human Rights System*. Brookfield, Vt.: Dartmouth, 1997.

Davis, Derek. "The Evolution of Religious Freedom as a Universal Human Right: Examining the Role of the 1981 United Nations Declaration on the Elimination of All Forms of Intolerance and of Discrimination Based on Religion or Belief." *Brigham Young University Law Review* (2002): 217–36.

Deane, Herbert A. *The Political and Social Ideas of St. Augustine*. New York: Columbia University Press, 1963.

de Baecque, Antoine, Wolfgang Schmale, and Michel Vovelle. *L'an I des droits de l'homme*. Paris: Presse du CNRS, 1988.

Debrunner, Hans. *A History of Christianity in Ghana*. Accra: Waterville Publishing House, 1967.

de Jong, Cornelis D. *The Freedom of Thought, Conscience and Religion or Belief in the United Nations (1946–1992)*. Antwerpen: Intersentia, 2000.

de la Hera, Alberto. "Relations with Religious Minorities: The Spanish Model." *Brigham Young University Law Review* (1998): 387–400.

de la Hera, Alberto and Rosa María Martínez de Codes. *Spanish Legislation on Religious Affairs*. Madrid: Ministerio de Justicia Centro de publicaciones, 1998.

della Rocca, Roberto Morozzo. *Vom Krieg zum Frieden. Mosambik: Geschichte einer Ungewöhnlichen Vermittlung*. Hamburg: Verlag Dienste in Übersee, 1997.

del Pilar Bellosillo, Maria, et al. "Women Appeal to the Pastors of the Church." *Pro Mundi Vita Bulletin* 108 (1987): 1–36.

del Russo, Alessandra Luini. *International Protection of Human Rights*. Washington, D.C: Lerner Law Book, 1971.

Dengerink, J. D. *Critisch-Historisch Onderzoek naar de Sociologische Ontwikkeling der Beginsel der "Souvereiniteit in Eigen Kring" in de 19e en 20e Eeuw*. Kampen: J. H. Kok, 1948.

"Developments in the Law—Judicial Control of Actions of Private Associations." *Harvard Law Review* 76 (1962–63): 983–1100.

"Developments in the Law—Nonprofit Corporations." *Harvard Law Review* 105 (1992): 1578–1699.

Dhammika, Ven. S. *The Edicts of King Ashoka: An English rendering*. Kandy, Sri Lanka: The Wheel Publication No. 386/387, 1993.
Dickson, Brice. "The UN and Freedom of Religion." *International and Comparative Law Quarterly* 44 (1995): 327–57.
Dietrich, Gabriele. *Reflections on the Women's Movement in India. Religion, Ecology, Development*. New Delhi: Horizon India Books, 1992.
Dinstein, Yoram. "Collective Human Rights of Peoples and Minorities." *International and Comparative Law Quarterly* 25 (1976): 102–3.
Dinstein, Yoram and Mala Tabory, eds. *The Protection of Minorities and Human Rights*. Boston: Martinus Nijhoff Publishers, 1992.
Doi, Abdur Rahman. *Shari'ah: The Islamic Law*. London: Ta Ha Publishers, 1984.
Donnelly, Jack. "Cultural Relativism and Universal Human Rights." *Human Rights Quarterly* 6 (1984): 400–19.
———. "International Human Rights: A Regime Analysis." *International Organization* 40 (summer 1986): 599–642.
Dooyeweerd, Herman. *A New Critique of Theoretical Thought*. Vol. 3. Jordan Station, Ontario: Padeia Press, 1969.
———. *De Strijd om het Souvereiniteitsbegrip in de Moderne Rechtsen Staatsleer*. Amsterdam: H. J. Paris, 1950.
———. *Verkenningen in de Wijsbegeerte, de Sociologie en de Rechtsgeschiedenis*. Amsterdam: Buijten & Schipperheijn, 1962.
Duijzings, Ger. *Religion and the Politics of Identity in Kosovo*. London: Hurst and Company, 2000.
Duran, Khalid. *The Children of Abraham: An Introduction to Islam for Jews*. Hoboken, N.J.: Ktav, 2001.
Durham, Cole. *Freedom of Religion or Belief: Laws Affecting the Structuring of Religious Communities*. Warsaw, Poland: OSCE/ODIHR, 1999.
Durham, W. Cole, Jr. *The Doctrine of Religious Freedom*. Provo, Utah: J. Reuben Clark Law School, Clark Memorandum, 2001.
Durham, W. Cole, Jr. and Lauren B. Homer. "Russia's 1997 Law on Freedom of Conscience and Religious Associations: An Analytical Appraisal." *Emory International Law Review* 12 (1998): 101–246.
Durham, W. Cole, Jr. and Silvio Ferrari, eds. *Religious Registration Laws in Post-Communist Europe*. Leuven: Peeters, forthcoming, 2004.
Dutch Center for Conflict Prevention, ed. *Prevention and Management of Conflicts. An International Directory*. Amsterdam: NCDO, 1996.
Eberly, Don E., ed.. *The Essential Civil Society Reader*. Oxford: Rowman & Littlefield, 2000.
Eide, Asbjørn and Gudmundur Alfredsson, eds. *The Universal Declaration of Human Rights: A Commentary*. New York: Scandinavian University Press, 1992.
Eidsvåg, Inge and Lena Larsen, eds. *Religion, livssyn og menneskerettigheter i Norge* (Religions, Life Stances, and Human Rights in Norway). Oslo: Universitetsforlaget, 1997.
El-Affendi, Abdelwahab. *Who Needs an Islamic State?* London: Grey Seal Books, 1991.
Eliah, Elaine. "Reaching for a Healthier Future: Uganda's Sabiny People." *Populi* 23, no. 1 (1996): 12–16.
Elton, Geoffrey R., ed. *New Cambridge Modern History*. 2d ed. Cambridge: Cambridge University Press, 1990.

Emiliou, Nicholas. *The Principle of Proportionality in European Law: A Comparative Study.* London: Kluwer Law International, 1996.
Enroth, Ronald. *The Lure of the Cults.* New York: Christian Herald, 1979.
Ermacora, Felix. "The Protection of Minorities Before the United Nations." *Recueil des Cours* 182, no. 4 (1983): 247–370.
Esbeck, Carl. "The Establishment Clause as a Structural Constraint on Governmental Power." *Iowa Law Review* 84 (1998): 1–113.
European Consortium for Church-State Research. *Conscientious Objection in the EC Countries.* Milan: Giuffrè, 1992.
———. *New Religious Movements and the Law in the European Union.* Vol. 15. Milan: Università degli Studi di ilano, 1997.
Evans, Carolyn. *Freedom of Religion under the European Convention on Human Rights.* Oxford: Oxford University Press, 2001.
Evans, Malcolm D. *Religious Liberty and International Law in Europe.* Cambridge: Cambridge University Press, 1997.
Fautré, Willie, ed. *The Belgian State and the Sects: A Close Look at the Work of the Parliamentary Commission of Inquiry on Sects' Recommendations to Strengthen the Rule of Law.* Vol. 10, 1/2. Brussels: Human Rights Without Frontiers, 1998.
Fawcett, James E. C. *The Application of the European Convention on Human Rights.* 2d ed. New York: Oxford University Press, 1987.
Fefferman, Dan, ed. *Religious Freedom and the New Millennium.* Falls Church, Va.: International Coalition for Religious Freedom, 2000.
Feinberg, Joel. *The Moral Limits of the Criminal Law.* 4 vols. New York: Oxford University Press, 1987–1990.
Feinburg, Nathan. *La Question des Minorités à la Conference de la Paix de 1919–1920 et l'action Juive en favour de la Protection International des Minorités.* Paris: Rousseau et Cie, 1929.
Feldman, Noah. "The Intellectual Origins of the Establishment Clause." *New York University Law Review* 77, no. 2 (May 2002): 346–428.
Ferrari, Silvio. "Concordats were Born in the West." *La Porta D'Oriente* 12/13 (1998): 37–44.
———. "The Emerging Pattern of Church and State in Western Europe: The Italian Model." *Brigham Young University Law Review* (1995): 421–37.
Ferrari, Silvio, W. Cole Durham, Jr., and Elizabeth A. Sewell, eds. *Law and Religion in Post-Communist Europe.* Leuven: Peeters, 2003.
Fishman, James J. "The Development of Nonprofit Corporation Law and an Agenda for Reform." *Emory Law Journal* 34 (1985): 617–83.
Flakk, Tommy. *Human Rights the Confucian Way. Towards International Consensus on Human Rights From Within Cultural Traditions.* University of Oslo: Department of Political Science, 2003.
Flynn, Gregory and Henry Farrell. "Piecing Together the Democratic Peace: The CSCE, Norms and the 'Construction' of Security in Post-Cold War Europe." *International Organization* 53, no. 3 (summer 1999): 505–35.
Foster, John G. *Enquiry into the Practice and Effects of Scientology.* London: Her Majesty's Stationary Office, 1971.
Fouques-Duparc, Jacques. *La Protection des Minorités de Race, de Langue et de Religion.* Paris: Libraire Dalloz, 1922.

Fowler, Alan. *The Virtuous Spiral: A Guide to Sustainability for NGOs in International Development*. London: Earthscan Publications, 2000.

Fox, Leslie M. and S. Bruce Schearer, eds. *Sustaining Civil Society: Strategies for Resource Mobilization*. Washington, D.C.: CIVICUS, 1997.

Fox, Matthew. *A Spirituality Named Compassion*. San Francisco: Harper and Row, 1990.

Fraser, Arvonne S. "Becoming Human: The Origins and Development of Women's Human Rights." *Human Rights Quarterly* (The Johns Hopkins University Press) 21 (1999): 853–906.

Fraser, Donald M. *Investigation of Korean-American Relations*. Washington, D.C.: U.S. House of Representatives, 1978.

Freeman, Michael. *Human Rights: An Interdisciplinary Approach*. Cambridge: Polity, 2002.

———. *The Moral Status of Children: Essays on the Rights of the Child*. The Hague: Martinus Nijhoff Publishers, 1997.

Frowein, Jochen A. "Freedom of Religion in the Practice of the European Commission and Court of Human Rights." *Zeitschrift für ausländisches öffentliches Recht und Völkerrecht* 46 (1986): 249.

Frowein, Jochen A. and Wolfgang Peukert. *Europäische Menschenrechtskonvention: EMRK Kommentar*. 2d ed. Kehl, Germany: N. P. Engel Verlag, 1996.

Fuhrmann, Willi. "Perspectives on Religious Freedom from the Vantage Point of the European Court of Human Rights." *Brigham Young University Law Review* (2000): 829–39.

Fukuyama, Francis. *The End of History and the Last Man*. New York: Free Press, 1992.

Fulbright, J. William. *The Arrogance of Power*. New York: Random House, 1966.

Furseth, Inger. *Samfunnsreligion i Norge? En analyse av nasjonal legitimering 1905–1980* (Civil Religion in Norway? An Analysis of National Legitimation 1905–1980). Oslo: University of Oslo, 1986.

Gales, Joseph, ed. *Annals of Congress*. Vol. 1. Washington, D.C.: Gales and Seaton, 1834.

Galey, Margaret E. "International Enforcement of Women's Rights." *Human Rights Quarterly* 6 (1984): 463–490.

Galtung, Johan. "The Role of Communication in Rethinking European Identity in Media Development." *Journal of the World Association for Christian Communication* 40, no. 4 (1993): 3–7.

Gampl, Inge, et al. *Österreichisches Staatskirchenrecht*. 2 vols. Vienna: Orac, 1990.

Garay, Alain. "La circulaire du 29 février 1996." *JCP*, no. 15 (10 April 1996).

———. *L'activisme anti-secte: de l'assistance à l'amalgame*. New York: Edwin Mellen Press, 1999.

———. "La liberté religieuse en Europe—restriction et protection." *Conscience et Liberté*, no. 59 (2000): 81–99.

Garvey, John H. "Churches and the Free Exercise of Religion." *Notre Dame Journal of Law, Ethics and Public Policy* 4 (1990): 567–89.

Gearty, Conor and Adam Tomkins, eds. *Understanding Human Rights*. London: Mansell, 1996.

Gedicks, Frederick Mark. *The Rhetoric of Church and State*. Durham, N.C.: Duke University Press, 1995.

———. "Toward a Constitutional Jurisprudence of Religious Group Rights." *Wisconsin Law Review* (1989): 99–169.

Gellner, Ernst. *Nations and Nationalism*. Oxford: Blackwell, 1993.
Gerstenblith, Patty. "Associational Structures of Religious Organizations." *Brigham Young University Law Review* (1995): 439–80.
Ghadially, Rehana, ed. *Women in Indian Society. A Reader.* New Delhi: Sage Publica tions, 1988.
Ghanea-Hercock, Nazila, ed. *Religious Discrimination*. Kluwer, forthcoming, 2004.
Giambalvo, Carol. *Exit Counselling: A Family Intervention: How to Respond to Cult-Affected Loved Ones.* Bonita Springs, Fla.: American Family Foundation, 1992.
Gibbon, Edward. *The Decline and Fall of the Roman Empire*. Edited by David Womersley. London: Allen Lane, 1994. First published in 1776.
Glendon, Mary Ann. *A World Made New: Eleanor Roosevelt and the Universal Declaration of Human Rights.* New York: Random House, 2001.
Goethals, Johan. *De sektencommissie. Het verhaal van een expert* (The sect commission. The story of an expert). Leuven: Uitgeverij van Halewijck, 1998.
Göle, Nilüfer. *The Forbidden Modern: Civilization and Veiling*. Ann Arbor, Mich.: The University of Michigan Press, 1996.
Greer, Steven. *The Margin of Appreciation: Interpretation and Discretion under the European Convention on Human Rights.* Strasbourg: Council of Europe, 2000.
Gregory, Brad S. *Salvation at Stake. Christian Martyrdom in Early Modern Europe.* Cambridge: Harvard University Press, 1999.
Greil, Arthur and Thomas Robbins, eds. *Between Sacred and Secular: Research and Theory on Quasi Religion*. Greenwich, Conn.: JAI Press, 1994.
Gremillion, Joseph, ed. *The Gospel of Peace and Justice. Catholic Social Teaching Since Pope John.* Maryknoll, N.Y.: Orbis Books, 1976.
Griffiths, Paul J. "Why We Need Religious Polemics." *First Things* 44 (June/July 1994): 31–37.
Gross, Brian. "A Bend in the Road to Civil Society: The Effect of Russian Anti-Extremism Legislation on Not-for-Profit Organizations." *International Journal of Not-for-Profit Law* 6 (September 2003): 1.
Gross, Oren and Fionnuala Ní Aoláin. "From Discretion to Scrutiny: Revisiting the Application of the Margin of Appreciation Doctrine in the Context of Article 15 of the European Convention on Human Rights." *Human Rights Quarterly* 23 (2001): 625–49.
Gross, Walter, ed. *Frauenordination. Stand der Diskussion in der katholischen Kirche.* München: Erich Wewel Verlag, 1996.
Gryson, Roger. *The Ministry of Women in the Early Church.* Collegeville, Minn.: Liturgical Press, 1976.
Gunn, T. Jeremy. "American Exceptionalism and Globalist Double Standards: A More Balanced Alternative." *Columbia Journal of Transnational Law* 41 (2002): 137–52.
———. "Caesar's Sword: The 1997 Law of the Russian Federation on the Freedom of Conscience and Religious Associations." *Emory International Law Review* 12 (1998): 43–99.
———. "The Complexity of Religion and the Definition of Religion in International Law." *Harvard Human Rights Journal* 16 (2003): 189–215.
———. "Majorities, minorities, and the rights of religion or belief." *Helsinki Monitor* 9, no. 3 (1998): 38–44.

Gunning, Isabelle R. "Arrogant Perception, World-Travelling and Multicultural Feminism: The Case of Female Genital Surgeries." *Columbia Human Rights Law Review* 23 (1992): 189–248.

Gustafson, Carrie and Peter Juviler, eds. *Religion and Human Rights: Competing Claims?* Armonk, N.Y.: M. E. Sharpe, 1999.

Gustafsson, Göran, ed. *Religiös förändring i Norden 1930–1980* (Religious Change in the Nordic Countries 1930–1980). Malmø: Liber, 1985.

Haas, Peter. "Introduction: Epistemic Communities and International Policy Coordination." *International Organization* 46, no.1 (winter 1992): 1–35.

Habermas, Jürgen. *Between Facts and Norms.* Translated by William Rehg. Cambridge: MIT Press, 1994.

Habermas, Jürgen and Norbert Elias. *Nasjonalisme og nasjonal identitet* (Nationalism and National Identity). Oslo: Cappelen akademiske forlag AS, 1994.

Hackett, Rosalind I. J., Mark Silk, and Dennis Hoover, eds. *Religious Persecution as a U.S. Policy Issue.* Hartford, Conn.: Center for the Study of Religion in Public Life, 2000.

Hadden, Jeffrey K, ed. *Religion on the Internet: Research Prospects and Promises.* New York: Elsevier Science, 2000.

Hamilton, Malcolm B., ed. *The Sociology of Religion: Theoretical and Comparative Perspectives.* London: Routledge, 1995.

Hannum, Hurst. "The Status of the Universal Declaration of Human Rights in National and International Law." *Georgia Journal of International and Comparative Law* 25 (1995/1996): 287–354.

Hansmann, Henry and Hugo Mattei. "The Functions of Trust Law: A Comparative Legal and Economic Analysis." *New York University Law Review* 73 (1998): 434–79.

———. "Trust Law in the United States: A Basic Study of its Special Contribution." *American Journal of Comparative Law* 46 (Supp. 1998): 133–49.

Hansmann, Henry and Reinier Kraakman. "The Essential Role of Organizational Law." *Yale Law Journal* 110 (2000): 387–440.

Harris, David J., Michael O'Boyle, and Chris Warbrick. *Law of the European Convention on Human Rights.* London: Butterworths, 1995.

Harris, David and Sarah Joseph, eds. *The International Covenant on Civil and Political Rights and United Kingdom Law.* Oxford: Clarendon Press, 1995.

Harris, David and Stephen Livingstone, eds. *The Inter-American System of Human Rights.* Oxford: Clarendon Press, 1998.

Harvey, Özlem Denli. *Islam and the Freedom of Religion or Belief: Perspectives from Contemporary Turkey.* Oslo: Institutt for Menneskerettigheter, 2000.

Hassan, Steven. *Combatting Cult Mind Control: Protection, Rescue and Recovery from Destructive Cults.* Wellingborough: Aquarian Press, 1988.

Hawley, John Stratton, ed. *Sati. The Blessing and the Curse. The Burning of Wives in India.* New York: Oxford University Press, 1994.

———, ed. *Fundamentalism and Gender.* New York: Oxford University Press, 1994.

Haynes, Charles C. and Oliver Thomas. *Finding Common Ground: A Guide to Religious Liberty in Public Schools.* Nashville, Tenn.: First Amendment Center, 2001.

Hazewinkel, Harm J. "Religious Freedom in the OSCE/CSCE Process." *Helsinki Monitor* 9, no. 3 (1998): 9–16.

Heinze, Eric, ed. *Of Innocence and Autonomy: Children, Sex and Human Rights.* Aldershot, England: Dartmouth, 2000.

Hefner, Robert W. *Civil Islam*. Princeton, N.J.: Princeton University Press, 2000.
Held, Gottfried. "Die Kleinen öffentlich-rechtlichen Religionsgemeinschaften im Staatskirchenrecht der Bundesrepublik." *Jus Ecclesiasticum* (Munich), vol. 22 (1974): 19.
Helmholz, R. H. "The Early Enforcement of Uses." *Columbia Law Review* 79 (1979): 1503–13.
Henkin, Louis. *The Age Of Rights*. New York: Columbia University Press, 1990.
———, ed. *The International Bill of Rights: The Covenant on Civil and Political Rights*. New York: Columbia University Press, 1981.
Henn, Harry G. and Jeffery H. Boyd. "Statutory Trends in the Law of Nonprofit Organizations: California, Here We Come!" *Cornell Law Review* 66 (1981): 1103–39.
Henn, Harry G. and Michael George Pfeiffer. "Nonprofit Groups: Factors Influencing Choice of Form." *Wake Forest Law Review* 11 (1975): 181.
Henriksen, Jan-Olav, ed. *Identitet og pluralitet* (Identity and Plurality). Oslo: Gyldendal akademiske, 2001.
Heringa, Aalt Willem. "Commentaar." *NJCM-Bulletin* 18 (1993): 1010.
Hernandéz-Forcada, Ricardo. "The Effect of International Treaties on Religious Freedom in Mexico." *Brigham Young University Law Review* (2002): 301–10.
Hill, Daniel G. *A Study of Mind Development Groups, Sects and Cults in Ontario*. Ontario: n.p., 1980.
Holborn, Hajo. *A History of Modern Germany: The Reformation*. New York: A. A. Knopf, 1959.
Holmes, Stephen. *Passions and Constraint. On the Theory of Liberal Democracy*. Chicago: The University of Chicago Press, 1995.
Homer, Lauren B. and Lawrence A. Uzzell. "Federal and Provincial Religious Freedom Laws in Russia: A Struggle for and Against Federalism and the Rule Of Law." *Emory International Law Review* 12 (1998): 247–312.
Houtart, François. "Gewalt im Namen der Religion." *Concilium* 33 (1997): 441–49.
Howe, Mark DeWolfe. "Foreword: Political Theory and the Nature of Liberty." *Harvard Law Review* 67 (1953): 91–95.
———. *The Garden and the Wilderness: Religion and Government in American Constitutional History*. Chicago: University of Chicago Press, 1965.
Howland, Courtney W. "The Challenge of Religious Fundamentalism to the Liberty and Equality Rights of Women: An Analysis under the United Nations Charter." *Columbia Journal of Transnational Law* 35 (1997): 271–377.
———, ed. *Religious Fundamentalisms and the Human Rights of Women*. London: Macmillan, 1999.
Hubmaier, Balthasar. *Schriften*. Edited by Gunnar Westin and Torsten Bergsten. Gütersloh: Mohn, 1962.
———. *Balthasar Hubmaier, Theologian of Anabaptism*. Translated by H. Wayne Pipkin and John H. Yoder. Scottdale, Pa.: Herald Press, 1989.
Human Rights Quarterly 7, no. 1 (1985).
Humphrey, John. "The International Bill of Rights: Scope and Implementation." *William and Mary Law Review* 17 (1976): 527–41.
———. *No Distant Millennium: The International Law Of Human Rights*. Paris: UNESCO, 1989.
Hunt, John. *Report on Sects and New Religious Movements*. Strasbourg: Council of Europe Parliamentary Assembly, 1991.

Hunter, Alan and Kim-Kwong Chan. *Protestantism in Contemporary China*. Cambridge: Cambridge University Press, 1993.

Huntington, Samuel P. "The Clash of Civilizations." *Foreign Affairs* 72, no. 3 (summer 1993): 22–49.

———. *The Clash of Civilizations and the Remaking of World Order.* New York: Simon and Schuster, 1996.

Hylland-Eriksen, Thomas, ed. *Flerkulturell forståelse* (Multicultural Understanding). Oslo: Tano Aschehoug, 1997.

Ilyasoglu, Aynur. *Örtulu Kimlik*. Istanbul: Metis Yayinlari, 1994.

Ingvardsson, Margó, Sonja Wallbom, and Lars Grip. *I God Tro: Samhället Och Nyandligheten.* Stockholm: Statens offentliga utredningar, Socialdepartementet, 1998.

Institut religii i prava. *Religioznye ob'edineniia svoboda sovesti i veroispovedaniia: Normativnye akti sudebnaia praktika*. Moscow: Yurisprudentsiia, 2001.

Introvigne, Massimo and J. Gordon Melton, eds. *Pour en finir avec les sectes. Le débat sur le rapport de commissions parlementaires.* Paris, Milan: Cesnur-Di Giovanni, 1996.

Isaacson, Scott E. "A Practical Comparison of the Laws of Religion of Colombia and Chile." *International Journal of Not-for-Profit Law* 6 (September 2003).

Isensee, Josef and Paul Kirchhof, eds. *Handbuch des Staatsrechts der Bundesrepublik Deutschland*. Vol. 6. Heidelberg: C. F. Müller, 1989.

Is Global Capitalism Working? A Foreign Affairs Reader. Washington, D.C.: Council on Foreign Relations, 1998.

Ishaq, Muhammad Ibn. *The Life of Muhammad.* Translated by A. Guillaume. Islamabad: Oxford University Press, 1967.

Iyer, V. R. Krishna. *Human Rights—A Judge's Miscellany.* New Delhi: B. R. Publishing Corporation, 1995.

Jackson, Vicki C. and Mark Tushnet. *Comparative Constitutional Law*. New York: Foundation Press, 1999.

Jacobs, Francis G. *The European Convention on Human Rights.* Oxford: Clarendon Press, 1975.

Jacobs, Francis G. and Robin C. A. White. *The European Convention on Human Rights.* 2d ed. New York: Oxford University Press, 1996.

Jacobson, Harold. *Networks of Interdependence: International Organizations and the Global Political System*. New York: A. A. Knopf, 1979.

Jayawickrama, Nihal. *The Judicial Application of Human Rights Law: National, Regional and International Jurisprudence*. Cambridge: Cambridge University Press, 2002.

Jeffery, Patricia and Amrita Basu, eds. *Appropriating Gender. Women's Activism and Politicized Religion in South Asia*. London: Routledge, 1998.

Jenkins, Pamela J. and Steve Kroll-Smith, eds. *Witnessing for Sociology: Sociologists in Court.* Westport, Conn.: Praeger, 1996.

Johnson, Eskil. "New Routes for Life and Peace." *New Routes* 6, no. 1 (2001): 35.

Johnston, Douglas and Cynthia Sampson, eds. *Religion, the Missing Dimension of State-craft.* New York: Oxford University Press, 1994.

Johnstone, E. H. *The Buddhacarita or Acts of the Buddha*. Calcutta, 1939.

Jones, Heidi, et al. "Female Genital Cutting Practices in Burkina Faso and Mali and Their Negative Health Outcomes." *Studies in Family Planning* 30 (1999): 219–30.

Jørstad, Guri. *Gemeinsam Leben Lernen* (Learning by living in community). Oslo: Norges forskningsråds KULT-serie, 1995.

Joseph, Sarah, Jenny Schultz, and Melissa Castan. *The International Covenant on Civil and Political Rights: Cases, Materials and Commentary.* Oxford: Oxford University Press, 2000.
Joubert, W. A. and J. A. Faris, eds. *The Law of South Africa.* Durban: Butterworths, 2001.
Kadish, Sanford H. "Complicity, Cause and Blame: A Study in the Interpretation of Doctrine." *California Law Review* 73 (1985): 323–410.
Kahn, Ellison, ed. *Fiat Iustitia: Essays in Memory of Oliver Deneys Schreiner.* Cape Town: Juta & Co., 1983.
Kalb, Herbert, et al. *Religionsgemeinschaftenrecht.* Vienna: Verlag Österreich, 1998.
Kälin, Walter. *Grundrechte im Kulturkonflikt, Freiheit und Gleichheit in der Einwanderungsgesellschaft.* Zürich: NZZ Verlag, 2000.
Kamaras, István. "Devotees of Krishna in Hungary." *ISKCON Communications Journal* 7, no. 2 (1999): 13–22.
Kandiyoti, Deniz, ed. *Women, Islam, and the State.* Basingstoke: Macmillan, 1991.
Kauper, Paul G. and Stephen C. Ellis. "Religious Corporations and the Law." *Michigan Law Review* 71 (1973): 1499–1574.
Kaushal, Rachana. *Women and Human Rights in India.* New Delhi: Kaveri Books, 2000.
Keck, Margaret E. and Kathryn Sikkink. *Activists Beyond Borders: Advocacy Networks in International Politics.* Ithaca: Cornell University Press, 1998.
Keohane, Robert O. and Joseph S. Nye, Jr. "Transgovernmental Relations and International Organizations." *World Politics* 27 (October 1974): 39–62.
———, eds. *Transnational Relations and World Politics.* Cambridge: Harvard University Press, 1971.
Kepel, Gilles. *Les banlieues de l'Islam.* Paris: Seuil, 1987.
Keyder, Caglar. *State and Class in Turkey: A Study in Capitalist Development.* London: Verso, 1987.
Khadduri, Majid. *War and Peace in the Law of Islam.* Baltimore: Johns Hopkins University Press, 1955.
Khan, Muhammad Zafrullah. *Islam and Human Rights.* Tilford: Islam International Publishers, 1989.
Killian, Johnny H. and Leland E. Beck, eds. *The Constitution of the United States of America: Analysis and Interpretation.* Washington, D.C.: Government Printing Office, 1987.
Kishwar, Madhu and Ruth Vanita, eds. *In Search of Answers. Indian Women's Voices From Manushi.* New Delhi: Manohar, 1996.
Kiss, Alexandre. "Commentary by the Rapporteur on the Limitation Provisions." *Human Rights Quarterly* 7, no. 1 (1985): 15–22.
Kiteme, Kamuti. *We, The Pan-Africans: Essays on the Global Black Experience.* New York: n.p., 1992.
Klostermaier, Klaus K. *A Survey of Hinduism.* 2d ed. Albany, N.Y.: State University of New York Press, 1994.
Kniola, Franz-Josef. *Zur Frage der Beobachtung der scientology-Organisation Durch die Verfassungsschutzbehörden.* Düsseldorf: Innenministerium des Landes Nrdrein-Westfalen, 1997.
Korey, William. *NGOs and the Universal Declaration of Human Rights: "A Curious Grapevine."* New York: St. Martin's Press, 1998.

Korey, William. *The Promises We Keep: Human Rights, the Helsinki Process, and American Foreign Policy.* New York: St. Martin's Press, 1993.
Kothari, Smitu and H. Sethni, eds. *Rethinking Human Rights: Challenges for Theory and Action.* New York: New Horizons Press, 1989.
Krasner, Stephen D. "Structural Causes and Regime Consequences: Regimes as Intervening Variables." *International Organization* 36 (spring 1982): 185–205.
Kratochwil, Friedrich and John Gerard Ruggie. "International Organization: A State of the Art on the Art of the State." *International Organization* 40, no. 4 (autumn 1986): 753–75
Kretzmer, David and Eckart Klein, eds. *The Concept of Human Dignity in Human Rights Discourse.* The Hague: Kluwer Law International, 2002.
Kriele, Martin. *Einführung in die Staatslehre. Die geschichtlichen Legitimationsgrundlagen des demokratischen Verfassungstaates.* 5th ed. Opladen: Westdeutscher Verlag, 1994.
Krishnaswami, Arcot. *Study of Discrimination in the Matter of Religious Rights and Practices.* New York: United Nations, 1960.
Kucsko-Stadlmayer, Gabriele. "Die Rechtsprechung des österreichischen Verfassungsgerichtshofs auf dem Gebiet der Glaubensfreiheit." *Europäische Grundrecht Zeitung* 26 (1999): 505.
Kulikov, A. *Inquiry on the Activities of Certain Foreign Religious Organizations.* Moscow: Ministry of Internal Affairs of the Russian Federation, 1996.
Kumar, Radha. *The History of Doing. An Illustrated Account of Movements for Women's Rights and Feminism in India 1800–1990.* London: Verso, 1993.
Küng, Hans. *Etikk for verdens fremtid.* Oslo: Gyldendal, 1991. (Norwegian translation of: Küng, Hans. *Global Responsibility. In Search of a New World Ethic.* London: SCM Press, 1991.)
Küng, Hans and Karl-Josef Kuschel, eds. *A Global Ethic: The Declaration of the Parliament of the World's Religions.* London: SCM Press, 1993.
Kunz, Josef. "The Status of the Holy See in International Law." *American Journal of International Law* 46 (1952): 308–14.
Kurdi, Abdulrahman Abdulkadir. *The Islamic State: A Study Based on the Islamic Holy Constitution.* London: Mansell, 1984.
Labuschagne, J. M. T. "Circumcision and Female Genital Mutilation: A Human Rights and Antropo-Legal Evaluation." *South Africa Public Law* 13 (1998): 277.
Lammers, J. G. *Pollution of International Watercourses: A Search for Substantive Rules and Principles of Law.* Dordrecht: Martinus Nijhoff Publishers, 1984.
Langbein, John. "The Contractarian Basis of the Law of Trusts." *Yale Law Journal* 105 (1995): 625–75.
Larkin, Maurice. *Church and State after the Dreyfus Affair: The Separation Issue in France.* London: Macmillan Press, 1974.
———. *Religion, Politics, and Preferment in France since 1890: La Belle Epoque and Its Legacy.* Cambridge: Cambridge University Press, 1995.
Larminaux, Gail. *The Silk Roads: Roads of Dialogue.* New York: UNESCO, 1997.
Lasson, Kenneth. "Racial Defamation as Free Speech: Abusing the First Amendment." *Columbia Human Rights Law Review* 17 (1985): 11–55.
Lauren, Paul Gordon. *The Evolution of International Human Rights.* Philadelphia: University of Pennsylvania Press, 1998.

Laycock, Douglas. "Towards a General Theory of the Religion Clauses: The Case of Church Labor Relations and the Right to Church Autonomy." *Columbia Law Review* 81 (1981): 1373–1417.

Leclerc, Joseph. "Die Religionsfreiheit im Lauf der Geschichte" (Freedom of Religion in the Course of History). *Concilium* 2 (1966): 572. The corresponding issue in English is *Concilium* 18 (1966).

Lederach, John Paul. *Building Peace: Sustainable Reconciliation in Divided Societies.* Washington, D.C.: United States Institute of Peace Press, 1999.

Leganger-Krogstad, Heid and Elisabeth Haakedal, eds. *Religiøse og pedagogiske idealer* (Religious and Pedagogical Ideals). Oslo: Norges forskningsråds KULTserie nr. 42, 1995.

Lehnhof, Lance. "Freedom of Religion Association: The Right of Religious Organizations to Obtain Legal Entity Status Under the European Convention." *Brigham Young University Law Review* (2002): 561–609.

Leirvik, Oddbjørn, ed. *Fellesskapsetikk i et flerkulturelt Norge* (Common Ethics in a Multi-Cultural Norway). Oslo: Universitetsforlaget, 1993.

Lerner, Natan. "Ethnic Cleansing." *Israel Yearbook on Human Rights* 24 (1994): 103–17.

———. "Group Libel Revisited." *Israel Yearbook on Human Rights* 17 (1987): 184–96.

———. *Group Rights and Discrimination in International Law.* 2d ed. The Hague: Kluwer Law International, 2003.

———. "Proselytism, Change of Religion, and International Human Rights." *Emory International Law Review* 12 (1998): 477–561.

———. "Protecting Religious Human Rights by Bilateral Arrangements." *La Porta D'Oriente* 12/13 (1998): 45–55.

———. *Religion, Beliefs and International Human Rights.* Maryknoll, N.Y.: Orbis Books, 2000.

———. "Towards a Draft Declaration against Religious Intolerance and Discrimination." *Israel Yearbook of Human Rights* 11 (1981): 82–105.

———. *The U.N. Convention on the Elimination of All Forms of Racial Discrimination.* Alphen aan den Rijn: Sijthoff & Noordhoff, 1980.

Les Inscriptions d'Asoka, traduites et commentées par Jules Bloch. Paris: Société d'Edition "Les Belles Lettres," 1950 (Collection Emile Senart).

Lheureux, N. L., et al. *Report on Discrimination against Spiritual and Therapeutical Minorities in France.* Paris: Coordination des Associations et Particuliers Pour la Liberté de Conscience, 2000.

Lillich, Richard B., ed. *International Human Rights Instruments.* 2d ed. New York: W. S. Hein, 1990.

Lillich, Richard B. and John M. Paxman. "State Responsibility for Injuries to Aliens Occasioned by Terrorist Activities." *American University Law Review* 26 (1977): 217–313.

Lindholm, Tore. "Menneskerettigheter og religioner: konflikt eller gjensidig støtte?" (Human rights and religions: Conflict or mutual reinforcement?) *Amnesty Nytt.* Oslo: Amnesty International Norway, Sept. 1998.

Lindholm, Tore and Kari Vogt, eds. *Islamic Law Reform and Human Rights: Challenges and Rejoinders.* Oslo: Nordic Human Rights Publications, 1993.

Listl, Joseph and Dietrich Pirson, eds. *Handbuch des Staatskirchenrechts der Bundesrepublik Deutschland.* 2d rev. ed. 2 vols. Berlin: Duncker &Humblot, 1994.

Little, David. "Rethinking Human Rights: Religion, Relativism, and Other Matters." *Journal of Religious Ethics* 27 (1999): 151–77.

Little, David. *Sri Lanka: The Invention of Enmity.* Washington, D.C.: United States Institute of Peace Press, 1994.

———. *Ukraine: The Legacy of Intolerance.* Washington, D.C.: United States Institute of Peace Press, 1991.

Little, David, John Kelsay, and Abdulaziz A. Sachedina. *Human Rights and Conflict of Cultures: Western and Islamic Perspectives on Religious Liberty.* Columbia, S.C.: University of South Carolina Press, 1988.

Llobell, J. "El derecho a un proceso equitativo. Notas a propósito de una sentencia de la Corte Europea de los Derechos Humanos sobre la homologación civil de una sentencia canónica de nulidad de matrimonio dictada en el marco del proceso documental canónico." *Revista General de Derecho Canónico y Derecho Eclesiástico del Estado*, no. 1 (2003).

Locke, John. *An Essay Concerning Human Understanding.* Edited by Roger Woolhouse. London: Penguin Books, 1997 (1689).

———. *A Letter Concerning Toleration.* Edited by John Horton and Susan Mendus. London and New York: Routledge, 1991.

Lockwood, Bert B., et al. "Working Paper for the Committee of Experts on Limitation Provisions." *Human Rights Quarterly* 7, no. 1 (1985): 35.

Loenen, Titia and Peter R. Rodrigues, eds. *Non-Discrimination Law: Comparative Perspectives.* The Hague: Martinus Nijhoff Publishers, 1999.

"LPI in Somalia: 7 Years Later." *New Routes* 4 (1999): 21.

Luhmann, Niklas. *The Differentiation of Society.* Translated by Stephen Holmes and Charles Larmore. New York: Columbia University Press, 1982.

Lunden, Kåre. *Nasjon eller union?* (Nation or Union?). Oslo: Det norske samlaget, 1993.

Lusage, Michel, ed. *Constitutions d'Europe centrale, orientale et balte.* Paris: La documentation française, 1995.

Macdonald, R. St. J., F. Matscher, and H. Petzold, eds. *The European System for the Protection of Human Rights.* Dordrecht: Martinus Nijhoff Publishers, 1993.

Maguire, Daniel C. *The Moral Revolution. A Christian Humanist Vision.* New York: Harper and Row, 1986.

Mahmoud, Mahgoub el-Tigani. "Islamic Law, Human Rights and International Law, A Critique of Mahmoud, Taha and Abdullahi Ahmed An-Na'im. *Islamica: The Journal of the Islamic Society of the London School of Economics* 2, no. 3 (summer 1996): 31–42.

Mahoney, Kathleen E. and Paul Mahoney, eds. *Human Rights in the Twenty-First Century.* Boston: Martinus Nijhoff Publishers, 1993.

Mahoney, Paul. "Marvellous Richness of Diversity or Invidious Cultural Relativism?" *Human Rights Law Journal* 19, no. 1 (1998): 5.

Mahoney, Paul, et al. "The Doctrine of the Margin of Appreciation under the European Convention on Human Rights: Its Legitimacy in Theory and Application in Practice." *Human Rights Law Journal* 19, no. 1 (1998): 1–36.

Maitland, Frederic William. *Collected Papers.* Cambridge: Cambridge University Press, 1911.

———. "The Corporation Sole." *Law Quarterly Review* 16 (1900): 335–54.

Mardin, Serif. *Türkiye'de Toplum ve Siyaset.* Istanbul: Iletisim Yayinlari, 1995.

Maresca, John J. *To Helsinki: The Conference on Security and Co-operation in Europe 1973–1975*. Duke Press Policy Studies. Durham: Duke University Press, 1987.
Markham, Ian S. *Plurality and Christian Ethics*. Rev. ed. New York: Seven Ridges Press, 1999.
Marks, Stephen P. "Emerging Human Rights: A New Generation for the 1980s?" *Rutgers Law Review* 33 (1981): 435–52.
Marshall, Paul. *Their Blood Cries Out: The Worldwide Tragedy of Modern Christians Who Are Dying for Their Faith*. Dallas: Word Publishing, 1997.
———, ed. *Religious Freedom in the World: A Global Report on Freedom and Persecution*. Nashville: Broadman & Holman, 2000.
Martin, David. *Does Christianity Cause War?* Oxford: Clarendon Press, 1997.
———. *Tongues of Fire: The Explosion of Protestantism in Latin America*. Oxford: Blackwell, 1990.
Martínez de Codes, Rosa María. "The Contemporary Form of Registering Religious Entities in Spain." *Brigham Young University Law Review* (1998): 369–85.
Martínez de Codes, Rosa M. and Jaime Rossell, eds. *Religious Freedom, Tolerance, and Non-Discrimination in Education*. Caceres: Universidad de Extremadura, 2001.
Martínez-Torrón, Javier. "Libertad de proselitismo en Europa: A propósito de una reciente sentencia del Tribunal europeo de derechos humanos." *Quaderni di diritto e politica ecclesiastica*, no. 1 (1994): 59–71.
———, ed. *La libertad religiosa y de conciencia ante la justicia constitucional: Actas del VIII Congreso Internacional de Derecho Eclesiástico del Estado*. Granada: Comares, 1998.
Marty, Martin E., and R. Scott Appleby, eds. *The Fundamentalism Project*. Chicago: University of Chicago Press, 1991.
Matlary, Janne Haaland. *Intervention for human rights in Europe*. Basingstoke: Palgrave, 2002.
Matscher, Franz and Wolfram Karl, eds. *Austrian–Soviet Round-Table on the Protection of Human Rights*. Kehl, Germany: N. P. Engel Verlag, 1992.
Matthews, Jessica T. "Power Shift." *Foreign Affairs* 76, no. 1 (1997).
Mayer, Ann Elizabeth. "A 'Benign' Apartheid: How Gender Apartheid Has Been Rationalized." *UCLA Journal of International Law and Foreign Affairs* 5 (2000): 237–338.
———. *Islam and Human Rights: Tradition and Politics*. 3d ed. Boulder, Colo.: Westview Press, 1999.
———. "Law and Religion in the Muslim Middle East." *American Journal of Comparative Law* 35 (1987): 127–84.
Mayeur, Jean-Marie. *La séparation des Eglises et de l'Etat*. Paris: Editions Ouvrières, 1991.
Mbiti, John S. *African Religions and Philosophy*. Garden City, N.Y.: Doubleday, 1970.
McConnell, Michael. "The Origins and Historical Understanding of Free Exercise of Religion." *Harvard Law Review* 103 (1990): 1409–1517.
McDougall, Walter A. *Promised Land, Crusader State: The American Encounter with the World Since 1776*. Boston: Houghton Mifflin Company, 1997.
McGoldrick, Dominic. *The Human Rights Committee: Its Role in the Development of the International Covenant on Civil and Political Rights*. New York: Oxford University Press, 1991.
McGuire, Meredith B. *Religion: The Social Context*. 4th ed. Belmont, Calif.: Wadsworth, 1997.

McKean, Warwick. *Equality and Discrimination Under International Law.* Oxford: Clarendon Press, 1983.
Mernissi, Fatima. *The Veil and the Male Elite: A Feminist Interpretation of Women's Rights in Islam.* Translated by Mary Jo Lakeland. Reading, Mass.: Perseus Books, 1991.
Meron, Theodor. "The Case for War Crimes Trials in Yugoslavia." *Foreign Affairs* 72 (summer 1993): 122–35.
———. *Human Rights Law-Making in the United Nations: A Critique of Instruments and Process.* Oxford: Clarendon Press, 1986.
———, ed. *Human Rights in International Law: Legal and Policy Issues.* Oxford: Clarendon Press, 1984.
Merton, Robert K. *Social Theory and Social Structure.* Glencoe, Ill.: The Free Press, 1957.
Messner, Francis, ed. *Les "sectes" et le droit en France.* Paris: PUF, 1999.
Messner, Francis, et. al., eds. *Traité de droit français des religions.* Paris: 2003.
Michalowski, Sabine and Lorna Woods. *German Constitutional Law: The Protection of Civil Liberties.* Aldershot, Hants, England: Dartmouth Publishing, 1999.
Militello, Cettina, ed. *Donne e Teologia. Bilancio di un secolo.* Bologna: Edizioni Dehoniane, 2001.
Miller, David H. *The Drafting of the Covenant.* 2 vols. New York: Putnam's Sons, 1928.
Miner, Christopher J. "Losing My Religion: Austria's New Religion Law in Light of International and European Standards of Religious Freedom." *Brigham Young University Law Review* (1998): 607–46.
Mingoen, Harriëtte, ed. *Report of the International Conference on Muslim Women and Development.* The Hague: Dutch Ministry of Foreign Affairs, 2001.
Mitter, Sara S. *Dharma's Daughters. Contemporary Indian Women and Hindu Culture.* New Brunswick, N.J.: Rutgers University Press, 1991.
Mnookin, Robert H. *In the Interests of Children.* New York: W. H. Freeman and Company, 1985.
Monshipouri, Mahmood. "The Muslim World Half a Century after the Universal Declaration of Human Rights: Progress and Obstacles." *Netherlands Quarterly of Human Rights* 16, no. 3 (September 1998): 287–314.
Montufar, Guillermo Garcia and Elvira Martinez Coco. "Antecedents, Perspectives, and Projections of a Legal Project about Religious Liberty in Peru." *Brigham Young University Law Review* (1999): 503–35.
Moreno, Pedro C., ed., *Handbook on Religious Liberty Around the World.* Charlottesville, Va.: The Rutherford Institute, 1996.
Morgan, Rod and Malcolm Evans. *Combating Torture in Europe.* Strasbourg: Council of Europe Press, 2001.
Morsink, Johannes. *The Universal Declaration of Human Rights: Origins, Drafting, and Intent.* Philadelphia: University of Pennsylvania Press, 1999.
Moskos, Charles C. and John Whiteclay Chambers II, eds. *The New Conscientious Objection: From Sacred to Secular Resistance.* New York: Oxford University Press, 1993.
Muhsin, Amina Wadud. *Qur'an and Woman: Rereading the Sacred Text from a Woman's Perspective.* New York: Oxford University Press, 1999.
Mukherjee, Prabhati. *Hindu Women. Normative Models.* New Delhi: Orient Longman, 1978.
Müller, Harald. *Das Zusammenleben der Kulturen: Ein Gegenentwurf zu Huntington.* Frankfurt: Fischer Taschenbuch Verlag, 1998.

Müllerson, Rein. *Human Rights Diplomacy.* New York: Routledge, 1997.
Munro, J. Forbes. *Colonial Rule Among the Kamba: Social Change in the Kenya Highlands 1889–1939.* New York: Oxford University Press, 1975.
Murray, John C. *Religious Liberty: Catholic Struggles with Pluralism.* Edited by J. Leon Hooper, S. J. Lousiville, Ky.: Westminster/Jon Knox Press, 1993.
Murray, Rachel and Malcolm Evans, eds. *Documents of the African Commission on Human and Peoples' Rights.* Oxford: Oxford, 2001.
Naber, Jonneke M. M., ed. *Freedom of Religion: A Precious Human Right.* Assen, The Netherlands: Van Gorkum, 2000.
Nagel, Ernest. *The Structure of Science: Problems in the Logic of Scientific Explanation.* London: Routledge, 1961.
Naldi, Gino J. *Documents of the Organizations of African Unity.* New York: Mansell, 1992.
Nanda, Ved P. "The Protection of the Rights of Migrant Workers." *Asian and Pacific Migration Journal* 2 (1993): 161.
Nastase, Adrian. *Illegal Activities of Sects.* Strasbourg: Council of Europe Parliamentary Assembly, 1998.
Navarro-Valls, Rafael and Javier Martínez-Torrón. *Las objeciones de conciencia en el derecho español y comparado.* Madrid: McGraw-Hill, 1997.
———. *Le obiezioni di coscienza: Profili di diritto comparato.* Torino: Giappichelli, 1995.
Neuhaus, Richard John. "A Continuing Survey of Religion and Public Life." *First Things* 46 (October 1994): 74–88.
Neussl, Peter. "Bosnia and Herzegovina still far from the rule of law/Basic facts and landmark decisions of the Human Rights Chamber." *Human Rights Law Journal* 20 (1999): 290.
Nichols, Joel A. "Mission, Evangelism, and Proselytism in Christianity: Mainline Conception as Reflected in Church Documents." *Emory International Law Review* 12 (1998): 563–656.
Nicolet, Claude. *L'idée républicaine en France.* Paris: Gallimard, 1982.
Noonan, John T. *The Lustre of Our Country: The American Experience of Religious Freedom.* Berkeley: The University of California Press, 1998.
Noonan, John T., Jr. *Contraception. A History of Its Treatment by the Catholic Theologians and Canonists.* Cambridge, Mass.: Harvard University Press, 1986.
Nowak, Manfred. "The Activities of the UN Human Rights Committee: Developments from 1 August 1992 to 31 July 1995." *Human Rights Law Journal* 16 (1995): 377.
———. "The Human Rights Chamber for Bosnia and Herzegovina Adopts Its First Judgements." *Human Rights Law Journal* 18 (1997): 174.
———. "Human Rights News." *Netherlands Quarterly of Human Rights* 12 (1994): 36.
———. U.N. Covenant on Civil and Political Rights: CCPR Commentary. Kehl: N. P. Engel Verlag, 1993.
———, ed. *World Conference on Human Rights: The Contributions of NGOs: Reports and Documents.* Wien: Manz, 1994.
Nozick, Robert. *Anarchy, State, and Utopia.* New York: Basic Books, 1974.
Nussbaum, Arthur. *A Concise History of the Law of Nations.* Rev. ed. New York: Macmillan, 1954.
Nussbaum, Martha. *Women and Human Development.* Cambridge: Cambridge University Press, 2000.

Nye, Joseph S., Jr. *Bound to Lead: The Changing Nature of American Power.* New York: Basic Books, 1990.

Nye, Joseph S., Jr. and William A. Owens. "America's Information Edge." *Foreign Affairs* 75, no. 2 (March/April 1996): 20–36.

Oaks, Dallin H. "Trust Doctrines in Church Controversies." *Brigham Young University Law Review* (1981): 805–907.

O'Brien, James C. "The International Tribunal for Violation of International Humanitarian Law in the Former Yugoslavia." *American Journal of International Law* 87 (1993): 639–59.

Odinkalu, Chidi Anselm and Camilla Christensen. "The African Commission on Human and Peoples' Rights: The Development of its Non-State Communication Procedures." *Human Rights Quarterly* 20 (1998): 235–80.

Office of the High Commissioner for Human Rights. *Final Document of the International Consultative Conference on School Education in Relation with Freedom of Religion and Belief, Tolerance and Non-Discrimination.* This document may be found at the Oslo Coalition site: <http://www.oslocoalition.org/html/project_school_education/final_document_madrid.html>

O'Hara, James B. "The Modern Corporation Sole." *Dickinson Law Review* 93 (1988): 23–39.

Olz, Martin A. "Non-Governmental Organizations in Regional Human Rights Systems." *Columbia Human Rights Law Review* 28 (winter 1997): 307–74.

Onuf, Nicholas G. and V. Spike Peterson. "Human Rights from an International Regimes Perspective." *Journal of International Affairs* 38 (winter 1984): 329–42.

Oommen, Tharaileth Koshy. "Religion as a Source of Violence: A Sociological Perspective." *Ecumenical Review* 53 (2001): 168–79.

Oosterveld, Valerie. "Refuge Status for Female Circumcision Fugitives: Building a Canadian Precedent." *University of Toronto Faculty of Law Review* 51 (1993): 277–303.

Orlin, Theodore S., Allan Rosas, and Martin Scheinin, eds. *The Jurisprudence of Human Rights Law: A Comparative Interpretive Approach.* Åbo, Turkey: Åbo Akademi University, 2000.

OSCE. *OSCE Handbook.* Vienna: Secretariat of the OSCE, 1999.

———. *OSCE Yearbook, 1998.* Baden: Nomos Verlagsgesellschaft, 1997.

———. *Seminar on Freedom of Religion or Belief in the OSCE Region: Challenges to Law and Practice.* The Hague: Ministerie van Buitenlandse Zaken, 26 June 2001.

Ostrander, Gilman Marston. *The Rights of Man in America, 1606–1861.* 2d ed. Columbia, Mo.: University of Missouri Press, 1969.

Packer, Corinne. "Defining and Delineating the Right to Reproductive Choice." *Nordic Journal of International Law* 67 (1998): 77–95.

Padilla, David. "The Inter-American Commission on Human Rights of the Organization of American States: A Case Study." *American University Journal of International Law and Policy* 9 (1993): 95–115.

Pal, R. M. and G. S. Bhargava, eds. *Human Rights of Dalits. Societal Violation.* New Delhi: Gyan Publishing House, 1999.

Palomino, Rafael. *Las objeciones de conciencia: Conflictos entre conciencia y ley en el derecho norteamericano.* Madrid: Montecorvo, 1994.

Pannenberg, Wolfhart. "How to Think About Secularism." *First Things* 64 (1996): 27–32.
Parliament of the World's Religions. *A Global Ethic: The Declaration of the Parliament of the World's Religions.* Edited by Hans Küng and Karl-Josef Kuschel. London: SCM Press, 1993.
Patrick, Ted and Tom Dulack. *Let Our Children Go.* New York: Ballantine, 1976.
People's Republic of China. *Li Hongzhi and His "Falun Gong": Deceiving the Public and Ruining Lives.* Beijing: New Star, 1999.
Perry, Michael J. *The Idea of Human Rights. Four Inquiries.* Oxford: Oxford University Press, 1998.
Perry, Richard L. and John C. Cooper, eds. *Sources of Our Liberties.* New York: New York University Press, 1972.
Peters, Julie and Andrea Wolper, eds. *Women's Rights, Human Rights. International Feminist Perspectives.* New York: Routledge, 1995.
Pfann, H. *A Short History of the Catholic Church in Ghana.* Cape Coast, 1965.
Phillipson, Coleman. *The International Law and Custom of Ancient Greece and Rome.* London: Macmillan, 1911.
Philpott, Daniel. "The Religious Roots of Modern International Relations." *World Politics* 52 (January 2000): 206–45.
Pinkham, Mildred Worth. *Woman in the Sacred Scriptures of Hinduism.* New York: AMS Press, 1967.
"*Playboy* Interview with Ted Patrick." *Playboy* (March 1979): 53.
Plesner, Ingvill T. "Religion-political models and models for religious and moral education." *Panorama: International Journal of Comparative Religious Education and Values* (edited by Peter Schreiner) 14, no. 2 (winter 2002): 111–22.
Podoprigora, Roman. "Religion in Kazakhstan: A General View." *Brigham Young University Law Review* (1999): 581–88.
Pope Gregory XVI. *Mirari vos* (On Liberalism and Religious Indifferentism). Encyclical promulgated on 15 August 1832.
Putnam, Robert D. "Diplomacy and Domestic Politics: The Logic of Two-Level Games." *International Organization* 42 (summer 1988): 429–60.
Quashigah, E. K. "Legislating Religious Liberty: The Ghanaian Experience." *Brigham Young University Law Review* (1999): 589–606.
Rabinove, Samuel. *Religious Rights and Freedoms: What They Mean for Jews.* New York: The American Jewish Committee, 1988.
Rader, Stanley R. *Against the Gates of Hell: The Threat to Religious Freedom in America.* New York: Everest House, 1980.
Rahman, Anika and Nahid Toubia, eds. *Female Genital Mutilation: A Guide to Laws and Policies Worldwide.* London: Zed Books, 2000.
Ramcharan, Bertrand G., ed. *Human Rights, Thirty Years After the Universal Declaration.* Boston: Martinus Nijhoff Publishers, 1979.
Raming, Ida. *The Exclusion of Women from the Priesthood: Divine Law or Sex Discrimination?* Metuchen, N.J.: Scarecrow Press, 1976.
Rawls, John. *Political Liberalism: The John Dewey Essays in Philosophy.* New York: Columbia University Press, 1993.
Raz, Joseph. *The Authority of Law.* Oxford: Clarendon Press, 1983.

Reynolds, Noel B. and W. Cole Durham, Jr., eds. *Religious Liberty in Western Thought.* Atlanta, Ga.: Scholars Press for Emory University, 1996.

Richardson, James T. "'Brainwashing' Claims and Minority Religions Outside the United States: Cultural Diffusion of a Questionable Concept in the Legal Arena." *Brigham Young University Law Review* (1996): 873–904.

Richardson, James T., Jan van der Lans, and Frans Derks. "Leaving and Labeling: Voluntary and Coerced Disaffiliation from Religious Social Movements." *Research in Social Movements, Conflicts and Change* 9 (1986): 97–126.

Richardson, James T. and Massimo Introvigne. "'Brainwashing' Theories in European Parliamentary and Administrative Reports on 'Cults' and 'Sects.'" *Journal for the Scientific Study of Religion* 40, no. 2 (2001): 143–68.

Rickard, Stephen. "Repression and Response." *SAIS Review* 18 (summer-fall 1998): 52–58.

Riffaut, Hélène. *Les valeurs des français.* Paris: PUF, 1994.

Risse, Thomas, Stephen C. Ropp, and Kathryn Sikkink, eds. *The Power of Human Rights: International Norms and Domestic Change.* Cambridge: Cambridge University Press, 1999.

Risse-Kappen, Thomas, ed., *Bringing Transnational Relations Back In: Non-state Actors, Domestic Structures, International Institutions.* Cambridge: Cambridge University Press, 1995.

Robbers, Gerhard, ed. *Church Autonomy: A Comparative Survey.* Frankfurt: Peter Lang, 2002.

———, ed. *State and Church in the European Union.* Baden-Baden: Nomos Verlagsgesellschaft, 1996.

Robbins, Thomas, ed. *In Gods We Trust: New Patterns of Religious Pluralism in America.* 2d ed. New Brunswick: Transaction, 1990.

Robbins, Thomas and Dick Anthony. "Deprogramming, Brainwashing and the Medicalization of Deviant Religious Groups." *Social Problems* 29 (1982): 283–97.

Robbins, Thomas and Roland Robertson, eds. *Church-State Relations: Tensions and Transitions.* London: Transaction, 1987.

Roberts, Adam and Richard Guelff, eds. *Documents on the Law of War.* 2d ed. Oxford: Clarendon Press, 1989.

Robertson, A. H. and J. G. Merrills. *Human Rights in the World.* 3d ed. Manchester: Manchester University Press, 1989.

Robinson, Catherine A. *Tradition and Liberation. The Hindu Tradition in the Indian Women's Movement.* England: Curzon Press, 1999.

Robinson, Jacob, et al. *Were the Minorities Treaties a Failure?* New York: Institute of Jewish Affairs, 1943.

Robinson, Nehemiah. *The Genocide Convention: A Commentary.* New York: Institute of Jewish Affairs, 1960.

———. *The Universal Declaration of Human Rights: Its Origin, Significance, Application, and Interpretation.* New York: Institute of Jewish Affairs, 1958.

Roca, María J. "La legislación sobre libertad religiosa en el Este de Europa: Especial referencia a Ucrania." *Anuario de Derecho Eclesiástico del Estado* 13 (1997): 189–221.

Rodley, Nigel. "The Work of Non-Governmental Organizations in the World-Wide Promotion and Protection of Human Rights." *UN Bulletin of Human Rights* 90, no. 1 (1991): 85.

Rosaldo, Michelle Z. and Louise Lamphère, eds. *Women, Culture and Society.* Stanford University Press, 1974.
Rouner, Leroy S., ed. *Human Rights and World Religions.* Notre Dame, Ind.: University of Notre Dame Press, 1988.
Rousseau, Jean-Jacques. *Du contrat social.* Edited by Bertrand de Jouvenel. Geneva: C. Bourquin, 1947.
Rousseau, Jean-Jacques. *The Social Contract.* Translated by G. D. H. Cole. New York: E. P. Dutton & Co., 1950.
Rousselle, Aline. *Porneia. On Desire and the Body in Antiquity.* Oxford: Basil Blackwell, 1988.
Roxin, Claus. *Täterschaft under Tatherrschaft.* Berlin: de Gruyter, 1975.
Roy, M. N. *New Humanism—A Manifesto.* Calcutta: Renaissance Publishers, 1953.
Rudolf, Susanne Hober and James Piscatori, eds. *Transnational Religion and Fading States.* Boulder, Colo.: Westview Press, 1997.
Ruether, Rosemary R. *Women and Redemption. A Theological History.* Minneapolis, Minn.: Fortress Press, 1998.
Ruggie, John Gerard. "Human Rights and the Future International Community." *Daedalus* 112 (fall 1983): 93–110.
Russell, Letty M., ed. *Feminist Interpretation of the Bible.* Philadelphia, Pa.: Westminster Press, 1985.
Russell, Ruth B. *A History of the United Nations Charter: the Role of the United States 1940–1945.* Washington, D.C.: The Brookings Institute, 1958.
Rutland, Robert A., et al., eds. *The Papers of James Madison.* Vol. 8. Chicago: University of Chicago Press, 1973.
Sangari, Kumkum and Sudesh Vaid, eds. *Recasting Women. Essays in Colonial History.* New Delhi: Kali for Women, 1989.
Saribay, Ali Yasar. *Postmodernizm, Sivil Toplum ve Islam.* Istanbul: Iletisim Yayinlari, 1995.
Sarkar, Tanika, and Urvashi Butalia, eds. *Women and Right-Wing Movements. Indian Experiences.* London: Zed Books, 1995.
Saunders, Anja, et al. *New Religious and Ideological Communities and Psychogroups in the Federal Republic of Germany: Final Report of the Enquete Commission on "So-Called Sects and Psychogroups."* Bonn: German Bundestag, 1998.
Schechter, Danny. *Falun Gong's Challenge to China: Spiritual Practice or "Evil Cult"?* New York: Akashuc, 2000.
Schirazi, Asghar. *The Constitution of Iran: Politics and the State in the Islamic Republic.* London: I. B. Tauris, 1997.
Schokkenbroek, Jeroen. "The Basis, Nature and Application of the Margin-of-Appreciation Doctrine in the Case-Law of the European Court of Human Rights: General Report." *Human Rights Law Journal* 19, no. 1 (1998): 30–36.
Schramm, Jürgen, ed. *The Role of Non-Governmental Organizations in the New European Order.* Baden-Baden: Nomos Verlaggesellschaft, 1995.
Schreiner, Peter. *Religious Education in Europe: A Collection of Basic Information about RE in European Countries.* Münster: Comenius Institut/Intereuropean Commission on Church and School, 2000.
Schuler, Margaret A., ed. *From Basic Needs to Basic Rights: Women's Claim to Human Rights.* Washington, D.C.: Institute for Women, Law, and Development, 1995.

Seligman, Adam. *The Idea of Civil Society*. New York: Free Press, 1992.

Selling, Joseph A. and Jan Jans, eds. *The Splendor of Accuracy. An Examination of the Assertions Made by Veritatis Splendor.* Grand Rapids, Mich.: Eerdmans Publishing, 1995.

Serritella, James A., et al., eds. *Religious Organizations in the United States: A Study of Identity, Liberty, and the Law*. Durham, N.C.: Carolina Academic Press, forthcoming, 2004.

Shapiro, Ian, ed. *The Rule of Law.* New York: New York University Press, 1994.

Sharma, Arvind. *Sati: Historical and Phenomenological Essays.* New Delhi: Motilal Barnasidass, 1988.

Shaskolsky-Sheleff, Leon. "Rabbi Captain Goldman's Yarmulke, Freedom of Religion and Conscience, and Civil (Military) Disobedience." *Israel Yearbook of Human Rights* 17 (1987): 206.

Shaw, Stanford J. and Ezel K. Shaw. *History of the Ottoman Empire and Modern Turkey.* Cambridge: Cambridge University Press, 1977.

Shea, Nina. *In the Lion's Den*. Nashville: Broadman & Holman Publishers, 1997.

Sheehan, James J. *Oxford History of Modern Europe: German History, 1770–1866.* Oxford: Clarendon Press, 1989.

Sheleff, Leon. "Tribal Rites and Legal Rights." *Israel Yearbook on Human Rights* 18 (1988): 153–72.

Shelton, Dinah. "Human Rights Within Churches: A Survey Concerning Discrimination Within Religious Organisations." *Human Rights Journal* 6 (1973): 526–57.

———. "The Jurisprudence of the Inter-American Court of Human Rights." *American University Journal of International Law and Policy* 10 (fall 1994): 333–72.

Shils, Edward. "The Virtues of Civil Society." *Government and Opposition* 26, no. 2 (winter 1991): 3–20.

Shipps, Jan. *Mormonism: The Story of a New Religious Tradition*. Champaign-Urbana, Ill.: University of Illinois Press, 1987.

Shropshire, Denys W. T. *The Church and Primitive Peoples.* London: SPCK, 1938.

Shterin, Marat and James T. Richardson. "Effects of the Western Anti-Cult Movement on Development of Laws Concerning Religion in Post-Communist Russia." *Journal of Church and State* 42, no. 2 (2000): 247–71.

Shupe, Anson D. and David G. Bromley. *The New Vigilantes: Deprogrammers, Anti-Cultists, and the New Religions.* Beverly Hills, Calif.: Sage Publications, 1980.

Shupe, Anson and David G. Bromley, eds. *Anti-Cult Movements in Cross-Cultural Perspective.* New York: Garland, 1994.

Sieghart, Paul. *The International Law of Human Rights.* New York: Oxford University Press, 1983.

Sigmund, Paul E., ed. *Religious Freedom and Evangelization in Latin America: The Challenge of Religious Pluralism*. Maryknoll, N.Y.: Orbis Books, 1999.

Singer, Margaret and Janja Lalich. *Cults in Our Midst: The Hidden Menace in Our Everyday Lives.* San Francisco: Jossey-Bass, 1995.

Slack, Alison T. "Female Circumcision: A Critical Appraisal." *Human Rights Quarterly* 10 (1988): 437–86.

Smith, Anthony D. *National Identity.* London: Penguin Books, 1991.

Smith, Hannah Clayson. "Liberté, Egalité, et Fraternité at Risk for New Religious Movements in France." *Brigham Young University Law Review* (2000): 1099–1151.

Smith, S. B. *Elements of Ecclesiastical Law.* 9th ed. New York: Benziger Brothers, 1887.

Smith, Sidonie. *A Poetics of Women's Autobiography: Marginality and the Fictions of Self-Representation*. Indianapolis, Ind.: Indiana University Press, 1987.
Smith, Steven D. *Foreordained Failure: The Quest for a Constitutional Principle of Religious Freedom*. New York: Oxford University Press, 1995.
Sohn, Louis B. "The Human Rights Law of the Charter." *Texas International Law Journal* 12 (1977): 129–40.
Soifer, Aviam. "Freedom of Association: Indian Tribes, Workers, and Communal Ghosts." *Maryland Law Review* 48 (1989): 350–83.
Sood, Sushma, ed. *Violence Against Women*. Jaipur, India: Arihant Publishers, 1990.
"Special Issue Freedom of Religion or Belief." *Helsinki Monitor* 9, no. 3 (1998).
Stahl, F. J. *Die Kirchenverfassung nach Lehre und Recht der Protestanten*. Erlangen: 2e Aufl., 1862.
———. *Der Protestantismus als politisches Prinzip*. Berlin: 2e Aufl., 1853.
Stahnke, Tad. "Proselytism and the Freedom to Change Religion in International Human Rights Law." *Brigham Young University Law Review* (1999): 251–350.
Stahnke, Tad and J. Paul Martin, eds. *Religion and Human Rights: Basic Documents*. New York: Center for the Study of Human Rights, Columbia University Press, 1998.
Standing Committee of the Municipal/Provincial People's Congress. "Five Provincial Level Official Regulations on Religious Affairs." *Chinese Law and Government* 36, no. 3 (May–June 2003): 49–80.
"State Power and Discrimination by Private Clubs: First Amendment Protection for Nonexpressive Associations." *Harvard Law Review* 104 (1991): 1835–56.
Stegeby, E. Kenneth. "An Analysis of the Impending Disestablishment of the Church of Sweden." *Brigham Young University Law Review* (1999): 703–67.
Stehle, Hans Jacob. *Geheimdiplomatie im Vatikan. Die Päpste und die Kommunisten*. Benzinger Verlag, 1993.
Steiner, Henry J. *Diverse Partners: Non-Governmental Organizations in the Human Rights Movement: The Report of a Retreat of Human Rights Activists*. Harvard Law School Human Rights Program Human Rights Internet, 1991.
———. "Ideals and Counter-Ideals in the Struggle for Autonomy Regimes for Minorities." *Notre Dame Law Review* 66 (1991): 1539–1566.
Steiner, Henry J. and Philip Alston. *International Human Rights in Context: Law, Politics, Morals*. 2d ed. Oxford: Oxford University Press, 2000.
Stone, Alec. *The Birth of Judicial Politics in France*. Oxford: Oxford University Press, 1992.
Sullivan, Donna J. "Advancing the Freedom of Religion or Belief through the UN Declaration on the Elimination of Religious Intolerance and Discrimination." *American Journal of International Law* 82 (1988): 487–520.
———. "Gender Equality and Religious Freedom: Toward a Framework for Conflict Resolution." *New York University Journal of International Law and Politics* 24 (1992): 795–856.
Svensson, Jonas. *Women's Human Rights and Islam. A Study of Three Attempts at Accommodation*. Sweden: Religionshistoriska avdelningen, Lunds universitet, 2000.
Swidler, Leonard. "Dialogue Decalogue: Ground Rules for Interreligious Dialogue." *Journal of Ecumenical Studies* 20, no. 1 (winter 1983): 1–4.
———, ed. *Religious Liberty and Human Rights in Nations and in Religions*. Philadelphia, Pa.: Ecumenical Press, 1986.

Symonides, Janusz, ed. *Human Rights: Concepts and Standards*. Aldershot, England: Ashgate, UNESCO Publishing, 2000.

Tahzib, Bahiyyih G. *Freedom of Religion and Belief: Ensuring Effective International Legal Protection*. Boston: Martinus Nijhoff Publishers, 1996.

Tahzib-Lie, Bahia G. "Applying a Gender Perspective in the Area of the Right to Freedom of Religion or Belief." *Brigham Young University Law Review* (2000): 967–87.

Tandem Project, The and the University of Minnesota Human Rights Resource Center. "Lifting the Spirit: Human Rights and Freedom of Religion or Belief: A Secondary School Curriculum to Promote Tolerance and Prevent Discrimination Based on Religion or Belief." 2002.

Tanör, Bülent. *Turkiye'nin Insan Haklari Sorunu*. Ankara: BDS Yayinlari, 1994.

Tapper, Richard, ed. *Islam in ModernTurkey*. London: I. B. Tauris, 1991.

Taricone, Fiorenza, ed. *Maschio e femmina li creò*. Italy: Il Segno dei Gabrielli Editori, 1998.

Tarkunde, V. M. *Radical Humanism, the Philosophy of Freedom and Democracy*. Delhi: Ajanta Publishers, 1983.

Taylor, Charles. "Modes of Civil Society." *Public Culture* 3, no. 1 (fall 1990): 95–118.

Thiemann, Ronald F. *Religion in Public Life: A Dilemma for Democracy*. Washington, D.C.: Georgetown University Press, 1996.

Thierstein, Joel and Yahya R. Kamalipour, eds. *Religion, Law and Freedom: A Global Perspective*. Westport, Conn.: Praeger Publishing, 2000.

Thornberry, Patrick. *International Law and the Rights of Minorities*. Oxford: Clarendon Press, 1993.

Thurfjell, Susanne. "Sermons of Sudan." *New Routes: A Journal of Peace Research and Action* 4, no. 4 (1999): 13.

Thurston, Patrick J. "The Development of Religious Liberty in Chile, 1973–2000." *Brigham Young University Law Review* (2000): 1185–1272.

Tibi, Bassam. *Krieg der Zivilisationene: Politik und Religion zwischen Vernunft und Fundamentalismus*. Hamburg: Hoffman und Campe, 1995.

Toebes, Brigit C. A. *The Right to Health as a Human Right in International Law*. Antwerp: Intersentia, 1998.

Tomasevski, Katrina. *Women and Human Rights*. London: Zed Books, 1993.

Tucker, St. George. *Blackstone's Commentaries*. Vol. 2. South Hackensack, N.J.: Rothman Reprints, 1969.

Tuttle, James, ed. *International Human Rights Law and Practice*. Chicago: American Bar Association, 1978.

Twiss, Sumner B. and Bruce Grelle, eds. *Explorations in Global Ethics. Comparative Religious Ethics and Interreligious Dialogue*. Boulder, Colo.: Westview Press, 1998.

Umozurike, U. Oji. *The African Charter on Human and People's Rights*. Boston: Martinus Nijhoff Publishers, 1997.

United Nations. *Human Rights: A Compilation of International Instruments* 1 (1994).

———. *Human Rights: A Compilation of International Instruments* 2 (1994).

———. *Human Rights: A Compilation of International Instruments*. New York: United Nations, 1993.

Valsecchi, Ambrogio. *Controversy. The birth control debate 1958–1968*. Geoffrey Chapman, 1968.

van Boven, Theo. "Religious Freedom in International Perspective: Existing and Future Standards." *Des Menschen Recht zwischen Freiheit under Verantwortung, Festschrift für Karl Josef Partsch* (1989): 103–13.

Van Bueren, Geraldine. *The International Law on the Rights of the Child.* Boston: Martinus Nijhoff Publishers, 1995.

Van Bueren, Geraldine, ed. *International Documents on Children.* 2d ed. Boston: Martinus Nijhoff Publishers, 1998.

van der Meer, Haye. *Women Priests in the Catholic Church? A Theological Historical Investigation.* Philadelphia, Pa.: Temple University Press, 1973.

Van der Molen, Gesina H. J. *Alberico Gentili and the Development of International Law.* 2d ed. Leyden: A. W. Sijthoff, 1968.

van der Vyver, Johan D. "Constitutional Free Speech and the Law of Defamation." *South African Law Journal* 112 (1995): 572–602.

———. "Constitutional Options for Post-Apartheid South Africa." *Emory Law Journal* 40 (1991): 745–835.

———. "The Function of Legislation as an Instrument of Social Reform." *South African Law Journal* 93 (1976): 56–67.

———. "Sovereignty and Human Rights in Constitutional and International Law." *Emory International Law Review* 5 (1991): 321–443.

———. "The State, the Individual and Society." *South African Law Journal* 94 (1977): 291–305.

van der Vyver, J. D. *Die Juridiese Funksie van Staat en Kerk: 'n Kritiese Analise van die Beginsel van Soewereiniteit in Eie Kring.* Durban: Butterworths, 1972.

van der Vyver, Johan D. and John Witte, Jr., eds. *Religious Human Rights in Global Perspective: Legal Perspectives.* The Hague: Martinus Nijhoff Publishers, 1995.

van Dijk, Pieter and Fried van Hoof. *Theory and Practice of the European Convention on Human Rights.* 3d ed. The Hague: Kluwer Law International, 1998.

VandeCreek, Larry, et al. "Patient and Family Perceptions of Hospital Chaplains." *Hospital and Health Services Administration* 36, no. 3 (fall 1991): 464.

———. "How Many Chaplains per 100 Inpatients? Benchmarks of Health Care Chaplaincy Departments." *The Journal of Pastoral Care,* 55, no. 3 (fall 2001): 295.

Vasak, Karel, ed. *The International Dimensions of Human Rights.* Vol. 1. Westport, Conn.: Greenwood Press, 1979.

Vernette, Jean and Claire Moncelon. *Dictionnaire des groupes religieux aujourd'hui.* Paris: Presses Universitaires de France, 1995.

Verwilghen, Michel J., ed. *Culture Chrétienne et Droits de l'Homme.* Bruylant, 1991.

Vivien, Alain. *Les Sectes En France: Expression De La Liberté.* Paris: La Documentation Française, 1985.

Vincent, Fernand and Piers Campbell. *Towards Greater Financial Autonomy: A Manual on Financing Strategies and Techniques for Development NGOs and Community Organizations.* Geneva: NGO Management Network, 1989.

Vincent, R. J., ed. *Foreign Policy and Human Rights: Issues and Responses.* Cambridge: Cambridge University Press, 1986.

Waldock, Humphrey. "Human Rights in Contemporary International Law and the Significance of the European Convention." *The European Convention of Human Rights* (British Institute for International and Comparative Law) (Ser. No. 5, 1965): 1.

Walkate, Jaap A. "The Right of Everyone to Change His Religion or Belief." *Netherlands International Law Review* 30 (1983): 146.
Walters, Francis P. *A History of the League of Nations.* 2 vols. London: Oxford University Press, 1952.
Waltzer, Michael. "The Idea of Civil Society." *Dissent* (spring 1991): 293–304.
Warner, Daniel, ed. *Human Rights and Humanitarian Law. The Quest for Universality.* Boston: Martinus Nijhoff Publishers, 1977.
Warnink, Hildegard, ed. *Legal Position of Churches and Church Autonomy.* Leuven: Uitgeverij Peeters, 2001.
Watanabe, Manabu. "Reactions to the Aum Affair: The Rise of the 'Anti-Cult' Movement in Japan." *Bulletin of the Nanzan Institute for Religion & Culture* 21 (1997): 43.
Waters, Malcolm. *Modern Sociological Theory.* London: Sage, 1994.
Weissbrodt, David. "The Three 'Theme' Special Rapporteur of the UN Commission on Human Rights." *American Journal of International Law* 80 (1986): 685–699.
Weissbrodt, David, Joan Fitzpatrick, and Frank Newman. *International Human Rights: Law, Policy and Process.* Cincinnati, Ohio: Anderson Publishing, 2001.
Welch, Claude E., Jr., ed. *NGOs and Human Rights: Promise and Performance.* Philadelphia: University of Pennsylvania Press, 2001.
Wessinger, Catherine. *How the Millennium Comes Violently: From Jonestown to Heaven's Gate.* Chappaqua, N.Y.: Seven Bridges Press, 2000.
Wernham, Richard B., ed. *New Cambridge Modern History.* Cambridge: Cambridge University Press, 1968.
Williams, Roger. *The Bloudy Tenent of Persecution for Cause of Conscience.* Providence, R.I.: Publications of the Narragansett Club, 1867.
Wilson, Bryan R., ed. *Religion: Contemporary Issues.* London: Bellew, 1992.
Witte, John, ed. *Soul Wars: The Problems of Proselytism in Russia.* Special Edition of *Emory International Law Review.* 3 vols. Atlanta, Ga.: Emory University School of Law, 1998.
Witte, John, Jr. and Johan D. van der Vyver, eds. *Religious Human Rights in Global Perspective: Religious Perspectives.* The Hague: Martinus Nijhoff Publishers, 1996.
Witte, John, Jr. and Michael Bourdeaux, eds. *Proselytism and Orthodoxy in Russia: The New War for Souls.* Maryknoll, N.Y.: Orbis Books, 1999.
Witteveen, Tobias A. M. *Overheid En Nieuwe Religeuze Bewegingen.* The Hague: Tweede Kamer, 1984.
Wright, Stuart, ed. *Armageddon in Waco: Critical Perspectives on the Branch Davidian Conflict.* Chicago: University of Chicago Press, 1995.
Youngman, Drew. *Double Standards: An Independent View of Religious Discrimination in Australia.* Australia: n.p., 1995.
Yourow, Howard Charles. *The Margin of Appreciation Doctrine in the Dynamics of the European Human Rights Jurisprudence.* The Hague: Kluwer Law International, 1996.
Zurcher, Erik J. *Turkey: A Modern History.* London: I. B. Tauris, 1993.

Index

Tore Lindholm, W. Cole Durham, Jr., Bahia G. Tahzib-Lie (eds.), Facilitating Freedom of Religion or Belief: A Deskbook, *977–1017.*

MIX
Papier aus verantwortungsvollen Quellen
Paper from responsible sources
FSC® C105338

If you have any concerns about our products,
you can contact us on
ProductSafety@springernature.com

In case Publisher is established outside the EU,
the EU authorized representative is:
Springer Nature Customer Service Center GmbH
Europaplatz 3, 69115 Heidelberg, Germany

Printed by Libri Plureos GmbH
in Hamburg, Germany